Lecture Notes in Computer Science

# Lecture Notes in Artificial Intelligence   16018

Founding Editor

Jörg Siekmann

Series Editors

Randy Goebel, *University of Alberta, Edmonton, Canada*
Wolfgang Wahlster, *DFKI, Berlin, Germany*
Zhi-Hua Zhou, *Nanjing University, Nanjing, China*

The series Lecture Notes in Artificial Intelligence (LNAI) was established in 1988 as a topical subseries of LNCS devoted to artificial intelligence.

The series publishes state-of-the-art research results at a high level. As with the LNCS mother series, the mission of the series is to serve the international R & D community by providing an invaluable service, mainly focused on the publication of conference and workshop proceedings and postproceedings.

Rita P. Ribeiro · Bernhard Pfahringer ·
Nathalie Japkowicz · Pedro Larrañaga ·
Alípio M. Jorge · Carlos Soares ·
Pedro H. Abreu · João Gama
Editors

# Machine Learning and Knowledge Discovery in Databases

## Research Track

European Conference, ECML PKDD 2025
Porto, Portugal, September 15–19, 2025
Proceedings, Part VI

*Editors*
Rita P. Ribeiro
University of Porto
Porto, Portugal

Nathalie Japkowicz
American University
Washington, D.C., WA, USA

Alípio M. Jorge
Departamento de Ciência de Computadores
University of Porto
Porto, Portugal

Pedro H. Abreu
University of Coimbra
Coimbra, Portugal

Bernhard Pfahringer
University of Waikato
Hamilton, Waikato, New Zealand

Pedro Larrañaga
Technical University of Madrid
Boadilla del Monte, Madrid, Spain

Carlos Soares
University of Porto
Porto, Portugal

João Gama
University of Porto
Porto, Portugal

ISSN 0302-9743 　　　　　ISSN 1611-3349　(electronic)
Lecture Notes in Artificial Intelligence
ISBN 978-3-032-06105-8 　　　ISBN 978-3-032-06106-5　(eBook)
https://doi.org/10.1007/978-3-032-06106-5

LNCS Sublibrary: SL7 – Artificial Intelligence

© The Editor(s) (if applicable) and The Author(s), under exclusive license
to Springer Nature Switzerland AG 2026

This work is subject to copyright. All rights are solely and exclusively licensed by the Publisher, whether the whole or part of the material is concerned, specifically the rights of translation, reprinting, reuse of illustrations, recitation, broadcasting, reproduction on microfilms or in any other physical way, and transmission or information storage and retrieval, electronic adaptation, computer software, or by similar or dissimilar methodology now known or hereafter developed.
The use of general descriptive names, registered names, trademarks, service marks, etc. in this publication does not imply, even in the absence of a specific statement, that such names are exempt from the relevant protective laws and regulations and therefore free for general use.
The publisher, the authors and the editors are safe to assume that the advice and information in this book are believed to be true and accurate at the date of publication. Neither the publisher nor the authors or the editors give a warranty, expressed or implied, with respect to the material contained herein or for any errors or omissions that may have been made. The publisher remains neutral with regard to jurisdictional claims in published maps and institutional affiliations.

This Springer imprint is published by the registered company Springer Nature Switzerland AG
The registered company address is: Gewerbestrasse 11, 6330 Cham, Switzerland

If disposing of this product, please recycle the paper.

# Preface

The 2025 edition of the European Conference on Machine Learning and Principles and Practice of Knowledge Discovery in Databases (ECML PKDD 2025) was held in the vibrant city of Porto, Portugal on September 15–19, 2025. This marks a significant return of the conference to Porto, following successful editions in 2005 and 2015, underscoring the city's enduring appeal as a hub for scientific exchange.

The annual ECML PKDD conference stands as a premier worldwide platform dedicated to showcasing the latest advancements and fostering insightful discussions in the fields of machine learning and knowledge discovery in databases. Held jointly since 2001, ECML PKDD has firmly established its reputation as the leading European conference in these disciplines. It provides researchers and practitioners with an unparalleled opportunity to exchange knowledge, share innovative ideas, and explore the latest technical advancements. Furthermore, the conference deeply values the synergy between foundational theoretical advances and groundbreaking practical data science applications, actively encouraging contributions that demonstrate how Machine Learning and Data Mining are being effectively employed to address complex real-world challenges.

## A Hub for Responsible AI and Cutting-Edge Research

As the technological landscape continues to evolve and societal needs shift, the conference remains committed to adapting to and reflecting these dynamic changes. This year's event saw a robust engagement from the global research community with a substantial increase in the number of submissions.

The three main conference days were organised into five distinct tracks:

- The Research Track received an impressive number of 924 submissions, with 226 papers ultimately accepted, reflecting a highly competitive acceptance rate of 24.5%.
- The Applied Data Science Track received a total of 299 submissions, accepting 74 papers, resulting in an acceptance rate of 24.7%.
- The Journal Track continued to bridge the gap between conference and journal publications, accepting 43 papers (27 for the Machine Learning journal and 16 for the Data Mining and Knowledge Discovery journal) out of 297 submissions.
- The Nectar Track, focusing on recent scientific advances at the frontier of machine learning and data mining, received 30 submissions.
- The Demo Track showcased practical applications and prototypes, accepting 15 papers from a total of 30 submissions.

These proceedings cover the papers accepted in the Research and Applied Data Science tracks.

The high quality and diversity of the accepted papers across all tracks underscore the continued vitality and intellectual breadth of the machine learning and data mining communities. We extend our sincere gratitude to all authors for their valuable contributions, to the program committee members and reviewers for their diligent efforts in ensuring the rigorous double-blind review process, and to the organising committee for their tireless work in making ECML PKDD 2025 a resounding success. We believe these proceedings will serve as a valuable resource, inspiring future research and innovation in these rapidly advancing fields.

This year's conference featured seven insightful keynote talks that focused on crucial and emerging areas within Responsible AI, including trustworthy AI, interpretability, and explainability. The keynotes also explored fundamental theoretical issues, covering causality, neural-symbolic systems, large language models (LLMs), and AI for science. We were honoured to host leading experts who shared their valuable perspectives:

- Cynthia Rudin (Duke University) presented on "Many Good Models Lead to …";
- Elias Bareinboim (Columbia University) discussed "Towards Causal Artificial Intelligence";
- Francisco Herrera (University of Granada) addressed "Not Just a Trend: Institutionalizing XAI for Responsible and Compliant AI Systems";
- Mirella Lapata (University of Edinburgh) explored "Compositional Intelligence: Coordinating Multiple LLMs for Complex Tasks";
- Nuria Oliver (ELLIS Alicante Foundation, Spain) spoke on "Towards a Fairer World: Uncovering and Addressing Human and Algorithmic Biases";
- Pedro Domingos (University of Washington) shared insights on "A Simple Unification of Neural and Symbolic AI"; and
- Sašo Džeroski (Jožef Stefan Institute, Slovenia) presented on "Artificial Intelligence for Science".

## Fostering Diversity and Inclusion

Our Diversity and Inclusion initiative proudly awarded 10 scholarship grants of €500 to early-career researchers. These grants enabled individuals from developing countries and communities underrepresented in science and technology to attend the conference, present their work, and become integral members of the ECML PKDD community.

## Acknowledging Our Contributors and Supporters

We extend our sincere gratitude to everyone who contributed to making ECML PKDD 2025 such a success. Our heartfelt thanks go to the authors, workshop and tutorial organisers, and all participants for their valuable scientific contributions.

An outstanding conference program would not be possible without the immense dedication and substantial time investment from our area chairs, program committee, and organising committee. The smooth execution of the event was also largely due to the hard work of our many volunteers and session chairs. A special acknowledgement goes to the local organisers for meticulously handling every detail, making the conference a truly memorable experience.

Finally, we are incredibly grateful for the generous financial support from our wonderful sponsors. We also appreciate Springer's ongoing support and Microsoft's provision of their CMT software for conference management, as well as their continued assistance. Our sincere thanks also go to the ECML PKDD Steering Committee for their invaluable advice and guidance over the past two years.

September 2025

João Gama
Pedro H. Abreu
Alípio M. Jorge
Carlos Soares
Rita P. Ribeiro
Pedro Larrañaga
Nathalie Japkowicz
Bernhard Pfahringer
Inês Dutra
Mykola Pechenizkiy
Sepideh Pashami
Paulo Cortez

# Organization

## Honorary Chair

Pavel Brazdil                          University of Porto, Portugal

## General Chairs

João Gama                           University of Porto, Portugal
Pedro H. Abreu                   University of Coimbra, Portugal
Alípio M. Jorge                    University of Porto, Portugal
Carlos Soares                      University of Porto, Portugal

## Research Track Program Chairs

Bernhard Pfahringer            University of Waikato, New Zealand
Nathalie Japkowicz             American University, USA
Pedro Larrañaga                Technical University of Madrid, Spain
Rita P. Ribeiro                    University of Porto, Portugal

## Applied Data Science Track Program Chairs

Inês Dutra                            University of Porto, Portugal
Mykola Pechenisky              TU Eindhoven, The Netherlands
Paulo Cortez                        University of Minho, Portugal
Sepideh Pashami                Halmstad University, Sweden

## Journal Track Chairs

Ana Carolina Lorena            Instituto Tecnológico de Aeronáutica, Brazil
Arlindo Oliveira                 Instituto Superior Técnico, Portugal
Concha Bielza                     Technical University of Madrid, Spain
Longbing Cao                      Macquarie University, Australia
Tiago Almeida                    Federal University of São Carlos, Brazil

## Nectar Track Chairs

Ricard Gavaldà  Amalfi Analytics, Spain
Riccardo Guidotti  University of Pisa, Italy

## Demo Track Chairs

Arian Pasquali  Faktion, Belgium
Nuno Moniz  University of Notre Dame, USA

## Local Chairs

Bruno Veloso  University of Porto, Portugal
Rita Nogueira  INESC TEC, Portugal
Shazia Tabassum  INESC TEC, Portugal

## Workshop Chairs

Irena Koprinska  University of Sydney, Australia
João Mendes Moreira  University of Porto, Portugal
Paula Branco  University of Ottawa, Canada

## Tutorial Chairs

Alicia Troncoso  Universidad Pablo de Olavide, Spain
Nikolaj Tatti  University of Helsinki, Finland

## PhD Forum Chairs

Raquel Sebastião  Polytechnic Institute of Viseu, Portugal
Yun Sing Koh  University of Auckland, New Zealand

## Awards Committee Chairs

| | |
|---|---|
| André Carvalho | University of São Paulo, Brazil |
| Amparo Alonso-Betanzos | University of A Coruña, Spain |
| Katharina Morik | TU Dortmund, Germany |
| Vítor Santos Costa | University of Porto, Portugal |

## Proceedings Chairs

| | |
|---|---|
| João Vinagre | European Commission (JRC), Spain |
| Miriam Santos | University of Porto, Portugal |
| Shazia Tabassum | INESC TEC, Portugal |

## Diversity and Inclusion Chairs

| | |
|---|---|
| Inês Sousa | Fraunhofer, Portugal |
| Zahraa Abdallah | University of Bristol, UK |

## Discovery Challenge Chairs

| | |
|---|---|
| Carlos Ferreira | Polytechnic Institute of Porto, Portugal |
| Peter van der Putten | Leiden University, The Netherlands |
| Rui Camacho | University of Porto, Portugal |

## Panel Chairs

| | |
|---|---|
| Pedro H. Abreu | University of Coimbra, Portugal |
| Paula Brito | University of Porto, Portugal |

## Publicity Chair

| | |
|---|---|
| Carlos Ferreira | Polytechnic Institute of Porto, Portugal |

## Sponsorship Chairs

| | |
|---|---|
| Mariam Berry | BNP Paribas, France |
| Nuno Moutinho | University of Porto, Portugal |
| Rui Teles | Accenture, Portugal |

## Social Media Chairs

| | |
|---|---|
| Luis Roque | ZAAI.ai, Portugal |
| Ricardo Pereira | University of Coimbra, Portugal |
| Dalila Teixeira | Creative Matter, USA |

## Web Chair

| | |
|---|---|
| Thiago Andrade | University of Porto, Portugal |

## Senior Program Committee – Research Track

| | |
|---|---|
| Adam Jatowt | University of Innsbruck, Austria |
| Andrea Passerini | University of Trento, Italy |
| Anthony Bagnall | University of Southampton, UK |
| Arno Knobbe | Leiden University, Netherlands |
| Arno Siebes | Universiteit Utrecht, Netherlands |
| Arto Klami | University of Helsinki, Finland |
| Bernhard Pfahringer | University of Waikato, New Zealand |
| Bettina Berendt | TU Berlin, Germany |
| Celine Robardet | INSA Lyon, France |
| Celine Vens | KU Leuven, Belgium |
| Cesar Ferri | Universitat Politècnica Valencia, Spain |
| Charalampos Tsourakakis | Boston University, USA |
| Chedy Raissi | Inria, France |
| Chen Gong | Nanjing University of Science and Technology, China |
| Danai Koutra | University of Michigan, USA |
| Dimitrios Gunopulos | University of Athens, Greece |
| Donato Malerba | Università degli Studi di Bari Aldo Moro, Italy |
| Dragi Kocev | Jožef Stefan Institute, Slovenia |
| Dunja Mladenic | Jožef Stefan Institute, Slovenia |
| Eirini Ntoutsi | Universität der Bundeswehr München, Germany |

| | |
|---|---|
| Emmanuel Müller | TU Dortmund, Germany |
| Ernestina Menasalvas | Universidad Politécnica de Madrid, Spain |
| Esther Galbrun | University of Eastern Finland, Finland |
| Evaggelia Pitoura | University of Ioannina, Greece |
| Evangelos Papalexakis | University of California, Riverside, USA |
| Fabio A. Stella | University of Milano-Bicocca, Italy |
| Fabrizio Costa | Exeter University, UK |
| Fragkiskos Malliaros | CentraleSupélec, France |
| Georg Krempl | Utrecht University, Netherlands |
| Georgiana Ifrim | University College Dublin, Ireland |
| Gustavo Batista | University of New South Wales, Australia |
| Heikki Mannila | Aalto University, Finland |
| Hendrik Blockeel | KU Leuven, Belgium |
| Henrik Bostrom | KTH Royal Institute of Technology, Sweden |
| Henry Gouk | University of Edinburgh, UK |
| Ioannis Katakis | University of Nicosia, Cyprus |
| Jan N. Van Rijn | LIACS, Leiden University, Netherlands |
| Jefrey Lijffijt | Ghent University, Belgium |
| Jerzy Stefanowski | Poznań University of Technology, Poland |
| Jesse Davis | KU Leuven, Belgium |
| Jesse Read | Ecole Polytechnique, France |
| Jessica Lin | George Mason University, USA |
| Jesus Cerquides | IIIA-CSIC, Spain |
| Jilles Vreeken | CISPA Helmholtz Center for Information Security, Germany |
| João Gama | INESC TEC - LIAAD, Portugal |
| Jörg Wicker | University of Auckland, New Zealand |
| José Hernández-Orallo | Universitat Politècnica de Valencia, Spain |
| Junming Shao | University of Electronic Science and Technology of China, China |
| Kai Puolamaki | University of Helsinki, Finland |
| Manfred Jaeger | Aalborg University, Denmark |
| Marius Kloft | TU Kaiserslautern, Germany |
| Marius Lindauer | Leibniz University Hannover, Germany |
| Mark Last | Ben-Gurion University of the Negev, Israel |
| Matthias Renz | University of Kiel, Germany |
| Matthias Schubert | Ludwig-Maximilians-Universität München, Germany |
| Michele Lombardi | University of Bologna, Italy |
| Michèle Sebag | LISN CNRS, France |
| Nathalie Japkowicz | American University, USA |
| Paolo Frasconi | Università degli Studi di Firenze, Italy |

| | |
|---|---|
| Parisa Kordjamshidi | Michigan State University, USA |
| Pasquale Minervini | University of Edinburgh, UK |
| Pauli Miettinen | University of Eastern Finland, Finland |
| Pedro Larrañaga | Technical University of Madrid, Spain |
| Peer Kroger | Christian-Albrechts-Universität Kiel, Germany |
| Peter Flach | University of Bristol, UK |
| Ricardo B. Prudencio | Universidade Federal de Pernambuco, Brazil |
| Rita P. Ribeiro | University of Porto and INESC TEC, Portugal |
| Salvatore Ruggieri | University of Pisa, Italy |
| Sebastijan Dumancic | TU Delft, Netherlands |
| Sibylle Hess | TU Eindhoven, Netherlands |
| Sicco Verwer | Delft University of Technology, Netherlands |
| Siegfried Nijssen | Université catholique de Louvain, Belgium |
| Sophie Fellenz | RPTU Kaiserslautern-Landau, Germany |
| Stefano Ferilli | University of Bari, Italy |
| Stratis Ioannidis | Northeastern University, USA |
| Szymon Jaroszewicz | Polish Academy of Sciences, Poland |
| Tijl De Bie | Ghent University, Belgium |
| Ulf Brefeld | Leuphana University of Lüneburg, Germany |
| Varvara Vetrova | University of Canterbury, New Zealand |
| Wannes Meert | KU Leuven, Belgium |
| Wei Ye | Tongji University, China |
| Wenbin Zhang | Florida International University, USA |
| Willem Waegeman | Universiteit Gent, Belgium |
| Wouter Duivesteijn | Technische Universiteit Eindhoven, Netherlands |
| Xiao Luo | University of California, Los Angeles, USA |
| Yun Sing Koh | University of Auckland, New Zealand |
| Zied Bouraoui | CRIL CNRS and Université d'Artois, France |

## Senior Program Committee – Applied Data Science Track

| | |
|---|---|
| Albrecht Zimmermann | Université de Caen Normandie, France |
| Andreas Hotho | University of Würzburg, Germany |
| Anirban Dasgupta | IIT Gandhinagar, India |
| Anna Monreale | University of Pisa, Italy |
| Annalisa Appice | University of Bari Aldo Moro, Italy |
| Bruno Cremilleux | Université de Caen Normandie, France |
| Carlotta Domeniconi | George Mason University, USA |
| Dejing Dou | BCG, USA |
| Fabio Pinelli | IMT Lucca, Italy |
| Fuzhen Zhuang | Beihang University, China |

| | |
|---|---|
| Gabor Melli | PredictionWorks, USA |
| Giuseppe Manco | ICAR-CNR, Italy |
| Glenn Fung | Independent Researcher, USA |
| Grzegorz Nalepa | Jagiellonian University, Poland |
| Hui Xiong | Hong Kong University of Science and Technology (Guangzhou), China |
| Inês Dutra | University of Porto, Portugal |
| Ioanna Miliou | Stockholm University, Sweden |
| Ira Assent | Aarhus University, Denmark |
| Jiayu Zhou | Michigan State University, USA |
| Jiliang Tang | Michigan State University, USA |
| Jingrui He | University of Illinois at Urbana-Champaign, USA |
| João Gama | INESC TEC - LIAAD, Portugal |
| Jose A. Gamez | Universidad de Castilla-La Mancha, Spain |
| Ke Liang | National University of Defense Technology, China |
| Kurt Driessens | Maastricht University, Netherlands |
| Lars Kotthoff | University of Wyoming, USA |
| Liang Sun | Alibaba Group, China |
| Martin Atzmueller | Osnabrück University and DFKI, Germany |
| Michael R. Berthold | KNIME, Germany |
| Michelangelo Ceci | University of Bari, Italy |
| Min-Ling Zhang | Southeast University, China |
| Mykola Pechenizkiy | TU Eindhoven, Netherlands |
| Myra Spiliopoulou | Otto-von-Guericke-Universität Magdeburg, Germany |
| Niklas Lavesson | Blekinge Institute of Technology, Sweden |
| Nikolaj Tatti | Helsinki University, Finland |
| Panagiotis Papapetrou | Stockholm University, Sweden |
| Paolo Frasconi | Università degli Studi di Firenze, Italy |
| Paulo Cortez | University of Minho, Portugal |
| Peggy Cellier | INSA Rennes, IRISA, France |
| Rayid Ghani | Carnegie Mellon University, USA |
| Sahar Asadi | King (Microsoft), UK |
| Sandeep Tata | Google, USA |
| Sepideh Pashami | Halmstad University, Sweden |
| Slawomir Nowaczyk | Halmstad University, Sweden |
| Sriparna Saha | IIT Patna, India |
| Thomas Liebig | TU Dortmund, Germany |
| Thomas Seidl | LMU Munich, Germany |
| Tom Diethe | AstraZeneca, UK |
| Tony Lindgren | Stockholm University, Sweden |

| | |
|---|---|
| Vincent S. Tseng | National Yang Ming Chiao Tung University, Taiwan |
| Vítor Santos Costa | Universidade do Porto, Portugal |
| Xingquan Zhu | Florida Atlantic University, USA |
| Yi Chang | Jilin University, China |
| Yinglong Xia | Meta, USA |
| Yongxin Tong | Beihang University, China |
| Yun Sing Koh | University of Auckland, New Zealand |
| Zhaochun Ren | Shandong University, China |
| Zheng Wang | Alibaba DAMO Academy, China |
| Zhiwei (Tony) Qin | Lyft, USA |

## Program Committee – Research Track

| | |
|---|---|
| Christoph Bergmeir | Monash University, Australia |
| A. K. M. Mahbubur Rahman | Independent University, Bangladesh |
| Abdulhakim Qahtan | Utrecht University, Netherlands |
| Abhishek A. | Fujitsu Research, India |
| Acar Tamersoy | Microsoft, USA |
| Ad Feelders | Universiteit Utrecht, Netherlands |
| Adam Goodge | I2R, A*STAR, Singapore |
| Adele Jia | China Agricultural University, China |
| Adem Kikaj | KU Leuven, Belgium |
| Aditya Mohan | Leibniz Universität Hannover, Germany |
| Ajay A. Mahimkar | AT&T, USA |
| Akka Zemmari | Université de Bordeaux, France |
| Akshay Sethi | MasterCard, USA |
| Alborz Geramifard | Meta, USA |
| Alessandro Antonucci | IDSIA, Switzerland |
| Alessandro Melchiorre | Johannes Kepler University Linz, Austria |
| Alexander Dockhorn | Leibniz University Hannover, Germany |
| Alexander Schiendorfer | Technische Hochschule Ingolstadt, Germany |
| Alexander Schulz | CITEC, Bielefeld University, Germany |
| Alexandre Termier | Université de Rennes 1, France |
| Alexandre Verine | Ecole Normale Supérieure - PSL, France |
| Alexandru C. Mara | Ghent University, Belgium |
| Ali Ayadi | University of Strasbourg, France |
| Ali Ismail-Fawaz | IRIMAS, Université de Haute-Alsace, France |
| Alicja Wieczorkowska | Polish-Japanese Academy of Information Technology, Poland |
| Alipio M. G. Jorge | INESC TEC/University of Porto, Portugal |

| | |
|---|---|
| Alireza Gharahighehi | KU Leuven, Belgium |
| Alistair Shilton | Deakin University, Australia |
| Alneu A. Lopes | University of São Paulo, Brazil |
| Alper Demir | Izmir University of Economics, Turkey |
| Alvaro Figueira | CRACS and Universidade do Porto, Portugal |
| Amal Saadallah | TU Dortmund, Germany |
| Aman Chadha | Stanford University and Amazon, USA |
| Amer Krivosija | TU Dortmund, Germany |
| Amir H. Payberah | KTH Royal Institute of Technology, Sweden |
| Ammar Shaker | NEC Laboratories Europe, Europe |
| Ana Rita Nogueira | INESC TEC, Portugal |
| Anand Paul | Louisiana State University HSC, USA |
| Anastasios Gounaris | Aristotle University of Thessaloniki, Greece |
| Andre V. Carreiro | Fraunhofer Portugal AICOS, Portugal |
| André C. P. L. F. de Carvalho | University of São Paulo, Brazil |
| Andrea Cossu | University of Pisa, Italy |
| Andrea Mastropietro | University of Bonn, Germany |
| Andrea Pugnana | University of Trento, Italy |
| Andrea Tagarelli | DIMES - UNICAL, Italy |
| Andreas Bender | LMU Munich, Germany |
| Andreas Nürnberger | Otto-von-Guericke-Universität Magdeburg, Germany |
| Andreas Schwung | Fachhochschule Südwestfalen, Germany |
| Andrei Paleyes | University of Cambridge, UK |
| Andrzej Skowron | University of Warsaw, Poland |
| Andy Song | RMIT University, Australia |
| Angelica Liguori | ICAR-CNR, Italy |
| Anirban Dasgupta | IIT Gandhinagar, India |
| Anke Meyer-Baese | Florida State University, USA |
| Anna Beer | University of Vienna, Austria |
| Anna Krause | Universität Wurzburg and Chair X Data Science, Germany |
| Anna Monreale | University of Pisa, Italy |
| Annelot W. Bosman | Universiteit Leiden, Netherlands |
| Antoine Caradot | Hubert Curien Laboratory, France |
| Antonio Bahamonde | University of Oviedo, Spain |
| Antonio Mastropietro | Università di Pisa, Italy |
| Antonio Pellicani | Università degli Studi di Bari, Aldo Moro, Italy |
| Antonis Matakos | Aalto University, Finland |
| Antti Laaksonen | University of Helsinki, Finland |
| Aomar Osmani | LIPN-UMR CNRS, France |
| Aonghus Lawlor | University College Dublin, Ireland |

| | |
|---|---|
| Aparna S. Varde | Montclair State University, USA |
| Apostolos N. Papadopoulos | Aristotle University of Thessaloniki, Greece |
| Aritra Konar | KU Leuven, Belgium |
| Arjun Roy | Freie Universität Berlin, Germany |
| Arthur Charpentier | UQAM, Canada |
| Arunas Lipnickas | Kaunas University of Technology, Lithuania |
| Atsuhiro Takasu | National Institute of Informatics, Japan |
| Aurora Esteban | University of Cordoba, Spain |
| Baosheng Zhang | Tsinghua University, China |
| Barbara Toniella Corradini | University of Florence and University of Siena, Italy |
| Bardh Prenkaj | Technical University of Munich, Germany |
| Barry O'Sullivan | University College Cork, Ireland |
| Beilun Wang | Southeast University, China |
| Benjamin Halstead | University of Auckland, New Zealand |
| Benjamin Paassen | Bielefeld University, Germany |
| Benjamin Quost | Université de Technologie de Compiègne, France |
| Benoit Frenay | University of Namur, Belgium |
| Bernardo Moreno Sanchez | University of Helsinki, Finland |
| Bernhard Pfahringer | University of Waikato, New Zealand |
| Bertrand Cuissart | University of Caen, France |
| Bin Liu | Chongqing University of Posts and Telecommunications, China |
| Bin Shi | Xi'an Jiaotong University, China |
| Bin Wu | Zhengzhou University, China |
| Bin Zhou | National University of Defense Technology, China |
| Bitao Peng | Guangdong University of Foreign Studies, China |
| Bo Kang | Ghent University, Belgium |
| Bogdan Cautis | Université Paris-Saclay, France |
| Bojan Evkoski | Central European University, Hungary |
| Boshen Shi | Institute of Computing Technology, Chinese Academy of Sciences, China |
| Boualem Benatallah | Dublin City University, Ireland |
| Brandon Gower-Winter | Utrecht University, Netherlands |
| Bunil K. Balabantaray | NIT Meghalaya, India |
| Carlos Ferreira | INESC TEC, Portugal |
| Carlos Monserrat-Aranda | Universitat Politècnica de Valencia, Spain |
| Carson K. Leung | University of Manitoba, Canada |
| Catarina Silva | University of Coimbra, Portugal |
| Cecile Capponi | Aix-Marseille University, France |
| Celine Rouveirol | LIPN Université de Sorbonne Paris Nord, France |

| | |
|---|---|
| Cesar H. G. Andrade | Porto University, Portugal |
| Chandrajit Bajaj | University of Texas, Austin, USA |
| Chang Rajani | University of Helsinki, Finland |
| Charlotte Laclau | Polytechnique Institute, Télécom Paris, France |
| Charlotte Pelletier | Université de Bretagne du Sud, France |
| Chen Wang | DATA61, CSIRO, Australia |
| Cheng Cheng | Carnegie Mellon University, USA |
| Cheng Xie | Yunnan University, China |
| Chenglin Wang | East China Normal University, China |
| Chenwang Wu | University of Science and Technology of China, China |
| Chiara Pugliese | IIT Institute of National Research Council, Italy |
| Chien-Liang Liu | National Chiao Tung University, Taiwan |
| Chihiro Maru | Chuo University, Japan |
| Chongsheng Zhang | Henan University, China |
| Christian Beecks | FernUniversität in Hagen, Germany |
| Christian M. M. Frey | University of Technology Nuremberg, Germany |
| Christian Hakert | TU Dortmund, Germany |
| Christine Largeron | LabHC Lyon University, France |
| Christophe Rigotti | INSA Lyon, France |
| Christophe Rodrigues | DVRC Pôle universitaire Léonard de Vinci, France |
| Christos Anagnostopoulos | University of Glasgow, UK |
| Christos Diou Harokopio | University of Athens, Greece |
| Chuan Qin | Chinese Academy of Sciences, China |
| Chunchun Chen | Tongji University, China |
| Chunyao Song | Nankai University, China |
| Claire Nedellec | INRAE, MaIAGE, France |
| Claudio Borile | CENTAI Institute, Italy |
| Claudio Gallicchio | University of Pisa, Italy |
| Claudius Zelenka | Kiel University, Germany |
| Colin Bellinger | NRC and Dalhousie University, Canada |
| Collin Leiber | Aalto University, Finland |
| Cong Qi | New Jersey Institute of Technology, USA |
| Congfeng Cao | University of Amsterdam, Netherlands |
| Corrado Loglisci | Università degli Studi di Bari, Aldo Moro, Italy |
| Cuicui Luo | University of Chinese Academy of Sciences, China |
| Cuneyt G. Akcora | University of Central Florida, USA |
| Cynthia C. S. Liem | Delft University of Technology, Netherlands |
| Dalius Matuzevicius | Vilnius Gediminas Technical University, Lithuania |

| | |
|---|---|
| Dan Li | Sun Yat-sen University, China |
| Danai Koutra | University of Michigan, USA |
| Dang Nguyen | Deakin University, Australia |
| Daniel Neider | TU Dortmund, Germany |
| Daniel Schlor | Universität Würzburg, Germany |
| Danil Provodin | TU Eindhoven, Netherlands |
| Danyang Xiao | Sun Yat-sen University, China |
| Dario Garcia-Gasulla | Barcelona Supercomputing Center (BSC), Spain |
| Dario Garigliotti | University of Bergen, Norway |
| Darius Plonis | Vilnius Gediminas Technical University, Lithuania |
| Dariusz Brzezinski | Poznań University of Technology, Poland |
| David Gomez | Universidad Politecnica de Madrid, Spain |
| David Holzmüller | University of Stuttgart, Germany |
| David Q. Sun | Apple, USA |
| Davide Evangelista | University of Bologna, Italy |
| Debo Cheng | University of South Australia, Australia |
| Deepayan Chakrabarti | University of Texas at Austin, USA |
| Deng-Bao Wang | Southeast University, China |
| Denilson Barbosa | University of Alberta, Canada |
| Denis Huseljic | University of Kassel, Germany |
| Denis Lukovnikov | Ruhr-Universität Bochum, Germany |
| Destercke Sebastien | UTC, France |
| Di Jin | TikTok, USA |
| Di Wu | Chongqing Institute of Green and Intelligent Technology, Chinese Academy of Sciences, China |
| Diana Benavides Prado | University of Auckland, New Zealand |
| Dianhui Wang | Independent Researcher, Australia |
| Diego Carrera | STMicroelectronics, Switzerland |
| Diletta Chiaro | Università degli Studi di Napoli Federico II, Italy |
| Dimitri Staufer | TU Berlin, Germany |
| Dimitrios Katsaros | University of Thessaly, Greece |
| Dimitrios Rafailidis | University of Thessaly, France |
| Dino Ienco | INRAE, France |
| Dmitry Kobak | University of Tübingen, Germany |
| Domenico Redavid | University of Bari, Italy |
| Dominik M. Endres | Philipps-Universität Marburg, Germany |
| Dominique Gay | Université de La Réunion, France |
| Dong Li | Baylor University, USA |
| Duarte Folgado | Fraunhofer Portugal AICOS, Portugal |
| Duo Xu | Georgia Institute of Technology, USA |

| | |
|---|---|
| Edoardo Serra | Boise State University, USA |
| Edouard Fouche | Karlsruhe Institute of Technology (KIT), Germany |
| Eduardo F. Montesuma | Université Paris-Saclay, France |
| Edward Apeh | Bournemouth University, UK |
| Edwin Simpson | University of Bristol, UK |
| Ehsan Aminian | INESC TEC, Portugal |
| Ekaterina Antonenko | Mines Paris - PSL, France |
| Eliana Pastor | Politecnico di Torino, Italy |
| Emanuela Marasco | George Mason University, USA |
| Emilio Dorigatti | LMU Munich, Germany |
| Emilio Parrado-Hernandez | Universidad Carlos III de Madrid, Spain |
| Emmanouil Krasanakis | CERTH, Greece |
| Emmanouil Panagiotou | Freie Universität Berlin, Germany |
| Emre Gursoy | Koc University, Turkey |
| Engelbert Mephu Nguifo | Université Clermont Auvergne, CNRS, LIMOS, France |
| Eran Treister | Ben-Gurion University of the Negev, Israel |
| Erasmo Purificato | Otto-von-Guericke Universität Magdeburg, Germany |
| Erik Novak | Jožef Stefan Institute, Slovenia |
| Erwan Le Merrer | Inria, France |
| Esra Akbas | Georgia State University, USA |
| Esther-Lydia Silva-Ramirez | Universidad de Cadiz, Spain |
| Evaldas Vaičiukynas | Kaunas University of Technology, Lithuania |
| Evangelos Kanoulas | University of Amsterdam, Netherlands |
| Evelin Amorim | INESC TEC, Portugal |
| Fabian C. Spaeh | Boston University, USA |
| Fabio Fassetti | Università della Calabria, Italy |
| Fabio Fumarola | Prometeia, Italy |
| Fabio Mercorio | University of Milan-Bicocca, Italy |
| Fabio Vandin | University of Padova, Italy |
| Fandel Lin | University of Southern California, USA |
| Federica Granese | Inria, Université Côte d'Azur, France |
| Federico Baldo | University of Bologna, Italy |
| Federico Sabbatini | National Institute for Nuclear Physics (INFN), Italy |
| Feifan Zhang | China Agricultural University, China |
| Felipe Kenji Nakano | KU Leuven, Belgium |
| Fernando Martinez-Plumed | Universitat Politècnica de Valencia, Spain |
| Filipe Rodrigues | Technical University of Denmark (DTU), Denmark |

| | |
|---|---|
| Flavio Giobergia | Politecnico di Torino, Italy |
| Florent Masseglia | Inria, France |
| Florian Beck | JKU Linz, Austria |
| Florian Lemmerich | University of Passau, Germany |
| Francesca Naretto | University of Pisa, Italy |
| Francesco Piccialli | University of Naples Federico II, Italy |
| Francesco Renna | Universidade do Porto, Portugal |
| Francisco Pereira | DTU, Denmark |
| Franco Raimondi | Gran Sasso Science Institute, Italy |
| Frederic Koriche | Université d'Artois, CRIL CNRS, France |
| Frederic Pennerath | CentraleSupélec - LORIA, France |
| Furong Peng | Shanxi University, China |
| Gabriel Marques Tavares | LMU Munich, Germany |
| Gabriele Sartor | University of Turin, Italy |
| Gabriele Venturato | KU Leuven, Belgium |
| Gaetan De Waele | Ghent University, Belgium |
| Gaia Saveri | University of Trieste, Italy |
| Gang Li | Deakin University, Australia |
| Gaoyuan Du | Amazon, USA |
| Gavin Smith | University of Nottingham, UK |
| Geming Xia | National University of Defense Technology, China |
| Geng Zhao | Heidelberg University, Germany |
| Gennaro Vessio | University of Bari Aldo Moro, Italy |
| Geoffrey I. Webb | Monash, Australia |
| Georgia Baltsou | Centre for Research & Technology, Greece |
| Geraldin Nanfack | Concordia University, Canada |
| Germain Forestier | University of Haute Alsace, France |
| Gerrit Grossmann | DFKI, Germany |
| Gerrit J. J. van den Burg | Alan Turing Institute, UK |
| Gherardo Varando | Universitat de Valencia, Spain |
| Giacomo Medda | University of Cagliari, Italy |
| Gilberto Bernardes | INESC TEC and University of Porto, Portugal |
| Giorgio Venturin | University of Padova, Italy |
| Giovanna Castellano | University of Bari Aldo Moro, Italy |
| Giovanni Ponti | ENEA, Italy |
| Giovanni Stilo | Università degli Studi dell'Aquila, Italy |
| Gisele Pappa | UFMG, Brazil |
| Giuseppe Manco | ICAR-CNR, IT, Italy |
| Gizem Gezici | Scuola Normale Superiore, Italy |
| Gjergji Kasneci | TU Munich, Germany |
| Goreti Marreiros | ISEP/GECAD, Portugal |

| | |
|---|---|
| Graziella De Martino | University of Bari, Aldo Moro, Italy |
| Grazina Korvel | Vilnius University, Lithuania |
| Grigorios Tsoumakas | Aristotle University of Thessaloniki, Greece |
| Guangyin Jin | National University of Defense Technology, China |
| Guangzhong Sun | University of Science and Technology of China, China |
| Guanjin Wang | Murdoch University, Australia |
| Guilherme Weigert | Cassales University of Waikato, New Zealand |
| Guillaume Derval | UC Louvain - ICTEAM, Belgium |
| Guorui Quan | University of Manchester, UK |
| Guoxi Zhang | Beijing Institute of General Artificial Intelligence, China |
| Gustau Camps-Valls | Universitat de Valencia, Spain |
| Gustav Sir | Czech Technical University, Czech Republic |
| Gustavo Batista | University of New South Wales, Australia |
| Hachem Kadri | Aix-Marseille University, France |
| Hadi Asghari | Humboldt Institute for Internet and Society, Germany |
| Haifeng Sun | University of Science and Technology of China, China |
| Haihui Fan | Institute of Information Engineering, Chinese Academy of Sciences, China |
| Haizhou Du | Shanghai University of Electric Power, China |
| Hajer Salem | AUDENSIEL, France |
| Hakim Hacid | TII, United Arab Emirates |
| Hamid Bouchachia | Bournemouth University, UK |
| Han Wang | Xidian University, China |
| Hang Yu | Shanghai University, China |
| Hanna Sumita | Institute of Science Tokyo, Japan |
| Hao Niu | KDDI Research, Japan |
| Hao Xue | University of New South Wales, Australia |
| Hao Yan | Carleton University, Canada |
| Haowen Zhang | Zhejiang Sci-Tech University, China |
| Harsh Borse | IIT Kharagpur, India |
| Heitor M. Gomes | Victoria University of Wellington, New Zealand |
| Helder Oliveira | FCUP and INESC TEC, Portugal |
| Helge Langseth | Norwegian University of Science and Technology, Norway |
| Hendrik Blockeel | KU Leuven, Belgium |
| Henrique O. Marques | University of Southern Denmark, Denmark |
| Henryk Maciejewski | Wroclaw University of Science and Technology, Poland |

| | |
|---|---|
| Hideaki Ishibashi | Kyushu Institute of Technology, Japan |
| Hilde J. P. Weerts | Eindhoven University of Technology, Netherlands |
| Holger Froening | University of Heidelberg, Germany |
| Holger Karl | HPI, Germany |
| Hongbo Bo | University of Bristol, UK |
| Hongyang Chen | Zhejiang Lab, China |
| Hua Chu | Xidian University, China |
| Huaiyu Wan | Beijing Jiaotong University, China |
| Huaming Chen | University of Sydney, Australia |
| Huandong Wang | Tsinghua University, China |
| Huanlai Xing | Southwest Jiaotong University, China |
| Hui Ji | University of Pittsburgh, USA |
| Hui (Wendy) Wang | Stevens Institute of Technology, USA |
| Huiping Chen | University of Birmingham, UK |
| Humberto Bustince | Universidad Publica de Navarra, Spain |
| Huong Ha | RMIT University, Australia |
| Idir Benouaret | Epita Research Laboratory, France |
| Ines Sousa | Fraunhofer AICOS, Portugal |
| Ingo Thon | Siemens AG, Germany |
| Inigo Jauregi Unanue | University of Technology Sydney, Australia |
| Ioannis Sarridis | Centre for Research & Technology, Greece |
| Issam Falih | Université Clermont Auvergne, CNRS, LIMOS, France |
| Ivan Vankov | iris.ai, Norway |
| Ivor Cribben | University of Alberta, Canada |
| Jaemin Yoo | KAIST, South Korea |
| Jakir Hossain | University at Buffalo, USA |
| Jakub Klikowski | Wroclaw University of Science and Technology, Poland |
| Jalaj Bhandari | Columbia University, USA |
| Jaleed Khan | University of Oxford, UK |
| James Goulding | University of Nottingham, UK |
| Jan Kalina | Czech Academy of Sciences, Czech Republic |
| Jan P. Mielniczuk | Polish Academy of Sciences, Poland |
| Jan Ramon | Inria, France |
| Jan Verwaeren | Ghent University, Belgium |
| Jannis Brugger | TU Darmstadt, Germany |
| Jean-Marc Andreoli | Naverlabs Europe, Netherlands |
| Jedrzej Potoniec | Poznań University of Technology, Poland |
| Jeronimo Arenas-Garcia | Universidad Carlos III de Madrid, Spain |
| Jhony H. Giraldo | Télécom Paris, Institut Polytechnique de Paris, France |

| | |
|---|---|
| Jia Cai | Guangdong University of Finance and Economics, China |
| Jiahui Jin | Southeast University, China |
| Jiang Zhong | Independent Researcher, China |
| Jianwu Wang | University of Maryland, Baltimore County, USA |
| Jiawei Chen | Tianjin University, China |
| Jiaxin Ding | Shanghai Jiao Tong University, China |
| Jidong Yuan | Beijing Jiaotong University, China |
| Jie Song | Zhejiang University, China |
| Jie Wu | Fudan University, China |
| Jie Yang | University of Wollongong, China |
| Jimeng Shi | Florida International University, USA |
| Jin Chen | Hong Kong University of Science and Technology, China |
| Jin Liang | South China Normal University, China |
| Jing Ren | NUDT, China |
| Jing Wang | Amazon, USA |
| Jinghui Zhong | South China University of Technology, China |
| Jingtao Ding | Tsinghua University, China |
| Jinli Zhang | Beijing University of Technology, China |
| Jiri Sima | Czech Academy of Sciences, Czech Republic |
| João Gama | University of Porto, Portugal |
| Joao Mendes-Moreira | University of Porto, Portugal |
| Joao Vinagre | European Commission (JRC), Spain |
| Joaquim Silva | NOVA LINCS, Universidade Nova de Lisboa, Portugal |
| Jochen De Weerdt | KU Leuven, Belgium |
| Joe Mellor | University of Edinburgh, UK |
| Johanne Cohen | LISN-CNRS, France |
| Johannes Jakubik | IBM Research, USA |
| John W. Sheppard | Montana State University, USA |
| Jonata Tyska Carvalho | Federal University of Santa Catarina, Brazil |
| Jordi Guitart | Barcelona Supercomputing Center (BSC), Spain |
| Joris Mattheijssens | Ghent University, Belgium |
| Jose M. Costa Pereira | University of Porto, Portugal |
| Jose Oramas | University of Antwerp, sqIRL/IDLab, imec, Belgium |
| Jose Tomas Palma | University of Murcia, Spain |
| Joydeep Chandra | Indian Institute of Technology, Patna, India |
| Juan A. Botia | University of Murcia, Spain |
| Juan Rodriguez | Universidad de Burgos, Spain |
| Jukka Heikkonen | University of Turku, Finland |

| | |
|---|---|
| Julien Delaunay | Inria, France |
| Julien Ferry | Polytechnique Montreal, Canada |
| Julien Perez | EPITA, France |
| Jun Zhuang | Boise State University, USA |
| Jun Yu Hou | Nanjing University, China |
| Junbo Zhang | JD Intelligent Cities Research, USA |
| Junze Liu | University of California, Irvine, USA |
| Jurgita Kapočiūtė-Dzikienė | Tilde SIA, University of Latvia and Tilde IT, Vytautas Magnus University, Lithuania |
| Justina Mandravickaitė | Vytautas Magnus University, Lithuania |
| Kamil Adamczewski | Max Planck Institute for Intelligent Systems, Germany |
| Kamil Michal Ksiazek | Jagiellonian University, Poland |
| Karim Radouane | Université Sorbonne Paris Nord, France |
| Kary Framing | Umeå University, Sweden |
| Katerina Taskova | University of Auckland, New Zealand |
| Katharina Dost | Jožef Stefan Institute, Slovenia |
| Kaushik Roy | University of South Carolina, USA |
| Kejia Chen | Nanjing University of Posts and Telecommunications, China |
| Ken Kobayashi | Tokyo Institute of Technology, Japan |
| Khaled Mohammed Saifuddin | Northeastern University, USA |
| Khalid Benabdeslem | Université de Lyon 1, France |
| Kim Thang Nguyen | LIG, University Grenoble-Alpes, France |
| Kira Maag | Heinrich-Heine-Universität Düsseldorf, Germany |
| Koji Maruhashi | Fujitsu Research, Japan |
| Koyel Mukherjee | Adobe Research, USA |
| Kristen M. Scott | KU Leuven, Belgium |
| Krzysztof Ruda | Polish Academy of Sciences, Poland |
| Krzysztof Slot | Lodz University of Technology, Poland |
| Kuldeep Singh | Cerence, Germany |
| Kushankur Ghosh | University of Alberta, Canada |
| Lamine Diop | EPITA, France |
| Latifa Oukhellou | IFSTTAR, France |
| Laurence Park | Western Sydney University, Australia |
| Laurens Devos | KU Leuven, Belgium |
| Len Feremans | Universiteit Antwerpen, Belgium |
| Lena Wiese | Goethe University Frankfurt, Germany |
| Lenaig Cornanguer | CISPA Helmholtz Center for Information Security, Germany |
| Lennert De Smet | KU Leuven, Belgium |
| Lev Reyzin | University of Illinois at Chicago, USA |

| | |
|---|---|
| Li Wang | National University of Defense Technology, China |
| Liang Du | Shanxi University, China |
| Lianyong Qi | China University of Petroleum (East China), China |
| Lijie Hu | King Abdullah University of Science and Technology, Saudi Arabia |
| Lijing Zhu | Bowling Green State University, USA |
| Lingling Zhang | Capital Normal University, China |
| Lingyue Fu | Shanghai Jiao Tong University, China |
| Linh Le Pham Van | Deakin University, Australia |
| Livio Bioglio | University of Turin, Italy |
| Lixing Yu | Yunnan University, China |
| Liyan Song | Harbin Institute of Technology, China |
| Longlong Sun | Chang'an University, China |
| Luca Corbucci | University of Pisa, Italy |
| Luca Ferragina | University of Calabria, Italy |
| Luca Romeo | University of Macerata, Italy |
| Lucas Pereira | LARSyS, Tecnico Lisboa, Portugal |
| Luciano Caroprese | ICAR-CNR, Italy |
| Ludovico Boratto | University of Cagliari, Italy |
| Luis Rei | Jožef Stefan Institute, Slovenia |
| Mahardhika Pratama | University of South Australia, Australia |
| Maiju Karjalainen | University of Eastern Finland, Finland |
| Makoto Onizuka | Osaka University, Japan |
| Manali Sharma | Samsung, South Korea |
| Maneet Singh | MasterCard, India |
| Manuel M. Garcia-Piqueras | Universidad de Castilla La Mancha, Spain |
| Manuele Bicego | University of Verona, Italy |
| Mao A. Cheng | University of California, Berkeley, USA |
| Marc Plantevit | EPITA, France |
| Marc Tommasi | Lille University, France |
| Marcel Wever | Leibniz University Hannover, Germany |
| Marcilio de Souto | LIFO/Université d'Orleans, France |
| Marco Lippi | University of Florence, Italy |
| Marco Loog | Radboud University, Netherlands |
| Marco Mellia | Politecnico di Torino, Italy |
| Marco Podda | University of Pisa, Italy |
| Marco Polignano | Università di Bari, Italy |
| Marco Viviani | Università degli Studi di Milano Bicocca, Italy |
| Maria Vasconcelos | Fraunhofer Portugal AICOS, Portugal |
| Maria Sofia Bucarelli | Sapienza University of Rome, Italy |

| | |
|---|---|
| Mariana Oliveira | Universidade do Porto, Portugal |
| Mariana Vargas Vieyra | MostlyAI, Austria |
| Marielle Malfante | CEA, France |
| Marina Litvak | Shamoon College of Engineering, Israel |
| Mario Antunes | Universidade de Aveiro, Portugal |
| Mario Andres Munoz | University of Melbourne, Australia |
| Marius Koppel | Johannes Gutenberg University Mainz, Germany |
| Mark Junjie Li | Shenzhen University, China |
| Marko Robnik-Sikonja | University of Ljubljana, Slovenia |
| Marta Soare | Université d'Orleans, France |
| Martin Holena | Czech Academy of Sciences, Czech Republic |
| Martin Pilat | Charles University, Czech Republic |
| Martino Ciaperoni | Aalto University, Finland |
| Marwan Hassani | TU Eindhoven, Netherlands |
| Masahiro Suzuki | University of Tokyo, Japan |
| Massimo Guarascio | ICAR-CNR, Italy |
| Matej Mihelcic | University of Zagreb, Croatia |
| Mathias Verbeke | KU Leuven, Belgium |
| Mathieu Lefort | Université de Lyon, France |
| Matteo Francobaldi | University of Bologna, Italy |
| Matteo Riondato | Amherst College, USA |
| Matteo Salis | University of Turin, Italy |
| Matthew B. Middlehurst | University of Southampton, UK |
| Matthia Sabatelli | University of Groningen, Netherlands |
| Mattia Cerrato | JGU Mainz, Germany |
| Mattia Setzu | University of Pisa, Italy |
| Mattis Hartwig | German Research Center for Artificial Intelligence, Germany |
| Matyas Bohacek | Stanford University, USA |
| Maximilian T. Fischer | University of Konstanz, Germany |
| Maximilian Münch | University of Applied Sciences, Würzburg-Schweinfurt, Germany |
| Maximilian Stubbemann | University of Hildesheim, Germany |
| Maximilian Thiessen | TU Wien, Austria |
| Maximilian von Zastrow | Southern Denmark University, Denmark |
| Megha Khosla | TU Delft, Netherlands |
| Meiyun Zuo | Renmin University of China, China |
| Meng Liu | National University of Defense Technology, China |
| Mengying Zhu | Zhejiang University, China |
| Michael Granitzer | University of Passau, Germany |
| Michael B. Ito | University of Michigan, USA |

| | |
|---|---|
| Michael G. Madden | National University of Ireland, Galway, Ireland |
| Michal Wozniak | Wroclaw University of Science and Technology, Poland |
| Michele Fontana | Università di Pisa, Italy |
| Michiel Stock | Ghent University, Belgium |
| Miguel Rocha | University of Minho, Portugal |
| Miguel Silva | INESC TEC, Portugal |
| Mike Holenderski | Eindhoven University of Technology, Netherlands |
| Milos Savic | University of Novi Sad, Serbia |
| Mina Rezaei | LMU Munich, Germany |
| Minh P. Nguyen | University of Texas, Austin, USA |
| Minyoung Choe | Korea Advanced Institute of Science and Technology, South Korea |
| Minyu Chen | Shanghai Jiaotong University, China |
| Miquel Perello-Nieto | University of Bristol, UK |
| Mira Kristin Jurgens | Ghent University, Belgium |
| Miriam Santos | University of Porto, Portugal |
| Mirko Bunse | TU Dortmund, Germany |
| Mirko Polato | University of Turin, Italy |
| Mitra Baratchi | LIACS, University of Leiden, Netherlands |
| Mohammed Elbamby | Telefonica Scientific Research, Spain |
| Moises Rocha dos Santos | University of Porto, Portugal |
| Monowar Bhuyan | Umeå University, Sweden |
| Morteza Rakhshaninejad | Ghent University, Belgium |
| Mounim A. El Yacoubi | Télécom SudParis, France |
| Muhammad Rajabinasab | University of Southern Denmark, Denmark |
| Muhao Guo | Arizona State University, USA |
| Mustapha Lebbah | Paris Saclay University-Versailles, France |
| Nabeel Hussain Syed | Rheinland-Pfälzische Technische Universität, Kaiserslautern-Landau, Germany |
| Nandyala Hemachandra | Indian Institute of Technology Bombay, India |
| Nannan Wu | Tianjin University, China |
| Nanqing Dong | Shanghai Artificial Intelligence Laboratory, China |
| Naresh Manwani | International Institute of Information Technology, Hyderabad, India |
| Natan Tourne | Ghent University, Belgium |
| Nate Veldt | Texas A&M, USA |
| Nathalie Japkowicz | American University, USA |
| Natthawut Kertkeidkachorn | Japan Advanced Institute of Science and Technology (JAIST), Japan |
| Ngoc-Son Vu | ENSEA, France |
| Nhat-Tan Bui | University of Arkansas, USA |

| | |
|---|---|
| Nian Li | Tsinghua University, China |
| Nick Lim | University of Waikato, New Zealand |
| Nico Piatkowski | Fraunhofer IAIS, Germany |
| Nicolas Roque dos Santos | University of São Paulo, Brazil |
| Niklas A. Strauss | LMU Munich, Germany |
| Nikolaj Tatti | Helsinki University, Finland |
| Nikolaos Nikolaou | University College London, UK |
| Nikolaos Stylianou | Information Technologies Institute, Greece |
| Nikos Kanakaris | University of Southern California, USA |
| Ning Xu | Southeast University, China |
| Nripsuta Saxena | University of Southern California, USA |
| Nuwan Gunasekara | Halmstad University, Sweden |
| Olga Kurasova | Vilnius University, Lithuania |
| Olga Slizovskaia | AstraZeneca, UK |
| Olivier Teste | IRIT, University of Toulouse, France |
| Oswald C. | NIT Trichy, India |
| Oswaldo Solarte-Pabon | Universidad del Valle, Colombia |
| Ozge Alacam | University of Bielefeld, Germany |
| P. S. Sastry | Indian Institute of Science, India |
| Pablo Olmos | Universidad Carlos III de Madrid, Spain |
| Panagiotis Karras | University of Copenhagen, Denmark |
| Panagiotis Symeonidis | University of the Aegean, Greece |
| Pance Panov | Jožef Stefan Institute, Slovenia |
| Paolo Bonetti | Politecnico di Milano, Italy |
| Paolo Merialdo | Università degli Studi Roma Tre, Italy |
| Paolo Mignone | University of Bari Aldo Moro, Italy |
| Pascal Welke | TU Wien, Austria |
| Patrick Y. Wu | American University, USA |
| Paul Caillon | LAMSADE Université Paris Dauphine - PSL, France |
| Paul Davidsson | Malmo University, Sweden |
| Paul Prasse | University of Potsdam, Germany |
| Paulo J. Azevedo | Universidade do Minho, Portugal |
| Pawel Teisseyre | Warsaw University of Technology, Poland |
| Pawel Zyblewski | Wroclaw University of Science and Technology, Poland |
| Pedro G. Ferreira | University of Porto, Portugal |
| Pedro Larrañaga | Technical University of Madrid, Spain |
| Pedro Ribeiro | University of Porto, Portugal |
| Pedro H. Abreu | CISUC, Portugal |
| Peijie Sun | Tsinghua University, China |
| Peng Wu | Shanghai Jiao Tong University, China |

| | |
|---|---|
| Pengpeng Qiao | Institute of Science Tokyo, Japan |
| Peter Karsmakers | KU Leuven, Belgium |
| Peter Schneider-Kamp | SDU, Denmark |
| Peter van der Putten | Leiden University, Netherlands |
| Petia Georgieva | University of Aveiro, Portugal |
| Philipp Vaeth | Technical University of Applied Sciences Würzburg-Schweinfurt and Universität Bielefeld, Germany |
| Philippe Preux | Inria, France |
| Phung Lai | SUNY-Albany, USA |
| Pierre Geurts | Montefiore Institute, University of Liège, Belgium |
| Pierre Monnin | Université Côte d'Azur, Inria, CNRS, I3S, France |
| Pierre Schaus | UC Louvain, Belgium |
| Pierre Wolinski | Paris Dauphine University - PSL, France |
| Pieter Robberechts | KU Leuven, Belgium |
| Pietro Sabatino | ICAR-CNR, Italy |
| Pingchuan Ma | HKUST, China |
| Piotr Habas | Amazon, USA |
| Piotr Lipinski | University of Wroclaw, Poland |
| Piotr Porwik | University of Silesia, Katowice, Poland |
| Prithwish Chakraborty | IBM Corporation, USA |
| Lucie Flek | Marburg University, Germany |
| Przemyslaw Biecek | Warsaw University of Technology, Poland |
| Qiang Sheng | Institute of Computing Technology, Chinese Academy of Sciences, China |
| Qiang Zhou | Nanjing University of Aeronautics and Astronautics, China |
| Rafet Sifa | Fraunhofer IAIS, Germany |
| Raha Moraffah | Arizona State University, USA |
| Raivydas Simanas | Vilnius University, Lithuania |
| Rajeev Rastogi | Amazon, USA |
| Ranya Almohsen | Baylor College of Medicine, USA |
| Raphael Romero | Ghent University, Belgium |
| Raquel Sebastiao | ESTGV-IPV & IEETA-UA, Portugal |
| Ravi Kolla | Sony Research India, India |
| Raza Ul Mustafa | Loyola University, USA |
| Remy Cazabet | Université de Lyon 1, France |
| Renhe Jiang | University of Tokyo, Japan |
| Reza Akbarinia | Inria, France |
| Ricardo P. M. Cruz | University of Porto (FEUP), Portugal |
| Ricardo B. Prudencio | Universidade Federal de Pernambuco, Brazil |
| Ricardo Rios | Federal University of Bahia, Brazil |

Ricardo Santos — Fraunhofer Portugal AICOS, Portugal
Riccardo Guidotti — University of Pisa, Italy
Robertas Damasevicius — Vytautas Magnus University, Lithuania
Roberto Corizzo — American University, USA
Roberto Interdonato — CIRAD, France
Rocio Chongtay — University of Southern Denmark, Denmark
Rohit Babbar — University of Bath, UK and Aalto University, Finland
Romain Tavenard — Université de Rennes, LETG/IRISA, France
Rosana Veroneze — LBiC, Italy
Ruggero G. Pensa — University of Turin, Italy
Rui Meng — BNU-HKBU United International College, USA
Rui Yu — University of Louisville, USA
Ruixuan Liu — Emory University, USA
Runqun Xiong — Southeast University, China
Runxue Bao — University of Pittsburgh, USA
Ruochun Jin — National University of Defense Technology, China
Ruta Juozaitiene — Vytautas Magnus University, Lithuania
Rytis Maskeliunas — Polsl, Poland
Salvatore Ruggieri — University of Pisa, Italy
Sam Verboven — Vrije Universiteit Brussel, Belgium
Sangkyun Lee — Korea University, South Korea
Sara Abdali — University of California, Riverside, USA
Sarah Masud — LCS2, IIIT-D, India
Sarwan Ali — Georgia State University, USA
Satoru Koda — Fujitsu Limited, Japan
Sebastian Buschjager — Lamarr Institute for ML and AI, Germany
Sebastian Jimenez — Ghent University, Belgium
Sebastian Meznar — Jožef Stefan Institute, Ljubljana, Slovenia
Sebastian Ventura Soto — University of Cordoba, Spain
Sebastien Razakarivony — Safran, France
Selpi Selpi — Chalmers University of Technology, Sweden
Sergio Greco — University of Calabria, Italy
Sergio Jesus — Feedzai, Portugal
Sha Lu — University of South Australia, Australia
Shalini Priya — Indian Institute of Technology Patna, India
Shanqing Guo — Shandong University, China
Shaofu Yang — Southeast University, China
Shazia Tabassum — INESCTEC, Portugal
Shengxiang Gao — Kunming University of Science and Technology, China

| | |
|---|---|
| Shichao Pei | University of Massachusetts, Boston, USA |
| Shin Matsushima | University of Tokyo, Japan |
| Shin-ichi Maeda | Preferred Networks, Japan |
| Shiwen Ni | Chinese Academy of Sciences, China |
| Shiyou Qian | Shanghai Jiao Tong University, China |
| Shu Zhao | Anhui University, China |
| Shuai Li | University of Cambridge, UK and University of Tokyo, Japan, Tsinghua University, China |
| Shuang Cheng | Institute of Computing Technology, Chinese Academy of Sciences, China |
| Shubhranshu Shekhar | Brandeis University, USA |
| Shurui Cao | Carnegie Mellon University, USA |
| Shuteng Niu | Mayo Clinic, USA |
| Siamak Ghodsi | Leibniz University of Hannover, Germany |
| Sihai Zhang | University of Science and Technology of China, China |
| Silvia Chiusano | Politecnico di Torino, Italy |
| Silviu Maniu | Université de Grenoble Alpes, France |
| Simon Gottschalk | L3S Research Center, Leibniz Universität Hannover, Germany |
| Simona Nistico | University of Calabria, Italy |
| Simone Angarano | Politecnico di Torino, Italy |
| Sinong Zhao | Nankai University, China |
| Siwei Wang | Intelligent Game and Decision Lab, China |
| Sofoklis Kitharidis | LIACS, Netherlands |
| Songlin Du | University of Melbourne, Australia |
| Songlin Du | Southeast University, China |
| Soumyajit Chatterjee | Nokia Bell Labs, USA |
| Sourav Dutta | Huawei Research Centre, China |
| Stefan Duffner | University of Lyon, France |
| Stefan Heindorf | Paderborn University, Germany |
| Stefan Kesselheim | Forschungszentrum Jülich, Germany |
| Stefano Bortoli | Huawei Research Center, China |
| Stefanos Vrochidis | Information Technologies Institute, CERTH, Greece |
| Steffen Thoma | FZI Research Center for Information Technology, Germany |
| Stephan Doerfel | Kiel University of Applied Sciences, Germany |
| Steven D. Prestwich | University College Cork, Ireland |
| Suman Banerjee | IIT Jammu, India |
| Sunil Aryal | Deakin University, Australia |
| Surabhi Adhikari | Columbia University, USA |

| | |
|---|---|
| Susan McKeever | TU Dublin, Ireland |
| Swati Swati | Universität der Bundeswehr München, Germany |
| Szymon Wojciechowski | Wroclaw University of Science and Technology, Poland |
| Talip Ucar | AstraZeneca, UK |
| Taro Tezuka | University of Tsukuba, Japan |
| Tatiana Passali | Aristotle University of Thessaloniki, Greece |
| Tatiane Nogueira Rios | UFBA, Brazil |
| Telmo M. Silva Filho | University of Bristol, UK |
| Teng Lin | Hong Kong University of Technology (Guangzhou), China |
| Teng Zhang | Huazhong University of Science and Technology, China |
| Thach Le Nguyen | Insight Centre, Ireland |
| Thang Duy Dang | Fujitsu Limited, Japan |
| Thanh-Son Nguyen | A*STAR, Singapore |
| Theresa Eimer | Leibniz University Hannover, Germany |
| Thiago Andrade | INESC TEC & University of Porto, Portugal |
| Thomas Bonald | Telecom Paris, France |
| Thomas Guyet | Inria, Centre de Lyon, France |
| Thomas Lampert | University of Strasbourg, France |
| Thomas L. Lee | University of Edinburgh, UK |
| Thomas Mortier | Ghent University, Belgium |
| Tianyi Chen | Boston University, USA |
| Tie Luo | University of Kentucky, USA |
| Tiehang Duan | Mayo Clinic, USA |
| Tijl De Bie | Ghent University, Belgium |
| Timilehin B. Aderinola | University College Dublin, Ireland |
| Timo Bertram | Johannes-Kepler Universität, Germany |
| Timo Ropinski | Ulm University, Germany |
| Tobias A. Hille | University of Kassel, Germany |
| Tom Hanika | University of Hildesheim, Germany |
| Tomas Kliegr | University of Economics, Prague, Czech Republic |
| Tomasz Michalak | University of Warsaw and Ideas NCBiR, Poland |
| Tomasz Walkowiak | Wroclaw University of Science and Technology, Poland |
| Tommaso Zoppi | University of Florence, Italy |
| Tong Li | Hong Kong University of Technology, China |
| Tong Mo | Peking University, China |
| Tongya Zheng | Hangzhou City University, China |
| Tonio Weidler | Maastricht University, Netherlands |
| Tony Lindgren | Stockholm University, Sweden |

| | |
|---|---|
| Tsunenori Mine | Kyushu University, Japan |
| Tuan Le | New Mexico State University, USA |
| Tuwe Lofstrom | Jönköping University, Sweden |
| Ulf Johansson | Jönköping University, Sweden |
| Vadim Ermolayev | Ukrainian Catholic University, Ukraine |
| Vahan Martirosyan | CentraleSupélec, Belgium |
| Vana Kalogeraki | Athens University of Economics and Business, Greece |
| Vanessa Gomez-Verdejo | Universidad Carlos III de Madrid, Spain |
| Vasileios Iosifidis | SCHUFA Holding, Germany |
| Vasilis Gkolemis | ATHENA RC, Greece |
| Victor Charpenay | Mines Saint-Etienne, France |
| Vincent Derkinderen | KU Leuven, Belgium |
| Vincent Lemaire | Orange Research, France |
| Vincenzo Pasquadibisceglie | University of Bari, Aldo Moro, Italy |
| Virginijus Marcinkevicius | Vilnius University, Lithuania |
| Vitor Cerqueira | University of Porto, Portugal |
| Vivek Kumar | Universität der Bundeswehr München, Germany |
| Vivek Srikumar | University of Utah, USA |
| Wagner Meira Jr. | UFMG, Brazil |
| Wei Wu | Ben Gurion University of the Negev, Israel |
| Weichen Li | RPTU Kaiserslautern-Landau, Germany |
| Weifeng Xu | Independent Researcher, China |
| Weike Pan | Shenzhen University, China |
| Weiwei Jiang | Beijing University of Posts and Telecommunications, China |
| Weiwei Sun | Carnegie Mellon University, USA |
| Weiwei Yuan | Nanjing University of Aeronautics and Astronautics, China |
| Weixiong Rao | Tongji University, China |
| Wen-Bo Xie | Southwest Petroleum University, China |
| Wenhao Li | Tongji University, China |
| Wenhao Zheng | Shopee, Singapore |
| Wenjie Feng | National University of Singapore, Singapore |
| Wenjie Xi | George Mason University, USA |
| Wenshui Luo | Nanjing University of Science and Technology, China |
| Wentao Yu | Nanjing University of Science and Technology, China |
| Wenzhe Yi | Wuhan University, China |
| Wenzhong Li | Nanjing University, China |
| Wojciech Rejchel | Nicolaus Copernicus University, Torun, Poland |

| | |
|---|---|
| Xi Jiang | Southern University of Science and Technology, China |
| Xiang Li | East China Normal University, China |
| Xiang Lian | Kent State University, USA |
| Xiao Ma | Beijing University of Posts and Telecommunications, China |
| Xiao Zhang | Shandong University, China |
| Xiaobing Zhou | Yunnan University, China |
| Xiaofeng Cao | University of Technology Sydney, Australia |
| Xiaofeng Gao | Shanghai Jiaotong University, China |
| Xiaojun Chen | Institute of Information Engineering, Chinese Academy of Sciences, China |
| Xiao-Jun Zeng | University of Manchester, UK |
| Xiaoming Zhang | Beihang University, China |
| Xiaoting Zhao | Etsy, USA |
| Xiaowei Mao | Beijing Jiaotong University, China |
| Xiaoyu Shi | Chinese Academy of Sciences, China |
| Xin Du | University of Edinburgh, UK |
| Xin Qin | California State University, Long Beach, USA |
| Xing Tang | Tencent, China |
| Xing Xing | Tongji University, China |
| Xinning Zhu | Beijing University of Posts and Telecommunications, China |
| Xinpeng Lv | National University of Defense Technology, China |
| Xintao Wu | University of Arkansas, USA |
| Xinyang Zhang | University of Illinois at Urbana-Champaign, USA |
| Xinyu Guan | Xi'an Jiaotong University, China |
| Xixun Lin | Chinese Academy of Sciences, China |
| Xiyue Zhang | University of Bristol, UK |
| Xuan-Hong Dang | IBM T.J. Watson Research Center, USA |
| Xue Li | University of Queensland, Australia |
| Xue Yan | Institute of Automation, Chinese Academy of Sciences, China |
| Xuefeng Chen | Chongqing University, China |
| Xuemin Wang | Guilin University of Electronic Technology, China |
| Yachuan Zhang | East China University of Science and Technology, China |
| Yan Zhang | Peking University, China |
| Yang Li | University of North Carolina at Chapel Hill, USA |
| Yang Shu | East China Normal University, China |
| Yang Wei | Nanjing University of Science and Technology, China |

| | |
|---|---|
| Yanhao Wang | East China Normal University, China |
| Yanmin Zhu | Shanghai Jiao Tong University, China |
| Yansong Y. L. Li | University of Ottawa, Canada |
| Yao-Xiang Ding | Nanjing University, China |
| Yaqi Xie | Carnegie Mellon University, USA |
| Yasutoshi Ida | NTT, Japan |
| Yaying Zhang | Tongji University, China |
| Ye Zhu | Deakin University, Australia |
| Yeon-Chang Lee | Ulsan National Institute of Science and Technology, South Korea |
| Yexiang Xue | Purdue University, USA |
| Yi Wang | Xinjiang Technical Institute of Physics and Chemistry, Chinese Academy of Sciences, China |
| Yifeng Gao | University of Texas, Rio Grande Valley, USA |
| Yilun Jin | Hong Kong University of Science and Technology, China |
| Yin Zhang | University of Electronic Science and Technology of China, China |
| Ying Chen | RMIT University, Australia |
| Yinsheng Li | Fudan University, China |
| Yong Li | Huawei European Research Center, China |
| Yongyu Wang | JD Logistics, China |
| Youhei Akimoto | University of Tsukuba/RIKEN AIP, Japan |
| You-Wei Luo | Sun Yat-sen University and Jiaying University, China |
| Yuchen Li | Baidu, China |
| Yuchen Yang | Harbin Institute of Technology, China |
| Yudi Zhang | Eindhoven University of Technology, Netherlands |
| Yuhao Li | University of Melbourne, Australia |
| Yuheng Jia | Southeast University, China |
| Yujia Zheng | CMU, USA |
| Yulong Pei | TU Eindhoven, Netherlands |
| Yuncheng Jiang | South China Normal University, China |
| Yuntao Shou | Xi'an Jiaotong University, China |
| Yunyun Wang | Nanjing University of Posts and Telecommunications, China |
| Yutong Ye | East China Normal University, China |
| Yuzhou Chen | University of California, Riverside, USA |
| Zahraa Abdallah | University of Bristol, UK |
| Zaineb Chelly Dagdia | UVSQ, Paris-Saclay, France |
| Zehua Cheng | University of Oxford, UK |
| Zeyu Chen | University of Auckland, New Zealand |

| | |
|---|---|
| Zhaocheng Ge | Huazhong University of Science and Technology, China |
| Zhe Yang | Soochow University, China |
| Zhen Liu | Guangdong University of Foreign Studies, China |
| Zheng Chen | Osaka University, Japan |
| Zhenghao Liu | Northeastern University, China |
| Zhenyu Yang | Macquarie University, Australia |
| Zhi Li | Tsinghua University, China |
| Zhichao Han | ETHZ, Switzerland |
| Zhihui Wang | Fudan University, China |
| Zhilong Shan | South China Normal University, China |
| Zhipeng Yin | Florida International University, USA |
| Zhipeng Zou | Nanjing University of Science and Technology, China |
| Zhiwen Xiao | Southwest Jiaotong University, China |
| Zhiwen Zhang | LocationMind, Japan |
| Zhixin Li | Guangxi Normal University, China |
| Zhiyong Cheng | Shandong Academy of Sciences, China |
| Zhong Chen | Southern Illinois University, USA |
| Zhong Li | Leiden University, Netherlands |
| Zhong Zhang | Tsinghua University, China |
| Zhongjing Yu | Peking University, China |
| Zhuang Liu | Dongbei University of Finance and Economics, China |
| Zhuo Cao | Forschungszentrum Jülich, Germany |
| Zhuoming Xie | Guangdong University of Technology, China |
| Zhuoqun Li | Louisiana State University, USA |
| Zicheng Zhao | Nanjing University of Science and Technology, China |
| Zichong Wang | Florida International University, USA |
| Zifeng Ding | University of Cambridge, UK |
| Ziheng Chen | Walmart, USA |
| Zijie J. Wang | Georgia Tech, USA |
| Zirui Zhuang | Beijing University of Posts and Telecommunications, China |
| Zixing Song | Chinese University of Hong Kong, China |
| Ziyu Wang | University of Tokyo, Japan |
| Ziyue Li | University of Cologne, Germany |
| Zongxia Xie | Tianjin University, China |
| Zongyue Li | LMU Munich, Germany |
| Zuojin Tang | Zhejiang University, China |

## List of Editors

| | |
|---|---|
| Bernhard Pfahringer | University of Waikato, New Zealand |
| Nathalie Japkowicz | American University, USA |
| Pedro Larrañaga | Technical University of Madrid, Spain |
| Rita P. Ribeiro | University of Porto, Portugal |
| Alípio M. Jorge | University of Porto, Portugal |
| Carlos Soares | University of Porto, Portugal |
| João Gama | University of Porto, Portugal |
| Pedro H. Abreu | University of Coimbra, Portugal |

## Program Committee – Applied Data Science Track

| | |
|---|---|
| Nasrullah Sheikh | IBM Research, USA |
| Aakarsh Malhotra | MasterCard, USA |
| Aakash Goel | Amazon, USA |
| Abdoulaye Sakho | Artefact, France |
| Abhijeet Pendyala | Ruhr-Universität Bochum, Germany |
| Abu Shad Ahammed | University of Siegen, Germany |
| Adi Lin | Didi, China |
| Aditya Gautam | Meta, USA |
| Ahmed K. Mohamed | Meta, USA |
| Akihiro Yoshida | Kyushu University, Japan |
| Akshay Sethi | MasterCard, USA |
| Alejandro Kuratomi | Stockholm University, Sweden |
| Alessandro Gambetti | Nova School of Business and Economics, Portugal |
| Alessandro Leite | INSA Rouen, Inria, France |
| Alessio Russo | Politecnico di Milano, Italy |
| Alex Beeson | University of Warwick, UK |
| Alexander Galozy | Halmstad University, Sweden |
| Alexander Karlsson | University of Skovde, Sweden |
| Alexander Kovalenko | Czech Technical University in Prague, Czech Republic |
| Alexey Zaytsev | Skoltech, Russia |
| Alina Bazarova | Forschungszentrum Jülich, Germany |
| Alix Lheritier | Amadeus SAS, France |
| Allan Tucker | Brunel University London, UK |
| Alvaro Figueira | CRACS and Universidade do Porto, Portugal |
| Aman Gulati | Amazon, USA |
| Amira Soliman | Halmstad University, Sweden |

| | |
|---|---|
| Ana Gjorgjevikj | Jožef Stefan Institute, Slovenia |
| Anders Holst | RISE SICS, Sweden |
| André C. P. L. F. de Carvalho | University of São Paulo, Brazil |
| Andrea Seveso | University of Milan-Bicocca, Italy |
| Andreas Bender | LMU Munich, Germany |
| Andreas Henelius | Independent Researcher, Finland |
| Andreas Holzinger | University of Natural Resources and Life Sciences, Vienna, Austria |
| Andrei Shelopugin | Independent Researcher, Brazil |
| Angelo Impedovo | Niuma, Italy |
| Aniket Chakrabarti | Amazon, USA |
| Animesh Prasad | Roku, USA |
| Anisio Lacerda | UFMG, Brazil |
| Anli Ji | Georgia State University, USA |
| Antoine Doucet | La Rochelle Université, France |
| Anton Borg | Blekinge Institute of Technology, Sweden |
| Antonio Bevilacqua | Meetecho, Italy |
| Antonis Klironomos | University of Mannheim, Germany |
| Aron Henriksson | Stockholm University, Sweden |
| Artur Chudzik | Polish-Japanese Academy of Information Technology, Poland |
| Arun Venkitaraman | EPFL, Switzerland |
| Arunabha Choudhury | ASML, Netherlands |
| Asem Omari | Higher Colleges of Technology, UAE |
| Ashman Mehra | Birla Institute of Technology and Science, India |
| Ashwani Rao | Amazon, USA |
| Asier Rodriguez | BBVA, Spain |
| Asma Atamna | Ruhr-Universität Bochum, Germany |
| Atiye Sadat Hashemi | Halmstad University, Sweden |
| Atul Anand Gopalakrishnan | SUNY Buffalo, USA |
| Avani Wildani | Emory University, USA |
| Aviv Rovshitz | Ben-Gurion University of the Negev, Israel |
| Axel Brando | Barcelona Supercomputing Center (BSC) and Universitat de Barcelona (UB), Spain |
| Azadeh Alavi | RMIT University, Australia |
| Beihong Jin | Institute of Software, China |
| Benoit Frenay | University of Namur, Belgium |
| Berkay Aydin | Georgia State University, USA |
| Bijaya Adhikari | University of Iowa, USA |
| Bin Li | Alibaba Group, China |
| Bo Pang | University of Auckland, New Zealand |
| Bogdan Ruszczak | Opole University of Technology, Poland |

| | |
|---|---|
| Bohao Qu | Agency for Science, China |
| Bruno Veloso | INESC TEC, FEP-UP, Portugal |
| Buyue Qian | Xi'an Jiaotong University, China |
| Camille Kurtz | Université Paris Cité, France |
| Cangbai Li | Guangdong University of Technology, China |
| Carlo Metta | ISTI CNR, Italy |
| Carlos N. Silla | Pontifical Catholic University of Paraná (PUCPR), Brazil |
| Cecile Bothorel | IMT Atlantique, France |
| Cesar Ferri | Universitat Politècnica Valencia, Spain |
| Chang Li | Apple, USA |
| Chang-Dong Wang | Sun Yat-sen University, China |
| Chaofan Li | Karlsruhe Institute of Technology, Germany |
| Chaoyuan Zuo | Nankai University, China |
| Chen Gao | Tsinghua University, China |
| Chen Li | Computer Network Information Center, China |
| Chen Zhao | Baylor University, USA |
| Chen-Wei Chang | Virginia Tech, USA |
| Chenxi Xue | Nanjing Normal University, China |
| Chongke Bi | Tianjin University, China |
| Christian M. Adriano | Hasso-Plattner Institute, Germany |
| Christophe Rodrigues | DVRC Pôle universitaire Léonard de Vinci, France |
| Chuan Li | Sorbonne University, LIPADE, France |
| Chunhui Zhang | Dartmouth College, USA |
| Cristina Soguero Ruiz | Rey Juan Carlos University, Spain |
| Daheng Wang | Amazon, USA |
| Daifeng Li | Sun Yat-sen University, China |
| Damien Fay | HPE Labs, Ireland |
| Dania Herzalla | Technology Innovation Institute, UAE |
| Daniel Lemire | University of Quebec (TELUQ), Canada |
| Daniel Trejo Banos | SDSC, USA |
| Daochen Zha | Rice University, USA |
| Dawei Cheng | Tongji University, China |
| Dayne Freitag | SRI International, USA |
| Di Yao | Institute of Computing Technology, China |
| Dimitris Nick Dimitriadis | Aristotle University of Thessaloniki, Greece |
| Diogo F. Soares | Universidade de Lisboa, Portugal |
| Dirk Pflueger | University of Stuttgart, Germany |
| Doheon Han | University of Notre Dame, USA |
| Dongxiang Zhang | Zhejiang University, China |
| Dongxiao Yu | Shandong University, China |

| | |
|---|---|
| Dugang Liu | Guangdong Laboratory of Artificial Intelligence and Digital Economy (Shenzhen), China |
| Ece Calikus | Uppsala University, Sweden |
| Edwyn Brient | Thales LAS/Mines Paris PSL, France |
| Efstathios Stamatatos | University of the Aegean, Greece |
| Elaine Faria | UFU, Brazil |
| Elio Masciari | University of Naples, Italy |
| Emilie Devijver | Université Grenoble Alpes, Inria, CNRS, Grenoble INP, LIG, France |
| Emmanuelle Claeys | IRIT, France |
| Enayat Rajabi | Halmstad University, Sweden |
| Enda Barrett | University of Galway, Ireland |
| Enyan Dai | Hong Kong University of Science and Technology (Guangzhou), China |
| Eric Peukert | ScaDS.AI, Germany |
| Eric Sanjuan | Avignon University, France |
| Erik Frisk | Linköping University, Sweden |
| Eui-Hong (Sam) Han | The Washington Post, USA |
| Eunil Park | Sungkyunkwan University, South Korea |
| Fabio Carrara | CNR-ISTI, Italy |
| Fabiola Pereira | Federal University of Uberlandia, Brazil |
| Fan Yang | Rice University, USA |
| Fangzhao Wu | MSRA, China |
| Fangzhou Shi | Didi Chuxing, China |
| Fathima Nuzla Ismail | State University of New York, USA |
| Flavio Bertini | University of Parma, Italy |
| Francesco Dente | EURECOM, France |
| Francesco Guerra | University of Modena e Reggio Emilia, Italy |
| Francesco Scala | CNR-ICAR, Italy |
| Francesco Spinnato | University of Pisa, Italy |
| Francesco Paolo Nerini | Sapienza University of Rome, Italy |
| Francisco P. Romero | UCLM, Spain |
| Franco Maria Nardini | ISTI-CNR, Italy |
| Francois Schwarzentruber | ENS Lyon, France |
| Fudong Lin | University of Delaware, USA |
| Gabriel Augusto Pinheiro | UNIFESP, Brazil |
| Gan Sun | South China University of Technology, China |
| Gargi Srivastava | Rajiv Gandhi Institute of Petroleum Technology Jais, India |
| Giacomo Boracchi | Politecnico di Milano, Italy |
| Giuseppe Garofalo | DistriNet, KU Leuven, Belgium |
| Giuseppina Andresini | University of Bari Aldo Moro, Italy |

| | |
|---|---|
| Goran Falkman | University of Skovde, Sweden |
| Grzegorz Nalepa | Jagiellonian University, Poland |
| Guanggang Geng | Jinan University, China |
| Guojun Liang | Halmstad University, Sweden |
| Haifang Li | Baidu, China |
| Haina Tang | University of Chinese Academy of Sciences, China |
| Hancheng Ge | Amazon, USA |
| Hao Li | National University of Defense Technology, China |
| Haohui Chen | CSIRO, Australia |
| Haomin Yu | Aalborg University, Denmark |
| Haoyi Xiong | Baidu, China |
| Hiba Najjar | DFKI, Germany |
| Hillol Kargupta | Agnik, USA |
| Hong Zhou | Meta, USA |
| Hongbin Pei | Xi'an Jiao Tong University, China |
| Hou-Wan Long | Chinese University of Hong Kong, China |
| Hua Wei | Arizona State University, USA |
| Huaiyuan Yao | Xi'an Jiaotong University, China |
| Huan Song | Amazon, USA |
| Hubert Baniecki | University of Warsaw, Poland |
| Hyunsung Kim | KAIST, Fitogether, South Korea |
| Ibtihal El Mimouni | Inria, France |
| Ildar Baimuratov | L3S Research Center, Germany |
| Ilir Jusufi | Blekinge Institute of Technology, Sweden |
| Inaam Ashraf | Bielefeld University, Germany |
| Ines Sousa | Fraunhofer AICOS, Portugal |
| Iris Heerlien | Saxion, Netherlands |
| Isak Samsten | Stockholm University, Sweden |
| Ishan Verma | TCS Research, India |
| Ismail Hakki Toroslu | METU, Turkey |
| Ivan Carrera | EPN, Ecuador |
| Jaakko Hollmen | Stockholm University, Sweden |
| Jairo Cugliari | Laboratoire ERIC, France |
| Jakub Nalepa | Silesian University of Technology, Poland |
| Jelica Vasiljević | Hoffmann-La Roche, Switzerland |
| Jens Lundstrom | Halmstad University, Sweden |
| Jesse Davis | KU Leuven, Belgium |
| Jiahui Bai | Meta, USA |
| Jiajun Gu | Carnegie Mellon University, USA |
| Jiali Pan | Department of Information Management, USA |

| | |
|---|---|
| Jian Yu | Auckland University of Technology, New Zealand |
| Jiangbin Zheng | Westlake University, China |
| Jianhua Yin | Shandong University, China |
| Jingbo Zhou | Baidu, China |
| Jingjing Liu | MD Anderson Cancer Center, USA |
| Jingwen Shi | Michigan State University, USA |
| Jingxuan Wei | University of Chinese Academy of Sciences, China |
| Jinyoung Han | Sungkyunkwan University, South Korea |
| Jiue-An Yang | City of Hope Beckman Research Institute, USA |
| Joao R. Campos | University of Coimbra, Portugal |
| Jochen De Weerdt | KU Leuven, Belgium |
| Joe Tekli | Lebanese American University, Lebanon |
| Joel Ky | University of Lorraine, CNRS, Inria, France |
| John McCall | Robert Gordon University, UK |
| John Mitros | University College Dublin, Ireland |
| Jonas Fischer | Ruhr-Universität Bochum, Germany |
| Jonas Nordqvist | Linnaeus University, Sweden |
| Joydeep Chandra | Indian Institute of Technology Patna, India |
| Julian Martin Rodemann | LMU Munich, Germany |
| Jun Shen | University of Wollongong, Australia |
| Junichi Tatemura | Google, USA |
| Junxuan Li | Microsoft, USA |
| Jyun-Yu Jiang | Amazon Science, USA |
| Kai Wang | Shanghai Jiao Tong University, China |
| Kaiping Zheng | National University of Singapore, Singapore |
| Kaiwen Dong | University of Notre Dame, USA |
| Katarzyna Bozek | University of Cologne, Germany |
| Katerina Schindlerova | UniVie, Austria |
| Katharina Dost | Jožef Stefan Institute, Slovenia |
| Katsiaryna Mirylenka | Zalando SE, Germany |
| Keith Burghardt | ISI, Germany |
| Klaus Brinker | Hamm-Lippstadt University of Applied Sciences, Germany |
| Koki Kawabata | Osaka University, Japan |
| Korbinian Randl | Stockholm University, Sweden |
| Krzysztof Krawiec | Poznań University of Technology, Poland |
| Krzysztof Kutt | Jagiellonian University, Poland |
| Kwan Hui Lim | Singapore University of Technology and Design, Singapore |
| Lamija Lemes | University of Zenica, Bosnia & Herzegovina |
| Le Nguyen | University of Oulu, Finland |

| | |
|---|---|
| Lei Li | Hong Kong University of Science and Technology (Guangzhou), China |
| Lei Liu | York University, Canada |
| Li Liu | Chongqing University, China |
| Li Zhang | University College London, UK |
| Liang Tang | Google, USA |
| Liang Tong | NEC Labs America, USA |
| Liang Wang | Alibaba Group, China |
| Lina Yao | University of New South Wales, Australia |
| Lingxiao Li | Michigan State University, USA |
| Lingyang Chu | McMaster University, Canada |
| Lixin Zou | Wuhan University, China |
| Lluis Garcia-Pueyo | Meta, USA |
| Lou Salaun | Nokia Bell Labs, USA |
| Luca Corbucci | University of Pisa, Italy |
| Luca Pappalardo | ISTI, Italy |
| Luca Romeo | University of Macerata, Italy |
| Luis Ferreira | Olympus Medical Products Portugal, Portugal |
| Luis Miguel Matos | ALGORITMI Centre, Portugal |
| Lukas Grasmann | TU Wien, Austria |
| Lukas Pensel | Johannes Gutenberg University Mainz, Germany |
| Maciej Grzenda | Warsaw University of Technology, Poland |
| Maciej Piernik | Poznań University of Technology, Poland |
| Madiraju Srilakshmi | Dream Sports, India |
| Mads C. Hansen | A.P. Moller-Maersk, Denmark |
| Mahardhika Pratama | University of South Australia, Australia |
| Mahmoud Rahat | Halmstad University, Sweden |
| Man Tianxing | Jilin University, China |
| Manish Gupta | Microsoft, USA |
| Manos Papagelis | York University, Canada |
| Manuel Lopes | Instituto Tecnico Superior, Portugal |
| Manuel Portela | Universitat Pompeu Fabra, Spain |
| Marc Tommasi | Lille University, France |
| Marco Fisichella | Leibniz Universität, Hannover, Germany |
| Maria Riveiro | Jonkoping University, Sweden |
| Maria Ulan | RISE Research Institutes of Sweden, Sweden |
| Marian Scuturici | LIRIS, France |
| Marianne Clausel | IECL, France |
| Mario Doller | University of Applied Sciences, Kufstein, Austria |
| Marius Schwammle | DLR/BT, Germany |
| Markus Gotz | Karlsruhe Institute of Technology (KIT), Germany |

| | |
|---|---|
| Markus Leyser | Technische Universität Dresden, Germany |
| Martin Boldt | Blekinge Institute of Technology, Sweden |
| Martin Mladenov | Google, USA |
| Martin Vita | Institute of Physics, Czech Academy of Sciences, Czech Republic |
| Matthias Demant | Fraunhofer ISE, Germany |
| Matthias Galipaud | SDSC, Switzerland |
| Matthias Petri | Amazon, USA |
| Matthieu Latapy | CNRS, France |
| Maurice Van Keulen | University of Twente, Netherlands |
| Maxime Cordy | University of Luxembourg, Luxembourg |
| Maxwell J. Jacobson | Purdue University, USA |
| Md Nahid Hasan | Miami University, USA |
| Md Zia Ullah | Edinburgh Napier University, UK |
| Mehtab Alam Syed | CIRAD, France |
| Melanie Neubauer | University of Leoben, Austria |
| Meng Chen | Shandong University, China |
| Mengxuan Zhang | Australian National University, Australia |
| Miao Fan | NavInfo, China |
| Michael Bain | University of New South Wales, Australia |
| Michele Bernardini | Uni eCampus.It, Italy |
| Michiel Dhont | EluciDATA Lab of Sirris, Belgium |
| Mickael Coustaty | L3i Laboratory, France |
| Miguel Couceiro | LORIA, France |
| Mihaela Mitici | Utrecht University, Netherlands |
| Min Lee | Singapore Management University, Singapore |
| Min Hun Lee | Singapore Management University, Singapore |
| Mina Rezaei | LMU Munich, Germany |
| Ming Ma | Inner Mongolia University, China |
| Minghao Chen | Tencent, China |
| Mirco Nanni | CNR-ISTI Pisa, Italy |
| Mirjam Wattenhofer | Google, USA |
| Mirko Marras | University of Cagliari, Italy |
| Mitra Heidari | University of Melbourne, Australia |
| Modesto Castrillon-Santana | Universidad de Las Palmas de Gran Canaria, Spain |
| Mohammadmehdi Saberioon | German Research Centre for Geosciences, Germany |
| Mohammed Amer | Fujitsu Research of Europe, Germany |
| Mohammed Ghaith Altarabichi | Halmstad University, Sweden |
| Mojgan Kouhounestani | University of Melbourne, Australia |
| Moonki Hong | Sogang University, South Korea |

| | |
|---|---|
| Munira Syed | Procter & Gamble, USA |
| Nan Li | Microsoft, USA |
| Narendhar Gugulothu | TCS Research, India |
| Nedra Mellouli | LIASD, Portugal |
| Ngoc Son Le | University of Hildesheim, Germany |
| Niklas Lavesson | Blekinge Institute of Technology, Sweden |
| Niraj Kumar | Fujitsu, Japan |
| Nitish Kumar | MasterCard, USA |
| Nuno Cruz Garcia | FCUL, Portugal |
| Nuno R. P. S. Guimaraes | INESC TEC, University of Porto, Portugal |
| Nuwan Gunasekara | Halmstad University, Sweden |
| Pablo Picazo-Sanchez | Halmstad University, Sweden |
| Pablo Torrijos Arenas | Universidad de Castilla-La Mancha, Spain |
| Pablo Jose Del Moral Pastor | Ekkono.ai, Finland |
| Pan He | Auburn University, USA |
| Panagiotis Kanellopoulos | University of Essex, UK |
| Panagiotis Papadakos | FORTH-ICS, Greece |
| Pandey Shourya Prasad | International Institute of Information Technology, Bangalore, India |
| Panpan Xu | Amazon AWS, USA |
| Paola Velardi | Sapienza University of Rome, Italy |
| Paolo Cintia | Kode, Italy |
| Pascal Plettenberg | Intelligent Embedded Systems, Italy |
| Paul Boniol | Inria, France |
| Pavel Blinov | Sber AI Lab, Russia |
| Pawel Parczyk | Wroclaw University of Science and Technology, Poland |
| Pedro M. Ferreira | University of Lisbon, Portugal |
| Pedro Seber | MIT, USA |
| Peng Qiao | NUDT, China |
| Pengyuan Wang | University of Georgia, USA |
| Petr Olegovich Sokerin | Skoltech, Russia |
| Philipp Bach | University of Hamburg, Germany |
| Philipp Froehlich | TU Darmstadt, Germany |
| Philipp Schmidt | Amazon Research, USA |
| Philipp Zech | University of Innsbruck, Austria |
| Pinar Karagoz | Middle East Technical University (METU), Turkey |
| Ping Luo | Chinese Academy of Sciences, China |
| Po Yang | University of Sheffield, UK |
| Pop Petrica | Technical University of Cluj-Napoca, Romania |
| Prathap Manohar Joshi R | Zoho Corporation, India |

| | |
|---|---|
| Praveen Borra | Florida Atlantic University, USA |
| Praveen Paruchuri | IIIT Hyderabad, India |
| Qian Li | Curtin University, Australia |
| Qihang Yao | Georgia Institute of Technology, USA |
| Qiwei Han | Nova School of Business and Economics, Portugal |
| Quentin Duchemin | Université Gustave Eiffel, France |
| Radu Tudor Ionescu | University of Bucharest, Romania |
| Rafal Kucharski | Jagiellonian University, Poland |
| Rafet Sifa | Fraunhofer IAIS & University of Bonn, Germany |
| Ramasamy Savitha | I2R A*STAR, Singapore |
| Ran Yu | DSIS Research Group, Singapore |
| Ranga Raju Vatsavai | North Carolina State University, USA |
| Raphael Couturier | University of Bourgogne Franche-Comte (UBFC), France |
| Renato M. Assuncao | ESRI, USA |
| Renaud Lambiotte | University of Oxford, UK |
| Reuben Kshitiz Borrison | ABB, Switzerland |
| Reza Shirvany | Zalando SE, Germany |
| Ricardo R. Pereira | Feedzai, Portugal |
| Riccardo Rosati | Università Politecnica delle Marche, Ancona, Italy |
| Richard Allmendinger | University of Manchester, UK |
| Richard Nordsieck | XITASO GmbH IT and Software Solutions, Germany |
| Richi Nayak | Queensland University of Technology, Australia |
| Roberto Trasarti | CNR, Italy |
| Rogerio Luis de C. Costa | Polytechnic of Leiria, Portugal |
| Romain Ilbert | Huawei Paris Research Center, France |
| Roy Ka-Wei Lee | Singapore University of Technology and Design, Singapore |
| Ruilin Wang | University of Aberdeen, UK |
| Sabrina Gaito | Università degli Studi di Milano, Italy |
| Sai Karthikeya Vemuri | Computer Vision Group Jena, Italy |
| Saisubramaniam Gopalakrishnan | Quantiphi, USA |
| Sajjad Shumaly | Max-Planck-Institut for Polymer Research, Germany |
| Salvatore Rinzivillo | KDD Lab, ISTI, CNR, Italy |
| Samaneh Shafee | LASIGE, Portugal |
| Sandra Wissing | Fachhochschule Münster, Germany |
| Sarwan Ali | Georgia State University, USA |
| Sebastian Becker | Fraunhofer ISST, Germany |

| | |
|---|---|
| Sebastian Honel | Linnaeus University, Sweden |
| Selin Colakhasanoglu | Saxion University of Applied Sciences, Netherlands |
| Senzhang Wang | Central South University, China |
| Sepideh Nahali | York University, Canada |
| Shahrooz Abghari | Blekinge Institute of Technology, Sweden |
| Shahroz Tariq | CSIRO, Australia |
| Shang Yanlei | BUPT, China |
| Shen Liang | Paris Cité University, France |
| Shengheng Liu | Southeast University, China |
| Shereen Elsayed | University of Hildesheim, Germany |
| Shi-ting Wen | NingboTech University, China |
| Shiv Krishna Jaiswal | Walmart Global Tech, USA |
| Shoujin Wang | Macquarie University, Australia |
| Shuai Li | University of Cambridge, UK and University of Tokyo, UK |
| Shuchu Han | Capital One Financial Group, Japan |
| Simon F. Weinberger | EssilorLuxottica, France |
| Siyuan Chen | Guangzhou University, China |
| Snehanshu Saha | BITS Pilani Goa Campus, India |
| Souhaib Ben Taieb | University of Mons, Abu Dhabi |
| Sriparna Saha | IIT Patna, India |
| Stefan Rueping | Fraunhofer IAIS, Germany |
| Stephane Chretien | Université Lyon 2, France |
| Sunil Aryal | Deakin University, Australia |
| Susana Ladra | University of A Coruña, Spain |
| Szymon Bobek | Jagiellonian University, Poland |
| Szymon Jaroszewicz | Institute of Computer Science, Poland |
| Szymon Wilk | Poznań University of Technology, Poland |
| Tanel Tammet | Tallinn University of Technology, Estonia |
| Thanh Thi Nguyen | Monash University, Australia |
| Thiago Zangato | Université Sorbonne Paris Nord, France |
| Theodora Tsikrika | Information Technologies Institute, Greece |
| Thibault Girardin | Université Jean Monnet, France |
| Thomas Czernichow | Darwinlabs, Portugal |
| Thorsteinn Rognvaldsson | Halmstad University, Sweden |
| Tiago Mendes-Neves | FEUP/INESC TEC, Portugal |
| Tianshu Yu | Chinese University of Hong Kong (Shenzhen), China |
| Ting Su | Imperial College London, UK |
| Tingrui Qiao | University of Auckland, New Zealand |
| Tobias Glasmachers | Ruhr-Universität Bochum, Germany |

| | |
|---|---|
| Tomas Olsson | RISE SICS, Sweden |
| Tome Eftimov | Jožef Stefan Institute, Slovenia |
| Topon Paul | Toshiba Corporation, Japan |
| Tsuyoshi Okita | Kyushu Institute of Technology, Japan |
| Unmesh Padalkar | Dream Sports, India |
| Vahid Shahrivari Joghan | Utrecht University, Netherlands |
| Valerio Bonsignori | Unipisa, Italy |
| Vanessa Borst | University of Würzburg, Germany |
| Venkata Sai Prakash Mukkamala | Quantiphi Analytics, USA |
| Veselka Boeva | Blekinge Institute of Technology, Sweden |
| Viacheslav Komisarenko | University of Tartu, Estonia |
| Vikas Gupta | HPCL, India |
| Vinayak Gupta | University of Washington, Seattle, USA |
| Vincent Auriau | Artefact Research Center, France |
| Vincenzo Pasquadibisceglie | University of Bari, Aldo Moro, Italy |
| Vincenzo Scotti | KASTEL, Germany |
| Vinothkumar Kolluru | Stevens Institute of Technology, USA |
| Vladimir Mic | Aarhus University, Denmark |
| Wang-Zhou Dai | Nanjing University, China |
| Wee Siong Ng | Institute for Infocomm Research, Singapore |
| Wei Cheng | NEC Laboratories America, USA |
| Wei Li | Harbin Engineering University, China |
| Wei Wang | Tsinghua University, China |
| Wei-Peng Chen | Fujitsu Research of America, USA |
| Wentao Wang | Michigan State University, USA |
| Wentao Wu | Microsoft Research, USA |
| Wray Buntine | VinUniversity, Vietnam |
| Xianchao Wu | Nvidia, USA |
| Xiang Lian | Kent State University, USA |
| Xianli Zhang | Xi'an Jiaotong University, China |
| Xiaobo Jin | Xi'an Jiaotong-Liverpool University, China |
| Xiaofei Zhou | University of Chinese Academy of Sciences, China |
| Xiaofeng Gao | Shanghai Jiaotong University, China |
| Xiaolin Han | Northwestern Polytechnical University, China |
| Xin Huang | Hong Kong Baptist University, China |
| Xin Liu | East China Normal University, China |
| Xing Tang | Tencent, China |
| Xiuqiang He | Tencent, China |
| Xiuyuan Hu | Tsinghua University, China |
| Xueping Peng | University of Technology Sydney, Australia |
| Yanchang Zhao | CSIRO, Australia |

| | |
|---|---|
| Yang Guo | Xidian University Hangzhou Institute of Technology, China |
| Yang Song | Apple, USA |
| Yijun Zhao | Fordham University, USA |
| Yinghui Wu | Case Western Reserve University, USA |
| Yingzhen Lin | Harbin Institute of Technology (Shenzhen), China |
| Yintao Yu | University of Illinois at Urbana-Champaign, USA |
| Yixiang Fang | Chinese University of Hong Kong, China |
| Yixuan Cao | Institute of Computing Technology, China |
| Yizheng Huang | York University, Canada |
| Yongchao Liu | Ant Group, China |
| Yu Huang | Indiana University, USA |
| Yu Wang | University of Oregon, USA |
| Yuantao Fan | Halmstad University, Sweden |
| Yucheng Zhou | University of Macau, China |
| Yue Shi | Meta, USA |
| Yueyuan Zheng | Beihang University, China |
| Yunchuan Shi | University of Sydney, Australia |
| Yunjun Gao | Zhejiang University, China |
| Yuting Ding | Southeast University, China |
| Yuzhuo Li | University of Auckland, New Zealand |
| Zahra Kharazian | Stockholm University, Sweden |
| Zahra Taghiyarrenani | Halmstad University, Sweden |
| Zahraa Abdallah | University of Bristol, UK |
| Zeyi Wen | Hong Kong University of Science and Technology (Guangzhou), China |
| Zeyu Zhu | National University of Defense Technology, China |
| Zhanyu Liu | Shanghai Jiao Tong University, China |
| Zhaogeng Liu | Jilin University, China |
| Zhaohui Liang | National Library of Medicine, USA |
| Zhen Zhang | Shandong University, China |
| Zhendong Chu | Squirrel Ai Learning, China |
| Zheng Zhang | University of California, USA |
| Zhengze Li | University of Göttingen, Germany |
| Zhibin Gu | Hebei Normal University, China |
| Zhuang Liu | Dongbei University of Finance and Economics, China |
| Ziyu Guan | Xidian University, China |
| Zoltan Miklos | Université de Rennes, France |
| Zunlei Feng | Zhejiang University, China |

## Program Committee – Demo Track

| | |
|---|---|
| Andrzej Wójtowicz | Adam Mickiewicz University, Poznań, Poland |
| Anna Sokol | University of Notre Dame, USA |
| Arian Pasquali | Faktion AI, Belgium |
| Bruno Veloso | INESC TEC - FEP-UP, Portugal |
| Chongsheng Zhang | Henan University, China |
| Christos Doulkeridis | University of Piraeus, Greece |
| Danqing Zhang | PathOnAI.org, USA |
| Fátima Rodrigues | INESC TEC, Portugal |
| Grigorii Khvatskii | University of Notre Dame, USA |
| Joe Germino | University of Notre Dame, USA |
| Jungwon Seo | University of Stavanger, Norway |
| Ke Li | University of Exeter, England |
| Manfred Jaeger | Aalborg University, Denmark |
| Marcin Luckner | Warsaw University of Technology, Poland |
| Mehwish Alam | Institut Polytechnique de Paris, France |
| Nuno Moniz | University of Notre Dame, USA |
| Tânia Carvalho | FCUP, Portugal |
| Vitor Cerqueira | FEUP, Portugal |
| Wei-Wei Du | National Yang Ming Chiao Tung University, Taiwan |

## Additional Reviewers

Andrea D'Angelo
Patrick Altmeyer
Guiseppina Adresini
Vedangi Bengali
Michele Bernardini
Zhi Cao
Louis Carpentier
Alessio Cascione
Lilia Chebbah
Meng Ding
Roberto Esposito
Alina Fastowski
Roger Ferrod
Michele Fontana
Chang Gong
Michal Grzejdziak-Zdziarski
Paul Hahn

Antonia Hain
Md Athikul Islam
Michael Ito
Philipp Jahn
Rahul Kumar
Bishal Lakha
Yuwen Liu
Jerry Lonlac
Shijie Luo
Francesca Naretto
Navid Nobani
Diego Coello de Portugal
Joana Santos
Francesco Scala
Richard Serrano
Nuno Silva
Francesco Spinnato

Pedro C. Vieira
Xiao Wang
Yunyun Wang
Qi Wen
Jianye Xie

Huaiyuan Yao
Yutong Ye
Obaidullah Zaland
Efstratios Zaradoukas
Nan Zhang

## Sponsors

### Diamond

### Platinum

liv  Organization

**Gold**

**Silver**

**Bronze**

**Other Sponsors**

**Partners**

# Keynotes

# Many Good Models Leads to …

Cynthia Rudin

Duke University, USA

**Abstract.** As it turns out, many good models leads to amazing things! The Rashomon Effect, coined by Leo Breiman, describes the phenomenon that there exist many equally good predictive models for the same dataset.

This phenomenon happens for many real datasets, and when it does it sparks both magic and consternation, but mostly magic. In light of the Rashomon Effect, my collaborators and I propose to reshape the way we think about machine learning, particularly for tabular data problems in the nondeterministic (noisy) setting. I'll address how the Rashomon Effect impacts (1) the existence of simple-yet-accurate models, (2) flexibility to address user preferences, such as fairness and monotonicity, without losing performance, (3) uncertainty in predictions, fairness, and explanations, (4) reliable variable importance, (5) algorithm choice, specifically, providing advanced knowledge of which algorithms might be suitable for a given problem, and (6) public policy. I'll also discuss a theory of when the Rashomon Effect occurs and why: interestingly, noise in data leads to a large Rashomon Effect. My goal is to illustrate how the Rashomon Effect can have a massive impact on the use of machine learning for complex problems in society.

# Towards Causal Artificial Intelligence

Elias Bareinboim

Columbia University, USA

**Abstract.** While a significant portion of AI scientists and engineers believe we are on the verge of achieving highly general forms of AI, I offer a critical appraisal of this view through a causal lens. In particular, building on foundational developments in the field, I will present my perspective on the relationship between intelligence and causality – and the central role of the latter in building intelligent systems and advancing credible data science.

I frame this discussion in terms of five core capabilities that we should expect from an intelligent AI system: performing causal reasoning and articulating explanations; making precise, surgical, and sample-efficient decisions; generalizing across changing conditions and environments; generating and simulating in a causally consistent manner; and learning causal structures and variables.

In this talk, I will elaborate on this perspective and share current progress toward building causally intelligent AI systems. A more detailed discussion of this thesis is provided in my forthcoming textbook, a draft of which is available here: https://causalai-book.net/.

# Not Just a Trend: Institutionalizing XAI for Responsible and Compliant AI Systems

Francisco Herrera

Granada University, Spain

**Abstract.** As artificial intelligence (AI) systems increasingly mediate decisions in high-stakes domains – from healthcare and finance to public policy – the demand for explainable AI (XAI) has grown rapidly. Yet many current XAI approaches remain disconnected from the practical needs of stakeholders and the requirements of emerging regulatory frameworks. This talk argues that XAI must not be treated as a passing trend or optional technical add-on, but as a foundational principle in the design and deployment of AI systems. We critically examine the state of the field, exposing the gap between model-centric explainability and stakeholder-centric accountability. In response, we propose a framework that aligns explainability with legal, ethical, and social responsibilities, emphasizing co-design with affected users, sensitivity to institutional contexts, and governance over opacity. Our goal is to advance XAI from superficial compliance toward deeply integrated transparency that fosters trust, accountability, and responsible innovation.

# Compositional Intelligence: Coordinating Multiple LLMs for Complex Tasks

Mirella Lapata

University of Edinburgh, UK

**Abstract.** Recent years have witnessed the rise of increasingly larger and more sophisticated language models (LMs) capable of performing every task imaginable, sometimes at (super)human level. In this talk, I will argue that in many realistic scenarios, solely relying on a single general-purpose LLM is suboptimal. A single LLM is likely to underrepresent real-world data distributions, heterogeneous skills, and task-specific requirements. Instead, I will discuss multi-LLM collaboration as an alternative to monolithic generative modeling. By orchestrating multiple LLMs, each with distinct roles, perspectives, or competencies, we can achieve more effective problem-solving while being more inclusive and explainable. I will illustrate this approach through two case studies: narrative story generation and visual question answering, showing how a society of agents can collectively tackle complex tasks while pursuing complementary subgoals. Additionally, I will explore how these agent societies leverage reasoning to improve performance.

# Towards a Fairer World: Uncovering and Addressing Human and Algorithmic Biases

Nuria Oliver

ELLIS Alicante Foundation, Spain

**Abstract.** In my talk, I will first briefly present ELLIS Alicante1, the only ELLIS unit that has been created from scratch as a non-profit research foundation devoted to responsible AI for Social Good. Next, I will provide an overview of AI with a focus on the ethical implications and limitations of today's AI systems, including algorithmic discrimination and bias. On this topic, I will present a few examples of our work on uncovering and mitigating both human and algorithmic biases with AI.

On the human front, I will present the body of work that we have carried out in the context of AI-based beauty filters that are so popular on social media. On the algorithmic front, I will explain the main approaches to address algorithmic discrimination and I will present three novel methods to achieve fairer decisions.

# Tensor Logic: A Simple Unification of Neural and Symbolic AI

Pedro Domingos

University of Washington, USA

**Abstract.** Deep learning has achieved remarkable successes in language generation and other tasks, but is extremely opaque and notoriously unreliable. Both of these problems can be overcome by combining it with the sound reasoning and transparent knowledge representation capabilities of symbolic AI. Tensor logic accomplishes this by unifying tensor algebra and logic programming, the formal languages underlying respectively deep learning and symbolic AI. Tensor logic is based on the observation that predicates are compactly represented Boolean tensors, and can be straightforwardly extended to compactly represent numeric ones. The two key constructs in tensor logic are tensor join and project, numeric operations that generalize database join and project. A tensor logic program is a set of tensor equations, each expressing a tensor as a series of tensor joins, a tensor project, and a univariate nonlinearity applied elementwise. Tensor logic programs can succinctly encode most deep architectures and symbolic AI systems, and many new combinations.

In this talk I will describe the foundations and main features of tensor logic, and present efficient inference and learning algorithms for it. A system based on tensor logic achieves state-of-the-art results on a suite of language and reasoning tasks. How tensor logic will fare on trillion-token corpora and associated tasks remains an open question.

# Artificial Intelligence for Science

Sašo Džeroski

Jožef Stefan Institute, Slovenia

**Abstract.** Artificial intelligence is already transforming science, with its future impact expected to be even greater. Realizing this potential requires addressing key scientific challenges, such as ensuring explainability (of models and their predictions), learning effectively from limited data, and integrating data with prior domain knowledge. It also requires the provision of support for open and reproducible science through formalizing and sharing scientific knowledge.

I will present an overview of my research on the development of AI methods suitable for use in science. These include methods for explainable machine learning – including multi-target prediction and relational learning – that deliver accurate yet interpretable models suitable for complex scientific domains. These methods have been applied in environmental science, life science and materials science. Learning from limited data is critical in science. I will discuss two complementary approaches: semi-supervised learning, which leverages unlabeled data directly, together with labeled data, and foundation models, which use representations learned from vast unlabeled data to support downstream tasks with minimal supervision, i.e., limited amounts of labeled data. Both paradigms expand AI's reach into data-scarce scientific problems.

I will then present our work on automated scientific modeling, where we learn interpretable models of dynamical systems – such as process-based models and differential equations – from time series data and domain knowledge. Finally, I will highlight the role of ontologies and semantic technologies in experimental computer science, including machine learning and optimization. In these areas, we have developed ontologies for the representation and annotation of both data and other artefacts produced by science, such as algorithms, models, and results of experiments.

# Contents – Part VI

**Recommender Systems**

Counterfactual Multi-player Bandits for Explainable Recommendation
Diversification ................................................................. 3
    *Yansen Zhang, Bowei He, Xiaokun Zhang, Haolun Wu, Zexu Sun,
    and Chen Ma*

RAE: A Rule-Driven Approach for Attribute Embedding in Property
Graph Recommendation ........................................................ 21
    *Sibo Zhao, Michael Bewong, Selasi Kwashie, Junwei Hu,
    and Zaiwen Feng*

**Reinforcement Learning**

Collaborative Value Function Estimation Under Model Mismatch:
A Federated Temporal Difference Analysis .................................. 41
    *Ali Beikmohammadi, Sarit Khirirat, Peter Richtárik,
    and Sindri Magnússon*

Reward Shaping for User Satisfaction ....................................... 59
    *Konstantina Christakopoulou, Can Xu, Sai Zhang, Sriraj Badam,
    Trevor Potter, Daniel Li, Hao Wan, Xinyang Yi, Ya Le, Chris Berg,
    Eric Bencomo Dixon, Ed H. Chi, and Minmin Chen*

Decentralizing Multi-agent Reinforcement Learning with Temporal
Causal Information ............................................................ 77
    *Jan Corazza, Hadi Partovi Aria, Hyohun Kim, Daniel Neider, and Zhe Xu*

De Novo Molecular Design Enabled by Direct Preference Optimization
and Curriculum Learning ...................................................... 95
    *Junyu Hou*

Hybrid Cross-Domain Robust Reinforcement Learning ................... 112
    *Linh Le Pham Van, Minh Hoang Nguyen, Hung Le, Hung The Tran,
    and Sunil Gupta*

Viability of Future Actions: Robust Safety in Reinforcement Learning
via Entropy Regularization .................................................. 129
    *Pierre-François Massiani, Alexander von Rohr, Lukas Haverbeck,
    and Sebastian Trimpe*

Continual Visual Reinforcement Learning with A Life-Long World Model .....  146
    *Minting Pan, Wendong Zhang, Geng Chen, Xiangming Zhu, Siyu Gao, Yunbo Wang, and Xiaokang Yang*

UCB-Driven Utility Function Search for Multi-objective Reinforcement Learning ............................................................  163
    *Yucheng Shi, David Lynch, and Alexandros Agapitos*

Efficient and Generalized End-to-End Autonomous Driving System with Latent Deep Reinforcement Learning and Demonstrations ...............  179
    *Zuojin Tang, Xiaoyu Chen, Yongqiang Li, and Jianyu Chen*

Generalization of Compositional Tasks with Logical Specification via Implicit Planning ....................................................  198
    *Duo Xu and Faramarz Fekri*

A Bilevel Reinforcement Learning Framework with Language Prior Knowledge ............................................................  216
    *Xue Yan, Yan Song, Xinyu Cui, Filippos Christianos, Haifeng Zhang, Jun Wang, and David Mguni*

**Representation Learning**

Learning from Stochastic Teacher Representations Using Student-Guided Knowledge Distillation ................................................  235
    *Muhammad Haseeb Aslam, Clara Martinez, Marco Pedersoli, Alessandro Lameiras Koerich, Ali Etemad, and Eric Granger*

BatMan-CLR: Making Few-Shots Meta-learners Resilient Against Label Noise .................................................................  254
    *Jeroen M. Galjaard, Robert Birke, Juan F. Pérez, and Lydia Y. Chen*

Spectral Distribution Alignment for Enhanced Generalization in Regression ...  272
    *Kaiyu Guo, Zijian Wang, Brian C. Lovell, and Mahsa Baktashmotlagh*

Prompting without Panic: Attribute-Aware, Zero-Shot, Test-Time Calibration ...........................................................  289
    *Ramya Hebbalaguppe, Tamoghno Kandar, Abhinav Nagpal, and Chetan Arora*

Leveraging Gradient Information for Out-of-Domain Performance Estimations ..........................................................  306
    *Ekaterina Khramtsova, Mahsa Baktashmotlagh, Guido Zuccon, Xi Wang, and Mathieu Salzmann*

Projective Pruning for Decoupling Weights .............................. 322
    Tommy Chu and Alexander Kovalenko

Two-Stage Temporal Knowledge Graph Completion Based
on Reinforcement Learning ............................................. 340
    Dong Li, Yong Wei, Xinyi Dong, Jingyou Sun, LinLin Ding, and Yue Kou

Beyond the Visible: Multispectral Vision-Language Learning for Earth
Observation .......................................................... 359
    Clive Tinashe Marimo, Benedikt Blumenstiel, Maximilian Nitsche,
    Johannes Jakubik, and Thomas Brunschwiler

Improving Temporal Knowledge Graph Reasoning with Hierarchical
Semantic-Aware Contrastive Learning .................................... 376
    Renning Pang, Yao Liu, Yanglei Gan, Tingting Dai, Yashen Wang,
    Xiaojun Shi, Tian Lan, and Qiao Liu

I-GLIDE: Input Groups for Latent Health Indicators in Degradation
Estimation ........................................................... 395
    Lucas Thil, Jesse Read, Rim Kaddah, and Guillaume Doquet

Learnable Diffusion for Wavelets in Scattering Networks: Towards
both Interpretability and Performance in Graph Representation Learning ...... 412
    Toan Van Tran and Hung Son Nguyen

Subgraph Gaussian Embedding Contrast for Self-supervised Graph
Representation Learning ............................................... 430
    Shifeng Xie, Aref Einizade, and Jhony H. Giraldo

Rethinking Graph Domain Adaptation: A Spectral Contrastive Perspective ..... 448
    Haoyu Zhang, Yuxuan Cheng, Wenqi Fan, Yulong Chen, and Yifan Zhang

Grouped Discrete Representation for Object-Centric Learning .............. 465
    Rongzhen Zhao, Vivienne Wang, Juho Kannala, and Joni Pajarinen

ETT-CKGE: Efficient Task-Driven Tokens for Continual Knowledge
Graph Embedding ...................................................... 481
    Lijing Zhu, Qizhen Lan, Qing Tian, Wenbo Sun, Li Yang, Lu Xia,
    Yixin Xie, Xi Xiao, Tiehang Duan, Cui Tao, and Shuteng Niu

**Resource Efficiency**

Unified Framework for Pre-trained Neural Network Compression
via Decomposition and Optimized Rank Selection ......................... 499
    Ali Aghababaei-Harandi and Massih-Reza Amini

Fine-Tune Smarter, Not Harder: Parameter-Efficient Fine-Tuning
for Geospatial Foundation Models .................................... 516
   *Francesc Marti Escofet, Benedikt Blumenstiel, Linus Scheibenreif,*
   *Paolo Fraccaro, and Konrad Schindler*

Transformer with Sparse Adaptive Mask for Network Dismantling ........... 533
   *Yu Liu, Fanghao Hu, Haojun Huang, and Bang Wang*

**Author Index** ....................................................... 551

# Recommender Systems

# Counterfactual Multi-player Bandits for Explainable Recommendation Diversification

Yansen Zhang[1], Bowei He[1], Xiaokun Zhang[1], Haolun Wu[2], Zexu Sun[3], and Chen Ma[1(✉)]

[1] Department of Computer Science, City University of Hong Kong, Hong Kong, China
{yanszhang7-c,boweihe2-c}@my.cityu.edu.hk, chenma@cityu.edu.hk
[2] School of Computer Science, McGill University, Montreal, QC, Canada
haolun.wu@mail.mcgill.ca
[3] Gaoling School of Artificial Intelligence, Renmin University of China, Beijing, China
sunzexu21@ruc.edu.cn

**Abstract.** Existing recommender systems tend to prioritize items closely aligned with users' historical interactions, inevitably trapping users in the dilemma of "filter bubble". Recent efforts are dedicated to improving the diversity of recommendations. However, they mainly suffer from two major issues: 1) a lack of explainability, making it difficult for the system designers to understand how diverse recommendations are generated, and 2) limitations to specific metrics, with difficulty in enhancing non-differentiable diversity metrics. To this end, we propose a **C**ounterfactual **M**ulti-player **B**andits (CMB) method to deliver explainable recommendation diversification across a wide range of diversity metrics. Leveraging a counterfactual framework, our method identifies the factors influencing diversity outcomes. Meanwhile, we adopt the multi-player bandits to optimize the counterfactual optimization objective, making it adaptable to both differentiable and non-differentiable diversity metrics. Extensive experiments conducted on three real-world datasets demonstrate the applicability, effectiveness, and explainability of the proposed CMB.

**Keywords:** Diversified recommendation · Counterfactual framework · Multi-armed bandits

## 1 Introduction

Recommendation systems (RS) are widely deployed on various online platforms, such as Google, Facebook, and Yahoo!, to mitigate information overload.

---

**Supplementary Information** The online version contains supplementary material available at https://doi.org/10.1007/978-3-032-06106-5_1.

However, existing recommendation methods [13,21,35] only prioritize recommending the most relevant items to users, which can have negative consequences for both users and service providers. Users may experience the "filter bubble" [20] problem, leading to limited content diversity, while content providers may face the "Matthew Effect" [18] where new content lacks exposure. Therefore, improving recommendation diversity is essential to enhance the overall user experience and maintain a healthy ecosystem for content providers.

Various approaches have been proposed to diversify the recommended items. Existing methods for diversification can be generally classified into three categories [31]: pre-processing, in-processing, and post-processing methods. Pre-processing methods involve modifying or selecting interaction data before model training [7,40]. In-processing methods, such as treating the need for diversity as a kind of regularization [5,29] or a ranking score [17], integrate diversification strategies into the training process directly. Post-processing methods, like MMR [22,27] and DPP [4,14,30], re-rank the recommended items based on relevance and diversity metrics after the model training.

Unfortunately, current methods still suffer from two main limitations. Firstly, current methods, such as [4,5,7,29,30,40], do not provide adequate explainability regarding how factors affect the diversity of recommendations at the (latent) feature level. This limitation makes it difficult for system designers to understand the underlying drivers of diversity, hindering efforts to enhance model diversity and potentially reducing user satisfaction. Secondly, most diversification methods, like [4,5,17,30,40], rely on diversity metrics to evaluate recommendation results, but they often fail to optimize these metrics directly because these metrics are mostly non-differentiable, as highlighted in a recent survey [31]. While several methods, such as those described in [33], strive to optimize some diversity metrics directly, they are only suitable for very few specific non-differentiable diversity metrics, like $\alpha$-nDCG [8], and cannot handle more commonly used metrics like Prediction Coverage or Subtopic Coverage [10].

To address the aforementioned challenges, we propose a counterfactual framework for explainable recommendation diversification. In response to the first limitation, we propose to identify the factors influencing diversity outcomes under the counterfactual framework. In this framework, perturbations are applied to the representation of items to adjust the diversity level of the ranking lists. Our goal is to identify the "minimal" changes to a specific factor in the factor space that can effectively switch the recommendation results to a desired level of diversity. Then in response to the second limitation, we design a gradient-free Counterfactual Multi-player Bandits (CMB) method to learn these perturbations by optimizing the diversity of recommended items, which is no longer constrained by diversity metrics and recommendation models. The bandit-based approach searches for the best perturbations applied to different factors, which also provides insights for explaining the recommendation diversification: *the factors with more perturbations have more potential to influence both the accuracy and diversity*. Finally, as there is a growing need to achieve a better trade-off between accuracy and diversity, we redesign the optimization objective considering accuracy and diversity metrics simultaneously. Overall, our proposed approach offers a more flexible and adaptable framework that can optimize various diversity metrics directly, and provides a promising solution to the explanation of recommendation diversification.

To summarize, the contributions of this work are as follows:

- To explain recommendation diversification, we employ the counterfactual framework to discover the meaningful factors that affect recommendation accuracy and diversity trade-off.
- To optimize a range of differentiable and non-differentiable diversity metrics, we propose a bandit-based diversity optimization approach that is agnostic to diversity metrics and recommendation models.
- To validate the applicability, effectiveness, and explainability of our method, we conducted extensive experiments on multiple real-world datasets and diversity metrics.

## 2 Related Work

### 2.1 Recommendation Diversification

To address the "filter bubble" and reduced provider engagement issues, it is crucial to recommend accurate and diverse items for a healthier online marketplace. Existing diversification methods are typically offline and categorized as pre-processing, in-processing, and post-processing methods [31]. Pre-processing methods [7,40] involve preparing interaction data before the model training. In-processing integrates diversity into the training process, using it as regularization [5,29] or a ranking score [17,33]. Post-processing, the most scalable, includes greedy-based methods like MMR [3,22,27] and DPP [4,14,30], which adjust item selection and rankings to balance relevance and diversity, and refinement-based methods [26], which modify positions or replace items based on diversity metrics. Other online methods, such as bandit strategies [9], treat diversity as part of the score on each arm (item or topic) in the bandit recommendation algorithms and reinforcement learning [23,39], continuously update based on user feedback for long-term optimization.

Although these methods enhance recommendation diversity, they do not provide explanations of the monopoly phenomenon of recommended items or the mechanisms behind their diversity improvements. Our work seeks to optimize recommendation diversity and offer explanations for these issues.

### 2.2 Explainable Recommendation

Explainable recommendations have attracted significant attention in academia and industry, aiming to enhance transparency, user satisfaction, and trust [28,36–38]. Early methods focused on generating individualized explanations, often customizing models and using auxiliary information [32,38]. For example, the Explicit Factor Model (EFM) [38] recommends products based on features extracted from user reviews. Other approaches decouple explanations from the recommendation model, making them post-hoc and model-agnostic [6,24]. Recently, counterfactual reasoning has been widely used to improve explainability. For instance, CEF [11] uses counterfactual reasoning to explain fairness in feature-aware recommendation systems.

This work focuses on explaining recommendation diversification. While existing approaches help interpret recommendation models, they overlook diversity, which is the main focus of our work.

## 3 Methodology

### 3.1 Preliminaries

**Problem Formulation.** Given a user set $\mathcal{U}$, an item set $\mathcal{V}$, and the corresponding user-item interactions set $\mathcal{T}$, the purpose of explainable diversification is to recommend accurate and also diverse items that meet user interests, while offering explainability to the diversification. Formally, we need to provide the diverse top-$K$ recommendation list $R^u \subset \mathcal{V}(|R^u| = K)$ to each user $u$, and analyze what leads to the diversified results.

**Base Recommendation Models.** Given the user latent feature matrix $\mathbf{P} \in \mathbb{R}^{d \times |\mathcal{U}|}$ and item latent feature matrix $\mathbf{Q} \in \mathbb{R}^{d \times |\mathcal{V}|}$, where $d$ is the dimension of the latent feature matrices. We define a base recommendation model $g$ that predicts the user-item ranking score $\hat{y}_{u,v}$ for user $u$ and item $v$ by:

$$\hat{y}_{u,v} = g(\mathbf{p}_u, \mathbf{q}_v \mid \mathbf{Z}, \mathbf{\Theta}), \tag{1}$$

where $\mathbf{p}_u \in \mathbb{R}^d$ and $\mathbf{q}_v \in \mathbb{R}^d$ are the latent feature vector of user $u$ and item $v$, respectively. The symbol $\mathbf{\Theta}$ denotes the model parameters, and $\mathbf{Z}$ represents all other auxiliary information. Since collaborative filtering (CF) methods are still mainstream in current recommendation systems, we mostly work on the factors with latent features of CF methods. Without loss of generality, we can also target the raw features (e.g., age, gender, etc.), which will be discussed in Sect. 4.4. We explore two popular and effective instances of $g$: **BPRMF** [21] and **LightGCN** [13]. The loss function for the base model adopts the Bayesian Personalized Ranking loss function.

**Diversity Metrics.** Among all diversity metrics, we discuss the following four most popular metrics [7,31]. **Novelty-biased Normalized Discounted Cumulative Gain ($\alpha$-nDCG)** [8], which is a subtopic-level metric derived from NDCG, accounting for subtopics and item redundancy, where $\alpha$ applies geometric penalization for redundancy. **Subtopic Coverage (SC)** [10], which is a subtopic-level coverage of a recommended item list $R^u$ in the whole item set. **Prediction Coverage (PC)** [10], which is an item-level coverage of all recommendation lists $R^u$ in the whole item set. **Intra-List Average Distance (ILAD)** [34], which is an item-level metric that measures diversity by averaging the dissimilarity between item pairs in the recommendation list $R^u$. We use cosine similarity for dissimilarity calculation.

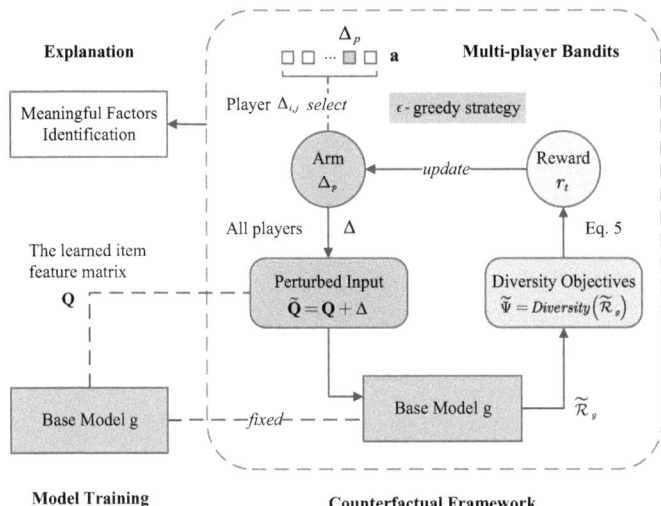

**Fig. 1.** The architecture of CMB. CMB consists of three major stages: the first stage of base model training, the second stage of counterfactual framework within multi-player bandits optimization, and the third stage of explanation. The $\mathbf{Q}$ is the learned item latent feature matrix from the base model $g$. The $\widetilde{\Psi}$ in the green part is alterable, which can be diversity or the trade-off between diversity and accuracy.

### 3.2 Counterfactual Framework for Explainable Diversification

Current diversification approaches generate diverse lists that are hard to explain and control. However, understanding the underlying diversity mechanism is crucial for making intelligent decisions in real-world applications. Inspired by counterfactual reasoning [11], we develop a perturbation-based framework for explaining the diversification of the recommendation lists.

The essential idea behind the proposed explanation model is to discover a perturbation matrix $\Delta$ on items' factors by solving a counterfactual optimization problem that maximizes diversity, as well as identify which factors are the underlying drive of diversified recommendations. After identifying these factors, it is easy to generate feature-based explanations for the given recommendation model $g$ and guide the system to make appropriate decisions that increase the recommendation diversity. Generally, given a recommendation model $g$, we have a certain recommendation result $\mathcal{R}_g = \{R^{u_1}, R^{u_2}, \cdots, R^{u_i}, \cdots, R^{u_{|\mathcal{U}|}}\} (|R^{u_i}| = K, i = 1, 2, \cdots, |\mathcal{U}|)$ containing all users' top-$K$ recommendation lists, where $R^{u_i}$ represents the top-$K$ items list recommended to user $u_i$ by the base model $g$. We denote the recommendation diversity of $g$ as,

$$\Psi = Diversity(\mathcal{R}_g), \qquad (2)$$

where $Diversity(\cdot)$ can be any of the previously introduced diversity measurements in Sect. 3.1.

Specifically, for the learned item latent feature matrix $\mathbf{Q} \in \mathbb{R}^{d \times |\mathcal{V}|}$ from $g$, we slightly intervene with an equal-size matrix $\Delta \in \mathbb{R}^{d \times |\mathcal{V}|}$. In detail, a small perturbation $\Delta_{i,j}$ will be added to feature $i$ of item $j$ ($\mathbf{Q}_{i,j}$) to obtained the perturbed input $\widetilde{\mathbf{Q}}$. That is,

$$\widetilde{\mathbf{Q}} = \mathbf{Q} + \Delta. \tag{3}$$

With this perturbed item latent feature matrix $\widetilde{\mathbf{Q}}$, the base model $g$ will change the recommendation from $\mathcal{R}_g$ to a new counterfactual result $\widetilde{\mathcal{R}}_g$ with a new diversity measure $\widetilde{\Psi}$,

$$\widetilde{\Psi} = Diversity(\widetilde{\mathcal{R}}_g). \tag{4}$$

Here, our goal is to find the minimum intervention on item factors that will result in the maximum improvement in terms of diversity. Thus, the objective function would be:

$$\max_{\Delta} \|\widetilde{\Psi}\|_2^2 - \lambda_1 \|\Delta\|_1, \tag{5}$$

where $\lambda_1$ is a hyperparameter that controls the balance between two terms: the first maximizes the predefined diversity, and the second constrains the perturbation by reflecting the distance between the original input and the counterfactuals. To minimize changes in item factors, we apply $L_1$ norm constraint on $\Delta$ and scale its absolute values between $[0, 1]$, encouraging more $\Delta$ as 0 and highlighting the factors that most influence diversity.

### 3.3 Multi-player Bandits for Diversity Optimization

According to certain needs of the diversity, various metrics can be used to optimize Eq. 5 for learning the perturbation $\Delta$. For example, $\alpha$-nDCG or SC metric can be employed to ensure broader coverage of subtopics in the recommendation list, while ILAD or PC metric can be used to enhance item-level diversity.

However, a significant challenge is that most diversity metrics are non-differentiable, making it difficult to define a proxy for their optimization [31, 33]. For instance, among the four metrics discussed in Sect. 3.1, only ILAD is differentiable, complicating the integration of non-differentiable metrics into gradient-based counterfactual frameworks. To overcome this, we propose a bandit-based method to learn the perturbation matrix $\Delta$, enabling the optimization of diverse objectives without relying on gradient computation.

The multi-armed bandit problem [2] models decision-making under uncertain rewards, where a player chooses among various options ("arms") to maximize cumulative payoff by balancing exploration and exploitation. This approach is well-suited for optimizing non-differentiable objectives within a counterfactual framework. Therefore, in our specific problem, each item feature is treated as a player, selecting an appropriate arm to construct the final perturbation matrix. Moreover, our problem can be further conceptualized as a multi-player bandit scenario [1], where players collaborate to optimize a shared reward, which serves as the objective in the counterfactual framework.

Specifically, we treat each variable $\Delta_{i,j}$ in $\Delta$ as a player; for simplicity, we denote it as $p(|p| = d \times |\mathcal{V}|)$, and then select a suitable arm $\Delta_p$ from arms $\mathbf{a}$ for every $p$ iteratively to maximize the objective in the counterfactual framework. Assume the total number of iterations for one player $p$ to select an arm is $T$; our problem can be formulated by maximizing the following $T$-step cumulative reward for each player:

$$V^T = \max \sum_{t=1}^{T} r_t, \quad (6)$$

where $r_t$ is the reward at the iteration step $t$ obtained from all players by selecting arms, as calculated by Eq. 5. In each iteration, every player selects a particular arm and gets $\Delta$ from all players to calculate the reward. This process continues as players select arms in subsequent iterations based on the obtained rewards. The iterative process repeats until the final iteration, where each player selects the optimal arm to achieve diversification. At this point, the value of the perturbation $\Delta$ can be justified.

More specifically, before commencing the algorithm, it is necessary to define the arm values from which the players can make their selections. To achieve this, we utilize the following method to initialize the arms $\mathbf{a}$ for each player $p$:

$$\mathbf{a} = \text{INIT}(A, n_A), \quad (7)$$

where $A$ and $n_A$ represent the perturbation threshold and the number of arms, respectively. The $\text{INIT}(\cdot)$ method samples $n_A$ values evenly from $[-A, A]$. For simplicity, this initialization is applied to each player, and the item latent feature matrix $\mathbf{Q}$ is scaled to $[-1, 1]$ using maximum absolute scaling ($\mathbf{Q} = \mathbf{Q}/|max(\mathbf{Q})|$). At each iteration $t$, players independently choose an arm $\Delta_p$ from $\mathbf{a}$ based on arm selection strategies like $\epsilon$-greedy or UCB [16,25], with experiments showing that $\epsilon$-greedy is more efficient and effective. The selection strategy of $\epsilon$-greedy strategy is as follows:

$$\Delta_p^t = \begin{cases} \arg\max_{\Delta_p \in \mathbf{a}}(V_\mathbf{a}^t) & \text{with probability } 1 - \epsilon, \\ \text{a random arm} & \text{with probability } \epsilon, \end{cases} \quad (8)$$

where $\Delta_p^t$ and $V_\mathbf{a}^t$ are the arm value selected by the player and the cumulative reward vector containing all arms for the player in the $t$ iteration, respectively.

When all players have selected the arm $\Delta_p^t$ based on the arm selection strategy, we can get the $\Delta$ and further the reward $r_t$ (Eq. 5) based on the counterfactual result $\widetilde{\mathcal{R}}_g$. To reduce the computational complexity, we update the cumulative reward value $V_{\Delta_p}^{t+1}$ of the corresponding arm $\Delta_p$ selected by each player $p$ in iteration $t+1$ by an incremental average method:

$$\begin{aligned}
V_{\Delta_p}^{t+1} &= \frac{1}{n}\sum_{i=1}^{n} r_i, \\
&= \frac{1}{n}\left(r_n^t + \sum_{i=1}^{n-1} r_i\right), \\
&= \frac{1}{n}\left(r_t + (n-1)\frac{1}{n-1}\sum_{i=1}^{n-1} r_i\right), \\
&= \frac{1}{n}\left(r_t + (n-1)V_{\Delta_p}^t\right), \\
&= \frac{1}{n}\left(r_t + nV_{\Delta_p}^t - V_{\Delta_p}^t\right), \\
&= V_{\Delta_p}^t + \frac{1}{n}\left(r_t - V_{\Delta_p}^t\right),
\end{aligned} \qquad (9)$$

where $n$ is the times that arm $\Delta_p$ has been selected by player $p$ till iteration $t$. Thus, the model iteratively learns and adjusts the $\Delta$ until convergence.

The challenge in diversified recommendation is to enhance diversity while preserving accuracy, i.e., maximizing diversity without significantly compromising accuracy. To better balance these two aspects, we propose a redesign of the optimization objective (Eq. 5), particularly the counterfactual diversity measurement $\widetilde{\Psi}$. As previously discussed, while a suitable diversity metric for $\widetilde{\Psi}$ can be chosen, it often leads to some loss in accuracy. To achieve an optimal balance, inspired by [3,4], we redesign $\widetilde{\Psi}$ to balance both accuracy and diversity simultaneously. Specifically,

$$\widetilde{\Psi} = \lambda_2 \times Accuracy(\widetilde{\mathcal{R}}_g) + (1-\lambda_2) \times Diversity(\widetilde{\mathcal{R}}_g), \qquad (10)$$

where $\lambda_2$ is a hyperparameter to control the trade-off between accuracy and diversity, and $Accuracy(\cdot)$ and $Diversity(\cdot)$ represent accuracy metrics (e.g., Recall@K, NDCG@K, etc.) and diversity metrics (Sect. 3.1), respectively.

**Time Complexity Analysis.** In the $\epsilon$-greedy strategy for multi-armed bandits, arm selection and incremental reward updates both have $O(1)$ time complexity in each step. However, if the reward update uses a complex equation (e.g., Eq. 5), the overall time complexity in each step will depend on that equation.

**Discussion.** 1) We mainly work on the latent features of items to explain the recommendation diversification. The key consideration is that current mainstream recommendation models still originate from collaborative filtering methods, which are based on latent features. These motivate us to work on the latent features for controlling the diversity level of recommendation results. It is worth noting that our model can both work raw and latent features. 2) The main reason why we decided to apply the perturbation $\Delta$ to the features of items is that perturbing at the items' feature level enables us to identify specific features that impact the diversity of the model at a more fine-grained feature level. 3) The multi-armed bandits method, unlike previous approaches, is primarily utilized in online recommendation scenarios. In our study, we employ this method to optimize the learning objective in the counterfactual framework, especially targeting and optimizing the non-differentiable diversity metrics directly.

### 3.4 Meaningful Factors Identification as Explanation

Once finishing optimization, we get the "minimal" changes $\Delta$ and the corresponding recommendation results under such changes. The values of $\Delta$ indicate the influence of item factors on the accuracy-diversity trade-off of the recommendation lists generated by the base model $g$. Specifically, compared with the initial item latent feature matrix $\mathbf{Q}$, after adding the values of $\Delta$, the model $g$ is supposed to generate more diverse lists. Therefore, the perturbation $\Delta$ provides insights for our explanation. In particular, larger absolute values of $\Delta$ correspond to a greater need for the corresponding factors to promote greater diversity.

Based on the above analysis, after we identify each factor's "ability" to incur the diversity of the recommendation list, we further select the most meaningful factors of the items affecting diversity and give insights into recommendation systems. We provide two perspectives on detecting the most meaningful factors here, namely CMB-Individual and CMB-Shared.

$$\begin{cases} \text{CMB-Individual,} & \textit{feature-level} \\ \text{CMB-Shared,} & \textit{item-level} \end{cases}$$

Specifically, the strategy of CMB-Individual is to directly select the factors corresponding to the higher absolute values of $\Delta$ on the factors as an explanation for each user. The CMB-Shared strategy is that we take the absolute values of $\Delta$, compute the mean value by rows, and compress the $\Delta$ into a vector $\Delta_v \in \mathbb{R}^d$,

$$\Delta_v = MEAN(|\Delta|, dim = 0), \tag{11}$$

and then choose the factors corresponding to the higher values of $\Delta_v$ as an explanation. After discovering the most meaningful factors, we can adjust the values of these factors to meet the corresponding needs of diversity.

### 3.5 Overall Procedure

The entire procedure contains three stages, as shown in Fig. 1. In the first stage, the base model $g$ introduced above will be trained. In the second stage, the counterfactual framework is first constructed. Based on this, the bandit algorithm is used to learn the perturbations by optimizing the diversity of the recommended top-$K$ lists. Our framework is model-agnostic and applicable to any recommendation model $g$. Meanwhile, our model is metric-agnostic since the optimization objective can be any diversity metric. In the final stage, two strategies are utilized to discover the most meaningful factors for recommendation diversification.

**Table 1.** The statistics of datasets.

| Dataset | #User | #Item | #Subtopic | #Interaction | Density |
|---------|-------|-------|-----------|--------------|---------|
| ML1M    | 5,950 | 3,125 | 18        | 573,726      | 0.0309  |
| ML10M   | 51,692| 7,135 | 19        | 4,752,578    | 0.0129  |
| CDs     | 13,364| 29,294| 30        | 371,204      | 0.0009  |

## 4 Experiments

In this section, we mainly focus on the following questions:

- **RQ1:** Does our method get better recommendation diversification effects than the state-of-art methods? Especially the trade-off between recommendation accuracy and diversity.
- **RQ2:** Do the selected top features play a significant role in diversification performance?
- **RQ3:** Are our generated feature-level diversification explanations reasonable and intuitive in real cases?

Given the limited space, for a more detailed experiment setup and the results, we invite the reader to check out the Appendix for the supplementary material.

### 4.1 Experiment Setup

**Datasets** We performed experiments on three widely used real-world datasets, *MovieLens 1M* [12] (*ML1M*), *MovieLens 10M* [12] (*ML10M*), and *Amazon CDs and Vinyl* [19] (*CDs*) to evaluate the models under different data scales and application scenarios. The statistics of the datasets are shown in Table 1.

For all datasets, we convert ratings to implicit feedback, treating ratings no less than four (out of five) as positive and all other ratings as missing entries. To optimize base models, we randomly sample 3 negative instances for each user's positive interaction. For the *CDs* dataset, we use the top 30 categories with the highest frequency as subtopic information according to the metadata. Each dataset is split 8:1:1 for training, test, and validation. We independently run all models five times and report the average results.

**Baselines.** To verify the effectiveness of our proposed CMB method, we compare it with the following representative baselines. Two vanilla recommendation models **BPRMF** [21] and **LightGCN** [13], which are introduced in Sect. 3.1. Two recommendation diversification methods **MMR** [3] and **DPP** [4]. In addition, we also explore the method **CMB**$^{\text{Gradient}}$, which represents our method is directly optimized for differentiable metrics (e.g., ILAD) by using the gradient method instead of the proposed bandit method.

**Evaluation Metrics.** In all experiments, we evaluate the recommendation performance using accuracy and diversity metrics on Top-$K$ ($K = 10, 20$) lists, where $K$ represents the list length as discussed earlier during training. For all metrics, the higher the value is, the better the performance is. **Accuracy:** we evaluate the accuracy of the ranking list using Recall@K and NDCG@K. **Diversity:** we evaluate the recommendation diversity by the $\alpha$-nDCG@K, SC@K, PC@K, and ILAD@K introduced previously.

**Implementation Details.** In our experiments, we employ BPRMF and LightGCN as the base model $g$, with LightGCN set to three layers of the graph neural network. For baselines, BPRMF calculates the relevance scores for MMR and constructs the kernel matrix for DPP. The trade-off parameter for MMR and DPP is empirically set to 0.9 after testing values from $\{0.1, 0.3, 0.5, 0.7, 0.9\}$, prioritizing guaranteeing the optimal accuracy performance as much as possible. All models have a latent feature dimension of 50, with $K$ set to 20 for counterfactual learning. The $\alpha$ in $\alpha$-nDCG is set to 0.5 same as [17,22,27,33], and model parameters are optimized by Adam [15] with a learning rate of 0.005. In the bandit algorithm, we set the threshold of arm values $A$ to 0.3, the number of arms $n_A$ to 61, and $\epsilon$ to 0.1. The hyperparameters $\lambda_1$, $\lambda_2$, and the total number of iterations $T$ are set to 5, 0.9, and 200, respectively. The source code is available at https://github.com/Forrest-Stone/CMB.

## 4.2 Performance Comparison (RQ1)

Tables 2, 3, and 4 compare the performance of different methods under two base models. Our model is denoted as CMB$_{\text{BPRMF}}$ when using BPRMF, and CMB$_{\text{LightGCN}}$ when using LightGCN. The * in CMB-* represents the specific objective $\widetilde{\Psi}$ optimized in Eq. 5. For instance, CMB-$\alpha$-nDCG means that we adopt the $\alpha$-nDCG metric for $\widetilde{\Psi}$, while CMB-$\alpha$-nDCG-NDCG means that we use the trade-off optimization objective (Eq. 10) of $\alpha$-nDCG and NDCG. When optimizing a single diversity metric, $\lambda_1$ is set to 0 for optimal results. BPRMF is the default base model $g$ unless otherwise specified. The observations from Tables 2, 3, and 4 are as follows.

**Trade-off Observations.** First, as shown in Table 2, CMB achieves a better balance between accuracy and diversity than other methods. While diversification methods like DPP improve diversity performance, they often significantly compromise accuracy performance. For example, DPP increases ILAD@10 on *ML1M* by 83.73% but causes a 75.43% drop in Recall@10, which is counterproductive to the primary goal of recommendation systems. In contrast, our method achieves an acceptable balance between accuracy and diversity. For instance, CMB$_{\text{BPRMF}}$-SC-Recall increases ILAD@10 by 11.74% on *ML1M* and 8.48% on *ML10M*, with only a 5.05% and 3.81% reduction in Recall@10, respectively. Similar trends are observed in other CMB variants, as evidenced in Tables 2 and 3, demonstrating the effectiveness of our trade-off objective.

**Table 2.** Comparisons of the accuracy and diversity performance. The base model $g$ here adopts BPRMF. The bold scores are the best in each column, and the underlined scores are the second best. The symbols ↑ and ↓, along with their preceding values, represent the percentage (% is omitted) improvement and decrease of a given method in the corresponding metric, in comparison to the base model $g$.

| Metric | Recall@10 | NDCG@10 | α-nDCG@10 | SC@10 | PC@10 | ILAD@10 |
|---|---|---|---|---|---|---|
| *ML1M* | | | | | | |
| BPRMF | **0.1465** | **0.2742** | 0.7035 | 0.4993 | 0.3206 | 0.2010 |
| MMR | 0.0441 (69.90↓) | 0.0741 (72.98↓) | 0.6980 (0.78↓) | 0.4692 (6.03↓) | 0.0970 (69.74↓) | 0.1709 (14.98↓) |
| DPP | 0.0360 (75.43↓) | 0.0689 (74.87↓) | **0.7186** (2.15↑) | **0.5558** (11.32↑) | **0.4554** (42.05↑) | **0.3693** (83.73↑) |
| CMB$_{BPRMF}$-α-nDCG-Recall | 0.1388 (5.26↓) | 0.2588 (5.62↓) | 0.7094 (0.84↑) | 0.5097 (2.08↑) | 0.3291 (2.65↑) | 0.2253 (12.09↑) |
| CMB$_{BPRMF}$-SC-Recall | <u>0.1391</u> (5.05↓) | <u>0.2594</u> (5.40↓) | 0.7078 (0.61↑) | 0.5102 (2.18↑) | 0.3307 (3.15↑) | 0.2246 (11.74↑) |
| CMB$_{BPRMF}$-PC-NDCG | 0.1388 (5.26↓) | 0.2584 (5.76↓) | 0.7093 (0.82↑) | 0.5107 (2.28↑) | 0.3286 (2.50↑) | 0.2247 (11.79↑) |
| CMB$_{BPRMF}$-ILAD-NDCG | 0.1387 (5.32↓) | 0.2587 (5.65↓) | <u>0.7109</u> (1.05↑) | <u>0.5127</u> (2.68↑) | <u>0.3313</u> (3.34↑) | 0.2246 (11.74↑) |
| *ML10M* | | | | | | |
| BPRMF | **0.1549** | **0.2648** | 0.7043 | 0.5483 | 0.2453 | 0.1886 |
| MMR | 0.0402 (74.05↓) | 0.0602 (77.27↓) | 0.7095 (0.74↑) | 0.5155 (5.98↓) | 0.0416 (83.04↓) | 0.1623 (13.94↓) |
| DPP | 0.0253 (83.67↓) | 0.0541 (79.57↓) | 0.6977 (0.94↓) | **0.6072** (10.74↑) | **0.3735** (52.26↑) | **0.3764** (99.58↑) |
| CMB$_{BPRMF}$-α-nDCG-Recall | 0.1488 (3.94↓) | 0.2531 (4.42↓) | **0.7126** (1.18↑) | 0.5544 (1.11↑) | 0.2475 (0.90↑) | 0.2045 (8.43↑) |
| CMB$_{BPRMF}$-SC-Recall | <u>0.1490</u> (3.81↓) | <u>0.2535</u> (4.27↓) | <u>0.7123</u> (1.14↑) | 0.5544 (1.11↑) | <u>0.2477</u> (0.98↑) | 0.2046 (8.48↑) |
| CMB$_{BPRMF}$-PC-NDCG | 0.1487 (4.00↓) | 0.2532 (4.38↓) | <u>0.7123</u> (1.14↑) | <u>0.5546</u> (1.15↑) | 0.2471 (0.73↑) | <u>0.2051</u> (8.75↑) |
| CMB$_{BPRMF}$-ILAD-NDCG | 0.1486 (4.07↓) | 0.2527 (4.57↓) | 0.7110 (0.95↑) | 0.5541 (1.06↑) | 0.2460 (0.29↑) | 0.2050 (8.70↑) |
| *CDs* | | | | | | |
| BPRMF | **0.0515** | **0.0457** | <u>0.7206</u> | 0.1700 | 0.1665 | 0.2332 |
| MMR | 0.0033 (93.59↓) | 0.0032 (93.00↓) | **0.7240** (0.47↑) | 0.1705 (0.29↑) | 0.0247 (85.17↓) | 0.2372 (1.72↑) |
| DPP | 0.0115 (77.67↓) | 0.0128 (71.99↓) | 0.7116 (1.25↓) | **0.2409** (41.71↑) | **0.3261** (95.86↑) | **0.4013** (72.08↑) |
| CMB$_{BPRMF}$-α-nDCG-NDCG | <u>0.0477</u> (7.38↓) | <u>0.0422</u> (7.66↓) | 0.7183 (0.32↓) | <u>0.1739</u> (2.29↑) | <u>0.1825</u> (9.61↑) | 0.2511 (7.68↑) |
| CMB$_{BPRMF}$-SC-NDCG | 0.0475 (7.77↓) | 0.0421 (7.88↓) | 0.7192 (0.19↓) | 0.1736 (2.12↑) | 0.1824 (9.55↑) | 0.2510 (7.63↑) |
| CMB$_{BPRMF}$-PC-Recall | 0.0476 (7.57↓) | 0.0421 (7.88↓) | 0.7180 (0.36↓) | 0.1737 (2.18↑) | 0.1816 (9.07↑) | 0.2509 (7.59↑) |
| CMB$_{BPRMF}$-ILAD-Recall | <u>0.0477</u> (7.38↓) | <u>0.0422</u> (7.66↓) | 0.7189 (0.24↓) | 0.1736 (2.12↑) | 0.1823 (9.49↑) | <u>0.2513</u> (7.76↑) |

Second, not only does the combined optimization objective help achieve a reasonable balance between accuracy and diversity, but also the single diversity objective does. For instance, as shown in Table 4, when compared to BPRMF, CMB$_{BPRMF}$-ILAD shows a decrease of 18.79% in Recall@10 and an increase of 40.62% in ILAD@10 on *ML10M*, while showing a decrease of 31.29% in NDCG@10 and an increase of 59.58% in PC@10 on *CDs*. These results demonstrate that the proposed single diversity objective can improve diversity performance while maintaining accuracy performance, and outperforming other diversity methods like MMR and DPP.

Finally, compared with the single diversity objective optimized by CMB, the combined optimization objective also achieves a better balance between accuracy and diversity. For example, according to Tables 2 and 4, on *ML10M* and *CDs*, the Recall@10 of CMB$_{BPRMF}$-SC-NDCG is 19.04% and 35.71% higher than CMB$_{BPRMF}$-SC, while the SC@10 only decreases by 5.06% and 10.33%, respectively. Similar findings can also be found in other cases. These results demonstrate the superiority of our proposed trade-off target in achieving a balance between accuracy and diversity.

**Diversification Observations.** First, the CMB model can effectively optimize various diversity metrics while yielding satisfactory results. For instance,

**Table 3.** Comparisons of the accuracy and diversity performance. The base model $g$ here adopts LightGCN. The bold scores are the best in each column, and the underlined scores are the second best. The symbols ↑ and ↓, along with their preceding values, represent the percentage (% is omitted) improvement and decrease of a given method in the corresponding metric, in comparison to the base model $g$.

| Metric | Recall@10 | NDCG@10 | α-nDCG@10 | SC@10 | PC@10 | ILAD@10 |
|---|---|---|---|---|---|---|
| *ML10M* | | | | | | |
| LightGCN | **0.1724** | **0.2912** | 0.7056 | **0.5680** | 0.1979 | 0.1480 |
| CMB$_{\text{LightGCN}}$-α-nDCG-NDCG | 0.1706 (1.04↓) | 0.2866 (1.58↓) | 0.7061 (0.07↑) | 0.5655 (0.44↓) | 0.2131 (7.68↑) | 0.1562 (5.54↑) |
| CMB$_{\text{LightGCN}}$-SC-NDCG | 0.1706 (1.04↓) | 0.2865 (1.61↓) | 0.7060 (0.06↑) | 0.5650 (0.53↓) | **0.2142** (8.24↑) | **0.1565** (5.74↑) |
| CMB$_{\text{LightGCN}}$-PC-Recall | 0.1704 (1.16↓) | 0.2866 (1.58↓) | 0.7062 (0.09↑) | 0.5664 (0.28↓) | 0.2122 (7.23↑) | 0.1562 (5.54↑) |
| CMB$_{\text{LightGCN}}$-ILAD-Recall | 0.1705 (1.10↓) | 0.2866 (1.58↓) | **0.7072** (0.23↑) | 0.5661 (0.33↓) | 0.2130 (7.63↑) | 0.1561 (5.47↑) |
| *CDs* | | | | | | |
| LightGCN | **0.0567** | **0.0500** | 0.7260 | 0.1616 | 0.0931 | 0.1659 |
| CMB$_{\text{LightGCN}}$-α-nDCG-Recall | 0.0554 (2.29↓) | 0.0490 (2.00↓) | 0.7240 (0.28↓) | 0.1643 (1.67↑) | **0.0938** (0.75↑) | **0.1751** (5.55↑) |
| CMB$_{\text{LightGCN}}$-SC-Recall | 0.0554 (2.29↓) | 0.0489 (2.20↓) | 0.7238 (0.30↓) | 0.1642 (1.61↑) | 0.0935 (0.43↑) | **0.1751** (5.55↑) |
| CMB$_{\text{LightGCN}}$-PC-NDCG | 0.0553 (2.47↓) | 0.0489 (2.20↓) | 0.7238 (0.30↓) | **0.1644** (1.73↑) | 0.0934 (0.32↑) | 0.1748 (5.36↑) |
| CMB$_{\text{LightGCN}}$-ILAD-NDCG | 0.0552 (2.65↓) | 0.0488 (2.40↓) | 0.7237 (0.32↓) | 0.1642 (1.61↑) | 0.0936 (0.54↑) | 0.1750 (5.49↑) |

as shown in Tables 2 and 4, CMB$_{\text{BPRMF}}$-α-nDCG outperforms the best baseline by 2.26% in α-nDCG@10 on *ML10M*. Additionally, from these two tables, we also observe that CMB$_{\text{BPRMF}}$ significantly improves all diversity metrics compared to the base model BPRMF when optimized individually.

Second, as illustrated in Tables 2 and 4, CMB$_{\text{BPRMF}}$-SC achieves the second-best SC@10 on *ML10M*, only 0.12% decrease compared to the best baseline. Similarly, CMB$_{\text{BPRMF}}$-PC also achieves the second-best performance in the PC metric on *ML10M* and *CDs*. These results demonstrate that CMB can achieve a satisfactory diversification. Moreover, while CMB sometimes trails DPP in diversity metrics, this is because DPP prioritizes diversity over accuracy. In contrast, our method balances both, leading to improved accuracy even if diversity scores are slightly lower when compared to the DPP.

**Application Observations**. First, from Table 4, by comparing CMB$_{\text{BPRMF}}^{\text{Gradient}}$-ILAD and CMB$_{\text{BPRMF}}$-ILAD, we observe that the gradient descent optimization method outperforms the bandit optimization method in terms of accuracy on *CDs*, while exhibiting better diversity results on *ML10M* for PC and ILAD metrics. Thus, the choice of which optimization method should be based on the specific application scenario (e.g., dataset, diversity level, etc.).

Second, as shown in Tables 2 and 4, compared to CMB$_{\text{Random}}$, CMB that only optimizes a single diversity metric also achieves good results on that metric, which shows that our bandit method is effective for optimizing different diversity metrics. Moreover, optimizing the combination of trade-off objectives simultaneously also achieves a good balance in accuracy and diversity, further highlighting the effectiveness of our combined optimization objectives. For example, NDCG@10 of CMB$_{\text{BPRMF}}$-SC-NDCG on *ML10M* and *CDs* is 18.88% and 34.08% higher than CMB$_{\text{BPRMF}}$-Random, respectively, while the SC@10 only decreases by 1.35% and 6.16%.

**Table 4.** Comparisons among the accuracy and diversity performance of CMB optimizes the single diversity metrics. The base model $g$ here adopts BPRMF. $\text{CMB}_{\text{ILAD}}^{\text{Gradient}}$ represents CMB that directly optimizes the differentiable metric ILAD by using the gradient method. $\text{CMB}_{\text{BPRMF}}$-Random represents CMB that chooses the arm randomly for each player. The bold scores are the best in each column.

| Metric | Recall@K | | NDCG@K | | α-nDCG@K | | SC@K | | PC@K | | ILAD@K | |
|---|---|---|---|---|---|---|---|---|---|---|---|---|
| | K=10 | K=20 | K=10 | K=20 | K=10 | K=20 | K=10 | K=20 | K=10 | K=20 | K=10 | K=20 |
| *ML10M* | | | | | | | | | | | | |
| $\text{CMB}_{\text{BPRMF}}$-Random | 0.1266 | 0.2032 | 0.2129 | 0.2217 | 0.7108 | 0.8045 | 0.5630 | 0.6930 | 0.2625 | 0.3514 | 0.2584 | 0.2787 |
| $\text{CMB}_{\text{BPRMF}}$-α-nDCG | **0.1267** | **0.2033** | **0.2138** | **0.2223** | **0.7467** | **0.8336** | 0.5794 | 0.7002 | 0.2620 | 0.3500 | 0.2554 | 0.2757 |
| $\text{CMB}_{\text{BPRMF}}$-SC | 0.1250 | 0.2024 | 0.2106 | 0.2201 | 0.7436 | 0.8295 | **0.6065** | **0.7253** | 0.2607 | 0.3496 | 0.2542 | 0.2751 |
| $\text{CMB}_{\text{BPRMF}}$-PC | 0.1259 | 0.2018 | 0.2135 | 0.2216 | 0.7104 | 0.8036 | 0.5726 | 0.7012 | 0.2714 | 0.3598 | 0.2582 | 0.2784 |
| $\text{CMB}_{\text{BPRMF}}$-ILAD | 0.1258 | 0.2021 | 0.2121 | 0.2209 | 0.7147 | 0.8073 | 0.5650 | 0.6928 | 0.2651 | 0.3556 | 0.2652 | 0.2843 |
| $\text{CMB}_{\text{BPRMF}}^{\text{Gradient}}$-ILAD | 0.1174 | 0.1914 | 0.1982 | 0.2086 | 0.6992 | 0.7948 | 0.5003 | 0.6279 | **0.3089** | **0.3780** | **0.2900** | **0.3034** |
| *CDs* | | | | | | | | | | | | |
| $\text{CMB}_{\text{BPRMF}}$-Random | 0.0353 | 0.0582 | 0.0314 | 0.0397 | 0.7053 | 0.8087 | 0.1850 | 0.2593 | 0.2659 | 0.3909 | 0.3081 | 0.3220 |
| $\text{CMB}_{\text{BPRMF}}$-α-nDCG | 0.0358 | 0.0583 | 0.0319 | 0.0400 | 0.7150 | **0.8155** | 0.1866 | 0.2593 | 0.2621 | 0.3859 | 0.3071 | 0.3209 |
| $\text{CMB}_{\text{BPRMF}}$-SC | 0.0350 | 0.0579 | 0.0310 | 0.0393 | 0.7043 | 0.8074 | **0.1936** | **0.2684** | 0.2649 | 0.3884 | 0.3064 | 0.3205 |
| $\text{CMB}_{\text{BPRMF}}$-PC | 0.0347 | 0.0572 | 0.0310 | 0.0391 | 0.7050 | 0.8086 | 0.1862 | 0.2610 | **0.2755** | **0.4050** | **0.3117** | **0.3255** |
| $\text{CMB}_{\text{BPRMF}}$-ILAD | 0.0354 | 0.0585 | 0.0314 | 0.0397 | 0.7046 | 0.8083 | 0.1855 | 0.2598 | 0.2657 | 0.3885 | 0.3102 | 0.3233 |
| $\text{CMB}_{\text{BPRMF}}^{\text{Gradient}}$-ILAD | **0.0524** | **0.0846** | **0.0458** | **0.0574** | **0.7164** | 0.8154 | 0.1717 | 0.2353 | 0.1768 | 0.2438 | 0.2788 | 0.2866 |

**Other Observations.** First, the accuracy and diversity trade-off exists widely. No method can achieve the best results in both accuracy and diversity since an increase in accuracy generally corresponds to a decrease in diversity. From the results in Table 2, DPP achieves the best results in SC@10, PC@10, and ILAD@10 on *ML1M* and *ML10M*, but it achieves the worst performance in Recall@10 and NDCG@10 on these datasets.

Second, generally, no single method demonstrates superior performance across all diversity metrics. For example, as shown in Table 2, DPP has the highest SC@10, PC@10, and ILAD@10 performance on *ML10M* and *CDs*, but has the lowest α-nDCG@K performance. This indicates the inherent gap between different diversity evaluation metrics, proving the necessity of optimizing different metrics in a general framework, which is just the focus of our work.

### 4.3 Validity Analysis of Explanations (RQ2)

As discussed in Sect.3.4, the values of $\Delta$ affect the diversity of recommendation lists generated by the base model $g$. To evaluate whether $\Delta$ can discover the meaningful factors that improve diversity or balance accuracy and diversity, we follow the widely deployed erasure-based evaluation criterion [11] from Explainable AI. Specifically, we erase the "most meaningful factors" from $\Delta$ (setting them to 0) and input this modified $\Delta$ into the pre-trained model $g$ to generate new recommendations. We then assess our model's effectiveness regarding the diversity and accuracy of these new results. We explore two erasure strategies, CMB-Individual (CMB-I) and CMB-Shared (CMB-S) – by erasing the top, least, or random $F$ factors, where $F$ is the number of erasing factors. For CMB-I, we erase the top/least/random-$F$ factors of each column of the absolute values of

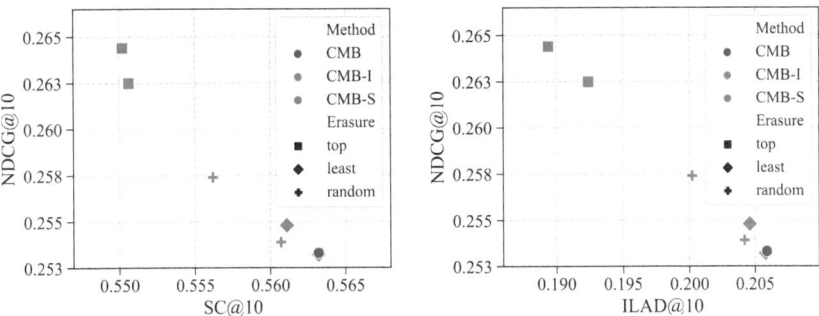

**Fig. 2.** Factor validity analysis on *ML10M* dataset when utilizing different erasure methods (CMB-I and CMB-S) with top/least/random manners.

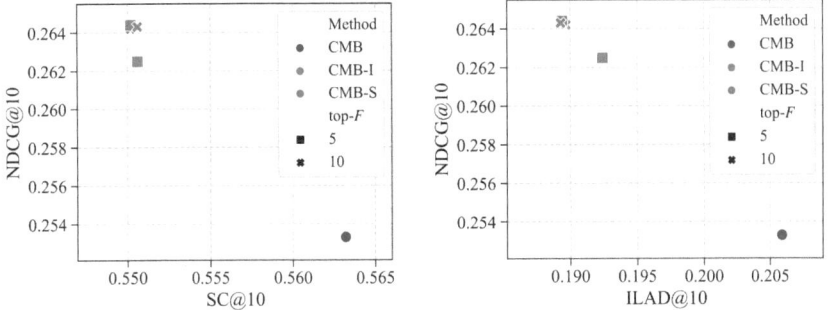

**Fig. 3.** Factor validity analysis on *ML10M* dataset when utilizing different erasure methods (CMB-I and CMB-S) with different $F$.

$\Delta$. For CMB-S, we average each row of the absolute values of $\Delta$, then erase the top/least/random-$F$ factors by row. Compared with the least/random manners in Fig. 2, we observe that omitting these meaningful factors by the top manner reduces the diversity scores much while increasing the accuracy measures a lot. And the least manner does little to alter the performance of diversity or accuracy. Therefore, it verifies that the meaningful factors we discover can benefit the trade-off between diversity and accuracy of recommendation results. Furthermore, as shown in Fig. 3, the results of the CMB-Shared approach with top-$F$ ($F = 5/10$) are highly equivalent, indicating that the CMB-Shared approach can identify only a few factors that significantly impact the model's diversity or accuracy. Observations from other approaches are similar.

### 4.4 Case Study of Explanations (RQ3)

The purpose of the case study is to demonstrate the applicability of our method to both latent and raw features. As described in Sect. 3.4, we illustrate how to generate explanations using raw features in this section. Following [11,38], we adopt the same method to extract the features and obtain the raw user and item

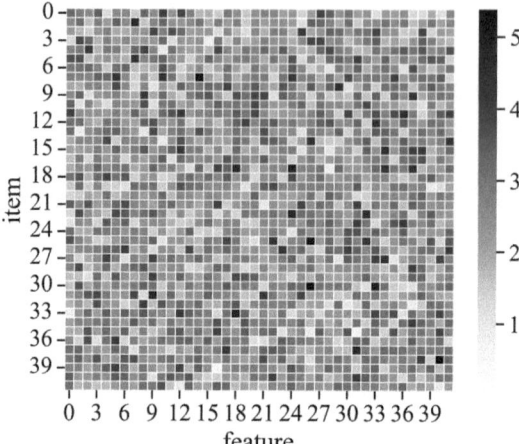

**Fig. 4.** The feature explanations of CMB-Individual-$\alpha$-nDCG-Recall. Only the results of partial items are shown.

**Table 5.** Top-5 feature-based explanations on *Phones* dataset.

| Method | Feature-based Explanations |
|---|---|
| CMB-Shared-SC-Recall | sound, volume, connector, headphone, protection |
| CMB-Shared-SC-NDCG | charger, button, flashlight, cable, protection |
| CMB-Shared-ILAD-Recall | connector, volume, pocket, charger, sound |
| CMB-Shared-ILAD-NDCG | port, headset, plug, volume, package |

feature matrices. Then, we apply two different feature-based explanations introduced in Sect. 3.4 on *Phones* dataset from Amazon. The explanation results are presented in Fig. 4 and Table 5. These findings support our idea that it is challenging to manually discover feature explanations for diversity in recommender systems. For example, as shown in Table 5, it is difficult to know how input features (such as sound, charger, and connector) would determine the diversity of phone recommendations. As a result, explainable diversity approaches like ours are necessary to discover such features in the recommendation.

## 5 Conclusion and Future Work

In this work, we propose CMB, a general bandit-based method, which optimizes the recommendation diversity while providing corresponding explanations. The method exhibits wide applicability and is agnostic to both recommendation models and diversity metrics. The proposed combination optimization target helps reach a more reasonable trade-off between recommendation accuracy and diversity performance. Besides, the explanations regarding diversification can be provided with the meaningfulness of the factors obtained from counterfactual optimization. Extensive experiments on real-world datasets demonstrate our method's applicability, effectiveness, and explainability. In the future, we plan to design more efficient methods for generating explanations.

**Acknowledgments.** This work was supported by the Early Career Scheme (No. CityU 21219323) and the General Research Fund (No. CityU 11220324) of the University Grants Committee (UGC), and the NSFC Young Scientists Fund (No. 9240127).

# References

1. Bistritz, I., Bambos, N.: Cooperative multi-player bandit optimization. In: NeurIPS, pp. 2016–2027 (2020)
2. Bubeck, S., Munos, R., Stoltz, G.: Pure exploration in multi-armed bandits problems. In: International Conference on Algorithmic Learning Theory, pp. 23–37 (2009)
3. Carbonell, J., Goldstein, J.: The use of MMR, diversity-based reranking for reordering documents and producing summaries. In: SIGIR, pp. 335–336 (1998)
4. Chen, L., Zhang, G., Zhou, E.: Fast greedy MAP inference for determinantal point process to improve recommendation diversity. In: NeurIPS, pp. 5627–5638 (2018)
5. Chen, W., Ren, P., Cai, F., Sun, F., de Rijke, M.: Improving end-to-end sequential recommendations with intent-aware diversification. In: CIKM, pp. 175–184 (2020)
6. Chen, Z., Silvestri, F., Wang, J., Zhu, H., Ahn, H., Tolomei, G.: Relax: reinforcement learning agent explainer for arbitrary predictive models. In: CIKM, pp. 252–261 (2022)
7. Cheng, P., Wang, S., Ma, J., Sun, J., Xiong, H.: Learning to recommend accurate and diverse items. In: WWW, pp. 183–192 (2017)
8. Clarke, C.L., et al.: Novelty and diversity in information retrieval evaluation. In: SIGIR, pp. 659–666 (2008)
9. Ding, Q., Liu, Y., Miao, C., Cheng, F., Tang, H.: A hybrid bandit framework for diversified recommendation. In: AAAI, pp. 4036–4044 (2021)
10. Ge, M., Delgado-Battenfeld, C., Jannach, D.: Beyond accuracy: evaluating recommender systems by coverage and serendipity. In: RecSys, pp. 257–260 (2010)
11. Ge, Y., et al.: Explainable fairness in recommendation. In: SIGIR, pp. 681–691 (2022)
12. Harper, F.M., Konstan, J.A.: The movielens datasets: History and context. TIIS **5**(4), 1–19 (2015)
13. He, X., Deng, K., Wang, X., Li, Y., Zhang, Y., Wang, M.: Lightgcn: simplifying and powering graph convolution network for recommendation. In: SIGIR, pp. 639–648 (2020)
14. Huang, Y., Wang, W., Zhang, L., Xu, R.: Sliding spectrum decomposition for diversified recommendation. In: KDD, pp. 3041–3049 (2021)
15. Kingma, D.P., Ba, J.: Adam: A method for stochastic optimization. arXiv preprint arXiv:1412.6980 (2014)
16. Li, L., Chu, W., Langford, J., Schapire, R.E.: A contextual-bandit approach to personalized news article recommendation. In: WWW, pp. 661–670 (2010)
17. Li, S., Zhou, Y., Zhang, D., Zhang, Y., Lan, X.: Learning to diversify recommendations based on matrix factorization. In: DASC/PiCom/DataCom/CyberSciTech. pp. 68–74 (2017)

18. Merton, R.K.: The matthew effect in science: the reward and communication systems of science are considered. Science **159**(3810), 56–63 (1968)
19. Ni, J., Li, J., McAuley, J.J.: Justifying recommendations using distantly-labeled reviews and fine-grained aspects. In: EMNLP-IJCNLP, pp. 188–197 (2019)
20. Pariser, E.: The filter bubble: How the new personalized web is changing what we read and how we think (2011)
21. Rendle, S., Freudenthaler, C., Gantner, Z., Schmidt-Thieme, L.: BPR: bayesian personalized ranking from implicit feedback. In: UAI, pp. 452–461 (2009)
22. Santos, R.L., Macdonald, C., Ounis, I.: Exploiting query reformulations for web search result diversification. In: WWW, pp. 881–890 (2010)
23. Shi, X., et al.: Relieving popularity bias in interactive recommendation: a diversity-novelty-aware reinforcement learning approach. TOIS **42**(2), 1–30 (2023)
24. Singh, J., Anand, A.: Exs: Explainable search using local model agnostic interpretability. In: WSDM, pp. 770–773 (2019)
25. Slivkins, A., et al.: Introduction to multi-armed bandits. Found. Trends® Mach. Learn. **12**(1-2), 1–286 (2019)
26. Tsukuda, K., Goto, M.: Dualdiv: diversifying items and explanation styles in explainable hybrid recommendation. In: RecSys, pp. 398–402 (2019)
27. Vargas, S., Castells, P., Vallet, D.: Intent-oriented diversity in recommender systems. In: SIGIR, pp. 1211–1212 (2011)
28. Wang, X., Chen, Y., Yang, J., Wu, L., Wu, Z., Xie, X.: A reinforcement learning framework for explainable recommendation. In: ICDM, pp. 587–596 (2018)
29. Wasilewski, J., Hurley, N.: Incorporating diversity in a learning to rank recommender system. In: FLAIRS, pp. 572–578 (2016)
30. Wilhelm, M., Ramanathan, A., Bonomo, A., Jain, S., Chi, E.H., Gillenwater, J.: Practical diversified recommendations on youtube with determinantal point processes. In: CIKM, pp. 2165–2173 (2018)
31. Wu, H., et al.: Result diversification in search and recommendation: a survey. In: TKDE (2024)
32. Wu, L., Quan, C., Li, C., Wang, Q., Zheng, B., Luo, X.: A context-aware user-item representation learning for item recommendation. TOIS **37**(2), 1–29 (2019)
33. Yu, H.: Optimize what you evaluate with: Search result diversification based on metric optimization. In: AAAI, pp. 10399–10407 (2022)
34. Zhang, M., Hurley, N.: Avoiding monotony: improving the diversity of recommendation lists. In: RecSys, pp. 123–130 (2008)
35. Zhang, Y., Hu, C., Dai, G., Kong, W., Liu, Y.: Self-adaptive graph neural networks for personalized sequential recommendation. In: ICONIP, pp. 608–619 (2021)
36. Zhang, Y., Zhang, X., Cui, Z., Ma, C.: Shapley value-driven data pruning for recommender systems. In: KDD (2025)
37. Zhang, Y., Chen, X., et al.: Explainable recommendation: A survey and new perspectives. Found. Trends® Inform. Retrieval **14**(1), 1–101 (2020)
38. Zhang, Y., Lai, G., Zhang, M., Zhang, Y., Liu, Y., Ma, S.: Explicit factor models for explainable recommendation based on phrase-level sentiment analysis. In: SIGIR, pp. 83–92 (2014)
39. Zheng, G., et al.: DRN: a deep reinforcement learning framework for news recommendation. In: WWW, pp. 167–176 (2018)
40. Zheng, Y., Gao, C., Chen, L., Jin, D., Li, Y.: DGCN: Diversified recommendation with graph convolutional networks. In: WWW, pp. 401–412 (2021)

# RAE: A Rule-Driven Approach for Attribute Embedding in Property Graph Recommendation

Sibo Zhao[1], Michael Bewong[2,3], Selasi Kwashie[2], Junwei Hu[1], and Zaiwen Feng[1,4,5,6(✉)]

[1] College of Informatics, Huazhong Agricultural University, Wuhan, China
Zaiwen.Feng@mail.hzau.edu.cn
[2] AI and Cyber Futures Institute, Charles Sturt University, Bathurst, Australia
[3] School of Computing, Mathematics and Engineering, Charles Sturt University, Wagga Wagga, Australia
[4] Hubei Key Laboratory of Agricultural Bioinformatics, Hubei, Wuhan, China
[5] Engineering Research Center of Agricultural Intelligent Technology, Ministry of Education, Hubei, Wuhan, China
[6] Hubei Three Gorges Laboratory, Hubei, Wuhan, China

**Abstract.** Recommendation systems are crucial in modern applications to enhance the user experience and drive business conversion rates through personalization. However, insufficient utilization of attribute information within the property graph remains a significant challenge. Most existing graph convolutional network (GCN) models do not consider attribute information, and those that do often employ a simplified triple format <users, items, attributes>, which fails to fully exploit the rich semantic structures of property graphs necessary for effective recommendations. To overcome these limitations, we introduce Rule-Driven Approach for Attribute Embedding (RAE), a novel methodology that enhances recommendation performance by effectively mining and utilizing semantic rules from property graphs. RAE applies a rule-mining process to extract meaningful rules that guide random walks in generating enriched attribute embeddings. These enriched embeddings are subsequently integrated into GCNs, surpassing conventional triple-based embedding techniques. We evaluate RAE on real-world datasets (e.g., Blogcatalog and Flickr) and demonstrate that RAE achieves an average improvement of 10.6% in both Recall@20 and NDCG@20 compared to state-of-the-art baselines, indicating superior relevance coverage and ranking rationality in top-20 recommendations. Additionally, RAE exhibits enhanced robustness against data sparsity and the attribute missingness problem. Our novel approach underscores the significant performance gains achieved in recommendation systems by fully leveraging attribute information within property graphs, enhancing both effectiveness and reliability.

**Keywords:** Recommendation Systems · Property Graphs · Rule Mining · Attribute Embedding · Graph Convolutional Network

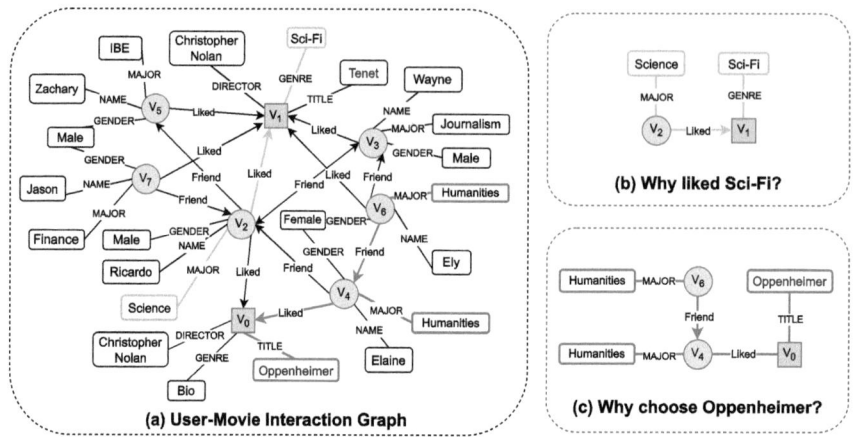

**Fig. 1.** Illustration of motivation of the proposed RAE

## 1 Introduction

Recommendation systems play an essential role in modern online applications, enhancing user experience by providing personalized content and services. These systems are crucial in e-commerce, social media, and entertainment platforms, helping users discover relevant items and mitigate information overload. Traditional recommendation algorithms primarily depend on users' historical behaviors, such as clicks and purchases, to predict preferences. However, as the volume and diversity of data continue to grow, conventional approaches increasingly encounter challenges in providing accurate and relevant recommendations.

In recent years, Graph Convolutional Networks (GCNs) have gained popularity due to their capacity to model complex relationships within user-item interaction networks, which have shown promising results in recommendation systems. Nevertheless, existing GCN-based models still suffer from the data sparsity problem. When there are limited user reviews or insufficient social information, such data sparsity restricts the models' ability to capture detailed user preferences, thereby reducing the effectiveness of recommendations.

To address data sparsity, researchers have explored the use of attributes as valuable side information. Attributes provide critical supplementary information in recommendation systems, especially for understanding user preferences and item characteristics, offering additional insights that can improve recommendation accuracy. Despite their potential, current attribute-enhanced models often underutilize these attributes [23,24], treating them merely as simple triples of the form `<users, items, attributes>`. Such representations do not fully exploit the rich semantic structures of attributes embedded within property graphs, where attributes originate from and can convey complex relationships and semantic meanings.

Motivated by the limitations of existing recommendation models in handling sparse and incomplete attribute data, we propose a novel **Rule-Driven Attribute Embedding (RAE)**[1] framework. RAE seeks to enhance recommendation performance by effectively mining and utilizing semantic rules from property graphs. In our work, a rule represents a dependency relationship between attributes in the graph, such as $x.a \rightarrow y.b$, indicating that attribute $a$ of node $x$ determines attribute $b$ of node $y$. For example, Fig. 1(a) represents a user-movie interaction graph, from which we can derive the rule $V_2.\text{MAJOR} \rightarrow V_1.\text{GENRE}$ (shown in Fig. 1(b)), implying that user $V_2$'s major in Science influences his preference for the Sci-Fi genre represented by movie $V_1$. Similarly, the rule $(V_6.\text{MAJOR} = V_4.\text{MAJOR} \wedge V_4.\text{MAJOR} = \text{Humanities} \rightarrow V_0.\text{TITLE})$ (Fig. 1(c)) suggests that the shared major in Humanities between users $V_6$ and $V_4$, along with their friendship, supports recommending the movie 'Oppenheimer' to user $V_6$. These rules capture the semantic dependencies between user attributes and movie attributes, which can enable a recommendation system to leverage attribute information meaningfully and ultimately produce more personalized and explainable recommendations.

Our approach begins with a rule mining process to extract relevant rules, which guide random walks for generating enriched attribute embeddings. These embeddings capture deeper semantic structures than conventional triple-based representations and are integrated into GCNs to improve recommendation quality. Our main contributions are as follows:

- We propose the Rule-Driven Attribute Embedding (RAE) framework, which encodes attribute information within property graphs to leverage rich semantic structures.
- We design a rule-based random walk process that generates attribute embeddings with enhanced semantic depth, outperforming traditional triple-based techniques.
- We integrate enriched attribute embeddings into GCNs, and conduct comprehensive evaluations on four real-world datasets, comparing RAE against five contemporary baselines. The results validate the framework's effectiveness, particularly in handling challenges of data sparsity and attribute missingness.

## 2 Related Work

### 2.1 Rule Discovery

In graph-structured data, rule discovery has often concentrated on pattern-based rules related to nodes, similar to graph pattern mining. Examples include graph evolution rules [1,2], link formation rules [3], and predictive graph rules [5], which are commonly mined using techniques such as gSpan [6]. Advanced models like RNNLogic [4] focus on learning path-based rules but lack logical conditions

---

[1] For more details: https://github.com/Sibo-Zhao/RAE.

related to attributes, limiting their ability to capture complex dependencies. In our approach, we aim to leverage attribute-related logical conditions to enhance rule discovery in graph-based recommendation systems. This approach is similar to methods like graph association rules (GARs) [8,12], graph functional dependencies (GFDs) [9], graph differential dependencies (GDDs) [10,31], and graph entity dependencies (GEDs) [11,28], which integrate both graph patterns and logic conditions through either mining-based levelwise traversal [9,10] or learning-based rule generation [7]. The integration of logic conditions allows for more expressive rules that can capture complex relationships and dependencies, which are especially beneficial in recommendation scenarios.

## 2.2 Property Graph Embedding

Existing property graph embedding methods primarily rely on factorization- and auto-encoder-based techniques. Factorization-based methods like BANE [18] and LQANR [17] improve storage efficiency by learning binary or low-bit-width embeddings, at the cost of accuracy. In contrast, auto-encoder-based methods use neural networks to learn embeddings by minimizing reconstruction loss, with various network structures and proximity matrices. Recent innovations, including SAGES [16] and PANE [13,14], aim to capture higher-order proximities and incorporate attribute data in property graphs. Of particular interest is PANE, which is similar to our approach in treating attributes as additional nodes within the graph for random walk-based embedding generation. Our approach extends this concept by incorporating logic rules during the random walk process, allowing the generation of more semantically enriched and contextually informed embeddings.

## 2.3 Graph-Based Recommendation

Recent advancements in contrastive learning have significantly improved recommender systems under sparse interaction settings. Methods such as LightGCL [32], SSLRec [33], and CGCL [34] apply data augmentation and self-supervised objectives over user-item bipartite graphs. However, they typically ignore the semantic structure from attribute information. In contrast, our RAE framework operates on property graphs, extracting semantic rules to guide attribute embedding, which is orthogonal to contrastive paradigms and potentially complementary.

Knowledge graph-based models, including RippleNet [35], KGCN [36], and RuleRec [37], enrich recommendation by leveraging external KGs via multi-hop propagation or symbolic rule induction. These methods depend on external resources and often require domain-specific construction. In contrast, RAE exploits attribute dependencies from the dataset's internal property graph, avoiding reliance on external KGs while enabling interpretable rule-based embedding.

Graph Convolutional Networks (GCNs) have proven highly effective in learning representations from non-Euclidean structures [21,22], making them increasingly popular in recommendation systems. LightGCN [19] streamlines GCN operations by omitting feature transformation and non-linear activations, optimizing for recommendation tasks. IMP-GCN [20] utilizes high-order graph convolutions within subgraphs to filter out irrelevant neighbor effects, enhancing embedding relevance. Attribute-aware GCNs such as AF-GCN [24] and $A^2$-GCN [23] integrate attributes through attention or unified graphs. Our work complements these models by incorporating rule-mined attribute embeddings into GCNs, addressing both data sparsity and missing attributes through structured semantic enrichment.

## 3 Preliminaries

### 3.1 Basic Definitions and Notions

**Property Graph:** Let $G = (V, E_v, R, E_R)$ denote a property graph, where $V$ is the set of nodes with cardinality $n$, $E_v$ is the set of edges with cardinality $m$ linking pairs of nodes in $V$, $R$ represents the set of attributes with cardinality $d$, and $E_R$ is the set of node-attribute associations. Each element in $E_R$ is a tuple $(v_i, r_j, w_{i,j})$, where $v_i \in V$ (e.g., $V_2$ in Fig. 1(a)) is directly associated with attribute $r_j \in R$ (e.g., "Science" in Fig. 1(a)) and $w_{i,j}$ (e.g., "MAJOR" in Fig. 1(a)) denotes the weight of this association, representing the attribute value. For generality, we assume $G$ is a directed graph; if $G$ is undirected, each undirected edge $(v_i, v_j)$ in $G$ is treated as two directed edges, $(v_i, v_j)$ and $(v_j, v_i)$, in opposite directions.

**Graph Patterns:** A graph pattern is defined as $Q[\bar{x}] = (V_Q, E_Q, L_Q, \mu)$, where: (1) $V_Q$ and $E_Q$ denote a set of pattern nodes and edges, respectively; (2) $L_Q$ is a function assigning each node $u \in V_Q$ a **label** $L_Q(u) \in L$, where $L$ is the set of possible labels, which are distinct from attributes. (3) $\bar{x}$ is an ordered list of distinct variables; and (4) $\mu$ is a bijective mapping from $\bar{x}$ to $V_Q$, meaning that each variable in $\bar{x}$ uniquely corresponds to a node $v \in V_Q$. The wildcard symbol '\_' is permitted as a special label in $Q[\bar{x}]$. For example, consider a pattern in Fig. 2(a) where a user $v_a$ is connected via a friend relationship to another user $v_b$, who in turn likes an entity $v_c$.

**Literals:** A literal in a graph pattern $Q[\bar{x}]$ can take one of the following forms:
- **Attribute literal** $x.A$: Specifies that the variable $x$ has an attribute $A$.
- **Edge literal** $\iota(x, y)$: Denotes an edge labeled $\iota$ directed from $x$ to $y$.
- **ML literal** $\mathcal{M}(x, y, \iota)$: Represents the prediction of an ML classifier regarding the existence of an edge labeled $\iota$ from $x$ to $y$.
- **Variable literal** $x.A = y.B$: Indicates that attribute $A$ of $x$ is equal to attribute $B$ of $y$.
- **Constant literal** $x.A = c$: Asserts that attribute $A$ of $x$ is equal to a constant value $c$.

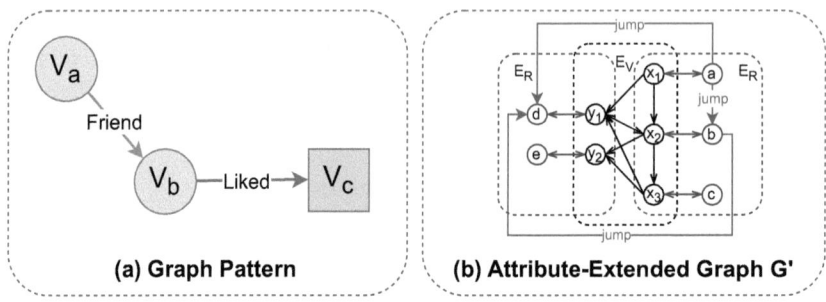

**Fig. 2.** A Graph Pattern and Attribute-Extended Graph $G'$.

**Rules in Graph:** A rule in a graph $\varphi$ is defined as: $Q[\bar{x}](X \to Y)$, where $Q[\bar{x}]$ denotes a graph pattern, and $X$ and $Y$ represent conjunctions of literals within $Q[\bar{x}]$. We refer to $Q[\bar{x}]$ as the *pattern* and $X \to Y$ as the *dependency* of $\varphi$. For instance, consider a rule (Fig. 1(c)) under Graph Pattern Fig. 2(a) ($V_a.major = Humanities \land V_a.major = V_b.major \implies V_c.Title = Oppenheimer$), suggesting that the common major in Humanities shared between users $V_6$ and $V_4$, alongside their established friendship, provides justification for recommending the film "Oppenheimer" to user $V_6$.

### 3.2 Problem Formulation

In this work, our goal is to effectively leverage the rich attribute information within property graphs to improve recommendation systems. The input consists of a set of user-item interactions $O^+ = \{(u,i) \mid u \in U, i \in I\}$ where $U = \{u_1, \ldots, u_M\}$ and $I = \{i_1, \ldots, i_N\}$ represent the sets of users and items, respectively, and a property graph $G = (V, E_v, R, E_R)$. Here, we focus on implicit feedback from interaction data, constructing a user-item interaction graph $G^I = \{(u, r_{ui}, i) \mid (u,i) \in O^+\}$, where $r_{ui}$ represents the interaction relation between user $u$ and item $i$. For instance, consider a scenario where the goal is to predict whether a user will like a movie. Using IMDB data containing user interactions with movies in the form of likes, we can generate a user-item interaction graph similar to the one shown in Fig. 1 (a). We can also rely on publicly available knowledge bases like Wikipedia to generate a property graph that represents movies under consideration. While existing work only relies on the information within the user-item interactions, our goal is to learn relevant rules from the property graph (*i.e.*, Wikipedia) to enhance the learning of a recommendation model from the user-item interactions (*i.e.*, IMDB).

In the property graph $G$, the node set $V$ includes both users and items, along with their associated attribute information. By integrating the user-item interaction graph $G^I$ with the property graph $G$, we aim to effectively utilize attributes to improve recommendation outcomes.

**Definition 1 (Problem Definition).** *Given a property graph G, our framework aims to develop an improved recommendation system that leverages rules to recommend items $I'_u$ to each user u based on both the enriched embeddings and the interaction history $I_u$.*

## 4 Methodology

In this section, we introduce our novel recommendation framework, **Rule-Driven Approach for Attribute Embedding (RAE)**, designed to fully leverage attribute information in property graphs. Our framework is composed of three main modules: (1) a rule mining module, which extracts significant attribute association rules to identify key relationships within the graph; (2) a rule-based random walk embedding module, where the mined rules guide random walks on the property graph to generate enriched node and attribute embeddings; and (3) a recommendation module, which integrates the generated embeddings into a GCN to improve recommendation accuracy. In the following, we detail the design and implementation of each module.

### 4.1 Rule Mining Module

Our approach leverages Graph Association Rules (GAR) [12] to extract relevant attribute association rules within property graphs. Specifically, we focus on three categories of literals: Attribute literals $(x.A)$, Variable literals $(x.A = y.B)$, and Constant literals $(x.A = c)$, which encapsulate essential attribute-based relationships critical for generating meaningful embeddings. By incorporating these literal types, we emphasize the effective application of these rules to create structured associations, rather than detailing the full inference mechanisms of GAR. These mined rules subsequently guide random walks, enriching attribute embeddings and enhancing recommendation performance.

### 4.2 Rule-Based Random Walk Embedding

To fully utilize the rich attribute information within property graphs, we introduce a rule-based random walk embedding approach. Our approach builds upon the concept of random walks in attributed network embedding [13], further guiding these walks using mined rules to capture deeper semantic relationships within the property graph.

**Attribute Matrix:** Given a limited embedding dimension $k \ll n$, each node $v \in V$ is represented by a vector of dimension $k$ to establish a **node embedding**. The primary aim of our property graph embedding approach is to construct an embedding $X_v$ for each node $v$, effectively capturing both the structural connections and the attributes associated with $v$. In line with prior research [13], we designate a portion of the embedding space, specifically $\frac{k}{2}$, for each attribute

$r \in R$. This allocation enables the formation of an **attribute embedding vector** of length $\frac{k}{2}$ per attribute, allowing our framework to efficiently integrate node interactions and attribute relations within the constrained embedding space.

In our work, matrices are represented by bold uppercase letters, such as $\mathbf{M}$. Specifically, $\mathbf{M}[v_i]$ indicates the row vector of $\mathbf{M}$ corresponding to $v_i$, while $\mathbf{M}[:, r_j]$ refers to the column vector associated with $r_j$. The entry at the intersection of the $v_i$-th row and $r_j$-th column in matrix $\mathbf{M}$ is denoted as $\mathbf{M}[v_i, r_j]$. Additionally, for any index set $S$, $\mathbf{M}[S]$ designates the submatrix that includes rows or columns as specified by $S$.

Let $\mathbf{A}$ denote the adjacency matrix for the property graph $G$, where $\mathbf{A}[v_i, v_j] = 1$ if there exists an edge $(v_i, v_j) \in E_v$, and $\mathbf{A}[v_i, v_j] = 0$ otherwise. We define $\mathbf{D}$ as the diagonal matrix of out-degrees for $G$, where each diagonal entry $\mathbf{D}[v_i, v_i] = \sum_{v_j \in V} \mathbf{A}[v_i, v_j]$ represents the out-degree of node $v_i$. The random walk matrix $\mathbf{P} = \mathbf{D}^{-1}\mathbf{A}$ is then constructed to represent the transition probabilities for a random walk moving from node $v_i$ to $v_j$.

To capture attribute-level interactions, we introduce an **attribute matrix** $\mathbf{R} \in \mathbb{R}^{n \times d}$, where each entry $\mathbf{R}[v_i, r_j] = w_{i,j}$ encodes the weight of association between node $v_i$ and attribute $r_j$, as specified in the property graph edge $(v_i, r_j, w_{i,j}) \in E_R$. The vector $\mathbf{R}[v_i]$ is termed the **attribute vector** of node $v_i$. Using $\mathbf{R}$, we derive row-normalized and column-normalized attribute matrices, denoted by $\mathbf{R}_r$ and $\mathbf{R}_c$, respectively, defined as follows:

$$\mathbf{R}_r[v_i, r_j] = \frac{\mathbf{R}[v_i, r_j]}{\sum_{r_l \in R} \mathbf{R}[v_i, r_l]}, \quad \mathbf{R}_c[v_i, r_j] = \frac{\mathbf{R}[v_i, r_j]}{\sum_{v_l \in V} \mathbf{R}[v_l, r_j]}. \quad (1)$$

**Rule-Based Random Walk:** Our approach leverages an *extended graph* $G'$ (Fig. 2(b)), which is an augmented version of the original graph $G$. The extended graph $G'$ is constructed by adding supplementary nodes and edges to $G$, which represent attribute associations and relationships. For example, Fig. 2(b) illustrates the extended graph $G'$ constructed from a given property input, where the black part represents the original graph $G$ and the blue part shows the added attribute associations $E_R$ within $G'$. The embedding generated for each vertex $v \in V$ encodes its *affinity* to the attribute set $R$, considering both attributes directly attached to $v$ and those reachable through longer paths in $E_V$. To capture such multi-hop relationships, we employ a random-walk-with-restart (RWR) [26,27] method specifically adapted to our directed extended graph $G'$. Because edge orientations matter, the procedure yields two complementary affinity scores: a forward measure, denoted $\mathbb{F}$, and a backward measure, denoted $\mathbb{B}$.

**Forward Affinity:** Given an attributed graph $G$, a vertex $v_i$, and a restart probability $\alpha$ with $0 < \alpha < 1$, a *forward random walk* begins at $v_i$. When the walker is currently located at vertex $v_l$, it will either stop at that vertex with probability $\alpha$ or, with probability $1 - \alpha$, traverse one outgoing edge chosen uniformly at random to an out-neighbour of $v_l$ contained in $E_V$.

Once the random walk terminates at a node $v_l$, an edge in $E_R$ is randomly selected to connect to an attribute $r_j$ based on the probability $\mathbf{R}_r[v_l, r_j]$, where $\mathbf{R}_r[v_l, r_j]$ represents a normalized edge weight as defined in Eq. 1. Upon reaching an attribute, we check whether it satisfies predefined rules. If a rule is satisfied, we examine the rule's left-hand side (LHS). If the LHS contains a single literal, we directly perform a **rule jump** to the right-hand side (RHS). For cases where the LHS contains multiple literals, we first propagate within the LHS before jumping to the RHS. This process yields more *node-to-attribute pairs* $(v_i, r_j)$ than previous random walks methods [14], and these pairs are collected in the set $S_f$.

Assume that every vertex $v_i$ contributes $n_r$ sampled node–attribute pairs. Under this setting, the cardinality of $S_f$ becomes $n_r \cdot n + \delta$, where $n$ is the number of vertices in $G$ and $\delta$ records extra pairs generated by rule jumps. Let $p'_f(v_i, r_j)$ denote the probability that a forward random walk starting from $v_i$ (with rule jumps enabled) outputs the pair $(v_i, r_j)$. We therefore define the *forward affinity* between $v_i$ and $r_j$ as

$$\mathbb{F}[v_i, r_j] = \log\left(\frac{n \cdot p'_f(v_i, r_j)}{\sum_{v_h \in V} p'_f(v_h, r_j)} + 1\right) \qquad (2)$$

To interpret this quantity, note that within $S_f$ the marginal probabilities satisfy $\mathbf{P}(v_i) = 1/n$, $\mathbf{P}(r_j) = \dfrac{\sum_{v_h \in V} p'_f(v_h, r_j)}{n + \delta}$, and the joint probability is $\mathbf{P}(v_i, r_j) = \dfrac{p'_f(v_i, r_j)}{n + \delta}$. Hence $\mathbb{F}[v_i, r_j]$ can be regarded as a *Shifted PMI* (SPMI) score, where the constant $+1$ guarantees non-negativity. A larger value indicates a stronger tendency for the node–attribute pair to co-occur in $S_f$.

**Backward Affinity:** For a directed, attributed graph $G$, an attribute $r_j$, and a restart probability $\alpha$ ($0 < \alpha < 1$), a *backward random walk* is defined as follows. First, a vertex $v_l$ is selected according to the distribution $\mathcal{R}_c[v_l, r_j]$ given in Eq. 1. The walk then proceeds from $v_l$; at each step it halts at the current node with probability $\alpha$ or traverses a uniformly sampled outgoing edge with probability $1 - \alpha$. Whenever the walk stops at vertex $v_i$, we record the pair $(r_j, v_i)$ and insert it into the multiset $\mathcal{S}_b$. Sampling $n_r$ such pairs for every attribute yields $|\mathcal{S}_b| = n_r \cdot d$, where $d$ is the number of distinct attributes.

Let $p_b(v_i, r_j)$ be the probability that a backward walk starting from $r_j$ terminates at $v_i$. Inside $\mathcal{S}_b$ we have $\mathbf{P}(r_j) = 1/d$, $\mathbf{P}(v_i) = \sum_{r_h \in \mathcal{R}} p_b(v_i, r_h)/d$, and $\mathbf{P}(v_i, r_j) = p_b(v_i, r_j)$. By the Shifted PMI (SPMI) scheme, the *backward affinity* [14] is defined as

$$\mathbb{B}[v_i, r_j] = \log\left(\frac{d \cdot p_b(v_i, r_j)}{\sum_{r_h \in \mathcal{R}} p_b(v_i, r_h)} + 1\right). \qquad (3)$$

**Objective Function:** Given the rule-based forward affinities $\mathbb{F}[v_i, r_j]$ and backward affinities $\mathbb{B}[v_i, r_j]$ (Eqs. 2, 3), we learn compact embeddings under a space budget $k$. Each vertex $v_i$ is assigned two vectors in $\mathbb{R}^{k/2}$: a forward embedding $\mathbf{X}_f[v_i]$ and a backward embedding $\mathbf{X}_b[v_i]$. Every attribute $r_j$ obtains a vector $\mathbf{Y}[r_j] \in \mathbb{R}^{k/2}$. The parameters are obtained by minimising the squared reconstruction error:

$$\mathcal{O} = \min_{\mathbf{X}_f, \mathbf{Y}, \mathbf{X}_b} \sum_{v_i \in V} \sum_{r_j \in \mathcal{R}} \left( \left( \mathbb{F}[v_i, r_j] - \mathbf{X}_f[v_i] \cdot \mathbf{Y}[r_j]^\top \right)^2 \right.$$
$$\left. + \left( \mathbb{B}[v_i, r_j] - \mathbf{X}_b[v_i] \cdot \mathbf{Y}[r_j]^\top \right)^2 \right). \tag{4}$$

The first term aligns the forward embeddings with forward affinities, while the second term enforces an analogous alignment for the backward direction, ensuring that the learned representations faithfully encode bidirectional nodeâĂŞattribute relationships within the prescribed dimensionality bound.

### 4.3 Item Recommendation Module

The enriched node and attribute embeddings generated from rule-based random walks are subsequently integrated into a GCN model adapted from [19]. This model leverages both structural and semantic information from the embeddings to predict user-item interactions more accurately. Specifically, we input both the forward and backward embedding vectors for each node, allowing the GCN model to capture transitive dependencies and attribute-based similarities. This integration enhances the model's ability to recommend relevant items to users based on their embedding proximity within the property graph.

To prepare the forward and backward embeddings for input into the GCN, we perform a series of operations, combining weighted summation, normalization, and scaling in a unified transformation. The combined embedding $\mathbf{X}_{\text{final}} \in \mathbb{R}^{n \times d}$ for each node is computed as follows:

$$\mathbf{X}_{\text{final}} = \frac{\alpha \cdot \mathbf{X}_f \odot \mathbf{Y} + \beta \cdot \mathbf{X}_b \odot \mathbf{Y} - \mu_{\text{sum}}}{\sigma_{\text{sum}}} \cdot \sqrt{\frac{2}{d_{\text{in}} + d_{\text{out}}}} \tag{5}$$

We feed the normalized and scaled embeddings $\mathbf{X}_{\text{final}}$ into the GCN model as the input layer. For training, we employ a pairwise loss function based on BPR, aiming to maximize the ranking of observed user-item interactions over unobserved ones. The optimization objective is defined as:

$$L_{BPR} = -\sum_{u=1}^{M} \sum_{i \in N_u} \sum_{j \notin N_u} \ln \sigma(\hat{y}_{ui} - \hat{y}_{uj}) + \lambda \|\mathbf{E}^{(0)}\|^2, \tag{6}$$

where $\sigma$ denotes the sigmoid function, $\hat{y}_{ui}$ and $\hat{y}_{uj}$ denote the predicted scores for an observed item $i$ and an unobserved (negative) item $j$ with respect to user $u$, respectively. Here, $M$ is the number of users, $N_u \subseteq I$ is the set of items user $u$ has interacted with, and $j \notin N_u$ indicates that $j$ is randomly sampled from the set of items not interacted with by $u$. This negative sampling process generates implicit contrastive pairs to guide the model toward ranking positive interactions higher than unobserved ones. The term $\lambda \|\mathbf{E}^{(0)}\|^2$ denotes $L_2$ regularization applied to the GCN input embeddings $\mathbf{E}^{(0)}$, constructed by combining rule-guided forward and backward node representations. We utilize the Adam optimizer for training, with mini-batch sampling to efficiently learn the model parameters.

This optimization approach, focusing on ranking-based recommendation, allows the GCN model to leverage both structural and attribute-based information from the embeddings to provide improved recommendations.

## 5 Experiments

### 5.1 Experimental Setup

Table 1. Summary of dataset statistics.

| Name | Type | $|V|$ | $|E_V|$ | $|R|$ | $|E_R|$ | Sparsity |
|---|---|---|---|---|---|---|
| Facebook | undirected | 4,039 | 88,234 | 1,283 | 33,301 | 0.00544 |
| Blogcatalog | undirected | 5,196 | 343,486 | 8,189 | 369,435 | 0.01272 |
| Flickr | undirected | 7,575 | 479,476 | 12,047 | 182,517 | 0.00836 |
| Citeseer | directed | 3,312 | 4,660 | 3,703 | 105,165 | 0.00053 |

Table 1 summarizes the datasets used in our experiments. The Facebook dataset consists of ego-networks where users interact with friends, and attributes are extracted from user profiles. The BlogCatalog dataset is a social network of bloggers with keywords as attributes. The Flickr dataset includes photos, with tags as attributes. Citeseer, a directed citation network, is used as a benchmark. $|V|$ and $|E_V|$ represent the number of nodes and edges, while $|R|$ and $|E_R|$ denote the number of attributes and node-attribute associations. The datasets vary in size and sparsity. Here, sparsity is defined as the ratio of the number of observed interactions to the total possible interactions between users and items. A lower sparsity value indicates a more incomplete interaction matrix, which often poses challenges for recommendations.

For our experiments, we split each dataset into 80% for training and 20% for testing. We compare our method against three baseline recommendation approaches: collaborative filtering (BPR-MF [25]), GCN-based methods (LightGCN [19] and IMP-GCN [20]), and attribute-enhanced methods (AF-GCN [24], $A^2$-GCN [23] ). All methods are optimized using a pair-wise learning strategy, with Recall@20 [29] and NDCG@20 [30] as evaluation metrics. Recall@20 measures the proportion of relevant items in the top 20 recommendations out of all relevant items a user interacted with. NDCG@20, denoting the normalized

**Table 2.** Performance of our RAE model and the competitors over four datasets. Values are reported as percentages ('%' omitted).

| Type | Method | Facebook | | Blogcatalog | | Flickr | | Citeseer | |
|---|---|---|---|---|---|---|---|---|---|
| | | R@20 | N@20 | R@20 | N@20 | R@20 | N@20 | R@20 | N@20 |
| **CF** | BPR-MF | 0.2342 | 0.2706 | 0.0976 | 0.1257 | 0.1372 | 0.1428 | 0.0609 | 0.0474 |
| **GCN** | LightGCN | 0.2462 | 0.3132 | 0.1406 | 0.1249 | 0.2092 | 0.1696 | <u>0.1246</u> | 0.0839 |
| | IMP-GCN | 0.2411 | 0.1578 | 0.1493 | 0.1361 | 0.1537 | 0.1537 | 0.1152 | <u>0.0879</u> |
| **Attr.** | AF-GCN | 0.2516 | 0.3173 | <u>0.1640</u> | <u>0.1495</u> | <u>0.2227</u> | <u>0.1792</u> | 0.1127 | 0.0793 |
| | $A^2$-GCN | <u>0.2554</u> | <u>0.3214</u> | 0.1429 | 0.1412 | 0.1987 | 0.1624 | 0.1169 | 0.0803 |
| **Our** | RAE | **0.2695** | **0.3381** | **0.1717** | **0.1588** | **0.2346** | **0.1853** | **0.1615** | **0.1005** |
| | Improvement | 5.52% | 5.22% | 4.72% | 6.21% | 5.36% | 3.35% | 29.64% | 14.41% |

Note: **Bold** and <u>underline</u> indicate best and second-best results, respectively.

discounted cumulative gain, evaluates the ranking quality by rewarding relevant items positioned higher in the list, with scores discounted logarithmically for lower ranks, normalized against the best possible ranking.

In implementation, we used TensorFlow, the Adam optimizer, a mini-batch size of 2048 (1024 for Citeseer), and explored learning rates from 0.01, 0.001, 0.0001. The L2 regularization coefficient was searched within $[10^{-5}, 10^{-2}]$. Latent vector dimensions were set to 64, stopping and validation strategies followed those used in LightGCN [19].

### 5.2 Performance Comparison

We evaluate our RAE method against five baselines, with results summarized in Table 2. Three key findings emerge from this evaluation.

GCN-based approaches (LightGCN, IMP-GCN) consistently outperform BPR-MF across all datasets, highlighting the importance of graph-based modeling in capturing complex user-item relationships through high-order connectivity. This demonstrates the superiority of GCN over traditional methods, underscoring its potential for improving recommendation systems. Models incorporating attribute data (AF-GCN, $A^2$-GCN) show significant performance improvements over non-attribute baselines. However, their performance is limited by simplistic attribute integration, as seen with AF-GCN's reliance on <users, items, attributes> triples, which fail to fully leverage the rich semantic structures inherent in property graphs.

RAE achieves state-of-the-art performance, with substantial improvements over the best baseline (AF-GCN). Its rule-mining mechanism enriches embeddings through semantic pattern discovery, significantly enhancing performance in challenging datasets. These results confirm RAE's effectiveness as a robust solution for real-world recommendation systems.

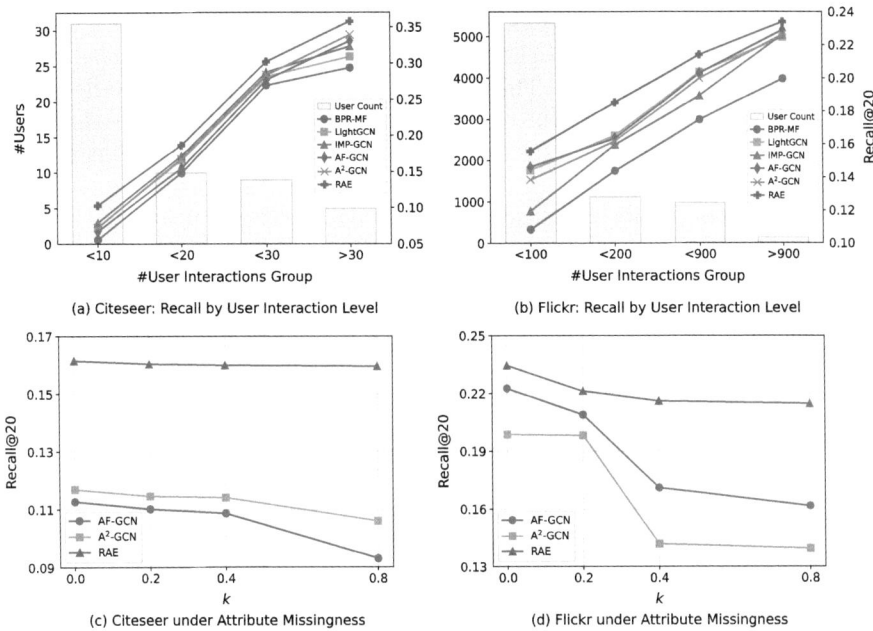

**Fig. 3.** (a)-(b) Perfomance comparison of the sparsity distribution of the user on different datasets. (c)-(d) Impact of attributes missing with attribute removed randomly in ratio of 0, 0.2, 0.4, 0.8. k is the ratio of removed attributes in each dataset.

### 5.3 Effects of Data Sparsity

Attribute information plays a crucial role in addressing data sparsity issues in recommendation systems. To examine the effectiveness of RAE under varying levels of user interaction sparsity, we divided users into four groups based on their interaction counts: fewer than 100, 200, 900, and more than 900 for the Flickr dataset, and fewer than 10, 20, 30, and more than 30 for the Citeseer dataset. Figure 3 (a)-(b) presents the Recall@20 results for each user group on Citeseer and Flickr.

In both datasets, models that leverage attribute information, such as AF-GCN and $A^2$-GCN, consistently outperform collaborative filtering methods like BPR-MF, highlighting the benefit of attributes in sparse settings. GCN-based models, such as LightGCN and IMP-GCN, also show enhanced performance compared to traditional CF methods, indicating the effectiveness of utilizing high-order connectivity within graph structures.

RAE consistently surpasses all baseline models across all sparsity levels in both datasets. This indicates that the rule-driven attribute embedding in RAE is particularly effective for capturing relationships in sparse data. For instance, on the Citeseer dataset, RAE achieves notable improvements in each interaction group, demonstrating its resilience and effectiveness even when interactions are extremely limited. Interestingly, the performance of RAE improves as the number of interactions increases. For example, in Citeseer, RAE's relative improvement over the best baseline method grows incrementally across groups with higher interaction counts. This trend suggests that while RAE is effective in very sparse scenarios, the presence of additional interactions enhances its ability to propagate attribute information within the graph structure, leading to even greater performance gains.

Overall, these results demonstrate that RAE effectively mitigates the challenges posed by data sparsity, outperforming baseline methods consistently by leveraging both attribute information and the graph structure. This robust performance in sparse datasets highlights RAE's potential for enhancing recommendation accuracy in real-world applications where user interactions are often limited.

### 5.4 Effects of the Attribute Missing Problem

In this section, we investigate the effects of missing attributes on attribute-aware recommendation methodologies. To simulate this scenario, we randomly removed attribute labels from the datasets at varying rates: 0%, 20%, 40%, and 80%. Specifically, a 20% missing rate indicates that 20% of the attribute labels were randomly omitted from the dataset. Due to constraints on space, we focus our presentation of results on the Citeseer and Flickr datasets, as shown in Fig. 3 (c)-(d). Notably, similar trends were observed across other datasets, reinforcing the robustness of our findings.

The results presented in Fig. 3 (c)-(d) for the Citeseer and Flickr datasets, show that RAE consistently outperforms the baselines AF-GCN and $A^2$-GCN across all missing attribute levels. While performance declines as more attributes are missing, RAE experiences a notably smaller decline. For example, on Citeseer, RAE's Recall@20 drops slightly from 0.161 to 0.160 at 80%, whereas AF-GCN and $A^2$-GCN show more significant reductions. Similar trends are observed on the Flickr dataset.

RAE's rule-driven embedding approach contributes to its robustness, as it effectively integrates attribute information and reduces dependency on complete data. This makes RAE particularly suitable for real-world recommendation tasks where attribute data may be incomplete, highlighting its practicality in such scenarios.

### 5.5 Ablation Study

We analyze the contribution of different components to the performance of our RAE model by comparing it with the following variants: **GCN**$_b$, which applies only GCN to the graph structure without rule-based random walks or attribute embeddings; **RAE**$_h$, which uses half of the available rules for the rule-based random walk to assess the impact of partial rule application; **RAE**$_n$, which employs regular random walks without rule guidance, serving as an embedding baseline; and **RAE**$_u$, where the random walk embeddings are fed directly into the GCN without further refinement.

**Table 3.** Performance Comparison of Different RAE Variants on Various Datasets

| Datasets | Blogcatalog | | Flickr | | Citeseer | |
|---|---|---|---|---|---|---|
| Methods | R@20 | N@20 | R@20 | N@20 | R@20 | N@20 |
| $GCN_b$ | 0.1406 | 0.1249 | 0.2092 | 0.1596 | 0.1246 | 0.0839 |
| $RAE_h$ | 0.1663 | 0.1537 | 0.2335 | 0.1789 | 0.1593 | 0.0991 |
| $RAE_n$ | 0.1659 | 0.1525 | 0.2322 | 0.1827 | 0.1575 | 0.0961 |
| $RAE_u$ | 0.1642 | 0.1485 | 0.2234 | 0.1792 | 0.1557 | 0.0636 |
| RAE | **0.1717** | **0.1588** | **0.2346** | **0.1853** | **0.1615** | **0.1005** |

Note: **Bold** indicates the best performance in each column.

The results, presented in Table 3, reveal that $RAE_h$ outperforms both $GCN_b$ and $RAE_u$, highlighting the significant enhancement brought by rule-based random walks, even with partial rule information. The improvement of RAE over $RAE_u$ confirms the importance of embedding refinement after the random walk. $RAE_n$, which uses traditional random walks, performs better than $GCN_b$ but still falls short of $RAE_h$ and the complete RAE model, emphasizing the added value of rule-based guidance.

In summary, the ablation study confirms that each component of RAE, including rule-based random walks and embedding refinement, contributes significantly to its superior performance, validating our design choices.

## 6 Conclusion

In this work, we introduced **RAE**, a novel *Rule-Driven Approach for Attribute Embedding*, designed to enhance recommendation systems by leveraging the semantic richness of property graphs. Through rule mining and rule-based random walks, RAE effectively utilizes attribute information within property graphs, overcoming the limitations of traditional Graph Convolutional Network (GCN) models that typically overlook the complex dependencies between attributes. Our extensive experiments demonstrate RAE's superior performance in recommendation tasks across various datasets, showing substantial improvements in recall and robustness compared to state-of-the-art baselines.

Beyond improving accuracy, RAE's design allows for better interpretability by tracing recommendations back to mined semantic rules, offering clearer insights into why items are suggested. This makes it particularly valuable in user-facing applications where transparency is critical. Overall, RAE provides a robust foundation for property graph-based attribute embedding and opens new directions for building more trustworthy, interpretable, and effective recommendation systems in real-world settings. Future work includes optimizing the computational efficiency of rule-based embedding and extending the framework to support dynamic attribute evolution in temporal or continuously evolving graphs.

**Acknowledgments.** The first author, affiliated with Huazhong Agricultural University, was funded by the Provincial Innovation and Entrepreneurship Training Program for Undergraduates under Grant No. S202310504323. The authors affiliated with institutions 1, 4, 5, and 6 were supported in part by the Hubei Key Research and Development Program of China under Grants 2024BBB055, 2024BAA008, and in part by the Fundamental Research Funds for the Chinese Central Universities under Grant 2662025XXPY005, and in part by the open funds of Hubei Three Gorges Laboratory under Grant SK232011.

# References

1. Berlingerio, M., Bonchi, F., Bringmann, B., Gionis, A.: Mining graph evolution rules. In: Buntine, W., Grobelnik, M., Mladenić, D., Shawe-Taylor, J. (eds.) ECML PKDD 2009. LNCS (LNAI), vol. 5781, pp. 115–130. Springer, Heidelberg (2009). https://doi.org/10.1007/978-3-642-04180-8_25
2. Scharwächter, E., Müller, E., Donges, J.F., Hassani, M., Seidl, T.: Detecting change processes in dynamic networks by frequent graph evolution rule mining. In: Proceedings of the IEEE International Conference on Data Mining (ICDM), pp. 1191–1196. (2016)
3. Leung, C.W., Lim, E.-P., Lo, D., Weng, J.: Mining interesting link formation rules in social networks. In: Proceedings of the ACM International Conference on Information and Knowledge Management (CIKM), pp. 209–218. (2010)
4. Qu, M., Chen, J., Xhonneux, L.-P.A.C., Bengio, Y., Tang, J.: RNNLogic: learning logic rules for reasoning on knowledge graphs. In: Proceedings of the International Conference on Learning Representations (ICLR). (2021)
5. Vaculík, K.: A versatile algorithm for predictive graph rule mining. In: Proceedings of the Information Technologies – Applications and Theory (ITAT), pp. 51–58. (2015)
6. Yan, X., Han, J.: gSpan: graph-based substructure pattern mining. In: Proceedings of the IEEE International Conference on Data Mining (ICDM), pp. 721–724. (2002)
7. Fan, W., Fu, W., Jin, R., Liu, M., Lu, P., Tian, C.: Making it tractable to catch duplicates and conflicts in graphs. Proc. ACM Manag. Data **1**(1), 86:1–86:28 (2023)
8. Fan, W., Fu, W., Jin, R., Lu, P., Tian, C.: Discovering association rules from big graphs. Proc. VLDB Endow. **15**(7), 1479–1492 (2022)
9. Fan, W., Hu, C., Liu, X., Lu, P.: Discovering graph functional dependencies. ACM Trans. Database Syst. **45**(3), 15:1–15:42 (2020)
10. Kwashie, S., Liu, J., Li, J., Liu, L., Stumptner, M., Yang, L.: Certus: an effective entity resolution approach with graph differential dependencies (GDDs). Proc. VLDB Endow. **12**(6), 653–666 (2019)
11. Zhou, G., et al.: FastAGEDs: fast approximate graph entity dependency discovery. In: Zhang, F., Wang, H., Barhamgi, M., Chen, L., Zhou, R. (eds.) Web Information Systems Engineering – WISE 2023: 24th International Conference, pp. 451–465. Springer, Berlin, Heidelberg (2023). https://doi.org/10.1007/978-981-99-7254-8_35
12. Fan, W., Liu, M., Liu, S., Tian, C.: Capturing more associations by referencing external graphs. Proc. VLDB Endow. **17**(6), 1173–1186 (2024). https://doi.org/10.14778/3648160.3648162

13. Yang, R., Shi, J., Xiao, X., Yang, Y., Liu, J., Bhowmick, S.S.: Scaling attributed network embedding to massive graphs. Proc. VLDB Endowment (PVLDB) **14**(1), 37–49 (2020). 10.14778/3421424.3421430
14. Yang, R., Shi, J., Xiao, X., Yang, Y., Bhowmick, S.S., Liu, J.: PANE: scalable and effective attributed network embedding. The VLDB J. **32**(6), 1237–1262,: Springer. Berlin, Heidelberg (2023). https://doi.org/10.1007/s00778-023-00790-4
15. Comon, P., Luciani, X., De Almeida, A.L.F.: Tensor decompositions, alternating least squares and other tales. J. Chemom. **23**, 393–405 (2009). https://doi.org/10.1002/cem.1236
16. Wang, J., Qu, X., Bai, J., Li, Z., Zhang, J., Gao, J.: Sages: scalable attributed graph embedding with sampling for unsupervised learning. IEEE Trans. Knowl. Data Eng., 1–1 (2022). https://doi.org/10.1109/TKDE.2022.3148272
17. Yang, H., Pan, S., Chen, L., Zhou, C., Zhang, P.: Low-bit quantization for attributed network representation learning. In: Proceedings of the 28th International Joint Conference on Artificial Intelligence (IJCAI'19), pp. 4047–4053. AAAI Press (2019)
18. Yang, H., Pan, S., Zhang, P., Chen, L., Lian, D., Zhang, C.: Binarized attributed network embedding. In: IEEE International Conference on Data Mining (ICDM), pp. 1476–1481. (2018). 10.1109/ICDM.2018.8626170
19. He, X., Deng, K., Wang, X., Li, Y., Zhang, Y., Wang, M.: LightGCN: simplifying and powering graph convolution network for recommendation. In: Proceedings of the 43rd International ACM SIGIR Conference on Research and Development in Information Retrieval (SIGIR '20), pp. 639–648. ACM, New York (2020). https://doi.org/10.1145/3397271.3401063
20. Liu, F., Cheng, Z., Zhu, L., Gao, Z., Nie, L.: Interest-aware message-passing GCN for recommendation. In: The Web Conference 2021 (WWW), pp. 1296–1305. ACM, New York (2021). https://doi.org/10.1145/3442381.3449986
21. Wang, X., He, X., Wang, M., Feng, F., Chua, T.-S.: Neural graph collaborative filtering. In: Proceedings of the 42nd International ACM SIGIR Conference on Research and Development in Information Retrieval (SIGIR), pp. 165–174. ACM, New York (2019). https://doi.org/10.1145/3331184.3331267
22. Ying, R., He, R., Chen, K., Eksombatchai, P., Hamilton, W.L., Leskovec, J.: Graph convolutional neural networks for web-scale recommender systems. In: KDD, London, UK, pp. 974–983. (2018). https://doi.org/10.1145/3219819.3219890
23. Liu, F., Cheng, Z., Zhu, L., Liu, C., Nie, L.: An attribute-aware attentive GCN model for attribute missing in recommendation. IEEE Trans. Knowl. Data Eng. **34**(9), 4077–4088 (2022). https://doi.org/10.1109/TKDE.2020.3040772
24. Yue, G., Xiao, R., Zhao, Z., Li, C.: AF-GCN: attribute-fusing graph convolution network for recommendation. IEEE Trans. Big Data **9**(2), 597–607 (2023). https://doi.org/10.1109/TBDATA.2022.3192598
25. Rendle, S., Freudenthaler, C., Gantner, Z., Schmidt-Thieme, L.: BPR: Bayesian personalized ranking from implicit feedback. In: UAI, pp. 452–461. (2009)
26. Jeh, G., Widom, J.: Scaling personalized web search. In: Proc. 12th International Conference on World Wide Web (WWW), pp. 271–279. ACM, New York (2003). 10.1145/775152.775191
27. Tong, H., Faloutsos, C., Pan, J.-Y.: Fast random walk with restart and its applications. In: 6th International Conference on Data Mining (ICDM), pp. 613–622. IEEE Computer Society, USA (2006). https://doi.org/10.1109/ICDM.2006.70
28. Liu, D., et al.: An efficient approach for discovering Graph Entity Dependencies (GEDs). Inf. Syst. **125**, 102421 (2024). https://doi.org/10.1016/j.is.2024.102421

29. He, X., Chua, T.-S.: Neural factorization machines for sparse predictive analytics. In: Proceedings of the 40th International ACM SIGIR Conference on Research and Development in Information Retrieval (SIGIR '17), pp. 355–364. ACM, New York, NY, USA (2017). https://doi.org/10.1145/3077136.3080777
30. Deshpande, M., Karypis, G.: Item-based top-N recommendation algorithms. ACM Trans. Inf. Syst. **22**(1), 143–177 (2004). https://doi.org/10.1145/963770.963776
31. Hu, J., et al.: When GDD meets GNN: a knowledge-driven neural connection for effective entity resolution in property graphs. Inf. Syst. **132**, 102551 (2025). https://doi.org/10.1016/j.is.2025.102551
32. Cai, X., Huang, C., Xia, L., Ren, X.: LightGCL: simple yet effective graph contrastive learning for recommendation. In: The Eleventh International Conference on Learning Representations (ICLR). (2023)
33. Ren, X., et al.: SSLRec: a self-supervised learning framework for recommendation. In: Proceedings of the 17th ACM International Conference on Web Search and Data Mining (WSDM), pp. 567–575. Mérida, Mexico (2024). https://doi.org/10.1145/3616855.3635814
34. He, W., Sun, G., Lu, J., Fang, X.S.: Candidate-aware graph contrastive learning for recommendation. In: Proceedings of the 46th International ACM SIGIR Conference on Research and Development in Information Retrieval (SIGIR), pp. 1670–1679. Taipei, Taiwan (2023). https://doi.org/10.1145/3539618.3591647
35. Wang, H., et al.: RippleNet: propagating user preferences on the knowledge graph for recommender systems. In: Proceedings of the 27th ACM International Conference on Information and Knowledge Management (CIKM), pp. 417–426. Torino, Italy (2018). https://doi.org/10.1145/3269206.3271739
36. Wang, H., Zhao, M., Xie, X., Li, W., Guo, M.: Knowledge graph convolutional networks for recommender systems. In: The World Wide Web Conference (WWW), pp. 3307–3313. San Francisco, CA, USA (2019). https://doi.org/10.1145/3308558.3313417
37. Ma, W., et al.: Jointly learning explainable rules for recommendation with knowledge graph. In: The World Wide Web Conference (WWW), pp. 1210–1221. San Francisco, CA, USA (2019). https://doi.org/10.1145/3308558.3313607

# Reinforcement Learning

# Collaborative Value Function Estimation Under Model Mismatch: A Federated Temporal Difference Analysis

Ali Beikmohammadi[1](✉), Sarit Khirirat[2], Peter Richtárik[2], and Sindri Magnússon[1]

[1] Department of Computer and Systems Sciences, Stockholm University, 16425 Stockholm, Sweden
{beikmohammadi,sindri.magnusson}@dsv.su.se
[2] King Abdullah University of Science and Technology (KAUST), Thuwal, Saudi Arabia
{sarit.khirirat,peter.richtarik}@kaust.edu.sa

**Abstract.** Federated reinforcement learning (FedRL) enables collaborative learning while preserving data privacy by preventing direct data exchange between agents. However, many existing FedRL algorithms assume that all agents operate in *identical environments*, which is often unrealistic. In real-world applications, such as multi-robot teams, crowd-sourced systems, and large-scale sensor networks, each agent may experience slightly different transition dynamics, leading to inherent model mismatches. In this paper, we first establish *linear convergence* guarantees for single-agent temporal difference learning (TD(0)) in *policy evaluation* and demonstrate that under a perturbed environment, the agent suffers a systematic bias that prevents accurate estimation of the true value function. This result holds under both *i.i.d.* and *Markovian* sampling regimes. We then extend our analysis to the federated TD(0) (FedTD(0)) setting, where multiple agents, each interacting with its own perturbed environment, *periodically* share value estimates to collaboratively approximate the true value function of a common underlying model. Our theoretical results indicate the impact of model mismatch, network connectivity, and mixing behavior on the convergence of FedTD(0). Empirical experiments corroborate our theoretical gains, highlighting that even moderate levels of information sharing significantly mitigate environment-specific errors.

**Keywords:** Federated Reinforcement Learning · Model Mismatch in Reinforcement Learning · Temporal Difference Learning · Policy Evaluation

## 1 Introduction

Reinforcement learning (RL) has been widely applied in various domains, including robotics, healthcare, finance, and game playing, where agents must learn

---

**Supplementary Information** The online version contains supplementary material available at https://doi.org/10.1007/978-3-032-06106-5_3.

to make sequential decisions in uncertain environments [43]. An agent in RL interacts with an unknown environment, observing states, taking actions, and receiving rewards, with the objective of learning an optimal policy that maximizes cumulative rewards. A key challenge in RL is learning the value function efficiently, especially when interactions with the environment are costly or time-consuming [4–6,45].

Recently, *federated reinforcement learning* (FedRL) has emerged as a promising framework to improve sample efficiency and reduce learning time by allowing multiple agents to learn in parallel while exchanging information [37,58]. In a typical FedRL setup, multiple agents operate independently in separate instances of an environment, collect data locally, and communicate periodically their learned value estimates or policies to a central server or peer-to-peer network [25,50]. By aggregating these estimates, FedRL can improve learning efficiency and robustness, particularly in distributed applications that exhibit data privacy or communication constraints [22,52].

However, existing literature in FedRL usually assumes that all agents interact with *identical* environments [2,17,25,29,39]. In practice, this assumption often fails to hold. In multi-robot teams, different robots may have slightly different actuators, sensors, or physical constraints, thus leading to variations in transition dynamics [56]. In crowdsourced RL tasks, different users experience distinct environments due to network conditions, device capabilities, or regional differences. Even in large-scale sensor networks, environmental fluctuations can introduce discrepancies in the transition dynamics observed by different sensors. These variations lead to *model mismatch*, where each agent experiences a perturbed version of the *true* environment [31,36].

In this paper, we study whether agents operating under *perturbed* transition dynamics can still collaboratively learn the true value function. Specifically, we focus on *policy evaluation*, which plays a fundamental role in RL as a precursor to improve the policy [7,42,46]. Our central research question is: *Can agents collaboratively learn the true value function while each leveraging information from a potentially different noisy model?* The presence of model mismatch introduces systematic bias in the learned value function, which does not necessarily vanish with more iterations [24,35,49,54]. While policy evaluation is a natural starting point, recent works [20,40] have shown that with minor modifications, similar analysis techniques can extend to control settings.

*Contributions.* Our work provides a comprehensive theoretical analysis of temporal difference (TD) learning [42,43] under model mismatch in both *single-agent* and *federated* settings, under both *i.i.d.* and *Markovian* sampling regimes:

- First, we analyze **single-agent TD(0) under model mismatch**. Under both *i.i.d.* and *Markovian* sampling regimes, single-agent TD(0) attains linear convergence with the model mismatch error, which does not vanish as the algorithm progresses or when the step size decreases.
- We extend our analysis to **federated TD(0) (FedTD(0))**, where $N$ agents, each with a different transition kernel, periodically exchange value estimates.

FedTD(0) achieves linear convergence with the model mismatch error that is reduced by the aggregation of value functions evaluated by multiple agents. Furthermore, our convergence bounds explicitly depend on the number of agents, degree of heterogeneity, and communication frequency.
– Finally, we corroborate our results with **numerical experiments**, showing that even moderate levels of collaboration significantly reduce bias and accelerate convergence to the true value function. Our experiments' code is publicly available at https://github.com/AliBeikmohammadi/FedRL.

## 2 Related Work

### 2.1 Single-Agent TD Learning Algorithms

Much of the existing literature on TD learning has focused on the single-agent setting. Foundational studies proved the *asymptotic* convergence of on-policy TD methods with function approximation, leveraging stochastic approximation theory [10,44,47]. More recent advances have generalized these guarantees to off-policy learning scenarios [30,55]. In parallel, a separate line of research has established *finite-sample* or *non-asymptotic* guarantees for TD learning. In the on-policy setting, TD learning was studied under i.i.d. sampling regime by [16,27], and Markovian sampling regime by [9,12,23,32,38,40]. In the off-policy setting, non-asymptotic convergence of TD learning was also derived in [11,12]. Notably, most of these studies assume linear function approximation to leverage techniques from stochastic approximation. Our work departs from these single-agent analyses by examining a *multi-agent federated* framework, where each agent interacts with its own perturbed environment and periodically shares updates with others. This setting poses additional challenges related to agent heterogeneity, multiple dynamics, and intermittent communication, thereby requiring a specialized analytical approach.

### 2.2 Distributed and Federated RL Algorithms

*Distributed RL.* Many distributed RL algorithms have emerged to address scalability and efficiency challenges. This progress is exemplified by the development of many distributed frameworks, such as asynchronous parallelization [34], the high-throughput IMPALA architecture [19], and decentralized gossip-based protocols [1]. Theoretical convergence properties of such distributed methods have expanded to include robustness against adversarial attacks [22,52] and communication compression [33]. Furthermore, several works derived sample complexities under i.i.d. sampling for distributed RL with linear function approximation [17,29], and actor-critic algorithms [14,39]. Further work extends to decentralized stochastic approximation [41,48,57], TD learning with linear function approximation [49], and off-policy TD actor-critic algorithms [13]. However, these analyses commonly rely on two key assumptions: agents synchronize updates through continuous communication (e.g., after every local iteration) and operate in *homogeneous* environments with identical dynamical properties across all participants.

*FedRL under Homogeneous Environments.* Parallel efforts in FedRL aim to reduce communication costs by allowing agents to perform multiple local updates between periodic synchronization rounds. This paradigm has been explored in contexts such as federated TD learning with linear function approximation [15,21,25], off-policy TD methods [25], and $Q$-learning [25], with further extensions to behavior-policy heterogeneity [51] and compressed communication [2]. However, a common limitation across all these approaches remains persistent: all agents are assumed to operate in identical Markov decision processes (MDPs) (*homogeneous* environments). This assumption fails to capture real-world scenarios where agents face environmental heterogeneity.

*FedRL under Heterogeneous Environments.* To our knowledge, only four works have studied FedRL under *heterogeneous* environments—a more closely related to our setting [24,49,53,54], but each differs substantially from ours. For instance, [24] focuses on tabular $Q$-learning, and [53] studies the asymptotic behavior of distributed $Q$-learning. Meanwhile, [54] considers SARSA with linear function approximation, modeling data heterogeneity via a worst-case total-variation distance between transition kernels. The most closely related work is [49], which analyzes TD learning under Markovian sampling and periodic communication in a heterogeneous setting, but the analysis relies on function approximation, employs a more restrictive multiplicative bound on transition-model deviation, and uses a norm-induced approach that differs from ours. We depart from these approaches by considering a tabular federated policy evaluation problem in which each agent's environment is drawn from a distribution centered on the true transition model, and the agents periodically communicate with a central server. Our framework handles both i.i.d. and Markovian sampling, and it explicitly quantifies how inter-agent collaboration mitigates the bias introduced by environment perturbations in estimating the true value function. To our knowledge, this is the first systematic treatment of *model mismatch* in a tabular RL setting for both the single-agent and federated scenarios.

## 3 Model and Background

Within this section, we formalize the MDP setting and key definitions.

*Discounted Infinite-horizon MDP.* We study a discounted infinite-horizon MDP formally defined as the tuple $\mathcal{M} = \langle \mathcal{S}, \mathcal{A}, \mathcal{R}, \mathcal{P}, \gamma \rangle$. Here, $\mathcal{S}$ and $\mathcal{A}$ are finite state and action spaces, respectively; $\mathcal{P}$ represents a set of the action-dependent transition probabilities; $\mathcal{R}$ is a bounded reward function; $\gamma \in (0,1)$ is the discount factor governing long-term reward trade-offs.

*Value Function and Bellman Operator.* Under a fixed policy $\mu \colon \mathcal{S} \to \mathcal{A}$, the MDP reduces to a Markov reward process (MRP) with transition matrix $P_\mu$ and reward function $r := R_\mu$. Here, $P_\mu(s, s')$ is the probability of transitioning from $s$ to $s'$ under action $\mu(s)$, and $r(s)$ denotes the expected immediate reward at state $s$. Our goal is to evaluate the value function $V$, which captures the expected discounted return when starting from any state $s$ and following $\mu$:

$$V(s) = \mathbb{E}\left[\sum_{t=0}^{\infty} \gamma^t r(s^{(t)}) \mid s^{(0)} = s\right], \quad \forall s \in \mathcal{S}, \tag{1}$$

where the expectation is taken over trajectories generated by the transition kernel $P_\mu$ (i.e., $s^{(t+1)} \sim P_\mu(\cdot \mid s^{(t)})$) for all $t \geq 0$.

A fundamental result in dynamic programming [7,8] states that $V$ is the unique fixed point of the policy-specific Bellman operator $T \colon \mathbb{R}^{|\mathcal{S}|} \to \mathbb{R}^{|\mathcal{S}|}$, defined as:

$$(TV)(s) = r(s) + \gamma \sum_{s' \in \mathcal{S}} P_\mu(s, s') V(s') \quad \forall s \in \mathcal{S}. \tag{2}$$

Equivalently, $V$ satisfies the Bellman equation: $TV = V$.

## 4 Single-Agent TD(0) under Model Mismatch

One popular approach for estimating the value function $V$ in a model-free setting (i.e., when the underlying MDP is unknown) is the TD(0) algorithm [42,43]. At each time step $t$, the agent observes a state $s^{(t)}$, receives reward $r^{(t)} := r(s^{(t)})$, transitions to a next state $s^{(t+1)}$, and updates its current value estimate $V^{(t)}(\cdot)$ by modifying only the coordinate at $s^{(t)}$. Specifically, TD(0) updates via:

$$V^{(t+1)}(s^{(t)}) = V^{(t)}(s^{(t)}) + \alpha \delta^{(t)} \text{ and } \delta^{(t)} = r^{(t)} + \gamma V^{(t)}(s^{(t+1)}) - V^{(t)}(s^{(t)}), \tag{3}$$

where $\alpha \in (0,1)$ is a step size, and $V^{(0)}$ is some initial guess. For states $s \neq s^{(t)}$, we simply set $V^{(t+1)}(s) = V^{(t)}(s)$. Under standard assumptions—such as a sufficiently small step size $\alpha$, bounded rewards, and ergodic state sampling—TD(0) converges to the unique fixed point of the Bellman operator $T$, which is precisely the true value function $V$ of the policy $\mu$ [10,43,47].

However, this holds when the agent interacts with the true transition probability $P_\mu$, which we aim to evaluate the policy for. Here, we instead consider scenarios where the agent interacts with a perturbed environment $\hat{P}$ rather than $P_\mu$, as explained in Algorithm 1. Specifically, we analyze the convergence of the single-agent TD(0) algorithm under the following model mismatch assumption.

**Assumption 1.** *Let the empirical transition matrix $\hat{P}$ be a perturbed transition matrix of $P_\mu$, which satisfies for $\Delta > 0$*

$$\left\|\hat{P} - P_\mu\right\|_2^2 \leq \Delta^2. \tag{4}$$

Assumption 1 implies the deviation of the empirical transition matrix $\hat{P}$ from the true transition matrix $P_\mu$. Small values of $\Delta$ imply that $\hat{P}$ is close to $P_\mu$. Furthermore, $\hat{P}$ can possibly be a biased estimate of $P_\mu$.

Next, we analyze the convergence of the single-agent TD(0) algorithm under model mismatch with both well-known sampling regimes, i.i.d. and Markovian, in Sects. 4.1 and 4.2, respectively.

**Algorithm 1.** Single-agent TD(0)
---
**Initialize:** Learning rate $\alpha \in (0, 1)$, Discount factor $\gamma \in (0, 1)$, Number of communication rounds $T$, Initial value function $V^{(0)}$.
**for** each time step $t = 0, 1, \ldots, T-1$ **do**
  Observe state $s^{(t)}$ according to the chosen sampling regime (i.i.d. or Markovian).
  Receive $r^{(t)}$ and get $s^{(t+1)} \sim \hat{P}(\cdot | s^{(t)})$.
  Update $V^{(t+1)}$ via
  $$V^{(t+1)}(s^{(t)}) = V^{(t)}(s^{(t)}) + \alpha[r^{(t)} + \gamma V^{(t)}(s^{(t+1)}) - V^{(t)}(s^{(t)})].$$
**end for**
---

## 4.1 Analysis for I.I.D. Setting

In the i.i.d. sampling regime, each state $s^{(t)}$ is independently drawn from the stationary distribution over $\mathcal{S}$. Although $s^{(t)}$ and $s^{(t-1)}$ are uncorrelated, we still generate a next state $s^{(t+1)} \sim \hat{P}(\cdot | s^{(t)})$ in TD(0) update (3) to perform one-step bootstrapping. Hence, while the *tuples* $(s^{(t)}, s^{(t+1)})$ are sampled i.i.d. from the stationary distribution, the actual *visited* states do not form a Markov chain. The i.i.d. sampling regime eliminates temporal correlations in the sampled states, and therefore simplifies the convergence analysis.

The following theorem establishes the linear convergence of single-agent TD(0) under i.i.d. sampling.

**Theorem 1 (Single-agent, i.i.d. sampling).** *Consider the single-agent TD(0) algorithm (Algorithm 1) under the i.i.d. sampling. Let a row-stochastic transition matrix $\hat{P}$ satisfy Assumption 1. Then, with probability at least $1 - \delta$,*

$$\|e^{(t)}\|_2 \leq [1 - \alpha(1-\gamma)]^t \|e^{(0)}\|_2 + \frac{\gamma \Delta \sqrt{|\mathcal{S}|}}{(1-\gamma)^2} + \frac{\alpha \sqrt{t}}{(1-\gamma)} \sqrt{32(\log(t/\delta) + 1/4)},$$

*where $e^{(t)} := V^{(t)} - V$, $|\mathcal{S}|$ is the number of states, and $\alpha \in (0, 1)$.*

*Remark 1.* From Theorem 1, the single-agent TD(0) algorithm ensures linear convergence with a high probability of its value function $V^{(t)}$ towards the unique true value function $V$ with the first error term due to the model mismatch $\Delta$ and the second error term of $\frac{\alpha \sqrt{t}}{(1-\gamma)} \sqrt{32(\log(t/\delta) + 1/4)}$ due to the i.i.d. sampling regime. Decreasing the step size $\alpha$ cannot reduce the first error term due to the model mismatch, while decreasing the second error term due to i.i.d. sampling at the price of a slow convergence rate. For instance, if we choose $\alpha = 1/T^\eta$ with $\eta \in (1/2, 1)$, $0 < t \leq T$, where $T$ is the given number of total iteration counts, then the algorithm converges at the rate:

$$\|e^{(t)}\|_2 \leq \exp\left(-\frac{t(1-\gamma)}{T^\eta}\right) \|e^{(0)}\|_2 + \mathcal{O}\left(\frac{\sqrt{t \log(t)}}{T^\eta}\right) + \frac{\gamma \Delta \sqrt{|\mathcal{S}|}}{(1-\gamma)^2},$$

with probability at least $1 - \delta$. In conclusion, the convergence bound for the algorithm contains the model mismatch error term $\frac{\gamma \Delta \sqrt{|\mathcal{S}|}}{(1-\gamma)^2}$.

## 4.2 Analysis for Markovian Setting

As a more realistic setting, we also study Algorithm 1 under a Markovian sampling regime. In this regime, the states follow a Markov chain defined by the transition matrix $\hat{P}$. Concretely, $s^{(t+1)} \sim \hat{P}(\cdot \mid s^{(t)})$ for each $t$, matching our earlier definition of MRP induced by a fixed policy. Although this better captures real-world dynamics, analyzing the corresponding TD(0) updates becomes more intricate due to the temporal correlations in $\{s^{(t)}\}$. To analyze the single-agent TD(0) algorithm under the Markovian sampling regime, we make an assumption on the Markov chain and define the mixing time $\tau_\epsilon$ in the single-agent setting.

**Assumption 2.** *The Markov chain induced by the policy $\mu$ is aperiodic and irreducible.*

**Definition 1.** *Let $\tau_\epsilon$ be the minimum time such that the following holds: $\|\xi^{(t)}\|_2 \leq \epsilon, \forall t \geq \tau_\epsilon$. Here, $\xi^{(t)} \in \mathbb{R}^{|\mathcal{S}|}$ is defined by $\xi^{(t)}(s) = \delta^{(t)} - \mathbb{E}\left[\delta^{(t)} \mid \mathcal{F}^{(t)}\right]$ when $s = s^{(t)}$, and $\xi^{(t)}(s) = 0$ for all other $s$, where $\mathcal{F}^{(t)}$ is the filtration up to $t$.*

This assumption implies that the Markov chain induced by $\mu$ admits a unique stationary distribution $\pi$, and mixes at a geometric rate [28]. The consequence of this assumption is that there exists some $T \geq 1$ such that $\tau_\epsilon \leq T \log(1/\epsilon)$.

The next theorem shows the linear convergence of the single-agent TD(0) algorithm under Markovian sampling.

**Theorem 2 (Single-agent, Markovian sampling).** *Consider the single-agent TD(0) algorithm (Algorithm 1) under Markovian sampling. Let a row-stochastic transition matrix $\hat{P}$ satisfy Assumption 1 and the Markov chain satisfy Assumption 2. Then,*

$$\|e^{(t)}\|_2 \leq [1 - \alpha(1-\gamma)]^t \|e^{(0)}\|_2 + \gamma \frac{\Delta \sqrt{|\mathcal{S}|}}{(1-\gamma)^2} + \frac{\alpha}{1-\gamma}(2\tau_\alpha + 1),$$

*where $e^{(t)} := V^{(t)} - V$, $|\mathcal{S}|$ is the number of states, $\alpha \in (0,1)$, and $\tau_\alpha$ is defined by Definition 1.*

*Remark 2.* The single-agent TD(0) algorithm under the Markovian sampling regime, similar to the i.i.d. sampling regime, achieves the linear convergence of its value function $V^{(t)}$ towards the fixed value function $V$ with two residual error terms. In particular, decreasing the step size $\alpha$ cannot reduce the first error term due to the model mismatch $\Delta$, while decreasing the second error term due to the mixing time $\tau_\alpha$ of the aperiodic and irreducible Markov chain at the price of slow convergence. For instance, the algorithm with $\alpha = 1/T^\eta$ for $\eta \in (1/2, 1)$ converges at the rate

$$\|e^{(t)}\|_2 \leq \exp\left(-\frac{t(1-\gamma)}{T^\eta}\right)\|e^{(0)}\|_2 + \mathcal{O}\left(\frac{1}{T^\eta}\right) + \frac{\gamma \Delta \sqrt{|\mathcal{S}|}}{(1-\gamma)^2}.$$

In conclusion, the single-agent TD(0) algorithm under both i.i.d sampling and Markovian sampling regimes converges with the model mismatch error term $\frac{\gamma \Delta \sqrt{|\mathcal{S}|}}{(1-\gamma)^2}$ that cannot be reduced by decreasing the step size. In the next section, we show that this model mismatch error term can be reduced by the benefits of multiple agents for running the TD(0) algorithm in the federated setting.

## 5 Extension to FedTD(0) under Model Mismatch

To show the benefits of multiple agents, we extend our results to the federated setting. We consider the FedTD(0) algorithm, where multiple agents collaboratively estimate the value function. In each communication round $t = 0, 1, \ldots, T-1$, each agent $i = 1, 2, \ldots, N$ receives the global value function estimate $V^{(t)}$ from the server, sets $V_i^{(t,0)} = V^{(t)}$, and updates its local estimate $V_i^{(t,k)}$ according to:

$$V_i^{(t,k+1)}(s_i^{(t,k)}) = V_i^{(t,k)}(s_i^{(t,k)}) + \alpha \delta_i^{(t,k)}, \quad \text{and}$$
$$\delta_i^{(t,k)} = r_i^{(t,k)} + \gamma V_i^{(t,k)}(s_i^{(t,k+1)}) - V_i^{(t,k)}(s_i^{(t,k)}) \text{ for } k = 0, 1, \ldots, K-1.$$

Here, the step size is denoted by $\alpha \in (0,1)$, $s_i^{(t,k)}$ is the observed state, $r_i^{(t,k)}$ is the received reward for each agent, and $s_i^{(t,k+1)}$ is drawn from the agent's transition probability conditioned on $s_i^{(t,k)}$. Then, the central server computes the average of the received estimate progress from all the agents $\frac{1}{N}\sum_{i=1}^{N}(V_i^{(t,K)} - V^{(t)})$, and updates the global value function estimate via:

$$V^{(t+1)} = V^{(t)} + \frac{\beta}{N}\sum_{i=1}^{N}(V_i^{(t,K)} - V^{(t)}),$$

where $\beta \in (0,1]$ is the federated tuning parameter. The description of FedTD(0) algorithm is provided in Algorithm 2. To demonstrate the benefit of multiple agents in FedTD(0), we impose the following model mismatch assumption.

**Assumption 3.** *Let the empirical transition matrices $\hat{P}_1, \hat{P}_2, \ldots, \hat{P}_N$ be the perturbed matrix of $P_\mu$, which satisfies Assumption 1 with $\Delta > 0$, and also*

$$\left\| \frac{1}{N}\sum_{i=1}^{N} \hat{P}_i - P_\mu \right\|_2^2 \leq \frac{\Lambda^2}{N}. \tag{5}$$

This assumption implies that as the number of agents $N$ grows, the average model $(1/N)\sum_{i=1}^{N} \hat{P}_i$ converges to the true model $P_\mu$ at the rate $\mathcal{O}(1/N)$. This captures the intuition that if agents have similar dynamics on average, their collective behavior also becomes more predictable. In particular, this assumption captures well when $\hat{P}_i$ are row-stochastic, i.e. $\|\hat{P}_i\|_2 \leq \|\hat{P}_i\|_1 \leq 1$, and are sampled under both i.i.d. and Markovian sampling regimes. On the one hand, if $\hat{P}_i$ are sampled under i.i.d. sampling, and satisfy $\mathbb{E}\|\hat{P}_i\|_2 = P_\mu$ and $\|\hat{P}_i\|_2 \leq 1$, then according to Lemma A.2. of [18], we obtain (5) with $\Lambda = [6(1+\sqrt{\log(1/\delta)})]^2$ with probability at least $1-\delta$. On the other hand, if $\hat{P}_i$ are sampled under Markovian sampling and satisfy $\|\hat{P}_i\|_2 \leq 1$, and the Markov chain satisfies Assumption 2 with the mixing time $\tau_\epsilon$, then according to Lemma A.6 of [18] we have (5) with $\Lambda = \tilde{\mathcal{O}}(\tau_\epsilon \lceil 2\log(N)\rceil)$ in expectation.

**Algorithm 2.** FedTD(0)

**Initialize:** Learning rate $\alpha \in (0,1)$, Federated parameter $\beta \in (0,1]$, Discount factor $\gamma \in (0,1)$, Number of agents $N$, Number of local steps $K$, Number of communication rounds $T$, Initial value function $V^{(0)}$.

**for** each communication round $t = 0, 1, \ldots, T-1$ **do**
    **for** each agent $i = 1, 2, \ldots, N$ **in parallel do**
        Set $V_i^{(t,0)} = V^{(t)}$, where $V^{(t)}$ is the global value estimate from the server.
        **for** $k = 0, 1, \ldots, K-1$ **do**
            Observe state $s_i^{(t,k)}$ according to the chosen sampling (i.i.d. or Markovian).
            Receive $r_i^{(t,k)}$ and get $s_i^{(t,k+1)} \sim \hat{P}_i(\cdot | s_i^{(t,k)})$.
            Update $V_i^{(t,k+1)}$ via

$$V_i^{(t,k+1)}(s_i^{(t,k)}) = V_i^{(t,k)}(s_i^{(t,k)}) + \alpha[r_i^{(t,k)} + \gamma V_i^{(t,k)}(s_i^{(t,k+1)}) - V_i^{(t,k)}(s_i^{(t,k)})].$$

        **end for**
        Send $V_i^{(t,k+1)} - V^{(t)}$ back to the server.
    **end for**
    Server computes and broadcasts global

$$V^{(t+1)} = V^{(t)} + \frac{\beta}{N} \sum_{i=1}^{N} (V_i^{(t,K)} - V^{(t)}).$$

**end for**

## 5.1 Analysis for I.I.D. Setting

FedTD(0) under i.i.d. sampling achieves linear convergence in high probability with a lower residual error than single-agent TD(0), as shown next.

**Theorem 3 (Federated, i.i.d. sampling).** *Consider FedTD(0) (Algorithm 2) under i.i.d. sampling. Let each row-stochastic transition matrix $\hat{P}_i$ of the $i^{\text{th}}$-agent satisfy Assumption 3. Then, with probability at least $1 - \delta$,*

$$\|e^{(t)}\|_2 \leq \rho^t \|e^{(0)}\|_2 + \frac{B_1}{\sqrt{N}} + \alpha^2 B_2 + \frac{4}{\sqrt{N}} \frac{\beta \alpha \sqrt{t} \sqrt{K} [A(\delta/(3Kt))]^3}{(1-\gamma)},$$

*where $e^{(t)} := V^{(t)} - V$, $\rho = (1-\beta) + \beta[(1-\alpha) + \alpha\gamma]^K$, $B_1 = \gamma \frac{\Lambda \sqrt{|\mathcal{S}|}}{(1-\gamma)^2(1-[1-\alpha(1-\gamma)]^K)}$, $B_2 = \gamma^2 \frac{C\Delta\sqrt{|\mathcal{S}|}}{(1-\gamma)(1-[1-\alpha(1-\gamma)]^K)}$, $A(\delta) = \sqrt{2(\log(1/\delta + 1/4)}$, $C = \exp(K(C_P + C_\mu))$ where $\|\hat{P}_i^l\|_2 \leq C_P$ and $\|P_\mu^l\|_2 \leq C_\mu$ for $l, C_P, C_\mu \geq 0$, and $\beta, \alpha \in (0,1)$.*

*Remark 3.* FedTD(0) under i.i.d. sampling achieves high-probability convergence at the linear rate with the $\frac{B_1}{\sqrt{N}}$ error term due to the model mismatch $\Lambda$, the $\alpha^2 B_2$ error term due to the model mismatch $\Delta$, and the $\frac{4}{\sqrt{N}} \frac{\beta \alpha \sqrt{t} \sqrt{K} [A(\delta/(3Kt))]^3}{(1-\gamma)}$ error term due to i.i.d. sampling. Unlike the single-agent case from Theorem 1, FedTD(0) achieves the $\sqrt{N}$-speedup, where $N$ is the number of agents.

*Remark 4.* The step size $\alpha$, the federated parameter $\beta$, the number of local steps $K$, and the number of agents $N$ impact the convergence rate and residual error terms of FedTD(0) under i.i.d. sampling. We can reduce the error term due to i.i.d. sampling at the price of slow convergence, either by decreasing $\alpha$ and $\beta$. For instance, we can reduce the error term due to i.i.d. sampling by choosing $\beta = \frac{1}{T^\eta}$ and $\alpha = \frac{1}{K^\eta}$ with $\eta \in (1/2, 1)$, which yields

$$\frac{\beta\alpha\sqrt{t}\sqrt{K}[A(\delta/(3t))]^3}{(1-\gamma)} = \mathcal{O}\left(\frac{\sqrt{t}(\log(Kt/\delta))^{3/2}}{T^\eta} \frac{1}{K^{\eta-1/2}}\right).$$

Furthermore, the error term due to $\Delta$ and $\Lambda$ can be decreased only by reducing $\alpha$ and only by increasing the number of agents $N$, respectively.

*Remark 5.* Under i.i.d. sampling, FedTD(0) can be shown to achieve a significantly more accurate value function $V^{(t)}$ than single-agent TD(0). We can show this by proving that FedTD(0) attains lower residual errors than single-agent TD(0). First, two error terms due to $\Lambda$ and i.i.d. sampling of FedTD(0), unlike single-agent TD(0), vanish, as $N$ approaches $+\infty$. Second, the error term due to $\Delta$ of FedTD(0) can be proved to be lower than single-agent TD(0) by a factor of $1/(1-\gamma)$ by setting $K \to +\infty$ and $\alpha = \sqrt{\frac{1}{\gamma C}}$ in Theorem 3. This yields

$$\alpha^2 \frac{\gamma^2 C \Delta \sqrt{|\mathcal{S}|}}{(1-\gamma)(1-[1-\alpha(1-\gamma)]^K)} \approx \alpha^2 \gamma^2 \frac{C \Delta \sqrt{|\mathcal{S}|}}{(1-\gamma)} = \frac{\gamma \Delta \sqrt{|\mathcal{S}|}}{(1-\gamma)} \stackrel{\gamma \in (0,1)}{\leq} \frac{\gamma \Delta \sqrt{|\mathcal{S}|}}{(1-\gamma)^2}.$$

In conclusion, as $N$ grows, FedTD(0) under i.i.d. sampling from Theorem 3 achieves the lower residual error than single-agent TD(0) from Theorem 1.

### 5.2 Analysis for Markovian Setting

Finally, we establish the convergence of FedTD(0) under Markovian sampling. To show this, we define the mixing time in the federated setting as follows.

**Definition 2.** *Let $\tau_\epsilon$ be the minimum time such that the following holds: For any agent, $k \geq 0$ and $t \geq \tau_\epsilon$, $\|\xi_i^{(t,k)}\|_2 \leq \epsilon$. Here, $\xi_i^{(t,k)} \in \mathbb{R}^{|\mathcal{S}|}$ is defined by $\xi_i^{(t,k)}(s) = \delta_i^{(t,k)} - \mathbb{E}[\delta_i^{(t,k)} \mid \mathcal{F}^{(t,k)}]$ when $s = s_i^{(t,k)}$, and $\xi_i^{(t,k)} = 0$ for all other $s$, where $\mathcal{F}^{(t,k)}$ is the filtration up to iterations $t, k$.*

We establish the convergence theorem of FedTD(0) under Markovian sampling, which achieves the same $\sqrt{N}$-speedup as FedTD(0) under i.i.d. sampling.

**Theorem 4 (Federated, Markovian sampling).** *Consider FedTD(0) (Algorithm 2) under i.i.d. sampling. Let each row-stochastic transition matrix $\hat{P}_i$ of the $i^{\text{th}}$-agent satisfy Assumption 3. Then,*

$$\|e^{(t)}\|_2 \leq \rho^t \|e^{(0)}\|_2 + \frac{B_1}{\sqrt{N}} + \alpha^2 B_2 + \beta \frac{1}{1-\gamma}\left(\frac{2\tau_\beta}{1-\gamma} + t\beta\right),$$

where $e^{(t)} := V^{(t)} - V$, $\rho = (1-\beta) + \beta[(1-\alpha) + \alpha\gamma]^K$, $B_1 = \gamma \frac{A\sqrt{|S|}}{(1-\gamma)^2(1-[1-\alpha(1-\gamma)]^K)}$, $B_2 = \gamma^2 \frac{C\Delta\sqrt{|S|}}{(1-\gamma)(1-[1-\alpha(1-\gamma)]^K)}$, $C = \exp(K(C_P + C_\mu))$ where $\|\hat{P}_i^l\|_2 \leq C_P$ and $\|P_\mu^l\|_2 \leq C_\mu$ for $l, C_P, C_\mu \geq 0$, $\tau_\beta$ is defined by Definition 2, and $\beta, \alpha \in (0,1)$.

*Remark 6.* FedTD(0) under Markovian sampling, similar to i.i.d. sampling, attains linear convergence with the $\frac{B_1}{\sqrt{N}}$ error term due to the model mismatch $\Lambda$, the $\alpha^2 B_2$ error term due to the model mismatch $\Delta$, and the $\beta \frac{1}{1-\gamma}\left(\frac{2\tau_\beta}{1-\gamma} + t\beta\right)$ error term due to Markovian sampling $\tau_\beta$. Unlike FedTD(0) under i.i.d. sampling, which achieves the $\sqrt{N}$-speedup for two error terms due to $\Lambda$ and i.i.d. sampling, FedTD(0) under Markovian sampling attains the $\sqrt{N}$-speedup only for the error term due to $\Lambda$.

*Remark 7.* The step size $\alpha$, the federated parameter $\beta$, the number of local steps $K$, and the number of agents $N$ influence the convergence rate and residual error terms of FedTD(0) under Markovian sampling. First, we can reduce the error term due to $\Delta$ at the price of slow convergence by decreasing $\alpha$. Second, decreasing $\beta$ lessens the error term due to Markovian sampling $\tau_\beta$ at the cost of slow convergence. For instance, the error term due to Markovian sampling can be lessened by choosing $\beta = \frac{1}{T^\eta}$ with $\eta \in (1/2, 1)$, as

$$\beta \frac{1}{(1-\gamma)}\left(\frac{2\tau_\beta}{1-\gamma} + t\beta\right) = \mathcal{O}\left(\frac{1}{T^\eta}\right) + \mathcal{O}\left(\frac{1}{T^{2\eta-1}}\right).$$

Third, increasing the number of agents $N$ decreases the error term due to $\Lambda$.

*Remark 8.* Under Markovian sampling, like i.i.d. sampling, FedTD(0) can be shown to achieve higher accuracy of value functions $V^{(t)}$ than single-agent TD(0). We show this by proving that under certain conditions, two residual error terms of FedTD(0) due to $\Lambda$ and $\Delta$ from Theorem 4 are lower than single-agent TD(0) from Theorem 2. First, the error term due to $\Lambda$ for FedTD(0) vanishes, as the number of agents $N$ goes to $+\infty$. Second, the error term due to $\Delta$ for FedTD(0) is lower than single-agent TD(0) by a factor of $1/(1-\gamma)$ for $\gamma \in (0,1)$ by choosing $K \to +\infty$ and $\alpha = \sqrt{\frac{1}{\gamma C}}$.

## 6 Experiments

### 6.1 Setup

We evaluate the empirical performance of FedTD(0) under varying levels of model mismatch. We consider a randomly generated MDP with 10 states, where the transition matrix $P_\mu$ is row-stochastic and generated using uniform distributions. The reward function $r$ also has a uniform $[0,1]$ distribution. To simulate heterogeneity among agents, we introduce small perturbations to the transition

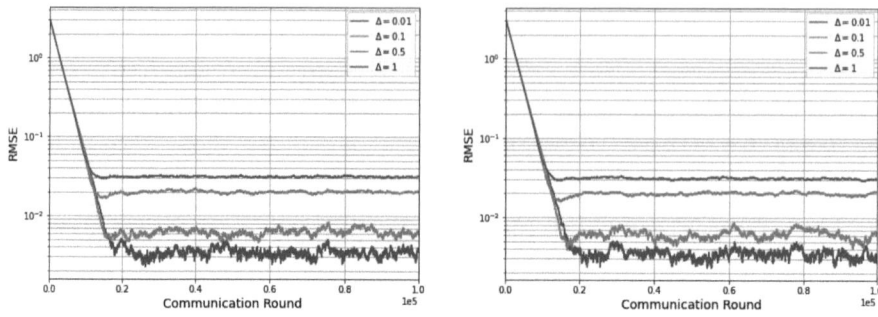

**Fig. 1.** Impact of the model mismatch $\Delta$ on the RMSE of the $V$-estimates for FedTD(0) with (**Left**) i.i.d sampling and (**Right**) Markovian sampling. Here, $N = 10$, $K = 5$, $\alpha = 0.01$, and $\beta = 0.4$.

matrix $P_\mu$, ensuring that each agent $i$ interacts with a slightly different transition model $\hat{P}_i$. The perturbation is controlled by a parameter $\Delta$, such that the Frobenius norm difference satisfies $\|\hat{P}_i - P_\mu\|_2 \leq \Delta$. This perturbation is followed by a projection step to ensure that each $\hat{P}_i$ remains row-stochastic. The reward function is kept identical across agents to isolate the effect of transition dynamics mismatch. To quantify the error in value function estimation, we compute the root mean square error (RMSE) between the global value estimate $V^{(t)}$ and the true value function $V$, where $V$ is computed via the Bellman fixed-point equation $(I - \gamma P_\mu)V = r$. We track the evolution of this metric over communication rounds $t$. The value function is initialized with zero entries ($V^{(0)} = 0$ for all $s$), and we set $\gamma = 0.8$. All experiments are repeated with five different seed numbers, and results are averaged for robustness.

### 6.2 Discussion

*Effect of Model Mismatch under I.I.D. and Markovian Sampling.* The model mismatch $\Delta$ affects the accuracy of value function estimates under both i.i.d. and Markovian sampling. From Fig. 1, increasing $\Delta$ leads to a higher RMSE in the estimated value function. Interestingly, the residual error behaves almost identically in both sampling regimes, as further illustrated in Appendix D.1, Fig. 5 and Appendix D.2, Fig. 6. This confirms our theoretical analysis in Theorems 3 and 4, which state that while the convergence dynamics differ under i.i.d. and Markovian sampling, the final bias due to model mismatch is primarily governed by $\Delta$. In particular, a large value of $\Delta$ results in a large residual error around the unique fixed value function $V$. These results highlight that FedRL methods must account for model mismatch effects rather than focusing solely on the sampling strategy of individual agents.

*Effect of the Number of Agents on Reducing Model Mismatch Bias.* From Fig. 2, FedTD(0) with the larger number of agents $N$ ensures that its estimated value

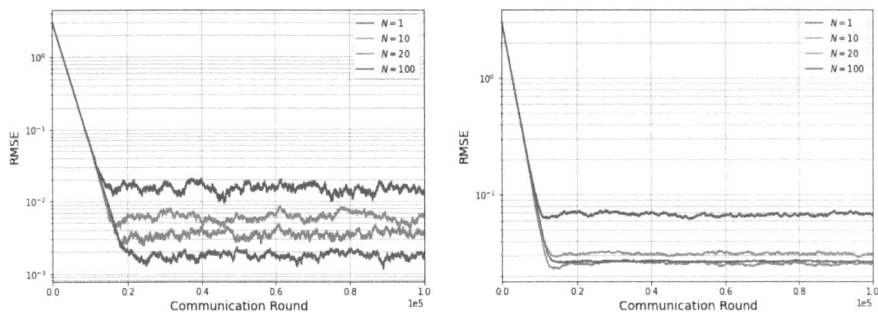

**Fig. 2.** Impact of the number of agents $N$ on the RMSE of $V$-estimates for FedTD(0) with Markovian sampling. Here, $K = 5$, $\alpha = 0.01$, and $\beta = 0.4$. (**Left**) Corresponds to a model mismatch of $\Delta = 0.1$, while (**Right**) considers a more severe mismatch of $\Delta = 1$.

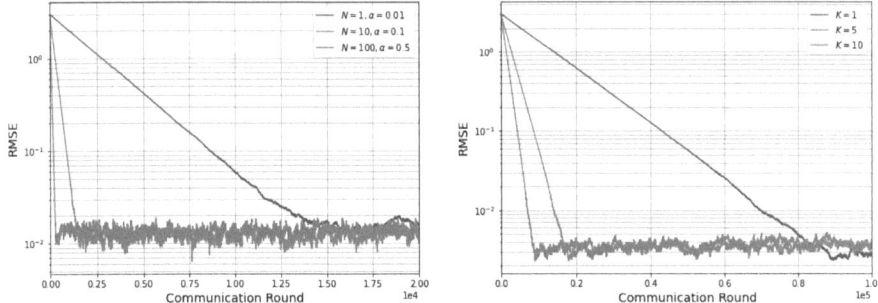

**Fig. 3.** RMSE of the $V$-estimates for FedTD(0) with Markovian sampling. (**Left**) Examines the effect of the number of agents $N$ and the learning rate $\alpha$ with $K = 5$. (**Right**) Studies the effect of the number of local steps $K$ while keeping $N = 20$ and $\alpha = 0.01$. Both cases use $\Delta = 0.1$ and $\beta = 0.4$.

function is closer to the true value function. This corroborates the $\sqrt{N}$-speedup in the convergence in Theorems 3 and 4. Further validation of this trend is provided in Appendix D.3, Fig. 7.

*Convergence Speedup with More Agents.* As shown in Fig. 3, more agents allow for a larger step size $\alpha$ without destabilizing the learning process. This is because federated averaging reduces variance in updates, enabling more aggressive updates without divergence. Consequently, FedTD(0) with more agents achieves similar accuracy in fewer iterations compared to a single-agent setting, making it a scalable solution for distributed RL applications. This aligns with the $\sqrt{N}$-speedup and the lower residual error by multiple agents from Theorems 3 and 4.

*Robustness to the Choice of Local Steps $K$: Communication Efficiency.* As shown in Fig. 3, increasing $K$ reduces communication overhead without significantly compromising final performance. Specifically, $K = 10$ achieves the same RMSE

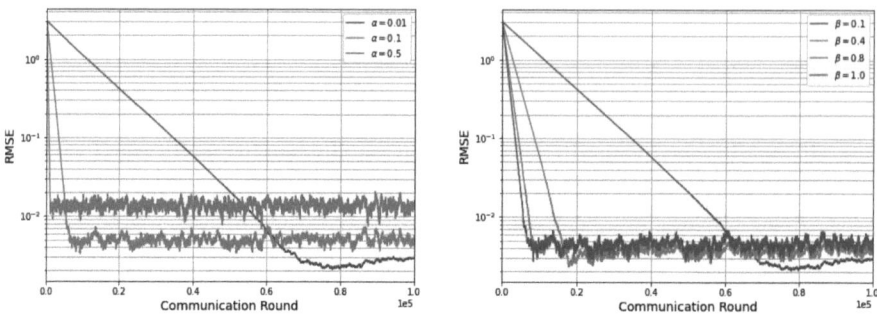

**Fig. 4.** RMSE of the $V$-estimates for FedTD(0) with Markovian sampling. (**Left**) Examines the effect of the learning rate $\alpha$ with $\beta = 0.1$. (**Right**) Studies the effect of the federated parameter $\beta$ while $\alpha = 0.01$. Both cases use $N = 20$, $K = 5$, and $\Delta = 0.1$.

as $K = 1$, but with a *10-fold reduction in communication rounds*. This suggests that increasing local updates can substantially improve efficiency in FedRL, making it particularly useful in scenarios where the communication cost is expensive.

*The Effect of Learning Rate $\alpha$ and Federated Parameter $\beta$.* Fig. 4 illustrates how $\alpha$ and $\beta$ impact the performance of FedTD(0). A smaller $\alpha$ slows convergence but stabilizes learning, whereas a larger $\alpha$ leads to faster convergence. Similarly, a large $\beta$ allows faster adaptation of the global value estimate. However, changes in $\alpha$ have a greater effect on residual error compared to adjustments in $\beta$, as supported by our non-asymptotic results (see Theorem 4), where the convergence of FedTD(0) consists of the two residual error terms, $\mathcal{O}(\alpha^2) + \mathcal{O}(\beta)$.

## 7 Conclusion

In this paper, we investigated FedTD(0) for *policy evaluation* under *model mismatch*, where multiple agents interact with perturbed environments and *periodically* exchange value estimates. We established *linear convergence* guarantees for single-agent TD(0) under both *i.i.d.* and *Markovian* sampling regimes and demonstrated how environmental perturbations introduce systematic bias in individual learning. Extending these results to the federated setting, we quantified the role of model mismatch, network connectivity, and mixing behavior in the convergence of FedTD(0). Our theoretical results indicate that even under heterogeneous transition dynamics, moderate levels of information sharing among agents can effectively mitigate environment-specific errors and improve convergence rates. Empirical results further support these findings, demonstrating that federated collaboration reduces individual bias and accelerates convergence to the true value function. These findings highlight the potential of FedRL for real-world applications where identical environment assumptions are impractical, such as multi-robot coordination and decentralized control in sensor networks. For future research, we aim to extend our framework beyond policy evaluation to control settings, such as federated $Q$-learning, and explore the effectiveness of FedRL in real-world tasks.

**Supplementary Material.** For comprehensive supplementary appendices and accompanying code, readers are directed to the full version of this paper, accessible via Springer Link and arXiv [3], along with the corresponding code repository hosted on GitHub: https://github.com/AliBeikmohammadi/FedRL.

**Acknowledgments.** This work was partially supported by the Swedish Research Council through grant agreement no. 2024-04058 and in part by Sweden's Innovation Agency (Vinnova). The computations were enabled by resources provided by the National Academic Infrastructure for Supercomputing in Sweden (NAISS) at Chalmers Centre for Computational Science and Engineering (C3SE) partially funded by the Swedish Research Council through grant agreement no. 2022-06725. The research reported in this publication was supported by funding from King Abdullah University of Science and Technology (KAUST): i) KAUST Baseline Research Scheme, ii) Center of Excellence for Generative AI, under award number 5940, iii) SDAIA-KAUST Center of Excellence in Artificial Intelligence and Data Science.

# References

1. Assran, M., Romoff, J., Ballas, N., Pineau, J., Rabbat, M.: Gossip-based actor-learner architectures for deep reinforcement learning. Adv. Neural Inform. Process. Syst. **32** (2019)
2. Beikmohammadi, A., Khirirat, S., Magnússon, S.: Compressed federated reinforcement learning with a generative model. In: Bifet, A., Davis, J., Krilavičius, T., Kull, M., Ntoutsi, E., Žliobaitė, I. (eds.) Machine Learning and Knowledge Discovery in Databases. Research Track: European Conference, ECML PKDD 2024, Vilnius, Lithuania, September 9–13, 2024, Proceedings, Part IV, pp. 20–37. Springer Nature Switzerland, Cham (2024). https://doi.org/10.1007/978-3-031-70359-1_2
3. Beikmohammadi, A., Khirirat, S., Richtárik, P., Magnússon, S.: Collaborative value function estimation under model mismatch: A federated temporal difference analysis (2025). https://arxiv.org/abs/2503.17454
4. Beikmohammadi, A., Magnússon, S.: Comparing NARS and reinforcement learning: an analysis of ONA and Q-learning algorithms. In: Hammer, P., Alirezaie, M., Strannegård, C. (eds.) Artificial General Intelligence: 16th International Conference, AGI 2023, Stockholm, Sweden, June 16–19, 2023, Proceedings, pp. 21–31. Springer Nature Switzerland, Cham (2023). https://doi.org/10.1007/978-3-031-33469-6_3
5. Beikmohammadi, A., Magnússon, S.: Ta-explore: teacher-assisted exploration for facilitating fast reinforcement learning. In: Proceedings of the 2023 International Conference on Autonomous Agents and Multiagent Systems, pp. 2412–2414 (2023)
6. Beikmohammadi, A., Magnússon, S.: Accelerating actor-critic-based algorithms via pseudo-labels derived from prior knowledge. Inf. Sci. **661**, 120182 (2024)
7. Bellman, R.: Dynamic programming, vol. 153. American Association for the Advancement of Science (1966)
8. Bertsekas, D., Tsitsiklis, J.N.: Neuro-dynamic programming. Athena Scientific (1996)

9. Bhandari, J., Russo, D., Singal, R.: A finite time analysis of temporal difference learning with linear function approximation. In: Conference on Learning Theory, pp. 1691–1692. PMLR (2018)
10. Borkar, V.S.: Stochastic approximation: a dynamical systems viewpoint, vol. 48. Springer (2009)
11. Chen, Z., Maguluri, S.T., Shakkottai, S., Shanmugam, K.: Finite-sample analysis of contractive stochastic approximation using smooth convex envelopes. Adv. Neural. Inf. Process. Syst. **33**, 8223–8234 (2020)
12. Chen, Z., Maguluri, S.T., Shakkottai, S., Shanmugam, K.: A lyapunov theory for finite-sample guarantees of asynchronous Q-learning and TD-learning variants. arXiv preprint arXiv:2102.01567 (2021)
13. Chen, Z., Zhou, Y., Chen, R.R.: Multi-agent off-policy TDC with near-optimal sample and communication complexities. Transactions on Machine Learning Research (2022)
14. Chen, Z., Zhou, Y., Chen, R.R., Zou, S.: Sample and communication-efficient decentralized actor-critic algorithms with finite-time analysis. In: International Conference on Machine Learning, pp. 3794–3834. PMLR (2022)
15. Dal Fabbro, N., Mitra, A., Pappas, G.J.: Federated TD learning over finite-rate erasure channels: linear speedup under markovian sampling. IEEE Control Systems Letters **7**, 2461–2466 (2023). https://doi.org/10.1109/LCSYS.2023.3287499
16. Dalal, G., Szörényi, B., Thoppe, G., Mannor, S.: Finite sample analyses for td (0) with function approximation. In: Proceedings of the AAAI Conference on Artificial Intelligence, vol. 32 (2018)
17. Doan, T., Maguluri, S., Romberg, J.: Finite-time analysis of distributed td (0) with linear function approximation on multi-agent reinforcement learning. In: International Conference on Machine Learning, pp. 1626–1635. PMLR (2019)
18. Dorfman, R., Levy, K.Y.: Adapting to mixing time in stochastic optimization with Markovian data. In: International Conference on Machine Learning, pp. 5429–5446. PMLR (2022)
19. Espeholt, L., et al.: Impala: Scalable distributed deep-rl with importance weighted actor-learner architectures. In: International Conference on Machine Learning, pp. 1407–1416. PMLR (2018)
20. Even-Dar, E., Mansour, Y., Bartlett, P.: Learning rates for q-learning. J. Mach. Learn. Res. **5**(1) (2003)
21. Fabbro, N.D., Mitra, A., Heath, R., Schenato, L., Pappas, G.J.: Over-the-Air federated TD learning. In: MLSys 2023 Workshop on Resource-Constrained Learning in Wireless Networks (2023)
22. Fan, X., Ma, Y., Dai, Z., Jing, W., Tan, C., Low, B.K.H.: Fault-tolerant federated reinforcement learning with theoretical guarantee. In: Ranzato, M., Beygelzimer, A., Dauphin, Y., Liang, P., Vaughan, J.W. (eds.) Advances in Neural Information Processing Systems, vol. 34, pp. 1007–1021. Curran Associates, Inc. (2021)
23. Hu, B., Syed, U.: Characterizing the exact behaviors of temporal difference learning algorithms using Markov jump linear system theory. Adv. Neural Inform. Process. Syst. **32** (2019)
24. Jin, H., Peng, Y., Yang, W., Wang, S., Zhang, Z.: Federated reinforcement learning with environment heterogeneity. In: International Conference on Artificial Intelligence and Statistics, pp. 18–37. PMLR (2022)
25. Khodadadian, S., Sharma, P., Joshi, G., Maguluri, S.T.: Federated reinforcement learning: Linear speedup under Markovian sampling. In: International Conference on Machine Learning, pp. 10997–11057. PMLR (2022)

26. Kohler, J.M., Lucchi, A.: Sub-sampled cubic regularization for non-convex optimization. In: International Conference on Machine Learning, pp. 1895–1904. PMLR (2017)
27. Lakshminarayanan, C., Szepesvari, C.: Linear stochastic approximation: How far does constant step-size and iterate averaging go? In: International Conference on Artificial Intelligence and Statistics, pp. 1347–1355. PMLR (2018)
28. Levin, D.A., Peres, Y.: Markov chains and mixing times, vol. 107. American Mathematical Soc. (2017)
29. Liu, R., Olshevsky, A.: Distributed td (0) with almost no communication. IEEE Control Syst. Letters **7**, 2892–2897 (2023)
30. Maei, H.R.: Convergent actor-critic algorithms under off-policy training and function approximation. arXiv preprint arXiv:1802.07842 (2018)
31. Mankowitz, D.J., et al.: Robust reinforcement learning for continuous control with model misspecification. In: International Conference on Learning Representations (2020)
32. Mitra, A.: A simple finite-time analysis of td learning with linear function approximation. IEEE Transactions on Automatic Control (2024)
33. Mitra, A., Pappas, G.J., Hassani, H.: Temporal difference learning with compressed updates: Error-feedback meets reinforcement learning. Transactions on Machine Learning Research (2024)
34. Mnih, V., et al.: Asynchronous methods for deep reinforcement learning. In: International Conference on Machine Learning, pp. 1928–1937. PMLR (2016)
35. Morimoto, J., Doya, K.: Robust reinforcement learning. Neural Comput. **17**(2), 335–359 (2005)
36. Pinto, L., Davidson, J., Sukthankar, R., Gupta, A.: Robust adversarial reinforcement learning. In: International Conference on Machine Learning, pp. 2817–2826. PMLR (2017)
37. Qi, J., Zhou, Q., Lei, L., Zheng, K.: Federated reinforcement learning: techniques, applications, and open challenges. Intell. Robot. **1**(1) (2021)
38. Samsonov, S., Tiapkin, D., Naumov, A., Moulines, E.: Improved high-probability bounds for the temporal difference learning algorithm via exponential stability. In: The Thirty Seventh Annual Conference on Learning Theory, pp. 4511–4547. PMLR (2024)
39. Shen, H., Zhang, K., Hong, M., Chen, T.: Towards understanding asynchronous advantage actor-critic: Convergence and linear speedup. IEEE Transactions on Signal Processing (2023)
40. Srikant, R., Ying, L.: Finite-time error bounds for linear stochastic approximation and td learning. In: Conference on Learning Theory, pp. 2803–2830. PMLR (2019)
41. Sun, J., Wang, G., Giannakis, G.B., Yang, Q., Yang, Z.: Finite-time analysis of decentralized temporal-difference learning with linear function approximation. In: International Conference on Artificial Intelligence and Statistics, pp. 4485–4495. PMLR (2020)
42. Sutton, R.S.: Learning to predict by the methods of temporal differences. Mach. Learn. **3**, 9–44 (1988)
43. Sutton, R.S., Barto, A.G., et al.: Reinforcement learning: An introduction, vol. 1. MIT press Cambridge (1998)
44. Tadić, V.: On the convergence of temporal-difference learning with linear function approximation. Mach. Learn. **42**, 241–267 (2001)
45. Tesauro, G., et al.: Temporal difference learning and td-gammon. Commun. ACM **38**(3), 58–68 (1995)

46. Tsitsiklis, J., Van Roy, B.: An analysis of temporal-difference learning with function approximation. IEEE Trans. Autom. Control **42**(5), 674–690 (1997)
47. Tsitsiklis, J., Van Roy, B.: Analysis of temporal-difference learning with function approximation. Adv. Neural Inform. Process. Syst. **9** (1996)
48. Wai, H.T.: On the convergence of consensus algorithms with Markovian noise and gradient bias. In: 2020 59th IEEE Conference on Decision and Control (CDC), pp. 4897–4902. IEEE (2020)
49. Wang, H., Mitra, A., Hassani, H., Pappas, G.J., Anderson, J.: Federated TD learning with linear function approximation under environmental heterogeneity. Transactions on Machine Learning Research (2024)
50. Woo, J., Joshi, G., Chi, Y.: The blessing of heterogeneity in federated Q-learning: Linear speedup and beyond. In: Proceedings of the 40th International Conference on Machine Learning, ICML'23, JMLR.org (2023)
51. Woo, J., Joshi, G., Chi, Y.: The blessing of heterogeneity in federated Q-learning: Linear speedup and beyond. In: International Conference on Machine Learning, pp. 37157–37216. PMLR (2023)
52. Wu, Z., Shen, H., Chen, T., Ling, Q.: Byzantine-resilient decentralized policy evaluation with linear function approximation. IEEE Trans. Signal Process. **69**, 3839–3853 (2021)
53. Xie, Z., Song, S.: FedKL: tackling data heterogeneity in federated reinforcement learning by penalizing KL divergence. IEEE J. Sel. Areas Commun. **41**(4), 1227–1242 (2023)
54. Zhang, C., Wang, H., Mitra, A., Anderson, J.: Finite-time analysis of on-policy heterogeneous federated reinforcement learning. In: The Twelfth International Conference on Learning Representations (2024)
55. Zhang, S., Liu, B., Yao, H., Whiteson, S.: Provably convergent two-timescale off-policy actor-critic with function approximation. In: International Conference on Machine Learning, pp. 11204–11213. PMLR (2020)
56. Zhao, W., Queralta, J.P., Westerlund, T.: Sim-to-real transfer in deep reinforcement learning for robotics: a survey. In: 2020 IEEE Symposium Series on Computational Intelligence (SSCI), pp. 737–744. IEEE (2020)
57. Zheng, Z., Gao, F., Xue, L., Yang, J.: Federated Q-learning: Linear regret speedup with low communication cost. In: The Twelfth International Conference on Learning Representations (2024)
58. Zhuo, H.H., Feng, W., Lin, Y., Xu, Q., Yang, Q.: Federated deep reinforcement learning. arXiv preprint arXiv:1901.08277 (2019)

# Reward Shaping for User Satisfaction

Konstantina Christakopoulou[1](✉), Can Xu[1], Sai Zhang[2], Sriraj Badam[2], Trevor Potter[2], Daniel Li[2], Hao Wan[3], Xinyang Yi[1], Ya Le[4], Chris Berg[2], Eric Bencomo Dixon[5], Ed H. Chi[1], and Minmin Chen[1]

[1] Google DeepMind, Mountain View, USA
{konchris,canxu,xinyang,edchi,minminc}@google.com
[2] Google, Mountain View, USA
{saisaizhang,srirajdutt,tpotter,chrisberg}@google.com
[3] Meta, Menlo Park, USA
[4] OpenAI, San Francisco, USA
[5] DoorDash, San Francisco, USA

**Abstract.** How might we design Reinforcement Learning (RL)-based recommenders that encourage aligning user trajectories with the underlying user satisfaction? Three research questions are key: (1) measuring user satisfaction, (2) combatting sparsity of satisfaction signals, and (3) adapting the training of the recommender agent to maximize satisfaction. For measurement, it has been found that surveys explicitly asking users to rate their experience with consumed items can provide valuable orthogonal information to the engagement/interaction data, acting as a proxy to the underlying user satisfaction. For sparsity, i.e., only being able to observe how satisfied users are with a tiny fraction of user-item interactions, *imputation models* can be useful in predicting satisfaction level for all items users have consumed. For learning satisfying recommender policies, we postulate that reward shaping in RL recommender agents is powerful for driving satisfying user experiences. Putting everything together, we propose to jointly learn a policy network and a satisfaction imputation network: The role of the imputation network is to learn which actions are satisfying to the user; while the policy network, built on top of REINFORCE, decides which items to recommend, with the reward utilizing the imputed satisfaction. We use both offline analysis and live experiments in an industrial large-scale recommendation platform to demonstrate the promise of our approach for satisfying user experiences.

## 1 Introduction

Recommender systems at heart aim at creating a good user experience by surfacing users with the right content at the right time and under the right context. It is thus critical for the system to identify what defines the user experience, more specifically the underlying user utilities of the platform. Most recent advances

---

H. Wan, Y. Le and B. Dixon—Work done while at Google.

in recommender systems have relied on implicit user feedback, such as clicks or dwell time, as proxies to capture user utilities [5,33]. Although this data measures *what users do*, it can fail to capture what users *say they want*—which are potentially very different [14]. As a result, recommender models learned solely based on user engagement data can be misaligned with the true user utilities.

Given a specified objective, or else *reward function*, which captures the long-term user utility, recommender systems can be formulated as Reinforcement Learning (RL) agents deciding on actions to take (i.e., contents to show to users) given certain user states (i.e., latent representation at a specific time/context), with the goal of maximizing said cumulative reward [3,13,15,35]. There are several challenges especially exacerbated in industrial recommendation settings which makes the application of RL for recommendation rather unique compared to other application areas like games [21,28] and robotics [10]. The action space is extremely large and ever-changing; user preferences change over time; and data are extremely sparse for the enormous action and state space. Only recently there have been major advances addressing these challenges and showcasing RL approaches for recommendation [3,15].

Besides addressing these challenges, the key in building recommender agents lies in defining the reward function guiding the learning of the agent policy. Although we do get to observe some proxy signals indicating when a recommendation, or a series of recommendations was successful (e.g., the user clicked on the recommended content, they shared it with their social network etc.), there is a disconnect between the implicit feedback we observe, and what the user really wants. The proximity between the proxy signals we include in the agent's reward function and the true user utility, will largely determine the extent to which the RL recommender can optimize for what users want.

However, despite the importance of the reward function for building recommendation agents, there has been relatively little work on reward shaping for RL recommenders. Most works treat the reward function as a black-box, which is given, and often assume that dense engagement signals are indicative of how much users value their experience. This assumption has been recently challenged in non-RL settings, underlying that post-engagement signals and/or satisfaction survey responses together with implicit behavioral signals give a clearer picture of user utilities [11,14,31].

In this paper, we put the reward front and center, and highlight it as a key tool for optimizing for what users actually want. Satisfaction data as collected by user responses to satisfaction surveys provide an important view as to how the user felt about the recommendation, as opposed to how they behaved while interacting with it. These surveys are shown uniformly to all users, and ask users to rate on a scale how satisfying they found a sampled item from their recent engagement history. In our systems, such survey data can offer more representativeness compared to post-engagement signals, as most users tend to not engage in post-click actions such as likes, dismissals. Furthermore, optimizing for satisfaction as measured by surveys can substantially move post-engagement related metrics as well. Based on the above, both behavioral signals, and satisfaction signals should be incorporated into the reward.

However, before we can utilize satisfaction signals into the reward, we need to highlight a major challenge inherently associated with them—*sparsity*. The volume of satisfaction data is orders of magnitude smaller compared with engagement data volume; in our case study, roughly *one out of thousands* of engagement signals will come with a satisfaction response. This is due to a number of reasons. First, it is disruptive to ask users about every item they recently consumed. Second, response rate can be very low in an environment where primary user intention is to consume content rather than providing feedback. As a result, we only have access to a small amount of survey responses covering an extremely small fraction of the user-item interaction pairs. Given this extreme sparsity, simply supplementing the existing reward signals that focus on engagement with the sparse satisfaction signals is not going to be effective in shifting towards optimizing for user satisfaction. Instead, personalized satisfaction models are required to impute for each user how they would rate their satisfaction level with each consumed item, had they responded to a survey.

Here, we propose augmenting a classic policy network trained with REINFORCE with a satisfaction imputation network to predict user satisfaction and include the prediction into the reward for the policy network, while training both networks concurrently in a multi-task learning setup.

Our contributions are threefold:

1. **Reward Shaping for User Utility Alignment:** We emphasize reward shaping as a crucial but underexplored technique for guiding RL-based recommenders to select satisfying actions (Sects. 4.2, 4.3 and 6), highlighting the inherent challenges in defining, measuring, and modeling user satisfaction.
2. **Scalable Satisfaction Imputation Networks:** We introduce satisfaction imputation networks to address the sparsity of satisfaction signals, demonstrating their integration into a top-K REINFORCE recommender with vast state and action spaces (Sect. 4.4). We also provide offline analysis on key design considerations for effective satisfaction imputation networks (Sect. 5).
3. **Demonstrated Benefits in Live Experiments:** Results from A/B tests on a large-scale platform with a two-stage recommendation system show that replacing a REINFORCE nominator with a dense engagement reward (without satisfaction imputation) with our proposed architecture (Fig. 2) increases satisfying nominations and decreases low-satisfaction nominations. This leads to a statistically significant improvement in satisfying user experiences and a reduction in unsatisfying ones (Sect. 6).

## 2 Related Work

Here, we give an overview of the most closely related works.

**Reinforcement Learning (RL).** Problems in which an agent learns to interact with the environment, with the interactions having long-term consequences, are a natural fit to be framed as Reinforcement Learning ones [29]. Classical approaches to RL problems include value-based approaches such as Q-learning [20], and policy-based ones such as policy gradient [32]. Deep RL combines the promise of deep neural networks to help RL achieve ground-breaking success in games and robotics applications [10,19,21,28]. We build our work on top of a policy-based approach, namely REINFORCE [32], following its prior success in recommendation settings [3]. The imputation network we introduce has deep connections with value learning approaches [20], where a state-action value network is learned. The estimations of this network are utilized as *part* of our policy's reward; as a result, we still need the off-policy correction component [3]. An alternative approach we leave for future work is employing Actor-Critic or its variants [19,27,30].

**Reinforcement Learning in Recommendation.** Although there have been many successes in RL for applications like games [21,28] and robotics [10], only recently some successes of RL for recommendation have been demonstrated [7]. The main work we build on top of is a policy-gradient-based approach correcting for off-policy skew with importance weighting [3]. This work demonstrated the value of REINFORCE and top-$K$ off-policy correction in a large-scale industrial recommendation platform with an extremely large action space. Other recent works have demonstrated the value of deep RL approaches for recommendation, such as Actor-Critic [15], Deep Q-learning [36], and hierarchical RL [34]. Also, novel RL approaches have been proposed for the more complicated problem of slate recommendation [13], as well as for page-wise recommendation [35]. Despite the recent promise of RL for recommendation, the majority of works do not draw attention to the important aspect of reward shaping, which is key for aligning system objectives with underlying user utilities; this is the focus of our paper.

*Reward Shaping.* The importance of reward shaping, i.e., shaping the original sparse, delayed reward signals as in-time credit assignment for successful RL algorithms has been emphasized early on [6,16,23]. This is a general term encompassing the incorporation of domain knowledge into RL to guide the policy learning. Carefully designing the reward function is critically important as: (i) a misspecified reward leads to sub-optimal policy; (ii) an under-specified reward leads to unexpected behavior [12]. While RL for robotics and games has relied on hand-crafted reward or imitation learning [26] to effectively guide the agent to success, the perils of a misspecified reward function in the design of recommender RL agents have not received a lot of attention. Motivated by the need to bridge the RL for recommendation line of work with the recent discussions on measuring and modeling user satisfaction to properly capture user experience [9,14,17,18], we provide a reward shaping approach for imputing user satisfaction into the reward of an RL recommender, along with using the ground truth engagement proxy signals.

## 3 Background

### 3.1 Recommendation as an RL Problem

The recommender system's goal is to decide which contents to recommend to the incoming user requests, given some representation of the user profile, the context, and their interaction history up to this point, as captured by the sequence of items (e.g. videos, news articles, products) they have interacted with, along with the corresponding feedback (e.g., time spent watching/reading), so as to maximize the cumulative rewards experienced by the users.

In RL terms, we formulate the recommendation problem as a Markov Decision Process (MDP), or better, a Partially Observable MDP (POMDP) as the states are unobserved:

| Recommendation MDP | |
|---|---|
| Action $a \in \mathcal{A}$ | item(s) available for recommendation |
| State $s \in \mathcal{S}$ | user interests and context |
| State Transition $s_{t+1} \sim \mathbf{P}(\cdot\|s_t, a_t)$ | unknown dynamics capturing how user state changes from $t$ to $t+1$, conditioned on $a_t$ and $s_t$ |
| Reward $r(s, a)$ | immediate reward obtained by performing action $a$ for state $s$ |

The goal is to find a policy $\pi(a|s)$ capturing the probability distribution over the action space, i.e., items to recommend, given the current user state $s \in \mathcal{S}$, so to maximize the expected cumulative reward,

$$\max_{\pi} \mathbf{E}_{\tau \sim \pi}[R(\tau)] \quad (1)$$

where $R(\tau) = \sum_{t=0}^{|\tau|} r(s_t, a_t)$, and the expectation $\mathbf{E}$ is taken over user trajectories $\tau$ obtained by acting according to the policy: $a_t \sim \pi(\cdot|s_t)$, $s_{t+1} \sim \mathbf{P}(\cdot|s_t, a_t)$.

We build our method on top of the REINFORCE recommender introduced in [32]. Let the policy $\pi$ assume a functional form, mapping states to actions, parameterized by $\theta \in \mathbf{R}^d$. Using the log-trick, the gradient of the expected cumulative reward with respect to the policy parameters $\theta$ can be derived analytically [32]:

$$\nabla_\theta \mathbf{E}_{\tau \sim \pi_\theta}[R(\tau)] = \mathbf{E}_{\tau \sim \pi_\theta}[R(\tau) \nabla_\theta \log \pi_\theta(\tau)]. \quad (2)$$

To reduce variance in the gradient estimate a common practice is to discount the future reward with a discount $\gamma$:

$$\sum_{\tau \sim \pi_\theta} [R(\tau) \nabla_\theta \log \pi_\theta(\tau)] \approx \sum_{\tau \sim \pi_\theta} \sum_{t=0}^{|\tau|} [R_t \nabla_\theta \log \pi_\theta(a_t|s_t)], \quad (3)$$

where

$$R_t = r(s_t, a_t) + \gamma r(s_{t+1}, a_{t+1}) + \gamma^2 r(s_{t+2}, a_{t+2}) + \ldots \\ + \gamma^{|\tau|-1-t} r(s_{|\tau|-1}, a_{|\tau|-1}). \quad (4)$$

Equation (3) gives an unbiased estimate of the policy gradient in *online RL*, where the gradient of the policy is computed on trajectories collected by the policy $\pi_\theta$ we are learning. In practice, due to infrastructure limitations or production concerns, the trajectories available for learning are collected from a different *logging* policy, or mixture of such policies, denoted by $\beta$ instead. Thus, we operate in an *offline RL* setting, making the policy gradient as given by Eq. (3) no longer unbiased. To address this skew, importance weighting is adopted [22]. In this work, we also operate in batch offline RL, applying top-$K$ off-policy correction, and we defer readers to [3] for details.

## 4 Imputing Satisfaction in Reward

We now turn to the main focus of this paper, i.e., shaping the reward of a REINFORCE recommender to drive user satisfaction. We start by describing how we parameterize the policy network (Sect. 4.1); next we highlight the role of reward in REINFORCE for capturing long-term user utility (Sect. 4.2); and emphasize the challenges associated with considering satisfaction as a proxy to user utility (Sect. 4.3). Motivated by these challenges, we propose to augment the policy network with a satisfaction imputation network (Sect. 4.4).

### 4.1 Policy Parameterization

We closely follow the setup in [1,3] to parameterize the policy. A Recurrent Neural Network (RNN) is used to encode the user's interaction history, capturing the changing user preferences. The output of the RNN is concatenated with the latent embeddings encoding context, which capture features like time of the day, device type. The concatenation of user sequential preferences and context embeddings is mapped to a lower dimensional representation via multiple Rectified Linear Units. This represents the user state $\mathbf{u}_s$. Conditioned on the user state $\mathbf{u}_s$, the policy $\pi_\theta(a|s)$ is then modeled with a softmax,

$$\pi_\theta(a|s) = \frac{\exp(\mathbf{u}_s^T \mathbf{v}_a / T)}{\sum_{a' \in \mathcal{A}} \exp(\mathbf{u}_s^T \mathbf{v}_{a'} / T)}, \quad (5)$$

where $\mathbf{v}_a$ are the action embeddings, and $T$ is a temperature term controlling the smoothness of the learned policy.

### 4.2 Reward

Reward plays a paramount role in determining the final learned policy. As shown in Eq. (3), the gradient from each state-action pair is weighted by the cumulative discounted reward $R_t$.

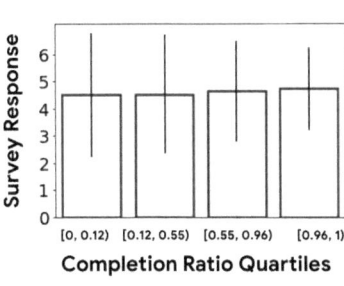
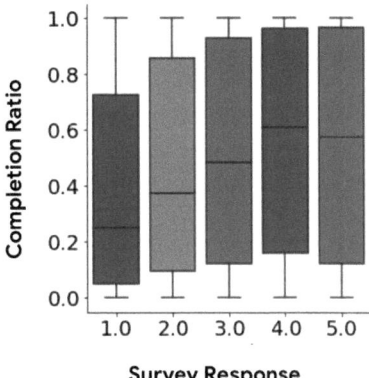

**Fig. 1.** Survey responses provide a different set of information compared to behavior signals. Interactions with the same completion ratio can have vastly different associated satisfaction levels.

As prescribed in Sect. 3.1, $R_t$ depends on the immediate rewards associated with the state-action pairs $r(s, a)$ as well as the discounting factor $\gamma$. In the absence of a user utility oracle, a key design choice is which *proxy signals* to use to define the immediate reward. For each recommendation, the user could leave different signals indicating their experience with the item. Examples include implicit engagement-related signals, such as click, time spent engaging (reading/ watching/ listening), post-engagement actions, e.g., shares/ likes/ dislikes/ comments, and they could leave explicit feedback in surveys asking them about their satisfaction level with the consumed item.

### 4.3 Value of Satisfaction Signals, and Challenges

It is easy to see that if the proxy signals used in the reward are solely engagement-focused, the policy will learn to choose actions that only drive engagement. This is not ideal as what users do (engagement) can be quite different from what they say they want (satisfaction), thus neglecting other important facets of the user experience.

Figure 1 illustrates this point. More than two million interactions with survey responses on a commercial recommendation platform were collected and analyzed. For the sake of this example, we consider completion ratio (e.g., time spent on the item out of total length of the item) as one useful behavioral signal, and study its relationship with satisfaction signals as measured by survey responses in the scale of one to five. As shown in (Fig. 1 *right*), grouping interactions by survey response rating, we find the higher the survey value, the higher the median completion ratio; however, we also see that per survey response value the range of associated completion ratios is quite large. This becomes more evident when grouping interactions with their associated survey responses based on the corresponding quantiles of completion ratios, (Fig. 1 *left*). Based on the plotted 95% confidence intervals, interactions belonging in the exact same quantile of completion ratios (i.e., same user behavior), have quite different associated satisfaction levels (Fig. 1 *left*).

It is worth pointing out that behavior signals alone fail to capture other sides of how the user felt about the interaction, e.g., did they find the content misleading, useful, did it provide some longer term value to them. It is therefore critical to consider both behavioral and satisfaction signals, and appropriately balance them when defining the reward.

Also, we opt for survey data rather than post-engagement signals as better proxies for user satisfaction as we have found that they can offer more representativeness—most users tend to not engage in post-click actions such as likes, dismissals. Having said that, although we demonstrate the effectiveness of reward shaping with imputation networks for survey signals, the same technique is equally applicable for other proxy reward signals exhibiting similar concerns, such as likes, dislikes, shares or dismissals. What is more, in our case study, we find that satisfaction as measured by survey responses highly correlates with goodness as measured by post-engagement signals. Thus, we are able to significantly increase likes, and decrease dislikes/dismissals, even without explicitly optimizing for them (Sect. 6).

If for each item the user interacted with in the trajectory, besides implicit engagement signals $r^e(s, a)$, we also had access to explicit satisfaction signals $r^u(s, a)$, we could define the immediate reward $r(s, a)$ as a function of the two, i.e.,

$$r(s, a) = f\left(r^u(s, a), r^e(s, a)\right), \qquad (6)$$

where $f(\cdot)$ can include operators such as transformations on the raw signal (e.g., raising to a power, hinge, sigmoid) and combination functions (e.g., addition, multiplication) on the two reward signals.

While the engagement signals $r^e$ are often dense, satisfaction signals $r^u$ are extremely sparse, as they are derived from user-provided responses to satisfaction surveys. These surveys are shown uniformly to all users, asking them to rate on a scale how satisfying they found a sampled item from their recent engagement history. In our case study, roughly *one out of thousands of engagement signals will come with a satisfaction response.* This is because in a primarily content consumption-focused recommender platform, it would be disruptive to ask users to rate *every* item consumed. Furthermore, users tend to not respond to surveys [4]— *response rate is around 2%* in our case.

### 4.4 Satisfaction Imputation Model

This inherent sparsity of a subset of signals makes simply including them in the reward when present, ineffective.

To address this challenge, we propose the use of an imputation network to densify the satisfaction signals, and include the imputed satisfaction signals in the reward instead.

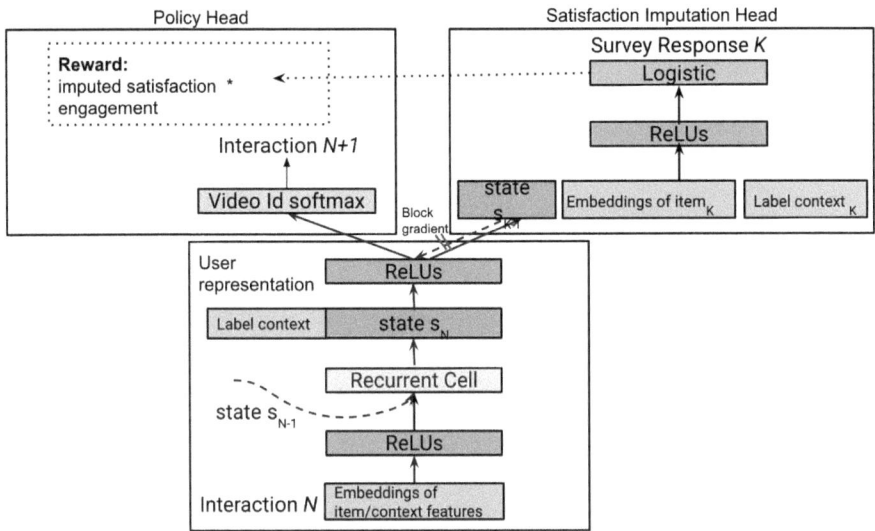

**Fig. 2.** Proposed architecture, where a satisfaction imputation head is added to learn goodness of actions based on sparse survey responses, conditioned on state, action and context embeddings learned from the policy. The reward utilizes the satisfaction imputations to guide the policy head to select actions that lead to satisfied engagement.

The role of the imputation network is to map user state and action pairs $(s, a)$ to satisfaction scores, i.e., survey responses $sr$ present in the satisfaction data $\mathcal{D}_{sr}$. One can imagine learning a completely separate imputation model on this data, and then utilize these imputations directly on the reward of the policy network. The alternative which we opt for is to extend the policy network with a satisfaction imputation head and have parameters shared between the two. This is quite appealing as given that the data used to train the policy head are of much higher volume compared to those used to train the imputation head, we hypothesize that transferring the learned user state and action embeddings from the dense task to the sparse one can be quite useful [24].

Concretely, we propose a multi-task shared-bottom architecture with two heads, the policy head and the satisfaction imputation head, each having their own task-specific parameters while sharing majorities of the state and action representations. As shown in Fig. 2 (bottom), the shared bottom encodes the sequential history of the user, as well as context information. The policy head in Fig. 2 (upper left) is identical to the standalone policy network described in Sect. 4.1, with the only change being in its reward. The imputation head in Fig. 2 (upper right) is used to infer the satisfaction score for each state-action pair $(s, a)$ in the collected trajectories. Then, the imputed satisfaction score combined with engagement signals forms the reward used to train the policy network.

We train the imputation head by gathering the corresponding state $\mathbf{u}_s$, and action embeddings $\mathbf{v}_a$ for any state-action pair associated with a survey response

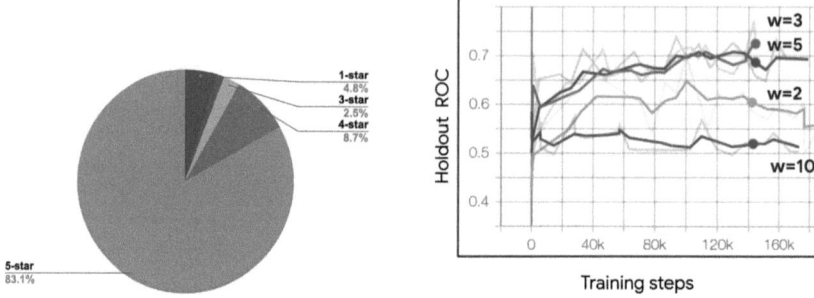

**Fig. 3.** Addressing class imbalance (*left*) by cost-sensitive learning (*right*). Upweighting the negative class survey responses (1/2/3 star responses) can significantly improve the holdout satisfaction AUC ROC of the imputation model. However, increasing the weight too much can lead to a satisfaction accuracy deterioration, and a negative effect on the policy head's accuracy.

in the batch, and learning a mapping $\hat{sr}_\phi$ from these embeddings to the corresponding survey response i.e., $\hat{sr}_\phi : (\mathbf{u}_s, \mathbf{v}_a) \rightarrow sr, \forall sr \in \mathcal{D}_{sr}$. As shown in Fig. 2 (upper right), we prevent the imputation head from influencing the policy parameterization by stopping its gradient from flowing to these shared-bottom embeddings. To give the imputation head its own parameters to learn the mapping $\hat{sr}_\phi$, we concatenate the embeddings, i.e., $[\mathbf{u}_s, \mathbf{v}_a]$, and send them through multiple Rectified Linear Units (ReLU), and a final dense layer to map to the ground truth survey response. The ReLU layers and the dense layer are learned by optimizing an appropriate loss function $\ell$. For our case study, $\mathcal{D}_{sr}$ consists of survey responses in the scale of 1 to 5, with user studies showing that values of 4 and 5 are considered satisfying, whereas lower values show dissatisfaction. So, we considered a logistic loss, with a sigmoid for the last layer, to predict satisfying versus unsatisfying:

$$\min_\phi \sum_{sr \in \mathcal{D}_{sr}} \ell\left(\hat{sr}_\phi(\mathbf{u}_s, \mathbf{v}_a), sr\right). \quad (7)$$

The policy head is learned via REINFORCE,

$$\nabla_\theta \pi_\theta = \sum_{\tau \sim \beta} \sum_{t=0}^{|\tau|} \left[ \frac{\pi_\theta(a_t|\mathbf{s}_t)}{\beta(a_t|\mathbf{s}_t)} \tilde{R}_t \nabla_\theta \log \pi_\theta(a_t|\mathbf{s}_t) \right] \quad (8)$$

where $\tilde{R}_t$ denotes the imputed reward, and $\frac{\pi_\theta(a_t|\mathbf{s}_t)}{\beta(a_t|\mathbf{s}_t)}$ does the off-policy importance weighting. We decompose $\tilde{R}_t$ as

$$\tilde{R}_t = R_t^e \times \tilde{R}_t^u, \quad (9)$$

i.e., the ground truth engagement reward $R_t^e$, and the satisfaction reward $\tilde{R}_t^u$ predicted by the imputation network.

The satisfaction imputation and the policy head are trained concurrently to optimize the (weighted) sum of the two losses. In practice, to prevent a poorly estimated imputation head from corrupting the policy head, we start the training of the policy head with engagement only reward $R^e$, and include the imputed $\tilde{R}^u$ only after the imputation head is properly trained.

## 5  What Makes a Good Satisfaction Imputation Model?

We now present some experimental findings on what makes a good satisfaction imputation model. To evaluate its predictive accuracy, we create a hold-out set consisting of user trajectories for users with at least one associated survey response. The AUC ROC achieved by the imputation model on the hold-out set is used as the offline evaluation metric.

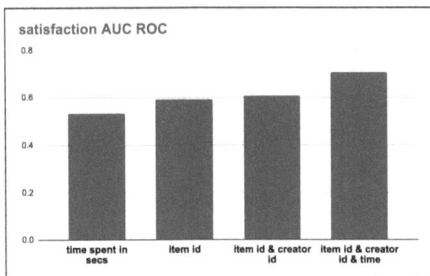 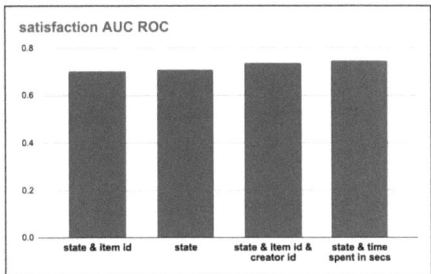

**Fig. 4.** *Left*: Using a set of features representing the item on the survey (i.e., item id & creator id & time spent on item in seconds), leads to an improved hold-out AUC ROC of the satisfaction imputation model, compared to using only individual action/item features. *Right*: Using only user state (as outputted by the RNN, and concatenated with context embeddings) performs equally well with when including all action feature embeddings, without user state (as shown in *top*). The satisfaction AUC ROC is further improved when including both user state and item-related features.

**Loss Function.** One challenge associated with the survey response data is the class imbalance problem. In our case study, the majority of responses recorded are in the higher spectrum (Fig. 3, *left*). One hypothesis is that users tend to respond to surveys about items they find highly satisfying [4,25]. This creates a natural imbalance of survey values in the satisfaction data, leading the model to focus more on survey responses of higher values. An under-specified model can predict every item to be satisfying as a result. One simple approach to address this is through cost-sensitive learning [8], in which the negative class of non-satisfying state-action pairs are weighted more. We calibrate the prediction after to reflect the ground-truth distribution of satisfying vs non-satisfying survey responses [2]. Figure 3 *right* compares the performance of the satisfaction head with different weights on the negative class. We found a weight of 3 or 5 perform the best according to the holdout AUC ROC.

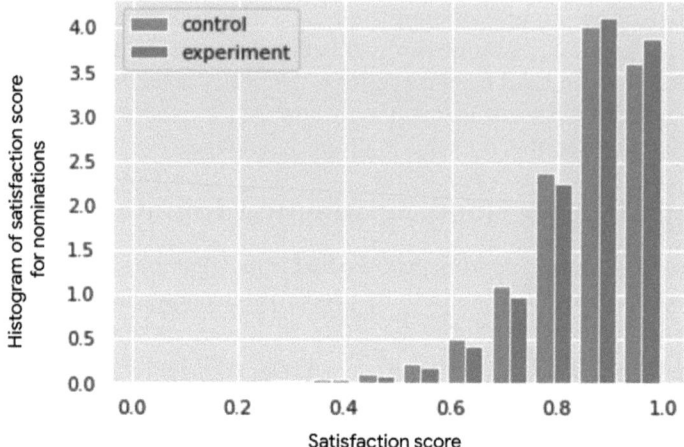

**Fig. 5.** Distribution of satisfaction scores for items nominated by model, for experiment arm (REINFORCE with satisfaction imputation model) versus control arm (REINFORCE without satisfaction in reward).

**Action Features.** Figure 4 *left* summarizes the predictive power of different action features, i.e., time spent, item id and creator id, on the quality of the satisfaction imputation head. We can see that when using a single feature to predict survey response, the continuous feature of the time the user spent interacting with the item is less informative compared to discrete features representing the item such as the embedding of the item id. The AUC ROC of a satisfaction imputation with item id as the only feature is further improved when including other features representing the item on the survey—we notice a slight improvement when including the creator id embedding, and a considerable improvement when also including time spent in seconds interacting with the item, on top of item id and creator id embeddings.

**User State.** We also evaluate the importance of including user state in learning the imputation model (Fig. 4 *right*). We can see that when using as features only the user state, as captured by the RNN over the sequence up until this point, concatenated with the label context embedding, we get the same hold out AUC ROC as the one achieved by using all features representing the action (Fig. 4 *left*, last bar). Concatenating the user state with action embeddings further improves the imputation model's predictive power. Thus, in what follows, our satisfaction imputation model will utilize both user state and action embeddings as features.

## 6 Live Experiments

Our case study involves a large scale two-stage recommender platform, where at the first stage multiple candidate generators retrieve potential candidates from

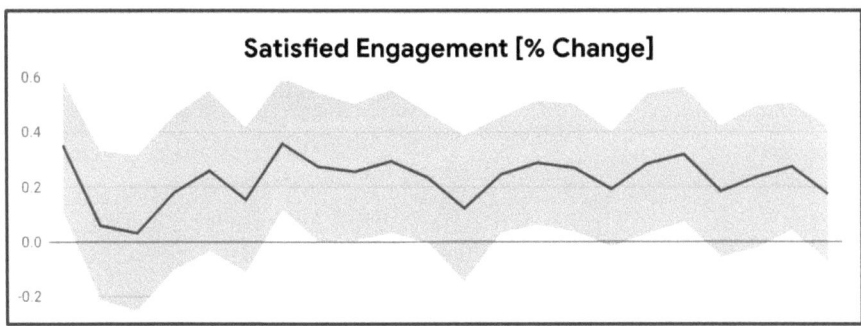

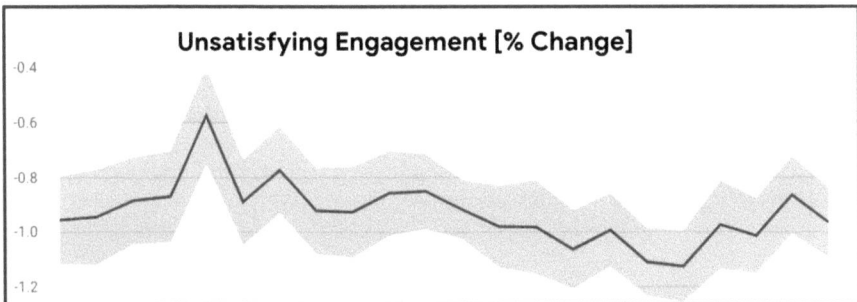

**Fig. 6.** Percentage improvements of online satisfaction metrics (y-axis) achieved by our proposed model over the course of a month (x-axis). On average, satisfied engagement is significantly increased by 0.23% (*top*), while unsatisfying engagement is significantly decreased by 0.93% (*bottom*), highlighting the value of our approach for driving user satisfaction.

the entire corpus; and the second stage involves a ranker model ranking the candidates and providing a final top-$K$ recommendation list to be shown to the user [5]. To study the extent to which our approach can improve real user experiences, we apply our reward shaping approach onto a RL-based candidate generator, and conducted a series of A/B experiments. The control arm runs a REINFORCE agent learned using engagement-only reward [3]. In the experiment arm, we test our proposed approach of augmenting the policy network with a satisfaction imputation head (Fig. 2), and utilizing the imputed satisfaction reward along with the ground truth behavioral signals into the policy's reward, described in Sect. 4.4. Experiments are run for over a month on a fixed set of randomly assigned user traffic to study the long-term effect. During this period, the model is trained continuously, with new interactions being used as training data with a lag under 24 h.

**Online Satisfied Engagement Metric.** For evaluating whether the user experiences are improved, one could look at ground truth survey responses. An experiment which increases the average survey response over the experiment period would be considered driving more user satisfaction. In fact our experi-

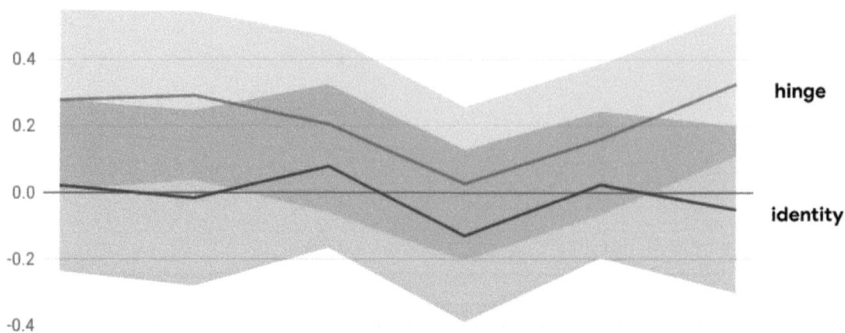

**Fig. 7.** Effect of choice of transformation function over the imputed satisfaction scores. Y axis denotes percentage improvements of online satisfied engagement metric, x-axis denotes the days over the course of the month, and the two lines refer to hinge and identity transformation. We find that filtering data with lower imputed satisfaction scores through the hinge function performed considerably better compared to raw imputations.

ment increases 5 star survey responses on average by **0.48%** and decreases 1 and 2 star survey responses by **1.89%**. However, we again run into the key challenge associated with survey responses which is sparsity. If we only measure on user-item pairs for which the users have responded to in a survey, we would only be looking at a very small percentage of the user interactions. To tackle this, we instead rely on a model-based metric predicting a survey response for each of the items the user has interacted with, and combining that with engagement metrics measured live. It is worth pointing out, the model used for measuring online satisfaction metric is independent of the imputation network we built, with a considerably different feature set and architecture. We cannot utilize the predictions of this model directly into our reward, due to infrastructure complexities and freshness requirements.

**Satisfaction Improvements.** In Fig. 5 we show how the distribution of ground truth satisfaction scores over nominations coming from the control model (REINFORCE with engagement-reward) versus the experiment (our approach optimizing for a combination of satisfaction and engagement) compare. The x-axis represents the ground truth satisfaction probability score (used to calculate the live satisfied engagement time metric, and distinct from our imputation model predictions), with scores close to 1.0 indicating users being satisfied with their interactions, and close to 0.0 being unsatisfied. We can see that in both experiment and control arms, the majority of interactions are predicted to have a score larger than 0.5, indicating satisfying experience. Nevertheless, we can clearly see that our experiment increases the number of nominations with satisfaction scores greater or equal to 0.9, and decreases respectively nominations with a score less than 0.9. This demonstrates that our proposed imputation head is able to identify items which are satisfying to the users and shift the policy to select more satisfying items, further validating its predictive accuracy.

Figure 6 compares the control and experiment arm on a live metric combining the model-based satisfaction metric and behavioral-based implicit engagement signals. We find that on average, satisfied engagement is increased by **0.23%**, while unsatisfying engagement is decreased by **0.93%**. Both results are statistically significant, signifying the value of reward shaping in driving user utility as specified by the reward. Furthermore, metrics orthogonal to the ground truth satisfaction scores, measuring other facets of user experience, significantly move towards the right direction: likes on items increase by **0.53%**, while dislikes are decreased by **1.11%** and dismissals decrease by **3.03%**. Note that we did not include these signals into the features or labels of our satisfaction imputation model. This further supports the point made in Sect. 1 that optimizing for satisfaction signals correlates well with improvements in post-engagement actions.

We found that an important design choice in the reward is the transformation function over the predicted satisfaction signal $r^u(s,a)$ by the imputation network, i.e., the probability of an item being satisfying to the user. Simply multiplying the engagement reward signals by the imputed probability of the item being satisfying (identity function) only decreases non-satisfied engagement, but did not lead to statistically significant improvements in satisfied engagement. It is critical to further differentiate highly satisfying items from less satisfying ones to allow the model to clearly prefer selecting such items. We found that in practice a simple hinge function performed the best, i.e., when imputed probability of an item being satisfying to the user is larger than a threshold, multiply with the probability, else completely zero out the engagement reward (Fig. 7). The threshold was tuned offline based on the ground truth response distribution, and the imputation network's predictions. We report results based on threshold set to 0.75.

Furthermore, we validated in live experiments some of our choices made offline. We found that predicting the probability of an item found satisfying by the user performed better than predicting the actual survey response they will give, i.e., cross-entropy loss gave better results compared to a square loss. We hypothesize that this could be the case due to better alignment with the loss used to train the model-based Satisfied Engagement live metric. Also, balancing the data to give more weight to unsatisfying survey responses and calibrating the prediction to account for the balancing (Fig. 3) was important for live improvements. Finally, we found that raising the satisfaction reward term to an exponent larger than 1 gave us slightly better results when using the identity transformation function; but for the hinge function, the improvement was not statistically significant.

## 7 Conclusions

This paper addresses the challenge of optimizing long-term user satisfaction in reinforcement learning-based recommenders. We advocate for reward shaping as a vital technique to align the recommender's goals with what users want. We argue that relying solely on engagement signals, as common in the current RL literature, does not adequately capture the nuances of user experience. Instead, incorporating user satisfaction signals is crucial. Recognizing the sparsity of these satisfaction signals, we propose improving a state-of-the-art REINFORCE recommender with a satisfaction imputation network to predict satisfaction scores for all interacted items. Through offline analysis and live A/B experiments on a large-scale commercial recommender platform, we demonstrate that integrating satisfaction imputation into the reward function effectively leads to more satisfying user experiences.

# References

1. Beutel, A., et al.: Latent cross: making use of context in recurrent recommender systems. In: Proceedings of the Eleventh ACM International Conference on Web Search and Data Mining, pp. 46–54 (2018)
2. Chapelle, O., Manavoglu, E., Rosales, R.: Simple and scalable response prediction for display advertising. ACM Trans. Intell. Syst. Technol. (TIST) **5**(4), 1–34 (2014)
3. Chen, M., Beutel, A., Covington, P., Jain, S., Belletti, F., Chi, E.H.: Top-k off-policy correction for a reinforce recommender system. In: Proceedings of the Twelfth ACM International Conference on Web Search and Data Mining, pp. 456–464 (2019)
4. Christakopoulou, K., et al.: Deconfounding user satisfaction estimation from response rate bias. In: Proceedings of the 14th ACM Conference on recommender systems, pp. 450–455 (2020)
5. Covington, P., Adams, J., Sargin, E.: Deep neural networks for YouTube recommendations. In: Proceedings of the 10th ACM Conference on Recommender Systems, pp. 191–198 (2016)
6. Dorigo, M., Colombetti, M.: Robot shaping: developing autonomous agents through learning. Artif. Intell. **71**(2), 321–370 (1994)
7. Dulac-Arnold, G., et al.: Deep reinforcement learning in large discrete action spaces. arXiv preprint arXiv:1512.07679 (2015)
8. Elkan, C.: The foundations of cost-sensitive learning. In: International joint Conference on Artificial Intelligence, vol. 17, pp. 973–978. Lawrence Erlbaum Associates Ltd (2001)
9. Garcia-Gathright, J., St. Thomas, B., Hosey, C., Nazari, Z., Diaz, F.: Understanding and evaluating user satisfaction with music discovery. In: The 41st International ACM SIGIR Conference on Research & Development in Information Retrieval, pp. 55–64 (2018)
10. Gu, S., Holly, E., Lillicrap, T., Levine, S.: Deep reinforcement learning for robotic manipulation with asynchronous off-policy updates. In: 2017 IEEE International Conference on Robotics and Automation (ICRA), pp. 3389–3396. IEEE (2017)
11. Guo, Q., Agichtein, E.: Beyond dwell time: estimating document relevance from cursor movements and other post-click searcher behavior. In: Proceedings of the 21st International Conference on World Wide Web, pp. 569–578 (2012)
12. Hadfield-Menell, D., Milli, S., Abbeel, P., Russell, S.J., Dragan, A.: Inverse reward design. In: Advances in neural information processing systems. pp. 6765–6774 (2017)

13. Ie, E., et al.: Slateq: a tractable decomposition for reinforcement learning with recommendation sets. In: Proceedings of the Twenty-eighth International Joint Conference on Artificial Intelligence (IJCAI-19), pp. 2592–2599. Macau, China (2019), see arXiv:1905.12767 for a related and expanded paper (with additional material and authors)
14. Lalmas, M.: Metrics, engagement & personalization. In: REVEAL workshop, The ACM Conference Series on Recommender Systems (2019)
15. Liu, F., et al.: Deep reinforcement learning based recommendation with explicit user-item interactions modeling. arXiv preprint arXiv:1810.12027 (2018)
16. Mataric, M.J.: Reward functions for accelerated learning. In: Machine learning proceedings 1994, pp. 181–189. Elsevier (1994)
17. Mehrotra, R., Lalmas, M., Kenney, D., Lim-Meng, T., Hashemian, G.: Jointly leveraging intent and interaction signals to predict user satisfaction with slate recommendations. In: Proceedings of The Web Conference 2019, pp. 1256–1267 (2019)
18. Mehrotra, R., McInerney, J., Bouchard, H., Lalmas, M., Diaz, F.: Towards a fair marketplace: Counterfactual evaluation of the trade-off between relevance, fairness & satisfaction in recommendation systems. In: Proceedings of the 27th ACM International Conference on Information and Knowledge Management, pp. 2243–2251 (2018)
19. Mnih, V., et al.: Asynchronous methods for deep reinforcement learning. In: International Conference on Machine Learning, pp. 1928–1937 (2016)
20. Mnih, V., et al.: Playing atari with deep reinforcement learning. arXiv preprint arXiv:1312.5602 (2013)
21. Mnih, V., et al.: Human-level control through deep reinforcement learning. Nature **518**(7540), 529–533 (2015)
22. Munos, R., Stepleton, T., Harutyunyan, A., Bellemare, M.: Safe and efficient off-policy reinforcement learning. In: Advances in Neural Information Processing Systems, pp. 1054–1062 (2016)
23. Ng, A.Y., Harada, D., Russell, S.: Policy invariance under reward transformations: Theory and application to reward shaping. In: ICML, vol. 99, pp. 278–287 (1999)
24. Pan, S.J., Yang, Q.: A survey on transfer learning. IEEE Trans. Knowl. Data Eng. **22**(10), 1345–1359 (2009)
25. Paulhus, D.L.: Measurement and control of response bias (1991)
26. Schaal, S.: Is imitation learning the route to humanoid robots? Trends Cogn. Sci. **3**(6), 233–242 (1999)
27. Schulman, J., Moritz, P., Levine, S., Jordan, M., Abbeel, P.: High-dimensional continuous control using generalized advantage estimation. arXiv preprint arXiv:1506.02438 (2015)
28. Silver, D., et al.: A general reinforcement learning algorithm that masters chess, shogi, and go through self-play. Science **362**(6419), 1140–1144 (2018)
29. Sutton, R.S., Barto, A.G.: Reinforcement learning: An introduction. MIT press (2018)
30. Sutton, R.S., McAllester, D.A., Singh, S.P., Mansour, Y.: Policy gradient methods for reinforcement learning with function approximation. In: Advances in neural information processing systems, pp. 1057–1063 (2000)
31. Wen, H., Yang, L., Estrin, D.: Leveraging post-click feedback for content recommendations. In: Proceedings of the 13th ACM Conference on Recommender Systems, pp. 278–286 (2019)
32. Williams, R.J.: Simple statistical gradient-following algorithms for connectionist reinforcement learning. Mach. Learn. **8**(3–4), 229–256 (1992)

33. Yi, X., Hong, L., Zhong, E., Liu, N.N., Rajan, S.: Beyond clicks: dwell time for personalization. In: Proceedings of the 8th ACM Conference on Recommender systems, pp. 113–120 (2014)
34. Zhang, J., Hao, B., Chen, B., Li, C., Chen, H., Sun, J.: Hierarchical reinforcement learning for course recommendation in MOOCs. In: Proceedings of the AAAI Conference on Artificial Intelligence, vol. 33, pp. 435–442 (2019)
35. Zhao, X., Xia, L., Zhang, L., Ding, Z., Yin, D., Tang, J.: Deep reinforcement learning for page-wise recommendations. In: Proceedings of the 12th ACM Conference on Recommender Systems, pp. 95–103 (2018)
36. Zheng, G., et al.: DRN: A deep reinforcement learning framework for news recommendation. In: Proceedings of the 2018 World Wide Web Conference, pp. 167–176 (2018)

# Decentralizing Multi-agent Reinforcement Learning with Temporal Causal Information

Jan Corazza[1(✉)], Hadi Partovi Aria[2], Hyohun Kim[2], Daniel Neider[1], and Zhe Xu[2]

[1] Research Center Trustworthy Data Science and Security of the University Alliance Ruhr, Department of Computer Science, TU Dortmund University, Dortmund, Germany
{jan.corazza,daniel.neider}@tu-dortmund.de
[2] Arizona State University, Tempe, USA
{hpartovi,hkim450,xzhe1}@asu.edu

**Abstract.** Reinforcement learning (RL) algorithms can find an optimal policy for a single agent to accomplish a particular task. However, many real-world problems require multiple agents to collaborate in order to achieve a common goal. For example, a robot executing a task in a warehouse may require the assistance of a drone to retrieve items from high shelves. In Decentralized Multi-Agent RL (DMARL), agents learn independently and then combine their policies at execution time, but often must satisfy constraints on compatibility of local policies to ensure that they can achieve the global task when combined. In this paper, we study how providing high-level symbolic knowledge to agents can help address unique challenges of this setting, such as privacy constraints, communication limitations, and performance concerns. In particular, we extend the formal tools used to check the compatibility of local policies with the team task, making decentralized training with theoretical guarantees usable in more scenarios. Furthermore, we empirically demonstrate that symbolic knowledge about the temporal evolution of events in the environment can significantly expedite the learning process in DMARL.

**Keywords:** Temporal Causality · Multi-Agent Reinforcement Learning · Reward Machines · Formal Methods

## 1 Introduction

One approach to solving a multi-agent problem is to learn a centralized policy that controls all agents simultaneously. Such a centralized controller is conceptually straightforward, but realizing it is often impractical [7] if the number of agents is large or there is an imposed need for decentralization. As the number of agents increases, the state space grows exponentially, making it less tractable to learn a centralized policy. Decentralization is imposed when agents are physically separated, communication is limited, or privacy is a concern. Centralized policies, by contrast, often assume seamless communication, which is unrealistic in many real-world scenarios. This challenge is further exacerbated by sparse reward signals with temporal dependencies, inherent in many real-world tasks.

Instead of learning a centralized policy, agents can learn decentralized policies that allow them to act independently and reduce the need for communication. These independent policies are then combined at execution time to solve the team task. To this end, Neary et al. [8] propose a DMARL algorithm called Decentralized Q-learning with Projected Reward Machines (DQPRM). DQPRM decomposes a global team task specification into a set of local task specifications, one for each individual agent. Agents are trained independently to learn policies based on their local task specifications. To ensure that the agents' local policies, when combined, satisfy the overall team task, DQPRM enforces strict **compatibility criteria** between the local and team specifications. In Sect. 3, we provide a brief overview of DQPRM.

Reward machines (RMs, formalized in Definition 1) are deterministic, finite-state automata that transduce sequences of relevant high-level events (labels) into sequences of rewards, thereby capturing the temporal nature of a sparse reward signal, and serving as specifications for RL tasks. Reward machines have been widely studied in literature [2,4–6,9,12], but the primary focus has been on the single-agent case. In multi-agent problems, communication limitations mean individual agents cannot sense all events, preventing them from accessing the full team state. DQPRM frames this limitation in terms of projected (local) RMs, that capture a particular agent's contribution to the team goal (with respect to events that the agent can sense).

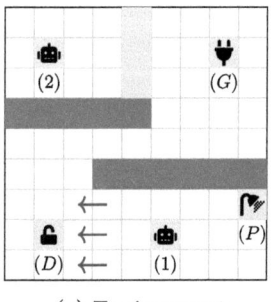

(a) Environment

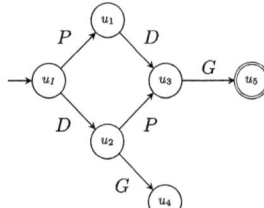

(b) Team Reward Machine

**Fig. 1.** *Generator Task.*

To illustrate the limitations of DQPRM's strict compatibility criteria, we will introduce a running example called the *Generator Task*, depicted in Fig. 1. In this task, two agents move on a gridworld (Fig. 1a), and must collaborate to power a generator during a flooding incident.

Agent 1's task is to prevent the flooding by closing the pipe ( , $P$), and to unlock the door ( , $D$) for agent 2 (in any order). The task for agent 2 is to wait for the door to be unlocked (🔓), i.e., for the yellow barrier to disappear, and then power the generator (🔌, $G$). The team reward machine, depicted in Fig. 1b, also specifies a failure condition: if agent 2 is let into the room and powers the generator *before* the flooding has been resolved, the team RM will enter an unsafe state, $u_4$, from which no further actions can result in a positive reward. The agents obtain a reward of 1 and end the task if their joint actions transition the team RM to into an accepting state, $u_5$, and 0 in all steps prior.

The challenge in this example arises from the agents' limited communication about the task's status. In particular, agent 1 does not communicate whether it is safe to power up the generator (i.e., whether event 🔌 has happened). In other words, agent 2 does not know whether the team is collectively in state $u_2$ (🔌 is unsafe) or $u_3$ (🔌 is safe and completes the task). Although both agents have an individual strategy that solves the team task, this specification fails to meet the requirements of DQPRM, which strictly prohibit outcomes to depend on local event synchronization.

Recent work in causal reinforcement learning [4,9] proposes methods that leverage causal knowledge of the long-term temporal evolution of high-level environmental events to improve the exploration-exploitation trade-off. Paliwal et al. [9] introduce Temporal Logic-based Causal Diagrams (TL-CDs), a formalism that captures such *temporal-causal* knowledge by enabling experts to specify causal relationships between $LTL_f$ formulas. During learning, temporal-causal knowledge expressed in TL-CDs is used to predict whether further exploration within a given episode is necessary and, if not, to short-circuit the exploration process. Unfortunately, this method lacks rigorous theoretical guarantees. Corazza et al. [4] extend this line of work with a provably correct method that directly integrates temporal-causal knowledge from TL-CDs into the reward machine. Ultimately, both methods expedite convergence to optimal policies by exploiting knowledge of temporal causality—i.e., the long-term evolution of high-level events within the MDP. In Sect. 4, we provide a brief overview of TL-CDs and their integration with reward machines.

Our paper connects these two lines of work (decentralized MARL and temporal-causal RL). In Sect. 5, we propose a method to exploit temporal-causal knowledge about the task at hand in order to (1) relax the theoretical compatibility criteria of DQPRM, broadening the scope of multi-agent tasks that can be decomposed and learned in a decentralized manner; and (2) short-circuit certain explorations during decentralized learning, improving the sample efficiency of the learning process even further. Moreover, we prove that our relaxed compatibility criterion is consistent with the original one, in the sense that passing the original criterion implies passing the relaxed one. In Sect. 6, we empirically demonstrate our method's effectiveness on the *Generator Task* and introduce the *Laboratory Task*, presenting experimental results for both. The appendix of our extended preprint [3] provides an analysis of a third case study, the *Buttons Task*. The code for our experiments and related materials is publicly available at https://github.com/corazza/tcdmarl.

## 2 Preliminaries

Aside from acting as a task specification, reward machines provide a form of finite memory for a team or an agent, tracking progress through the task. We assume that during the agents' interaction with the MDP, relevant high-level events are labeled. Reward machines use these event labels as inputs to transition between states and determine the appropriate rewards. By modeling the temporal dependencies within the task, RMs guide agents through complex environments, especially in situations where rewards are sparse. We first introduce the general definitions of Event-based Reward Machines (RMs) and RM-based Markov Decision Processes (RM-MDPs), which provide a foundational framework for handling task specification and reward functions. In Sect. 3, we will extend this formalism to the multi-agent setting, where decentralized coordination becomes crucial.

**Definition 1. (Event-based Reward Machine).** *An event-based RM $\mathcal{R} = \langle U, u_I, \Sigma, \delta, \sigma, F \rangle$ is a tuple where $U$ is a finite set of states with an initial state $u_I \in U$, $\Sigma$ is the set of events, $\delta : U \times \Sigma \to U$ is a (partial) transition function, $\sigma : U \times U \to \mathbb{R}$ is a (partial) function mapping transitions to rewards, and $F \subseteq U$ is a set of terminal states that signal the end of the interaction.*

When the RM is in state $u \in U$ and reads an event $e \in \Sigma$ such that $(u, e) \in \text{Dom}(\delta)$, it transitions into a new state $u' = \delta(u, e)$ and outputs a reward $\sigma(u, u')$. Otherwise, the RM remains in the same state and outputs a reward of 0. For finite event sequences, we define $\delta(u, \epsilon) = u$ and $\delta(u, \xi e) = \delta(\delta(u, \xi), e)$, where $\epsilon$ is the empty sequence, $\xi \in (\Sigma)^*$, and $e \in \Sigma$. Note that $\delta$ and $\sigma$ are partial functions, i.e., we do not require the transition function to be defined for every input event from every state. The term *event-based RM* is a deliberate departure from prior work [8], which conflated event-driven RMs with propositional RMs under the generic "RM" label. We focus on *task completion* RMs which output a reward of 1 upon reaching a terminal state $u \in F$, and 0 otherwise. For brevity, we refer to task completion event-based reward machines simply as reward machines throughout the remainder of this work.

To connect an RM with the MDP (with set of states $S$), we use a labeling function $L: S \times U \times S \to 2^\Sigma$. The codomain of $L$ is $2^\Sigma$ to model the possibility that certain events may occur concurrently. We restrict the labeling function so that only one event may occur per step, per agent.[1] Because of this restriction and the compatibility criterion defined in Sect. 3, the order an RM reads simultaneous events does not matter. In other words, if an RM reads an event sequence $\xi \in \text{Perm}(L(s, u, s'))$, the resulting state $u' = \delta(u, \xi)$ is well-defined (independent of the permutation of $\xi$).

**Definition 2. (RM-MDP).** *A Reward Machine-based Markov Decision Process is a tuple $\mathcal{M} = \langle S, s_I, A, p, \gamma, \mathcal{R}, L \rangle$ consisting of a finite state space $S$, an*

---

[1] We explain this assumption in Sect. 3, where we provide background for decentralized MARL.

initial state $s_I \in S$, a finite set of actions $A$, a probabilistic transition function $p\colon S \times U \times A \times S \to [0,1]$, a discount factor $\gamma \in (0,1]$, a reward machine $\mathcal{R}$ which captures the reward function, and a labeling function $L\colon S \times U \times S \to 2^{\Sigma}$. Note that the transition probabilities $p(s' \mid s, u, a)$ are conditioned on the state of the reward machine $u \in U$.

Intuitively, if the MDP and the RM are in a joint state $(s, u) \in S \times U$, and the agent chooses an action $a \in A$, the MDP transitions to a new state $s' \sim p(s, u, a)$. The labeling function then outputs a set of simultaneous events $L(s, u, s')$, which the RM reads in any order, and transitions into $u' = \delta(u, L(s, u, s'))$.

We say that a trajectory $s_0 u_0 a_0 \cdots a_{n-1} s_n u_n$ is attainable within an RM-MDP $\mathcal{M} = \langle S, s_I, A, p, \gamma, \mathcal{R}, L \rangle$ when $(s_0, u_0) = (s_I, u_I)$, and for all $i = 0, 1, \ldots, n-1$ we have $p(s_i, u_i, a_i, s_{i+1}) > 0$ and $u_{i+1} = \delta(u_i, L(s_i, u_i, s_{i+1}))$. An event sequence $\xi = e_1 \ldots e_n$ is attainable if it can be obtained using a finite number of concatenation and swap operations from the label sequence $\ell_i = L(s_i, u_i, s_{i+1})$ of an attainable trace.

The reward function of an RM-MDP is induced by the reward machine $\mathcal{R}$ via $R((s, u), a, (s', u')) = \sigma(u, u')$. Because $R$ is Markovian over the product space $S \times U$, one may use Q-learning to find an optimal policy in an RM-MDP.

## 3 Decentralized Multi-agent Reinforcement Learning

In this section, we outline the baseline DQPRM algorithm proposed by Neary et al. [8], including its assumptions and theoretical guarantees. In decentralized MARL with reward machines, the overall team task is specified by an RM $\mathcal{R}$ defined over a global set of events $\Sigma$ (all events that may occur in the MDP). However, not every agent can observe all events from $\Sigma$. In order to capture this limitation, we define a local event set $\Sigma_i$ for each agent $i = 1, \ldots, N$, where $N$ is the number of agents. We assume that $\Sigma = \bigcup_{i=1}^{N} \Sigma_i$.

In the *Generator Task* from Fig. 1, the local event set of agent 1 is $\Sigma_1 = \{P, D\}$, modeling the capabilities to fix the pipe (observe 🔧) and open the door (observe 🔒). The local event set of agent 2 is $\Sigma_2 = \{D, G\}$, modeling the capabilities to observe the door being unlocked (🔒) and power the generator (🔌). As demonstrated by the event $D$, local event sets may overlap, i.e., there may be events that can be sensed by more than one agent. We call such events *shared events*, and write $I_e = \{i \mid e \in \Sigma_i\}$ for the set of agents that share event $e$. When $|I_e| > 1$ for some $e \in \Sigma$, a synchronization mechanism ought to be simulated during decentralized training episodes. For example, since the event $D$ is under the control of agent 1, during decentralized training of agent 2, we simulate the communication of this event with probability $p > 0$ at every time-step.

In decentralized MARL, we train each agent independently to avoid the exponential blow-up of a centralized policy. The primary benefit of this approach is sample efficiency, as centralized policies induce a state space that grows exponentially with the number of agents. Other benefits include privacy (limiting shared knowledge), and the fact that centralized policies may be infeasible due to practical concerns (differing capabilities, limited communication).

To facilitate decentralized training, we first need to capture the individual contribution of each agent towards the team goal in terms of the agent's local event set. This can be achieved with the notion of *Projected* Reward Machines, which we will now introduce. We also refer to projected reward machines as *local RMs*, to highlight that the projection is defined in terms of the local event set.

To define the projection of the team RM $\mathcal{R} = \langle U, u_I, \Sigma, \delta, \sigma, F \rangle$ along a local event set $\Sigma_i \subseteq \Sigma$, we first introduce an equivalence relation $\sim_i$ over states of $\mathcal{R}$. Informally, two states $u_1, u_2 \in U$ are $\sim_i$-equivalent if agent $i$ can not distinguish between them based on events in $\Sigma_i$. Formally, $\sim_i$ is the smallest equivalence relation such that for all $u_1, u_2, u_1', u_2' \in U$ we have (1) $u_1 \sim_i u_2$ if there exists an event $e \in \Sigma \setminus \Sigma_i$ such that $u_2 = \delta(u_1, e)$; and (2) if $u_1 \sim_i u_1'$ and there exists an event $e \in \Sigma_i$ such that $\delta(u_1, e) = u_2$ and $\delta(u_1', e) = u_2'$, then $u_2 \sim_i u_2'$. We denote the set of equivalence classes of $\sim_i$ with $U/\sim_i$, and we will write $[u]_i$ for the $\sim_i$-equivalence class of $u \in U$.

Condition (1) ensures that two states of $\mathcal{R}$ are indistinguishable for agent $i$ if a transition between them is triggered by an event outside of $\Sigma_i$. Condition (2) (congruence) ensures that an event $e \in \Sigma_i$ may only trigger transitions to a unique successor equivalence class. An algorithm to compute this equivalence relation with runtime $O(|U|^7|\Sigma_i|^2 + |U|^5|\Sigma_i| + |U|^4)$ is provided in appendix C of Wong [11]. Using $\sim_i$, we formalize the notion of a projected RM in Definition 3. Figure 2 depicts the projections of the team RM from the *Generator Task* along the local event sets of agents 1 and 2.

**Definition 3. (Projected Reward Machine).** *Given a reward machine $\mathcal{R} = \langle U, u_I, \Sigma, \delta, \sigma, F \rangle$ and local event set $\Sigma_i$, the projection of $\mathcal{R}$ along $\Sigma_i$ is the RM $\mathcal{R}_i = (U_i, u_I^i, \delta_i, \Sigma_i, F_i)$ where $U_i = U/\sim_i$, $u_I^i = [u_I]_i$, $\delta_i : U_i \times \Sigma_i \to U_i$ is defined as $u_2^i = \delta_i(u_1^i, e)$ for $e \in \Sigma_i$ if and only if there exist $u_1, u_2 \in U$ such that $[u_1] = u_1^i$, $[u_2] = u_2^i$ and $u_2 = \delta(u_1, e)$ (and undefined otherwise), $F_i = \{u^i \in U_i \mid \exists u \in F, u^i = [u]_i\}$, and $\sigma_i(u_1^i, u_2^i) = \mathbb{1}_{u_2^i \in F_i \wedge u_1^i \notin F_i}$.*

(a) $\Sigma_1 = \{P, D\}$      (b) $\Sigma_2 = \{D, G\}$

**Fig. 2.** Projections of the RM from Fig. 1b along local event sets of agents 1 (Left) and 2 (Right).

We model a multi-agent system with $N$ agents as an RM-MDP $\mathcal{M} = \langle S, s_I, A^N, p, \gamma, \mathcal{R}, L \rangle$ where the state space $S$ is a Cartesian product of local state spaces, $S = S_1 \times \cdots \times S_N$, the action space $A^N$ is a product of individual action spaces (the same for each agent) $A \times \cdots \times A$, and the transition function $p: S \times U \times A^N \times S$ can be decomposed as a product $p(s, u, a, s') = \prod_{i=1}^{N} p_i(s_i, u^i, a_i, s'_i)$, where $u^i = [u]_i$ is the projection of the team state from $\mathcal{R}$ to the local RM state of agent $i$. The dynamics $p_i$ of agent $i$ depend only on the agent's individual state and action, $(s_i, a_i)$, and the events that the agent can sense (i.e., the state of its local RM $\mathcal{R}_i$).

To fully capture the local dynamics of each agent, DQPRM relies on the notion of local labeling functions $L_i : S_i \times U_i \times S_i \to 2^\Sigma$, where $S_i$ is the local state space of agent $i$, and $U_i = U/\sim_i$ are the states of its local RM. Intuitively, $L_i(s_i, u^i, s'_i)$ outputs events that *could* be occurring from the perspective of agent $i$, given that the rest of the team state is unknown. We note that local labeling functions must output at most a single event $\{e\}$ (which corresponds to the assumption that only one event may occur per agent per time step), and that $L(s, u, s')$ outputs event $e$ if and only if $L_i(s_i, u^i, s'_i)$ output $e$, for all $i \in I_e$. We call such label functions decomposable with respect to $\Sigma_1, \ldots, \Sigma_N$ (or just decomposable if the family $\{\Sigma_i\}_{i=1}^{N}$ is clear from the context).[2] We define the projection of a finite event sequence $\xi \in \Sigma^*$ onto the local event set $\Sigma_i$ as $P_i(\xi'\ell) = P_i(\xi')e$ if $\xi = \xi'e$ and $e \in \Sigma_i$, and $P_i(\xi e) = P_i(\xi)$ otherwise (for the empty word $\epsilon$, $P_i(\epsilon) = \epsilon$ for all $i = 1, \ldots, N$).

A key requirement for the task decomposition to be successful is that policies induced by projected RMs must combine to form a policy that satisfies the team RM. This requirement is satisfied if the team RM is bisimilar to the parallel composition of its projections, which we refer to as the *strict decomposition criterion*. Intuitively, two reward machines $\mathcal{R}$ and $\mathcal{P}$ are bisimilar ($\mathcal{R} \cong \mathcal{P}$) if there exists a relation between their states such that the transition behavior of related states is the same (initial and final states must be related). The parallel composition of two RMs $\mathcal{R}_1$ and $\mathcal{R}_2$ is an RM $\mathcal{R}_1 \| \mathcal{R}_2$ whose states are the Cartesian product of states of $\mathcal{R}$ and $\mathcal{P}$, initial (terminal) states are pairs of initial (terminal) states, and transitions are defined component-wise.[3] Using the notions of bisimilarity and parallel composition of RMs, we can formalize the strict decomposition criterion for the team RM $\mathcal{R}$ and local RMs $\mathcal{R}_1, \ldots, \mathcal{R}_N$. The criterion holds if $\mathcal{R} \cong \|_{i=1}^{N} \mathcal{R}_i$. In that case, decentralized training of local policies will yield a combined policy with guaranteed bounds on the probability of solving the team task. By definition, if local RMs $\mathcal{R}_i$ output 1 (for all $i = 1, \ldots, N$), then their parallel composition also outputs 1. And because their parallel composition is bisimilar to the team RM, the team task is satisfied as well. The converse also holds: if the team RM outputs a reward, then each local RM will output a reward. This is formalized in Theorem 1 [8].

**Theorem 1. (Strict Decomposition Criterion).** *If RM $\mathcal{R}$ and projections $\mathcal{R}_1, \ldots, \mathcal{R}_N$ satisfy the strict decomposition criterion, then $\forall \xi \in \Sigma^*$, $\mathcal{R}(\xi) = 1$ if and only if $\mathcal{R}_i(P_i(\xi)) = 1, \forall i = 1, \ldots, N$. Here, $P_i(\xi)$ is the projection of $\xi$ to $\Sigma_i$ defined earlier.*

---

[2] For more details on constructing local labeling functions see Neary et al. [8].
[3] Formal definitions and visual explanation in the appendix of our extended preprint. [3].

We provide the pseudocode for DQPRM in Algorithm 1. In brief, DQPRM runs $N$ concurrent episodes, where each agent moves independently, receiving observations, events, and rewards decoupled from the state of the other $N-1$ agents. When acting in a team setting during testing, agents must synchronize on shared events. This is the only communication channel necessary to execute single-agent policies, found by DQPRM, in a multi-agent RM-MDP. When the local labeling function $L_i$ outputs a shared event $e$, synchronization ensures that $\mathcal{R}_i$ reads $e$ iff. $L_j$ outputs the same event $e$ for all $j \in I_e$. To account for this fact during decentralized training, DQPRM simulates the synchronization signal with probability $p > 0$ (Line 18). We summarize the guarantees for team performance in Theorem 2.

---

**Algorithm 1:** Decentralized training with DQPRM

**Input**: Team RM $\mathcal{R}$, local event sets $\Sigma_1, \ldots, \Sigma_N$, local labeling functions $L_1, \ldots, L_N$

**Output**: Policies $\pi_1, \ldots, \pi_N$

1 Project $\mathcal{R}$ along local event sets $\Sigma_i$ to obtain projected RMs $\mathcal{R}_1, \ldots, \mathcal{R}_N$;
2 **if** $\mathcal{R} \not\cong \mathcal{R}_1 \| \cdots \| \mathcal{R}_N$ **then**
3     Reject: the strict decomposition criterion does not hold;
4 **end**
5 Initialize$(\pi_1, \ldots, \pi_N)$;
6 **for** $m = 1$ **to** $numEpisodes$ **do**
7     **for** $i = 1$ **to** $N$ **do**
8        $s_i \leftarrow s_I^i,\ u_i \leftarrow u_I^i$;
9     **end**
10    **for** $t = 1$ **to** $numSteps$ **do**
11       **for** $i = 1$ **to** $N$ **do**
12          **if** $TaskComplete_i(u_i)$ **then**
13            continue;
14          **end**
15          $a_i \leftarrow \text{Sample}(\pi_i(s_i, u_i))$;
16          $s' \leftarrow \text{Step}_i(s_i, u_i, a_i),\ u' \leftarrow u_i,\ r_i \leftarrow 0$;
                   // $L_i(s_i, u_i, s')$ is either $\emptyset$ or $\{e\} \in \Sigma_i$
17          **for** $e \in L_i(s_i, u_i, s')$ **do**
18            **if** $|I_e| = 1$ **or** $Rand(0,1) \leq p$ **then**
19              $u' \leftarrow \delta(u_i, e);\ r_i \leftarrow r_i + \sigma(u_i, u');\ u_i \leftarrow u'$;
20            **end**
21          **end**
22          PolicyUpdate$(\pi_i, s_i, u_i, a_i, s', r_i)$;
23          $s_i \leftarrow s'$;
24       **end**
25    **end**
26 **end**
27 **return** $(\pi_1, \ldots, \pi_N)$;

**Theorem 2. (Decomposition Viability).** *Given a team RM $\mathcal{R}$, local event sets $\Sigma_1, \ldots, \Sigma_N$, a decomposable label function $L$, and local labeling functions $L_1, \ldots, L_N$, assume that agents synchronize on shared events and $\mathcal{R} \cong \|_{i=1}^{N} \mathcal{R}_i$. Then for all team trajectories $s_0 u_0 \cdots s_k u_k$ and local trajectories $\{s_0^i u_0^i \cdots s_k^i u_k^i\}_{i=1}^{N}$, we have $\mathcal{R}(L(s_0 u_0 \cdots s_k u_k)) = 1$ if and only if $\mathcal{R}_i(L_i(s_0^i u_0^i \cdots s_k^i u_k^i)) = 1$ for all $i = 1, \ldots, N$. Furthermore, let $V^\pi(s_I)$ denote the team success probability and $V_i^\pi(s_I^i)$ the success probability of agent $i$. Then $\max\{0, V_1^\pi(s_I) + \cdots + V_N^\pi(s_I) - (N-1)\} \leq V^\pi(s_I) \leq \min\{V_1^\pi(s_I), \ldots, V_N^\pi(s_I)\}$.*

Formal proofs of Theorems 1 and 2 can be found in Neary et al. [8]. Informally, Theorem 2 states that if a task specification respects the strict decomposition criterion, decentralized training will yield local agent policies which, when combined, satisfy the team task (depending on the probability that each agent performs its own part of the task). This result depends critically on Theorem 1, which guarantees a correspondence between solving local tasks and solving the team task, and the assumption that the agents synchronize on shared events.

## 4 Modeling Temporal-Causal Knowledge with TL-CDs

In this section, we lay the groundwork for modeling temporal-causal knowledge in RM-MDPs, and extend the notion of Temporal Logic-based Causal Diagrams (TL-CDs), proposed in Paliwal et al. [9], to Event-based Reward Machines. Linear temporal logic over finite sequences (LTL$_f$) is a formal reasoning system that can capture causal and temporal properties of event sequences and RM-MDPs. Aside from Boolean operators like $\neg$ and $\vee$, LTL$_f$ introduces temporal operators such as $\mathbf{G}\psi$ (true if and only if $\psi$ holds for every element in the sequence), $\mathbf{X}\psi$ (true iff. $\psi$ holds for the next element of the sequence), and $\psi \mathbf{U} \varphi$ (true iff. $\psi$ holds until $\varphi$ becomes true, and $\varphi$ is true in some element of the sequence). We also rely on the weak until operator $\psi \mathbf{W} \varphi$ (true iff. $\psi$ holds until $\varphi$ becomes true, but $\varphi$ is not required to become true).

TL-CDs are directed graphs where nodes are labeled with LTL$_f$ formulas and edges represent causal relationships between them, providing a structured notation to express temporal-causal knowledge. To give the semantics of TL-CD $\mathcal{C}$, one can construct an equivalent LTL$_f$ formula, $\varphi^\mathcal{C}$, which captures the temporal-causal knowledge encoded in the graph. The formula induced by the TL-CD in Fig. 3a, $\mathbf{G}(D \to \mathbf{G}(\neg \mathbf{X} P))$, models sequences in which the event $P$ never follows the event $D$. In other words, it captures the effect of the one-way ramp (represented by blue arrows ← in Fig. 1a), which blocks agent 1 from returning to the region of the MDP containing the pipe (🪠) after unlocking the door (🔒).

To capture the semantics of a given TL-CD $\mathcal{C}$ over event sequences in $\Sigma^*$, we construct an equivalent LTL$_f$ formula, $\Psi_\Sigma^\mathcal{C}$, as the conjunction $\Psi_\Sigma^\mathcal{C} \equiv \varphi^\mathcal{C} \wedge \psi_\Sigma$. The formula $\varphi^\mathcal{C}$ encodes the temporal-causal knowledge expressed in $\mathcal{C}$, and is defined as $\varphi^\mathcal{C} \equiv \bigwedge_{\varphi \blacktriangleright \psi} \mathbf{G}(\varphi \to \psi)$, where $\varphi \blacktriangleright \psi$ iterates over edges that connect

**Fig. 3.** TL-CD for the Routing Door Task (Left) and respective Causal DFA (Right).

formulas $\varphi$ and $\psi$ in the TL-CD. The formula $\psi_\Sigma = \mathbf{G}(\bigvee_{e \in \Sigma}(e \wedge (\bigwedge_{e' \in \Sigma \setminus \{e\}} \neg e')))$ restricts models of $\Psi_\Sigma^\mathcal{C}$ to event sequences in $\Sigma^*$. If $\Psi_\Sigma^\mathcal{C}$ is true for an event sequence $\xi = e_1 \ldots e_n$, we will write $\xi \models \Psi_\Sigma^\mathcal{C}$. We will say that a TL-CD $\mathcal{C}$ holds for an MDP $\mathcal{M}$ if for every event sequence $\xi$ attainable in $\mathcal{M}$, we have $\xi \models \Psi_\Sigma^\mathcal{C}$. In order to simplify working with TL-CDs, we leverage the notion of deterministic finite automata (DFAs), formalized in Definition 4.

**Definition 4. (Deterministic Finite Automaton).** *A DFA is a tuple* $\mathsf{C} = (Q, q_I, \Sigma, \delta, F)$ *consisting of a finite set of states $Q$ with an initial state $q_I$, input alphabet $\Sigma$, deterministic transition function $\delta : Q \times \Sigma \to Q$, and a set of accepting states $F \subseteq Q$.*

If the run of the DFA $\mathsf{C}$ on an input string $\xi$ ends in an accepting state $q \in F$, we will write $\xi \in \mathcal{L}(\mathsf{C})$. Every TL-CD $\mathcal{C}$ can be converted into an equivalent DFA $\mathsf{C}$ [9], in the sense that for every $\xi$, we have $\xi \in \mathcal{L}(\mathsf{C}) \iff \xi \models \Psi_\Sigma^\mathcal{C}$. We will refer to $\mathsf{C}$ as the *causal DFA*. When illustrating causal DFAs, we will only consider the fragment constructed from $\varphi^\mathcal{C}$, as the contribution of $\psi_\Sigma$ is always the same and serves a technical purpose. One can obtain the full causal DFA from the parallel composition of automata for $\varphi^\mathcal{C}$ and $\psi_\Sigma$. In Fig. 3b, we illustrate the DFA induced by the TL-CD which holds for the *Generator Task*.

## 5 Causal DQPRM

We enhance decentralized multi-agent RL by integrating temporal-causal knowledge through TL-CDs in two key ways. *First*, we enable valid decomposition of tasks rejected by DQPRM through causal constraints, preserving performance guarantees. *Second*, we accelerate learning by short-circuiting redundant exploration using TL-CD predictions, significantly improving sample efficiency in decentralized training.

### 5.1 Relaxing the Decomposition Criterion in DQPRM

The main assumption of the method proposed in Neary et al. [8] is that the team RM is bisimilar to the parallel composition of the projected RMs. As demonstrated by the decomposition in Fig. 2, this assumption is not always satisfied. To illustrate this point, consider the event sequence $\xi = DGP$, which induces a reward of 1 in both projections, but 0 in the team RM. Unfortunately, this means that Theorem 2 no longer guarantees a viable decomposition into local

RMs. As such, one can not expect DQPRM to solve the *Generator Task* (at least not before results analogous to Theorem 1 are shown to hold).

On the other hand, by constructing a strategy for each agent manually, one can see that decentralized learning ought to yield satisfactory results. The reason for this lies in the fact that 🏁 ($P$) and 🔓 ($D$) are separated by a one-way ramp (Fig. 1a). Once agent 1 visits 🔓, then due to this one-way ramp, no attainable trajectory leads to 🏁. In other words, while agent 1 satisfies its local task (Fig. 2a) by observing $P$ and $D$ in any order, the structure of the MDP does not permit orders of the form $P \to \cdots \to D$. Therefore, Q-learning, equipped with knowledge of the current RM state of agent 1, ought to converge to a policy which avoids such paths.

As TL-CDs overapproximate the set of attainable event sequences within the MDP, they enable experts to encode temporal-causal knowledge—for instance, the fact that problematic sequences like $\xi = DGP$ are unattainable. Given a team task RM $\mathcal{R}$ and local event sets $\Sigma_1, \ldots, \Sigma_N$ where $\mathcal{R} \not\cong \|_{i=1}^N \mathcal{R}_i$, our method leverages TL-CD $\mathcal{C}$ to validate whether decomposition remains viable under the causal constraints of the RM-MDP.

To relax the strict bisimilarity assumption ($\mathcal{R} \cong \|_{i=1}^N \mathcal{R}_i$) from Theorem 1, we introduce a modified bisimulation check: $\mathcal{R}\|\mathsf{C} \cong \mathcal{P}\|\mathsf{C}$, where $\mathcal{P} = \|_{i=1}^N \mathcal{R}_i$ represents the parallel composition of projected RMs, and $\mathcal{R}\|\mathsf{C}$, $\mathcal{P}\|\mathsf{C}$ denote their respective compositions with the causal DFA $\mathsf{C}$ derived from $\mathcal{C}$.

The parallel composition of an RM and a causal DFA synchronizes their transitions, meaning that $\mathcal{R}\|\mathsf{C}$ and $\mathcal{P}\|\mathsf{C}$ do not reward event sequences which do not satisfy the TL-CD $\mathcal{C}$. In Theorem 3 we show that our relaxed decomposition criterion yields the same guarantees as the strict one, and in Theorem 4 we show that the two are compatible (provided $\mathcal{C}$ holds for the RM-MDP).

As $\mathcal{R}$ and $\mathcal{P}$ are both deterministic finite automata, if $\mathcal{R} \not\cong \mathcal{P}$, the issue is caused by event sequences $\xi$ such that $\mathcal{R}(\xi) \neq \mathcal{P}(\xi)$ [1]. At its core, our method allows experts to exploit temporal-causal knowledge by finding a TL-CD $\mathcal{C}$ such that (1) $\mathcal{C}$ holds for the RM-MDP, i.e., for every event sequence $\xi$ attainable in $\mathcal{M}$, we have $\xi \models \Psi_\Sigma^\mathcal{C}$; and (2) $\mathcal{R}$, $\mathcal{P}$, and the causal DFA $\mathsf{C}$ of the TL-CD $\mathcal{C}$ pass the relaxed decomposition criterion, i.e. $\mathcal{R}\|\mathsf{C} \cong \mathcal{P}\|\mathsf{C}$.

The first property ensures that the TL-CD overapproximates the RM-MDP and expresses correct causal knowledge about the environment. The second property ensures that the causal knowledge added by the TL-CD is complete, in the sense that for every event sequence $\xi$ such that $\mathcal{P}(\xi) \neq \mathcal{R}(\xi)$, we have $\xi \not\models \Psi_\Sigma^\mathcal{C}$ (i.e. $\xi$ is not an attainable event sequence in the RM-MDP).

We use these properties to recover the important result that underpins team performance guarantees, and formalize our relaxed decomposition criterion in Theorem 3. In Theorem 4 we show that the relaxed and strict decomposition criteria are compatible, and in Theorem 5 we provide a lower and upper bound on the team success probability, analogous to Theorem 2. The proofs for the theorems in this subsection are provided in the appendix of our extended preprint [3].

**Theorem 3. (Relaxed Decomposition Criterion).** *Let $\mathcal{R}$ be the team task RM, and $\mathcal{R}_1, \ldots, \mathcal{R}_N$ be the projections of $\mathcal{R}$ onto the local event sets $\Sigma_1, \ldots, \Sigma_N$,* respectively. If $\mathcal{C}$ is a TL-CD with causal DFA C such that $\mathcal{R} \| \mathsf{C} \cong (\|_{i=1}^{N} \mathcal{R}_i) \| \mathsf{C}$, then for all $\mathcal{M}$-attainable event sequences $\xi$, we have $\mathcal{R}(\xi) = 1$ if and only if $\mathcal{R}_i(P_i(\xi)) = 1$ $(\forall i = 1, \ldots, N)$.

Theorem 3 states that if one can find a TL-CD $\mathcal{C}$ which satisfies the two properties outlined above, then the team task RM can be decomposed into local task RMs such that on all attainable sequences, the team RM and the parallel composition of local RMs output the same reward. Intuitively, if agents 1 through $N$ satisfy their local tasks (induce a reward of 1 in projected RMs), then their combined behavior also induces a reward of 1 in the parallel composition of projected RMs (which is bisimilar to the team RM).

If the strict decomposition criterion holds, it is not immediately clear that the relaxed criterion will also hold (given an arbitrary TL-CD that holds for the MDP). In other words, Theorem 1 and Theorem 3 present two different criteria for decomposing the team task RM (C1 and C2, respectively), and it is natural to ask whether these criteria are compatible. Table 1 summarizes the possible outcomes of comparing the two criteria.

**Table 1.** Results from Theorems 3 & 4

| C1 | C2 | Explanation |
|----|----|-------------|
| ⊘ | ⊘ | No decomposition (neither met) |
| ⊘ | ✓ | New decomposition (our method) |
| ✓ | ⊘ | *Claim:* Impossible combination |
| ✓ | ✓ | Known decomposition (both met) |

**Theorem 4. (Criterion Compatibility).** *Given a team task RM $\mathcal{R}$, a family of local event sets $\Sigma_1, \ldots, \Sigma_N$, and a TL-CD $\mathcal{C}$ with causal DFA C, let $\mathcal{P} = \|_{i=1}^{N} \mathcal{R}_i$ be the parallel composition of local task DFAs. Then $\mathcal{R} \cong \mathcal{P} \Rightarrow \mathcal{R} \| \mathsf{C} \cong \mathcal{P} \| \mathsf{C}$. In other words, the additional parallel composition with the causal DFA will not change the bisimulation decision if the original parallel composition is bisimilar to the team task DFA.*

In Theorem 4 we show that a parallel composition with an appropriate causal DFA introduced by our method will not make a task RM, that was originally decomposable, *not* decomposable. In other words, the relaxed criterion is a generalization of the original criterion, and so the two criteria are compatible. Once the relationship between the two criteria has been established, the main result is given by Theorem 5, which provides lower and upper bounds on the probability of combined action success, analogous to Theorem 2. In order to derive the results, we also assume that agents synchronize on shared events in the team setting, and that the team labeling function $L$ is decomposable with respect to the local event sets with corresponding labeling functions $L_i$.

**Theorem 5. (Relaxed Decomposition Viability).** *Given a team RM $\mathcal{R}$, local event sets $\Sigma_1, \ldots, \Sigma_N$, a decomposable label function $L$, and local labeling functions $L_1, \ldots, L_N$, assume that agents synchronize on shared events and $\mathcal{R} \| \mathsf{C} \cong (\|_{i=1}^{N} \mathcal{R}_i) \| \mathsf{C}$. Then for all team trajectories $s_0 u_0 \cdots s_k u_k$ and local trajectories $\{s_0^i u_0^i \cdots s_k^i u_k^i\}_{i=1}^{N}$, we have $\mathcal{R}(L(s_0 u_0 \cdots s_k u_k)) = 1$ if and only if $\mathcal{R}_i(L_i(s_0^i u_0^i \cdots s_k^i u_k^i)) = 1$ for all $i = 1, \ldots, N$. Furthermore, we retain the bounds for the team success probability $V^\pi(s_I)$, i.e. $\max\{0, V_1^\pi(s_I) + \cdots + V_N^\pi(s_I) - (N-1)\} \leq V^\pi(s_I) \leq \min\{V_1^\pi(s_I), \ldots, V_N^\pi(s_I)\}$.*

## 5.2 Expediting RL with Temporal-Causal Knowledge

In the *Generator Task* from Fig. 1, if agent 1 unlocks the door 🔓 before fixing the pipe 🔧, it will not be able to return and fix the pipe later, because its path is blocked by a one-way ramp. Unfortunately, agent 1's projected reward machine, illustrated in Fig. 2a, does not capture this information. Due to this mismatch, during decentralized training episodes, agent 1 will tend to waste a large portion of time steps exploring trajectories which do not lead to a positive reward.

As discussed in Sect. 4, one can use high-level symbolic knowledge in the form of the TL-CD on Fig. 3 a to capture this information. While we first exploited this knowledge to check if the task specification for the *Generator Task* is decomposable into local task specifications, we will now use it to expedite decentralized training for agent 1. Note that the same TL-CD has been applied for both purposes: this is not always the case. In our second case study, which covers the *Laboratory Task*, we use a separate TL-CD to expedite decentralized training for two agents at once, but a different one to prove that the task specification passes the relaxed decomposition criterion.

Designing task specifications using reward machines is an error-prone and time-consuming task, and it is challenging to accommodate all possible scenarios and causal structures in advance. Moreover, manually updating reward machines can lead to unintended consequences, ultimately inducing a different optimal policy. Therefore, we investigate how to extend DQPRM to automatically incorporate temporal-causal knowledge about the environment, and help agents achieve a better balance exploration and exploitation, without adversely affecting performance in the original task.

To this end, we adapt the method proposed in Corazza et al. [4] to Event-based task-completion RMs. The method relies on finding *rejecting sink states* in the causal DFA $\mathsf{C}$, i.e., states $q_{\text{r.s.}} \in Q^{\mathsf{C}} \setminus F^{\mathsf{C}}$ such that $\delta_{\mathsf{C}}(q_{\text{r.s.}}, e) = q_{\text{r.s.}}$ for all $e \in \Sigma$. We implicitly consider causal DFAs to have at most one rejecting sink state $q_{\text{r.s.}}$, and that an accepting state is reachable from all other states. This can be achieved by minimization [10]. On Fig. 3 b, that is the state $q_2$. At its core, the method exploits the fact that once a label sequence $\xi$ induces a transition into $q_{\text{r.s.}}$, there is no continuation $\xi \cdot \xi'$ that will exit it, and are therefore, all such label sequences unattainable.

In order to identify explorations that will not be rewarded, the method computes $\tilde{\mathcal{R}}_i$, a modification of agent $i$'s projected RM $\mathcal{R}_i$ that induces the same optimal policy [4], but embeds the temporal-causal knowledge captured by $\mathcal{C}$. The states of $\tilde{\mathcal{R}}_i$ are elements of $U^i \times Q^{\mathsf{C}}$ (the Cartesian product of the states of $\mathcal{R}_i$ and the causal DFA of $\mathcal{C}$), while the transition function $\tilde{\delta}_i$ is defined as $\tilde{\delta}_i((u,q),e) = (\delta_i(u,e), \delta_{\mathsf{C}}(q,e))$. The reward function $\tilde{\sigma}_i$ is defined as $\tilde{\sigma}_i((u,q),(u',q')) = \sigma_i(u,u')$ if $q \neq q_{\text{r.s.}}$, and $-1$ otherwise.[4]

Because only unattainable label sequences (such as $DGP$ in the *Generator Task*) induce transitions into rejecting sink states, setting the reward to $-1$ when reaching such states does not affect the optimal policy. The final step relies on computing the solution to the Bellman optimality equation over the states of $\tilde{\mathcal{R}}_i$, $V^*(u,q) = \max_{e \in \Sigma_i, u' = \tilde{\delta}_i(u,e)} (\sigma((u,q),(u',q')) + V^*(u',q'))$. In every step, the maximum possible return from the current episode is bounded from above by $V^*(u,q)$ and 0 from below (by definition of task-completion RMs). If $\tilde{\mathcal{R}}_i$ reaches a state $(u,q)$ such that $V^*(u,q) = 0$ during decentralized training, then all policies induce the same return thereon, and the learning can stop.

We summarize our method in Algorithm 2, which we call Causal DQPRM. The inputs for Causal DQPRM include a TL-CD $\mathcal{C}$ which is used to ensure the task specification passes the relaxed decomposition criterion, along with a family of TL-CDs $\mathcal{C}_1, \ldots, \mathcal{C}_N$ (possibly a different one for each agent). In Algorithm 2, $q_i$ ranges over the states of causal DFA $\mathsf{C}_i$, and $(u_i, q_i)$ over the states of $\tilde{\mathcal{R}}_i$, the recomputed task specification for agent $i$. In our experiments, we use $p = 0.3$.

## 6 Case Studies

We performed three case studies, validating our approach in the *Generator Task*, described extensively throughout this paper, and two new domains: the *Laboratory Task* and the *Buttons Task*. This section will detail the results on the *Generator Task* and the *Laboratory Task*, while the *Buttons Task* is described in the appendix of our extended preprint [3].

### 6.1 Case Study 1: Generator Task

Our first case study is an ablation of our approach on the *Generator Task*, with results shown in Fig. 4. We compare the average steps needed for task completion per training step. The baseline we compare against is a centralized controller found with Q-learning, corresponding to the *No TL-CD* plot on Fig. 4, *Centralized*.

Adding temporal-causal information improves team performance, even with centralized training. Decentralized training, enabled by our relaxed decomposition check, is significantly more efficient, taking an order of magnitude fewer steps to converge. In our two additional case studies, we perform the same analysis for the *Laboratory Task* and the *Buttons Task*.

---

[4] To justify this we note that, for task-completion RMs, $-1$ satisfies the reward bounds computed in Corazza et al. [4].

**Algorithm 2:** Decentralized training with Causal DQPRM

**Input** : Team RM $\mathcal{R}$, local event sets $\Sigma_1, \ldots, \Sigma_N$, local labeling functions $L_1, \ldots, L_N$, TL-CDs $\mathcal{C}, \mathcal{C}_1, \ldots, \mathcal{C}_N$
**Output**: Policies $\pi_1, \ldots, \pi_N$

1  Project $\mathcal{R}$ along local event sets $\Sigma_i$ to obtain projected RMs $\mathcal{R}_1, \ldots, \mathcal{R}_N$;
2  **if** $\mathcal{R}\|\mathsf{C} \not\cong (\|_{i=1}^{N} \mathcal{R}_i)\|\mathsf{C}$ **then**
3  | Reject: the relaxed decomposition criterion does not hold;
4  **end**
5  **for** $i = 1$ **to** $N$ **do**
6  | Compute $\tilde{\mathcal{R}}_i$ via value iteration over $\mathcal{R}_i\|\mathsf{C}_i$ ;
7  | $s_i \leftarrow s_I^i$, $(u_i, q_i) \leftarrow (u_I^i, q_I^i)$, $\text{steps}_i \leftarrow 0$;
8  **end**
9  Initialize$(\pi_1, \ldots, \pi_N)$;
10 **for** $t = 1$ **to** numEpisodes $*$ numSteps **do**
11 | **for** $i = 1$ **to** $N$ **do**
12 | | **if** $\text{steps}_i >$ numSteps **or** $V_i^*(u_i, q_i) = 0$ **then**
13 | | | $s_i \leftarrow s_I^i$, $(u_i, q_i) \leftarrow (u_I^i, q_I^i)$, $\text{steps}_i \leftarrow 0$;
14 | | **end**
15 | | $a_i \leftarrow \text{Sample}(\pi_i(s_i, u_i))$;
16 | | $s' \leftarrow \text{Step}_i(s_i, u_i, a_i)$, $(u', q') \leftarrow (u_i, q_i)$, $r_i \leftarrow 0$;
17 | | **foreach** $e \in L_i(s_i, u_i, s')$ **do**
18 | | | **if** $|I_e| = 1$ **or** $\text{Rand}(0, 1) \leq p$ **then**
19 | | | | $(u', q') \leftarrow \tilde{\delta}((u_i, q_i), e)$;
20 | | | | $r_i \leftarrow r_i + \tilde{\sigma}((u_i, q_i), u')$;
21 | | | | $(u_i, q_i) \leftarrow (u', q')$;
22 | | | **end**
23 | | **end**
24 | | PolicyUpdate$(\pi_i, s_i, u_i, a_i, s', r_i)$;
25 | | $s_i \leftarrow s'$, $\text{steps}_i \leftarrow \text{steps}_i + 1$;
26 | **end**
27 **end**
28 **return** $(\pi_1, \ldots, \pi_N)$;

## 6.2 Case Study 2: Laboratory Task

In the *Laboratory Task*, two agents are tasked with aiding with an accident that occurred in a laboratory. There are two possible types of accidents that may have occurred: a fire, represented by 🔥, or a radioactive spill, represented by ☢. Agent 1 is equipped with heat sensors, but not with radiation sensors, vice-versa for agent 2.

The two accident types are mutually exclusive. Once the agents enter the conveyor belt, represented by ⚙, which leads them to the laboratory, either agent 1 will observe 🔥, or agent 2 will observe ☢ (with 50% probability each). Once inside, the agents must, depending on the type of the accident, converge to a tool which will provide aid (🔨 in case of fire, and ⛑ in case of radiation).

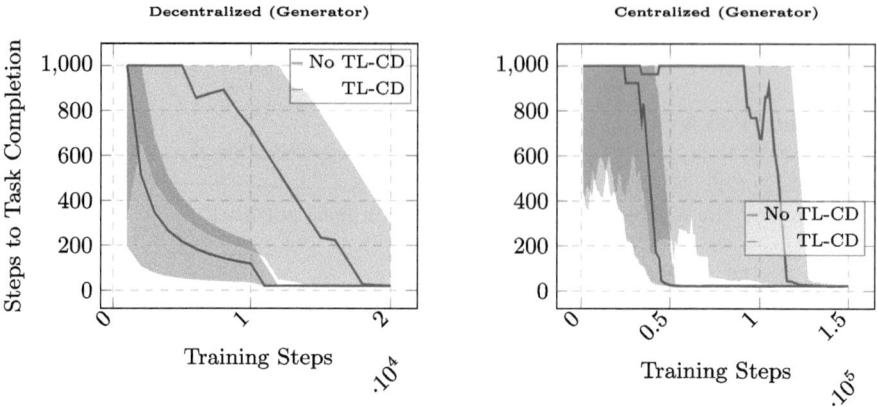

**Fig. 4.** *Generator Task* study. Aggregated results from 50 independent runs..

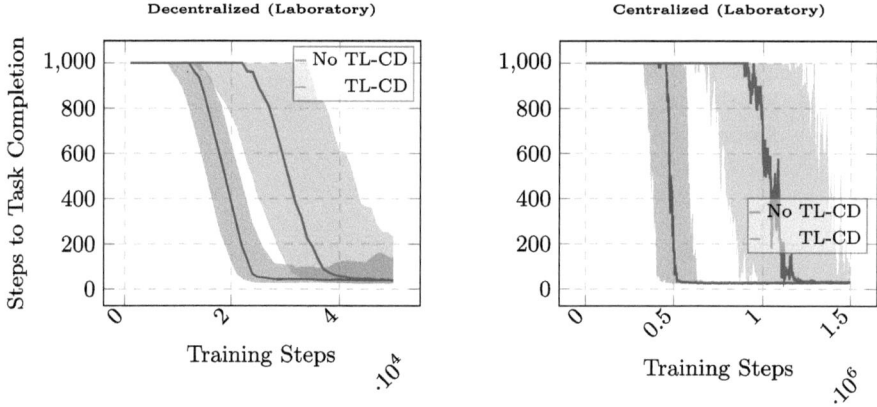

**Fig. 5.** *Laboratory Task* study. Aggregated results from 50 independent runs.

We illustrate the environment for the *Laboratory Task* in Fig. 6a, and the team reward machine which provides the task specification in Fig. 6b. As shown by the results in Fig. 5, Causal DQPRM is able to solve this task, and leverages temporal-causal information to significantly increase sample efficiency compared to a centralized controller.

On Fig. 7, we illustrate the local reward machines of agents 1 and 2 in the *Laboratory Task*.

Our experiments were conducted on a single machine with AMD Ryzen 7 5825U and 7 GB of RAM, except for the centralized case of the Buttons task, where we used a machine with AMD EPYC 7742 64-Core Processor and 515 GB of RAM, due to the extremely large state space.

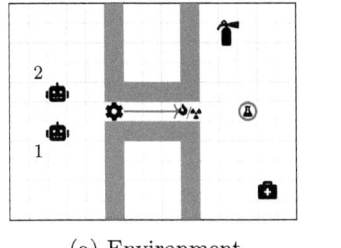 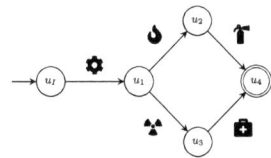

(a) Environment  (b) Team Reward Machine

**Fig. 6.** *Laboratory Task*

(a) $\Sigma_1 = \{C, F, E, M\}$  (b) $\Sigma_2 = \{C, R, E, M\}$

**Fig. 7.** Projections of the RM from Fig. 5b along local event sets of agents 1 (Left) and 2 (Right).

## 7 Conclusion

We introduced a framework for integrating temporal-causal knowledge, formalized via TL-CDs, into decentralized multi-agent reinforcement learning, enabling both relaxed task decomposition and accelerated policy learning. Experimentally validated across three case studies, our method improves the applicability of decentralized training guarantees while achieving higher success rates and sample efficiency compared to baseline approaches. By automating the incorporation of expert knowledge into task specifications and learning processes, this work enables scalable solutions to complex, temporally structured multi-agent tasks.

**Acknowledgments.** This work was supported in part by the National Science Foundation (NSF) under Grants CNS 2304863 and CNS 2339774, and in part by the Office of Naval Research (ONR) under Grant N00014-23-1-2505.

**Disclosure of Interests.** The authors have no competing interests to declare that are relevant to the content of this article.

## References

1. Almeida, M., Moreira, N., Reis, R.: Testing the equivalence of regular languages. Electron. Proc. Theoretical Comput. Sci. **3**, 47–57 (2009). https://doi.org/10.4204/EPTCS.3.4, http://arxiv.org/abs/0907.5058v1

2. Azran, G., Danesh, M.H., Albrecht, S.V., Keren, S.: Contextual pre-planning on reward machine abstractions for enhanced transfer in deep reinforcement learning. In: Proceedings of the AAAI Conference on Artificial Intelligence, vol. 38, no. 10, pp. 10953–10961 (2024). https://doi.org/10.1609/aaai.v38i10.28970, https://ojs.aaai.org/index.php/AAAI/article/view/28970
3. Corazza, J., Aria, H.P., Kim, H., Neider, D., Xu, Z.: Decentralizing multi-agent reinforcement learning with temporal causal information (2025). https://arxiv.org/abs/2506.07829
4. Corazza, J., Aria, H.P., Neider, D., Xu, Z.: Expediting reinforcement learning by incorporating knowledge about temporal causality in the environment. In: Locatello, F., Didelez, V. (eds.) Proceedings of the Third Conference on Causal Learning and Reasoning. In: Proceedings of Machine Learning Research, vol. 236, pp. 643–664. PMLR (2024). https://proceedings.mlr.press/v236/corazza24a.html
5. Dohmen, T., Topper, N., Atia, G., Beckus, A., Trivedi, A., Velasquez, A.: Inferring probabilistic reward machines from non-markovian reward processes for reinforcement learning (2022)
6. Icarte, R.T., Klassen, T.Q., Valenzano, R.A., McIlraith, S.A.: Reward machines: exploiting reward function structure in reinforcement learning. CoRR **abs/2010.03950** (2020), https://arxiv.org/abs/2010.03950
7. Kazemi, M., Perez, M., Somenzi, F., Soudjani, S., Trivedi, A., Velasquez, A.: Assume-guarantee reinforcement learning (2023)
8. Neary, C., Xu, Z., Wu, B., Topcu, U.: Reward Machines for Cooperative Multi-Agent Reinforcement Learning (2021). https://doi.org/10.5555/3463952.3464063, http://arxiv.org/abs/2007.01962, arXiv:2007.01962 [cs]
9. Paliwal, Y., et al.: Reinforcement learning with temporal-logic-based causal diagrams (2023)
10. Sipser, M.: Introduction to the Theory of Computation. MA, third edn, Course Technology, Boston (2013)
11. Wong, K.C.: On the complexity of projections of discrete-event systems. Discrete Event Dynamic Syst. (1998). https://api.semanticscholar.org/CorpusID:17637223
12. Xu, Z., et al.: Joint inference of reward machines and policies for reinforcement learning. In: Proceedings of the International Conference on Automated Planning and Scheduling, vol. 30, pp. 590–598 (2020). https://doi.org/10.1609/icaps.v30i1.6756, http://dx.doi.org/10.1609/icaps.v30i1.6756

# De Novo Molecular Design Enabled by Direct Preference Optimization and Curriculum Learning

Junyu Hou(✉)

School of Computer Science, Nanjing University, Nanjing, China
221220151@smail.nju.edu.cn

**Abstract.** De novo molecular design has extensive applications in drug discovery and materials science. The vast chemical space renders direct molecular searches computationally prohibitive, while traditional experimental screening is both time- and labor-intensive. Efficient molecular generation and screening methods are therefore essential for accelerating drug discovery and reducing costs. Although reinforcement learning (RL) has been applied to optimize molecular properties via reward mechanisms, its practical utility is limited by issues in training efficiency, convergence, and stability. To address these challenges, we adopt Direct Preference Optimization (DPO) from NLP, which uses molecular score-based sample pairs to maximize the likelihood difference between high- and low-quality molecules, effectively guiding the model toward better compounds. Moreover, integrating curriculum learning further boosts training efficiency and accelerates convergence. A systematic evaluation of the proposed method on the GuacaMol Benchmark yielded excellent scores. For instance, the method achieved a score of 0.883 on the Perindopril MPO task, representing a 6% improvement over competing models. And subsequent target protein binding experiments confirmed its practical efficacy. These results demonstrate the strong potential of DPO for molecular design tasks and highlight its effectiveness as a robust and efficient solution for data-driven drug discovery. The code is available at https://github.com/SiliconMangrove/MolDPO.

**Keywords:** De Novo Molecular Design · DPO · Curriculum Learning

## 1 Introduction

De novo molecular design is one of the core tasks in fields such as catalyst design, energy materials design, and pharmaceutical research, aiming to generate novel molecules from scratch that satisfy specified physicochemical properties and biological activity requirements [21]. This process plays a pivotal role in new drug discovery, materials science, and synthetic chemistry. Traditional methods for candidate molecule screening and optimization typically rely on extensive experimental synthesis and biological assays, which are both time- and labor-intensive and require substantial financial investment [7]. Moreover, the chemical space is astronomically vast–estimated to contain more than $10^{60}$

potential molecules [4] –making exhaustive exploration by manual means virtually impossible. Consequently, computer-aided drug design (CADD) has emerged as a prominent research focus, leveraging mathematical models, statistical techniques, and advanced computational technologies to efficiently search and optimize within this enormous chemical space [8,28,31,33].

In recent years, molecular conditional generation has played a critical role in drug development and materials design [22], and reinforcement learning (RL) has gradually been introduced into the field of molecular design [16,24,25]. By employing molecular scoring functions as reward signals, RL enables generative models to continuously adjust and improve their generation strategies toward predefined objectives–such as enhancing biological activity, optimizing physicochemical properties, and improving synthetic accessibility–thereby demonstrating enormous potential [30,34].

However, RL-based methods still face several challenges: **(1) Convergence Challenges and Training Instability**: The high-dimensional and non-convex nature of molecular generation makes RL models prone to slow convergence and local optima. For instance, REINVENT [3] exhibits volatile policy updates and noisy rewards, requiring extensive training before reliably generating molecules that satisfy multiple objectives.

**(2) Exploration Inefficiency and Limited Coverage**: The vast chemical space limits the effectiveness of traditional RL approaches, which often get trapped in narrow structural regions. DrugEx [18], for example, generates molecules meeting specific activity criteria but lacks sufficient scaffold diversity.

**(3) Multi-Objective Optimization and Reward Design Challenges**: Designing effective reward functions for molecular optimization is complex and often requires empirical tuning. For example, to simultaneously maximize logP, TPSA, and structural similarity, some studies have employed multi-layered, nonlinear composite reward models, increasing both implementation complexity and limiting generalizability across different tasks [15,27,29].

To address these challenges, we draw inspiration from two established methodologies in machine learning. Direct Preference Optimization (DPO), originally developed in NLP, has shown strong optimization capabilities in reinforcement learning tasks by leveraging paired samples to optimize likelihood differences, eliminating the need for explicit reward modeling [6,26]. Meanwhile, Curriculum Learning, which gradually increases task complexity, has been adopted to enhance molecular generation [2,11]. By starting with simpler tasks and progressively optimizing bioactivity, physicochemical properties, and synthetic feasibility, this approach improves model learning [10,23].We contend that integrating DPO with curriculum learning can both accelerate model convergence and substantially improve the overall performance of the generated molecules.

In this study, we first employ traditional autoregressive training to train a prior model, which is then assigned to four agent models. These agent models are responsible for sampling and constructing paired samples, which are subsequently trained using DPO and curriculum learning to optimize the molecular

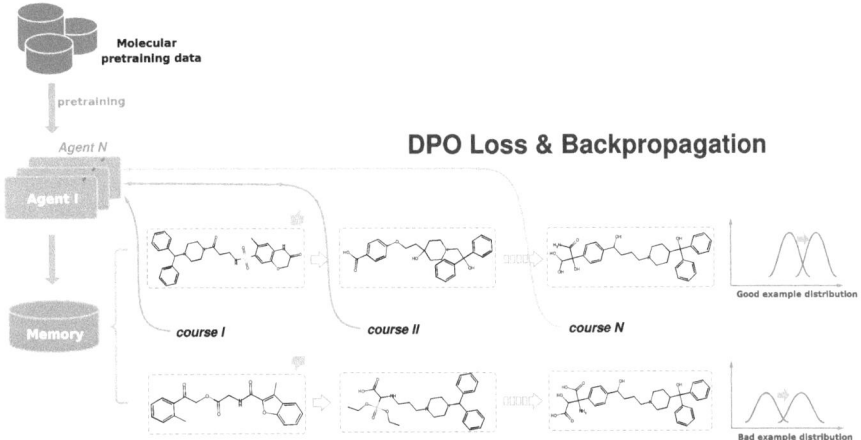

**Fig. 1. Structure of the DPO+Curriculum Learning model.** The model is initially pre-trained, followed by optimization using Direct Preference Optimization. As curriculum learning progresses, the molecular scores of the collected compounds steadily increase while the distinction between superior and inferior molecules gradually narrows. Ultimately, the process yields molecules that meet the predefined quality criteria.

generation process, ultimately yielding molecules that satisfy the desired properties. The overall architecture of our proposed method is illustrated in Fig. 1. We evaluate our method on the Guacamol benchmark [5] and target protein binding experiments, where experimental results demonstrate that our approach achieves superior performance across multiple evaluation metrics, validating its effectiveness in molecular conditional generation tasks.

The primary objective of this study is to investigate the application of DPO combined with curriculum learning in molecular conditional generation, aiming to improve the molecular generation process through a more efficient and stable approach. By integrating these two methods, we aim to improve molecular discovery and optimization efficiency while providing strong technological support for drug development. Our main contributions are threefold:

- We propose a novel de novo molecular design framework that combines Direct Preference Optimization (DPO) with curriculum learning.
- Our method has achieved high scores on the GuacaMol benchmark and demonstrated outstanding performance in target protein docking experiments.
- The proposed framework exhibits strong potential for scalability in terms of multi-objective optimization, training stability, and computational efficiency.

## 2 Related Work

In recent years, computationally driven de novo molecular design has witnessed rapid advancements, primarily evolving along three key directions: **(1) continuous optimization of reinforcement learning frameworks, (2) cross-domain adaptation of large language models (LLMs), and (3) efficiency improvements in preference learning paradigms**. These innovations have enhanced chemical space exploration and multi-objective optimization, laying a stronger foundation for drug discovery.

### 2.1 Reinforcement Learning-Based Molecular Generation

Reinforcement learning (RL)-based generative models have established a systematic paradigm for molecular design [19,34]. Among them, REINVENT [20] integrates recurrent neural networks (RNNs) with policy gradient algorithms to enable targeted chemical space exploration. Another notable approach [24] leverages prior knowledge to constrain the reward function, optimizing molecular properties while maintaining synthetic feasibility. However, traditional RL approaches face challenges when handling high-dimensional chemical spaces, including inefficient policy updates and susceptibility to local optima.

### 2.2 Curriculum Learning Strategies

To enhance training efficiency in complex tasks, researchers have introduced curriculum learning frameworks into de novo molecular design. Guo et al. [10] proposed a strategy that gradually increases task difficulty: the model initially focuses on generating simpler chemical structures, thereby establishing a solid foundation, and then progressively tackles more challenging optimization tasks. This staged approach not only accelerates convergence but also improves the diversity and quality of the generated molecules, demonstrating the effectiveness of curriculum learning in refining generative models for molecular design.

### 2.3 Large Language Models for Molecular Generation

Large Language Models (LLMs) have recently been applied to molecular design, offering novel strategies for molecule generation. Liu et al. [17] explored the adaptation of ChatGPT for molecular tasks, demonstrating its ability to capture chemical patterns and generate valid molecular representations through language modeling. Similarly, Hu et al. [12] introduced MolRL-MGPT, which integrates a GPT-based generative strategy with reinforcement learning to enhance molecular diversity and optimize target-directed properties. These studies highlight the promising potential of LLMs to provide scalable and effective approaches for molecular design.

## 2.4 Preference Optimization in Molecular Design

Preference learning techniques provide an efficient pathway for strategy optimization in molecular generation. Rafailov et al. proposed direct preference optimization (DPO) [26], which employs implicit reward modeling to bypass the complexity of explicit reward function design in traditional RL. This paradigm has recently been successfully adapted to molecular design [6,9]: Widatalla et al. utilized experimental data to construct preference pairs, enabling DPO to directly optimize protein stability [32]. Experimental results show that ProteinDPO performs exceptionally well in protein stability prediction and demonstrates strong generalization capabilities for large proteins and multi-chain complexes. This suggests that it has effectively learned transferable insights from its biophysical alignment data.

# 3 Methodology

Our molecular generation framework is built upon three core technical components integrated through a structured training pipeline: (1) Pretraining establishes chemical validity by learning SMILES syntax from large-scale datasets; (2) Direct Preference Optimization (DPO) replaces reward modeling with contrastive learning to align generation with target objectives; (3) Curriculum Learning introduces progressive difficulty levels for gradual chemical space exploration. To synergistically combine these components, we design a two-stage training procedure: pretraining initializes molecular priors, followed by DPO fine-tuning guided by curriculum-constructed preference pairs. The following subsections detail each component.

## 3.1 Pretrain on Large Molecular Dataset

In this study, we adopt the same model architecture as MolRL-MGPT by building a multi-agent GPT model with 8 layers and 8 attention heads [12]. Two distinct prior models were pre-trained on different datasets: one on the GuacaMol dataset (a subset of ChEMBL) for benchmark evaluation and another on the ZINC dataset (containing approximately 100 M molecules) for general-purpose molecular generation tasks [13]. The primary objective during pretraining is to enable the model to deeply learn the syntax rules of SMILES representations, thereby allowing it to generate valid SMILES structures one character at a time and effectively capture the distribution of the chemical space. This pretraining strategy not only demonstrates the model's capability in efficiently generating chemically valid molecules but also lays a solid foundation for subsequent task-specific optimization and performance enhancement.

To rigorously train our prior models on SMILES representations, we employ an autoregressive framework that decomposes each sequence into a series of incremental prediction tasks. Let $S = (c_1, c_2, \ldots, c_L)$ denote a SMILES sequence of length $L$, where each $c_i$ represents a character from the SMILES vocabulary

$\mathcal{V}$. In our autoregressive training approach, we generate training pairs $(x_i, y_i)$ for $i = 1, 2, \ldots, L-1$, where

$$x_i = (c_1, c_2, \ldots, c_i) \quad \text{and} \quad y_i = (c_1, c_2, \ldots, c_i, c_{i+1}). \tag{1}$$

The model parameterized by $\theta$ learns a conditional probability distribution $P_\theta(c_{i+1} \mid c_1, \ldots, c_i)$ such that the joint probability of the sequence can be expressed as:

$$P_\theta(S) = \prod_{i=1}^{L} P_\theta(c_i \mid c_1, \ldots, c_{i-1}), \tag{2}$$

with the convention that $P_\theta(c_1 \mid \cdot) = P_\theta(c_1)$.

The training objective is to minimize the cross-entropy loss over the entire training set, which for a single sequence is given by:

$$\mathcal{L}(\theta) = -\sum_{i=1}^{L-1} \log P_\theta(c_{i+1} \mid c_1, \ldots, c_i). \tag{3}$$

This objective encourages the model to assign high probabilities to the correct next character at each step. Parameter updates are performed using gradient descent:

$$\theta \leftarrow \theta - \eta \nabla_\theta \mathcal{L}(\theta), \tag{4}$$

where $\eta$ is the learning rate. This autoregressive framework enables the model to learn the syntax rules of SMILES representations, thereby generating valid molecular structures character by character.

The model trained on the Guacamol dataset for approximately 3 h, achieving an 97% validity rate for the generated molecular structures, demonstrating that it had effectively learned the SMILES generation rules. The model trained on the ZINC dataset for approximately 70 h, achieving a 99.6% validity rate for the generated molecules, further validating its generalization capability. All pretraining experiments were conducted on a single A100 GPU.

## 3.2 DPO for Molecular Optimization

Building upon the pretrained molecular generation capability, we introduce Direct Preference Optimization (DPO) to align molecular generation with chemical preferences. DPO is a contrastive learning approach that optimizes the generation policy without explicitly modeling a reward function. Instead of using reinforcement learning with human feedback (RLHF) methods that first train a reward model and then optimize the policy using algorithms like PPO, DPO directly optimizes the policy by enforcing preference constraints.

The training data consists of triplets $(x, y_w, y_l)$, where: $x$ represents the input. $y_w$ is the preferred (or "winning") response. $y_l$ is the less preferred (or "losing") response.

DPO is built upon the idea that an optimal policy $\pi^*$ should satisfy the following preference ratio constraint:

$$\frac{\pi^*(y_w|x)}{\pi^*(y_l|x)} = \exp(r(y_w|x) - r(y_l|x))$$

where $r(y \mid x)$ is an implicit reward function that ranks different responses. Instead of explicitly learning this reward function, DPO directly optimizes the policy ratio by defining the following log preference probability:

$$\log \sigma(\beta \cdot (\log \pi_\theta(y_w|x) - \log \pi_\theta(y_l|x)))$$

where $\sigma(z) = \frac{1}{1+e^{-z}}$ is the sigmoid function, and $\beta$ is a temperature hyperparameter controlling sensitivity to preference differences.

The final DPO objective function is:

$$\mathcal{L}(\theta) = \mathbb{E}_{(x,y_w,y_l) \sim D} [\log \sigma(\beta \cdot (\log \pi_\theta(y_w|x) - \log \pi_\theta(y_l|x)))]$$

In our molecular generation task, there is no explicit input $x$. Furthermore, whereas other DPO tasks often require human annotation of preference samples, which is costly, our task does not rely on human annotations to determine response quality. Instead, we leverage a chemical computation library to evaluate the quality of generated molecules, thereby streamlining the preference learning process.

### 3.3 Curriculum Learning for Structured Molecular Optimization

To address the challenge of learning complex chemical spaces, we integrate DPO with curriculum learning. Curriculum learning is a machine learning strategy inspired by the human learning process, where the model begins with simple tasks and gradually progresses to more complex ones. By organizing training samples in order of increasing difficulty, the model builds a solid foundation with easier examples, leading to more efficient learning, better generalization, and ultimately enhanced performance on challenging tasks.

Aligned with this progressive approach, our pair construction process incrementally increases the difficulty of the learning task. Initially, the score gap between the superior and inferior samples is large, making it straightforward for the model to distinguish high-quality molecules. As training advances, this gap is gradually reduced, requiring the model to discern more subtle differences. This strategy reinforces the curriculum learning paradigm and refines the model's fine-grained discrimination of molecular quality, ultimately enhancing the validity of the generated compounds.

Furthermore, we adopt a multi-stage learning mechanism to enhance model performance. Specifically, during training, high-quality molecules collected by the model are stored in memory. Subsequently, all agents are reinitialized to the pre-trained model and continue training by constructing new sample pairs from the high-scoring molecules in memory. The primary objective of this strategy is to mitigate potential biases introduced during early exploration, preventing the model from converging to suboptimal solutions. By leveraging previously identified high-quality molecules, the model can effectively restart its learning process in a more optimized direction, ultimately improving the quality of generated molecules.

As illustrated in the Fig. 2, our training process is divided into three stages. In the first stage, the model learns the fundamental requirements of the task and rapidly identifies high-scoring molecules from the vast chemical space. In the second stage, the model fine-tunes molecular scaffolds to further refine its understanding. Finally, in the third stage, the model modifies functional groups based on the optimal molecular scaffolds stored in memory, further optimizing molecular structures. This multi-stage approach significantly enhances molecular design efficiency, leading to a remarkable score of 0.993 on the GSK3B+DRD2 task.

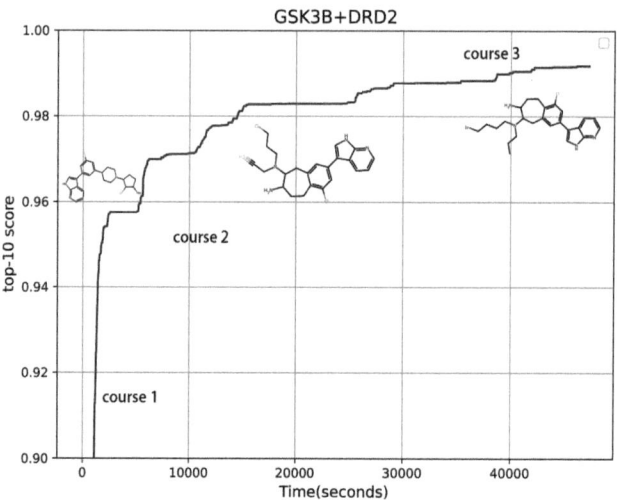

**Fig. 2. In the GSK3B+DRD2 docking experiment, the model achieved good performance through curriculum learning.** In Course 1, the model learns the fundamental requirements of the task. In Course 2, it fine-tunes the molecular scaffold. In Course 3, it adjusts functional groups to optimize molecular structures.

## 3.4 Training Procedure

---
**Algorithm 1.** Direct Preference Optimization (DPO) Training
---
1: **procedure** DPO_TRAIN($F_{\text{score}}, k$)
   **Initialize:**
2:     Load pretrained prior $p_{\text{ref}} \leftarrow \text{GPT}(\theta_{\text{prior}})$
3:     Initialize agents $\{\pi_i\}_{i=1}^N$ with $\theta_i \sim \mathcal{N}(0, 0.02)$
4:     **for** $t \leftarrow 1$ to $T$ **do**
5:        **AgentLoop**
6:            **for** each agent $\pi_i$ **do**
7:                **Sampling**
8:                    $\mathcal{D}_i \leftarrow \text{SampleSMILES}(\pi_i, m_{\text{batch}})$
9:                    $\mathbf{s} \leftarrow F_{\text{score}}(\mathcal{D}_i)$
10:                  $\mathcal{M} \leftarrow \text{UpdateMemory}(\mathcal{D}_i, \mathbf{s})$
11:              **EndSampling**
12:              POSITIVE SELECTION:

$$\mathbf{x}^w \sim p_{\mathcal{M}}(x) \propto \exp(s/\tau) // \textit{ top-weighted historical samples}$$

13:              NEGATIVE SELECTION:

$$\mathbf{x}^l \sim \text{Uniform}(\mathcal{D}_t) // \textit{ current batch negatives}$$

14:              Compute log-ratios for each sample:

$$\log r_\theta(x) = \log \pi_\theta(x) - \log \pi_{\text{ref}}(x)$$

15:              Optimize loss:

$$\mathcal{L}_{\text{DPO}} = -\mathbb{E}\left[\log \sigma\left(\beta(r_\theta(x^w) - r_\theta(x^l))\right)\right]$$

16:              Gradient step: $\theta \leftarrow \theta - \eta \nabla_\theta \mathcal{L}_{\text{DPO}}$
17:           **end for**
18:        **EndAgentLoop**
19:        Log $\max \mathcal{M}.\mathbf{s}$, $\text{top}_k\text{-mean}(\mathcal{M}.\mathbf{s})$
20:     **end for**
21:     **return** $\text{Top}_k(\mathcal{M}.\mathbf{x}, \mathcal{M}.\mathbf{s})$
22: **end procedure**

---

Integrating DPO with curriculum learning, we design a two-stage training protocol, as illustrated in Algorithm 1. The process begins with pre-training to obtain the prior model, followed by reinforcement fine-tuning using DPO and curriculum learning.

In the pre-training phase, the model learns to generate valid SMILES strings and capture the chemical space distribution, forming a prior model.

During reinforcement fine-tuning, the agents–initialized from the prior generates molecules, which are evaluated by a task-specific scoring function. Preference pairs are then constructed by selecting the top-k highest-scoring molecules (k varies across agents) as "preferred samples" and randomly sampling lower-quality ones as "dispreferred samples". These pairs are used to optimize the policy via DPO, progressively aligning the model's generation strategy with the target objectives.

As training progresses, the scores of the generated molecules steadily improve while the gap between preferred and dispreferred samples narrows, indicating an increase in training difficulty. Initially, the model makes broad scaffold-level adjustments to identify promising frameworks; as scaffolds stabilize, it shifts to fine-tuning functional groups to further optimize molecular properties.

## 4 Experiments

To validate the effectiveness of our model, we designed and conducted a series of experiments, including the Guacamol benchmark evaluation, target protein binding experiments, and impact analysis. The experimental results demonstrate that our model is not only capable of handling classical molecular design tasks but also performs exceptionally well in tasks that are more closely aligned with real-world drug discovery. Furthermore, the impact analysis, which examines model performance under different parameter settings, helping us identify the optimal parameter settings.

### 4.1 GuacaMol Benchmark

**Guacamol Introduction.** Guacamol Benchmark, proposed by BenevolentAI in 2019 [5], is a standardized framework for evaluating molecular generation models in terms of diversity, synthetic feasibility, and goal-directed optimization. It comprises 20 tasks covering key challenges in molecular design.

These tasks can be broadly categorized into rediscovery and similarity-based optimization, isomer generation, and molecular property balancing. Additionally, multi-parameter optimization (MPO) tasks focus on improving physicochemical properties of known drugs, while SMARTS-constrained tasks enforce structural constraints. Lastly, scaffold hopping and decorator hopping tasks assess the model's ability to modify core structures and substituents.

**Baselines.** To comprehensively evaluate our approach, we compare it against several representative baselines: **SMILES LSTM** [29]: An LSTM-based model trained via maximum likelihood estimation to generate SMILES strings. **Graph GA** [14]: A graph-based genetic algorithm that optimizes molecular structures through crossover and mutation. **Reinvent** [3]: A model combining recurrent neural networks with reinforcement learning, using reward functions to enhance both bioactivity and physicochemical properties. **GEGL** [1]: An approach that integrates graph neural networks with reinforcement learning to directly optimize molecular graphs. **MolRL-MGPT** [12]: A hybrid model that fuses GPT-based generative strategies with reinforcement learning to boost molecular diversity and target-specific performance.

**Experimental Details.** First of all, we pre-trained the model using the training set provided by Guacamol. The pre-training was conducted for 15 epochs on a single A100 GPU over a duration of 3 h. After pre-training, the model achieved a molecular validity of **97%**, demonstrating its high accuracy in molecular structure generation.

Subsequently, we further trained the model on 20 tasks from the Guacamol benchmark to evaluate its performance across different objectives. The **hyperparameter** settings used in this stage were as follows: **Batch size** = 50, **n_steps** = 1000, **num_agents** = 4, **Learning rate** = 1e-4, **Memory size** = 1000.

The complete training of the 20 benchmark tasks required 60 h, whereas MolRL-MGPT took 400 h under the same conditions (both on a single A100 GPU). Our model demonstrated a training speed nearly 6 times faster, highlighting the advantages of DPO's stable training and faster convergence, which significantly reduces training costs.

**Table 1.** Scores of DPO&CL and baselines on the GuacaMol benchmark. (All task scores are rounded to three decimal places.)

|  | SMILES-LSTM | GraphGA | Reinvent | GEGL | MolRL-MGPT | **DPO&CL** |
|---|---|---|---|---|---|---|
| Celecoxib rediscovery | 1.000 | 1.000 | 1.000 | 1.000 | 1.000 | 1.000 |
| Troglitazone rediscovery | 1.000 | 1.000 | 1.000 | 0.552 | 1.000 | 1.000 |
| Thiothixene rediscovery | 1.000 | 1.000 | 1.000 | 1.000 | 1.000 | 1.000 |
| Aripiprazole similarity | 1.000 | 1.000 | 1.000 | 1.000 | 1.000 | 1.000 |
| Albuterol similarity | 1.000 | 1.000 | 1.000 | 1.000 | 1.000 | 1.000 |
| Mestranol similarity | 1.000 | 1.000 | 1.000 | 1.000 | 1.000 | 1.000 |
| $C_{11}H_{24}$ | 0.993 | 0.971 | 0.999 | 1.000 | 1.000 | 1.000 |
| $C_9H_{10}N_2O_2PF_2Cl$ | 0.879 | 0.982 | 0.877 | 1.000 | 0.939 | 1.000 |
| Median molecules 1 | 0.438 | 0.406 | 0.434 | **0.455** | 0.449 | **0.455** |
| Median molecules 2 | 0.422 | 0.432 | 0.395 | **0.437** | 0.422 | 0.422 |
| Osimertinib MPO | 0.907 | 0.953 | 0.889 | 1.000 | 0.977 | 0.990 |
| Fexofenadine MPO | 0.959 | 0.998 | 1.000 | 1.000 | 1.000 | 1.000 |
| Ranolazine MPO | 0.855 | 0.920 | 0.895 | 0.933 | 0.939 | **0.950** |
| Perindopril MPO | 0.808 | 0.792 | 0.764 | 0.833 | 0.810 | **0.883** |
| Amlodipine MPO | 0.894 | 0.894 | 0.888 | 0.905 | **0.906** | **0.906** |
| Sitagliptin MPO | 0.545 | **0.891** | 0.539 | 0.749 | 0.823 | 0.838 |
| Zaleplon MPO | 0.669 | 0.754 | 0.590 | 0.763 | 0.790 | **0.797** |
| Valsartan SMARTS | 0.978 | 0.990 | 0.095 | 1.000 | 0.997 | 0.994 |
| deco hop | 0.996 | 1.000 | 0.994 | 1.000 | 1.000 | 1.000 |
| scaffold hop | 0.998 | 1.000 | 0.990 | 1.000 | 1.000 | 1.000 |
| Total | 17.340 | 17.983 | 16.350 | 17.627 | 18.052 | **18.235** |

As shown in Table 1, our model achieved the best performance on multiple tasks, with its overall score surpassing all other baselines. Specifically, our method achieved top performance on 16 out of 20 benchmark tasks, demonstrating strong competitiveness in molecular generation. Compared to GEGL, our model exhibited higher stability across diverse tasks, achieving consistently superior performance rather than excelling in only a subset of cases.

The GuacaMol benchmark [5] consists of 20 tasks designed to comprehensively evaluate molecular generative models across rediscovery, similarity, isomer generation, scaffold hopping, and multi-parameter optimization (MPO). The molecules used in these tasks span diverse chemical classes, including drug-like compounds such as Celecoxib and Aripiprazole, small aliphatic molecules like $C_{11}H_24$, and highly specific drug targets such as Osimertinib and Ranolazine. This diversity ensures a rigorous assessment of the model's ability to generalize across different molecular properties and structural features. Most of the tasks require not only the reproduction of known actives but also the generation of novel molecules that satisfy specific structural constraints, pharmacophoric features, or physicochemical profiles.

In terms of dataset size, GuacaMol includes over 1.5 million molecules drawn from the ChEMBL database, filtered to ensure drug-likeness and chemical feasibility. The challenge lies in generating valid, novel, and property-compliant molecules from this vast and structurally heterogeneous chemical space.

Our model's effectiveness is particularly evident in chemically challenging tasks. For instance, in the Perindopril MPO task, which requires optimizing multiple pharmacokinetic and structural constraints simultaneously, our method achieved a score of 0.883, significantly outperforming existing methods by a margin of 0.05. This indicates strong optimization capabilities in complex molecular design settings. Another compelling example is the Ranolazine MPO task, where MolRL-MGPT–previously the best-performing model–surpassed its closest competitor by only 0.006. However, our model further improved upon MolRL-MGPT by an additional 0.011, demonstrating its ability to break through performance plateaus and generate high-quality, novel candidates in narrow, high-density regions of the chemical space.

These results highlight that our model not only performs well on standard rediscovery and similarity tasks but also maintains robustness and adaptability when facing multi-objective constraints and structurally diverse target molecules. Moreover, these findings validate the effectiveness of the DPO method and curriculum learning in guiding the generative process toward chemically meaningful and practically valuable solutions, laying a strong foundation for future applications in real-world drug discovery.

## 4.2 Molecular Generation for High Binding Affinity to Target Proteins

In this experiment, we utilized a prior model pretrained on the ZINC dataset. The evaluation was conducted on six tasks: JNK3, GSK3B, DRD2, and their pairwise combinations (JNK3+GSK3B, JNK3+DRD2, GSK3B+DRD2).

The model performance was evaluated using the oracle function provided by TDC. For multi-objective optimization tasks, we used the arithmetic mean of the individual target scores as the final score to assess the overall performance of the generated molecules across multiple targets.

**Table 2.** The scores of the generated molecules on JNK3, GSK3$\beta$, DRD2, and pairwise combination tasks.

|              | top 1 | top 10 mean | top 100 mean |
|--------------|-------|-------------|--------------|
| JNK3         | 1.000 | 1.000       | 1.000        |
| GSk3B        | 1.000 | 1.000       | 1.000        |
| DRD2         | 1.000 | 1.000       | 1.000        |
| JNK3+GSK3B   | 0.944 | 0.943       | 0.938        |
| JNK3+DRD2    | 0.925 | 0.925       | 0.920        |
| GSK3B+DRD2   | 0.993 | 0.992       | 0.989        |

As shown in the Table 2, our model successfully generated molecules with strong binding potential to JNK3, GSK3B, and DRD2, demonstrating its effectiveness in molecular generation tasks. These results indicate that our model not only performs well on the Guacamol benchmark but also excels in real-world drug discovery tasks, providing a solid foundation for future research in molecular design and generation.

### 4.3 Impact Analysis

This study suggests that multiple factors, including the learning rate, the number of agents, the sampling-to-training ratio, and the DPO parameter $\beta$, may influence model performance. Through preliminary analysis, we identified that the number of agents and the sampling-to-training ratio have a particularly significant impact. To validate this hypothesis, we conducted a systematic impact analysis experiment focusing on these two key parameters. The experimental results demonstrate that appropriately adjusting the number of agents and the sampling-to-training ratio can significantly enhance model performance, providing valuable theoretical insights and practical guidance for further model optimization.

**Agents Num.** Experimental results in Fig. 3 indicate that the model achieves optimal performance when employing 2 to 4 agents. When the number of agents is too small, the model's expressive capacity is limited, making it difficult to effectively learn complex patterns. Conversely, an excessive number of agents may introduce redundant information and increase optimization complexity, thereby lowering the model's performance upper bound and slowing down convergence. Moreover, the number of agents also affects the score distribution of molecules stored in memory: fewer agents lead to a more concentrated distribution, whereas

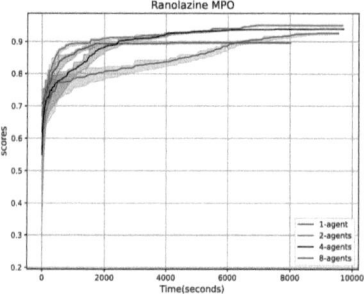
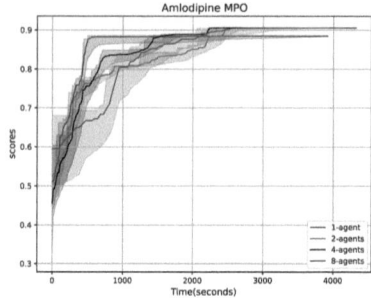

**Fig. 3.** Model performance on Ranolazine MPO and Amlodipine MPO tasks under different numbers of agents. (The curve represents the Top-10 score, while the shaded region indicates the score distribution of the top 100 molecules.)

a larger number of agents result in a more dispersed distribution. Due to differences in the learning configurations of individual agents, their capabilities diverge as training progresses, leading to an increasingly diverse molecular distribution. This broader distribution facilitates the optimization of DPO training and enhances the model's generalization capability.

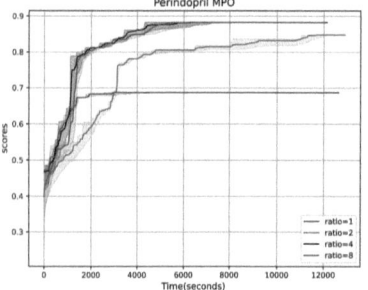
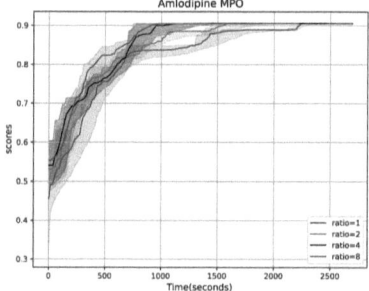

**Fig. 4.** Model performance on Perindopril MPO and Amlodipine MPO tasks under different Sampling-to-Training Ratios. (The curve represents the Top-10 score, while the shaded region indicates the score distribution of the top 100 molecules.)

**Sampling-To-Training Ratio.** As shown in the Fig. 4, increasing the sampling-to-training ratio within a certain range can improve the model's performance upper bound and accelerate convergence. If the ratio is too small, the weights assigned to a few high-quality molecules obtained by chance become excessively large, causing the model to shift towards them–even when they do not represent the optimal direction–ultimately leading to a suboptimal solution. Conversely, if the ratio is too large, the model remains in the sampling phase for an extended period, collecting a large number of redundant molecules while lacking sufficient training. This results in inadequate gradient updates and significantly prolongs the model's convergence time.

## 5 Conclusion

This study proposes a molecule generation method based on DPO and curriculum learning, and achieves favorable experimental results on the Guacamol benchmark and several target tasks. The experiments demonstrate that the proposed method has significant advantages in tasks that generate molecules with specified properties.

**Disclosure of Interests.** The authors have no competing interests to declare that are relevant to the content of this article.

## References

1. Ahn, S., Kim, J., Lee, H., Shin, J.: Guiding deep molecular optimization with genetic exploration. Adv. Neural. Inf. Process. Syst. **33**, 12008–12021 (2020)
2. Bengio, Y., Louradour, J., Collobert, R., Weston, J.: Curriculum learning. In: Proceedings of the 26th Annual International Conference On Machine Learning, pp. 41–48 (2009)
3. Blaschke, T., et al.: Reinvent 2.0: an AI tool for de novo drug design. J. Chemical Inf. Modeling **60**(12), 5918–5922 (2020)
4. Bohacek, R.S., McMartin, C., Guida, W.C.: The art and practice of structure-based drug design: a molecular modeling perspective. Med. Res. Rev. **16**(1), 3–50 (1996)
5. Brown, N., Fiscato, M., Segler, M.H., Vaucher, A.C.: Guacamol: benchmarking models for de novo molecular design. J. Chemical Inf. Modeling **59**(3), 1096–1108 (2019)
6. Cheng, X., Zhou, X., Yang, Y., Bao, Y., Gu, Q.: Decomposed direct preference optimization for structure-based drug design. arXiv preprint arXiv:2407.13981 (2024)
7. DiMasi, J.A., Grabowski, H.G., Hansen, R.W.: Innovation in the pharmaceutical industry: new estimates of r&d costs. J. Health Econ. **47**, 20–33 (2016)
8. Gómez-Bombarelli, R., et al.: Automatic chemical design using a data-driven continuous representation of molecules. ACS Cent. Sci. **4**(2), 268–276 (2018)
9. Gu, S., et al.: Aligning target-aware molecule diffusion models with exact energy optimization. Adv. Neural. Inf. Process. Syst. **37**, 44040–44063 (2025)
10. Guo, J., et al.: Improving de novo molecular design with curriculum learning. Nat. Mach. Intell. **4**(6), 555–563 (2022)
11. Hacohen, G., Weinshall, D.: On the power of curriculum learning in training deep networks. In: International Conference On Machine Learning, pp. 2535–2544. PMLR (2019)
12. Hu, X., Liu, G., Zhao, Y., Zhang, H.: De novo drug design using reinforcement learning with multiple gpt agents. Adv. Neural. Inf. Process. Syst. **36**, 7405–7418 (2023)

13. Irwin, J.J., Shoichet, B.K.: Zinc- a free database of commercially available compounds for virtual screening. J. Chemical Inf. Modeling **45**(1), 177–182 (2005)
14. Jensen, J.H.: A graph-based genetic algorithm and generative model/monte carlo tree search for the exploration of chemical space. Chem. Sci. **10**(12), 3567–3572 (2019)
15. Jin, W., Barzilay, R., Jaakkola, T.: Junction tree variational autoencoder for molecular graph generation. In: International Conference On Machine Learning, pp. 2323–2332. PMLR (2018)
16. Jin, W., Barzilay, R., Jaakkola, T.: Multi-objective molecule generation using interpretable substructures. In: International Conference On Machine Learning, pp. 4849–4859. PMLR (2020)
17. Liu, S., Wang, J., Yang, Y., Wang, C., Liu, L., Guo, H., Xiao, C.: Chatgpt-powered conversational drug editing using retrieval and domain feedback. arXiv preprint arXiv:2305.18090 (2023)
18. Liu, X., Ye, K., van Vlijmen, H.W., Emmerich, M.T., IJzerman, A.P., van Westen, G.J.: Drugex v2: de novo design of drug molecules by pareto-based multi-objective reinforcement learning in polypharmacology. J. Cheminf. **13**(1), 85 (2021)
19. Liu, X., Ye, K., van Vlijmen, H.W., IJzerman, A.P., van Westen, G.J.: Drugex v3: scaffold-constrained drug design with graph transformer-based reinforcement learning. J. Cheminf. **15**(1), 24 (2023)
20. Loeffler, H.H., He, J., Tibo, A., Janet, J.P., Voronov, A., Mervin, L.H., Engkvist, O.: Reinvent 4: modern ai-driven generative molecule design. J. Cheminform **16**(1), 20 (2024)
21. Mandal, S., Mandal, S.K., et al.: Rational drug design. Eur. J. Pharmacol. **625**(1–3), 90–100 (2009)
22. Meyers, J., Fabian, B., Brown, N.: De novo molecular design and generative models. Drug Discovery Today **26**(11), 2707–2715 (2021)
23. Narvekar, S., Peng, B., Leonetti, M., Sinapov, J., Taylor, M.E., Stone, P.: Curriculum learning for reinforcement learning domains: a framework and survey. J. Mach. Learn. Res. **21**(181), 1–50 (2020)
24. Olivecrona, M., Blaschke, T., Engkvist, O., Chen, H.: Molecular de-novo design through deep reinforcement learning. J. Cheminform. **9**, 1–14 (2017)
25. Popova, M., Isayev, O., Tropsha, A.: Deep reinforcement learning for de novo drug design. Sci. Adv. **4**(7), eaap7885 (2018)
26. Rafailov, R., Sharma, A., Mitchell, E., Manning, C.D., Ermon, S., Finn, C.: Direct preference optimization: your language model is secretly a reward model. Adv. Neural Inform. Process. Syst. **36** (2024)
27. Sanchez-Lengeling, B., Aspuru-Guzik, A.: Inverse molecular design using machine learning: generative models for matter engineering. Science **361**(6400), 360–365 (2018)
28. Schneider, G., Fechner, U.: Computer-based de novo design of drug-like molecules. Nat. Rev. Drug Discovery **4**(8), 649–663 (2005)
29. Segler, M.H., Kogej, T., Tyrchan, C., Waller, M.P.: Generating focused molecule libraries for drug discovery with recurrent neural networks. ACS Cent. Sci. **4**(1), 120–131 (2018)
30. Simm, G., Pinsler, R., Hernández-Lobato, J.M.: Reinforcement learning for molecular design guided by quantum mechanics. In: International Conference on Machine Learning, pp. 8959–8969. PMLR (2020)
31. Stokes, J.M., et al.: A deep learning approach to antibiotic discovery. Cell **180**(4), 688–702 (2020)

32. Widatalla, T., Rafailov, R., Hie, B.: Aligning protein generative models with experimental fitness via direct preference optimization. bioRxiv, pp. 2024–05 (2024)
33. Zhavoronkov, A., et al.: Deep learning enables rapid identification of potent ddr1 kinase inhibitors. Nat. Biotechnol. **37**(9), 1038–1040 (2019)
34. Zhou, Z., Kearnes, S., Li, L., Zare, R.N., Riley, P.: Optimization of molecules via deep reinforcement learning. Sci. Rep. **9**(1), 10752 (2019)

# Hybrid Cross-Domain Robust Reinforcement Learning

Linh Le Pham Van[1]($\boxtimes$), Minh Hoang Nguyen[1], Hung Le[1], Hung The Tran[2], and Sunil Gupta[1]

[1] Deakin Applied Artificial Intelligence Initiative, Deakin University, Geelong, Australia
{l.le,s223669184,thai.le,sunil.gupta}@deakin.edu.au
[2] Hanoi University of Science and Technology, Hanoi, Vietnam
hungtt@soict.hust.edu.vn

**Abstract.** Robust reinforcement learning (RL) aims to learn policies that remain effective despite uncertainties in its environment, which frequently arise in real-world applications due to variations in environment dynamics. The robust RL methods learn a robust policy by maximizing value under the worst-case models within a predefined uncertainty set. Offline robust RL algorithms are particularly promising in scenarios where only a fixed dataset is available and new data cannot be collected. However, these approaches often require extensive offline data, and gathering such datasets for specific tasks in specific environments can be both costly and time-consuming. Using an imperfect simulator offers a faster, cheaper, and safer way to collect data for training, but it can suffer from dynamics mismatch. In this paper, we introduce HYDRO, the first Hybrid Cross-Domain Robust RL framework designed to address these challenges. HYDRO utilizes an online simulator to complement the limited amount of offline datasets in the non-trivial context of robust RL. By measuring and minimizing performance gaps between the simulator and the worst-case models in the uncertainty set, HYDRO employs novel uncertainty filtering and prioritized sampling to select the most relevant and reliable simulator samples. Our extensive experiments demonstrate HYDRO's superior performance over existing methods across various tasks, underscoring its potential to improve sample efficiency in offline robust RL. [1] https://github.com/linhlpv/Hybrid-Cross-domain-Robust-Reinforcement-Learning.

**Keywords:** Hybrid cross-domain · Distributionally robust · Offline source - Online target · Reinforcement Learning · Transfer Learning

## 1 Introduction

Reinforcement learning (RL) has shown remarkable success in real-world applications [20,21], but deploying RL policies is often challenged by fluctuations in environment dynamics. Many existing methods assume consistency between training and deployment environments, an assumption frequently violated in practice due to such fluctuations. For instance, a robot operating in a dynamic real-world environment may encounter variations in mass, friction, and sensor noise compared to its training environment, leading to performance degradation [1,11]. The Robust Markov Decision Process (RMDP) framework [27] addresses this challenge by modeling uncertain test environments as a set of possible models around a training model, which is often called the nominal model. Robust RL aims to learn an optimal policy that maximizes performance under the worst-case scenario within this uncertainty set, using only the nominal model.

Since its introduction [27,28], the RMDP framework has been extensively studied in the context of planning problems [29]. Recently, many robust RL algorithms, learning robust policies from unknown nominal models, have also been proposed [34,35]. Still, all these works are limited to the online setting, where policy learning requires online interactions with the environment. Recent success in offline RL [23–25,53] has motivated the development of offline robust RL methods [37–40] to alleviate this restriction. Despite this progress, offline robust RL methods rely on large datasets, and current offline robust RL struggles when the amount of training data is reduced. As shown in Fig. 1, the robustness performance of the robust RL method drops significantly when the amount of data decreases. This raises a natural question: *Can we reduce the required offline training data without sacrificing the performance of the learn policy under uncertain deployment environments?*

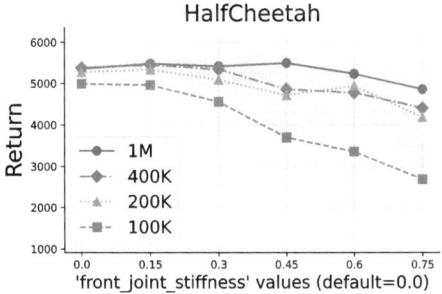

**Fig. 1.** Problem of existing offline robust RL model: Robustness performance drops significantly when training data decreases. Figure illustrates performance comparison under 'front_joint_stiffness' perturbation of offline robust RL [37] with different training data sizes from HalfCheetah medium dataset (D4RL).

To address the challenge of scarce data in offline RMDP, we propose a method that utilizes a simulator (source domain), an imperfect model but a faster, cheaper, and safer place to collect data for training the agent. We aim to leverage the interaction with this simulator to mitigate performance degradation caused by the limited offline nominal (target) dataset. A simulator enables unrestricted exploration and access to abundant, diverse data, potentially compensating for limited coverage of offline datasets. The potential of using an additional source environment to bring sample efficiency has sparked research interest with numerous methods proposed in the Markov Decision Process (MDP) setting, often referred to as cross-domain RL [51]. However, naively combining source and target data may lead to performance degradation due to dynamics mismatches [6]. Thus, in the normal MDP setting, prior methods measure the domain gap directly between target and source domains using corresponding datasets. This approach cannot be directly applied to RMDPs where we optimize for *worst-case* performance while only having access to nominal model data. To the best of our knowledge, our work is the first to study the combination of online source and offline nominal dataset in the robust RL setting.

In this paper, we introduce HYDRO, the first Hybrid Cross-Domain Robust RL framework. HYDRO measures the performance gap caused by the dynamics mismatch between the simulator and the worst-case model in an uncertainty set around the nominal target model. Using this measurement, HYDRO uses a novel uncertainty based filtering mechanism and priority sampling scheme to select reliable and relevant samples from the simulator, minimizing performance degradations. Our contributions are:

- We are the first to address the Hybrid cross-domain Robust RL setting, which is a novel problem, and develop a method to improve the sample efficiency for the offline robust RL.
- We perform a theoretical analysis of our novel problem setting and use it to propose HYDRO, a practical and effective algorithm for solving this problem via novel uncertainty filtering and priority sampling.
- Through comprehensive experiments, we demonstrate that our method consistently outperforms existing approaches across diverse tasks.

## 2 Related Works

### 2.1 Offline Robust Reinforcement Learning

The RMDP framework was first introduced by [27,28] to address the parameter uncertainty problem. The initial works mainly focused on planning problems and have been well-studied [29–31]. Recently, robust RL in RMDP has gained much attention, with many works that have studied this problem in online [34,35], and offline [36,38–40] in both tabular settings [32,33,36] and large state-action space RMDP setting [37,39]. We focus on offline robust RL in large state and action spaces. Despite recent successes in such settings [37], offline robust RL methods rely on the coverage of the offline dataset. This means their robustness performance, similar to non-robust offline RL algorithms, highly depends on the amount of available offline data [37]. In practice, obtaining datasets with extensive coverage is often infeasible. Therefore, improving the sample efficiency of offline robust RL algorithms is a critical research challenge.

### 2.2 Cross-Domain Reinforcement Learning

Cross-domain RL seeks to improve sample efficiency by leveraging data from additional source environments. Domain discrepancies can arise from differences in the observation space [41,42], transitional dynamics [4,7]. In this work, we focus on the mismatch in the transition dynamics. Many approaches have been proposed to deal with dynamics mismatches, such as system identification [14–16], domain randomization [11–13], or meta-RL [17–19]. However, these methods often require environment models or careful selection of randomized parameters. Recently, several methods attempted to measure dynamics discrepancy using domain classifiers [4,7], learned dynamics models [5], or feature representation mismatch [10]. Many approaches to utilize source data have been developed, such as reward modification [7,10], support constraint [5] for purely online [8,9], purely offline [5,6], or hybrid setting [2,3]. However, these methods have primarily focused on standard RL setting. In contrast, we study the *hybrid* cross-domain problem in the *distributionally robust* RL setting, aiming to leverage online source simulators to improve sample efficiency for offline robust RL methods. To this end, we propose a novel approach using uncertainty filtering and priority sampling specifically designed for this hybrid robust setting.

### 2.3 Other Robust RL

Recently, adversarial robust RL [26,46] and risk-sensitive RL [47,48] in online and offline settings also address robustness problems under different frameworks that are independent of RMDP. Additionally, the corruption-robust offline RL problem, where an adversary can modify a fraction of the training dataset, has been studied in [49,50]. However, their goal is still to find the optimal policy for the nominal model.

## 3 Preliminaries

We denote an MDP as $\mathcal{M} = (\mathcal{S}, \mathcal{A}, \gamma, r, d_0, P)$, where $\mathcal{S}, \mathcal{A}$ are the state and action spaces. The parameter $\gamma \in (0,1)$ is the discounted factor, $r : \mathcal{S} \times \mathcal{A} \to \mathbb{R}$ is the reward function, $d_0$ is the initial state distribution and $P$ is the transition dynamics. We denote a policy $\pi : \mathcal{S} \to \Delta(\mathcal{A})$ as a map from state space $\mathcal{S}$ to a probability distribution over actions space $\mathcal{A}$. Given a policy $\pi$ and a transition dynamics (model) $P$, we denote discounted state-action occupancy as $d_P^\pi(s,a) = (1-\gamma)\mathbb{E}_{\pi,P}\left[\sum_{t=0}^{\infty} \gamma^t \mathbb{1}(s_t = s, a_t = a)\right]$. We define value function $V^{\pi,P}$ and state-action value function $Q^{\pi,P}$ for a policy $\pi$ and a transition dynamics $P$ as follows:

$$V^{\pi,P}(s) = \mathbb{E}_{\pi,P}\Big[\sum_{t=0}^{\infty} \gamma^t r(s_t, a_t) | s_0 = s\Big], \text{ and}$$
$$Q^{\pi,P}(s,a) = \mathbb{E}_{\pi,P}\Big[\sum_{t=0}^{\infty} \gamma^t r(s_t, a_t) | s_0 = s, a_0 = a\Big]. \quad (1)$$

We adopt the following notation: $|\mathcal{X}|$ for the cardinality of a set $\mathcal{X}$, $\Delta(\mathcal{X})$ for the set of probability distributions over $\mathcal{X}$, $(x)_+$ for $\max(x,0)$ where $x \in \mathbb{R}$, and $\mathbb{E}_P[f(s')]$ as a short notation for $\mathbb{E}_{s' \sim P(s'|s,a)}[f(s')]$.

## 3.1 Distributionally Robust Reinforcement Learning

We introduce the distributionally robust MDP (RMDP) as $\mathcal{M}_r = \{\mathcal{S}, \mathcal{A}, \gamma, r, \mathcal{U}_\rho^\sigma(P^o)\}$. RMDP allows the transition dynamics to be chosen arbitrarily from a predefined uncertainty set $\mathcal{U}_\rho^\sigma(P^o)$ centered around a nominal model $P^o$ w.r.t a metric $\rho$. In particular, the uncertainty set is specified as:

$$\mathcal{U}_\rho^\sigma(P^o) := \otimes \, \mathcal{U}_\rho^\sigma(P^o(.|s,a)), \\ \text{with } \mathcal{U}_\rho^\sigma(P^o(.|s,a)) := \{P(.|s,a) \in \Delta(\mathcal{S}) : \rho(P(.|s,a), P^o(.|s,a)) \leq \sigma\}, \quad (2)$$

where $\otimes$ denotes the Cartesian product. In RMDP, we focus on the worst-case performance of a policy $\pi$ over all the transition models in the uncertainty set. Formally, we define the robust value functions for all $s, a \in \mathcal{S} \times \mathcal{A}$ as follows:

$$V^{\pi,\sigma}(s) := \inf_{P \in \mathcal{U}_\rho^\sigma(P^o)} V^{\pi,P}(s), \, Q^{\pi,\sigma}(s,a) := \inf_{P \in \mathcal{U}_\rho^\sigma(P^o)} Q^{\pi,P}(s,a). \quad (3)$$

We also have the following equations held in RMDP:

$$Q^{\pi,\sigma}(s,a) = r(s,a) + \gamma \inf_{P \in \mathcal{U}_\rho^\sigma(P^o)} \mathbb{E}_{s' \sim P}\left[V^{\pi,\sigma}(s')\right]. \quad (4)$$

In RMDP, there exists at least one deterministic policy that maximizes robust value function [27]. We denote optimal robust value function, and optimal robust policy, which satisfies the following:

$$\forall s \in \mathcal{S} : V^{*,\sigma}(s) := V^{\pi^*,\sigma}(s) = \max_\pi V^{\pi,\sigma}, \\ \forall s, a \in \mathcal{S} \times \mathcal{A} : Q^{*,\sigma}(s,a) := Q^{\pi^*,\sigma}(s,a) = \max_\pi Q^{\pi,\sigma}(s,a). \quad (5)$$

Similar to the normal MDP, we have the robust Bellman operator as follows:

$$\forall (s,a) \in \mathcal{S} \times \mathcal{A} : \mathcal{T}^\sigma Q(s,a) := r(s,a) + \gamma \inf_{\mathcal{P} \in \mathcal{U}_\rho^\sigma(P_{s,a}^0)} \mathcal{P}V, \quad V(s) := \max_a Q(s,a). \quad (6)$$

It is known that $\mathcal{T}^\sigma$ is a contraction mapping w.r.t. the infinity norm, and has a unique fix point solution as $Q^{*,\sigma}$. The *fitted* procedure $Q_{k+1} = \mathcal{T}^\sigma Q_k$ can be used to find the fixed point solution $Q^{*,\sigma}$.

## 3.2 RMDP with Offline Data

Offline Robust RL addresses learning robust policies for RMDPs using only an offline nominal dataset $\mathcal{D} = \{(s_i, a_i, r_i, s_i')\}_{i=1}^N$, where $(s_i, a_i) \sim \mu$, $s_i' \sim P^o(.|s_i, a_i)$. The fundamental challenge is that applying the robust Bellman operator in Eq (6) requires computing expectations over all dynamic models $P \in \mathcal{U}_\rho^\sigma$, while only samples from the nominal model $P^o$ are available.

A common approach is to leverage a dual reformulation of the robust Bellman operator, replacing the expectation over all transition dynamics in $\mathcal{U}_\rho^\sigma(P^o)$ with one over nominal model $P^o$ [37–39]. Specifically, [37] studied uncertainty sets with TV distance and proposed RFQI algorithm. To overcome the difficulty of estimating the robust Bellman operator, RFQI proposed the dual reformulation of the second term in the robust Bellman operator.

**Proposition 1.** Let $D_{TV}$ be the total variation distance corresponding to the TV uncertainty set $\mathcal{U}_{TV}^\sigma(P^o)$, then

$$\inf_{P \in \mathcal{U}_{TV}^\sigma(P^o)} \mathbb{E}_P[V(s)] = -\inf_{\eta \in [0, \frac{2}{\sigma(1-\gamma)}]} (\mathbb{E}_{P^o}[(\eta - V(s))_+] + \sigma((\eta - \inf_{\tilde{s} \in \mathcal{S}} V(\tilde{s}))_+ - \eta) \tag{7}$$

They made the 'fail-state' assumption to overcome the issue of finding $\inf_{s'' \in \mathcal{S}} V(s'')$ when $\mathcal{S}$ is large.

**Assumption 1.** *(Fail-state) The RMDP $\mathcal{M}$ has a 'fail-state' $s_f$, such that $\forall a \in \mathcal{A}, \forall P \in \mathcal{U}_{TV}^\sigma(P^o), r(s_f, a) = 0$ and $P(s_f | s_f, a) = 1$.*

Under Proposition 1 and Assumption 1, RFQI reformulates the robust Bellman operator as follows:

$$\mathcal{T}^\sigma Q(s,a) := r(s,a) - \gamma \inf_{\eta \in [0, \frac{2}{\sigma(1-\gamma)}]} \left( \mathbb{E}_{s' \sim P_{s,a}^o}[(\eta - V(s'))_+] - \eta(1 - \sigma) \right), \tag{8}$$

where $\eta \in [0, \frac{2}{\sigma(1-\gamma)}]$ is the dual variable. To deal with large state and action space problems, RFQI frames the problem as a function approximation task. Specifically, they learn the dual variable network $g_\theta$ via the loss function $L_{dual} = \mathbb{E}_{s,a,s' \sim \mathcal{D}}[(g_\theta(s,a) - \max_{a'} Q_\phi(s', a'))_+ - (1 - \sigma)g_\theta(s,a)]$.

They also define the operator $\mathcal{T}^{\sigma,g} Q(s,a) = r(s,a) - \gamma(\mathbb{E}_{P^o}[(g(s,a) - \max_{a'} Q(s', a'))_+] - g(s,a)(1 - \sigma))$. Then, the value function $Q_\phi$ is learned with the following objective $L_{RFQI} = \mathbb{E}_{s,a,s' \sim \mathcal{D}}\left[(\hat{\mathcal{T}}^{\sigma,g} \hat{Q}_\phi(s,a) - Q_\phi(s,a))^2\right]$, where $\hat{Q}_\phi$ is the value function from the last iteration, and $\hat{\mathcal{T}}^{\sigma,g}$ is the empirical $\mathcal{T}^{\sigma,g}$ that only backs up a single sample.

## 4 Hybrid Cross-Domain Robust Reinforcement Learning

### 4.1 Problem Setting

We consider the offline RMDP problem $\mathcal{M}_r$ with the uncertainty set around the nominal model $P^o$. For clarity, **we will refer to this nominal model as the target model throughout the paper**. In our work, we study the RMDPs with total variation (TV) uncertainty set $\mathcal{U}_{TV}^\sigma(P^o)$ and in the large state, action spaces setting. Specifically, we study the setting with limited offline data collected from the target model, i.e. $\mathcal{D} = \{(s_i, a_i, r_i, s_i')\}_{i=1}^N$, where $(s_i, a_i) \sim \mu$, $\mu$ is some data generating distribution, and $s_i' \sim P^o(.|s_i, a_i)$. For computational tractability, we adopt the fail-state assumption established in function approximation settings [37]. We note that the 'fail-state' is natural in many real-world systems such as robotics [37] where the collapse of the robot can be seen as a fail state.

Along with the offline dataset from the target model, we also have access to an imperfect online simulator which we call a *source environment*. The source environment $\mathcal{M}_{src}$ shares the same state space $\mathcal{S}$, action space $\mathcal{A}$, reward function $r$, discounted factor $\gamma$ and initialized state distribution $d_0$ with target domain, and only differs in its transition model, i.e. $P_{src} \neq P^o$. Our goal is to utilize online simulator $\mathcal{M}_{src}$ and limited offline target dataset $\mathcal{D}$ to learn a policy that is robust under the uncertainty set around target model $P^o$.

## 4.2 Domain Gap for Hybrid Cross-Domain Robust RL

Naively combining source data to train robust target policies can lead to performance degradation due to dynamics mismatch, a challenge also noted in cross-domain RL [2,6]. Therefore, caution is necessary when utilizing source data from a different dynamics model. We begin with a theoretical analysis of the performance gap caused by this dynamics mismatch between the two domains, followed by convergence guarantees for value functions in hybrid cross-domain robust RL settings. We provide detailed proof in Appendix 2 due to the space limit.

**Theorem 1 (Performance Bound).** *Let $\mathcal{M}_{src}$ and $\mathcal{M}_r$ be the source MDP and the target RMDP with different dynamics $P_{src}$ and $P^o$ respectively. Consider the RMDP with the TV uncertainty set. Denote:*

$$A = D_{TV}(P^{\pi,\mathcal{U}_{TV}^\sigma(P^o)}, P^{\pi,\mathcal{U}_{TV}^\sigma(\hat{P}^o)}), B = \left|\mathbb{E}_{P_{src}}[V_{\hat{P}^o}^{\pi,\sigma}(s')] - \inf_{P \in \mathcal{U}^\sigma(\hat{P}^o)} \mathbb{E}_P[V_{\hat{P}^o}^{\pi,\sigma}(s')]\right|$$

*where, given a policy $\pi$, $P^{\pi,\mathcal{U}_{TV}^\sigma(P^o)}$, $P^{\pi,\mathcal{U}_{TV}^\sigma(\hat{P}^o)}$ denote the worst case model w.r.t. the uncertainty set around the target model $P^o$ and the estimated target model $\hat{P}^o$ from offline dataset $\mathcal{D}$, respectively.*

*The performance difference of any policy $\pi$ on the source domain and the RMDP target can be bounded as follows:*

$$\mathbb{E}_{s \sim d_0}[V^{\pi,\sigma}(s)]$$
$$\geq \mathbb{E}_{s \sim d_0}[V^{\pi,src}(s)] - \frac{2\gamma r_{max}}{(1-\gamma)^2}\mathbb{E}_{d_{P^{\pi,\mathcal{U}_{TV}^\sigma(\hat{P}^o)}}^{\pi}}[A] - \frac{\gamma}{1-\gamma}\mathbb{E}_{d_{P_{src}}^{\pi}}[B]. \quad (9)$$

The second term $A$ in the Ineq (9) is caused by the offline dataset and can be reduced by offline Robust RL algorithms via pessimism [37,38,40]. The third term $B$ represents the gap between the worst case model $P^{\pi,\mathcal{U}_{TV}^\sigma(\hat{P}^o)}$ and the source model $P_{src}$, which can be reduced by our proposed method. Specifically, Theorem 1 provides the intuition that the robust performance in the target model could be guaranteed if values of robust value function are consistent when evaluating in the source environment and the worst-case model.

Next, we analysis the value function's convergence. Denote the source dataset as $\mathcal{D}_{src}$, we consider the following approach using both source and target data:

$$Q^{k+1} \leftarrow \underset{Q}{\arg\min}\, \kappa \mathbb{E}_{s,a,s' \sim \mathcal{D}}[(\hat{\mathcal{T}}^{\sigma,g}Q^k - Q)^2] + (1-\kappa)\mathbb{E}_{s,a,s' \sim \mathcal{D}_{src}}[(\hat{\mathcal{T}}Q^k - Q)^2], \quad (10)$$

where $\kappa \in [0,1]$ is the combination weight, $k$ denotes training iteration, and $\hat{\mathcal{T}}$ is the empirical Bellman operator. We denote $\mu$ and $\nu$ as the state-action distributions of target and source datasets. We analyze the convergence guarantee of the value function. To maintain simplicity, we assume the source and the target datasets have the same state-action distribution, i.e. $\mu(s,a) = \nu(s,a), \forall s, a \in \mathcal{S} \times \mathcal{A}$. This assumption can hold easily when the source data $\mathcal{D}_{src}$ is generated via a simulator, as it allows flexibility in selecting the transition starting points. We note that the source and target dynamics remain distinct ($P_{src} \neq P^o$). Below, we present the convergence guarantee in the following theorem.

**Theorem 2 (Convergence).** *Let $Q^*$ denote the optimal robust value function for the RMDP of the nominal model $P^o$, and define $Q^0 = 0$. Denote*

$$\xi = \max_Q \max_{s,a \in \mathcal{S} \times \mathcal{A}} |T^{\sigma,g}Q(s,a) - T^\sigma Q(s,a)|,$$
$$\zeta = \max_Q \max_{s,a \in \mathcal{S} \times \mathcal{A}} |TQ(s,a) - T^\sigma Q(s,a)|. \quad (11)$$

*Assume $\mu(s,a) = \nu(s,a), \forall s, a \in \mathcal{S} \times \mathcal{A}$, we have the following result holds:*

$$\|Q^* - Q^{k+1}\|_\infty \leq \frac{\gamma^{k+1} r_{max}}{1-\gamma} + \frac{1-\gamma^{k+1}}{1-\gamma}(\kappa\xi + (1-\kappa)\zeta). \quad (12)$$

Term $\xi$ arises from offline target dataset and can be reduced via offline robust RL algorithms, while $\zeta$ reflects the gap between worst-case target and source models. Theorem 2 guarantees that the learned Q function converges near the optimal robust $Q^*$, with a bound determined by the domain gaps and the combination weight. Theorem 2 suggests that target robust performance can be ensured by carefully using the *most* relevant, reliable source data that minimizes domain gaps during training, thus controlling the second term in Ineq (12).

### 4.3 Incorporating Source Data in Target Robust Training

In this section, we present our proposed method, which involves the priority sampling method to select relevant source data for training and uncertainty filtering to keep reliable source samples.

***Source Data Selection with Priority Sampling.*** Motivated by the performance bound in Theorem 1, we focus on controlling the third term in Ineq (9). We propose selecting source transitions that induce minimal value discrepancies when incorporating the source environment for training. This requires computing the domain gap between transition pairs starting from the same source state-action pair $(s_{src}, a_{src})$. Specifically, given $(s_{src}, a_{src})$, we aim to estimate the domain gap between next states $s'$, defined as follows:

$$\Lambda(s_{src}, a_{src}) = \left| \mathbb{E}_{P_{src}}[V^{\pi,\sigma}_{\hat{P}^o}(s')] - \inf_{P \in \mathcal{U}^\sigma(\hat{P}^o)} \mathbb{E}_P[V^{\pi,\sigma}_{\hat{P}^o}(s')] \right|. \quad (13)$$

Computing $\Lambda(s_{src}, a_{src})$ for a given source state-action pair $(s_{src}, a_{src})$ requires the worst-case model w.r.t. uncertainty set $\mathcal{U}^\sigma(\hat{P}^o)$, which is challenging because we only have offline dataset $\mathcal{D}$. However, using Proposition 1 and Assumption 1, we can rewrite $\Lambda(s_{src}, a_{src})$ as follows:

$$\Lambda(s_{src}, a_{src}) = \left| \mathbb{E}_{P_{src}}[V^{\pi,\sigma}_{\hat{P}^o}(s')] + \inf_{\eta \in [0, \frac{2}{\sigma(1-\gamma)}]} \left( \mathbb{E}_{\hat{P}^o}[(\eta - V^{\pi,\sigma}_{\hat{P}^o}(s'))_+] - \eta(1-\sigma) \right) \right|. \quad (14)$$

With Eq (14), given $(s_{src}, a_{src})$ from the source environment, we can approximately compute $\Lambda(s_{src}, a_{src})$ using the offline dataset $\mathcal{D}$. In practice, we compute

$\Lambda(s_{src}, a_{src})$ for each source state-action pair $(s_{src}, a_{src})$ using the robust value function, estimated target model $\hat{P}^o$, and dual variable $\eta$. We learn the estimated dynamics model $\hat{P}^o$ from offline dataset $\mathcal{D}$. For a given $(s_{src}, a_{src})$, we generate the next state $s'_{tar}$ using the learned target dynamics model. The learned dual network $g_\theta$ gives approximated values for dual variable $\eta$. We then introduce a gap-measurement function approximating $\Lambda(s_{src}, a_{src})$ by estimating the value function for next state $s'$ as $V_{\hat{P}^o}^{\pi,\sigma}(s') := Q_\phi(s', a')|_{a' \sim \pi(.|s')}$:

$$\hat{\Lambda}(s_{src}, a_{src}) = \big|Q_\phi(s'_{src}, a') + (g_\theta(s_{src}, a_{src}) - Q_\phi(s'_{tar}, a'))_+ \\ - g_\theta(s_{src}, a_{src})(1 - \sigma)\big|. \quad (15)$$

As our objective is to select the source samples with small gaps to tighten the bound in Ineq (9), we introduce the following *priority score function* $\psi(s, a) = 1/(1 + \hat{\Lambda}(s, a))$. This priority score guides our sampling process during training. The sampling probability for each source transition is defined as:

$$p^i(s, a, s', r) = \psi^i(s, a) / \sum_k \psi^k(s, a), \quad (16)$$

where $\psi^i(s, a)$ is the priority score of the source transition.

**Uncertainty Filtering.** To address the uncertainty of the offline dataset, we employ a quantifier to compute uncertainty values for each source sample. Source samples with high uncertainty can lead to unreliable estimation scores, potentially hindering the training process if included. Conversely, reliable source state-action pairs with low uncertainty can serve as valuable augmented data for training the dual network $g_\theta$. Therefore, we propose removing source samples with high uncertainty values. Inspired by prior works [44,45], we train an ensemble of $N$ dynamics model $\{\hat{P}_i^o(s'|s, a) = \mathcal{N}(\mu_\varphi(s, a), \Sigma_\varphi(s, a))\}_{i=1}^N$. Each model in the ensemble is trained using offline target dataset $\mathcal{D}_{tar}$ via the maximum log-likelihood (MLE) as follows: $\mathcal{L}_\varphi = \mathbb{E}_{(s,a,r,s') \sim \mathcal{D}}[\log \hat{P}^o(s' \mid s, a)]$.

Then, we use the max pairwise difference as our uncertainty quantifier, i.e. $u(s, a) = \max_{i,j} \|\mu_\varphi^i(s, a) - \mu_\varphi^j(s, a)\|^2$, where $\|.\|_2$ is the L2-norm and $\mu_\varphi^i(s, a)$, $\mu_\varphi^j(s, a), i, j \in \{1, \ldots, N\}$ are the mean vectors of the Gaussian distributions in the ensemble dynamics model. For the uncertainty threshold, instead of naively setting a constant threshold, we measure the uncertainty on all samples in the offline dataset $\mathcal{D}$. Then, we take the maximum uncertainty in the dataset and set the uncertainty threshold as follows: $\epsilon_u = \frac{1}{\alpha} \max_{s,a \in \mathcal{D}} u(s, a)$,

where $\alpha \in \mathbb{R}_+$ is a hyperparameter to control the threshold value. Then, for any source transition $(s, a, s', r)_{src}$, we add them to the source replay buffer if its uncertainty value is less than the uncertainty threshold $\epsilon_u$. Otherwise, we remove them.

During training, we sample a batch of source data from the source replay buffer with probabilities defined by Eq. (16). Based on Theorems 1 and 2, we prioritize the most relevant source samples while carefully controlling combination weight $\kappa$. We recompute scores for these samples, select the top-k highest-scoring samples to update the value function, and adjust priorities accordingly.

**Algorithm 1.** HYbrid cross-Domain RObust RL - HYDRO

1: **Input:** Source $\mathcal{M}_{src}$, offline target dataset $\mathcal{D}$, the source replay buffer $\mathcal{D}_{src} = \emptyset$, robust value function $Q_\phi$ and dual variable functions $g_\theta$.
2: Train $\{\hat{P}_i^o(s'|s,a) = \mathcal{N}(\mu_\varphi(s,a), \Sigma_\varphi(s,a))\}_{i=1}^N$ via MLE on $\mathcal{D}$.
3: **for** $t = 1, \ldots,$ num iterations **do**
4:    **for** $i = 1, \ldots, h$ **do**
5:       Rollout with $\mathcal{M}_{src}$, compute $u_i(s_i, a_i) = \max_{j,k} \|\mu_\varphi^j(s_i, a_i) - \mu_\varphi^k(s_i, a_i)\|^2$.
6:       **if** $u_i \le \epsilon_u$ **then**
7:          $\mathcal{D}_{src} \leftarrow \mathcal{D}_{src} \bigcup (s_i, a_i, r_i, s_i')$.
8:       **end if**
9:    **end for**
10:   Sample $\{(s,a,r,s')_{src}^i\}_{i=1}^N$ with probability $p^i(s,a,s')$ via Eq (16) from $\mathcal{D}_{src}$.
11:   Sample $\{(s,a,r,s')_{tar}^i\}_{i=1}^N$ uniformly from $\mathcal{D}$.
12:   Update transition priority in $\{(s,a,r,s')_{src}^i\}_{i=1}^N$.
13:   Update $g_\theta$ via Eq (18) using source, target data.
14:   Update $Q_\phi$ via Eq (17) using $\{(s,a,r,s')_{src}^i\}_{i=1}^N$ and $\{(s,a,r,s')_{tar}^i\}_{i=1}^N$.
15: **end for**
16: **return** $Q_\phi$.

The robust value function is trained using both source and target data as follows:

$$Q_\phi \leftarrow \underset{Q_\phi}{\arg\min}\, \mathbb{E}_{s,a,s' \sim \mathcal{D}}[(\hat{\mathcal{T}}^{\sigma,g} \hat{Q}_\phi - Q_\phi)^2] + \mathbb{E}_{s,a,s' \sim \mathcal{D}_{src}}[\omega(s,a,s')(\hat{\mathcal{T}} \hat{Q}_\phi - Q_\phi)^2] \tag{17}$$

, where source data sampled via priority sampling after the uncertainty filter, $w(s,a,s') = \mathbb{1}(\psi(s,a) > \psi_{k\%})$, and $\mathcal{T}$ and $\mathcal{T}^\sigma$ is the normal and robust Bellman operator respectively. We use the offline target data $(s_{tar}, a_{tar}, s'_{tar})$ along with the augmented sample $(s_{src}, a_{src}, s'_{tar})$, where $s'_{tar} \sim \hat{P}^o(s'|s_{src}, a_{src})$, for training dual network $g_\theta$. Specifically, we update the dual network $g_\theta$ as follows:

$$\begin{aligned}\theta \leftarrow \underset{\theta}{\arg\min}\, &\mathbb{E}_{s,a,s' \sim \mathcal{D}}\left[(g_\theta(s,a) - V(s'))_+ - (1-\sigma)g_\theta(s,a)\right] \\ &+ \mathbb{E}_{s,a \sim \mathcal{D}_{src}, s' \sim \hat{P}^o}\left[(g_\theta(s,a) - V(s'))_+ - (1-\sigma)g_\theta(s,a)\right].\end{aligned} \tag{18}$$

***Algorithm.*** We summarize the above steps as our proposed method HYDRO in Algorithm 1.

## 5 Experiments

In this section, we present the empirical evaluation to answer the following questions: **1)** Can HYDRO enhance data efficiency and improve robustness performance in scarce data settings? **2)** Why is using HYDRO more advantageous than just naively merging the source data? **3)** How do different components of HYDRO contribute to its performance?

***Environments.*** We conduct our experiments on three MuJoCo environments (HalfCheetah-v3, Walker2d-v3, Hopper-v3), utilizing the Medium datasets from

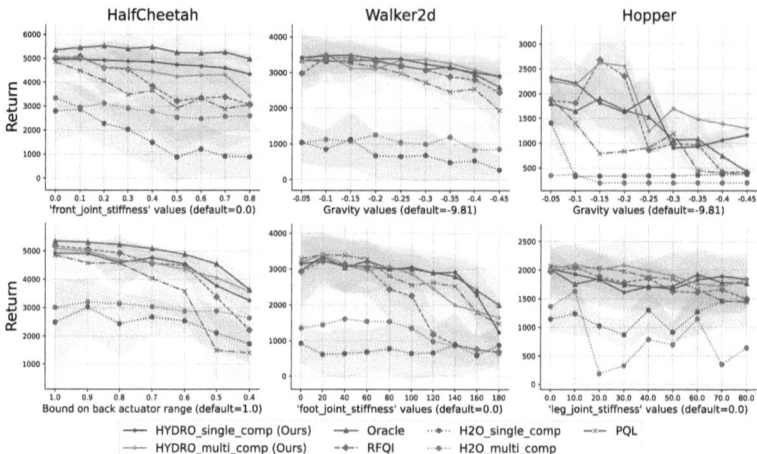

**Fig. 2.** Cumulative rewards of different methods in three Mujoco benchmarks under perturbation. The lines are the average returns over 30 different seeded runs, and the shaded areas represent standard deviation.

D4RL [43] as our offline datasets [37]. To create the scarce data settings, we only use 10% of these datasets for training, i.e. 100K target transitions from D4RL. The source environments are created by modifying the morphology of the agents in the Mujoco XML file. We consider two types of modifications: single-comp, modifying a single agent component, and multi-comp, altering multiple components. For robustness evaluation, we perturb each Mujoco environment by altering its physical parameters.

***Metric.*** In the cross-domain robust setting, we evaluate the agent's return on the target domain under perturbations.

***Baselines.*** We compare HYDRO against the following baselines: *RQFI* [37], the current state-of-the-art in offline robust RL; *H2O* [2], an only recent state-of-the-art method with available public code for non-robust hybrid cross-domain transfer that uses importance sampling to correct the dynamics shift between source and target environments; *PQL* [22], a non-robust offline RL algorithm and a practical state-of-the-art variant of FQI with neural architecture. Finally, we train RFQI agent with a full offline target dataset, which we refer to as *Oracle*. Due to limited space, we defer more details about the environment and baseline settings to Appendix 4 and provide more experiment results in Appendix 5.

### 5.1 Robustness Performance Evaluation

In this section, we answer the first question, showing that our method, HYDRO, can enhance data efficiency and improve robust performance in scarce data settings. Figure 2 presents the performance of our method and the baselines across three Mujoco environments under model parameter perturbations. Notably, the robust performance of RFQI degrades substantially with reduced training data. In the scarce data setting (10% target data), RFQI's performance drops notably with increasing perturbations, resembling the non-robust offline method PQL. H2O performs poorly across all settings, as its performance is heavily reliant on the amount of training target data and struggles in scarce data scenarios [2]. We believe the lack of target samples causes the inferior performance of H2O, which also was observed in [52]. In contrast, HYDRO consistently demonstrates robust performance, surpassing RFQI and non-robust methods across all tasks. While baseline methods exhibit substantial performance drops with increasing environmental changes, HYDRO maintains robustness. Table 1 presents the average returns of all methods under various environment parameter perturbations. As the table illustrates, our method improves upon RFQI across all tasks, with the most significant improvement reaching approximately 36%. Statistical testing (please see Appendix 5.1) confirms HYDRO significantly outperforms all baselines. Importantly, compared to Oracle, HYDRO exhibits the smallest degradation in robust performance across all tasks.

**Table 1.** Average returns over different environment parameter perturbations for Mujoco tasks over 30 different seeded runs. We **bold** the best results (except Oracle). "-m": multi comp, "-s" single comp, "B-" Back.

|         | Halfcheetah          |                    | Walker2d   |                      | Hopper     |                    |
|---------|----------------------|--------------------|------------|----------------------|------------|--------------------|
|         | Front joint stiffness | B-actuator ctrlrange | Gravity   | Foot joint stiffness | Gravity   | Leg joint stiffness |
| Oracle  | 5332±287             | 4866±184           | 3150±481   | 2871±684             | 1316±373   | 1804±398           |
| RFQI    | 4016±1219            | 4264±557           | 3062±537   | 2056±672             | 1374±358   | 1769±361           |
| PQL     | 3644±1437            | 3508±828           | 2865±340   | 2710±506             | 920±151    | 1823±323           |
| H2O-m   | 2814±606             | 2974±350           | 1043±778   | 1208±770             | 235±3      | 794±334            |
| H2O-s   | 1710±1013            | 2431±854           | 701±585    | 733±655              | 466±47     | 1187±316           |
| HYDRO-m | 4456±872             | **4480±350**       | 3225±487   | 2652±703             | **1858±468** | **1933±468**     |
| HYDRO-s | **4781±476**         | 4399±382           | **3273±284** | **2790±623**       | 1551±309   | 1814±469           |

## 5.2 Ablation Study

***Naively Combining Source Data.*** To address the second question, we compare the performance of RFQI trained on target data only versus RFQI trained on combined target and source data (cross-domain data), as well as our proposed method. For the cross-domain data experiment, we simply merge target and source data without any further processing and use this combined dataset to train RFQI. Figure 3a demonstrates that simply incorporating additional source data does not enhance robustness and can also lead to poor performance compared to using only the limited target data (100K). We argue that the primary reason for this is the dynamics mismatch between the source and worst-case

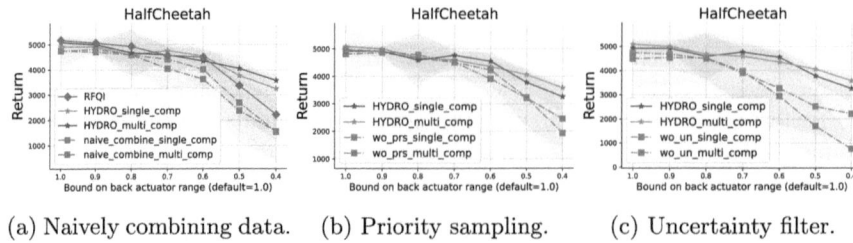

(a) Naively combining data.  (b) Priority sampling.  (c) Uncertainty filter.

**Fig. 3.** (a) Robust performance comparison between HYDRO, RFQI, and its variations using naive combination of source and target data. (b-c) Robust performance comparison between HYDRO and its variants without priority sampling and uncertainty filter.

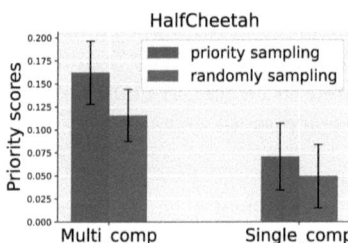

**Fig. 4.** Average priority scores of random and priority sampling.

model, which hinders the simple merging cross-domain data approach. On the other hand, our method handles this mismatch by selecting the *most* reliable source data with a small gap to tighten Ineq (9) and control the learn robust Q function as motivated by Theorem 2. The results highlight the effectiveness of our approach compared to both RFQI and the naive combination strategy.

To address the third question, we perform a comprehensive ablation study on HYDRO, analyzing the contribution of each component to its performance.

***Priority Sampling.*** To evaluate priority sampling's impact, we compare against a variant without this component. Figure 3b shows a significant decrease in robust performance when priority sampling is excluded. The enhanced performance stems from the increased utilization of source samples with greater proximity to the worst-case target model. Figure 4 confirms this hypothesis, demonstrating that priority sampling significantly increases the mean priority score of selected samples compared to random sampling. These results confirm that priority sampling plays a crucial role in enhancing the robustness of our method.

***Uncertainty Filter.*** To assess the impact of the uncertainty filter, we compare our method to a variant that excludes this component. Figure 3c reveals a significant decrease in robustness when the uncertainty filter is omitted, highlighting its crucial role in our approach. We hypothesize that the significant performance gains observed when incorporating the uncertainty filter arise from the strategic exclusion of source samples with high uncertainty levels, allowing the model to focus on more informative data points, leading to improved performance.

### 5.3 More Experiment Results

We conduct additional experiments to explore the potential of HYDRO. Please see Appendix 5 for more results.

***HYDRO with different domain-gaps measurement.*** To emphasize the distinction between HYDRO and *standard* cross-domain RL methods, we evaluate HYDRO's performance using an alternative domain-gaps measurement. We replace our measurement, which quantifies the discrepancy between worst-case target and source models, with standard cross-domain RL measurements quantifying the discrepancy between nominal target and source models using domain classifiers from DARC [7]. Results in Appendix 5.4 illustrate this substitution leads to significant performance degradation. These results underscore the inadequacy of standard domain-gap measurement in *robust* RL settings and highlight the critical role and effectiveness of HYDRO's tailored measurement approach.

***How HYDRO performs under harder limited target data settings?*** To further understand H2O's performance, we analyze HYDRO's behavior under increasingly challenging, data-limited target settings. The results in Appendix 5.5 show RFQI's robust performance decreases substantially as target data decreases, while HYDRO maintains consistently strong performance with only minimal degradation. These results demonstrate HYDRO's effectiveness in overcoming data scarcity challenges.

## 6 Conclusion

In this paper, we have addressed the problem of Hybrid cross-domain robust reinforcement learning, which is widely encountered in many real-world problems. To the best of our knowledge, this is the first work to tackle the hybrid setting of online source and offline target under Robust MDPs. We introduce HYDRO, a novel method that effectively leverages source domain data by selecting relevant and reliable data points with respect to the worst-case model in an uncertainty set, utilizing priority sampling and an uncertainty filter. We have demonstrated the superior performance of our method through extensive experiments. The limitation of our approach is its dependence on an estimated target transition model. Although we have demonstrated our method's effectiveness empirically, a theoretical analysis of how the estimated target model impacts the performance of the learned policy can be a promising direction for future research. Another promising research direction is extending HYDRO to fully online settings.

## References

1. Sünderhauf, et al.: The limits and potentials of deep learning for robotics. Int. J. Robot. Res. **37**(4–5), 405–420 (2018)
2. Niu, H., et al.: When to trust your simulator: dynamics-aware hybrid offline-and-online reinforcement learning. NeurIPS **35**, 36599–36612 (2022)
3. Niu, H., et al.: H2O+: An Improved Framework for Hybrid Offline-and-Online RL with Dynamics Gaps. arXiv preprint arXiv:2309.12716 (2023)
4. Liu, J., et al.: DARA: Dynamics-Aware Reward Augmentation in Offline Reinforcement Learning. In: ICLR (2022)
5. Liu, J., et al.: Beyond OOD state actions: supported cross-domain offline reinforcement learning. AAAI **38**, 13945–13953 (2024)
6. Wen, X., et al.: Contrastive Representation for Data Filtering in Cross-Domain Offline Reinforcement Learning. In: Forty-first ICML (2024)
7. Eysenbach, B., et al.: Off-Dynamics Reinforcement Learning: training for transfer with Domain Classifiers. In: ICLR (2021)
8. Pham Van Linh, L., et al.: Policy Learning for Off-Dynamics RL with Deficient Support. In: AAMAS, pp. 1093–1100 (2024)
9. Xu, K., et al.: Cross-domain policy adaptation via value-guided data filtering. NeurIPS **36** (2024)
10. Lyu, J., et al.: Cross-Domain policy adaptation by capturing representation mismatch. In: ICML (2024)
11. Peng, X.B., et al.: Sim-to-real transfer of robotic control with dynamics randomization. In: ICRA, pp. 3803–3810 (2018)
12. Tobin, J., et al.: Domain randomization for transferring deep neural networks from simulation to the real world. In: IROS, pp. 23–30 (2017)
13. Sadeghi, F., et al.: CAD2RL: Real Single-Image Flight Without a Single Real Image. Science and Systems XIII, Robotics (2017)
14. Werbos, P.J.: Neural networks for control and system identification. In: Proceedings of the 28th IEEE Conference on Decision and Control, pp. 260–265 (1989)
15. Zhu, S., et al.: Fast model identification via physics engines for data-efficient policy search. In: IJCAI, pp. 3249–3256 (2018)
16. Chebotar, Y., et al.: Closing the sim-to-real loop: adapting simulation randomization with real world experience. In: ICRA, pp. 8973–8979 (2019)
17. Finn, C., et al.: Model-agnostic meta-learning for fast adaptation of deep networks. In: ICML, pp. 1126–1135 (2017)
18. Nagabandi, A., et al.: Learning to Adapt in Dynamic, Real-World Environments through Meta-Reinforcement Learning. In: ICLR (2018)
19. Wu, Z., et al.: Zero-shot policy transfer with disentangled task representation of meta-reinforcement learning. In: ICRA, pp. 7169–7175 (2023)
20. Mnih, V., et al.: Human-level control through deep reinforcement learning. Nature **518**(7540), 529–533 (2015)
21. Schrittwieser, J., et al.: Mastering Atari, go, chess and shogi by planning with a learned model. Nature **588**(7839), 604–609 (2020)
22. Liu, Y., et al.: Provably good batch off-policy reinforcement learning without great exploration. NeurIPS **33**, 1264–1274 (2020)
23. Kumar, A., et al.: Conservative q-learning for offline reinforcement learning. NeurIPS **33**, 1179–1191 (2020)
24. Lyu, J., et al.: Mildly conservative q-learning for offline reinforcement learning. NeurIPS **35**, 1711–1724 (2022)

25. Levine, S., et al.: Offline reinforcement learning: tutorial, review, and perspectives on open problems, arXiv preprint arXiv:2005.01643 (2020)
26. Rigter, M., et al.: Rambo-RL: Robust adversarial model-based offline reinforcement learning. NeurIPS **35**, 16082–16097 (2022)
27. Iyengar, G.N.: Robust dynamic programming. Math. Oper. Res. **30**(2), 257–280 (2005)
28. Nilim, A., et al.: Robust control of Markov decision processes with uncertain transition matrices. Oper. Res. **53**(5), 780–798 (2005)
29. Xu, H., et al.: Distributionally robust Markov decision processes. NeurIPS **23** (2010)
30. Wang, Y., et al.: Policy gradient method for robust reinforcement learning. In: ICML, pp. 23484–23526 (2022)
31. Wang, Q., et al.: On the convergence of policy gradient in robust MDPS. arXiv preprint arXiv:2212.10439, vol. 5 (2022)
32. Yang, W., et al.: Toward theoretical understandings of robust Markov decision processes: Sample complexity and asymptotics. Ann. Stat. **50**(6), 3223–3248 (2022)
33. Xu, Z., et al.: Improved sample complexity bounds for distributionally robust reinforcement learning. In: AISTATS, pp. 9728–9754 (2023)
34. Wang, Y., et al.: Online robust reinforcement learning with model uncertainty. NeurIPS **34**, 7193–7206 (2021)
35. Dong, J., et al.: Online policy optimization for robust MDP. arXiv preprint arXiv:2209.13841 (2022)
36. Zhou, Z., et al.: Finite-sample regret bound for distributionally robust offline tabular reinforcement learning. In: AISTATS, pp. 3331–3339 (2021)
37. Panaganti, K., et al.: Robust reinforcement learning using offline data. NeurIPS **35**, 32211–32224 (2022)
38. Shi, L., et al.: Distributionally robust model-based offline reinforcement learning with near-optimal sample complexity. arXiv preprint arXiv:2208.05767 (2022)
39. Ma, X., et al.: Distributionally robust offline reinforcement learning with linear function approximation, arXiv preprint arXiv:2209.06620 (2022)
40. Blanchet, et al.: Double pessimism is provably efficient for distributionally robust offline reinforcement learning: generic algorithm and robust partial coverage. NeurIPS **36** (2024)
41. Bousmalis, K., et al.: Using simulation and domain adaptation to improve efficiency of deep robotic grasping. In: ICRA, pp. 4243–4250 (2018)
42. Higgins, I., et al.: Darla: improving zero-shot transfer in reinforcement learning. In: ICML, pp. 1480–1490 (2017)
43. Fu, J., et al.: D4RL: datasets for deep data-driven reinforcement learning. arXiv preprint arXiv:2004.07219 (2020)
44. Wu, F., et al.: OCEAN-MBRL: offline conservative exploration for model-based offline reinforcement learning. AAAI **38**, 15897–15905 (2024)
45. Kidambi, R., et al.: Morel: model-based offline reinforcement learning. NeurIPS **33**, 21810–21823 (2020)
46. Pinto, L., et al.: Robust adversarial reinforcement learning. In: ICML (2017)
47. Fei, Y., et al.: Exponential bellman equation and improved regret bounds for risk-sensitive reinforcement learning. NeurIPS **34**, 20436–20446 (2021)
48. Rigter, M., et al.: One risk to rule them all: a risk-sensitive perspective on model-based offline reinforcement learning. In: NeurIPS, vol. 36 (2024)
49. Zhang, X., et al.: Corruption-robust offline reinforcement learning. In: AISTATS (2022)

50. Ye, C., et al.: Corruption-robust offline reinforcement learning with general function approximation. NeurIPS (2024)
51. Niu, H., et al.: A comprehensive survey of cross-domain policy transfer for embodied agents. In: IJCAI (2024)
52. Daoudi, P., et al.: A conservative approach for few-shot transfer in off-dynamics reinforcement learning. In: IJCAI (2024)
53. Nguyen, M., et al.: Beyond the Known: decision making with counterfactual reasoning decision transformer. ArXiv Preprint ArXiv:2505.09114 (2025)

# Viability of Future Actions: Robust Safety in Reinforcement Learning via Entropy Regularization

Pierre-François Massiani[1], Alexander von Rohr[1,2(✉)], Lukas Haverbeck[1], and Sebastian Trimpe[1]

[1] Institute for Data Science in Mechanical Engineering, RWTH Aachen University, Aachen, Germany
{massiani,lukas.haverbeck,trimpe}@dsme.rwth-aachen.de
[2] Learning Systems and Robotics Lab, Technical University of Munich, Munich, Germany
alex.von.rohr@tum.de

**Abstract.** Despite the many recent advances in reinforcement learning (RL), the question of learning policies that robustly satisfy state constraints under unknown disturbances remains open. In this paper, we offer a new perspective on achieving robust safety by analyzing the interplay between two well-established techniques in model-free RL: entropy regularization, and constraints penalization. We reveal empirically that entropy regularization in constrained RL inherently biases learning toward maximizing the number of future viable actions, thereby promoting constraints satisfaction robust to action noise. Furthermore, we show that by relaxing strict safety constraints through penalties, the constrained RL problem can be approximated arbitrarily closely by an unconstrained one and thus solved using standard model-free RL. This reformulation preserves both safety and optimality while empirically improving resilience to disturbances. Our results indicate that the connection between entropy regularization and robustness is a promising avenue for further empirical and theoretical investigation, as it enables robust safety in RL through simple reward shaping.

## 1 Introduction

Safety is the ability of a policy to keep the system away from a failure set of undesirable states. Robustness extends the notion to adversarial or noisy settings; robust policies remain outside of the failure set in spite of the noise or adversary. While robust reinforced learning (RL) may be formulated as a constrained optimization

---

P.-F. Massiani and A. von Rohr—Equal contribution.

**Supplementary Information** The online version contains supplementary material available at https://doi.org/10.1007/978-3-032-06106-5_8.

problem [1], there is a strong appeal in achieving robustly safe policies through reward shaping alone, given the numerous algorithms available for unconstrained RL. The purpose of this work is to reveal how robustly safe policies arise naturally from two common practices in RL; namely, maximum-entropy RL [2] and failure penalization [3]. Our results support that the maximum-entropy RL objective together with failure penalties enable safe operation at testing under action noise stronger than that seen at training; a property we call *robustness*.

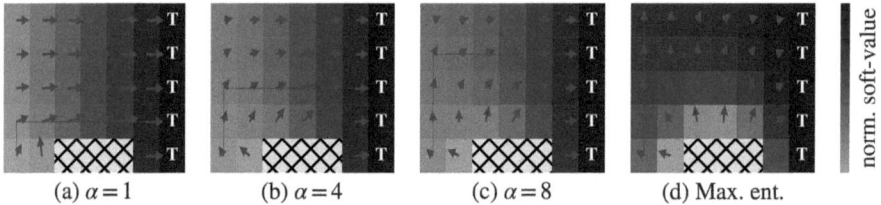

Fig. 1. **Fenced cliff—Robustness as a function of** $\alpha$: An entropy-regularized policy avoids states with fewer actions available (d). The degree is controlled by the temperature parameter $\alpha$. As it increases (a–c), the policy moves away from the constraints, getting more robust but taking longer to reach the target. The mode of the policy is shown as a thin blue line. (Color figure online)

Since "robustness" is a highly overloaded term in RL, we emphasize the notion of robustness in this paper differs from those of previous studies [4–6]. Indeed, they guarantee that entropy regularization preserves a high return under changes in the reward or dynamics. In other words, the *return* is robust to such changes. In contrast, we want that *safety constraints are still satisfied* under changes in the dynamics (namely, the level of action noise). These two types of objectives are complementary since safety and optimality are generally separate concerns in optimal control, where the goal is to act optimally while abiding by safety constraints. Similarly, the term "entropy-regularized RL" is used in the literature to refer to various formulations of regularized MDPs [7]. In this paper, we use it specifically to refer to methods that optimize the soft RL objective (3) as in [8], which are often referred to as maximum-entropy RL. From here on, we reserve the term "maximum-entropy" for the special case where the reward is identically zero and the agent solely maximizes entropy.

Our approach builds on two key contributions. First, we empirically show that entropy regularization in a *constrained* environment induces robustness to action noise. We do this by first showing that agents optimizing the entropy-regularized objective may sacrifice reward to avoid constraints boundaries, with the degree of avoidance modulated by the temperature parameter. This is illustrated in Fig. 1, where higher temperatures yield policies whose mode stays farther from constraints. Then, we provide empirical evidence that this constraints avoidance translates to robustness to action noise, i.e., policies preserving the long-term number of viable actions are generally more robust.

This general behavior aligns with the viability-based notion of robustness (called "safety" therein) introduced by [8,9] (cf. [10]), where the robustness of a state is quantified by the number of viable actions—those that allow indefinite constraint satisfaction. We interpret the cumulative discounted entropy of a policy as a proxy for the long-term number of safe actions it considers, and thus entropy regularization naturally encourages avoidance of states with few viable options.

Our second contribution shows that this constrained setting can be approximated arbitrarily well using failure penalties. For penalties above a finite threshold, the *mode* of the resulting policy matches that of the constrained problem, offering a practical reward-shaping strategy for learning robustly safe policies.

Making this observation relevant to state-of-the-art RL requires relating the unconstrained and state-constrained optimization problems, as most applications focus on the former [11]. This is the role of *constraints penalization* or, more concisely, of penalties. In the absence of entropy regularization, they are known to make constraints violations suboptimal, and large enough penalties guarantee that policies optimal for the penalized problem are also optimal for the constrained problem [3]. We add entropy regularization to this analysis. Furthermore, penalties above a *finite* threshold recover the mode of the constrained policy.

Our observations emphasize a benefit of entropy regularization that differs from what is commonly mentioned in the literature. Indeed, algorithms such as soft actor-critic (SAC) [2] are often praised for their excellent exploration and their robustness to the choice of hyperparameters [2]. Although crucial in practice, these strengths are relevant *during* learning. In contrast, we focus on the optimal policy, that is, on what occurs *after* successful learning.

*Contributions.* We reveal how robust optimal controllers arise from the combination of entropy regularization together with sufficient constraints penalties. Specifically:

1. We identify empirically that constraints repel trajectories of optimal controllers in the presence of entropy regularization, by favoring controllers maximizing the number of future viable actions.
2. We prove that failure penalties approximate this constrained problem arbitrarily closely.
3. Finally, we show that we can extract a safe policy from the optimal solution to the penalized problem and demonstrate that this policy is robustly safe.

The first contribution strongly supports that the mode of entropy-regularized policies is robust to action noise, as the most-likely trajectory is "repelled" by the constraints. We confirm robustness to action noise empirically, and further theoretical investigation is a promising avenue for future work. Together, our results enable achieving reward-shaping-based robustness, and a novel interpretation of the temperature coefficient in the presence of constraints as a tunable robustness parameter.

The article is organized as follows. We discuss other approaches to robustness in RL in Sect. 2. We then expose necessary preliminaries in Sect. 3, and formalize the problem we consider in Sect. 4. Section 5 contains our theoretical results, with first a high-level interpretation of the constrained, entropy-regularized problem, and our main theorem guaranteeing approximation with penalties. The empirical evidence on robustness follows in Sect. 6, together with further empirical validation of our theoretical results.

A complete version of this paper together with its appendix is available at this address: www.doi.org/10.48550/arXiv.2506.10871

## 2 Related Work

*Viability and safety in RL.* There is a variety of definitions of safety in RL [11]. We consider the case of avoiding state constraints with certainty (level 3 in [11]). Such a definition of safety falls into the general problem of viability [10]. Many specialized algorithms were developed to solve this safe RL problem, both model-free and model-based [12]. It has been shown in [3] that sufficient failure penalties enforce equivalence between the unconstrained and safety-constrained problems, making safe RL amenable to unconstrained algorithms. This idea falls in the class of *penalty methods*, a general idea in optimization which has been studied in the context of optimal control [13,14]; a reformulation of the results of [3] is that the discounted risk is an exact penalty function. Our results show that it is no longer the case for entropy-regularized RL, as no finite penalty exactly recovers the constrained problem. Yet, we show it can be approximated arbitrarily closely. Regardless, the above works only guarantee safety and neglect robustness. We extend the analysis and proof methods of [3] to entropy-regularized RL, which naturally yields robustness in addition to safety.

*Robustness in optimal control.* Robustness is a well-studied topic in optimal control [15] and consists of preserving viability despite *model uncertainties*. Classical approaches consist of robust model predictive control [16,17] and Hamilton-Jacobi reachability analysis [18]. They provide *worst-case* guarantees, mainly through constraints tightening. The robustness of entropy-regularized controllers does not fit directly in this category, as their full support makes them explore the whole viability kernel. Instead, they seem to exhibit a form of "expected" constraints tightening, which translates into robustness to action noise of the mode, as we illustrate empirically. Finally, alternative methods such as scenario optimization [19] address quantitative uncertainty instead of worst-case, but the connection to the robustness discussed in this article is still open.

*Robustness in RL.* Achieving robustness for RL policies is an active area of research [1]. A common formalization is that of a two-player game between the agent and an adversary [20,21]. This setup is akin to that of Hamilton-Jacobi reachability analysis, only with a discounted cost. These approaches achieve robustness through an adversary controlling, for instance, disturbances [21] or action noise [22], yielding worst-case robustness. However, such adversarially-robust RL requires specialized algorithms and training the adversary. In contrast, entropy-regularized RL is a popular framework with many standard implementations, which, as we show, also yields robustness solely through reward shaping.

The work of [9] introduces a state-dependent safety measure based on the number of viable actions available in each state. Our work extends this notion to robust safety of policies. A detailed discussion on the connection with the safety measure therein is in Appendix C.

We are not the first to report that entropy-regularization leads to robustness. Some empirical [4,5] and theoretical works [6] highlight the inherent robustness of entropy-regularized RL. As mentioned above, however, their definition of robustness differs: [6] consider robustness of the return to changes in the dynamics, whereas we are interested in preserving constraints satisfaction.

The observation that action noise during training can lead to more robust behavior was already made in [23, Example 6.6] on the famous cliff walking gridworld. There, $\varepsilon$-greedy action selection resulted in more robust behavior for the case of on-policy learning (SARSA), whereas Q-learning (an off-policy method) learns to the optimal, non-robust, policy. We take the same example in Fig. 1 and observe that entropy regularization leads to robust behavior in off-policy RL. Similarly, the G-learning algorithm exhibits the same robust behavior on the cliff environment [24]. Our results and interpretation provide a general explanation for this observation.

## 3 Preliminaries

We introduce concepts to frame the optimization problems and their constraints. In particular, we address entropy-regularized RL and viability.

### 3.1 Entropy-Regularized RL

We consider finite sets $\mathcal{X}$ and $\mathcal{A}$ called the state and action spaces, respectively, and deterministic dynamics $f : \mathcal{Q} \to \mathcal{X}$, where $\mathcal{Q} = \mathcal{X} \times \mathcal{A}$ is the state-action space. A policy $\pi : \mathcal{Q} \to [0, 1]$ is a map whose partial evaluation in any $x \in \mathcal{X}$ is a probability mass function on $\mathcal{A}$; we write $\pi(\cdot \mid x)$, and $\Pi$ is the set of all policies. The state at time $t \in \mathbb{N}$ from initial state $x \in \mathcal{X}$ and following $\pi \in \Pi$ is $X(t; x, \pi)$, and the action taken by $\pi$ at that time is $A(t; x, \pi)$. If the policy and initial state are unambiguous, we simply write $X_t$ and $A_t$.

We also consider $r : \mathcal{Q} \to \mathbb{R}$ a bounded reward function. The return of $\pi \in \Pi$ from initial state $x \in \mathcal{X}$ is then

$$G(x, \pi) = \sum_{t=0}^{\infty} \gamma^t r(X_t, A_t), \quad (1)$$

where $\gamma \in (0, 1)$ is the discount factor. A smaller $\gamma$ disregards delayed rewards, but can be overcome if the said rewards have large magnitude. The expected return is $\bar{G}(x, \pi) = \mathbb{E}[G(x, \pi)]$. With $\mathcal{H}$ as the entropy, we introduce the discounted cumulative entropy of $\pi \in \Pi$ from $x \in \mathcal{X}$ as

$$S(x, \pi) = \sum_{t=0}^{\infty} \gamma^t \mathcal{H}(\pi(\cdot \mid X_t)), \quad (2)$$

and its expectation $\bar{S}(x, \pi) = \mathbb{E}[S(x, \pi)]$. The objective of entropy-regularized RL is then to find an optimal policy, that is, a policy $\pi_{\text{opt}} \in \Pi$ such that

$$\pi_{\text{opt}} \in \arg\max_{\pi \in \Pi} \bar{G}(x, \pi) + \alpha \bar{S}(x, \pi), \quad \forall x \in \mathcal{X}, \tag{3}$$

where $\alpha \in \mathbb{R}_{\geq 0}$ is a design parameter called the *temperature*. It is known that there exists an optimal policy [2]. Specifically, one can be computed by leveraging the optimal soft-$Q$-value function $q : \mathcal{Q} \to \mathbb{R}$, which satisfies for all $(x, a) \in \mathcal{Q}$ [25]:

$$q(x, a) = r(x, a) + \gamma \alpha \ln \left[ \sum_{b \in \mathcal{A}} \exp\left( \frac{1}{\alpha} q(x', b) \right) \right], \tag{4}$$

where we defined the shorthand $x' = f(x, a)$. An equivalent definition is [25, Theorem 16]

$$q(x, a) = \max_{\pi \in \Pi} r(x, a) + \gamma \bar{G}(x', \pi) + \alpha \gamma \bar{S}(x', \pi). \tag{5}$$

Once $q$ is known, the softmax policy solves (3):

$$\pi_{\text{opt}}(a \mid x) = \text{softmax}\left[ \frac{1}{\alpha} q(x, \cdot) \right](a) \quad \forall (x, a) \in \mathcal{Q}. \tag{6}$$

Finally, for any policy $\pi \in \Pi$, its *mode* is the policy

$$\hat{\pi}(a \mid x) = \frac{1}{|\arg\max \pi(\cdot \mid x)|} \delta_{\arg\max \pi(\cdot \mid x)}(a), \tag{7}$$

where $|A|$ is the cardinality and $\delta_A(a)$ is the indicator function of a set $A \subset \mathcal{A}$.

### 3.2 Viability

We consider a set of failure states $\mathcal{X}_C \subset \mathcal{X}$ that the system should never visit. Avoiding $\mathcal{X}_C$ is a dynamic concern, and some states that are not in $\mathcal{X}_C$ themselves may still lead there inevitably. We address this through viability theory [10, Chapter 2].

**Definition 1 (Viability kernel).** *The viability kernel $\mathcal{X}_V$ is the set of states from where $\mathcal{X}_C$ can be avoided at all times almost surely:*

$$\mathcal{X}_V = \{ x \in \mathcal{X} \mid \exists \pi \in \Pi, \forall t \in \mathbb{N}_{>0}, \mathbb{P}[X_t \notin \mathcal{X}_C] = 1 \}.$$

By definition, any state that is not in the viability kernel leads to $\mathcal{X}_C$ in finite time. Such states are called *unviable*. The viability kernel is therefore the largest set that enables recursive feasibility of the problem of avoiding transitions into $\mathcal{X}_C$. A closely related concept is the *viable set*, which is the set of state-action pairs that preserve viability [8]:

$$\mathcal{Q}_V = \{ (x, a) \in \mathcal{Q} \mid x \in \mathcal{X}_V \wedge f(x, a) \in \mathcal{X}_V \}.$$

We also define the unviable set $\mathcal{Q}_U = \mathcal{Q} \setminus \mathcal{Q}_V$, and the critical set $\mathcal{Q}_{\text{crit}} = \mathcal{Q}_U \cap (\mathcal{X}_V \times \mathcal{A})$ [26].

**Definition 2.** Let $\pi \in \Pi$. We say that $\pi$ is safe from the state $x \in \mathcal{X}$ if $\mathbb{P}[X_t \notin \mathcal{X}_C] = 1$ for all $t \in \mathbb{N}_{>0}$. We say that $\pi$ is safe if it is safe from any $x \in \mathcal{X}_V$. For $\delta > 0$, we say that $\pi$ is $\delta$-safe if $\max_{\mathcal{Q}_{\mathrm{crit}}} \pi \leq \delta$. We denote the set of policies safe from the state $x$ by $\Pi_V(x)$ and that of safe policies by $\Pi_V = \bigcap_{x \in \mathcal{X}_V} \Pi_V(x)$.

By definition of the viability kernel, the condition for a safe policy can be replaced with $\mathbb{P}[X_t \in \mathcal{X}_V] = 1$ for all $t \in \mathbb{N}$.

*Remark 1.* Another meaningful definition of $\delta$-safety could be that the policy assigns at most $\delta$ of probability mass to unviable actions, that is, $\sum_{a \in \mathcal{Q}_{\mathrm{crit}}[x]} \pi(a \mid x) \leq \delta$ for all $x \in \mathcal{X}_V$, where $\mathcal{Q}_{\mathrm{crit}}[x]$ is the $\mathcal{X}$-slice of $\mathcal{Q}_{\mathrm{crit}}$ in $x$. This is equivalent to Definition 2 up to the choice of $\delta$, since a $\delta$-safe policy satisfies $\sum_{a \in \mathcal{Q}_{\mathrm{crit}}[x]} \pi(a \mid x) \leq \delta \cdot |\mathcal{Q}_{\mathrm{crit}}[x]|$.

In the next section, we consider an RL problem over the set of safe policies and dual relaxations thereof. To allow for general such relaxations, we introduce dynamic indicators.

**Definition 3 (Dynamic indicator).** Let $c : \mathcal{Q} \to \mathbb{R}_{\geq 0}$ and the associated discounted risk

$$\rho(x, \pi) = \sum_{t=0}^{\infty} \gamma^t c(X_t, A_t). \tag{8}$$

We say that $c$ is a dynamic indicator of $\mathcal{X}_C$ if, for all $x \in \mathcal{X}_V$, $\mathbb{E}[\rho(x, \pi)] > 0$ if, and only if, $\pi \notin \Pi_V(x)$.

The notion is independent of $\gamma \in (0, 1)$. A simple example is the composition of the indicator function of $\mathcal{X}_C$ with the dynamics; it is a dynamic indicator of $\mathcal{X}_C$ [3, Lemma 1]. While this one is always available, more elaborate dynamic indicators help penalize unviable states earlier in the Lagrangian relaxation and lower required penalties, eventually leading to better conditioning.

*Remark 2 (Recovering from constraints violation).* Our results hold in the two settings where visiting $\mathcal{X}_C$ terminates the episode or not. The second case is fully consistent with the setup of infinite time-horizon RL that precedes. Then, actions taken from $\mathcal{X}_C$ may map back into $\mathcal{X}_V$: trajectories leaving $\mathcal{X}_V$ may only return there *after* visiting $\mathcal{X}_C$. We even have $\mathcal{X}_C \cap \mathcal{X}_V \neq \emptyset$ in general, and the intersection is composed of states with actions that map in $\mathcal{X}_V \setminus \mathcal{X}_C$. The first case, however, is not naturally framed in infinite time-horizon. Indeed, while adding an absorbing state with null reward and dynamic indicator as in [3] effectively cuts the sums in $G(x, \pi)$ and $\rho(x, \pi)$, the sum in $S(x, \pi)$ cannot be handled similarly without additional notation. In the interest of conciseness and clarity, we thus only introduce formally the case of non-terminal $\mathcal{X}_C$. We emphasize that this is the more challenging case, as forbidding entropy collection after failure effectively further penalizes failure states.

## 4 Problem Formulation

We consider a standard constrained RL problem with dynamics $f$, constraint set $\mathcal{X}_C$, viability kernel $\mathcal{X}_V$, return $G$, and entropy regularization with temperature $\alpha > 0$, as defined in Sect. 3:

$$\max_{\pi \in \Pi_V} \bar{G}(x, \pi) + \alpha \bar{S}(x, \pi). \tag{9}$$

We investigate the following questions:

*Question 1.* In what sense can we interpret (9) as a robust control problem?

*Question 2.* Can we make (9) amenable to unconstrained algorithms?

We provide an empirical answer to Question 1 by identifying that the constraints repel trajectories of optimal controllers to an extent controlled by $\alpha$, using tools from viability theory. The higher $\alpha$, the stronger the repulsion. We then interpret this repulsion as a form of robustness to action noise, as the mode of the solution to (9) favors visiting states where adversarial action noise takes longer to bring the agent to states with constraints. We support this high-level interpretation with empirical demonstrations on toy examples and standard RL benchmarks. We then answer Question 2 through constraints penalties: we show that the solutions of (9) are approximated arbitrarily closely by solving a Lagrangian relaxation of the constraint $\pi \in \Pi_V$. Provided that one can solve the resulting unconstrained problem in practice (using for instance classical RL algorithms such as SAC), our results provide a model-free way to approximate robustly-safe controllers arbitrarily closely with a tunable degree of robustness, as well as a clear interpretation of the temperature and penalty parameters.

## 5 Theoretical Results

In this section, we explain on a high level why entropy regularization causes constraints to repel trajectories of optimal controllers and state our theoretical results on how to approximate (9) with a classical unconstrained problem. The proofs are in Appendix D.

### 5.1 Preserving Future Viable Options

*Explanation.* Our starting point to understand the claimed phenomenon is the observation that, for $x \in \mathcal{X}_V$, the maximum immediate entropy achievable by a *safe* controller is limited by the number of unsafe actions available in $x$. Specifically, it follows immediately from properties of $\mathcal{H}$ that

$$\forall \pi \in \Pi_V, \ \mathcal{H}(\pi(\cdot \mid x)) \leq \ln|\mathcal{Q}_V[x]|. \tag{10}$$

Since $\bar{S}$ is the (expected discounted) sum of the left-hand side of (10) along trajectories, it is meaningful that entropy-regularized, safe optimal controllers avoid states for which this upper bound is low, i.e., where $|Q_V[x]|$ is low. On the other hand, completely forbidding actions leading to such states is also harmful, since it "propagates" the constraints backwards along trajectories, enforcing a similar upper bound on the immediate entropy obtainable in those previous states as well. In other words, entropy-regularized controllers limit the probability of actions that eventually lead to states with a low bound in (10), without completely avoiding such actions to avoid loss of immediate entropy. The more steps it takes to reach states with many constraints, the less pronounced this effect of the constraints is. It follows from this reasoning that trajectories that go towards states with many constraints generally have lower probability than trajectories that go away from them.

This discussion supports on a high level that entropy regularization with constraints promotes constraints avoidance by preserving the long-term number of future viable options. Next, we identify this behavior as a form of robustness to action noise of the mode policy. Indeed, the mode policy tends to minimize the long-term proportion of actions unavailable because of constraints, and thus the probability that action noise selects such an action is also approximately minimized. We leave a precise formalization of this idea to future work, and support it with empirical evidence in Sect. 6.

*A metric of robustness.* This discussion highlights that, for any $\pi \in \Pi_V$ and $x \in \mathcal{X}_V$, the quantity $\bar{S}(x, \pi)$ captures the *long-term number of viable actions* that $\pi$ considers from $x$. A controller achieving a high $\bar{S}(x, \pi)$ successfully avoids highly-constrained states. This motivates taking the cumulative entropy as a quantitative measurement of robustness, which enables comparing the robustness of controllers.

**Definition 4.** *We say that $\pi_1 \in \Pi_V$ is less S-robust than $\pi_2 \in \Pi_V$, and write $\pi_1 \preceq \pi_2$, if*

$$\bar{S}(x, \pi_1) \leq \bar{S}(x, \pi_2), \quad \forall x \in \mathcal{X}_V. \tag{11}$$

*Behavior for increasing temperatures.* For $\alpha = 0$, (9) recovers the constrained, unregularized problem

$$\max_{\pi \in \Pi_V} \bar{G}(x, \pi). \tag{12}$$

We are then maximizing the return over viable policies with no concerns about robustness. As $\alpha$ increases, entropy is more and more prevalent in the objective of (9), whose solution converges to the maximum entropy policy $\pi^\star_{\text{ent}}$

$$\pi^\star_{\text{ent}} = \arg\max_{\pi \in \Pi_V} \bar{S}(x, \pi), \quad \forall x \in \mathcal{X}_V. \tag{13}$$

This is best seen through the soft-value function.

**Theorem 1.** *Consider the soft-Q-value functions $Q_{\text{ent}}$ and $Q_\alpha$ of (13) and (9), respectively and for all $\alpha \in \mathbb{R}_{\geq 0}$. Then, $\max_{Q_V} |\frac{1}{\alpha} Q_\alpha - Q_{\text{ent}}| \to 0$ as $\alpha \to \infty$.*

**Corollary 1.** *Denote by $\pi_{\text{ent}}^{\star}$ and $\pi_{\alpha}^{\star}$ the solutions of (13) and (9), respectively and for all $\alpha \in \mathbb{R}_{\geq 0}$. Then, the map $\alpha \mapsto \pi_{\alpha}^{\star}$ is monotonic for $\preceq$ and $\max_{\mathcal{Q}_V}|\pi_{\alpha}^{\star} - \pi_{\text{ent}}^{\star}| \to 0$ as $\alpha \to \infty$.*

Corollary 1 formalizes that the solution of (9) becomes more $S$-robust and approaches that of (13) as $\alpha$ increases. The mode of (9) thus gets robust to action noise by the preceding explanations and empirical evidence of Sect. 6.

### 5.2 Relaxing Safety Constraints with Penalties

A practical consequence of our observation is that solving (9) yields controllers that preserve a safe distance to the constraints with high probability. An important drawback, however, is that the problem involves the viable set $\mathcal{Q}_V$, which is unknown in model-free situations. We now leverage a Lagrangian relaxation of these viability constraints to make the problem amenable to model-free algorithms. The results in this section extend those of [3] to the case of an entropy-regularized objective.

In this section, we consider $c$ a dynamic indicator function of $\mathcal{X}_C$ and $\rho$ the associated discounted risk (Definition 3). We are interested in the following penalized problem

$$\pi_{\alpha,p}^{\star} = \arg\max_{\pi \in \Pi} \bar{G}(x, \pi) + \alpha \bar{S}(x, \pi) - p\rho(x, \pi), \tag{14}$$

where $p \in \mathbb{R}_{\geq 0}$ is a penalty parameter. It is known that in the case $\alpha = 0$, (14) and (9) share the same solutions if $p$ is large enough [3, Theorem 2]. Unfortunately, this result does not directly carry to the case $\alpha > 0$: from (6), $\pi_{\alpha,p}^{\star}(a \mid x) > 0$ for all $(x, a) \in \mathcal{Q}$, and thus in particular $\pi_{\alpha,p}^{\star} \notin \Pi_V$. However, scaling the penalty remains possible if one accepts to trade viability for $\delta$-safety.

**Theorem 2.** *For any $\delta > 0$, $\epsilon > 0$, and $\alpha > 0$, there exists $p^{\star} \in \mathbb{R}_{\geq 0}$ such that, for all $p > p^{\star}$, the optimal policy of (14) $\pi_{\alpha,p}^{\star}$ is $\delta$-safe and*

$$\max_{\mathcal{Q}_V}|\pi_{\alpha,p}^{\star} - \pi_{\alpha}^{\star}| < \epsilon. \tag{15}$$

*Proof (Sketch of proof).* The penalty enforces an upper-bound on the soft $Q$-value of state-actions in $\mathcal{Q}_{\text{crit}}$ (Lemma 2). Values there thus decrease arbitrarily low as the penalty increases, while it remains lower-bounded on $\mathcal{Q}_V$. This, in turn, shows $\delta$-safety of $\pi_{\alpha,p}^{\star}$ for $p$ large enough. Therefore, the value function of (14) approximates to that of (9) on $\mathcal{Q}_V$, and $\pi_{\alpha,p}^{\star}$ gets arbitrarily close to $\pi_{\alpha}^{\star}$.

### 5.3 Safe Policies from the Relaxed Problem

It follows from Theorem 2 that the solution $\pi_{\alpha,p}^{\star}$ to the penalized problem (14) is a $\delta$-safe policy and the *mode* of $\pi_{\alpha,p}^{\star}$ is safe if the penalty is sufficient.

**Corollary 2.** *Under the same notations as Theorem 2, there exists $\bar{\delta} \in (0, 1)$ such that, if $\delta \in (0, \bar{\delta})$, then the policy $\hat{\pi}_{\alpha,p}$ following the mode (7) of $\pi_{\alpha,p}^{\star}$ is safe.*

*Proof.* This directly follows from Theorem 2.

We empirically investigate the robustness of this policy in the next section.

*Conclusion on the questions.* Finally, we are able to answer Questions 1 and 2 based on the following arguments. Entropy regularization in the presence of constraints biases the learning problem towards policies that avoid constraints to preserve a high number of viable options, with the temperature coefficient monotonically controlling the degree of $S$-robustness. Furthermore, the viability constraints of (9) can be relaxed by a Lagrangian formulation at the price of trading viability for $\delta$-safety. Specifically, the solution of (14) approximates arbitrarily closely that of (9), provided that the penalty is sufficiently high. In particular, penalties above a finite threshold recover the mode of (9) exactly and the policy following that mode is therefore safe. Put together, these results provide a model-free way to approximate safe and robust controllers with tunable degrees of robustness.

## 6 Empirical Results

We provide in this section the empirical evidence that entropy regularization with constraints yields policies whose mode avoids constraints and is robustly safe under increased action noise, and that penalties enable approximating these constraints. We start with a discrete grid world, where we can solve the constrained problem numerically, to showcase how constraints repel trajectories in the presence of entropy regularization. Second, we introduce failure penalties to reveal how they recover the constraints. Finally, we illustrate the claimed robustness to increased action noise on MuJoCo benchmarks[1]. These experimental results confirm our interpretation of the two hyperparameters: penalties control the probability of failure, while the temperature controls the degree of robustness.

### 6.1 Cliff Walking

Our gridworld (Fig. 1) is an adaptation of the cliff environment [23, Example 6.6]. Three states in the middle of the bottom row represent the cliff; the failure set $\mathcal{X}_C$ the agent should robustly avoid. The right column represents the target of escaping the cliff. The failure and target states are invariant under all actions. Otherwise, the dynamics follow the direction of the chosen action, or map back into the current state if the agent hits a border. Actions outside of the cliff or target get a $-1$ reward.

**Interaction of Constraints and Entropy.** The constrained version of the environment—the fenced cliff—only offers three actions to an agent neighboring the cliff, imposing a lower upper-bound on the entropy in those states as per (10). This observation is key in understanding why entropy regularization avoids states with unviable actions, yielding robustness (Fig. 1.d).

---

[1] The code to reproduce results is available at www.github.com/Data-Science-in-Mechanical-Engineering/entropy_robustness.

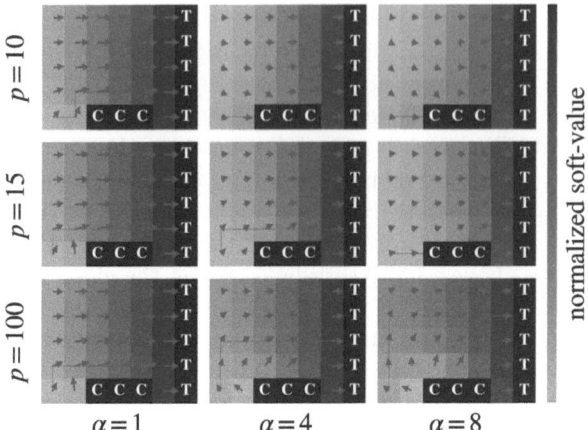

**Fig. 2. Unconstrained cliff—Safety and robustness as functions of $\alpha$ and $p$:** Safety and robustness can be achieved by penalizing ($p$) the constraints $\mathcal{X}_C$ and adjusting the temperature ($\alpha$).

Indeed, when maximizing entropy only (Fig. 1.d), the optimal policy favors transitioning away from states neighboring the constraints due to the aforementioned upper bound on immediate entropy. In turn, the immediate entropy of the policy in the 2-step neighbors is also reduced since some transitions are less desirable. The same logic applies recursively "outwards" from states with unviable actions, and the policy generally pushes trajectory away from the constraints; that is, towards the top corners. When initialized on the right, the policy aims at reaching the invariant target states where full entropy is available. When initialized on the left, the mode of the policy favors the top-left corner to avoid the low entropy of states close to the constraints, overcoming the long-term benefit of the target state. This trade-off between short- and long-term entropy depends on the discount factor $\gamma$.

In contrast, finite temperatures (Fig. 1.a–c) further encourage reaching the goal state to avoid the negative reward. The agent thus takes more risks to collect rewards while preserving some distance from the constraints. This trade-off between performance and robustness is controlled by the temperature parameter $\alpha$: high values favor entropy (and, thus, robustness by what precedes), whereas lower ones favor performance. While high robustness may be desirable, it comes at the price of suboptimality. Too high a temperature may entirely prevent task completion for the mode policy if the path thereto is inherently risky, leading to unsuccessful learning outcomes due to poor choice of hyperparameters.

**Interaction of Penalties and Entropy.** Sufficient penalties enable solving the constrained problem (Fig. 2), consistently with Theorem 2. The example shows the robustness–performance trade-off with different temperatures and penalties. Importantly, entropy and penalties are now competing, and any fixed penalty is eventually overcome by high temperatures, degrading safety (Fig. 3). The penalty thus needs to scale with the temperature to ensure $\delta$-safety with a low $\delta$.

The minimum sufficient value for the penalty depends not only on $\alpha$, but also on other hyperparameters such as the reward function, discount factor, and dynamic indicator. For instance, if the dynamic indicator is simply the indicator function of the constraints set, then the minimum penalty scales exponentially with the longest trajectory contained in $\mathcal{X} \setminus (\mathcal{X}_V \cup \mathcal{X}_C)$. Other choices of dynamic indicators may improve this dependency by incurring the penalty earlier in the trajectory, but choosing the penalty remains a problem-specific concern. While theory suggests picking it as high as possible, too high a penalty may introduce numerical instabilities when combined with value function approximators outside of tabular methods. We refer to [3] for an extended discussion.

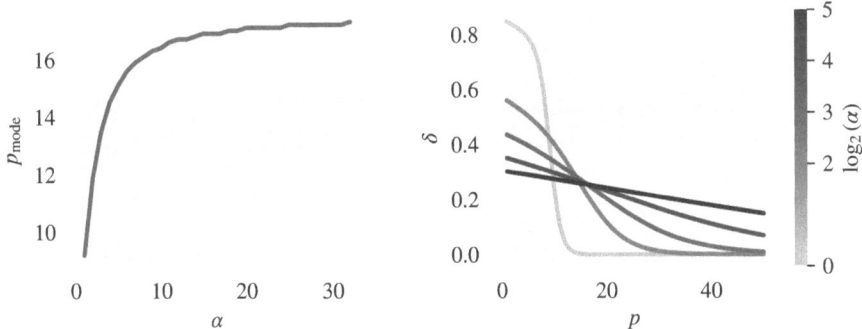

**Fig. 3. Effect of the temperature on the minimum safe penalty $p_{\text{mode}}$ (left) and $\delta$-safety (right) on the cliff:** *Left:* The minimum penalty such that the mode of the stochastic policy is safe. *Right:* The minimum $\delta$ such that the policy is $\delta$-safe as functions of $p$ and $\alpha$. Policies get safer as $p$ increases, but less safe as $\alpha$ does.

### 6.2 Reinforcement Learning Benchmarks

We now illustrate on standard RL benchmarks that this constraints avoidance translates into increased robustness to action noise. For this, we train entropy-regularized agents on two popular MuJoCo benchmarks, namely the Pendulum-v1 and the Hopper-v4 environment [27], with various temperatures. We then evaluate the mode of the learned policy under additional external action noise, whereas training is noise-free. The action noise is sampled from a uniform distribution $\mathcal{U}(-\epsilon, \epsilon)$. For each value of the temperature, we evaluate the frequency of successful constraints avoidance over 100 episodes. Further details on the setup are in Appendix B and additional results are in Appendix A.

Consistently with our theoretical results, we find that (i) entropy-regularization decreases the return by avoiding high-value states with many unviable actions; and (ii) the mode of entropy-regularized policies is more robust to disturbances as the training temperature increases.

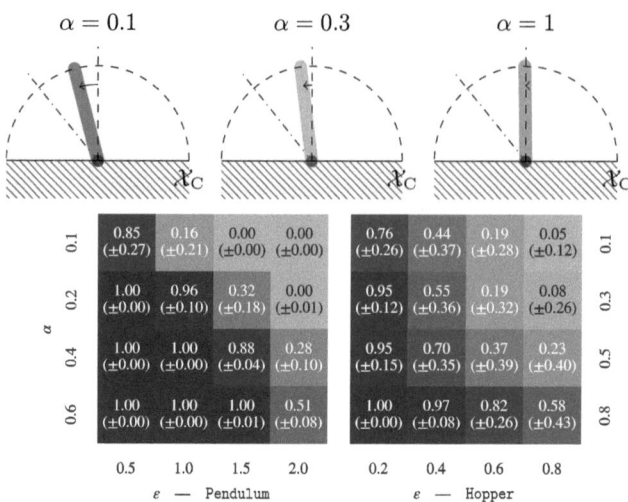

**Fig. 4. Learning robust policies with SAC** *Top:* With a target angle at 40° (dashed-dotted line) the agent learns to stabilize at different angles depending on the training temperature. For higher temperatures, the agent stabilizes the pendulum further away from the failure set $\mathcal{X}_C$. *Bottom:* Rate of successful failure avoidance on the disturbed Pendulum-v1 (left heat map) and Hopper-v4 (right heat map) environments. As the temperature increases the mode of the stochastic policy is robust to higher levels of action noise $\epsilon$.

**Pendulum.** We modify the Pendulum-v1 environment as follows to incorporate robustness concerns: (i) the initial state is the still, upright position; (ii) the constraints consist of angles with magnitude beyond 90° and the penalty is 90; and (iii) the reward is the squared angular difference to a target angle of 40°, which is outside of the viability kernel since the agent exerts bounded torque.

The results are shown in Fig. 4. All policies lean towards the target state but avoid leaving the viability kernel and reaching the constraints. The sufficient penalty emulates the boundary of the viability kernel, which reduces the effective number of available actions when leaning to one side. This pushes entropy-regularized policies away from the target state, and they learn to stabilize angles closer to 0 as $\alpha$ increases—the maximum entropy policy keeps the pendulum upright. The results show a robustness–performance trade-off between staying upright and leaning as far as possible towards the target, which is controlled by the temperature $\alpha$. Furthermore, the mode of the entropy-regularized policy can cope with significantly higher action disturbances when trained with higher temperatures.

**Hopper.** We repeat the same experiment as in the previous section for a modified Hopper-v4 environment [27]. We modify the environment by penalizing the "unhealthy" states with a penalty of $p = 500$. The results are shown in Fig. 4. Increasing the temperature improves the robustness to additional action noise. However, the learned gait is slower, hinting at a performance–robustness trade-off for this environment (see Appendix A.2). Interestingly, as the temperature is increased, the training finds two distinct robust behaviors: one is the intended hopping forward; the other is standing still and only collecting the healthy reward, which is arguably the most robust behaviour.

Our experiments inform hyperparameter settings for RL practitioners: while entropy regularization leads to robustly safe policies, high temperatures (or minimum entropy constraints [28]) can make parts of the state space unreachable, lead to conservative policies, and may even entirely prevent task completion as seen in the Hopper example.

## 7 Conclusion

We study the interaction between entropy regularization and state constraints in RL and reveal empirically that this favors policies that are constraints-avoiding and robust to increased action noise, as they preserve an expected long-term number of viable actions. We also show both in theory and in practice how to approximate the constraints with failure penalties. In particular, the mode of the policy—which is often what is deployed after training completion—is recovered exactly by penalties above a finite threshold.

The connection between entropy regularization with constraints and control-theoretic robustness is novel, to the best of our knowledge. This study identifies the phenomenon, its relevance for RL, and opens many interesting avenues for future work. A particularly promising one is the systematic study of the identified robustness. Indeed, we hypothesize that entropy regularization with constraints induces a kind of *soft constraints tightening*; that is, restricts the optimization domain to controllers that go away from the constraints with at least some given probability. Such a result would enable identifying "softly invariant sets": subsets of the viability kernel that are control invariant under a robustly safe controller (but not directly under entropy-regularized controllers, as they have full action support) and contain the entropy-regularized controller's trajectory with high probability. This would draw a clear theoretical bridge between entropy-regularized constrained RL and robust control through constraints tightening. An alternative would be identifying a noise model to which the modes of entropy-regularized, constrained policies are robust. More generally, it would be interesting to find other regularization terms that promote robustness and that are amenable to RL beyond the cumulative entropy, following ideas from [7]. Such regularizers could enable novel robustness properties with rigorous guarantees, and perhaps help training policies that are less sensitive to the sim-to-real gap.

In the meantime, we expect our findings to inform practitioners when applying RL algorithms such as SAC. While entropy regularization has mainly been developed as an exploration mechanism [2], it biases the policy to robustness to action noise if one uses constraints penalties. This understanding enables principled decisions when tuning the temperature and penalties, for instance by discouraging the common practice of annealing the temperature if robustness is a concern.

**Acknowledgments.** The authors thank Zeheng Gong for help with the empirical results. Simulations were performed with computing resources granted by RWTH Aachen University under project rwth1626. This work has been supported by the Robotics Institute Germany, funded by BMBF grant 16ME0997K.

**Disclosure of interests.** The authors have no competing interests to declare.

# References

1. Moos, J.: Robust reinforcement learning: a review of foundations and recent advances. Mach. Learn. Knowl. Extraction **4**(1), 276–315 (2022). https://doi.org/10.3390/make4010013
2. Haarnoja, T., Zhou, A., Abbeel, P., Levine, S.: Soft actor-critic: off-policy maximum entropy deep reinforcement learning with a stochastic actor. In: International conference on machine learning, pp. 1861–1870. PMLR (2018)
3. Massiani, P.F., Heim, S., Solowjow, F., Trimpe, S.: Safe Value Functions. IEEE Trans. Autom. Control (2023)
4. Haarnoja, T., et al.: Composable deep reinforcement learning for robotic manipulation. In: IEEE International Conference on Robotics and Automation, pp. 6244–6251 (2018). https://doi.org/10.1109/ICRA.2018.8460756
5. Haarnoja, T., et al.: Learning to walk via deep reinforcement learning. In: Proceedings of Robotics: Science and Systems (2019). https://doi.org/10.15607/RSS.2019.XV.011
6. Eysenbach, B., Levine, S.: Maximum entropy RL (provably) solves some robust RL problems. In: International Conference on Learning Representations (2022)
7. Geist, M., Scherrer, B., Pietquin, O.: A theory of regularized Markov decision processes. In: Proceedings of the 36th International Conference on Machine Learning, vol. 97, pp. 2160–2169 (2019)
8. Heim, S., Badri-Spröwitz, A.: Beyond basins of attraction: quantifying robustness of natural dynamics. IEEE Trans. Rob. **35**(4), 939–952 (2019)
9. Heim, S., Rohr, A., Trimpe, S., Badri-Spröwitz, A.: A Learnable Safety Measure. In: Conference on Robot Learning, pp. 627–639. PMLR (2020)
10. Aubin, J.P., Bayen, A.M., Saint-Pierre, P.: Viability theory: new directions. Springer Science and Business Media (2011)
11. Brunke, L.: Safe learning in robotics: from learning-based control to safe reinforcement learning. Ann. Rev. Control Robot. Auton. Syst. **5**, 411–444 (2022)
12. Achiam, J., Held, D., Tamar, A., Abbeel, P.: Constrained policy optimization. In: International conference on machine learning, pp. 22–31. PMLR (2017)
13. Kerrigan, E.C., Maciejowski, J.M.: Soft constraints and exact penalty functions in model predictive control. In: Control 2000 Conference, Cambridge, pp. 2319–2327 (2000)
14. Xing, A.Q., Wang, C.L.: Applications of the exterior penalty method in constrained optimal control problems. Optimal Control Appl. Methods **10**(4), 333–345 (1989)
15. Zhou, K., Doyle, J., Glover, K.: Robust and optimal control. Prentice Hall (1996)
16. Grüne, L., Pannek, J.: Nonlinear Model Predictive Control. Springer, 2nd edn. (2017)

17. Limon, D., et al.: Input-to-state stability: a unifying framework for robust model predictive control. Nonlinear Model Predictive Control: Towards New Challenging Applications, pp. 1–26 (2009)
18. Bansal, S., Chen, M., Herbert, S., Tomlin, C.J.: Hamilton-jacobi reachability: a brief overview and recent advances. In: Conference on Decision and Control, pp. 2242–2253 (2017)
19. Calafiore, G.C., Campi, M.C.: The scenario approach to robust control design. IEEE Trans. Autom. Control **51**(5), 742–753 (2006)
20. Morimoto, J., Doya, K.: Robust reinforcement learning. Neural Comput. **17**(2), 335–359 (2005). https://doi.org/10.1162/0899766053011528
21. Pinto, L., Davidson, J., Sukthankar, R., Gupta, A.: Robust adversarial reinforcement learning. In: Precup, D., Teh, Y.W. (eds.) Proceedings of the 34th International Conference on Machine Learning. Proceedings of Machine Learning Research, vol. 70, pp. 2817–2826 (2017)
22. Tessler, C., Efroni, Y., Mannor, S.: Action robust reinforcement learning and applications in continuous control. In: Chaudhuri, K., Salakhutdinov, R. (eds.) Proceedings of the 36th International Conference on Machine Learning. vol. 97, pp. 6215–6224 (2019)
23. Sutton, R.S., Barto, A.G.: Reinforcement learning: An introduction. MIT press (2018)
24. Fox, R., Pakman, A., Tishby, N.: Taming the noise in reinforcement learning via soft updates. In: 32nd Conference on Uncertainty in Artificial Intelligence, pp. 202–211 (2016)
25. Nachum, O., Norouzi, M., Xu, K., Schuurmans, D.: Bridging the gap between value and policy based reinforcement learning. Advances Neural Inf. Process. Syst. **30** (2017)
26. Massiani, P.F., Heim, S., Trimpe, S.: On exploration requirements for learning safety constraints. In: Learning for Dynamics and Control, pp. 905–916. PMLR (2021)
27. Towers, M., et al.: Gymnasium (2023). https://doi.org/10.5281/zenodo.8127026, https://zenodo.org/record/8127025
28. Haarnoja, T., et al.: Soft actor-critic algorithms and applications. arXiv preprint arXiv:1812.05905 (2018)
29. Huang, S., et al.: CleanRL: high-quality single-file implementations of deep reinforcement learning algorithms. J. Mach. Learn. Res. **23**(274), 1–18 (2022). http://jmlr.org/papers/v23/21-1342.html
30. Todorov, E., Erez, T., Tassa, Y.: Mujoco: a physics engine for model-based control. In: 2012 IEEE/RSJ international conference on intelligent robots and systems, pp. 5026–5033. IEEE (2012)

# Continual Visual Reinforcement Learning with A Life-Long World Model

Minting Pan, Wendong Zhang, Geng Chen, Xiangming Zhu, Siyu Gao, Yunbo Wang[✉], and Xiaokang Yang

MoE Key Lab of Artificial Intelligence, AI Institute,Shanghai Jiao Tong University,Shanghai, China
{panmt53,diergent,yunbow,xkyang}@sjtu.edu.cn

**Abstract.** Learning physical dynamics in a series of non-stationary environments is a challenging but essential task for model-based reinforcement learning (MBRL) with visual inputs. It requires the agent to consistently adapt to novel tasks without forgetting previous knowledge. In this paper, we present a new continual learning approach for visual dynamics modeling and explore its efficacy in visual control. The key assumption is that an ideal world model can provide a non-forgetting environment simulator, which enables the agent to optimize the policy in a multi-task learning manner based on the imagined trajectories from the world model. To this end, we first introduce the *life-long world model*, which learns task-specific latent dynamics using a mixture of Gaussians and incorporates generative experience replay to mitigate catastrophic forgetting. Then, we further address the value estimation challenge for previous tasks with the *exploratory-conservative behavior learning* approach. Our model remarkably outperforms the straightforward combinations of existing continual learning and visual RL algorithms on DeepMind Control Suite and Meta-World benchmarks with continual visual control tasks. Code available at https://github.com/WendongZh/continual_visual_control

## 1 Introduction

Recent advances in reinforcement learning (RL) have demonstrated remarkable success in mastering complex visual environments through world models [7,10,29]. However, these approaches typically assume a static task distribution and fixed environmental dynamics, which fundamentally break down in real-world scenarios where agents must adapt to continuously evolving conditions. In domains such as kitchen robotics, autonomous systems, or dynamic clinical environments, as shown in Fig. 1, agents are required to learn incrementally from non-stationary data streams while retaining and building upon prior knowledge–a capability central to continual learning.

A critical challenge in this setting is catastrophic forgetting, where neural networks overwrite previously acquired skills when trained on new tasks. This issue is exacerbated in visual RL, where agents must process pixel-based observations that encode both task-specific and task-agnostic features. Unlike the previous efforts to integrate standard solutions for catastrophic forgetting into model-free RL methods [30,37,38,43], it is impractical to retain a large data

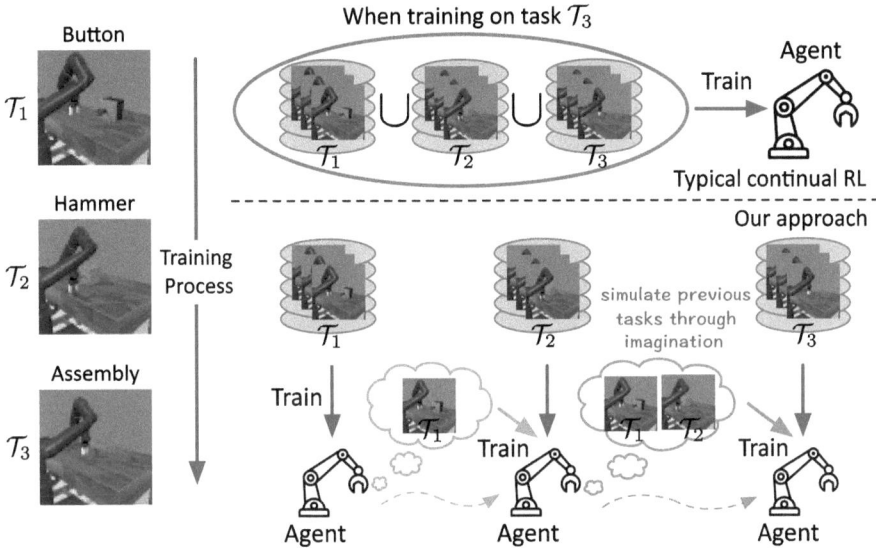

**Fig. 1. Left:** The problem setting of continual visual control. **Top Right:** Existing continual RL solutions typically retain large amounts of previous data in a replay buffer to train model-free RL models. **Bottom Right:** We employ model-based RL to alleviate catastrophic forgetting in continual visual control. The key insight is to simulate past tasks using a lifelong world model (LLWM).

buffer for each previous task. In this paper, we suggest that the key challenge is rooted in combating the distribution shift in dynamics modeling. The basic assumption of our approach is that *an ideal world model can be viewed as a natural remedy against catastrophic forgetting in continual RL scenarios, because it can replay the previous environments through "imagination", allowing multi-task policy optimization.*

To cope with the dynamics shift, we introduce a novel life-long world model (LLWM) architecture, which lies a dynamically expandable state representation space governed by task index in the lifelong learning. Specially, it learns a mixture of Gaussian priors to capture task-specific latent dynamics based on a set of categorical task variables. Building upon LLWM, we formulate an experience replay mechanism to synthesize fictitious trajectories of previous tasks, avoiding huge raw pixel observation storage. To achieve that, we need to train an additional generative model to reproduce the initial video frames in previous tasks and then feed them into the learned LLWM to generate subsequent image sequences for data rehearsal. The training process alternates between (i) *generating rehearsal data with the frozen world model learned on previous tasks* and (ii) *training the entire model with both rehearsal data and current real data.*

However, a straightforward use of the experience replay mechanism is less effective. In world model learning, the mechanism's replay of previous task trajectories suffers from excessive homogeneity, inducing an overfitting issue in the reward prediction that may overestimate or underestimate the true reward. Moreover, as shown in Fig. 2, the value network increasingly overestimates the true value functions of previous tasks during behavior learning as the number of sequential tasks grows. This issue is fundamentally rooted in the constrained diversity of replayed data. To solve these issues, we propose the *exploratory-conservative behavior learning* approach, which improves the aforementioned solution in two aspects. First, in representation learning, we use the $\epsilon$-greedy exploration and introduce an action-shuffling technique to augment the replayed observation-action-reward trajectories, thereby preventing the reward predictor of the world model from overfitting the narrow distribution of replayed data. Second, to alleviate value overestimation in behavior learning, we use the value network learned in the previous task to constrain the target of value estimation on replayed data. This learning strategy balances the exploration and constraints of value functions in historical tasks, *i.e.*, it encourages the agent to learn a conservative policy over a broader distribution of observation-action-reward pairs.

We evaluate our approach on DeepMind Control [36] and Meta-World [41] environments. For the DeepMind Control, we construct sequential tasks with different robotic physical or environmental properties. For the Meta-World, we collect various tasks with distinct control policies and spatiotemporal data patterns. Experiments on these two benchmarks show that our approach remarkably outperforms the naïve combinations of existing continual learning algorithms and visual MBRL models.

In summary, the main technical contributions of this paper are as follows:

- We present a novel architecture of *life-long world model* within the MBRL framework, which learns task-specific Gaussian priors and performs generative replay to mitigate catastrophic forgetting.
- We propose the *exploratory-conservative behavior learning method* to mitigate reward overfitting and value overestimation issues in continual RL.

## 2 Related Work

**Continual RL.** Continual RL has become a hot topic in recent years [9,18,30,37]. To overcome catastrophic forgetting, a straightforward way is to explicitly retain pre-learned knowledge, which includes storage-based approaches that directly save task-dependent parameters [1] or priors [26,34,40], distillation based approaches [16,22,42] that leverages knowledge distillation [15] to recall previous knowledge, and the rehearsal based approaches that simply save trajectories [5,25] or compact representations [32] for re-training. Besides, previous approaches [38,43] mainly consider Markov decision processes (MDP) with compact state space, which leaves the control tasks with high-dimensional visual inputs unexplored. Inspired by the success of continual visual forecasting [4], our work proposes a new generative framework to tackle the forgetting issues in continual visual control tasks. Instead of storing extensive trajectories, our method preserves only a single set of model parameters and leverages the world model with an experience replay mechanism to retain past knowledge, ensuring a more efficient and effective approach. Besides knowledge retention, there are also approaches using shared structures to learn non-forgetting RL agents [27,28].

**RL for visual control.** In visual control tasks, agents can only access high-dimensional observations. Previous approaches can be roughly summarized into two categories, that is, model-free approaches [20,23,39] and model-based approaches [11,14,33]. Compared with MFRL approaches, the MBRL approaches explicitly learn the dynamic transitions and generally obtain higher sample efficiency. Ha and Schmidhuber proposed the World Model [7] with a two-stage training procedure that first learns latent transitions of the environment with self-supervision and then performs behavior learning on the states generated by the world model. PlaNet [11] introduces the *recurrent state-space model* (RSSM) to optimize the policy over its recurrent states. The same architecture is also adopted by DreamerV1-V3 [10,12,13], where behavior learning is conducted on the latent imagination of RSSM. Recently, several studies [2,3,24,29,35], such as Iso-Dream [29] and TWISTER [3], further have explored different ways to produce more robust dynamics representations for MBRL. In this paper, we make three improvements to adapt MBRL to continual visual control, *i.e.*, the world model architecture, the world model learning scheme, and behavior learning.

## 3 Approach

Given a stream of tasks $\{\mathcal{T}_1, \ldots, \mathcal{T}_K\}$, we formulate continual visual control as a partially observable Markov decision process (POMDP) in sequential domains. At a particular task $\mathcal{T}_k$ where $k$ represents the task index, the POMDP contains high-dimensional visual observations and scalar rewards $(o_t^k, r_t^k) \sim p(o_t^k, r_t^k | o_{<t}^k, a_{<t}^k)$ that are provided by the environment, and continuous actions $a_t^k \sim p(a_t^k | o_{\leq t}^k, a_{<t}^k)$ that are drawn from the action model. The goal is to maximize the expected total payoff on all tasks $\mathbb{E}_\pi(\sum_k \sum_t r_t^k)$.

Compared to previous RL approaches, we aim to build an agent that can learn the state transitions in different tasks, such that

$$\hat{o}_t, \hat{z}_t, \hat{r}_t \sim \mathcal{M}(o_{t-1}, a_{t-1}, k), \quad a_t \sim \pi(\hat{z}_t, k), \tag{1}$$

where $\mathcal{M}$ and $\pi$ are respectively the world model and the action model, and $\hat{o}_t$, $\hat{z}_t$ and $\hat{r}_t$ are respectively the generated next observation, the extracted latent state, and the predicted reward.

In this section, we present the details of our approach, which mainly consist of two parts: *life-long world model* and *exploratory-conservative behavior learning*. In Sect. 3.1, we first discuss the overall pipeline of our method and its basic motivations. In Sect. 3.2 to Sect. 3.3, we respectively introduce the technical details of the two components.

## 3.1 Overall Pipeline

Our overall pipeline is built upon DreamerV2 method [12], which involves two iterative stages: (i) world model learning of latent state transitions and reward predictions and (ii) behavior learning via latent imagination. To adapt DreamerV2 to the continual RL setup, we make improvements in three aspects: the world model architecture, the world model learning scheme, and behavior learning. As shown in Fig. 1, we first initialize the agent, including the life-long world model $\mathcal{M}$, the actor $\pi$, the critic $v$, and an image generator $\mathcal{G}$. Since the agent is not allowed to access real data of previous tasks, we will retain a copy of the current models after finishing the training process of a particular task, termed as $\mathcal{M}'$, $\pi'$, $v'$, and $\mathcal{G}'$. These frozen models generate replay trajectories for previous tasks through imagined rollouts using images synthesized by $\mathcal{G}'$. In other words, we train the models on sequential tasks but continually update one copy of them to involve increasingly more previous knowledge for rehearsal. This pipeline is at the heart of our approach. For the control tasks, ideally reproducing prior knowledge as latent imagination is a cornerstone for alleviating the forgetting issues in behavior learning. Besides, the requirement of ideally reproducing prior knowledge also guides the detailed world model design.

## 3.2 Life-Long World Model

The proposed *life-long world model* (LLWM) incorporates Gaussian mixture representations. We improve the world model $\mathcal{M}$ in DreamerV2 [12] from the perspective of multimodal spatiotemporal modeling, which serves as the cornerstone to overcome catastrophic forgetting in continual visual control.

As discussed in Sect. 1, the key challenge for the world model lies in how to be aware of the distribution shift. To address this challenge, we exploit mixture-of-Gaussian variables to capture the multimodal distribution of both visual dynamics in the latent space and spatial appearance in the input/output observation space. Accordingly, the world model can be written as:

$$
\begin{aligned}
\text{Representation module:} \quad & z_t \sim q_\phi(o_t^k, z_{t-1}, a_{t-1}^k, k) \\
\text{Transition module:} \quad & \hat{z}_t \sim p_\psi(z_{t-1}, a_{t-1}^k, k) \\
\text{Observation module:} \quad & \hat{o}_t = p_{\theta_1}(z_t, k) \\
\text{Reward module:} \quad & \hat{r}_t = p_{\theta_2}(z_t, k).
\end{aligned}
\tag{2}
$$

The representation module aims to encode observations and actions to infer the latent state $z_t$. It also takes the categorical task variable $k \in \{1, \ldots, K\}$ as an extra input to handle the covariate shift in input space. The transition module is also aware of the categorical task variable and tries to predict latent state $\hat{z}_t$ to approximate the posterior state $z_t$. These modules are jointly optimized with the Kullback-Leibler divergence to learn the posterior and prior distributions of $z_t$. The observation and reward modules take as inputs $z_t$ along with the task variable $k$ to reconstruct images and predict corresponding rewards.

In this model, the task-specific latent variables $z_t$ and $\hat{z}_t$ have the form of Gaussian mixture distributions conditioned on $k$, which shares a similar motivation with the Gaussian mixture priors proposed in existing unsupervised learning methods [6,17,31]. Compared with these methods, LLWM leverages multimodal priors to model spatiotemporal dynamics more effectively. For task $\mathcal{T}_k$, the objective function of the world model combines the reconstruction loss of the input frames, the prediction loss of the rewards, and the KL divergence:

$$\mathcal{L}_\mathcal{M} = \mathbb{E}\big[\sum_{t=1}^{H} - \log p(\hat{o}_t \mid z_t, k) - \log p(\hat{r}_t \mid z_t, k) \\ - \alpha D_{KL}(q(z_t \mid o_t^k, z_{t-1}, a_{t-1}^k, k) \,\|\, p(\hat{z}_t \mid z_{t-1}, a_{t-1}^k, k)\big], \quad (3)$$

where $\alpha$ equals to 1.0, and $(o_t^k, a_t^k, r_t^k)_{t=1}^H$ represents a training trajectory sampled from the data buffer for the current task or produced by the following experience replay mechanism for the historical tasks.

**Generative experience replay.** We train LLWM under a generative experience replay scheme, which additionally employs an image generator to produce the initial frames in the replayed trajectories of previous tasks. To overcome the covariant shift of the image appearance in time-varying environments, the image generator also uses Gaussian mixture distributions to form the latent priors, denoted by $e$. Specifically, after training on the previous task, we first retain a copy of the image generator $\mathcal{G}$, the world model $\mathcal{M}$, and the action model $\pi$. These copies are respectively denoted as $\mathcal{G}'$, $\mathcal{M}'$, and $\pi'$. Then, for each previous task $\mathcal{T}_{\tilde{k}<k}$, we use $\mathcal{G}'$ to generate the initial frames of the rehearsal trajectories. Along with a zero-initialized action $a_0$, we iteratively perform $\mathcal{M}'$ and $\pi'$ to generate future sequences:

$$\hat{o}_0^{\tilde{k}} \leftarrow \mathcal{G}'(\tilde{k}), \quad \hat{o}_t^{\tilde{k}}, \hat{z}_t, \hat{r}_t^{\tilde{k}} \leftarrow \mathcal{M}'(\hat{o}_{t-1}^{\tilde{k}}, \hat{a}_{t-1}^{\tilde{k}}, \tilde{k}), \quad \hat{a}_t^{\tilde{k}} \leftarrow \pi'(\hat{z}_t, \tilde{k}). \quad (4)$$

Finally, the replay trajectories $(\hat{o}_t^{\tilde{k}}, \hat{a}_t^{\tilde{k}}, \hat{r}_t^{\tilde{k}})_{t=1}^H$ and the real trajectories at the current task $\mathcal{T}_k$ are mixed to train the generator and the agent in turn, and $\mathcal{G}'$, $\mathcal{M}'$, and $\pi'$ will be frozen and continually updated until the task stream ends. Since the world model is also involved in the replay process and plays a key role, the proposed experience replay mechanism is significantly different from all previous generative replay methods. During task $\mathcal{T}_k$, the world model $\mathcal{M}$ is trained by minimizing

$$\mathcal{L}_\mathcal{M} = \sum_{\tilde{k}=1}^{k-1} \mathcal{L}_\mathcal{M}^{\tilde{k}}(\hat{o}_{1:H}^{\tilde{k}}, \hat{a}_{1:H}^{\tilde{k}}, \hat{r}_{1:H}^{\tilde{k}}) + \mathcal{L}_\mathcal{M}^k(o_{1:H}^k, a_{1:H}^k, r_{1:H}). \quad (5)$$

The objective function of the image generator $\mathcal{G}$ can be written as

$$\mathcal{L}_\mathcal{G} = \mathbb{E}_{q(e \mid o_1^k, k)} \log p(o_1^k \mid e, k) - \beta D_{KL}(q(e \mid o_1^k, k) \,\|\, p(\hat{e} \mid k)) \\ + \sum_{\tilde{k}=1}^{k-1} \big[\mathbb{E}_{q(e \mid \hat{o}_1^{\tilde{k}}, \tilde{k})} \log p(\hat{o}_1^{\tilde{k}} \mid e, \tilde{k}) - \beta D_{KL}(q(e \mid \hat{o}_1^{\tilde{k}}, \tilde{k}) \,\|\, p(\hat{e} \mid \tilde{k}))\big], \quad (6)$$

where we use the $\ell_2$ loss for reconstruction and set $\beta$ equals to $10^{-4}$ through an empirical grid search.

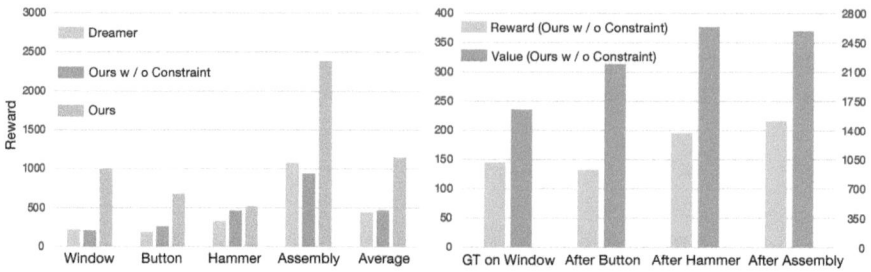

**Fig. 2.** Motivating examples. **Left:** Effect of the proposed behavior learning method. We evaluate the model obtained after the last training task (*i.e.*, *Assembly* on Meta-World) on each of the tasks represented on the X-axis. The task order is *Window-open* → *Button-press* → *Hammer* → *Assembly*. "Constraint" represents the exploratory-conservative behavior learning. **Right:** Reward predictions and value estimations in the naïve solution. We use 100 batches of trajectories of *Window-open* to evaluate models trained after each subsequent task. We use the model trained on *Window-open* to calculate the "ground truth" of the state values. The X-axis represents different models that just finished training on corresponding tasks. The left and right Y-axes represent reward and value, respectively.

### 3.3 Exploratory-Conservative Behavior Learning

**Preliminary findings and motivations.** The life-long world model serves as a naïve solution to handle continual visual control tasks. However, as shown in Fig 2(left), on the Meta-World benchmark, we can observe that this naïve solution (indicated by the blue bars) can not mitigate the forgetting issue and may even degenerate the control performance on some tasks compared with Dreamer, such as the task *Window-open*. We find that the performance degeneration is rooted in two closely related overfitting problems that happen respectively in world model learning and behavior learning. Both of them lead to the erroneous estimation of the value functions for previous tasks. As shown in Fig. 2(right), we use the same trajectory batches from the very first task (*i.e.*, *Window-open*) to evaluate the outputs of the reward predictor and those of the value network after training these models on each subsequent task. These issues form a vicious cycle: biased reward predictions amplify value estimation errors, while overestimated values further distort policy optimization. It motivates our dual focus on enhancing the robustness of the reward model in the world model and constraining value extrapolation for stable continual learning.

**Solutions.** To tackle these problems, we propose the exploratory-conservative behavior learning method (see Alg. 1), which simultaneously enhances the world model's reward prediction capability and stabilizes value estimation in actor-critic optimization. First, we introduce specific data augmentation for the reward predictor during experience replay. The key insight lies in that we want the world model to experience more diverse observation-action pairs to keep it from overfitting the limited rehearsal data and thus underperforming for out-of-distribution samples. On one hand, we exploit the $\epsilon$-greedy strategy to improve action exploration to generate trajectories of previous tasks $(\hat{o}_t^k, \hat{a}_t^k, \hat{r}_t^k)_{t=1}^H$. On the other hand, we randomly shuffle the generated actions and reuse the learned world model at the previous task $\mathcal{M}'$ to predict new rewards, which results in a new trajectory $(\hat{o}_t^k, \tilde{a}_t^k, \tilde{r}_t^k)_{t=1}^H$. Notably, these augmented trajectories are only used to train the reward predictor. They break the temporal biases in the distribution of rehearsal data and prevent the reward prediction from overfitting issues. Assuming $\tilde{z}_t$ represents the latent state extracted from the augmented data, the objective function of the world model in Eq. (3) can be rewritten as:

$$\mathcal{L}_\mathcal{M} = \mathbb{E}\Big[\sum_{t=1}^H -\log p(\hat{o}_t \mid z_t, k) - \log p(\hat{r}_t \mid z_t, k) \\ - \delta \log p(\tilde{r}_t \mid \mathbf{sg}(\tilde{z}_t), k) - \alpha D_{KL}(q(z_t \mid o_t^k, \cdot) \,\|\, p(\hat{z}_t \mid \cdot))\Big], \quad (7)$$

where $\mathbf{sg}$ is the stop-gradient operation and $\delta$ equals to 0.5 in all experiments.

Second, we constrain the target of the value model when performing behavior learning on the replayed data, which is inspired by *conservative Q-learning* (CQL) [21]. Given the world model that captures the latent dynamics, the behavior learning stage is performed on the task-specific latent imagination. We use $t'$ to denote the time index of the imagined states. Starting at the posterior latent state $z_t$ inferred from the visual observation, we exploit the transition module, the reward predictor, and the action model to predict the following states and corresponding rewards in imagination, which are all guided by the explicit task label $k$. Then, the action model and the value model will be optimized on the imagined trajectories:

$$\text{Action model:} \quad a_t^k \sim \pi(z_t, k) \\ \text{Value model:} \quad v(z_{t'}, k) \approx \mathbb{E}_{\pi(\cdot \mid z_{t'}, k)} \sum_{t'=t}^{t+L} \gamma^{t'-t} r_{t'}, \quad (8)$$

where $L$ is the imagination time horizon and $\gamma$ is the reward discount. The action model is optimized to maximize the value estimation, while the value model is optimized to approximate the expected imagined rewards. The training target for the value model on real data is:

$$V_t = r_t + \lambda_t \begin{cases} (1-\lambda)v(z_{t+1}) + \lambda V_{t+1} & \text{if } t < L, \\ v(z_L) & \text{if } t = L, \end{cases} \quad (9)$$

where $\lambda$ equals to 0.95. We adopt the objective functions from DreamerV2 [12] to train these models. However, when learning on the replayed data, this objective

---
**Algorithm 1:** Exploratory-conservative behavior learning
---
1 **Input:** Task stream $\mathcal{T}_1, \ldots, \mathcal{T}_K$
2 **Output:** World model $\mathcal{M}$, generator $\mathcal{G}$, and actor $\pi$
3 Initial buffer $\mathcal{B}_1$ at $\mathcal{T}_1$ with random episodes
4 **while** *not converged* **do**
5     Train $\mathcal{G}$ at $\mathcal{T}_1$ according to Eq. (6) with $k=1$
6     Perform dynamics learning at $\mathcal{T}_1$ according to Eq. (3)
7     Perform behavior learning at $\mathcal{T}_1$ according to Eq. (9)
8     Add interaction experience to buffer $\mathcal{B}_1$
9 **end**
10 **for** $k = 2, \ldots, K$ **do**
11     Initial buffer $\mathcal{B}_k$ at $\mathcal{T}_k$ with random episodes
12     Retain a copy of previous model as $\mathcal{M}'$, $\mathcal{G}'$, $\pi'$, and $v'$
13     Generate replayed trajectory $\tau_1$ and augmented data $\tau_2$
14     // Mix replayed data at $\mathcal{T}_{1:k-1}$ and real data at $\mathcal{T}_k$
15     $\mathcal{B}'_k \leftarrow \tau_1 \cup \mathcal{B}_k$
16     **while** *not converged* **do**
17         Train $\mathcal{G}$ on $\mathcal{B}'_k$ according to Eq. (6)
18         Perform dynamics learning on $\mathcal{B}'_k$ with Eq. (3)
19         Perform behavior learning on $\mathcal{B}_k$ with Eq. (9)
20         // Use reward augmentation
21         Train reward module on $\tau_2$ with Eq. (7)
22         // Use conservative value target
23         Perform behavior learning on $\tau_1$ with Eq. (10)
24         Append interaction experience to $\mathcal{B}_k$
25     **end**
26 **end**
---

may result in the overestimation problem as shown in Fig. 2. Therefore, we reuse the learned value model to update the target when training on replayed data. Given a replayed trajectory $(\hat{o}_t^k, \hat{a}_t^k, \hat{r}_t^k)_{t=1}^H$, we first calculate the training target $V_t$ according to Eq. (9). We then retain a copy of the value model $v'$ that was learned on the previous task and use the same trajectory as above to produce another conservative target $\widetilde{V}_t$ with the same function. We use $\widetilde{V}_t$ to constrain the current value model to tackle the value overestimation problem for previous tasks. The final target for training the value model on the rehearsal data is

$$V'_t = \begin{cases} V_t & if \quad V_t < \widetilde{V}_t, \\ \widetilde{V}_t & if \quad V_t \geq \widetilde{V}_t. \end{cases} \quad (10)$$

Alg. 1 gives the full training procedure of the exploratory-conservative behavior learning. With the above two improvements, it successfully extends MBRL algorithms to sequential visual control tasks.

**Fig. 3.** Showcases of the sequential visual control tasks.

## 4 Experiments

### 4.1 Implementations

**Benchmarks.** We exploit two RL platforms with rich visual observations to perform the quantitative and qualitative evaluation for continual control tasks:

- **Continual DeepMind Control Suite** [36]. The DeepMind Control Suite (DMC) is a popular RL environment that contains various manually designed control tasks with an articulated-body simulation. We use the *Walker* as the base agent and construct a task stream including four different tasks, *i.e.*, *Walk* → *Uphill* → *Downhill* → *Nofoot*. *Nofoot* represents the task in which we cannot control the right foot of the robot.
- **Continual Meta-world** [41]. The Meta-World environment contains 50 distinct robotic manipulation tasks with the same embodied agent. We select four tasks to form a task stream for evaluation: *Window-open* → *Button-press* → *Hammer* → *Assembly*.

We provide some showcases in Fig. 3. We assume that the task label in the test phase is provided for all experiments. We use the same task order for comparisons between different methods, and without loss of generality, our approach is practical to different task orders (see Sect. 4.4).

**Compared methods.** We compare our method with the following baselines:

- **DreamerV2 (DV2)** [12]: It is an MBRL method that learns the policy directly from latent states in the world model.
- **CURL** [23]: It is a model-free RL framework that exploits unsupervised representation learning to help high-level feature extraction from visual inputs. We use the version that uses SAC [8] for policy optimization.
- **RL with EWC** [19]: It is a mainstream parameter-constrained continual learning method. We apply it to both DreamerV2 and CURL.

**Training details.** In all environments, the input image size is set to 64 × 64, the batch size is 50, and the imagination horizon is 50. For each task in Meta-World, we train our method for 200K iterations with action repeat equal to 1, which results in 200K environment steps. For each task in DMC, we train our method for 500K iterations with action repeat equals to 2, which results in 1M environment steps. The probability in the $\epsilon$-greedy exploration is set to 0.2 for all experiments.

**Table 1.** Results on the DeepMind Control Suite: The task order is *Walk* → *Uphill* → *Downhill* → *Nofoot*. We evaluate the models on all tasks after completing training on the last task (*Nofoot*). The last two rows represent baseline models: one is a model jointly trained on all tasks, and the other is a model trained independently on a single task.

| Method | Walk | Uphill | Downhill | Nofoot | Average |
|---|---|---|---|---|---|
| DV2 | 239 ± 156 | 181 ± 19 | 444 ± 178 | 936 ± 32 | 450 |
| CURL | 539 ± 170 | 132 ± 64 | 133 ± 63 | 919 ± 46 | 431 |
| DV2+EWC (hyper-1) | **744 ± 36** | 27 ± 12 | 70 ± 29 | 49 ± 40 | 223 |
| DV2+EWC (hyper-2) | 705 ± 39 | 351 ± 133 | 292 ± 139 | 423 ± 182 | 443 |
| CURL+EWC (hyper-3) | 206 ± 125 | 119 ± 90 | 186 ± 113 | 433 ± 322 | 236 |
| CURL+EWC (hyper-4) | 222 ± 143 | 101 ± 59 | 409 ± 88 | 887 ± 75 | 405 |
| Ours | 606 ± 365 | **734 ± 346** | **954 ± 30** | **951 ± 19** | **812** |
| Multi-task | 951 ± 16 | 581 ± 120 | 903 ± 34 | 950 ± 16 | 846 |
| Single-task | 759 ± 24 | 343 ± 97 | 934 ± 24 | 929 ± 35 | 741 |

### 4.2 Continual DeepMind Control

We run the continual learning procedure with 3 seeds and report the mean rewards and standard deviations of 10 episodes. As shown in Table 1, our method achieves significant improvements compared with existing model-based and model-free RL approaches on all tasks. For example, our model performs nearly 2.5× higher than DreamerV2 on the first learning task *Walk*, and the performance on the task *Downhill* is almost 7× higher than CURL. Additionally, our model generally outperforms the straightforward combinations of EWC and popular RL approaches. For each combination, we present the results using two different sets of hyper-parameters termed "hyper-1" to "hyper-4". For DV2+EWC, EWC coefficients are ($\omega_1 = 10^9$, $\omega_2 = 10^7$, $\omega_3 = 10^8$) for "hyper-1" and ($10^7, 10^5, 10^6$) for "hyper-2", where $\omega_1, \omega_2, \omega_3$ correspond to actor, value and world model losses respectively. For CURL+EWC, "hyper-3" uses ($10^6, 10^3, 10^7$) while "hyper-4" employs ($10^5, 10^2, 10^6$), with $\omega_3$ now regulates contrastive loss. We can observe that the performance may change sharply when using different hyper-parameter sets. The reason may be that additional constraints on the feature extraction module from visual inputs make it difficult to preserve pre-learned knowledge in its parameters. Furthermore, our approach outperforms the results of both multi-task joint training and single-task training on three of four tasks. Considering the average rewards on all tasks, our model outperforms the single training results by a large margin (811.5 vs. 741.3). It shows that our approach not only mitigates catastrophic forgetting issues but also improves the pre-learned tasks.

We also conduct visual forecasting experiments on the DMC benchmark to explore whether the learned world model can preserve the pre-learned visual dynamics during the continual learning procedure. After training the models on the last task *Nofoot*, we randomly collect sequences of frames and actions

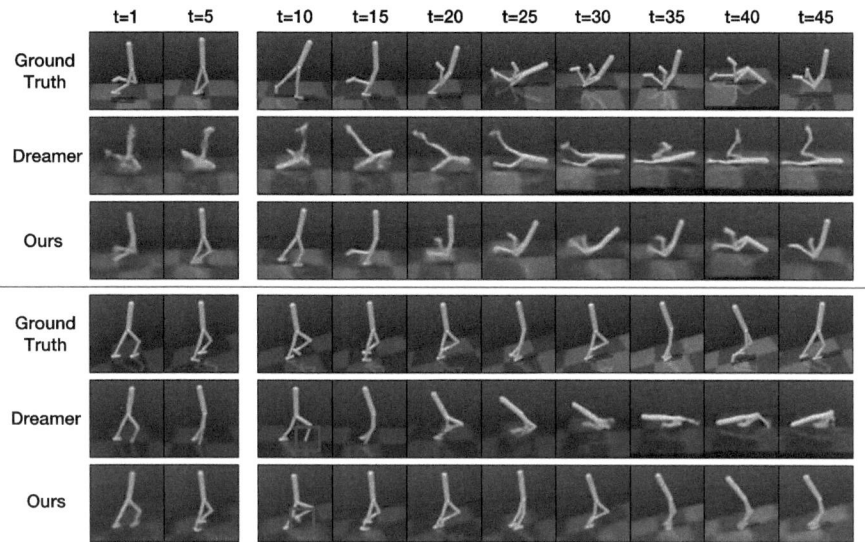

**Fig. 4.** Visual forecasting results on the task *Walk* (**upper**) and *Uphill* (**bottom**) after the model trained on the last task *Nofoot*. For each sequence, we use the first 5 images as context frames and predict the next 45 frames given actions. The world model in our method effectively alleviates catastrophic forgetting, while DreamerV2 makes predictions similar to those in the last task.

during the test phases of the first two tasks *Walk* and *Uphill*. We input the first five frames to the learned world model and ask it to predict the next 45 frames with actions input. The prediction results are shown in Fig. 4. From these prediction results, we can observe that although these models have been continually trained on different tasks, the world model in our method still remembers the visual dynamics in previous tasks. It successfully forecasts future frames given the corresponding action inputs without forgetting. On the contrary, the results predicted by DreamerV2 suffer from severe blur effects and share a similar appearance with trajectories of the last task *Nofoot*. These results show that the world models in MBRL methods can not handle catastrophic forgetting.

### 4.3 Continual Meta-world

We can also find similar observations on the Meta-World benchmark in Table 2. Our approach consistently outperforms previous RL methods and their direct combinations with the continual learning EWC method on all tasks. For instance, our model achieves near 3× average rewards compared with DreamerV2 and about 2.5× average rewards compared with CURL. Notably, the result on the final task *Assembly* shows that our method can effectively use the pre-learned knowledge to further improve the performance on the latter tasks. For the *Assembly* task, our model outperforms the single training results by a large margin and

**Table 2.** Results on Meta-World: The task order is *Window-open → Button-press → Hammer → Assembly*. We evaluate the models on all tasks after completing training on the last task (*Assembly*).

| Method | Window-open | Button-press | Hammer | Assembly | Average |
|---|---|---|---|---|---|
| DV2 | 220 ± 33 | 195 ± 232 | 331 ±196 | 1075 ± 37 | 451 |
| CURL [23] | 152 ± 37 | 51 ± 9 | 491 ± 38 | 862 ± 151 | 389 |
| DV2+EWC | 549 ± 990 | 267 ± 105 | 448 ± 55 | 206 ± 10 | 367 |
| CURL+EWC | 462 ± 450 | 265 ± 157 | 480 ± 41 | 202 ± 17 | 352 |
| Ours | **1004 ± 1251** | **681 ± 546** | **524 ± 333** | **2389 ± 676** | **1149** |
| Multi-task | 2119 ± 1528 | 2722 ± 516 | 2499 ± 895 | 2310 ± 418 | 2412 |
| Single-task | 3367 ± 954 | 2642 ± 840 | 950 ± 109 | 1283 ± 66 | 2060 |

**Table 3.** Ablation studies of each component in our model on the average rewards across all tasks in the DMC benchmark. "Replay" denotes the use of the experience replay mechanism. "Action shuffling" indicates using action shuffling in exploratory-conservative behavior learning. "Value regulation" means that the agent takes the previous value model to constrain the value estimation.

| Replay | ϵ-Greedy | Action shuffling | Value regulation | Reward |
|---|---|---|---|---|
| ✗ | ✗ | ✗ | ✗ | 450 |
| ✓ | ✗ | ✗ | ✗ | 525 |
| ✓ | ✓ | ✗ | ✗ | 616 |
| ✓ | ✓ | ✓ | ✗ | 788 |
| ✓ | ✓ | ✓ | ✓ | 812 |

even outperforms the joint training results. Combined with the results in the DMC benchmark, it seems that our framework has a huge potential in improving the forward transfer performance in continual visual control.

### 4.4 Ablation Studies

We conduct ablation studies on the DMC benchmark to evaluate different components on the average rewards across all tasks. In Table 3, the first row provides the results of the baseline model, which only contains the life-long world model. In the second row, we train the baseline model with the experience replay mechanism, and we observe that the improvements are limited. As suggested in Sect. 3.3, the main reason lies in the fact that training on the replay data only will result in overfitting problems on both the reward prediction and the value estimation. Then, as shown in the third row and the fourth row, we further improve the experience replay with the exploration-conservative behavior learning scheme. We gradually introduce the $\epsilon$-greedy exploration strategy and the data augmentation on the frame-action pairs and use them to regularize the learning of the reward module on replay trajectories. We can observe significant

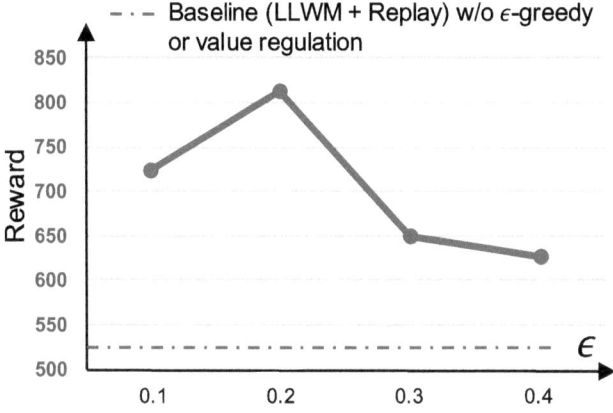

**Fig. 5.** Ablation study of different $\epsilon$ in the $\epsilon$-greedy exploration on DMC.

improvement compared with the pure replay scheme. Finally, in the bottom row, we reuse the pre-learned value model to introduce the constraint on the value estimation during the behavior learning stage. It also shows a large performance boost. We also experiment with different $\epsilon$ values in the $\epsilon$-greedy exploration and show the average rewards in Fig. 5. On one hand, slightly increasing the probability to introduce random actions can significantly improve the performance. On the other hand, excessively raising the $\epsilon$ value may introduce too much noise and degenerate the performance.

Finally, we evaluate our continual MBRL approach over 3 random task orders on the DMC benchmark to analyze whether our model can effectively alleviate catastrophic forgetting regardless of the task order. The mean reward with standard deviation is $801 \pm 35$, which shows that the proposed techniques, including the life-long world model and the experience replay mechanism, are still effective despite the change of training order.

## 5 Conclusion and Discussion

In this paper, we studied the continual learning problem of sequential visual control tasks, which is challenging due to the dynamics shift. The main contributions of our method can be viewed in two aspects. First, it presents the life-long world model that captures task-specific visual dynamics in a Gaussian mixture latent space, incorporating an experience replay mechanism to overcome the forgetting issue in the world model. Second, it further presents a pilot model-based RL approach for continual visual control by involving the exploratory-conservative behavior learning scheme to overcome the overfitting problems within both the world model and the policy models. Our approach has shown competitive results on both DeepMind Control and Meta-World benchmarks, achieving remarkable improvements over the straightforward combinations of existing continual learning and reinforcement learning approaches.

In the future, extending the framework to handle more drastic domain shifts or out-of-distribution tasks encountered in lifelong learning scenarios would enhance its robustness and applicability. Investigating mechanisms that improve transfer learning and mitigate catastrophic forgetting across highly dissimilar tasks is a key direction.

**Acknowledgments.** This work was supported by the National Natural Science Foundation of China (62250062), the Smart Grid National Science and Technology Major Project (2024ZD0801200), the Shanghai Municipal Science and Technology Major Project (2021SHZDZX0102), and the Fundamental Research Funds for the Central Universities.

**Disclosure of Interests.** The authors have no competing interests to declare that are relevant to the content of this article.

# References

1. Ammar, H.B., Eaton, E., Ruvolo, P., Taylor, M.: Online multi-task learning for policy gradient methods. In: International Conference on Machine Learning, pp. 1206–1214 (2014)
2. Bharadhwaj, H., Babaeizadeh, M., Erhan, D., Levine, S.: Information prioritization through empowerment in visual model-based RL. In: International Conference on Learning Representations (2022)
3. Burchi, M., Timofte, R.: Learning transformer-based world models with contrastive predictive coding. In: International Conference on Learning Representations (2025)
4. Chen, G., et al.: Continual predictive learning from videos. In: Proceedings of the IEEE/CVF Conference on Computer Vision and Pattern Recognition
5. Daniels, Z.A., et al.: Model-free generative replay for lifelong reinforcement learning: Application to starcraft-2. In: Conference on Lifelong Learning Agents, pp. 1120–1145 (2022)
6. Dilokthanakul, N., et al.: Deep unsupervised clustering with gaussian mixture variational autoencoders. arXiv preprint arXiv:1611.02648 (2016)
7. Ha, D., Schmidhuber, J.: Recurrent world models facilitate policy evolution. In: Advances in neural information processing syste, vol. 31 (2018)
8. Haarnoja, T., Zhou, A., Abbeel, P., Levine, S.: Soft actor-critic: off-policy maximum entropy deep reinforcement learning with a stochastic actor. In: International conference on machine learning
9. Hadsell, R., Rao, D., Rusu, A.A., Pascanu, R.: Embracing change: continual learning in deep neural networks. Trends Cogn. Sci. **24**(12), 1028–1040 (2020)
10. Hafner, D., Lillicrap, T., Ba, J., Norouzi, M.: Dream to control: learning behaviors by latent imagination. In: International Conference on Learning Representations (2020)
11. Hafner, D., et al.: Learning latent dynamics for planning from pixels. In: International Conference on Machine Learning, pp. 2555–2565 (2019)
12. Hafner, D., Lillicrap, T.P., Norouzi, M., Ba, J.: Mastering atari with discrete world models. In: International Conference on Learning Representations (2021)
13. Hafner, D., et al.: Learning latent dynamics for planning from pixels. In: International Conference on Machine Learning, pp. 2555–2565 (2019)

14. Hansen, N., Lin, Y., Su, H., Wang, X., Kumar, V., Rajeswaran, A.: Modem: accelerating visual model-based reinforcement learning with demonstrations. arXiv preprint arXiv:2212.05698 (2022)
15. Hinton, G., Vinyals, O., Dean, J.: Distilling the knowledge in a neural network. arXiv preprint arXiv:1503.02531 (2015)
16. Igl, M., Farquhar, G., Luketina, J., Böhmer, J., Whiteson, S.: Transient non-stationarity and generalisation in deep reinforcement learning. In: International Conference on Learning Representations (2021)
17. Jiang, Z., Zheng, Y., Tan, H., Tang, B., Zhou, H.: Variational deep embedding: an unsupervised and generative approach to clustering (2017)
18. Khetarpal, K., Riemer, M., Rish, I., Precup, D.: Towards continual reinforcement learning: a review and perspectives. J. Artif. Intell. Res. **75**, 1401–1476 (2022)
19. Kirkpatrick, J.: Overcoming catastrophic forgetting in neural networks. Proc. Natl. Acad. Sci. **114**(13), 3521–3526 (2017)
20. Kostrikov, I., Yarats, D., Fergus, R.: Image augmentation is all you need: regularizing deep reinforcement learning from pixels. arXiv preprint arXiv:2004.13649 (2020)
21. Kumar, A., Zhou, A., Tucker, G., Levine, S.: Conservative q-learning for offline reinforcement learning. In: Advances in neural information processing system (2020)
22. Lan, Q., Pan, Y., Luo, J., Mahmood, A.R.: Memory-efficient reinforcement learning with knowledge consolidation. arXiv preprint arXiv:2205.10868 (2022)
23. Laskin, M., Srinivas, A., Abbeel, P.: CURL: contrastive unsupervised representations for reinforcement learning. In: International conference on machine learning, pp. 5639–5650 (2020)
24. Li, J., et al.: Open-world reinforcement learning over long short-term imagination. In: International Conference on Learning Representations (2025)
25. Liotet, P., Vidaich, F., Metelli, A.M., Restelli, M.: Lifelong hyper-policy optimization with multiple importance sampling regularization. In: Proceedings of the AAAI Conference on Artificial Intelligence, pp. 7525–7533. No. 7 (2022)
26. Liu, B., Liu, X., Jin, X., Stone, P., Liu, Q.: Conflict-averse gradient descent for multi-task learning. In: Advances in Neural Information Processing Systems, pp. 18878–18890 (2021)
27. Mendez, J.A., Eaton, E.: How to reuse and compose knowledge for a lifetime of tasks: a survey on continual learning and functional composition. arXiv preprint arXiv:2207.07730 (2022)
28. Mendez, J.A., van Seijen, H., Eaton, E.: Modular lifelong reinforcement learning via neural composition. arXiv preprint arXiv:2207.00429 (2022)
29. Pan, M., Zhu, X., Wang, Y., Yang, X.: Iso-dream: Isolating and leveraging noncontrollable visual dynamics in world models. In: Advances in Neural Information Processing Systems (2022)
30. Powers, S., Xing, E., Kolve, E., Mottaghi, R., Gupta, A.: Cora: benchmarks, baselines, and metrics as a platform for continual reinforcement learning agents. In: Conference on Lifelong Learning Agents, pp. 705–743 (2022)
31. Rao, D., Visin, F., Rusu, A.A., Teh, Y.W., Pascanu, R., Hadsell, R.: Continual unsupervised representation learning. In: Advances in Neural Information Processing Systems (2019)
32. Riemer, M., Klinger, T., Bouneffouf, D., Franceschini, M.: Scalable recollections for continual lifelong learning. In: Proceedings of the AAAI conference on artificial intelligence. vol. 33, pp. 1352–1359 (2019)

33. Sekar, R., Rybkin, O., Daniilidis, K., Abbeel, P., Hafner, D., Pathak, D.: Planning to explore via self-supervised world models. In: International conference on machine learning, pp. 8583–8592 (2020)
34. Shi, G., Azizzadenesheli, K., O'Connell, M., Chung, S.J., Yue, Y.: Meta-adaptive nonlinear control: Theory and algorithms. In: Advances in Neural Information Processing Systems, pp. 10013–10025 (2021)
35. Sun, R., Zang, H., Li, X., Islam, R.: Learning latent dynamic robust representations for world models. In: ICML (2024)
36. Tassa, Y., et al.: Deepmind control suite. arXiv preprint arXiv:1801.00690 (2018)
37. Wolczyk, M., Zajac, M., Pascanu, R., Kucinski, L., Milos, P.: Continual world: a robotic benchmark for continual reinforcement learning. In: Advances in Neural Information Processing Systems, pp. 28496–28510 (2021)
38. Xie, A., Finn, C.: Lifelong robotic reinforcement learning by retaining experiences. In: Conference on Lifelong Learning Agents, pp. 838–855 (2022)
39. Yarats, D., Zhang, A., Kostrikov, I., Amos, B., Pineau, J., Fergus, R.: Improving sample efficiency in model-free reinforcement learning from images. In: Proceedings of the AAAI Conference On Artificial Intelligence, vol. 35, pp. 10674–10681 (2021)
40. Yu, T., Kumar, S., Gupta, A., Levine, S., Hausman, K., Finn, C.: Gradient surgery for multi-task learning. In: Advances in Neural Information Processing Systems, pp. 5824–5836 (2020)
41. Yu, T., et al.: Meta-world: a benchmark and evaluation for multi-task and meta reinforcement learning. In: Conference on robot learning, vol. 100, pp. 1094–1100 (2019)
42. Zhang, T., Wang, X., Liang, B., Yuan, B.: Catastrophic interference in reinforcement learning: a solution based on context division and knowledge distillation. In: IEEE Transactions on Neural Networks and Learning Systems (2022)
43. Zhou, W., et al.: Forgetting and imbalance in robot lifelong learning with off-policy data. In: Conference on Lifelong Learning Agents, pp. 294–309 (2022)

# UCB-Driven Utility Function Search for Multi-objective Reinforcement Learning

Yucheng Shi[1], David Lynch[2], and Alexandros Agapitos[2](✉)

[1] Trinity College Dublin, Dublin, Ireland
shiy2@tcd.ie
[2] Huawei Ireland Research Centre, Dublin, Ireland
{david.lynch1,alexandros.agapitos}@huawei.com

**Abstract.** In Multi-objective Reinforcement Learning (MORL) agents are tasked with optimising decision-making behaviours that trade-off between multiple, possibly conflicting, objectives. MORL based on decomposition is a family of solution methods that employ a number of utility functions to decompose the multi-objective problem into individual single-objective problems solved simultaneously in order to approximate a Pareto front of policies. We focus on the case of linear utility functions parametrised by weight vectors **w**. We introduce a method based on Upper Confidence Bound to efficiently search for the most promising weight vectors during different stages of the learning process, with the aim of maximising the hypervolume of the resulting Pareto front. The proposed method demonstrates consistency and strong performance across various MORL baselines on Mujoco benchmark problems. The code is released in: https://github.com/SYCAMORE-1/ucb-MOPPO

**Keywords:** Multi-objective Reinforcement Learning · Upper Confidence Bound · Mujoco benchmark problems

## 1 Introduction

In many real-world control and planning problems, multiple and often conflicting objectives arise. These objectives are interrelated, requiring trade-offs that significantly affect the overall quality of decision-making [24,30]. Such learning objectives are usually represented as weighted reward signals, where conflicting rewards can lead to divergent optimisation directions [35]. Consequently, the classic reinforcement learning (RL) methods are inadequate, as training individual policies to align with each preference weight vector across multiple rewards results in an impractical computational burden [10,13]. Therefore, Multi-objective reinforcement learning (MORL) has become an increasingly

---

**Supplementary Information** The online version contains supplementary material available at https://doi.org/10.1007/978-3-032-06106-5_10.

recognised methodology for handling tasks with conflicting objectives, enabling the simultaneous optimisation of multiple criteria [3,31,36]. In cases where the objectives conflict with each other, the best trade-offs among the objectives are defined in terms of Pareto optimal. A policy $\pi$ is said to dominate $\pi'$ if $\left(\forall i : \mathbf{V}_i^\pi \geq \mathbf{V}_i^{\pi'}\right) \wedge \left(\exists i : \mathbf{V}_i^\pi > \mathbf{V}_i^{\pi'}\right)$, and it is Pareto optimal if there is no other policy that dominates it. The set of Pareto optimal policies is called the Pareto front (PF). In many real-world applications, an approximation to the PF is required by a decision maker in order to select a preferred policy [13]. A real-world use case is the multi-objective optimisation of wireless networks [11]. In this case, four primary objective classes, i.e.,throughput, coverage, energy efficiency and utilisation are considered. This is a very challenging problem that motivates further research to advance the state-of-the-art (SOTA) in MORL.

One prevalent category of MORL approaches is Multi-Objective Reinforcement Learning with Decomposition (MORL/D) [10]. A Pareto-optimal solution to a multi-objective sequential decision-making problem can be interpreted as an optimal solution to a single-objective problem, defined with respect to a utility function $u : \mathbb{R}^m \to \mathbb{R}$. This utility function aggregates $m$ objectives into a scalar reward, mapping the multi-objective value of the policy into a scalar value, expressed as $V_u^\pi = u(\mathbf{V}^\pi)$ [8]. Therefore, the approximation of the PF can be reformulated as a set of scalar reward sub-problems, each defined by a utility function. This approach unifies MORL methods [13] with decomposition-based multi-objective optimisation techniques [34], collectively termed MORL/D.

MORL/D offers several advantages, including scalability to many objectives, flexibility in employing various scalarisation techniques, and the ability to parallelise sub-problem training, thereby reducing computational overhead [9,10]. SOTA MORL/D methods can be broadly categorised into single-policy and multi-policy approaches [10]. Single-policy methods [1,2,18,32] aim to learn a single policy conditioned on the parameters of the utility function, i.e., scalarisation vector $\mathbf{w}$, where $\forall i : w_i \geq 0$, and $\sum_i w_i = 1.0$. However, these methods face two major challenges: (1) single-policy methods require large neural networks and extensive training time to accurately reconstruct the optimal PF; and (2) they may struggle to generalise effectively to unseen $\mathbf{w}$ [33]. In contrast, multi-policy approaches maintain a separate policy for each $\mathbf{w}$ [17,19]. Parameter sharing improves the sample efficiency of single-policy methods and enhances generalisation to new objective preferences [1,32]. However, multi-policy methods often require maintaining various suboptimal policies to adequately cover the preference space, which can be highly memory-intensive [17]. Existing MORL/D approaches share common limitations. As the number of objectives increases or the granularity of the weight space becomes finer, the total preference space grows exponentially. This exponential growth renders prefixed scalarisation weights inefficient and degrades the quality of the approximated PF.

To address the limitations of MORL/D, particularly in the multi-policy paradigm, this work introduces an Upper Confidence Bound (UCB) acquisition function to identify promising scalarisation vectors $\mathbf{w} \in \mathbf{W}$ at different learning stages, guided by the Pareto front quality metric of *hypervolume* (HV) [9]. Extending [1], we use a weight-conditioned Actor-Critic network $\pi_\theta(s, w)$

trained with Proximal Policy Optimisation (PPO) [26] for $C$ iterations, instead of a Q-network $Q_\theta(s, a, \mathbf{w})$.

We adopt a multi-policy approach, each $\pi_\theta(s, w)$ specialises in a sub-space of $\mathbf{W}$, enabling time-efficient and parallel optimisation with a compact parameter size. Inspired by [17], we frame HV maximisation as a surrogate-assisted optimisation problem, where a data-driven surrogate predicts changes in objective values to select weight vectors that improve HV. We extend [17] by incorporating prediction uncertainty into the UCB acquisition function, balancing exploration and exploitation. Further, we replace large Pareto archives with scalarisation-vector-conditioned policies $\pi_\theta(s, w)$, reducing memory overhead while ensuring efficient PF coverage.

In summary, two contributions distinguish our work from previous systems of MORL/D:

1. A two-layer decomposition enables policies to specialize in different subspaces of the scalarisation vector space, with conditioning refining sub-problems within each subspace. This facilitates generalisation across local scalarisation neighbourhoods, enhancing HV metrics [9].
2. The use of a UCB acquisition function for selecting from a finite set of evenly distributed scalarisation vectors to balance exploration and exploitation.

The rest of the paper is structured as follows. Background knowledge is introduced in Sect. 2. Prior work on gradient-based MORL is reviewed in Sect. 3. The proposed method is described in Sect. 4. Experiment configurations on six multi-objective benchmark problems are outlined in Sect. 5, and SOTA results on these problems are discussed in Sect. 6. Finally, we conclude in Sect. 7 with directions for future research.

## 2 Preliminaries

### 2.1 Policy-Gradient Reinforcement Learning

Policy gradient methods are a class of RL algorithms that optimise policies directly by computing gradients of an objective function with respect to the policy parameters. The objective function $J(\theta)$ for a parameterised policy $\pi_\theta(a|s)$ can be expressed as the expected return, the policy gradient is then computed as:

$$\nabla_\theta J(\theta) = \mathbb{E}_{\tau \sim \pi_\theta} \left[ \nabla_\theta \log \pi_\theta(a_t|s_t) \hat{A}_t \right],$$

where $\hat{A}_t$ is the advantage function [29], which measures the relative value of taking action $a_t$ in state $s_t$.

Proximal Policy Optimisation (PPO) [26] improves upon traditional policy gradient methods by introducing a surrogate objective that prevents overly large policy updates, ensuring stable learning. The PPO objective is defined as:

$$L^{\text{PPO}}(\theta) = \mathbb{E}_t \left[ \min \left( r_t(\theta) \hat{A}_t, \text{clip}(r_t(\theta), 1 - \epsilon, 1 + \epsilon) \hat{A}_t \right) \right],$$

where $r_t(\theta) = \frac{\pi_\theta(a_t|s_t)}{\pi_{\theta_{\text{old}}}(a_t|s_t)}$ is the probability ratio, and $\epsilon$ is a hyperparameter controlling the clipping range. By clipping the ratio, PPO limits deviations from the current policy, leading to improved stability and sample efficiency. These advancements have made PPO one of the most widely used algorithms for continuous and high-dimensional control tasks.

### 2.2 Definition of MORL

A multi-objective sequential decision making problem can be formulated as a multi-objective Markov Decision Process (MOMDP) defined by the tuple $\langle S, A, P, \gamma, \rho_0, \mathbf{r} \rangle$ with state space $S$, action space $A$, state transition probability $P : S \times A \times S \to [0,1]$, discount factor $\gamma$, initial state distribution $\rho_0$, and vector-valued reward function $\mathbf{r} : S \times A \to \mathbb{R}^m$ specifying one-step reward for each of the $m$ objectives. A decision-making policy $\pi : S \to A$ maps states into actions, for which a vector-valued value function $\mathbf{V}^\pi$ is defined as:

$$\mathbf{V}^\pi = \mathbb{E}\left[\sum_{t=0}^{H} \gamma^t \mathbf{r}(s_t, \alpha_t) | s_0 \sim \rho_0, a_t \sim \pi\right] \quad (1)$$

where $H$ is the length of the horizon.

The space of utility functions for a MORL problem is typically populated by linear and non-linear functions of $\mathbf{V}^\pi$. In this work we focus on the highly prevalent case where the utility functions are linear, taking the form of $u(\mathbf{V}^\pi) = \mathbf{w}^\top \mathbf{V}^\pi$, where scalarisation vector $\mathbf{w}$ provides the parametrisation of the utility function. Each element of $\mathbf{w} \in \mathbb{R}^m$ specifies the relative importance (preference) of each objective. The space of linear scalarisation vectors $\mathbf{W}$ is the m-dimensional simplex: $\sum_i w_i = 1, w_i \geq 0, i = 1, \ldots, m$. For any given $\mathbf{w}$, the original MOMDP is reduced to a single-objective MDP.

### 2.3 Convex Coverage Set (CCS)

Linear utility functions enable MORL to generate a Convex Coverage Set (CCS) of policies, which is a subset of all possible policies such as there exists a policy $\pi$ in the set that is optimal with respect to any linear scalarisation vector $\mathbf{w}$:

$$CCS \equiv \left\{\mathbf{V}^\pi \in \Pi \mid \exists \mathbf{w} \text{ s.t. } \forall \mathbf{V}^{\pi'} \in \Pi, \mathbf{V}^\pi \mathbf{w}^\top \geq \mathbf{V}^{\pi'} \mathbf{w}^\top\right\} \quad (2)$$

CCS is a subset of PF defined for monotonically increasing utility functions [13]. At the same time, the underlying linear utility function space (space of scalarisation vectors $\mathbf{W}$) is easier to search than that of arbitrarily-composed utility functions, where one has to search for the overall function composition out of primitive function elements. The sampling of scalarisation vectors $\mathbf{w} \in \mathbf{W}$ impacts the quality of the CCS in approximating the PF. Vectors can be sampled uniformly at random [1,6,18,20,32], selected from a predefined set [4,17], or adapted via search methods [2,19]. A small step size is required for high-quality CCS when using predefined vectors [25].

## 3 Related Work

A thorough review of MORL can be found in [13]. In this section we highlight previous work that employs gradient-based with a linear utility function, which can be classified into three main categories.

In the first category, a single policy [21,27] is trained using a linear scalarisation function when the user's preferences are known in advance. For example, [4] proposes a novel algorithm that trains a single universal network to cover the entire preference space. The approach utilises preferences to guide network parameter updates and employs a novel parallelisation strategy to enhance sample efficiency.

In the second category, when user preferences are unknown or difficult to define, a CCS of policies is computed by training multiple independent policies with different scalarisation vectors to capture various trade-offs between objectives [16,18]. The work of [19] proposes Optimistic Linear Support, a method that adaptively selects the weights of the linear utility function via the concepts of corner weights and estimated improvement to prioritise those corner weights. [2] introduces a sample-efficient MORL algorithm that leverages Generalised Policy Improvement (GPI) to prioritize training on specific preference weights. By focusing on corner weights with higher GPI priority, the method iteratively learns a set of policies whose value vectors approximate the CCS. The work of [17] maintains a Pareto archive of policies by focusing on those scalarisation vectors that are expected to improve the hypervolume and sparsity metrics of the resulting PF the most.

The third category of methods maintains a single policy conditioned on the scalarisation vector $\mathbf{w}$. Several works aim to train such policies for few-shot adaptation to varying objective preferences [1,6,32]. [1] uses a scalarisation-vector-conditioned Q-network trained on randomly sampled $\mathbf{w}$ to solve single-objective RL sub-problems, generalizing across changing objective preferences. Similarly, [32] applies Envelope Q-learning to train a Q-network for few-shot adaptation to new scalarisation vectors. [6] proposes a PPO-based meta-policy trained collaboratively with data from policies specialized to sampled scalarisation vectors, enabling PF construction via few-shot fine-tuning. Other works directly approximate the CCS using a single scalarisation-conditioned policy. [18] enhances Soft Actor Critic with an entropy term to train scalarisation-conditioned policies and Q-networks, while [4] extends [17] by incorporating scalarisation-conditioning, replacing a Pareto archive with a single policy.

Existing methods demonstrate notable strengths but face challenges in scalability, computational cost, generalisation, and performance consistency. By comparing these methods to UCB-MOPPO, we highlight its key advantages: 1) Preference space decomposition enables scalable, efficient parallel training with compact policies. 2) The UCB-driven surrogate model selects scalarisation vectors to maximise hypervolume. 3) Integration of PPO enhances stability and sample efficiency. 4) The weight-conditioned network reduces memory overhead.

## 4 Methods

The key technical characteristics of the proposed MORL/D algorithm, named UCB-MOPPO, are as follows:

**MORL/D as scalar RL sub-problems.** The overall scalarisation weight $\mathbf{W}$ is divided into $K$ sub-spaces as shown in Fig. 2a. A separate policy $\pi_k$ is trained for each sub-problem, conditioned on scalarisation vectors sampled from the corresponding sub-space $\mathbf{W}_k \subset \mathbf{W}$, where $k = 1, \ldots, K$.

**Scalarisation-vector-conditioned Actor-Critic.** A policy network $\pi_\theta$, a value network $v_\phi^\pi$, and a scalarisation vector $\mathbf{w}$ ($\sum_i w_i = 1, w_i \geq 0, i = 1, \ldots, m$) are used to maximise the weighted-sum of expected rewards, denoted as $J(\theta, \phi, \mathbf{w}) = \sum_{i=1}^{m} w_i V_i^\pi$. Following [1,18,32], both $\pi_\theta(s, \mathbf{w})$ and $v_\phi^\pi(s, \mathbf{w})$ are conditioned on $\mathbf{w}$. This enables a single policy to express different trade-off between objectives by generalising across a neighbourhood of scalarisation vectors.

**Surrogate-assisted maximisation of CCS hypervolume.** An acquisition function based on UCB [28] is used to select scalarisation vectors for training from each sub-space $\mathbf{W}_k$. During training, the chosen scalarisation vectors are those expected to maximise the hypervolume of the resulting CCS most effectively.

### 4.1 Two-layer Decomposition of MORL Problem Into Scalar RL Sub-Problems

At the first layer of problem decomposition, a set of $K$ evenly distributed scalarisation vectors, named as *pivots*, are defined within the scalarisation vector space $\mathbf{W}$. These pivot vectors effectively divide $\mathbf{W}$ into $K$ different sub-spaces as shown in Fig. 2a. The system allows to independently train multiple pivot policies with different random seeds in order to improve the density of the resulting CCS. At the second layer of problem decomposition, for each sub-space $\mathbf{W}_k, k = 1, \ldots, K$, a number of $M$ evenly distributed scalarisation vectors are defined in turn. Therefore the overall MORL problem is decomposed into a total of $K * M$ scalar RL sub-problems, defined as follows for a fixed $\mathbf{w}$:

$$\pi(\cdot, \mathbf{w}) = \underset{\pi'(\cdot, \mathbf{w})}{\arg\max} \mathbb{E}\left[\sum_{t=1}^{H} \gamma^t \mathbf{w}^\top \mathbf{r}(s_t, \alpha_t)\right] \quad (3)$$

A separate policy $\pi_k$ (i.e., *pivot* policy) is independently trained for each sub-space $\mathbf{W}_k \subset \mathbf{W}$ by conditioning on the corresponding scalarisation vectors. As an example, for a bi-objective problem with $\mathbf{w} = [w_1, w_2]$ in Fig. 2a, for two sub-spaces $\mathbf{W}_i, \mathbf{W}_j$ with $i > j$, $\left(w_1^{i,n} > w_1^{j,n}\right) \wedge \left(w_2^{i,n} < w_2^{j,n}\right)$, $n = 1, \ldots, M$. The solutions of the $K * M$ sub-problems compose a CCS.

### 4.2 Scalarisation-Vector-Conditioned Actor-Critic

The neural network(NN) architecture of the Actor-Critic is illustrated in Fig. 1. The state vector $\mathbf{s}$ concatenated with the scalarisation vector $\mathbf{w}$ form the input layer. **w** is also concatenated with the last shared layer through a residual connection [14]. Residual connections aim at improving the sensitivity of NN output to changes in **w** in a similar vein with reward-conditioned policies in [15].

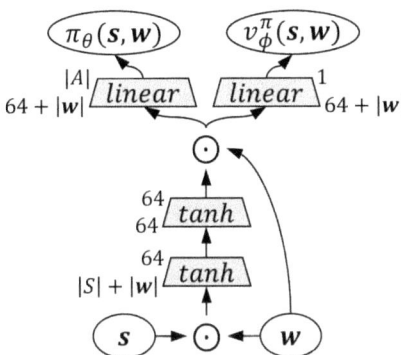

**Fig. 1.** Scalarisation vector **w** conditioned actor-critic network.

### 4.3 Surrogate-Assisted Maximisation of CCS Hypervolume

**Overview** The learning algorithm proceeds in stages of $C$ iterations each. At every stage, $K$ pivot policies $\pi_k$, $k = 1, \ldots, K$ are trained in parallel using PPO, each conditioned on a subset of $N$ scalarisation vectors out of $M$ in total that are defined for each corresponding sub-space $\mathbf{W}_k$, $k = 1, \ldots, K$, with $N \ll M$. The selection of $N$ scalarisation vectors to train on at each stage is performed via surrogate-assisted maximisation of the hypervolume of the CCS. First, a data-driven uncertainty-aware surrogate model is built in the scalarisation vector space to predict the expected change in each objective after training $\pi_k$ conditioned on said scalarisation vectors for $C$ iterations. Second, an acquisition function is defined as the UCB of the CCS hypervolume that is expected by including a scalarisation vector to the policy's conditioning set at each training stage. Maximising the acquisition function selects the scalarisation vectors that are expected to improve CCS hypervolume the most. Pseudo code can is provided in supplementary material, Sect. 1, algorithm 3.

**Warm-Up Phase.** The algorithm starts with a warm-up stage performed using Algorithm 1. For an $m$-objective problem, a set of $K$ evenly distributed pivot vectors $\{\mathbf{w}_i\}_{i=1}^K$ are generated, where $\sum_i w_i = 1, w_i \geq 0, i = 1, \ldots, m$. Accordingly, a set of $K$ pivot policies, each conditioned on a separate pivot vector, is trained using Algorithm 1 for a number of epochs.

**Surrogate Model.** Let $\pi_{k,z+1}$ be the policy that results from the $k^{th}$ policy $\pi_{k,z}$ during the $z^{th}$ training stage of $C$ iterations. Let $\Delta V_{j,\mathbf{w}}^{\pi_k,(z \to z+1)} = V_{j,\mathbf{w}}^{\pi_{k,z+1}} - V_{j,\mathbf{w}}^{\pi_{k,z}}$ be the change in the value of the $j^{th}$ objective for the $k^{th}$ policy conditioned on scalarisation vector **w** trained with PPO for $C$ iterations. For each pivot policy $\pi_k$, $k = 1, \ldots, K$, and for each objective $j = 1, \ldots, m$, a separate dataset $D_{surrogate}^{k,j}$ is created using policy's $\pi_k$ evaluation data of objective $j$ that are collected from the simulation environment during a number of consecutive training stages $Z$, as follows:

$$D_{surrogate}^{k,j} = \left\{ \left(\mathbf{w}, \left(V_{j,\mathbf{w}}^{\pi_k, z+1} - V_{j,\mathbf{w}}^{\pi_k, z}\right)\right) \right\}_{z=1}^{Z} \tag{4}$$

A surrogate model $f_{bagging}^{k,j} : \mathbb{R}^m \rightarrow \mathbb{R}$ is trained on $D_{surrogate}^{k,j}$ to predict $\Delta V_{j,\mathbf{w}}^{\pi_k, (z \rightarrow z+1)}$ as a function of the scalarisation vector $\mathbf{w}$, for $m$ number of objectives. The training is incremental while additional tuples are appended to $D_{surrogate}$ from consecutive training stages. The surrogate model takes the form of Bagging [5] of linear models $f_\psi(\mathbf{w}) = \sum_{i=1}^{m} \psi_i w_i + \psi_0$ with elastic net regularisation [37]. Bagging trains independently $B$ linear models $\{f_\psi^b\}_{b=1}^{B}$ on $B$ bootstrap samples of the original training data and predicts using their average, that is $f_{bagging}^{k,j}(\mathbf{w}) = \frac{1}{B} \sum_{i=1}^{B} f_\psi^b(\mathbf{w})$. An estimate of the epistemic uncertainty of the prediction can be computed using the variance of the component model predictions [12], that is $\sigma_{k,j}^2(\mathbf{w}) = \frac{1}{B} \sum_{i=1}^{B} \left(f_\psi^b(\mathbf{w}) - f_{bagging}^{k,j}(\mathbf{w})\right)^2$.

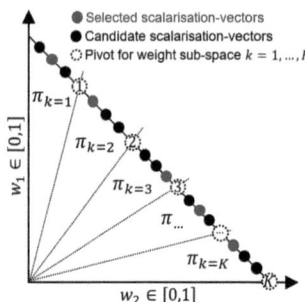
(a) Decomposition of MORL problem into scalar sub-problems.

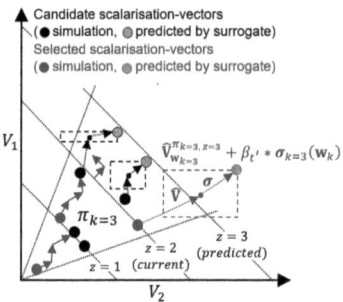
(b) Surrogate-assisted maximisation of CCS hypervolume.

**Fig. 2.** Overview of the proposed approach for UCB-driven utility function search for MORL/D.

**UCB Acquisition Function Maximisation.** For each policy $k$ and each objective $j$ a surrogate model can predict the expected objective values by conditioning a policy on scalarisation vector $\mathbf{w}$ during a training stage $z$ as follows:

$$\hat{V}_{j,\mathbf{w}}^{\pi_k, z+1} = V_{j,\mathbf{w}}^{\pi_k, z} + f_{bagging}^{k,j}(\mathbf{w}) \tag{5}$$

with a corresponding vectorised prediction, denoted as $\hat{\mathbf{V}}_{\mathbf{w}}^{\pi_k,z+1} = \mathbf{V}_{\mathbf{w}}^{\pi_k,z} + \mathbf{f}_{bagging}^k(\mathbf{w})$ over $j$ objectives and the accompanying vectorised uncertainty estimate $\boldsymbol{\sigma}_k^2(\mathbf{w})$.

At the beginning of each training stage $z$ the algorithm needs to select those $N$ scalarisation vectors out $M$ evenly distributed vectors in each sub-space $\mathbf{W}_k$, $k = 1, \ldots, K$ that are predicted via the surrogate model to improve the hypervolume of the resulting $\text{HV}(CCS)$ the most. $\text{HV}(\cdot)$ is a function that computes hypervolume as in [9]. The scalarisation vectors are selected one at a time without replacement in a sequence of $N$ invocations of a process that maximises a UCB acquisition function defined on $\text{HV}(CCS)$ as:

$$\mathbf{w}_k^* = \underset{\mathbf{w}_{k,j} \in \{\mathbf{w}_{k,j}\}_{j=1}^M}{\operatorname{argmax}} \text{HV}\big(\text{Pareto}(\mathbf{V}_{k,j})\big), \tag{6}$$

$$\mathbf{V}_{k,j} = \hat{\mathbf{V}}_{\mathbf{w}_{k,j}}^{\pi_k,z+1} + \beta_{t'} \cdot \boldsymbol{\sigma}_k(\mathbf{w}_{k,j}), \quad k = 1, \ldots, K.$$

where $\text{Pareto}(\cdot)$ is a function computing the CCS from a set of objective vectors. The dynamic parameter of current training step, i.e., $\beta_{t'} = \sqrt{\frac{\log(2t')}{t'}}$ ensures that scalarisation vector with higher uncertainty (standard deviation) are explored early, but the focus shifts towards exploiting the ones with high mean rewards as confidence improves, assuming maximisation of objectives. Once selected, a scalarisation vector $\mathbf{w}_k^*$ is removed from the candidate set $\{\mathbf{w}_{k,j}\}_{j=1}^M$ for the current training stage. The process of selecting scalarisation vectors that are expected to maximise the hypervolume of the resulting CCS is illustrated in Fig. 2b.

### 4.4 Baseline Methods

---

**Algorithm 1.** Fixed-MOPPO

---
1: **Input:** State $s_t$, weights $\mathbf{w}$
2: **Initialize:** $K$ Actor-Critic networks $\pi_k$, $v^{\pi_k}$; scalarisation spaces $\mathbf{W}_k$; buffer $\mathcal{E}$ of size $D$.
3: **for** $k = 1$ **to** $K$ **do**
4:     **for** $t = 1$ **to** $D$ **do**
5:         $\mathbf{w}_{\text{pivot}} \leftarrow \text{get\_pivot\_weight}(\mathbf{W}_k)$
6:         $a_t \sim \pi_k(s_t, \mathbf{w}_{\text{pivot}})$, $s_{t+1}, \mathbf{r}_t \leftarrow \text{simulator}(s_t, a_t)$
7:         $\mathcal{E} \leftarrow \mathcal{E} \cup \langle s_t, a_t, \mathbf{w}_{\text{pivot}}, \mathbf{r}_t, s_{t+1} \rangle$, $s_t \leftarrow s_{t+1}$
8:     **end for**
9:     Sample $\langle s_t, a_t, \mathbf{w}_{\text{pivot}}, \mathbf{r}_t, s_{t+1} \rangle \sim \mathcal{E}$
10:     $\theta \leftarrow \theta + \eta \nabla_\theta \log \pi_\theta(s_t, a_t; \mathbf{w}_{\text{pivot}}) A^\pi(s_t, a_t; \mathbf{w}_{\text{pivot}})$
11:     $\phi \leftarrow \phi + \eta \|V^{\pi_k}(s_t; \mathbf{w}_{\text{pivot}}) - (\mathbf{r}_t + \gamma V^{\pi_k}(s_{t+1}; \mathbf{w}_{\text{pivot}}))\|^2$
12:     $\mathcal{E} \leftarrow \emptyset$
13: **end for**

Seven baseline methods are introduced for comparison, including three proposed **MOPPO** baseline methods for ablation studies and four SOTA MORL methods: 1) **PG-MORL** [17], 2) **PD-MORL** [4], 3) **CAPQL** [18], and 4) **GPI-LS** [2]. These baselines are used to evaluate the benefits introduced by PPO and the UCB-driven search of the scalarisation vector space. A brief description of the proposed **MOPPO baselines** is as follows:

**Fixed-MOPPO** in Algorithm 1, which trains $K$ policies, each conditioned on a fixed scalarisation vector $\mathbf{w}_{pivot} \in \mathbf{W}_k$ corresponding to subspace $k$ (see Fig. 2a).

**Random-MOPPO** (see supplementary material, Sect. 1, algorithm 2) which is similar to Fixed-MOPPO, $K$ policies are trained, with each $\pi_k$ conditioned on scalarisation vectors uniformly sampled from $\mathbf{W}_k$. These vectors are periodically re-sampled to ensure diversity during training.

**Mean-MOPPO** which is identical to UCB-MOPPO, except that the acquisition function ignores uncertainty by setting $\beta_{t'} := 0, \forall t'$ in Eq. 6.

## 5 Experiment Setup

We evaluate the performance of all seven baselines on six continuous control multi-objective RL problems: **Swimmer-V2**, **Halfcheetah-V2**, **Walker2d-V2**, **Ant-V2**, **Hopper-V2**, and **Hopper-V3** (the only problem with three objectives). Detailed descriptions of the objectives, as well as the state and action spaces, are provided in the supplementary material, Sect. 2. Each method is evaluated on three different random seeds for each problem, consistent with [17]. For a fair comparison, we use raw reward outputs and assess the results using the *hypervolume* (HV) and *Expected Utility* (EU) metrics [2].

Table 1. Decomposition setup for two-objective and three-objective problems.

| Parameter | Objective | UCB | Mean | Random | Fixed |
|---|---|---|---|---|---|
| $K$ (pivot vectors) | 2-objective | 10 | 10 | 10 | 10 |
|  | 3-objective | 36 | 36 | 36 | 36 |
| $N$ (sub-space selection) | 2-objective | 10 | 10 | 10 | 1 |
|  | 3-objective | 10 | 10 | 10 | 1 |
| $M$ (sub-space vectors) | 2-objective | 100 | 100 | 10 | 10 |
|  | 3-objective | 117 | 117 | 36 | 36 |
| Step-size (layer 1) | 2-objective | 0.1 | 0.1 | 0.1 | 0.1 |
|  | 3-objective | 0.1 | 0.1 | 0.1 | 0.1 |
| Step-size (layer 2) | 2-objective | 0.01 | 0.01 | 0.1 | 0.1 |
|  | 3-objective | 0.05 | 0.05 | 0.1 | 0.1 |

For UCB-MOPPO and the proposed MOPPO baselines, hyperparameters for policy neural network initialisation and PPO are aligned with the values recommended in Stable-Baselines3 [22]. Detailed hyperparameters are provided in the supplementary material, Sect. 3. Proposed problem decomposition is based on scalarisation vectors generated via discretisation of space **W** with a fixed step size. The overall parameters of problem decomposition for 2- and 3-objective problems are summarised in Table 1. SOTA baselines are reproduced using the MORL-Baseline library [9].

## 6 Results Analysis

### 6.1 Quality of Pareto Front

Pareto front(PF) are evaluated in **HV and EU**, which are reported in Table 2. **PF coverage** and **HV convergence speed** are visualized in Fig. 3.

**Table 2.** Evaluation of HV and EU metrics for continuous MORL tasks over three independent runs. Due to table size limitations, environment and method names are **abbreviated**, and only **mean** values from three runs are reported. The full detailed table is provided in supplementary material, Sect. 4.

|  | Metric | UCB | Mean | Rand- | Fix- | PG- | PD- | CAP- | GPI- |
|---|---|---|---|---|---|---|---|---|---|
| Swimmer | HV ($10^4$) | **5.60** | 4.72 | 4.56 | 4.45 | 1.67 | 1.77 | 2.40 | 4.75 |
|  | EU ($10^2$) | **2.18** | 2.16 | 2.08 | 2.11 | 1.23 | 1.24 | 1.79 | 2.14 |
| Halfcheetah | HV ($10^7$) | 1.78 | 1.60 | 1.21 | 1.12 | 0.58 | 0.62 | **2.20** | 2.16 |
|  | EU ($10^3$) | 3.88 | 3.58 | 3.55 | 3.44 | 2.30 | 2.42 | **4.47** | 4.30 |
| Walker2d | HV ($10^7$) | **1.40** | 1.29 | 1.15 | 1.13 | 0.44 | 0.56 | 0.18 | 1.22 |
|  | EU ($10^3$) | **3.54** | 3.42 | 3.34 | 3.30 | 1.98 | 2.24 | 1.50 | 3.40 |
| Ant | HV ($10^7$) | **1.07** | 0.92 | 0.65 | 0.60 | 0.61 | 0.66 | 0.45 | 0.81 |
|  | EU ($10^3$) | **2.96** | 2.61 | 2.35 | 2.21 | 2.28 | 2.41 | 2.03 | 2.84 |
| Hopper2d | HV ($10^7$) | **0.84** | 0.81 | 0.79 | 0.76 | 0.23 | 0.25 | 0.25 | 0.80 |
|  | EU ($10^3$) | 2.77 | **2.84** | 2.77 | 2.71 | 1.48 | 1.51 | 1.46 | 2.75 |
| Hopper3d | HV ($10^{10}$) | **3.62** | 2.83 | 2.90 | 2.64 | 0.63 | 0.11 | 0.31 | 0.65 |
|  | EU ($10^3$) | 3.20 | 3.19 | **3.28** | 2.90 | 1.70 | 1.74 | 1.52 | 2.14 |

**UCB-MOPPO** delivers consistent performance and outperforms all baselines except in Halfcheetah-V2. Notably, **PGMORL** produces a dense PF by accumulating a large number of policies in the archive, yet it achieves significantly lower HV and EU compared to the proposed MOPPO baselines. **PDMORL** achieves slightly higher HV and EU than PGMORL while using only a single network; however, it struggles with three-objective problems. **CAPQL** achieves the best performance in Halfcheetah-V2 but struggles significantly on Walker2d-V2 and Hopper-V3 due to learning only a limited dynamics of those problems. **GPI-LS** delivers the most competitive results and requires the longest GPU time for training. it performs better than the proposed MOPPO baselines

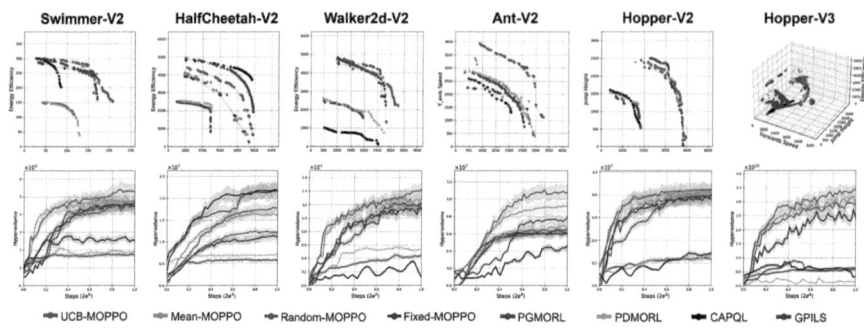

**Fig. 3.** Comparison of PF and HV evaluation for six MORL tasks. The top row shows PF plots, and the bottom row shows HV comparisons. Shaded areas in HV plots represent the standard deviation over three seeds.

in Halfcheetah-V2; however, it fails to explore a spread CCS in the Ant-V2 and Hopper-2d/-3d environments.

The consistent performance of the proposed method can be partially attributed to the integration of PPO, which provides enhanced stability and sample efficiency by employing trust region enforcement compared to vanilla policy gradient methods. As shown in Fig. 3, UCB-MOPPO demonstrates superior convergence across most tasks (except for HalfCheetah-V2). The proposed method achieves rapid early-stage convergence by efficiently identifying scalarisation vectors that improve hypervolume. Additionally, the MOPPO baselines exhibit stable convergence without overfitting and dropping, ensuring robust performance across diverse multi-objective tasks.

### 6.2 Analysis of Ablation Experiments

**Fixed-MOPPO** is the simplest baseline, conditioning policies on pivot scalarisation vectors. It provides quick insights into a new MORL problem but results in a sparse PF.

**Random-MOPPO** achieves higher hypervolume and a denser PF than Fixed-MOPPO by randomly selecting scalarisation vectors under sub-space during training. However, it is inefficient, failing to explore promising regions effectively.

**Mean-MOPPO** improves search efficiency but yields a less dense PF than UCB-driven methods. The less coverage of PF can be attributed to the greedy selection of scalarisation vectors based solely on the mean predicted hypervolume improvement from the surrogates, without awareness of the uncertainty.

### 6.3 Comparison of the Policy Archive

UCB-MOPPO constructs a satisfactory PF with a consistently low number of policies compared to the baselines across all tested environments. The total number of policies after convergence is shown in Table 3. Some challenging problems

**Table 3.** Number of archived policies after the hypervolume converges.

| Environment   | PGMORL | CAPQL | GIPLS | UCB-MOPPO |
|---------------|--------|-------|-------|-----------|
| Swimmer-v2    | 168    | 33    | 41    | 30        |
| Halfcheetah-v2| 285    | 35    | 83    | 30        |
| Walker2d-v2   | 412    | 51    | 52    | 30        |
| Ant-v2        | 64     | 26    | 27    | 30        |
| Hopper-v2     | 206    | 30    | 45    | 30        |
| Hopper-v3     | 4023   | 82    | 89    | 108       |

result in a large number of policies in the archive (e.g., Walker2d-V2 and Hopper-V3).

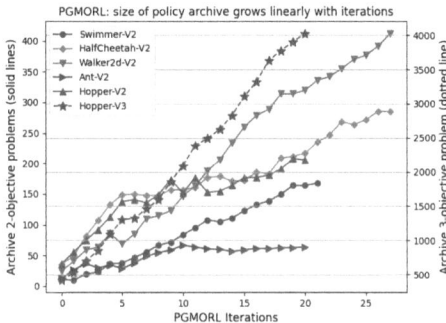

**Fig. 4.** Growth in policy archive size in PGMORL.

A key advantage of all the MOPPO methods is that they maintain a small, fixed set of policies, unlike PGMORL, where the policy archive size grows linearly, as depicted in Fig. 4. Therefore, an efficient search in UCB-MOPPO is complemented by a memory-efficient implementation, which can be an important consideration in production environments with tight resource constraints.

### 6.4 Interpolating in Scalarisation Vectors Spaces

An analysis was carried out to assess the ability of policies trained via UCB-MOPPO to interpolate in a more fine-grained discretisation of vector space $\mathbf{W}$, discretised using smaller step-sizes than those considered during training.

Each of the $K$ policies, corresponding to the $K$ sub-spaces, is evaluated on $N = \{10, 20, \ldots, 50\} \cup \{100, 150, \ldots, 500\}$ scalarisation vectors. The results are shown in Fig. 5, where we present the hypervolume and sparsity curves. The plots reveal a general trend: as $N$ increases, the hypervolume improves, indicating a better approximation of the PF. Simultaneously, sparsity decreases,

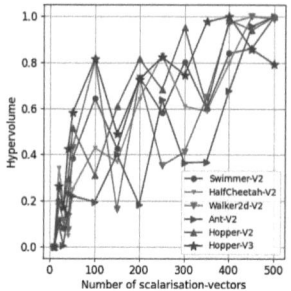 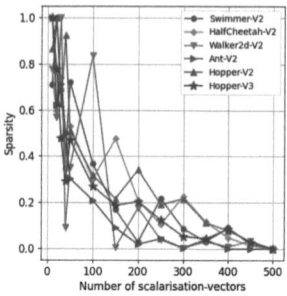

**Fig. 5.** Hypervolume and sparsity achieved by UCB-MOPPO improve with more scalarisation vectors conditioning the policies.

signifying a more uniform PF coverage. This suggests that increasing the granularity of scalarisation vectors leads to a more comprehensive and higher-quality representation of the PF, all without requiring additional training. This advantage is not shared by PGMORL or other MORL/D approaches, which often need further training to achieve similar results. Thus, the proposed method offers a distinct benefit in improving PF quality with minimal computational overhead.

## 7 Conclusion

This paper presents a method for efficiently searching scalarisation vectors that maximize the quality of the CCS. The key findings are: (1) the proposed method outperforms competitive baselines in terms of CCS hypervolume and Expected Utility in most cases, (2) it requires maintaining a minimal number of policies to produce high-quality CCS, making it well-suited for resource-constrained environments, and (3) the CCS hypervolume and sparsity metrics improve as the scalarisation vector step-size decreases, demonstrating effective generalisation across scalarisation vector neighbourhoods. For future work, we plan to explore acquisition functions that leverage additional Pareto front quality indicators [7] and search algorithms designed for non-linear utility function spaces [23].

## References

1. Abels, A., Roijers, D., Lenaerts, T., Nowé, A., Steckelmacher, D.: Dynamic weights in multi-objective deep reinforcement learning. In: International conference on machine learning, pp. 11–20. PMLR (2019)
2. Alegre, L.N., Bazzan, A.L., Roijers, D.M., Nowé, A., da Silva, B.C.: Sample-efficient multi-objective learning via generalized policy improvement prioritization. arXiv preprint arXiv:2301.07784 (2023)
3. Basaklar, F., Sen, T.: Multi-objective reinforcement learning: methods and applications. Expert Syst. Appl. **202**, 117016 (2022)
4. Basaklar, T., Gumussoy, S., Ogras, U.Y.: Pd-morl: preference-driven multi-objective reinforcement learning algorithm. arXiv preprint arXiv:2208.07914 (2022)

5. Breiman, L.: Bagging predictors. Mach. Learn. **24**, 123–140 (1996). https://api.semanticscholar.org/CorpusID:47328136
6. Chen, X., Ghadirzadeh, A., Björkman, M., Jensfelt, P.: Meta-learning for multi-objective reinforcement learning. In: 2019 IEEE/RSJ International Conference on Intelligent Robots and Systems (IROS), pp. 977–983 (2019). https://doi.org/10.1109/IROS40897.2019.8968092
7. Falcón-Cardona, J.G., Coello, C.A.C.: Indicator-based multi-objective evolutionary algorithms: a comprehensive survey. ACM Comput. Surv. (CSUR) **53**(2), 1–35 (2020)
8. Feinberg, E.A., Shwartz, A.: Constrained markov decision models with weighted discounted rewards. Math. Oper. Res. **20**, pp. 302–320 (1995). https://api.semanticscholar.org/CorpusID:16510079
9. Felten, F., et al.: A toolkit for reliable benchmarking and research in multi-objective reinforcement learning. In: Neural Information Processing Systems (2023). https://api.semanticscholar.org/CorpusID:268042105
10. Felten, F., Talbi, E.G., Danoy, G.: Multi-objective reinforcement learning based on decomposition: a taxonomy and framework. J. Artif. Intell. Res. **79**, 679–723 (2024)
11. Gao, X., Yi, W., Agapitos, A., Wang, H., Liu, Y.: Coverage and capacity optimization in star-riss assisted networks: a machine learning approach. In: 2023 IEEE Wireless Communications and Networking Conference (WCNC), pp. 1–6. IEEE (2023)
12. Gawlikowski, J., et al.: A survey of uncertainty in deep neural networks. Artif. Intell. Rev. **56**(Suppl 1), 1513–1589 (2023)
13. Hayes, C.F., et al.: A practical guide to multi-objective reinforcement learning and planning. Auton. Agent. Multi-Agent Syst. **36**(1), 1–59 (2022). https://doi.org/10.1007/s10458-022-09552-y
14. He, K., Zhang, X., Ren, S., Sun, J.: Deep residual learning for image recognition. In: Proceedings of the IEEE conference on computer vision and pattern recognition, pp. 770–778 (2016)
15. Kumar, A., Peng, X.B., Levine, S.: Reward-conditioned policies. arXiv preprint arXiv:1912.13465 (2019)
16. Li, K., Zhang, T., Wang, R.: Deep reinforcement learning for multiobjective optimization. In: IEEE Transactions on Cybernetics **51**, pp. 3103–3114 (2019). https://api.semanticscholar.org/CorpusID:174802898
17. Liu, F., Qian, C.: Prediction guided meta-learning for multi-objective reinforcement learning. In: 2021 IEEE Congress on Evolutionary Computation (CEC), pp. 2171–2178 (2021). https://api.semanticscholar.org/CorpusID:236981140
18. Lu, H., Herman, D., Yu, Y.: Multi-objective reinforcement learning: convexity, stationarity and pareto optimality. In: International Conference on Learning Representations (2023). https://api.semanticscholar.org/CorpusID:260108193
19. Mossalam, H., Assael, Y.M., Roijers, D.M., Whiteson, S.: Multi-objective deep reinforcement learning (2016)
20. Natarajan, S., Tadepalli, P.: Dynamic preferences in multi-criteria reinforcement learning. In: Proceedings of the 22nd international conference on Machine learning (2005). https://api.semanticscholar.org/CorpusID:15370837
21. Pan, A., Xu, W., Wang, L., Ren, H.: Additional planning with multiple objectives for reinforcement learning. Knowl.-Based Syst. **193**, 105392 (2020)
22. Raffin, A., Hill, A., Gleave, A., Kanervisto, A., Ernestus, M., Dormann, N.: Stable-baselines3: reliable reinforcement learning implementations. J. Mach. Learn. Res. **22**(268), 1–8 (2021)

23. Reymond, M., Hayes, C.F., Steckelmacher, D., Roijers, D.M., Nowé, A.: Actor-critic multi-objective reinforcement learning for non-linear utility functions. Auton. Agent. Multi-Agent Syst. **37**(2), 23 (2023)
24. Roijers, D.M., Vamplew, P., Whiteson, S., Dazeley, R.: A survey of multi-objective sequential decision-making. J. Artif. Intell. Res. **48**, 67–113 (2013)
25. Roijers, D.M., Whiteson, S., Oliehoek, F.A.: Point-based planning for multi-objective pomdps. In: International Joint Conference on Artificial Intelligence (2015). https://api.semanticscholar.org/CorpusID:9116349
26. Schulman, J., Wolski, F., Dhariwal, P., Radford, A., Klimov, O.: Proximal policy optimization algorithms. arXiv preprint arXiv:1707.06347 (2017)
27. Siddique, U., Weng, P., Zimmer, M.: Learning fair policies in multi-objective (deep) reinforcement learning with average and discounted rewards. In: International Conference on Machine Learning, pp. 8905–8915. PMLR (2020)
28. Srinivas, N., Krause, A., Kakade, S.M., Seeger, M.: Gaussian process optimization in the bandit setting: no regret and experimental design. arXiv preprint arXiv:0912.3995 (2009)
29. Sutton, R.S., McAllester, D., Singh, S., Mansour, Y.: Policy gradient methods for reinforcement learning with function approximation. In: Proceedings of the 12th International Conference on Neural Information Processing Systems, pp. 1057–1063 (2000)
30. Vamplew, P., Dazeley, R., Foale, C., Firmin, S., Mummery, S.: Empirical evaluation methods for multiobjective reinforcement learning algorithms. Mach. Learn. **84**(1), 51–80 (2011)
31. Xu, Y., Zhou, B., Sun, X.: Reinforcement learning for multi-objective optimization: a survey. Artif. Intell. Rev. **53**(6), 4123–4156 (2020)
32. Yang, R., Sun, X., Narasimhan, K.: A generalized algorithm for multi-objective reinforcement learning and policy adaptation. In: Neural Information Processing Systems (2019). https://api.semanticscholar.org/CorpusID:201319046
33. Yang, Y., Roijers, D.M., Foster, C.: Generalized multiple objectives for reinforcement learning. In: Advances in Neural Information Processing Systems (NeurIPS). vol. 32, pp. 5194–5204 (2019)
34. Zhang, Q., Li, H.: Moea/d: a multiobjective evolutionary algorithm based on decomposition. IEEE Trans. Evol. Comput. **11**(6), 712–731 (2007)
35. Zhang, Z., Yang, Y., Wang, J., Roijers, D.M., Nowé, A., Foster, C.: Convex hull value iteration for multi-objective reinforcement learning. Adv. Neural. Inf. Process. Syst. **33**, 20837–20848 (2020)
36. Zhu, W., Li, Q., Wang, Z.: A survey on multi-objective reinforcement learning: advances and challenges. ACM Comput. Surv. **55**(1), 1–32 (2023)
37. Zou, H., Hastie, T.: Regularization and variable selection via the elastic net. J. R. Stat. Soc. Ser. B (Stat. Method.) **67**(2), 301–320 (2003)

# Efficient and Generalized End-to-End Autonomous Driving System with Latent Deep Reinforcement Learning and Demonstrations

Zuojin Tang[1,2], Xiaoyu Chen[3], Yongqiang Li[4], and Jianyu Chen[1,3(✉)]

[1] Shanghai Qizhi Institute, Shanghai, China
jianyuchen@tsinghua.edu.cn
[2] College of Computer Science and Technology, Zhejiang University, Hangzhou, China
[3] Institute for Interdisciplinary Information Sciences, Tsinghua University, Beijing, China
[4] Mogo Auto Intelligence and Telematics Information Technology Co., Ltd, Beijing, China

**Abstract.** An intelligent driving system should dynamically formulate appropriate driving strategies based on the current environment and vehicle status while ensuring system security and reliability. However, methods based on reinforcement learning and imitation learning often suffer from high sample complexity, poor generalization, and low safety. To address these challenges, this paper introduces an efficient and generalized end-to-end autonomous driving system (EGADS) for complex and varied scenarios. The RL agent in our EGADS combines variational inference with normalizing flows, which are independent of distribution assumptions. This combination allows the agent to capture historical information relevant to driving in latent space effectively, thereby significantly reducing sample complexity. Additionally, we enhance safety by formulating robust safety constraints and improve generalization and performance by integrating RL with expert demonstrations. Experimental results demonstrate that, compared to existing methods, EGADS significantly reduces sample complexity, greatly improves safety performance, and exhibits strong generalization capabilities in complex urban scenarios. Particularly, we contributed an expert dataset collected through human expert steering wheel control, specifically using the G29 steering wheel. Our code is available: https://github.com/Mark-zjtang/EGADS?tab=readme-ov-file.

## 1 Introduction

An intelligent autonomous driving systems must be able to handle complex road geometry and topology, complex multi-agent interactions with dense surrounding dynamic objects, and accurately follow the planning and obstacle avoidance. Current, autonomous driving systems in industry are mainly using a highly

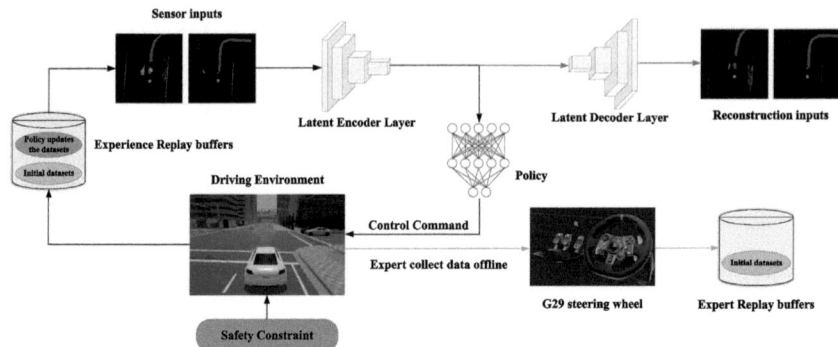

**Fig. 1.** Overview of the efficient and generalized end-to-end autonomous driving system with latent deep reinforcement learning and demonstrations.

modularized hand-engineered approach, for example, perception, localization, behavior prediction, decision making and motion control, etc. [40] and [41]. Particularly, the autonomous driving decision making systems are focusing on the non-learning model-based methods, which often requires to manually design a driving policy [14] and [31]. However, the manually designed policy could have two several weaknesses: 1) Accuracy. The driving policy of human heuristics and pre-training model can be suboptimal, which will lead to either conservative or aggressive driving policies. 2) Generality. For different scenarios and complicated tasks, we might need to be redesigned the model policy manually for each new scenario.

To solve those problems, existing works such as imitation learning (IL) is most popular approach, which can learn a driving policy by collecting the expert driving data. However, those methods can suffer from the following shortcomings for imitation learning: (1) High training cost and sample complexity. (2) Conservation. Due to the collect driving data from the human expert, which can only learn driving skills that are demonstrated in the datasets. (3) Limitation of driving performance. What's more, the driving policy based on reinforcement learning (RL) is also popular method in recent years, which can automatically learn and explore without any human expert data in various kinds of different driving cases, and it is possible to have a better performance than imitation learning. However, the existing methods also have some weakness: (1) Existing methods in latent space are based on specific distribution assumptions, whereas distributions in the real world tend to be more flexible, resulting in a failure to learn more precisely about belief values. (2) High costs of learning and exploration. (3) The safety and generalization of intelligent vehicles need further improvement.

Combining the advantages of RL and IL, the demonstration of enhanced RL is not only expected to accelerate the initial learning process, but also gain the potential of experts beyond performance. In this paper, we introduce an efficient and generalized end-to-end autonomous driving system (EGADS) for complex and varied scenarios. The RL agent in our EGADS combines variational inference with normalizing flows independent of distribution assumptions, allowing it to sufficiently and flexibly capture historical information useful for driving in latent space, thereby significantly reducing sample complexity. In addition, unlike traditional methods that constrain policy actions directly, we integrate safety constraints into the reward function, which allows the agent to consider safety during training, thereby improving its robustness and generalization. To further increase the upper limit of the overall system, we further enhance the RL search process with a dataset of human experts. In particular, we contributed a dataset of human experts to driving by driving the G29 steering wheel. The experimental results show that compared with the existing methods, our EGADS greatly improves the safety performance, shows strong generalization ability in multiple test maps, and significantly reduces the sample complexity. In summary, our contributions are:

- We present an EGADS framework designed for complex and varied scenarios.
- The RL agent in EGADS uses variational inference with normalizing flows (NFRL), independent of distribution assumptions, to capture historical driving information in latent space, significantly reducing sample complexity.
- we incorporate Safety Constraints (SC) directly into the reward function to enable the agent to account for safety considerations during training.
- By fine-tuning with a small amount of human expert dataset via using the G29 steering wheel, NFRL agents can learn more general driving principles, significantly improving generalization and sample efficiency.

## 2 Related Work

Imitation learning, which utilizes an efficient supervised learning approach, has gained widespread application in autonomous driving research due to its simplicity and effectiveness. For instance, imitation learning has been employed in end-to-end autonomous driving systems that directly generate control signals from raw sensor inputs [1,5,8,27].

Deep reinforcement learning (DRL) has demonstrated its strength in addressing complex decision-making and planning problems, leading to a series of breakthroughs in recent years. Researchers have been trying to apply deep RL techniques to the domain of autonomous driving. Lillicarp et.al [24] introduced a continuous control DRL algorithm that trains a deep neural network policy for autonomous driving on a simulated racing track. Wolf et.al [43] used Deep Q-Network to learn to steer an autonomous vehicle to keep in the track in simulation. Chen et.al [4] developed a hierarchical DRL framework to handle driving scenarios with intricate decision-making processes, such as navigating traffic lights. Kendall et.al [22] marked the first application of DRL in real-world autonomous driving, where they trained a deep lane-keeping policy using only a single front-view camera image as input. Chen et.al [3] proposed an interpretable DRL method for end-to-end autonomous driving. Nehme et.al [30] proposed safe navigation. Murdoch et.al [29] propose a partial end-to-end algorithm that decouples the planning and control tasks. Zhou et.al [46] proposes a method to identify and protect unreliable decisions of a DRL driving policy. Zhang et.al [44] a framework of constrained multi-agent reinforcement learning with a parallel safety shield for CAVs in challenging driving scenarios. Liu et.al [26] propose the Scene-Rep Transformer to enhance RL decision-making capabilities.

By combining the advantages of RL and IL is also a relatively popular method in recent years. The techniques outlined in [38,42,45,47] have proven to be efficient in merging demonstrations and RL for improving learning speed. Liu et.al [25] propose a novel framework combining RL and expert demonstration to learn a motion control strategy for urban scenarios. Huang et.al [19] introduces a predictive behavior planning framework that learns to predict and evaluate from human driving data. Huang et.al [20] propose an enhanced human in-the-loop reinforcement learning method, while they rely on human expert performance and can only accomplish simple scenario tasks. DPAG [32] combines RL and imitation learning to solve complex dexterous manipulation problems. Our approach utilizes the potential for reinforcement learning and normalization flows to learn useful information from historical trajectory information, further learning expert demonstrations through DPAG methods.

## 3 Methodology

The proposed framework of our EGADS is illustrated in Fig. 1. Firstly, human experts collect demonstrations offline using the G29 steering wheel. These expert demonstrations are then utilized as the RL fine-tuning experience replay buffers for training the entire model. Subsequently, a pre-training process is conducted to establish a model with human expert experience that does not update environmental data during training. The resulting model, enriched with human expert experience, is then used to fine-tune the policy for RL agent. Additionally, we have designed safety constraints for the intelligent vehicle, enhancing its safety performance.

### 3.1 Preliminaries

We model the control problem as a Partially Observable Markov Decision Process (POMDP), which is defined using the 7-tuple: $(S, A, T, R, \Omega, O, \gamma)$, where $S$ is a set of states, $A$ is a set of actions, $T$ is a set of conditional transition probabilities between states, $R$ is the reward function, $\Omega$ is a set of observations, $O$ is a set of conditional observation probabilities, and $\gamma$ is the discount factor. The goal of the RL agent is to maximize expected cumulative reward $E[\sum_{t=0}^{\infty} \gamma_t r_t]$. After having taken action $a_{t-1}$ and observing $o_t$, an agent needs to update its belief state, which is defined as the probability distribution of the environment state conditioned on all historical information: $b(s_t) = p(s_t \mid \tau_t, o_t)$, where $\tau_t = \{o_1, a_1, \ldots, o_{t-1}, a_{t-1}\}$.

### 3.2 Latent Dynamic Model for Autonomous Driving

We propose the use of latent variables to solve problems in end-to-end autonomous driving. This potential space is used to encode complex urban driving environments, including visual inputs, spatial features, and road conditions.

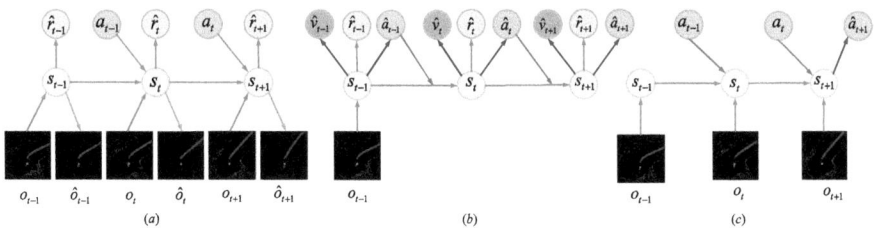

**Fig. 2.** (a) RL agent learns potential dynamics from past experience datasets. (b) RL agent predicts driving action in an imaginary space. (c) RL agent interacts with driving environment. Where $o$ is observation, $a$ is action, $s$ is latent state, $\hat{r}_t$ is reward, $\hat{o}_t$ is reconstructed and $\hat{v}_t$ is value.

Historical high-dimensional raw observation data is compressed into this low-dimensional latent space and learned through a sequential latent environment model that learns in conjunction with the maximum entropy RL process. We introduce RL agent model consists of components can be constructed the probabilistic graphical model of POMDP as follow:

$$\begin{aligned} \text{State transition model:} \quad & p_\theta(s_t|s_{t-1}, a_{t-1}) \\ \text{Reward model:} \quad & p_\theta(r_t|s_t) \\ \text{Observation model:} \quad & p_\theta(o_t|s_t) \end{aligned} \quad (1)$$

where $p$ is prior probability, $q$ is posterior probability, $o$ is observation, $a$ is action, is latent state and $\theta$ is the parameter of the model.

### 3.3 RL Agent in the Latent Space

Visual control [2,34,39] can be defined as a POMDP. The traditional components of agents that learn through imagination include dynamics learning, behavior learning, and environment interaction [16,17]. The RL agent in the latent space in our EGADS mainly includes the following:

(1) RL agent learns potential dynamics from past experience datasets of autonomous vehicle. As shown in Fig. 2(a), using $p$ to represent prior probability, $q$ to represent posterior probability, agent learns to encode observation and action into compact latent state, and $\hat{o}_t$ is reconstructed with $q(\hat{o}_t|s_t)$ while $s_t$ is determined via $p(s_t|s_{t-1}, a_{t-1}, o_t)$.

(2) RL agent predicts driving action in an imaginary space. As shown in Fig. 2(b), RL agent is in a close latent state space where it can predict value $\hat{v}_t$, reward $\hat{r}_t$ and action $\hat{a}_t$ based on current input $o_{t-1}$ with $q(\hat{v}_t, \hat{r}_t, \hat{a}_t|s_t)$, $p(s_t|s_{t-1}, \hat{a}_{t-1})$, $q(\hat{a}_{t-1}|s_{t-1})$.

(3) RL agent interacts with driving environment. As shown in Fig. 2(c), RL agent predicts next action values $\hat{a}_{t+1}$ by encoding historical trajectory information via $q(\hat{a}_{t+1}|s_{t+1})$, $p(s_{t+1}|s_t, a_t, o_{t+1})$.

## 3.4 Normalizing Flow for Inferred Belief

Existing latent RL models in autonomous driving either suffer from the curse of dimensionality or make some assumptions and only learn approximate distributions. This approximation imposes strong limitations and is problematic, whereas distributions in the real world tend to be more flexible. In the continuous and dynamic space, existing methods based on normalizing flows (NF) [10], [18,33] can learn more flexible and generalized beliefs. These methods provide a solid foundation for RL agents to accurately predict future driving actions. Inspired by [7], we added a belief inference model: $q_\theta(s_t|\tau_t, o_t)$, where $\theta$ is the parameter of the model. The belief model can be substituted for the probability density with NF in the KL-divergence term of Eq. 2.

$$q_K(s_t|\tau_t, o_t) = \log q_0(s_t|\tau_t, o_t) - \sum_{k=1}^{K} |\det \frac{\partial f_{\psi_k}}{\partial s_{t,k-1}}|$$

$$p_K(s_t|\tau_t) = \log p_0(s_t|\tau_t) - \sum_{k=1}^{K} |\det \frac{\partial f_{\omega_k}}{\partial s_{t,k-1}}|$$

(2)

where $q_0 = q_\theta$, $q_K = q_{\theta,\psi}$, $p_0 = p_\theta$, $p_K = p_{\theta,\omega}$, $\psi$ and $\omega$ are the parameters of a series of mapping transformations of the posterior and prior distributions. Where $\tau_t = \{o_1, a_1, \cdots, o_{t-1}, a_{t-1}\}$. The input images $o_{1:t}$ and actions $a_{1:t-1}$ are encoded with $q_\theta(s_t|\tau_t, o_t)$. Then the final inferred belief is obtained by propagating $q_\theta(s_t|\tau_t, o_t)$ through a set of NF mappings denoted $f_{\psi_K} \ldots f_{\psi_1}$ to get a posterior distribution $q_{\theta,\psi}(s_t|\tau_t, o_t)$. The final prior is obtained by propagating $p_\theta(s_t|\tau_t)$ through a set of NF mappings denoted $f_{\omega_K} \ldots f_{\omega_1}$ to get a prior distribution $p_{\theta,\omega}(s_t|\tau_t)$. Where $p_K(s_t|\tau_t) = p_K(s_t|s_{t-1}, a_{t-1})$, given the sampled $s_{t-1}$ from $q_K(s_{1:t}|\tau_t, o_t)$. Finally, our NF inference RL model (NFRL) is optimized by variational inference method, in which the evidence lower bound (ELBO) [9,21] is maximized. The loss function is defined as:

$$\mathcal{M}_{\text{model}}(\theta, \psi, \omega) = \sum_{t=1}^{T} \left( \mathbb{E}_{q(s_t|o_{\leq t}, a_{<t})} [\log p_\theta(o_t \mid s_t) + \log p_\theta(r_t \mid s_t)] - \mathbb{E}_{q_K(s_{1:T}|o_{1:T}, a_{1:T-1})} [D_{\text{KL}}(q_K(s_t \mid \tau_t, o_t) \| p_K(s_t \mid \tau_t, o_t))] \right)$$

(3)

## 3.5 Policy Optimization

The action model implements the policy and is designed to predict the actions that are likely to be effective in responding to the simulated environment. The value model estimates the expected reward generated by the behavior model at each state $s_\tau$.

$$a_\tau \sim q_\phi(a_\tau|s_\tau), \quad v_\eta(s_\tau) = \mathbb{E}_{q_\phi}[\sum_{t=t}^{t+H} \gamma^{\tau-t} r_\tau]$$

(4)

where $\phi, \eta$ are the parameters of the approximated policy and value. The obejective of the action model is to use high value estimates to predict action that result in state trajectories

$$\mathcal{M}_{\text{actor}}(\phi) = \mathbb{E}_{q_\phi}(\sum_{\tau=t}^{t+H} V_\tau^\lambda) \tag{5}$$

To update the action and value models, we calculate the value estimate $v_\eta(s_\tau)$ for all states $s_\tau$ along the imagined trajectory. $V_\tau^\lambda$ can be defined as follow:

$$V_\tau^\lambda = (1-\tau)v_\eta(s_{\tau+1}) + \lambda V_{\tau+1}^\lambda, \quad \tau < t+H \tag{6}$$

Then we can train the critic to regress the TD($\lambda$) [35] target return via a mean squared error loss:

$$\mathcal{M}_{\text{critic}}(\eta) = \mathbb{E}\left[\sum_{\tau=t}^{t+H} \frac{1}{2}\left(v_\eta(s_\tau) - V_\tau^\lambda\right)^2\right] \tag{7}$$

where $\eta$ denote the parameters of the critic network and $H$ is the prediction horizon. Then the loss function is as follows:

$$\min_{\psi,\eta,\phi,\theta,\omega,\eta} \alpha_0 \mathcal{M}_{\text{critic}}(\eta) - \alpha_1 \mathcal{M}_{\text{actor}}(\phi) - \alpha_2 \mathcal{M}_{\text{model}}(\theta,\psi,\omega) \tag{8}$$

we jointly optimize the parameters of model loss $\psi, \theta, \omega$, critic loss $\eta$ and actor loss $\phi$, where $\alpha_0, \alpha_1, \alpha_2$ are coefficients for different components.

### 3.6 Safety Constraint

In the Gym-Carla benchmark, the reward function proposed by Chen et.al [6] is denoted as $f_1$. To ensure the intelligent vehicle operates safely and smoothly in complex environments, we incorporated additional safety and robustness constraints into $f_1$, denoted as $f_2 = f_1 + 200r_{ft} + 50r_{lt} + 2r_{sc}$. $r_{ft}$ is the front time to collision. $r_{lt}$ is lateral time to collision. $r_{sc}$ is the smoothness constraint.

(1) Front time to collision. When around vehicles are within the distance of ego vehicle (our agent vehicle) head in our setting, then we can calculate the front time to collision between ego vehicle and around vehicles. Firstly, the speed and steering vector $(s_\tau, a_\tau) \in \mathbb{S}$ of the ego vehicle are defined, where $s_\tau$ represents the angle vector of vehicle steering and $a_\tau$ represents the acceleration vector of the vehicle in local coordinate system. Secondly, two waypoints closest to the current ego vehicle are selected from the given navigation routing as direction vectors $w_p$ for the entire route progression, where $\rightarrow$ indicates a vector in world coordinates. The position vectors for both ego vehicle and around vehicles are represented by $(x_t^*, y_t^*)$, respectively.

Finally, $\delta_e$ and $\delta_a$ representing angles between position vectors for ego vehicle and around vehicles with respect to $w_p$ are calculated respectively.

$$w_p = [(\frac{w_{t+1}^x - w_t^x}{2}) - (w_t^x), (\frac{w_{t+1}^y - w_t^y}{2}) - (w_t^y)]$$
$$\delta_e = \frac{[v_t^{x*}, v_t^{y*}] \cdot w_p}{\|v_t^{x*}, v_t^{y*}\|_2 \; \|w_p\|_2}, \delta_a = \frac{[v_t^x, v_t^y] \cdot w_p}{\|v_t^x, v_t^y\|_2 \; \|w_p\|_2} \quad (9)$$

where, $l$ is the length of the set of waypoints $\mathbb{W}$ stored. The variable $t \in \tau$, and $w_t^x \in \mathbb{W}_1$ represents the $x$ coordinate of the first navigation point closest to the intelligent vehicle on its current route at time $t$. Similarly, $w_{t+1}^x \in \mathbb{W}_2$. Furthermore, it is possible to calculate the $F_{ttc}$ as follows:

$$F_{ttc} = \frac{\|x_t - x_t^*, y_t - y_t^*\|_2}{|\|v_t^{x*}, v_t^{y*}\|_2 sin(\delta_e) - \|v_t^x, v_t^y\|_2 sin(\delta_a)|} \quad (10)$$

(2) Lateral time to collision. When around vehicles are not within the distance of ego vehicle head in our setting, we consider significantly the $L_{ttc}$. The calculation method for $L_{ttc}$ and $F_{ttc}$ is the same. However, the collision constraint effect of $L_{ttc}$ on intelligent vehicle is limited, mainly due to the slow reaction time of intelligent vehicle to $L_{ttc}$, lack of robustness and generalization ability. Therefore, we have implemented a method of assigning values to different intervals for $L_{ttc}$ as follows:

$$\begin{cases} \min(z_\tau, c_\tau + 1.0), & \nu_g \leq (c_\tau - 1.5) \text{ and } \mu_a \leq (c_\tau - 0.5). \\ \min(z_\tau, c_\tau - 1.8), & \nu_g \leq (c_\tau - 3.0) \text{ and } \mu_a \leq (c_\tau - 2.0). \\ \min(z_\tau, c_\tau - 3.0), & \nu_g \leq (c_\tau - 3.5) \text{ and } \mu_a \leq (c_\tau - 3.0). \end{cases} \quad (11)$$

where $c_\tau$ is the empirical const of $L_{ttc}$ in our setting at (5,7), $z_\tau$ is the ttc based on their combined speed. $\nu_g$ is the ttc obtained by calculating the longitudinal velocity. $\mu_a$ is the ttc obtained by calculating the lateral velocity.

(3) Smooth steering is defined as $|s_t^\delta - s_t^{*\delta}| \in e_c$. $s_t^\delta$ is the actual steering angle. $s_t^{*\delta}$ is the predicted steering angle based on policy $\pi$. The range of $e_c$ can be established based on empirical data.

## 3.7 Augmenting RL Policy with Demonstrations

Though, NFRL can significantly reduce complexity, and reward design based on safety constraints can enhance safety. Demonstrations can mitigate the need for painstaking reward shaping, guide exploration, further reduce sample complexity, and help generate robust, natural behaviors. We propose the demonstration augmented RL agent method which incorporates demonstrations into NFRL agent in two ways:

(1) Pretraining with behavior cloning. We use behavior cloning to provide a policy $\pi^*$ via expert demonstrations and then to train a model $\mathcal{M}_{expert}$ with some expert ability.

$$\mathcal{M}_{\text{expert}} = \underset{\xi}{\text{maximize}} \sum_{(s',a') \in \pi^*(\mathcal{D}_e)} \ln \pi_\xi^*(a'_\tau | s'_\tau) \quad (12)$$

where $\mathcal{D}_e$ is a human expert dataset obtained from driving G29 steering.
(2) RL fine-tuning with augmented loss: we employ $\mathcal{M}_{\text{expert}}$ to initialize a model trained by deep RL policies, which reduces the sampling complexity of the deep RL policy. The training loss of the actor model as follows:

$$\mathcal{M}_{\hat{\text{actor}}}(\phi, \xi) = \mathcal{M}_{\text{actor}}(\phi) + k \ln \pi_\xi^*(a'_\tau | s'_\tau), (a'_\tau, s'_\tau) \in \mathcal{D}_e \quad (13)$$

where $k$ represents the balance between the behavior cloning policy and NFRL policy, and is set as a constant based on empirical data. We only changed the actor model of NFRL, and the optimization of the other parts is exactly the same.

## 4 Experiment

### 4.1 Experiment Setup

Models were trained on an NVIDIA RTX 3090 GPU using Python 3.8. Our experiments were conducted on a benchmark called Gym-carla, a third-party environment for OpenAI gym that is used with the CARLA simulator [11]. In our experiments, as shown in Fig. 3, the NFRL series models and baseline methods were trained in Town03 (random) and evaluated across four scenarios: Town03, Town04, Town05, and Town06. These scenarios are abbreviated as Town03-Town06, encompassing both random and roundabout modes. Town03 simulates a realistic urban environment with diverse features such as tunnels, intersections, roundabouts, curves, and turnaround bends. Here, "random" refers to randomly selected intersections and driving scenarios, while "roundabout" focuses specifically on roundabout intersections. Town04, a small town embedded in the mountains with a special infinite highway. Town05, squared-grid town with cross junctions and a bridge. Town06, long many lane highways with many highway entrances and exits.

**Fig. 3.** The road networks of the CARLA include routes for Town03, Town04, Town05, and Town06

## 4.2 Comparison Settings

In order to evaluate the performance of our autonomous driving system more effectively, we have conducted various comparisons with existing methods such as DDPG [24], SAC [15], TD3 [12], DQN [28], Latent_SAC [3], Dreamer [16], CQL [23]. We decomposed EGADS into three components: NFRL, Safety Constraint (SC) and augmenting RL policy with demonstrations (Demo). We then conducted evaluations using four comparison settings, NFRL, NFRL+SC, BC+Demo, NFRL+SC+Demo. BC+Demo indicates the use of behavioral cloning to imitate the expert dataset, while NFRL+SC+Demo involves using expert datasets to augment the NFRL policy combined with SC.

## 4.3 Hyperparameter Settings

$\mathcal{M}_{model}$, the KL regularizer is clipped below 3.0 free nats for imagination range $H = 15$ using the same trajectories for updating action and value models separately with $\lambda = 0.99$ and $\lambda = 0.95$, while $k = 1.5$. The size of all our trainig and evaluating images is $128 \times 128 \times 3$. A random seed $S = 5$ is used to collect datasets for the *ego* vehicle before updating the model every $C = 100$ steps during training process.

All baseline methods share a model size of 32 but differ in other hyperparameters: conventional RL algorithms (DDPG, SAC, TD3, DQN) and Latent_SAC use a larger batch size of 256 with 5 evaluation episodes and action repeat of 2, while NFRL-based methods (NFRL, NFRL+SC, BC+Demo, NFRL+SC+Demo) and Dreamer adopt a smaller batch size of 32 with 10 evaluation episodes and action repeat of 1.

Regarding learning rates: The standard RL methods (DDPG, SAC, TD3, DQN) and Latent_SAC share identical learning rate configurations, with model learning rate at $1 \times 10^{-4}$, and both actor and value learning rates at $3 \times 10^{-4}$. The model-based approaches (Dreamer, NFRL series methods and BC+Demo) demonstrate different patterns, using a higher model learning rate of $1 \times 10^{-3}$, while maintaining lower actor and value learning rates at $8 \times 10^{-5}$. Notably, all NFRL variants (NFRL, NFRL+SC, NFRL+SC+Demo) and BC+Demo maintain identical learning rate configurations with the Dreamer method.

## 4.4 Measure Driving Performance Metrics

In the Gym-Carla benchmark, an episode terminates under any of the following conditions: the number of collisions exceeds one, the maximum number of time steps is reached, the destination is reached, the cumulative lateral deviation from the lane exceeds 10 m, or the vehicle remains stationary for 50 s. EGADS is an end-to-end autonomous driving system. We implemented our trained model on an autonomous vehicle for urban navigation, assessing performance through five standard metrics: Off-road Rate (OR), Episode Completion Rate (ER), Average Safe Driving Distance (ASD), Average Reward (AR) using the reward function from Chen et.al [6] that accounts for driving dynamics (yaw, collisions, speeding, and lateral velocity), and Driving Score (DS): a composite metric calculated as DS = ER × AR in accordance with CARLA Leaderboard standards. During model selection, we focused on checkpoints that simultaneously optimized DS and AR, while implementing the remaining metrics (ER, OR, AR, ASD) based on the methodology from Gao et.al [13] and Tang et.al [37] [36]. As below:

$$OR = \frac{N_{\text{off\_road\_events}}}{N_{\text{total\_episodes}}}, ER = \frac{N_{\text{completed\_steps}}}{N_{\text{total\_steps}}}, AR = \frac{\sum_{i=1}^{N_{\text{episodes}}} \text{rewards}_i}{N_{\text{total\_episodes}}} \quad (14)$$

$$ASD = \frac{\sum_{i=1}^{N_{\text{episodes}}} \text{distance}_i}{N_{\text{total\_episodes}}}, DS = ER \times AR \quad (15)$$

where $N_{\text{off\_road\_events}}$ is the number of times the vehicle went off-road, and $N_{\text{total\_steps}}$ is the total number of episodes. Where $N_{\text{total\_episodes}}$ is the total number of episodes in the test. Where $\text{distance}_i$ is the distance driven during the $i$-th safe driving episode. Where $N_{\text{completed\_steps}}$ is the number of successfully completed steps, and $N_{\text{total\_steps}}$ is the total number of steps in the episode. Where $AR$ is the average reward $f$ collected during the episode.

### 4.5 Collect Expert Datasets

CARLA can be operated and controlled through using the python API. Figure 4 shows that we establish a connection between the Logitech G29 steering wheel and the CARLA, and then human expert can collect the datasets of teaching via the G29 steering wheel. Specifically, we linearly map accelerator pedals, brake pedals, and turning angles into *accel[0,3](min,max), brake[-8,0] (min,max), steer[-1,1](left,right)*. The tensors are written into user-built Python scripts and combined with CARLA built-in Python API so that users can provide input from their steering wheels to autonomous driving cars in CARLA simulator for $\mathcal{D}_{expert}$ collection. Particularly, we contributed a dataset collected through human expert steering wheel control.

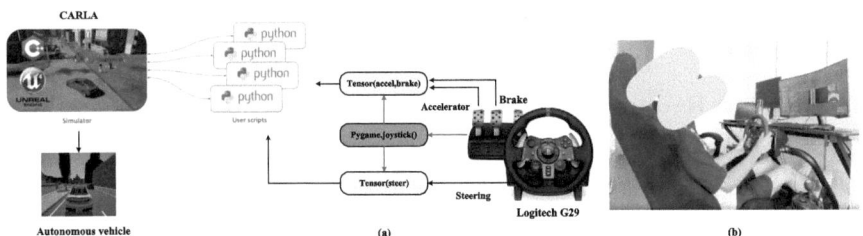

**Fig. 4.** (a) CARLA connects with the G29 steering wheel (b) Human expert collects the datasets via the G29 steering wheel

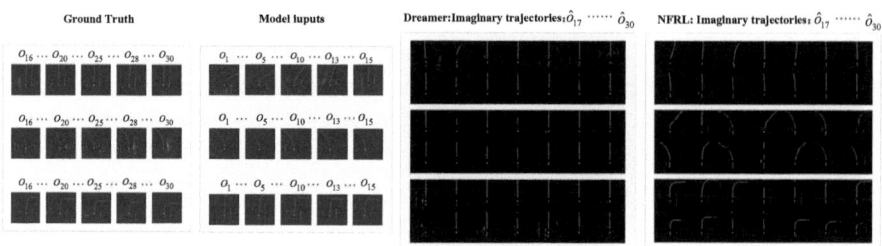

**Fig. 5.** Randomly sample sensor inputs Lidar_noground $o_1, o_2, \cdots, o_{15}$, and then our model can imagine driving behaviors $\hat{o}_{16}, \hat{o}_{17}, \cdots, \hat{o}_{30}$.

**Table 1.** In training, all methods were compared under different RL baselines in Town03 (random), with episodes of 500 steps. $+\infty$ indicates failure to reach the baseline within the maximum tested runtime of 250 GPU hours.

| Method | ASD=50 m | | ASD=100 m | |
|---|---|---|---|---|
| | episodes↓ | times↓ | episodes↓ | times↓ |
| DDPG | $+\infty$ | $+\infty$ | $+\infty$ | $+\infty$ |
| SAC | $+\infty$ | $+\infty$ | $+\infty$ | $+\infty$ |
| TD3 | $\geq 161$ | $\geq 192$h | $+\infty$ | $+\infty$ |
| DQN | $\geq 163$ | $\geq 53$h | $+\infty$ | $+\infty$ |
| Latent_SAC | $\geq 167$ | $\geq 43$h | $\geq 352$ | $\geq 105$h |
| Dreamer | $+\infty$ | $+\infty$ | $+\infty$ | $+\infty$ |
| NFRL(our) | $\geq 141$ | $\geq \mathbf{21}$**h** | $\geq 121$ | $\geq \mathbf{65}$**h** |

### 4.6 Results on Trajectory Prediction

In order to accurately evaluate our model prediction of driving actions for intelligent vehicle, this problem can be viewed as a special POMDP problem with the reward value maintained at 0. As shown in Fig. 5, the comparison with ground-truth data demonstrates that our NFRL model achieves higher accuracy and greater diversity than Dreamer, with no mode collapse and significantly reduced blurring effects.

### 4.7 How to Reduce Sampling Complexity ?

To evaluate the sampling complexity of different methods, we used the average ASD as the test threshold and set three distinct checkpoints at 50 m, 100 m, and 200 m. We measured the GPU hours required for each method to reach the corresponding ASD threshold, with a maximum testing duration capped at 250 GPU hours, as shown in Tables 1 and 2. Notably, in Table 1, although different methods require varying numbers of episodes to reach the ASD threshold, the actual time consumed differs significantly. This is because each episode has a fixed length of 500 steps. Some methods remain stationary for most of the episode, yet the episode does not terminate early, leading to prolonged total runtime. In

**Table 2.** In training, all methods were compared under different NFRL baselines in Town03 (random), with episodes of 500 steps. $+\infty$ indicates failure to reach the baseline within the maximum tested runtime of 250 GPU hours.

| Method | ASD=50 m | | ASD=100 m | | ASD=200 m | |
|---|---|---|---|---|---|---|
| | episodes↓ | times↓ | episodes↓ | times↓ | episodes↓ | times↓ |
| NFRL | ≥141 | ≥21h | ≥121 | ≥65h | $+\infty$ | $+\infty$ |
| NFRL+SC | ≥71 | ≥12h | ≥301 | ≥40h | ≥1100 | ≥146h |
| NFRL+SC+Demo | ≥21 | ≥1.3h | ≥58 | ≥3h | ≥321 | ≥48h |

**Table 3.** Performance Comparison Across multiple Towns (Trained in Town03, Evaluated in Town04-Town06, hereinafter referred to as T04-T06)

| Method | DS ↑ | | | AR ($f_1$) ↑ | | | EC (%) ↑ | | | OR (%) ↓ | | | ASD (m) ↑ | | |
|---|---|---|---|---|---|---|---|---|---|---|---|---|---|---|---|
| | T04 | T05 | T06 | T04 | T05 | T06 | T04 | T05 | T06 | T04 | T05 | T06 | T04 | T05 | T06 |
| DDPG | −0.10 | −0.01 | −0.08 | −10.01 | −10.1 | −10.02 | 0.00 | 0.01 | 0.00 | - | - | - | 0.00 | 0.00 | 0.00 |
| DQN | 17.50 | 60.67 | 69.09 | 76.37 | 174.89 | 206.66 | 11.38 | 15.84 | 16.34 | 11.83 | 11.83 | 15.26 | 20.29 | 31.01 | 36.83 |
| TD3 | −15.89 | −2.24 | −25.62 | −131.36 | −84.83 | −195.60 | 9.18 | 8.16 | 5.82 | 33.32 | 16.94 | 16.02 | 6.17 | 10.05 | 4.50 |
| SAC | −20.56 | −14.89 | −15.02 | −14.08 | −18.92 | −16.67 | 4.95 | 69.07 | 85.60 | 0.00 | 0.00 | 0.00 | 6.71 | 6.07 | 8.03 |
| L_SAC | 102.61 | 110.66 | 21.52 | 170.79 | 8.70 | 145.77 | 15.09 | 12.78 | 12.21 | 1.05 | 4.96 | 4.64 | 15.97 | 21.24 | 42.15 |
| Dreamer | −0.01 | −0.03 | −0.03 | −15.10 | −15.10 | −15.20 | 0.00 | 0.12 | 0.20 | - | - | - | 0.01 | 0.01 | 0.00 |
| NFRL (base) | **326.78** | **390.54** | **431.44** | **1509.90** | **785.92** | **947.26** | **15.81** | 22.61 | 29.59 | 30.88 | 12.05 | 16.50 | **220.18** | **123.24** | **143.61** |

contrast, other methods may collide or deviate from the lane, triggering early termination of the episode Table 4.

As shown in Table 1, our proposed NFRL method significantly improves training time efficiency, achieving at least a 2-fold acceleration in reaching the 50-meter and 100-meter baselines compared to existing reinforcement learning methods. However, due to frequent collision issues observed in experiments, the method fails to surpass the 150-meter baseline. To address this limitation, we innovatively design a reward function incorporating Safety Constraints (SC). Experimental results, as presented in Table 2, show that the enhanced NFRL+SC method not only successfully achieves the 200-meter baseline but also improves training efficiency by at least 1.5 times compared to the original NFRL method. To further optimize performance, we introduce expert datasets for fine-tuning. Experimental data indicate that the NFRL+SC+Demo method achieves a remarkable 3-fold improvement in training efficiency over the NFRL+SC method when reaching the 200-meter baseline.

The performance improvements are primarily driven by three key mechanisms: (1) The NFRL framework employs Normalizing Flow technology to reconstruct training data distributions, aligning them more closely with real-world driving scenarios. This technique enables both accurate future trajectory prediction and comprehensive coverage of possible trajectories across diverse driving situations. Such high-quality data representation allows the model to rapidly learn correct behavioral patterns. (2) The Safety Constraint (SC) module dynamically limits the policy exploration scope to safe regions, thereby minimizing costly divergent behaviors. (3) Demonstration data accelerates reward

**Table 4.** Evaluation results for different methods in CARLA Town03 (random) and Town03 (roundabout): we denote RND as random and RBT as roundabout. For a fair comparison, all reward functions are in the form of $f_1$. Particularly, − indicates that valid data could not be obtained because the episode completion rate for this method is close to 0.

| Method | DS ↑ | | AR ($f_1$) ↑ | | EC(%) ↑ | | OR(%) ↓ | | ASD(m) ↑ | |
|---|---|---|---|---|---|---|---|---|---|---|
| | RND | RBT | RND | RBT | RND | RBT | RND | RBT | RND | RBT |
| DDPG | −0.11 | −0.08 | −10.01 | −10.02 | 0.01 | 0.00 | − | − | 0.00 | 0.00 |
| DQN | 30.64 | 36.33 | 86.50 | 121.24 | 17.02 | 16.42 | 8.52 | 11.83 | 21.68 | 26.27 |
| TD3 | 2.40 | −6.60 | −18.15 | −129.52 | 6.91 | 4.07 | 51.53 | 49.32 | 7.51 | 3.12 |
| SAC | −7.57 | −20.56 | −19.90 | −24.74 | **63.76** | **67.95** | **0.00** | **0.65** | 6.27 | 6.71 |
| L_SAC | 125.95 | 31.59 | 161.24 | 84.13 | 11.98 | 10.50 | 14.72 | 1.14 | 31.31 | 13.87 |
| Dreamer | −0.03 | −0.02 | −15.12 | −15.12 | 0.01 | 0.02 | − | − | 0.01 | 0.01 |
| NFRL (base) | **170.03** | **48.73** | **424.60** | **249.17** | 24.04 | 10.88 | 20.93 | 18.11 | **72.16** | **46.27** |

**Table 5.** During the evaluation, an ablation study of EGADS's three modules across scenarios was conducted (Trained in Town03, Evaluated in Town04-Town06, hereinafter referred to as T04-T06)

| Method | DS ↑ | | | AR ($f_1$) ↑ | | | EC (%) ↑ | | | OR (%) ↓ | | | ASD (m) ↑ | | |
|---|---|---|---|---|---|---|---|---|---|---|---|---|---|---|---|
| | T04 | T05 | T06 | T04 | T05 | T06 | T04 | T05 | T06 | T04 | T05 | T06 | T04 | T05 | T06 |
| NFRL | 326.78 | 390.54 | 431.44 | 1509.90 | 785.92 | 947.26 | 15.81 | 22.61 | 29.59 | 30.88 | 12.05 | 16.50 | **220.18** | **123.24** | 143.61 |
| NFRL+SC | 649.46 | 213.17 | 1234.89 | 418.22 | 381.39 | 1571.85 | 48.70 | 38.80 | 63.42 | **0.00** | **0.00** | **0.00** | 91.34 | 50.42 | 195.36 |
| NFRL+SC+Demo | **1174.16** | **723.90** | **2155.40** | 1329.89 | **894.58** | **2294.30** | **57.41** | **46.85** | **82.47** | 3.25 | 11.51 | 6.05 | 159.42 | 116.96 | **265.92** |

function discovery by injecting domain-specific prior knowledge. This co-design enables EGADS to achieve efficient convergence in complex autonomous driving scenarios, establishing it as a paradigm for sample-efficient reinforcement learning.

### 4.8 Ablation Study

In the ablation study of the EGADS system, we evaluated the contributions of each module in cross-domain scenarios (evaluated in Town04, Town05 and Town06, trained in Town03) to validate the generalization performance of the NFRL, SC and Demo modules, as shown in Tables 5. The driving score (DS) served as the primary comprehensive metric, with other indicators providing supplementary reference. The addition of the SC module significantly improves the cross-scenario performance of NFRL (e.g. NFRL vs. NFRL + SC), demonstrating the effectiveness of our SC module design. Further incorporating the Demo learning module on top of NFRL+SC, the experimental results show that NFRL+SC+Demo achieves the highest scores in Town04 (1174.16), Town05 (723.90), and Town06 (2155.40), with substantial improvements over both the baseline NFRL and NFRL+SC configurations. This proves that the Demo module enhances cross-domain generalization through expert knowledge.

**Table 6.** Evaluation results for different methods in CARLA Town03 (random) and Town03 (roundabout): we denote RND as random and RBT as roundabout. For a fair comparison, all reward functions are in the form of $f_1$. Particularly, − indicates that valid data could not be obtained because the episode completion rate for this method is close to 0.

| Method | DS ↑ | | AR ($f_1$) ↑ | | EC(%) ↑ | | OR(%) ↓ | | ASD(m) ↑ | |
|---|---|---|---|---|---|---|---|---|---|---|
| | RND | RBT | RND | RBT | RND | RBT | RND | RBT | RND | RBT |
| L_SAC | 125.95 | 31.59 | 161.24 | 84.13 | 11.98 | 10.50 | 14.72 | 1.14 | 31.31 | 13.87 |
| Dreamer | −0.03 | −0.02 | −15.12 | −15.12 | 0.01 | 0.02 | − | − | 0.01 | 0.01 |
| NFRL | 170.03 | 48.73 | 424.60 | 249.17 | 24.04 | 10.88 | 20.93 | 18.11 | 72.16 | 46.27 |
| L_SAC+SC | 156.23 | 64.76 | 284.02 | 148.50 | 13.98 | 15.91 | 10.64 | 12.88 | 50.52 | 18.67 |
| Dreamer+SC | 98.12 | 50.02 | 124.74 | 74.98 | 10.42 | 11.20 | 18.08 | 16.35 | 42.85 | 16.90 |
| NFRL+SC | 192.84 | 101.29 | 341.56 | 181.28 | 38.46 | 34.66 | **5.87** | **4.04** | 80.21 | 50.24 |
| BC+Demo | −6.30 | −1.63 | −62.43 | −27.92 | 9.22 | 10.31 | 15.49 | 15.57 | 14.78 | 15.34 |
| CQL+Demo | 8.52 | 4.35 | 42.10 | 49.06 | 10.58 | 8.21 | 13.45 | 19.08 | 19.25 | 16.01 |
| NFRL+Demo | 203.26 | 143.03 | 478.04 | 26.15 | 25.71 | 20.66 | 10.50 | 12.82 | 81.32 | 64.80 |
| NFRL+SC+Demo | **485.92** | **380.17** | **720.27** | **653.21** | **44.25** | **36.63** | 7.69 | 5.48 | **100.13** | **84.92** |

As shown in Table 6, we conducted comprehensive comparisons with various mainstream baselines (online RL methods such as L_SAC and Dreamer; offline or imitation learning approaches including BC+Demo and CQL+Demo) across two challenging scenarios (Town03 RND and RBT). The multi-dimensional evaluation metrics clearly demonstrate that: 1) The NFRL framework itself surpasses existing online RL methods; 2) The SC module universally and significantly enhances both safety and overall performance across all methods, including baselines; 3) The NFRL framework effectively utilizes demonstration data, achieving far superior results compared to imitation learning and offline RL baselines; 4) The final NFRL+SC+Demo solution comprehensively outperforms all methods, including enhanced baselines, across nearly all positive metrics (DS, AR, EC, ASD) while maintaining excellent safety performance. These results fully validate the absolute superiority of our proposed method, the effectiveness of each module, and the powerful synergistic effects of their combination.

### 4.9 How to Improve Generalization Capabilities ?

The EGADS system enhances cross-scenario generalization through the co-design of the NFRL framework, SC module, and Demo module. NFRL decouples state representation from policy learning, establishing a transferable foundation for driving policies. As shown in Table 3, in the cross-town evaluation (Town04-Town06), NFRL achieves a significantly higher DS value compared to traditional reinforcement learning methods, demonstrating robust generalization capabilities.

As evidenced in Tables 5 and 6, the SC module effectively mitigates high-risk behaviors through trajectory smoothing, improving overall DS values compared to standalone NFRL and enhancing system robustness. Meanwhile, the Demo module accelerates policy convergence and optimizes exploration via imitation learning. As shown in Tables 5 and 6, the NFRL+SC+Demo configuration demonstrates significant improvements across multiple metrics including DS and AR , confirming that demonstration data effectively reduces inefficient sampling.

The synergy between the SC module and Demo data can be summarized as follows: the SC module establishes safety boundaries to prevent the policy from entering hazardous or suboptimal states, while Demo data alleviates the conservatism of the SC module. EGADS integrates imitation learning (BC loss) and reinforcement learning (NFRL loss), dynamically balancing their weights to enable the agent to leverage expert knowledge while exploring autonomously within safe limits. This balanced mechanism enhances the policy's generalization capability and environmental adaptability, enabling efficient task execution across diverse scenarios and rapid adaptation to new challenges.

## 5 Conclusion

In summary, our EGADS framework effectively enhances sample efficiency, safety, and generalization in autonomous driving systems. The inclusion of safety constraints significantly enhances vehicle safety. NFRL, our proposed method, accurately predicts future driving actions, reducing sample complexity. By fine-tuning with a small amount of expert data, NFRL agents learn more general driving principles, which greatly improve generalization and sample complexity reduction, offering valuable insights for autonomous driving system design.

## References

1. Bansal, M., Krizhevsky, A., Ogale, A.: ChauffeurNet: learning to drive by imitating the best and synthesizing the worst. arXiv preprint arXiv:1812.03079 (2018)
2. Bengtsson, T., Bickel, P., Li, B.: Curse-of-dimensionality revisited: collapse of the particle filter in very large scale systems. In: Probability and statistics: Essays in honor of David A. Freedman, vol. 2, pp. 316–335. Institute of Mathematical Statistics (2008)
3. Chen, J., Li, S.E., Tomizuka, M.: Interpretable end-to-end urban autonomous driving with latent deep reinforcement learning. IEEE Trans. Intell. Transp. Syst. **23**(6), 5068–5078 (2021)
4. Chen, J., Wang, Z., Tomizuka, M.: Deep hierarchical reinforcement learning for autonomous driving with distinct behaviors. In: 2018 IEEE Intelligent Vehicles Symposium, pp. 1239–1244. IEEE (2018)
5. Chen, J., Yuan, B., Tomizuka, M.: Deep imitation learning for autonomous driving in generic urban scenarios with enhanced safety. In: 2019 IEEE/RSJ International Conference on Intelligent Robots and Systems, pp. 2884–2890. IEEE (2019)
6. Chen, J., Yuan, B., Tomizuka, M.: Model-free deep reinforcement learning for urban autonomous driving. In: 2019 IEEE Intelligent Transportation Systems Conference, pp. 2765–2771. IEEE (2019)

7. Chen, X., Mu, Y.M., Luo, P., Li, S., Chen, J.: Flow-based recurrent belief state learning for POMDPs. In: International Conference on Machine Learning, pp. 3444–3468. PMLR (2022)
8. Codevilla, F., Müller, M., López, A., Koltun, V., Dosovitskiy, A.: End-to-end driving via conditional imitation learning. In: 2018 IEEE International Conference on Robotics and Automation, pp. 4693–4700. IEEE (2018)
9. De Cao, N., Aziz, W., Titov, I.: Block neural autoregressive flow. In: Uncertainty in Artificial Intelligence, pp. 1263–1273. PMLR (2020)
10. Dinh, L., Sohl-Dickstein, J., Bengio, S.: Density estimation using real NVP. arXiv preprint arXiv:1605.08803 (2016)
11. Dosovitskiy, A., Ros, G., Codevilla, F., Lopez, A., Koltun, V.: CARLA: an open urban driving simulator. In: Conference on Robot Learning, pp. 1–16. PMLR (2017)
12. Fujimoto, S., Hoof, H., Meger, D.: Addressing function approximation error in actor-critic methods. In: International Conference on Machine Learning, pp. 1587–1596. PMLR (2018)
13. Gao, Z., et al.: Enhance sample efficiency and robustness of end-to-end urban autonomous driving via semantic masked world model. IEEE Trans. Intell. Transp. Syst. **25**(10), 13067–13079 (2024)
14. González, D., Pérez, J., Milanés, V., Nashashibi, F.: A review of motion planning techniques for automated vehicles. IEEE Trans. Intell. Transp. Syst. **17**(4), 1135–1145 (2015)
15. Haarnoja, T., Zhou, A., Abbeel, P., Levine, S.: Soft actor-critic: off-policy maximum entropy deep reinforcement learning with a stochastic actor. In: International Conference on Machine Learning, pp. 1861–1870. PMLR (2018)
16. Hafner, D., Lillicrap, T., Ba, J., Norouzi, M.: Dream to control: learning behaviors by latent imagination. arXiv preprint arXiv:1912.01603 (2019)
17. Hafner, D., et al.: Learning latent dynamics for planning from pixels. In: International Conference on Machine Learning, pp. 2555–2565. PMLR (2019)
18. Huang, C.W., Krueger, D., Lacoste, A., Courville, A.: Neural autoregressive flows. In: International Conference on Machine Learning, pp. 2078–2087. PMLR (2018)
19. Huang, Z., Liu, H., Wu, J., Lv, C.: Conditional predictive behavior planning with inverse reinforcement learning for human-like autonomous driving. IEEE Trans. Intell. Transp. Syst. **24**(7), 7244–7258 (2023)
20. Huang, Z., Sheng, Z., Ma, C., Chen, S.: Human as AI mentor: enhanced human-in-the-loop reinforcement learning for safe and efficient autonomous driving. arXiv preprint arXiv:2401.03160 (2024)
21. Jordan, M.I., Ghahramani, Z., Jaakkola, T.S., Saul, L.K.: An Introduction to Variational Methods for Graphical Models. In: Learning in Graphical Models, pp. 105–161 (1998)
22. Kendall, A., et al.: Learning to drive in a day. In: 2019 International Conference on Robotics and Automation, pp. 8248–8254. IEEE (2019)
23. Kumar, A., Zhou, A., Tucker, G., Levine, S.: Conservative Q-learning for offline reinforcement learning. Adv. Neural. Inf. Process. Syst. **33**, 1179–1191 (2020)
24. Lillicrap, T.P., et al.: Continuous control with deep reinforcement learning. arXiv preprint arXiv:1509.02971 (2015)
25. Liu, H., Huang, Z., Lv, C.: Improved deep reinforcement learning with expert demonstrations for urban autonomous driving. In: 2022 IEEE Intelligent Vehicles Symposium (IV), pp. 921–928 (2021). https://api.semanticscholar.org/CorpusID: 231951804

26. Liu, H., Huang, Z., Mo, X., Lv, C.: Augmenting reinforcement learning with transformer-based scene representation learning for decision-making of autonomous driving. arXiv preprint arXiv:2208.12263 (2022)
27. Mero, L.L., Yi, D., Dianati, M., Mouzakitis, A.: A survey on imitation learning techniques for end-to-end autonomous vehicles. IEEE Trans. Intelligent Transp. Syst. **23**, 14128–14147 (2022). https://api.semanticscholar.org/CorpusID:246539766
28. Mnih, V., et al.: Human-level control through deep reinforcement learning. Nature **518**(7540), 529–533 (2015)
29. Murdoch, A., Schoeman, J.C., Jordaan, H.W.: Partial end-to-end reinforcement learning for robustness against modelling error in autonomous racing. arXiv preprint arXiv:2312.06406 (2023)
30. Nehme, G., Deo, T.Y.: Safe navigation: training autonomous vehicles using deep reinforcement learning in Carla. arXiv preprint arXiv:2311.10735 (2023)
31. Paden, B., Čáp, M., Yong, S.Z., Yershov, D., Frazzoli, E.: A survey of motion planning and control techniques for self-driving urban vehicles. IEEE Trans. Intell. Veh. **1**(1), 33–55 (2016)
32. Rajeswaran, A., et al.: Learning complex dexterous manipulation with deep reinforcement learning and demonstrations. arXiv preprint arXiv:1709.10087 (2017)
33. Rezende, D., Mohamed, S.: Variational inference with normalizing flows. In: International Conference on Machine Learning, pp. 1530–1538. PMLR (2015)
34. Silver, D., Veness, J.: Monte-Carlo planning in large POMDPs. Adv. Neural Info. Process. Syst. **23** (2010)
35. Sutton, R.S., Barto, A.G.: Reinforcement Learning: An Introduction. MIT Press (2018)
36. Tang, Z., Chen, X., Li, Y., Chen, J.: Efficient and generalized end-to-end autonomous driving system with latent deep reinforcement learning and demonstrations. arXiv preprint arXiv:2401.11792 (2024)
37. Tang, Z., Hu, B., Zhao, C., Ma, D., Pan, G., Liu, B.: How to build a pre-trained multimodal model for simultaneously chatting and decision-making? arXiv preprint arXiv:2410.15885 (2024)
38. Theodorou, E., Buchli, J., Schaal, S.: Reinforcement learning of motor skills in high dimensions: a path integral approach. In: 2010 IEEE International Conference on Robotics and Automation, pp. 2397–2403. IEEE (2010)
39. Thrun, S.: Monte Carlo POMDPs. Adv. Neural Info. Process. Syst. **12** (1999)
40. Thrun, S., et al.: Stanley: the robot that won the DARPA grand challenge. J. field Robot. **23**(9), 661–692 (2006)
41. Urmson, C., et al.: Autonomous driving in urban environments: boss and the urban challenge. J. field Robot. **25**(8), 425–466 (2008)
42. Van Hoof, H., Hermans, T., Neumann, G., Peters, J.: Learning robot in-hand manipulation with tactile features. In: 2015 IEEE-RAS 15th International Conference on Humanoid Robots (Humanoids), pp. 121–127. IEEE (2015)
43. Wolf, P., et al.: Learning how to drive in a real world simulation with deep q-networks. In: 2017 IEEE Intelligent Vehicles Symposium, pp. 244–250. IEEE (2017)
44. Zhang, Z., Han, S., Wang, J., Miao, F.: Spatial-temporal-aware safe multi-agent reinforcement learning of connected autonomous vehicles in challenging scenarios. In: 2023 IEEE International Conference on Robotics and Automation, pp. 5574–5580. IEEE (2023)
45. Zhao, C., Zhou, Z., Liu, B.: On context distribution shift in task representation learning for online meta RL. In: International Conference on Intelligent Computing, pp. 614–628. Springer (2023)

46. Zhou, W., Cao, Z., Deng, N., Jiang, K., Yang, D.: Identify, estimate and bound the uncertainty of reinforcement learning for autonomous driving. IEEE Trans. Intell. Transp. Syst. **24**(8), 7932–7942 (2023)
47. Zhou, Z., Hu, B., Zhao, C., Zhang, P., Liu, B.: Large language model as a policy teacher for training reinforcement learning agents. arXiv preprint arXiv:2311.13373 (2023)

# Generalization of Compositional Tasks with Logical Specification via Implicit Planning

Duo Xu(✉) and Faramarz Fekri

Georgia Institute of Technology, Atlanta, GA 30332, USA
dxu301@gatech.edu

**Abstract.** In this study, we address the challenge of learning generalizable policies for compositional tasks defined by logical specifications. These tasks consist of multiple temporally extended sub-tasks. Due to the sub-task inter-dependencies and sparse reward issue in long-horizon tasks, existing reinforcement learning (RL) approaches, such as task-conditioned and goal-conditioned policies, continue to struggle with slow convergence and sub-optimal performance in the generalization of compositional tasks. To overcome these limitations, by decomposing the given task into reach-avoid sub-tasks, we introduce a new hierarchical RL framework that trains a high-level planner to select optimal sub-tasks and zero-shot generalizes to other tasks in the sub-task level, which enhances the efficiency and optimality of task generalization. At the high level, we present an implicit planner specifically designed for generalizing compositional tasks. This planner selects the next sub-task and estimates the multi-step return for completing the remaining task from the current state. It learns a latent transition model and performs planning in the latent space to select sub-tasks based on a graph neural network (GNN). Subsequently, the sub-task assigned by the high level guides the low-level module to effectively handle long-horizon tasks, while the estimated return encourages the low-level policy to account for future sub-task dependencies, enhancing its optimality and densifying the sparse rewards. We conduct comprehensive experiments to demonstrate the framework's advantages over previous methods in terms of both efficiency and optimality.

## 1 Introduction

In real-world applications, such as robotics and control system, task completion often involves achieving multiple subgoals that are spread over time and must follow user-specified temporal order constraints. For instance, a service robot on a factory floor may need to gather components in specific sequences based on the product being assembled, all while avoiding unsafe conditions. These complex tasks are defined through logic-based compositional languages, which have long been essential for objective specification in sequential decision-making [7].

Using domain-specific properties as propositional variables, formal languages like Linear Temporal Logic (LTL) [28] and SPECTRL [13] encode intricate temporal patterns by combining these variables with temporal operators and logical connectives.

**Supplementary Information** The online version contains supplementary material available at https://doi.org/10.1007/978-3-032-06106-5_12.

These languages provide clear semantics and support semantics-preserving transformations into deterministic finite-state automata (DFA), which reveal the discrete structure of an objective to a decision-making agent. Generalizing across multiple tasks is crucial for deploying autonomous agents in various real-world scenarios [33]. In this work, we tackle the problem of generalizing compositional tasks where, at test time, the trained agent is given a DFA description of an unseen task and is expected to accomplish the task without further training.

While reinforcement learning (RL) algorithms have achieved remarkable success across numerous fields [26,27,29,38], they still face challenges in generalizing to compositional tasks, which differ significantly from typical problems addressed by conventional RL methods. Previous works on compositional task generalization [2,8,17,24, 35] trained generalizable agents with satisfying success rate. Some approaches [2,8,24] tackle unseen compositional tasks by leveraging trained reusable skills or options. However, these methods train each option to achieve a specific subgoal independently, thereby risking the loss of global optimality in task completion when sub-tasks are dependent on each other. Additionally, methods that train policies directly conditioned on task formulas [17,35] proposed an effective framework for temporal logic task generalization, which can reach the global optimality in generalization. However, these methods tend to exhibit slow convergence in complex tasks or environments, as they lack task decomposition and miss out on the compositional structure of such tasks. Another recent paper [40] pre-trains embeddings for reach-avoid DFAs of the task, which enables the zero-shot generalization of goal-conditioned RL agent to other tasks. However, this work still treated the given compositional task as a whole and does not address the spare reward issue specifically. Before introducing the proposed framework, we will first present two motivating examples to show the importance of considering sub-task dependencies.

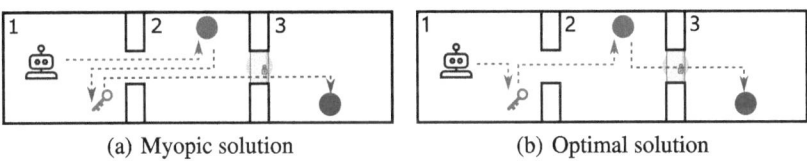

(a) Myopic solution        (b) Optimal solution

**Fig. 1.** Motivating example 1. Task: first go to red ball, and then blue ball. Red: reaching red ball. Blue: reaching blue ball. (Color figure online)

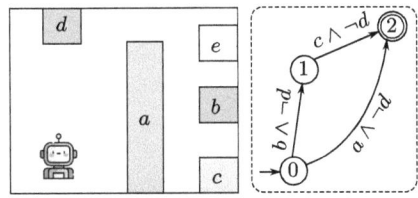

**Fig. 2.** Motivating example 2. Left: map. Right: task automaton with self loops omitted.

**Motivating Examples.** The first example, shown in Fig. 1, involves a robot starting in room 1 with a locked door between rooms 2 and 3. This door can only be opened using the key located in room 1. The task is to visit the red ball first, then the blue ball. Previous option-based methods train options for reaching each ball independently, disregarding dependencies between subgoals. This approach results in the myopic solution illustrated in Fig. 1(a), where the robot wastes additional steps retrieving the key compared to the optimal solution shown in Fig. 1(b).

The second example, illustrated in Fig. 2 with the task automaton on the right, assigns rewards of 1 and 10 for reaching areas "a" and "c", respectively, while other areas yield no rewards. The optimal solution for completing the task with maximal rewards is to reach "b" first, then "c", while avoiding "a" and "d". However, if task-conditioned policies are trained using previous methods [17,35,40], the agent often ends up reaching "a" and avoiding "d" since it is easier and still completes the task, producing sub-optimal solution for the given task. This occurs because the task-conditioned policy is not explicitly trained to avoid "a" while reaching "b" at the initial automaton state 0. The resulting sub-optimality arises from overlooking dependencies of sub-tasks in different branches (i.e. paths to task completion): reaching "a" from the state 0 can directly accomplish the task, making "b" and "c" inaccessible and hence getting sub-optimal rewards for completing the task. In addition, the rewards of achieving some sub-tasks may also be dependent on each other. For example, if the agent first completes the sub-task "b" and then achieves "a", it will get a higher reward than directly achieving "a". This is because the user may prefer some patterns to others in the task specifications.

In this work, in order to address the sub-task dependencies and sparse reward issue in the generalization of compositional tasks, we introduce a hierarchical RL framework which trains a high-level planner to select the optimal reach-avoid sub-task for the low-level module to complete, achieving zero-shot generalization to other tasks in the sub-task level. Unlike previous methods which treat any given compositional task as a whole, our approach decomposes the given task into reach-avoid sub-tasks to resolve the sparse reward issue, and trains a novel implicit planner to select optimal target sub-task for the low-level module to complete by taking sub-task dependencies into consideration. In addition to selecting target sub-tasks, the high-level module also estimates the multi-step return of completing the remaining task for the low-level module, which can guide the low-level module while accounting for dependencies among future sub-tasks. The low-level module is responsible for choosing primitive actions to accomplish the assigned sub-task, with its decisions conditioned on both the current and upcoming sub-tasks required to complete the remaining task.

Specifically, in the high-level module, the implicit planner learns a latent transition model for sub-task transitions, which encodes environmental observations into latent states and predicts the latent state when the input sub-task is complete. By decomposing any given task into sub-tasks and applying a graph neural network (GNN) over predicted latent states of completing sub-tasks, the high-level module generates an embedding vector representing the future situations of completing the remaining task. This embedding vector serves as input to the implicit planner, guiding it to predict the next sub-task and estimate the return for the low-level module. The low-level module is a variant of the agent module in [35], which is conditioned on any sub-task assigned by the high-level module and future sub-tasks to complete.

In experiments, we demonstrate the advantages of the proposed framework over baselines in three environments, including both discrete and continuous state and action spaces. Based on comprehensive experiments, we show the proposed framework outperforms baselines in terms of both optimality and learning efficiency.

## 2 Preliminary

### 2.1 Task Specification Language

A compositional task considered in this work is described by a logic specification formula $\phi$, a Boolean function that determines whether the objective formula is satisfied by the given trajectory or not [28]. In this work, we adopt the specification language SPECTRL [13] to express the logic and temporal relationships of subgoals in tasks. A specification $\phi$ in SPECTRL is a logic formula applied to trajectories, determining whether a given trajectory $\zeta = (s_0, s_1, \dots)$ successfully accomplishes the task specified by $\phi$. For rigor of math, $\phi$ can be described as a function $\phi : \mathcal{Z} \to \{0,1\}$ producing binary outputs, where $\mathcal{Z}$ is the set of all the trajectories.

Specifically, a specification is defined based on a set of atomic propositions $\mathcal{P}_0$. For each proposition $p \in \mathcal{P}_0$, the MDP state $s$ of the agent satisfies $p$ (denoted as $s \models p$) when $p \in L(s)$ and $L$ is labeling function. The set of symbols $\mathcal{P}$ is composed by conjunctions of atomic propositions in $\mathcal{P}_0$.

Based on definitions above, the grammar for formulating SPECTRL specifications can be written as:

$$\phi ::= \text{achieve } b \mid \phi_1 \text{ ensuring } b \mid \phi_1; \phi_2 \mid \phi_1 \text{ or } \phi_2 \tag{1}$$

where $b \in \mathcal{P}$. Here "achieve" and "ensuring" correspond to "eventually" and "always" operators in LTL [2,28]. Given any finite trajectory $\zeta$ with length $h$, the satisfaction of a SPECTRL specification are defined as:

1. $\zeta \models \text{achieve } b$ if $\exists i \leq h, s_i \models b$ (or $b \in L(s_i)$)
2. $\zeta \models \phi \text{ ensuring } b$ if $\zeta \models \phi$ and $\forall i \leq h, s_i \models b$
3. $\zeta \models \phi_1; \phi_2$ if $\exists i < h, \zeta_{0:i} \models \phi_1$ and $\zeta_{i+1;h} \models \phi_2$
4. $\zeta \models \phi_1 \text{ or } \phi_2$ if $\zeta \models \phi_1$ or $\zeta \models \phi_2$

Specifically, the statement 1) signifies that the trajectory should eventually reach a state where the symbol $b$ holds true. The statement 2) means that the trajectory should satisfy specification $\phi$ while always remaining in states where $b$ is true. The statement 3) signifies that the trajectory should sequentially satisfy $\phi_1$ and then $\phi_2$. The statement 4) says that the trajectory should satisfy either $\phi_1$ or $\phi_2$. We say a trajectory $\zeta$ satisfies specification $\phi$ if there is a time step $h$ such that the prefix $\zeta_{0:h}$ satisfies $\phi$.

In addition, every SPECTRL specification $\phi$ is guaranteed to have an equivalent directed acyclic graph (DAG), termed as abstract graph [13]. An abstract graph $\mathcal{G}$ is defined as $\mathcal{G} ::= (Q, E, q_0, F, \kappa)$, where $Q$ is the set of nodes, $E \subseteq Q \times Q$ is the set of directed edges, $q_0 \in Q$ denotes the initial node, $F \subseteq Q$ denotes the accepting nodes, subgoal region mapping $\beta : Q \to 2^S$ which denotes the subgoal region for every node in $Q$, and safe trajectories $\mathcal{Z}_{\text{safe}} = \cap_{e \in E} \mathcal{Z}^e_{\text{safe}}$ where $\mathcal{Z}^e_{\text{safe}}$ denotes the safe trajectories for any edge $e \in E$. Note that the environmental MDP $\mathcal{M}$ is connected with task specification $\phi$ and $\mathcal{G}_\phi$ by $\beta$ and $\mathcal{Z}^e_{\text{safe}}$ which may change for different tasks.

Furthermore, the function $\kappa$ labels each edge $e := q \to q'$ with the symbol $b_e$ (labeled edge denoted as $e := q \xrightarrow{b_e} q'$). Given $\kappa$, the agent transits from node $q$ to $q'$ when the states $s_i$ and $s_{i+l}$ of trajectory $\zeta$ satisfy $s_i \in \beta(q)$ and $b_e \subseteq L(s_{i+l})$ for some $l \geq 0$.

Given a task specification $\phi$, the corresponding abstract graph $\mathcal{G}_\phi$ can be constructed based on its definition, such that, for any trajectory $\zeta \in \mathcal{Z}$, we have $\zeta \models \phi$ if and only if $\zeta \models \mathcal{G}_\phi$. Hence, the RL problem for task $\phi$ can be equivalent to the reachability problem for $\mathcal{G}_\phi$. It is obvious that every task DAG has a single initial node in SPECTRL language, which can be converted into a tree.

**Sub-task Definition.** Given the DAG $\mathcal{G}_\phi$ corresponding to task specification $\phi$, we can define sub-tasks based on edges of the DAG. Formally, an edge from node $q$ to $p \in Q$ can define a reach-avoid sub-task specified by the following SPECTRL formula:

$$\text{Sub-Task}(q,p) := \text{achieve}(b_{(q,p)}) \text{ ensuring} \left( \bigwedge_{r \in \mathcal{N}(q), r \neq p} \neg b_{(q,r)} \right) \quad (2)$$

where $b_{(q,p)}$ is the propositional formula labeled over the edge $(q,p)$ in the DAG, and $\mathcal{N}(q)$ is the set of neighboring nodes to which the out-going edges of $q$ point in the DAG. For instance, in Fig. 2, the propositional formula over the edge $(q_0, q_2)$ is $b_{(q_0,q_2)} = \neg d \wedge a$. When $e = (q, p)$, the notation Sub-Task$(e)$ is same as Sub-Task$(q, p)$ defined in (2), e.g., Sub-Task$(q_0, q_2) := $ achieve$(a)$ensuring$(\neg b \wedge \neg d)$ in Fig. 2 after some algebra.

For each Sub-Task$(q, p)$ and any MDP state $s_0 \in \mathcal{S}$, there is a policy $\pi_{(q,p)}$ which can guide the agent to produce a trajectory $s_0 s_1 \ldots s_n$ in MDP. It induces the path $qqq \ldots qp$ in the DAG, meaning that the agent's DAG state remains at $q$ until it transits to $p$, i.e., $s_n \in \beta(p)$ and $s_i \notin \beta(p)$ for $i < n$. In this work, since we consider the dependencies of sub-tasks, the policy $\pi_{(q,p)}$ is also dependent on the future sub-tasks to complete.

Given the environmental MDP $M$, for any SPECTRL task specification $\phi$, the agent first transforms $\phi$ to its corresponding DAG (abstract graph) $\mathcal{G}_\phi = (Q, E, q_0, F, \beta, \mathcal{Z}_{\text{safe}}, \kappa)$. Then, the sub-tasks of all the edges can be obtained from $\mathcal{G}_\phi$ based on (2). In this work, we assume that for every edge sub-task of the DAG, the achieve part only has conjunction of propositions (denoted as $p_+$ for reaching) and the ensuring part only has conjunctions of negated propositions (denoted as $p_-$ for avoidance). The propositions in $p^+$ of sub-task $\eta$ are regarded as subgoals of $\eta$. This is because achieving any negated propositions in the safety condition is assumed infeasible. For example, for the sub-task achieve$(b)$ensuring$(\neg a \wedge \neg d)$ (i.e., $b \wedge \neg a \wedge \neg d$), we have $p_+ = \{b\}$ and $p_- = \{a, d\}$. Whenever the achieve part in (2) contains disjunction, this sub-task will decomposed further into sub-tasks in parallel edges, until every sub-task only achieves conjunction of propositions.

**Remark.** For example, based on our assumptions, if the DFA in Fig. 2 has $b_{q_0, q_1} = b \wedge \neg d$ and $b_{q_0, q_2} = a \wedge \neg f$, then Sub-Task$(q_0, q_1) :=$ achieve$(b)$ensuring$\neg a \wedge \neg d \wedge \neg f$. Although (2) could yield $f$ in the ensuring part, our assumption ignores the achievement of any propositions which are negated in the safety condition, hence discarding $f$.

## 2.2 Problem Formulation

We introduce the labeled MDP as the working environment in Appendix, where propositions and labeling function are defined. Given the labeled MDP $M$ with unknown state transition dynamics and reward function, a SPECTRL specification $\phi$ represents the logic compositional task consisting of temporally extended sub-tasks, and $\mathcal{G}_\phi$ is the DAG (abstract graph) corresponding to the task $\phi$.

The target of this work is to train an reinforcement learning (RL) agent in a data-efficient manner which can be generalized to complete any unseen SPECTRL task $\phi$ without further training. In addition to task completion, we also consider the optimality of the found solution for the unseen task $\phi$, maximizing the discounted accumulated environmental rewards, i.e. return, during task completion. Specifically, the reward function of MDP $\mathcal{M}$ is unknown to the agent, and the reward of any state $s$ is available to the agent only whenever $s$ is visited.

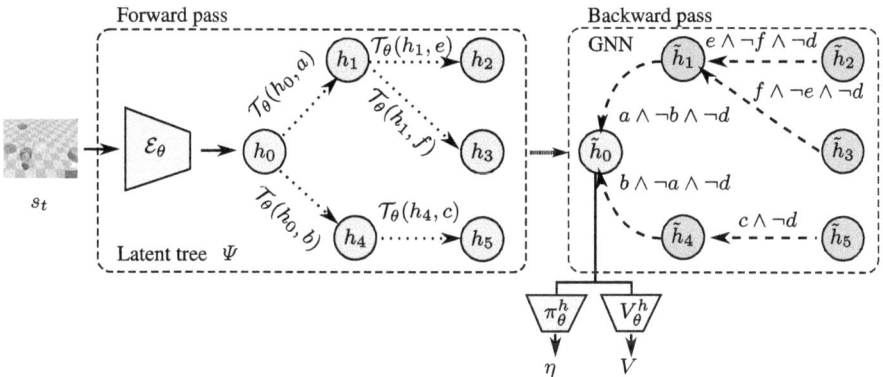

**Fig. 3.** Diagram of implicit planner as the high-level agent. The DAG (abstract graph) of the task is shown in the Fig. 4. The latent tree is spanned by the encoder $\mathcal{E}_\theta$ and latent transition model $\mathcal{T}_\theta$ in the forward pass, while the feature of future sub-tasks ($\tilde{h}_0$) is extracted by GNN ($\mathcal{M}_\theta, \mathcal{U}_\theta$) in the backward pass. The sub-task $\eta$ and estimated return $V$ are predicted by policy $\pi_\theta^h$ and value networks $V_\theta^h$, respectively, which are realized by MLPs with feature $\tilde{h}_0$ as input. Note that in GNN, every edge is labeled by a corresponding sub-task derived from the task DAG, and the feature of a edge is the binary encoding of positive ($p^+$) and negative ($p_-$) propositions of the corresponding sub-task.

## 3 Methodology

In the following sections, we first detail the modules and operational mechanisms of the proposed framework. Next, we outline the training algorithm, describing the training processes for both low-level and high-level modules. We also propose specific training techniques aimed at enhancing robustness and data efficiency throughout the learning process, including curriculum, experience relabeling and proposition avoidance, which are introduced in Appendix.

## 3.1 Architecture

The proposed framework consists of high-level and low-level modules. The high-level module is essentially an implicit planner which selects the next sub-task for the low-level agent to complete. Based on the feature of future sub-tasks, the implicit planner is directly trained to predict the best selection of next sub-task and also estimate the return for completing the rest of task, which are passed to the low-level agent for guidance. The low-level module is trained to achieve the assigned sub-task together with the estimated return which makes the low-level policy look into the future sub-tasks. This approach fastens the training of the low-level module, improving the learning efficiency in long-horizon tasks.

**High-level Module.** When the dependencies among sub-tasks are accounted for, the planning problem of selecting the next high-level sub-task no longer adheres to the Markovian property. This limitation prevents the use of the commonly applied value iteration (VI) method for sub-task selection, as VI relies on Bellman equations [32] to compute the value function and is effective only when the Markovian property holds. To address this, we introduce an implicit planner that directly predicts the optimal next sub-task and estimates the expected return for completing the remaining task based on an embedding that represents future sub-tasks and observations. This embedding is generated by a graph neural network (GNN) [30,41] and a latent transition model [16,36], described below. As shown in Fig. 3, the proposed implicit planner consists of an encoder $\mathcal{E}_\theta$, a latent state transition model $\mathcal{T}_\theta$, a GNN ($\mathcal{M}_\theta, \mathcal{U}_\theta$), a policy network $\pi_\theta^h$ and a value network $V_\theta^h$. All components of the implicit planner are trained together end-to-end, so their trainable parameters are collectively represented as $\theta$. The implicit planner operates through both forward and backward passes. The task DAG corresponding to Fig. 3 is shown in Fig. 4.

**Forward Pass.** In the forward pass, the planner generates latent representations of the current and future states by using the encoder $\mathcal{E}_\theta$ and the latent dynamic model $\mathcal{T}_\theta$, iteratively constructing a tree $\Psi$ whose node features are predicted latent representations of states. Given the current environmental state $s_t$, the encoder first derives its latent representation, denoted as $h_0 := \mathcal{E}_\theta(s_t)$, which serves as the root of the latent tree $\Psi$. Following the structure of the task directed acyclic graph (DAG) $\mathcal{G}_\phi$, the tree $\Psi$ is expanded from $h_0$ until every accepting node in $F$ of the DAG $\mathcal{G}_\phi$ is included in $\Psi$.

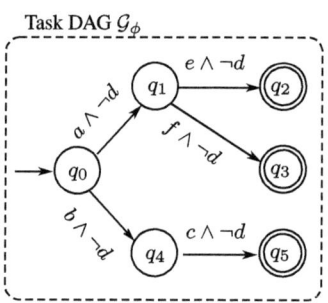

**Fig. 4.** Task DAG of Fig. 3.

Expanding $\Psi$ from a node $n$ entails adding all nodes in $\mathcal{G}_\phi$ connected through edges that originate from $n$. Specifically, the latent state of node $n$ (i.e., $h_n$) and the subgoals associated with its outgoing edges in $\mathcal{G}_\phi$ are input to the latent transition dynamics model $\mathcal{T}_\theta$, which then predicts the subsequent latent states. These predicted states serve as features for new nodes, which are added to $\Psi$ as the children of node $n$. This expansion process iterates until all subgoals in $\mathcal{G}_\phi$ are incorporated into $\Psi$. An example is illustrated in Fig. 3. It is worth noting that $\Psi$ is built based on the subgoals (positive propositions of sub-tasks) associated with edges in $\mathcal{G}_\phi$, rather than directly from sub-tasks.

**Backward Pass.** In the backward pass, the GNN component operates over a graph modified from the latent tree $\Psi$ to extract an embedding vector, $\tilde{h}_0$, which represents the completion of the remaining task, encoding future sub-tasks and predicted states. Specifically, the direction of each edge in the latent tree $\Psi$ is reversed and labeled with the sub-task which is derived from related edges in the task DAG $\mathcal{G}_\phi$ based on its definition in (2), resulting in a new graph. A multi-layer GNN is then applied to this new graph to extract an embedding vector that encapsulates future sub-tasks and predicted states in the remaining task, denoted by the node feature $\tilde{h}_0$. An example of this process is illustrated in Fig. 3. Finally, based on $\tilde{h}_0$, the policy and value function determine the selection of the next sub-task and estimate the return for the low-level agent.

It's important to note that, in the backward pass, the sub-task on each edge of the graph is derived based on (2) and differs from the sub-task in the task DAG $\mathcal{G}_\phi$. This distinction is because the derived sub-task explicitly incorporates conditions to avoid accidentally completing any neighboring sub-tasks, which is not explicitly addressed in the original task DAG $\mathcal{G}_\phi$, as shown in the example of Fig. 2.

**Encoder.** The encoder function, $\mathcal{E}_\theta : \mathcal{S} \to \mathbb{R}^d$, takes an environmental state as input and outputs its latent representation. The encoder's neural architecture is tailored to the environment: a CNN is employed for pixel-based environments, while an MLP is used for environments with continuous observations.

**Latent Transition Model.** The latent transition function, $\mathcal{T}_\theta : \mathbb{R}^d \times \mathcal{P} \to \mathbb{R}^d$, predicts the next latent state by using the latent of the current state and the subgoals (positive propositions of the sub-task). Given the current state $s$ and sub-task $\eta$, the next latent state is predicted as $\mathcal{E}_\theta(s) + \mathcal{T}_\theta(\mathcal{E}_\theta(s), p_\eta^+)$, where $p_\eta^+$ is the binary encoding of the subgoals of sub-task $\eta$. This function models the changes in the latent state caused by completing a sub-task. In implementation, $\mathcal{T}_\theta$ is typically realized using an MLP.

**Graph Neural Network.** The GNN is employed to generate an embedding that represents the progress toward completing the remaining tasks. For each node $k$ in the GNN, it first gathers a set of incoming messages from each connected node $j$ with an edge $(j, k)$ directed from $j$ to $k$. This is achieved using the message-passing function $\mathcal{M}_\theta$, which takes as input the features of nodes $k$ and $j$ ($\tilde{h}_k$ and $\tilde{h}_j$) along with the edge feature $e(j, k)$. The initial feature of each node is its latent state $h_k$, predicted by $\mathcal{T}_\theta$ during the forward pass, and it is subsequently updated with the incoming messages using the update function $\mathcal{U}_\theta$.

The edge feature $e_{(j,k)}$ is a binary encoding of the sub-task $b_{(k,j)}$ associated with the edge $(j, k)$. Specifically, this feature is created by concatenating two binary vectors that separately represent the positive and negative propositions of the sub-task.

In every layer of GNN, the incoming messages of node $k$ are first aggregated by summation as below,

$$m_k = \bigoplus_{j \in \mathcal{N}(\tilde{h})} \mathcal{M}_\theta(\tilde{h}_j, \tilde{h}_k, e_{(j,k)}) \tag{3}$$

Then, the node feature $\tilde{h}_k$ is updated with incoming message, i.e., $\tilde{h}_k \leftarrow \mathcal{U}_\theta(\tilde{h}_k, m_k)$. In implementation, both $\mathcal{M}_\theta$ and $\mathcal{U}_\theta$ are realized by MLPs.

Since the direction of each edge in $\Psi$ is reversed in the graph used for the backward pass, multiple iterations of applying the functions $\mathcal{M}_\theta$ and $\mathcal{U}_\theta$ in the GNN enable information from each future sub-task to back-propagate to the root node. Consequently, the root node feature, denoted as $\tilde{h}_0$, encapsulates the status of completing future sub-tasks within the remaining task.

**Policy and Value Function.** The policy function $\pi_\theta^h : \mathbb{R}^d \to [0,1]^{|\mathcal{P}|}$ maps the embedding $\tilde{h}_0$ extracted by GNN to a distribution of *feasible* next sub-tasks. The next sub-task assigned to the low-level agent is sampled from this output distribution. The value function $V_\theta^h : \mathbb{R}^d \to \mathbb{R}$ maps the embedding $\tilde{h}_0$ to the estimated return for completing the remaining task starting from the current state.

**Remark.** Previous approaches to planning for logic-based compositional tasks have utilized value iteration [2,3], Dijkstra's algorithm [10], and heuristic-based search algorithms [9,15]. These methods rely on the assumption that the cumulative rewards for completing each sub-task are independent of others, meaning the Markovian property must hold. However, as illustrated in the examples in Sect. 1, this work considers dependencies between sub-tasks, where the cumulative rewards for completing one sub-task depend on future sub-tasks, breaking the Markovian property and making standard planning algorithms inapplicable. To address this, we leverage the generalization capabilities of GNNs to train a value function for sub-tasks and states through supervised learning, enabling the high-level policy to be trained using the PPO algorithm [31].

**Low-Level Module.** The target of low-level module is to complete the sub-task $\eta$ specified by the high-level module, considering the dependencies of future sub-tasks. As discussed in the Sub-task Definition of Sect. 2.1, every sub-task in SPECTRL language is a reach-avoid task, and can be decomposed into positive proposition (to achieve) and negative propositions (to avoid), stored in the sets $p_+$ and $p_-$, respectively. Hence, the low-level policy and value functions, denoted as $\pi_\omega^l$ and $V_\omega^l$, are conditioned on $p_+$ and $p_-$ encoded into binary vectors. The diagram of processing inputs to the low-level agent is in Fig. 5.

**Remark.** This low-level module is essentially a variant, where the agent model in [35] is made conditioned on the target sub-task $\eta$. Since the high-level module gives an estimate return $V$ upon the completion of every sub-task, the training of the low-level module in this work should be much more efficient than that in [35]. The original model in [35] only has outcome-based reward signals about the whole task.

To account for dependencies of future sub-tasks, both $\pi_\omega^l$ and $V_\omega^l$ are conditioned on the DAG of the remaining task $\phi'$, denoted as $\mathcal{G}_{\phi'}$. Here, $\phi'$ represents the remainder of the task $\phi$ after completing sub-task $\eta$. Essentially, $\phi'$ is the progression [19,35] of task $\phi$ once sub-task $\eta$ is achieved. For example, in the task shown in Fig. 2, if sub-task $b \wedge \neg a \wedge \neg d$ (on the edge from state 0 to 1) is completed, the progression of the task becomes $c \wedge \neg d$, indicating the remaining part of the task to be accomplished.

**DAG Processing.** However, the functions $\pi_\omega^l$ and $V_\omega^l$ cannot directly process a DAG. To address this, similar as LTL2Action [35], we use a GNN to generate an embedding

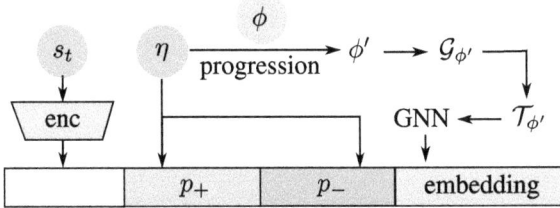

**Fig. 5.** Diagram of processing inputs to the low-level policy $\pi_\omega^l$ and value function $V_\omega^l$. $\eta$ is the sub-task assigned by the high-level module. $\phi$ is the target task to complete. $\phi'$ is the progression of $\phi$ with $\eta$. The embedding is the representation of $\phi'$ produced by the GNN. $s_t$ is the environmental observation. "enc" is the encoder mapping the raw observation into a latent vector.

from the tree representation of the DAG $\mathcal{G}_{\phi'}$, which can be directly used as input to $\pi_\omega^l$ and $V_\omega^l$. Since any DAG with a single source node can be equivalently converted into a tree, we first convert the DAG of $\phi'$, denoted $\mathcal{G}_{\phi'}$, into its corresponding tree $\mathcal{T}_{\phi'}$.

This tree $\mathcal{T}_{\phi'}$ differs from the high-level latent tree $\Psi$. Given that the low-level policy operates at every time step, it's essential to keep the low-level module as streamlined as possible. Thus, the latent transition model is omitted, and each node's initial feature is set to an all-zero vector. Additionally, we ignore the negative propositions of future sub-tasks, using only the binary encoding of the positive propositions (i.e. subgoals) as the edge feature. However, the negative propositions of the current sub-task $\eta$ are still encoded as a binary vector $p_-$, as shown in Fig. 5.

With these defining node and edge features, a multi-layer GNN is applied to $\mathcal{T}_{\phi'}$, with the direction of each edge reversed. The embedding at the root node then represents the characteristics of all future subgoals to accomplish. The process of obtaining $p_+$, $p_-$, and the embedding for future subgoals is illustrated in Fig. 5. Note that this low-level GNN differs from the one used at the high level and is trained alongside other low-level components only.

### 3.2 Algorithm

The high-level and low-level modules are trained independently. In the high level, all components are trained end-to-end to predict the optimal selection of the next sub-task to complete and to estimate the return for completing the remainder of the task. In the low level, the module is trained to accomplish the assigned sub-task while accounting for dependencies from future sub-tasks. To enhance the sample efficiency of the learning process, several training techniques are introduced, including a training curriculum, experience replay, and proposition avoidance. The training of low-level module is introduced in Appendix.

**High-level Transition Data.** We define a high-level transition tuple as $(s, \phi, \eta, R, s', \phi')$, which indicates that starting from state $s$, the agent completes the sub-task $\eta$ and reaches state $s'$. Here, $\phi'$ is the progression of task $\phi$ after sub-task $\eta$ is completed, representing the remaining part of the task, and $R$ is the accumulated discounted reward earned while completing $\eta$. The high-level transition buffer $\Gamma^h$ stores these transition tuples collected from all trajectories, but only includes transitions where completing the sub-task $\eta$ resulted in progression over $\phi$ (i.e., $\phi' \neq \phi$). For a trajectory $\zeta = (s_l, a_l, r_l)_{l=0}^{H-1}$, where $K_\zeta$ sub-tasks are completed sequentially, we denote these sub-tasks as $\eta_0, \eta_1, \ldots, \eta_{K_\zeta - 1}$, with the time steps at which they are completed as $t_0, t_1, \ldots, t_{K_\zeta - 1}$. The accumulated rewards obtained for completing each sub-task $\eta_i$ are defined as $R_i := \sum_{\tau=t_{i-1}}^{t_i} \gamma^{\tau - t_{i-1}} r_\tau$, where $r_\tau$ represents the environmental reward at time step $\tau$.

**High-Level Training.** The effectiveness of the high-level module depends on the embedding vector that represents the remaining task, which is extracted by the latent transition model and GNN. Therefore, it is essential to train the encoder, latent transition model, and GNN effectively. Drawing inspiration from previous work on learning latent dynamic spaces [4,16], we utilize the TransE [16] loss to train the encoder $\mathcal{E}_\theta$ and the latent transition function $\mathcal{T}_\theta$ together. For any high-level transition data $(s, \phi, \eta, R, s', \phi')$ and a negatively sampled state $\tilde{s}$, the TransE loss can be expressed as below:

$$\mathcal{L}_{\text{TransE}}((s, \eta, s'), \tilde{s}; \theta) = d(\mathcal{E}_\theta(s) + \mathcal{T}_\theta(\mathcal{E}_\theta(s), \eta), \mathcal{E}_\theta(s')) \\ + \max(0, \xi - d(\mathcal{E}_\theta(s), \mathcal{E}_\theta(\tilde{s}))) \qquad (4)$$

where $\theta$ are the trainable parameters, $d$ is the distance function which is chosen as the Euclidean distance in this work, and $\xi$ is a positive hyper-parameter. The tasks $\phi, \phi'$ and reward $R$ are not used in the training loss of $\mathcal{E}_\theta$ and $\mathcal{T}_\theta$.

For the GNN part, models $\mathcal{M}_\theta$ and $\mathcal{U}_\theta$ are trained together with policy $\pi_\theta^h$ and value networks $V_\theta^h$ in an end-to-end manner. Since the training curriculum is designed to start from simple tasks, there is no need to pre-train the GNN part.

The components of the high-level module are jointly trained using the PPO algorithm [31] with a set of feasible sub-tasks serving as the action space. Based on the high-level transition buffer $\Gamma^h$, the PPO loss is calculated by evaluating the outputs of the policy and value networks through the forward and backward passes, as detailed in Sect. 3.1. One iteration of training the high-level module can be summarized as the following steps:

1. Sample trajectories $\zeta$ from the replay buffer $\mathcal{B}$ which forms the high-level transition dataset $\Gamma^h$;
2. Based on transition tuples in $\Gamma^h$, compute the PPO [31] and TransE (4) losses, where the negative samples $\tilde{s}$ in (4) are randomly sampled from states in $\Gamma^h$;
3. Update parameters $\theta$ of all the components in the high-level module together, with gradients of the following loss function:

$$\mathcal{L}(\Gamma^h; \theta) = \mathcal{L}_{\text{PPO}}(\Gamma^h; \theta) + \lambda \sum_i \mathcal{L}_{\text{TransE}}((s_{t_i}, \eta_i, s_{t_{i+1}}), \tilde{s}_i; \theta) \qquad (5)$$

where $\lambda$ is a hyper-parameter to balance two loss terms, chosen as 0.01 in this work.

Note that since $V_\theta^h$ is trained with $R_i$ in the value loss of PPO, where $R_i$ is a discounted accumulated rewards in multiple steps and hence $V_\theta^h$ is essentially updated by a multi-step Bellman operator (BO) [32].

## 4 Experiments

Our experiments aim to evaluate the performance of a multi-task RL agent trained using the proposed framework, focusing on learning efficiency, optimality, and generalization. Specifically, the section on overall performance examines whether the proposed framework outperforms baselines in terms of optimality and learning efficiency when sub-task dependencies are present. Next, ablation studies in Appendix investigate the impact of considering future sub-tasks within the low-level module, the contribution of experience relabeling to learning efficiency and the effect of latent transition model.

Before presenting the experiment results, we will first introduce the environments. Finally, the experiments about overall performance comparison will be demonstrated. The training setup and baselines are introduced in Appendix. Other experiment results and algorithmic details are deferred to Appendix.

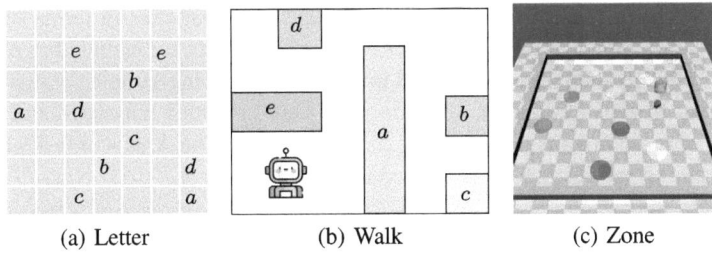

(a) Letter        (b) Walk        (c) Zone

**Fig. 6.** Environments. The details of environments are introduced in Appendix.

### 4.1 Environments and Setup

We conducted experiments in various environments featuring both discrete and continuous action and state spaces. Each environment is procedurally generated, with object layouts and positions randomized upon reset. The agent does not know the positions or properties of objects in advance, making it impossible to solve these environments using simple tabular-based methods. Each task is defined by a SPECTRL specification, expressed through symbolic propositions given by the labeling function. The agent's goal is to complete the specified task while maximizing accumulated rewards. The example screen shots of environments are shown in Fig. 6. The detailed introduction of environments are in Appendix.

**Sub-task Dependencies.** In our experiments, sub-task dependencies can arise from various factors, including avoidance requirements, aliasing states, and subgoal reward functions. First, successfully completing one sub-task may necessitate avoiding the subgoals of another, thereby introducing dependencies between them. (Note that here, "sub-task" is defined by (2), which may not be explicitly represented in the task DAG.) Second, multiple states in the environment may be mapped to a single symbol through the labeling function, leading to aliasing states (e.g., multiple cells labeled with the same letter in Fig. 6(a) and example in Fig. 1). Because the agent must choose which state to visit conditioned on a particular subgoal symbol, these aliasing states cause the low-level policy of one sub-task to depend on future sub-tasks, thereby creating sub-task dependencies. Third, subgoal reward functions can induce dependencies if certain task specifications are more favorable to the user; for instance, in the Walk domain depicted in Fig. 6(b), visiting "b" before "c" may yield a higher reward than going directly to "c," correlating the "b" and "c" sub-tasks. Additional experiments illustrating a wider range of sub-task dependencies are provided in the Appendix.

Note that the sub-task dependencies are unknown to the agent initially and the agent has to learn to adapt to these dependencies via interacting with the environment. The first two types of dependencies are at the low level, while the third type operates at a higher (subgoal) level.

### 4.2 Overall Performance

In this section, we present the overall performance comparisons in terms of average return for completing testing tasks. Other experiment results are included in Appendix. In each plot, the evaluation is conducted in every 10K training samples drawn from the environment. In each evaluation, 10 testing tasks are randomly generated and the average return of these tasks is used as the y-axis of the plot. The details of task generation for both training and testing are presented in Appendix.

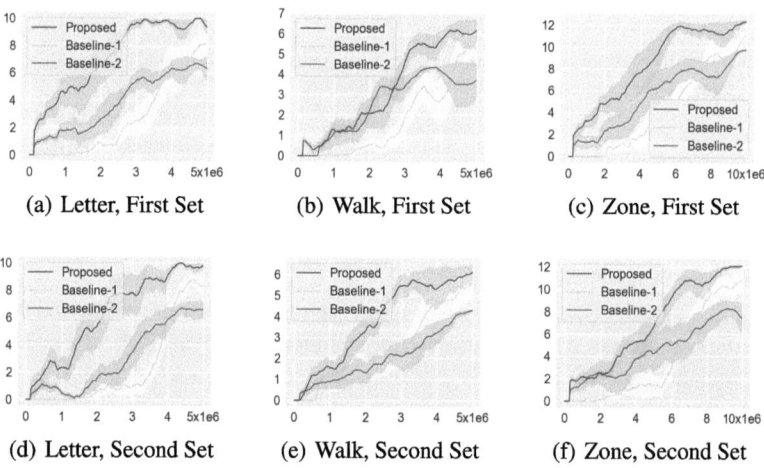

**Fig. 7.** Performance Comparisons. The x-axis is the environmental step, and the y-axis is the average episodic return. In the first set of experiments, the reward is only given at the completion of the given task. In the second set, the reward of achieving a subgoal is dependent other subgoals achieved previously.

In Fig. 7, the proposed method is compared with two baselines introduced in Appendix. In the first set of experiments, the trained agent is evaluated on completing testing tasks with the minimum number of steps. Here, the reward is only provided upon completion of the task, and the agent must avoid any propositions specified in the safety condition. This set of experiments focuses on low-level sub-task dependencies, specifically requiring the agent to avoid subgoals of other sub-tasks and to reach designated subgoals while accounting for future subgoals. In the second set of experiments, in addition to task completion, rewards are also granted for achieving some subgoals under ordering constraints. Specifically, the reward for certain subgoals depends on previously achieved subgoals within the same episode, introducing sequential sub-task dependencies. Detailed information on rewards of sub-task dependencies is provided in the Appendix. In addition, we conduct the third set of experiments with parallel sub-task dependencies, which is presented in Appendix.

In Fig. 7, we observe that the proposed framework outperforms Baseline-1 (LTL2Action [35]) in terms of learning efficiency. Unlike the proposed method, Baseline-1 relies solely on a task-conditioned policy and does not decompose the task to leverage its compositional structure, which hinders its learning efficiency. The faster convergence of the proposed framework results from the multi-step return estimation performed by the high-level module, which backpropagates rewards for each sub-task and provides return estimates to the low-level module upon the completion of each sub-task. In contrast, Baseline-1 propagates rewards step-by-step, resulting in slower learning convergence of its value function.

As shown in Fig. 7, the proposed method outperforms Baseline-2 (Logic Option Framework [2]) in terms of both average return and learning efficiency. In Baseline-2, the low-level policy is specifically trained for each assigned sub-task, aiming to reach positive propositions and avoid negative propositions relevant to that sub-task, without regard to other sub-tasks. This lack of awareness of dependencies compromises global optimality in low-level behavior. Additionally, when subgoal rewards depend on one another, Baseline-2's high-level planning can only myopically select next sub-tasks to complete the rest of the task. This is because conventional planning methods, which is value iteration (VI) [2] in Baseline-2, cannot handle non-Markovian rewards of sub-tasks. These limitations explain Baseline-2's lower average return in both first and second sets of experiments.

## 5 Related Work

Applying the RL paradigm to solve logic compositional tasks has been explored in numerous prior studies. These methods typically start by converting the compositional task formula into an equivalent automaton representation and then create a product MDP by combining the environmental MDP with the task automaton [37]. Prominent approaches utilizing product MDPs include Q-learning for reward machines (Q-RM) [5,11,12], LPOPL [34], and geometric LTL (G-LTL) [23]. Additionally, [14] introduced the DiRL framework, which uses hierarchical RL to accomplish LTL tasks by integrating graph-based planning on the automaton to guide exploration for task satisfaction. However, these approaches are tailored to specific task formulas, requiring policies to be retrained from scratch for each new task. Thus, they lack zero-shot generalization.

Previous approaches have sought to train reusable skills or options to facilitate generalization in compositional task settings [1,2,20,21]. In these methods, agents fulfill unseen tasks by sequentially combining pre-trained option policies through value iteration over potential subgoal choices, achieving satisfying success rate. However, they overlook inter-dependencies between subgoals, which can lead to suboptimal solutions when sub-tasks are dependent on each other, as demonstrated in Figs. 1 and 2. Although [19] considers causal dependencies among sub-tasks, it requires these dependencies to be explicitly provided. In contrast, our framework does not require the agent to know sub-task dependencies beforehand, making it applicable to scenarios with general and implicit sub-task dependencies.

In [17,35,40], the authors propose task-conditioned policies to enable zero-shot generalization in compositional tasks by conditioning the policy on task embeddings extracted through recurrent graph neural networks [17] or graph neural networks [35, 40]. These methods can learn optimal policies for generalization with sufficient training. However, they did not address sparse reward and long horizon issues of DFA tasks specifically, so their learning efficiency was still not satisfying. This arises because they did not decompose tasks into sub-tasks or leverage the inherent compositional structure of these tasks. In this work, we introduce a hierarchical RL framework for zero-shot generalization that decomposes DFA task into reach-avoid sub-tasks and train the RL agent to generalize across different sub-tasks, addressing the issues of sparse reward and long horizon specifically.

In addition, authors in [18] proposed to compute successor features of propositional symbols as policy bias to guide the generalization of unseen LTL tasks. However, the successor features are only about the achievement of next symbols and do not encode any dependencies of sub-tasks to be completed in the future. So, their approach still ignores the sub-task dependencies and cannot achieve the optimality in zero-shot generalization.

Goal-conditioned reinforcement learning (GCRL) has long focused on training a unified policy for reaching arbitrary single goals within a specified goal space [25]. However, GCRL typically addresses scenarios where agents need to reach only a single goal per episode. In contrast, the compositional tasks in our work require achieving multiple subgoals under specific temporal order constraints. While some GCRL approaches introduce hierarchical frameworks that generate multiple subgoals within an episode [6,22], these frameworks primarily aid exploration, with subgoals achieved in any order. This lack of temporal constraints makes these GCRL methods incompatible with our setting, so that these methods are not compared against the proposed framework.

There is a recent work [39] proposing to use future-dependent options to improve the optimality and learning efficiency of the generalization of compositional tasks. It is a similar work, but it does not consider safety issue and avoiding negative propositions of sub-tasks. This work proposes a new architecture and trains the agent to avoid negative propositions for the safety guarantee.

# 6 Conclusion

In this work, we propose a new hierarchical framework for generalizing compositional tasks in the SPECTRL language to address the sub-task dependencies and sparse reward issue. In the high level, we propose to use an implicit planner to select next sub-task optimally for the low-level module to complete. In the low level, the module is trained to complete the assigned sub-task, conditioned on the remaining task to complete. By transforming the given task into a DAG of reach-avoid sub-tasks, the sub-task dependencies are considered in the sub-task selection via an embedding of future sub-tasks extracted by a GNN, and the spare reward issue is resolved by the estimated return passed to the low-level module upon the completion of every sub-task. With comprehensive experiments, we demonstrate the advantages of the proposed framework over baselines in terms of optimality and learning efficiency. In the future, we plan to investigate the generalization of tasks specified by probabilistic logic language.

**Acknowledgment.** This work is supported by ARO grant under Award #W911NF-23-1-0146 and a gift by Open Philanthropy.

# References

1. Andreas, J., Klein, D., Levine, S.: Modular multitask reinforcement learning with policy sketches. In: *International Conference on Machine Learning*, pp. 166–175. PMLR (2017)
2. Araki, B., Li, X., Vodrahalli, K., DeCastro, J., Fry, M., Rus, D.: The logical options framework. In: *International Conference on Machine Learning*, pp. 307–317. PMLR (2021)
3. Araki, B., Vodrahalli, K., Leech, T., Vasile, C.I., Donahue, M.D., Rus, D.L.: Learning to plan with logical automata (2019)
4. Bordes, A., Usunier, N., Garcia-Duran, A., Weston, J., Yakhnenko, O.: Translating embeddings for modeling multi-relational data. *Adv. Neural Info. Process. Syst.* **26** (2013)
5. Camacho, A., Icarte, R.T., Klassen, T.Q., Valenzano, R.A., McIlraith, S.A.: Formal languages for reward function specification in reinforcement learning. In: IJCAI, Ltl and beyond (2019)
6. Chane-Sane, E., Schmid, C., Laptev, I.: Goal-conditioned reinforcement learning with imagined subgoals. In: *International Conference on Machine Learning*, pp. 1430–1440. PMLR (2021)
7. De Giacomo, G., Vardi, M.Y.: Linear temporal logic and linear dynamic logic on finite traces. In: *IJCAI'13 Proceedings of the Twenty-Third International Joint Conference on Artificial Intelligence*, pp. 854–860. Association for Computing Machinery (2013)
8. Hengst, F.D., François-Lavet, V., Hoogendoorn, M., van Harmelen, F.: Reinforcement learning with option machines. In: *Proceedings of the Thirty-First International Joint Conference on Artificial Intelligence, IJCAI-22*, pp. 2909–2915. International Joint Conferences on Artificial Intelligence Organization (2022)
9. Gujarathi, D., Saha, I.: Mt*: multi-robot path planning for temporal logic specifications. In: *2022 IEEE/RSJ International Conference on Intelligent Robots and Systems (IROS)*, pp.13692–13699. IEEE (2022)
10. He, K., Lahijanian, M., Kavraki, L.E., Vardi, M.Y.: Towards manipulation planning with temporal logic specifications. In: *2015 IEEE International Conference on Robotics and Automation (ICRA)*, pp. 346–352. IEEE (2015)
11. Icarte, R.T., Klassen, T., Valenzano, R., McIlraith, S.: Using reward machines for high-level task specification and decomposition in reinforcement learning. In: *International Conference on Machine Learning*, pp. 2107–2116. PMLR (2018)
12. Icarte, R.T., Klassen, T.Q., Valenzano, R., McIlraith, R.S.: Exploiting reward function structure in reinforcement learning: reward machines. *J. Artif. Intell. Res.* **73**, 173–208 (2022)

13. Jothimurugan, K., Alur, R., Bastani, O.: A composable specification language for reinforcement learning tasks. *Adv. Neural Info. Process. Syst.* **32** (2019)
14. Jothimurugan, K., Bansal, S., Bastani, O., Alur, R.: Compositional reinforcement learning from logical specifications. Adv. Neural. Inf. Process. Syst. **34**, 10026–10039 (2021)
15. Khalidi, D., Gujarathi, D., Indranil Saha, T: A heuristic search based path planning algorithm for temporal logic specifications. In: *2020 IEEE International Conference on Robotics and Automation (ICRA)*, pp. 8476–8482. IEEE (2020)
16. Kipf, T., van der Pol, E., Welling, M.: Contrastive learning of structured world models. In: *International Conference on Learning Representations* (2020)
17. Kuo, Y., Katz, B., Barbu, A.: Encoding formulas as deep networks: Reinforcement learning for zero-shot execution of LTL formulas. In: *2020 IEEE/RSJ International Conference on Intelligent Robots and Systems (IROS)*, pp. 5604–5610. IEEE (2020)
18. Kuric, D., Infante, G., Gómez, V., Jonsson, A., van Hoof, H.: Planning with a learned policy basis to optimally solve complex tasks. In: Proceedings of the International Conference on Automated Planning and Scheduling vol. 34, pp. 333–341 (2024)
19. Kvarnström, J., Doherty, P.: Talplanner: a temporal logic based forward chaining planner. Ann. Math. Artif. Intell. **30**, 119–169 (2000)
20. G León, B., Shanahan, M., Belardinelli, F.: Systematic generalisation through task temporal logic and deep reinforcement learning. arXiv preprint arXiv:2006.08767 (2020)
21. G León, B., Shanahan, M., Belardinelli, F.: In a nutshell, the human asked for this: latent goals for following temporal specifications. In: *International Conference on Learning Representations* (2021)
22. Li, S., Zhang, J., Wang, J., Yu, Y., Zhang, C.: Active hierarchical exploration with stable subgoal representation learning. arXiv preprint arXiv:2105.14750, 2021
23. Littman, M.L., Topcu, U., Fu, J., Isbell, C., Wen, M., MacGlashan, J.: Environment-independent task specifications via GLTL. arXiv preprint arXiv:1704.04341, 2017
24. Xinyu Liu, J., Shah, A., Rosen, E., Konidaris, G., Tellex, S.: Skill transfer for temporally-extended task specifications. arXiv preprint arXiv:2206.05096, 2022
25. Liu, M., Zhu, M., Zhang, W.: Goal-conditioned reinforcement learning: Problems and solutions. arXiv preprint arXiv:2201.08299, 2022
26. Mnih, V.: Playing atari with deep reinforcement learning. arXiv preprint arXiv:1312.5602 (2013)
27. Mnih, V., et al.: Human-level control through deep reinforcement learning. *Nature* **518**(7540), 529–533 (2015)
28. Pnueli, A.: The temporal logic of programs. In: *18th Annual Symposium on Foundations of Computer Science (SFCS 1977)*, pp. 46–57. IEEE (1977)
29. Ray, A., Achiam, J., Amodei, D.: Benchmarking safe exploration in deep reinforcement learning. arXiv preprint arXiv:1910.01708, 7:1 (2019)
30. Scarselli, F., Gori, M., Tsoi, A.C., Hagenbuchner, M., Monfardini, G.: The graph neural network model. *IEEE Trans. Neural Netw.* **20**(1), 61–80 (2008)
31. Schulman, J., Wolski, F., Dhariwal, P., Radford, A., Klimov, O.: Proximal policy optimization algorithms. arXiv preprint arXiv:1707.06347 (2017)
32. Sutton, R.S., Barto, R.G.: *Reinforcement Learning: An Introduction*. MIT Press (2018)
33. Taylor, M.E., Stone, P.: Transfer learning for reinforcement learning domains: a survey. *J. Mach. Learn. Res.* **10**(7) (2009)
34. Icarte, R.T., Klassen, T.Q., Valenzano, R., McIlraith, S.A.: Teaching multiple tasks to an RL agent using LTL. In: *Proceedings of the 17th International Conference on Autonomous Agents and MultiAgent Systems*, pp. 452–461 (2018)
35. Vaezipoor, P., Li, A.C., Icarte, R.A.C., Mcilraith, S.A.: Ltl2action: generalizing LTL instructions for multi-task RL. In: *International Conference on Machine Learning*, pp. 10497–10508. PMLR (2021)

36. van der Pol, E., Kipf, T., Oliehoek, F.A., Welling, M.: Plannable approximations to MDP homomorphisms: equivariance under actions. In: *Proceedings of the 19th International Conference on Autonomous Agents and Multiagent Systems, AAMAS 2020*, vol. 2020. International Foundation for Autonomous Agents and Multiagent Systems (IFAAMAS) (2020)
37. Voloshin, C., Verma, A., Yue, Y.: Eventual discounting temporal logic counterfactual experience replay. In: *International Conference on Machine Learning*, pp. 35137–35150. PMLR (2023)
38. Wang, X., et al.: Deep reinforcement learning: a survey. IEEE Trans. Neural Netw. Learn. Syst. **35**(4), 5064–5078 (2022)
39. Xu, D., Fekri, F.: Generalization of temporal logic tasks via future dependent options. *Mach. Learn.*, pp. 1–32 (2024)
40. Yalcinkaya, B., Lauffer, N., Vazquez-Chanlatte, M., Seshia, S.: Compositional automata embeddings for goal-conditioned reinforcement learning. Adv. Neural. Inf. Process. Syst. **37**, 72933–72963 (2024)
41. Zhou, J., et al.: Graph neural networks: a review of methods and applications. AI open **1**, 57–81 (2020)

# A Bilevel Reinforcement Learning Framework with Language Prior Knowledge

Xue Yan[1,2], Yan Song[3], Xinyu Cui[1,2], Filippos Christianos[4], Haifeng Zhang[1,2], Jun Wang[3(✉)], and David Mguni[5(✉)]

[1] The Key Laboratory of Cognition and Decision Intelligence for Complex Systems, Institute of Automation, Chinese Academy of Sciences, Beijing, China
{yanxue2021,cuixinyu2021,haifeng.zhang}@ia.ac.cn
[2] School of Artificial Intelligence, University of Chinese Academy of Sciences, Beijing, China
[3] AI Centre, Department of Computer Science, University College London, London, UK
yan.song.24@ucl.ac.uk, jun.wang@cs.ucl.ac.uk
[4] Huawei Technologies, London, UK
[5] Queen Mary University, London, UK
davidmguni@hotmail.com

**Abstract.** Large language models (LLMs) demonstrate their promise in tackling complicated practical challenges by combining action-based policies with chain of thought (CoT) reasoning. Having high-quality prompts on hand, however, is vital to the framework's effectiveness. Currently, these prompts are handcrafted utilising extensive human labor, resulting in CoT policies that frequently fail to generalise. Human intervention is also required to develop grounding functions that ensure low-level controllers appropriately process CoT reasoning. In this paper, we propose a comprehensive end-to-end training framework for complex task-solving that utilises language prior knowledge embedded within LLMs or from human experts. To that purpose, we offer a new leader-follower reinforcement learning framework that incorporates a prompt policy, a CoT process, and an action policy. The prompt policy is employed to ask pertinent questions based on historical observations, leading the CoT process to consider the anticipated goals and generate state-adaptive thoughts that lead to decisive, high-performing actions. To induce these high-quality actions, the prompt policy has its own objective in our system, encouraging it to adapt to the behavior of the action policy. The action policy subsequently learns to comprehend and integrate the CoT outputs to take precise actions. Empirical results demonstrate that our framework outperforms leading methods in 6 popular decision-making benchmark environments, including Overcooked and ALFWorld.

**Supplementary Information** The online version contains supplementary material available at https://doi.org/10.1007/978-3-032-06106-5_13.

**Keywords:** Reinforcement learning · Bilevel optimisation · Language priors

## 1 Introduction

Large language models (LLMs) with Chain-of-thought (CoT) prompts [28,29] have achieved impressive performance improvements for solving complex natural language processing (NLP) tasks. Moreover, techniques such as reward incentives and tree search [12,32] have enhanced the quality of CoT reasoning for addressing intricate decision-making tasks, ultimately inducing the step-by-step problem-solving process. This involvement of CoT reasoning has given rise to the promise of unlocking the power of LLMs to be able to assist in performing complex reasoning and acting in real-world environments.

While LLMs such as GPT-4 possess a wealth of human knowledge, in general, current prompt-engineering based language agents [16,32] and prior knowledge distillation approaches [33,36] heavily depend on meticulously crafted prompts designed by humans for each specific task. The dependence on high-quality, task-specific crafted prompts limits the generalization of these methods, while manually designing (high-quality) prompts is an arduous and expensive task. Additionally, despite the obvious potential of using CoT reasoning for guiding a low-level control policy, human-intelligible CoT reasoning can often be ambiguous for a downstream control policy, such as a rule-based planning method [23,34] and an action policy trained by a reinforcement learning (RL) algorithm [4,27]. As such, a natural consideration is the need to generate CoT outputs that are interpretable to the action policy, and provably reduce the uncertainty of the action policy in making decisions. Therefore, the ambition of embedding CoT reasoning appropriately within a generalist artificial intelligence (AI) framework has presented a series of critical challenges that have yet to be fully resolved.

In this paper, we propose a fully unified decision-making framework that adaptively incorporates CoT reasoning to assist in tackling complex tasks. In order to achieve this goal, both the prompt design and the action policy to be executed have to be sufficiently flexible and useful so as to adapt to the current task at hand. To this end, we introduce a comprehensive end-to-end decision-making framework that follows the *question, reason, then act* pipeline. Specifically, it learns to ask pertinent *questions*, performs CoT reasoning, and then learns to take the best actions in the environment. The first component of the framework is enacted by a *prompt policy* that learns a suitable prompt question given the environment observations. These prompts serve as inputs to a *CoT process*, allowing the framework to perform state-related and meaningful reasoning. The CoT outputs are then integrated into the *action policy*, which learns to find solutions to tasks that may require both interaction experience and human knowledge embedded in CoT reasoning to solve.

Learning how to generate in-demand prompts for the CoT process produces formidable challenges. One such challenge is to ensure that the resulting CoT outputs enhance the performance of an action policy. We resolve this challenge by designing a *leader-follower Bilevel* optimisation [19] structure, called

Bilevel-LLM and illustrated in Fig. 1, that generates mutually adaptive policies. Each policy is endowed with its own objective—the prompt policy observes the effect of its prompt and subsequent CoT reasoning on the action policy and learns to generate useful prompts. In particular, the prompts are chosen so as to minimise the uncertainty of the action policy i.e. minimise the entropy of the action policy. The action policy, on the other hand, learns to maximise the environmental reward while taking into account the outputs of the CoT process. Ultimately, the generated thoughts serve to learn a more effective action policy, providing additional information beyond the observation of the environment. These natural language insights embody human knowledge, reducing the need for redundant exploration compared to traditional RL algorithms, which typically require extensive exploration of specific environments to train a competent agent.

To minimise human intervention in task-related prompt design, we implement a prompt policy based on a set of predefined prompt candidates. This approach also helps avoid the dilemma of the scarcity of high-quality, supervised data for prompt generation and the instability risks associated with exploring an unrestricted prompt space. In many task environments, expert prompt data is available, such as well-defined sets of subtasks [23,30]. In environments where such prompt candidates are not available, our experimental results have shown that GPT-3.5 can generate high-quality prompts based on task descriptions, enabling Bilevel-LLM to achieve comparable performance to that rely on human-written prompts. Additionally, we demonstrate that Bilevel-LLM successfully learns to select the state-adaptive prompt from a global set of candidates.

The contributions of this paper can be summarised as follows:

- A new framework for dynamically adjusting prompts for decision-making tasks. An integral component is a prompt policy trained to select prompts that induce low uncertainty in the action policy, which receives thoughts generated by the CoT process triggered by the prompts. Therefore, the prompt policy (and hence the CoT process) behaves adaptively toward the needs of the action policy.
- Embedding CoT reasoning into the resolution of complicated decision-making tasks, where the outputs of the CoT process guide a policy that takes actions within an environment. This leverages the benefits of natural language models and CoT reasoning that encapsulate worldly experience and the capacity for deductive reasoning, while efficiently tuning the thought process by adjusting the prompt policy.
- A new bilevel optimisation framework that integrates prompt-tuning with the learning of a CoT output-based action policy. In this framework, the prompt and action policies mutually influence each other and are concurrently trained to converge.

## 2 Problem Formulation

In this setting, an agent aims to solve some task by performing a sequence of actions in an environment. Formally, the problem is described by a partially observable Markov decision process (POMDP), which is defined by the following tuple $\langle \mathcal{S}, \mathcal{A}, P, \mathcal{O}, T, \mathcal{R}, \rangle$, where $\mathcal{S}$ is the finite set of environment states, $\mathcal{A}$ is the set of actions for the agent, $P: \mathcal{S} \times \mathcal{A} \to \Delta(\mathcal{S})$ is the state transition kernel for the environment, $\mathcal{O}$ is the finite set of observations. The states, observations, and actions can be described in natural language. The function $\mathcal{R}: \mathcal{S} \times \mathcal{A} \to \mathbb{R}$ is the reward function, which returns a scalar reward conditioned on a state-action pair whose realisation at time step $t$ we denote by $r_t \sim R$. Lastly, the observation function is $T: \mathcal{S} \times \mathcal{A} \to \mathcal{O}$ which is a mapping from the environment state, action to the observation set. Since the exact form of the observation and state spaces varies between environments, we provided a general description of the POMDP setting for introducing the general problem setting.[1] In complex decision-making problems, standard methods such as RL struggle to solve these tasks in a sample efficient way. To solve these problems, an agent may required to deductive reasoning in order to resolve the challenge of finding an optimal policy. To tackle these challenges, we propose a bilevel decision-making framework as illustrated in Fig. 1, which can be split into three components:

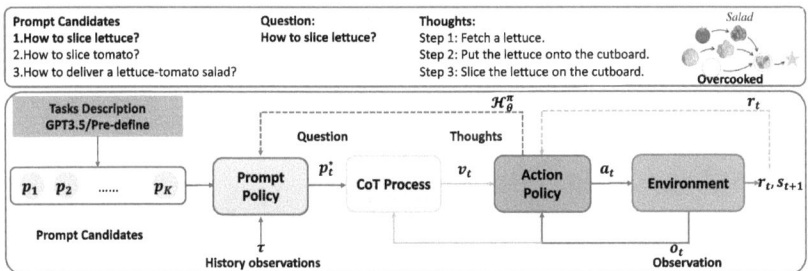

**Fig. 1.** *Top:* Example of the workflow from prompt candidates to CoT reasoning on Overcooked. The prompt policy first selects a prompt question from the candidate set. Subsequently, the CoT process generates complex reasoning guided by the prompt and the current state observation to assist in subsequent action performing. *Bottom:* The illustration of our bilevel optimisation framework.

- First, a *prompt policy* $\pi_\phi : (\mathcal{O})^{j<\infty} \to \Delta(\mathcal{P})$. Denote the $\mathcal{P}$ as the prompt space containing finite prompt questions. This policy learns to tune prompts after observing (a window of) $j < \infty$ observations.
- Second, a *CoT process* $\pi^{\text{re}} : \mathcal{O} \times \mathcal{P} \to \mathcal{T}$—a fixed language model that reasons about the task at the particular state observations and prompts questions. Denote that $\mathcal{T}$ is the space of textual sentences based on the vocabulary set

---
[1] In the MDP setting, the observation space is equivalent to the state space.

$\mathcal{V}$ (with finite words in it). Bilevel-LLM is a plug-and-play framework that supports various options, including universal LLMs, task-specific knowledge distillation [36], and environment-provided expert feedback [6], for performing CoT reasoning. In our experiments, we employ either GPT-3.5[2] or expert feedback provided by the environment [6]. Examples of prompt questions and CoT reasoning are illustrated in Fig. 1.

- Lastly, an *action policy* $\pi_\theta : \mathcal{O} \times \mathcal{T} \to \Delta(\mathcal{A})$. The action policy takes the observation of the environment and the CoT thought as inputs then executes actions in the environment.

Concretely, at times $t = 0, 1, \ldots$, a prompt $p_t$ is selected by the prompt policy i.e. $p_t \sim \pi_\phi(\cdot|o_t, \ldots, o_{t-j \wedge 0})$. The prompt is then used by the CoT process whose output is a thought $v_t \in \mathcal{T}$. Last, the action policy samples an action given the observation and the thought $a_t \sim \pi_\theta(\cdot|o_t, v_t)$. Therefore, the sequence of events proceeds as follows:

1. At time $t$, the system is at an environment state $s_t \in \mathcal{S}$.
2. A prompt $p_t$ is chose by the prompt policy i.e. $p_t \sim \pi_\phi(\cdot|o_t, \ldots, o_{t-j \wedge 0})$, $p_t \in \mathcal{P}$.
3. An action $a_t \sim \pi_\theta(\cdot|o_t, v_t)$ is taken given the output of the CoT process $v_t \sim \pi^{\text{re}}(p_t, o_t)$.
4. The environment state transitions according to $s_{t+1} \sim P(\cdot|s_t, a_t)$. Figure ?? in Appendix shows a step by step inference example of Bilevel-LLM on the Overcooked task.

To tackle the problem of learning how to tune prompts while learning the action policy, we structure the problem as a leader-follower *bilevel optimisation* [7]. This allows the prompt policy to learn how its decisions affect the action policy while the action policy learns both how to interpret the CoT outputs and take desirable actions. Since LLMs already contain a vast amount of world knowledge, we here fix the CoT process $\pi^{\text{re}}$. We update the prompt policy and action policy concurrently. The prompt policy aims to precisely adjust prompts minimise the uncertainty of the action policy, while the action policy aims to maximise the environmental return, taking the CoT outputs into account. The optimisation objective can be expressed as a bilevel optimisation problem:

$$(\pi_\theta^*, \pi_\phi^*) \in \arg\max_{(\pi_\theta, \pi_\phi) \in \Pi_\theta \times \Pi_\phi}$$

$$\mathbb{E}_{\pi_\theta, \pi_\phi, v_t \sim \pi^{\text{re}}}\left[-\sum_{t \geq 0} \gamma^t \mathcal{H}^{\pi_\theta}(y_t) | y_t = (o_t, v_t)\right]$$

$$\text{s.t. } \pi_\theta^* \in \arg\max_{\pi_\theta \in \Pi_\theta} \mathbb{E}_{\pi_\theta, p_t \sim \pi_\phi, \pi^{\text{re}}}\left[\sum_{t \geq 0} \gamma_I^t r_t\right],$$

where $\mathcal{H}^{\pi_\theta}(y_t) = -\sum_{a_t \in \mathcal{A}} \pi_\theta(a_t|y_t) \log \pi_\theta(a_t|y_t)$ is the entropy of the action policy $\pi_\theta$, $y_t = (o_t, v_t)$, and $\gamma_I, \gamma \in [0, 1)$ are the discount factors for the action

---
[2] The version of GPT-3.5 used in this work is GPT-3.5-turbo.

and prompt generation policies respectively and $r_t \sim \mathcal{R}$ is the environment reward. Here, we explain the bilevel optimisation:

**In the inner loop**, the action policy $\pi_\theta$ learns to take optimal actions, i.e. to maximisie environment reward, based on both observations and CoT reasoning, which contains task-solving prior knowledge.

**In the outer loop**, the prompt policy $\pi_\phi$ aims to minimise the entropy of the action policy. *The motivation for using the negative entropy of the action policy as a objective can be explained as follows.* It learns to find appropriate prompts that subsequently lead to CoT reasoning, enabling the action policy to take high-performing actions more certainly.

---

**Algorithm 1.** Bilevel-LLM

---
**Input:** Initialise parameters of policies $\pi_\theta$, $\pi_\phi$. Prompt candidate set $\mathcal{P}$. Set the data buffer $D = \emptyset$.
**Output:** $\pi_\theta^*$, and $\pi_\phi^*$.
1: **while** not done **do**
2:    #Rollout trajectories with $\pi_\theta, \pi^{\text{re}}, \pi_\phi$.
3:    **for** $i = 1, 2, .., $ step **do**
4:       Generate prompt given historical observations: $p_t \sim \pi_\phi(\cdot|o_t, \ldots, o_{t-j\wedge 0})$.
5:       Perform CoT reasoning given prompt and observation: $v_t \sim \pi^{\text{re}}(\cdot|p_t, o_t)$.
6:       Sample action according to the CoT reasoning and observation: $a_t \sim \pi_\theta(\cdot|o_t, v_t)$.
7:       Apply action $a_t$ to the environment, sample the reward $r_t$ and next step observation $o_{t+1}$.
8:       Calculate the entropy of the action policy: $h_t = \mathcal{H}\left(\pi_\theta(\cdot|s_t, v_t)\right)$.
9:       Add to data buffer: $D = D \cup (o_t, p_t, v_t, a_t, r_t, h_t, o_{t+1})$
10:    **end for**
11:    Update the action policy $\pi_\theta$ by optimising Eq. (2).
12:    Update the prompt policy $\pi_\phi$ by optimising Eq. (1).
13: **end while**

---

## 3 Methodology

In this section, we describe the training procedure of the proposed bilevel framework. The action policy is optimised to maximise environmental rewards, while the prompt policy is designed to assist the action policy in performing optimal actions more certainly by minimising its entropy. In the bilevel framework, the prompt and action policies are concurrently optimised until convergence. The overall framework is illustrated in Fig. 1.

*Prompt Policy Training.* When meticulously crafted prompts are provided, CoT reasoning has proven to be effective in aiding decision-making tasks. However, crafting prompts that effectively trigger reasonable CoTs for various long-term decision-making tasks is challenging, given the vast state space and the multifaceted skills these tasks demand. Therefore, we aim to develop a prompt policy that can dynamically adjust the prompts for different states while minimising reliance on extensive human labor.

Due to the limited availability of supervised data for high-quality prompts and the potential instability of exploring an unlimited prompt space, we opt not to train a model to autonomously generate prompts. Instead, we use predefined prompt candidates for each specific task, crafted either by humans or generated by powerful LLMs like GPT-3.5 with task descriptions given. Additionally, we conducted an experiment comparing the performance of our method using LLM-generated prompts with those designed by humans, as shown in Fig. 6(b).

Given a prompt candidate set $\mathcal{P} = \{p^{(1)}, p^{(2)}, \cdots p^{(K)}\}$, we aim to train a prompt policy that selects state-adaptive prompts from the candidate set. To implement the prompt policy, we use a pre-trained LLM, Flan-T5 Small [21] or Flan-T5 Large in this paper, as the backbone. The prompt LLM policy selects an appropriate prompt question for the current state given historical observation information and prompt candidates as inputs. This process is formally represented as: $p_t \sim \pi_\phi(\cdot|o_t, \ldots, o_{t-j\wedge 0}, \mathcal{P})$. For simplicity, we denote this as $p_t \sim \pi_\phi(\cdot|o_t, \ldots, o_{t-j\wedge 0})$, ignoring the $\mathcal{P}$ which are the same for all states. The prompt policy is updated via PPO, with the negative entropy of the action policy serving as the reward. The detailed procedure is described as below:

- For a decision-making task, we employ GPT-3.5, along with the provided task description, to generate appropriate prompt candidates. As a second case, we utilise the natural subtask structure [30] and human-crafted assists to generate valuable prompt candidates.
- With these $K$ prompts, the prompt policy is optimised to maximise the minus action policy entropy. The objective function is given by:

$$\arg\max_{\phi} \mathbb{E}_{\pi_\theta, \pi_\phi, v_t \sim \pi^{\text{re}}} \left[ -\sum_{t\geq 0} \gamma^t \mathcal{H}^{\pi_\theta}(y_t) | y_t = (o_t, v_t) \right] \quad (1)$$

When optimising the prompt policy $\pi_\phi$ through Eq. (1), we update only the parameters $\phi$, keeping the action policy $\pi_\theta$ fixed. The entropy $\mathcal{H}^{\pi_\theta}(y_t)$ of the action policy is treated as a scalar, non-differentiable reward.

**CoT Reasoning with Prompts.** With the selected prompt $p_t$, the CoT reasoning is obtained by $v_t \sim \pi^{\text{re}}(\cdot|p_t, o_t)$, where the CoT process $\pi^{\text{re}}$ is implemented by a powerful LLM such as GPT-3.5 or environment-integrated language feedback (for ALFWorld [6]). The motivation of integrating the CoT reasoning into our bilevel framework is to use human prior knowledge to provide a high-level guideline for solving complicated decision-making tasks. For example, as shown in Fig. 1, in the Overcooked game, the CoT process can generate a sequence of solving steps -"picking up the lettuce, placing it on the cutting board, and then slicing it"- related to a prompt question "how to slice lettuce".

During implementation, to reduce the inference time and costs for frequent queries, we store the CoT outputs for each state. Additionally, in Overcooked, which has a vast state space (up to $9.8 \times 10^{21}$), we abstract states into representative situations via a rule-based method and store CoT outputs accordingly. Specifically, we preserve the materials situation while disregarding the items' map positions.

**Action Policy Training.** Existing works [4,15,36] utilise LLMs as the action policy and fine-tune these LLMs to adapt to decision-making tasks, taking advantage of the comprehensive capabilities of LLMs. In our work, we also utilise an LLM as the action policy. In implementation, the action LLM takes the textual observations and the CoT reasoning as input and output an distribution over the action space. To regulate the action LLM to output executable actions, we fine-tune the action LLM, denoted as $\pi_\theta$, using PPO [22]. The objective of the action policy is to maximise the environmental return:

$$\arg\max_\theta \mathbb{E}_{a_t \sim \pi_\theta, p_t \sim \pi_\phi, v_t \sim \pi^{\text{re}}} \left[ \sum_{t \geq 0} \gamma_I^t r_t \right] \quad (2)$$

We use the same pre-trained LLM as the backbone for both the prompt and action policies. The PPO algorithm is employed to train both policies, with the prompt policy aiming to minimize the entropy of the action policy. Despite this, the exploration ability of the action policy is still preserved, thanks to the exploration-encouraging term in PPO.

**Bilevel Optimisation.** In our leader-follower Bilevel LLM framework, the prompt policy and the action policies are trained alternately, with the other policy being kept frozen. On the one hand, the prompt policy selects an appropriate prompt for the CoT process, the output of which is expected to assist the action policy in solving complex tasks. Thus, the goal of the prompt policy is to reduce the uncertainty of the action policy when it encounters challenging scenarios. On the other hand, the action policy is trained to effectively solve specific decision-making tasks while benefiting from CoT reasoning and the experience gathered during exploration. The overall training process of the Bilevel framework is detailed in Algorithm 1.

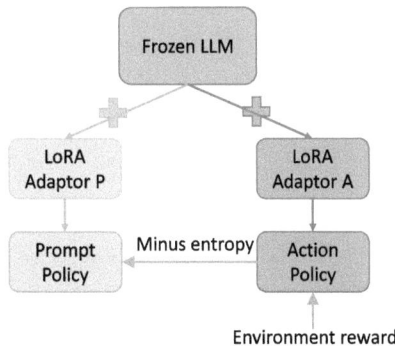

**Fig. 2.** The training structure of Bilevel-LLM using LoRA.

Inspired by the success of LoRA [14], which achieves comparable performance by training only a few parameters instead of fine-tuning all parameters, and considering that our prompt and action policies are based on the same LLM, we train two different LoRA adaptors for the two policies to enhance computational efficiency. The overall training structure of Bilevel-LLM is illustrated in Fig. 2.

## 4 Experiments

In this section, we validate that our bilevel framework, which integrates prompt tuning, CoT reasoning, and action policy learning, is beneficial for decision-making. Additionally, our bilevel framework supports utilising prompt candidates from GPT-3.5 while also automatically interpreting CoT reasoning, thereby avoiding the need for extensive human labor compared to prompt-engineering-based LLM agents [20,34]. Further details of experimental settings, such as hyperparameter and environment settings, and more ablation study results can be found in Appendix.

### 4.1 Environments

In this work, we incorporate six language decision-making environments involving various skills, including reasoning and navigation abilities, detailed statistics are shown in Table ?? in Appendix C. The six environments are the following: **Tower of Hanoi** [13], a classical logic reasoning game. **Frozen Lake** and **ChainWorld** are POMDP environments, where only the agent's position is accessible. **FourRoom** is a POMDP task, where the agent should navigate through hallways to reach the goal. **ALFWorld** is a widely recognized benchmark for LLM agents [24,32], is also a POMDP task. We utilise the environment as implemented by LLF-Bench, which provides off-the-shelf prompt questions and language feedback. We compare baselines across 50 tasks. For **Overcooked**, we consider three different layouts: *Overcooked(Tomato)*: deliver a chopped tomato with the map size of $5 \times 4$; *Overcooked(Salad)*: deliver a tomato-lettuce salad with a map size of $5 \times 4$; *Overcooked(Large)*: deliver tomato-lettuce salad with a map size of $7 \times 7$. Note that the state space of *Overcooked(Large)* reaches $9.8 \times 10^{21}$, making it challenging to explore. Standard RL environments, such as Frozen Lake and Overcooked, are converted into text-based environments using predefined rule-based transitions. More detailed environment descriptions can be found in Appendix C.

### 4.2 Baselines

We evaluate Bilevel-LLM against five baselines: **GFlan**, which utilises the Flan-T5 model as the action policy and optimises it with PPO based on textual state representation; **Vanilla PPO**, which uses an MLP network with symbolic state embeddings; and **GPT-3.5** in a zero-shot setting with task instructions, observations, and action candidates. An enhanced version, **GPT-3.5 with CoT**

**prompt**, includes step-by-step reasoning examples from human interactions. **ReAct(GPT-4)** employs GPT-4-turbo for generating actions after reasoning with historical data. Bilevel-LLM combines a prompt policy, CoT process, and action policy to improve decision-making in complex tasks. The Flan-T5 Small model is used in five environments for GFlan and Bilevel-LLM, except in ALF-World, where a fine-tuned Flan-T5 Large, based on expert trajectories from 10 tasks, is employed due to the task's complexity. Further details on the baselines are available in Appendix C.

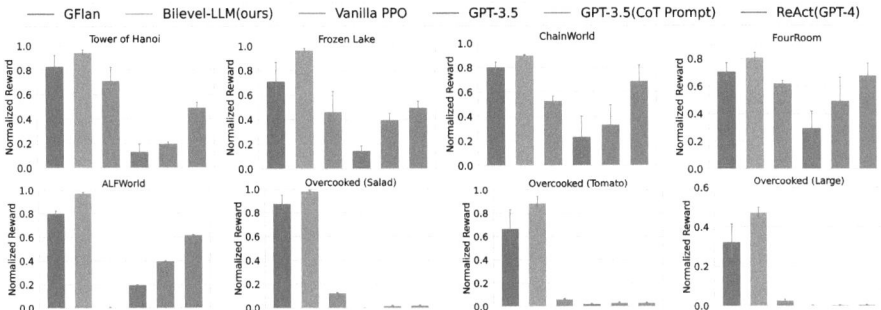

**Fig. 3.** Results of comparison with baselines. We plot the mean and standard error of the normalized cumulative reward. For inference baselines, the normalized reward is averaged over 20 episodes. For trainable baselines, we plot the normalized rewards averaged over the final third of the training processes across 5 random seeds. All cumulative rewards are normalized within the range of $[0, 1]$.

**Table 1.** Comparison of query costs on the Tower of Hanoi. We present the query cost for training Bilevel-LLM and running 20 episodes for ReAct. Bilevel-LLM incurs less cost while achieving better performance than ReAct (GPT-4).

| Baselines | Performance | Tokens |
|---|---|---|
| Bilevel-LLM(GPT-3.5) | **0.95** | 56K |
| ReAct(GPT-4) | 0.49 | 334K |

**Comparison With Baselines.** The results of comparisons with baselines are shown in Fig. 3. Bilevel-LLM outperforms other baselines on all environments and exhibits a smaller standard error than the suboptimal GFlan. This indicates that Bilevel-LLM, incorporating state-adaptive language prior knowledge, can improve the task-solving ability and convergence rate. In addition, GFlan consistently surpasses Vanilla PPO, especially on Overcooked. This suggests that using a pre-trained LLM as an action policy is beneficial for decision-making due to its rich prior knowledge and strong ability to reason about world rules. The

**Table 2.** Comparison of training resource requirements of baselines necessary to reach convergence (achieving a 95% win rate) on Frozen Lake. Our method requires fewer episode examples and comparable computational resources to achieve convergence.

| Baselines | Time(min) | GPU | Episodes |
|---|---|---|---|
| GFlan | 10.8 | 3598 MB | 1600 |
| Bilevel-LLM(ours) | 8.7 | 4658 MB | **800** |
| Direct-Prompt-LLM | 8.3 | 4378 MB | 1300 |

**training curves** can be found in Fig. 4, where our algorithm outperforms all other baselines and converges smoothly in most tasks.

Furthermore, inference baselines, including GPT-3.5, GPT-3.5 (CoT Prompt), and ReAct (GPT-4), struggle with most decision-making tasks. This may be because, although powerful models like GPT-3.5/4 can generate useful high-level task solutions, they still face challenges in long-term decision-making due to complex world models and rules. For example, in the Tower of Hanoi, GPT-3.5 can identify valid moves but struggles to generate the correct move sequence from start to goal, as detailed in Appendix D. Moreover, as shown in Table 1, Bilevel-LLM incurs a tolerable cost for querying LLMs compared to inference baselines.

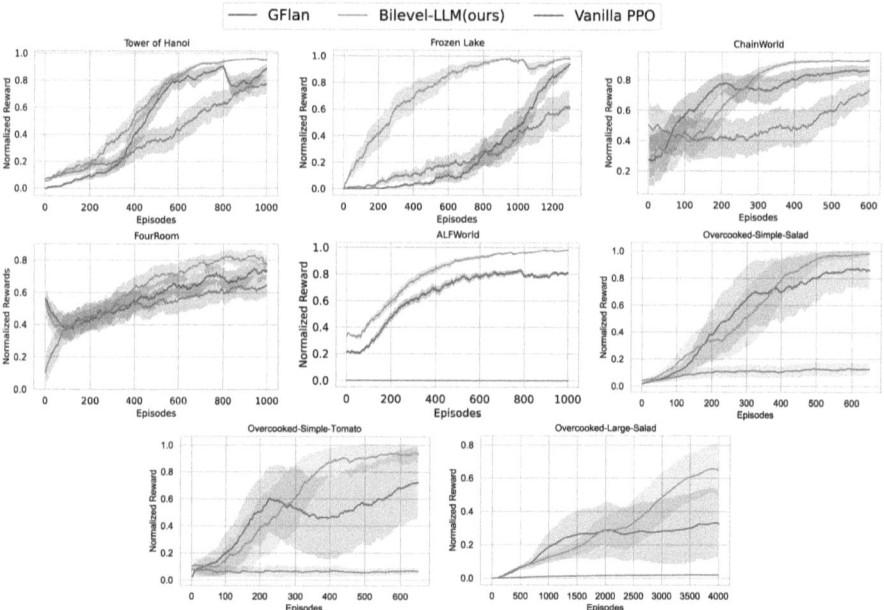

**Fig. 4.** Training curves of baselines. We plot the average and standard error of normalized rewards over 5 seeds.

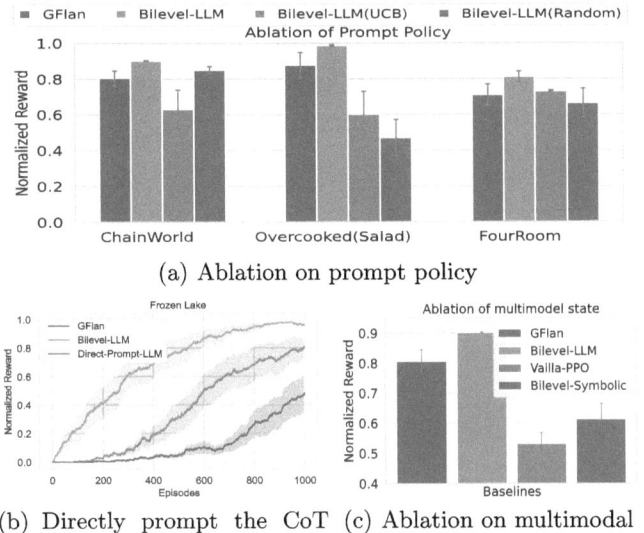

(a) Ablation on prompt policy

(b) Directly prompt the CoT LLM

(c) Ablation on multimodal

**Fig. 5.** Ablation studies. We include GFlan for reference purposes. (a) The effect of different prompt generation strategies. (b) Direct-Prompt-LLM lets the LLM(GPT-3.5) directly generate state-specific prompts and corresponding thought answers. (c) Verification of the effectiveness of Bilevel-LLM under multimodal state representations on ChainWorld.

### 4.3 Ablation Studies

We conducted a series of ablation studies to confirm the usefulness of the components of Bilevel-LLM. In the following, we modified components of Bilevel-LLM in order to validate the following claims:

**Does the Prompt Policy Trained Through Reinforcement Learning Improve Performance?.** To validate the claim that the prompts generated by Bilevel-LLM lead to improved performance, we have also tried different ways to implement the prompt policy other than RL and present the comparative results in Fig. 5(a). Bilevel-LLM (Random) naively selects prompt candidates randomly, Bilevel-LLM (UCB) views the prompt selection from a candidate set as the multi-armed bandit problem and the selection follows Upper Confidence Bound (UCB) over action choices. As shown in Fig. 5(a), Bilevel-LLM outperforms all other prompt policy versions on all environments. The poor performance of Bilevel-LLM (UCB) might be attributed to the lack of consideration for environmental observations.

**Does Action Behavior-Guided Prompt Tuning Improve Performance?.** We compare our method to the variant *Direct-Prompt-LLM*, which inquires the GPT-3.5 for the prompt question and corresponding CoT on the current state, and learn an action interpreter to decode CoT output. This method involves more automation but compromises performance at the same time, as shown in Fig. 5(b). *Direct-Prompt-LLM* surpasses GFlan due to the injection of domain prior knowledge but performs worse than our Bilevel-LLM. This is likely because our approach adjusts the prompt question according to the action policy's behavior, reflecting the experience gained from interaction with the environment. As shown in Table 2, Our Bilevel-LLM requires less online sampled episodes to train a proficient action policy, demonstrating greater sample efficiency than the other two baselines. Additionally, our method maintains acceptable training time and GPU usage requirements, thanks to the LoRA technique.

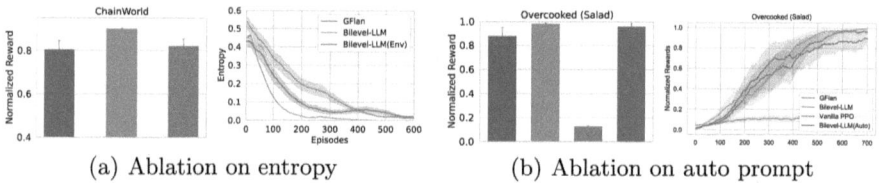

(a) Ablation on entropy  (b) Ablation on auto prompt

**Fig. 6.** Ablation studies. (a)Ablation of the entropy objective on Chainworld. *Left:* Normalized reward. *Right:* Entropy of the action policy. (b)Automatically generated prompt candidates on Overcooked(Salad). *Left:* Normalized reward. *Right:* Rewards during training.

**Can Bilevel-LLM Framework Accommodate Multimodal State Representation?.** We designed a baseline, Bilevel-LLM-*Symbolic*, where the action policy is replaced by that of Vanilla PPO, and it takes both the sentence embedding of the CoT output and symbolic environment observation as inputs. As shown in Fig. 5(c), Bilevel-LLM outperforms GFlan, and Bilevel-LLM-Symbolic surpasses Vanilla-PPO. This indicates that the use of CoT reasoning, triggered by dynamically tuned prompt questions, enhances the performance of action policies.

**Does the Entropy Objective Improve Performance?.** To validate that the entropy objective leads to more certainty in action policy decisions, we tested Bilevel-LLM against the variant Bilevel-LLM *(Env)*, which replaces the negative entropy with the environment reward. As shown in Fig. 6(a), Bilevel-LLM outperforms Bilevel-LLM *(Env)* and exhibits lower entropy of the action policy.

**Can Bilevel-LLM Learn From Automatically Generated Prompts?.** For most environments, we utilise the prompt candidates set generated by GPT-3.5 with the task description given, demonstrating that the learning framework can operate with minimum human intervention. In the tasks of ALFWorld, we directly adapt the candidates provided automatically by the LLF-Bench environment. In experiments on Overcooked and FourRoom tasks, we use the environmental well-structured subtasks as prompt questions for simplicity purposes. To further verify the effectiveness of automatically generated prompt candidates, we compare Bilevel-LLM to the variant Bilevel-LLM-*Auto*, which uses the prompt candidates automatically generated by GPT-3.5. As shown in Fig. 6(b),

*Bilevel-LLM-Auto* achieve similar rewards compared to those using human-crafted prompt candidates in the Overcooked task. These results also demonstrate that our plug-and-play framework can accommodate various sources of domain-specific prior knowledge, including that from pre-trained LLMs and human experts. Examples of automatically generated prompts can be found in Appendix C.

## 5 Related Work

**LLMs for RL.** A series of studies have attempted to incorporate LLMs into planning algorithms to address decision-making tasks. ICPI [3] solves a number of simple interactive RL tasks through in-context learning from historical interactions, thereby the need for expert demonstrations or gradient computations, The study [5] leverages historical trajectories to prompt LLM to generate the next step actions on the TextWorld game. LFG [23] utilises an LLM with a polling strategy to recommend and subsequently rank subgoals. Recent studies, Reflect-RL [36] and Retrosformer [33], learn a smaller model to distill valuable and critical human prior knowledge using an offline CoTs dataset collected from powerful LLMs such as GPT-4. Then use the distilled model for the subsequent action policy to take actions. In our work, we integrate complex CoT reasoning into RL to enhance the quality of actions while eliminating the need for meticulous engineering to interpret LLM outputs.

**Entropy in RL.** Entropy has been used extensively in RL as a tool for regularisation [1,18]. The policy in actor-critic methods is often trained with an additional term that aims to maximise the entropy of the learned actions, with the goal of exploring the environment without having a policy collapse early to suboptimal actions [18]. More formal use of entropy is explored in maximum entropy reinforcement learning [9,11], where the optimisation objective aims to learn the optimal policy that has the maximum entropy. In this work, we take a different approach, and look at finding prompts that minimise the entropy of the action policy. Intuitively, this would push the CoT process to provide reasoning that makes the policy sure about its action. Such minimisation of the entropy has also been explored: HIDIO [35] formulates a hierarchical approach to intrinsic options, where entropy is minimised to improve the option sub-trajectories, and the work [2] considers entropy for decision making in the exploration-exploitation trade-off.

**Automated Prompt Engineering.** The quality of prompts plays a crucial role in determining the output quality of LLMs. Many works hand-craft desirable prompts such as the Generative Agents [20] and ProAgent [34]. Apart from completely using human-crafted prompts, there are other studies that adopt different degrees of automation when generating meaningful prompts. For example, APE [37] and DLN [26] generate prompts from multiple examples and utilise LLM to rank the prompt candidates. PromptPG [17] trained a prompt selection network using the policy gradient to choose from a predefined set of examples. Unlike PromptPG, which selects prompts for one-step supervised data, we introduce a method to select state-adaptive prompts for multi-step decision-making tasks. Bilevel-LLM optimises the prompt policy by adapting it to the action policy's performance within interactive environments.

## 6 Conclusion

We introduce Bilevel-LLM, a bilevel framework that is capable of learning appropriate questions (in the form of prompts), and then performing complex reasoning for guiding actions executed by an action policy. The bilevel nature of the framework enables the accommodation of separate objectives for the two learning components, namely the prompt policy uses an action policy entropy minimisation objective which enables it to induce unambiguous and useful prompts to be fed to the action policy. Meanwhile, the action policy learns how to perform actions in the environment while making use of the CoT thoughts which it learns to interpret. We showed that this leads to a powerful framework that outperforms leading baselines in complex benchmark environments. We believe our framework takes an important step towards generalist artificial intelligence that is capable of introspection and complex decision-making.

**Limitations and Future Work.** In this work, we only explore our framework for solving single-agent decision-making tasks, but neglect the prevalent multi-agent setting. Further work will extend our framework to encompass decision-making in multi-agent scenarios, possibly exploring the potential of leveraging the reasoning abilities of LLMs to uncover cooperation patterns or to model the behaviors of opponents.

**Acknowledgments.** Haifeng Zhang thanks IPT Project 2024002.

## References

1. Albrecht, S.V., Christianos, F., Schäfer, L.: Multi-Agent Reinforcement Learning: Foundations and Modern Approaches. MIT Press (2023). https://www.marl-book.com
2. Allahverdyan, A.E., Galstyan, A., Abbas, A.E., Struzik, Z.R.: Adaptive decision making via entropy minimization. Int. J. Approx. Reas. **103**, 270–287 (2018)
3. Brooks, E., Walls, L., Lewis, R.L., Singh, S.: In-context policy iteration. arXiv preprint arXiv:2210.03821 (2022)
4. Carta, T., Romac, C., Wolf, T., Lamprier, S., Sigaud, O., Oudeyer, P.Y.: Grounding large language models in interactive environments with online reinforcement learning. arXiv preprint arXiv:2302.02662 (2023)
5. Chen, L., et al.: Introspective tips: large language model for in-context decision making. arXiv preprint arXiv:2305.11598 (2023)
6. Cheng, C.A., Kolobov, A., Misra, D., Nie, A., Swaminathan, A.: LLF-Bench: benchmark for interactive learning from language feedback. arXiv preprint arXiv:2312.06853 (2023)
7. Colson, B., Marcotte, P., Savard, G.: An overview of bilevel optimization. Ann. Oper. Res. **153**, 235–256 (2007)

8. Côté, M.A., et al.: TextWorld: a learning environment for text-based games. In: Computer Games: 7th Workshop, CGW 2018, Held in Conjunction with the 27th International Conference on Artificial Intelligence, IJCAI 2018, Stockholm, Sweden, July 13, 2018, Revised Selected Papers 7, pp. 41–75. Springer (2019)
9. Eysenbach, B., Levine, S.: Maximum entropy RL (provably) solves some robust RL problems. arXiv preprint arXiv:2103.06257 (2021)
10. Gao, L., et al.: Pal: program-aided language models. In: International Conference on Machine Learning, pp. 10764–10799. PMLR (2023)
11. Haarnoja, T., et al.: Soft actor-critic algorithms and applications. arXiv preprint arXiv:1812.05905 (2018)
12. Hao, S., et al.: Reasoning with language model is planning with world model. arXiv preprint arXiv:2305.14992 (2023)
13. Hinz, A.M., Klavžar, S., Milutinović, U., Petr, C.: The tower of Hanoi-Myths and Maths. Springer (2013)
14. Hu, E.J., et al.: Lora: low-rank adaptation of large language models. In: International Conference on Learning Representations
15. Jang, Y., Lee, J., Kim, K.E.: Gpt-Critic: offline reinforcement learning for end-to-end task-oriented dialogue systems. In: International Conference on Learning Representations (2021)
16. Lin, B.Y., et al.: SwiftSage: a generative agent with fast and slow thinking for complex interactive tasks. Adv. Neural Info. Process. Syst. **36** (2024)
17. Lu, P., et al.: Dynamic prompt learning via policy gradient for semi-structured mathematical reasoning. arXiv preprint arXiv:2209.14610 (2022)
18. Mnih, V., et al.: Asynchronous methods for deep reinforcement learning. In: International Conference on Machine Learning (2016)
19. Pakseresht, M., Mahdavi, I., Shirazi, B., Mahdavi-Amiri, N.: Co-reconfiguration of product family and supply chain using leader-follower Stackelberg game theory: bi-level multi-objective optimization. Appl. Soft Comput. **91**, 106203 (2020)
20. Park, J.S., O'Brien, J.C., Cai, C.J., Morris, M.R., Liang, P., Bernstein, M.S.: Generative agents: interactive simulacra of human behavior. arXiv preprint arXiv:2304.03442 (2023)
21. Rae, J.W., et al.: Scaling language models: methods, analysis and insights from training gopher. arXiv preprint arXiv:2112.11446 (2021)
22. Schulman, J., Wolski, F., Dhariwal, P., Radford, A., Klimov, O.: Proximal policy optimization algorithms. arXiv preprint arXiv:1707.06347 (2017)
23. Shah, D., Equi, M.R., Osiński, B., Xia, F., Levine, S., et al.: Navigation with large language models: semantic guesswork as a heuristic for planning. In: 7th Annual Conference on Robot Learning (2023)
24. Shinn, N., Cassano, F., Gopinath, A., Narasimhan, K., Yao, S.: Reflexion: language agents with verbal reinforcement learning. Adv. Neural Info. Process. Syst. **36** (2024)
25. Shridhar, M., Yuan, X., Côté, M.A., Bisk, Y., Trischler, A., Hausknecht, M.: ALFWorld: aligning text and embodied environments for interactive learning. arXiv preprint arXiv:2010.03768 (2020)
26. Sordoni, A., et al.: Deep language networks: joint prompt training of stacked LLMs using variational inference. arXiv preprint arXiv:2306.12509 (2023)
27. Tan, W., Zhang, W., Liu, S., Zheng, L., Wang, X., Bo, A.: True knowledge comes from practice: aligning large language models with embodied environments via reinforcement learning. In: The Twelfth International Conference on Learning Representations (2024)

28. Wang, X., et al.: Self-consistency improves chain of thought reasoning in language models. arXiv preprint arXiv:2203.11171 (2022)
29. Wei, J., et al.: Chain of thought prompting elicits reasoning in large language models. arXiv preprint arXiv:2201.11903 (2022)
30. Yan, X., Guo, J., Lou, X., Wang, J., Zhang, H., Du, Y.: An efficient end-to-end training approach for zero-shot human-ai coordination. Adv. Neural Info. Process. Syst. **36** (2024)
31. Yao, S., et al.: Tree of thoughts: deliberate problem solving with large language models. arXiv preprint arXiv:2305.10601 (2023)
32. Yao, S., et al.: React: synergizing reasoning and acting in language models. arXiv preprint arXiv:2210.03629 (2022)
33. Yao, W., et al.: RetroFormer: retrospective large language agents with policy gradient optimization. arXiv preprint arXiv:2308.02151 (2023)
34. Zhang, C., et al.: ProAgent: building proactive cooperative AI with large language models. arXiv preprint arXiv:2308.11339 (2023)
35. Zhang, J., Yu, H., Xu, W.: Hierarchical reinforcement learning by discovering intrinsic options. arXiv preprint arXiv:2101.06521 (2021)
36. Zhou, R., Du, S.S., Li, B.: Reflect-RL: two-player online RL fine-tuning for LMS. arXiv preprint arXiv:2402.12621 (2024)
37. Zhou, Y., et al.: Large language models are human-level prompt engineers. arXiv preprint arXiv:2211.01910 (2022)

# Representation Learning

# Learning from Stochastic Teacher Representations Using Student-Guided Knowledge Distillation

Muhammad Haseeb Aslam[1(✉)], Clara Martinez[2], Marco Pedersoli[1], Alessandro Lameiras Koerich[1], Ali Etemad[3], and Eric Granger[1]

[1] LIVIA, Department of Systems Engineering, ETS Montreal, Montreal, Canada
muhammad-haseeb.aslam.1@ens.etsmtl.ca,
{marco.pedersoli,alessandro.koerich,eric.granger}@etsmtl.ca
[2] CentraleSupélec, Universite Paris Saclay, Paris, France
[3] Aiim Lab, Queen's University, Kingston, Canada
ali.etemad@queensu.ca

**Abstract.** Advances in self-distillation have shown that when knowledge is distilled from a teacher to a student using the same deep learning (DL) model, student performance can surpass the teacher, particularly when the model is over-parameterized and the teacher is trained with early stopping. Alternatively, ensemble learning also improves performance, although training, storing, and deploying multiple DL models becomes impractical as the number of models grows. Even distilling a deep ensemble to a single student model or weight averaging methods first requires training of multiple teacher models and does not fully leverage the inherent stochasticity for generating and distilling diversity in DL models. These constraints are particularly prohibitive in resource-constrained or latency-sensitive applications on, e.g., wearable devices. This paper proposes to train only one model and generate multiple diverse teacher representations using *distillation-time dropout*. However, generating these representations stochastically leads to noisy representations that are misaligned with the learned task. To overcome this problem, a novel stochastic self-distillation (SSD) training strategy is introduced for filtering and weighting teacher representation to distill from task-relevant representations only, using student-guided knowledge distillation. The student representation at each distillation step is used to guide the distillation process. Experimental results[4](Code and supplementary available at: https://github.com/haseebaslam95/SSD) on real-world affective computing, wearable/biosignal (UCR Archive), HAR, and image classification datasets show that the proposed SSD method can outperform state-of-the-art methods without increasing the model size at both training and testing time. It incurs negligible computational complexity compared to ensemble learning and weight averaging methods.

**Supplementary Information** The online version contains supplementary material available at https://doi.org/10.1007/978-3-032-06106-5_14.

**Keywords:** Deep Learning · Self Distillation · Dropout · Time-Series · Student-Guided Knowledge Distillation

## 1 Introduction

Wearable technology has many applications, primarily in healthcare monitoring, such as activity and exercise tracking, sleep analysis, stress detection, and fall detection. It also includes applications like chronic disease management, personalized health insights, and human behavior and physiology research by continuously tracking metrics like heart rate, steps taken, body temperature, and movement patterns over time. Time-series signals such as electrocardiogram (ECG), respiration rate, and other biosignals are often multi-dimensional, noisy, and collected in real time from resource-constrained devices. These signals require efficient processing methods that balance accuracy with computational efficiency. Cumbersome methods for performance boosting are less effective for this application. Knowledge distillation (KD) is typically used for transferring knowledge from a large, well-trained teacher model to a more compact student model for deployment, thereby enhancing the latter's accuracy without incurring significant computational costs [12].

Self-distillation is a specialized case in KD, where the teacher and student have the same DL architecture, and the student typically surpasses the teacher's performance particularly where the model is over-parameterized i.e., has sufficient capacity and the teacher is trained with early-stopping. This increase in performance is typically associated with the fact that, with DL models, the teacher and the student have learned separate discriminative features, and self-distillation implicitly ensembles the two models [1]. Diversity in the feature space is a critical factor that enhances the robustness and accuracy of machine learning models. Diverse representations provide a comprehensive understanding of the input data, mitigating overfitting and improving generalization across various tasks [9,17].

Approaches for ensemble learning leverage the independent training of multiple diverse models to learn more robust decision boundaries, leading to significant improvements in predictive accuracy. Despite these advantages, deploying deep ensembles introduces substantial computational and storage overhead, as each model in the ensemble requires independent training, parameter storage, and inference pipelines. These constraints are particularly prohibitive in resource-constrained embedded systems as employed in wearable applications.

State-of-the-art (SOTA) approaches [1] that distill diverse ensemble-based representations involve the cumbersome process of training the teacher model multiple times or utilizing complex ensemble learning methods to generate a pool of diverse teacher models for effective knowledge transfer. These methods are computationally intensive and may not fully leverage the potential of stochasticity inherent in DL models for generating diversity.

This paper introduces a KD training strategy called Stochastic Self-Distillation (SSD) to capitalize on *distillation-time* dropout, thereby inducing stochasticity in a single, pre-trained teacher model. SSD generates multiple stochastic feature representations, effectively simulating a diverse ensemble of DL models without requiring extensive teacher re-training. This technique aligns with the principles of Monte Carlo dropout [11]. Moreover, a Student-Guided Knowledge Distillation (SGKD) is introduced to distill the most relevant knowledge (or filter out noisy representations) to the student model using student-guided attention. This mechanism allows the student to selectively focus on the most informative representations within the teacher's output space, facilitating a more efficient and targeted knowledge transfer. Subsequently, feature-level KD is employed to align the student's feature representations with the filtered and attention-weighted teacher feature representation.

The main contributions of this paper are summarized as follows.
**(1)** We propose SSD, a novel distillation-time dropout strategy to generate diverse stochastic representations from a single, pre-trained teacher model.
**(2)** Within SSD, a novel SGKD mechanism enables the student model to selectively distill knowledge from the most informative teacher representations. Feature-based KD is used to align the student's internal feature space with the teacher, promoting a more granular knowledge transfer.
**(3)** Our extensive experiments on challenging affective computing benchmark datasets (Biovid Pain and StressID), biosignal/wearable datasets (from the UCR Archive), the HAR dataset, and benchmark image classification datasets (CIFAR-10 and CIFAR-100) show that our SSD training strategy allows training models that can achieve SOTA performance while maintaining computational efficiency.

## 2 Related Work

**Knowledge Distillation.** Originally introduced by [5,12], the KD domain has evolved with several refinements in its application and architecture. Romero et al. [29] introduced the concept of distilling from feature representations instead of logits. The idea of transferring the attention maps from the teacher model to the student model was studied by Zagoruyko and Komodakis [41]. Relational KD proposed by Park et al. [27] studied the benefits of utilizing structural information for more fine-grained KD. The KD domain was extended to multi-task, semi-supervised, and unsupervised learning by Lopez et al. [23]. KD has also been studied in multimodal systems, particularly with applications like cross-modal KD [30] privileged KD [3], federated learning [21], are a few examples of the widespread application of KD in real-world systems.

**Deep Ensembles and Model Soups.** Ensembling methods improve predictive performance, generalization in neural networks, and uncertainty estimation. Deep ensemble is a simple yet effective technique where a simple aggregation of independently trained models harnesses the diversity, leading to better performance than each model. Lakshminarayanan et al. [17] demonstrated the effectiveness of deep ensembles for uncertainty estimation, showing that they outperform many Bayesian approaches in terms of both calibration and robustness. Deep theoretical insights on ensemble diversity were provided by Fort et al. [9]. Moreover, Ovadia et al. [26] highlight the advantages of deep ensembles in handling distributional shifts, reinforcing their utility in real-world scenarios. Despite their advantages, deep ensembles are computationally expensive, requiring the training and storage of multiple models, which motivates research into alternative methods that capture similar benefits with reduced complexity. More recently, parameter-efficient fine-tuning techniques like low-rank adaptation (LoRA) [13] have enabled efficient fine-tuning of large models. For example, Li et al. [20] introduced Ensembles of Low-Rank Expert Adapters. However, these techniques still require i) careful adaptation of each model, and ii) storing all the models for inference.

Model soups [39], is a technique for improving model generalization by averaging the weights of multiple fine-tuned models. Instead of selecting a single best model, model soups combine the parameters of different models fine-tuned with different hyperparameters, datasets, or random seeds, resulting in a more robust model. Two variations of the model soups were proposed: $(i)$ uniform soup averages the weights of all fine-tuned models equally, and $(ii)$ greedy soup, where models are added iteratively using a greedy approach. Model soup does not increase the model size for inference/deployment, yet it incurs significant additional train-time computational cost by fine-tuning models multiple times.

**Self-distillation.** This term has been used in the literature in two different contexts: distilling knowledge from deeper layers in a model to shallower layers of the same model's instance or through the use of an auxiliary network [19,42], and knowledge distilled from a model to another instance of the model with the same architecture [1,10,25]. In this work, 'self-distillation' refers to the latter. Furlanello et al. [10] proposed born-again neural networks, a seminal work exploring KD using the same model for teacher and student, showing that the student can outperform the teacher. Iterative distillation from the trained student, used as a teacher for the subsequent student model, also improved performance. Dong et al. [?] showed that early stopping is crucial in harnessing dark knowledge in self-distillation settings. Dark knowledge is the hidden class relationships encoded in the teacher model's soft probability outputs, which provide more information than hard labels. This nuanced information helps the student model learn better generalization and richer representations. A direct correlation between the diversity in the teacher predictions and student performance was studied in depth by Zhang et al. [43]. The authors enhanced the predictive diversity through a novel instance-specific label smoothing.

The concept of self-distillation in a regression setting was first studied by Mohabi et al. [25], in which the authors provided a theoretical analysis of self-distillation where only the soft labels from the teachers were used to train the student. Multi-round self-distillation settings limit the number of basic functions that must be learned. Borup et al. [4] build upon the previous analysis by including the weighted-ground truth targets in the self-distillation procedure. They show that for fixed distillation weights, the ground-truth targets lessen the sparsification and regularization effect of the self-distilled solution. Stanton et al. [32] studied the paradigm of KD through the lens of fidelity. Their key takeaway regarding KD and ensembles was that the highest-fidelity student is the best calibrated, even when it is not the most accurate. The closest work to SSD was proposed by Allen-Zhu and Li [1], who explored the concept of self-distillation in conjunction with the *multi-view* structure of the input data. In this case, the student model was trained on the ground truth labels with additional supervision from the ensemble of multiple teachers' soft labels. Multiple teachers were trained with random seed initialization.

In contrast to these methods, our proposed SSD training strategy obviates the need for such data augmentations or random seed initialization to generate diversity in the teacher space. SSD operates in the feature space, using dropout as a tool to introduce diversity and student-guided attention to distill relevant information for the student. Consequently, SSD requires significantly less complexity for training when compared to traditional ensemble learning and weight-averaging methods, and without increasing model size at deployment time.

## 3 Proposed Method

**Notation:** Let $\mathcal{T}$ be a teacher model with model parameters $\theta^{\mathcal{T}}$ and $\mathcal{S}$ be a student model with parameters $\theta^{\mathcal{S}}$. For given inputs $\mathcal{X} = [x_1, x_2, \ldots, x_m]$, we obtain the feature vectors $f^{\mathcal{T}} = \mathcal{T}(\mathcal{X}; \theta^{\mathcal{T}}) \in \mathbb{R}^{d \times m}$ and $f^{\mathcal{S}} = \mathcal{S}(\mathcal{X}; \theta^{\mathcal{S}}) \in \mathbb{R}^{d \times m}$, where $d$ is the dimension of the feature vector and $m$ is the number of input samples. Let $\mathcal{F}^{\mathcal{T}}(x) = [f_1^{\mathcal{T}}(x), f_2^{\mathcal{T}}(x), \ldots, f_n^{\mathcal{T}}(x)]$ represents the multiple stochastic teacher representations generated through $n$ forward passes through $\mathcal{T}(\mathcal{X}; \theta^{\mathcal{T}})$ for the same input sample $x \in \mathcal{X}$.

**Problem Definition:** Given a trained teacher model $\mathcal{T}$, the challenge is to effectively transfer its knowledge to a student model $\mathcal{S}$ such that its generalization performance is maximized. Standard self-distillation techniques often treat the teacher's outputs as deterministic, failing to exploit the inherent stochasticity that can provide richer and more diverse information. On the other hand, stochastically obtaining the teacher representations introduces diversity but at the cost of generating noisy representations. The problem, therefore, is to design a KD framework that leverages the variability in the teacher's representations, generated through stochastic mechanisms like dropout, while ensuring that the student learns task-relevant information in a computationally efficient manner. The main aim of our paper is to filter out the noisy representations from $\mathcal{F}^{\mathcal{T}}(x)$ and obtain weighted teacher representation $\hat{f}^{\mathcal{T}}(x)$ to selectively distill from the relevant teacher representations.

### 3.1 Stochastic Self-distillation

The proposed SSD training strategy generates multiple diverse representations per sample and uses the current student representation as a reference to rank, select, and weigh (using student-guided attention) the teacher representations before distilling. Further, SSD enforces the attention weights of the meaningful representations to be spread out through temperature scaling, this implicitly

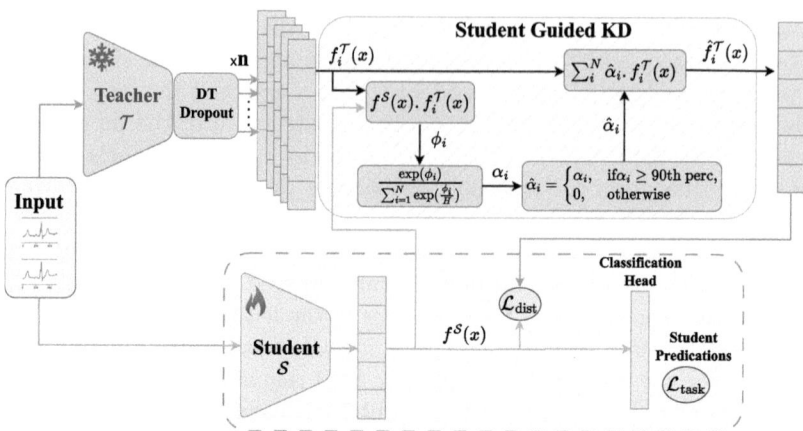

**Fig. 1.** Illustration of the proposed SSD training strategy. The teacher $\mathcal{T}$ is trained, and its parameters are frozen except for the dropout layers in the student training stage. In SGKD, for each input $x \in \mathcal{X}$, $n$ stochastic teacher representations $f_i^{\mathcal{T}}(x)$, $i = 1, 2, ..., n$, and one student representation is obtained $f^{\mathcal{S}}$, which are fed to the SSD module that outputs $\hat{f}^{\mathcal{T}}(x)$. Feature-based KD is then applied on $\hat{f}^{\mathcal{T}}(x)$ and $f^{\mathcal{S}}(x)$, with addition of $\mathcal{L}_{\text{task}}$, and the student model parameters $\theta_{\mathcal{S}}$ are updated. The part inside the dashed orange block is kept at inference.

models the feature ensemble to harness diversity. The student representation guides each distillation step because it is initialized with the same weights as the main trained teacher. Figure 1 illustrates the proposed SSD method. The remainder of this section provides details on the SSD training strategy.

**Teacher Training.** The first step is to train the teacher model and get trained teacher parameters $\theta^{\mathcal{T}'}$. This step is needed for two purposes: i) because the trained teacher model is used to generate the stochastic teacher representations $\mathcal{F}^{\mathcal{T}}(x)$, and ii) because these weights are also used to initialize the student model parameters in the student training step.

**Student Parameters Initialization.** After the teacher model is trained, the student model parameters are initialized with the trained teacher weights. This initialization is also crucial in the proposed training strategy. The proposed method relies on student guidance to obtain the attended teacher feature vector $\hat{f}^{\mathcal{T}}(x)$. The initialization of the student parameters with trained teacher weights lets the student serve as authority to weigh the teacher representations. As mentioned earlier, the stochastic nature of $\theta^{\mathcal{T}'}$, necessitates that some of the generated representations would be misaligned with the learned task-specific representation and hence would act as noise for the student model. This phenomenon is studied in detail in Sect. 4.3

## 3.2 Student-Guided Knowledge Distillation

Traditionally, in KD methods, the teacher representation(s) are informative and serve as additional supervision for the student model. However, if the teacher representations are generated through a stochastic process, they are not aligned with the learned class boundary and can be noise for the student model. Therefore, we use the current student representation as authority to select representations aligned with the learned class boundary. The student representation at each distillation step can be used as the guiding mechanism because the student model is initialized with the learned weights from the teacher network. This initialization allows the student to make use of its intermediate representation $f^S(x)$ as an anchor to rank the teacher representation $f_i^T(x) \in \mathcal{F}^T$.

To guide the distillation process using the current student representation, we first calculate the dot product ($\phi_i$) between the current student representation $f^S(x)$ and each teacher representation $f_i^T(x) \in \mathcal{F}^T(x)$ and compute attention weights using:

$$\alpha_i = \frac{\exp(\phi_i/h)}{\sum_{i=1}^{N} \exp(\phi_i/h)} \quad (1)$$

where $N$ is the number of teacher representations and $h$ is a regularization factor used to smooth the attention weights to ensure that the attended teacher feature vector $\hat{f}^T(x)$ is not heavily influenced only by a single teacher representation. This regularization step is crucial since it dictates the attention weights for teacher representations. Since the way these teacher representations are ranked is through dot product between current student representation $f^S(x)$ and each of the stochastic teacher representation $f_i^T(x)$, the value $\phi_i$ naturally would be the highest for the teacher representation that is the most similar to the student representation. This renders the entire framework ineffective because $\hat{f}^T(x)$ becomes overly similar to $f^S(x)$.

The SSD method relies on selecting teacher representations that would mimic an ensemble of independently trained teacher models. In other words, it masks out the representations that are too different from the current student representations. A direct way of selecting such representations would be to use the top-$k$ strategy at each distillation step. Although this strategy can work, it relies on $k$ a hyperparameter that is agnostic to the distribution of $f_i^T(x) \in \mathcal{F}^T$ at each distillation step. To avoid a manual selection of meaningful representations using a top-$k$ strategy, $\alpha_i$ is masked for all indices falling outside of the $\epsilon$-th percentile, denoted by $\hat{\alpha}_i$.

$$\hat{\alpha}_i = \begin{cases} \alpha_i, & \text{if } \alpha_i \geq \epsilon, \\ 0, & \text{otherwise.} \end{cases} \quad (2)$$

where $\epsilon \in [0, 100]$ is the threshold value for masking. Section 4.3 provides a more detailed discussion. After obtaining the regularized attention weights $\hat{\alpha}_i$, the original teacher feature representations $f_i^T(x)$ are weighed using $\hat{\alpha}_i$ to obtain the attended teacher feature vector $\hat{f}^{\mathcal{T}}(x)$ as:

$$\hat{f}^{\mathcal{T}}(x) = \sum_{i=1}^{N} \hat{\alpha}_i \cdot f_i^{\mathcal{T}}(x) \tag{3}$$

The attended feature vector $\hat{f}^{\mathcal{T}}(x)$ is used to distill the information using the mean squared error loss:

$$\mathcal{L}_{\text{dist}} = \frac{1}{d} \sum_{j=1}^{d} \left( f^{\mathcal{S}}(x_j) - \hat{f}^{\mathcal{T}}(x_j) \right)^2 \tag{4}$$

The total loss for the student is shown in Eq. 5,

$$\mathcal{L}_{\text{total}} = \mathcal{L}_{\text{task}} + \lambda \mathcal{L}_{\text{dist}} \tag{5}$$

where $\lambda$ is the weighting parameter for the distillation loss. The method also allows for the additional constraint for logit-level distillation and can be added to $\mathcal{L}_{\text{total}}$. For the unsupervised/contrastive loss-based methods, we use the intermediate teacher representations to obtain the $\hat{f}^{\mathcal{T}}(x)$. In case of augmented views of the input sample, we average the distillation loss from both views. The pseudocode for the SSD training procedure is shown in Algorithm 1.

---

**Algorithm 1 - SSD Training Procedure.**

---
**Require:** Teacher model $\mathcal{T}$ with parameters $\theta^{\mathcal{T}}$, student model $\mathcal{S}$ with parameters $\theta^{\mathcal{S}}$, input samples $\mathcal{X} = [x_1, x_2, \ldots, x_m]$, weighting parameter $\lambda$.
**Ensure:** Trained student model $\mathcal{S}$.
1: Extract teacher feature vectors $f^{\mathcal{T}} = \mathcal{T}(\mathcal{X}; \theta^{\mathcal{T}}) \in \mathbb{R}^{d \times m}$.
2: Extract student feature vectors $f^{\mathcal{S}} = \mathcal{S}(\mathcal{X}; \theta^{\mathcal{S}}) \in \mathbb{R}^{d \times m}$.
3: **for** each input sample $x \in \mathcal{X}$ **do**
4:     Generate $n$ stochastic teacher representations $\mathcal{F}_i^{\mathcal{T}}(x) = [f_1^{\mathcal{T}}(x), \ldots, f_n^{\mathcal{T}}(x)]$.
5:     Compute **dot products** $\phi_i = f^{\mathcal{S}}(x) \cdot f_i^{\mathcal{T}}(x)$ for $i = 1, 2, \ldots, n$.
6:     Compute **attention weights**: $\alpha_i$ for $i = 1, 2, \ldots, n$ using Eq. (1)
7:     **Mask** $\alpha_i$ for all indices outside the $\epsilon$-th percentile using Eq. (2)
8:     Compute **attended teacher feature vector**: $\hat{f}^{\mathcal{T}}(x)$ using Eq. (3)
9:     Compute distillation loss $\mathcal{L}_{\text{dist}}$ using Eq. (4)
10: **end for**
11: Compute total loss $\mathcal{L}_{\text{total}}$ using Eq. (5)
12: Update parameters $\theta^{\mathcal{S}}$ using backpropagation

---

## 4 Results and Discussion

### 4.1 Experiment Setup

SSD is validated on: (i) real-world affective computing datasets: the Biovid Heat Pain Database [35] and StressID dataset [6], (ii) wearable and biosignal datasets from the UCR Archive [8], (iii) Human Activity Recognition (HAR) dataset set from the UCI Archive [2], and (iv) on benchmark image classification datasets. Appendix A.1 provides details on these datasets, while Appendix A.3 provides implementation details and results on the CIFAR-10 and CIFAR-100 datasets.

**Biovid Heat Pain Database.** For Biovid, we use the EDA modality and LOSO cross-validation. The proposed method is tested with a SOTA method on the dataset using the Pain Attention Net [24], which is a transformer-based physiological signal classification network comprised of a multi-scale convolutional network, as SE residual network, and a transformer encoder block. The batch size used for teacher training was 128, and the network was optimized using the Adam optimizer with a learning rate of 0.001. The network was trained over 100 epochs with early stopping. The total number of folds was 87, corresponding to the total number of subjects. For student training, we keep the same setting as the teacher. We manually activate dropout layers with a $p$-value of 0.2 while keeping the teacher model in inference mode. The total number of repetitions for generating diverse teacher representations was 30.

**StressID Dataset.** For the StressID dataset, use the EDA and RR modalities and apply feature concatenation to fuse the backbone representations. The EDA backbone was Pain Attention Net [24], and the RR backbone was a 1D CNN with three 1D conv layers with 16, 32, and 64 channels, respectively, with a kernel size of 5, and stride equal to 1, followed by three batch normalization layers. Following the original dataset authors [6], we apply an $80 - 20$ split for the train and test set and further divide the train data and keep 20% of that for model selection. The batch size used for both teacher and student training was 128, with the learning rate of 0.001 using the Adam optimizer. The total number of repetitions was 30. The dropout layer was activated before the feature concatenation module with a $p$-value of 0.2.

**UCR Archive.** For the datasets in the UCR Archive, the proposed method was applied to two SOTA techniques – TS2Vec and SoftCLT – for unsupervised time-series representation learning. We follow the same experimental methodology proposed in TS2Vec [40] and SoftCLT [18]. For the TS2Vec method, the number of stochastic teacher representations was 15, with a teacher dropout rate $p$ of 0.2, and the student dropout rate was set to 0.1. The value of $H$ was 5. For loss weighting, $\lambda$ was set to 0.2. For softCLT, all the parameters were kept the same as those for TS2Vec except for the value of $H$, which was set to 15.

**Computing Infrastructure.** All experiments were performed on the NVIDIA A100-SXM4-40GB GPUs with the $\epsilon$ value of 90.

### 4.2 Comparison Against State-of-the-Art Methods

**Affective Computing Datasets.** Table 1 reports the results of SSD and SOTA methods on Biovid. SSD improves accuracy by 2.5% over the selected baseline (PAN without SSD) and 1.7% over the current SOTA. Specifically, accuracy on

**Table 1.** Accuracy of SSD against state-of-the-art methods on Biovid data. Baseline results were obtained using the network architecture without applying the proposed SSD method (without distillation).

| Method | | Modality | CV Scheme | Accuracy |
|---|---|---|---|---|
| Werner et al. [38] | ICPR 2014 | Physio + Vision | 5-fold | 0.8060 |
| Werner et al. [37] | IEEE TAC 2016 | Video | LOSO | 0.7240 |
| Kachele et al. [16] | IEEE IJSTSP 2016 | EDA, ECG, EMG | LOSO | 0.8273 |
| Lopez et al. [23] | ACII 2017 | EDA, ECG | 10-fold | 0.8275 |
| Lopez et al. [22] | EMBC 2018 | EDA | LOSO | 0.7421 |
| Thiam et al. [33] | Sensors 2019 | EDA | LOSO | 0.8457 |
| Wang et al. [36] | EMBC 2020 | EDA, ECG, EMG | LOSO | 0.8330 |
| Pouromran et al. [28] | PLoSONE 2021 | EDA | LOSO | 0.8330 |
| Thiam et al. [34] | Frontiers 2021 | EDA, ECG, EMG | LOSO | 0.8425 |
| Shi et al. [31] | ICOST 2022 | EDA | LOSO | 0.8523 |
| Ji et al. [14] | ACM SAC 2023 | EDA | LOSO | 0.8040 |
| Jiang et al. [15] | ESWA 2024 | EDA | LOSO | 0.8458 |
| Baseline (w/o SSD) | – | EDA | LOSO | 0.8459 |
| **SSD (ours)** | – | **EDA** | **LOSO** | **0.8690** |

Biovid increases from 84.59% (using the EDA modality without SSD) to 86.90% with the proposed SSD method.

Table 2 compares the performance of the proposed method with SOTA on the StressID dataset. We achieve 0.74±0.02 for the F1-score and 0.74±0.03 accuracy without applying SSD. The proposed method improves 3% for the F1-score and 4% in accuracy for the binary classification task over the SOTA. This increase in predictive performance shows that the proposed method can perform well on real-world time-series dataset tasks by effectively harnessing task-relevant diversity from stochastic teacher representations.

**Table 2.** Performance of the SSD against state-of-the-art methods on the StressID dataset. (MM: Multimodal, NR: Not Reported.)

| Method | Modality | 2-class problem | | 3-class problem | |
|---|---|---|---|---|---|
| | | F1-score | Accuracy | F1-score | Accuracy |
| HC + RF | Physio | 0.73 ± 0.02 | 0.72 ± 0.03 | 0.55 ± 0.04 | 0.56 ± 0.03 |
| HC + SVM | Physio | 0.71 ± 0.02 | 0.71 ± 0.02 | 0.59 ± 0.04 | 0.59 ± 0.03 |
| HC + MLP | Physio | 0.70 ± 0.03 | 0.70 ± 0.03 | 0.54 ± 0.04 | 0.53 ± 0.04 |
| AUs + kNN | Vision | 0.70 ± 0.04 | 0.69 ± 0.04 | 0.54 ± 0.05 | 0.53 ± 0.05 |
| AUs + SVM | Vision | 0.69 ± 0.04 | 0.69 ± 0.04 | 0.55 ± 0.05 | 0.54 ± 0.04 |
| AUs + MLP | Vision | 0.70 ± 0.03 | 0.70 ± 0.03 | 0.55 ± 0.03 | 0.55 ± 0.03 |
| HC + kNN | Audio | 0.67 ± 0.06 | 0.60 ± 0.05 | 0.53 ± 0.04 | 0.52 ± 0.04 |
| HC + SVM | Audio | 0.61 ± 0.06 | 0.54 ± 0.03 | 0.53 ± 0.08 | 0.48 ± 0.04 |
| wav2vec 2.0 | Audio | 0.70 ± 0.02 | 0.66 ± 0.03 | 0.56 ± 0.04 | 0.52 ± 0.04 |
| Mordacq et al. | MM | 0.69 | 0.76 | NR | NR |
| Baseline (w/o SSD) | Physio | 0.74 ± 0.02 | 0.74 ± 0.03 | 0.61 ± 0.01 | 0.59 ± 0.01 |
| **SSD (ours)** | **Physio** | **0.77 ± 0.03** | **0.77 ± 0.03** | **0.63 ± 0.02** | **0.60 ± 0.02** |

**Time-Series Datasets (UCR Archive).** Table 3 shows the performance of SSD against the TS2Vec baseline on 12 wearable/biosignal datasets from the UCR Archive. The student model achieves an average accuracy score of 0.8441.

**Table 3.** Accuracy of SSD applied to TS2Vec and SoftCLT baselines for the wearable biosignal datasets in the UCR Archive.

| Dataset | TS2Vec [40] AAAI '22 | TS2Vec + SSD (Ours) | SoftCLT [18] ICLR '24 | SoftCLT + SSD (Ours) |
| --- | --- | --- | --- | --- |
| ECG200 | 0.9000 | **0.9100** | 0.8800 | **0.9300** |
| ECG5000 | 0.9348 | **0.9411** | 0.9400 | **0.9413** |
| TwoLeadECG | 0.9789 | **0.9877** | 0.9762 | **0.9798** |
| NIFetalECGThorax1 | 0.9277 | **0.9318** | 0.9201 | **0.9394** |
| NIFetalECGThorax2 | **0.9389** | 0.9343 | 0.9435 | **0.9480** |
| Chinatown | **0.9737** | 0.9708 | **0.9737** | 0.9708 |
| UWaveGestureLibraryX | 0.7995 | **0.8079** | 0.8001 | **0.8143** |
| UWaveGestureLibraryY | 0.7152 | **0.7317** | 0.7169 | **0.7266** |
| UWaveGestureLibraryZ | 0.7624 | **0.7660** | 0.7674 | **0.7682** |
| MedicalImages | **0.8092** | 0.8078 | **0.8171** | 0.7710 |
| DodgerLoopDay | 0.5125 | **0.5250** | 0.5500 | 0.5500 |
| DodgerLoopGame | 0.7826 | **0.8405** | 0.8260 | **0.8695** |
| Total | 0.8350 | **0.8441** | 0.8426 | **0.8508** |

**Comparison with Traditional Ensembles and Model Soups.** Table 4 compares the performance of SSD against traditional ensembles and weight-averaging methods. For simplicity in experimentation and to make sure the results are not biased by the internal mechanisms of architecture, this comparison is performed on bare-bones 1D CNN architecture, which serves as the teacher network for SSD and is also used in the ensembles as well as weight-averaging results.

SSD aims to minimize the space and computational complexity both during training and testing. Figure 2 compares the performance gain in terms of model size at inference. We compare traditional ensembles (majority voting and averaging), stochastic weight averaging, uniform soup (uniform weight averaging), and greedy soup (a greedy approach for weight averaging). The marker size in Fig. 2 denotes the model size at inference; since traditional ensembles require storing all of the trained models for inference, it becomes impractical to deploy for inference on wearable devices. It can be observed from Fig. 2 that both majority vote and averaging-based ensembles increase the model performance, but the model size proportionally increases; essentially, for an ensemble model with 25 models, it would become **25×** the size of the baseline model. On the other hand, model soups do not increase the model size at inference but are still computationally expensive in terms of train-time FLOPs as shown in Appendix B. The total

**Table 4.** Accuracy of the SSD against state-of-the-art methods with a 1D CNN and traditional ensembles on the HAR dataset.

| Model | Accuracy |
|---|---|
| 1D CNN (Baseline) | 0.9002 |
| Ensemble Majority Vote (25 Models) | 0.9135 |
| Ensemble Average (25 Models) | 0.9128 |
| Model Soup (10 Models) | 0.9101 |
| Model Soup (25 Models) | 0.9183 |
| SSD (Student) | 0.9182 |

number of FLOPs increases from $\approx$ **0.87 G-FLOPs** to $\approx$ **21.8 G-FLOPs**. In contrast, the proposed method achieves comparable performance to the traditional approaches, i.e., 1.8% increase in the accuracy over the baseline, while keeping the model size the same as the baseline model, and the train-time computation is significantly less since SSD requires the model to be trained twice, once in the teacher training process and second for student training.

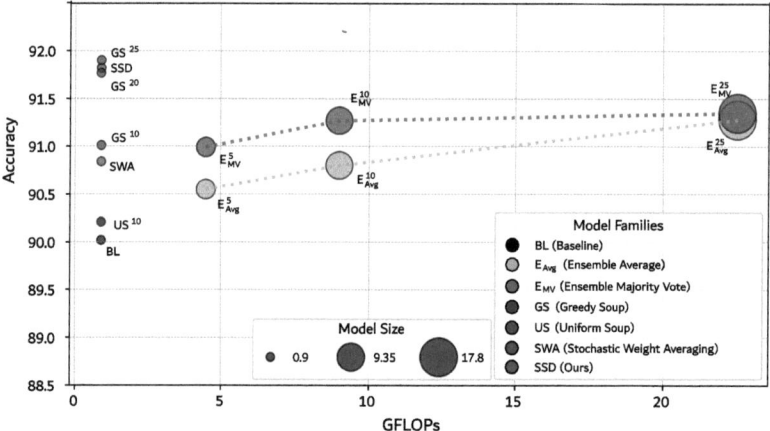

**Fig. 2.** Comparison of the SSD method with baseline (BL), traditional ensembles with majority vote ($E_{MV}$) and average ($E_{Avg}$), uniform soup (US) and greed soups (GS) on HAR dataset in terms of accuracy and model size at inference.

### 4.3 Ablations

**Number of Stochastic Representations.** As discussed before, meaningful diversity in the teacher space is crucial for the superior performance of an ensemble and, by extension, also crucial in SSD, since it also implicitly ensembles

**Table 5.** Comparison of schemes for selecting teacher representations on the StressID dataset. (DS: Dynamic selection. NA: Not available.)

| Scheme | # Representations | # Selected | F1-Score | Accuracy |
|---|---|---|---|---|
| Distill All | 10 | All | 0.74 ± 0.02 | 0.74 ± 0.02 |
| Distill All | 30 | All | ↓ 0.72 ± 0.02 | 0.72 ± 0.02 |
| top-$k$ | 10 | 3 | ↑ 0.75 ± 0.02 | 0.74 ± 0.02 |
| top-$k$ | 20 | 10 | ↑ 0.76 ± 0.03 | 0.76 ± 0.02 |
| top-$k$ | 30 | 15 | ↑ 0.76 ± 0.04 | 0.76 ± 0.04 |
| top-$k$ | 50 | 30 | ↓ 0.72 ± 0.02 | 0.73 ± 0.02 |
| **DS** | **30** | **NA** | **↑ 0.77 ± 0.03** | **0.77 ± 0.03** |
| **DS** | **50** | **NA** | **↑ 0.77 ± 0.03** | **0.77 ± 0.04** |

teacher representations. The number of repetitions dictates how diverse $f_i^\mathcal{T}(x)$ is. We evaluated with different settings and reported the results in Table 5. Distill All - the first two rows show the results without applying SSD and learning from all stochastic representations. This could also be seen as an alternative way of teaching students to drop out. Rows 3–6 show results with an increasing number of total repetitions and selected representations. As the total number of representations becomes too large, the performance drops even when applying SSD. This leads us to believe that when you select a more significant number of representations, the noisy representations bypass through the filtering mechanism and become part of the distillation process. This problem also indicates a simple top-$k$ selection is not the best strategy in this case. Hence, dynamic selection is applied based on $\epsilon$-th percentile thresholding.

**Dropout Rate.** The extent of diversity in the teacher space is directly related to the distillation-time dropout rate. To study how the probability value of each neuron to be deactivated affects the teacher representation space, we plot and compare the t-SNE plots with different dropout rates. Figures 3(a)-(d) are plotted with dropout rates 0.1, 0.2, 0.5 and 0.9 respectively. It is observed that for smaller dropout rates (Fig. 3(a)), the teacher can maintain its discriminative ability; however, the three teacher representations $f_1^\mathcal{T}(x)$ (triangle), $f_2^\mathcal{T}(x)$ (circle), $f_3^\mathcal{T}(x)$ (square) mostly overlap each other, effectively meaning there is not enough diversity in the teacher space. For dropout rate 0.2 (Fig. 3(b)), the three representations are diverse while maintaining the original structure, which shows that the teacher space has become diverse while maintaining the discriminative ability. In Fig. 3(c), the three representations are adequately spaced, but the model loses its discriminative ability.

To further analyze the impact dropout rate on both variance and overall performance, we conducted an ablation study on the HAR dataset. Figure 4 shows the effect of dropout rates on the student performance (dashed/black line) and the variance across teacher representations (colored/solid lines). Variance increases with the teacher dropout rate. For each dropout rate, the highest

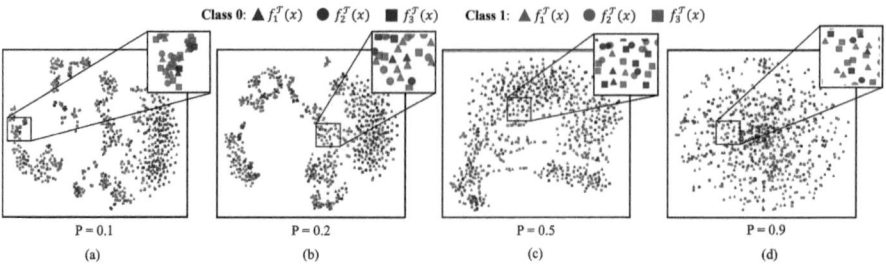

**Fig. 3.** t-SNE plots of three teacher representations $f_1^T(x)$ [triangle], $f_2^T(x)$ [circle], $f_3^T(x)$ [square] over various dropout rates $P$ showing the effect of the stochastic representations on the learned feature space.

variance is observed for the lowest number of repetitions. Conversely, the lowest variance for each dropout rate is observed with the highest number of reps. Results suggest that when the number of forward passes is greater, the overall variance decreases. It may also indicate a more accurate approximation of the true variance because it is calculated with more samples. In the latter case, it can be observed that for lower dropout rates, the variances across different number of repetitions are more accurate approximation of the true variance. In terms of performance, the model peaks at a dropout rate of 0.2, and the performance starts deteriorating beyond a dropout rate of 0.5. This phenomenon can be further explained from Fig. 3 where the t-SNE plots show the model starting to lose its discriminative ability at higher dropout rates.

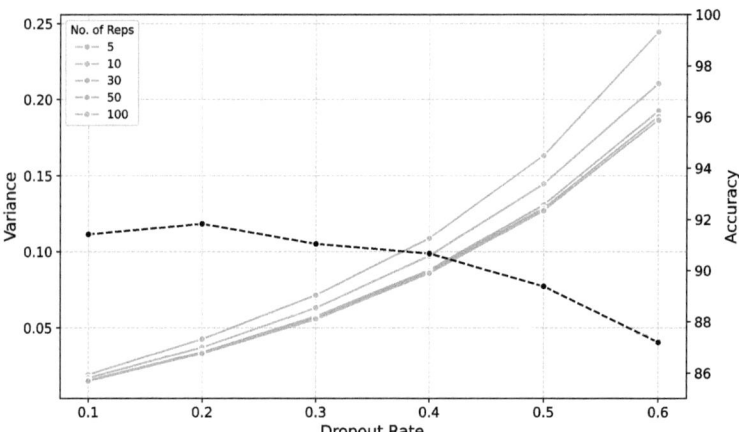

**Fig. 4.** Effect of various dropout rates on the performance and variance quantification among teacher representations. Accuracy (black/dashed line), and variance for various no. of reps (colored/solid lines) are plotted against dropout rates on the HAR dataset

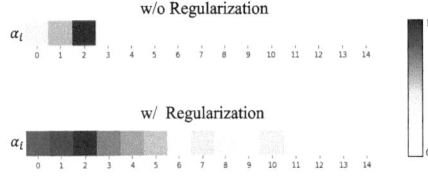
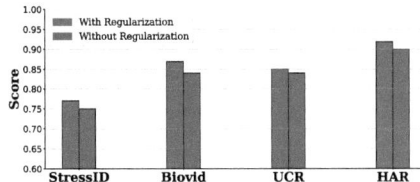

(a) Visualization of attention weights $\alpha_i$ for two input samples $x_1 \in \mathcal{X}$ and $x_2 \in \mathcal{X}$ with and without regularization.

(b) Performance comparison with and without attention weights $\alpha_i$ regularization on various datasets.

**Fig. 5.** Effect of attention weights $\alpha_i$ regularization on student performance

**Effect of Attention Weights Regularization.** SSD heavily relies on the diversity in the $\hat{f}^\mathcal{T}(x)$, implicitly mimicking the ensemble of task-relevant embeddings from the teacher space. If the attention weights are not regularized, the $\hat{f}^\mathcal{T}(x)$ would be highly influenced by one of the teacher embeddings, which is closest to the current $f^\mathcal{S}(x)$, essentially rendering the proposed methodology ineffective. Figure 5a shows the attention weights of an input sample $x \in \mathcal{X}$. It can be observed from Fig. 5a that, without regularization, the attention weight is extremely high for $\alpha_2$. On the other hand, the weights are more spread out with regularization, showing that the student model trained with SSD leverages the diversity in the meaningful teacher representations. Figure 5b shows the results obtained with and without regularization of $\alpha_i$. In all instances, regularization improves accuracy.

**Effect of Student Parameters Initialization with Teacher Weights.** The current student representation guides the distillation process at each step. This section investigates the impact of student parameter initialization with the trained teacher weights $\theta^{\mathcal{T}'}$. Figure 6 shows the results obtained by the student model with the baseline, random initialization, and student parameter initialization with trained teacher weights. It can be observed from the figure that in each instance, the random initialization performs even worse than the baseline. This shows the effectiveness of the proposed method, because if the student model is not initialized with $\theta^{\mathcal{T}'}$, the $\phi_i$ calculated would be ineffective since the current $f^\mathcal{S}(x)$ is not task aligned. Hence adding the additional constraint in the $\mathcal{L}_{total}$ term breaks the performance. See Appendix C.1 for detailed results.

### 4.4 Discussion

**Analysis of Performance on Teacher Network Architecture.** SSD can improve performance quite significantly on real-world datasets, particularly with models that have multiple dropout layers built into the architecture. Methods like PAN [24] and the fusion-based architecture used for Biovid and StressID datasets, respectively, have multiple dropout layers throughout backbones and various modules; in contrast, models for HAR and CIFAR datasets are 1D and

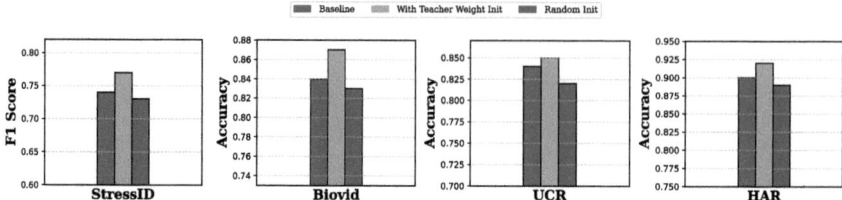

**Fig. 6.** Performance of SSD with and without student parameters initialization with trained teacher weights $\theta^{T'}$ on various datasets.

2D-Conv ResNet-based architectures with only one dropout layer. One direct correlation between the performance and the capacity to generate stochastic representations can be drawn. The models with a higher number of dropout layers naturally have a greater capacity to generate stochastic representations with more diversity, which allows the proposed method to form a more informative $\hat{f}^T(x)$, consequently leading to a student model with a significant performance boost over the teacher model.

**Supervised vs. Unsupervised Setting.** The proposed method can enhance performance both in supervised and unsupervised settings. The performance boost observed in the supervised setting is slightly higher than in the unsupervised setting; this could be because the unsupervised contrastive loss-based methods are already equipped with the ability to learn generalized representation. The augmented views of the input data in both TS2Vec and SoftCLT methods lead to more generalized representations.

**Why is SSD Different from Just Teaching *Dropout* to the Student Model?.** Intuitively, it seems that the proposed method might be an alternative way of teaching the student model to drop out. However, during both the teacher training step and student training, the standard *training-time* dropout is activated, but the performance boost is not observed. The performance boost can be explained by the filtering of the teacher representations, where *teaching the student to drop out* would be equivalent to distilling from all stochastic representations $f_i^T(x)$ instead of the attended teacher representation $\hat{f}^T(x)$, which is then filtered through the proposed SSD method (see Appendix D for a detailed discussion). This explanation is also supported by the results in Table 5 where we first distill from all $f_i^T(x)$, and the student performance does not improve.

## 5 Conclusion

In this work, we introduced SSD, a novel approach to enhancing diversity in the teacher space by leveraging the stochastic nature of DL models using *distillation-time* dropout and applying SGKD to learn meaningful representations. It employs the student's current representation as a guide to select meaningful representations, implicitly mimicking an ensemble of task-relevant representations. Extensive experiments on real-world time-series data, complemented by validation on a benchmark vision dataset, show the effectiveness of SSD in improving representation learning. While SSD outperforms SOTA methods, its current evaluation is limited to architectures that already incorporate dropout. Given that SSD operates in the latent space, we hypothesize that the proposed SGKD framework could be extended to other settings where diversity is introduced through perturbations in the feature space or noise injection. This presents an compelling avenue for future research and a promising alternative to deep ensembles. It also provides an alternative for learning generalized representations for time-series data, paving the way for more efficient and robust representation learning in a wide range of applications.

**Acknowledgments.** This research endeavor was partially supported by the Natural Sciences and Engineering Research Council of Canada (NSERC), Fonds de recherche du Québec – Santé (FRQS), Canada Foundation for Innovation (CFI), and the Digital Research Alliance of Canada.

**Disclosure of Interests.** The authors have no competing interests to declare that are relevant to the content of this article.

# References

1. Allen-Zhu, Z., Li, Y.: Towards understanding ensemble, knowledge distillation and self-distillation in deep learning. ICLR (2020)
2. Anguita, D., Ghio, A., Oneto, L., Parra, X., Reyes-Ortiz, J.L.: A public domain dataset for human activity recognition using smartphones. In: ESANN (2013)
3. Aslam, M.H., Osama Zeeshan, M., Pedersoli, M., Koerich, A.L., Bacon, S., Granger, E.: Privileged knowledge distillation for dimensional emotion recognition in the wild. In: IEEE/CVF CVPRw (2023)
4. Borup, K., Andersen, L.N.: Even your teacher needs guidance: ground-truth targets dampen regularization imposed by self-distillation. arXiv 2102.13088 (2021)
5. Bucilua, C., Caruana, R., Niculescu-Mizil, A.: Model compression. In: Proceedings of the 12th ACM SIGKDD. Association for Computing Machinery (2006)
6. Chaptoukaev, H., Strizhkova, V., et al., M.P.: StressID: a multimodal dataset for stress identification. In: Neural IPS Datasets and Benchmarks Track (2023)
7. Chen, Y., Wang, N., Zhang, Z.: DarkRank: accelerating deep metric learning via cross sample similarities transfer (2017)
8. Dau, H.A., et al.: The UCR time series archive. IEEE/CAA J. Autom. Sinica **6**(6), 1293–1305 (2019)
9. Fort, S., Hu, H., Lakshminarayanan, B.: Deep ensembles: a loss landscape perspective. arXiv 1912.02757 (2020)
10. Furlanello, T., Lipton, Z.C., Tschannen, M., Itti, L., Anandkumar, A.: Born again neural networks. In: ICML (2018)
11. Gal, Y., Ghahramani, Z.: Dropout as a Bayesian approximation: representing model uncertainty in deep learning. ICML **48** (2016)
12. Hinton, G., Vinyals, O., Dean, J.: Distilling the knowledge in a neural network. arXiv 1503.02531 (2015)
13. Hu, E.J., et al.: LORA: low-rank adaptation of large language models (2021)

14. Ji, X., Zhao, T., Li, W., Zomaya, A.: Automatic pain assessment with ultra-short electrodermal activity signal. SAC '23. In: ACM (2023)
15. Jiang, M., Rosio, R., et al., S.S.: Personalized and adaptive neural networks for pain detection from multi-modal physiological features. ESWA **235** (2024)
16. Kächele, M., Thiam, P., Amirian, M.E.A.: Methods for person-centered continuous pain intensity assessment from bio-physiological channels. IEEE JSTSP **10**(5), 854–864 (2016)
17. Lakshminarayanan, B., Pritzel, A., Blundell, C.: Simple and scalable predictive uncertainty estimation using deep ensembles. In: NeurIPS (2017)
18. Lee, S., Park, T., Lee, K.: Soft contrastive learning for time series. In: ICLR (2024)
19. Li, S., Lin, M., Wang, Y., Wu, Y., Tian, Y., Shao, L., Ji, R.: Distilling a powerful student model via online knowledge distillation. IEEE TNNLS **34**(11), 8743–8752 (2023)
20. Li, Y. et al.: Ensembles of low-rank expert adapters (2025)
21. Lin, T., et al: Ensemble distillation for robust model fusion in fed. learning (2021)
22. Lopez-Martinez, D., Picard, R.: Continuous pain intensity estimation from autonomic signals with recurrent neural networks. In: IEEE EMBC 2018
23. Lopez-Martinez, D., Picard, R.: Multi-task neural networks for personalized pain recognition from physiological signals. In: IEEE ACIIw (2017)
24. Lu, Z., Ozek, B., Kamarthi, S.: Transformer encoder with multiscale deep learning for pain classification using physiological signals. Front. Phys. **14** (2023)
25. Mobahi, H., Farajtabar, M., Bartlett, P.L.: Self-distillation amplifies regularization in hilbert space. arXiv 2002.05715 (2020)
26. Ovadia, Y., Fertig, E., et al., J.J.R.: Can you trust your model's uncertainty? Evaluating predictive uncertainty under dataset shift. In: NeurIPS 2019
27. Park, W., Kim, D., Lu, Y., Cho: Relational knowledge distillation. In: CVPR '19
28. Pouromran, F., Radhakrishnan, S., Kamarthi, S.: Exploration of physiological sensors, features, and ml models for pain intensity estimation. PlusOne J. **16**(7), e0254108 (2021)
29. Romero, A., Ballas, N., Kahou, S.E., Chassang, A., Gatta, C., Bengio, Y.: FitNets: hints for thin deep nets. In: ICLR (2015)
30. Sarkar, P., Etemad, A.: XKD: cross-modal knowledge distillation with domain alignment for video representation learning. AAAI **38**(13), 14875–14885 (2024)
31. Shi, H., Chikhaoui, B., Wang, S.: Tree-Based Models for Pain Detection from Biomedical Signals. Springer International Publishing, ICOST (2022)
32. Stanton, S., Izmailov, P., Kirichenko, P., Alemi, A.A., Wilson, A.G.: Does knowledge distillation really work? arXiv 2106.05945 (2021)
33. Thiam, P., Bellmann, P., Kestler, H.A., Schwenker, F.: Exploring deep physiological models for nociceptive pain recognition. Sensors **19**, 4503 (2019)
34. Thiam, P., Hihn, H., Braun, D.A., Kestler, H.A., Schwenker, F.: Multi-modal pain intensity assessment based on physiological signals. Front. Physiol. (2022)
35. Walter, S., Werner, E.A.: The biovid heat pain database: data for the advancement and systematic validation of an automated pain recognition. In: IEEE ICC (2013)
36. Wang, R., Xu, K., Feng, H., Chen, W.: Hybrid RNN-ANN based deep physiological network for pain recognition. In: 42nd IEEE EMBC (2020)
37. Werner, P., Al-Hamadi, A., Limbrecht-Ecklundt, K., Walter, S., Gruss, S., Traue, H.C.: Automatic pain assessment with facial activity descriptors. IEEE TAC **99**, 1 (2016)
38. Werner, P., Al-Hamadi, A., Niese, R., Walter, S., Gruss, S., Traue, H.C.: Automatic pain recognition from video and biomedical signals. In: ICPR (2014)

39. Wortsman, M., Ilharco, G., Gadre, S.Y., et al., R.R.: Model soups. arXiv 2203.05482 (2022)
40. Yue, Z., Wang, Y., Duan, J., Yang, T., Huang, C., Tong, Y., Xu, B.: TS2Vec: towards universal representation of time series. In: AAAI (2021)
41. Zagoruyko, S., Komodakis, N.: Paying more attention to attention: improving the performance of CNNs via attention transfer. arXiv 1612.03928 (2017)
42. Zhang, L., Bao, C., Ma, K.: Self-distillation: towards efficient and compact neural networks. IEEE T-PAMI **44**(8), 4388–4403 (2021)
43. Zhang, Z., Sabuncu, M.R.: Self-distillation as instance-specific label smoothing **2006**, 05065 (2020)

# BatMan-CLR: Making Few-Shots Meta-learners Resilient Against Label Noise

Jeroen M. Galjaard[1(✉)], Robert Birke[2], Juan F. Pérez[3], and Lydia Y. Chen[1,4]

[1] Delft University of Technology, Mekelweg 5, 2628 CC Delft, The Netherlands
{J.M.Galjaard,Y.Chen-10}@tudelft.nl
[2] University of Turin, Via Pessinetto 12, 10149 Turin, Italy
robert.birke@unito.it
[3] Universidad de los Andes, Cra 1 #18A-12, Bogotá, Colombia
jf.perez33@uniandes.edu.co
[4] Université de Neuchâtel, Rue Emile-Argand 11, 2000 Neuchâtel, Switzerland
lydiaychen@ieee.org

**Abstract.** The negative impact of label noise is well studied in classical supervised learning yet remains an open research question in meta-learning. Meta-learners aim to adapt to unseen tasks by learning a good initial model in meta-training and fine-tuning it to new tasks during meta-testing. In this paper, we present an extensive analysis of the impact of label noise on the performance of meta-learners, specifically gradient-based $N$-way $K$-shot learners. We show that the accuracy of Reptile, iMAML, and foMAML drops by up to 34% when meta-training is affected by label noise on the three representative datasets: Omniglot, CifarFS, and MiniImageNet. To strengthen the resilience against label noise, we propose two sampling techniques, namely manifold (Man) and batch manifold (BatMan), which transforms the noisy supervised learners into semi-supervised learners to increase the utility of noisy labels. We construct $N$-way 2-contrastive-shot tasks through augmentation, learn the embedding via a contrastive loss in meta-training, and perform classification through zeroing on the embeddings in meta-testing. We show that our approach can effectively mitigate the impact of meta-training label noise. Even with 60% wrong labels BatMan and Man can limit the meta-testing accuracy drop to 2.5, 9.4, 1.1% points with existing meta-learners across Omniglot, CifarFS, and MiniImageNet, respectively. We provide our code online: https://gitlab.ewi.tudelft.nl/dmls/publications/batman-clr-noisy-meta-learning.

## 1 Introduction

Few-Shot Learning (FSL) poses the problem where learners need to quickly adapt to new unseen tasks by using a low number of samples. Meta-learning [6,21] emerged as a promising solution to this problem. Like humans, meta-learners learn the information at a higher abstraction or meta-level, providing the inductive bias to adapt to new tasks quickly. Among existing meta-learners, gradient-based few-shot learners, e.g., iMAML [20] and foMAML(+ZO) [6,8], have been shown effective to solve $N$-way $K$-shot $(N, K)$ problems, that need to learn $N$ classes for each way given only $K$ samples each. Such few-shot learners are composed of two stages, each with their own labeled support and query sets. The meta-training stage learns a meta-model using two nested optimization loops. The inner-loop tunes the model to a specific task via supervised learning on the support set. The outer-loop uses the task-specific model and query set to update the meta-model. The meta-testing stage verifies how well the meta-model performs on new tasks. Using a similar structure, it uses supervised learning to adapt the meta-model to an unseen task via a test support set. Then, it computes the learner's accuracy on the test query set comparing given and predicted labels. Each way's class labels are thus crucial in both meta-training and meta-testing.

Label noise is more the norm than a rarity and can significantly degrade the performance of supervised learners [23]. Prior studies address label noise mainly in classical supervised learners. In this context, samples hold labels different from the underlying ground truth. In the context of FSL, label noise means that a shot (example) may not correspond to the way (class) it was provided with. This yields a degenerate $N$-way $K$-shot problem where ways become indistinguishable since they contain shots of the same ground truth. Such noise may appear in the support sets of meta-training and meta-testing and the query set of meta-training.

Despite the importance of labels in meta-training and meta-testing, only a few studies [14–16] address the challenge of noisy labels in FSL and only at the meta-testing support set level. However, label noise can appear in all support and query sets, affecting both meta-testing and meta-training, and little is known on its impact and resolution. As the number of samples per way is very limited, e.g., five to ten shots, the task adaptation step can be easily over-parameterized by label noise, leading to significant degradation. Moreover, existing meta-learners that account for label noise still require clean data to learn a meta-objective [10, 26].

In this paper, we first empirically show that gradient-based FSL methods, i.e., Reptile [19], Eigen-Reptile [4], iMAML [20], and foMAML+ZO [8], are significantly affected by label noise in both query and support sets during meta-training. To counter the effect of label noise, we propose Man and BatMan, which turn any supervised few-shot learner into a semi-supervised learner by a novel (batch) manifold sampling and contrastive learning. Specifically, we turn a noisy $N$-way $K$-shot problem into a self-cleansed $N$-way 2-*contrastive* shot problem. We first augment the original shots and construct contrastive pairs, ensuring the shots are from the same class. We then sample such pairs from the $N$ ways, termed manifold (Man) samples. To lower the probability of an update seeing only noisy $N$-ways, i.e., overlapping classes for different ways, we draw a batch of such Man samples, termed BatMan sampling. Combining this approach with a self-supervised contrastive loss, we can effectively learn the embedding of the initial model, which can then be adapted in meta-testing to a new $N$-way $K$-shot task. The specific contributions of this paper are:

1. An extensive study on the impact of label noise in meta-training for representative gradient-based meta-learners.
2. A generic, self-cleansing framework, BatMan-CLR, which turns meta-learners into semi-supervised ones by manifold sampling $N$-way 2-contrastive shots.
3. Extensive evaluation on four meta-learners, Reptile, Eigen-Reptile, iMAML, and foMAML, shows nearly no performance degradation under the presence of up to 60% label noise.

**Table 1.** Meta-learning algorithm's meta-test accuracies (mean with 95% confidence for 3 runs) on clean $\mathcal{D}_{test}$ under varying levels of $\mathcal{D}_{train}$ label noise. Evaluated on increasing strengths of label noise $\epsilon \in \{0.0, 0.3, 0.6\}$, corresponding to clean (0%), 30% and 60% *dataset-level* noise.

(a) Few-shot results with increasing noise on CifarFS [2], and Omniglot [12].

|  | CifarFS | | | Omniglot | | |
|---|---|---|---|---|---|---|
| Algorithm | $\epsilon = 0.0$ | $\epsilon = 0.3$ | $\epsilon = 0.6$ | $\epsilon = 0.0$ | $\epsilon = 0.3$ | $\epsilon = 0.6$ |
| foMAML | 69.5±0.26 | 65.2±0.27 | 40.3±0.21 | 99.3±0.04 | 97.7±0.07 | 90.3±0.15 |
| iMAML | 64.0±0.24 | 55.9±0.26 | 46.3±0.24 | 96.9±0.11 | 91.0±0.18 | 82.6±0.19 |
| Reptile | 65.5±0.24 | 58.6±0.26 | 51.8±0.25 | 92.5±0.13 | 79.7±0.21 | 71.5±0.24 |
| Eigen-Reptile | 65.3±0.24 | 58.1±0.27 | 52.7±0.24 | 93.6±0.12 | 83.6±0.19 | 73.4±0.24 |

(b) Few-shot results under increasing noise on MiniImageNet [24].

| Algorithm | $\epsilon = 0.0$ | $\epsilon = 0.3$ | $\epsilon = 0.6$ |
|---|---|---|---|
| foMAML | 52.2±0.22 | 37.1±0.18 | 28.2±0.15 |
| iMAML | 53.9±0.22 | 45.5±0.21 | 20.0±0.08 |
| Reptile | 54.2±0.21 | 27.8±0.14 | 24.6±0.14 |
| Eigen-Reptile | 58.7±0.25 | 44.8±0.20 | 24.8±0.14 |

## 2 Preliminary and Related Work

**Preliminary on FSL.** FSL considers the setting where a learned model must adapt to new tasks leveraging only few samples. We consider the $N$-way $K$-shot classification problem, which consists of a family of tasks, each comprised of $N$ classes with $K$ samples—termed $(N, K)$-FSL tasks. We focus on gradient-based meta-learners, which use an iterative two-step meta-training algorithm to find a meta-model parameterized by $\theta$ capable of quickly adapting towards a task-specific parameterization $\phi$. Each meta-training epoch $t$, starts by randomly drawing a task $\mathcal{T}$ from a collection of meta-training tasks and samples two disjoint sets, support $\mathcal{D}^{\mathcal{T}}_{\text{support}}$ and query $\mathcal{D}^{\mathcal{T}}_{\text{query}}$, from the training data $\mathcal{D}^{\mathcal{T}}_{\text{train}}$ associated with $\mathcal{T}$. Next, the inner loop of meta-training transforms $\theta_t$ in task-specific parameters $\phi$ by minimizing a supervised loss function $\mathcal{L}_{sup}$ over the input-output pairs $(X_s, Y_s) \in \mathcal{D}^{\mathcal{T}}_{\text{support}}$. Then, the meta-training outer loop uses $\phi$, $\mathcal{L}_{sup}$ and the data $(X_q, Y_q) \in \mathcal{D}^{\mathcal{T}}_{\text{query}}$ to obtain $\theta_{t+1}$ for the next iteration. Note that while the support set $\mathcal{D}^{\mathcal{T}}_{\text{support}}$ is used during an inner-loop to train for a specific task, the query set $\mathcal{D}^{\mathcal{T}}_{\text{query}}$ is used in an outer-loop to learn initialization of the meta-model. Meta-testing evaluates the ability of a trained meta-model with parameters $\theta^*$ to adapt to new tasks. Analogous to meta-training, meta-testing first randomly selects a task $\mathcal{T}_{test}$ for testing and samples $\mathcal{D}^{\mathcal{T}_{test}}_{\text{support}}$ and $\mathcal{D}^{\mathcal{T}_{test}}_{\text{query}}$ from the associated test data $\mathcal{D}_{\text{test}}$. Next, the adaptation step uses $\mathcal{D}^{\mathcal{T}_{test}}_{\text{support}}$ to fine tune $\theta^*$ into task-specific parameters $\phi^*$. Finally, $\phi^*$ is tested on the query set $(X_q, Y_q) \in \mathcal{D}^{\mathcal{T}_{test}}_{\text{query}}$ by comparing its predictions $\hat{Y}_q$ against known labels $Y_q$.

**Gradient-Based Meta-learners.** MAML [6], the father of gradient-based meta-learners, updates the meta-model via gradient descent through gradient descent. As this operation is very resource intensive and sensitive to hyperparameters [6,18,20], many works propose approximations outperforming the original MAML. iMAML and foMAML+ZO approximate the meta-gradient with respect to $\theta_t$ by leveraging the first-order gradient on $\mathcal{D}_{\text{query}}$ with respect to $\phi_u$. This drops the need for gradient descent through gradient descent. iMAML considers that it can compute the meta-gradient using more adaptation steps and weight regularization. foMAML+ZO assumes that the higher-order meta-gradient components can be ignored altogether. Reptile drops $\mathcal{D}_{\text{query}}$ during meta-training by estimating the meta-gradient by stepping towards $\phi_u$ to find $\theta_{t+1}$. Eigen-Reptile further decomposes parameterization of the inner-learners optimization path from $\phi_0 = \theta_t$ to $\phi_u$ following $u$ optimization steps, i.e., $[\phi_0, \phi_1, \ldots, \phi_u]$, and steps towards the direction with the largest variance.

**Label Noise in FSL.** Label noise poses a major challenge to meta-learners, especially in the absence of clean data that can be used as ground truth during meta-training. Although a large collection of work on robust supervised learning exists [13,25,28], these are not directly applicable to meta-learners due to the limited number of samples. Related studies [10,14,14–16,26] mainly focus on distilling the label noise in *meta-testing* by explicitly studying the noise patterns [14,15,26], using soft-relabeling [16] through clustering or re-weighting suspicious samples [10] based on additional *clean* data. To our best knowledge, Eigen-Reptile [4] is the only study that addresses noisy *training data* by updating only along the highest variance direction. Such an approach lacks generalization to other meta-learners. Alternatively, UMTRA [9] and CACTUS [7] assume labels are unavailable during meta-training and propose to syntheticly generate support and query sets from $N \times K$ images from pre-generated clusters of training data. Although these methods show promising results, they have considerably larger compute and memory requirements for training on considerably larger batch sizes (256+) and are unable to exploit (noisy) label information during (meta-)training.

**The Impact of Label Noise.** We motivate the need for noise resilience in FSL via an empirical study on three representative datasets, CifarFS [2], Omniglot [11], and MiniImageNet [24], in a (5, 5)-FSL setting with a query set of 15 samples per class. We consider symmetric label noise and train four gradient-based meta-learners, i.e., Reptile (Rp) [19], Eigen-Reptile (ER) [4], foMAML+ZO (fM) [8], and iMAML (iM) [20], using hyperparameters comparable to the ones in the corresponding paper (details in Sect. 4). We remark that we assume that meta-learners have no access to clean data—including validation data, while original works report accuracies of meta-validated models, which are expected to score higher. Table 1 shows the meta-test accuracy across 2048 (5, 5)-FSL tasks of 15 samples obtained by each meta-learner under 0% (no), 30%, and 60% corrupted training labels. Across datasets, meta-learners show significant performance degradation as the noise ratio increases. With CifarFS, accuracy drops across all meta-learners on average by 10.1% and 27.4% under 30% and 60% corrupted labels, respectively. Omniglot shows similar trends but more limited in amplitude, with 8.1% and 17.0% average degradation. This is due to the fact that the Omniglot dataset is easier to learn (without noise all meta-learners achieve above 90% accuracy). Lastly, MiniImageNet shows a lower initial accuracy without label noise due to its more challenging nature, with a mean deterioration of 15.6% at 30% noise, and close to random guessing (20%) at 60% noise. Although ER is the sole meta-learner that explicitly aims to counter noise, it is not always the most robust one. Under moderate noise, i.e., 30%, foMAML+ZO is the least affected. Only on CifarFS and 60% noise, ER is the least affected with only a 0.9% margin. More in general, Reptile, ER and iMAML show a higher but almost linear impact of noise, while foMAML+ZO degrades less with 30% noise but gets much worse under 60% noise. Overall, the results underline the need for better noise resilience across all considered meta-learners.

## 3 Proposed Method

The core challenge of dealing with noise is that labels lose meaning and misguide meta-learners. This challenge is amplified in the FSL setting as the limited number of samples (shots) in each class (way) makes it harder to isolate noise from the signal in each class. In other words, the few clean samples— those corresponding to the original uncorrupted class—may not be enough to appropriately guide the gradient descent algorithm. Thus, our approach aims to build clean ways and shots—so that each way is more likely to have samples with valid ground truths for FSL. Specifically, the core of the proposed Man sampling is to use data augmentation to create replacement shots for each way rather than leveraging *other* shots of the same way. This guarantees that the underlying ground truth label for the shots of way is effectively the same. BatMan sampling further introduces batches to increase the likelihood of observing all $N$ classes in a single inner-loop

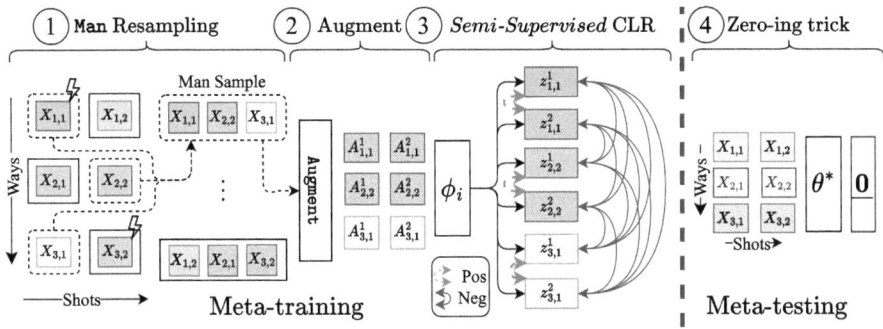

**Fig. 1.** Illustration of meta-learning with BatMan on a noisy 3-way 2-shot few-shot learning task, i.e., a (3, 2)-FSL. The task is provided to the learner as containing three classes (ways): red, purple, and yellow, with two supporting samples (shots) each. Colors indicate the *true* underlying class (ground-truth), while lightning bolts indicate shots provided with a mismatched label (i.e., noisy) (way 1 shot 1, and way 3 shot 2). Steps: ① Man sampling (Algorithm 2) creates a batch of (3, 1)-FSL manifold samples; ② Augment creates semi-supervised (3, 2)-FSL sub-tasks via independent random augmentations; ③ a contrastive loss jointly optimizes all sub-tasks via (Pos)itive and (Neg)ative pairs; ④ trained meta-model $\theta^*$ is meta-tested in a supervised way by appending a zero-ed out linear layer. (Color figure online)

step. Figure 1 shows the four main steps of our proposed method: ① resampling, either with Man or BatMan, ② shot augmentation with random independent transformations, ③ 'semi'-supervised meta-training with a contrastive loss, and ④ classification of new tasks (meta-testing) leveraging a zeroing trick. One major benefit of our approach is that these steps can be incorporated into *existing meta-learning algorithms* to achieve label noise robustness.

***Step ①–②: (Batched) Manifold sampling and data augmentation.*** We start with an $(N, K)$-FSL problem with noisy labels and observe that we can frame it as a set of $(N, 2)$-FSL problems. For each $(N, K)$-FSL, we methodically select and augment one shot from each $N$ ways, constructing a new $N$-way 2-shot problem. More formally, each adapted FSL sample is created by independently augmenting sub-sampled shots,

$$M_i = \bigcup_{j=1}^{N} \left\{ (\texttt{Augment}(X_j^y), \texttt{Augment}(X_j^y)) \mid X_j^y \sim D_{(\cdot)}^{\mathcal{T}}, y = j \right\},$$

where $X_j^y$ represents a random shot the $j^{\text{th}}$ way of a task's set $\mathcal{D}_{(\cdot)}^{\mathcal{T}}$, and Aug a random augmentation function. As a result, we end up with two samples with the same label for each way in each constructed Manifold FSL problem—i.e., the augmentation for each sampled way's shot. Since we sample $N$ observations from all $N \times K$ samples in $\mathcal{D}_{\text{query}}$, we end up with *up to $N$ actual classes*, as selected shots from different ways may share their underlying ground-truth class due to label noise. We coin this sampling approach Manifold (Man) sampling.

---

**Algorithm 1.** BatMan-CLR inner-loop style for gradient-based meta-learners.

**Require:** Inner-learner parameters $\phi$, support set $\mathcal{D}_{\text{support}}$, query set $\mathcal{D}_{\text{query}}$, inner-learning rate $\alpha$, BatMan sample hyper-parameter $N$, inner-loop steps $u$.

1: **function** BATMAN-CLR
2:    **for** $B_i \in [\text{BatMan}(\mathcal{D}_{sup}, N)]_{i=1}^{u}$ **do**
     ▷ ③ *Joint **inner-loop** Manifold optimization.*
3:      $\phi \leftarrow \phi - \frac{\alpha}{|B_i|} \nabla_\phi \sum_{i=1}^{|B_i|} \mathcal{L}_{con}(\phi, M_i)$
4:    $B_{\text{query}} \leftarrow \text{BatMan}(\mathcal{D}_{\text{query}}, N)$
     ▷ ③ *Joint **outer-loop** Manifold optimization.*
5:    **return** $\phi, \sum_{M_j \in B_{\text{query}}} \mathcal{L}_{con}(\phi, M_j)$

---

**Algorithm 2.** Pseudocode for BatMan Sampling.

**Require:** Augment input augmentation function, meta train/test set $\mathcal{D}$, number of manifold batches $B$.

1: **function** BATMAN
2:    $M = \{\}$
3:    **for** $j \in [1, \ldots, B]$ **do**
     ▷ ① *Sample single shot each way.*
4:      $X \leftarrow rand\,((X,y) \in \mathcal{D} \mid y = j)$
     ▷ ② *Augment selected samples.*
5:      $M \leftarrow M \cup \{(\text{Augment}(X), j)\}_1^2$
6:    **return** $M$

---

We propose a Batched Manifold, as shown in Algorithm 2, sampling as an extension of Man sampling, where multiple Man samples are grouped to employ more samples in a single step. Multiple 'sub-problems' can be jointly optimized by leveraging a batch of individually created Man samples. More formally, this allows for the joint optimization of,

$$\frac{1}{N} \sum_{M_j \in \text{BatMan}(\mathcal{D}_*, B)} \mathcal{L}_{con}(\phi_i, M_j),$$

for both the support and query samples, using a BatMan batch size of $B$, as label information is only leveraged to construct the manifold samples. Herein, $\mathcal{L}_{con}$ is the contrastive loss used to optimize a learner $\phi$. on the sampled manifold samples $M_j$ jointly, and BatMan is a function that returns a batched manifold sample for a given support/query set and batch size, as seen in Algorithm 2. Additionally, this increases the likelihood of considering *all* the provided queries' shots together while calculating meta-gradients.

We illustrate this process in Fig. 1 on a 3-way 2-shot FSL task with label noise. The samples $X_{q,r}$ are ordered such that each row index $q$ represents a 'way' and a column index $r$ a corresponding shot. The underlying classes—i.e., ground-truth labels—in the few-shot task are illustrated using different colors. The corrupted two shots are highlighted with lightning bolts: a red one $X_{1,1}$ is provided as green, and a purple $X_{3,2}$ one appears yellow. The (3, 2)-FSL task in this example is thus provided to the learner to discern between 'green', 'purple', and 'yellow' samples. A Man sample is generated by sampling 1 shot from each of the 3 ways and augmenting it twice. To speed up the process, the Man sampler can sample augmentations from a set of pre-fetched augmentations. For BatMan, these steps are repeated to create a batch of such manifold sub-tasks.

In the presence of noise, class clean-up is necessary as shots from two separate ways may share the same ground-truth class. Suppose in the simplest case with 2 classes and a probability $p = 1-\epsilon$ that a sample has a ground truth label, the classes resulting from the Man sampling process belong to different classes with probability $p^2 + (1-p)^2$, as either both lack noise or both are noisy. On the contrary, the 2 samples belong to the same class with probability $2p(1-p)$. In general, with $N$ classes, there are $N!$ combinations in which the Man samples actually correspond to the $N$ *different* classes while there are $N^N$ combinations to select the $N$ samples, with replacement. Let us consider the case of symmetric noise, where a sample is mislabeled with probability $(1-p)/(N-1)$. The probability of obtaining a clean selection of classes can then be posed as the probability of obtaining one of the $N!$ combinations in which this occurs. To represent each possible selection we employ permutation matrices. Let $P_N^i$ be the $N \times N$ $i$th permutation matrix out of the $N!$ such matrices. For instance, in the $N = 3$ case, we have 6 different permutation matrices, i.e.,

$$\begin{bmatrix} 1 & 0 & 0 \\ 0 & 1 & 0 \\ 0 & 0 & 1 \end{bmatrix}, \begin{bmatrix} 1 & 0 & 0 \\ 0 & 0 & 1 \\ 0 & 1 & 0 \end{bmatrix}, \begin{bmatrix} 0 & 1 & 0 \\ 1 & 0 & 0 \\ 0 & 0 & 1 \end{bmatrix}, \ldots, \begin{bmatrix} 0 & 0 & 1 \\ 0 & 1 & 0 \\ 1 & 0 & 0 \end{bmatrix}.$$

Let us also define the $N \times N$ matrix $Q$ with entries $q_{ij}$ such that $q_{ii} = p$ and $q_{ij} = (1-p)/(N-1)$ for $i \neq j$. The probability of obtaining one of these valid permutations under Man sampling can thus be obtained as the trace of the matrix $P_N^i Q$. As a result, the probability of obtaining a clean selection of ways is given by: $\sum_{i=1}^{N!} \text{trace}(P_N^i Q)$, considering all possible valid sample selections that lead to a set with $N$ different classes. As this probability becomes smaller with increasing label noise, BatMan sampling helps by introducing additional samples that increase the likelihood of observing all $N$ classes in a single meta-epoch.

***Step ③: Semi-supervised meta-training with contrastive loss.*** Although re-sampling allows for *likely valid* (N, 2)-FSL sub-problems, *which exact classes* they contain remains unknown. These sub-tasks can be considered as *semi-supervised*, as there are now *at most* $N$ classes in each manifold. To allow for (meta-)learning with the semi-supervised sub-problems, we incorporate a contrastive loss to allow for joint optimization of potentially semantically misaligned sub-tasks. Note that we artificially build positive and negative pairs from the sampled augmentations obtained via steps ①–②. These positive and negative pairs can be optimized under a contrastive learning strategy. We use the Decoupled Contrastive Loss (DCL) [27] as contrastive loss function, an adaptation of the infoNCE loss [5],

$$\mathcal{L}_{\text{DCL}} = -\frac{1}{N}\sum_{i=1}^{N}\log\left(\exp(\langle z_i^{(1)}|z_i^{(2)}\rangle)\right)$$
$$-\log\left(\sum_{j=1}^{2N}\mathbb{1}\left[z_j \notin \{z_i^{(1)}, z_i^{(2)}\}\right]\exp(\langle z_i^{(1)}|z_j\rangle)\right), \quad (1)$$

where $\langle z|z'\rangle$ is the (normalized) cosine-similarity between embedding vectors $z, z'$, and $\mathbb{1}[\cdot]$ the indicator function returning 1 when its clause $[\cdot]$ holds else 0. By design, the decoupled contrastive loss is particularly well-suited for smaller batch sizes, although alternative contrastive losses can replace it. Once samples are augmented and BatMan sampling applied, the batches are used in the meta-training step where the embeddings $z$ are computed and contrasted using a contrastive loss.

**Step ④: Classification of new tasks.** The meta-model $\theta^*$ trained using the contrastive loss produces embeddings instead of class logits as output. To solve this, we append the meta-model with a fully connected layer $C_0 = (\boldsymbol{W}, \boldsymbol{b})$ with $\boldsymbol{W} = \boldsymbol{0}$ and $\boldsymbol{b} = \boldsymbol{0}$. This approach decouples the embedding learning from the classification task. Similar to [8], this allows us to treat the model as a semi-supervised meta-learned backbone. The resulting meta-model $\theta^{*\prime} = C_0 \circ \theta^*$ can then be treated as a supervised learner utilizing the cross-entropy (CE) classification loss. We found that applying the Zeroing Out trick on the *classification* layer significantly impacts the learner's performance because it allows leveraging the optimized embedding from the pre-trained meta-model $\theta^*$. This is because the stochastic gradient descent will directly use the embeddings as activations without noise introduced by randomly initialized weights.

For conceptual clarity, the algorithm above differs slightly in two points from our implementation of BatMan-CLR, prioritizing efficiency during dataloading while training. First, we change the order of operations from constructing manifolds and then augmenting them to creating augmentations and sampling (batches of) manifolds. This approach enables parallel pre-fetching of FSL tasks with $A$ augmentations for each way's shots. By creating a fixed set of augmentations, the BatMan sub-sampler can randomly sample $N \times K \frac{A(A-1)}{2}!$ Man-samples for each FSL problem. Second, all samples of a BatMan sample are forwarded as a single batch in our BatMan-CLR implementation for each inner-loop and meta-adaptation step—line 3–6 and line 7–8 in Algorithm 1, using masking and vectorization. Through these design considerations, the BatMan-CLR meta-learners can efficiently perform each (meta-)adaptation step.

## 4 Evaluation Results

We present the effectiveness of BatMan-CLR in enhancing the noise resilience for a total of four gradient-based meta-learners, Eigen-Retipe, Reptile, iMAML,

**Table 2.** Meta-test accuracy with 95th Confidence Interval ($\overline{acc} \pm CI95$) of Meta-Pretrained models (5, 5)-FSL with varying degrees of label noise $\epsilon \in \{0.0, 0.3, 0.6\}$ during training.

(a) Few-shot results with increasing noise on CifarFS [2], and Omniglot [12].

| Algorithm | Sampler | CifarFS $\epsilon$=0.0 | CifarFS $\epsilon$=0.3 | CifarFS $\epsilon$=0.6 | Omniglot $\epsilon$=0.0 | Omniglot $\epsilon$=0.3 | Omniglot $\epsilon$=0.6 |
|---|---|---|---|---|---|---|---|
| foMAML | BatMan | 66.6±0.167 | 65.2±0.17 | 64.8±0.16 | 98.2±0.07 | 98.2±0.06 | 98.0±0.07 |
| | Man | 66.2±0.16 | 64.8±0.17 | 64.0±0.17 | 98.1±0.06 | 98.1±0.06 | 98.1±0.06 |
| iMAML | BatMan | 64.2±0.185 | 62.7±0.25 | 62.9±0.20 | 97.5±0.08 | 98.1±0.07 | 98.3±0.06 |
| | Man | 62.8±0.17 | 62.6±0.17 | 61.7±0.17 | 97.8±0.08 | 98.2±0.07 | 98.2±0.06 |
| Reptile | BatMan | 66.5±0.17 | 65.0±0.17 | 64.1±0.17 | 97.9±0.07 | 97.3±0.08 | 96.2±0.10 |
| | Man | 61.8±0.18 | 62.0±0.18 | 61.4±0.17 | 97.8±0.07 | 97.8±0.07 | 97.7±0.07 |
| Eigen-Reptile | BatMan | 66.3±0.17 | 64.4±0.17 | 63.8±0.18 | 92.6±0.13 | 93.0±0.12 | 93.2±0.12 |
| | Man | 58.0±0.25 | 57.9±0.24 | 58.1±0.24 | 93.7±0.12 | 93.9±0.11 | 94.0±0.11 |

(b) Few-shot results under increasing noise on MiniImageNet [24].

| Algorithm | Sampler | MiniImageNet $\epsilon$=0.0 | MiniImageNet $\epsilon$=0.3 | MiniImageNet $\epsilon$=0.6 |
|---|---|---|---|---|
| foMAML | BatMan | 50.4±0.22 | 50.5±0.22 | 50.4±0.21 |
| | Man | 51.6±0.22 | 51.4±0.22 | 51.2±0.22 |
| iMAML | BatMan | 50.9±0.15 | 50.5±0.15 | 50.5±0.14 |
| | Man | 50.1±0.21 | 50.3±0.22 | 50.2±0.22 |
| Reptile | BatMan | 53.2±0.16 | 52.8±0.15 | 52.1±0.15 |
| | Man | 50.8±0.20 | 51.6±0.21 | 51.9±0.20 |
| Eigen-Reptile | BatMan | 51.5±0.22 | 51.2±0.22 | 51.5±0.22 |
| | Man | 48.5±0.20 | 48.7±0.20 | 49.2±0.20 |

and foMAML, under varying levels of label noise. We include Eigen-Reptile specifically as a noise-aware FSL [4].

**Setup.** We consider three data sets in a (5, 5)-FSL setting: Omniglot, CifarFS, and MiniImageNet. We emulate training label noise by adding symmetric uniform random noise to $\mathcal{D}_{\text{train}}$ with 30% and 60% corrupted labels on the underlying datasets, i.e., *prior* to the few-shot tasks are randomly sampled. For instance, for experiments with 60% noise, we randomly select 60% samples of each class in $\mathcal{D}_{\text{train}}$ and assign them to a different class *within the same split* with equal probability. Reported meta-test results are on *clean* data, to evaluate the learners under a base-case scenario. The support set size is 5 (15), and query set size is 15 (Reptile learners), following [6,19]. All experiments ran on machines with 128 GB RAM, dual 16-Core AMD CPUs, and an Nvidia A4000 16 GB GPU. We used cross-entropy loss for supervised meta-training and meta-testing. Each learner uses a ConvNet-4 architecture with 64 filters and a linear layer with output dimension $\mathbb{R}^{128}$. On Omniglot, the number of filters was increased to 128. iMAML uses weight decay centered around $\theta_t$ [20] and foMAML+ZO resets its final layer to zero at the beginning of each inner-loop. Learners were trained with the original papers' hyper-parameters, except for the following changes. Eigen-Reptile and Reptile run with 7 inner-loop steps, iMAML with 12 (16 for Omniglot), and foMAML with 5. iMAML's proximal decay was set to 0.5 (2.0 for Omniglot). Each learner was meta-tested after 5K, 15K (10K), 15K (10K), training outer-loop steps (iMAML), respectively, for Omniglot, CifarFS, and MiniImageNet. To augment the samples before Manifold sampling, we use a set of independently random augmentations to each image. On CifarFS and MiniImageNet, we use the augmentations proposed in [1], consisting of: cropping, random horizontal flip, random color jitter, random grayscale, random blurring, and normalization. For Omniglot, we follow the augmentation scheme in [3], applying one of: random crop, affine transform, or perspective transform to the source image. During meta-testing, the task-specific model is fine-tuned for 10 steps (Omniglot and CifarFS) and 20 steps (MiniImageNet). When applying Man-CLR or BatMan-CLR, we keep the same model sizes with the addition of a larger output dimension: $\mathbb{R}^{128}$ rather than $\mathbb{R}^N$. The batch size of BatMan is 5 for all inner-loop adaptations, resulting in mini-batching [19] for (Eigen) Reptile, and 15 for the meta-gradient calculation of iMAML and foMAML. For each task's support set, we create five random augmentations for each shot. Each query sample is augmented twice, allowing the inner loop to sample more varied tasks. Results are averaged over 3 runs, using 2048 tasks sampled from $\mathcal{D}_{\text{test}}$.

**Meta-test Accuracy.** Table 2 summarizes the BatMan-CLR results on noisy CifarFS, Omniglot, and MiniImageNet with both Man and BatMan under 0% (no), 30% and 60% noisy training labels. One can easily observe that BatMan-CLR clearly strengthens the resilience of all learners to noise across all three datasets. Only marginal decreases in testing accuracy occur under increasing label noise. On Omniglot when encountering the label noise in meta-training, all learners can still learn effective initial models for task adaptation, which for most is around 97% and slightly worse for Eigen-Reptile. All learners display an accuracy under label noise similar to that without label noise. On CifarFS, we observe similar results, where most learners reach a test accuracy between 62–64%, which remains almost constant under increasing noise levels. Finally, even on MiniImageNet, the most difficult dataset of the three, consisting of more diverse classes and larger inputs, the testing accuracy of all meta-learners is limited to drops in the range between 0.5–1% points under BatMan-CLR. These results strongly validate the effectiveness of BatMan, which self-cleanses the shots by creating contrastive pairs and ways in batched Man samples. The only exception is Man sampling on Eigen-Reptile on Omniglot and MiniImageNet, where we observe a minor increase of 0.3–0.7% points under 60% noise. We speculate that this is because Eigen-Reptile's meta-gradient approximation is performed by selecting the optimization direction with the highest variance. However, a high noise level introduces a high variance in the optimization di-

**Table 3.** Meta-test accuracy with 95th confidence intervals ($\overline{acc} \pm CI_{95}$), meta-trained on (5, 5)-FSL tasks with label noise $\epsilon \in \{0.0, 0.3, 0.6\}$ on Omniglot and CifarFS, and different Inner/Outer-loop samplers: Random Manifold (R), and BatMan (B). SSL represents a self-supervised meta-trained model trained without information. Results from Table 2 are highlighted.

(a) Omniglot MAML-like.

| Alg. | $\epsilon$ | B/B | B/R | R/B | R/R |
|---|---|---|---|---|---|
| foMAML | SSL | | 94.7±0.11 | | |
| | 0.0 | 98.2±0.07 | 94.1±0.12 | 98.3±0.05 | 94.5±0.12 |
| | 0.3 | 98.2±0.06 | 96.9±0.09 | 98.4±0.05 | 96.7±0.09 |
| | 0.6 | 98.0±0.07 | 97.9±0.07 | 98.4±0.05 | 98.0±0.07 |
| iMAML | SSL | | 97.0±0.09 | | |
| | 0.0 | 97.5±0.08 | 94.9±0.11 | 98.1±0.07 | 94.5±0.12 |
| | 0.3 | 98.1±0.07 | 96.5±0.10 | 98.3±0.07 | 96.7±0.09 |
| | 0.6 | 98.3±0.06 | 97.8±0.08 | 98.2±0.07 | 97.9±0.07 |

(b) Omniglot Reptile-like.

| Alg. | $\epsilon$ | B/- | R/- |
|---|---|---|---|
| Reptile | SSL | | 96.0±0.10 |
| | 0.0 | 97.9±0.07 | 65.3±0.29 |
| | 0.3 | 97.3±0.08 | 69.5±0.27 |
| | 0.6 | 96.2±0.10 | 73.1±0.27 |
| Eigen-Reptile | SSL | | 95.1±0.13 |
| | 0.0 | 92.6±0.13 | 82.5±0.21 |
| | 0.3 | 93.0±0.12 | 71.9±0.27 |
| | 0.6 | 93.2±0.12 | 73.5±0.26 |

(c) CifarFS MAML-like.

| Alg. | $\epsilon$ | B/B | B/R | R/B | R/R |
|---|---|---|---|---|---|
| foMAML | SSL | | 52.8±0.16 | | |
| | 0.0 | 66.6±0.17 | 58.4±0.24 | 62.0±0.23 | 58.0±0.24 |
| | 0.3 | 65.2±0.17 | 59.7±0.23 | 61.8±0.24 | 59.7±0.23 |
| | 0.6 | 64.8±0.16 | 60.5±0.24 | 61.1±0.24 | 60.5±0.24 |
| iMAML | SSL | | 54.5±0.24 | | |
| | 0.0 | 64.2±0.19 | 58.0±0.24 | 60.9±0.30 | 56.9±0.29 |
| | 0.3 | 62.7±0.25 | 59.2±0.24 | 60.3±0.23 | 58.3±0.29 |
| | 0.6 | 62.9±0.20 | 59.7±0.24 | 60.3±0.29 | 60.0±0.29 |

(d) CifarFS Reptile-like.

| Alg. | $\epsilon$ | B/- | R/- |
|---|---|---|---|
| Reptile | SSL | | 55.0±0.17 |
| | 0.0 | 66.5±0.17 | 53.9±0.22 |
| | 0.3 | 65.0±0.17 | 55.3±0.22 |
| | 0.6 | 64.1±0.17 | 56.4±0.22 |
| Eigen-Reptile | SSL | | 54.5±0.16 |
| | 0.0 | 66.3±0.17 | 57.2±0.27 |
| | 0.3 | 64.4±0.17 | 57.8±0.23 |
| | 0.6 | 63.8±0.18 | 58.8±0.23 |

rections, making it harder to select an appropriate direction even with the use of Man. By employing the less noisy BatMan sampling strategy, the learner has higher chances to see more diverse shots and can better select an optimization direction, achieving performance closer to Reptile with Man sampling.

In terms of comparison between BatMan and Man, there is a visible advantage in using BatMan, especially on the more challenging MiniImageNet and CifarFS. This suggests that taking steps with more information, as in BatMan, provides greater benefits than taking a larger number of simpler steps, as in Man. Zooming into the performance of different learners on CifarFS and MiniImageNet, the difference in testing accuracy between Man and BatMan is smaller with foMAML and iMAML, compared to Reptile and Eigen-Reptile. This can be explained by the fact that in our experiments, the MAML style learners use BatMan to calculate the meta-gradient, resulting in more informative meta-updates.

Reptile-style learners do not calculate their meta-gradients using query data but directly using the inner-optimization *direction*.

**Ablations.** We consider three types of ablation studies using the Omniglot and CifarFS (and MiniImageNet) datasets. First, we consider the impact of supervised task generation by training meta-learners in a self-supervised learning (SSL) setting. Similar to UMTRA [9] and CACTUS [7], we construct $(5,5/15)$-FSL tasks (MAML/Reptile) by drawing 5 random images from $\mathcal{D}_{\text{train}}$. To construct the required shots, $K + Q$ augmentations are created and divided into support and query sets, with $|\mathcal{D}_{\text{support}}| = K$ and $|\mathcal{D}_{\text{query}}| = Q$. Table 3 provides the results in the rows indicated with SSL. We use the same hyper-parameters and loss function as for BatMan-CLR, with the meta-batch size increased to 25 (from 5), so that all learners see a comparable number of expected unique ways per meta-update. Although this approach shows similar performance to BatMan-CLR on Omniglot (see Table 3a and b), on CifarFS (see Table 3c and d) there is a considerable gap of 11–13.8% points compared to BatMan-CLR (gray columns). Indicating that BatMan-CLR benefits from performing a joint optimization of more ways and shots in the inner-loop.

Second, we replace BatMan with a random manifold batch sampler (Rand) to investigate the impact of the BatMan sampling strategy. This Rand-sampler differs from BatMan by *uniformly sampling from* the FSL task, i.e., allowing multiple instances from the same way to be selected in a single random manifold. We pair Rand (R) with BatMan (B) sampling in different configurations for the inner and outer-loop, marked as (inner)/(outer) in the column names in Table 3a and c. Reptile and Eigen-Reptile only use a support set during meta-training, so we only replace their inner-sampling strategy (see Table 3b and d). We keep the same hyper-parameters as used in the corresponding BatMan-CLR setting. In general, the learners trained with random sampling in the outer-loop show an increased accuracy as the noise level increases. Learners show an increase in accuracy of around 2–8% and 2–3% on Omniglot and CifarFS, respectively, comparing the $\epsilon = 0$ (no) and $\epsilon = 0.6$ noise levels, whereas BatMan sees a slight drop. Even so, it stays ahead of Rand across the board. This shows that BatMan has the capability to self-clean. An interesting exception is Omniglot combined with Eigen-Reptile when increasing the noise level from 0 to 0.3 (Table 3b). This is expected as higher noise levels increase the *expected* number of unique ground-truth classes in a task, yielding fewer false negatives in each Rand manifold during contrastive learning. Replacing only the inner or outer-loop sampler for iMAML and foMAML with Rand, we see that the contribution of the inner-loop is less significant than the outer-loop. This shows that BatMan-CLR is also an effective strategy when replacing only the outer-loop (R/B).

Lastly, we consider the impact of the meta-testing label noise on meta-learned supervised and BatMan-CLR models. While meta-train label noise exists at the dataset level, meta-testing lies at the task level. Task-level noise is added by corrupting an original $(5,5)$-FSL problem, where a fraction ($\epsilon_{test}$) of shots from each way within the FSL problem is remapped to a different class. As such, the meta-test error models class confusion—e.g., for an $(3,*)$-FSL problem a

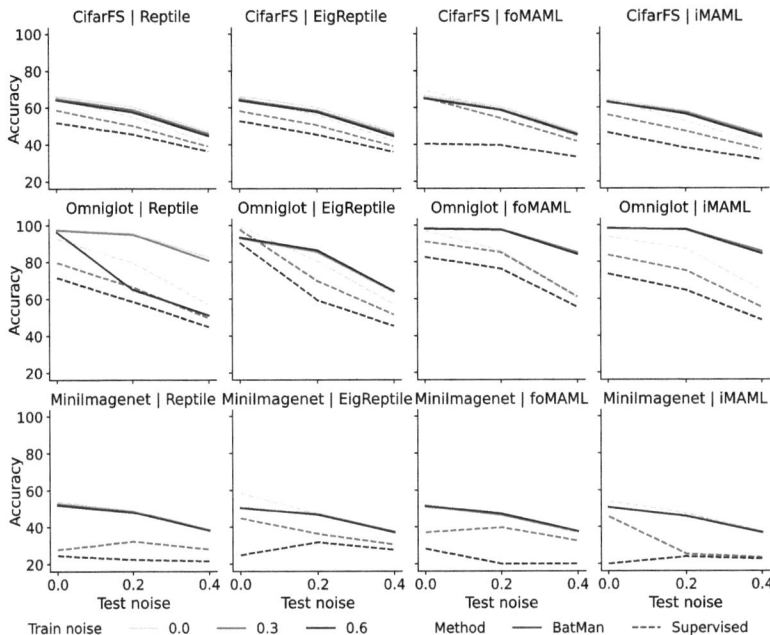

**Fig. 2.** Meta-test accuracy of supervised and BatMan-CLR meta-trained models with different meta-learners, training, and testing noise levels. Results shown meta-trained with dataset-level label noise ($\epsilon \in \{0.0, 0.3, 0.6\}$) and meta-testing label noise ($\epsilon \in \{0.0, 0.2, 0.4\}$) at task-level.

fraction ($\epsilon_{test}$) of class 'car' gets re-labeled as 'truck', 'truck' to 'plane', and 'plane' to 'car'. We consider different noise levels during both meta-training ($\epsilon_{train} \in \{0.0, 0.3, 0.6\}$), and meta-testing ($\epsilon_{test} \in \{0.0, 0.2, 0.4\}$). Here, we evaluate the impact of meta test-noise under supervised and BatMan-CLR. In Fig. 2, we show the accuracy curves of the learners under varying noise configurations.

Generally, in Fig. 2, we observe a negative trend across all configurations as both meta-train and meta-test noise increase. Additionally, the impact of meta-training noise is more pronounced in the baseline learners, compared against the BatMan-CLR learned results—consistent with the results from Table 1 and Table 2. Moreover, this performance difference remains stable as testing noise increases, resulting in a larger vertical spread for the baseline results than for the BatMan-CLR results, corresponding with improved robustness against training label noise. An exception to this is the performance of Reptile paired with BatMan-CLR with an $\epsilon_{train} = 0.6$, where the learner's meta-testing accuracy degrades around the level of its baseline counterpart with training noise of $\epsilon = 0.3$.

On the CifarFS and (Omniglot) datasets—top and (middle) row in Fig. 2— the BatMan-CLR meta-learned models showcase a reduced sensitivity to testing noise compared to their supervised counterparts. We see that the BatMan-CLR meta-learned models at $\epsilon_{test} = 0.2$ have an accuracy loss reduction of 2.1–5.7% (4.5–16.0%) and at $\epsilon_{test}$ of 4.6–5.5% (6.1–25.6%) compared to the supervised learned models. Nonetheless, the BatMan-CLR learners see a degradation as the meta-testing noise increases, of 5.5–6.6% (0.5–31.1%) at $\epsilon = 0.2$ and 18.6–19.7% (12.6–45.0%) with $\epsilon = 0.4$. MiniImagenet results (bottom row in Fig. 2) show that the BatMan-CLR meta-learned models under test noise perform similarly to the cleanly pre-trained meta-learner. Whereas the supervised baseline models with $\epsilon_{train} > 0$ on MiniImagenet show a drastic deterioration in performance, the BatMan-CLR trained models perform on-par with the baseline trained without meta-training noise.

## 5 Conclusion

Motivated by the ubiquitous presence of label noise, we empirically unveil the impact of label noise on existing few-shot meta-learners, with a particular focus on noise in meta-training. As the number of shots per way is low, the label noise can be exceedingly detrimental to meta-learners and highly challenging to address. To enhance the resilience against label noise for few-shot learners, we propose BatMan—a generic approach that turns supervised few-shot tasks into semi-supervised ones. BatMan is capable of self-cleansing noisy $N$-way $K$-shots instances by (i) batch manifold sampling that re-constructs $N$-way 2-contrastive-shots via augmentation and (ii) introducing the DCL [27] contrastive loss. Our results on three datasets, Omniglot, CifarFS, and MiniImageNet, show that Bat-Man can maintain the effectiveness of few-shot learners independent of noise levels, i.e., recouping up to 30% accuracy degradation (20% on average under 60% noise).

As future work, we aim to explore further (label noisy) meta-testing paired with BatMan-CLR and adding class awareness [9,22]. Herein, the impact of alternative augmentation strategies can also be explored. Further exploring the utility of BatMan-CLR under the meta-testing setting would be valuable, as well as considering the incorporation of other loss functions, such as ProtoCLR [17]. Lastly, we leave the consideration of other types of noise for future work, such as out-of-domain noise, asymmetric noise, or task-level corruption [26].

**Acknowledgments.** This research is part of the Priv-GSyn project, 200021E_229204 of Swiss National Science Foundation and the DEPMAT project, P20-22/N21022, of the research programme Perspectief, which is partly financed by the Dutch Research Council (NWO). This research was partly funded by the Spoke "FutureHPC & BigData" of the ICSC-Centro Nazionale di Ricerca in "High Performance Computing, Big Data and Quantum Computing", funded by the European Union - NextGenerationEU, and by the DYMAN project funded by the European Union - European Innovation Council under G.A. n. 101161930.

# References

1. Bachman, P., Hjelm, R.D., Buchwalter, W.: Learning representations by maximizing mutual information across views. In: Wallach, H.M., Larochelle, H., Beygelzimer, A., D'Alché-Buc, F., Fox, E.B., Garnett, R. (eds.) Advances in Neural Information Processing Systems 32: Annual Conference on Neural Information Processing Systems 2019, NeurIPS 2019, 8–14 December 2019, Vancouver, BC, Canada, pp. 15509–15519 (2019)
2. Bertinetto, L., Torr, P.H., Henriques, J., Vedaldi, A.: Meta-learning with differentiable closed-form solvers. In: 7th International Conference on Learning Representations, ICLR 2019 (2019)
3. Boutin, V., Singhal, L., Thomas, X., Serre, T.: Diversity vs. recognizability : human-like generalization in one-shot generative models. ArXiv (2022)
4. Chen, D., Wu, L., Tang, S., Yun, X., Long, B., Zhuang, Y.: Robust meta-learning with sampling noise and label noise via eigen-reptile. In: Chaudhuri, K., Jegelka, S., Song, L., Szepesvari, C., Niu, G., Sabato, S. (eds.) Proceedings of the 39th International Conference on Machine Learning. Proceedings of Machine Learning Research, vol. 162, pp. 3662–3678. PMLR (2022)
5. Chen, T., Kornblith, S., Norouzi, M., Hinton, G.: A simple framework for contrastive learning of visual representations. In: 37th International Conference on Machine Learning, ICML 2020, vol. PartF16814, pp. 1575–1585 (2020)
6. Finn, C., Abbeel, P., Levine, S.: Model-agnostic meta-learning for fast adaptation of deep networks. 34th International Conference on Machine Learning, ICML 2017, vol. 3, pp. 1856–1868 (2017)
7. Hsu, K., Levine, S., Finn, C.: Unsupervised Learning via Meta-Learning. In: 7th International Conference on Learning Representations, ICLR 2019, New Orleans, LA, USA, 6–9 May 2019. OpenReview.net (2019)
8. Kao, C.H., Chiu, W.C., Chen, P.Y.: MAML is a noisy contrastive learner in classification. In: The Tenth International Conference on Learning Representations, ICLR 2022, 25–29 April 2022, Virtual Event (2021)
9. Khodadadeh, S., Bölöni, L., Shah, M.: Unsupervised meta-learning for few-shot image classification. In: Wallach, H.M., Larochelle, H., Beygelzimer, A., D'Alché-Buc, F., Fox, E.B., Garnett, R. (eds.) Advances in Neural Information Processing Systems 32: Annual Conference on Neural Information Processing Systems 2019, NeurIPS 2019, 8–14 December 2019, Vancouver, BC, Canada, vol. 32, pp. 10132–10142 (2019)
10. Killamsetty, K., Li, C., Zhao, C., Chen, F., Iyer, R.: A nested bi-level optimization framework for robust few shot learning. In: Proceedings of the AAAI Conference on Artificial Intelligence, no. 7, pp. 7176–7184. OpenReview.net (2022)
11. Lake, B.M., Salakhutdinov, R., Gross, J., Tenenbaum, J.B.: One shot learning of simple visual concepts. In: Proceedings of the Annual Meeting of the Cognitive Science Society, vol. 33, no. 33 (2011)
12. Lake, B.M., Salakhutdinov, R., Tenenbaum, J.B.: Human-level concept learning through probabilistic program induction. Science **350**(6266), 1332–1338 (2015)
13. Li, M., Soltanolkotabi, M., Oymak, S.: Gradient descent with early stopping is provably robust to label noise for overparameterized neural networks. In: Chiappa, S., Calandra, R. (eds.) The 23rd International Conference on Artificial Intelligence and Statistics, AISTATS 2020, 26–28 August 2020, Online, Palermo, Sicily, Italy. Proceedings of Machine Learning Research, vol. 108, pp. 4313–4324. PMLR (2020)

14. Liang, K.J., Rangrej, S.B., Petrovic, V., Hassner, T.: Few-shot learning with noisy labels. In: CVPR (2022)
15. Lu, J., Jin, S., Liang, J., Zhang, C.: Robust few-shot learning for user-provided data. IEEE Trans. Neural Netw. Learn. Syst. **32**(4), 1433–1447 (2021)
16. Mazumder, P., Singh, P., Namboodiri, V.P.: RNNP: a robust few-shot learning approach. In: IEEE Winter Conference on Applications of Computer Vision, WACV 2021, Waikoloa, HI, USA, 3–8 January 2021, pp. 2663–2672. IEEE (2021)
17. Medina, C., Devos, A., Grossglauser, M.: Self-supervised prototypical transfer learning for few-shot classification. CoRR (2020)
18. Muhammad Abdullah Jamal, Wang, L., Gong, B.: A lazy approach to long-horizon gradient-based meta-learning. In: International Conference on Computer Vision, pp. 6577–6586 (2021)
19. Nichol, A., Achiam, J., Schulman, J.: On first-order meta-learning algorithms. CoRR, pp. 1–15 (2018)
20. Rajeswaran, A., Finn, C., Kakade, S.M., Levine, S.: Meta-learning with implicit gradients. In: Wallach, H.M., Larochelle, H., Beygelzimer, A., D'Alché-Buc, F., Fox, E.B., Garnett, R. (eds.) Advances in Neural Information Processing Systems 32: Annual Conference on Neural Information Processing Systems 2019, NeurIPS 2019, 8–14 December 2019, Vancouver, BC, Canada, pp. 113–124. NeurIPS (2019)
21. Schmidhuber, J.: Evolutionary principles in self-referential learning, or on learning how to learn: the meta-meta-... hook. Diploma thesis, Institute of Informatics at the Technical University of Munich (1987)
22. Shirekar, O.K., Singh, A., Rad, H.J.: Self-attention message passing for contrastive few-shot learning. In: IEEE/CVF Winter Conference on Applications of Computer Vision, WACV 2023, Waikoloa, HI, USA, 2–7 January 2023, pp. 5414–5425. IEEE (10 2023)
23. Song, H., Kim, M., Park, D., Shin, Y., Lee, J.G.: Learning from noisy labels with deep neural networks: a survey. IEEE Trans. Neural Netw. Learn. Syst. 1–19 (2022)
24. Vinyals, O., Blundell, C., Lillicrap, T., Kavukcuoglu, K., Wierstra, D.: Matching networks for one shot learning. In: Advances in Neural Information Processing Systems, vol. 29, pp. 3637–3645 (2016)
25. Wang, Z., Hu, G., Hu, Q.: Training noise-robust deep neural networks via meta-learning. In: 2020 IEEE/CVF Conference on Computer Vision and Pattern Recognition, CVPR 2020, Seattle, WA, USA, 13–19 June 2020, pp. 4523–4532. Computer Vision Foundation/IEEE (2020)
26. Yao, H., et al.: Meta-learning with an adaptive task scheduler. In: Advances in Neural Information Processing Systems, vol. 9, pp. 7497–7509 (2021)

27. Yeh, C.H., Hong, C.Y., Hsu, Y.C., Liu, T.L., Chen, Y., LeCun, Y.: Decoupled contrastive learning. In: Avidan, S., Brostow, G.J., Cissé, M., Farinella, G.M., Hassner, T. (eds.) ECCV 2022, Part XXVI. LNCS, vol. 13686, pp. 668–684. Springer, Cham (2022). https://doi.org/10.1007/978-3-031-19809-0_38
28. Yu, X., Liu, T., Gong, M., Zhang, K., Batmanghelich, K., Tao, D.: Label-noise robust domain adaptation. In: Proceedings of the 37th International Conference on Machine Learning, ICML 2020, 13–18 July 2020, Virtual Event. Proceedings of Machine Learning Research, vol. 119, pp. 10913–10924. PMLR (2020)

# Spectral Distribution Alignment for Enhanced Generalization in Regression

Kaiyu Guo, Zijian Wang, Brian C. Lovell, and Mahsa Baktashmotlagh[✉]

University of Queensland, Brisbane 4072, Australia
uqkguo1@uq.edu.au, zijian.wang@uq.edu.au, lovell@itee.uq.edu.au,
m.baktashmotlagh@uq.edu.au

**Abstract.** While several techniques have been proposed to enhance the generalization of deep learning models for classification problems, limited research has been conducted on improving generalization for regression tasks. This is primarily due to the continuous nature of regression labels, which makes it challenging to directly apply classification-based techniques to regression tasks. In this paper, we introduce a novel generalization method for regression tasks based on the metric learning assumption that the distance between features and labels should be proportional. Unlike previous approaches that solely consider the prediction of this proportion as constant and disregard its variation among samples, we argue that this proportion can be defined as a mapping function. Additionally, we propose minimizing the error of this function and stabilizing its fluctuating behavior by smoothing out its variations. To further enhance Out-of-Distribution (OOD) generalization, we leverage the characteristics of the spectral norm (*i.e.*, the sub-multiplicativity of the spectral norm of the feature matrix can be expressed as Frobenius norm of the output), and align the maximum singular value of the feature matrices across different domains. We conduct experiments on 5 datasets for OOD generalization in regression, and our method consistently outperforms state-of-the-art approaches in the majority of cases. Our code is released at https://github.com/workerbcd/SCR.

**Keywords:** Out-of-Distribution Generalization · Representation learning · Regression

## 1 Introduction

Continuous label prediction, known as regression, finds widespread application across various domains, including computer vision [8,49], medical testing [1,18], and financial analysis [22]. Unlike classification, which aims to determine optimal decision boundaries, regression involves fitting outputs to a continuous function [30]. On the other hand, out-of-distribution generalization has received considerable attention in classification [40]; however, the exploration of regression generalization remains relatively limited. Specifically, existing representation learning-based methods [2,4,14,16,17] are predominantly tailored for classification tasks. Although these methods can be adapted for regression generalization, their efficacy is constrained as they fail to fully account for the inherent proportional interdependence between features and labels.

In light of the above discussion, we argue that, when addressing challenges such as uncertainty estimation [25] and generalization [46] in regression, it is crucial to consider the relationships between the labels. To this end, we introduce a metric learning loss specifically designed for regression. Different from the previous method RankSim [20] to regularize the distribution with the order of label distance, our proposed loss not only takes the distance order into account but also constrains the feature distribution by discriminating the ratio between feature distance and label distance. This idea can efficiently solve the discontinuity of feature distribution caused by the discrete ranking order in RankSim. In addition, contrary to the assumption in Regression Metric Loss (RML) [7] that the ratio between feature distance and label distance is constant, we show that this ratio varies and only equals a constant under certain ideal conditions. We argue that RML, by overlooking the variability in this ratio, may obscure the pattern of feature distributions in certain cases. As demonstrated in Fig. 1, our metric loss can significantly discriminate the pattern, while maintaining the continuity of feature distribution.

To improve the OOD generalization, we design a method to align the discriminative feature pattern in different distributions. Motivated by augmentation-based techniques [39,44,48] for OOD generalization in classification, we further leverage the method mixing pairs of training data [46] to generate new distributions. For each distribution, we create a metric penalty to identify discriminative patterns within the feature distribution. The real and synthesized distributions are aligned by minimizing the difference between the spectral norms of their feature representations. According to the spectral norm property, the minimization process ensures that the Frobenius norm of outputs remains consistent, thereby reducing the upper bound of distribution discrepancy in regression tasks. The main contributions of this paper are three-folded:

- We introduce a tailored metric loss for regression, bringing features closer if their label distances are small and pushing them apart if distances are large. This facilitates pattern recognition in regression and improves generalization performance. We depart from previous approaches by modeling the feature-label distance proportion as a variable mapping function and mitigating instability caused by its fluctuations.
- According to the theory of domain adaptation in regression, we theoretically present the relation between the spectral norm of feature matrix and the upper bound of the distribution discrepancy in regression. Based on our theory, we expand the training distribution by generating samples with new distribution and then align the real and synthesized distributions by minimizing the difference between the spectral norm of their feature representations, to enhance OOD generalization in regression.

– We conduct experiments on five regression datasets and show that our method outperforms the state-of-the-art in most cases. The t-SNE visualization of the feature embedding illustrates the effectiveness and stability of our proposed metric loss.

## 2 Related Work

### 2.1 Metric Learning

Metric learning has been shown to be effective when related to methods that rely on distances and similarities [28]. Traditionally, methods like PCA and KNN are widely used in the area of machine learning. With the development of deep learning, networks [38] related to pair distances are designed to correlate among samples while using shared weights in deep learning [26]. Then, prototype-based metric losses [13,41] were proposed based on contrastive motivation. In regression tasks, the metric learning loss has not been well-defined because it is hard to build the connection between the metric distance and continuous labels. Recently, RML [7] has been proposed based on the assumption that there is a constant proportion between the feature distance and the label distance. However, the method based on this assumption only considers the scale of the feature matrix, ignoring fluctuations in the proportion map. To solve this issue, we assume that the proportion is a mapping function in the training process and propose a metric loss to smooth fluctuations.

### 2.2 Out-of-Distribution Generalization

Out-of-distribution (OOD) generalization aims at generalizing the model from the training distribution to an unseen distribution. Mostly, the methods can be divided into 3 parts [40]: data augmentation, representation learning, and training strategy. Data augmentation methods [48,50] utilize linear interpolation to fill the distribution gap, and some methods [39,44] also generate a new distribution to enrich the convex hull supported by the source distributions. Representation learning [3,4] aims at generating distribution-invariant feature representations from source distributions. Recently, methods like SWAD [6] proposed some novel training and model selection strategies, significantly improving performance in OOD generalization. However, most methods above are designed for classification. There are limited methods [4,46] designed for regression tasks.

### 2.3 Generalization in Regression

Recent research targeting generalization in regression tasks is based on data augmentation in which mixup pairs are selected based on the probability related to label distances [45,46]. Even though limited research has been proposed on this topic, some methods designed for regression tasks can be transferred to generalization purposes. For instance, due to the function of metric learning, the metric loss in regression [7,20,47] can be regarded as an in-distribution generalization method. Also, distribution alignment methods in regression [11, 34] can be updated as OOD generalization methods. However, these distribution alignment methods are not related to the proportion between features and labels, which are supposed to be very important in regression tasks.

## 3 Methodology

### 3.1 Problem Definition

Let $\{(x_i, y_i)\}_{i=1}^{N}$ be the dataset with $N$ samples, with $x_i \in \mathcal{X}$ being the input sample $i \in \mathbb{R}^+$ and $y_i \in \mathcal{Y}$ its corresponding label, and $\mathcal{X}$ and $\mathcal{Y}$ denoting the input space and the continuous label space, respectively. In the training phase, the network learns a projection function $g : \mathcal{X} \to \mathcal{F}$ and a regression function $\varphi : \mathcal{F} \to \mathcal{Y}$. The projection function $g$ transforms the input data into the feature space, and the regression function $\varphi$ maps the compact feature representation to the label space. The objective of the regressor is to bring the output prediction $\hat{y}_i$ close to the ground truth label $y_i$. Ideally, the optimal predictor $\varphi$ is a fully connected layer that satisfies $y_i = \hat{y}_i = W_\varphi^* f_i + b_\varphi^*$, where $f_i = g(x_i)$ is the extracted feature, $W_\varphi^*$ is the optimal weight, and $b_\varphi^*$ is the optimal bias.

**Distribution Discrepancy in Regression.** A theory of learning from different distributions in regression is defined in [12]. Given the hypothesis $h$ being a map from input space $\mathcal{X}$ to the label space $\mathcal{Y}$, the discrepancy distance $disc$ between two distributions $P$ and $Q$ is defined as:

$$disc(P, Q) = \max_{h, h' \in H} |\mathcal{L}_P(h', h) - \mathcal{L}_Q(h', h)|$$

Here, the hypothesis $H$ is a subspace of the reproducing kernel Hilbert space (RKHS) $\mathbb{H}$ and $\mathcal{L}_D(h', h) = E_{x \sim D}[L(h(x), h'(x))]$, with $L$ being a MSE loss. In this paper, we only consider the situation of finite dimension, thus, Euclidean space can be considered as a Hilbert space with a linear kernel.

### 3.2 Proportional Metric Loss

By leveraging the discrete labels to define sample pairs in classification models, metric learning aims to learn feature representations with low intra-class variance and high inter-class separation, which can improve the generalization ability of the learned model [9,28]. However, this motivation is based on the fact that the labels are discrete [34]. In regression tasks, given an input-label pair of $(x_i, y_i)$, $\forall \epsilon > 0$, with input $x_{i+\epsilon}$ and its continuous label $y_{i+\epsilon}$, it's proven that $\varphi$ should be a continuous bijection [7], with homeomorphic label and feature distributions. Intuitively, there is an optimal relationship between the distances of labels and distances of features - as the distance between two labels increases, the distance between their corresponding features should also increase, meaning that when two examples have labels that are farther apart, their representations in feature space should also be farther apart, and vice versa for labels that are closer together.

**Remark 1.** $d(y_i, y_j) < d(y_i, y_k) \iff d(f_i, f_j) < d(f_i, f_k), \forall i, j, k \in \mathbb{R}^+$

For any bounded open subset in $\mathcal{F}$, $\varphi$ should be convergent and bounded, which means $\varphi$ should be uniformly continuous on any bounded open subset [36]. Thus, we conclude Remark 2.

**Remark 2.** $d(y_i, y_j) < d(y_t, y_k) \iff d(f_i, f_j) < d(f_t, f_k), \forall i, j, k, t \in \mathbb{R}^+$

Building upon Remark 1, since $\mathcal{F}$ is a compact space and label $\mathcal{Y}$ is continuous, then for $\forall \epsilon > 0$, we can find labels $y', y''$ with $d(y', y'') = \epsilon$. Then, $\exists \delta = d(f', f'') > 0$, such that $\forall d(f_a, f_b) < \delta$, we have $d(y_a, y_b) < \epsilon$. So, Remark 2 keeps $\varphi$ uniformly continuous.

In light of the discussion above, we argue that the distance between labels can not be ignored in the regression tasks. In particular, we propose learning a feature-label proportional distance instead of the traditional distance, e.g., Euclidean distance between features:

$$d_r(f_i, f_j) = \frac{d(f_i, f_j)}{d(y_i, y_j)}, \tag{1}$$

Here, $d(\cdot, \cdot)$ represents Euclidean distance and $d_r(\cdot, \cdot)$ denotes the proportional distance induced from $d(\cdot, \cdot)$. In addition, $d_r(\cdot, \cdot)$ should be a bounded distance, which can be illustrated by the following Proposition.

**Proposition 1.** *Given any two data points $(x_i, y_i)$ and $(x_j, y_j)$, we have $\|f_i - f_j\|_p \leq \|W_\varphi^{*-1}\|_p |y_i - y_j|$. Here, $W_\varphi^*$ is the optimal weight of the fully connected layer. $f_i, f_j$ are the features extracted from $x_i, x_j$ through model $g$, and $\|\cdot\|_p$ is the norm under $L_p$ space.*

**Proof 1.** *Given the optimal weight $W_\varphi^*$, bias $b_\varphi^*$ and data $(x_i, y_i), (x_j, y_j)$, we have*

$$y_i = W_\varphi^* f_i + b_\varphi^*, y_j = W_\varphi^* f_j + b_\varphi^*$$

*where $f_i, f_j$ are extracted features from $x_i, x_j$, respectively. Then,*

$$\|f_i - f_j\|_p = \|W_\varphi^{*\dagger}(y_i - y_j)\|_p \leq \|W_\varphi^{*\dagger}\|_p |y_i - y_j|$$

*where $\dagger$ represents Moore–Penrose inverse*

Proposition 1 gives the upper bound of $d_r(\cdot, \cdot)$ which is $\|W_\varphi^{*\dagger}\|_2$. In addition, when the equal sign in Proposition 1 holds, it can explain the assumption of regression metric loss [7] that the distance between the features should be proportional to the distance between their corresponding labels. Specifically, [7] uses a learnable parameter to restrain the proportion between feature distance and label distance. However, according to Proposition 1, this proportion should be related to the optimal weight $W_\varphi^*$, and the equation may not hold when the labels are continuous. Moreover, representing this proportion with a constant ignores its fluctuations and variances among different samples. To alleviate this issue, we formulate this proportion as a mapping function and minimize its standard deviation to constrain the distance between the features to be uniform along the samples.

According to Proposition 1, the result of $d_r(\cdot,\cdot)$ should be a bounded proportion map and can be a constant function in some ideal situation. Hence, we minimize the standard deviation of $d_r(\cdot,\cdot)$ to acquire a flatter proportion map in a mini-batch. The proportional metric loss function should be:

$$L_{pml} = \sqrt{\frac{1}{N_b^2 - 1} \sum_i^{N_b} \sum_j^{N_b} (d_r(f_i, f_j) - \bar{d}_r)} \qquad (2)$$

Here, $\bar{d}_r$ is a constant function equal to the mean of the relative distances in the batch and $N_b$ is the batch size. $L_{pml}$ constrains the predictor $\varphi$ as a Lipschitz continuous function satisfying Remarks 1 and 2. $L_{pml}$ is based on the assumption that the target label is univariate. For the multivariate regression task with a $D$ dimensional target label $y \in \mathbb{R}^D$, the loss can be updated as:

$$\hat{L}_{pml} = \sum_{i=1}^{D} L_{pml}^i \qquad (3)$$

with $L_{pml}^i = L_{pml}$ if $D = 1$.

**Superiority of $L_{pml}$ over SOTA** RankSim [20] is the SOTA method to regularize the feature distance in regression by aligning the feature distance order with the label distance order. We argue that the consistency between the orders of label distance and feature distances is insufficient to regularize the feature distribution with continuous labels, especially for unseen labels.[1] With the consideration of the proportion between label distance and feature distance, $L_{pml}$ can mitigate this problem with continuous feature distribution.

### 3.3 Spectral Alignment of Domains

Existing works [43,44] in domain generalization have demonstrated that the diversity and amount of training examples are positively correlated with the generalizability of a machine learning model. To expand the training set, we employ the data augmentation technique of C-Mixup [46] to generate additional samples from unseen distributions. However, without imposing a constraint of domain invariance, the learned feature space might include domain-specific information and thus become noisy [32]. This could hinder obtaining the optimal generalization power of the model.

---

[1] In the 1-D space, given seen labels $l_s = \{1, 2, 10, 11\}$, the feature can be distributed as $f_s = \{1, 2, 100, 101\}$ according to [20]. But, according to the pigeonhole principle, there must be at least two unseen labels in [2, 10] with label distance equal to 0.5 (default to $\{4, 4.5\}$), whose feature distance is larger than 1 (default to $\{6, 7.1\}$). However, the features $f = \{1, 2, 6, 7.1, 100, 101\}$ with labels $l = \{1, 2, 4, 4.5, 10, 11\}$ are ill-distributed according to [20].

To impose domain invariance constraint, the existing work of [11] suggests not to minimize the difference between the Frobenius norm of feature representations of different domains. However, this may cause unstable performance. We argue that this instability can come from the fact that the Frobenius norm may encode the average of variances (i.e., singular values) along all orthogonal feature projections, and that, the transferability of the feature representations mainly lies in aligning the highest variability directions corresponding to the largest singular values [10]. Therefore, in our formulation, the Frobenius norm is substituted by the spectral norm, which only encodes the highest variability direction. We further show that the difference between spectral norms of features can be related to domain discrepancy.

**Notations.** The expected loss in regression is $\mathcal{L}_D(h', h) = E_{x \sim D}[L(h(x), h'(x))]$ with $L$ being the MSE loss [12]. We have the $\mathcal{L}_D(h, 0) = \frac{1}{N} \|\hat{Y}_D^h\|_F^2$, with $N$ being the number of samples, and $\hat{Y}_D^h$ being the output with hypothesis $h$ under distribution $D$. 0 represents the hypothesis mapping to zero element in $\mathcal{Y}$.

**Proposition 2.** *Given two distributions $P$ and $Q$, we have*

$$disc(P, Q) \leq \frac{1}{N} \max_{h \in H} |\|\hat{Y}_P^h\|_F^2 - \|\hat{Y}_Q^h\|_F^2|,$$

*where disc represents the difference between distributions and $N$ denotes the number of the samples.*

**Proof 2.** *Generally speaking, we have*

$$\mathcal{L}(h', h) = \mathcal{L}(h - h', 0)$$

*Since $h, h'$ are in the subspace $H$ of Hilbert Space $\mathbb{H}$, we have $h'' = h - h' \in H$. Then, we have*

$$\forall h'' \in \mathbb{H}, disc(P, Q) \leq \max_{h'' \in H} |\mathcal{L}_P(h'', 0) - \mathcal{L}_Q(h'', 0)|$$

*So, the proof is concluded.*

Proposition 2 shows the relation between the difference of feature representations and their distribution discrepancy. To determine the relation between the norm of the feature matrix and the output scale[2], we consider the spectral norm of the feature space, $\|F\|_2 = \sup_{w \neq 0} \frac{\|Fw\|_2}{\|w\|_2}$. If $W_i$ is a row vector of the weight $W$ in the fully connected layer, then $\|\hat{Y}_i^h\|_2 \leq \|\hat{Y}_i^h - b_i\|_2 + |b_i| \leq \|F\|_2\|W_i\|_2 + |b_i|$, $\hat{Y}_i^h$, and $\hat{Y}_i^h$ is the $i$-th vector of the output matrix $\hat{Y}^h$ and $b_i$ is the $i$-th value of the bias vector $b$ in the fully connected layer. If we define $\lambda_i(F) = \|F\|_2\|W_i\|_2 + |b_i|$, we will have $\|\hat{Y}^h\|_F \leq \|\lambda(F)\|_2$.

---

[2] The Frobenius norm of the output $\|\hat{Y}_P^h\|_F$ represents the scale of the output in distribution $P$. Unlike classification, in regression, the target label for each sample can be a vector. That means, if we have $N$ samples, each with $M$ dimensional target vectors, then $\hat{Y}_P^h$ is an $N \times M$ matrix.

From the discussion above, the spectral norm is related to the upper bound of the output scale. So aligning the spectral norms can prevent the output scales from differing greatly, which can also align two distributions as per Proposition 2. Therefore, we propose the spectral alignment loss based on singular value decomposition (SVD) as follows:

$$L_{sa} = |max(s^{real}) - max(s^{syn})|, \quad (4)$$

where $s_{real}$ and $s_{syn}$ are the set of the singular values of the feature matrices from the real and synthesized distributions. The largest singular values of matrices are selected for calculating the loss. Note that $\|F\|_2 = max(s_F)$, where $s_F$ is the set of the singular values of matrix $F$.

### 3.4 Overall Objective Function

We combine our objectives for proportional metric loss and spectral alignment, and optimize them in an end-to-end training fashion. Formally, we have:

$$L = L_{mse} + \alpha \hat{L}_{pml} + \beta L_{sa}, \quad (5)$$

where $\alpha$ and $\beta$ represent hyper-parameters to balance the contribution of their corresponding loss functions. We further optimize the supervised loss of $L_{mse}$, formulated as:

$$L_{mse} = \frac{1}{N}(\sum_{i=1}^{N}(\varphi(g(x_i^{real})) - y_i^{real})^2 + \sum_{i=1}^{N}(\varphi(g(x_i^{syn})) - y_i^{syn})^2) \quad (6)$$

with $\varphi(g(x_i^{real}))$ and $\varphi(g(x_i^{syn}))$ being the prediction of input $x_i^{real}$ and the augmented sample $x_i^{syn}$ with C-Mixup [46], respectively. Here, $y_i^{real}$ and $y_i^{syn}$ denote the ground truth label corresponding to $x_i^{real}$ and $x_i^{syn}$, respectively.

## 4 Experimental Results

### 4.1 Implementation Details

Recent research [27,29] reveals a phenomenon that fine-tuning the whole network on a new task can improve the in-distribution (ID) performance of the new task, at the price of its out-of-distribution (OOD) accuracies. This is because fine-tuning the whole network changes the feature space spanned by the training data of a new task, which distorts the pretrained features. While linear probing can be an alternative solution to fine-tuning, due to its inability to adapt the features to the downstream task, it may degenerate the performance on in-distribution tasks. To mitigate this ID-OOD trade-off, motivated by the discussion in [27,29], we freeze the top of the C-Mixup [46] pretrained network (excluding the last block and the linear layers) during the training process. Specifically, we only fine-tune the bottom layer to preserve the low-level features from the pretrained model and unfreeze the last block to avoid degeneracy in the ID tasks.

**Table 1.** Comparison on out-of-distribution datasets. The **bold** number is the best result and the underline number is the second best result. The results of methods with † are reported by [46]. ERM is the baseline method using only MSE loss. The results of methods with * are reproduced based on the provided source code

|  | RCF-MNIST | DTI | |
|---|---|---|---|
|  | RMSE↓ | $R$ ↑ | |
|  | Avg. | Avg. | Worst |
| ERM† | 0.162 | 0.464 | 0.429 |
| ERM* | 0.160 | 0.475 | 0.438 |
| IRM† [4] † | 0.153 | 0.478 | 0.432 |
| IB-IRM† [2] | 0.167 | 0.479 | 0.435 |
| CORAL† [31] | 0.163 | 0.483 | 0.432 |
| GroupDRO† [37] | 0.232 | 0.442 | 0.407 |
| Mixup† [48] | 0.176 | 0.465 | 0.437 |
| C-Mixup* [46] | 0.153 | 0.483 | 0.449 |
| C-Mixup† [46] | 0.146 | <u>0.498</u> | 0.458 |
| RML* [7] | 0.167 | 0.480 | 0.446 |
| RankSim* [20] | 0.239 | 0.479 | <u>0.464</u> |
| Full model w/o $L_{sa}$ | <u>0.145</u> | 0.491 | **0.479** |
| Full model w/o $L_{pml}$ | 0.147 | 0.481 | 0.447 |
| Full model | **0.143** | **0.500** | 0.448 |

### 4.2 Generalization in Univariate Regression

**Datasets.** The generalization ability of models in regression tasks with univariate output is evaluated over two datasets, namely Drug-target Interactions (DTI) [24] and RCF-MNIST [46]. **DTI** is a real world dataset designed to predict the binding activity score between each small molecule and the corresponding target protein by collecting 232,458 data on the drug and target protein information. The whole dataset is divided into different domains according to the years of data collection. **RCF-MNIST** is a dataset with 60,000 images built on FashionMNIST [42] with spurious correlations between colours and rotation angles (label).

**Experimental Settings.** We evaluate our method on two datasets, namely RCF-MNIST and DTI. We leverage Resnet18 [23] as the feature extractor for RCF-MNIST, and employ DeepDTA [35] on DTI.

Following the original paper of DTI [24], we evaluate the methods on $R$ value. Same as C-Mixup [46], we report both average and worst-domain performance for the experiments on DTI. For RCF-MNIST, the evaluation metric is Root Mean Square Error (RMSE). Our full model is trained with three losses, $L_{mse}$, $L_{sa}$ and $L_{pml}$. The fine-tuning strategy mentioned in Sect. 4.1 is also applied in the experiments on univariate regression in our models. All the experiments are run over 3 seeds.

**Performance Comparison.** The performance of OOD robustness on the two datasets is shown in Table 1. We compare our methods with not only the OOD generalization methods, *i.e.* C-Mixup [46], CORAL [31], but also some metric loss in regression, *i.e.* RankSim [20] and RML [7]. Note that RankSim is a method designed for age prediction where the continuity of the target label is not required. ERM is the baseline training strategy, where the objective is to minimize the Mean Squared Error (MSE) loss Similar to our proposed losses, the fine-tuning method is applied for the models with RankSim and RML. As the table shows, our method can achieve superior performance in most cases. For the datasets with small sizes, the pretrained model plays an important role in improving generalization, since the scarcity of data and the lack of variety is the key problem in these datasets. In addition, we find that $L_{pml}$ can also generalize the spurious correlation, as shown by the results of RCF-MNIST. We assume that the spurious correlation increases the variance in the proportion, which can be generalized by $L_{pml}$.

**t-SNE Visualization.** According to our discussion, $L_{pml}$ is trying to get a flatter $d_r$, which means the feature distribution should follow a discriminative pattern with less variance. To test the effect of the losses in regression on embedding space, we visualize the feature distribution without metric loss, with RML, and with $L_{pml}$ on Fig. 1. This visualization can strongly support our assumption and discussion above. As Fig. 1 shows, the feature distribution is more compact and the distribution pattern is clearer with $L_{pml}$. In addition, as we discussed, RML focuses on learning a scale of the matrix feature and ignores the variance in the proportion. So, in some situations, the pattern will be blurred with RML, which is the same as the one shown in Fig. 1. Note that $L_{pml}$ maintains the property of being Lipschitz continuous for the predictor, which enhances the continuity of the feature distribution with less steep slopes. Figures 1c and 1d illustrate this difference: unlike $L_{pml}$, RankSim [20], which focuses solely on the distance between orders, does not preserve Lipschitz continuity. This characteristic might contribute to $L_{pml}$'s superior performance over RankSim in most scenarios, as shown in Table 1. It will also contribute to the frequent breakpoints in Fig. 1c, which supports this hypothesis.

$L_{pml}$ *v.s. Ranksim*: The t-SNE visualization highlights two primary distinctions between the methods: the pattern of $L_{pml}$ appears rougher than that of RankSim; and $L_{pml}$ exhibits significantly fewer breakpoints compared to RankSim. This is likely due to the penalty mechanism of RankSim, which aligns feature distances more loosely in accordance with label distances, allowing for a broader spread with fewer disruptions. This accounts for the rougher appearance of the $L_{pml}$ pattern. However, such stretching of patterns might result in extremely varied feature distances, potentially causing poorly distributed patterns, particularly for unseen labels as noted in Footnote 1. Consequently, the t-SNE visualization of RankSim reveals more breakpoints than that of $L_{pml}$, explaining the suboptimal performance of RankSim in DTI and RCF-MNIST.

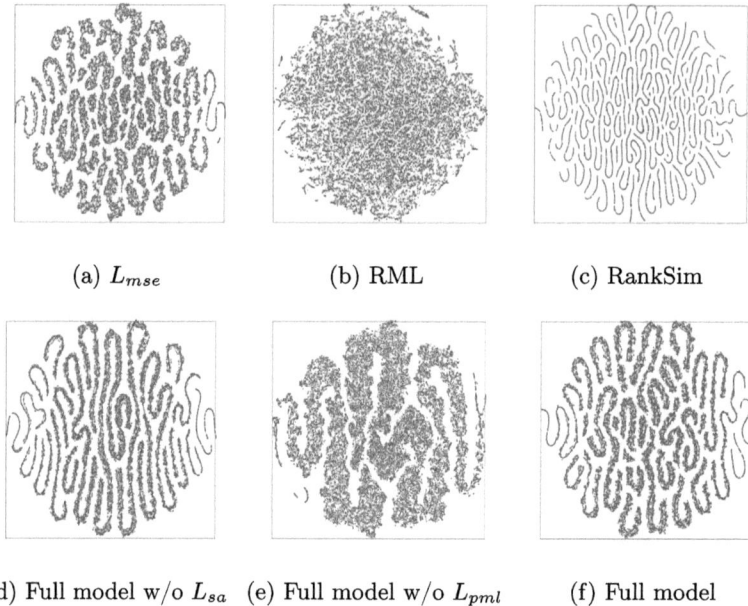

**Fig. 1.** T-SNE visualization of the embedding space on DTI dataset. The visualizations from le to right are (a) The baseline model that is fine-tuned to minimize MSE loss, (b) The model that is fine-tuned to minimize both MSE and RML objectives, (c) the model that is fine-tuned to minimize both MSE and RankSim, (d) The model that is fine-tuned to optimize full model without $L_{sa}$, (e) The model that is fine-tuned to optimize full model without $L_{pml}$. (f) The model that is fine-tuned to optimize full model. Red points represent the features extracted from the train set and the blue points represent the features extracted from the test set.

### 4.3 Generalization in Multivariate Regression

**Datasets.** The out-of-distribution (OOD) generalization ability of models in multivariate regression is evaluated over three datasets, including dSprites [33], MPI3D [19] and BiwiKinect [15] which are widely used for domain adaptation tasks in computer vision [11,34]

**dSprites** is a synthetic dataset of three domains, namely Color(**c**), Scream(**s**) and Noisy(**n**), which are generated by adding colors or noise in the real images. Each domain comprises 737,280 images. Following the setup in [11], the orientation factors in the dataset are excluded.

**MPI3D** is a benchmark dataset of 1,036,800 images with three distributions to predict intrinsic factors. The dataset contains real data (domain Real (**rl**)) and synthetic data (domain Toy (**t**) and Realistic (**rc**)). In our experiments, we only consider the prediction of the rotation around a vertical and horizontal axis.

**BiwiKinect** is a real-world dataset of head poses recorded by a Microsoft Kinect sensor. The dataset can be divided into 2 domains: Female (**F**) with 5,874

**Table 2.** Comparison on MPI3D and dSprites dataset with the setting of domain generalization under the MSE index. The **bold** number is the best and the underline number is the second best result. The unseen domains are on the top.

|  | MPI3D-MSE | | | MPI3D-MAE | | |
|---|---|---|---|---|---|---|
|  | rc | rl | t | rc | rl | t |
| ERM | 0.08132 | 0.09819 | 0.007004 | 0.3163 | 0.3511 | 0.0922 |
| C-Mixup | 0.09226 | 0.10495 | 0.014453 | 0.3367 | 0.3666 | 0.1296 |
| RML | 0.08596 | 0.09412 | 0.020132 | 0.3315 | 0.3448 | 0.1661 |
| Nuclear-norm | 0.09490 | 0.09536 | 0.011940 | 0.3270 | 0.3313 | 0.1181 |
| F-norm | 0.09565 | 0.10548 | 0.008318 | 0.3226 | 0.3411 | 0.0985 |
| Full model w/o $L_{sa}$ | **0.07829** | <u>0.08262</u> | 0.006996 | 0.3149 | 0.3478 | 0.0919 |
| Full model w/o $L_{pml}$ | <u>0.07942</u> | 0.08355 | **0.006016** | **0.3016** | <u>0.3225</u> | **0.0856** |
| Full model | 0.07956 | **0.07885** | <u>0.006017</u> | <u>0.3058</u> | **0.3137** | <u>0.0858</u> |
|  | dSprites-MSE | | | dSprites-MAE | | |
|  | c | s | n | c | s | n |
| ERM | 0.04904 | 0.4903 | 0.4108 | 0.3071 | 0.9793 | 0.8977 |
| C-Mixup | 0.08769 | 0.5087 | **0.3672** | 0.4144 | 0.9846 | **0.8596** |
| RML | 0.08037 | 0.5860 | 0.4348 | 0.4147 | 1.054 | 0.9115 |
| Nuclear-norm | 0.2076 | 0.7718 | 0.4970 | 0.3270 | 0.3313 | 0.1181 |
| F-norm | 0.06709 | 0.4856 | 0.5868 | 0.3035 | 0.9234 | 1.067 |
| Full model w/o $L_{sa}$ | <u>0.03480</u> | <u>0.4589</u> | 0.4051 | <u>0.2626</u> | <u>0.9413</u> | 0.8953 |
| Full model w/o $L_{pml}$ | 0.03721 | 0.4861 | <u>0.3954</u> | 0.2711 | 0.9650 | <u>0.8859</u> |
| Full model | **0.03479** | **0.4569** | 0.4030 | **0.2620** | **0.9396** | 0.8942 |

images and Male (**M**) with 9,804 images. The Euler angles of the head, namely yaw, pitch and roll angles are used to evaluate our method.

**Experimental Settings.** We analyze our method under the setting of domain generalization on the three datasets, which is a benchmark dataset for Domain Adaptation in Regression. We adapt a domain generalization setting [21] by evaluating our method over three generalization tasks on the three datasets: 1) dSprites: **c, s → n; c, n → s; s, n → c**; 2) MPI3D: **rl, rc → t; t, rc → rl; rl, t → rc**; 3) Biwikinect: **F → M; M → F**. We use the test sets of source distributions as the validation sets for the model selection. All the experiments are run over three random seeds, and we follow [6] for random seed and hyper-parameter seed selection.

The evaluation metrics on this task are Mean Square Error (MSE) and Mean Absolute Error (MAE). The variances over seeds of the methods are reported in the supplementary. We do not use our fine-tuning method on the three datasets and there is no frozen parameter during the training process on these three datasets. Since RankSim does not provide the algorithm for multivariate regression, we do not include it in the experiments for multivariate regression.

**OOD generalization with Multiple Source Domains.** The MSE and MAE results on dSprites and MPI3D are shown in Table 2. The comparison between $L_{pml}$ and RML [7] shows the advantage of modeling the proportion as a fluctuating map rather than a fixed constant. In addition, the performance also shows that the alignment with $L_{sa}$ can significantly improve the generalization ability in some cases. We also provide the results of alignment with Nuclear-norm $\|\cdot\|_*$ and Frobenius norm $\|\cdot\|_F$. With norm equivalence [5], $\|\cdot\|_2 \leq \|\cdot\|_F \leq \|\cdot\|_*$, the spectral norm can give a tighter upper bound. This can explain the reason that $L_{sa}$ can get the best performance among them. In addition, compared with $L_{pml}$, $L_{sa}$ makes more significant improvement in generalization tasks, which illustrates the importance of distribution alignment in OOD generalization.

Table 2 shows that the C-Mixup performs very well, when the Noisy domain is the unseen domain on dSprites. We assume that the mix-up distribution is very similar to the noisy domain. When the other distributions are involved, the well-built distribution is damaged, which may complicate the training process.

**Table 3.** Comparison on BiwiKinect dataset with the setting of domain generalization under MSE and MAE index. The **bold** number is the best and the underline number is the second best result. The unseen domains are on the top.

|  | BiwiKinect-MSE | | BiwiKinect-MAE | |
| --- | --- | --- | --- | --- |
|  | F | M | F | M |
| ERM | 0.3953 | 0.4949 | 0.7907 | 0.8879 |
| C-Mixup | 0.3542 | 0.4908 | 0.7555 | 0.8795 |
| RML | 0.4139 | 0.4923 | 0.8125 | 0.8833 |
| Nuclear-norm | 0.4792 | 0.5967 | 0.8771 | 0.9902 |
| F-norm | 0.3472 | 0.4735 | 0.7394 | 0.8489 |
| Full model w/o $L_{sa}$ | 0.3486 | 0.4744 | 0.7401 | <u>0.8424</u> |
| Full model w/o $L_{pml}$ | **0.3376** | **0.4683** | **0.7257** | 0.8585 |
| Full model | <u>0.3391</u> | <u>0.4695</u> | <u>0.7276</u> | **0.8419** |

**OOD Generalization with Single Source Domain.** We also evaluate our method on single OOD generalization on BiwiKinect dataset. Table 3 shows the MSE and MAE results on BiwiKinect. From the result of F-norm and $L_{sa}$, it seems that the distribution alignment methods can contribute more to the improvement of the performance on single domain generalization because of the lack of diversity in the source distribution.

### 4.4 Hyper-parameter Sensitivity Analysis

We analyze the hyper-parameters on $\alpha$ and $\beta$ in Eq. 5. When the values of $L_{pml}$ and $L_{sa}$ are much larger than $L_{mse}$, the total loss $L_{mse}$ is hard to converge

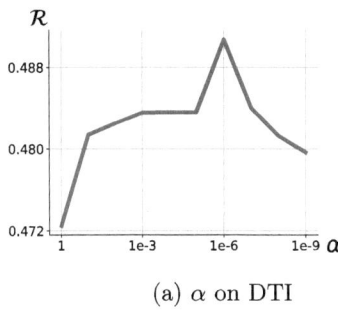
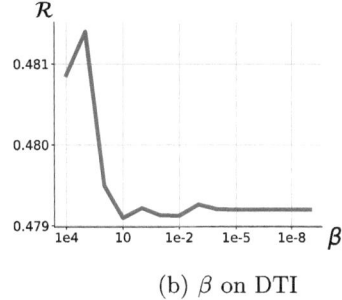

(a) $\alpha$ on DTI  (b) $\beta$ on DTI

**Fig. 2.** (a) and (b) shows the hyper-parameter analysis on DTI datasets. The larger $\mathcal{R}$ value means the better result.

and the performance will drop dramatically. So, we analyze the trend of the performance of $L_{pml}$ and $L_{sa}$ with $\alpha$ and $\beta$ in the range between $[1e^{-9}, 1]$ and $[1e^{-9}, 1e^{4}]$ respectively. Figure 2 shows the sensitivity of the hyper-parameters on out-of-distribution dataset DTI. We find that the $L_{pml}$ is much more sensitive since the value of $L_{pml}$ is usually much larger than $L_{mse}$ and $L_{sa}$.

## 5 Conclusion

This paper discusses two main objectives that are required to improve generalization in regression. For In-Distribution generalization, we propose proportional metric loss, based on the assumption that the distance between features and their corresponding labels should be correlated. We assume that the proportion between feature distance and label distance is a mapping function. Through this loss, we show that the variance in the embedding space is decreased, resulting in more discriminative patterns. To improve the transferability of the model on out-of-distribution data, we propose to augment the original data and then align the synthesized and real distributions through minimizing the difference between spectral norm of features.

**Acknowledgments.** This work is partially supported by Australian Research Council Project FT230100426.

## References

1. Agatston, A., Janowitz, W., Hildner, F.J., Zusmer, N.R., Viamonte, M., Detrano, R.: Quantification of coronary artery calcium using ultrafast computed tomography. J. Am. Coll. Cardiol. **15**(4), 827–832 (1990)
2. Ahuja, K., et al.: Invariance principle meets information bottleneck for out-of-distribution generalization. In: Proceedings of the Conference Neural Information Processing System, vol. 34, 3438–3450 (2021)

3. Albuquerque, I., Monteiro, J., Darvishi, M., Falk, T.H., Mitliagkas, I.: Generalizing to unseen domains via distribution matching. arXiv:1911.00804 (2019)
4. Arjovsky, M., Bottou, L., Gulrajani, I., Lopez-Paz, D.: Invariant risk minimization. arXiv preprint arXiv:1907.02893 (2019)
5. Cai, T.T., Ren, Z., Zhou, H.H.: Estimating structured high-dimensional covariance and precision matrices: Optimal rates and adaptive estimation (2016)
6. Cha, J., Chun, S., Lee, K., Cho, H.C., Park, S., Lee, Y., Park, S.: Swad: domain generalization by seeking flat minima. In: Proceeding of the Conference on Neural Information Processing Systems, pp. 34, pp. 22405–22418 (2021)
7. Chao, H., Zhang, J., Yan, P.: Regression metric loss: Learning a semantic representation space for medical images. arXiv preprint arXiv:2207.05231 (2022)
8. Chen, W., Fu, Z., Yang, D., Deng, J.: Single-image depth perception in the wild. In: Proceeding of the Conference on Neural Information Processing Systems (2016)
9. Chen, W., Chen, X., Zhang, J., Huang, K.: Beyond triplet loss: a deep quadruplet network for person re-identification. In: Proceedings of the IEEE/CVF Conference on Computer Vision and Pattern Recognition, pp. 403–412 (2017)
10. Chen, X., Wang, S., Long, M., Wang, J.: Transferability vs. discriminability: Batch spectral penalization for adversarial domain adaptation. In: Chaudhuri, K., Salakhutdinov, R. (eds.) Proceedings of International Conference on Machine Learning. Proceedings of Machine Learning Research, vol. 97, pp. 1081–1090. PMLR (09–15 Jun 2019), https://proceedings.mlr.press/v97/chen19i.html
11. Chen, X., Wang, S., Wang, J., Long, M.: Representation subspace distance for domain adaptation regression. In: International Conference on Machine Learning, pp. 1749–1759 (2021)
12. Cortes, C., Mohri, M.: Domain adaptation in regression. In: International Conference on Algorithmic Learning Theory, pp. 308–323. Springer (2011)
13. Deng, J., Guo, J., Xue, N., Zafeiriou, S.: Arcface: additive angular margin loss for deep face recognition. In: Proceedings of the IEEE/CVF Conference on Computer Vision and Pattern Recognition, pp. 4690–4699 (2019)
14. Deshmukh, A.A., Lei, Y., Sharma, S., Dogan, U., Cutler, J.W., Scott, C.: A generalization error bound for multi-class domain generalization. arXiv preprint arXiv:1905.10392 (2019)
15. Fanelli, G., Dantone, M., Gall, J., Fossati, A., Van Gool, L.: Random forests for real time 3d face analysis. Int. J. Comput. Vision **101**(3), 437–458 (2013). https://doi.org/10.1007/s11263-012-0549-0
16. Ganin, Y., Lempitsky, V.: Unsupervised domain adaptation by backpropagation. In: International Conference on Machine Learning, pp. 1180–1189. PMLR (2015)
17. Ganin, Y., et al.: Domain-adversarial training of neural networks. J. Mach. Learn. Res. **17**(59), 1–35 (2016)
18. Gilsanz, V., Ratib, O.: Hand Bone Age: A Digital Atlas of Skeletal Maturity. Springer, Berlin Heidelberg (2011)
19. Gondal, M.W., et al.: On the transfer of inductive bias from simulation to the real world: a new disentanglement dataset. In: Wallach, H., Larochelle, H., Beygelzimer, A., d'Alché-Buc, F., Fox, E., Garnett, R. (eds.) Advances in Neural Information Processing Systems, vol. 32. Curran Associates, Inc. (2019)
20. Gong, Y., Mori, G., Tung, F.: Ranksim: Ranking similarity regularization for deep imbalanced regression. arXiv preprint arXiv:2205.15236 (2022)
21. Gulrajani, I., Lopez-Paz, D.: In search of lost domain generalization. In: International Conference on Learning Representations (2021)
22. Happersberger, D.: Advancing Systematic and Factor Investing Strategies Using Alternative Data and Machine Learning. Lancaster University (2021)

23. He, K., Zhang, X., Ren, S., Sun, J.: Deep residual learning for image recognition. In: Proceedings of the IEEE/CVF Conference on Computer Vision and Pattern Recognition (June 2016)
24. Huang, K., et al.: Therapeutics data commons: Machine learning datasets and tasks for drug discovery and development. arXiv:2102.09548 (2021)
25. Hüllermeier, E., Waegeman, W.: Aleatoric and epistemic uncertainty in machine learning: An introduction to concepts and methods. Mach. Learn. **110**, 457–506 (2021)
26. Kaya, M., Bilge, H.Ş: Deep metric learning: a survey. Symmetry **11**(9), 1066 (2019)
27. Kirichenko, P., Izmailov, P., Wilson, A.G.: Last layer re-training is sufficient for robustness to spurious correlations. In: International Conference on Learning Representations (2023). https://openreview.net/forum?id=Zb6c8A-Fghk
28. Kulis, B., et al.: Metric learning: a survey. Found. Trends® Mach. Learn. **5**(4), 287–364 (2013)
29. Kumar, A., Raghunathan, A., Jones, R., Ma, T., Liang, P.: Fine-tuning can distort pretrained features and underperform out-of-distribution. arXiv preprint arXiv:2202.10054 (2022)
30. Lee, C., Landgrebe, D.A.: Feature extraction based on decision boundaries. Trans. Pattern Anal. Mach. Intell. **15**(4), 388–400 (1993)
31. Li, H., Pan, S.J., Wang, S., Kot, A.C.: Domain generalization with adversarial feature learning. In: Proceedings of the IEEE/CVF Conference on Computer Vision and Pattern Recognition, pp. 5400–5409 (2018)
32. Liu, Y., et al.: Promoting semantic connectivity: dual nearest neighbors contrastive learning for unsupervised domain generalization. In: Proceedings of the IEEE/CVF Conference on Computer Vision and Pattern Recognition, pp. 3510–3519 (2023)
33. Matthey, L., Higgins, I., Hassabis, D., Lerchner, A.: dsprites: disentanglement testing sprites dataset. https://github.com/deepmind/dsprites-dataset/ (2017)
34. Nejjar, I., Wang, Q., Fink, O.: Dare-gram : Unsupervised domain adaptation regression by aligning inversed gram matrices. In: Proceedings of the IEEE/CVF Conference on Computer Vision and Pattern Recognition (2023)
35. Öztürk, H., Özgür, A., Ozkirimli, E.: Deepdta: deep drug-target binding affinity prediction. Bioinformatics **34**(17), i821–i829 (2018)
36. Rudin, W.: Principles of Mathematical Analysis. International series in pure and applied mathematics, McGraw-Hill (1976)
37. Sagawa, S., Koh, P.W., Hashimoto, T.B., Liang, P.: Distributionally robust neural networks for group shifts: On the importance of regularization for worst-case generalization. arXiv preprint arXiv:1911.08731 (2019)
38. Schroff, F., Kalenichenko, D., Philbin, J.: Facenet: A unified embedding for face recognition and clustering. In: Proceedings of the IEEE/CVF Conference on Computer Vision and Pattern Recognition, pp. 815–823 (2015)
39. Sicilia, A., Zhao, X., Hwang, S.J.: Domain adversarial neural networks for domain generalization: When it works and how to improve. Machine Learning, pp. 1–37 (2023)
40. Wang, J., et al.: Generalizing to unseen domains: A survey on domain generalization. IEEE Transactions on Knowledge and Data Engineering (2022)
41. Wen, Y., Zhang, K., Li, Z., Qiao, Yu.: A discriminative feature learning approach for deep face recognition. In: Leibe, B., Matas, J., Sebe, N., Welling, M. (eds.) ECCV 2016. LNCS, vol. 9911, pp. 499–515. Springer, Cham (2016). https://doi.org/10.1007/978-3-319-46478-7_31
42. Xiao, H., Rasul, K., Vollgraf, R.: Fashion-mnist: a novel image dataset for benchmarking machine learning algorithms. arXiv preprint arXiv:1708.07747 (2017)

43. Xu, Q., Zhang, R., Fan, Z., Wang, Y., Wu, Y.Y., Zhang, Y.: Fourier-based augmentation with applications to domain generalization. Pattern Recogn. **139**, 109474 (2023)
44. Xu, Q., Zhang, R., Zhang, Y., Wang, Y., Tian, Q.: A Fourier-based framework for domain generalization. In: Proceedings of the IEEE/CVF Conference on Computer Vision and Pattern Recognition, pp. 14383–14392 (2021)
45. Yang, Y., Zha, K., Chen, Y., Wang, H., Katabi, D.: Delving into deep imbalanced regression. In: International Conference on Machine Learning, pp. 11842–11851. PMLR (2021)
46. Yao, H., Wang, Y., Zhang, L., Zou, J., Finn, C.: C-mixup: Improving generalization in regression. In: Proceeding of the Conference on Neural Information Processing Systems (2022)
47. Zha, K., Cao, P., Son, J., Yang, Y., Katabi, D.: Rank-n-contrast: learning continuous representations for regression. In: Thirty-seventh Conference on Neural Information Processing Systems (2023)
48. Zhang, H., Cisse, M., Dauphin, Y.N., Lopez-Paz, D.: mixup: beyond empirical risk minimization. In: International Conference on Learning Representations (2018)
49. Zhang, X., Sugano, Y., Fritz, M., Bulling, A.: Appearance-based gaze estimation in the wild. In: Proceedings of the IEEE/CVF Conference on Computer Vision and Pattern Recognition, pp. 4511–4520 (2015)
50. Zhou, K., Yang, Y., Qiao, Y., Xiang, T.: Domain generalization with mixstyle. In: International Conference on Learning Representations (2021)

# Prompting without Panic: Attribute-Aware, Zero-Shot, Test-Time Calibration

Ramya Hebbalaguppe[1,2(✉)], Tamoghno Kandar[2], Abhinav Nagpal[1], and Chetan Arora[1]

[1] IIT Delhi, New Delhi, India
ramya.murthy@gmail.com
[2] TCS Research Labs, New Delhi, India
https://promptwithoutpanic.github.io/

**Abstract.** Vision language models (VLMs) have become effective tools for image recognition, primarily due to their self-supervised training on large datasets. Their performance can be enhanced further through test-time prompt tuning (TPT). However, TPT's singular focus on accuracy improvement often leads to a decline in confidence calibration, restricting its use in safety-critical applications. In this work, we make two contributions: **(1)** We posit that random or naive initialization of prompts leads to overfitting on a particular test sample, and is one of the reasons for miscalibration of VLMs after TPT. To mitigate the problem, we propose careful initialization of test time prompt using prior knowledge about the target label attributes from a large language model (LLM). **(2)** We propose a novel regularization technique to preserve prompt calibration during test-time prompt tuning (TPT). This method simultaneously minimizes intraclass distances while maximizing interclass distances between learned prompts. Our approach achieves significant calibration improvements across multiple CLIP architectures and 15 diverse datasets, demonstrating its effectiveness for TPT. We report an average expected calibration error (ECE) of 4.11 with our method, TCA, compared to 11.7 for vanilla TPT [29], 6.12 for C-TPT [55] (ICLR'24), 6.78 for DiffTPT [8] (CVPR'23), and 8.43 for PromptAlign [44] (NeurIPS'23). The code is publicly accessible at https://github.com/rhebbalaguppe/TCA_PromptWithoutPanic.

## 1 Introduction

**VLMs and Confidence calibration.** Vision-Language Models (VLMs) have unlocked transformative applications across a wide range of fields, from healthcare diagnostics [52] to assistive solutions for visually impaired [53]. However,

---

R. Hebbalaguppe and T. Kandar—Equal contribution.

**Supplementary Information** The online version contains supplementary material available at https://doi.org/10.1007/978-3-032-06106-5_17.

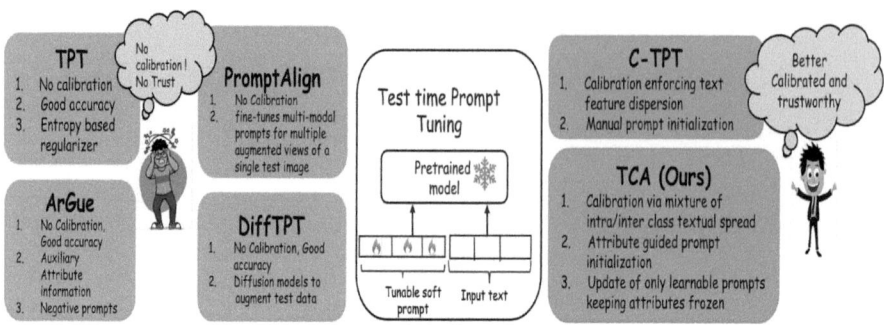

**Fig. 1. Conceptual comparison between our proposed TCA vs. the contemporaries.** Test-time prompt tuning methods, such as TPT [29], learn test-time prompts through parameter optimization. However, these methods often face performance disadvantages in calibration, as they struggle to dynamically adapt to varying textual feature distributions, limiting effective prompt calibration. Methods, ArgGue [46], DiffTPT [8], and PromptAlign [44] do not explicitly optimize for calibration. Although C-TPT [55] introduces enhancements in calibration, it still falls short in capturing *nuanced visual attributes* that contribute to precise prompt conditioning leading to suboptimal prompt specificity. Our method termed **T**est-time **C**alibration via **A**ttribute Alignment (TCA) infuses relevant attribute information providing context via LLMs and captures intra/inter-class textual attribute spread improving prompt calibration. **Note:** TCA works in zero-shot and test-time settings without any labeled data, making it very practical for real-world deployment where data annotation is infeasible. No model fine-tuning required: Only prompts are updated at test time; base vision and text encoders are kept frozen.

recent findings [47] reveal that VLMs suffer from miscalibration, which can hinder model trustworthiness in critical applications. Traditional calibration methods rely on large labeled datasets, posing significant limitations for settings like test-time adaptation, where the labeled data is unavailable or infeasible to obtain. Inspired by the success of VLMs in generalizing to unseen data in a zero-shot setting [55], in this paper we focus on zero-shot setting, and adapt these models using prompt tuning.

**Prompt Tuning.** Test-time prompt tuning (TPT) has emerged as a promising approach to improve generalization of VLMs, offering a way to adapt prompts to specific contexts without requiring any labeled data from the target domain. Hard prompts [32], often composed of fixed vocabulary tokens from standard templates like "A photo of a {class name}" can simplify prompt creation. However, [55] indicate that more flexible prompt designs, such as soft prompts or learned embeddings, can significantly enhance a model's adaptability and effectiveness. On the other hand, domain-specific prompt creation for image-text models requires substantial expertise and time, with no guarantee of optimal results despite extensive engineering efforts [43]. Shu et al.[29] suggested a TPT technique (hereinafter referred to as Vanilla TPT (VTPT)) which aims to enhance the accuracy of CLIP based models by minimizing the entropy in the prediction distribution as a self-supervision signal during test time. However, a reduction in entropy leads the model to generate overconfident predictions, a characteristic often observed in models trained with cross-entropy loss [10,55]. Figure 1 illustrates the conceptual distinction between existing prompt tuning approaches and the method proposed in this work.

**Contributions.** This work focuses on TPT strategy to improve model's calibration. At first, this may seem infeasible since various calibration techniques employed in standard supervised training of neural networks require substantial amounts of labeled training data, which restricts their applicability in test-time prompt tuning scenarios for CLIP based models. Here, we come up with a clever workaround, by extracting label attributes using a LLM, and leveraging them in TPT instead of label supervision.

1. **Attribute-Aware Prompting for Improved Calibration:** Unlike the contemporary methods that directly attach soft prompts before class names, we append the model with precise visual attributes produced by an LLM that provide rich context. The visual attributes are sorted by their **relevance**. It may be noted that a particular attribute may be relevant for more than one labels. Hence, by aligning the visual embeddings with the chosen attributes allows a model to not only demonstrate that it recognizes features that are crucial for distinguishing the correct class from others, but also allows the model to express its prediction uncertainty in terms of the ambiguous attributes. Multiple relevant attributes also enhance the compositional nature of visual data as they serve as semantic anchors. Their incorporation in soft prompt design improves image-text alignment scores as they establish interpretable correspondences between visual and linguistic embeddings.
2. **Regularization Loss:** Proposed visual attributes-based prompt initialization allows the model a much better starting point compared to random initialization and prevents overfitting in the presence of limited variations in the single sample (and its augmentation) based training. However, the gradient-based update of the prompts may still overfit the prompts to the sample. Hence, we propose a loss on text prompt embeddings to minimize intra-class text feature dispersion, while maximizing inter-class dispersion. The idea is inspired from contrastive learning [20] in supervised training where the intra-class distance w.r.t. anchor is minimized and inter-class distance w.r.t. negative sample is maximized. The proposed loss can be combined with other prompt tuning methods for e.g. PromptAlign [44], DiffTPT [8], TDA [19], BoostAdapter [57] could integrate TCA for prompt calibration. In supplementary, we show gains in accuracy and ECE when we incorporate TCA on top of PromptAlign [44] and DiffTPT [8].
3. **Superior Performance:** We perform extensive experiments across various datasets and CLIP based models, incorporating our proposed attributes aware prompt initialization, and proposed loss. We report an average performance on 11 benchmark datasets improving the model calibration by 7.5% over the baseline TPT [29] and 2.01% in terms of ECE over C-TPT [55] respectively.

## 2 Related Works

**Miscalibration in Neural Network.** Accurate estimation of predictive uncertainty, often referred to as model calibration, is a critical aspect of deploying neural networks in safety-sensitive applications. Proper calibration ensures that the confidence associated with a model's predictions aligns with its true accuracy, thereby facilitating more reliable decision-making. However, recent studies have highlighted frequent instances of miscalibration in modern neural network architectures, indicating a concerning trend: despite improvements in predictive performance, newer and more accurate models tend to produce poorly calibrated probability estimates [10, 48].

**Calibration Techniques.** Calibration techniques can be broadly classified as train-time methods and post-hoc methods. Train-time techniques typically used additional loss terms along with the NLL (cross-entropy) loss during training. Some representative works include: [9, 12–14, 34, 36, 37, 41]. These techniques are not practical in our setting as it requires retraining the neural network with the regularization terms. Post-hoc calibration are applied after the model has been trained and often require a validation set to fine-tune the output probabilities. Some common post-hoc calibration techniques include: TS [38], DC [23] etc.

**Prompt Tuning for VLMs.** To efficiently adapt the large foundational models, prompting [26] has emerged as a resource-efficient method. Prompt tuning typically uses static or learnt prompts as part of the input text to guide the model in performing specific tasks in a zero-shot, or few-shot manner. Handcrafted prompts consisting of predefined vocabulary tokens, or hard prompts, may not be optimal in various settings. Hence, there is a growing focus on techniques that regard prompts as learnable vectors which can be optimized through gradient descent [27]. For instance, CoOp [59] tunes the prompts in CLIP using labeled training samples to improve its classification accuracy. However, CoCoOp [58] identified that CoOp struggles with generalizing to out-of-distribution data and recommends conditioning the prompt on input images. While effective, these methods require access to annotated training data, which limits the zero-shot adaptation of pre-trained models like ours. To tackle this challenge, recent research has introduced a TPT technique [29], which enables adaptive prompt learning at the inference time, using just one test sample. TPT optimizes the prompt by minimizing the entropy with confidence selection so that the model has consistent predictions for each test sample. DiffTPT [8] innovates test-time prompt tuning by leveraging pre-trained diffusion models to augment the diversity of test data samples used in TPT. PromptAlign [44] fine-tunes multi-modal prompts at test-time by aligning the distribution statistics obtained from multiple augmented views of a single test image with the training data distribution statistics. Although previous studies [2, 29, 58, 59] have primarily concentrated on refining prompt templates to improve accuracy, they have largely neglected calibration [10], except for [55].

Our paper focuses on the critical and under-explored challenge of calibrating VLMs in a **zero-short, test-time setting**. To maintain the efficiency and practicality, we develop our solution within prompt tuning framework.

## 3 Proposed Method

### 3.1 Preliminaries

**Confidence Calibration.** Given a data distribution $\mathcal{D}$ of $(x, y) \in \mathcal{X} \times \{0, 1\}$, let $c$ denote the predictive confidence of a predictor $f : \mathcal{X} \to [0, 1]$. The predictor is said to be calibrated [5], if:

$$\mathbb{E}_{(x,y) \sim \mathcal{D}}\big[y \mid f(x) = c\big] = c, \quad \forall c \in [0, 1]. \tag{1}$$

Intuitively, if a network predicts a class "cancer" for an image with a score of 0.9, then a network is calibrated, if the probability that the image actually contains a cancer is 0.9. Expected Calibration Error (ECE) is a common metric used for measuring calibration, and evaluates how well the predicted confidence of a model align with its accuracy. To compute ECE, the confidence interval $[0, 1]$ is divided into a fixed number of bins. Each bin encompasses a range of predicted confidence. ECE value is then computed as [30]:

$$\text{ECE} = \sum_{k=1}^{K} \frac{|B_k|}{m} \left| \text{acc}(B_k) - \text{conf}(B_k) \right|,$$

where $K$ is the number of bins, $B_k$ is the set of samples, $|B_k|$ is the number of samples, $\text{acc}(B_k)$ is the prediction accuracy, and $\text{conf}(B_k)$ is the average predictive confidence in bin $k$. A lower ECE is preferred.

**Zero-Shot Classification with CLIP.** Let $\mathcal{X}$ be the image space, and $\mathcal{Y}$ be the label space. Let $t \in T$ be the text prompt corresponding to an image sample $x \in \mathcal{X}$. CLIP [40] architecture is composed of two distinct encoders: a visual encoder denoted by: $f$, and a text encoder $g$. In the vanilla zero-shot inference with CLIP, we attach a manually designed prompt prefix, $\mathbf{p}$ (e.g., $\mathbf{p}$ = "a photo of a") to each possible class $y_i \in \mathcal{Y} = \{y_1, y_2, \ldots, y_K\}$, generating class-specific textual descriptions $t_i = [\mathbf{p}; y_i]$. Here, $K$ denotes the number of classes. Next, we generate text features $g(t_i)$, and image features $f(x)$ by passing the relevant inputs to the respective encoders. This allows to compute the similarity between text feature, and image features as: $s_i = s\left(f(x), g(t_i = [\mathbf{p}; y_i])\right)$, where $s(\cdot)$ refers to the cosine similarity. The probability of predicting class $y_i$ for the test image $x$ can be computed as:

$$p(y_i | x) = \frac{\exp\big(s\big(g(t_i), f(x)\big)/\tau\big)}{\sum_{j=1}^{K} \exp\big(s\big(g(t_j), f(x)\big)/\tau\big)},$$

where $\tau$ is the temperature for the softmax function. The predicted class is $\widehat{y} = \arg\max_{y_i} p(y_i \mid x)$, with predicted confidence $\widehat{p} = \max_{y_i} p(y_i \mid x)$.

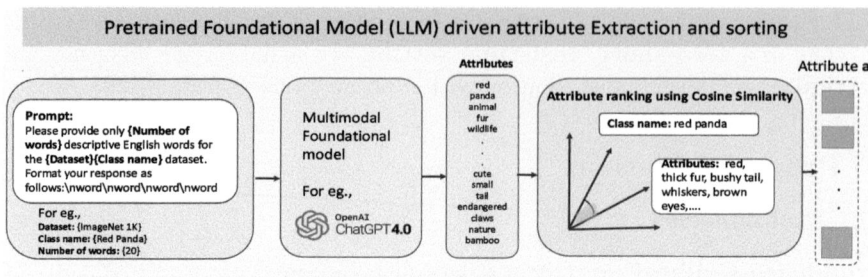

**Fig. 2.** Visual attributes are extracted by prompting a multimodal foundational model as shown in the leftmost block. The extracted attributes (shown in red) are ranked based on their similarity to the Class name in the Dataset (e.g., the top 20 attributes for "red panda" in ImageNet1K dataset). This offline process aids model calibration by identifying relevant attributes. The relevant attributes $a \subset \{a_i\}_{i=1}^{N}$ by identifying the attribute similarity with respect to a class name. Here $a_i$ is the set of attributes returned for a particular class by pretrained LLM.

**Test-time Prompt Tuning.** Several researchers have demonstrated the efficacy of few shot prompt tuning in general [18,21,24,54,56], as well as for CLIP based models [2,11,58,59]. Test-time prompt tuning (Vanilla TPT (VTPT)) introduced by [29] aims to benefit from the rich knowledge of CLIP to boost its generalization in a zero-shot manner. optimizes prompts without requiring labeled data. During inference, $N$ augmented views, $x^j$, of the test sample $x$ are generated. Predictions with entropy values below a predefined threshold are retained, while those with higher entropy are discarded through a confidence selection filter. The entropy of the remaining predictions is then averaged, and this value is used to update the prompts in an unsupervised manner using back-propagation from the following the objective function [29].

$$\mathcal{L}_{\text{TPT}} = -\sum_{i=1}^{K} \bar{p}(y_i) \log \bar{p}(y_i), \quad \text{where } \bar{p}(y_i) = \frac{1}{N}\sum_{j=1}^{N} p(y_i \mid x^j). \quad (2)$$

Here, $\bar{p}(\cdot)$ represents the mean of vector class probabilities produced by the model across different augmented views preserved after the confidence selection filter. Additionally, it has been shown that test-time prompt tuning can be effectively combined with few-shot prompt tuning techniques (during train time), further boosting vanilla VTPT's performance [29].

**Attribute Alignment Using an LLM.** In VLMs, attribute alignment in prompt tuning guides the model to generate outputs matching specific visual or textual attributes. Authors in [39] use LLMs to create descriptive sentences highlighting key features of image categories. An attribute extractor identifies relevant domain-specific information like color or context [31,39,46], and the prompt is adjusted accordingly. This aligned prompt improves inference accuracy by tailor-

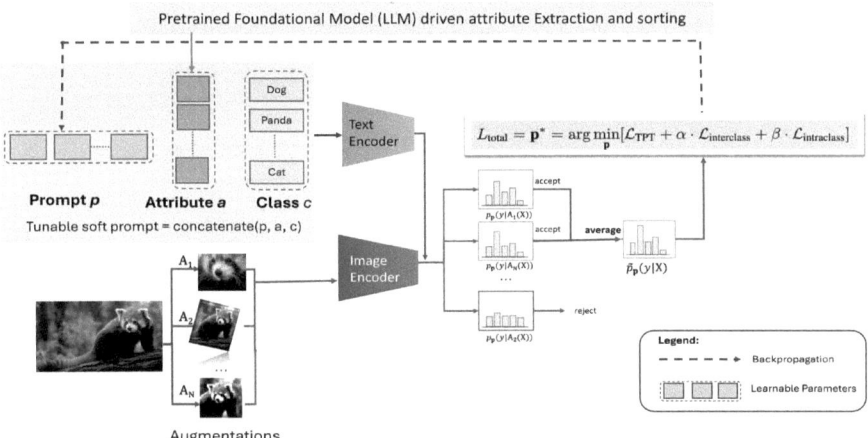

**Fig. 3. Calibration using Test-time Attribute Alignment for zero-shot image classification:** In a typical test time prompt tuning for image classification, a category label is prefixed with a template text, such as "a photo of a" (e.g., "a photo of a red panda") to generate the prompt for tuning. Our approach differs in the following ways: **(a)** Visual attributes are extracted as shown in Fig. 2. **(b)** Our approach takes an image and its augmentations $(A_1, A_2, ...A_N)$ as the input. In contrast to TPT [29], we utilize the attribute vector **a** concatenated with template text **p** and class name $c_i$ to initialize the prompt. We introduce two auxiliary terms in the objective function for test-time calibration via attribute alignment: $L_{\text{interclass}}$ to maximize mean text features between classes and $L_{\text{intraclass}}$ to minimize intra-class variance of textual attributes during prompt tuning to improve alignment between predicted and actual class probabilities, enhancing model calibration. This allows us to tune adaptive prompts on the fly with a single test sample, and without the need for additional training data or annotations. Both visual and text encoders are kept frozen while prompt tuning.

ing the model to the task. Unlike the train-time techniques above, our approach focuses on test-time calibration.

### 3.2 Test Time Calibration via Attribute Alignment

Our proposed attribute-aware prompt tuning procedure comprises of two steps, namely, **(a)** relevant attribute extraction (See Fig. 2); **(b)** enhancing calibration via test-time loss on textual features separation/contraction (See Fig. 3).

Figure 2 depicts the first step, we obtain visual attributes that provide context by prompting LLMs with inquiries about the visual characteristics of specific classes. The LLM input exclusively consists of class names from a dataset. Formally, given any label $y_i \in \mathcal{Y}$, we retrieve its corresponding class name, $c_i$, and a list of attributes $\mathbf{a}_{y_i} = \gamma(y_i)$ where $\gamma$ is any language model like GPT4. The template for prompting LLM has been pre-defined (see Fig. 2). The attributes are subsequently ranked in descending order of relevance by sorting based on the cosine similarity between the class name and attribute names. We then store $M$

**Algorithm 1.** Test-time Calibration via Attribute Alignment (**Inference**)

1: Initialize manual prompt, **p** = "a photo of a"
2: Attribute $a$ and class $= c$
3: **for** each class $i \in \{1, \ldots, K\}$ **do**
4:     **for** each attribute $j \in \{1, \ldots, M\}$ **do**
5:         Form text embedding $t_{ij} = \mathbf{p} \oplus \mathbf{a}_j \oplus c_i$
6:     **end for**
7:     Compute the mean of text embeddings for each class $\bar{t}_{y_i} = \frac{1}{M}\sum_{j=1}^{M} g(t_{ij})$, where $g(\cdot)$ is the CLIP text encoder.
8:     Calculate mean text attribute spread (MTAS) for class $y_i$: $\text{MTAS}(y_i) = \frac{1}{M}\sum_{j=1}^{M} \|g(t_{ij}) - \bar{t}_{y_i}\|_2$
9:     $\mathcal{L}_{\text{intra-class}}(y_i) = \text{MTAS}(y_i)$
10: **end for**
11: Compute the mean of text embeddings for all classes, $\bar{\bar{t}} = \frac{1}{K}\sum_{i=1}^{K} \bar{t}_{y_i}$
12: Calculate Average Text Feature Dispersion (ATFD) [55] across all classes: $\text{ATFD} = \frac{1}{K}\sum_{i=1}^{K} \|\bar{\bar{t}} - \bar{t}_{y_i}\|_2$.
13: $\mathcal{L}_{\text{inter-class}} = -\text{ATFD}$
14: $\mathcal{L}_{\text{total}} = \mathcal{L}_{\text{TPT}} + \alpha.\mathcal{L}_{\text{inter-class}} + \beta.\mathcal{L}_{\text{intra-class}}$.

most relevant attributes in the attribute vector $\mathbf{a}_c$ (we use top 2 attribute in our implementation based on our ablation study). In Fig. 2 we illustrate this with an example of a "red panda" image. The attributes thus generated are appended to the tunable prompt, $\mathbf{p}^1$, along with the class names, such that tunable prompt = concatenate(**p**, **a**, c)) (also see the block diagram corresponding to yellow box in Fig. 3. The full prompt text including the attributes are shown in the json file for Caltech 101 dataset included in the supplementary material. In step (**b**), to enforce effective calibration, we employ a contrastive loss at test-time, and a test-time calibration process as specified in Algorithm 1.

We start with the initialized prompts as described earlier, and then for every class $i$ and attribute $j$, we form the text embedding $\mathbf{p} \oplus a_j \oplus c_i$ and then compute the centroid of these text embeddings. We then minimize the distance between class centroid and textual embeddings corresponding to class (generated using different class attributes). This is referred to as intra-class loss and serves to learn most discriminative features of a class. Similar to C-TPT [55], we also increase the distance between text embeddings of distinct classes and this loss is referred to as inter-class loss. For this, we first take the mean of the embeddings corresponding to different attributes of a specific class. This represents the textual feature corresponding to a class. We then maximise the distance between these representative features of each class so that all classes are well separated. The overall loss used to tune the prompts is the summation of vanilla test time prompt tuning loss $\mathcal{L}_{\text{TPT}}$ [29], and the above two loss terms. Note that the back-propagated gradients only update tokens corresponding to **p**, whereas **a**, and $c_i$ tokens remain frozen, to prevent overfitting on the test sample.

---
[1] Recall **p** is generated from manual template text, such as "a photo of".

## 3.3 Understanding the Role of TCA in Enhancing Calibration

TCA improves representation quality by leveraging contrastive learning principles thus enabling the generation of high-quality, meaningful, and discriminative embeddings that effectively capture semantic similarity. This is achieved through a contrastive test-time loss with inter-class ($\mathcal{L}_{\text{inter-class}}$) and intra-class ($\mathcal{L}_{\text{intra-class}}$) loss terms. The model classifies new samples by aligning them with the closest class embeddings while simultaneously distinguishing them from other classes. We believe this alignment enhances calibration during test-time.

Specifically, recall that calibration aims to align predictive probabilities with the true likelihood of an event. TCA addresses this by aligning similar representations while simultaneously mitigating overconfidence, a key factor contributing to miscalibration. The use of the term (See Algorithm 1 line 12) plays a critical role in this process by explicitly penalizing embedding overlap for dissimilar classes. This discourages the model from assigning overly confident probabilities to incorrect predictions, ensuring that extreme predictive probabilities (close to 0 or 1) are only assigned when the different classes are well-separated. (See Algorithm 1 lines 8 and 9) takes care of aligning similar textual embeddings.

### 3.4 Difference Between TCA and Other Contemporary Techniques

Although prompt tuning through C-TPT [55] introduces enhancements in calibration, it still falls short in capturing nuanced class specific features which are important to disambiguate between classes, and thus necessary for uncertainty calibration. Though the sample specific labels are absent in the test time setting as ours, however we make a observation, and note that even then class specific information is indeed available. We make use of LLMs to generate class attributes and then use the proposed technique to choose most representative attributes. In another big difference, we choose not to update these attribute features. In C-TPT, firstly the text prompt initialization is same for all the classes, and then all of them get updated updated by the test-time loss, leading to overfitting on the sample, and less than ideal calibration. In our case, the frozen attribute based features provide adequate grounding and prevent overfitting, whereas other learnable prompts allow to adapt to the particular sample, thus leading to better calibration through proposed TCA over the current state-of-the-art, C-TPT. Our approach also differs from that of TPT [29], as they do not incorporate attribute auxiliary information from LLMs, nor do they explicitly optimize for calibration. As a result, their method exhibits sub-optimal calibration performance.

## 4 Experiments

This section outlines the benchmarks for assessing our method and the experimental results. Consistent with previous research on the prompt tuning of vision-language models [2,29,58,59], our evaluation is centered on two primary aspects:

**Table 1. Fine-Grained Classification.** Results for CLIP-RN50 and CLIP-ViT-B/16 are reported, providing the **Accuracy** (↑) and **ECE** (↓) metrics for different experimental configuration (please see main test for configuration details). The values highlighted in **bold** indicate the lowest ECE achieved following test-time prompt tuning and underline is the second best. **Note:** The full table, which includes comparisons with other contemporary methods, can be found in the supplementary material due to space limitations in the main paper - we ablate TCA loss with promptAlign [44] and DiffTPT [8] to show gains on top of contemporary methods PromptAlign (NeurIPS'24) and DiffTPT (ICCV'23)

| Method | Metric | ImageNet | Caltech | Pets | Cars | Flower | Food101 | Aircraft | SUN397 | DTD | EuroSAT | UCF101 | Average |
|---|---|---|---|---|---|---|---|---|---|---|---|---|---|
| CLIP-RN50$_{HardPrompt}$ | Acc. | 58.1 | 85.8 | 83.8 | 55.7 | 61 | 74 | 15.6 | 58.6 | 40 | 23.7 | 58.4 | 55.9 |
| | ECE | 3.83 | 4.33 | 5.91 | 4.7 | 3.19 | 3.11 | 6.45 | 3.54 | 9.91 | 15.4 | 3.05 | 5.61 |
| +TPT$_{HardPrompt}$ | Acc. | 60.7 | 87 | 84.5 | 58 | 62.5 | 74.9 | 17 | 61.1 | 41.5 | 28.3 | 59.5 | 57.7 |
| | ECE | 11.4 | 5.04 | 3.65 | 3.76 | 13.4 | 5.25 | 16.1 | 9.24 | 25.7 | 22.5 | 12.4 | 11.7 |
| +TPT$_{HardPrompt}$+C-TPT | Acc. | 60.2 | 86.9 | 84.1 | 56.5 | 65.2 | 74.7 | 17 | 61 | 42.2 | 27.8 | 59.7 | 57.8 |
| | ECE | 3.01 | 2.07 | 2.77 | 1.94 | 4.14 | 1.86 | 10.7 | 2.93 | 19.8 | 15.1 | 3.83 | 6.2 |
| +TPT$_{HardPrompt}$+TCA (2 Attribute) | Acc. | 58.72 | 86.69 | 86.21 | 55.95 | 64.47 | 75.38 | 17.04 | 60.02 | 39.59 | 31.32 | 61.04 | 57.85 |
| | ECE | 1.76 | 1.79 | 5.43 | 3.35 | 3.7 | 2.45 | 4.48 | 4.32 | 8.16 | 5.5 | 4.33 | 04.11 |
| +TPT$_{Ensemble}$ | Acc. | 61.1 | 87.4 | 83.2 | 59.2 | 61.4 | 76.2 | 17.9 | 62 | 42.8 | 28.4 | 60.2 | 58.2 |
| | ECE | 11.2 | 4.29 | 4.79 | 3.08 | 14.1 | 5.27 | 14.6 | 7.68 | 22.2 | 18.9 | 11.1 | 10.7 |
| +TPT$_{Ensemble}$+C-TPT | Acc. | 61.2 | 87.4 | 84 | 57.3 | 65.3 | 76 | 17.5 | 62.1 | 43.1 | 29.4 | 60.7 | 58.5 |
| | ECE | 4.13 | 2.15 | 2.71 | 1.68 | 3.6 | 1.47 | 10.9 | 2.96 | 15.7 | 8.7 | 3.27 | 5.2 |
| +TPT$_{Ensemble}$+TCA (2 Attributes) | Acc. | 68.1 | 93.26 | 90.13 | 65.94 | 68.9 | 84.23 | 25.38 | 65.84 | 43.91 | 47.17 | 67.72 | 65.50 |
| | ECE | 1.88 | 3.09 | 4.38 | 3.93 | 3.57 | 1.91 | 3.36 | 6.02 | 4.36 | 9.36 | 2.71 | 4.05 |
| CLIP-ViT-B/16$_{HardPrompt}$ | Acc. | 66.7 | 92.9 | 88 | 65.3 | 67.3 | 83.6 | 23.9 | 62.5 | 44.3 | 41.3 | 65 | 63.7 |
| | ECE | 2.12 | 5.5 | 4.37 | 4.25 | 3 | 2.39 | 5.11 | 2.53 | 8.5 | 7.4 | 3.59 | 4.43 |
| +TPT$_{HardPrompt}$ | Acc. | 69 | 93.8 | 87.1 | 66.3 | 69 | 84.7 | 23.4 | 65.5 | 46.7 | 42.4 | 67.3 | 65 |
| | ECE | 10.6 | 4.51 | 5.77 | 5.16 | 13.5 | 3.98 | 16.8 | 11.3 | 21.2 | 21.5 | 13 | 11.6 |
| +TPT$_{HardPrompt}$+C-TPT | Acc. | 68.5 | 93.6 | 88.2 | 65.8 | 69.8 | 83.7 | 24 | 64.8 | 46 | 43.2 | 65.7 | 64.8 |
| | ECE | 3.15 | 4.24 | 1.9 | 1.59 | 5.04 | 3.43 | 4.36 | 5.04 | 11.9 | 13.2 | 2.54 | 5.13 |
| +TPT$_{HardPrompt}$+TCA (2 Attribute) | Acc. | 67.37 | 92.86 | 90.51 | 65.92 | 69.18 | 69.18 | 25.32 | 65.5 | 44.73 | 45.58 | 66.9 | 63.91 |
| | ECE | 2.27 | 3.01 | 6.3 | 7.85 | 3.67 | 5.28 | 3.6 | 7.17 | 5.48 | 8.37 | 2.82 | 5.07 |
| CLIP-ViT-B/16$_{Ensemble}$ | Acc. | 68.2 | 93.4 | 86.3 | 65.4 | 65.7 | 85.2 | V23.5 | 64 | 45.6 | 43 | 66.1 | 64.2 |
| | ECE | 3.7 | 6.16 | 4.88 | 7.09 | 6.01 | 3.78 | 4.56 | 4.01 | 13.8 | 6.01 | 4.05 | 5.82 |
| +TPT$_{Ensemble}$ | Acc. | 69.6 | 94.1 | 86.1 | 67.1 | 67.6 | 85.1 | 24.4 | 66.5 | 47.2 | 44 | 68.5 | 65.5 |
| | ECE | 9.82 | 4.48 | 5.72 | 4 | 13.9 | 4.27 | 14.6 | 9.01 | 18.6 | 14.1 | 10.5 | 9.91 |
| +TPT$_{Ensemble}$+C-TPT | Acc. | 69.3 | 94.1 | 87.4 | 66.7 | 69.9 | 84.5 | 23.9 | 66 | 46.8 | 45.8 | 66.7 | 65.8 |
| | ECE | 4.48 | 3.14 | 1.54 | 1.84 | 5.77 | 2.38 | 6.4 | 3.09 | 13.7 | 5.49 | 3.04 | 4.62 |
| +TPT$_{Ensemble}$+TCA 2 attributes | Acc. | 68.1 | 93.26 | 90.13 | 65.94 | 68.9 | 84.23 | 25.38 | 65.84 | 43.91 | 47.17 | 67.72 | 65.5 |
| | ECE | 1.88 | 3.09 | 4.38 | 3.93 | 3.57 | 1.91 | 3.36 | 6.02 | 4.36 | 9.36 | 2.71 | 4.05 |

(1) a range of fine-grained classifications and (2) the natural distribution shift. **Note:** In particular, given our objective to enhance calibration in the context of test-time prompt tuning, our experimental framework emphasizes prompt optimization in the absence of labeled training data.

**Datasets.** For fine-grained classification, we utilize a diverse set of datasets, including ImageNet [6], Caltech101 [7], OxfordPets [35], StanfordCars [22], Flowers102 [31], Food101 [1], FGVCAircraft [28], SUN397 [51], UCF101 [45], DTD [4], and EuroSAT [15]. For the out-of-distribution (OOD) generalization task, we define ImageNet [6] as the in-distribution (source) dataset and extend evaluation to four OOD variants: ImageNetV2 [42], ImageNet-Sketch [49], ImageNet-A [17], and ImageNet-R [16].

**Implementation Details.** We report results in following experimental configurations. The initialized prompt is set to a hard prompt 'a photo of a' (CLIP$_{HardPrompt}$) and the corresponding 4 tokens are optimized based on a single test image using TPT (TPT$_{HardPrompt}$) or jointly using TPT and our proposed technique TCA (TPT$_{HardPrompt}$+TCA). We also include an ensemble setting where we average the logits from 4 different hard-prompt initialization using 'a photo of a', 'a photo of the', 'a picture of a', 'a picture of the' (CLIP$_{Ensemble}$). Similarly, we optimize using TPT as well (TPT$_{Ensemble}$), or jointly using TPT and TCA (TPT$_{Ensemble}$+TCA) on each of the hard-prompt initialization and average the resulting logits. We have tried to use 1, 2, and 3 attribute initialization. **Hyperparameters $\alpha$ and $\beta$:** We employ a test-time prompt tuning strategy, which does not allow access to data for hyperparameter tuning. We perform a grid search over $\alpha$ and $\beta$ to balance the calibration loss for the least ECE using Caltech 101 dataset and apply the same values for 11 datasets following a setup similar to C-TPT [55]. We obtain $(\alpha, \beta)$ as $(10, 35)$, respectively. Using 2 attributes gave the best ECE values on majority of the datasets for finegrained classification. For Natural distribution shifts, we obtained, $(\alpha, \beta)$ as $(45, 15)$. For TPT [29], we optimize the prompt in one step using the AdamW optimizer with a learning rate of 0.005. Our method runs on a single NVIDIA Tesla V100 GPU with 32 GB of memory, except for the ImageNet, ImageNet-A, and ImageNet V2 datasets, which use two GPUs for evaluation.

### 4.1 Comparison on Fine Grained Classification

For the fine-grained classification task, we compare contemporary methods against hard prompt and benchmark approaches, such as TPT [29] and C-TPT [55]. Table 1 summarizes the results: accuracy and ECE values. Our evaluation includes multiple CLIP architectures, specifically CLIP RN-50 and ViT-B/16. The results show that our method significantly outperforms the hard prompt configuration. When comparing the average performance of C-TPT across all 11 datasets, our method achieves a similar average predictive accuracy while notably reducing the average ECE. For CLIP RN-50, the ECE decreases from 5.6 to 4.11. Similarly, for ViT-B/16, the ECE is reduced from 5.82 to 4.05.

### 4.2 Robustness to Natural Distribution Shifts

We follow the setting in Radford et al.[40] and evaluate model's robustness to natural distribution shifts on 4 ImageNet Variants which have been considered as OOD for ImageNet in previous works. We report the results in Table 2. The table shows that we outperform contemporary methods (TPT, and C-TPT) in terms of ECE on 3 out of 4 datasets.

### 4.3 Ablation Study

We investigate the factors contributing to calibration— whether it is driven by the inclusion of attributes or by the choice of loss function. To examine this, we conducted an experiment under two conditions. In the first condition, we incorporate attributes into the prompts and evaluate the method using the TPT loss function. In the second, we again incorporate attributes into the prompts but evaluate using the combined TPT +TCA loss function on 3 datasets.

**Relative Contribution of Attribute Initialization and Proposed Loss.** To better understand the contribution we conduct the ablation experiments on DTD dataset using ResNet50 feature extractor and report (Acc $\uparrow$, ECE $\downarrow$). We

**Table 2. Natural Distribution Shifts.** Results for CLIP-RN50 and CLIP-ViT-B/16 are reported, providing the **Acc.** (↑) and **ECE** (↓) metrics for different experimental configurations (please refer to the main text for details of configurations). Dataset abbreviations: ImageNet-V2 (IN-V2), ImageNet-A (IN-A), ImageNet-R (IN-R), and ImageNet-Sketch (IN-S). Values highlighted in **bold** indicate the lowest ECE achieved after test-time prompt tuning.

| Methods | Metric | IN-A | IN-V2 | IN-R | IN-S | Avg. |
|---|---|---|---|---|---|---|
| CLIP-RN50$_{HardPrompt}$ | Acc. | 21.7 | 51.4 | 56 | 33.3 | 40.6 |
|  | ECE | 21.3 | 3.33 | 2.07 | 3.15 | 7.46 |
| +TPT$_{HardPrompt}$ | Acc. | 25.2 | 54.6 | 58.9 | 35.1 | 43.5 |
|  | ECE | 31.0 | 13.1 | 9.18 | 13.7 | 16.7 |
| +TPT$_{HardPrompt}$+C-TPT | Acc. | 23.4 | 54.7 | 58 | 35.1 | 42.8 |
|  | ECE | 25.4 | 8.58 | 4.57 | 9.7 | 12.1 |
| **+TPT$_{HardPrompt}$+TCA (2 Attributes)** | Acc. | 20.77 | 51.74 | 54.83 | 32.83 | 40.04 |
|  | ECE | **22.53** | **4.39** | **1.25** | **6.22** | **8.59** |
| CLIP-RN50_Ensemble | Acc. | 22.7 | 52.5 | 57.9 | 34.7 | 42 |
|  | ECE | 17 | 2.68 | 5.64 | 10.9 | 9.06 |
| +TPT$_{Ensemble}$ | Acc. | 26.9 | 55 | 60.4 | 35.6 | 44.5 |
|  | ECE | 29.1 | 12.7 | 7.5 | 14 | 15.8 |
| +TPT$_{Ensemble}$+C-TPT | Acc. | 25.6 | 54.8 | 59.7 | 35.7 | 44 |
|  | ECE | 27 | 9.84 | 5.17 | 12.2 | 13.6 |
| **+TPT$_{Ensemble}$+TCA (2 Attributes)** | Acc. | 21.12 | 51.8 | 55.57 | 33.11 | 40.4 |
|  | ECE | **22.99** | **3.69** | **0.94** | **5.37** | **8.24** |
| CLIP-ViT-B/16$_{HardPrompt}$ | Acc. | 47.8 | 60.8 | 74 | 46.1 | 57.2 |
|  | ECE | 8.61 | 3.01 | 3.58 | 4.95 | 5.04 |
| +TPT$_{HardPrompt}$ | Acc. | 52.6 | 63 | 76.7 | 47.5 | 59.9 |
|  | ECE | 16.4 | 11.1 | 4.36 | 16.1 | 12 |
| +TPT$_{HardPrompt}$+C-TPT | Acc. | 51.6 | 62.7 | 76 | 47.9 | 59.6 |
|  | ECE | **8.16** | 6.23 | **1.54** | **7.35** | **5.82** |
| **+TPT$_{HardPrompt}$+TCA (2 Attributes)** | Acc. | 46.95 | 59.94 | 72.78 | 45.1 | 56.19 |
|  | ECE | 8.59 | **4.95** | 5.1 | 8.62 | 6.81 |
| CLIP-ViT-B/16$_{Ensemble}$ | Acc. | 50.9 | 62 | 74.5 | 46 | 58.4 |
|  | ECE | 8.85 | 3.01 | 2.85 | 9.7 | 6.1 |
| +TPT$_{Ensemble}$ | Acc. | 54.2 | 63.9 | 78.2 | 48.5 | 61.2 |
|  | ECE | 13.5 | 11.2 | 3.64 | 15.3 | 10.9 |
| +TPT$_{Ensemble}$+C-TPT | Acc. | 52.9 | 63.4 | 78 | 48.5 | 60.7 |
|  | ECE | 10.9 | 8.38 | **1.4** | 12.6 | 8.32 |
| **+TPT$_{Ensemble}$+TCA (2 attributes)** | Acc. | 47.36 | 60.85 | 72.74 | 45.72 | 56.66 |
|  | ECE | **5.21** | **1.81** | 3.42 | **4.81** | **3.81** |

have 3 variants: (a) +TPT$_{HardPrompt}$ (41.5, 25.7), (b) +TPT$_{HardPrompt}$+ initialization with 2 attributes (40.96, 20.45), (c) +TPT$_{HardPrompt}$ + initialization with 2 attributes + proposed TCA loss (42.79, 5.59). The key observations with ablation are as follows: **(1.) Attribute Initialization:** When initialized with 2 attributes, there was a 20.6% reduction in ECE compared to the hard prompt model; **(2.) TCA Loss:** Introduction of the TCA loss resulted in a 3.65× reduction in ECE, bringing ECE down from 25.7 to 5.59, significantly improving the model's calibration. **(3.) Combined Effect of Both:** When both attribute initialization and TCA loss were used together, the ECE reduction was even more pronounced, with an overall 4.59× reduction in ECE, yielding the lowest ECE

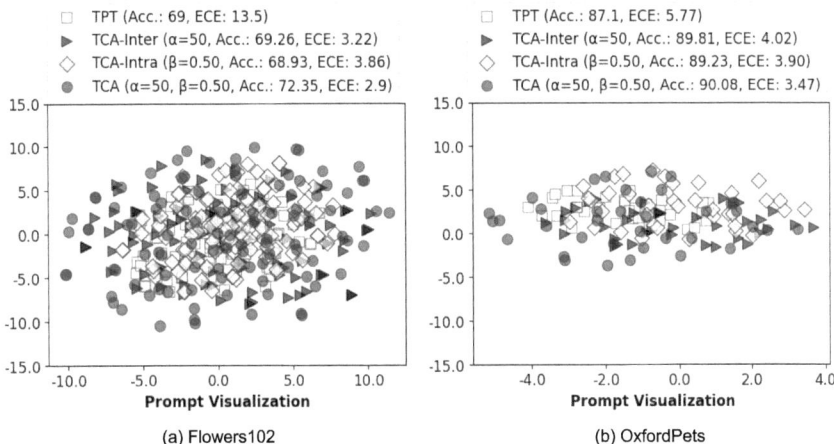

**Fig. 4.** The t-SNE plot shows Class-specific Text Embeddings on tuned prompts. We conduct ablation on each term of $L_{\text{total}} = \mathbf{p}^* = \arg\min_{\mathbf{p}}[\mathcal{L}_{\text{TPT}} + \alpha.\mathcal{L}_{\text{inter-class}} + \beta.\mathcal{L}_{\text{intra-class}}]$ to understand its relative contribution empirically. In (a) and (b), notice that incorporating all three terms in $L_{\text{total}}$ results in the lowest ECE and highest feature dispersion or spread.

value of 5.59 and maximum accuracy of 42.79. Thus, both proposed contributions, attribute initialization strategy, as well as the proposed loss play significant roles in improving model calibration. The proposed loss is particularly effective in reducing ECE, and combining it with attribute initialization leads to the most significant improvement in both accuracy and calibration. Refer to Fig. 4, which illustrates the comparison of feature dispersion, found to be inversely correlated with ECE. When both inter- and intra-loss terms are utilized, we observe the maximum Class-specific Text Embedding dispersion and the lowest ECE, consistent with the findings of [55]. See suppl. for details on how the plot was obtained.

### 4.4 Discussion

**Confidence Calibration and TCA:** Here, we provide an intuitive understanding of our proposed loss function, formulated as: $L_{\text{total}} = \mathbf{p}^* = \arg\min_{\mathbf{p}}[\mathcal{L}_{\text{TPT}} + \alpha.\mathcal{L}_{\text{inter-class}} + \beta.\mathcal{L}_{\text{intra-class}}]$. To assess the significance of each component within this formulation, we conduct a systematic ablation study. This includes t-SNE visualizations, which facilitate the analysis of the impact of individual loss terms on feature separability and clustering. Additionally, we compare our approach against state-of-the-art test-time calibration methods in the zero-shot setting, thereby demonstrating its effectiveness and robustness.

**Need for Intra-inter Class Losses:** TCA improves representation quality by leveraging contrastive principles thus enabling the generation of high-quality, discriminative embeddings that effectively capture semantic similarity/dissimilarity. TCA addresses calibration by aligning similar classes, and the use of the dispersion term explicitly penalizes the embedding overlap for dissimilar classes. This discourages the model from assigning overly confident probabilities to incorrect predictions, ensuring that extreme predictive probabilities (near 0 or 1) are only assigned when the different classes are well-separated. Figure 4 shows an ablation over individual loss terms' impact on calibration: Using both $\mathcal{L}_{\text{intra}}$ and $\mathcal{L}_{\text{inter}}$ in $\mathcal{L}_{\text{total}}$ leads to the lowest ECE and greatest text feature dispersion.

**Conceptual Differences Between TCA Loss and Contemporaries:** The recent contemporary method, DAPT [3] targets improved accuracy in few-shot settings, whereas we focus on zero-shot calibration. DAPT uses exponential inter- and intra-dispersion on both vision and text embeddings, while our method relies on $L_2$ norm distance between the test sample and mean text embeddings. $L_2$ norm is easier to interpret as it measures the Euclidean distance between embeddings, making it more intuitive and transparent, especially when comparing distances in high-dimensional spaces, but less sensitive to outliers and computationally efficient. [25] facilitates calibration using temperature scaling on the ImageNet validation set. However, when applying TS with TCA loss on the Caltech 101 dataset (ViT B-16), we observe a degradation in (Accuracy,ECE) from 93.02, 12.92 with TS vs. 92.45, 3.89 without TS, suggesting a decrease in performance with TS. [50] uses Distribution aware calibration for fine-tuned VLM calibration, while our focus is on zero-shot settings like C-TPT [55]. Finally, [33] involves few-shot finetuning, making it not directly comparable to our approach.

**Vizualisation of Class-Specific Text Embeddings on Tuned Prompts.** Please refer to the supplemental materials for t-SNE plots across multiple datasets, which illustrate the lower ECE and the highest dispersion indicating better class separability of TCA relative to contemporaneous methods.

**Supplementary Material.** details the factors behind TCA's superior performance, datasets, metrics, feature extractor, experimental setup, hyperparameters, and t-SNE comparisons with PromptAlign [44], DiffTPT [8].

## 5 Conclusions and Future Directions

In this work, we introduced two key insights to enhance the effectiveness of test time prompt tuning. First, we demonstrated that attribute-aware prompting, wherein relevant visual attributes are appended to the prompts. This allows the model to better align its visual embeddings with discriminative features, resulting in improved predictive uncertainty handling and class-separation. Second, we proposed a regularization loss that encourages the model to minimize intra-class text feature dispersion while maximizing inter-class dispersion, inspired by contrastive learning principles. This ensures that the learned prompts do not overfit to individual samples, even when limited data is available.

This work opens up new possibilities for leveraging unsupervised attribute information to improve model performance in low-data or test-time settings, paving the way for more robust and adaptable models in real-world applications. In future, it would be interesting to study the effectiveness on other VLM architectures apart from CLIP such as Flamingo.

# References

1. Bossard, L., Guillaumin, M., Gool, L.: Food-101 – mining discriminative components with random forests. In: Fleet, D., Pajdla, T., Schiele, B., Tuytelaars, T. (eds.) ECCV 2014. LNCS, vol. 8694, pp. 446–461. Springer, Cham (2014). https://doi.org/10.1007/978-3-319-10599-4_29
2. Chen, G., Yao, W., Song, X., Li, X., Rao, Y., Zhang, K.: PLOT: prompt learning with optimal transport for vision-language models. In: ICLR (2023)
3. Cho, E., Kim, J., Kim, H.J.: Distribution-aware prompt tuning for vision-language models. In: Proceedings of the IEEE/CVF ICCV, pp. 22004–22013 (2023)
4. Cimpoi, M., Maji, S., Kokkinos, I., S., Vedaldi, A.: Describing textures in the wild. In: CVPR, pp. 3606–3613 (2014)
5. Dawid, A.P.: The well-calibrated Bayesian. J. Am. Stat. Assoc. (1982)
6. Deng, J., Dong, W., Socher, R., Li, L., Li, K., Fei-Fei, L.: Imagenet: a large-scale hierarchical image database. In: CVPR, pp. 248–255 (2009)
7. Fei-Fei, L., Fergus, R., Perona, P.: Learning generative visual models from few training examples: an incremental Bayesian approach tested on 101 object categories. In: CVPR Workshops, p. 178 (2004)
8. Feng, C.M., Yu, K., Liu, Y., Khan, S., Zuo, W.: Diverse data augmentation with diffusions for effective test-time prompt tuning. ICCV (2023)
9. Ghosal, S., Hebbalaguppe, R., Manocha, D.: Better features, better calibration: a simple fix for overconfident networks. In: Joint European Conference on Machine Learning and Knowledge Discovery in Databases. Springer (2025)
10. Guo, C., Pleiss, G., Sun, Y., Weinberger, K.Q.: On calibration of modern neural networks. In: ICML, vol. 70, pp. 1321–1330 (2017)
11. Hantao Yao, Rui Zhang, C.X.: Visual-language prompt tuning with knowledge-guided context optimization. In: CVPR (2023)
12. Hebbalaguppe, R., Baranwal, M., Anand, K., Arora, C.: Calibration transfer via knowledge distillation. In: Proceedings of the Asian Conference on Computer Vision, pp. 513–530 (2024)
13. Hebbalaguppe, R., Ghosal, S.S., Prakash, J., Khadilkar, H., Arora, C.: A novel data augmentation technique for out-of-distribution sample detection using compounded corruptions. In: Joint European Conference on Machine Learning and Knowledge Discovery in Databases, pp. 529–545. Springer (2022)
14. Hebbalaguppe, R., Prakash, J., Madan, N., Arora, C.: A stitch in time saves nine: a train-time regularizing loss for improved neural network calibration. In: Proceedings of the IEEE/CVF Conference on Computer Vision and Pattern Recognition (CVPR), pp. 16081–16090 (2022)
15. Helber, P., Bischke, B., Dengel, A., Borth, D.: Eurosat: a novel dataset and deep learning benchmark for land use and land cover classification. IEEE J. Sel. Top. Appl. Earth Obs. Remote. Sens. **12**(7), 2217–2226 (2019)
16. Hendrycks, D., et al.: The many faces of robustness: a critical analysis of out-of-distribution generalization. ICCV (2021)
17. Hendrycks, D., Zhao, K., Basart, S., Steinhardt, J., Song, D.: Natural adversarial examples. CVPR (2021)

18. Jia, M., et al.: Visual prompt tuning. In: ECCV, pp. 709–727 (2022)
19. Karmanov, A., Guan, D., Lu, S., El Saddik, A., Xing, E.: Efficient test-time adaptation of vision-language models. In: Proceedings of the IEEE/CVF Conference on Computer Vision and Pattern Recognition, pp. 14162–14171 (2024)
20. Khosla, P., et al.: Supervised contrastive learning. In: NeurIPS, vol. 33, pp. 18661–18673 (2020)
21. Koo, G., Yoon, S., Yoo, C.D.: Wavelet-guided acceleration of text inversion in diffusion-based image editing. arXiv preprint arXiv:2401.09794 (2024)
22. Krause, J., Stark, M., Deng, J., Fei-Fei, L.: 3D object representations for fine-grained categorization. In: IEEE Workshop on 3D Representation and Recognition (3dRR-13) (2013)
23. Kull, M., Perello Nieto, M., Kängsepp, M., Silva Filho, T., Song, H., Flach, P.: Beyond temperature scaling: obtaining well-calibrated multi-class probabilities with dirichlet calibration. In: NeurIPS, vol. 32 (2019)
24. Lester, B., Al-Rfou, R., Constant, N.: The power of scale for parameter-efficient prompt tuning. In: EMNLP, pp. 3045–3059 (2021)
25. LeVine, W., Pikus, B., Raja, P., Gil, F.A.: Enabling calibration in the zero-shot inference of large vision-language models. arXiv preprint arXiv:2303.12748 (2023)
26. Liu, P., Yuan, W., Fu, J., Jiang, Z., Hayashi, H., Neubig, G.: Pre-train, prompt, and predict: a systematic survey of prompting methods in natural language processing. ACM Comput. Surv. **55**(9), 1–35 (2023)
27. Liu, X., et al.: P-tuning V2: prompt tuning can be comparable to fine-tuning universally across scales and tasks (2022)
28. Maji, S., Kannala, J., Rahtu, E., Blaschko, M., Vedaldi, A.: Fine-grained visual classification of aircraft. Technical report (2013)
29. Manli, S., et al.: Test-time prompt tuning for zero-shot generalization in vision-language models. In: NeurIPS (2022)
30. Naeini, M.P., Cooper, G.F., Hauskrecht, M.: Obtaining well calibrated probabilities using Bayesian binning. In: AAAI, pp. 2901–2907 (2015)
31. Nilsback, M., Zisserman, A.: Automated flower classification over a large number of classes. In: ICVGIP, pp. 722–729 (2008)
32. Niu, S., et al.: Efficient test-time model adaptation without forgetting. In: ICLR, vol. 162, pp. 16888–16905 (2022)
33. Oh, C., et al.: Towards calibrated robust fine-tuning of vision-language models. Adv. Neural. Inf. Process. Syst. **37**, 12677–12707 (2024)
34. Park, H., Noh, J., Oh, Y., Baek, D., Ham, B.: ACLS: adaptive and conditional label smoothing for network calibration. In: ICCV, pp. 3936–3945 (2023)
35. Parkhi, O., Vedaldi, A., Zisserman, A., Jawahar, C.V.: Cats and dogs. In: CVPR (2012)
36. Patra, R., Hebbalaguppe, R., Dash, T., Shroff, G., Vig, L.: Calibrating deep neural networks using explicit regularisation and dynamic data pruning. In: Proceedings of the IEEE/CVF Winter Conference on Applications of Computer Vision (WACV), pp. 1541–1549 (2023)
37. Pereyra, G., Tucker, G., Chorowski, J., Kaiser, Ł., Hinton, G.: Regularizing neural networks by penalizing confident output distributions. arXiv preprint arXiv:1701.06548 (2017)
38. Platt, J.C.: Probabilistic outputs for support vector machines and comparisons to regularized likelihood methods. In: Advances in Large Margin Classifiers, pp. 61–74. MIT Press (1999)

39. Pratt, S., Covert, I., Liu, R., Farhadi, A.: What does a platypus look like? Generating customized prompts for zero-shot image classification. In: ICCV, pp. 15691–15701 (2023)
40. Radford, A., et al.: Learning transferable visual models from natural language supervision. In: ICML, pp. 8748–8763 (2021)
41. Rawat, M., Hebbalaguppe, R., Vig, L.: Pnpood: out-of-distribution detection for text classification via plug andplay data augmentation. arXiv preprint arXiv:2111.00506 (2021)
42. Recht, B., Roelofs, R., Schmidt, L., Shankar, V.: Do imagenet classifiers generalize to imagenet? In: ICML, pp. 5389–5400 (2019)
43. S., G., Basu, S., Feizi, S., Manocha, D.: Intcoop: interpretability-aware vision-language prompt tuning. In: EMNLP (2024)
44. Samadh, A.: Align your prompts: test-time prompting with distribution alignment for zero-shot generalization. In: NeurIPS, vol. 36 (2024)
45. Soomro, K., Zamir, A.R., Shah, M.: UCF101: a dataset of 101 human actions classes from videos in the wild. CoRR abs/1212.0402 (2012)
46. Tian, X., Zou, S., Yang, Z., Zhang, J.: Argue: attribute-guided prompt tuning for vision-language models. In: CVPR, pp. 28578–28587 (2024)
47. Tu, W., Deng, W., Campbell, D., Gould, S., Gedeon, T.: An empirical study into what matters for calibrating vision-language models (2024)
48. Wang, D.B., Feng, L., Zhang, M.L.: Rethinking calibration of deep neural networks: Do not be afraid of overconfidence. In: NeurIPS, vol. 34, pp. 11809–11820 (2021)
49. Wang, H., Ge, S., Lipton, Z., Xing, E.P.: Learning robust global representations by penalizing local predictive power. In: NeurIPS (2019)
50. Wang, S., Wang, J., Wang, G., Zhang, B., Zhou, K., Wei, H.: Open-vocabulary calibration for fine-tuned clip. arXiv preprint arXiv:2402.04655 (2024)
51. Xiao, J., Hays, J., Ehinger, K.A., Oliva, A., Torralba, A.: Sun database: large-scale scene recognition from abbey to zoo. In: CVPR, pp. 3485–3492 (2010)
52. Yildirim, N.: Multimodal healthcare AI: identifying and designing clinically relevant vision-language applications for radiology. In: CHI Conference on Human Factors in Computing Systems (2024)
53. Yi, Z., Yilin, Z., Rong, X., Jing, L., Hillming, L.: Vialm: a survey and benchmark of visually impaired assistance with large models. arXiv preprint arXiv:2402.01735 (2024)
54. Yoon, E., Yoon, H.S., Harvill, J., Hasegawa-Johnson, M., Yoo, C.D.: INTapt: information-theoretic adversarial prompt tuning for enhanced non-native speech recognition (2023)
55. Yoon, H.S., Yoon, E., Tee, J.T.J., Hasegawa-Johnson, M.A., Li, Y., Yoo, C.D.: C-TPT: calibrated test-time prompt tuning for vision-language models via text feature dispersion. In: ICLR (2024)
56. Yoon, S., Koo, G., Hong, J.W., Yoo, C.D.: Neutral editing framework for diffusion-based video editing. arXiv preprint arXiv:2312.06708 (2023)
57. Zhang, T., Wang, J., Guo, H., Dai, T., Chen, B., Xia, S.T.: Boostadapter: improving vision-language test-time adaptation via regional bootstrapping. arXiv preprint arXiv:2410.15430 (2024)
58. Zhou, K., Yang, J., Loy, C.C., Liu, Z.: Conditional prompt learning for vision-language models. In: CVPR (2022)
59. Zhou, K., Yang, J., Loy, C.C., Liu, Z.: Learning to prompt for vision-language models. IJCV (2022)

# Leveraging Gradient Information for Out-of-Domain Performance Estimations

Ekaterina Khramtsova[1]([✉]), Mahsa Baktashmotlagh[1], Guido Zuccon[1], Xi Wang[2], and Mathieu Salzmann[3]

[1] The University of Queensland, Brisbane, Australia
{e.khramtsova,m.baktashmotlagh,g.zuccon}@uq.edu.au
[2] Neusoft, Shenyang, China
wxi@neusoft.com
[3] École Polytechnique Fédérale de Lausanne, Lausanne, Switzerland
mathieu.salzmann@epfl.ch

**Abstract.** One of the limitations of applying machine learning methods in real-world scenarios is the existence of a domain shift between the source (i.e., training) and target (i.e., test) datasets, which typically entails a significant performance drop. This is further complicated by the lack of annotated data in the target domain, making it impossible to quantitatively assess the model performance. As such, there is a pressing need for methods able to estimate a model's performance on unlabeled target data. Most of the existing approaches addressing this train a linear performance predictor, taking as input either an activation-based or a performance-based metric. As we will show, however, the accuracy of such predictors strongly depends on the domain shift. Recent research highlights the significance of network weights in understanding model generalizability. The early work of [46] proposes a method to predict out-of-distribution error by comparing the weights of the original model and fine-tuned model on the target data. However, this process is computationally demanding, especially for large models and input sizes. To address this, we propose an efficient approach for assessing a model's performance on target datasets by leveraging the gradients and Hessian of a model as indicators of weight differences. Our approach builds on the idea that lower norms of gradient and Hessian matrices signify a flatter training landscape and better adaptability to new data. Our extensive experiments on standard object recognition benchmarks, using diverse network architectures, demonstrate the benefits of our method, outperforming both activation-based and performance-based baselines by a large margin. It also outperforms [46]'s weight-based approach in efficiency by avoiding parameter updates and effectively estimates out-of-domain performance. Our code is available in the following repository: https://github.com/khramtsova/hessian_performance_estimator/.

**Keywords:** Performance Prediction · Generalisability Estimation

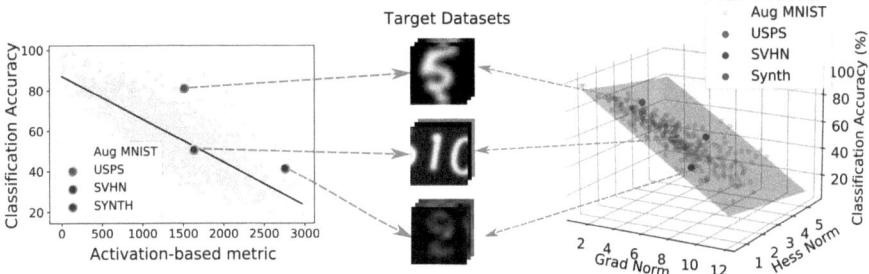

**Fig. 1.** Correlation between classification accuracy and different metrics: Hessian and Gradient norms (right, our method) and Fréchet Insepiton Distance (left, [13]). Note that our method yields a more reliable performance estimator, as evidenced by the points corresponding to the target datasets lying closer to the decision boundary. The light-blue points correspond to sample sets from the meta-dataset.

## 1 Introduction

Being able to estimate how well a trained deep network would generalize to new target, unlabeled datasets would be a key asset in many real-world scenarios, where acquiring labels is too expensive or unfeasible. When the training and target data follow the same distribution, this can easily be achieved by setting aside a validation set from the training data. However, such a performance estimator fails in the presence of a domain shift, i.e., when the target data differs significantly from the source one.

Recent studies [11,13] address this by creating a meta-dataset incorporating multiple variations of the source data obtained by diverse augmentation techniques, such as background change, color variation, and geometric transformations, so as to mimic different domain shifts. Target datasets can then be sampled from this meta-dataset, and their ground-truth performance obtained by evaluating the source-trained network on them. In essence, this provides data to train a linear performance predictor, which in turn can be applied to the real target data.

The aforementioned studies differ in the quantities they use as input to this linear performance predictor. Specifically, Deng et al. [13] rely on the Fréchet distance between the network activations obtained from the source samples and the target ones, whereas the authors of [11] exploit the performance of the source network on the task of rotation prediction. Unfortunately, while the resulting linear predictors perform well within the meta-dataset, their generalization to some real target datasets remains unsatisfactory, depending on the gap between the source and real target data. This is illustrated by the left plot of Fig. 1, where the red point indicating the true performance on USPS lies far from the activation-based linear predictor shown as a black line.

Recent studies show that the network weights provide valuable insights into model uncertainty [31], model complexity [40], model compressibility [2], and in-domain generalization [4,16,35,43]. The early work of [46] in the field of out-of-domain generalization analyzes the extent to which network weights change when fine-tuned on target data with a supervised loss. It confirms that the greater the domain gap between source and target datasets, the more substantial the changes needed in the network to bridge this gap. Building on this concept, [46] proposes predicting out-of-distribution error by fine-tuning the model on the target data using a cross-entropy loss and then calculating the distance between the weights of the original and the fine-tuned models. Despite the more accurate estimation achieved with the proposed weight-based metric in [46], the process of fine-tuning and comparing weights can be computationally intensive and time-consuming, particularly for large models.

To take advantage of the weight-based metric while avoiding its high computational cost, we propose an efficient alternative that captures the key aspects of weight differences without needing to update network parameters. Our method focuses on examining the gradients and the Hessian of the network, acting as a substitute for weight changes. Our approach is based on the intuition that a smaller norm of the gradient and Hessian matrices indicates a flatter landscape of the training objective. This flatness is strongly correlated with better generalization, suggesting that networks with flatter landscapes are more likely to generalize effectively to new data. Our approach avoids the significant complexity, memory, and time demands usually involved in updating network weights. This makes it especially suitable for large models and large batch sizes.

Our results demonstrate that the proposed metric provides more reliable performance estimates than those based on activation and score. Compared to the weight-based approach of [46], our method is not only more efficient because it does not require parameter updates, but it is also effective in bridging the domain gap for estimating out-of-domain performance. This is illustrated in the right plot of Fig. 1, where the points corresponding to the three real target datasets all lie close to the linear predictor. While alternative, more complex measures may also be viable, our work shows that even a basic gradient-based approach surpasses other methods, which we evidence on several benchmark datasets and using different network architectures.

## 2 Related Work

Various methods have been proposed to estimate the performance of a model on an unlabeled dataset under a domain shift. We categorize the existing works into two main groups: Activation-based and performance-based methods.

**Activation-based approaches** aim to find a criteria for performance estimation based on network activations. For example, Garg et al. [18] propose Average Threshold Confidence (ATC) score based on the negative entropy of networks predictions. The authors acknowledge that ATC returns inconsistent estimates on certain types of distribution shifts. Another approach in this category [41] explores various statistics derived from a prediction score to estimate the accuracy on the target domain. Elsahar et al. [15] also provide a similar analysis for NLP tasks. An alternative entropy-based approach was proposed by Guillory et al. [19], who discover a correlation between the classification accuracy and the difference of entropy between the network activations on the source and target data. However, the success of this approach to produce consistent estimations depends on how calibrated the network is.

Chen et al. [6] develop an evaluation framework, Mandoline, that adapts importance weighting to settings with distribution shifts between source and target domains. Their approach leverages prior knowledge about the nature of the shift, which can be a strength when such information is available, though it may limit applicability in fully unsupervised scenarios.

In contrast with the above-mentioned approaches that focus on the network output, Deng et al. [13] analyze feature representations. The authors create augmented source datasets and train a linear regression model to predict accuracy based on the Fréchet distance between source and augmented feature representations. In our experiments, while there is a strong linear correlation between accuracy on the augmented datasets and the Fréchet distance, real target datasets do not consistently follow this pattern, leading to poor accuracy estimates.

**Performance-based approaches** evaluate the classification accuracy of the network using its performance on self-supervised tasks. For instance, Deng et al. [11] propose to learn a correlation between the rotation prediction accuracy and the classification accuracy. The works of [8,26] show that test error can be estimated by training the same network multiple times on the source dataset and measuring the disagreement on the target dataset. Building on this work, Chen et al. [5] learn an ensemble of models to identify misclassified points from the target dataset based on the disagreement between the models, and use self-training to improve this ensemble.

The aforementioned methods require access to the model during training. For example, in the work of Deng et al. [11], the network architecture needs to be upgraded with the second head and trained on both tasks. The works of [5,8,26] require re-training of the source model to find the samples with disagreement. This might be undesirable for a large source dataset where training is time consuming. Note that our approach requires neither architecture alterations nor re-training on the source data.

In this work, we focus on analyzing the network weights and gradients, which was proven to be useful for various in-domain and out-of-domain tasks. For example Nagarajan et al. [35] show that the distance of trained weights from random initialization is implicitly regularized by SGD and has a negative correlation with the proportion of noisy labels in the data. Hu et al. [24] further use the distance of trained weights from random initialization as a regularization method for training with noisy labels. Yu et al. [46] introduce a projection norm and show its correlation with out-of-distribution error.

By contrast, here, we study the relationship between the first and second-order derivative of the network w.r.t an unsupervised loss function, and performance on the target data. Our approach compares favorably to the SOTA accuracy estimation methods. We emphasize that our method requires neither prior knowledge of the nature of the distribution shift, nor target labels.

## 3 Methodology

Let us now introduce our approach to estimating how well a model trained on a source dataset would generalize to a target dataset from a different domain, in the absence of target supervision. Instead of predicting performance from the activation difference between the source and target samples or from the network performance on a different task, we propose to exploit the model's weights perturbations from an unsupervised loss. Specifically, we consider the Gradient Norm and the Hessian Norm, obtained by differentiating the network with an unsupervised loss function calculated on the target dataset. We empirically show that these metrics display a strong linear correlation with the model performance on the target task. We therefore learn this correlation with a linear regressor trained on augmented versions of the source data, which we use to predict the target data performance.

### 3.1 Problem Definition

Let $\mathcal{P}^S$ and $\mathcal{Q}^T$ be the probability distributions of the source and target domains, respectively, $\mathcal{D}_S : \{x_s, y_s\}^{n_s} \sim \mathcal{P}^S$ be a labeled source dataset with $n_s$ samples, and $\mathcal{D}_T : \{x_t\}^{n_t} \sim \mathcal{Q}^T$ be an unlabeled target dataset with $n_t$ samples. A model $f_\theta$ is trained on the source dataset $\mathcal{D}_S$ to predict a correct label: $f_\theta : x_i \to \hat{y}_i; x_i \sim \mathcal{D}^S$. Our goal then is to estimate the accuracy of the trained model $f_\theta$ on the unlabeled target dataset $\mathcal{D}_T$.

### 3.2 Gradient-Based Performance Estimation

In this paper, we propose predicting model performance on target data by examining the norm of the first and second-order derivatives of the unsupervised loss function with respect to the target dataset. This is motivated by the intuition that large domain gaps would lead to larger gradient variations and also to lower accuracy than small domain gaps. Below, we first introduce the intuition behind analysing the weight dynamics for estimating the performance on unlabeled target dataset; we then propose an approach for approximating the the degree of the network changes via the gradient. Finally, we show how the proposed approximating can be used to build an effective and efficient accuracy predictor.

Due to the high-dimensionality of the network weight space, comparing the network weights and gradients is non-trivial and may suffer from the curse of dimensionality. The impact of backpropagation is not equally distributed across the network, with the last layers typically being affected more than the first ones [29]. Furthermore, computing the second-order derivative is both resource-intensive and time-consuming, making it less suitable for deep networks. Therefore, we limit our gradient calculations to the classifier part of the network, which includes only the final fully connected layer.

*From Magnitude of Network Updates to Difference Between Weights.* In this section, we provide a detailed analysis of weight updates from the perspective of gradients.

Consider a network with parameters $\theta$ optimized by minimizing an unsupervised entropy loss $L$, using a learning rate $\alpha$. We will use the following notations:

- $\theta^{(k)}$ - the weights of the network at step $k$,
- $g_i^{(k)} = \nabla L^{(i)}(\theta^{(k)})$ - the gradient of the loss $L$ at step $i$ w.r.t. $\theta^{(k)}$,
- $H_i^{(k)} = \nabla_\theta^2 L^{(i)}(\theta^{(k)})$ - the Hessian at step $i$ w.r.t. $\theta^{(k)}$.

The aim of this section is to express the dynamics of the network updates after k steps of fine-tuning (from $\theta^{(0)}$ to $\theta^{(k)}$) using the gradients and Hessians computed at $\theta^{(0)}$. This will allow us to assess the model's generalizability by calculating the derivatives only once.

Let us consider the change in the weights after one step of gradient descent. Naturally, it corresponds to the gradient at step 0:

$$\theta^{(0)} - \theta^{(1)} = \alpha g_0^{(0)} \tag{1}$$

After the second gradient descent step, the distance between the weights has an additional gradient $g_1^{(1)}$, calculated at step 1 w.r.t. the updated weights $\theta^{(1)}$:

$$\theta^{(0)} - \theta^{(2)} = \alpha g_0^{(0)} + \alpha g_1^{(1)} \tag{2}$$

Following the works of [37] and [42], we can approximate $g_1^{(1)}$ using First-order Taylor series as follows:

$$g_1^{(1)} = g_0^{(1)} - \alpha H_0^{(1)} g_0^{(0)} + \mathcal{O}(\alpha^2). \tag{3}$$

This allows us to approximate the gradients at $\theta^{(1)}$ in terms of the gradients and Hessians at $\theta^{(0)}$. This approximation is due to the fact that we are not updating the network, which makes $\theta^{(1)}$ unknown at step 1. Plugging 3 back into 2:

$$\theta^{(0)} - \theta^{(2)} = \alpha g_0^{(0)} + \alpha(g_0^{(1)} - \alpha H_0^{(1)} g_0^{(0)}) = \alpha(g_0^{(0)} + g_0^{(1)}) - \alpha^2 H_0^{(1)} g_0^{(0)} + \mathcal{O}(\alpha^3) \tag{4}$$

Finally, after $k$ steps of gradient descent, the gradient is:

$$g_k^{(k)} = g_0^{(k)} - \alpha H_0^{(k)} \sum_{i=0}^{k-1} g_i^{(i)} + \mathcal{O}(\alpha^2) \tag{5}$$

The weight difference after $k$ steps of fine-tuning is:

$$\theta^{(0)} - \theta^{(k)} = \alpha \sum_{i=0}^{k-1} g_i^{(i)} = \alpha \sum_{s=0}^{k-1} g_0^{(s)} - \alpha^2 \sum_{i=1}^{k-1} H_0^{(i)} \sum_{j=0}^{i-1} g_0^{(j)} + \mathcal{O}(\alpha^3) \tag{6}$$

The norm of the weight difference $||\theta^{(0)} - \theta^{(k)}||$ has been shown to correlate with model accuracy [46]. However, our approach diverges from this weight-based approximation, opting instead to work directly with gradients. By taking a norm of 6, we obtain:

$$||\theta^{(0)} - \theta^{(k)}|| \leq \alpha || \sum_{s=0}^{k-1} g_0^{(s)} || + \alpha^2 || \sum_{i=1}^{k-1} H_0^{(i)} || \cdot || \sum_{j=0}^{i-1} g_0^{(j)} || \quad (7)$$

In Eq. 7, two main components have emerged. We will now explain how these two components of the model updates, namely the magnitude and the curvature of the loss function, are related to model generalizability.

- *Magnitude of the network updates:* The magnitude of the network updates required to optimize an unsupervised loss function is encapsulated in its average gradient w.r.t. $\theta^{(0)}$, i.e., $|| \sum_{s=0}^{k-1} g_0^{(s)} ||$. The gradient's magnitude reflects the flatness of the loss function and can be regarded as an indicator of convergence [47].
- *Curvature of the loss surface.* In addition to evaluating the magnitude of network updates, we can assess the sensitivity of the loss function to changes in model parameters by examining the Hessian, which provides insights into the curvature of the loss surface. Large Hessian norm, $|| \sum_{i=1}^{k-1} H_0^{(i)} ||$, implies that slight modifications in the parameters $\theta$ might lead to substantial changes in loss, indicating a sharp minimum [27]. On the other hand, a Hessian with small values implies that the parameters reside in a flatter region.

*Accuracy Predictor.* The right-hand side plot in Fig. 1, corroborated by our experimental results, reveals a linear relationship between the newly proposed gradient-based metrics and the accuracy achieved on a target dataset. This suggests that the accuracy for a given target dataset can be effectively predicted using a linear regression model. Specifically, we compute both the norm of the cumulative Hessians and the norm of the cumulative gradients across the target dataset. These computed norms serve as inputs to the linear regression model, where $w_0$, $w_1$, and $w_2$ represent the model's learnable parameters.

To train these parameters, we follow [13] and create a meta-dataset consisting of a collection of datasets obtained by performing different augmentations of the source data. Specifically, a sample set $\hat{\mathcal{D}}_s^j$ in the meta-dataset is built as follows. First, a set of $m$ possible transformations $T = \{T_1, T_2, .., T_m\}$, corresponding to background change, geometric transformations, or color variations, is created. Then, $l$ images are randomly selected from the validation set $\{v_s\}$ of the source data, leading to a set $\{v_s^j\}^l \subset \{v_s\}$. A random selection of $t$ transformations $\tau = \{T_i\}_{i=1}^t$ is then applied to these images, resulting in the sample set $\hat{\mathcal{D}}_s^j = \tau[v_s^j]$. By repeating this process $k$ times, we create a collection of sample sets, which form the meta-dataset.

As each sample set originally comes from the source data, we can compute its true performance under model $f_\theta$. Similarly, we can calculate the model's gradients on each sample set using the entropy loss function. Altogether, this gives us supervised data, consisting of pairs of gradients and true accuracy, from which we can learn the weights $w_0$, $w_1$ and $w_2$ of the linear regressor.

### 3.3 Accuracy Prediction on Target Data

We can use the trained linear regressor to estimate the network performance on any unlabeled target dataset. Specifically, given a target dataset $\mathcal{D}_T : \{x_t\}^{n_t}$, we first split it into $k$ subsets of size $l$,

$$\mathcal{D}_t = \{\mathcal{D}_t^1, \mathcal{D}_t^2, ..., \mathcal{D}_t^k\}, \quad k = \left\lfloor \frac{n_t}{l} \right\rfloor,$$

so that the size of each subset matches the size of the validation sample sets. This procedure standardizes gradient scales across varying dataset sizes.

Then, we calculate the gradient $g$ and the Hessian $H$ on $\mathcal{D}_t^j, \forall j \in [1, .., k]$ with our unsupervised loss, and estimate the change using a gradient-based measure. Given the obtained metrics $g$ and $H$, we use the trained linear regressor to predict the accuracy of $\mathcal{D}_t^j$ as $acc_j = w_2 \cdot g + w_1 \cdot H + w_0$. The final accuracy for the target dataset is calculated as the average accuracy of its subsets.

## 4 Experiments

We conduct extensive experiments on both Single-Source and Multi- Source Datasets to evaluate the effectiveness of the proposed approach.

**Single-Source Datasets** include Digits, CIFAR10 and ImageNet.

*Digits* consists of one source domain, MNIST [33], with 60K training and 10K test images of handwritten digits from 10 classes, and three target datasets: USPS [14], SVHN [36], and SYNTH [17]. The target datasets also consist of digit images, but they differ in terms of colors, styles, and backgrounds. USPS and SVHN represent natural shifts, while SYNTH represents a synthetic shift.

*CIFAR10* contains one source domain, CIFAR10 [30], with natural images from 10 classes, divided between 50K training samples and 10K test samples, and one target domain, CIFAR10.1 [38] with 2K test images from the TinyImages dataset [44]. *ImageNet.* The source domain is a large-scale dataset of natural images, Imagenet [10], with 1.2M training and 50K validation images. The target dataset ImageNetV2 [39] contains three test sets with 10K images each, representing a natural domain shift.

**Multi-source Datasets** For a more realistic evaluation, we include multi-source datasets, fMoW [7], Camelyon17 [1] and iWildCam [3], from the WILDs benchmark [28], and PACS and DomainNet from Domain Bed [21], where we employ leave-one-domain-out cross-validation.

*fMoW* includes satellite images categorized into 62 classes. The domains are categorized based on the year the image was taken and the geographical region.

*Camelyon17* includes patches from 50 whole-slide images of a lymph node section from a patient with potentially metastatic breast cancer. The training set consists of 30 WSIs from 3 hospitals, with an OOD-validation split of 10 WSIs from another hospital and a test split of 10 WSIs from the last hospital. The task is to predict whether the patch contains a tumor.

*PACS* consists of 4 domains, each representing a unique visual style; within each domain, there are 7 categories.

*DomainNet* has 6 domains, each separated into 345 object categories. These domains cover a diverse range of image types, including clipart, real-world photos, sketches, infographics, artistic paintings, and quickdraw drawings.

**Networks** We utilize the LeNet architecture [32] for the Digits setup. For the CIFAR10 dataset, we follow [46] and fine-tune the pretrained on Image-Net ResNet50 [22] model. For ImageNet, we utilize the ResNet50 model with the same hyperparameters described in [22]. For both the fMoW and Camelyon17 datasets, we adopt the Densenet-121 [25] architecture; for iWildCam we use the ResNet50 architecture; and follow the ERM training procedure from the WILDs benchmark [28]. For Pacs and DomainNet, we use ResNet50 [22] and follow the training procedure from DomainBed benchmark [21].

For multi-source datasets we adopt a standard domain generalization training approach, where training is conducted on all available domains except for the test domain.

### 4.1 Baselines and Metrics

The considered baselines can be divided into three groups: score-based, activation-based and weight-based.

Score-based methods rely on the validation set of the source data to establish a threshold on a certain metric, and evaluate each sample of the target data w.r.t. that threshold. The score-based methods are: Entropy Score, AC [23], DoC [20], COT [34] and Nuclear Norm [12]. Entropy score considers the prediction to be correct if its entropy is smaller than a certain threshold $\tau \in [0, 1]$. In other words, the prediction $\hat{y}$ is considered to be correct if $H(\hat{y}) \leq \tau * \log(C)$, where $C$ is the number of classes. Average Confidence (AC), proposed by Hendrycks et al. [23], calculates the model's performance by determining the maximum confidence value from softmax probabilities on the target data. DOC [20] calculates the difference in probabilities between the source and target datasets. The final accuracy prediction for the target set is determined by subtracting the difference in confidences from the source accuracy. COT [34] uses the Earth Mover's Distance to measure the dissimilarity between the softmax probability distributions of samples from the source and target domains. Nuclear Norm [12] quantify the dispersity and confidence of the prediction matrix with Nuclear Norm.

Activation-based approaches analyze the hidden representations within the network. We consider the FID baseline [13], wherein the authors propose creating a collection of augmented source datasets. They further learn a linear regression model to predict accuracy on these sets based on the Fréchet distance between the source and augmented feature representations. We have also considered the Negative Dispersion Score [45], which analyzes feature separability. However, the results across all natural shifts were unsatisfactory; therefore, we have included it only for the CIFAR dataset in Fig. 2.

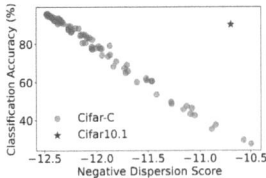 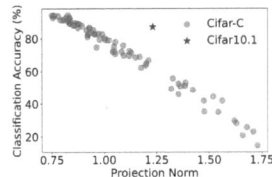 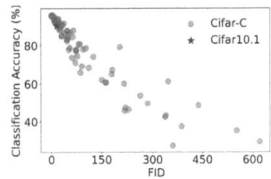

**Fig. 2.** Correlation between the accuracy of CIFAR-Corrupted and CIFAR10.1 across various metrics, including Negative Dispersion Score, Projection Norm, and FID. Note that while the Dispersion Score and Proj. Norm exhibit a stronger linear correlation on CIFAR-Corrupted compared to FID, they are less effective on CIFAR10.1, which represents natural shift.

Weight-based approaches rely on analyzing the dynamics of the network's weights. We refer to Projection Norm [46] as a weight-based baseline; this method involves fine-tuning the network using pseudo-labels and calculating the distance between the original and fine-tuned weights. The original implementation of Projection Norm does not support direct prediction of accuracy but instead provides a correlation between the norm of weights and accuracy. To adapt it to our task, we employ the meta-set pipeline used in [13] and our own method.

The construction of a Meta-set involves creating a collection of augmented sets from the validation split of the corresponding source dataset. For the comparison to the baselines to be fair, we use the same augmentation strategy for all the methods, which results in identical meta-datasets for every experimental setup. The data is augmented once, prior to the network updates.

As MNIST contains grayscale images, we create binary masks from the MNIST samples. We then select a test sample from the COCO dataset, and mine patches to match the size of the binary masks. Finally, we invert the values of the patches in the location of the MNIST binary masks.

For the COCO and CIFAR10 datasets, we use the RandAugment [9] automated augmentation strategy. For each sample set, we randomly select an augmentation magnitude and three transformations from the following pool of transformation types: `cutout, auto_contrast, contrast, brightness, equalize, sharpness, solarize, color, posterize, translate`. Differently from [13], we do not apply a computationally expensive background replacement on the COCO dataset. In fact, we show that even with these simple transformations, our approach is able to capture a variety of domain shifts.

It is worth noting that the applied augmentations primarily induce covariate shift, as they modify the input distribution P(X) without altering the label distribution P(Y|X). This limits our current setup to shifts that do not affect the label semantics (i.e., no concept shift). Incorporating other shift types— particularly concept shift, where the relationship between features and labels changes—could potentially improve robustness and help explain some of the method's observed limitations. We leave the exploration of such shift types for future work (Fig. 3).

**Table 1.** Results on Single-Source Setups. Values Represent Absolute Error, MAE: Mean Absolute Error.

|  | Digits | | | | ImageNet | | | | CIFAR10 |
| --- | --- | --- | --- | --- | --- | --- | --- | --- | --- |
|  | SVHN | USPS | SYNTH | MAE ↓ | MFreq | Thresh | TopIm | MAE ↓ | CIFAR10.1 |
| Ground Truth Accuracy | 41.59 | 81.46 | 50.66 |  | 63.13 | 72.29 | 77.61 |  | 88.65 |
| Entropy Score $\tau=0.1$ | 39.82 | 27.85 | 30.46 | 32.71 | 13.16 | 13.01 | 14.28 | 13.48 | 3.25 |
| Entropy Score $\tau=0.3$ | 36.84 | 7.52 | 15.94 | 20.10 | 11.56 | 8.23 | 9.03 | 9.61 | 10.90 |
| AC | 9.41 | 5.03 | 13.17 | 9.2 | 5.41 | 0.15 | 1.61 | 2.39 | 2.61 |
| DoC | 9.77 | 4.67 | 12.82 | 9.08 | 4.72 | 0.54 | 0.92 | 2.06 | 1.94 |
| COT | 10.49 | 2.97 | 9.88 | 7.78 | 2.45 | 2.89 | 1.32 | 2.22 | 1.32 |
| Nuc | 0.08 | 4.46 | 20.37 | 8.3 | 11.33 | 4.01 | 6.34 | 7.23 | 4.3 |
| FID | 13.94 | 26.26 | 1.76 | 14.04 | 12.02 | 2.82 | 2.38 | 5.74 | 8.90 |
| ProjNorm | 14.87 | 33.99 | 6.83 | 18.56 | 13.74 | 4.65 | 2.23 | 6.87 | 26.66 |
| Hess & Grad Norm | 6.1 | 7.46 | 0.57 | 4.71 | 1.21 | 0.09 | 0.96 | 0.76 | 0.85 |

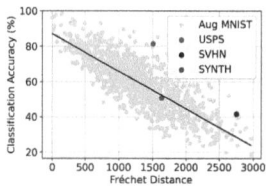
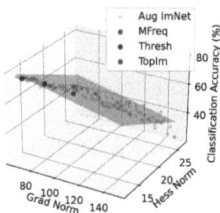

**Fig. 3.** Single-Source Datasets results. Correlation between classification accuracy and the FID measure for the Digits setup (Left), as well as our proposed gradient-based approach on ImageNet.

**Results on Single-Source Datasets.** The results for Single-Source setup are summarized in Table 1. We start our analysis with the discussion of the criteria for assessing the effectiveness of accuracy prediction. Our findings indicate that relying solely on the correlation between an input metric (for instance, FID or Projection Norm, see Fig. 2) and accuracy within a meta-dataset falls short of providing a comprehensive assessment. This limitation arises because this method of evaluation may not accurately represent the correlation with target datasets, particularly when faced with natural distribution shift.

We further highlight that applying a single threshold derived from entropy scores is not effective across various datasets. Specifically, a higher threshold improves the prediction for the Digits dataset, while a lower one is more suitable for CIFAR-10, suggesting a need for adjustments tailored to each dataset.

In single-source setups, we observed that score-based methods, that estimate the threshold based on the validation set of the source data (e.g. DoC, ATC, COT, and Nuc) consistently outperform both activation-based and weight-based methods. Among these, the COT method emerged as the most effective benchmark across all three experimental setups. This superiority is attributed to the

**Table 2.** Results on PACS and Wilds Benchmark. Values represent Absolute Error, MAE: Mean Absolute Error

|  | Wilds | | | | PACS | | | |
| --- | --- | --- | --- | --- | --- | --- | --- | --- |
|  | Camelyon | IWildCam | FMoW | MAE | Art Painting | Cartoon | Photo | Sketch | MAE |
| Ground Truth Accuracy | 72.91 | 67.69 | 52.90 |  | 81.45 | 76.79 | 93.29 | 76.48 | |
| Entropy Score $\tau=0.1$ | 54.52 | 0.94 | 25.34 | 26.94 | 5.32 | 0.21 | 2.81 | 0.31 | 2.16 |
| Entropy Score $\tau=0.3$ | 19.31 | 21.41 | 0.45 | 13.72 | 5.81 | 11.18 | 1.98 | 10.82 | 7.45 |
| AC | 16.13 | 2.11 | 5.69 | 7.98 | 7.13 | 11.8 | 0.48 | 7.29 | 6.68 |
| DOC | 14.44 | 1.41 | 3.26 | 6.37 | 6.68 | 11.07 | 0.25 | 6.61 | 6.15 |
| COT | 2.95 | 14.83 | 0.01 | 5.93 | 0.73 | 3.28 | 24.49 | 16.63 | 11.28 |
| Nucl | 14.45 | 7.13 | 4.05 | 8.54 | 9.28 | 13.06 | 0.44 | 3.63 | 6.60 |
| FID | 1.69 | 8.39 | 4.89 | 4.99 | 1.81 | 10.15 | 32.3 | 16.65 | 15.22 |
| ProjNorm | 16.47 | 10.95 | 7.83 | 11.75 | 3.02 | 3.82 | 28.8 | 36.48 | 18.03 |
| Hess & Grad Norm | 2.23 | 3.59 | 3.66 | 3.16 | 5.63 | 0.42 | 1.57 | 4.1 | 2.93 |

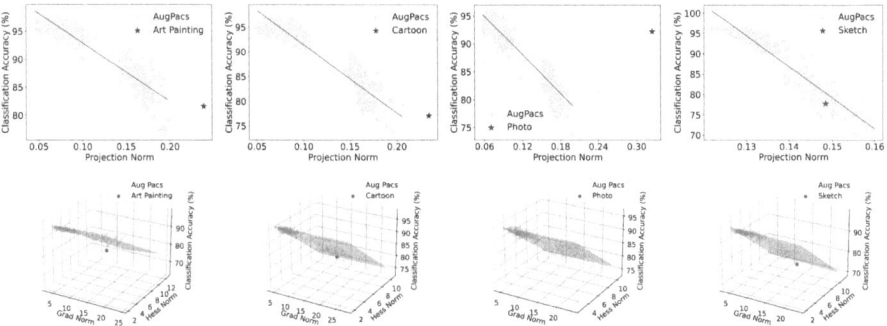

**Fig. 4.** Multi-Source results. Correlation between the classification accuracy of PACS datasets and the Projection Norm (Top), as well as our proposed gradient-based approach (Bottom).

model's tendency to overfit on the training data, making even the validation set from the same domain an effective estimator for the level of uncertainty.

The final baselines, Projection Norm and Fréchet Inception Distance (FID), exhibited a clear linear correlation with the accuracy of the meta-set; however, there was notable variability in the distribution of points across datasets. For instance, in the Digits setup, predictions of FID for the Synth dataset closely matched the ground truth, with an Absolute Error (AE) of only 1.76. However, for the USPS and SVHN datasets, the deviations from the main trend were substantial, leading to inaccurate predictions.

Finally, our gradient-based approach outperforms all other methods across all three experimental setups. By integrating both Hessian and gradient norms, we successfully developed a Linear Regressor capable of capturing the correlation with classification accuracy not only within the meta-dataset but also across the target datasets. The superiority of our method is demonstrated by the results presented in Table 1, which indicate that our method's predictions

**Table 3.** Results on DomainNet accross various domain shifts. Values represent Absolute Error, MAE: Mean Absolute Error.

| | Clipart | Infographics | Paintings | QuickDraw | Real | Sketches | MAE |
|---|---|---|---|---|---|---|---|
| Ground Truth Accuracy | 58.22 | 19.92 | 45.80 | 12.64 | 58.36 | 47.98 | |
| AC | 3.15 | 12.88 | 6.61 | 24.17 | 5.96 | 7.84 | 10.10 |
| DOC | 2.89 | 12.29 | 6.17 | 24.26 | 5.47 | 7.28 | 9.72 |
| COT | 4.2 | 4.85 | 1.05 | 51.83 | 31.99 | 0.3 | 15.70 |
| Nucl | 7.21 | 18.54 | 10.38 | 19.47 | 10.6 | 12.59 | 13.13 |
| FID | 19.19 | 19.58 | 13.36 | 12.64 | 33.65 | 8.67 | 17.84 |
| ProjNorm | 18.95 | 19.92 | 3.61 | 12.64 | 5.93 | 2.94 | 10.66 |
| Hess&Grad | 1.18 | 8.39 | 5.97 | 9.1 | 9.33 | 6.65 | 6.77 |

for the target datasets are more accurate than those produced by alternative approaches. Specifically, we observed an average absolute error of only 4.71% for Digits, 0.76% for ImageNet-V2 and 0.85% for CIFAR10.1.

**Results on Multi-Source Datasets.** Next, we proceed to the multi-source setups, where instead of having a single domain available during training, the network is exposed to multiple domains. This generally leads to the development of more robust models than single-source setups. The results for datasets from Wilds benchmark and PACS dataset are detailed in Table 2, the results for DomainNet are shown in Table 3.

Our analysis reveals that the COT method is unstable across different datasets. For example, it achieves nearly perfect predictions on the FMoW dataset, with an AE of 0.01, as well as on the Sketch target set from DomainNet. It also performs well on the Art Painting subset of the PACS dataset, with an AE of less than 1%. However, its performance declines on the iWildCam dataset, where the AE reaches 14.83%. On the other hand, the FID metric represents a more robust baseline, particularly for datasets within the Wilds benchmark. Notably, it outperforms all other baselines in the evaluation of the Camelyon dataset.

The performance of the Projection Norm in multi-source setups is unsatisfactory. This is attributed to the fact that the reference model is not consistently capable of converging to a local minimum. As illustrated in Fig. 4, Top, when the Photo test set is used in the PACS setup, the network fine-tuned on the test data continues to change even after the meta-set weights have stabilized. This leads to a larger Projection Norm for the target dataset compared to the meta-set, resulting in poor performance estimation.

Crucially, our proposed method outperforms existing approaches, achieving the lowest MAE across all evaluated multi-source datasets. The closest competitor to our method is the Projection Norm. However, in addition to inferior performance, the Projection Norm also demands greater computational complexity due to the requirement of fine-tuning the entire network (see Table 4).

**Table 4.** Comparison of Time Complexity. The values indicate the time (in seconds) required to compute a Projection Norm and our proposed Hess&Grad on a set of 1000 samples, evaluated using a single A100 GPU.

|              | ImageNet | PACS | IWildCam | FMoW  | DomainNet |
|--------------|----------|------|----------|-------|-----------|
| Proj Norm    | 100.1    | 47.5 | 235.7    | 114.2 | 48.64     |
| Our Approach | 2.6      | 2.1  | 4.8      | 3.9   | 2.9       |

## 5 Conclusion

In this work, we tackle the problem of predicting the performance of a network on unlabeled target data whose distribution differs from that of the source training data. To this end, we build on the findings of recent work [46] that estimates the performance of the network from the degree of weight changes incurred by fine-tuning the network on the target dataset with a self-supervised loss. In contrast, our method avoids the time-consuming process of updating network weights and relies on analyzing gradients and the Hessian matrix to capture weight differences efficiently. Our extensive experiments show that our approach effectively and efficiently predicts the accuracy across a variety of domain shifts and network architectures.

**Acknowledgments.** This work is partially supported by Australian Research Council Project FT230100426.

## References

1. Bándi, P., et al.: From detection of individual metastases to classification of lymph node status at the patient level: the camelyon17 challenge. IEEE Trans. Med. Imaging **38**, 550–560 (2019)
2. Barsbey, M., Sefidgaran, M., Erdogdu, M.A., Richard, G., Simsekli, U.: Heavy tails in SGD and compressibility of overparametrized neural networks. In: NeurIPS (2021)
3. Beery, S., Agarwal, A., Cole, E., Birodkar, V.: The iwildcam 2021 competition dataset. arXiv preprint arXiv:2105.03494 (2021)
4. Birdal, T., Lou, A., Guibas, L.J., cSimcsekli, U.: Intrinsic dimension, persistent homology and generalization in neural networks. In: NeurIPS (2021)
5. Chen, J., Liu, F., Avci, B., Wu, X., Liang, Y., Jha, S.: Detecting errors and estimating accuracy on unlabeled data with self-training ensembles. In: NeurIPS (2021)
6. Chen, M., Goel, K., Sohoni, N., Poms, F., Fatahalian, K., Re, C.: Mandoline: model evaluation under distribution shift. In: International Conference of Machine Learning (ICML) (2021)
7. Christie, G., Fendley, N., Wilson, J., Mukherjee, R.: Functional map of the world. In: CVPR, pp. 6172–6180 (2018)
8. Chuang, C.Y., Torralba, A., Jegelka, S.: Estimating generalization under distribution shifts via domain-invariant representations. In: ICML (2020)

9. Cubuk, E.D., Zoph, B., Shlens, J., Le, Q.: Randaugment: practical automated data augmentation with a reduced search space. In: NeurIPS, vol. 33, pp. 18613–18624 (2020)
10. Deng, J., Dong, W., Socher, R., Li, L.J., Li, K., Fei-Fei, L.: Imagenet: a large-scale hierarchical image database. In: CVPR, pp. 248–255 (2009)
11. Deng, W., Gould, S., Zheng, L.: What does rotation prediction tell us about classifier accuracy under varying testing environments? In: ICML (2021)
12. Deng, W., Suh, Y., Gould, S., Zheng, L.: Confidence and dispersity speak: Characterising prediction matrix for unsupervised accuracy estimation. In: ICML (2023)
13. Deng, W., Zheng, L.: Are labels always necessary for classifier accuracy evaluation? In: CVPR (2021)
14. Denker, J., et al.: Neural network recognizer for hand-written zip code digits. In: NeurIPS, vol. 1 (1989)
15. Elsahar, H., Gallé, M.: To annotate or not? predicting performance drop under domain shift. In: EMNLP-IJCNLP, pp. 2163–2173 (2019)
16. Franchi, G., Yu, X., Bursuc, A., Aldea, E., Dubuisson, S., Filliat, D.: Latent discriminant deterministic uncertainty. arXiv abs/2207.10130 (2022)
17. Ganin, Y., Lempitsky, V.: Unsupervised domain adaptation by backpropagation. In: International Conference of Machine Learning (2015)
18. Garg, S., Balakrishnan, S., Lipton, Z.C., Neyshabur, B., Sedghi, H.: Leveraging unlabeled data to predict out-of-distribution performance. In: ICLR (2022)
19. Guillory, D., Shankar, V., Ebrahimi, S., Darrell, T., Schmidt, L.: Predicting with confidence on unseen distributions. In: ICCV, pp. 1114–1124 (2021)
20. Guillory, D., Shankar, V., Ebrahimi, S., Darrell, T., Schmidt, L.: Predicting with confidence on unseen distributions. In: ICCV, pp. 1114–1124 (2021)
21. Gulrajani, I., Lopez-Paz, D.: In search of lost domain generalization. In: ICLR (2021)
22. He, K., Zhang, X., Ren, S., Sun, J.: Deep residual learning for image recognition. In: CVPR, pp. 770–778 (2016)
23. Hendrycks, D., Gimpel, K.: A baseline for detecting misclassified and out-of-distribution examples in neural networks. arXiv abs/1610.02136 (2016)
24. Hu, W., Li, Z., Yu, D.: Simple and effective regularization methods for training on noisily labeled data with generalization guarantee. In: ICLR (2020)
25. Huang, G., Liu, Z., Van Der Maaten, L., Weinberger, K.Q.: Densely connected convolutional networks. In: CVPR, pp. 2261–2269 (2017)
26. Jiang, Y., Nagarajan, V., Baek, C., Kolter, J.Z.: Assessing generalization of SGD via disagreement. arXiv abs/2106.13799 (2022)
27. Keskar, N.S., Mudigere, D., Nocedal, J., Smelyanskiy, M., Tang, P.T.P.: On large-batch training for deep learning: Generalization gap and sharp minima. In: ICLR (2017)
28. Koh, P.W., et al.: Wilds: a benchmark of in-the-wild distribution shifts. In: ICML, vol. 139, pp. 5637–5664 (2021)
29. Kornblith, S., Chen, T., Lee, H., Norouzi, M.: Why do better loss functions lead to less transferable features? In: NeurIPS (2020)
30. Krizhevsky, A., Hinton, G.: Learning multiple layers of features from tiny images. University of Toronto, Technical report (2009)
31. Lacombe, T., Ike, Y., Umeda, Y.: Topological uncertainty: monitoring trained neural networks through persistence of activation graphs. In: IJCAI (2021)
32. Lecun, Y., Bottou, L., Bengio, Y., Haffner, P.: Gradient-based learning applied to document recognition. Proc. IEEE **86**(11), 2278–2324 (1998)

33. LeCun, Y., Cortes, C., Burges, C.: Mnist handwritten digit database. ATT Labs. http://yann.lecun.com/exdb/mnist. **2** (2010)
34. Lu, Y., Wang, Z., Zhai, R., Kolouri, S., Campbell, J., Sycara, K.P.: Predicting out-of-distribution error with confidence optimal transport. In: ICLR Workshop (2023)
35. Nagarajan, V., Kolter, J.Z.: Generalization in deep networks: The role of distance from initialization. arXiv abs/1901.01672 (2019)
36. Netzer, Y., Wang, T., Coates, A., Bissacco, A., Wu, B., Ng, A.Y.: Reading digits in natural images with unsupervised feature learning. In: NIPS Workshop on Deep Learning and Unsupervised Feature Learning (2011)
37. Nichol, A., Achiam, J., Schulman, J.: On first-order meta-learning algorithms. arXiv abs/1803.02999 (2018)
38. Recht, B., Roelofs, R., Schmidt, L., Shankar, V.: Do cifar-10 classifiers generalize to cifar-10? (2018)
39. Recht, B., Roelofs, R., Schmidt, L., Shankar, V.: Do imagenet classifiers generalize to imagenet? In: ICML (2019)
40. Rieck, B., Togninalli, M., Bock, C., Moor, M., Horn, M., Gumbsch, T., Borgwardt, K.: Neural persistence: a complexity measure for deep neural networks using algebraic topology. In: ICLR (2019)
41. Schelter, S., Rukat, T., Biessmann, F.: Learning to validate the predictions of black box classifiers on unseen data. In: ACM SIGMOD International Conference on Management of Data, pp. 1289–1299. SIGMOD (2020)
42. Shi, Y., Seely, J., Torr, P.N.S., Hannun, A., Usunier, N., Synnaeve, G.: Gradient matching for domain generalization. In: ICLR (2022)
43. Simsekli, U., Sener, O., Deligiannidis, G., Erdogdu, M.A.: Hausdorff dimension, heavy tails, and generalization in neural networks. J. Stat. Mech. Theory Exp. (2020)
44. Torralba, A., Fergus, R., Freeman, W.T.: 80 million tiny images: a large data set for nonparametric object and scene recognition. IEEE Trans. Pattern Anal. Mach. Intell. **30**(11), 1958–1970 (2008)
45. XIE, R., Wei, H., Feng, L., Cao, Y., An, B.: On the importance of feature separability in predicting out-of-distribution error. In: NeurIPS (2023)
46. Yu, Y., Yang, Z., Wei, A., Ma, Y., Steinhardt, J.: Predicting out-of-distribution error with the projection norm. In: International Conference on Machine Learning (ICML), vol. 162, pp. 25721–25746 (2022)
47. Zhang, X., Xu, R., Yu, H., Zou, H., Cui, P.: Gradient norm aware minimization seeks first-order flatness and improves generalization. In: CVPR, pp. 20247–20257 (2023)

# Projective Pruning for Decoupling Weights

Tommy Chu and Alexander Kovalenko

Faculty of Information Technology, Czech Technical University, Thákurova 9, 160 00 Prague, Czech Republic
{alexander.kovalenko,chutommy}@fit.cvut.cz

**Abstract.** This paper proposes Projective Pruning, a structured deep neural network sparsification technique that removes highly correlated weights, as they provide a minimal contribution to the parameter subspace. Due to the inefficiencies in deep neural networks caused by excessive overparametrization and highly correlated weights, the method enables parameter compression while maintaining the high performance of the models. The approach incorporates a redistribution mechanism to preserve model performance and expressiveness. Evaluations on multiple vision and language benchmarks, including large language model architectures, demonstrate that, unlike most other pruning methods, Projective Pruning delivers reliable compression while ensuring stable model performance. Applying this method improves retrainability and achieves competitive results compared to existing structured pruning methods.

**Keywords:** Model compression · Structured pruning · Sparsification

## 1 Introduction

In recent years, deep learning has profoundly transformed many disciplines such as computer vision, natural language processing, speech recognition, recommendation systems, and computational biology. These advancements have enabled unprecedented capabilities in pattern recognition, content generation, and decision-making systems across various domains [13, 24].

The most performing models, however, often have billions of parameters and prohibitively high training costs [21, 47]. For instance, state-of-the-art large language models (LLM) such as GPT-4 are estimated to have over 1.8 trillion parameters [39], requiring thousands of GPU-years for training and costing tens of millions of dollars [5].

The environmental impact of such computational demands is highly concerning. Training a single large transformer model can produce carbon emissions equivalent to the lifetime emissions of five automobiles [44]. The energy consumption of modern AI systems has been increasing exponentially, with energy usage doubling approximately every 3.4 months between 2012 and 2022 [46]. This trajectory raises significant sustainability concerns about the future development of deep learning technologies.

This challenge gave rise to the paradigm of foundation models, which are pretrained on vast, generic datasets, and can be reusably fine-tuned for various downstream tasks [2]. This approach amortizes the initial training costs across multiple applications, improving overall efficiency.

Moreover, while training constitutes a substantial initial energy investment, it is the inference process–the deployment and repeated use of trained models– that accounts for the majority of the total energy consumption over a model's lifetime. Recent studies indicate that inference operations represent up to 90% of the total computational cost for widely deployed models [35,49]. This imbalance is particularly pronounced in commercial applications of LLM that serve millions of queries daily.

Nevertheless, even after training, large models require substantial compute, and memory resources for inference [10,15]. The memory footprint alone can exceed the capabilities of many edge devices, limiting AI deployment in resource-constrained environments such as mobile phones, IoT devices, and autonomous vehicles [3].

One of the possible solutions to reduce the inference and/or training cost of deep learning models is model pruning. The concept of pruning builds upon the observation that neural networks are typically over-parameterized, containing significantly more parameters than necessary to represent their learned functions [6]. This redundancy creates an opportunity for compression without substantial performance degradation.

Therefore, in this paper, we propose a new flexible neural pruning method that decouples weights in deep learning models. Projective Pruning uses a dependency graph [9] to group weights, and prune them based on redundancy computed by their relative distance to orthogonal projections on the subspace spanned by other parameters in the same group. The pruned weights are then used to redistribute lost signals to the remaining parameters to maintain the model's representational capacity. We test our method on various convolutional and attention-based models against other pruning algorithms. On average, Projective Pruning outperforms existing methods in terms of post-pruning retrainability, and raw performance retention.

## 2 Background

Model compression has a rich history, tracing back to the late 1980s with pioneering pruning techniques such as Optimal Brain Damage [25] and Optimal Brain Surgeon [16]. These early methods aimed to compress neural networks by systematically removing parameters based on their significance using second-derivative and magnitude-based criteria. Initially, such pruning approaches were driven primarily by necessity due to the severely limited computing resources available at the time.

As deep learning architectures and hardware capabilities evolved throughout the decades, the field of model compression expanded significantly, with Han et al.'s Deep Compression [14] marking a pivotal advancement in modern approaches. Contemporary research has refined these techniques and established a temporal classification framework for pruning methodologies. According to recent surveys [4], modern pruning methods are typically applied at one of three distinct stages in a model's lifecycle:

- **Pruning before training** [27,29]: The network is pruned at initialization, before training begins. This approach is motivated by improved convergence speed and reduced memory costs of sparse training.
- **Pruning during training** [8,30]: Pruning is integrated into the training process, and the model's size is iteratively reduced as it learns. The large number of parameters initially helps the model recover from poor initialization [11], and quickly traverse to the low area of the loss landscape [28]. At the same time, the iterative pruning reduces the model's size, and improve its generalization.
- **Pruning after training** [1,11,12,37]: The model is fully trained first, then pruned, and finally fine-tuned to regain any lost performance. This strategy targets existing pretrained models like vision and large language models with computationally intensive convolutional or transformer-based architectures.

Beyond pruning, the model compression landscape encompasses several complementary approaches. Knowledge distillation [19,42] transfers information from a larger "teacher" model to a smaller "student" network by training the smaller network using the output logits of the fully converged larger model. Low-rank approximation [20] replaces large matrices with products of smaller matrices to reduce parameter counts while preserving essential representational capacity. Quantization [40] achieves speedups and memory savings by reducing the numerical precision of weights and activations without necessarily changing the network architecture.

The structural nature of pruning operations represents another important classification dimension. Unstructured pruning involves setting individual parameters to zero while maintaining the original network architecture. This approach yields a sparse network that often demonstrates improved generalization capabilities but primarily benefits from specialized hardware such as FPGAs [14,45]. A significant limitation of unstructured pruning is that the overall dimensions of weight matrices remain unchanged, resulting in minimal speedup on conventional computing hardware despite the reduction in non-zero parameters.

Structured pruning, by contrast, systematically removes entire groups of parameters, such as neurons, layers, or channels. This approach directly reduces the model's dimensions, leading to concrete improvements in both inference speed and memory utilization across standard hardware platforms. Between these approaches lies semi-structured pruning, which removes individual parameters within organized structural groups. Given that structured sparsity patterns are increasingly supported by GPU manufacturers, these approaches can deliver substantial improvements in both training and inference performance [12].

Through this systematic progression of techniques, model compression has evolved from a necessity imposed by hardware constraints to a sophisticated field focused on optimizing the efficiency-performance trade-off across diverse neural network architectures and application domains.

## 3 Related Work

Pruning has significantly advanced network acceleration, with numerous studies demonstrating its effectiveness across various architectural paradigms. This section outlines key pruning methodologies that form the foundation of modern network compression techniques.

### 3.1 Magnitude-Based Pruning Approaches

Magnitude-based pruning represents one of the most widely adopted approaches due to its simplicity and effectiveness. Han et al. introduced Deep Compression [14], which established simple structured magnitude pruning as a strong baseline by removing weights based on their L2 norms. Recent comprehensive surveys have confirmed that this straightforward approach remains competitive with many newer techniques [4].

Building upon this foundation, Layer-Adaptive Magnitude-based Pruning (LAMP) [26] offers a notable advancement by dynamically adjusting layerwise sparsity based on L2 distortion metrics. This approach eliminates the need for extensive hyperparameter tuning, making pruning more accessible and practical for widespread implementation.

### 3.2 Alternative Pruning Criteria

Interestingly, research has revealed that random pruning produces surprisingly effective results. Studies by Liu et al. [31] and Sui et al. [29] demonstrate that random weight elimination can offer competitive performance comparable to more sophisticated techniques, challenging assumptions about the necessity of complex pruning criteria.

Network Slimming [32] takes a different approach by enforcing channel-level sparsity through the addition of scaling factors to channel-wise parameters. This technique effectively identifies and removes entire channels with minimal impact on network performance.

Filter Pruning via Geometric Median (FPGM) [18] diverges from mainstream approaches by focusing on redundancy rather than magnitude. Instead of eliminating low-magnitude weights, FPGM identifies and removes filters that are most redundant within the representational space of each layer, preserving unique feature extractors.

### 3.3 Advanced Mathematical Frameworks

EigenDamage [48] introduces a more sophisticated mathematical framework by leveraging Kronecker-factored eigenbases for structured pruning. This approach aims for more precise weight removal by analyzing the eigenvalues of the Hessian matrix, targeting parameters that contribute minimally to the loss landscape.

### 3.4 Architecture-Agnostic Methods

DepGraph [9] represents a significant advancement by enabling general structural pruning across diverse architectures, including Convolutional Neural Networks (CNNs), Recurrent Neural Networks (RNNs), Graph Neural Networks (GNNs), and Transformers. By modeling inter-layer dependencies through a graph-based approach, DepGraph ensures structural integrity through grouped norm pruning while providing a flexible framework that can accommodate arbitrary pruning criteria.

### 3.5 Transformer-Specific Techniques

As transformer architectures have become increasingly dominant, specialized pruning methods have emerged. SliceGPT [1] employs Principal Component Analysis (PCA)-based projections to identify and remove weights associated with the smallest singular values in transformer models. While highly effective for large language models, this approach has limitations: it can only prune dimensions that do not directly interact with nonlinear structures and requires coordinated pruning across multiple layers to maintain architectural consistency.

These pruning methodologies collectively demonstrate the evolution from simple heuristic approaches to sophisticated, architecture-specific techniques that leverage advanced mathematical concepts to optimize neural network efficiency while preserving performance.

## 4 Methodology

We first introduce Projective Pruning for fully connected layers and then extend the concept to arbitrary learning structures. Projective Pruning decouples weights by identifying neurons with high redundancy based on their projection onto the subspace formed by other neurons in the same layer. If a neuron's signal can be closely represented as a linear combination of others, it is pruned, and its weights are redistributed across the remaining neurons. The strength of the redistributed signal varies for each parameter and is proportional to the coefficients of the linear combination. This approach minimizes the impact on the model's overall expressiveness while compensating for the lost information.

### 4.1 Fully Connected Layers

Consider two adjacent fully connected layers with weights $\boldsymbol{W} \in \mathbb{R}^{n,m}$, bias $\boldsymbol{b} \in \mathbb{R}^n$ in the first layer and $\boldsymbol{V} \in \mathbb{R}^{k,n}$, $\boldsymbol{a} \in \mathbb{R}^k$ in the second layer. The forward pass through these two layers is given by

$$\boldsymbol{h}_{i+1} = \sigma(\boldsymbol{W}\boldsymbol{h}_i + \boldsymbol{b}), \tag{1}$$

$$\boldsymbol{h}_{i+2} = \sigma(\boldsymbol{V}\boldsymbol{h}_{i+1} + \boldsymbol{a}), \tag{2}$$

where $\sigma$ is a nonlinear activation function, and $\boldsymbol{h}_i \to \boldsymbol{h}_{i+1} \to \boldsymbol{h}_{i+2}$ are hidden states that transition from $\mathbb{R}^m$ to $\mathbb{R}^n$ to $\mathbb{R}^k$. Projective Pruning decreases the shared dimension $n$ by removing redundant neurons (output dimension) in the first layer and input dimension in the second.

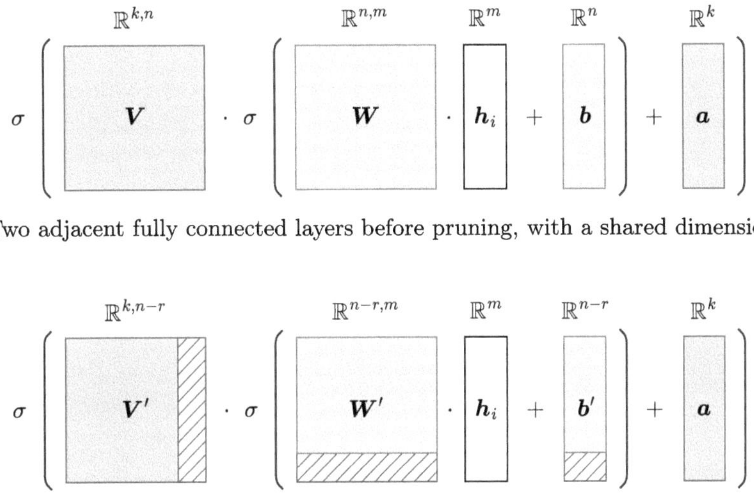

(a) Two adjacent fully connected layers before pruning, with a shared dimension $n$.

(b) The same layers after pruning $r$ redundant neurons, reducing the shared dimension to $n - r$ while preserving the input dimension $m$ and output dimension $k$.

**Fig. 1.** Illustration of pruning a dense layer.

Pruning a single neuron corresponds to removing a row in $\boldsymbol{W}$, its associated element in $\boldsymbol{b}$, and a column in $\boldsymbol{V}$. Initially, the overall mapping of these two layers is $\sigma(\boldsymbol{V} \cdot \sigma(\boldsymbol{W}\boldsymbol{h}_i + \boldsymbol{b}) + \boldsymbol{a})$, as illustrated in Fig. 1a. After pruning $r$ rows, we get $\sigma(\boldsymbol{V}' \cdot \sigma(\boldsymbol{W}'\boldsymbol{h}_i + \boldsymbol{b}') + \boldsymbol{a})$ with reduced weights $\boldsymbol{W}' \in \mathbb{R}^{n-r,m}$, $\boldsymbol{b}' \in \mathbb{R}^{n-r}$, $\boldsymbol{V}' \in \mathbb{R}^{k,n-r}$ as shown in Fig. 1b. The pruned composite function maintains the same domain $\mathbb{R}^m$ and codomain $\mathbb{R}^k$, so no structural changes are required.

### 4.2 Projective Pruning

Our goal is to determine the reduced weights $\boldsymbol{W}', \boldsymbol{b}', \boldsymbol{V}'$, so that the new composite transformation approximates the original one ($\boldsymbol{a}$ is unaffected, and thus ignored):

$$\forall \boldsymbol{h}_i \in \mathcal{D}: \quad \boldsymbol{V}' \cdot \sigma(\boldsymbol{W}'\boldsymbol{h}_i + \boldsymbol{b}') \stackrel{\text{approx.}}{\approx} \boldsymbol{V} \cdot \sigma(\boldsymbol{W}\boldsymbol{h}_i + \boldsymbol{b}). \quad (3)$$

The nonlinear function $\sigma$ prevents us from simply merging the two layers into one $(\boldsymbol{V}\boldsymbol{W})\boldsymbol{h}_i + (\boldsymbol{V}\boldsymbol{b} + \boldsymbol{a})$ and pruning the entire layer losslessly. Minimizing the difference between the left and the right side of the Eq. 3 requires either some training data or assumptions about its distribution (over which domain to minimize). Unlike data-dependent methods, Projective Pruning prioritizes general expressivity over data fitness, and does not use any data assumptions.

*Criterion.* Neurons are pruned iteratively one at a time. The most redundant neuron (row) in $\boldsymbol{W}$ is identified as the one which is closest to its projection onto the subspace spanned by the other neurons. This heuristic assumes that highly correlated neurons can be fully replaced by strengthening the signal of similar neurons.

Although this assumption holds only partially as neurons are not active all the time or the activation function may not have a linear form (similar to ReLU, GELU, Swish), pruning under this assumption encourages weights to better utilize the full parameter range. The reliance on this assumption can be regulated by the parameters $\alpha$, $\beta$, $\gamma$ (discussed in Subsect.4.4) which control the amount of the pruned signal to be redistributed.

### 4.3 Orthogonal Projection

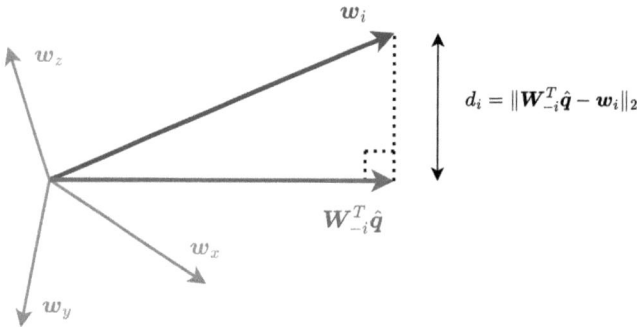

**Fig. 2.** Assuming the vector set $(\boldsymbol{w}_i^T, \boldsymbol{w}_x^T, \boldsymbol{w}_y^T, \boldsymbol{w}_z^T, \ldots)$ in $\boldsymbol{W}$ is linearly independent: The figure shows the projection of $\boldsymbol{w}_i^T$ onto the subspace spanned by the other rows. The projection $\boldsymbol{W}_{-i}^T \hat{\boldsymbol{q}}$ resides within the subspace $\langle \boldsymbol{w}_x, \boldsymbol{w}_y, \boldsymbol{w}_z, \ldots \rangle$ and its distance from $\boldsymbol{w}_i$ defines the redundancy score $d_i$.

Let $\boldsymbol{w}_i^T$ denote the $i$-th row of $\boldsymbol{W}$, and let $\boldsymbol{W}_{-i}$ be $\boldsymbol{W}$ without this row. The projection of $\boldsymbol{w}_i^T$ onto the subspace spanned by the rows of $\boldsymbol{W}_{-i}$ is found by solving:

$$\hat{\boldsymbol{q}} = \arg\min_{\boldsymbol{q}} \|\boldsymbol{W}_{-i}^T \boldsymbol{q} - \boldsymbol{w}_i\|_2, \qquad (4)$$

where $\hat{\boldsymbol{q}}$ represents the coefficients of the linear combination of the projection. Equivalently, $\boldsymbol{q}$ is the solution $\hat{\boldsymbol{q}}$ only if $\boldsymbol{W}_{-i}^T \boldsymbol{q} - \boldsymbol{w}_i$ is orthogonal to the span $\langle \boldsymbol{w}_1, \ldots, \boldsymbol{w}_{i-1}, \boldsymbol{w}_{i+1}, \ldots, \boldsymbol{w}_n \rangle$. This yields the normal equation $\boldsymbol{W}_{-i}(\boldsymbol{W}_{-i}^T \hat{\boldsymbol{q}} -$

$w_i) = 0$ with a closed-form solution $\hat{q} = \left(W_{-i}W_{-i}^T\right)^{-1} W_{-i}w_i$. The redundancy is then quantified by the norm of the difference between the original vector and its projection $d_i = \|W_{-i}^T \hat{q} - w_i\|_2$, as illustrated in Fig. 2.

We introduce a parameter $\lambda$ to stabilize the matrix inverse. The full expression of the criterion for selecting the neuron to prune is therefore given by

$$\arg\min_i \|W_{-i}^T \left(W_{-i}W_{-i}^T + \lambda \mathbb{I}\right)^{-1} W_{-i}w_i - w_i\|_2. \tag{5}$$

### 4.4 Redistribution Mechanism

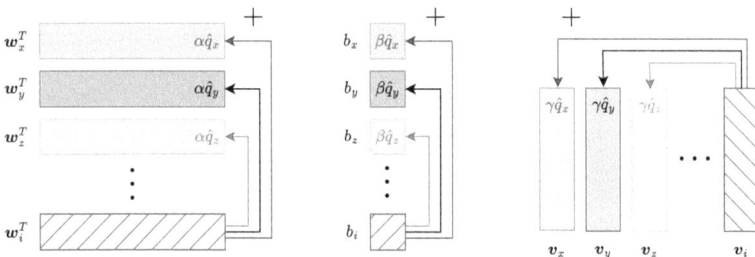

**Fig. 3.** The redistribution schema in which $w_i$ is pruned, with its weights readjusting unpruned parameters using the coefficients $\hat{q}$ of the orthogonal projection.

After identifying the neuron, we remove its row from $W$, its bias element from $b$, and its associated column from $V$. This keeps the unpruned signals properly aligned while maintaining the model's overall structure. We also reuse the coefficients of the linear combination to proportionally reinforce the remaining weights (Fig. 3):

$$\forall j \neq i: \quad w_j \leftarrow w_j \cdot (1 + \alpha \hat{q}_j), \tag{6}$$
$$b_j \leftarrow b_j \cdot (1 + \beta \hat{q}_j), \tag{7}$$
$$v_j \leftarrow v_j \cdot (1 + \gamma \hat{q}_j), \tag{8}$$

where $w_j^T$, $b_j$, $v_j$ are elements of $W$, $b$, $V$, and $\alpha$, $\beta$, and $\gamma$ determines the amount of signal redistributed back.

### 4.5 Generalization to Other Structures

Projective Pruning can also be applied to 2D convolutional layers by reshaping the weights into a matrix, where each row represents a flattened filter. The pruning criterion and the mathematical framework stay the same: redundancy is measured across filters within the same layer (Subsect. 4.3).

Conceptually, this can be viewed as shifting the vector space from $\mathbb{R}^n$ to $\mathbb{R}^{d,h,w}$, where $d$ is the input channel, and $(h, w)$ is the kernel size. The pruned dimension corresponds to the shared channel dimension between consecutive layers. This concept extends naturally to other types of convolutions.

More generally, flattening weights allows this analogy to extend to any deep learning structure where prunable units form a vector space of the same dimension. For example, in attention layers, Projective Pruning targets the key-query matrices. Projections are computed on joint key-query pairs, and pruning is applied to the shared key-query dimension.

## 5  Efficient Implementation

A naive implementation of the algorithm is computationally prohibitive. It requires inverting a large matrix for each neuron at every pruning step. To make this approach feasible, we introduce three key optimizations: a fast method for matrix inversion, a lazy update scheme for iterative pruning, and the use of weight masking.

### 5.1  Fast Matrix Inversion

To identify which neuron to prune, we evaluate expression (5), which requires the inverse of a different matrix $\mathbf{G}_{-i} := \mathbf{W}_{-i}\mathbf{W}_{-i}^T + \lambda \mathbb{I} \in \mathbb{R}^{n-1,n-1}$ for each of the $n$ candidate rows. However, these inverses do not need to be computed independently.

Instead, we first compute the inverse of the full matrix $\mathbf{G} := \mathbf{W}\mathbf{W}^T + \lambda \mathbb{I}$. We then derive each required sub-matrix inverse $\mathbf{G}_{-i}^{-1}$ from the blocks of $\mathbf{G}^{-1}$. Let the symmetric positive-definite matrices $\mathbf{G}$ and $\mathbf{G}^{-1}$ be permuted and partitioned as follows:

$$\mathbb{P}_{i,n}\mathbf{G}\mathbb{P}_{i,n} = \begin{pmatrix} \mathbf{G}_{-i} & \mathbf{G}_i \\ \mathbf{G}_i^T & \mathbf{G}_{ii} \end{pmatrix} =: \begin{pmatrix} \mathbf{A} & \mathbf{B} \\ \mathbf{B}^T & \mathbf{C} \end{pmatrix}, \qquad (9)$$

$$\mathbb{P}_{i,n}\mathbf{G}^{-1}\mathbb{P}_{i,n} = \begin{pmatrix} \mathbf{g}_{-i} & \mathbf{g}_i \\ \mathbf{g}_i^T & \mathbf{g}_{ii} \end{pmatrix} =: \begin{pmatrix} \mathbf{a} & \mathbf{b} \\ \mathbf{b}^T & \mathbf{c} \end{pmatrix}, \qquad (10)$$

where $\mathbb{P}_{i,n}$ is a permutation matrix. The block $\mathbf{G}_{-i}$ is the matrix $\mathbf{G}$ with the $i$-th row and column removed, and $\mathbf{G}_i \in \mathbb{R}^{n-1}$ is the removed column excluding the $i$-th element $\mathbf{G}_{ii} \in \mathbb{R}$. The blocks of $\mathbf{G}^{-1}$ are defined analogously.

From the identity $\mathbb{I}_n = (\mathbb{P}_{i,n}\mathbf{G}\mathbb{P}_{i,n})(\mathbb{P}_{i,n}\mathbf{G}^{-1}\mathbb{P}_{i,n})$, we can establish a relationship between the blocks:

$$\begin{pmatrix} \mathbb{I}_{n-1} & 0 \\ 0 & 1 \end{pmatrix} = \begin{pmatrix} \mathbf{A}\mathbf{a} + \mathbf{B}\mathbf{b}^T & \mathbf{A}\mathbf{b} + \mathbf{B}\mathbf{c} \\ \mathbf{B}^T\mathbf{a} + \mathbf{C}\mathbf{b}^T & \mathbf{B}^T\mathbf{b} + \mathbf{C}\mathbf{c} \end{pmatrix} \qquad (11)$$

The upper blocks give $\mathbf{Aa} + \mathbf{Bb}^T = \mathbb{I}_{n-1}$, and $\mathbf{Ab} + \mathbf{Bc} = 0$, from which we derive:

$$\mathbf{Bb}^T = \mathbf{B}(\mathbf{cc}^{-1})\mathbf{b}^T = (\mathbf{Bc})\mathbf{c}^{-1}\mathbf{b}^T = -\mathbf{Abc}^{-1}\mathbf{b}^T \tag{12}$$

$$\mathbf{Aa} + \mathbf{Bb}^T = \mathbf{Aa} - \mathbf{Abc}^{-1}\mathbf{b}^T = \mathbf{A}(\mathbf{a} - \mathbf{bc}^{-1}\mathbf{b}^T) = \mathbb{I}_{n-1} \tag{13}$$

The first equation in (12) is valid because $\mathbf{c}$, a diagonal element of a positive-definite matrix, is guaranteed to be strictly positive ($\mathbf{c} \neq 0$). The final equation in (13) provides a direct formula for the required inverse:

$$\mathbf{G}_{-i}^{-1} = \mathbf{A}^{-1} = \mathbf{a} - \frac{1}{\mathbf{c}}\mathbf{bb}^T = \mathbf{g}_{-i} - \frac{1}{g_{ii}}\mathbf{g}_i \mathbf{g}_i^T. \tag{14}$$

This efficient formulation allows us to derive all necessary inverses from the sub-blocks of the single inverse $\mathbf{G}^{-1}$, and avoid explicit matrix inversions inside a loop.

## 5.2 Iterative Pruning with Lazy Updates

After pruning a neuron, the weight matrix $\mathbf{W}$ changes, which in turn invalidates the previously computed matrix $\mathbf{G}$ and its inverse. Recomputing $\mathbf{G}^{-1}$ and the associated $\mathbf{G}_{-i}^{-1}$ matrices at every step remains expensive. The lazy update scheme avoids this by tracking changes without modifying the underlying weight matrices until the end.

We track the cumulative multiplicative updates for each neuron using coefficient vectors, $\boldsymbol{u}_\phi^{(t)}$ for $\phi \in \{\alpha, \beta, \gamma\}$, initialized as vectors of ones. At each pruning step $t$, the coefficient vector for the unpruned neurons is updated in-place:

$$\boldsymbol{u}_\phi^{(t+1)} \leftarrow \boldsymbol{u}_\phi^{(t)} \odot \left(1 + \phi \hat{\boldsymbol{q}}_i^{(t)}\right), \tag{15}$$

where $\odot$ is the element-wise product and $\hat{\boldsymbol{q}}_i^{(t)}$ is the coefficient vector of the linear combination of the projection of the pruned row $\boldsymbol{w}_i^T$. To maintain its validity for subsequent steps, we apply a similar update:

$$\forall j \text{ not pruned}: \quad \hat{\boldsymbol{q}}_j^{(t+1)} \leftarrow \hat{\boldsymbol{q}}_j^{(t)} \odot \frac{1}{1 + \phi \hat{\boldsymbol{q}}_i^{(t)}} \tag{16}$$

The final weight updates are applied only once after all $r$ pruning iterations are complete:

$$\forall j \text{ not pruned}: \quad \boldsymbol{w}'_j \leftarrow \boldsymbol{w}_j \cdot \left(\boldsymbol{u}_\alpha^{(r)}\right)_j, \tag{17}$$

$$\boldsymbol{b}'_j \leftarrow \boldsymbol{b}_j \cdot \left(\boldsymbol{u}_\beta^{(r)}\right)_j, \tag{18}$$

$$\boldsymbol{v}'_j \leftarrow \boldsymbol{v}_j \cdot \left(\boldsymbol{u}_\gamma^{(r)}\right)_j. \tag{19}$$

## 5.3 Masking and Views

To support the lazy update scheme, pruned rows are not physically removed from data structures during the iteration. Instead, a binary mask tracks the status of each neuron.

Operations with weights and coefficients are performed efficiently on unpruned elements via masking (Eqs. 16, 17) and views (Eq. 14). By preserving the shape of the underlying matrices, this method avoids costly memory reallocations while maintaining the relevant coefficients up-to-date.

## 6 Experimental Results

We evaluate Projective Pruning on various deep learning architectures and datasets covering both computer vision (image and point cloud classification) and language modeling (next-token prediction). All experiments are conducted in a pruning-after-training scenario, with results reported either with or without recovery fine-tuning. The former evaluates model trainability after the compression, while the latter evaluates the pruning method's ability to retain accuracy on its own.

Additionally, we analyze the impact of redistribution parameters $\alpha$, $\beta$, $\gamma$, and the regularization term $\lambda$ on model performance. Overall, the results indicate that Projective Pruning is a viable alternative to existing structured pruning algorithms. The code is available at github.com/bnjpm/projective-pruning.

### 6.1 Vision Tasks

We evaluate Projective Pruning on image classification tasks using the CIFAR-10/100 and ImageNet datasets [22,23], and on point cloud classification with ModelNet40 [50]. Architectures include VGG-19 [43], ResNet56 [17], MobileNetV2 [41], ViT [7], and PointNet [36]. Projective Pruning is compared against eight baselines: random pruning, MagnitudeL2, Slimming [32], FPGM [18], EigenDamage [48], LAMP [26], DepGraph, and DepGraph-SL [9]. Models are pruned globally at 2× and 3× FLOPs reduction using dependency graph-based grouping [9].

Results in Table 1 demonstrate that Projective Pruning achieves state-of-the-art performance on common benchmark computer vision datasets. On CIFAR-10, it outperforms competitors for ResNet56 at 3× FLOPs reduction (0.9402 vs. 0.9401 for DepGraph-SL) and MobileNetV2 at 3× FLOPs reduction (0.9051 vs. 0.9041 for MagnitudeL2). For CIFAR-100, it attains the highest accuracy on VGG-19 at 3× FLOPs speedup (0.7387 vs. 0.7352 for DepGraph-SL) and ResNet56 at 2× FLOPs reduction (0.7256 vs. 0.7239 for DepGraph-SL). On ModelNet40, Projective Pruning dominates PointNet at both 2× (0.8966) and 3× (0.8963) reduction, surpassing all baselines.

Key strengths of Projective Pruning include its superiority on lightweight architectures (e.g., MobileNetV2) and high pruning ratios (3× speedup). For example, on MobileNetV2 (CIFAR-100, 3×), it achieves 0.6911 accuracy vs.

**Table 1.** Models are pretrained, globally pruned, and fine-tuned on CIFAR-10/100 and ModelNet40. The results show the top-1 accuracy of pruned models with 2/3× FLOPs reduction.

| | CIFAR-10 | | | | | |
|---|---|---|---|---|---|---|
| Model | VGG-19 | | ResNet56 | | MobileNetV2 | |
| Accuracy | 0.9368 | | 0.9392 | | 0.8938 | |
| Method | 2× | 3× | 2× | 3× | 2× | 3× |
| Random | 0.7538 | 0.6338 | 0.9295 | 0.8963 | 0.8561 | 0.8884 |
| MagnitudeL2 | <u>0.9398</u> | 0.9356 | 0.9346 | 0.9315 | 0.8997 | <u>0.9041</u> |
| Slimming | 0.9387 | 0.9367 | **0.9408** | 0.9389 | **0.9064** | 0.9030 |
| FPGM | 0.9388 | 0.9363 | 0.9340 | 0.9241 | 0.9025 | 0.9011 |
| EigenDamage | 0.9367 | 0.9361 | 0.9292 | 0.9108 | 0.9005 | 0.8981 |
| LAMP | 0.9389 | 0.9383 | 0.9297 | 0.9133 | 0.9019 | 0.9021 |
| DepGraph | **0.9402** | 0.9370 | 0.9362 | 0.9313 | 0.9010 | 0.9000 |
| DepGraph-SL | 0.9392 | **0.9387** | <u>0.9407</u> | <u>0.9401</u> | 0.9045 | 0.8977 |
| **Projective (ours)** | 0.9388 | <u>0.9384</u> | 0.9403 | **0.9402** | <u>0.9061</u> | **0.9051** |

| | CIFAR-100 | | | | | |
|---|---|---|---|---|---|---|
| Model | VGG-19 | | ResNet56 | | MobileNetV2 | |
| Accuracy | 0.7377 | | 0.7269 | | 0.6699 | |
| Method | 2× | 3× | 2× | 3× | 2× | 3× |
| Random | 0.7049 | 0.6558 | 0.7099 | 0.6708 | **0.7068** | 0.6042 |
| MagnitudeL2 | 0.7318 | 0.7227 | 0.7143 | 0.6900 | 0.6843 | 0.6823 |
| Slimming | 0.7380 | 0.7350 | 0.7213 | **0.7257** | 0.6892 | <u>0.6865</u> |
| FPGM | 0.7357 | 0.7181 | 0.7076 | 0.6919 | 0.6856 | 0.6848 |
| EigenDamage | <u>0.7403</u> | 0.7284 | 0.6739 | 0.6369 | 0.6792 | 0.6848 |
| LAMP | **0.7414** | 0.7308 | 0.6750 | 0.6378 | 0.6824 | 0.6862 |
| DepGraph | 0.7326 | 0.7237 | 0.7177 | 0.6925 | 0.6847 | 0.6849 |
| DepGraph-SL | 0.7366 | <u>0.7352</u> | <u>0.7239</u> | <u>0.7253</u> | 0.6873 | 0.6129 |
| **Projective (ours)** | 0.7396 | **0.7387** | **0.7256** | 0.7242 | <u>0.6995</u> | **0.6911** |

| | ModelNet40 | |
|---|---|---|
| Model / Accuracy | PointNet / 0.9238 | |
| Method | 2× | 3× |
| Random | 0.8517 | 0.8840 |
| MagnitudeL2 | 0.8902 | 0.8886 |
| Slimming | 0.8936 | <u>0.8934</u> |
| FPGM | 0.8878 | 0.8870 |
| EigenDamage | 0.8912 | 0.8851 |
| LAMP | 0.8906 | 0.8849 |
| DepGraph | 0.8898 | 0.8886 |
| DepGraph-SL | <u>0.8938</u> | 0.8926 |
| **Projective (ours)** | **0.8966** | **0.8963** |

0.6865 for the Slimming method. Additionally, without fine-tuning, Projective Pruning retains expressiveness better than heuristic methods, as shown by its post-pruning accuracy on ViT models (Fig. 4). This underscores its mathematical advantage in preserving critical signal pathways during redundancy removal, even for complex architectures.

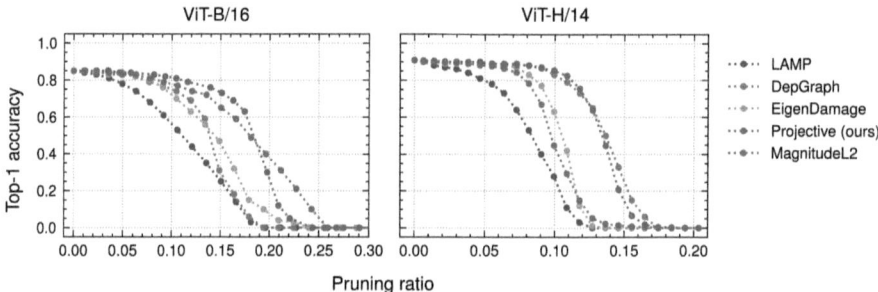

**Fig. 4.** Pretrained (PytorchHub) vision transformers evaluated on ImageNet. The models are pruned uniformly across all layers. Top-1 accuracy is reported with no recovery fine-tuning.

### 6.2 Language Modeling

We evaluate the effectiveness of Projective Pruning on the GPT-2 model using the Penn Treebank [33] and WikiText-2 [34] datasets with pre-trained weights (OpenAI) [38]. Table 2 presents the perplexity scores of the pruned models without fine-tuning. The results demonstrate that Projective Pruning consistently outperforms other methods, particularly for small to medium-sized models (124M, 355M, and 774M parameters) at moderate pruning rates (10% and 20%). For instance, on the Penn Treebank dataset with a 20% pruning ratio, Projective Pruning achieves a perplexity of 46.66 for the 124M model, significantly lower than Random (70.32), MagnitudeL2 (459.13), and DepGraph-SL (85.97). Similarly, on WikiText-2, Projective Pruning maintains strong performance, with perplexities of 39.13 (124M) and 26.26 (355M) at 20% pruning, showing its ability to retain model expressiveness after significant weight reduction.

However, at higher pruning rates (30%) and for larger models (1.5B parameters), random pruning shows competitive performance, occasionally surpassing Projective Pruning. This suggests that for highly overparametrized models, Random Pruning is seemingly a valid option due to the high level of redundancy in weights.

The key strength of Projective Pruning lies in its ability to preserve model performance at moderate pruning levels, especially for smaller architectures, as its mathematical foundation in redundancy identification and weight redistribution ensures minimal loss of information. This makes it particularly suitable for resource-constrained environments where maintaining accuracy while reducing model size is critical.

**Table 2.** Perplexity of the pretrained GPT-2 model after pruning on the Penn Treebank and WikiText-2 datasets. Projective Pruning on average outperforms other pruning methods across S/M/L model sizes, while random pruning shows the best performance retention in the XL model.

| Ratio | Method | Penn Treebank | | | | WikiText-2 | | | |
|---|---|---|---|---|---|---|---|---|---|
| | | 124M | 355M | 774M | 1.5B | 124M | 355M | 774M | 1.5B |
| 0% | None | 35.86 | 27.18 | 23.14 | 21.10 | 29.94 | 21.71 | 19.44 | 17.40 |
| 10% | Random | <u>49.75</u> | 35.39 | 24.45 | <u>22.05</u> | <u>45.32</u> | <u>25.74</u> | <u>20.88</u> | <u>18.14</u> |
| | MagnitudeL2 | 248.64 | 466.72 | 59.79 | 37.80 | 217.69 | 540.25 | 50.62 | 29.84 |
| | DepGraph-SL | 53.67 | **28.31** | <u>23.52</u> | 24.94 | 57.91 | 29.86 | 21.39 | 18.31 |
| | **Projective** | **38.50** | <u>29.43</u> | **23.92** | **21.91** | **31.79** | **22.75** | **20.14** | **17.89** |
| 20% | Random | <u>70.32</u> | 43.34 | 28.18 | <u>23.57</u> | <u>67.29</u> | <u>42.30</u> | <u>22.48</u> | **18.83** |
| | MagnitudeL2 | 459.13 | 685.59 | 101.99 | 56.20 | 494.08 | 911.08 | 93.29 | 44.18 |
| | DepGraph-SL | 85.97 | <u>41.92</u> | <u>26.19</u> | 26.01 | 81.71 | 44.19 | 22.71 | <u>18.91</u> |
| | **Projective** | **46.66** | **35.69** | **26.10** | **23.27** | **39.13** | **26.26** | **21.81** | 18.96 |
| 30% | Random | 131.55 | 86.41 | 31.91 | **26.49** | 118.68 | 81.58 | 27.43 | **20.65** |
| | MagnitudeL2 | 687.52 | 1053.79 | 152.41 | 91.55 | 858.36 | 1399.66 | 154.61 | 70.28 |
| | DepGraph-SL | <u>121.88</u> | <u>79.21</u> | **29.16** | 32.72 | <u>104.12</u> | <u>51.49</u> | **24.19** | <u>21.13</u> |
| | **Projective** | **66.31** | **51.77** | <u>31.64</u> | <u>26.66</u> | **62.37** | **37.90** | <u>25.78</u> | 21.48 |

### 6.3 Hyperparameter Analysis

*Redistribution parameters.* $\alpha$, $\beta$, and $\gamma$ regulate the redistribution of pruned signals. To study their impact, we use a simple feedforward network with two convolutional layers and four dense layers (extended LeNet) on the FashionMNIST dataset [51]. In Fig. 5, pruning is applied equally across dense layers, and performance is compared against Magnitude-$L_2$ pruning, random pruning, and variations of Projective Pruning with different weight readjustments. Pruning is assessed without retraining to measure accuracy retention directly.

*Regularization term.* $\lambda$ stabilizes the inverse of $\boldsymbol{W}_{-i}\boldsymbol{W}_{-i}^T$. While this matrix is typically well-conditioned, it can become ill-conditioned when rows are highly correlated. In widening fully connected layers, $\boldsymbol{W}_{-i}\boldsymbol{W}_{-i}^T$ is always singular, in which case the inverse is undefined. Adding a small value to the diagonal introduces a bias towards $\boldsymbol{0}$ for $\hat{\boldsymbol{q}}$ (flattens redundancy scores), but it ensures that the matrix is always full rank, and the inverse is well-defined. $\lambda$ represents a trade-off between bias and stability (Fig. 5).

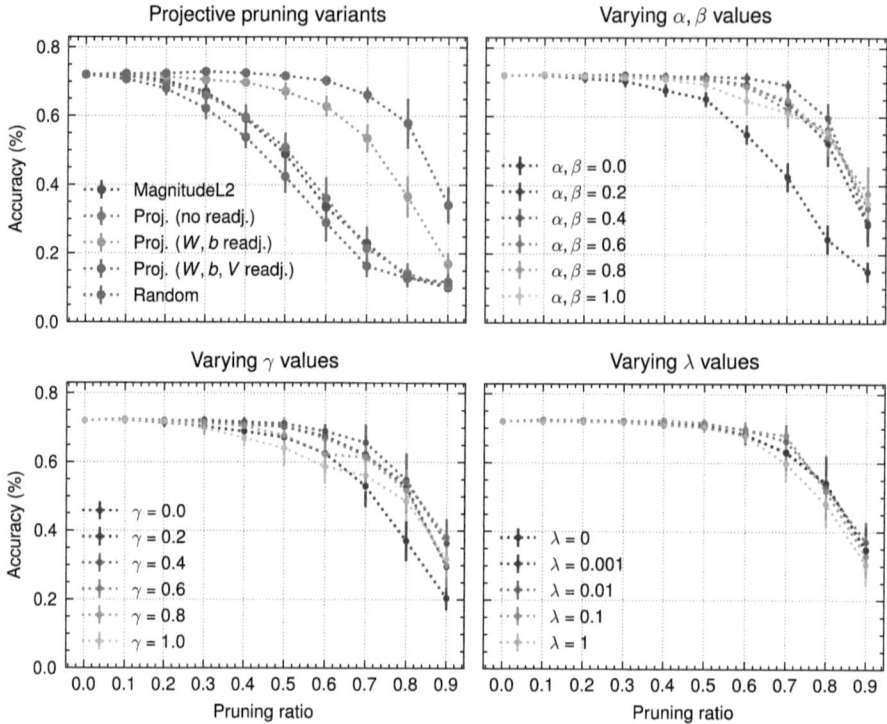

**Fig. 5.** (upper left) Comparison of Projective Pruning variants on FashionMNIST. Accuracy is reported after training and pruning with no retraining. Error bars show the 95% confidence interval. Other subfigures show impact of hyperparameters on model accuracy with varying $\alpha/\beta$ (upper right), $\gamma$ (lower left), and $\lambda$ (lower right). Non-varying parameters are set to default values: 0.5 for $\alpha$, $\beta$, $\gamma$, and $10^{-3}$ for $\lambda$.

## 7 Conclusion

We introduced Projective Pruning, a structured pruning algorithm for neural compression that minimizes weight co-adaptation by removing linearly redundant parameters. Additionally, we designed a redistribution scheme that preserves model performance by reallocating the pruned weights' signal. Our method was evaluated against state-of-the-art pruning techniques across diverse domains, including standard vision and language modeling benchmarks. The results show that Projective Pruning retains model expressiveness effectively, the method performs consistently across different model sizes and pruning ratios, with particularly strong performance in scenarios involving relatively small parameter counts and aggressive pruning conditions.

**Acknowledgments.** This work was supported by the 2024 Student Summer Research Program at the Faculty of Information Technology, Czech Technical University in Prague. We extend our gratitude for this opportunity and the resources provided to make this work possible.

**Disclosure of Interests.** The authors have no competing interests to declare that are relevant to the content of this article.

# References

1. Ashkboos, S., Croci, M.L., do Nascimento, M.G., Hoefler, T., Hensman, J.: Slicegpt: compress large language models by deleting rows and columns (2024)
2. Bommasani, R., et al.: On the opportunities and risks of foundation models. arXiv preprint arXiv:2108.07258 (2021)
3. Cai, H., Gan, C., Wang, T., Zhang, Z., Han, S.: Once-for-all: train one network and specialize it for efficient deployment. In: International Conference on Learning Representations (2020)
4. Cheng, H., Zhang, M., Shi, J.Q.: A survey on deep neural network pruning: taxonomy, comparison, analysis, and recommendations. In: IEEE Transactions on Pattern Analysis and Machine Intelligence pp. 1–20 (2024)
5. Cottier, B., Rahman, R., Fattorini, L., Maslej, N., Besiroglu, T., Owen, D.: The rising costs of training frontier AI models. arXiv preprint arXiv:2405.21015 (2024)
6. Denil, M., Shakibi, B., Dinh, L., Ranzato, M., De Freitas, N.: Predicting parameters in deep learning. Adv. Neural Inf. Proc. Syst. **26** (2013)
7. Dosovitskiy, A., et al.: An image is worth $16 \times 16$ words: transformers for image recognition at scale (2021)
8. Evci, U., Gale, T., Menick, J., Castro, P.S., Elsen, E.: Rigging the lottery: making all tickets winners (2021)
9. Fang, G., Ma, X., Song, M., Mi, M.B., Wang, X.: Depgraph: towards any structural pruning (2023)
10. Frankle, J., Carbin, M.: The lottery ticket hypothesis: finding sparse, trainable neural networks. In: International Conference on Learning Representations (2019)
11. Frankle, J., Carbin, M.: The lottery ticket hypothesis: finding sparse, trainable neural networks (2019)
12. Frantar, E., Alistarh, D.: SparseGPT: Massive language models can be accurately pruned in one-shot. In: Krause, A., Brunskill, E., Cho, K., Engelhardt, B., Sabato, S., Scarlett, J. (eds.) Proceedings of the 40th International Conference on Machine Learning. Proceedings of Machine Learning Research, vol. 202, pp. 10323–10337. PMLR (2023)
13. Goodfellow, I., Bengio, Y., Courville, A.: Deep learning. MIT Press (2016)
14. Han, S., Mao, H., Dally, W.J.: Deep compression: compressing deep neural networks with pruning, trained quantization and huffman coding (2016)
15. Han, S., Pool, J., Tran, J., Dally, W.: Learning both weights and connections for efficient neural network. In: Advances in Neural Information Processing Systems. vol. 28 (2015)
16. Hassibi, B., Stork, D.: Second order derivatives for network pruning: optimal brain surgeon. In: Hanson, S., Cowan, J., Giles, C. (eds.) Advances in Neural Information Processing Systems. vol. 5. Morgan-Kaufmann (1992)
17. He, K., Zhang, X., Ren, S., Sun, J.: Deep residual learning for image recognition. In: 2016 IEEE Conference on Computer Vision and Pattern Recognition (CVPR), pp. 770–778 (2016)
18. He, Y., Liu, P., Wang, Z., Hu, Z., Yang, Y.: Filter pruning via geometric median for deep convolutional neural networks acceleration. In: Proceedings of the IEEE/CVF Conference on Computer Vision and Pattern Recognition (CVPR) (2019)

19. Hinton, G.E., Vinyals, O., Dean, J.: Distilling the knowledge in a neural network. CoRR **abs/1503.02531** (2015)
20. Idelbayev, Y., Carreira-Perpinan, M.A.: Low-rank compression of neural nets: learning the rank of each layer. In: 2020 IEEE/CVF Conference on Computer Vision and Pattern Recognition (CVPR), pp. 8046–8056 (2020)
21. Jiang, A.Q., et al.: Mistral 7b (2023)
22. Krizhevsky, A., Nair, V., Hinton, G.: Cifar-10 (canadian institute for advanced research)
23. Krizhevsky, A., Sutskever, I., Hinton, G.E.: Imagenet classification with deep convolutional neural networks. In: Pereira, F., Burges, C., Bottou, L., Weinberger, K. (eds.) Advances in Neural Information Processing Systems. vol. 25. Curran Associates, Inc. (2012)
24. LeCun, Y., Bengio, Y., Hinton, G.: Deep learning. Nature **521**(7553), 436–444 (2015)
25. LeCun, Y., Denker, J., Solla, S.: Optimal brain damage. In: Touretzky, D. (ed.) Advances in Neural Information Processing Systems. vol. 2. Morgan-Kaufmann (1989)
26. Lee, J., Park, S., Mo, S., Ahn, S., Shin, J.: Layer-adaptive sparsity for the magnitude-based pruning. In: International Conference on Learning Representations (2021)
27. Lee, N., Ajanthan, T., Torr, P.H.S.: Snip: single-shot network pruning based on connection sensitivity (2019)
28. Li, H., Xu, Z., Taylor, G., Studer, C., Goldstein, T.: Visualizing the loss landscape of neural nets. In: Bengio, S., Wallach, H., Larochelle, H., Grauman, K., Cesa-Bianchi, N., Garnett, R. (eds.) Advances in Neural Information Processing Systems. vol. 31. Curran Associates, Inc. (2018)
29. Li, Y., Adamczewski, K., Li, W., Gu, S., Timofte, R., Gool, L.V.: Revisiting random channel pruning for neural network compression (2022)
30. Liu, S., et al.: Sparse training via boosting pruning plasticity with neuroregeneration. In: Proceedings of the 35th International Conference on Neural Information Processing Systems. NIPS '21, Curran Associates Inc., Red Hook, NY, USA (2024)
31. Liu, S., et al.: The unreasonable effectiveness of random pruning: return of the most naive baseline for sparse training. In: International Conference on Learning Representations (2022)
32. Liu, Z., Li, J., Shen, Z., Huang, G., Yan, S., Zhang, C.: Learning efficient convolutional networks through network slimming. In: 2017 IEEE International Conference on Computer Vision (ICCV), pp. 2755–2763 (2017)
33. Marcus, M.P., Santorini, B., Marcinkiewicz, M.A.: Building a large annotated corpus of english: the penn treebank. Comput. Linguist. **19**(2), 313–330 (1993)
34. Merity, S., Xiong, C., Bradbury, J., Socher, R.: Pointer sentinel mixture models (2016)
35. Patterson, D., et al.: Carbon emissions and large neural network training. arXiv preprint arXiv:2104.10350 (2021)
36. Qi, C.R., Yi, L., Su, H., Guibas, L.J.: Pointnet++: deep hierarchical feature learning on point sets in a metric space. In: Guyon, I., et al (eds.) Advances in Neural Information Processing Systems. vol. 30. Curran Associates, Inc. (2017)
37. Radford, A., Narasimhan, K., Salimans, T., Sutskever, I.: Improving language understanding by generative pre-training (2018)
38. Radford, A., Wu, J., Child, R., Luan, D., Amodei, D., Sutskever, I.: Language models are unsupervised multitask learners. OpenAI (2019)

39. Raiaan, M.A.K., et al.: A review on large language models: architectures, applications, taxonomies, open issues and challenges. IEEE access **12**, 26839–26874 (2024)
40. Sabih, M., Hannig, F., Teich, J.: Utilizing explainable AI for quantization and pruning of deep neural networks. CoRR **abs/2008.09072** (2020)
41. Sandler, M., Howard, A., Zhu, M., Zhmoginov, A., Chen, L.C.: Mobilenetv2: inverted residuals and linear bottlenecks. In: Proceedings of the IEEE Conference on Computer Vision and Pattern Recognition (CVPR) (2018)
42. Sanh, V., Debut, L., Chaumond, J., Wolf, T.: Distilbert, a distilled version of BERT: smaller, faster, cheaper and lighter. ArXiv **abs/1910.01108** (2019)
43. Simonyan, K., Zisserman, A.: Very deep convolutional networks for large-scale image recognition. CoRR **abs/1409.1556** (2014)
44. Strubell, E., Ganesh, A., McCallum, A.: Energy and policy considerations for deep learning in NLP. In: Proceedings of the 57th Annual Meeting of the Association for Computational Linguistics, pp. 3645–3650 (2019)
45. Sun, M., Liu, Z., Bair, A., Kolter, J.Z.: A simple and effective pruning approach for large language models. In: The Twelfth International Conference on Learning Representations (2024)
46. Thompson, N.C., Greenewald, K., Lee, K., Manso, G.F.: Deep learning's diminishing returns. IEEE Spectr. **59**(10), 34–39 (2022)
47. Touvron, H., et al.: Llama: open and efficient foundation language models (2023)
48. Wang, C., Grosse, R.B., Fidler, S., Zhang, G.: Eigendamage: structured pruning in the kronecker-factored eigenbasis. ArXiv **abs/1905.05934** (2019)
49. Wu, C.J., et al.: Sustainable AI: environmental implications, challenges and opportunities. In: Proceedings of Machine Learning and Systems. vol. 4, pp. 795–813 (2022)
50. Wu, Z., et al.: 3d shapenets: a deep representation for volumetric shapes. In: 2015 IEEE Conference on Computer Vision and Pattern Recognition (CVPR), pp. 1912–1920 (2015)
51. Xiao, H., Rasul, K., Vollgraf, R.: Fashion-mnist: a novel image dataset for benchmarking machine learning algorithms (2017)

# Two-Stage Temporal Knowledge Graph Completion Based on Reinforcement Learning

Dong Li[1], Yong Wei[1], Xinyi Dong[1], Jingyou Sun[1], LinLin Ding[1(✉)], and Yue Kou[2]

[1] Liaoning University, Shenyang, China
dinglinlin@lnu.edu.cn
[2] Northeastern University, Shenyang, China

**Abstract.** Knowledge graphs have become an indispensable technology for organizing and processing vast amounts of information, with applications spanning intelligent robotics, risk management, recommender systems, and healthcare analytics. However, the effectiveness of knowledge graphs in downstream tasks is often limited by inherent structural incompleteness. To address this issue, we propose TS-TKGC (Two-Stage Temporal Knowledge Graph Completion), a novel reinforcement learning-based method. Our TS-TKGC method consists of two key stages: clue search and temporal reasoning. In the first stage, reinforcement learning is employed to identify informative clues. In the second stage, the method integrates Gated Recurrent Units (GRU) for temporal reasoning, alongside a multi-dimensional reward mechanism to optimize the training strategy. Finally, experimental results validate the feasibility and effectiveness of the proposed key technique, demonstrating the model's capability to enhance temporal knowledge graph completion.

**Keywords:** Temporal Knowledge Graphs · Two-Stage Knowledge Completion · Reinforcement Learning · Clue Search · Gated Recurrent Units

## 1 Introduction

In the digital era, the information explosion has provided abundant data resources for intelligent services. However, such data are often characterized by high redundancy, structural heterogeneity, and low utilization efficiency, necessitating the construction of domain-specific knowledge bases with refined management. As an extension of traditional knowledge graphs, temporal knowledge graphs incorporate timestamps to evolve fact representations from static triples $(h, r, t)$ to dynamic quadruples $(h, r, t, \tau)$. By not only modeling entity-relationship structures but also capturing their temporal dynamics, temporal knowledge graphs enable advanced capabilities such as trend analysis, temporal querying, and event prediction. These enhancements significantly empower applications in decision support, risk assessment, and cybersecurity, among other domains.

Temporal knowledge graph completion enhances dynamic knowledge representation by modeling facts as timestamped quadruples $(h, r, t, \tau)$. This approach captures both explicit event occurrences and implicit temporal patterns, enabling sophisticated temporal reasoning capabilities. Despite its practical value, current temporal knowledge graph completion approaches exhibit significant limitations: rule-based methods are hindered by poor scalability from rule explosion and ineffective temporal modeling; GNN-based techniques struggle with frequent entity/relation changes and long-term dependency capture; while reinforcement learning frameworks face challenges in reward mechanism design and suffer from sparse feedback-induced learning inefficiency. Crucially, existing methods fail to effectively bridge temporal evolution with structural semantics, creating a disconnect between dynamic patterns and graph topology. Although reinforcement learning offers interpretable temporal reasoning, fundamental challenges remain unresolved, particularly the joint modeling of temporal dynamics and semantic relationships, coupled with severe training inefficiencies stemming from inadequate reward signals in sparse environments.

In this paper, we propose a temporal knowledge graph completion model that incorporates reinforcement learning to address these challenges. The main contributions of this paper include: (1) We propose a novel temporal knowledge graph completion framework integrating clue searching and temporal reasoning to jointly model temporal information and structural characteristics; (2) We propose an interpretable reinforcement learning mechanism for enhanced performance in complex temporal reasoning; (3) We design a collaborative training mechanism that synchronizes clue searching and temporal reasoning, allowing adaptive optimization under varying temporal constraints; (4) Extensive experiments on multiple benchmark datasets validate the model's effectiveness, achieving better performance on temporal knowledge graph completion tasks.

## 2 Related Work

In this section, we review related work on temporal knowledge graph completion and highlight our technical contributions. Existing temporal knowledge graph completion approaches fall into three main categories: rule-based approaches, graph neural network (GNN)-based approaches, and reinforcement learning-based approaches.

### 2.1 Rule-Based Temporal Knowledge Graph Completion

In static environments, rule-based temporal knowledge graph completion demonstrates strong interpretability and reliability. Early approaches relied on manually defined temporal logic rules for reasoning. For instance, the approach proposed in [1] achieved 89.6% prediction precision in biomedical event forecasting by designing 14 temporal clause rules through multi-path dependency analysis. Subsequent work by Bai et al. [2] enhanced this framework using Bayesian pruning strategies, maintaining temporal confidence scores above 0.85. Recent advances have focused on automated rule extraction. For example, the ALREIR model [3] leverages temporal attention mechanisms to autonomously discover logical patterns, achieving a 23.7% improvement in F1-score over manual rule-engineering methods while preserving model interpretability.

## 2.2 GNN-Based Temporal Knowledge Graph Completion

GNN-based approaches have significantly advanced temporal knowledge graph completion by jointly learning structural and temporal entity representations. RENET [4] pioneered this direction with multi-relational graph aggregation for structural feature extraction. Subsequent innovations in variants of GNN-based approaches have further enhanced temporal modeling. For example, the method proposed in [5] incorporates GRU gates conditioned on event frequency to capture temporally inactive dependencies. REGCN [6] employs autoregressive GRU networks to model temporal event dynamics. DACHA [7] introduces architectural innovation through dual-graph convolutional networks, synchronizing information flow between primal graphs and their edge-graph counterparts. Notably, Zhu et al. [8] propose an advanced framework with implicit knowledge propagation, enabling concurrent future event prediction via three synergistic modules: entity vocabulary pattern recognition, temporal transaction recurrence detection, and known fact reference mechanisms.

## 2.3 Reinforcement Learning-Based Temporal Knowledge Graph Completion

Recent advances in reinforcement learning for temporal knowledge graph completion have highlighted the critical importance of sophisticated reward design [9], where early binary reward mechanisms [10] established performance baselines while subsequent innovations progressively addressed reward sparsity through temporal pattern encoding and exploration optimization. Notable developments include path diversity rewards [11] for multi-pattern exploration, Dirichlet temporal allocation [12] for time-aware reward distribution, and LSTM-enhanced beam rewards [13] for sequential decision optimization.

Compared with the above models, our proposed TS-TKGC model makes three significant advances: first, it adopts a unified framework integrating clue searching with temporal reasoning to jointly capture semantic dependencies and temporal evolution patterns; second, it utilizes a two-stage collaborative learning mechanism that effectively mitigates the persistent challenge of reward sparsity in reinforcement learning; third, it implements dynamic temporal constraint-aware path adjustment to simultaneously enhance exploration efficiency and task performance in complex scenarios.

# 3 Problem Definition

This section mainly introduces the concepts involved in temporal knowledge graph completion and then formally defines the problem of temporal knowledge graph completion.

**Definition 1.** (*Quadruple*) *A quadruple $(h, r, t, timestamp)$ consists of four parts: head entity, relation, tail entity, and timestamp. The quadruple represents a fact triplet with temporal information, indicating that at time t, the triplet $(h, r, t)$ holds.*

**Definition 2.** (*Temporal Knowledge Graph*) *A temporal knowledge graph is an extension of traditional knowledge graph in the temporal dimension, aiming to record the relationships and evolution processes of things over time.*

In temporal knowledge graphs, each fact is represented by a quadruple consisting of a head entity, a relation, a tail entity, and a timestamp associated with the fact. By incorporating temporal attributes, temporal knowledge graphs can reflect the states and changes of things at different time points.

Temporal knowledge graph uses entities as nodes, relationships to represent connections between entities, and timestamps to indicate the temporal attributes of current facts. They can be represented by the quadruple $G = (E, R, T, F)$, where $E$ denotes the set of entities (e.g., Xiaomi Company, Li Auto, China, Physics), $R$ denotes the set of relationships between entities (e.g., father-son, bordering, possession), $T$ denotes the set of timestamps (e.g., 2021, March 2nd, 8 a.m.), and $F$ denotes the set of quadruples (e.g., (COVID-19, outbreak, Wuhan, Hubei Province, December 2019), (Alibaba Group, acquires, Ele.me, April 2, 2018), (Tencent stock price, is, 400 yuan, April 30, 2023)).

**Definition 3.** (*Temporal Knowledge Graph Completion*) *Temporal knowledge graph completion refers to the process of using algorithms and technical means to complete or supplement missing entities, relationships, or quadruples in temporal knowledge graph with temporal labels.*

Temporal knowledge graph completion addresses evolving entity-relationship dynamics by inferring valid missing facts. For example, in a corporate leadership knowledge graph tracking directors' positions across time intervals, temporal gaps may exist in role transition records. Temporal knowledge graph completion predicts such missing position changes and their precise timestamps by leveraging existing temporal patterns.

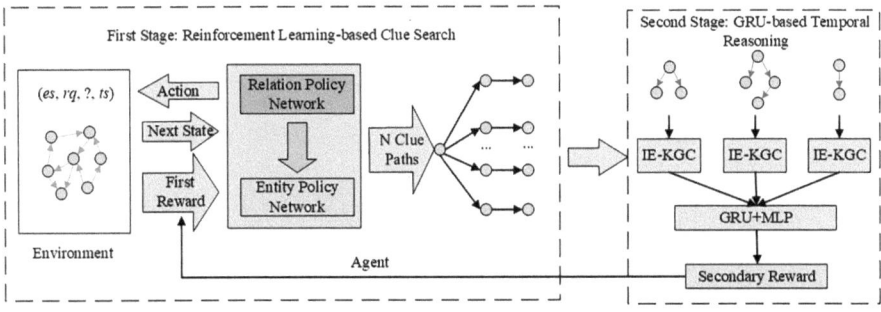

**Fig. 1.** Model Overview

It is to infer the missing components of quadruples in a given temporal knowledge graph G, based on the existing fact quadruples $\{(e_h, r, e_t, t) \in F\}$. Specifically, it aims to predict the missing tail entity in quadruples of the form $(e_h, r, ?, t)$, the missing head entity in quadruples of the form $(?, r, e_t, t)$, or the missing relation in quadruples of the form $(e_h, ?, e_t, t)$.

The proposed model operates in two stages: 1) clue searching: identifies temporally constrained clue paths relevant to the query, capturing rich semantic information for reasoning. 2) temporal reasoning: processes clue paths and candidate entities to capture temporal dependencies and generate final predictions. This integrated approach maintains information accuracy while handling temporal dynamics, improving prediction precision (Fig. 1).

## 4 Temporal Knowledge Graph Completion Model

### 4.1 Model Architecture

In the first stage, the clue searching process is formulated as a Markov Decision Process (MDP), incorporating two specialized reasoning agents: one focuses on relationship-based inference, and the other on entity-based reasoning. First, the relationship agent conducts preliminary reasoning on the relationships associated with the current entity to identify potential target entities. Subsequently, based on the candidate relationships provided by the relationship agent, the entity agent performs a more refined reasoning process to determine the next action. Ultimately, this process generates $N$ informative clue paths.

The temporal reasoning stage begins by reorganizing the identified clue paths into timestamp-ordered quadruples, which are then chronologically sorted to construct a temporal graph sequence. The model initializes each graph structure through comprehensive integration of entities and relationships, followed by temporal feature extraction using GRU networks to capture evolutionary patterns. Multi-layer perceptrons then process these temporal representations to either generate final predictions or produce stage feedback rewards that optimize the clue searching process through a cross-stage reinforcement mechanism. This integrated approach not only enhances path discovery efficiency but also effectively mitigates reward sparsity, ultimately improving overall model performance through coordinated temporal-structural learning.

### 4.2 Clue Searching Based on Reinforcement Learning

The goal of the first stage of clue searching is to find and summarize clue paths related to the given query from historical information. For a given query $(e_s, r_q, ?, t_s)$, where $e_s$ denotes the head entity, $r_q$ denotes the query placeholder, ? represents the unknown tail entity placeholder, and $t_s$ is the timestamp of the query, the first stage aims to obtain several candidate entities close to the target entity $e_p$ and their paths.

The TS-TKGC model employs a reinforcement learning system with two agents in the first stage to reason over paths in historical knowledge. First, the model constructs a candidate relationship set by aggregating all relationships associated with the current entity. Subsequently, the relationship policy network directs the relationship agent to select the optimal next-hop relationship. Finally, the entity policy network calculates and selects the next target entity.

This reasoning process continues until the target entity $e_p$ is reached, marking the end of the reasoning task. This dual-agent strategy enables the model to conduct knowledge reasoning with higher accuracy and efficiency. The first stage aims to discover and aggregate clue paths relevant to the query quadruple $(e_s, r_q, ?, t_s)$ from historical knowledge. Thus, developing a learnable and efficient clue searching strategy is critical. The first stage is formulated as a sequential decision-making problem that is solved by the reinforcement learning system.

Static quadruples are transformed into entity nodes with timestamps to construct a temporal graph structure. Nodes (entity, timestamp) are connected via bidirectional edges: forward edges retain original relations while reverse edges use inverse relations for semantic symmetry, with an entity-to-temporal-nodes mapping dictionary established. Action spaces are dynamically generated for each current entity state and query time: only strictly preceding events are accessible when current time equals query time; otherwise, preceding or concurrent events are permitted. State-transition actions are (relation, entity, timestamp) triples including NO-OP (stay) and PAD (padding) actions. Reverse chronological sorting is used to prioritize the latest events. Batch action spaces are standardized by truncating earliest events when exceeding capacity, padding with PAD when undersized, and disabling NO-OP at initial steps using a first-step policy, yielding reinforcement learning tensors with consistent dimensions.

The reinforcement learning system in TS-TKGC consists of an agent and an environment, formalized as a Markov Decision Process (MDP). This standard RL framework models agent-environment interactions to discover $N$ optimal clue paths that satisfy the query constraints. Starting from the initial state, the agent selects actions according to a policy to traverse to new entities, continuing until reaching the maximum step length $I$ or the target entity. Formally, the MDP is defined by four components:

**State.** Each state $s_i = (e_i, t_i, e_s, r_q, t_s) \in ST$ is a tuple, where ST is the set of all available states; $e_i(e_0 = e_s)$ is the entity visited by the agent at step $i$; $t_i(t_0 = t_s)$ is the timestamp when the agent took the action in the previous step.

**Action.** The action is represented as the set of relationships, tail entities, and timestamps that the agent might reach at step $i$, including the next entity in the quadruple. Let $A_i \in A$, $A$ be the set of all possible actions. in Eq. 4.1:

$$A_i = \{(r', e', t') | (e_i, r', e', t') \in G_{t-1}\} \tag{4.1}$$

Among them, $G_{t-1}$ denotes the set of possible quadruples that the entity $e_i$ may reach in the next step, $r'$ denotes the relation, $e'$ denotes the tail entity, and $t'$ denotes the timestamp.

**Transition.** The transition function $\delta : ST \times A \rightarrow ST$, and $ST$ is deterministic in the context of temporal knowledge graph, simply updating the state to the new entity associated with the action chosen by the agent.

**Reward.** At the end of the search process, the agent receives a final reward consisting of primary and secondary components. Specifically, the primary reward is 1 for correct target entity $e_p$ identification in the $N$ candidate entities generated by the entity agent, 0 otherwise. If $e_p$ is correctly identified, the agent also receives a secondary reward from the second stage. This reward is designed to drive the agent to locate the target entity more accurately and promote seamless collaboration between the two stages.

### (1) Relationship Policy Network

When constructing the relationship policy network, a Gated Recurrent Unit (GRU) is employed to encode historical reasoning paths. This encoding process combines historical information with the current node state to serve as the input for preliminary relationship reasoning in the network. This design enables the proposed model to fully leverage historical information, thereby enhancing reasoning accuracy and efficiency. The detailed architecture of the relationship policy network is shown in Fig. 2a.

The GRU encodes historical path-searching information by taking the previous historical state encoding $H_{t-1}$, current node information $e_s$, and query relation $r_q$ as inputs to compute the current historical state $H_t$. Notably, the initial state $H_0$ is defined as the current node $e_s$. The specific calculation is detailed in Eq. 4.2. This strategy effectively integrates historical context, providing a richer basis for the reasoning process.

$$H_t = GRU([e_s \oplus r_q], H_{t-1}) \tag{4.2}$$

The historical state information $H_t$ at the current time step t is concatenated with the current node information $e_s$ and the given query $r_q$ to form a fusion vector. This fusion vector is then passed through a ReLU function and multiplied with the set of candidate relationships, followed by a softmax activation function to obtain the probability distribution of the current node $e_s$ over the set of candidate relationships. The relationship agent can select the relationship with the highest score according to this probability distribution as the next action for the agent. The calculation process of the relationship policy network in this method is shown in Eq. 4.3, where $R_t$ represents the set of candidate relationships connected to the current entity, $W_1$ and $W_2$ are different weights.

$$\pi_\theta^h(r_t|s_t) = softmax(R_t W_2 ReLU(W_1[H_t, e_s, r_q])) \tag{4.3}$$

After constructing the relationship policy network $\pi_\theta^h$, we apply a Dropout algorithm that randomly discards a subset of candidate relationships, yielding a filtered relationship policy network $\pi_\theta^h$, as shown in Eq. 4.4.

$$\pi_\theta^{h'}(r_t|s_t) = \pi_\theta^h(r_t|s_t) b_i \tag{4.4}$$

Here, $b_i$ represents a binary variable sampled from a Bernoulli distribution. After obtaining the final relationship policy network $\pi_\theta^{h'}$, the relationships connected to the current node are probabilistically assigned to guide the relationship agent in selecting the next relationship.

**(2) Entity Policy Network**

Similar to the relationship policy network, the entity policy network takes the current node $e_s$, the given query relationship $r_q$, the historical search encoding $H_{t-1}$, and the relationship $r_t$ obtained from the relationship policy network as inputs. The entities connected to the selected relationship by the relationship agent in the current node are used as the candidate action set for the entity policy network to construct the preliminary entity policy network $\pi_\theta^l$. The final entity policy network $\pi_\theta^{l'}$ is obtained by randomly discarding some nodes in $\pi_\theta^l$ using the Dropout algorithm. The entity policy network is shown in Fig. 2b.

The calculation process of the entity policy network in this paper is shown in Eq. 4.5 and Eq. 4.6, where $A_i$ represents the action set of the current entity $e_s$, and $W_3$ and $w_4$ are different weights.

$$\pi_\theta^l(e_s|s_t) = softmax(A_i W_4 ReLU(W_3 \lceil H_t, e_s, r_q, r_t \rceil)) \qquad (4.5)$$

$$\pi_\theta^{l'}(e_s|s_t) = \pi_\theta^l(e_s|s_t) b_i \qquad (4.6)$$

After successfully constructing the entity policy network $\pi_\theta^{l'}(e_s|s_t)$, the entity agent can select the entity with the highest probability as the next action based on this probability distribution. This process ensures that the entity agent can make more accurate and effective entity selections based on the relationship chosen by the relationship agent, and continuously optimize its decision-making process through the reward mechanism.

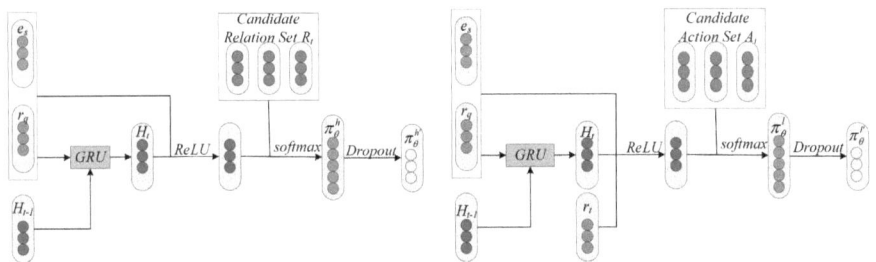

(a) Relationship Policy Network    (b) Entity Policy Network

**Fig. 2.** Relationship and Entity Policy Network

### 4.3 Temporal Reasoning Based on Gated Recurrent Units

To comprehensively model the temporal dependencies between clue facts at different timestamps and the structural correlations among simultaneously occurring clue facts, the second stage first reorganizes all clue facts in chronological order, then transforms them into a temporal graph sequence. Specifically, all clue facts are reorganized into a set of quadruples, and quadruples sharing the same timestamp are aggregated to form multi-relational temporal graphs. Each graph is composed of clue facts with timestamps $j \in \{0, 1, \ldots, t_s - 1\}$, where $t_s$ denotes the query timestamp.

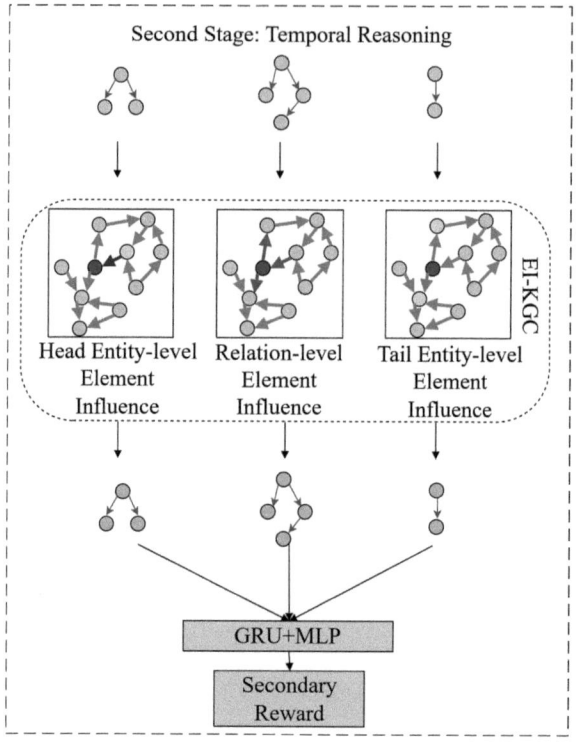

**Fig. 3.** The Basic Idea of Temporal Reasoning

After obtaining multiple reorganized graphs, we adopt this approach. We define intra-graph interaction vectors for head entities, relations, and tail entities. These vectors are computed using Graph Neural Networks (GNNs) to integrate structural information and node semantics from the knowledge graph. **Initialization Step**: For each temporal graph, the model computes initial node and relation embeddings using GNN message passing. **Iterative Update**: For each entity in the graph, the model computes three interaction vectors capturing: Head entity-to-tail entity influences, Relation-to-entity influences, and Tail entity-to-head entity influences. These vectors enable the model to capture semantic dependencies between triplets and extract implicit information within the graph. The updated entity embedding is obtained by merging these interaction vectors with the original entity embedding, as defined in Eq. 4.7:

$$e'_s = e_s + g_s^{head} + g_s^{rel} + g_s^{tail} \qquad (4.7)$$

Here, $e'_s$ represents the updated embedding of entity $e_s$ in the multi-relational graph, while $g_s^{head}$, $g_s^{rel}$ and $g_s^{tail}$ represent the influences between head entity-level elements, relation-level elements, and tail entity-level elements, respectively.

A secondary iterative refinement is applied to the current entity to effectively capture and aggregate interaction features from neighboring nodes. Taking the first-iteration updated entities as input, a second-round information aggregation is performed via iterative message passing, enabling each entity to fully integrate the semantic and structural information within its local neighborhood. The mathematical formulation for the secondary iteration is detailed in Eq. 4.8:

$$e_s^2 = e'_s + (g_s^{head})^1 + (g_s^{rel})^1 + (g_s^{tail})^1 \tag{4.8}$$

Here, $e_s^2$ represents the secondary embedding of entity $e_s^2$, while $(g_s^{head})^1$, $(g_s^{tail})^1$ and $(g_s^{tail})^1$ represent the influences between head entity-level elements, relation-level elements, and tail entity-level elements for $e_s$ in the first layer, respectively.

The embeddings are fed into the GRU to obtain the final output of the GRU, denoted as $H_j$, as shown in Eq. 4.9. $H_j$ and $W_{mlp}$ are then passed into a multi-layer perceptron (MLP) to obtain the final scores for all entities, as shown in Eq. 4.10.

$$H_j = GRU([e_s \oplus g_j \oplus r_q], H_{j-1}) \tag{4.9}$$

$$p(e|e_s, r_q, t_s) = \sigma(H_j W_{mlp}) \tag{4.10}$$

Finally, the candidate entities are re-ranked based on the obtained scores. To provide positive feedback for the clue paths that lead to the answer, the second stage offers a secondary reward to the first stage, which is equal to the final score obtained. The architecture of the temporal reasoning process is shown in Fig. 3.

### 4.4 Training Strategy and Multi-Dimensional Rewards

In the first stage, the search strategy network is trained by maximizing the expected return for all queries in the training set. Since the first and second stages are interrelated, they are trained jointly. Before the joint training process, the first stage is pre-trained using binary rewards. then, the second stage is trained while the parameters of the first stage are frozen. Finally, both stages are trained together. The final reward function is shown in Eq. 4.11, where $J(\theta)$ represents the final reward, $R(e_I|e_s, r_q, t_s)$ represents the reward obtained when reaching the maximum number of steps, and $E_{(a_0 \ldots a_{I-1})}$ represents the action chosen at the maximum step. The relationship policy network and entity policy network guide the relationship agent and entity agent, respectively, in selecting the next relationship and action. By using an interactive reward mechanism, the interaction between these two policies is strengthened, ensuring that the agents maximize their rewards. This approach enhances the model's reasoning accuracy.

$$J(\theta) = E_{(a_0 \ldots a_{I-1})}[R(e_I|e_s, r_q, t_s)] \tag{4.11}$$

Reinforcement learning is applied to the task of temporal knowledge graph completion. To avoid performance degradation caused by sparse rewards, a new reward mechanism is constructed to calculate reward weights from multiple dimensions. The rewards are mainly divided into two parts. In the first stage, an interactive reward function is constructed for clue searching to give timely rewards for the choices made by the relationship and entity agents. In the second stage, a secondary reward is returned if the correct result is ultimately obtained

The rewards in the first stage are primarily obtained by calculating the similarity scores between the candidate relationships or entities selected by the two agents and the target quadruple using a scoring function score $f(e_t, r_{t+1}, e_{t+1}, t_s)$. These similarity scores are used as the reward scores for the agents' choices, facilitating interaction between the relationship and entity agents. When the agents find the target relationship or entity, a global reward is given, as $R_g^h = 1$ and $R_t^l = 1$; if the target is not found and the maximum reasoning step length is not reached, the similarity score calculated by the scoring function is used as the reward for the agents' choices. The calculation methods for the interactive reward functions are shown in Eq. 4.12 and Eq. 4.13.

$$R_t^h = R_g^h + (1 - R_g^h)f(e_t, r_{t+1}, e_{t+1}, t_s) \qquad (4.12)$$

$$R_t^l = R_g^l + (1 - R_g^l)f(e_t, r_{t+1}, e_{t+1}, t_s) \qquad (4.13)$$

Here, $R_t^h$ and $R_t^l$ are the interactive reward functions for the relationship agent and the entity agent, respectively, while $R_g^h$ and $R_g^l$ serve as the global reward. When the relationship agent and the entity agent find the target relationship and the target entity, respectively, a reward of +1 is given; otherwise, the reward is 0. If the reward is 0, the similarity between the choices made by the two agents can be calculated using a scoring function based on the embedding model, and this score is used as the reward for the agents' choices.

In the first stage, embedding-based models provide intermediate rewards by computing cosine similarity between candidate actions (i.e., relations and entities) and the target quadruple at each step. This mechanism offers progressive feedback during the search process–for instance, immediately evaluating a relation's semantic match with the target rather than delaying reward until termination. The second stage generates secondary rewards from final prediction scores, which are fed back to the first stage as evaluation signals. Correct path verification triggers additional rewards, forming an interstage reinforcement loop: effective clue searching improves temporal reasoning accuracy, while accurate reasoning enhances search capability. This cross-stage reward loop dynamically adapts the first stage's search strategy to the second stage's reasoning needs, propagating global feedback for end-to-end policy optimization.

## 5 Temporal Knowledge Graph Completion Algorithm

This section describes the algorithm for the policy network in the TS-TKGC model. The algorithm takes the current entity embedding $e_s$, the given query relation $r_q$, the set of candidate relationships $R_t$, and the set of candidate actions $A_i$ as inputs. By computing the relationship policy network and the entity policy network, the algorithm ultimately generates clue paths, which are then outputted as the final result. The specific calculation process is shown in Algorithm 1.

Step 1: Obtain the candidate relationships for the current entity. First, acquire the historical state information $H_t$ of the current entity $e_s$; then obtain the relationship policy network; filter the relationship policy network; and finally, get the candidate relationships $r_t$.

Step 2: Obtain the candidate entities for the current entity. First, acquire the entity policy network for the current entity $e_s$; then filter the entity policy network; and finally, get the candidate entities $e_t$.

---

**Algorithm 1:** Policy Network Construction Algorithm

**Input**: Current moment entity embedding $e_s$, given query relation $r_q$, relation candidate set $R_t$ and candidate action set $A_i$
**Output**: $N$ search paths

1. **for** $i < N$ **do**
2.    **while** *step $< I$ and not success* **do**
3.       $H_t = GRU([e_s \oplus r_q], H_{t-1})$ //Obtain the current state
4.       $\pi_\theta^h(r_t|s_t) = softmax(R_t W_2 ReLU(W_1[H_t, e_s, r_q]))$ //Obtain relation strategy network
5.       $\pi_\theta^l(e_s|s_t) = softmax(A_i W_4 ReLU(W_3[H_t, e_s, r_q, r_t]))$ //Obtain entity strategy network
6.       $\pi_\theta^{l'}(r_t|s_t) = \pi_\theta^l(e_t|s_t)b_i$ //Perform filtering
7.       select $e_t$ from $\pi_\theta^{l'}$ //Obtain candidate entity
8.       Obtain a candidate triple for the current entity $(e_s, r_t, e_t)$
9.    **end**
10.   Obtain a candidate path $(e_s, r_t, e_t, r_{t+1}, e_{t+1}, ..., r_I, e_I)$
11. **end**

---

## 6 Experiment and Analysis

### 6.1 Datasets and Experimental Settings

This section introduces the five temporal KG datasets used in experiments: GDELT (Global Database of Events, Language, and Tone [14]), ICEWS14, ICEWS05-15, ICEWS18 (sourced from the Integrated Crisis Early Warning System [15]) and YAGO. Dataset statistics are provided in Table 1.

**Table 1.** Statistical Summary of Temporal Knowledge Graph Datasets

| Dataset | ICEWS14 | ICEWS05-15 | ICEWS18 | GDELT | YAGO |
|---|---|---|---|---|---|
| entity | 7128 | 10,488 | 23,033 | 7,691 | 10,623 |
| relation | 230 | 251 | 256 | 240 | 10 |
| train triple | 74,845 | 368,868 | 373,018 | 1,734,399 | 136,770 |
| valid triple | 8,514 | 46,302 | 45,995 | 238,765 | 10,000 |
| test triple | 7,371 | 46,159 | 49,545 | 305,241 | 14,770 |
| time interval | 24 h | 24 h | 24 h | 15 mins | 1 year |

While static knowledge graph filtering effectively removes known facts from corrupted rankings during training/validation/testing, it is unsuitable for temporal knowledge graph reasoning under extrapolation. To enable more accurate evaluation of temporal knowledge graph completion methods, this paper adopts a time-aware filtering approach. This method filters out only quadruples occurring at the specific query timestamp during metric calculation, ensuring evaluation accuracy and reliability. The hyperparameters used in the model affect both the training process and accuracy of the final model predictions. In the experiments, the model's accuracy was boosted by continuously tuning the hyperparameters. The main hyperparameter settings for the TS-TKGC model are shown in Table 2. **Note**: Except for the learning rate ($\alpha$) and dimension of the GRU vectors, which may vary across the four datasets, all other parameters are the same across the datasets.

**Table 2.** TS-TKGC Model Parameters

| Parameter | Value |
|---|---|
| I | 2 |
| $\alpha$ | 0.5/0.5/0.4/0.3 |
| learning rate | 0.001 |
| vector dimension | 100 |
| number of GRU layers | 2 |
| number of EI-KGC layers | 2 |
| maximum GRU sequence length | 10 |
| GRU vector dimension | 100/100/100/200 |

We utilize Mean Reciprocal Rank (MRR), Hits@N, and Mean Absolute Error (MAE) for evaluation. MRR and Hits@N provide complementary performance assessment, while MAE specifically evaluates temporal sensitivity in time prediction experiments.

### 6.2 Comparative Experiment

For entity prediction experiments, we first replace the entity in the quadruple $(e_h, r, e_t, t)$ participating in the test with each element in the entity set, and then calculate the scores of each quadruple according to the scoring function. After obtaining all scores, arrange the quadruple in ascending order in the score order to obtain the score table, and obtain the correct quadruple position.

**Table 3.** Results of Entity Prediction Experiment on ICEWS14 Dataset

| Model | MRR | Hits@1 | Hits@3 | Hits@10 |
|---|---|---|---|---|
| RE-NET | 0.367 | 0.226 | 0.332 | 0.481 |
| CyGNet | 0.264 | 0.172 | 0.371 | 0.403 |
| TiRGN | 0.439 | 0.343 | 0.502 | **0.586** |
| RE-GCN | 0.253 | 0.162 | 0.478 | 0.532 |
| **TS-TKGC(ours)** | **0.452** | **0.341** | **0.504** | 0.572 |

**Table 4.** Results of Entity Prediction Experiment on ICEWS05-15 Dataset

| Model | MRR | Hits@1 | Hits@3 | Hits@10 |
|---|---|---|---|---|
| RE-NET | 0.417 | 0.276 | 0.432 | 0.581 |
| CyGNet | 0.384 | 0.292 | 0.371 | 0.483 |
| TiRGN | 0.337 | 0.232 | 0.382 | 0.542 |
| RE-GCN | 0.351 | 0.312 | 0.478 | 0.539 |
| **TS-TKGC(ours)** | **0.443** | **0.342** | **0.525** | **0.584** |

We compare our model with previous classic temporal knowledge graph completion models, including RE-NET, CyGNet [16], TiRGN [17], RE-GCN, to verify the effectiveness of the TS-TKGC model. To evaluate the performance of these models, the TS-TKGC model conducted detailed comparative experiments on the ICEWS14, ICEWS05-15, ICEWS18, GDELT and YAGO dataset. MRR, Hits@1, Hits@3 and Hits@10 are selected as evaluation indicators.

As shown in Tables Tables 3 - 7: 1) On the ICEWS14 and YAGO datasets, TS-TKGC model obtains optimal performance in the MRR, Hits@1 and Hits@3 metrics compared to other baseline models. 2) On the ICEWS05-15 and ICEWS18, compared with other baseline models, the TS-TKGC model obtains the optimal performance in the MRR, Hits@1, Hits@3 and Hits@10 metrics. 3) On the GDELT dataset, compared with other baseline models, the TS-TKGC model

**Table 5.** Results of Entity Prediction Experiment on ICEWS18 Dataset

| Model | MRR | Hits@1 | Hits@3 | Hits@10 |
|---|---|---|---|---|
| RE-NET | 0.286 | 0.208 | 0.312 | 0.481 |
| CyGNet | 0.269 | 0.172 | 0.271 | 0.403 |
| TiRGN | 0.322 | 0.201 | 0.388 | 0.511 |
| RE-GCN | 0.251 | 0.162 | 0.288 | 0.432 |
| **TS-TKGC(ours)** | **0.325** | **0.211** | **0.395** | **0.561** |

**Table 6.** Results of Entity Prediction Experiment on GDELT Dataset

| Model | MRR | Hits@1 | Hits@3 | Hits@10 |
|---|---|---|---|---|
| RE-NET | 0.177 | 0.111 | 0.332 | 0.342 |
| CyGNet | 0.154 | 0.102 | 0.271 | 0.331 |
| TiRGN | **0.194** | 0.113 | 0.212 | 0.343 |
| RE-GCN | 0.161 | 0.102 | 0.278 | 0.298 |
| **TS-TKGC(ours)** | 0.192 | **0.117** | **0.344** | **0.389** |

**Table 7.** Results of Entity Prediction Experiment on YAGO Dataset

| Model | MRR | Hits@1 | Hits@3 | Hits@10 |
|---|---|---|---|---|
| RE-NET | 0.177 | 0.111 | 0.332 | 0.342 |
| CyGNet | 0.759 | 0.730 | 0.779 | 0.798 |
| TiRGN | 0.871 | 0.113 | 0.212 | 0.343 |
| RE-GCN | 0.809 | 0.843 | 0.902 | **0.929** |
| **TS-TKGC(ours)** | **0.877** | **0.853** | **0.912** | 0.905 |

obtains optimal performance in the Hits@1, Hits@3 and Hits@10 indicators compared with other baseline models.

The five comparative experiments verify that the proposed TS-TKGC model, with its two-stage clue search and temporal reasoning modules, effectively mines the interplay between temporal information and entity relations in temporal knowledge graphs, achieving superior knowledge graph completion performance.

### 6.3 Ablation Study

To evaluate the effects of different stages and agents in first stage of the TS-TKGC model, an ablation study was conducted on ICEWS18 and YAGO dataset. The variants of the TS-TKGC model are: using only relation agent in first stage, using only entity agent in first stage, and using only first stage of the model.

As shown in Table 8 and Table 9, the most vital impact on experimental results was observed when the second stage was completely removed, with the greatest decrease in all indicators. For the first stage, both agents have a certain

**Table 8.** Ablation Study Results on ICEWS18

| Model | MRR | Hits@1 | Hits@10 |
|---|---|---|---|
| TS-TKGC(ours) | 0.325 | 0.211 | 0.561 |
| -First Stage (Relation Agent) | 0.312 | 0.187 | 0.464 |
| -First Stage (Entity Agent) | 0.321 | 0.202 | 0.401 |
| -Second Stage | 0.302 | 0.182 | 0.352 |

**Table 9.** Ablation Study Results on YAGO

| Model | MRR | Hits@1 | Hits@10 |
|---|---|---|---|
| TS-TKGC(ours) | 0.877 | 0.853 | 0.905 |
| -First Stage (Relation Agent) | 0.855 | 0.833 | 0.794 |
| -First Stage (Entity Agent) | 0.861 | 0.829 | 0.783 |
| -Second Stage | 0.803 | 0.816 | 0.718 |

degree of impact on final results. Thus, experiments have proven that each part of two stages in the TS-TKGC model has an impact on the overall model, which validates the effectiveness of each component in the model.

### 6.4 Relation Prediction Experiment

To assess the effectiveness of the TS-TKGC model in relation prediction, we conducted a relation prediction experiment on temporal knowledge graphs. The TITer [18], RE-GCN, and CluSTeR [19] models were selected as baseline comparisons. For evaluation, MRR was useed as the primary metric in this section to ensure a focused and consistent evaluation of predictive accuracy. The detailed results of the relation prediction experiment are visualized in Fig. 4a.

TS-TKGC consistently outperforms baselines, exhibiting narrower performance margins in relation prediction owing to the limited candidate relation pool. Analysis of the GDELT dataset reveals inherent limitations: abstract concepts (e.g., "government") lack contextual anchors (e.g., national affiliation), which restricts temporal reasoning and leads to performance plateaus across models. TS-TKGC's two-stage temporal-graph integration architecture demonstrates superior noise resilience to such contextual ambiguities, achieving state-of-the-art results on both ICEWS14 and GDELT while significantly outperforming structure-centric baselines such as RE-GCN. This highlights the critical role of joint temporal-structural modeling in learning precise relational embeddings under incomplete contextual constraints.

### 6.5 Time Prediction Experiment

For the time prediction experiment, given a test quadruple $(h, r, t, t')$, the goal is to predict the expected time of next occurrence of fact $(h, r, t)$. The Mean Absolute Error(MAE) between predicted time and actual time is used as evaluation metric, measured in hours. The specific results are shown in Fig. 4b.

In contrast to RE-GCN, which employs relation-aware GCN to capture structural dependencies in knowledge graphs, TS-TKGC utilizes a two-stage temporal reasoning framework to better capture temporal dynamics. Unlike TAgent (binary terminal rewards) and TITer (Dirichlet distribution-based temporal rewards), TS-TKGC adopts a multi-dimensional reward mechanism to address the sparse reward problem and facilitate accurate temporal modeling. In the

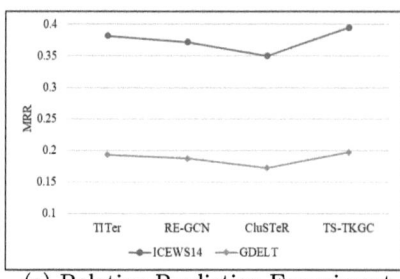 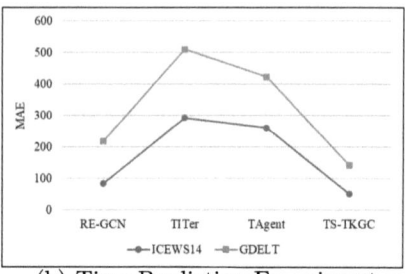

(a) Relation Prediction Experiment   (b) Time Prediction Experiment

**Fig. 4.** Results of the Relation Prediction and the Time Prediction Experiment

time prediction experiment, the proposed TS-TKGC achieved state-of-the-art performance, demonstrating its capability to effectively model dynamic temporal dependencies in temporal knowledge graphs.

### 6.6 Sensitivity Analysis Experiment

To optimize the model effectively, this paper investigates how TS-TKGC's performance varies with different hyperparameters. We designed experiments to analyze the impact of two key hyperparameters: the maximum reasoning steps $I$ and the reward balancing factor $\alpha$. MRR served as the primary evaluation metric, with detailed results tabulated in Tables 10 and 11.

As shown in Table 10, TS-TKGC exhibits significant performance degradation when the maximum reasoning steps exceed 3, aligning with findings in prior RL-based TKGC literature. This phenomenon can be attributed to the accumulation of noise in multi-step reasoning: while early steps capture relevant temporal dependencies, longer reasoning chains introduce compounding errors that ultimately impair prediction accuracy.

Table 11 lists the optimal reward balancing factors for the four datasets: 0.5 for ICEWS14, 0.5 for ICEWS05-15, 0.4 for ICEWS18, and 0.3 for GDELT. The ICEWS subsets prioritize semantic-level learning rewards, indicating that when temporal KG datasets share similar temporal granularity, dataset scale shows a positive correlation with semantic-level adaptive rewards.

**Table 10.** Impact of Maximum Reasoning Steps $I$ on Model Performance

| $I$ | ICEWS14 | ICEWS05-15 | ICEWS18 | GDELT |
|---|---|---|---|---|
| 2 | **0.452** | **0.443** | **0.325** | **0.192** |
| 3 | 0.442 | 0.431 | 0.320 | 0.187 |
| 4 | 0.431 | 0.419 | 0.315 | 0.172 |
| 5 | 0.413 | 0.402 | 0.295 | 0.163 |

**Table 11.** Impact of Reward Balancing Factor $\alpha$ on Model Performance

| $\alpha$ | ICEWS14 | ICEWS05-15 | ICEWS18 | GDELT |
|---|---|---|---|---|
| 0.2 | 0.435 | 0.426 | 0.298 | 0.182 |
| 0.3 | 0.442 | 0.431 | 0.307 | **0.192** |
| 0.4 | 0.448 | 0.439 | **0.325** | 0.179 |
| 0.5 | **0.452** | **0.443** | 0.318 | 0.176 |
| 0.6 | 0.439 | 0.440 | 0.312 | 0.168 |

# 7 Conclusion

Current temporal knowledge graph completion models over-rely on timestamp correlations while neglecting joint modeling of temporal dynamics and semantic relationships. To address this limitation, we propose TS-TKGC, which features two synergistic stages: **Clue Search**: A reinforcement learning module identifies temporally constrained semantic pathways; **Temporal Reasoning**: GRU networks model temporal clue evolution patterns. Joint training enables synergistic integration of temporal and structural features. Experiments on four benchmark datasets demonstrate that TS-TKGC consistently outperforms state-of-the-art baselines. For future research, we suggest integrating large language models for temporal information extraction or developing more efficient mining strategies to address current limitations in existing approaches.

**Acknowledgments.** This work was supported by the National Natural Science Foundation of China (62472204), the Social Science Planning Fund Program of Liaoning Province (L23BJY018), the Research Program of the Liaoning Liaohe Laboratory (LLL24KF-01–04).

**Disclosure of Interests.** We declare that we have no competing financial interests.

# References

1. Li, N., E, H.: TR-rules: rule-based model for link forecasting on temporal knowledge graph considering temporal redundancy. In: Findings of the Association for Computational Linguistics: EMNLP 2023, pp. 7885–7894. Association for Computational Linguistics, Singapore (2023)
2. Bai, L.: Multi-hop temporal knowledge graph reasoning with temporal path rules guidance. Expert Syst. Appl. **223**, 119804 (2023)
3. Mei, X., Yang, L.: An adaptive logical rule embedding model for inductive reasoning over temporal knowledge graphs. In: Proceedings of the 2022 Conference Onempirical Methods In Natural Language Processing, pp. 7304–7316 (2022)
4. Jin, W., Qu, M.: Recurrent event network: autoregressive structure inferenceover temporal knowledge graphs. In: Proceedings of the 2020 Conference on Empirical Methods in Natural Language Processing (EMNLP), pp. 6669–6683. Association for Computational Linguistics, Online (2020)

5. Wu, J.: Temp: temporal message passing for temporal knowledge graph completion. arXiv preprint arXiv:2010.03526 (2020)
6. Li, Z., Jin, X.: Temporal knowledge graph reasoning based on evolutional representation learning. In: Proceedings of the 44th International ACM SIGIR Conference On Research And Development In Information Retrieval,pp. 408–417 (2021)
7. Chen, L.: Dacha: a dual graph convolution based temporal knowledge graph representation learning method using historical relation. ACM Trans. Knowl- edge Discov. Data (TKDD) **16**(3), 1–18 (2021)
8. Zhu, C., Chen, M.: Learning from history: mdeling temporal knowledge graphs with sequential copy-generation networks. In: Proceedings of the AAAI Conference On Artificial Intelligence,pp. 4732–4740 (2021)
9. Hu, J.: A blockchain-based reward mechanism for mobile crowdsensing. IEEE Trans. Comput. Soc. Syst. **7**(1), 178–191 (2020)
10. Tao, Y., Li, Y.: Temporal link prediction via reinforcement learning. In: ICASSP 2021-2021 IEEE International Conference on Acoustics, Speech and Signal Processing (ICASSP),pp. 3470–3474. IEEE (2021)
11. Bai, L.: Multi-hop reasoning over paths in temporal knowledge graphs using reinforcement learning. Appl. Soft Comput. **103**, 107144 (2021)
12. Sun, H., Zhong, J., Ma, Y.: Timetraveler: rinforcement learning for temporal knowledge graph forecasting. arXiv preprint arXiv:2109.04101 (2021)
13. Li, Z., Jin, X., Guan, S.: Search from history and reason for future: to-stage reasoning on temporal knowledge graphs. arXiv preprint arXiv:2106.00327 (2021)
14. Leetaru, K.: Gdelt: Global data on events, location and tone, 1979-2012 (2013)
15. Jäger, K.: The limits of studying networks via event data: Evidence from the ICEWS dataset. J. Global Secur. Stud. **3**(4), 498–511 (2018)
16. Li, Y., Sun, S.: Tirgn: Time-guided recurrent graph network with local-global historical patterns for temporal knowledge graph reasoning. In: Proceedings of the Thirty-First International Joint Conference on Artificial Intelligence, IJCAI 2022, Vienna, Austria, 23-29 July 2022,pp. 2152–2158 (2022)
17. Zhu, C., Chen, M.: Learning from history: mdeling temporal knowledge graphs with sequential copy-generation networks. In: AAAI (2021)
18. Sun, H., Zhong, J.: Timetraveler: reinforcement learning for temporal knowledge graph forecasting. In: EMNLP (2021)
19. Li, Z., Jin, X.: Search from history and reason for future: two-stage reasoning on temporal knowledge graphs. arXiv preprint arXiv:2106.00327 (2021)

# Beyond the Visible: Multispectral Vision-Language Learning for Earth Observation

Clive Tinashe Marimo[1], Benedikt Blumenstiel[2(✉)], Maximilian Nitsche[1], Johannes Jakubik[2], and Thomas Brunschwiler[2]

[1] IBM Germany, Ehningen, Germany
[2] IBM Research Europe, Zurich, Switzerland
benedikt.blumenstiel@ibm.com

**Abstract.** Vision-language models for Earth observation (EO) typically rely on the visual spectrum of data as the only model input, thus failing to leverage the rich spectral information available in the multispectral channels recorded by satellites. Therefore, we introduce Llama3-MS-CLIP—-the first vision-language model pre-trained with contrastive learning on a large-scale multispectral dataset and report on the performance gains due to the extended spectral range. Furthermore, we present the largest-to-date image-caption dataset for multispectral data, consisting of one million Sentinel-2 samples and corresponding textual descriptions generated using Llama3-LLaVA-Next and Overture Maps data. We develop a scalable captioning pipeline, which is validated by domain experts. We evaluate Llama3-MS-CLIP on multispectral zero-shot image classification and retrieval using three datasets of varying complexity. Our results demonstrate that Llama3-MS-CLIP significantly outperforms other RGB-based approaches, improving classification accuracy by +6.77% on average and retrieval performance by +4.63% mAP compared to the second-best model. Our results emphasize the relevance of multispectral vision-language learning. The image-caption dataset, code, and model weights are available at https://github.com/IBM/MS-CLIP.

**Keywords:** Multispectral Data · Vision-Language Model · Earth Observation

## 1 Introduction

Vision-language models (VLM) have transformed computer vision, enabling powerful zero-shot learning and cross-modal retrieval capabilities [10,20]. By learning joint representations of images and text, these models generalize across

---

C. T. Marimo and B. Blumenstiel—Equal contribution.

**Supplementary Information** The online version contains supplementary material available at https://doi.org/10.1007/978-3-032-06106-5_21.

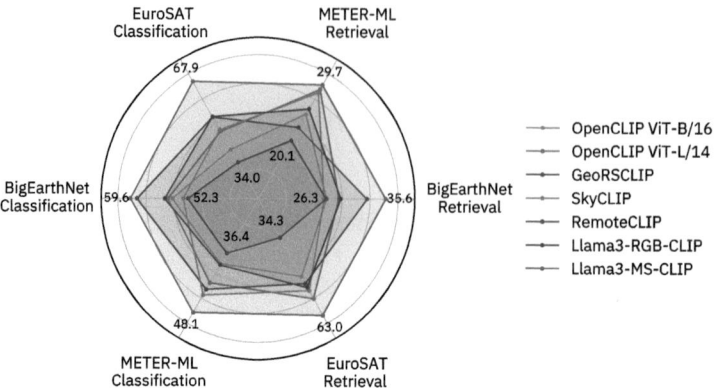

**Fig. 1.** Zero-shot classification and text-to-image retrieval results, measured in accuracy (%) ↑ and mAP@100 (%) ↑, respectively. We applied a smoothed min-max scaling and annotated the lowest and highest scores. The multispectral CLIP is outperforming other RGB-based models on most benchmarks.

tasks without requiring task-specific training data. However, existing VLMs, such as CLIP [20], are predominantly trained on natural RGB images, limiting their applicability to specialized domains such as Earth observation(EO) [16,25,28]. Conversely, effectively utilizing multispectral input data in VLMs represents an interesting and underexplored research topic in the machine learning community.

EO relies on satellite imagery to monitor environmental changes, urban expansion, and agriculture [30]. To use VLMs for such EO applications, researchers proposed a range of domain-specific EO adaptations of CLIP [15, 16,25,28]. Those models have been trained on up to five million remote sensing images with aligned image captions. Despite impressive performance, these models rely only on RGB input channels instead of leveraging the full spectral range available in multispectral (MS) satellite data for maximum effectiveness. Satellites like Sentinel-2 provide up to 13 spectral bands, capturing rich information far beyond visible wavelengths. Yet, until today, no large-scale multispectral dataset with image captions is publicly available for the research community.

To address this gap, we generate approximately one million captions for a popular, multispectral EO dataset derived from the Sentinel satellites called SSL4EO-S12 [24]. We develop an automated captioning approach using metadata tags from Overture maps and the multimodal large language model (MLLM) Llama3-LLaVA-Next-8B [12]. These captions provide semantic grounding for contrastive learning, allowing the model to align multispectral image representations with natural language. We then perform continual pre-training on OpenCLIP [10], adapting the model to the EO domain. Our model, Llama3-MS-CLIP[1], outperforms other VLMs on a range of downstream applications as depicted in Fig. 1. The results demonstrate that multispectral data significantly

---

[1] Built with Meta Llama 3. While the model itself is not based on Llama 3 but OpenCLIP B/16, it is trained on captions generated by a Llama 3-derivative model.

enhances vision-language learning in EO, unlocking capabilities that RGB-based models fail to capture.

Our contributions are threefold: (1) We create the largest multispectral image-caption dataset for EO, (2) we present the first multispectral EO VLM, surpassing current state-of-the-art performance, and (3) we propose novel best practices for model development and image captioning with multispectral data. The dataset, code, and model weights are available at https://github.com/IBM/MS-CLIP under a permissive license.

## 2 Related Work

Vision-language models have successfully enabled zero-shot learning and cross-modal retrieval by aligning image and text embeddings through contrastive learning. CLIP [20], OpenCLIP [10], and ALIGN [11] are among the most prominent models in this space, trained on vast datasets of internet-scale image-text pairs. These models excel at general vision tasks but are inherently biased toward natural RGB images. Their ability to generalize to remote sensing imagery is limited due to the domain gap between natural images and satellite imagery [20,28]. Spectral information beyond the visible range is key for applications like vegetation and disaster monitoring, as well as urban planning, which benefit from near-infrared and short-wave infrared reflectance measurements [23].

One of the major challenges in EO vision-language learning is the lack of large-scale image-text datasets with multispectral data [26]. Unlike natural images, satellite images do not inherently come with descriptive text. Most EO datasets provide only categorical labels or metadata, making it challenging to train models that require diverse textual supervision. While some approaches have attempted to generate captions for EO images, they often rely on metadata-based descriptions [25] or manually curated annotations [16]. These approaches do not scale to the large volumes of data required to train robust vision-language models. UCMC [19], RSICD [17], and RSITMD [27] are some famous examples of human-curated EO datasets that are often limited by their small size. RS5M [28] collected five million images from eleven source datasets and used BLIP-2 [13] to generate captions for the RGB images. RSCLIP [15] introduced a pseudo-labeling technique that automatically generates pseudo-labels from unlabeled data. ChatEarthNet [26] is the first multispectral dataset with over 100k samples, using ChatGPT-3.5 to generate captions. However, the captions are solely based on a small set of land-cover classes without visual input for the LLM.

Recent approaches have adapted VLMs to EO by continual pre-training on domain-specific RGB datasets. For instance, SkyCLIP [25], RSCLIP [15], and RemoteCLIP [16] built large-scale image-text datasets and adapted CLIP-based backbones. GeoRSCLIP [28] was pre-trained on RS5M, the largest known image-test dataset in the domain with five million images. GRAFT [18] utilized co-located street-view images to correlate satellite imagery with language. Despite

---

Therefore, the model name starts with Llama 3 following its license (https://github.com/meta-llama/llama3/blob/main/LICENSE).

these advancements, all these methods rely solely on RGB data, ignoring the rich spectral information available in multispectral EO imagery. We further note the emergence of autoregressive approaches that generate language output based on optical or radar images, like in TerraMind [4].

In contrast to prior work, we introduce a self-supervised approach based on multimodal large language models (MLLM) and Overture annotations to automatically generate captions for multispectral EO imagery (i.e., Sentinel-2 images). By fine-tuning OpenCLIP on this dataset, we enable multispectral vision-language learning, allowing the model to leverage spectral information beyond the visible spectrum.

## 3 Automated Captioning

The effectiveness of vision-language models relies heavily on the availability of high-quality image-text datasets. Thus, we introduce Llama3-SSL4EO-S12 captions, a novel dataset of text data aligned with SSL4EO-S12 v1.1 [2]. It provides detailed natural language descriptions required for contrastive learning of multispectral vision-language models.

SSL4EO-S12 v1.1 [2] consists of 975k co-registered images of optical data from Sentinel-2 L1C (top-of-atmosphere) and Sentinel-2 L2A (bottom-of-atmosphere) as well as synthetic aperture radar (SAR) data from Sentinel-1 GRD. The dataset covers 244k global locations centered around urban areas, with a 264 × 264 pixel size at 10 m resolution, each including samples from four seasons.

We generate captions by employing a multimodal large language model, specifically Llama-LLaVA-Next-8B. The model was selected based on a qualitative comparison and a quantitative evaluation of three MLLM models using METEOR (Metric for Evaluation of Translation with Explicit Ordering) [8], comparing ground truth captions with generations. We tested BLIP2 [13], used for the captioning in the RS5M [28] dataset, Llama3-LLaVA-Next-8B [12], and RS-LLaVA [1], a domain-specific adaptation of LLaVA 1.5. We assessed these models using UCM Captions [19], RSICD [17], and RSITMD [27] that provide human-annotated captions. Llama3-LLaVA-Next-8B reaches an average METEOR score of 0.20 compared to 0.16 for RS-LLaVA and 0.10 for BLIP2. All scores and some examples are provided in the supplementary material.

The captioning process consists of the following steps: First, we extract the RGB channels from S-2 L2A data and scale it to a uint8 value range of 0—-255 as no publicly available MLLM supports multispectral inputs. The images are resized to 224 × 224 pixels as input for the captioning model. We then extract geographical tags from the Overture Maps base layer[2] that provides additional contextual information about land cover, infrastructure, and other features in the satellite image. The geographical instances are then sorted and filtered by size, i.e., all features smaller than 2500 square meters (5 × 5 pixels) are omitted. We use all tags of each instance as they include additional information,

---
[2] Overture Maps: https://docs.overturemaps.org (Version: 2024-03-12-alpha.0).

like intermittent rivers. We further add the names of places to avoid hallucinations. Otherwise, we observe that the model often refers to popular places incorrectly, like labeling most universities as *Harvard* or *Berkeley*. Finally, we prompt the MLLM to generate captions in a structured manner by following a chain-of-thought approach. First, the model is prompted to generate three relevant question-answer pairs, guiding the model in producing the final caption. The prompt includes further instructions to avoid hallucinations and increase the caption quality. We repeat the generation if any Q&A pair or the caption is missing in the output. We include the prompt and other details on the captioning process in the supplementary material.

Figure 2 shows example images and their corresponding generated captions. While we do observe several hallucinations in the generated captions, they are also more diverse and include more details than other image-caption datasets such as SkyScript or RS5M, which are based on heuristics [25] or the much simpler MLLM BLIP2 [14,28] (see supplementary material for examples). Figure 2 includes three examples with hallucinations to showcase their different forms. For example, the model sometimes imagines landmasses in ocean patches, man-made or water features, and provides wrong counts or length estimations.

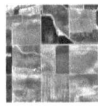
The image is a satellite view of a diverse landscape, featuring agricultural fields, orchards, scrubland, and forested areas. A waterway, possibly a stream or river, is also visible in the image. The land appears to be in a dry condition.

The image is a satellite view of a wetland area, featuring several water bodies such as rivers, lakes, and ponds. The wetland area is green, indicating that it is healthy and thriving.

A satellite image of a landscape featuring a long, winding waterway, scattered residential areas, farmland, and orchards.

The image shows a satellite view of an irregularly shaped landmass with a complex coastline, surrounded by a mix of blue and green ocean waters. The vegetation on the landmass is a mix of green and brown, indicating a combination of healthy and dying plants.

The image shows a brown land surface with distinct patterns and textures, including rocky areas and patches of dirt. There are objects and structures visible on the land surface, including a building and a road.

The image is a satellite view of a landscape featuring a river, a lake, and brown land. The river is approximately 500 kilometers long and is surrounded by land. There are two bodies of water visible in the image.

**Fig. 2.** Examples of image-caption pairs of high quality (left) and hallucination examples (right) of our generated pre-training dataset. We highlight hallucinations in red. (Color figure online)

We evaluate the captions quantitatively by comparing our validation set with manually labeled EO datasets: RSITMD [27], RSICD [17], and UCM Captions [19]. The generated captions exhibit a much higher average n-gram diversity of 0.75 compared to only 0.48 to 0.49 in the three human-annotated datasets. The similarity between captions is also lower, showing a higher lexical variety in the SSL4EO-S12-captions.

To assess the quality of our dataset, we asked domain experts[3] to conduct a manual evaluation using a random subset with more than one thousand captions from the validation split. Domain experts rated the captions based on

---
[3] 14 researchers from the FAST-EO project working in the Earth observation domain.

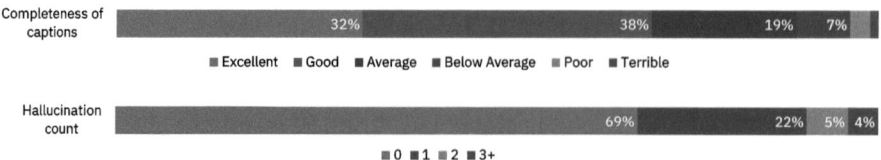

**Fig. 3.** Evaluation results of the caption quality in the Llama3-SSL4EOS12 dataset based on 1.3k captions reviewed by domain experts. Completeness evaluates if all relevant features of an image are mentioned in the caption, while hallucinations are the number of incorrect features.

completeness and presence of hallucinations. The caption completeness represents whether all relevant features in the image are covered in the caption and is measured on a scale from 0 (Terrible) to 5 (Excellent). Additionally, the experts counted hallucinations. Figure 3 presents the distribution of expert ratings, indicating that over 85% of the captions are considered to include most of the relevant features in the image. The human assessment further demonstrates that two-thirds of the evaluated data is free from hallucinations. If hallucinations are present, we typically observe only one hallucinated feature within an image. We provide details of the quantitative comparison and the human evaluation in the supplementary material.

The manual evaluation of the generated captions demonstrates that automated captioning with a general-purpose MLLM and additionally provided tags is feasible and leads to mostly correct captions. Furthermore, the quantitative assessment of the full validation set indicates that the captioning model uses a more diverse vocabulary than existing human-annotated datasets. Different from datasets like ChatEarthNet [26] or SkyScript [25] that do not use multimodal LMMs, our pipeline can capture scene-specific features like snow, clouds, or colors. While we do want to highlight the challenge of hallucinations in the dataset, our experiments show that VLMs can learn semantic concepts from the correct annotations. Furthermore, the alignment with S-1 GRD data in SSL4EO-S12 and the question-answer pairs provides additional potential for the EO community.

## 4 Llama3-MS-CLIP

Llama3-MS-CLIP is trained with self-supervised contrastive language-image pre-training (CLIP) [20], visualized in Fig. 4. We modified the input layer to handle Sentinel-2's spectral bands beyond RGB by extending the patch embedding for the additional channels. We initialize the corresponding weights with zero tensors so that during continual pre-training, the model starts from RGB input and can iteratively include additional channels based on optimizing the loss landscape. Hence, the model can slowly learn to leverage the additional information. Our initial experiments suggest that this initialization strategy outperforms random initialization, where the continual pre-training would be disrupted due to the noise that originates from the random weights for the additional channels.

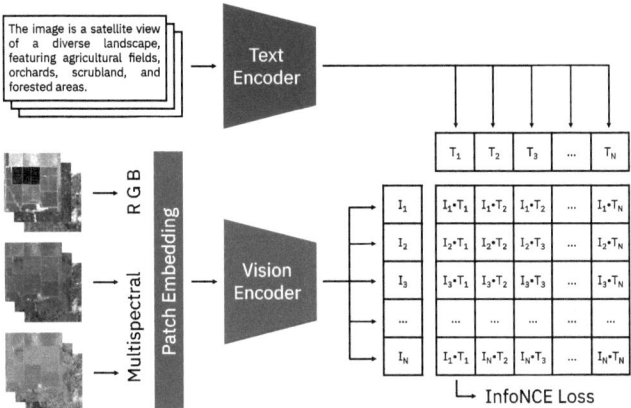

**Fig. 4.** The CLIP model consists of two encoders for text and images [20]. We extended the RGB patch embeddings to multispectral input and initialized the weights of the additional input channels with zeros. During the continual pre-training, the images and texts of each batch are encoded and combined. The loss increases the similarity of matching pairs while decreasing other combinations.

Following CLIP, we utilize the InfoNCE loss, a contrastive loss function, to align embeddings of semantically similar samples while separating semantically dissimilar ones through cross-modal supervision. The InfoNCE loss encourages the embeddings of matching (positive) pairs $(x_i, y_i)$ to be similar, while pushing apart non-matching (negative) pairs $(x_i, y_j)$ with $j \neq i$. Here, $\text{sim}(\cdot, \cdot)$ is a pairwise similarity measure, and $\tau$ is a temperature parameter that scales the logits. Minimizing the loss thus maximizes the similarity of each positive pair relative to all negative pairs. We summarize the training objective in Eq. 1.

$$\mathcal{L}_{\text{InfoNCE}} = -\frac{1}{2N} \sum_{i=1}^{N} \left[ \log \frac{e^{\text{sim}(x_i, y_i)/\tau}}{\sum_{j=1}^{N} e^{\text{sim}(x_i, y_j)/\tau}} + \log \frac{e^{\text{sim}(y_i, x_i)/\tau}}{\sum_{j=1}^{N} e^{\text{sim}(y_i, x_j)/\tau}} \right] \quad (1)$$

## 5 Experimental Setup

In the following, we outline our pre-training and evaluation setting, including the downstream datasets and benchmark models.

**Pre-training.** We use the implementation and model weights provided by OpenCLIP [10] and perform continual pre-training of the ViT-B/16 using the SSL4EO-S12-captions. The model has 150 million parameters, split between the image and text encoders, and was initially pre-trained on LAION-2B, an English subset of the LAION-5B [21] dataset. While many EO models use the ViT-B/32 version with a patch size of 32 [16,25,28], we find a patch size of 16 more appropriate for low-resolution images with many details. We used an AdamW optimizer with a learning rate of 4e-5, 50 warm-up steps, and a cosine decay scheduler that updated after each training step. The model was trained for up to five epochs on NVIDIA-A100 GPUs with a global batch size of 1200. The final model was selected based on the lowest validation loss reached after one epoch for the multispectral version and two epochs for the RGB version. Based on prior experiments, all layers are unfrozen during the pre-training of Llama3-MS-CLIP, but only the projection layers are trained for the RGB data.

**Benchmark Models.** We evaluate OpenCLIP [6] ViT-B/16 and ViT-L/14 as well as three RGB-based EO-specific models based on ViT-B/32 backbones. SkyCLIP [25] used remote sensing images with rich semantics covered in Open Street Map to construct a dataset comprising 2.6 million images and generated captions with a simple heuristic by just listing all Open Street Map tags. They performed fully unfrozen continual pre-training using the ViT B/32 backbone initialized from the LAION 2B weights by OpenCLIP [10]. RemoteCLIP [16] proposed a data scaling approach to existing datasets via annotation unification. For images with bounding box annotations, a box-to-caption generation approach was applied. The mask-to-box conversion method was used to generate captions for datasets with available semantic segmentation. The resulting high-resolution dataset consisted of 165k images, each accompanied by five captions. RemoteCLIP is based on the OpenAI CLIP weights [20] and was adapted with fully unfrozen weights. The authors of GeoRSCLIP [28] used the images from BigEarthNet [22] and ten other datasets. They generated captions based on the annotations and metadata using BLIP-2 [13]. Subsequently, they fine-tuned the OpenAI ViT B/32 and ViT H/14 models applying parameter-efficient fine-tuning techniques.

**Downstream Datasets.** Our zero-shot evaluation focuses on low-resolution Sentinel-2 imagery from EuroSAT [9], BigEarthNet [22], and METER-ML [29]. EuroSAT includes 64 × 64 patches from ten land-use/land-cover (LULC) classes. BigEarthNet consists of S-2 L2A patches with 19 multi-labels covering a more diverse set of LULC classes and has an input size of 120 × 120 pixels. Finally, METER-ML covers images with seven classes of different methane sources like *landfills*, *coal mines*, or *natural gas processing plants*. METER-ML includes S-2 images of size 72 × 72 and high-resolution RGB images from NAIP with size 720 × 720. Methane is visible in the SWIR S-2 bands (bands 11 and 12) and, therefore, is an especially interesting downstream task. Since EuroSAT and METER-ML only include S-2 L1C data, we downloaded L2A data for their test sets to better align the inputs with the pre-training data. We observed improvements for METER-ML and therefore evaluated on L2A data for this task. We perform additional experiments with the METER-ML-NAIP data and the RESISC45 [5] dataset. The latter includes RGB images of size 256 × 256 with a spatial resolution ranging from 30 m to 0.2 m. The 45 scene classes range from landscapes like *wetland* to large objects like *airplane*.

**Evaluation.** We assess our model's zero-shot capabilities on previously unseen EO datasets. Specifically, we evaluate two tasks: zero-shot classification and text-to-image retrieval. We adopt a template-based approach that leverages multiple prompts of the form *a satellite photo of {class name}* and averages these for the class embedding. For zero-shot classification, we compute the similarity between each image and all possible class labels, assigning the class with the highest similarity score. The zero-shot classification performance is measured using macro top-1 accuracy. We use the test set defined by CLIP for EuroSAT [20] and the official test split for all other datasets.

For the multi-label dataset BigEarthNet, we transform each class into a binary classification task. For each class, we calculate the similarity between the image embedding and the respective text embedding of that class and compare it to the mean similarity between the image and all other classes, as formulated in Eq. 2. Here, $\hat{y}_i$ is the predicted label for class $i$, $x$ is the image embedding, $c_i$ is the class embedding, $\text{sim}(\cdot, \cdot)$ is the dot-product similarity, and $K$ is the total number of classes. We also compare this method to a negative-class approach (e.g., *"other features"*), which boosts accuracy but substantially lowers recall and the F1 score (results in the supplementary material).

$$\hat{y}_i = \begin{cases} 1, & \text{if } \text{sim}(x, c_i) > \frac{1}{K-1} \sum_{j \neq i} \text{sim}(x, c_j), \\ 0, & \text{otherwise} \end{cases} \quad (2)$$

For text-to-image retrieval, we calculate the similarity between a given class label and all test images, rank these scores in descending order, and then compute the mean average precision over the top 100 results (mAP@100). We report the average mAP@100 across all classes. As this retrieval procedure is class-based, it naturally extends to both single-label and multi-label datasets.

## 6 Results

We first analyze Llama3-MS-CLIP's performance and compare it against RGB-based EO models. Next, we evaluate our RGB-only model on two high-resolution tasks. Finally, we present ablation studies to investigate the effects of multispectral continual pre-training.

Table 1 presents the zero-shot classification and retrieval results for Llama3-MS-CLIP, OpenCLIP baselines, and other RGB-based EO VLMs. Llama3-RGB-CLIP is an ablation trained using only the RGB channels of SSL4EO-S12 v1.1. Llama3-MS-CLIP achieves an average top-1 accuracy of 58.54% for classification, surpassing the untuned baseline by +14.48% points (pp), followed by GeoRSCLIP [28] with 51.77%. In text-to-image retrieval, Llama3-MS-CLIP outperforms all other models as well, exhibiting a 9.43pp improvement over its base model, OpenCLIP ViT-B/16. Domain-specific approaches generally outperform general-purpose baselines in zero-shot tasks, except for RemoteCLIP.

These findings underscore the effectiveness of our curated dataset and the importance of multispectral pre-training. While our RGB-based variant yields

**Table 1.** Evaluation results on EuroSAT, BigEarthNet, METER-ML, and the overall average. We report zero-shot classification results in accuracy (%) ↑ and text-to-image retrieval results in mAP@100 (%) ↑. The best-performing model is highlighted in bold, and the second-best model is underlined.

| Model | Zero-shot classification | | | | Text-to-image retrieval | | | |
|---|---|---|---|---|---|---|---|---|
| | ESAT | BEN | M-ML | Avg | ESAT | BEN | M-ML | Avg |
| OpenCLIP B/16 [20] | 39.36 | 54.28 | 38.54 | 44.06 | 48.77 | 26.70 | 24.62 | 33.36 |
| OpenCLIP L/14 [20] | 46.90 | 54.85 | 42.28 | 48.01 | <u>56.92</u> | 28.57 | <u>28.99</u> | <u>38.16</u> |
| GeoRSCLIP [28] | 52.92 | <u>58.80</u> | 43.59 | <u>51.77</u> | 51.36 | <u>32.80</u> | 22.33 | 35.50 |
| SkyCLIP [25] | 47.54 | 52.88 | <u>44.70</u> | 48.37 | 53.96 | 26.29 | 28.41 | 36.22 |
| RemoteCLIP [16] | 34.02 | 52.28 | 36.42 | 40.91 | 34.34 | 26.62 | 20.08 | 27.01 |
| Llama3-RGB-CLIP | <u>52.96</u> | 55.23 | 38.74 | 48.98 | 52.72 | 28.84 | 25.60 | 35.72 |
| Llama3-MS-CLIP | **67.86** | **59.63** | **48.13** | **58.54** | **63.03** | **35.62** | **29.72** | **42.79** |

only a minor improvement over the baseline, incorporating multispectral channels leads to a substantial performance gain. Notably, GeoRSCLIP [28], despite being adapted with five times more training samples, still falls short of bridging the gap created by the missing multispectral information.

We provide example predictions from Llama3-MS-CLIP in Fig. 5 to illustrate common behavior. On EuroSAT, the model is nearly always correct for general classes like *residential*, *sea/lake*, or *industrial*, but it confuses certain pairs such as *permanent crop* and *annual crop*. On METER-ML, samples are often mistakenly classified as *wastewater treatment plants*. In contrast, *concentrated animal feedings operations* (COFAs) like farms and *other features* (negative class) are mostly correctly identified.

In BigEarthNet's multi-label scenario, our approach tends to produce numerous false positives. However, these misclassifications are usually semantically correlated (e.g., *inland waters* or *beaches* predictions for *marine waters*). Introducing an extra negative class (*other features*) mitigates false positives but leads to many more false negatives. This results in higher accuracy overall, but the F1 score drops for six of the seven models. Since F1 reflects both precision and recall, we report the original method here and the alternative strategy in the supplementary material. In both cases, MS-CLIP achieves the highest F1 and significantly outperforms five other models in accuracy.

We further analyse the embedding space of the single-label datasets EuroSAT and METER-ML in Fig. 6 and compare Llama3-MS-CLIP with the base model. While many EuroSAT classes overlap in the OpenCLIP UMAP visualization, the clusters are more distinct for Llama3-MS-CLIP. Differentiating between classes in METER-ML is much more difficult, which is reflected in the lower accuracy and the embedding space visualization with no large clusters for any model. However, some classes like *wastewater treatment* or *refineries and terminals* form small clusters in the Llama3-MS-CLIP plot, while being more distributed for OpenCLIP.

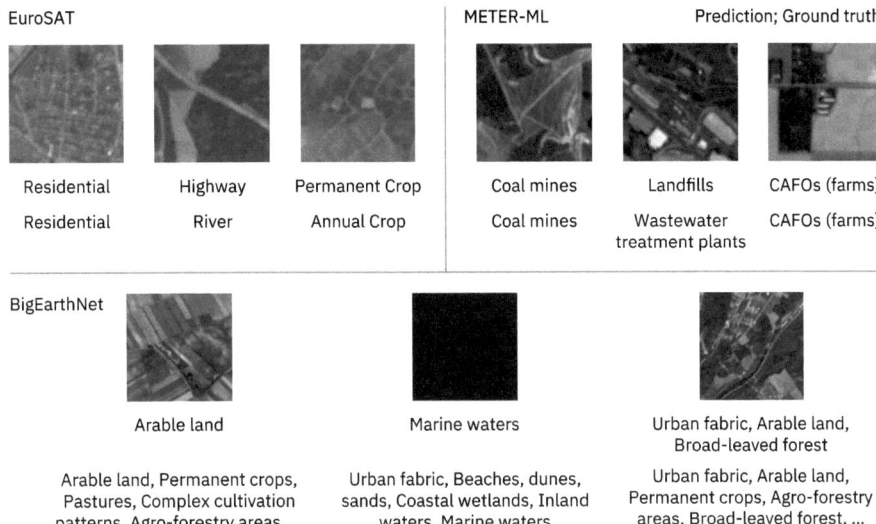

**Fig. 5.** Prediction examples from Llama3-MS-CLIP.

## 6.1 RGB Experiments

We conduct additional experiments on two RGB datasets that feature high-resolution imagery, aiming to assess the generalization capabilities of our models trained solely on low-resolution Sentinel-2 data. Table 2 shows that Llama3-RGB-CLIP achieves results on par with the untuned base model. While it scores 1.71pp lower for METER-ML-NAIP classification, it outperforms the baseline in all other tasks. GeoRSCLIP achieves the best zero-shot classification but underperforms in retrieval tasks, and RemoteCLIP again delivers the lowest results across metrics.

Comparing performance on METER-ML for both Sentinel-2 and NAIP data reveals that all models benefit from the higher resolution, with improvements ranging from 3pp to 17pp in both classification and retrieval. Our RGB variant is 5.25pp more accurate than its multispectral version in classification using S-2 imagery. Although high-resolution imagery clearly enhances VLM performance, its public availability is limited, whereas Sentinel-2 data is openly accessible every five days. Notably, relying on low-resolution data for domain adaptation does not reduce performance on high-resolution tasks, and other domain-specific approaches, even those trained on high-resolution data, only show marginal improvements over the baseline.

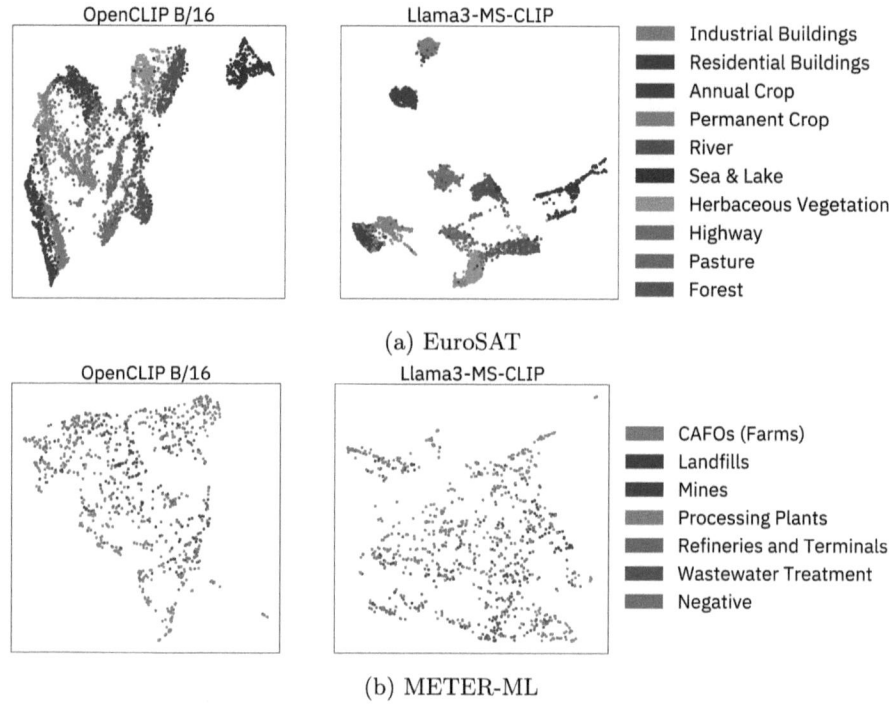

**Fig. 6.** UMAP plot of the embedding spaces from OpenCLIP B/16 and Llama3-MS-CLIP for EuroSAT and METER-ML using the S-2 test images. The UMAP settings are 10 nearest neighbors and min distance 0.0.

### 6.2 Ablation Studies

We conduct several ablation experiments to study various design choices systematically. Specifically, we investigate prompt templates, weight initialization for the patch embedding, different input bands, and strategies for freezing/unfreezing model layers.

Our initial prompt templates follow RS5M, which are already adapted for EO and outperform the original CLIP templates used for EuroSAT (see Table 3). Extending and refining these prompts leads to a gain of on average 3.47pp in classification and 1.16pp in retrieval, relative to the baseline.

Figure 7(a) compares two approaches to initialize the multispectral patch embeddings. While a naive solution is to set each new channel's weights to the mean of the RGB ones, we find that zero-initialization produces superior performance in all six tasks. We hypothesize that starting from zero with a short warm-up phase lets the model adjust gradually to the additional input channels instead of the more sudden interruption with mean initialization.

We analyse the weights of the patch embedding before and after continual pre-training. The absolute values of the patch embedding for the multispectral channels are much lower than for the RGB channels, showing that the

**Table 2.** Zero-shot evaluation results for the high-resolution RGB datasets METER-ML NAIP and RESISC45. We report zero-shot classification results in accuracy (%) ↑ and text-to-image retrieval results in mAP@100 (%) ↑. The two best-performing models are highlighted in bold and underlined.

| Model | Zero-shot classification | | | Text-to-image retrieval | | |
|---|---|---|---|---|---|---|
| | M-ML-N | RESISC45 | Avg | M-ML-N | RESISC45 | Avg |
| OpenCLIP B/16 [20] | <u>55.09</u> | 67.45 | 61.27 | 37.43 | 64.30 | 50.87 |
| OpenCLIP L/14 [20] | 53.48 | **72.82** | <u>63.15</u> | **42.55** | **70.88** | **56.72** |
| GeoRSCLIP [28] | **59.03** | <u>68.28</u> | **63.66** | 34.93 | 60.04 | 47.49 |
| SkyCLIP [25] | 53.88 | 67.68 | 60.78 | <u>39.02</u> | <u>66.79</u> | <u>52.91</u> |
| RemoteCLIP [16] | 39.35 | 66.90 | 53.13 | 23.80 | 56.88 | 40.34 |
| Llama3-RGB-CLIP | 53.38 | 68.26 | 60.82 | 38.50 | 66.49 | 52.50 |

**Table 3.** Zero-shot evaluation results for different text templates using the Llama3-MS-CLIP model. We report zero-shot classification results in accuracy (%) ↑ and text-to-image retrieval results in mAP@100 (%) ↑. The best-performing method is highlighted in bold.

| Templates | Zero-shot classification | | | | Text-to-image retrieval | | | |
|---|---|---|---|---|---|---|---|---|
| | ESAT | BEN | M-ML | Avg | ESAT | BEN | M-ML | Avg |
| CLIP templates [20] | 67.64 | 60.25 | 37.33 | 55.07 | 61.14 | 34.31 | 29.45 | 41.63 |
| RS5M templates [28] | 67.28 | **60.17** | 47.02 | 58.15 | 60.19 | 34.69 | **30.99** | 41.95 |
| MS-CLIP templates | **67.86** | 59.63 | **48.13** | **58.54** | **63.03** | **35.62** | 29.72 | **42.79** |

model did not fully adapt to the additional input due to the limited number of weight updates with only one million samples. At the same time, changes in the multispectral channels are ∼2800 times higher than the changes in the RGB weights, which are adjusted by only 0.03% compared to the OpenCLIP weights. This shows the additional information Llama3-MS-CLIP leverages from the multispectral channels and highlights the need for even larger multispectral EO datasets for longer pre-training without overfitting.

In Fig. 7(b), we examine the effect of using three, ten, or all twelve Sentinel-2 bands. Although using all bands might seem beneficial, certain tasks decline in performance compared to using only the RGB bands. Omitting bands 1 and 10 and training on ten bands leads to the overall best results. The dropped bands both have a 60 m spatial resolution, and their information might not align well with the other bands. Dropping these bands is common among EO models (e.g., in [7]), suggesting low meaningful information for many use cases.

We further compare various strategies for freezing and unfreezing model layers in Table 4. The patch embedding was unfrozen in every setting to adapt to the multispectral input. Freezing layers can, in principle, reduce the risk of catastrophic forgetting. Yet, our experiments show that fully unfreezing the image and text encoders leads to the best results when adapting to multispec-

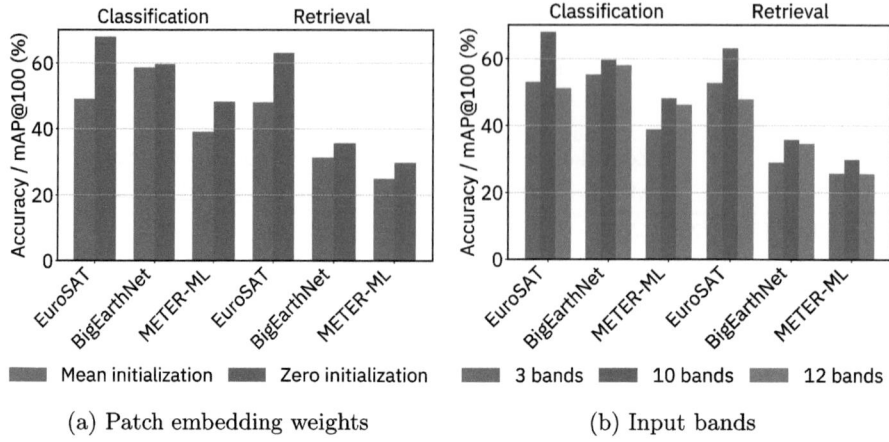

**Fig. 7.** Ablation experiments for the initialization of additional patch embedding channels (a) and the selected input bands (b). The final setting is in blue. (Color figure online)

**Table 4.** Ablation experiment with different unfrozen layers. We either unfreeze the attention layers, projection layers, or all layers in the image and text encoders. We report zero-shot classification results in accuracy (%) ↑ and text-to-image retrieval results in mAP@100 (%) ↑. The best-performing method is highlighted in bold.

| Image enc. | Text enc. | Zero-shot classification | | | | Text-to-image retrieval | | | |
|---|---|---|---|---|---|---|---|---|---|
| | | ESAT | BEN | M-ML | Avg | ESAT | BEN | M-ML | Avg |
| Attention l. | Attention l. | 56.12 | 58.05 | 45.30 | 53.15 | 48.76 | 33.80 | 24.96 | 35.84 |
| Projection l. | Projection l. | 32.00 | 56.25 | 43.49 | 43.91 | 34.70 | 34.47 | 21.44 | 30.20 |
| All layers | None | 65.82 | 58.87 | **48.63** | 57.77 | 55.46 | 34.19 | 29.08 | 39.57 |
| All layers | All layers | **67.86** | **59.63** | 48.13 | **58.54** | **63.03** | **35.62** | **29.72** | **42.79** |

tral data. By contrast, selectively fine-tuning only the projection layer yields lower performance than the baseline. We performed a similar ablation study for Llama3-RGB-CLIP with contrary results. Fine-tuning only the projection layer resulted in the best performance. Keeping the earlier layers frozen avoids forgetting pre-trained features with RGB input, but it cannot capture the multispectral information when including the additional multispectral channels.

## 7 Discussion and Limitations

In this work, we demonstrate the benefit of leveraging MLLMs for accelerating image captioning in order to curate datasets for subsequent vision-language model training. While MLLMs are already able to digest and caption RGB representations of remote sensing images themselves, they cannot leverage multispectral data—leaving room for specialized models for Earth observation. We address this gap by coupling the automated caption generation on RGB imagery with multi-spectral data for the Llama3-MS-CLIP. However, we acknowledge limitations when using MLLMs to generate synthetic image captions. First, we understand that there exists a risk of propagating errors or biases (e.g., in the form of hallucinations) of the MLLM further into the self-supervised models that are trained on top of the synthetic data. It will be relevant to identify such ripple effects that result from training self-supervised models on synthetically generated data of MLLMs in order to understand how errors and biases are propagated, reduced, or reinforced by downstream models. Second, we note that the existing dataset likely benefits from increased diversity, as the word count graph in the supplementary section highlights a trend of similar topics in many of the captions. Third, we advocate for considering human-in-the-loop systems during the caption generation process in settings where errors by the MLLMs are not acceptable.

Based on the synthetically generated captions, Llama3-MS-CLIP demonstrates the benefit of using multi-spectral data during pretraining. Even though we observe significant performance improvements when leveraging multi-spectral data instead of RGB data, our experiments also show that the model is potentially not yet saturated. This is indicated by comparably low weights in the patch embedding of Llama3-MS-CLIP for the non-visible channels compared to the visible RGB spectrum. Overall, this experiment reinforces our expectation that the performance of the model will further improve with longer continuous pretraining, leveraging a larger and more diverse training corpus.

Finally, we see a possibility for future research to work on integrating and merging pixel-level training strategies with the image-level training we employ in this work. This merge could improve the model's capability to capture detailed image nuances and help differentiate between closely related classes. Pixel-level understanding might also unlock additional progress on other tasks that we did not explore in this work, including semantic segmentation and object detection.

## 8 Conclusion

We introduce a multispectral vision-language dataset of low-resolution, multispectral Sentinel-2 data with corresponding captions. Our automated captioning strategy scales easily, reducing the need for costly human annotations. On top of this dataset, we build Llama3-MS-CLIP, the first CLIP-like multispectral VLM. Our experiments show that our model significantly improves zero-shot classification and retrieval compared to other methods, even domain-specific adaptations trained on larger datasets. We see significant potential in leveraging the open-sourced Llama3-MS-CLIP in downstream applications and as a vision encoder for building multispectral MLLMs.

**Acknowledgments.** We thank the remote sensing experts for reviewing the generated captions and Niklas Kopp for providing the embedding space analysis.

**Disclosure of Interests.** This work is part of the FAST-EO project funded by the European Space Agency (ESA), contract number 4000143501/23/I-DT.

# References

1. Bazi, Y., Bashmal, L., Al Rahhal, M.M., Ricci, R., Melgani, F.: Rs-llava: A large vision-language model for joint captioning and question answering in remote sensing imagery. Remote Sens. **16**(9) (2024). https://doi.org/10.3390/rs16091477
2. Blumenstiel, B., Braham, N.A.A., Albrecht, C.M., Maurogiovanni, S., Fraccaro, P.: Ssl4eo-s12 v1. 1: A multimodal, multiseasonal dataset for pretraining, updated. arXiv preprint arXiv:2503.00168 (2025)
3. Blumenstiel, B., Jakubik, J., Kühne, H., Vössing, M.: What a mess: multi-domain evaluation of zero-shot semantic segmentation. Adv. Neural. Inf. Process. Syst. **36**, 73299–73311 (2023)
4. Jakubik, J., et al.: TerraMind: Large-scale generative multimodality for Earth observation (2025). arXiv preprint arXiv:2504.11171
5. Cheng, G., Han, J., Lu, X.: Remote sensing image scene classification: benchmark and state of the art. Proc. IEEE **105**(10), 1865–1883 (2017)
6. Cherti, M., et al.: Reproducible scaling laws for contrastive language-image learning. In: Proceedings of the IEEE/CVF Conference on Computer Vision and Pattern Recognition, pp. 2818–2829 (2023)
7. Cong, Y., et al.: Satmae: pre-training transformers for temporal and multi-spectral satellite imagery. Adv. Neural. Inf. Process. Syst. **35**, 197–211 (2022)
8. Denkowski, M., Lavie, A.: Meteor universal: Language specific translation evaluation for any target language. In: Proceedings of the Ninth Workshop on Statistical Machine Translation, pp. 376–380 (2014)
9. Helber, P., Bischke, B., Dengel, A., Borth, D.: Eurosat: a novel dataset and deep learning benchmark for land use and land cover classification. IEEE J. Selected Topics Appl. Earth Observ. Remote Sens. **12**(7), 2217–2226 (2019)
10. Ilharco, G., et al.: Openclip (2021). https://doi.org/10.5281/zenodo.5143773
11. Jia, C., et al.: Scaling up visual and vision-language representation learning with noisy text supervision. In: International Conference on Machine Learning, pp. 4904–4916. PMLR (2021)
12. Li, B., et al.: Llava-next: Stronger LLMs supercharge multimodal capabilities in the wild (2024). https://llava-vl.github.io/blog/2024-05-10-llava-next-stronger-llms/
13. Li, J., Li, D., Savarese, S., Hoi, S.: Blip-2: Bootstrapping language-image pre-training with frozen image encoders and large language models. In: International Conference on Machine Learning, pp. 19730–19742. PMLR (2023)
14. Li, J., Li, D., Xiong, C., Hoi, S.: Blip: Bootstrapping language-image pre-training for unified vision-language understanding and generation. In: International Conference on Machine Learning, pp. 12888–12900. PMLR (2022)
15. Li, X., Wen, C., Hu, Y., Zhou, N.: RS-clip: Zero shot remote sensing scene classification via contrastive vision-language supervision. Int. J. Appl. Earth Obs. Geoinf. **124**, 103497 (2023)
16. Liu, F., et al.: Remoteclip: A vision language foundation model for remote sensing. IEEE Transactions on Geoscience and Remote Sensing (2024)
17. Lu, X., Wang, B., Zheng, X., Li, X.: Exploring models and data for remote sensing image caption generation. IEEE Trans. Geosci. Remote Sens. **56**(4), 2183–2195 (2017)

18. Mall, U., Phoo, C.P., Liu, M.K., Vondrick, C., Hariharan, B., Bala, K.: Remote sensing vision-language foundation models without annotations via ground remote alignment. arXiv preprint arXiv:2312.06960 (2023)
19. Qu, B., Li, X., Tao, D., Lu, X.: Deep semantic understanding of high resolution remote sensing image. In: 2016 International Conference on Computer, Information and Telecommunication Systems (Cits), pp. 1–5. IEEE (2016)
20. Radford, A., et al.: Learning transferable visual models from natural language supervision. In: International Conference on Machine Learning, pp. 8748–8763. PmLR (2021)
21. Schuhmann, C., et al.: LAION-5b: An open large-scale dataset for training next generation image-text models. In: Thirty-sixth Conference on Neural Information Processing Systems Datasets and Benchmarks Track (2022)
22. Sumbul, G., Charfuelan, M., Demir, B., Markl, V.: Bigearthnet: a large-scale benchmark archive for remote sensing image understanding. In: IGARSS IEEE international geoscience and remote sensing symposium, pp. 5901–5904. IEEE (2019)
23. Szwarcman, D., et al.: Prithvi-eo-2.0: A versatile multi-temporal foundation model for earth observation applications. arXiv preprint arXiv:2412.02732 (2024)
24. Wang, Y., Braham, N.A.A., Xiong, Z., Liu, C., Albrecht, C.M., Zhu, X.X.: Ssl4eo-s12: a large-scale multimodal, multitemporal dataset for self-supervised learning in earth observation [software and data sets]. IEEE Geosci. Remote Sens. Mag. **11**(3), 98–106 (2023)
25. Wang, Z., Prabha, R., Huang, T., Wu, J., Rajagopal, R.: Skyscript: A large and semantically diverse vision-language dataset for remote sensing. In: Proceedings of the AAAI Conference on Artificial Intelligence. vol. 38, pp. 5805–5813 (2024)
26. Yuan, Z., Xiong, Z., Mou, L., Zhu, X.X.: Chatearthnet: a global-scale image-text dataset empowering vision-language geo-foundation models. Earth Syst. Sci. Data Discuss. **2024**, 1–24 (2024)
27. Yuan, Z., et al.: Exploring a fine-grained multiscale method for cross-modal remote sensing image retrieval. arXiv preprint arXiv:2204.09868 (2022)
28. Zhang, Z., Zhao, T., Guo, Y., Yin, J.: Rs5m and georsclip: A large scale vision-language dataset and a large vision-language model for remote sensing. IEEE Transactions on Geoscience and Remote Sensing (2024)
29. Zhu, B., et al.: Meter-ml: a multi-sensor earth observation benchmark for automated methane source mapping. arXiv preprint arXiv:2207.11166 (2022)
30. Zhu, X.X., et al.: deep learning in remote sensing: a comprehensive review and list of resources. IEEE Geosci. and Remote Sens. Mag. **5**(4) (2017)

# Improving Temporal Knowledge Graph Reasoning with Hierarchical Semantic-Aware Contrastive Learning

Renning Pang[1], Yao Liu[1], Yanglei Gan[1], Tingting Dai[1], Yashen Wang[2], Xiaojun Shi[2], Tian Lan[1(✉)], and Qiao Liu[1]

[1] School of Computer Science and Engineering, University of Electronic Science and Technology of China, Chengdu, China
{prn,yangleigan}@std.uestc.edu.cn, {liuyao,lantian,qliu}@uestc.edu.cn
[2] Artificial Intelligence Institute of CETC, Beijing, China

**Abstract.** Temporal Knowledge Graph (TKG) reasoning seeks to infer the future evolution of incomplete facts from observed historical data. Although supervised contrastive learning has recently enhanced query representations for TKG reasoning, two critical challenges remain. First, current methods uniformly treat all negative samples, overlooking their semantic and temporal correlations. Second, these approaches do not fully exploit the hierarchical relationships between fine-grained events and higher-level event categories, thereby missing crucial event taxonomies. To address these limitations, we propose a Hierarchical Semantic-aware Contrastive Learning (HSCL) framework. Specifically, our Instance-level objective introduces a dynamic adaptive weighting mechanism that differentiates negative samples based on semantic similarity, while our Category-level objective incorporates ontology-guided clustering to represent hierarchical event semantics. This dual-level design encourages cohesive embeddings within the same event category and clear separation across different categories. Extensive experiments on four real-world benchmarks demonstrate that HSCL consistently outperforms state-of-the-art baselines([1]The code is available at https://github.com/AONE-NLP/TKGR-HSCL.

**Keywords:** Temporal knowledge graph · Contrastive learning · Graph Neural Network

## 1 Introduction

Temporal Knowledge Graphs (TKGs) extend traditional Knowledge Graphs (KGs) by incorporating temporal information, associating event facts with timestamps or time intervals to indicate their validity periods. Unlike static KGs,

**Supplementary Information** The online version contains supplementary material available at https://doi.org/10.1007/978-3-032-06106-5_22.

which represent facts as triples (subject, relation, object), TKGs add a temporal dimension, forming quadruples $<s, r, o, t>$, where $t$ specifies when the fact holds, such as $<$ USA, negotiate, Japan, 2019-6-29 $>$.

Reasoning over TKGs involves inferring missing facts based on observed quadruples within a specified time range $[t_0, t_T]$. It is categorized into interpolation [2,3,11], which infers missing facts within the historical range ($t_0 \leq t \leq t_T$), and extrapolation [7,28,32], which predicts facts beyond the observed range ($t > t_T$). This study focuses on the extrapolation setting, emphasizing its forward-looking significance.

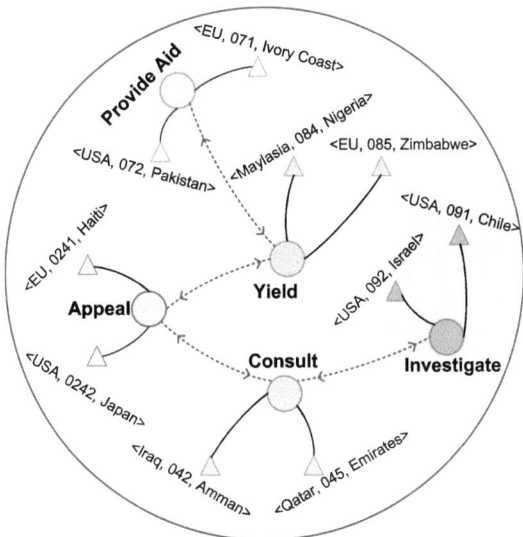

**Fig. 1.** An illustrative example highlighting the importance of capturing the hierarchical semantics related to the query. Event codes have been replaced with corresponding numbers from the codebook to emphasize the structured categorization. △ denotes fine-grained events, while ○ denotes coarse-grained events.

Accurately predicting future facts requires a thorough understanding of the developmental patterns embedded within historical facts. Existing research primarily focuses on aggregating structural information from adjacent entities and integrating temporal dynamics to construct historical representations of entities and relations [32,37,38]. These representations are then utilized within scoring functions, such as ConvTransE [52], to estimate the likelihood of future event facts. Building upon these foundational methods, recent advancements have introduced contrastive learning to enhance TKG reasoning by leveraging the discriminative capability of contrasting diverse types of information, such as local and global historical contexts [39], or historical and non-historical dependencies [36]. These techniques aim to refine feature representations by emphasizing the distinctions between positive and negative samples.

Despite the significant progress of contrastive learning in TKG reasoning, these methods exhibit inherent limitations. **First, they uniformly treat all negative samples, failing to capture essential semantic and temporal correlations among queries** [36,39]. This uniform treatment overlooks critical distinctions necessary for optimal feature representation and contradicts the alignment principle of feature representations [42–44], which aims to position semantically similar samples closer together. As illustrated in Fig. 1, events within the same coarse-grained category are treated uniformly as negative samples, ignoring their internal semantic and temporal relationships and potentially leading to suboptimal representations. **Second, existing approaches fail to account for the hierarchical relations between fine-grained events and their broader categories**, as defined in the widely used CAMEO ontology, thereby preventing the model from capturing hierarchical semantic structures [48,50]. Consider the event *"Investigate"* in Fig. 1, which encompasses the fine-grained events *"091"* (*"Investigate crime, corruption"*) and *"092"* (*"Investigate human rights abuses"*). While these fine-grained events exhibit distinct characteristics, they share the broader semantic context of *"Investigate"*. We argue that incorporating these hierarchical semantics into contrastive learning objective would enable capture of latent semantic, resulting in more robust and generalized representations.

To bridge these gaps, we propose a Hierarchical Semantic-aware Contrastive Learning (HSCL) framework for TKG reasoning. Specifically, HSCL integrates short and long term sequence encoders with an entity-aware attention mechanism to capture query-specific temporal dynamics. Additionally, we design a hierarchical contrast module for short and long term queries. The instance-level contrastive learning refines representations by directly comparing individual event embeddings, distinguishing semantically similar and dissimilar events, and enabling the model to discern fine-grained differences between queries and their contexts; meanwhile, the category-level contrastive learning captures hierarchical relationships between detailed events and broader categories, encouraging events of the same type to cluster while keeping distinct types separated. This higher-level grouping enhances the generalization of the representations and supports the model in inferring broader patterns and relationships. The contribution of our work are three-fold:

- We propose two optimization objectives to maximize the mutual information of query-specific information in different granularities.
- We introduce a hierarchical contrastive learning framework in which an instance-level objective distinguishes subtle differences between events, while a category-level objective enforces hierarchical grouping into broader categories, enhancing generalization and robustness.
- Evaluations across four benchmark datasets highlight the effectiveness of the proposed method compared to the current state-of-the-art baselines in terms of reasoning accuracy and representation capability.

## 2 Related Work

Temporal Knowledge Graph (TKG) reasoning seeks to predict facts at future timestamps by modeling observed historical facts. This task typically operates under two settings interpolation and extrapolation with our primary focus on the extrapolation scenario. Existing approaches mainly concentrate on either learning temporal patterns [28,32] or capturing structural information [26,34] to enrich entity and relation representations. RE-NET [28] models long-term historical interactions of target entities as sequences, integrating a Recurrent Neural Network (RNN) and a relational Graph Convolutional Network (GCN) to capture both temporal and structural dependencies. RE-GCN [32] similarly encodes temporal and relational dependencies among entities, leveraging graph convolutions to capture complex interactions. $L^2TKG$ [40] exploits both intra-time relations (co-occurring entities at the same timestamp) and inter-time relations (entities appearing at different timestamps). DaeMon [55] adaptively retrieves temporal path information between query subjects and object candidates over time without relying on entity representations. TiPNN [54] constructs a unified history temporal graph to comprehensively represent past information, using query-aware temporal paths for historical path modeling. In addition, Tlogic [56] enhances interpretability through a symbolic framework built on temporal logical rules extracted via temporal random walks. Despite these achievements, existing methods often have shortcomings when modeling both long and short term temporal dependencies, as they frequently overlook explicit dependencies among distinct entities across different timestamps in long-term histories.

To address above limitation, TiRGN [35] proposes a global history encoder to identify entities associated with historical or unseen facts, complemented by a time-guided decoder. HGLS [38] directly connects the same entity at each timestamp to capture long and short term dependencies. CRAFT [41] leverages candidate-specific historical context via dual-attention-enhanced path encoding for long-term relevance, while using frequency-based contextual modeling for short-term repetitive patterns. Similarly, MGESL [58] incorporates a multi-granularity history module, capturing long-term coarse-grained multi-hop history alongside short-term fine-grained repetitive patterns. Building on these strategies, recent work integrates contrastive learning to merge historical and non-historical dependencies for enhanced temporal reasoning. CENET [36] applies historical contrastive learning in temporal knowledge graphs to improve entity prediction and event reasoning. LogCL [39] unifies local and global temporal embeddings through a contrastive loss function, ensuring robust historical context fusion. Dejavu [21] proposes a unified PLM-based framework that employs contrastive learning to model historical contextual information, effectively balancing temporal information and textual knowledge.

Despite these advances, existing contrastive learning methods often treat all negative samples uniformly, overlooking crucial semantic and temporal correlations that may arise across different queries. Moreover, they fail to leverage the hierarchical relationships between fine-grained events and their broader categories, thus limiting their ability to capture nuanced event structures.

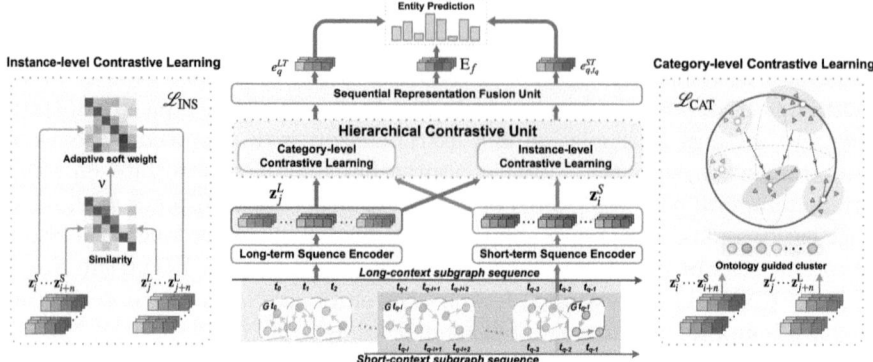

**Fig. 2.** Model overview of HSCL. Given a query $< s, r, ?, t+\Delta t >$, HSCL employs long and short term sequence encoders to capture query-specific temporal dynamics. The instance-level contrastive module refines representations by distinguishing subtle differences between individual events, while the category-level module organizes events into broader semantic groups. then the sequential representation fusion unit integrates the long and short term representations via a cross-attention to generate the final probability distribution over entities.

## 3 Methods

In this section, we detail our proposed framework, as shown in Fig. 2 We begin by formulating the preliminaries of Temporal Knowledge Graph (TKG) reasoning. A TKG is formally represented as a sequence of snapshots $G = \{G_1, G_2, \ldots, G_{t-1}\}$, where each snapshot $G_{t_i}$ encompasses all quadruples that occur at timestamp $t_i$. Each fact within a snapshot is denoted as a quadruple $(e_s, r, e_o, t_i)$, indicating that the subject entity $e_s$ interacts with the object entity $e_o$ through relation $r$ at time $t_i$. To ensure comprehensive representation [53], inverse relation quadruples $(e_s, r^{-1}, e_o, t_i)$ are incorporated into $G$. The aim of TKG reasoning is to predict either the missing object $(e_s, r, ?, t)$ or subject $(?, r, e_o, t)$ at future timestamp by leveraging the historical snapshots $\{G_{t-l}, G_{t-l+1}, \ldots, G_{t-1}\}$ spanning the preceding $l$ timestamps.

### 3.1 Sequential Representation Learning

To comprehensively capture the diverse temporal dynamics inherent in TKGs, we propose modeling both long-term and short-term representations of historical quadruple sequences. Long-term representations provide the essential context required to understand the evolution of entity relationships and interactions over extended periods. In contrast, short-term representations focus on recent interactions and transient relationships, which may indicate emerging trends or temporary states within the TKG.

**Long-Term Sequence Encoder.** To model the long-term temporal dynamics, we adopt the R-GCN [9] as the encoder to capture historical subgraphs information. Given a query $(e_q, r_q, ?, t_q)$ and its corresponding temporal knowledge graph $G^{t_q} = \{G_1, G_2, \ldots, G_{t_q-1}\}$, we first extract all one-hop historical facts associated with the query. Subsequently, for each of these target entities, we expand the sub-graph to include two-hop relational patterns to model historical long-term temporal information. The aggregated representation obtained from this expanded structure is then used for downstream processing.

To effectively encode the structural and semantic information embedded in this sub-graph, we update the entity embeddings at layer $l$ as follows:

$$e_o^l = \sigma_1 \left( \frac{1}{c_o} \sum_{(e_s, r) \in \mathcal{E}_o} W_1 \left( e_s^{l-1} + r \right) \right) \tag{1}$$

where $(e_s, r) \in \mathcal{E}_o$ represents the neighbors connected to the target node via edge $c_o$, and $W_1 \in \mathbb{R}^{d \times d}$ is the trainable parameter matrix at layer $l$ layer for feature aggregation. $\sigma_1$ denotes the ReLU activation function, and $e_o^l$ represents weighted summation of the neighboring entitys and relations by R-GCN at layer $l-1$. And for simplicity, the output of the R-GCN at the final layer $L$ is represented as $e^L$.

To further exploit the long-term facts relevant to queries, we deploy an attention aggregation mechanism, as follows:

$$e_q^{LT} = \sigma_2(W_2 e^L + e') \cdot e^L \tag{2}$$

where $W_2 \in \mathbb{R}^{d \times d}$ is learnable weight matrix, while $\sigma_2$ denotes the RReLU activation function. $e_q^{LT}$ denotes the final long-term representations with respect to the query.

**Short-Term Sequence Encoder.** To capture the recent interactions and transient relationships with respect to the query. At timestamp $t$ and in context $c$, the representation message $e_o^l \in \mathbb{R}^d$ received by an object $o$ at the $l$-th layer of graph propagation is defined as:

$$e_{o,t}^l = \sigma_2 \left( \frac{1}{c_o} \sum_{(s,r), \exists(s,r,o) \in \mathcal{E}_t} W_3 \left( e_{s,t}^{l-1} + r \right) + W_4 e_{o,t}^{l-1} \right) \tag{3}$$

where $\mathcal{E}_t$ denotes the set of edges for timestamp $t$; $e_{s,t}^{l-1}$ is the representation of a neighboring entity $e_s$ in $(l-1)$-th layer at timestamp $t$. $W_3, W_4 \in \mathbb{R}^{d \times d}$ are learnable parameters for feature aggregation and self-loop connections. For simplicity, the output of the R-GCN at the final layer $L$ is denoted as $e_t^L$.

To update entity representations over time, we employ a Gated Recurrent Unit (GRU) [4] to model short-term sequence dynamics:

$$E_{t+1} = \text{GRU}(e_t, e_t^L) \tag{4}$$

Additionally, we apply a time gate unit over the relation embedding at $t-1$ to obtain the updated relation representation:

$$R_t = U_t \cdot R_t^w + (1 - U_t) \cdot R_{t-1}; \tag{5}$$
$$U_t = \sigma_3(W_5 R_t^w + b) \tag{6}$$

where $U_t \in \mathbb{R}^{d \times d}$. $\sigma_3$ denotes sigmoid function, $W_5$ is learnable weight matrix. $R_t^w$ denotes the relation representation at time $t$, calculated by aggregating the representations of entities interacting with the relation at time $t$:

$$R_t^w = Meanpool(E_{s,r}) + r, \forall e_s \in \mathcal{N}_r^t \tag{7}$$

where $E_{s,r}$ is the embedding associated with $r$, $Meanpool(\cdot)$ aggregates the embeddings of entities in the set $\mathcal{N}_r^t$ that interact with relation $r$ at time $t$.

Subsequently, we refine the entity embeddings using an attention mechanism to emphasize the importance of query-relevant KG snapshots. For a query at timestamp $t_q$, the query-specific features representation $e_{t_q}$ is calculated as:

$$e_{t_q} = W_6 \left[ Meanpool(r_{t_q}) \parallel e_q \right] \tag{8}$$

where $e_q$ denotes query entity, $r_{t_q}$ denotes relations associated with $e_{t_q}$, $W_6$ is learnable weight matrix, and $\parallel$ represents the concatenation operation.

For entity and relation within a time window $T_{\text{win}} = \{\tau \mid \tau \in [t_q - (p-1) \ldots t_q]\}$, we apply an attention mechanism to weight the importance of query-relevant features:

$$\begin{aligned} e_{q,t_q}^{ST} &= e_{t_q} + \sum_{\tau \in T_{\text{win}} \setminus \{t_q\}} \delta e_\tau \\ \delta &= \sigma_3 \left( W_7 \left( e_\tau^L + e_{t_q} \right) \right), \tau \in T_{\text{win}} \setminus \{t_q\} \end{aligned} \tag{9}$$

where $e_{q,t_q}^{ST}$ is the final representation of the short-term sequence, $\delta$ denotes attention scores for historical snapshots within $T_{\text{win}}$, then $\sigma_3$ is the Softmax function, and $W_7$ is learnable weight matrix. $e_\tau$ is representation of the entity associated with the query at historical timestamp $\tau$.

### 3.2 Hierarchical Contrastive Learning

To improve the discriminative power and generalization of the embeddings, we propose a hierarchical contrastive learning unit comprising two complementary objectives: instance-level and category-level contrastive learning. These objectives address the challenges of capturing semantic correlations and hierarchical relationships, respectively.

**Instance-level Contrastive Learning.** To overcome the uniform treatment of negative samples, we incorporate a dynamic adaptive weighting mechanism into the instance-level contrastive learning objective. This mechanism differentiates negative samples based on semantic relations, thereby improving the model's ability to learn informative gradients. The short-term contextual embeddings $e_i^S$

and the long-term contextual embeddings $e_j^L$ are first projected into the same latent space using a shared projection model:

$$\mathbf{z}_i^S = \mathrm{Norm}(\mathrm{Proj}(e_{q,t_q}^{ST})); \qquad \mathbf{z}_j^L = \mathrm{Norm}(\mathrm{Proj}(e_q^{LT})) \tag{10}$$

where $\mathrm{Proj}(\cdot)$ is multi-layer perceptron (MLP), and $\mathrm{Norm}(\cdot)$ denotes $L_2$ normalization. The adaptive soft weight $\mathcal{V}$ learned by 2-layer MLP according to the samples under the long and short term sequences, formulated as:

$$\mathcal{V} = \sigma_3(W_8(\sigma_4(W_9 \cdot [\mathbf{z}_i^S \parallel \mathbf{z}_j^L] + b_1)) + b_2) \tag{11}$$

where $W_8, W_9$ are earnable parameter matrices, while $b_1, b_2$ are bias vectors, $\sigma_4$ is the Tanh activation function. The instance-level contrastive loss is then defined as:

$$\mathcal{L}_{\mathrm{INS}} = -\frac{1}{|B|} \sum_{i \in B} \log \frac{\exp\left(\mathbf{z}_i^S \cdot \mathbf{z}_i^L / \tau\right)}{\sum_{j \in B} \mathcal{V} \cdot \exp\left(\mathbf{z}_i^S \cdot \mathbf{z}_j^L / \tau\right)} \tag{12}$$

Where $\tau$ is a temperature parameter, $B$ denotes batch size.

**Category-Level Contrastive Learning.** To capture hierarchical relationships and semantic context, we propose a Category-level contrastive learning task that models the relationships between fine-grained events and their broader categories. Specifically, We employ ontology-guided K-means clustering to group event based on their event types. The centroid $C_c$ for each event type $c$ is computed as:

$$\mathbf{C}_c = \frac{1}{|S_c|} \sum_{i \in S_c} \mathbf{z}_i, \tag{13}$$

where $S_c$ denotes the set of events associated with type $c$, and $\mathbf{z}_i$ represents the embedding of event $i$. Each event embedding $z_i$ treats its category centroid $\mathbf{C}_{c_i}$ as the positive sample, and the centroids of other categories $\mathbf{C}_{c(c \neq c_i)}$ as negative samples. The cosine similarity between event embedding and category centroid is computed as:

$$\mathrm{sim}\left(\mathbf{z}_i, \mathbf{C}_c\right) = \frac{\mathbf{z}_i \cdot \mathbf{C}_c}{\|\mathbf{z}_i\| \|\mathbf{C}_c\|} \tag{14}$$

we dynamically select the hardest negative sample as the centroid with the highest similarity among negative categories. The category-level contrastive loss is then defined as:

$$\mathcal{L}_{\mathrm{CAT}} = \frac{1}{N} \sum_{i=1}^{N} \max(0, \Delta_i) \tag{15}$$

$$\Delta_i = \gamma\text{-}\mathrm{sim}\left(\mathbf{z}_i, \mathbf{C}_{c_i}\right) + \max_{c \neq c_i} \mathrm{sim}\left(\mathbf{z}_i, \mathbf{C}_c\right)$$

where $\gamma$ is a hyper-parameter to control the hardness of probability assignment. This loss ensures that embeddings of events within the same type are closer together, while those of different categories are further apart, capturing hierarchical semantic structures.

### 3.3 Sequential Representation Fusion Unit

To capture latent signals from sequential representations, we introduce a weight-shared attention layer to optimally fuse diverse embeddings. For a clear explanation we denote the linearly-transformed long-term and short-term embeddings from $e_q^{LT}$ and $e_{q,t_q}^{ST}$ as $E^L$ and $E^S$, respectively. We then evaluate the relevance between each event embedding in one set and the other using a cross-attention mechanism:

$$E_c^{SL} = \text{MHA}(\underbrace{E^S}_{Q}, \underbrace{E^L}_{K}, \underbrace{E^L}_{V}); E_c^{LS} = \text{MHA}(\underbrace{E^L}_{Q}, \underbrace{E^S}_{K}, \underbrace{E^S}_{V}) \tag{16}$$

where $\text{MHA}(Q, K, V)$ denotes multi-head attention operator, $Q$, $K$ and $V$ are derived from the respective embedding sets.

These two features $E_c^{SL}$ and $E_c^{LS}$ are subsequently combined using a fusion layer to obtain the final representation:

$$E_f = W_9 \odot E_c^{LS} + W_{10} \odot E_c^{SL} \tag{17}$$

$W_9, W_{10}$ are learnable weight matrices, $E_f$ deliver a holistic representation for reasoning.

### 3.4 Inference and Training

We utilize ConvTransE [10] to derive the representation of the query, we calculate the prediction scores for all candidate entities given the query at time $t_q$ as follows:

$$\phi(e_q, r_q, e, q) = \sigma_3 \left( E_{t_q}^{e_q} \text{ConvTransE} \left( \hat{E}_{t_q}^{e_q}, r_{t_q} \right) \right) \tag{18}$$

$$\hat{E}_{t_q}^{e_q} = \lambda \hat{e}_q^{LT} + (1-\lambda) \hat{e}_{q,t_q}^{ST} + \hat{E}_f \tag{19}$$

where $\lambda$ is a variable factor that is set at [0,1].

TKG reasoning task can be regarded as a multi-classification task. Following the past works [32], we employs Cross-Entropy as the loss function:

$$\mathcal{L}_{tkg} = \sum_{t=0}^{T} \sum_{(c_s,r,c,t) \in \mathcal{F}_t} \sum_{e \in \mathcal{E}} y_t^e \log \phi(e_s, r, e, t) \tag{20}$$

where $\phi(e_s, r, e, t)$ is the entity prediction probabilistic scores $\mathbf{y}_t^e \in \mathbb{R}^{|\mathcal{E}|}$ is the label [0, 1]. The final loss is then computed as:

$$\mathcal{L} = \mathcal{L}_{tkg} + \lambda_1 \mathcal{L}_{CAT} + \lambda_2 \mathcal{L}_{INS} \tag{21}$$

where $\lambda_1$ and $\lambda_2$ are the parameters that control the contrastive loss terms.

## 4 Experiments

### 4.1 Experimental Settings

**Datasets.** We leverage four real-world event-based benchmark datasets to evaluate our proposed methods. The datasets include four from the Integrated Crisis Early Warning System (ICEWS) [3]: ICEWS14, ICEWS18, ICEWS05-15 and one from the Global Database of Events, Language, and Tone (GDELT) [27]. Following previous works [35,37], all datasets are split into training, validation, and test sets in proportions of 80%, 10%, 10%. Detailed statistics for all datasets are presented in Table 1.

**Table 1.** Dataset Statistics, with "Unseen Events" showing the proportion of test queries involving unseen events.

| Dataset | ICEWS14 | ICEWS18 | ICEWS05-15 | GDELT |
|---|---|---|---|---|
| Training Facts | 74,845 | 373,018 | 368,868 | 1,734,399 |
| Validation Facts | 8,514 | 45,995 | 46,302 | 238,765 |
| Test Facts | 7,371 | 49,545 | 46,159 | 305,241 |
| Entities | 6,869 | 10,094 | 23,033 | 7,691 |
| Relations | 230 | 256 | 251 | 240 |
| Time Interval | 1 day | 1 day | 1 day | 15 mins |
| Timestamps | 365 | 365 | 4017 | 2975 |
| Unseen Events | 58.43% | 55.69% | 39.82% | 43.72% |

**Evaluation Metrics.** We evaluate our approach on the task of entity prediction, where the objective is to predict the missing object entity given an entity-relation pair. The evaluation metrics include Mean Reciprocal Ranking (MRR), and Hits@1/3/10. Following standard practices in recent works [7,34,38], we report results under the time-aware filtered setting, which excludes quadruples occurring at the query time.

**Baselines.** To provide a comprehensive comparison and intuitive proof, we compare it against with interpolation methods including TTransE [2], TA-DisMult [3] and DE-SimIE [11], as well as extrapolation methods RE-NET [28], CyGNet [29], TITer [31], RE-GCN [32], CEN [33], TiRGN [35], HisMatch [34], RETIA [37], CENET [36], HGLS [38], $L^2$TKG [40], CRAFT [41], THCN [6], LogCL [39]. We provide detailed model descriptions in Appendix A.

**Implementation Details.** All experiments are conducted on NVIDIA A100 GPUs. We utilize Adam as the optimizer with a learning rate of 0.001. The embedding size $d$ is set to 200. R-GCN layers on encoders is set to 2 and the dropout rate for each layer is set to 0.2. The optimal local historical KG snapshots sequences lengths of all datasets are set to 7. The number of heads of the multi-attention mechanism is set to 8, dropout is set to 0.3. The optimal temperature coefficient of all datasets are set to 0.05, 0.05, 0.03, 0.05.

**Table 2.** The prediction performance of MRR and Hit@{1/3/10} are on all datasets with time-aware metrics. The best results are highlighted in **bold**, while the second-best results are underlined. All results are retrieved from [7,39]. To highlight the effectiveness of our proposed HSCL method, we report its relative performance improvement in the final row of the table.

| Models | ICEWS14 | | | | ICEWS18 | | | | ICEWS05-15 | | | | GDELT | | | |
|---|---|---|---|---|---|---|---|---|---|---|---|---|---|---|---|---|
| | MRR | Hit@1 | Hit@3 | Hit@10 | MRR | Hits@1 | Hit@3 | Hit@10 | MRR | Hit@1 | Hit@3 | Hit@10 | MRR | Hit@1 | Hit@3 | Hit@10 |
| TTransE | 13.72 | 2.98 | 17.70 | 35.74 | 8.31 | 1.92 | 8.56 | 21.89 | 15.57 | 4.80 | 19.24 | 38.29 | 5.50 | 0.48 | 4.94 | 15.25 |
| TA-DisMult | 25.80 | 16.94 | 29.74 | 42.99 | 16.75 | 8.61 | 18.41 | 33.59 | 24.31 | 14.58 | 27.92 | 44.21 | 12.00 | 5.76 | 12.94 | 23.54 |
| DE-SimIE | 33.36 | 24.85 | 37.15 | 49.82 | 19.30 | 11.53 | 21.86 | 34.80 | 35.02 | 25.91 | 38.99 | 52.75 | 19.70 | 12.22 | 21.39 | 33.70 |
| RE-NET | 36.93 | 26.83 | 39.51 | 54.78 | 28.81 | 19.05 | 32.44 | 47.51 | 43.32 | 33.43 | 47.77 | 63.06 | 19.62 | 12.42 | 21.00 | 34.01 |
| CyGNet | 35.05 | 25.73 | 39.01 | 53.55 | 24.93 | 15.90 | 28.82 | 42.61 | 36.81 | 26.61 | 41.63 | 56.22 | 18.48 | 11.52 | 19.57 | 31.98 |
| RE-GCN | 40.39 | 30.66 | 44.96 | 59.21 | 30.58 | 21.01 | 34.34 | 48.75 | 48.03 | 37.33 | 53.85 | 68.27 | 19.64 | 12.42 | 20.99 | 34.81 |
| CEN | 42.20 | 32.08 | 46.07 | 61.31 | 31.50 | 21.70 | 35.44 | 50.59 | 46.84 | 36.38 | 52.45 | 67.40 | 20.39 | 12.69 | 21.77 | 37.67 |
| TiRGN | 44.04 | 33.48 | 48.95 | 63.84 | 33.19 | 23.91 | 37.90 | 54.22 | 50.71 | 41.62 | 56.10 | 70.71 | 21.67 | 13.53 | 23.37 | 37.60 |
| HisMatch | 46.42 | 35.91 | 51.63 | 66.84 | 33.99 | 23.91 | 37.90 | 53.94 | 52.85 | 42.01 | 59.05 | 73.28 | 22.01 | 14.45 | 23.80 | 36.61 |
| CENET | 39.02 | 29.62 | 43.23 | 57.49 | 27.85 | 18.15 | 31.63 | 46.93 | 47.13 | 37.25 | 47.13 | 67.61 | 20.23 | 12.69 | 21.70 | 34.92 |
| L²TKG | 45.89 | 34.63 | - | 68.47 | 31.63 | 21.17 | - | 53.01 | 52.42 | 40.09 | - | 75.86 | 20.16 | 12.49 | - | 35.83 |
| HGLS | 47.00 | 35.06 | - | <u>70.41</u> | 29.32 | 19.21 | - | 49.83 | 46.21 | 35.32 | - | 67.12 | 19.04 | 11.79 | - | 33.23 |
| RETIA | 42.76 | 33.28 | 47.77 | 62.75 | 34.23 | 22.83 | 36.48 | 52.94 | 47.26 | 36.64 | 52.90 | 67.76 | 21.16 | 14.25 | 21.70 | 34.94 |
| CRAFT | 45.71 | 35.05 | 51.83 | 65.21 | 34.21 | 23.96 | 38.53 | 54.11 | 50.14 | 39.56 | 56.18 | 70.09 | <u>23.78</u> | <u>15.38</u> | <u>26.23</u> | 40.15 |
| THCN | 45.39 | 36.58 | 50.84 | 66.07 | 35.63 | <u>24.90</u> | 39.26 | 56.76 | 51.94 | 40.32 | 57.79 | 72.18 | 23.46 | 15.18 | 25.21 | 39.03 |
| LogCL | <u>48.87</u> | <u>37.76</u> | <u>54.71</u> | 70.26 | <u>35.67</u> | 24.53 | <u>40.32</u> | <u>57.74</u> | <u>57.04</u> | <u>46.07</u> | <u>63.72</u> | <u>77.87</u> | 23.75 | 14.64 | 25.60 | <u>42.33</u> |
| **HSCL** | **50.03** | **39.24** | **55.65** | **71.29** | **36.52** | **25.37** | **41.61** | **58.22** | **58.98** | **48.33** | **65.93** | **79.62** | **25.08** | **15.51** | **27.31** | **44.40** |
| Improv. | 2.37% | 3.92% | 1.72% | 1.47% | 2.46% | 1.89% | 3.20% | 0.82% | 3.40% | 4.91% | 3.47% | 2.25% | 5.47% | 0.84% | 4.12% | 4.89% |

### 4.2 Main Results

The experimental results for TKG reasoning are presented in Table 2, evaluated using time-aware filtered MRR and Hit@{1/3/10}. These results highlight the effectiveness of our proposed model, demonstrating robust performance and confirming the effectiveness of HSCL in addressing TKG reasoning tasks. Our model consistently outperforms all baseline methods, achieving state-of-the-art (SOTA) performance across the four TKG benchmark datasets. Notably, extrapolation models outperform interpolation models on all datasets. This is attributed to HSCL's ability to incorporate the temporal features of events, enabling it to predict future missing facts. When compared to models under the extrapolation setting, our method consistently achieves superior results in both MRR and Hit scores, with improvements ranging from 0.82% to 5.47%. These results confirm that our hierarchical contrastive learning strategy effectively leverages both temporal and structural information, enabling the model to learn customized, query-specific representations that enhance overall reasoning accuracy. Furthermore, it is noteworthy that HSCL exhibits relatively better performance on ICEWS05-15 and GDELT compared to ICEWS14 and ICEWS18. This phenomenon may be due to more complex dynamic interactions among entities and relations in the ICEWS18 and GDELT datasets, underscoring HSCL's capability to model intricate temporal fact interactions.

**Table 3.** Ablation study of HSCL on ICEWS14 and ICEWS18.

| Models | ICEWS14 | | ICEWS18 | |
|---|---|---|---|---|
| | MRR | Hit@1 | MRR | Hit@1 |
| HSCL-w/o-CL | 46.58 | 34.28 | 35.20 | 24.06 |
| HSCL-w/o-$\mathcal{L}_{\text{INS}}$ | 47.08 | 35.66 | 35.25 | 24.20 |
| HSCL-w/o-$\mathcal{L}_{\text{CAT}}$ | 47.42 | 35.96 | 35.38 | 24.36 |
| HSCL-w/o-fusion | 48.61 | 37.41 | 35.97 | 25.01 |
| **HSCL** | **50.03** | **39.24** | **36.52** | **25.37** |

### 4.3 Ablation Studies

To verify the effectiveness of each module in HSCL, ablation studies are carried out with ICEWS14 and ICEWS18, as shown in Table 3. Compared with HSCL-w/o-CL, which achieved an MRR of 46.58 and Hit@1 of 34.28 on ICEWS14, the full HSCL model improved these metrics to 50.03 and 36.52, respectively, demonstrating the positive impact of contrastive learning. Specifically, removing either the instance-level (HSCL-w/o-$\mathcal{L}_{\text{INS}}$) or category-level (HSCL-w/o-$\mathcal{L}_{\text{CAT}}$) loss led to decreases in performance of MRR dropped to 47.08 and 47.42 on ICEWS14, respectively, illustrating the complementary roles of both contrastive components, which certificates that incorporating hierarchical semantics into contrastive learning objective would enable capture of latent semantic, resulting in more robust and generalized representations. Furthermore, HSCL-w/o-fusion, which recorded 48.61 on MRR and 37.41 on Hit@1 on ICEWS14, was outperformed by the full model. The fusion unit, integrating long and short term sequence representations via cross-attention, contributed an absolute improvement of over 2.4% in MRR and nearly 3% in Hit@1 on ICEWS14. These improvements underscore how contrastive learning enhances feature differentiation and sample separation at dual semantic levels while the fusion unit facilitates positive knowledge interactions, ultimately leading to more robust reasoning.

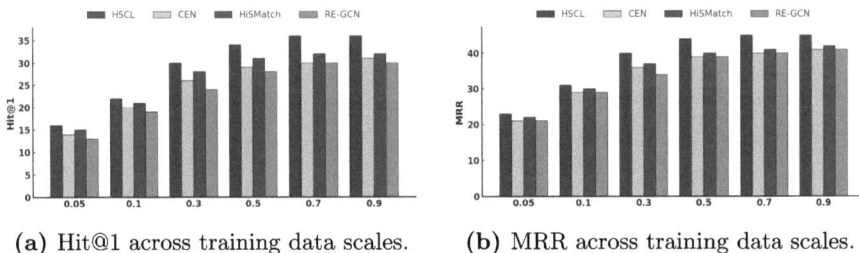

(a) Hit@1 across training data scales.  (b) MRR across training data scales.

**Fig. 3.** Performance of HSCL in terms of MRR and Hit@1 on ICEWS14 under different training data scale settings.

## 4.4 Performance Under Low-Resource Setting

In this section, we analyze the impact of different scales of training data setting. We randomly generate different proportions $r\%$ ($5\%, 10\%, 20\%, 30\%, 50\%, 90\%$) of training data to study the influence of the size of the training set and use the original vaild and test set for evaluation. As shown in Fig. 3, we compare the performance of HisMatch, CEN and RE-GCN in various size of training set. Generally, predictions under low-resource conditions yield poorer results due to the greater difficulty in optimizing representations from limited data. However, HSCL consistently outperforms all baselines across various $r\%$ settings in terms of MRR and Hit@1. This performance can be attributed to the hierarchical contrastive learning module, which is particularly effective in low-resource scenarios. The hierarchical contrastive learning module operates by leveraging both instance-level and category-level distinctions to refine representations. Under data scarcity, the instance-level contrastive objective encourages the model to discern subtle differences between facts using dynamic adaptive weighting, which magnifies important relational and temporal cues even when direct examples are few. Simultaneously, the category-level contrastive component groups events into broader semantic categories, allowing the model to draw on shared structural and temporal patterns across similar events.

**Table 4.** Performance on predicting unseen events in terms of MRR and Hit@1 on both ICEWS14 and ICEWS18 datasets.

| Models | ICEWS14 | | ICEWS18 | |
|---|---|---|---|---|
| | MRR | Hit@1 | MRR | Hit@1 |
| RE-GCN | 23.26 | 13.91 | 15.08 | 7.09 |
| CEN | 22.06 | 13.28 | 15.41 | 8.20 |
| RETIA | 24.17 | 14.67 | 16.62 | 9.08 |
| HisMatch | 27.49 | 19.04 | 17.51 | 11.13 |
| LogCL | 29.19 | 18.72 | 18.40 | 11.74 |
| **HSCL** | **30.73** | **20.00** | **19.43** | **12.17** |
| Improv. | 5.28% | 5.04% | 5.60% | 3.66% |

## 4.5 Performance Under Inductive Setting

To further validate HSCL's capacity for learning discriminative and generalized query-specific representations, we evaluate its performance on ICEWS14 and ICEWS18 datasets featuring unseen events absent from historical TKGs. Chosen for their higher rate of unseen events, as shown in Table 1, these datasets pose a rigorous test for generalization. Experimental results in Table 4 demonstrate that HSCL outperforms all SOTA baselines, with relative improvements of 5.28% and 5.60% on MRR and 5.04% and 3.66% on Hit@1 for ICEWS14 and ICEWS18, respectively. This underscores HSCL's ability to integrate both structural dependencies and temporal dynamics of entities and relations. Its superior performance on unseen events suggests that HSCL's hierarchical contrastive learning effectively captures underlying patterns, enabling robust reasoning even when encountering unfamiliar events. By synthesizing structural information with evolving temporal patterns, HSCL constructs nuanced, query-specific representations that differentiate subtle semantic variations and relational changes critical for reasoning in unseen events.

### 4.6 Sensitivity Analysis

We run our model with two sets of different important hyper-parameters to explore weight impacts. The temperature coefficient $\tau$ is crucial in contrastive learning, affecting how aggressively the model differentiates between positive and negative pairs. A smaller $\tau$ encourages more assertive separation of negative pairs, which can accelerate learning but may also lead to instability or overfitting. To assess the training stability of HSCL, we conducted a sensitivity analysis of $\tau$ across a range from 0.01 and 0.09 on both ICEWS14 and ICEWS18 datasets. As shown in Figs. 4a and Fig. 4b, our findings reveal that the model's effectiveness remains consistent across various settings, without any significant decline in performance metrics in terms of MRR and Hit@$\{1/3/10\}$. Furthermore, we analyze the impact of the loss balancing terms $\lambda_1$ and $\lambda_2$ within our multi-task learning paradigm. To systematically investigate these terms, we conducted experiments varying $\lambda_1$ and $\lambda_2$ from 0.1 to 0.9 in increments of 0.1 as depicted in Figs. 4c and Fig. 4d. Our findings confirm that appropriate balancing of task contributions is crucial for maximizing model effectiveness, with optimal performance observed when $\lambda_1$ and $\lambda_2$ are set to 0.3 and 0.4, respectively.

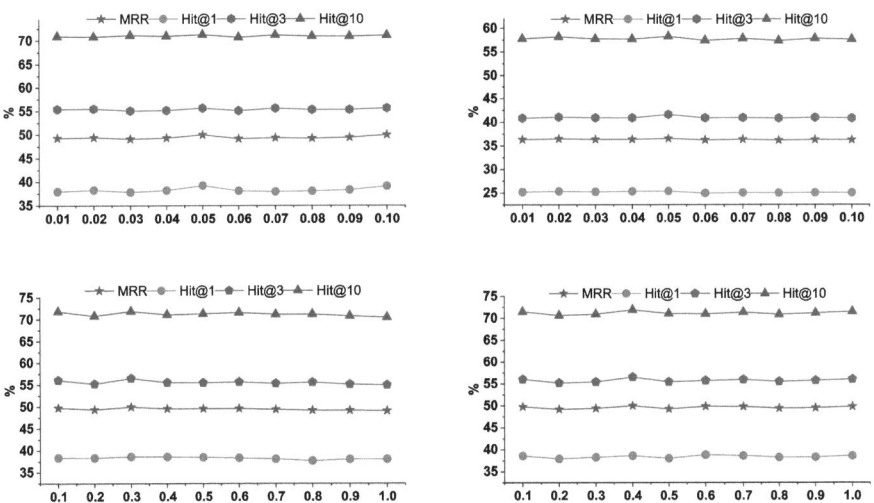

**Fig. 4.** Performance of HSCL under different hyper-parameters

## 5 Conclusion

In this study, we propose a novel Hierarchical Semantic-aware Contrastive Learning (HSCL) framework for TKG reasoning. HSCL leverages two complementary contrastive objectives that operate at different semantic levels to effectively address the challenges of fine-grained differentiation and broader hierarchical structuring. Specifically, the instance-level contrastive objective refines representations by distinguishing subtle differences between individual events, ensuring that semantically similar events remain adequately differentiated. Meanwhile, the category-level contrastive objective clusters events into broader semantic groups, capturing hierarchical relationships among events and improving generalization. Our empirical evaluations across four benchmarks confirm HSCL's superior representation capability and inference accuracy under various experimental setups.

**Acknowledgments.** We would like to thank the reviewers for their constructive comments. This project is supported by the National Natural Science Foundation of China (U2336204, U22B2061), Key Development Projects of the Sichuan Provincial Science and Technology Plan (2024YFG0005), Natural Science Foundation of Sichuan, China (2024NSFSC0496).

## References

1. Chen, T., Kornblith, S., Norouzi, M., Hinton, G.: A simple framework for contrastive learning of visual representations. In: International Conference on Machine Learning, (pp. 1597–1607) (2020, November) PMLR
2. Leblay, J., Chekol, M.W.: Deriving validity time in knowledge graph. In: Companion Proceedings of the Web Conference 2018, (pp. 1771–1776) (2018 April)
3. García-Durán, A., Dumančić, S., Niepert, M.: Learning sequence encoders for temporal knowledge graph completion (2018). arXiv preprint arXiv:1809.03202
4. Chung, J., Gulcehre, C., Cho, K., Bengio, Y.: Empirical evaluation of gated recurrent neural networks on sequence modeling (2014). arXiv preprint arXiv:1412.3555
5. Van der Maaten, L., Hinton, G.: Visualizing data using t-SNE. J. Mach. Learn. Res. **9**(11), 2579–2605 (2008)
6. Chen, T., Long, J., Wang, Z., Luo, S., Huang, J., Yang, L.: THCN: a Hawkes process based temporal causal convolutional network for extrapolation reasoning in temporal knowledge graphs. IEEE Transactions on Knowledge and Data Engineering (2024)
7. Cai, Y., et al.: Predicting the unpredictable: uncertainty-aware reasoning over temporal knowledge graphs via diffusion process. Find. Assoc. Comput. Linguist. ACL **2024**, 5766–5778 (2024)
8. Vashishth, S., Sanyal, S., Nitin, V., Talukdar, P.: Composition-based multi-relational graph convolutional networks (2019). arXiv preprint arXiv:1911.03082
9. Schlichtkrull, M., Kipf, T.N., Bloem, P., Berg, R., Titov, I., Welling, M.: Modeling relational data with graph convolutional networks. In: Gangemi, A., et al. (eds.) ESWC 2018. LNCS, vol. 10843, pp. 593–607. Springer, Cham (2018). https://doi.org/10.1007/978-3-319-93417-4_38

10. Shang, C., Tang, Y., Huang, J., Bi, J., He, X., Zhou, B.: End-to-end structure-aware convolutional networks for knowledge base completion. In: Proceedings of the AAAI Conference on Artificial Intelligence, (vol. 33, pp. 3060-3067) (2019)
11. Goel, R., Kazemi, S. M., Brubaker, M., Poupart, P.: Diachronic embedding for temporal knowledge graph completion. In: Proceedings of the AAAI Conference on Artificial Intelligence, vol. 34, No. 04, pp. 3988–3995 (2020)
12. Ren, X., Wu, Z., He, W., Qu, M., Voss, C. R., Ji, H., Abdelzaher, T. F., & Han, J. (2017). Cotype: Joint extraction of typed entities and relations with knowledge bases. In Proceedings of the 26th international conference on world wide web (pp. 1015-1024)
13. Ma, Y., Ye, C., Wu, Z., Wang, X., Cao, Y., Chua, T.S.: Context-aware event forecasting via graph disentanglement. In: Proceedings of the 29th ACM SIGKDD Conference on Knowledge Discovery and Data Mining, (pp. 1643–1652) (2023)
14. Zheng, S., Chen, W., Zhao, P., Liu, A., Fang, J., Zhao, L.: When hardness makes a difference: multi-hop knowledge graph reasoning over few-shot relations. In Proceedings of the 30th ACM International Conference on Information and Knowledge Management (pp. 2688–2697) (2021)
15. Wang, R., et al.: Metahkg: Meta hyperbolic learning for few-shot temporal reasoning. In: Proceedings of the 47th International ACM SIGIR Conference on Research and Development in Information Retrieval, pp. 59–69 (2024)
16. Sun, H., Geng, S., Zhong, J., Hu, H., He, K.: Graph Hawkes transformer for extrapolated reasoning on temporal knowledge graphs. In: Proceedings of the 2022 Conference on Empirical Methods in Natural Language Processing, pp. 7481–7493) (2022)
17. Ding, Z., Wu, J., He, B., Ma, Y., Han, Z., Tresp, V.: Few-shot inductive learning on temporal knowledge graphs using concept-aware information. arXiv preprint arXiv:2211.08169 (2022)
18. Liu, K., Zhao, F., Chen, H., Li, Y., Xu, G., Jin, H.: Da-net: distributed attention network for temporal knowledge graph reasoning. In: Proceedings of the 31st ACM International Conference on Information & Knowledge Management, pp. 1289–1298 (2022)
19. Gao, Y., Feng, L., Kan, Z., Han, Y., Qiao, L., Li, D.: Modeling precursors for temporal knowledge graph reasoning via auto-encoder structure. In: Proceedings of the International Joint Conference on Artificial Intelligence, pp. 2044–2051) (2022)
20. Wang, R., Li, Z., Sun, D., Liu, S., Yin, B., Abdelzaher, T.: Learning to sample and aggregate: few-shot reasoning over temporal knowledge graphs. In: Advances in Neural Information Processing Systems, vol. 35, pp. 16863–16876 (2022)
21. Peng, M., Liu, B., Xu, W., Jiang, Z., Zhu, J., Peng, M.: Deja vu: contrastive historical modeling with prefix-tuning for temporal knowledge graph reasoning. In: Findings of the Association for Computational Linguistics: NAACL 2024, pp. 1178–1191 (2024)
22. Feng, X., Liu, X., Yang, Y., Wang, W., Wang, J.: Learning rules in knowledge graphs via contrastive learning. In: International Conference on Database Systems for Advanced Applications, pp. 408–424. Springer (2024)
23. Li, J., Selvaraju, R.R., Gotmare, A.S., Joty, S., Xiong, C., Hoi, S.C.H.: Align before fuse: vision and language representation learning with momentum distillation. Adv. Neural. Inf. Process. Syst. **34**, 9694–9705 (2021)
24. Gunel, B., Du, J., Conneau, A., Stoyanov, V.: Supervised contrastive learning for pre-trained language model fine-tuning (2020). arXiv preprint arXiv:2011.01403

25. Wu, J., et al.: Self-supervised graph learning for recommendation. In: Proceedings of the 44th International ACM SIGIR Conference on Research and Development in Information Retrieval, pp. 726–735 (2021)
26. Han, Z., Ding, Z., Ma, Y., Gu, Y., Tresp, V.: Learning neural ordinary equations for forecasting future links on temporal knowledge graphs. In: Proceedings of the 2021 Conference on Empirical Methods in Natural Language Processing, pp. 8352–8364 (2021)
27. Trivedi, R., Dai, H., Wang, Y., Song, L.: (2017). Know-evolve: deep temporal reasoning for dynamic knowledge graphs. In: International Conference on Machine Learning, pp. 3462–3471) (2017). PMLR
28. Jin, W., Qu, M., Jin, X., Ren, X.: Recurrent event network: autoregressive structure inference over temporal knowledge graphs (2019). arXiv preprint arXiv:1904.05530
29. Zhu, C., Chen, M., Fan, C., Cheng, G., Zhang, Y.: Learning from history: modeling temporal knowledge graphs with sequential copy-generation networks. In: Proceedings of the AAAI Conference on Artificial Intelligence, vol. 34, No. 04, pp. 3988–3995 (2020)
30. Han, Z., Chen, P., Ma, Y., Tresp, V.: Explainable subgraph reasoning for forecasting on temporal knowledge graphs. In: International Conference on Learning Representations (2021)
31. Sun, H., Zhong, J., Ma, Y., Han, Z., He, K.: Timetraveler: Reinforcement learning for temporal knowledge graph forecasting (2021). arXiv preprint arXiv:2109.04101
32. Li, Z., et al.: Temporal knowledge graph reasoning based on evolutional representation learning. In: Proceedings of the 44th International ACM SIGIR Conference on Research and Development in Information Retrieval, (pp. 408–417) (2021)
33. Li, Z., et al.: Complex evolutional pattern learning for temporal knowledge graph reasoning (2022). arXiv preprint arXiv:2203.07782
34. Li, Z., Hou, Z., Guan, S., Jin, X., Peng, W., Bai, L., Lyu, Y., Li, W., Guo, J., & Cheng, X. (2022). Hismatch: Historical structure matching based temporal knowledge graph reasoning. arXiv preprint arXiv:2210.09708
35. Li, Y., Sun, S., Zhao, J.: TiRGN: Time-guided recurrent graph network with local-global historical patterns for temporal knowledge graph reasoning. In: Proceedings of the International Joint Conference on Artificial Intelligence, pp. 2152–2158 (2022)
36. Xu, Y., Ou, J., Xu, H., & Fu, L. (2023). Temporal knowledge graph reasoning with historical contrastive learning. In Proceedings of the AAAI Conference on Artificial Intelligence (Vol. 37, No. 4, pp. 4765-4773)
37. Liu, K., Zhao, F., Xu, G., Wang, X., Jin, H.: RETIA: relation-entity twin-interact aggregation for temporal knowledge graph extrapolation. In: 2023 IEEE 39th International Conference on Data Engineering (ICDE), pp. 1761–1774. IEEE (2023)
38. Zhang, M., Xia, Y., Liu, Q., Wu, S., Wang, L.: Learning long-and short-term representations for temporal knowledge graph reasoning. In: Proceedings of the ACM Web Conference 2023, pp. 2412–2422 (2023)
39. Chen, W., et al.: Local-global history-aware contrastive learning for temporal knowledge graph reasoning. In: 2024 IEEE 40th International Conference on Data Engineering (ICDE), (pp. 733–746). IEEE (2023)
40. Zhang, M., Xia, Y., Liu, Q., Wu, S., Wang, L.: Learning latent relations for temporal knowledge graph reasoning. In: Proceedings of the 61st Annual Meeting of the Association for Computational Linguistics (Volume 1: Long Papers), pp. 12617–12631 (2024)

41. Zhang, S., Wei, W., Huang, R., Xie, W., Chen, D.: Modeling historical relevant and local frequency context for representation-based temporal knowledge graph forecasting. In: Findings of the Association for Computational Linguistics: EMNLP 2024, pp. 7675–7686 (2024)
42. Wang, T., Isola, P.: Understanding contrastive representation learning through alignment and uniformity on the hypersphere. In: International Conference on Machine Learning, pp. 9929–9939. PMLR (2020)
43. Luo, D., et al.: Synergistic anchored contrastive pre-training for few-shot relation extraction. In: Proceedings of the AAAI Conference on Artificial Intelligence, vol. 38, No. 17, pp. 18742–18750 (2024)
44. Xu, H., et al.: Seed the views: hierarchical semantic alignment for contrastive representation learning. IEEE Trans. Pattern Anal. Mach. Intell. **45**(3), 3753–3767 (2022)
45. Yang, C., Wu, Q., Jin, J., Gao, X., Pan, J., Chen, G.: Trading hard negatives and true negatives: a debiased contrastive collaborative filtering approach (2022). arXiv preprint arXiv:2204.11752
46. Kalantidis, Y., Sariyildiz, M.B., Pion, N., Weinzaepfel, P., Larlus, D.: Hard negative mixing for contrastive learning. Adv. Neural. Inf. Process. Syst. **33**, 21798–21809 (2020)
47. Zhang, H., Zhang, J., Molybog, I.: HaSa: Hardness and Structure-Aware Contrastive Knowledge Graph Embedding. In: Proceedings of the ACM Web Conference 2024 (2024), pp. 2116–2127 (2024)
48. Liu, Y., Shu, L., Chen, C., Zheng, Z.: Fine-grained semantics enhanced contrastive learning for graphs. IEEE Transactions on Knowledge and Data Engineering (2024)
49. Guo, Q., Guo, Y., Zhao, J.: HRCL: hierarchical relation contrastive learning for low-resource relation extraction. IEEE Trans. Neural Netw. Learn. Syst. **35**(1), 1–12 (2024). https://doi.org/10.1109/TNNLS.2024.3281234
50. Wang, J., et al.: HCL: Improving graph representation with hierarchical contrastive learning. In: International Semantic Web Conference, pp. 108–124. Springer (2022)
51. Boschee, E., Lautenschlager, J., O'Brien, S., Shellman, S., Starz, J., Ward, M.: CAMEO.CDB.09b5.pdf. In: ICEWS Coded Event Data (Version V37). Harvard Dataverse (2015). https://doi.org/10.7910/DVN/28075/SCJPXX
52. Dettmers, T., Minervini, P., Stenetorp, P., & Riedel, S. (2018). Convolutional 2D knowledge graph embeddings. In Proceedings of the AAAI Conference on Artificial Intelligence (Vol. 32, No. 1)
53. Kazemi, S. M., Poole, D.: Simple embedding for link prediction in knowledge graphs. In: Advances in Neural Information Processing Systems, pp. 4284–4295 (2018)
54. Dong, H., Wang, P., Xiao, M., Ning, Z., Wang, P., Zhou, Y.: Temporal inductive path neural network for temporal knowledge graph reasoning. Artif. Intell. **329**, 104085 (2024). https://doi.org/10.1016/j.artint.2024.104085
55. Dong, H., et al.: Adaptive path-memory network for temporal knowledge graph reasoning. In: Proceedings of the Thirty-Second International Joint Conference on Artificial Intelligence pp. 2086–2094 (2023)
56. Liu, Y., Ma, Y., Hildebrandt, M., Joblin, M. Tresp, V.: Tlogic: temporal logical rules for explainable link forecasting on temporal knowledge graphs. In: Proceedings of the AAAI Conference on Artificial Intelligence, vol. 36, No. 4, pp. 4120–4127 (2022)
57. He, Y., Zhang, P., Liu, L., Liang, Q., Zhang, W., Zhang, C.: Hip network: historical information passing network for extrapolation reasoning on temporal knowledge graph (2024). arXiv preprint arXiv:2402.12074

58. Mingcong, S., Zhu, C., Zhang, D., Wen, S., Qing, L.: Multi-granularity history and entity similarity learning for temporal knowledge graph reasoning. In: Proceedings of the 2024 Conference on Empirical Methods in Natural Language Processing, pp. 5232–5243 (2024).
59. Chen, B., Xiao, C., Zhou, F.: Natural evolution-based dual-level aggregation for temporal knowledge graph reasoning. In: Findings of the Association for Computational Linguistics: EMNLP 2024, pp. 9274–9284 (2024)

# I-GLIDE: Input Groups for Latent Health Indicators in Degradation Estimation

Lucas Thil[1,2](✉), Jesse Read[1], Rim Kaddah[2], and Guillaume Doquet[3]

[1] LIX Ecole Polytechnique, Palaiseau, France
thil@lix.polytechnique.fr, jesse.read@polytechnique.edu
[2] IRT SystemX, Palaiseau, France
lucas.thil@irt-system.fr, rim.kaddah@irt-systemx.fr
[3] Safran Tech, Châteaufort, France
guillaume.doquet@safrangroup.com

**Abstract.** Accurate remaining useful life (RUL) prediction hinges on the quality of health indicators (HIs), yet existing methods often fail to disentangle complex degradation mechanisms in multi-sensor systems or quantify uncertainty in HI reliability. This paper introduces a novel framework for HI construction, advancing three key contributions. First, we adapt Reconstruction along Projected Pathways (RaPP) as a health indicator (HI) for RUL prediction for the first time, showing that it outperforms traditional reconstruction error metrics. Second, we show that augmenting RaPP-derived HIs with aleatoric and epistemic uncertainty quantification (UQ)—via Monte Carlo dropout and probabilistic latent spaces—significantly improves RUL-prediction robustness. Third, and most critically, we propose indicator groups, a paradigm that isolates sensor subsets to model system-specific degradations, giving rise to our novel method, I-GLIDE which enables interpretable, mechanism-specific diagnostics. Evaluated on data sourced from aerospace and manufacturing systems, our approach achieves marked improvements in accuracy and generalizability compared to state-of-the-art HI methods while providing actionable insights into system failure pathways. This work bridges the gap between anomaly detection and prognostics, offering a principled framework for uncertainty-aware degradation modeling in complex systems.

**Keywords:** Health Indicator · Latent Space · Degradation Modeling

## 1 Introduction

Accurate RUL prediction is critical for enabling condition-based maintenance in complex engineering systems. A cornerstone of this task lies in deriving interpretable Health Indicators (HIs) that reliably capture subsystem degradation

---

**Supplementary Information** The online version contains supplementary material available at https://doi.org/10.1007/978-3-032-06106-5_23.

patterns. While autoencoder (AE)-based reconstruction errors have emerged as a popular HI-construction method, existing approaches suffer from two key limitations: (1) sensitivity to noise and epistemic uncertainty, which obscures degradation signals, and (2) a lack of granularity in disentangling subsystem-specific degradation behaviors. This work addresses these gaps by introducing a novel Ensemble of Indicators framework, which advances traditional AE architectures through multi-head encoders and decoders designed to isolate degradation patterns across subsystems (e.g., fan, high-pressure compressor). We call this method I-GLIDE: Input Groups for Latent Health Indicators in Degradation Estimation.

Contrary to prior studies that treat UQ as an auxiliary feature, our proposed method I-GLIDE leverages this uncertainty to enhance HI robustness while maintaining explainability. We rigorously benchmark our approach against established latent-space HI methods—including Reconstruction along Projected Pathways (RaPP) [17,29] and Monte Carlo (MC) dropout-based uncertainty estimation [9] demonstrating superior RUL prediction accuracy on the NASA C-MAPSS turbofan dataset [28] and the MILL NASA degradation dataset [2]. Our contributions are threefold:

1. **Systematic Analysis:** We identify and characterize critical limitations of existing AE derived HIs, notably their vulnerability to noise and inability to isolate subsystem-level degradation.
2. **Uncertainty-Aware Benchmarking:** By integrating aleatoric and epistemic UQ into latent-HI construction, we improve RUL estimation.
3. **I-GLIDE Framework:** We propose a multi-head AE architecture where each encoder-decoder pair targets distinct subsystems, enabling granular, explainable HI extraction, achieving state-of-the-art RUL prediction while providing insights into degradation mechanisms.

Table 1. Notation used in the paper.

| Symbol | Description |
|---|---|
| $\sigma_a, \sigma_e$ | Aleatoric, Epistemic uncertainty |
| $\mathcal{F}$ | Function mapping HIs to a RUL |
| $\mathcal{X}$ | Input data set with entries $x$ |
| $\hat{x}$ | reconstruction of input $x$, also noted as the target variable $y$ |
| $W_D$ | Decoder weight parameters |
| $g \in G$ | Set of sub-complex systems indices $g$ |
| $z$ | Latent space of the AE |
| $y$ | Target variable |
| $h_{g,l}$ | hidden layer of group $g$ $h_g$, at position $l$ |
| $d_g(x)$ | specific distance vector of groups $h_g(x) - h_g(\hat{x})$ |

## 2 Background and Related Works

### 2.1 RUL Prognostics and Health Indicators

Most industrial complex systems are built by the interdependencies of sub-complex systems; degradation in one component can propagate cascading effects, triggering operational disruptions, escalating costs, safety risks, and—in extreme cases—catastrophic system-wide failures. As a result, the accurate RUL estimation of a complex system is heavily studied in engineering, particularly where costs and safety are associated. Early methodologies relied on stochastic approaches, such as threshold-based degradation signatures or empirical lifetime metrics (e.g., flight cycles or mileage) [8]. While methods prioritized identifying failure precursors or tracking cumulative usage they lacked adaptability to complex, non-linear degradation patterns. Timely and precise RUL prognostics not only curtails downtime and waste but also enables proactive maintenance, aligning operational decisions with evolving system health.

### 2.2 Evolution of HI Extraction

Early HI derivation prioritized interpretability through handcrafted statistical features (e.g., signal variance) or physics-based models. Using a Bayesian framework enriched by expert knowledge to estimate failure probabilities, Lacaille [19] proposed a normalization pretreatment to derive standardized signatures interpretable as HIs by domain experts. However, such approaches depended heavily on predefined failure patterns and manual refinement, limiting their adaptability to heterogeneous operational conditions in non-stationary environments [6]. Hybrid approaches combined Kalman filters with NNs to model state-of-charge degradation [12], while others used neural networks (NNs) to learn a RUL representation to derive syncretic HIs [32]. Zhao et al. [34] used degradation pattern learning in the case of turbofan engines to predict the RUL. They extracted degradation patterns that helped characterize the nature of the degradation, which can itself be seen as a HI. Furthermore, their method was shown to improve the predictive capability of a NN towards RUL estimation.

AEs later emerged as a cornerstone method, using reconstruction errors from healthy-state training as implicit HIs [10,13,23]. Despite progress, these methods often assumed linear degradation trends or predefined failure modes, limiting adaptability to non-stationary systems. Other NN approaches later enabled data-driven prognostics, with Long Short-Term Memory (LSTM) architectures capturing temporal degradation in batteries [30] and turbofans [21]. However, early frameworks often bundled HI estimation with RUL prediction, risking conflated objectives where HIs were implicitly tuned to downstream tasks rather than intrinsic degradation patterns. This coupling became particularly evident in methods that embedded domain assumptions directly into HI design. For example, Jing et al. [15] incorporated exponential normalization of sensor data as an inductive bias in a Variational Autoencoder (VAE), aligning the HI with the CMAPSS dataset's predefined degradation trends. While this yielded robust RUL predictions, it effectively tied the HI to the target degradation profile, limiting adaptability to systems with non-exponential behaviors. Pillai and Vadakkepat [26] addressed this issue more directly, proposing a two-stage architecture that decoupled HI feature discovery from RUL regression. Their approach improved generalizability by isolating degradation modeling from task-specific optimization, though challenges persisted in interpretability and subsystem-specific analysis.

**Latent-Space HI Refinement.** More recent advances focused on refining HI quality through latent-space analysis. Kim et al. [17] introduced the RaPP method, projecting latent representations from an AE's encoder to compute distance metrics that outperformed classical reconstruction errors. González-Muñiz et al. [11] validated this paradigm shift, demonstrating that latent-space metrics from RaPP consistently surpass input-space approaches in HI quality. Their work highlighted the latent space between encoder and decoder as a rich source of degradation signals, though subsystem-specific trends remained obscured by holistic aggregation. Despite these innovations, mapping HIs to RUL remains fraught with challenges. Many approaches employ black-box models or simplistic linear mappings [22], neglecting context-dependent HI interpretations under varying operational conditions. For instance, a high reconstruction error might indicate severe degradation in one context but sensor noise in another—a nuance often lost in end-to-end frameworks. Recent benchmarking by Rombach et al. [27] underscores this gap, advocating for feature engineering to improve HI interpretability while maintaining correlation with ground truth degradation.

### 2.3 Uncertainty-Aware Subsystem Modeling

Uncertainty quantification in NNs can be achieved through MC dropout [1]. Variational AEs (VAEs) [3], can disentangle aleatoric uncertainty (inherent data noise) and epistemic uncertainty (model ambiguity) to isolate distinct sources of unpredictability. While probabilistic frameworks optimize maintenance via confidence intervals [24], UQ is often treated as a post-hoc refinement rather than a core HI component. Deterministic AEs, for instance, cannot isolate aleatoric uncertainty due to fixed latent spaces—a limitation addressed by variational architectures [31]. Ensemble methods further reduce uncertainty [33], yet their application to subsystem-aware HIs remains underexplored.

### 2.4 Monotonicity and Degradation Dynamics

RUL is typically modeled as a monotonic function of the State of Health (SOH), declining from 100% (pristine) to 0% (failure). While mechanical wear rarely reverses, subsystem interactions (e.g., turbine degradation accelerating fan wear) introduce non-stationary dynamics [4]. This necessitates HIs that isolate localized degradation while preserving system-wide coherence—a gap addressed by our subsystem-aware architecture. Similarly, we model RUL estimation as a function $\mathcal{F}$ of the HIs, mapping their values to the corresponding RUL.

## 3 Proposed Approach: I-GLIDE

In order to produce better HIs, we build on foundational assumptions about degradation dynamics and their statistical relationships to RUL established earlier, and we begin by formalizing our UQ for prognostic tasks. We then introduce a novel architecture that disentangles subsystem-specific degradation signatures by managing sensor groups and operational variabilities at the component level, while adapting the RaPP method to mitigate cross-component interference. Finally, we propose a data-driven strategy to validate constructed HIs through direct RUL estimation, demonstrating their prognostic utility. Each phase is rigorously evaluated via empirical case studies (Sect. 4), ensuring robustness across diverse degradation scenarios. Our notation is summarized in Table 1.

### 3.1 Uncertainty Quantification

Uncertainty in prognostics arises from two primary sources: aleatoric ($\sigma_a$), inherent to data noise and irreducible even with additional observations, and epistemic ($\sigma_e$), stemming from model limitations and reducible through improved architectures or training [14,16].

In order to produce high-quality HIs we make use of the UQ capabilities of AE architectures with an underlying change. Our epistemic UQ focuses on the scalar reconstruction error $\epsilon = \|x - \hat{x}\|_2$ instead of the full-dimensional decoder output $\hat{x} = y$. This aligns with prognostics frameworks where $\epsilon$ serves as a health indicator (HI), reducing dimensionality for easier integration with downstream RUL prediction models (e.g., $\mathcal{F}$). We avoided using raw $y$ (the reconstruction) as a standalone HI directly because it is 1) outperformed by RaPP methods [11,17] and 2) our RUL predictor model $\mathcal{F}$ showed high variance in selecting the best variables when both RaPP and $y$ were fed as inputs. Thus we dropped $y$ as a HI and instead focused in introducing MC dropout to quantify $\epsilon$ uncertainties as a HI which showed to be a better complement. Therefore, the disentangled UQ is performed through the aggregation of our $\epsilon_1..\epsilon_n$ over $n$ MC samples in our VAE architecture:

$$\sigma_a = \text{Var}\,(\epsilon_1, \ldots, \epsilon_n | \text{ fixed } W_D), \quad \sigma_e = \text{Var}\,(\epsilon_1, \ldots, \epsilon_n | \text{ fixed } z).$$

As $z$ is deterministic, aleatoric uncertainty $\sigma_a$ cannot be isolated in AEs, rendering it undefined. Thus, we can only compute $\sigma_e$ in the case of a vanilla AE. This highlights the advantage of VAEs for joint uncertainty estimation.

### 3.2 Architecture

Building on the above foundations, our proposed architecture extends the traditional AE and VAE frameworks by introducing multiple encoder-decoder pairs for each sensor group, which are then integrated through a shared latent space, as illustrated in Fig. 1 (3.2). This design addresses the non-stationarity of sensor signals by disentangling subsystem-specific degradation dynamics in the latent space. This separation allows us to apply the RaPP [17] method individually to each encoder. By projecting the activations of the hidden spaces $h_g(x)$ corresponding to isolated sensor groups $g \in G$, we aim to achieve more comprehensive feature extraction, enabling the construction of specific health indicators (HIs).

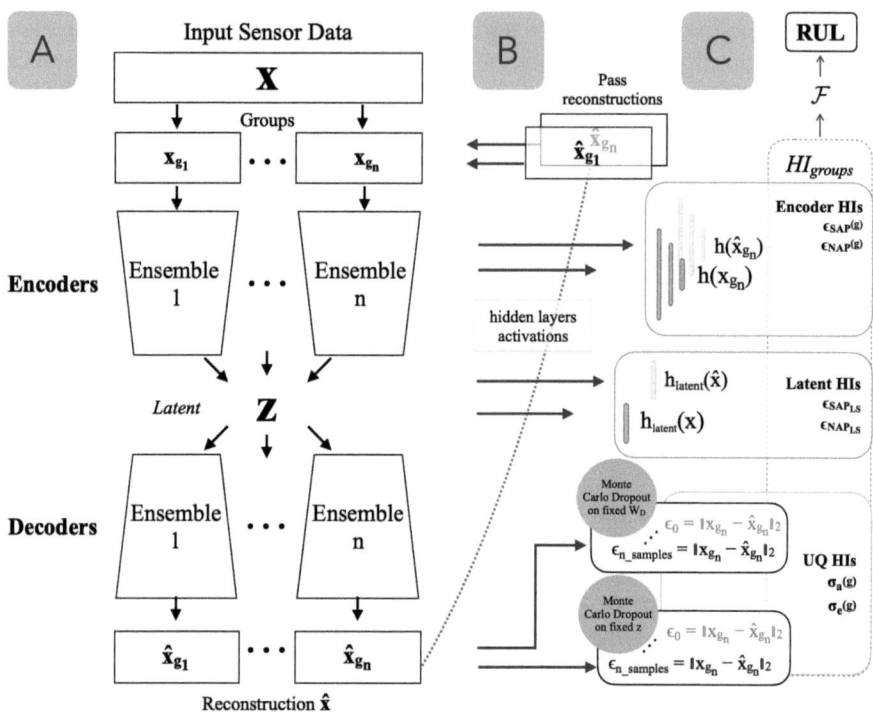

**Fig. 1.** I-GLIDE Architecture Framework – **A:** Subsystem-specific encoder-decoder heads learn distinct latent representations, fused into a shared latent space $z$ via reconstruction loss (trained on healthy data). **B:** HIs are extracted using RaPP metrics [11] and UQ [18] over full trajectories. **C:** Aggregated HIs are used to predict RUL, trained via a Random Forest (RF) regressor $\mathcal{F}$.

We derive this architecture with two different latent spaces: the first one being in the way of traditional AE named I-GLIDE$_{AE}$, and in the second version where the latent is a Gaussian type distribution in the manner of VAEs named I-GLIDE$_{VAE}$. In the latter, we can leverage the variational inference aspect of the architecture.

### 3.3 Adapting Domain-Specific Latent Space Health Indicators

A main novelty of I-GLIDE is to adapt RaPP [17], traditionally used in monolithic architectures, for each subsystem in our multi-autoencoder framework. By moving away from the monolithic approach, I-GLIDE computes group-specific health indicators (HIs) for each sensor group $g$. Unlike the original RaPP framework, which operates on a single encoder-decoder pair, our architecture independently calculates $\epsilon_{\text{SAP}(g)}$ and $\epsilon_{\text{NAP}(g)}$ for each group $g$, leveraging dedicated encoders and decoders per subsystem. These components share a cohesive latent space $z$, preserving global system coherence while isolating localized anomalies. For a sensor group $g$, let $h_{g,l}(x) \in \mathbb{R}^{n_l}$ denote the activations of the $l$-th encoder layer (with $n_l$-dimensional output) for input $x$, and $h_{g,l}(\hat{x}_g)$ represent the reconstructed activations across $L$ layers ($l = 1, \ldots, L$).

We redefine two HIs per sensor group:

$$\epsilon_{\text{SAP}(g)}(x) = \|h_g(x) - h_g(\hat{x})\|_2 \qquad (1)$$

which computes the first RaPP metric: the Simple Aggregation along Pathway (SAP) [17] as the Euclidean distance between original and reconstructed activations across all layers $l$. For the second RaPP metric, Normalized Aggregation along Pathway (NAP), we first derive the group-specific distance vector $d_g(x) = h_g(x) - h_g(\hat{x})$, where $h_g(x) = [h_{g,1}(x), \ldots, h_{g,L}(x)]$ concatenates activations across all layers $l$. Given a training set $\mathcal{X}$, let $D_g$ be a matrix whose rows correspond to $d_g(x_i)$ for $x_i \in \mathcal{X}$, and let $\bar{D}_g$ denote the column-wise centered version of $D_g$. The NAP metric for group $g$ is then:

$$\epsilon_{\text{NAP}(g)}(x) = \left\|(d_g(x) - \mu_\mathcal{X})^\top V_g \Sigma_g^{-1}\right\|_2. \qquad (2)$$

Here, $\mu_{\mathcal{X}_g} \in \mathbb{R}^{n_l \cdot L}$ is the column-wise mean of $D_g$, $\Sigma_g \in \mathbb{R}^{k \times k}$ is a diagonal matrix containing the singular values of $\bar{D}_g$, and $V_g \in \mathbb{R}^{(n_l \cdot L) \times k}$ contains the right singular vectors from the singular value decomposition (SVD) of $\bar{D}_g$, with $k$ denoting the rank of $\bar{D}_g$.

This design allows the model to isolate sensor group contributions, where anomalies in specific sensor groups are preserved without being diluted by nominal signals from other groups and this results in enhanced interpretability as HIs directly map to physical sensor groups, aiding root-cause analysis.

Building on González et al. [11], where latent-space RaPP metrics outperform encoder-derived counterparts for HI construction, our method integrates both approaches. We compute latent-space $z$ metrics ($\epsilon_{\text{NAP}_{\text{LS}}}, \epsilon_{\text{SAP}_{\text{LS}}}$), with $\epsilon_{\text{SAP}_{\text{LS}}}$ derived from all the data and not by individual groups.

### 3.4 Final Set of HIs

The full set of HIs produced by I-GLIDE are then aggregated with our UQ as the set $\text{HI}_{\text{groups}} = \{\epsilon_{\text{SAP}(g)}, \epsilon_{\text{NAP}(g)}, \epsilon_{\text{SAP}_{\text{LS}}}, \epsilon_{\text{NAP}_{\text{LS}}}, \sigma_{a(g)}, \sigma_{e(g)}\} \forall g \in G$ where $\sigma_{a(g)}, \sigma_{e(g)}$ are respectively the aleatoric and espitemic uncertainties computed for each group g. We also compare with the monilithic architecture where the inputs $x$ are not divided into subgroups, and thus our set of HIs is defined as $\text{HI}_{\text{mono}} = \{\epsilon_{\text{SAP}}, \epsilon_{\text{NAP}}, \epsilon_{\text{SAP}_{\text{LS}}}, \epsilon_{\text{NAP}_{\text{LS}}}, \sigma_a, \sigma_e\}$.

To evaluate their predictive capabilities, we train a meta regressor $\mathcal{F}(.)$ on the task of RUL estimation. We also compare with the previous set of RaPP indicators from Gonzàlez by define $\text{HI}_{\text{Gonz\'alez}} = \{\epsilon_{\text{NAP}_{\text{LS}}}, \epsilon_{\text{SAP}_{\text{LS}}}\}$ [11].

## 4 Experiments

We aim to find out whether augmenting latent space HIs (RaPP metrics) with UQ, contributes to better understanding of degradation mechanisms in complex system in the perspective of RUL estimation. In a second step, we'd like to test whether introducing an architecture able to disentangle sub-systems degradation mechanisms can further improve this RUL estimation, through better understanding of the system from data, and minimal domain-knowledge. Our code is available at: https://github.com/LucasStill/I-GLIDE for reproduction purposes.

**Table 2.** The four C-MAPSS dataset subsets and their description, with associated number of operating conditions and amount of degradation fault modes origins.

|                    | FD001 | FD002 | FD003 | FD004 |
|--------------------|-------|-------|-------|-------|
| Train trajectories | 100   | 260   | 100   | 248   |
| Test trajectories  | 100   | 259   | 100   | 249   |
| Conditions         | 1     | 6     | 1     | 6     |
| Fault modes        | 1     | 1     | 2     | 2     |

### 4.1 Datasets

We evaluate our framework on two datasets. The C-MAPSS dataset [28] a benchmark for degradation modeling, contains simulated run-to-failure trajectories of jet engines generated using NASA's C-MAPSS simulator. Each multivariate time series corresponds to a unique engine operating under varying conditions, divided into four subsets (FD001–FD004; see Table 2). During training, we focus on samples with RUL $\leq 80$ timesteps ($R_{early} = 80$) to prioritize early degradation signals while retaining healthy-state representations. For testing, we follow the established protocol by prior works with $R_{early} = 125$ to enable direct comparison. The test set contains truncated trajectories that stop before the point of failure, and the task is to predict this last available value on the trajectory. We present the partitioning of the different groups in Table 3.

To further validate our approach and compare the effects of subsystem group separation, we test on the MILL NASA dataset, which records 167 unique tool wear progression during milling experiments under varied conditions (depth of cut, feed rate, material). Sensor signals (acoustic, vibration, current) track wear, with failure defined at wear $= 0.70$ (initial wear $= 0$). We classify samples as healthy (wear $\leq 0.20$) during training and evaluate degradation over three test phases: complete trajectories, moderate degradation (wear $> 0.20$), and severe degradation (wear $> 0.50$). Each sensor contains a total of 9000 entries, but some have missing data which we fill through interpolation with neighboring values.

For both datasets, we will apply our method to create our sets of HIs and measure their predictive capabilities over RUL prediction, using RMSE metric which is commonly used on these datasets [7].

### 4.2 Experimental Methodology

To validate our framework, we adopt a prognostics-centric evaluation protocol that directly benchmarks HIs by their ability to predict RUL—the ultimate objective of HI construction. We first compare the RaPP-based HIs proposed by González et al. ($HI_{González}$) [11] against a enhanced variants: $HI_{mono}$, which integrates encoder-level RaPP metrics [17], with UQ. We use a single timestep for each created HI. Critically, we bypass classical HI metrics like monotonicity or trendability, which often fail to correlate with actionable prognostic value,

Table 3. Grouping of sensors in the CMAPS dataset.

| Group | Sensor ID | Description |
|---|---|---|
| Fan | s_1 | Total temperature at fan inlet (°R) |
| | s_5 | Pressure at fan inlet (psia) |
| | s_8 | Physical fan speed (rpm) |
| | s_13 | Corrected fan speed (rpm) |
| | s_18 | Demanded fan speed (rpm) |
| | s_19 | Demanded corrected fan speed (rpm) |
| LPC | s_2 | Total temperature at LPC outlet (°R) |
| HPC | s_3 | Total temperature at HPC outlet (°R) |
| | s_7 | Total pressure at HPC outlet (psia) |
| | s_11 | Static pressure at HPC outlet (psia) |
| Core | s_9 | Physical core speed (rpm) |
| | s_14 | Corrected core speed (rpm) |
| Pressure Turbine | s_4 | Total temperature at LPT outlet (°R) |
| | s_20 | HPT coolant bleed (lbm/s) |
| | s_21 | LPT coolant bleed (lbm/s) |
| Other | s_6 | Total pressure in bypass-duct (psia) |
| | s_10 | Engine pressure ratio (P50/P2) (-) |
| | s_12 | Ratio of fuel flow to Ps30 (pps/psia) |
| | s_15 | Bypass Ratio (-) |
| | s_16 | Burner fuel-air ratio (-) |
| | s_17 | Bleed Enthalpy (-) |

and instead train a random forest (RF) regressor $\mathcal{F}$ to map HIs to RUL. This choice reflects a key design principle: HI quality should be first judged by its downstream utility in prognostics.

We then introduce our I-GLIDE architecture, instantiated as I-GLIDE$_{AE}$ and I-GLIDE$_{VAE}$, which generates subsystem-specific HIs (HI$_{groups}$) by isolating sensor-group degradation patterns. These are benchmarked against monolithic AE/VAE counterparts under identical RF training protocols, ensuring fair comparison. By using a simple, non-temporal model like RF, we deliberately decouple HI quality from algorithmic sophistication, isolating how architectural choices (monolithic vs. subsystem-specific) impact prognostics performance.

### 4.3 Results

When comparing the RUL estimation capabilities of HI$_{González}$ and HI$_{mono}$ as shown in Table 4, we find that HI$_{mono}$ consistently outperforms HI$_{González}$ across all C-MAPSS subsets (FD001-FD004). For example, HI$_{mono}$ derived from AEs reduces RMSE by 22.95% on average compared to HI$_{González}$, with particularly notable gain on FD002 (15.71 vs 22.91) and FD003 (8.07 vs 12.03). Similar trends hold for VAEs, where HI$_{mono}$ achieves a 28.44% average RMSE improvement, underscoring the value of UQ in stabilizing HI quality. The same can be observed for the MILL dataset in Table 5. This ablation study demonstrates that a broader coverage of latent HIs with UQ, collectively strenghtens RUL predictive capabilities, even before subsytem-specific modeling.

Next, we deploy I-GLIDE, which explicitly disentangles subsytem degradation (e.g., HPC, fan, turbine in C-MAPSS) by grouping sensor signals into functionally coherent components (exacts group choices are presented in the appendix). Compared to monolithic architectures, I-GLIDE achieves superior robustness, as evidenced by its 39.96% reduction of standard deviation in RMSE across C-MAPSS subsets from AE-based HIs (6). For VAEs, gains are even more pronounced: I-GLIDE$_{VAE}$ reduces RMSE by 39.03% and standard deviation by 56.07%, resolving the instability seen in monolithic VAEs (e.g., FD002/FD003 variance). This subsystem isolation proves critical on FD004-the most complex C-MAPSS subset-where I-GLIDE's average results set a new state-of-the-art performance with a RMSE of 14.19 despite using only a RF regressor for RUL prediction.

On the MILL dataset, I-GLIDE's subsytem-specific HIs improve RUL prediction across all degradation phases (healthy, moderate, severe), with I-GLIDE$_{AE}$-driven HIs achieving the lowest RMSE in every scenario. VAE gains are subtler, likely due to MILL's lower inherent complexity, or high dimensional space which limits the benefits of variational inference.

**Table 4.** Comparison of sets of HIs extracted from different architectures to predict the RUL RMSE on C-MAPSS test dataset using a Random Forest for $\mathcal{F}$. Best models shown.

| HI Extractor | HI Set for $\mathcal{F}(.)$ | FD001 | FD002 | FD003 | FD004 | Avg. |
|---|---|---|---|---|---|---|
| AE | $HI_{González}$ [11] | 11.43 | 22.91 | 12.03 | 16.78 | 15.79 |
|  | $HI_{mono}$ | 10.53 | **15.71** | **8.07** | 14.35 | 12.17 |
| VAE | $HI_{González}$ [11] | 27.56 | 28.62 | 24.36 | 22.33 | 25.72 |
|  | $HI_{mono}$ | 18.77 | 19.44 | 15.59 | 19.81 | 18.40 |
| I-GLIDE$_{AE}$ | $HI_{groups}$ | **9.47** | 16.18 | 8.29 | 12.32 | 11.57 |
| I-GLIDE$_{VAE}$ | $HI_{groups}$ | 12.33 | 16.76 | 8.5 | **11.4** | 12.25 |

**Table 5.** RUL MILL Dataset Benchmark on three wear levels. I-GLIDE HIs consistently outperform the monolithic counterpart in RMSE for RUL prediction [2]

| Model Name, HI set for RF | Wear 0.0–0.70 | Wear 0.20–0.70 | Wear 0.50–0.70 |
|---|---|---|---|
| AE, $HI_{González}$ [11] | 23.78 | 24.34 | 22.33 |
| AE, $HI_{mono}$ | 16.14 | 16.47 | 16.25 |
| I-GLIDE$_{AE}$, $HI_{groups}$ | **13.64** | **14.37** | **16.17** |
| VAE, $HI_{González}$ [11] | 27.84 | 27.92 | 27.14 |
| VAE, $HI_{mono}$ | 22.32 | 22.46 | 23.47 |
| I-GLIDE$_{VAE}$, $HI_{groups}$ | **21.76** | **22.29** | **23.13** |

**Table 6.** Average model performances across 10 runs over C-MAPSS subsets using RMSE (mean ± standard deviation). Bold: best results per subset; underline: outperforms methods without HIs. Last column provides average improvement over the previous row.

| Model, HI Set | FD001 | FD002 | FD003 | FD004 | Avg. | Improvement |
|---|---|---|---|---|---|---|
| AE, $HI_{González}$ [11] | 19.00 ±4.78 | 25.69 ±4.19 | 18.38 ±6.18 | 19.46 ±2.46 | 20.63 ±4.40 | – |
| AE, $HI_{mono}$ | 13.14 ±2.50 | 20.35 ±3.46 | 13.87 ±5.07 | 17.73 ±3.56 | 16.27 ±3.65 | +21.13% +17.15% |
| I-GLIDE$_{AE}$, $HI_{groups}$ | **12.11** ±2.72 | 22.01 ±2.88 | **10.23** ±1.85 | <u>14.92</u> ±1.31 | 14.82 ±2.19 | +8.94% +39.96% |
| VAE, $HI_{González}$ [11] | 34.13 ±3.71 | 31.05 ±1.89 | 27.25 ±2.58 | 25.23 ±2.03 | 29.42 ±2.55 | – |
| VAE, $HI_{mono}$ | 27.19 ±5.97 | 22.81 ±2.86 | 24.64 ±5.26 | 22.89 ±1.82 | 24.38 ±3.98 | +17.10% −55.83% |
| I-GLIDE$_{VAE}$, $HI_{groups}$ | 15.32 ±2.08 | **18.83** ±1.51 | 11.12 ±2.29 | <u>14.19</u> ±1.11 | 14.87 ±1.75 | +39.03% +56.07% |

## 5 Discussion

Remarkably, when looking at the best produced models, even with a RF-a model far simpler than deep learning baselines-our HIs match or exceed prior SOTA on three out of four C-MAPSS benchmarks as shown in Table 7. This paradox highlights that HI quality, not model complexity, drives prognostics success. When looking at the expected accuracies of the different models, we see that I-GLIDE has lower standard deviations, being more robust to prediction, which explains why in two cases the best model was a monolithic AE: despite showing great performance on a single set, its high standard deviation shown in Table 6 indicates it would not be robust on a broader test set, or in real-life conditions. This is why I-GLIDE offers solid perspectives towards more robust predictions.

**Table 7.** Comparison of I-GLIDE method for HI extraction benchmarked to predict a RUL, compared with best known approaches. In bold are the best results for each subset. Most previous methods were predicting a RUL from transformed sensor data without producing HIs, contrarily to our method which does provide HIs.

| Model | FD001 | FD002 | FD003 | FD004 |
|---|---|---|---|---|
| MLP [35] | 37.56 | 80.03 | 37.39 | 77.37 |
| CNN [35] | 18.45 | 30.29 | 19.82 | 29.16 |
| CNN-LSTM [25] | 11.17 | – | 9.99 | – |
| MS-DCNN [20] | 11.44 | 19.35 | 11.67 | 22.22 |
| VAE + RNN [5] | 11.44 | 24.12 | 14.88 | 26.54 |
| MLE(4X)+CCF [26] | 11.57 | 18.84 | 11.83 | 20.78 |
| RVE [5] | 13.42 | 14.92 | 12.51 | 16.37 |
| Probabilistic RUL CNN [7] | 12.42 | **13.72** | 12.16 | 15.95 |
| I-GLIDE$_{AE}$ + RF (ours) | **9.47** | 16.18 | **8.29** | 12.32 |
| I-GLIDE$_{VAE}$ + RF (ours) | 12.33 | 16.76 | 8.5 | **11.4** |

Monolithic AEs struggle to disentangle subsystem-specific degradation, which we illustrate with a HI plot of the trajectories in Fig. 2. For Engine 1 (FD001), where HPC degradation is the source, HI$_{mono}$ shows weak latent-space ($z$) sensitivity to subsystem dynamics. This occurs because deeper layers in monolithic AEs compress sensor signals into a global representation, obscuring non-stationary interactions (e.g., HPC wear indirectly altering turbine behavior). In contrast, Fig. 3 reveals how I-GLIDE isolates these dynamics: the HPC encoder HI exhibits a clear upward trend, while the turbine HI shifts abruptly as degradation propagates—a causal linkage masked in monolithic architectures. Notably, the shared latent $z$ in I-GLIDE still captures the composite degradation trend, and subsystem-specific decoders also localize fault origins (e.g., rising epistemic uncertainty in HPC vs. stable turbine estimates). This explains why HI$_{mono}$ underperforms—it conflates cross-subsystem effects into a single noisy signal, while our I-GLIDE overcomes these restrains. In future work, we would like to formalize methods to interpret such causal relationships between HIs, identify noise patterns in the degradation signals, and apply it to maintenance tasks.

Traditional HI metrics (monotonicity, trendability, prognosability) often produce misleading scores (e.g., near-perfect prognosability) that poorly correlate with actual RUL prediction. Worse, they ignore subsystem-specific degradation, obscuring actionable insights. Our framework addresses this by directly linking HI quality to RUL prediction accuracy—a metric aligned with real-world decision-making. By disentangling subsystem trends (e.g., turbine wear vs. fan imbalance), I-GLIDE enables targeted fault diagnosis and maintenance planning.

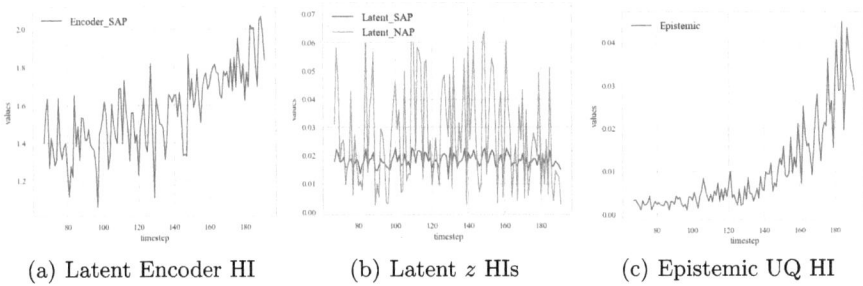

(a) Latent Encoder HI  (b) Latent $z$ HIs  (c) Epistemic UQ HI

**Fig. 2.** AE HI trajectories for Engine 1 for the monolithic architecture. We can observe that the HIs model a degradation, but cannot distinguish sub-system components. We only show the SAP metric for the encoder HIs because NAP shows extreme values.

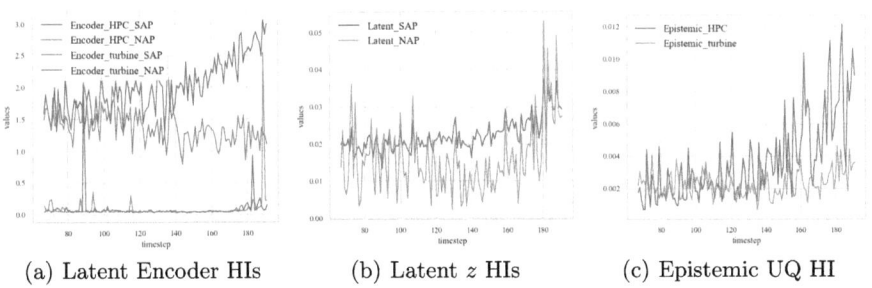

(a) Latent Encoder HIs  (b) Latent $z$ HIs  (c) Epistemic UQ HI

**Fig. 3.** I-GLIDE$_{AE}$ HI trajectories for Engine 1, comparing degradation effects on HPC and Turbine. Latent encoder HIs (a) show rising HPC degradation and reduced Turbine HIs due to cross-component effects. System-wide latent $z$ HIs trends are in (b). Epistemic uncertainty (c) rises sharply for HPC as degradation progresses, remaining stable for the Turbine until late-cycle HPC interference. UQ confirms causal cross-component effects without confusing intrinsic health states.

While our framework advances subsystem-aware HIs, several constraints merit consideration. First, it is worth noting that both the C-MAPSS and MILL datasets model exponential degradation patterns, which oversimplify real-world scenarios where industrial systems often exhibit linear or piecewise degradation trends. Real-world applications also introduce complex noise profiles (e.g., cyclic sensor artifacts) and heterogeneous failure modes that our method may not optimally capture without tailored adaptations.

Readers should be aware that our architecture assumes strictly monotonous degradation, limiting its ability to model recovery phases—a critical shortcoming for systems where transient improvements occur, such as medical devices supporting patient recovery or aircraft exiting high-stress environments. Furthermore, our subsystem groupings rely on domain heuristics; while this aligns with prior work, poorly defined sensor groupings could propagate biases into the latent representations, undermining HI interpretability.

## 6 Conclusion and Future Work

This work establishes the first prognostics benchmark for evaluating Health Indicators (HIs) generated via the RaPP methods, demonstrating that integrating uncertainty quantification significantly enhances their predictive capabilities. Building on this foundation, we introduce I-GLIDE, a novel framework that learns subsystem-specific latent representations through dedicated encoder-decoder pairs. By isolating degradation mechanisms (e.g., HPC degradation vs. turbine wear) while maintaining global system dynamics via a shared latent space, I-GLIDE captures nuanced failure modes without compromising system-level coherence. The resulting high-quality HIs achieve state-of-the-art performance on the C-MAPSS dataset, surpassing existing deep learning benchmarks using only a simple Random Forest regressor.

Our subsystem-specific HIs advance prognostics but invite refinement. Temporal improvements—like extending observation windows—could better resolve slow degradation signatures and transient noise, aligning HI trajectories with real-world failure timelines. Coupling uncertainty-specific t-SNE visualizations with expert annotations could map latent clusters to physical degradation stages, bridging data-driven insights with domain knowledge.

A promising direction involves modeling causal subsystem interactions via architectures like graph neural networks, trained on fused HIs to disentangle degradation propagation (e.g., turbine-to-compressor wear). This would scale prognostics to systems with complex interdependencies.

Critically, our results show that high-quality HIs paired with simple models (e.g., RF) outperform deep learning on raw data—a "data is gold" paradigm. Future efforts should prioritize refining physics-aware HI representations—grounded in subsystem dynamics and enriched with UQ to unlock generalizable, trustworthy RUL prediction across grounded industrial domains.

**Acknowledgments.** This work has been supported by the French government under the "France 2030" program, as part of the SystemX Technological Research Institute within the JNI3 project.

**Disclosure of Interests.** The authors have no competing interests to declare that are relevant to the content of this article.

# References

1. Abdar, M., et al. A review of uncertainty quantification in deep learning: techniques, applications and challenges. Inf. Fusion **76**, 243–297 (2021). https://linkinghub.elsevier.com/retrieve/pii/S1566253521001081
2. Agogino, A., Goebel, K.: Milling data set. NASA Prognostics Data Repository, NASA Ames Research Center, Moffett Field (2007)
3. Akbari, A., Jafari, R.: Personalizing activity recognition models through quantifying different types of uncertainty using wearable sensors. IEEE Trans. Biomed. Eng. **67**, 2530–2541 (2020,9), https://ieeexplore.ieee.org/document/8949726/
4. Amini, A., Soleimany, A., Karaman, S., Rus, D.: Spatial uncertainty sampling for end-to-end control. arXiv (2018). https://arxiv.org/abs/1805.04829
5. Costa, N., Sánchez, L.: Variational encoding approach for interpretable assessment of remaining useful life estimation. Reliabil. Eng. Syst. Saf. **222**, 108353 (2022). https://linkinghub.elsevier.com/retrieve/pii/S0951832022000321
6. Côme, E.: Aircraft engine health monitoring using self-organizing maps. In: 10th Industrial Conference, ICDM 2010, Berlin, Germany, pp. 405–417 (2010)
7. De Pater, I., Mitici, M.: Novel metrics to evaluate probabilistic remaining useful life prognostics with applications to turbofan engines. In: PHM Society European Conference, vol. 7, pp. 96–109 (2022). https://papers.phmsociety.org/index.php/phme/article/view/3320
8. Fink, O., Wang, Q., Svensén, M., Dersin, P., Lee, W., Ducoffe, M.: Potential, challenges and future directions for deep learning in prognostics and health management applications. Eng. Appl. Artif. Intell. **92**, 103678 (2020). https://linkinghub.elsevier.com/retrieve/pii/S0952197620301184
9. Gal, Y., Ghahramani, Z.: Dropout as a Bayesian approximation: representing model uncertainty in deep learning (2016). https://arxiv.org/abs/1506.02142
10. Gherbi, E., Hanczar, B., Janodet, J., Klaudel, W. An encoding adversarial network for anomaly detection. In: Proceedings of the Eleventh Asian Conference On Machine Learning, vol. 101, pp. 188–203 (2019). https://proceedings.mlr.press/v101/gherbi19a.html
11. González-Muñiz, A., Díaz, I., Cuadrado, A., García-Pérez, D.: Health indicator for machine condition monitoring built in the latent space of a deep autoencoder. Reliabil. Eng. Syst. Saf. **224**, 108482 (2022)
12. He, W., Williard, N., Chen, C., Pecht, M.: State of charge estimation for Li-ion batteries using neural network modeling and unscented Kalman filter-based error cancellation. Int. J. Electr. Power Energy Syst. **62**, 783–791 (2014). https://linkinghub.elsevier.com/retrieve/pii/S0142061514002646
13. Huang, L., Pan, X., Liu, Y., Gong, L.: An unsupervised machine learning approach for monitoring data fusion and health indicator construction. Sensors **23**, 7239 (2023). https://www.mdpi.com/1424-8220/23/16/7239

14. Hüllermeier, E., Waegeman, W.: Aleatoric and epistemic uncertainty in machine learning: an introduction to concepts and methods. arXiv (2019). https://arxiv.org/abs/1910.09457
15. Jing, T., Zheng, P., Xia, L., Liu, T.: Transformer-based hierarchical latent space VAE for interpretable remaining useful life prediction. Adv. Eng. Inform. **54**, 101781 (2022). https://linkinghub.elsevier.com/retrieve/pii/S1474034622002397
16. Kendall, A., Gal, Y.: What uncertainties do we need in bayesian deep learning for computer vision?. arXiv (2017). https://arxiv.org/abs/1703.04977
17. Ki Hyun, K., Sangwoo, S., Yongsub, L.: RaPP: novelty detection with reconstruction along projection pathway (2019)
18. Kingma, D., Welling, M.: Auto-encoding variational bayes. arXiv (2013). https://arxiv.org/abs/1312.6114
19. Lacaille, J. Standardized failure signature for a turbofan engine. In: 2009 IEEE Aerospace Conference, pp. 1–8 (2009). http://ieeexplore.ieee.org/document/4839670/
20. Li, H., Zhao, W., Zhang, Y., Zio, E.: Remaining useful life prediction using multi-scale deep convolutional neural network. Appl. Soft Comput. **89**, 106113 (2020). https://linkinghub.elsevier.com/retrieve/pii/S1568494620300533
21. Li, X., Ding, Q., Sun, J.: Remaining useful life estimation in prognostics using deep convolution neural networks. Reliabil. Eng. Syst. Saf. **172**, 1-11 (2018). https://linkinghub.elsevier.com/retrieve/pii/S0951832017307779
22. Liu, D., Zhou, J., Liao, H., Peng, Y., Peng, X.: A health indicator extraction and optimization framework for lithium-ion battery degradation modeling and prognostics. IEEE Trans. Syst. Man Cybern.: Syst. **45**, 915-928 (2015). http://ieeexplore.ieee.org/document/7018028/
23. Martinelli, M., Tronci, E., Dipoppa, G., Balducelli, C.: Electric power system anomaly detection using neural networks. Knowl.-Based Intell. Inf. Eng. Syst. **3213**, 1242–1248 (2004). http://link.springer.com/10.1007/9783540301325168
24. Mitici, M., De Pater, I., Barros, A., Zeng, Z.: Dynamic predictive maintenance for multiple components using data-driven probabilistic RUL prognostics: the case of turbofan engines. Reliabil. Eng. Syst. Saf. **234**, 109199 (2023). https://linkinghub.elsevier.com/retrieve/pii/S095183202300114X
25. Peng, C., Chen, Y., Chen, Q., Tang, Z., Li, L., Gui, W.: A remaining useful life prognosis of turbofan engine using temporal and spatial feature fusion. Sensors **21**, 418 (2021). https://www.mdpi.com/1424-8220/21/2/418
26. Pillai, S., Vadakkepat, P.: Two stage deep learning for prognostics using multi-loss encoder and convolutional composite features. Expert Syst. Appl. **171**, 114569 (2021). https://linkinghub.elsevier.com/retrieve/pii/S0957417421000105
27. Rombach, K., Michau, G., Bürzle, W., Koller, S., Fink, O.: Learning informative health indicators through unsupervised contrastive learning. IEEE Trans. Reliabil. 1–13 (2024). https://ieeexplore.ieee.org/document/10531793/
28. Saxena, A., Goebel, K., Simon, D., Eklund, N. Damage propagation modeling for aircraft engine run-to-failure simulation. In: 2008 International Conference on Prognostics and Health Management, pp. 1–9 (2008). http://ieeexplore.ieee.org/document/4711414/
29. Thil, L., Read, J., Kaddah, R., Doquet, G.: Uncertainty quantification as a complementary latent health indicator for remaining useful life prediction on turbofan engines. In: 13th IMA International Conference On Modelling In Industrial Maintenance And Reliability (MIMAR) (2025). https://hal.science/hal-05093810

30. Wang, S., Fan, Y., Jin, S., Takyi-Aninakwa, P., Fernandez, C.: Improved anti-noise adaptive long short-term memory neural network modeling for the robust remaining useful life prediction of lithium-ion batteries. Reliabil. Eng. Syst. Saf. **230**, 108920 (2023). https://linkinghub.elsevier.com/retrieve/pii/S095183202200535X
31. Wang, Y., et al.: Uncertainty quantification and reduction in aircraft trajectory prediction using Bayesian-Entropy information fusion. Reliabil. Eng. Syst. Saf. **212**, 107650 (2021). https://linkinghub.elsevier.com/retrieve/pii/S0951832021001915
32. Wei, M., Ye, M., Wang, Q., Xinxin-Xu, Twajamahoro, J.: Remaining useful life prediction of lithium-ion batteries based on stacked autoencoder and gaussian mixture regression. J. Energy Storage **47**, 103558 (2022). https://linkinghub.elsevier.com/retrieve/pii/S2352152X21012378
33. Zhang, C., Lim, P., Qin, A., Tan, K.: Multiobjective deep belief networks ensemble for remaining useful life estimation in prognostics. IEEE Trans. Neural Netw. Learn. Syst. **28**, 2306–2318 (2017). http://ieeexplore.ieee.org/document/7508982/
34. Zhao, Z., Liang, B., Wang, X., Lu, W.: Remaining useful life prediction of aircraft engine based on degradation pattern learning. Reliabil. Eng. Syst. Saf. **164**, 74–83 (2017). https://linkinghub.elsevier.com/retrieve/pii/S0951832017302454
35. Zheng, S., Ristovski, K., Farahat, A., Gupta, C.: Long short-term memory network for remaining useful life estimation. In: 2017 IEEE International Conference On Prognostics And Health Management (ICPHM), pp. 88–95 (2017). http://ieeexplore.ieee.org/document/7998311/

# Learnable Diffusion for Wavelets in Scattering Networks: Towards both Interpretability and Performance in Graph Representation Learning

Toan Van Tran[1(✉)] and Hung Son Nguyen[2]

[1] Hanoi University of Science and Technology, Hanoi, Vietnam
toantranvan1203@gmail.com, toan.tv214932@sis.hust.edu.vn
[2] University of Warsaw, Warsaw, Poland
son@mimuw.edu.pl

**Abstract.** Scattering networks are deep convolutional architectures that use predefined wavelets for feature extraction and representation. They are mathematically well-understood, and have proven effective for classification tasks in limited training data scenarios, where traditional deep learning methods struggle. However, the opposite holds in larger data regimes, resulting in a performance gap between well-understood learning architectures and non-transparent yet highly effective paradigms. Our work addresses this gap on the domain of graphs by adapting the choice of diffusion operator that constructs the scattering network to the data, allowing better task-wise geometric representation. The resulting architecture preserves stability guarantees with respect to input perturbations. Continuous diffusion is applied in the learning process for more refined weight updates. Numerical experiments on benchmark datasets show that our approach consistently outperforms traditional graph scattering with predefined wavelets, expanding the scenarios where interpretable scattering architectures are competitive or superior to deep learning methods, and further reducing their aforementioned performance disparity.

**Keywords:** Graph learning · Scattering networks · Interpretability

## 1 Introduction

Euclidean scattering networks are deep convolutional architectures analogous to Convolutional Neural Networks (CNNs). Unlike standard CNNs, which employ learnable filters at each layer, these networks are equipped with mathematically predefined wavelets selected from a multi-resolution filter bank [3, 15]. This distinction allows Euclidean scattering networks to serve as mathematically well-understood models that capture the principles underlying the empirical success

---

**Supplementary Information** The online version contains supplementary material available at https://doi.org/10.1007/978-3-032-06106-5_24.

of CNNs. Specifically, they exhibit proven robustness to small perturbations that are close to translations in the underlying domain [3]. For classification, these models serve as efficient feature extractors, requiring only the classifier to be trained. This is especially beneficial with limited data, enabling state-of-the-art performance while maintaining efficiency comparable to learned deep networks on simpler datasets.

The increasing focus on graph-structured data has spurred interest in adapting CNN architectures to these domains, leading to the development of effective graph convolutional models and variants (e.g. [14,26]). Naturally, proposals on extending the theoretical and practical benefits of Euclidean scattering networks to geometric data follow. [33] first introduced graph scattering networks using spectral wavelets [13,22] and analyzed their stability with respect to permutations of the nodes and perturbations on the spectrum of the underlying graph domain. Subsequently, [10] established improved stability bounds for this family of graph scattering transforms, applicable to more general graphs and independent of their spectral characteristics. Alternatively, [9] introduced graph scattering employing diffusion wavelets [6], using the lazy diffusion operator induced from normalized adjacency, and analyzing stability using diffusion metrics [5,18]. Following this, [11] proposed an alternative graph scattering transform based on lazy random walk diffusion, demonstrating expressivity through extensive empirical evaluations.

A fundamental characteristic shared by all these scattering architectures is the use of fixed, often manually selected filters. This contributes to scattering networks' mathematical interpretability, and in low data scenarios helps them achieve higher classification performance than deep learning methods considered as black boxes. In larger data regimes, the performance of scattering architectures plateaus, while deep learning's becomes much higher than any predefined representations [20]. This work aims to bridge the performance gap between these interpretable and non-transparent learning paradigms in graph domains.

In particular, we consider diffusion graph scattering network [9], constructed from wavelets [6] which extract multiscales information in a single geometric diffusion process. Given a dataset, different diffusion operators can extract different properties via the use of diffusion map [7]. The selection of diffusion, which can be labor-intensive if manually done, is thus critical to the performance of the scattering network. Our approach for the diffusion scattering is thus to make the corresponding diffusion operator learnable, training it at the same time with the classifier. One operator is used throughout the network, making the number of additional parameters small. Our method also preserves expressivity and stability properties of the resulting architecture, maintaining the interpretability aspect of the original scattering.

The paper is organized as follows. In Sect. 2 we discuss related works. Section 3 provides the necessary background. Section 4 discusses the framework for defining diffusion wavelets and metrics (Sect. 4.1) and constructing the diffusion-based graph scattering transform (Sect. 4.2). Section 5 demonstrates the importance of diffusion operator selection with examples, introduces a learnable operator design (Sect. 5.1), establishes energy conservation bounds for wavelets

(Sect. 5.2), provides a stability analysis of the resulting learnable diffusion scattering transform (Sect. 5.4), and complexity analysis (Sect. 5.5). Section 6 presents numerical results for graph classification tasks on low to medium data regimes.

## 2 Related Works

The performance gap between scattering architectures and deep learning methods in larger data regimes has been widely discussed, particularly in the context of Euclidean scattering, but remains less explored for graphs. For geometric data, [24] introduced a scale-adaptive extension of the lazy random walk diffusion scattering transform, enabling adaptive wavelet scale adjustment. Their approach demonstrated competitive performance compared to popular GNNs and the original graph scattering network.

For Euclidean image, [20] showed that the initial layers of a CNN can be replaced with a scattering network, forming a hybrid architecture that achieves competitive performance. [31] further demonstrated that learning in later CNN layers can be reduced to a dictionary matrix that computes a positive sparse $l^1$ code. Their model outperformed AlexNet on ImageNet 2012 while remaining mathematically interpretable. Additionally, [30] introduced a scattering-based model, in which only $1 \times 1$ convolutional tight frames are learned for scattering feature projection. This approach delivered performance comparable to ResNet-18. The authors of [12] investigated the role of non-linearity in deep CNNs and identified a phenomenon called "phase collapsing". They applied this into a Learned Scattering with $1 \times 1$ complex convolutional operators to achieve performance of ResNets of similar depths.

Adaptive diffusion for GNNs has also been explored in prior works [23,32]. These studies consider the weighted sum of outputs from each step of a predefined diffusion process as multiscale information and propose learning these weights for adaptivity. In contrast, our approach focuses on adapting the diffusion operator, while multiscale feature extraction is handled by the scattering architecture using wavelets [6]. Unlike previous methods that emphasize multi-hop aggregation, we focus on improving how the diffusion process extracts information.

## 3 Preliminaries

We start with some background that will be used throughout the paper (most of which can be found in standard textbooks (e.g. [16,21])):

**Metric Space:** A metric space is a tuple consisting of a set $X$ and a distance function $d$, which satisfies the metric properties: $\forall x, y, z \in X$: (i) positivity: $d(x, y) > 0$, $\forall x \neq y$; (ii) reflexivity: $d(x, x) = 0$; (iii) symmetry: $d(x, y) = d(y, x)$, and (iv) triangle inequality: $d(x, y) \leq d(x, z) + d(z, y)$. A weighted undirected connected graph $G = (V, E, W)$, where $W$ assigns positive weights to the edges, is an example of a metric space with the distance between two nodes $x$ and $y$ defined by $d(x,y) = \inf_{p_{x,y}} \sum_{e \in p_{x,y}} w_e$, where $p_{x,y}$ is a path connecting $x$ and $y$.

**Measure Space:** A measure space is a triple $(X, \Sigma, \mu)$, where $X$ is a set, $\Sigma$ is a $\sigma$-algebra on $X$ (a nonempty collection of subsets of $X$ closed under set-theoretic operations: complement, countable union, and countable intersection) and $\mu$ is a measure on $(X, \Sigma)$. A **metric measure space** is a triple $(X, d, m)$ of a space $X$, metric $d$ and a Borel measure $m$. For a finite graph $G$, mostly considered is the counting measure $\mu$ where $\mu\{u\} = 1$, $\forall u \in V$.

**Multiresolution Analysis:** A multiresolution analysis of $\mathcal{L}^2$ of a metric measure space $(X, d, \mu)$ is a sequence of subspaces $\{V_j\}_{j \in \mathbb{Z}}$, each of which is called an **approximation space**. In the case of $\mathcal{L}^2(\mathbb{R})$, the sequence $\{V_j\}_{j \in \mathbb{Z}}$ satisfies the properties:

(i) $\lim_{j \to -\infty} V_j = \bigcup_{j=-\infty}^{+\infty} V_j = \mathcal{L}^2(\mathbb{R})$
(ii) $\lim_{j \to +\infty} V_j = \bigcap_{j=-\infty}^{+\infty} V_j = \{0\}$
(iii) $V_{j+1} \subseteq V_j$, $\forall j \in \mathbb{Z}$
(iv) There exists a Riesz basis that spans $V_0$.

The **detail space** $W_j$ is defined as the orthogonal complement of $V_j$ in $V_{j-1}$; in other words, $V_{j-1} = V_j \oplus^\perp W_j$, $\forall j \in \mathbb{Z}$. The orthogonal projection of a signal $x$ on $V_{j-1}$ can thus be decomposed as $P_{V_{j-1}} x = P_{V_j} x + P_{W_j} x$. The projection of a signal $x$ on $W_j$ captures the "details" of $x$ that are present in the finer-scale space $V_{j-1}$ but absent in the coarser-scale $V_j$. Given a mother wavelet $\psi$, the translations of $\psi$ after being dilated onto scale $2^j$, denoted as $\{\psi_{j,n}\}_{n \in \mathbb{Z}} = \{\frac{1}{\sqrt{2^j}} \psi(\frac{t - 2^j n}{2^j})\}_{n \in \mathbb{Z}}$, compose an orthonormal basis of $W_j$. On said basis, the projection of $x$ on $W_j$ can be obtained by a partial expansion: $P_{W_j} x = \sum_{n=-\infty}^{+\infty} \langle x, \psi_{j,n} \rangle \psi_{j,n}$.

**Scattering Transform** is a mapping which takes an input signal $x$ and returns a representation $\Phi(x)$, calculated based on a deep convolutional architecture, stable to small deformations while preserving high-frequency information. $\Phi(x)$ is computed by applying sequentially three elements: A **filter bank** of band-pass wavelets $\{\{\psi_{j,k}\}_{k=0}^{K-1}\}_{j=1}^{J}$, a **pointwise nonlinearity** $\rho$ (modulus or ReLU), and an **average operator** $U$. In the Euclidean setting, the filter bank consists of rotated and dilated versions $\psi_{j,k}$ of a mother wavelet $\psi$ with scaling parameter $j$ and angle parameter $k$, with the angle $\theta \in \{2\pi k/K\}_{k=0,\ldots,K-1}$. The scattering representation of $x$ is defined as:

$$\Phi(x) = [S_0(x), S_1(x), \ldots, S_{m-1}(x)], \text{ where}$$
$$S_k(x) = \left[ U \Pi_{i=0}^{k} (\rho \psi_{\alpha_i})(x) \right]_{\alpha_0, \alpha_1, \ldots, \alpha_k} \quad (1)$$
$$= [U(\rho(\ldots \rho(\rho(x * \psi_{\alpha_0}) * \psi_{\alpha_1}) \ldots * \psi_{\alpha_k}))]_{\alpha_0, \alpha_1, \ldots, \alpha_k}.$$

where $\alpha_i$, $i = 0, \ldots, k$ represent the scale parameters.

## 4 Graph Diffusion Scattering Transform

### 4.1 Graph Diffusion Wavelets and Diffusion Distances

The works in [6,8] introduce a framework for multiscale and multiresolution analysis on the domain of graphs, based on polyadic powers of a diffusion operator. We consider an undirected, weighted, and connected graph $G = (V, E, W)$, with $|V| = n$ nodes, edges set $E$ and adjacency matrix $W \in \mathbb{R}^{+n \times n}$. The random walk matrix $T = WD^{-1}$ of $G$ defines an induced diffusion process on its nodes, where $D = \text{diag}(d_1, ..., d_n)$, and $d_i, i = 1, ..., n$ are the degrees of the nodes of $G$. For stability, the lazy diffusion $P = \frac{1}{2}(I + T)$ can be employed. Given that $P$ is left-stochastic and guaranteed to have positive entries at indices $(u, v)$ whenever $(u, v) \in E$, it can also be interpreted as a transition matrix of a random walk process on $G$.

The operator $P$ is mass-preserving (i.e. $\sum_{(u,v) \in E} P[v, u] = 1$ for any fixed $u$), contractive ($\|P\| \leq 1$), and positivity-preserving ($x \geq 0 \Rightarrow Px \geq 0$). Consider a random walk on $G$ with $P$ as the transition matrix, the probability distribution starting from an initial $p_0$ (e.g. a Dirac delta $\delta_u$ at any node $u$ of $G$) becomes increasingly "smoothed out" as over time, as observed from the fact that $P^t p_0$ converges to a stationary distribution when $t \to \infty$, and this distribution is independent of $p_0$.

Based on this "smoothening" property, $P$ can be interpreted as a dilation operator, acting on signals on $\mathcal{L}^2(G)$. An analog to the multiresolution analysis can thus be constructed, as proposed in [6]. In a more general perspective, we consider a diffusion semigroup $\{A^t\}_{t \geq 0}$ induced by a general diffusion operator $A$ acting on $\mathcal{L}^2(X, \mu)$ which satisfies the following properties:

(i) $\|A^t\|_p \leq 1$, for every $1 \leq p \leq +\infty$.
(ii) $A^t x \geq 0$, for every $x \geq 0$

Semigroups as such are referred to as Markovian semigroups. We fix a precision level $\epsilon < 1$. Define $A\mathcal{L}^2(X) = \text{span}\{x \in \mathcal{L}^2(X) : \|x\| \leq 1, \frac{\|Ax\|}{\|x\|} \geq \epsilon\}$. Let $\lambda_{min} = \inf_{x \in \mathcal{L}^2(X), \|x\| \leq 1} \frac{\|Ax\|}{\|x\|}$, and $\lambda_{max} = \sup_{x \in \mathcal{L}^2(X), \|x\| \leq 1} \frac{\|Ax\|}{\|x\|}$. As $\|A\| \leq 1$, it follows that $\dim(A\mathcal{L}^2(X)) \leq \dim(\mathcal{L}^2(X))$. The operator $A$ contracts the functional space $\mathcal{L}^2(X)$ after each application. The inequality may be strict, as there are signals in some parts of $\mathcal{L}^2(X)$ have their norm contracted by $\lambda_{min}$, which may already be smaller than $\epsilon$.

At times $t_j = \gamma^{j+1}$, where $\gamma > 1$ (commonly set to 2), we discretize $\{A^j\}$ following classical wavelet theory, having wavelets are dilated at scales of polyadic powers. We define the approximation spaces $V_j$ analogous to a multiresolution analysis of $\mathcal{L}^2(X)$ as $A^{t_j} \mathcal{L}^2(X)$. We also conventionally define $V_{-1} = \mathcal{L}^2(X)$. A family of multiresolution filters, analogous to the wavelet filter bank in the Euclidean setting, can thus be defined as:

$$\psi_0 = I - A \, , \, \psi_i = A^{t_{i-2}} - A^{t_{i-1}} = A^{2^{i-1}} - A^{2^i} \, (i > 0) \tag{2}$$

These filters can be understood as projecting a signal $x$ onto the complement of $V_j$ in $V_{j+1}$, analogous to the partial expansion of $x$ in the wavelet basis $\{\psi_{j,n}\}$ of $W_j$ [9], thereby extracting the details of $x$ at coarser scales as $j$ increases.

A diffusion distance can also be constructed on the operator $A$ [5]. If $A$ is left-stochastic (i.e. it can be considered as a transition matrix of a Markov chain) and positivity-preserving, then the diffusion distances at time $t$ between two nodes $u$ and $v$ is given by: $d_t(u,v) = \|A^t \delta_u - A^t \delta_v\|$, with the norm induced from the inner product weighted by $1/\pi_A$. This distance considers all paths of length $t$ between $u$ and $v$. If there are many connecting short paths between the two nodes, then $d_t(u,v)$ will be small. It is, as a consequence, robust to noise, unlike the shortest path distance. An additional consequence is that $d_t(u,v)$ is small if $u$'s and $v$'s neighborhoods are similar.

A distance between two graphs of equal size can also be defined based on this node-level one. Given two graphs $G = (V, E, W)$ and $G' = (V', E', W')$ with $|V| = |V'| = n$ and respective symmetric diffusion operators $A_G$ and $A_{G'}$, the normalized diffusion distance between $G$ and $G'$ at time $t$ is defined in [9] as:

$$\tilde{d}_t(G, G') = \inf_{\Pi \in \Pi_n} \|(A_G^t)(A_G^t)^* - \Pi^{-1}(A_{G'}^t)(A_{G'}^t)^* \Pi\| \tag{3}$$

where $\Pi_n$ is the space of all $n \times n$ permutation matrices, $A^*$ is the adjoint of operator $A$. $(A_G^t)(A_G^t)^*$ is the Gram matrix of the system $A_G^t \delta_u{}_{u \in V}$. The distance thus compares the 2 vector systems intrinsic to $G$ and $G'$ at time $t$, and is invariant to permutation and orthonormal transformation. It is also robust to noise similarly to the node-level one. For simplicity, we consider $t = 1$ in this work. As random walk matrices are not generally symmetric in the same inner product, a weighted variant of (3) can be considered:

$$\begin{aligned} d(G, G') &= \inf_{\Pi \in \Pi_n} \|(A_G) D_{A_G}(A_G)^* - \Pi^{-1}(A_{G'}) D_{A_{G'}}(A_{G'})^* \Pi\| \\ &= \inf_{\Pi \in \Pi_n} d(G, G', \Pi) \end{aligned} \tag{4}$$

where $D_A = \mathrm{diag}(\pi)$ where $\pi$ is the limiting distribution of $A$.

Each entry of $(A_G^2)(A_G^2)^*$ is $(W^2)_{u,v}/\deg(u)\deg(v)$, representing a form of local normalization, thus using (3) focuses on structural equivalence. In contrast, a global normalization takes the form $(W^2)_{u,v}/\mathrm{vol}(G)^2$, where $\mathrm{vol}(G) = \sum_{u \in V} \deg(u)$, giving more weights to important nodes (i.e. those with high degree). The distance in (4) normalizes by $\sqrt{\deg(u)\deg(v)}\mathrm{vol}(G)$, thereby balancing between the two. In this work, we consider the distance on graphs of equal sizes; however, it can be naturally extended to graphs of different sizes by replacing permutation matrices with soft-correspondences, as in [2] [9].

### 4.2 Graph Scattering Transform

The construction of the multiresolution analysis, and thus an analog of the wavelet filter bank on the domain of graphs, paves the way for the extension of graph scattering transform. Let $\Psi_n : \mathcal{L}^2(X) \to (\mathcal{L}^2(X))^{J_n}$ be the wavelet

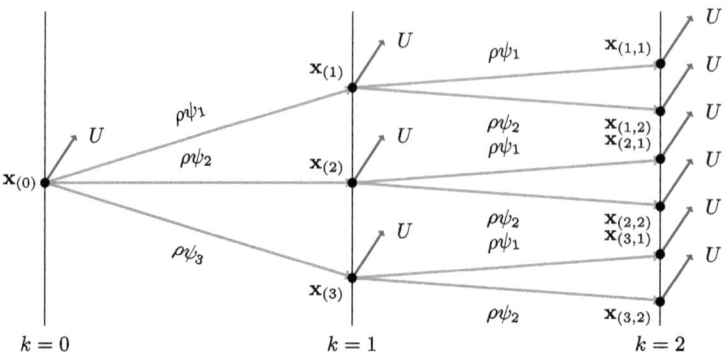

**Fig. 1.** Illustration of graph scattering transform with $m = 3$ layers, scales $J_1 = 3$ and $J_2 = 2$.

decomposition operator that maps $x$ to $(\psi_j x)_{j=0,\ldots,J_n-1}$, with $\psi_j$ defined as in the previous subsection. Following the Euclidean setting described in Sect. 3, the diffusion graph scattering transform $\Phi_G(x)$ is also defined from three components: the wavelet decomposition operator at each layer $k$: $\Psi_k$; a pointwise nonlinearity $\rho$; and a low-pass operator $U$. The representation $\Phi(x)$ is calculated analogously to the scattering transform in Sect. 1 (see Fig. 1).

In [9], $\Phi_G(x)$ is introduced with the multiresolution filters being constructed from the intrinsic lazy normalized symmetric adjacency $\overline{P} = \frac{1}{2}(I + M)$ of $G = (V, E, W)$, where $M = D^{-1/2}WD^{-1/2}$. Although $\overline{P}$ is not mass-preserving, there is a spectral theory to this operator, with respect to the canonical inner product on $\mathcal{L}^2(G)$. This is desirable in many cases - for example, when constructing a diffusion embedding such that the Euclidean distance in the embedding space corresponds to the diffusion distance in the original graph space [7]. Moreover, since $\overline{P}$ is contractive (due to its self-adjointness and having spectral radius $\rho(\overline{P}) \leq 1$) and positivity preserving, the multiresolution analysis construction remains valid. The average operator $U$ is taken to be the infinite-time diffusion limit $\lim_{t\to\infty} \overline{P}^t$, expressible as $Ux = \langle \mathbf{v}^\mathsf{T}, x \rangle$, where $\mathbf{v} = \frac{\mathbf{d}^{1/2}}{\|\mathbf{d}^{1/2}\|_2} = (\frac{\mathbf{d}}{\|\mathbf{d}\|_1})^{1/2}$ is the eigenvector of $\overline{P}$ corresponding to the eigenvalue 1, $\mathbf{d}$ being the degree vector of $G$, and $\mathbf{x}^{1/2}$ is the vector with square root of every entry of $\mathbf{x}$.

## 5 Graph Scattering Networks with Learnable Diffusion

In this section, we first discuss examples of how different diffusion kernels can capture different properties of a dataset via the use of diffusion maps, as part of our motivation. We then propose a formulation of a learnable diffusion operator that we will use in our experiments as an example to demonstrate the enhanced performance. In subsequent parts, expressivity and stability bounds for wavelets and scattering networks constructed from said operator are established.

## 5.1 Learnable Diffusion Kernels and Diffusion Operators

We consider some examples of $X$ approximately lying on some submanifolds $\mathcal{M}$ of $\mathbb{R}^n$, characterized by a density function $p(x)$, to show how different kernels can captures different properties, e.g. the intrinsic geometry of the data points, its distribution density, or a combination of both [7]. This feature extraction is done via the use of diffusion map [5]. Between two points $x$, $y$ of $X$, let $k(x,y)$ be the "affinity function" that is symmetric, positivity-preserving, and positive semi-definite. $k(x,y)$ can be interpreted as the analog of edges weight between graph nodes. Let $d(x) = \int_X k(x,y)\mu(y)$ be an analog of degrees of nodes, where $\mu$ is a probability measure. The random walk diffusion operator $A$ can thus be defined as $As(x) = \int_X a(x,y)s(y)d\mu(y)$, where $s$ is a signal on $X$, and $a(x,y) = \frac{k(x,y)}{d(y)}$.

Two examples of diffusion kernels are given in [7], one accounting for the density of the points in $X$, and the other captures the geometry irrespective of density. Consider the random walk diffusion $A_\epsilon$ constructed from an isotropic kernel $k_\epsilon(x,y) = \exp(-\|x-y\|^2/\epsilon)$. If $p(x)$ is uniform, $A_\epsilon$ approximates the Laplacian-Beltrami operator $\Delta$ on $\mathcal{M}$, as $\epsilon \to 0$ [1]. On the other hand, if $p(x)$ is not, $A_\epsilon$ tends to a more general operator of the form $\Delta + Q$, where $Q(x) = \frac{\Delta p(x)}{p(x)}$ acts as a potential term, reflecting the influence of the non-uniform density.

An alternative normalization is introduced that captures the geometry of the data points by taking into account the non-uniformity of $p(x)$: Let $p_\epsilon(x) = \int_X k_\epsilon(x,y)p(y)dy$, and define the new kernel $\hat{k}_\epsilon(x,y) = k_\epsilon(x,y)/p_\epsilon(x)p_\epsilon(y)$. The corresponding random walk diffusion $\hat{A}_\epsilon$ then serves as an approximation of the Laplace-Beltrami operator at time $\epsilon$, regardless of density variations.

These examples show that the embeddings obtained are highly sensitive to the choice of kernel. Depending on the task, one may prefer this diffusion to another. For example, the second kernel discussed above are used for segmentation with spectral clustering [28], while the first one can be used for analysis solely on the topology of the domain. Thus, there are cases where data-driven diffusion is naturally preferable.

For each node $u$ of a graph $G$, we define the **descriptor** $g_u$ to be a vector that has the characteristics of $u$, e.g. its node degree. Between every two adjacent nodes $u$ and $v$, let $k(u,v)$ be the kernel that quantifies the affinity between the two, being positive if $u$ and $v$ are adjacent. Taking inspiration from attentional diffusion in [4], we propose the affinity kernel between two distinct, adjacent nodes to be given by:

$$k(u,v) = \exp\left(\frac{\langle W(g_u), W(g_w) \rangle}{\|W(g_u)\|.\|W(g_v)\|} k_1\right) \quad (5)$$

where $\|\cdot\|$ is the vector norm, $W$ is a mapping from the descriptor space $\mathcal{G}$ to an embedding space $W(\mathcal{G})$, and $k_1$ is a hyperparameter to be tuned. This formulation differs from the affinity used in scale-dot attention [25], which is given by $k_{sd}(u,v) = \exp(\frac{(W_K g_u)^\top W_Q g_v}{d_e})$, in two key aspects: First, $k$ is symmetrized by letting $W_K = W_Q$, where both mappings can be nonlinear transformations (e.g. a simple MLP), thereby preserving generalization capability. Second, the inner product is normalized to be the cosine-similarity. In our experiments, we found out that the resulting attention weights without normalization tend to be "extreme", i.e. one neighbor would dominate, causing the attention values to be reduced to either 0 or 1. As cosine similarity is at most 1, we introduce a relaxing hyperparameter $k_1 \in [0, \infty)$, to extend the possible magnitude range of the affinity function. One can apply random walk normalization to $k$ to construct the diffusion kernel. However, for stability and convergence reasons, we reformulate the diffusion kernel $a(u, v)$ between any two nodes (either adjacent or identical) as follows:

$$\begin{aligned} a(u,v) &= \left[k(u,v)/K_u\right] * \left[\sigma(\alpha(u)) * (1 - k_2) + k_2/2\right] \text{ if } u \neq v, \\ a(u,u) &= 1 - \left[\sigma(\alpha(u)) * (1 - k_2) + k_2/2\right] \end{aligned} \quad (6)$$

where $K_u = \sum_{v \in \mathcal{N}(u)} k(u,v)$, $\sigma$ denotes the sigmoid function, $k_2 \in [0,1]$ is an additional hyperparameter, and $\alpha(u) = \langle W(g_u), \alpha \rangle$, with $\alpha$ is a learnable vector of dimension $\dim(W(\mathcal{G}))$. We introduce $\alpha$ to also allow learnability into self-diffusion, which is necessary for the convergence of the diffusion process. $k_2$ here is used to control the possible range of $a(u,u)$, thereby preventing it becomes too "extreme". We would like to remark that $k_1$ and $k_2$ can be interpreted as regularization hyperparameters, as setting $k_1 = 0$ and $k_2 = 1$ recovers the standard random walk diffusion kernel for the unweighted version of the graph $G$.

Let $\mathbf{A} : \mathcal{G} \to (\mathcal{L}^2(G))^2$ be the operator which maps $g$ to a diffusion matrix $A$ of $g$. By definition, $A$ is left-stochastic. To enhance stability during the training process, we employ a multi-head attention mechanism analogous to that introduced in [25,26] by taking the average across the heads: $\mathbf{A}(g) = \frac{\sum_{k=0}^{h-1} \mathbf{A}_k(g)}{h}$. This matrix can then be used directly as diffusion operator $A = \mathbf{A}(g)$.

However, modeling the diffusion in graph neural networks (GNNs) as a continuous-time process has been shown to enhance both training stability and performance [27]. The same approach could thus be done for the above formula. One could discretize update step between two consecutive powers of $A$ by taking fractional temporal difference. Temporal discretization schemes for continuous process, such as Euler or Runge-Kutta, can be used for such purposes. A quick discussion of these schemes is given in the supplementary materials[1]. Further experiments are presented and discussed in Sect. 6.

### 5.2 Wavelets with Learnable Diffusion

The construction of wavelets, in general, relies on the framework of multiresolution analysis, which we have mentioned in Sect. 4.1. For such construction to be possible, the diffusion operator used must have a single limiting distribution. This condition is satisfied, as our diffusion operator $A$ above is irreducible (since the underlying domain $G$ is connected and $a(u,v) > 0$ if $(u,v) \in E$) and

---

[1] Supplementary materials are provided at https://github.com/toanvtran/learnable-diffusion-scattering.

aperiodic ($\exists u : A(u,u) > 0$). This is a basic result from the theory of Markov processes.

Having our multiresolution analysis, constructed using $A$ with the filters in Sect. 4.1, we can now obtain a wavelet decomposition operator $\Psi$ for the proposed adaptive scattering network. We now prove $\Psi$ is a frame analysis operator, i.e. it defines a frame. This ensures expressivity guarantees on the representation returned by $\Psi$. Notationally, $\langle x, y \rangle_{D_A} = x^T D_A y$ is a weighted inner product, where $D_A = \text{diag}(\pi_A)$ and $\pi_A$ are the stationary distribution of $A$. $\|\cdot\|_{D_A}$ refers to the weighted $\ell^2$-norm induced by this inner product. $\langle \cdot \rangle$ and $\|\cdot\|$ refers to the canonical inner product and $\ell^2$-norm, respectively.

**Proposition 1.** *On a connected domain $G$, let $\Psi$ be the wavelet decomposition operator on $\mathcal{L}^2(G)$ based on the non-negative matrix $A$ defined as above. Assume that for every $x \in \mathcal{L}^2(G)$ satisfying $\langle x, \pi_A \rangle_{D_A} = 0$, $\frac{\|Ax\|_{D_A}}{\|x\|_{D_A}} < 1$. Let $\beta_A = \inf_x (1 - \frac{\|Ax\|_{D_A}}{\|x\|_{D_A}})$. Then, there exists constants $M(\beta_A), N(\beta_A) > 0$ depending only on $\beta_A$ such that for any $x$ as above:*

$$M(\beta_A)\|x\|_{D_A}^2 \leq \sum_{j=0}^{J-1} \|\psi_j x\|_{D_A}^2 \leq N(\beta_A)\|x\|_{D_A}^2 \qquad (7)$$

The proof is presented in the supplementary materials. The existence of the two bounds is a necessary and sufficient condition that there exists a bounded inverse for each decomposition on the image space $\text{Im}(\Psi)$. This means $\Psi$ defines on $\mathcal{L}^2(G, \mu_{\pi_A})$ a complete and stable representation.

According to the general Perron-Frobenius theory, any irreducible and aperiodic matrix $A$ with non-negative elements has a unique eigenvector $\pi_A$ corresponding to its largest eigenvalue, 1, up to a constant multiple. Furthermore, the remaining eigenvalues of $A$, considered in the unitary space, have strictly smaller moduli. However, there is no guarantee that the orthogonal complements $M_{\pi_A}$ of span($\pi_A$) in $\mathcal{L}^2(G)$ will remain invariant under the action of $A$. As every signal which is a multiple of $\pi_A$ lose all of its information under the wavelet decomposition, to prevent unnecessary information loss, we would want to design $A$ such that $AM_{\pi_A} \subseteq M_{\pi_A}$. A straightforward family of matrices satisfying this property is the class of self-adjoint matrices. Ensuring symmetry in the affinity function $k$, as in our construction, is a sufficient condition for this.

It is also worth noting that the condition that $G$ be connected can be relaxed. Specifically, $G$ can consist of $p$ connected components that are pairwise disconnected, provided $p \ll |V| = n$. This condition is necessary because each component can have its own stationary distribution, making the subspace of stationary distributions of $A$ on $\mathcal{L}^2(G)$ of multiple dimensions, with a maximum dimension of $p$. Any signal in this subspace will lose all of its information upon applying $\Psi$, thus rendering $\Psi$ useless for such signals. For simplicity, we continue to consider the case where $G$ has only 1 connected component.

## 5.3 Graph Scattering Transform with Learnable Diffusion

We construct our adaptive variant of Graph Scattering Transform similarly to the one in Sect. 4.2 by replacing the fixed decomposition operator with the adaptive version we defined above. Additionally, we employ the average mean pooling operator $U$, which is independent of $A$: $Ux = \langle 1/\mathbf{n}, x \rangle$. In particular, on a connected graph $G$ with a graph signal $x$, the transformation at each layer is given by:

$$\phi_k = U(\rho\Psi)^k x = \left[ U \Pi_{i=0}^k (\rho \psi_{j_i})(x) \right]_{j_0, j_1, \dots, j_k} \qquad (8)$$
$$= [U\rho\psi_{j_k} \dots \rho\psi_{j_1} \rho\psi_{j_0} x]_{j_0, j_1, \dots, j_k}.$$

where $\{\psi_{j_i}\}_{j_i}$ are multiresolution filters constructed using the adaptive operator $A$. Thus, the scattering representation obtained from an $m$-layer network is:

$$\Phi(x) = [Ux, \phi_1(x), \dots, \phi_{m-1}(x)] = [Ux, U\rho\Psi x, \dots, U(\rho\Psi)^{m-1} x] \qquad (9)$$

In the following we provide the stability analysis of the adaptive graph scattering transforms using our learnable diffusion operators:

## 5.4 Stability Analysis

A robust and meaningful signal representation should exhibit stability to noise, meaning that a small change in the input signal yields proportionally small variations in the output representation. As mentioned in Sect. 4.1, the matrix $A$, being a random walk operator, naturally induces a graph-level diffusion distance. We begin by establishing the stability of the wavelet decomposition operator in the following lemma.

**Lemma 1.** *On two distinct graphs $G$ and $G'$ with $|V| = |V'| = n$, let $\Psi_G$ and $\Psi_{G'}$ be the wavelet decomposition operators induced from respectively $A_G$ and $A_{G'}$. Consider all signals $x$ with both $\frac{\|A_G x\|}{\|x\|}$ and $\frac{\|A_{G'} x\|}{\|x\|} < 1$. Let $\beta = \min\{\inf_x (1 - \frac{\|A_G x\|}{\|x\|}), \inf_x (1 - \frac{\|A_{G'} x\|}{\|x\|})\}$. Let $\delta_\pi = \max\{\min_i\{\pi_{A_G, i}\}, \min_j\{\pi_{A_{G'}, j}\}\}$. Assume that the spectra of $A_G$ and $-A_{G'}$ are disjoint, where every pair of eigenvalues are at least $\delta$ from each other. We have:*

$$\inf_{\Pi \in \Pi_n} \|\Psi_G - \Pi \Psi_{G'} \Pi^\mathsf{T}\| \le C_{A_G, A_{G'}} d_1(G, G') \qquad (10)$$

*where $d_1(G, G') = \inf_{\Pi \in \Pi_n} \left[ d(G, G', \Pi) + (1-\beta)^2 \|\pi_{A_G} - \Pi \pi_{A_{G'}} \Pi^{-1}\|_\infty \right]$, $C_{A_G, A_{G'}} = \frac{\sqrt{2C_1 + 4C_2}}{\delta_\pi}$, $C_1 = n \frac{\kappa(D_{A_G}) \kappa(D_{A_{G'}})}{\delta}^2$, $C_2 = \frac{(1-\beta)^2 (2 - 2\beta + \beta^2)}{(2\beta - \beta^2)^3}$, $D_A = \text{diag}(\pi_A)$, $\kappa(D_A) = \sqrt{\frac{\max_i \pi_A}{\min_i \pi_A}}$, and $d(G, G', \Pi)$ as presented in Sect. 4.1.*

The complete proof is presented in the supplementary materials. Since $A_G$ and $A'_G$ may not be symmetric with respect to the same weighted inner product, an additional term is introduced to measure the discrepancy between their stationary distributions. If this discrepancy is small, then the bound can be characterized as linear in $d(G, G')$, which is discussed in Sect. 4.1. This lemma serves as the primary tool in proving the next result, which establishes stability bounds for an $m$-layer graph scattering network under small perturbations to the graph structure:

**Theorem 1.** *Let $x \in \mathbb{R}^n$ and $\Phi_G(x)$ be the $m$-layer scattering representation of a signal $x$ on a graph $G$, and let $\Phi_{G'}(x)$ be the same respectively on graph $G'$. With the same assumption and notation as in Lemma 1, let $N = \max\{N(\beta_{A_G})\kappa(D_{A_G}), N(\beta_{A_{G'}})\kappa(D_{A_{G'}})\}$, $N(\beta_A)$ be as in Proposition 1. We have:*

$$\|\Phi_G(x) - \Phi_{G'}(x)\|^2 \leq \sum_{k=0}^{m-1} \left[kN^{k-1}C_{A_G,A_{G'}}d_1(G,G')\right]^2 \|x\|^2 \quad (11)$$

The proof is presented in detail in the supplementary materials. Theorem 1 provides the stability bound for the scattering representations of the same signal $x$ on two different graphs $G$ and $G'$. Each graph has its own multiresolution analysis, and if the distance $d_1(G, G')$ between the two graphs is small, then the discrepancy between the resulting representations will also be small. Since $m \leq 5$ in most applications (as the scattering energy rapidly diminishes in deeper layers with increasing $m$ [3], the change in the learnable scattering representations due to a small topological perturbation is effectively characterized by a linear dependence on $d_1(G, G')$.

### 5.5 Complexity

**Number of Parameters:** In this work, we adopt the traditional architecture of the scattering transform, where the same wavelet decomposition operator is used throughout, and all of its wavelets are generated from a single mother wavelet. Consequently, only one filter needs to be learned across the entire scattering network. The additional number of parameters compared to traditional scattering is $\mathcal{O}(KPH)$, where $K$ is the size of each descriptor, $P$ is the number of parameters in the mapping $W$, and $H$ is the number of heads. This does not depend on the size of the scattering network or the size of the graph $G$.

**Memory Requirement:** We consider a scattering network of $m$ layers, and each layer has $k$ wavelets. Since the model has to store the attributes in each wavelet scale for doing low-pass averaging and diffusion in subsequent layer, the memory requirement is $\mathcal{O}(Ck^mN)$, where $C$ is the number of input channels, $N = |V|$ is the number of graph nodes. Since $m$ and $k$ are predefined hyperparameters, with $m \leq 5$ in most applications, the memory requirement effectively scales linearly with the number of graph nodes.

## 6 Numerical Experiments

In this section, we empirically demonstrate the discriminative power of the scattering transform with learnable diffusion in classification tasks on two types of datasets: social networks and bioinformatics, particularly in low- to medium-data regimes. Our results show the method extends the scenarios where interpretable models are competitive to non-transparent deep learning methods in term of performance.

**Table 1.** Classification accuracies as a function of percentage of training data used in the social network dataset (IMDB-BINARY) and the bioinformatics dataset (MUTAG). The highest, second-highest, and third-highest accuracies are highlighted in blue, orange, and red, respectively.

| | Training amount | Deep learning | | Traditional scattering | | Ours |
|---|---|---|---|---|---|---|
| | | GIN-0 (MLP-sum) | UGformer | GS-SVM | GSN +MLP | LD-GSN +MLP |
| IMDB-BINARY | $1\%_{(10)}$ | $58.52 \pm 5.37$ | $56.96 \pm 2.33$ | $59.81 \pm 5.27$ | $60.21 \pm 4.17$ | $63.03 \pm 3.70$ |
| | $2.5\%_{(25)}$ | $63.45 \pm 7.18$ | $60.71 \pm 3.63$ | $61.27 \pm 3.45$ | $62.79 \pm 3.15$ | $65.17 \pm 3.20$ |
| | $5\%_{(50)}$ | $65.40 \pm 2.07$ | $64.52 \pm 2.15$ | $61.88 \pm 1.98$ | $64.70 \pm 2.40$ | $66.83 \pm 1.96$ |
| | $7.5\%_{(75)}$ | $67.63 \pm 1.47$ | $65.99 \pm 1.93$ | $63.45 \pm 1.68$ | $64.84 \pm 1.64$ | $68.15 \pm 2.06$ |
| | $10\%_{(100)}$ | $68.36 \pm 1.52$ | $67.92 \pm 0.94$ | $65.62 \pm 2.93$ | $65.15 \pm 1.99$ | $68.58 \pm 1.02$ |
| | $20\%_{(200)}$ | $70.51 \pm 0.97$ | $70.20 \pm 0.92$ | $66.46 \pm 1.56$ | $66.56 \pm 3.43$ | $70.90 \pm 4.63$ |
| MUTAG | $2\%_{(3)}$ | $70.90 \pm 3.24$ | $68.82 \pm 7.35$ | $70.08 \pm 2.74$ | $70.55 \pm 2.72$ | $71.85 \pm 4.36$ |
| | $2.5\%_{(4)}$ | $71.78 \pm 3.40$ | $69.28 \pm 8.93$ | $71.65 \pm 2.95$ | $71.11 \pm 1.98$ | $72.87 \pm 2.52$ |
| | $5\%_{(9)}$ | $75.51 \pm 3.20$ | $72.41 \pm 2.25$ | $72.84 \pm 3.56$ | $74.86 \pm 3.47$ | $77.08 \pm 3.85$ |
| | $7.5\%_{(14)}$ | $77.89 \pm 3.07$ | $76.84 \pm 3.15$ | $75.24 \pm 2.61$ | $75.63 \pm 3.17$ | $79.41 \pm 2.77$ |
| | $10\%_{(18)}$ | $79.04 \pm 3.81$ | $78.91 \pm 2.78$ | $75.47 \pm 2.61$ | $77.24 \pm 3.80$ | $80.83 \pm 3.17$ |
| | $20\%_{(37)}$ | $82.98 \pm 2.34$ | $80.50 \pm 3.13$ | $77.11 \pm 2.27$ | $79.51 \pm 2.22$ | $81.51 \pm 2.36$ |

* Percentage of dataset used for training, followed by the actual number of samples

We conduct experiments on well-known social network and bioinformatics datasets as described in [17]. To maintain consistency with our theoretical framework, we restrict our experiments to 2 datasets comprising connected graphs, namely, IMDB-BINARY and MUTAG, and perform graph-level classification on them with varying amounts of training data. A detailed description of these datasets is provided in the supplementary materials. For each node $u$, the descriptor $g_u$ is chosen to be a vector consisting of topological features of $u$ and its neighborhood: degree, eccentricity, clustering coefficient, number of triangles contains $u$ as a vertex, core number, clique number, and PageRank. While MUTAG provides intrinsic node features, which can be used as input to the diffusion process, we use the descriptors as proxies for the featureless IMDB-BINARY dataset.

Some discussion on the alternative usage of node features in place of descriptor can also be found in the supplementary materials.

For the classification task, we employ a model that integrates our learnable diffusion graph scattering network as a feature extractor with a simple MLP as the classifier, denoted as LD-GSN+MLP. Using the MLP allows the learning of the kernel weights in our model via backpropagation. As a baseline, we implement the same architecture but with a lazy random walk operator $\frac{1}{2}(I+WD^{-1})$, referred to as GSN+MLP. We compared our method against traditional scattering methods (GSN+MLP, GS-SVM [11]), graph transformer (UGformer [19]), and graph neural network (GIN-0 (MLP-sum) [29]). These models were chosen for their publicly available implementations.

**Performance:** Table 1 presents classification accuracy as a function of training data percentage, with the rest used for validation. Further experimental details are provided in the supplementary materials. As expected, increasing training data generally improves accuracy across all models. LD-GSN+MLP consistently outperforms competitors, whether when traditional scattering surpasses deep learning or when deep models regain dominance with more data. The only exception is MUTAG at 20% training data, where deep learning begins to recover its advantage. LD-GSN ranks second, with a statistically minimal gap to the top-performing GIN-0.

LD-GSN benefits from the stability of scattering networks while improving adaptability through learnable diffusion, regulated via parameters introduced in Sect. 5.1. This adaptivity, shown by our experiments, results in a consistent performance advantage over both deep learning and traditional scattering approaches in low to medium data regimes, further expanding the applicability of interpretable models for graph data.

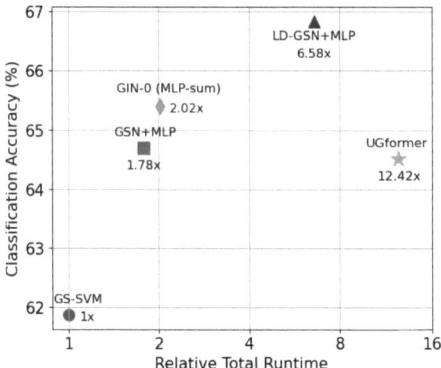

**Fig. 2.** Total running time versus classification accuracy on IMDB-BINARY with 2.5% data for training.

**Running Time:** We compare the end-to-end runtime of the five models using 2.5% of IMDB-BINARY as training data on an NVIDIA A100 40 GB GPU

(Fig. 2, logarithmic scale). GIN-0, UGformer, and LD-GSN+MLP require adding node features, while GS-SVM and GSN+MLP also extract scattering representations. Neural networks train for 200 epochs, whereas GS-SVM is fitted once. LD-GSN+MLP runs ≈3.5× slower than GSN+MLP and GIN-0 due to backpropagation through the scattering architecture but achieves significantly higher accuracy.

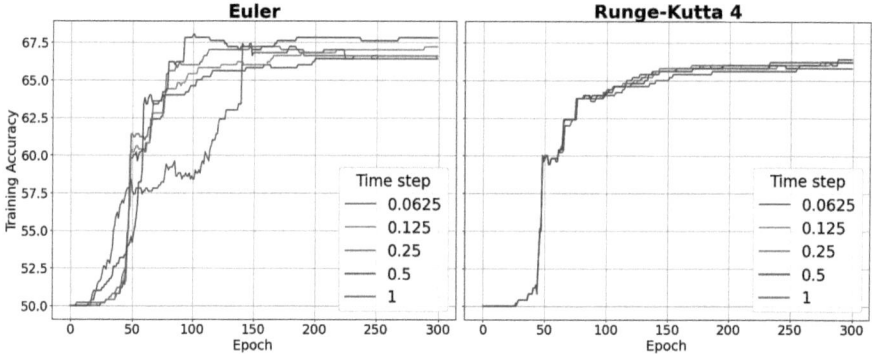

**Fig. 3.** Training accuracies as a function of epoch for different time step and approximation scheme choices on IMDB-BINARY with otherwise same configuration and initialization.

**Effect of Temporal Discretization Schemes:** As mentioned in Sect. 5.1, the diffusion process can be modeled as a continuous one. We perform additional experiments to investigate how the choice of time step or temporal discretization schemes affect the stability of the training process (Fig. 3). Increasing the time step or employing discretization schemes with higher numerical accuracy improves the numerical precision of each weight update, resulting in a more stable and refined training curve, similarly to adjusting the learning rate. However, in our case, due to the highly non-convex nature of the optimization problem, this does not necessarily translate to better performance as observed in [27] for linear GCNs. A balance should be achieved between stability and the ability to escape local minima. Consequently, we treat the time step as a hyperparameter in our experiments.

## 7 Conclusions

In this work, we introduced a framework to incorporate learnable diffusion into a graph scattering network, allowing for data-driven feature extraction. The model is mathematically interpretable, with expressivity and stability guarantees maintained. We show that our approach expands the scenarios where scattering architectures are competitive with deep learning in terms of performance and reduce the performance gap between well-understood and non-transparent learning paradigms on larger data regimes, via graph classification experiments on social network and bioinformatics datasets.

Our results open up several promising research directions. One is to explore more designs of learnable operators beyond the self-adjoint constraint. Another is developing scattering-based models with interpretable later modules, akin to the Euclidean case, while integrating learnable diffusion into the scattering transform. For completeness, we note that preliminary experiments on much larger data regimes, which are not discussed in detail here, indicate that the current scattering framework does not maintain a performance advantage compared to deep learning in those settings and is still outperformed by a significant, albeit narrowed, margin. We leave further investigation to future work.

**Acknowledgments.** Computing resources were sponsored by Intelligent Integration Co., Ltd. (INT2), Viet Nam. We thank the reviewers and meta-reviewer for their insightful suggestions which contributed to improving this paper.

**Disclosure of Interests.** The authors have no competing interests to declare that are relevant to the content of this article, beyond the computing resources provided by INT2, already acknowledged above.

# References

1. Belkin, M., Niyogi, P.: Laplacian eigenmaps for dimensionality reduction and data representation. Neural Comput. **15**(6), 1373–1396 (2003)
2. Bronstein, A.M., Bronstein, M.M., Kimmel, R., Mahmoudi, M., Sapiro, G.: A Gromov-Hausdorff framework with diffusion geometry for topologically-robust non-rigid shape matching. Int. J. Comput. Vis. **89**(2), 266–286 (2010)
3. Bruna, J., Mallat, S.: Invariant scattering convolution networks. IEEE Trans. Pattern Anal. Mach. Intell. **35**(8), 1872–1886 (2013)
4. Chamberlain, B., Rowbottom, J., Gorinova, M.I., Bronstein, M., Webb, S., Rossi, E.: Grand: graph neural diffusion. In: International Conference on Machine Learning, pp. 1407–1418. PMLR (2021)
5. Coifman, R.R., Lafon, S.: Diffusion maps. Appl. Comput. Harmon. Anal. **21**(1), 5–30 (2006)
6. Coifman, R.R., Maggioni, M.: Diffusion wavelets. Appl. Comput. Harmonic Anal. **21**(1), 53–94 (2006). Special Issue: Diffusion Maps and Wavelets
7. Coifman, R., et al.: Geometric diffusions as a tool for harmonic analysis and structure definition of data: diffusion maps. PNAS **102**(21) (2005)
8. Coifman, R., et al.: Geometric diffusions as a tool for harmonic analysis and structure definition of data: multiscale methods. PNAS **102**(21) (2005)
9. Gama, F., Ribeiro, A., Bruna, J.: Diffusion scattering transforms on graphs. In: International Conference on Learning Representations (2019)
10. Gama, F., Ribeiro, A., Bruna, J.: Stability of graph scattering transforms. In: Advances in Neural Information Processing Systems, vol. 32 (2019)
11. Gao, F., Wolf, G., Hirn, M.: Geometric scattering for graph data analysis. In: International Conference on Machine Learning, pp. 2122–2131. PMLR (2019)

12. Guth, F., Zarka, J., Mallat, S.: Phase collapse in neural networks. In: International Conference on Learning Representations (2022)
13. Hammond, D.K., Vandergheynst, P., Gribonval, R.: Wavelets on graphs via spectral graph theory. Appl. Comput. Harmon. Anal. **30**(2), 129–150 (2011)
14. Kipf, T.N., Welling, M.: Semi-supervised classification with graph convolutional networks. In: 5th International Conference on Learning Representations, ICLR 2017, Toulon, France, 24–26 April 2017, Conference Track Proceedings. OpenReview.net (2017)
15. Mallat, S.: Group invariant scattering. Commun. Pure Appl. Math. **65**(10), 1331–1398 (2012)
16. Mallat, S.: A Wavelet Tour of Signal Processing, Third Edition: The Sparse Way, 3rd edn. Academic Press Inc., USA (2008)
17. Morris, C., Kriege, N.M., Bause, F., Kersting, K., Mutzel, P., Neumann, M.: Tudataset: a collection of benchmark datasets for learning with graphs. In: ICML 2020 Workshop on Graph Representation Learning and Beyond (GRL+ 2020) (2020)
18. Nadler, B., Lafon, S., Kevrekidis, I., Coifman, R.: Diffusion maps, spectral clustering and eigenfunctions of Fokker-Planck operators. In: Advances in Neural Information Processing Systems, vol. 18 (2005)
19. Nguyen, D.Q., Nguyen, T.D., Phung, D.: Universal graph transformer self-attention networks. In: Companion Proceedings of the Web Conference 2022, pp. 193–196 (2022)
20. Oyallon, E., Zagoruyko, S., Huang, G., Komodakis, N., Lacoste-Julien, S., Blaschko, M., Belilovsky, E.: Scattering networks for hybrid representation learning. IEEE Trans. Pattern Anal. Mach. Intell. **41**(9), 2208–2221 (2018)
21. Rudin, W.: Real and Complex Analysis, 3rd edn. McGraw-Hill Inc., USA (1987)
22. Shuman, D.I., Wiesmeyr, C., Holighaus, N., Vandergheynst, P.: Spectrum-adapted tight graph wavelet and vertex-frequency frames. IEEE Trans. Signal Process. **63**(16), 4223–4235 (2015)
23. Sun, C., Hu, J., Gu, H., Chen, J., Yang, M.: Adaptive graph diffusion networks (2022). https://arxiv.org/abs/2012.15024
24. Tong, A., et al.: Learnable filters for geometric scattering modules. IEEE Trans. Signal Process. (2024)
25. Vaswani, A., et al.: Attention is all you need. In: Guyon, I., et al. (eds.) Advances in Neural Information Processing Systems, vol. 30. Curran Associates, Inc. (2017)
26. Veličković, P., Cucurull, G., Casanova, A., Romero, A., Liò, P., Bengio, Y.: Graph attention networks. In: International Conference on Learning Representations (2018)
27. Wang, Y., Wang, Y., Yang, J., Lin, Z.: Dissecting the diffusion process in linear graph convolutional networks. In: Advances in Neural Information Processing Systems, vol. 34, pp. 5758–5769 (2021)
28. Weiss, Y.: Segmentation using eigenvectors: a unifying view. In: Proccedings of the Seventh IEEE International Conference on Computer Vision, vol. 2, pp. 975–982 (1999). https://doi.org/10.1109/ICCV.1999.790354
29. Xu, K., Hu, W., Leskovec, J., Jegelka, S.: How powerful are graph neural networks? In: International Conference on Learning Representations (2018)
30. Zarka, J., Guth, F., Mallat, S.: Separation and concentration in deep networks. In: 9th International Conference on Learning Representations, ICLR 2021 (2021)
31. Zarka, J., Thiry, L., Angles, T., Mallat, S.: Deep network classification by scattering and homotopy dictionary learning. In: 8th International Conference on Learning Representations, ICLR 2020 (2020)

32. Zhao, J., Dong, Y., Ding, M., Kharlamov, E., Tang, J.: Adaptive diffusion in graph neural networks. In: Advances in Neural Information Processing Systems, vol. 34, pp. 23321–23333 (2021)
33. Zou, D., Lerman, G.: Graph convolutional neural networks via scattering. arXiv preprint arXiv:1804.00099 (2018)

# Subgraph Gaussian Embedding Contrast for Self-supervised Graph Representation Learning

Shifeng Xie[ID], Aref Einizade[ID], and Jhony H. Giraldo[✉][ID]

LTCI, Télécom Paris, Institut Polytechnique de Paris, Palaiseau, France
{shifeng.xie,aref.einizade,jhony.giraldo}@telecom-paris.fr

**Abstract.** Graph Representation Learning (GRL) is a fundamental task in machine learning, aiming to encode high-dimensional graph-structured data into low-dimensional vectors. Self-Supervised Learning (SSL) methods are widely used in GRL because they can avoid expensive human annotation. In this work, we propose a novel Subgraph Gaussian Embedding Contrast (SubGEC) method. Our approach introduces a subgraph Gaussian embedding module, which adaptively maps subgraphs to a structured Gaussian space, ensuring the preservation of input subgraph characteristics while generating subgraphs with a controlled distribution. We then employ optimal transport distances, more precisely the Wasserstein and Gromov-Wasserstein distances, to effectively measure the similarity between subgraphs, enhancing the robustness of the contrastive learning process. Extensive experiments across multiple benchmarks demonstrate that SubGEC outperforms or presents competitive performance against state-of-the-art approaches. Our findings provide insights into the design of SSL methods for GRL, emphasizing the importance of the distribution of the generated contrastive pairs.

**Keywords:** Subgraph Gaussian embeddings · graph representation learning · self-supervised learning · optimal transport

## 1 Introduction

Graph Representation Learning (GRL) is a fundamental task in machine learning and data mining, aiming to encode high-dimensional, sparse graph-structured data into low-dimensional dense vectors [25]. Effective GRL techniques enable downstream applications such as node classification, link prediction, and community detection. Self-Supervised Learning (SSL) has emerged as a promising approach for GRL by reducing the dependence on extensive human annotation [22]. Among SSL methods, contrastive learning has gained significant attention due to its ability to learn meaningful representations by distinguishing similarities and differences among data samples. In contrastive learning, positive sample pairs typically consist of two augmented views of the same data point, which

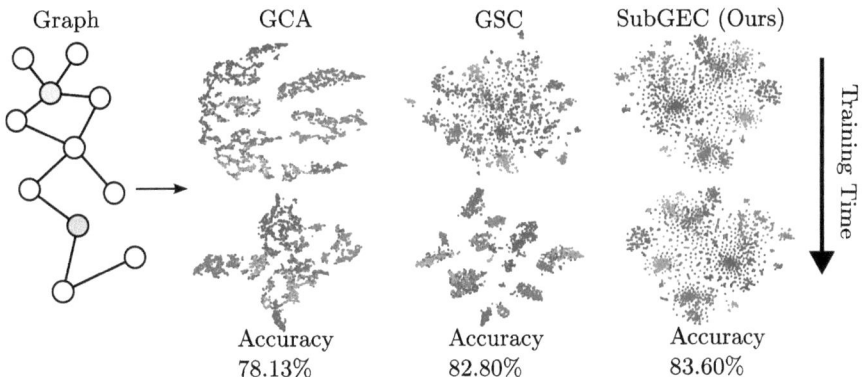

**Fig. 1.** t-stochastic neighbor embedding (t-SNE) visualizations of previous graph representation learning methods based on contrastive learning: GCA [53], GSC [17], and our method SubGEC. Each point corresponds to a node representation with reduced dimensionality, with colors indicating classes. Unlike GCA and GSC, which exhibit sharp boundaries, SubGEC maps node representations into a dense, uniform, and linearly separable space.

should be mapped close in the representation space, whereas negative sample pairs are formed by comparing different data points [5].

Existing graph-based contrastive learning methods primarily generate positive and negative pairs through structural perturbations [41,52,53] or learnable transformations [17,54]. However, Fig. 1 shows t-stochastic neighbor embedding (t-SNE) visualizations of previous SSL methods, such as GCA [53] and GSC [17], where we observe uneven node distributions, sharp boundaries, and erroneous clusters. These issues suggest that existing approaches struggle to maintain smooth and meaningful representations, negatively impacting their performance in GRL tasks.

In this paper, we propose the **Sub**graph **G**aussian **E**mbedding **C**ontrast (SubGEC) model, a novel framework for graph contrastive learning. Our method introduces the Subgraph Gaussian Embedding (SGE) module, which maps input subgraphs to a structured Gaussian space, ensuring that the output features follow a Gaussian distribution using Kullback–Leibler (KL) divergence. This learnable mapping effectively controls the distribution of embeddings, improving representation quality. The generated subgraphs are then paired with the original subgraphs to form positive and negative contrastive pairs, and similarity is measured using Optimal Transport (OT) distances. By leveraging the Wasserstein and Gromov-Wasserstein distances, our approach enhances robustness and mitigates mode collapse (also called positive collapse [24]), where the embeddings shrink into a low-dimensional subspace, by controlling the embedding distribution.

Gaussian distributions provide several properties that make them useful in SSL for graphs. For example, they preserve important mathematical structures, such as displacement interpolation, which helps in clustering and interpolation tasks [13,51]. Gaussian smoothing also improves robustness by reducing noise and stabilizing learned representations [13]. Additionally, their simple parameterization using means and covariances makes them computationally efficient, enabling scalability to high-dimensional spaces while avoiding excessive computational costs [6,51]. These properties make Gaussian-based OT a valuable tool in fields such as machine learning, physics, and statistical inference [10]. In this work, we theoretically and empirically prove the benefits of using Gaussian embeddings in contrastive learning.

The primary contributions of this paper are as follows:

- We introduce SubGEC, a novel framework that outperforms or remains competitive with state-of-the-art methods across eight benchmark datasets.
- We theoretically and empirically highlight the importance of mapping the distribution of contrastive pairs into a Gaussian space and analyze its impact on GRL.
- We conduct extensive ablation and validation studies to demonstrate the effectiveness of each component of SubGEC.

## 2 Related Work

GRL has gained significant attention due to its ability to encode structured data into meaningful representations. Here, we review the recent advancements in Graph Neural Networks (GNNs), SSL on graphs, and contrastive learning techniques.

**GNNs** [49] have been widely adopted for learning representations that capture both node features and graph topology [25]. Several architectures have been proposed to improve their learning capabilities. For example, Graph Convolutional Networks (GCNs) [29] leverage a simplification of graph filters to aggregate information from neighboring nodes. GraphSAGE [16] introduced an inductive learning framework with multiple aggregation functions, enabling generalization to unseen nodes. Furthermore, Graph Attention Networks (GAT) [47] integrate attention mechanisms to dynamically weigh node relationships, improving feature propagation. However, these models require supervised training.

**SSL on graphs** aims to design and solve learning tasks that do not require labeled data, avoiding costly supervised learning methodologies. Based on how these tasks are defined, SSL methods can be categorized into two main types: *predictive* and *contrastive* approaches.

Predictive methods focus on learning useful representations by generating perturbed versions of the input graph. For example, BGRL [41] learns node representations by encoding two perturbed versions of a graph using an online encoder and a target encoder. The online encoder is optimized to predict the target encoder's representation, while the target encoder is updated as an exponential moving average of the online encoder. BNLL [33] improves upon BGRL by introducing additional positive node pairs based on a homophily assumption, where neighboring nodes tend to share the same label. This is achieved by incorporating cosine similarity between a node's online representation and the weighted target representations of its neighbors. VGAE [28] adopts a variational autoencoder framework to reconstruct the input graph and its features.

**Contrastive methods**, which are the focus of this paper, generally outperform predictive methods in SSL for graphs. These methods can be classified based on how data pairs are defined: node-to-node, graph-to-graph, and node-to-graph comparisons. For example, GRACE [52] generates two perturbed graph views and applies contrastive learning at the node level. MUSE [50] refines this approach by extracting multiple embeddings—semantic, contextual, and fused—to enhance node-to-node contrastive learning. However, node-level contrastive learning is often suboptimal as it struggles to capture the overall structural information of the graph.

At the subgraph level, DGI [46] employs node-to-graph contrast, where it extracts node embeddings from the original and perturbed graphs and adjusts their agreement levels using a readout function. Spectral polynomial filter methods like GPR-GNN [7] and ChebNetII [19] offer greater flexibility than GCNs by adapting to different homophily levels. However, they often underperform when used as encoders for traditional SSL methods. To address this, PolyGCL [4] constrains polynomial filter expressiveness to construct high-pass and low-pass graph views while using a simple linear combination strategy for optimization. Unlike DGI, PolyGCL applies this contrastive approach to both high- and low-frequency embeddings extracted with shared-weight polynomial filters.

Subg-Con [23] extends DGI by performing contrastive learning at the subgraph level. It selects anchor nodes and extracts subgraphs using the personalized PageRank algorithm, adjusting the agreement between anchor nodes and their corresponding subgraphs for positive and negative pairs. However, methods like DGI and Subg-Con rely on a readout embedding to represent entire graphs, which disregards structural information. GSC [17] addresses this limitation by applying subgraph-level contrast using Wasserstein and Gromov-Wasserstein distances from OT to measure subgraph similarity, ensuring a more structurally-aware contrastive learning process. From another point of view, FOSSIL [38] uses the fused Gromow-Wasserstein distance [2,42] in the loss function to benefit from both node and subgraph-level features.

SubGEC leverages OT distance metrics to effectively measure subgraph dissimilarity as in [17]. However, unlike previous OT-based models such as GSC [17], our approach introduces a novel mapping of subgraphs into a structured Gaussian space. This design choice is driven by the properties of Gaussian embeddings, which enhance representation quality. Our work provides both theoretical justification and empirical validation for the effectiveness of this approach.

## 3 Preliminaries

### 3.1 Mathematical Notation

Consider an undirected graph $G = (\mathcal{V}, \mathcal{E})$ with vertex set $\mathcal{V}$ and edge set $\mathcal{E}$. The feature matrix $\mathbf{X} = [\mathbf{x}_1, \ldots, \mathbf{x}_N]^\top \in \mathbb{R}^{N \times C}$ contains node features $\mathbf{x}_i \in \mathbb{R}^C$, where $N$ is the number of nodes and $C$ is the feature dimension. The adjacency matrix $\mathbf{A} \in \mathbb{R}^{N \times N}$ represents the graph topology, and $\mathbf{D}$ is the diagonal degree matrix. For the $i$-th node, let $G^i = (\mathcal{V}^i, \mathcal{E}^i)$ be its induced Breadth-First Search [3] (BFS) subgraph with $k^i$ nodes with adjacency matrix $\mathbf{A}^i \in \mathbb{R}^{k^i \times k^i}$ and feature matrix $\mathbf{X}^i \in \mathbb{R}^{k^i \times C}$. Our method embeds this subgraph (with the same sets of nodes and edges) producing adjacency matrix $\tilde{\mathbf{A}}^i$ and feature matrix $\tilde{\mathbf{X}}^i \in \mathbb{R}^{k^i \times F}$. In this work, we preserve the subgraph topology, so that $\tilde{\mathbf{A}}^i = \mathbf{A}^i$.

The KL divergence [44] is an asymmetry measure between two probability distributions $P$ and $Q$. It quantifies the informational loss that occurs when distribution $Q$ is utilized to approximate distribution $P$. The KL divergence is defined as:

$$D_{KL}(P\|Q) = \sum_{x \in \mathcal{X}} P(x) \log\left(\frac{P(x)}{Q(x)}\right), \quad (1)$$

where $P(x)$ and $Q(x)$ are the probability masses of $P$ and $Q$ at each point $x$ in the sample space $\mathcal{X}$.

### 3.2 Problem Formulation for Self-supervised Graph Representation

The goal of self-supervised graph representation learning is to learn graph embeddings $\mathbf{R}$ through an encoder $\varepsilon: \mathbb{R}^{N \times N} \times \mathbb{R}^{N \times C} \to \mathbb{R}^{N \times F}$, where $\mathbf{R} = \varepsilon(\mathbf{A}, \mathbf{X}; \boldsymbol{\theta})$ is parametrized by some learnable parameters $\boldsymbol{\theta}$ and $F$ represents the dimension of the embeddings (representation). This procedure is unsupervised, i.e., it does not use labels. In this paper, $\varepsilon(\cdot)$ is a GNN [25], aiming to effectively capture both the graph's feature and topology information within the representation space.

### 3.3 Optimal Transport Distance

The Wasserstein distance [37], commonly used in OT, serves as a robust metric to compare the probability distributions defined over metric spaces. For subgraphs $G^i$ and $G^j$, their corresponding feature matrices are denoted as $\mathbf{X}^i \in \mathbb{R}^{k^i \times C}$ and $\mathbf{X}^j \in \mathbb{R}^{k^j \times C}$. $\mathbf{x}_m^i \in \mathbb{R}^C$ and $\mathbf{x}_n^j \in \mathbb{R}^C$ respectively denote the feature vector of the $m$-th and $n$-th node in the subgraphs $G^i$ and $G^j$, where $m = 1, 2, \ldots, k^i$ and $n = 1, 2, \ldots, k^j$. The $r$-Wasserstein distance between the feature distributions of these subgraphs is defined as [30, 48]:

$$W_r(\mathbf{X}^i, \mathbf{X}^j) := \left(\min_{\mathbf{T} \in \pi(u,v)} \sum_{m=1}^{k^i} \sum_{n=1}^{k^j} \mathbf{T}_{(m,n)} d(\mathbf{x}_m^i, \mathbf{x}_n^j)^r\right)^{\frac{1}{r}}, \quad (2)$$

where $\pi(u, v)$ represents the set of all valid possible transport plans with probability distributions $u$ and $v$ responsible for generating $\mathbf{x}_m^i$ and $\mathbf{x}_n^j$, respectively. These distributions capture the node feature distributions in subgraphs $G^i$ and $G^j$. The matrix $\mathbf{T} \in \pi(u, v)$ is the OT plan that matches the node pairs of the

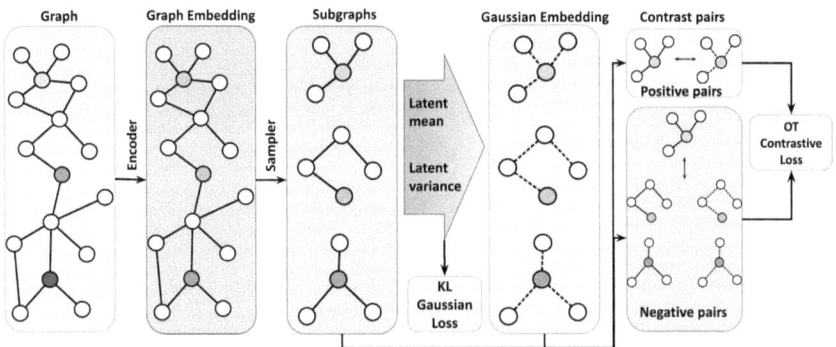

**Fig. 2.** Overview of the SubGEC method. Our model employs a graph encoder to obtain graph embeddings. We randomly select a set of nodes and then extract corresponding subgraphs using BFS sampling. Therefore, we use the proposed subgraph Gaussian embedding module using a KL loss to generate contrastive samples. Finally, we leverage OT distances for contrastive learning.

two subgraphs. $\mathbf{T}_{(m,n)}$ is value of the transportation plan between nodes $m$ and $n$, and $d(\mathbf{x}_m^i, \mathbf{x}_n^j)$ represents a valid distance metric.

Similarly, the Gromov-Wasserstein distance [1,45] extends this idea to compare graph-structured data, where internal distances between nodes are taken into account. For two subgraphs $G^i$ and $G^j$ with adjacency matrices $\mathbf{A}^i$ and $\mathbf{A}^j$, and feature matrices $\mathbf{X}^i$ and $\mathbf{X}^j$, the Gromov-Wasserstein distance is defined as [45]:

$$GW_r(\mathbf{A}^i, \mathbf{A}^j, \mathbf{X}^i, \mathbf{X}^j)$$
$$:= \left( \min_{\mathbf{T} \in \pi(u,v)} \sum_{m,\tilde{m},n,\tilde{n}} \mathbf{T}_{(m,n)} \mathbf{T}_{(\tilde{m},\tilde{n})} \left| d(\mathbf{x}_m^i, \mathbf{x}_{\tilde{m}}^i)^r - d(\mathbf{x}_n^j, \mathbf{x}_{\tilde{n}}^j)^r \right| \right)^{\frac{1}{r}}, \quad (3)$$

where $d(\mathbf{x}_m^i, \mathbf{x}_{\tilde{m}}^i)$ and $d(\mathbf{x}_n^j, \mathbf{x}_{\tilde{n}}^j)$ represent valid distance metrics between node pairs $(m, \tilde{m})$ in subgraph $G^i$, and $(n, \tilde{n})$ in subgraph $G^j$, respectively. Note that the node neighborhoods are considered by the term $\mathbf{T}$, thus relying on the graph topology.

In this work, for both the Wasserstein and Gromov-Wasserstein distances, we set $r = 1$ and define $d(\mathbf{x}_m^i, \mathbf{x}_n^j) = \exp\left(-\frac{\langle \mathbf{x}_m^i, \mathbf{x}_n^j \rangle}{\tau}\right)$, where $\langle \cdot, \cdot \rangle$ denotes the cosine similarity between node features, and $\tau$ is a temperature parameter.

## 4 Subgraph Gaussian Embedding Contrast (SubGEC)

Figure 2 shows an overview of our methodology, where our process begins with an encoder of the input graph. Subsequently, we obtain subgraphs utilizing BFS sampling. The embedded node representations within these subgraphs are thus embedded into a Gaussian latent space, enforced by the KL divergence regularization. Finally, we use the Wasserstein and Gromov-Wasserstein distances to measure the dissimilarities in the subgraphs for contrastive learning. Our methodology is described in more detail in the following sections.

### 4.1 Graph Encoder

We begin by employing a graph encoder to preprocess the graph data [17,27]. The output feature matrix of the graph encoder is the desired graph representation. The graph encoder comprises some graph convolution layers. Further details on the implementation of these layers are provided in the Appendix A.

### 4.2 Subgraph Gaussian Embedding (SGE)

Constructing positive and negative pairs is crucial in graph contrastive learning [26]. The SGE module offers diversity to prevent mode collapse [24]. It also avoids generated subgraphs from becoming overly similar to the input subgraphs [14]. The SGE module comprises a GraphSAGE [16,31] network and then two GAT [47] models, representing the mean and variance for the KL loss. The first step in SGE is as follows:

$$\mathbf{H}_{\text{GSA}} = \text{GraphSAGE}\left(\mathbf{H}_{\text{conv}}, \mathbf{A}\right), \tag{4}$$

where $\mathbf{H}_{\text{conv}}$ represents the output of the graph encoder. Following GraphSAGE, GAT employs its attention mechanism to assign weights to the relationships between each node and its neighbors. The hidden means and variances are managed by separate GAT networks and processed as follows:

$$\boldsymbol{\mu} = \text{GAT}_{\mu}\left(\mathbf{H}_{\text{GSA}}, \mathbf{A}\right), \quad \log \boldsymbol{\sigma} = \text{GAT}_{\sigma}\left(\mathbf{H}_{\text{GSA}}, \mathbf{A}\right). \tag{5}$$

In this configuration, $\boldsymbol{\mu}$ and $\log \boldsymbol{\sigma}$ are matrices of mean and variance vectors $\boldsymbol{\mu}_i$ and $\boldsymbol{\sigma}_i$ for $i = 1, \ldots, N$, respectively. In our approach, the embedded matrix $\tilde{\mathbf{X}}$ is generated using the reparametrization trick [28] to facilitate the differentiation and optimization of our model as follows:

$$\tilde{\mathbf{X}} = \boldsymbol{\mu} + \boldsymbol{\sigma} \odot \boldsymbol{\epsilon}, \tag{6}$$

where $\odot$ states the element-wise multiplication, and the matrix $\boldsymbol{\epsilon} = [\boldsymbol{\epsilon}_1, \ldots, \boldsymbol{\epsilon}_N]^\top$, where $\boldsymbol{\epsilon}_i \sim \mathcal{N}(\mathbf{0}, \mathbf{I})$ for $i = 1, \ldots, N$, represents Gaussian (normal) noise.

### 4.3 Kullback-Leibler Gaussian Regularization Loss

In our approach, we introduce a regularization to the SGE module to guide the embedded subgraph node features toward a Gaussian distribution. This regularization is implemented using the KL divergence. The prior $p(\tilde{\mathbf{X}}) = \prod_{i=1}^{N} p(\tilde{\mathbf{x}}_i)$ is taken as a product of independent normal distributions for each latent variable

$\tilde{\mathbf{x}}_i$, i.e., the embedded feature vector of the $i$-th node. Similarly, by benefiting from Gaussianity on the posterior distribution $q(\tilde{\mathbf{x}}_i|\mathbf{X},\mathbf{A}) = \mathcal{N}(\boldsymbol{\mu}_i, \text{diag}(\boldsymbol{\sigma}_i^2))$ [29], we express it on the whole data as:

$$q(\tilde{\mathbf{X}}|\mathbf{X},\mathbf{A}) = \prod_{i=1}^{N} q(\tilde{\mathbf{x}}_i|\mathbf{X},\mathbf{A}) = \prod_{i=1}^{N} \mathcal{N}(\boldsymbol{\mu}_i, \text{diag}(\boldsymbol{\sigma}_i^2)), \tag{7}$$

where $\text{diag}(\mathbf{a})$ is a diagonal matrix with the elements of the vector $\mathbf{a}$ on its main diagonal, and $\boldsymbol{\sigma}_i^2$ obtains by element-wise power operation on the vector. The expression for the regularization then simplifies to (details in the Appendix B):

$$\mathcal{L}_R = \beta \, \text{KL}\left(q(\tilde{\mathbf{X}}|\mathbf{X},\mathbf{A}) \| p(\tilde{\mathbf{X}})\right). \tag{8}$$

Here, $\beta$ is a hyperparameter modulating the influence of the regularization term relative to the contrastive loss, which we introduce in Sect. 4.4, enabling precise control over the balance between data fidelity and distribution alignment.

### 4.4 Optimal Transport Contrastive and Model Loss

In terms of the architectures available for the contrastive learning loss function, options include the Siamese network loss [18], the triplet loss [20], and the noise contrastive estimation loss [15]. Given the presence of multiple sets of negative pairs in our model, we opt for the InfoNCE loss [34]. Our contrastive loss function integrates the Wasserstein and Gromov-Wasserstein distances into the InfoNCE loss formulation [34], addressing the complexities of graph-based data. The Wasserstein distance captures feature distribution representation within subgraphs. Furthermore, the Gromov-Wasserstein distance captures structural discrepancies, providing a topology-aware similarity measure. We define $W_{(\tau)}(\mathbf{X}^i, \tilde{\mathbf{X}}^i) := W(\mathbf{X}^i, \tilde{\mathbf{X}}^i)/\tau$, and $GW_{(\tau)}(\mathbf{A}^i, \mathbf{X}^i, \mathbf{A}^i, \tilde{\mathbf{X}}^i) := GW(\mathbf{A}^i, \mathbf{X}^i, \mathbf{A}^i, \tilde{\mathbf{X}}^i)/\tau$, where $\tau$ is a temperature hyperparameter. The Wasserstein ($\mathcal{L}_W$) and Gromov-Wasserstein ($\mathcal{L}_{GW}$) contrastive losses are given as follows:

$$\mathcal{L}_W = -\sum_{i \in \mathcal{S}} \log \frac{e^{-W_{(\tau)}(\mathbf{X}^i, \tilde{\mathbf{X}}^i)}}{\sum_{j \in \mathcal{S}, j \neq i}^{N} \left(e^{-W_{(\tau)}(\mathbf{X}^i, \tilde{\mathbf{X}}^j)} + e^{-W_{(\tau)}(\mathbf{X}^i, \mathbf{X}^j)}\right)},$$

$$\mathcal{L}_{GW} = -\sum_{i \in \mathcal{S}} \log \frac{e^{-GW_{(\tau)}(\mathbf{A}^i, \mathbf{X}^i, \mathbf{A}^i, \tilde{\mathbf{X}}^i)}}{\sum_{j \in \mathcal{S}, j \neq i}^{N} \left(e^{-GW_{(\tau)}(\mathbf{A}^i, \mathbf{X}^i, \mathbf{A}^j, \tilde{\mathbf{X}}^j)} + e^{-GW_{(\tau)}(\mathbf{A}^i, \mathbf{X}^i, \mathbf{A}^j, \mathbf{X}^j)}\right)},$$

(9)

where $\mathcal{S}$ is the set of sampled nodes. The model loss $\mathcal{L}$ incorporates the contrastive and regularization components as follows:

$$\mathcal{L} = \alpha \mathcal{L}_W + (1-\alpha)\mathcal{L}_{GW} + \mathcal{L}_R, \tag{10}$$

where $\alpha$ is a hyperparameter that balances the emphasis on feature distribution and structural fidelity.

### 4.5 Theoretical Analysis of the Loss Function

The following theorem illustrates the effect of adding the term $\text{KL}(\cdot)$ to the overall loss function $\mathcal{L}$ in (10) with the input $x$ and latent variable $z$.

**Theorem 1.** *By increasing the number of subgraphs (and consequently their associate node feature matrices), minimizing InfoNCE loss $\mathcal{L}_W(\cdot)$ in (9) and also the KL divergence in (10), the SubGEC model implicitly minimizes:*

$$\mathbb{E}_{\mathbf{X} \sim p(\mathbf{X}|\tilde{\mathbf{X}})} \left[ KL\left( q_\phi(\tilde{\mathbf{X}}|\mathbf{X}, \mathbf{A}) \| p(\tilde{\mathbf{X}}|\mathbf{X}, \mathbf{A}) \right) \right]. \qquad (11)$$

*Proof.* Firstly, the following theorem from [34] outlines the relationship between minimizing the InfoNCE loss and maximizing mutual information between the input $x$ and latent variable $z$, i.e., $I(x, z)$.

**Proposition 1. (From [34]).** *The equivalence of maximizing the mutual information between the input $x$ and latent variable $z$ and minimizing $\mathcal{L}_{InfoNCE(N)}(x, z)$ becomes tighter by increasing the number of input data $N$ as:*

$$I(x, z) \geq \log(N) - \mathcal{L}_{InfoNCE(N)}(x, z). \qquad (12)$$

Next, by minimizing $\text{KL}\left(q_\phi(z|x) \| p(z)\right)$ leading to $q_\phi(z|x) \approx p(z)$, one can write:

$$I(x,z) = \int\int p(x,z) \log\left(\frac{p(x,z)}{p(x)p(z)}\right) dx\,dz = \int\int \overbrace{p(x,z)}^{p(x|z)p(z)} \log\left(\frac{p(z|x)}{p(z)}\right) dx\,dz$$

$$= \int p(x|z) \left[ \int q_\phi(z|x) \log\left(\overbrace{\frac{p(z|x)}{q_\phi(z|x)}}^{-\text{KL}(q_\phi(z|x)\|p(z|x))}\right) dz \right] dx = -\mathbb{E}_{x \sim p(x|z)}\left[\text{KL}\left(q_\phi(z|x)\|p(z|x)\right)\right]. \qquad (13)$$

where we have used the mathematical expectation formula $\mathbb{E}_{x \sim p(x)}[f(x)] = \int f(x) p(x) dx$ for the last equality. Therefore, by increasing the number of inputs, minimizing $\mathcal{L}_{\text{InfoNCE}(N)}(x, z)$ and also KL divergence $\text{KL}\left(q_\phi(z|x) \| p(z)\right)$, the network implicitly minimizes $\mathbb{E}_{x \sim p(x|z)}\left[\text{KL}\left(q_\phi(z|x) \| p(z|x)\right)\right]$, which means that the average distance over the samples from $p(x|z)$ between the parametric probability distribution $q_\phi(z|x)$ and $p(z|x)$ is minimized. Now, by replacing $\mathcal{L}_{\text{InfoNCE}(N)}(x, z)$, $q_\phi(z|x)$, $p(z)$, $p(z|x)$, and $p(x|z)$ with $\mathcal{L}_W$, $q_\phi(\tilde{\mathbf{X}}|\mathbf{X}, \mathbf{A})$, $p(\tilde{\mathbf{X}})$, $p(\tilde{\mathbf{X}}|\mathbf{X}, \mathbf{A})$, and $p(\mathbf{X}|\tilde{\mathbf{X}})$, respectively, the proof is completed.

SubGEC is driven by two key principles: (i) maximizing the mutual information between the input and latent variables and (ii) designing a robust encoder that generates latent embeddings closely aligned with the true latent distribution. Theorem 1 formally establishes that enforcing the joint minimization of the OT and KL losses in the overall loss (10) leads to the minimization of the expected KL divergence $\mathbb{E}_{\mathbf{X} \sim p(\mathbf{X}|\tilde{\mathbf{X}})} \left[ \text{KL}\left( q_\phi(\tilde{\mathbf{X}}|\mathbf{X}, \mathbf{A}) \| p(\tilde{\mathbf{X}}|\mathbf{X}, \mathbf{A}) \right) \right]$, ensuring an accurate estimation of the true conditional distribution $p(\tilde{\mathbf{X}}|\mathbf{X}, \mathbf{A})$. Simultaneously, this optimization strategy increases the mutual information between the input $\mathbf{X}$ and the latent embedding $\tilde{\mathbf{X}}$, thereby reinforcing the encoder's capacity to preserve essential input characteristics. Theorem 1 thus provides the theoretical foundation for SubGEC's design. Moreover, it highlights a crucial insight: minimizing the KL divergence alone does not necessarily maximize mutual information and may result in suboptimal performance, an observation we empirically validate in Sect. 5.2.

## 5 Experimental Evaluation

In this section, we present the empirical assessment of SubGEC by comparing its performance against current state-of-the-art methodologies across various public datasets. Additionally, through ablation studies, we verify the efficacy of our method. These studies analyze the contribution of individual SubGEC components to the overall performance. Finally, we analyze the computational cost to show our method's scalability to larger graphs. We also explore the sensitivity of the loss balance hyperparameter $\beta$ and the size of the subgraph on the model's performance in Appendix C.

**Datasets.** We select several widely used datasets for graph node classification to evaluate SubGEC. These datasets encompass various types of networks, including academic citation networks, collaboration networks, and web page networks, providing diverse challenges and characteristics. Table 1 summarizes the basic statistics of these datasets.

Table 1. Overview of selected datasets used in the study.

| Dataset | Nodes | Edges | Features | Avg. degree | Classes |
|---|---|---|---|---|---|
| Cora [29] | 2,708 | 5,429 | 1,433 | 4.0 | 7 |
| Citeseer [11] | 3,312 | 4,732 | 3,703 | 2.9 | 6 |
| Pubmed [39] | 19,717 | 44,338 | 500 | 4.5 | 3 |
| Coauthor [40] | 18,333 | 163,788 | 6,805 | 17.9 | 15 |
| Squirrel [36] | 5,201 | 217,073 | 2,089 | 83.5 | 5 |
| Chameleon [35] | 2,277 | 36,101 | 2,325 | 31.7 | 5 |
| Cornell [8] | 183 | 298 | 1,703 | 3.3 | 5 |
| Texas [8] | 183 | 325 | 1,703 | 3.6 | 5 |

**Implementation Details.** We implement SubGEC using `PyG` and `PyTorch`. Our approach adopts a self-supervised scheme evaluated via linear probing. The model is trained using the official training subsets of the referenced datasets. Hyperparameter tuning involves a random search on the validation set to determine optimal values for the hyperparameters. The best configuration in validation is subsequently employed for tests on the dataset. We train our model with the Adam optimizer. We train our models on GPU architectures, including the RTX 3060 and A40.

**Hyperparameter Random Search.** Informed by the findings of [9,12,43], which indicate the sensitivity of GNNs to hyperparameter settings, we undertake random searches for hyperparameter optimization. The training proceeds on the official splits of the train datasets, with the random search conducted on the validation dataset to pinpoint the best configurations. These settings are then implemented to evaluate the model on the test dataset. The ranges of the hyperparameters explored and our code implementation are available[1] and will be made public after acceptance to facilitate replication and further research.

### 5.1 Classification Results

In our study, we compared our model against five state-of-the-art self-supervised node classification algorithms: POLYGCL [4], GREET [32], GRACE [52], GSC [17], and MUSE [50]. Additionally, we include three classic SSL algorithms for a comprehensive comparison: DGI [46], GCA [53], and GraphMAE [21]. To provide a broader context, we also report the training results from two supervised learning models: GCN [29] and GAT [47].

**Table 2.** Performance comparison of self-supervised and supervised graph representation learning methods across eight benchmark datasets.

| Method | Cora | Citeseer | Pubmed | Coauthor | Squirrel | Chameleon | Cornell | Texas |
|---|---|---|---|---|---|---|---|---|
| GCN | $81.40_{\pm 0.50}$ | $70.30_{\pm 0.50}$ | $76.80_{\pm 0.70}$ | $93.03_{\pm 0.31}$ | $53.43_{\pm 1.52}$ | $64.82_{\pm 2.32}$ | $60.54_{\pm 3.30}$ | $67.57_{\pm 4.80}$ |
| GAT | $83.00_{\pm 0.52}$ | $72.50_{\pm 0.30}$ | $79.00_{\pm 0.24}$ | $92.31_{\pm 0.24}$ | $42.72_{\pm 3.27}$ | $63.90_{\pm 2.19}$ | $76.00_{\pm 3.63}$ | $78.87_{\pm 3.78}$ |
| MUSE | $69.90_{\pm 0.41}$ | $66.35_{\pm 0.40}$ | $79.95_{\pm 0.59}$ | $90.75_{\pm 0.39}$ | $40.15_{\pm 3.04}$ | $55.59_{\pm 2.21}$ | $83.78_{\pm 3.42}$ | $83.78_{\pm 2.79}$ |
| POLYGCL | **$84.89_{\pm 0.62}$** | **$76.28_{\pm 0.85}$** | $81.02_{\pm 0.27}$ | $93.76_{\pm 0.08}$ | $55.29_{\pm 0.72}$ | **$71.62_{\pm 0.96}$** | $77.86_{\pm 3.11}$ | $85.24_{\pm 1.80}$ |
| GREET | $84.40_{\pm 0.77}$ | $74.10_{\pm 0.44}$ | $80.29_{\pm 0.24}$ | **$94.65_{\pm 0.18}$** | $39.76_{\pm 0.75}$ | $60.57_{\pm 1.03}$ | $78.36_{\pm 3.77}$ | $78.03_{\pm 3.94}$ |
| GRACE | $83.30_{\pm 0.74}$ | $72.10_{\pm 0.60}$ | **$86.70_{\pm 0.16}$** | $92.78_{\pm 0.04}$ | $52.10_{\pm 0.94}$ | $52.29_{\pm 1.49}$ | $60.66_{\pm 11.32}$ | $75.74_{\pm 2.95}$ |
| GSC | $82.80_{\pm 0.10}$ | $71.00_{\pm 0.10}$ | $85.60_{\pm 0.20}$ | $91.88_{\pm 0.11}$ | $51.32_{\pm 0.21}$ | $64.02_{\pm 0.29}$ | $93.56_{\pm 1.73}$ | $88.64_{\pm 1.21}$ |
| DGI | $81.99_{\pm 0.95}$ | $71.76_{\pm 0.80}$ | $77.16_{\pm 0.24}$ | $92.15_{\pm 0.63}$ | $38.80_{\pm 0.76}$ | $58.00_{\pm 0.70}$ | $70.82_{\pm 7.21}$ | $81.48_{\pm 2.79}$ |
| GCA | $78.13_{\pm 0.85}$ | $67.81_{\pm 0.75}$ | $80.63_{\pm 0.31}$ | $93.10_{\pm 0.20}$ | $47.13_{\pm 0.61}$ | $56.54_{\pm 1.07}$ | $53.11_{\pm 9.34}$ | $81.02_{\pm 2.30}$ |
| GraphMAE | $84.20_{\pm 0.40}$ | $73.40_{\pm 0.40}$ | $81.10_{\pm 0.40}$ | $80.63_{\pm 0.15}$ | $48.26_{\pm 1.21}$ | $71.05_{\pm 0.36}$ | $61.93_{\pm 4.59}$ | $67.80_{\pm 3.37}$ |
| SubGEC | $83.60_{\pm 0.10}$ | $73.14_{\pm 0.14}$ | $84.60_{\pm 0.10}$ | $92.34_{\pm 0.04}$ | **$56.39_{\pm 0.57}$** | $69.14_{\pm 1.12}$ | **$94.57_{\pm 2.13}$** | **$92.38_{\pm 0.81}$** |

The results in Table 2 highlight the strong performance of SubGEC across diverse datasets. Our model outperforms other state-of-the-art algorithms on three out of eight benchmarks while demonstrating competitive results on the remaining datasets. Notably, it achieves the highest accuracy on the strongly heterophilic Squirrel, Cornell, and Texas datasets, exceeding GSC, POLYGCL, and other baselines. This suggests that the proposed design is particularly robust in settings where node connectivity patterns deviate from typical homophilic assumptions. Although POLYGCL slightly surpasses Sub-GEC on certain homophilic datasets (e.g., Cora and Citeseer), SubGEC remains

---
[1] https://github.com/ShifengXIE/SubGEC/tree/main.

**Table 3.** Ablation study on KL regularization and other components. **Reg.** denotes the type of regularization applied, with possible choices including no regularization (✗), KL divergence (**KL**), and dropout (**D.**). **L1** indicates whether the L1 norm was used as a reconstruction loss. **De.** represents whether a decoder was included in the model. **Cons.** refers to whether contrastive loss was incorporated.

| Reg. | L1 | De. | Cons. | Cora | Citeseer | Pubmed | Coauthor | Squirrel | Chameleon | Cornell | Texas |
|---|---|---|---|---|---|---|---|---|---|---|---|
| ✗ | ✗ | ✗ | ✓ | $83.00_{\pm0.07}$ | $71.88_{\pm0.07}$ | $85.46_{\pm0.04}$ | $91.96_{\pm0.09}$ | $42.99_{\pm0.17}$ | $64.25_{\pm0.21}$ | $94.58_{\pm0.22}$ | $75.72_{\pm0.40}$ |
| KL | ✓ | ✗ | ✗ | $78.78_{\pm1.09}$ | $68.33_{\pm1.00}$ | $75.56_{\pm1.65}$ | $88.86_{\pm0.25}$ | $30.52_{\pm0.48}$ | $48.12_{\pm0.63}$ | $68.43_{\pm0.55}$ | $73.83_{\pm1.20}$ |
| KL | ✗ | ✓ | ✓ | $82.80_{\pm0.07}$ | $73.00_{\pm0.08}$ | $80.26_{\pm0.37}$ | $92.03_{\pm0.13}$ | $35.47_{\pm0.21}$ | $60.30_{\pm0.21}$ | $93.56_{\pm0.64}$ | $88.98_{\pm0.52}$ |
| KL | ✓ | ✗ | ✓ | $81.60_{\pm0.99}$ | $69.60_{\pm0.10}$ | $67.54_{\pm0.35}$ | $87.03_{\pm0.65}$ | $30.52_{\pm0.48}$ | $43.26_{\pm0.66}$ | $53.29_{\pm0.13}$ | $63.45_{\pm0.48}$ |
| D. | ✗ | ✗ | ✓ | $79.00_{\pm0.21}$ | $70.60_{\pm3.52}$ | $80.84_{\pm0.05}$ | $91.52_{\pm0.37}$ | $44.24_{\pm0.50}$ | $58.94_{\pm0.72}$ | $85.76_{\pm0.24}$ | $87.98_{\pm0.15}$ |
| KL | ✗ | ✗ | ✓ | $\mathbf{83.60}_{\pm0.10}$ | $\mathbf{73.14}_{\pm0.14}$ | $84.60_{\pm0.10}$ | $\mathbf{92.34}_{\pm0.04}$ | $\mathbf{56.39}_{\pm0.57}$ | $\mathbf{69.14}_{\pm1.12}$ | $94.57_{\pm2.13}$ | $\mathbf{92.38}_{\pm0.81}$ |

comparably strong there. Overall, these results highlight SubGEC's robustness in handling heterophilic structures while maintaining strong performance on homophilic graphs, demonstrating its versatility across diverse graph topologies.

### 5.2 Ablation Studies

**KL Divergence and Contrastive Loss.** The first ablation study is concerned with analyzing some elements of SubGEC such as the architectural choices, the KL regularization, and the contrastive loss. The outcomes of this ablation study are presented in Table 3.

The first row in Table 3 analyzes the case where we drop the KL loss from SubGEC. We observe that in overall the performance decreases, demonstrating the importance of the KL loss as theoretically proved in Sect. 4.5. On the contrary, the second row in Table 3 includes only the KL loss and L1 reconstruction loss without including the contrastive loss. This effectively models a Variational Autoencoder (VAE) type method, where we observe a loss in performance. This result also aligns with the theoretical findings in Theorem 1, where we show that solely relying on the minimization of the KL loss does not guarantee the accurate estimation of the encoder distribution and can lead to performance degradation compared to using both the KL and contrastive loss functions.

The third model in Table 3 incorporates a decoder into SubGEC, *i.e.*, we use a VAE-type architecture to generate contrastive pairs. The decoder consists of two fully connected multi-layer perceptrons. This model achieves competitive results only on specific databases, illustrating that SubGEC is not merely a combination of a VAE generative model and contrastive learning training methodologies. The fourth model includes a norm-1 reconstruction loss, calculated as the norm of the difference between input and output features, adding a constraint to enforce similarity between input and output features. The results indicate that enforcing such similarity is not reasonable. Finally, the fifth model in Table 3 replaces the KL divergence with the commonly used regularization technique, dropout. The results show that our method outperforms dropout.

**Contrastive Loss.** The second ablation study examines the impact of the distance metric used in our contrastive loss, specifically comparing OT distances with alternative approaches. Table 4 presents the results of this study, evaluating models with Wasserstein-only, Gromov-Wasserstein-only, and L1-only metrics, as well as SubGEC. Our findings indicate that excluding OT distances leads to suboptimal performance, particularly on heterophilic datasets. Additionally, we observe that the Gromov-Wasserstein distance slightly outperforms the Wasserstein distance on homophilic datasets. Most importantly, incorporating both Wasserstein and Gromov-Wasserstein distances in the contrastive loss consistently yields the best performance across all datasets.

### 5.3 Running Time

We employ a subgraph sampling strategy to avoid the high computational complexity of OT computations. Figure 3 shows the average time to compute the loss per iteration. The running time can vary due to server performance fluctuations, leading to non-monotonic timing variations. We observe that the running time remains low, increasing modestly as the graph size grows from 100 to 2,500 nodes, with times ranging from 0.1 to 0.2 s. We attribute this increase in computational

**Table 4.** Ablation studies on the choice of the distance metric in the contrastive loss. **W** indicates the use of the Wasserstein distance. **GW** indicates the use of the Gromov-Wasserstein distance. **L1** indicates the use of a simple L1 distance.

| W | GW | L1 | Cora | Citeseer | Pubmed | Coauthor | Squirrel | Chameleon | Cornell | Texas |
|---|---|---|---|---|---|---|---|---|---|---|
| ✓ | ✗ | ✗ | 77.00$_{\pm 0.81}$ | 66.80$_{\pm 1.39}$ | 78.24$_{\pm 1.22}$ | 88.65$_{\pm 0.62}$ | 49.02$_{\pm 0.85}$ | 62.50$_{\pm 0.49}$ | 91.29$_{\pm 0.10}$ | 87.67$_{\pm 0.09}$ |
| ✗ | ✓ | ✗ | 76.20$_{\pm 1.56}$ | 68.98$_{\pm 0.23}$ | 80.20$_{\pm 1.42}$ | 91.08$_{\pm 0.28}$ | 45.16$_{\pm 0.55}$ | 56.17$_{\pm 0.28}$ | 90.16$_{\pm 1.52}$ | 88.47$_{\pm 0.89}$ |
| ✗ | ✗ | ✓ | 79.84$_{\pm 0.68}$ | 69.80$_{\pm 0.64}$ | 79.20$_{\pm 2.54}$ | 82.23$_{\pm 1.51}$ | 47.10$_{\pm 0.58}$ | 58.35$_{\pm 0.92}$ | 90.33$_{\pm 1.08}$ | 84.59$_{\pm 0.80}$ |
| ✓ | ✓ | ✗ | **83.60**$_{\pm 0.10}$ | **73.14**$_{\pm 0.14}$ | **84.60**$_{\pm 0.10}$ | **92.34**$_{\pm 0.04}$ | **56.39**$_{\pm 0.57}$ | **69.14**$_{\pm 1.12}$ | **94.57**$_{\pm 2.13}$ | **92.38**$_{\pm 0.81}$ |

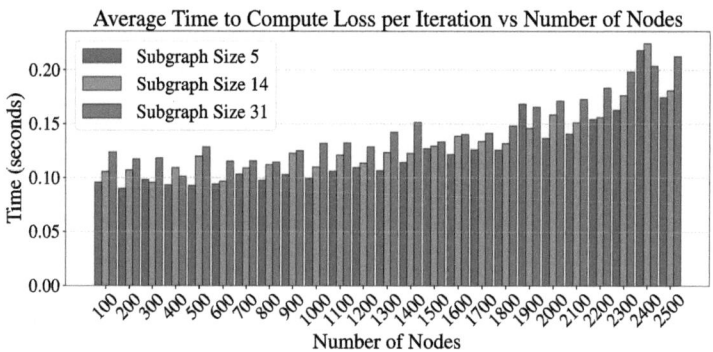

**Fig. 3.** Average time to compute loss per iteration as a function of the number of nodes. The figure compares the computation times for three different subgraph sizes (5, 14, and 31).

time to the higher dimensionalities of the adjacency matrices when subgraphs are sampled. Overall, SubGEC keeps a low running time even for increasing graph sizes, potentially enabling applications in large-scale graph SSL tasks.

## 6 Conclusion

This paper introduces the SubGEC, a novel GRL framework that leverages subgraph Gaussian embeddings for self-supervised contrastive learning. Our approach maps subgraphs into a Gaussian space, ensuring a controlled distribution while preserving essential subgraph characteristics. We also incorporate the OT Wasserstein and Gromov-Wasserstein distances into our contrastive loss. From a theoretical perspective, we demonstrated that our method minimizes the KL divergence between the learned encoder distribution and the Gaussian distribution while maximizing mutual information between input and latent variables. Our experiments on multiple benchmark datasets validate these theoretical insights and show that SubGEC outperforms or presents competitive performance against previous state-of-the-art models. Our findings emphasize the importance of controlling the distribution of contrastive pairs in SSL.

**Acknowledgment.** This research was supported by DATAIA Convergence Institute as part of the «Programme d'Investissement d'Avenir», (ANR-17-CONV-0003) operated by the center Hi! PARIS. This work was also supported by the ANR French National Research Agency under the JCJC projects DeSNAP (ANR-24CE23-1895-01).

## A Graph Convolutional Network

The graph encoder uses two graph convolution layers, which are mathematically represented as follows:

$$\mathbf{H}_1 = \sigma\left((\mathbf{D}^{-\frac{1}{2}}(\mathbf{A}+\mathbf{I})\mathbf{D}^{-\frac{1}{2}}\mathbf{X}\Theta_1)\right), \quad \mathbf{H}_2 = \sigma\left(\mathbf{D}^{-\frac{1}{2}}(\mathbf{A}+\mathbf{I})\mathbf{D}^{-\frac{1}{2}}\mathbf{H}_1\Theta_2\right). \tag{14}$$

## B Details of the KL Divergence in Subgraph Gaussian Embedding

The KL divergence between these two distributions has a well-known closed-form expression. In our setting, we write [27]:

$$\mathrm{KL}\big(q(\tilde{\mathbf{X}}|\mathbf{X},\mathbf{A})\,\|\,p(\tilde{\mathbf{X}})\big) = \frac{1}{2|\mathcal{P}|}\sum_{i\in\mathcal{P}}\sum_{j=1}^{d}\Big(\mu_{ij}^2 + \sigma_{ij}^2 - 1 - 2\log\sigma_{ij}\Big), \tag{15}$$

where $\mu_{ij}$ and $\sigma_{ij}$ represent the $j$-th components of the latent mean and latent standard deviation for node $i$. The set $\mathcal{P}$ indexes the nodes in the induced subgraphs under consideration, and $d$ is the dimensionality of the latent space.

## C  Sensitivity Analysis

To investigate the impact of the regularization constraint on our method, experiments were conducted on the Cora dataset. The influence of regularization within the loss function was controlled by varying the hyperparameter $\beta$, which ranged from $10^{-6}$ to $10^2$. The results, as illustrated in Fig. 4a, indicate sensitivity to changes in $\beta$. Specifically, we observe that values of $\beta$ greater than or equal to $10^{-5}$ have a pronounced effect on the model's performance. Optimal results on the Cora dataset are achieved when $\beta$ was set within $10^{-3}$.

To evaluate the sensitivity of SubGEC to the subgraph size hyperparameter, we conducted a sensitivity analysis on the Cora dataset using subgraph sizes $k = 5, 15, 25$, and 35. As shown in Fig. 4b, the model exhibits robust performance across a wide range of subgraph sizes, with competitive mean test accuracy and low variability observed for $k = 5$ to 25. While $k = 15$ achieves marginally higher accuracy, the minimal differences in performance across this range suggest that the model is not overly sensitive to precise subgraph size selections. A gradual decline in performance at $k = 35$ highlights the upper bound of robustness, likely due to increased noise from redundant structural information.

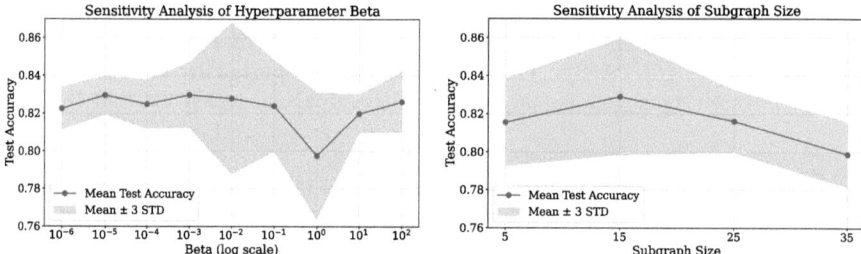

(a) Sensitivity analysis of hyperparameter beta $\beta$.

(b) Sensitivity analysis of subgraph size $k^i$.

**Fig. 4.** The plot displays the mean test accuracy (solid blue line) along with a shaded confidence region representing the mean ±3 standard deviations. The analysis illustrates the sensitivity of test accuracy to variations in hyperparameter beta and subgraph sizes. (Color figure online)

## References

1. Arya, S., Auddy, A., Clark, R.A., Lim, S., Memoli, F., Packer, D.: The Gromov–Wasserstein distance between spheres. Found. Comput. Math. 1–56 (2024)
2. Brogat-Motte, L., Flamary, R., Brouard, C., Rousu, J., d'Alché Buc, F.: Learning to predict graphs with fused Gromov-Wasserstein barycenters. In: International Conference on Machine Learning (2022)
3. Bundy, A., Wallen, L.: Breadth-first search. Catalogue Artif. Intell. Tools 13 (1984)

4. Chen, J., Lei, R., Wei, Z.: PolyGCL: graph contrastive learning via learnable spectral polynomial filters. In: International Conference on Learning Representations (2024)
5. Chen, T., Kornblith, S., Norouzi, M., Hinton, G.: A simple framework for contrastive learning of visual representations. In: International Conference on Machine Learning (2020)
6. Chen, Y., Georgiou, T.T., Tannenbaum, A.: Optimal transport for Gaussian mixture models. IEEE Access **7**, 6269–6278 (2018)
7. Chien, E., Peng, J., Li, P., Milenkovic, O.: Adaptive universal generalized PageRank graph neural network. In: International Conference on Learning Representations (2021)
8. Craven, M., et al.: Learning to extract symbolic knowledge from the World Wide Web. In: AAAI Conference on Artificial Intelligence (1998)
9. Gasteiger, J., Weiß enberger, S., Günnemann, S.: Diffusion improves graph learning. In: Advances in Neural Information Processing Systems (2019)
10. Genevay, A., Cuturi, M., Peyré, G., Bach, F.: Stochastic optimization for large-scale optimal transport. In: Advances in Neural Information Processing Systems (2016)
11. Giles, C.L., Bollacker, K.D., Lawrence, S.: CiteSeer: an automatic citation indexing system. In: ACM Conference on Digital Libraries (1998)
12. Giraldo, J.H., Skianis, K., Bouwmans, T., Malliaros, F.D.: On the trade-off between over-smoothing and over-squashing in deep graph neural networks. In: ACM International Conference on Information and Knowledge Management (2023)
13. Goldfeld, Z., Greenewald, K.: Gaussian-smoothed optimal transport: metric structure and statistical efficiency. In: International Conference on Artificial Intelligence and Statistics (2020)
14. Grill, J.B., et al.: Bootstrap your own latent: a new approach to self-supervised learning. In: Advances in Neural Information Processing Systems (2020)
15. Gutmann, M., Hyvärinen, A.: Noise-contrastive estimation: a new estimation principle for unnormalized statistical models. In: International Conference on Artificial Intelligence and Statistics (2010)
16. Hamilton, W., Ying, Z., Leskovec, J.: Inductive representation learning on large graphs. In: Advances in Neural Information Processing Systems (2017)
17. Han, Y., Hui, L., Jiang, H., Qian, J., Xie, J.: Generative subgraph contrast for self-supervised graph representation learning. In: European Conference on Computer Vision (2022)
18. He, A., Luo, C., Tian, X., Zeng, W.: A twofold Siamese network for real-time object tracking. In: IEEE/CVF Conference on Computer Vision and Pattern Recognition (2018)
19. He, M., Wei, Z., Wen, J.R.: Convolutional neural networks on graphs with Chebyshev approximation, revisited. In: Advances in Neural Information Processing Systems (2022)
20. Hermans, A., Beyer, L., Leibe, B.: In defense of the triplet loss for person re-identification. arXiv preprint arXiv:1703.07737 (2017)
21. Hou, Z., et al.: GraphMAE: self-supervised masked graph autoencoders. In: ACM SIGKDD Conference on Knowledge Discovery and Data Mining (2022)
22. Jaiswal, A., Babu, A.R., Zadeh, M.Z., Banerjee, D., Makedon, F.: A survey on contrastive self-supervised learning. Technologies **9**(1), 2 (2020)
23. Jiao, Y., Xiong, Y., Zhang, J., Zhang, Y., Zhang, T., Zhu, Y.: Sub-graph contrast for scalable self-supervised graph representation learning. In: IEEE International Conference on Data Mining (2020)

24. Jing, L., Vincent, P., LeCun, Y., Tian, Y.: Understanding dimensional collapse in contrastive self-supervised learning. In: International Conference on Learning Representations (2022)
25. Ju, W., et al.: A comprehensive survey on deep graph representation learning. Neural Netw. (2024)
26. Ju, W., et al.: Towards graph contrastive learning: a survey and beyond. arXiv preprint arXiv:2405.11868 (2024)
27. Kingma, D.P., Welling, M.: Auto-encoding variational bayes. In: International Conference on Learning Representations (2014)
28. Kipf, T.N., Welling, M.: Variational graph auto-encoders. In: Advances in Neural Information Processing Systems - Workshop (2016)
29. Kipf, T.N., Welling, M.: Semi-supervised classification with graph convolutional networks. In: International Conference on Learning Representations (2017)
30. Kolouri, S., Park, S.R., Thorpe, M., Slepcev, D., Rohde, G.K.: Optimal mass transport: signal processing and machine-learning applications. IEEE Signal Process. Mag. **34**(4), 43–59 (2017)
31. Liu, J., Ong, G.P., Chen, X.: GraphSAGE-based traffic speed forecasting for segment network with sparse data. IEEE Trans. Intell. Transp. Syst. **23**(3), 1755–1766 (2020)
32. Liu, Y., Zheng, Y., Zhang, D., Lee, V.C., Pan, S.: Beyond smoothing: unsupervised graph representation learning with edge heterophily discriminating. In: Proceedings of the AAAI Conference on Artificial Intelligence (2023)
33. Liu, Y., Zhang, H., He, T., Zheng, T., Zhao, J.: Bootstrap latents of nodes and neighbors for graph self-supervised learning. In: European Conference on Machine Learning and Knowledge Discovery in Databases (2024)
34. van den Oord, A., Li, Y., Vinyals, O.: Representation learning with contrastive predictive coding. arXiv preprint arXiv:1807.03748 (2018)
35. Pei, H., Wei, B., Chang, K.C.C., Lei, Y., Yang, B.: Geom-GCN: geometric graph convolutional networks. In: International Conference on Learning Representations (2020)
36. Rozemberczki, B., Allen, C., Sarkar, R.: Multi-scale attributed node embedding. J. Complex Netw. **9**(2) (2021)
37. Rüschendorf, L.: The Wasserstein distance and approximation theorems. Probab. Theory Relat. Fields **70**(1), 117–129 (1985). https://doi.org/10.1007/BF00532240
38. Sangare, A.S., Dunou, N., Giraldo, J.H., Malliaros, F.D.: A fused Gromov-Wasserstein approach to subgraph contrastive learning. Trans. Mach. Learn. Res. (2025)
39. Sen, P., Namata, G., Bilgic, M., Getoor, L., Galligher, B., Eliassi-Rad, T.: Collective classification in network data. AI Mag. **29**(3), 93 (2008)
40. Shchur, O., Mumme, M., Bojchevski, A., Günnemann, S.: Pitfalls of graph neural network evaluation. In: Advances in Neural Information Processing Systems - Workshops (2018)
41. Thakoor, S., et al.: Large-scale representation learning on graphs via bootstrapping. In: International Conference on Learning Representations (2021)
42. Titouan, V., Courty, N., Tavenard, R., Flamary, R.: Optimal transport for structured data with application on graphs. In: International Conference on Machine Learning, pp. 6275–6284 (2019)
43. Topping, J., Giovanni, F.D., Chamberlain, B.P., Dong, X., Bronstein, M.M.: Understanding over-squashing and bottlenecks on graphs via curvature. In: International Conference on Learning Representations (2022)

44. Van Erven, T., Harremos, P.: Rényi divergence and Kullback-Leibler divergence. IEEE Trans. Inf. Theory **60**(7), 3797–3820 (2014)
45. Vayer, T., Chapel, L., Flamary, R., Tavenard, R., Courty, N.: Fused Gromov-Wasserstein distance for structured objects. Algorithms **13**(9), 212 (2020)
46. Veličković, P., Fedus, W., Hamilton, W.L., Liò, P., Bengio, Y., Hjelm, R.D.: Deep graph infomax. In: International Conference on Learning Representations (2019)
47. Veličković, P., Cucurull, G., Casanova, A., Romero, A., Liò, P., Bengio, Y.: Graph attention networks. In: International Conference on Learning Representations (2018)
48. Villani, C.: Topics in Optimal Transportation, vol. 58. American Mathematical Society (2021)
49. Wu, Z., Pan, S., Chen, F., Long, G., Zhang, C., Philip, S.Y.: A comprehensive survey on graph neural networks. IEEE Trans. Neural Netw. Learn. Syst. **32**(1), 4–24 (2020)
50. Yuan, M., Chen, M., Li, X.: MUSE: multi-view contrastive learning for heterophilic graphs. In: ACM International Conference on Information and Knowledge Management (2023)
51. Zhu, J., Xu, K., Tannenbaum, A.: Optimal transport for vector Gaussian mixture models. In: Advances in Neural Information Processing Systems - Workshops (2023)
52. Zhu, Y., Xu, Y., Yu, F., Liu, Q., Wu, S., Wang, L.: Deep graph contrastive representation learning. In: International Conference on Machine Learning - Workshops (2020)
53. Zhu, Y., Xu, Y., Yu, F., Liu, Q., Wu, S., Wang, L.: Graph contrastive learning with adaptive augmentation. In: Proceedings of the Web Conference (2021)
54. Zhuo, J., et al.: Unified graph augmentations for generalized contrastive learning on graphs. In: Advances in Neural Information Processing Systems (2024)

# Rethinking Graph Domain Adaptation: A Spectral Contrastive Perspective

Haoyu Zhang[1], Yuxuan Cheng[2], Wenqi Fan[3], Yulong Chen[1], and Yifan Zhang[1(✉)]

[1] City University of Hong Kong (Dongguan), Dongguan, China
{haoyu.zhang,yifan.zhang}@cityu-dg.edu.cn
[2] Huazhong Agricultural University, Wuhan, China
hxwxss@webmail.hzau.edu.cn
[3] The Hong Kong Polytechnic University, Hong Kong, China

**Abstract.** Graph neural networks (GNNs) have achieved remarkable success in various domains, yet they often struggle with domain adaptation due to significant structural distribution shifts and insufficient exploration of transferable patterns. One of the main reasons behind this is that traditional approaches do not treat global and local patterns discriminatingly so that some local details in the graph may be violated after multi-layer GNN. Our key insight is that domain shifts can be better understood through spectral analysis, where low-frequency components often encode domain-invariant global patterns, and high-frequency components capture domain-specific local details. As such, we propose FracNet (**Fr**equency **A**ware **C**ontrastive Graph **Net**work) with two synergic modules to decompose the original graph into high-frequency and low-frequency components and perform frequency-aware domain adaption. Moreover, the blurring boundary problem of domain adaptation is improved by integrating with a contrastive learning framework. Besides the practical implication, we also provide rigorous theoretical proof to demonstrate the superiority of FracNet. Extensive experiments further demonstrate significant improvements over state-of-the-art approaches.

**Keywords:** Graph Neural Networks · Domain Alignment · Frequency Aware

## 1 Introduction

Graph-structured data has become increasingly ubiquitous across various domains, from social networks to molecular structures [16, 17, 40]. The ability to effectively analyze and understand these complex graph structures is crucial for numerous applications, including drug discovery, protein structure analysis, and material science. Graph Neural Networks (GNNs) have emerged as powerful tools for learning representations from such structured data, demonstrating exceptional capabilities in capturing complex topological patterns [7, 20, 36, 39]. While GNNs have achieved remarkable success in various graph-related tasks, they typically require substantial amounts of labeled training data to achieve optimal performance. However, in many real-world scenarios, particularly in specialized domains such as drug discovery [8] and materials science [4],

---

H. Zhang, Y. Cheng and Y. Chen—Equal contribution.

© The Author(s), under exclusive license to Springer Nature Switzerland AG 2026
R. P. Ribeiro et al. (Eds.): ECML PKDD 2025, LNAI 16018, pp. 448–464, 2026.
https://doi.org/10.1007/978-3-032-06106-5_26

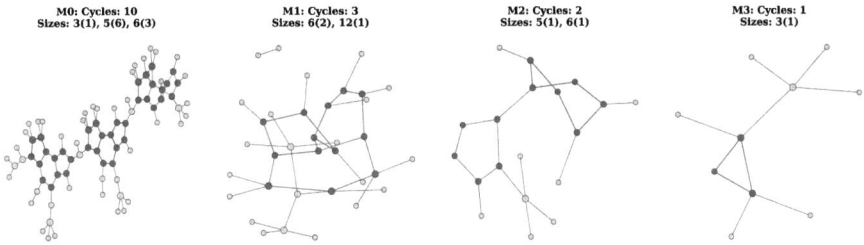

**Fig. 1.** Molecular topological structures of four compounds.

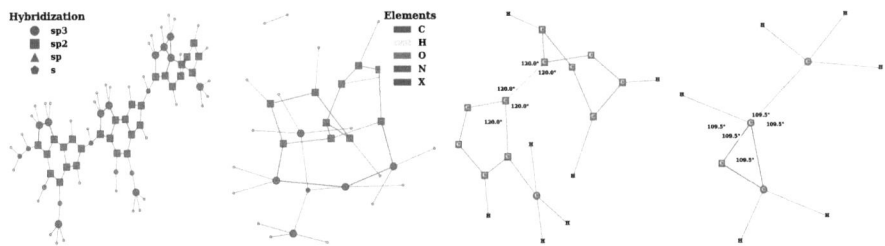

**Fig. 2.** Molecular properties of four compounds.

obtaining labeled data can be expensive and time-consuming. This challenge has led to increasing interest in domain adaptation techniques, which aim to transfer knowledge from label-rich source domains to label-scarce target domains [5] (Fig. 1).

However, existing efforts treat the graph as a holistic entity without distinguishing its properties in global and local patterns [22], which may lead to inaccurate performance due to overlooking crucial local structural features. For example, consider representative molecules from different domains of the Mutagenicity dataset, as shown in Fig. 2. While M0 contains multiple cyclic structures (10 cycles in total, including 6 five-membered rings and 3 six-membered rings), M1 exhibits fewer but larger cycles (3 cycles, including 2 six-membered rings and 1 twelve-membered ring). These structural differences are further emphasized by their hybridization states and bond angles. M0 is rich in $sp^2$ hybridized carbons forming planar geometries with $120°$ bond angles, characteristic of aromatic rings with delocalized $\pi$-electrons. In contrast, M3 contains predominantly $sp^3$ hybridized carbons with tetrahedral geometry and $109.5°$ bond angles, forming more flexible single bonds. These distinct local structural motifs, particularly the type and number of cyclic systems, significantly influence molecular reactivity, electron distribution, and biological properties. Traditional GNNs, primarily focusing on topological connectivity, often fail to effectively capture these critical local geometric features that determine molecular behavior across different domains.

This observation naturally introduces our key insight: domain shifts in graph data can be better understood and addressed through spectral analysis. When projecting graphs into the frequency domain, different structural patterns—such as the $sp^2$-rich aromatic systems in M0 versus the $sp^3$-dominated structures in M3—manifest as distinct frequency components with varying degrees of transferability across domains. Specifically, low-frequency components often correspond to groups of strongly connected nodes with similar features, capturing **global**, potentially transferable patterns like the basic carbon scaffolds common across domains. In contrast, high-frequency components reflect rapid variations in node features between neighborhoods, often representing domain-specific **local** details such as the specific ring sizes, hybridization states, and bond angles that differentiate molecular domains. This frequency-domain perspective provides a principled way to understand and address domain shifts in molecular graph datasets.

Based on these observations, we propose FracNet, a new framework that combines frequency decomposition with contrastive learning for better domain adaptation. Our method first breaks down graph structures into high- and low-frequency parts, which helps us understand different structural patterns in molecular graphs. The low-frequency parts show us the overall structure that tends to be similar across different domains, while the high-frequency parts capture detailed local features that might be domain-specific. Given the decomposed components, we then improve the conventional Maximum Mean Discrepancy (MMD), a popularly used method for domain alignment, from the following two perspectives: (1) mitigate the problem of blurring class boundaries in binary classification tasks [6]; (2) extend it into the frequency domain, considering multiple frequency components. To this end, we use contrastive learning [12] to maintain clear class separation while aligning domains to achieve the first enhancement. And the second one is addressed by designing a new kernel to integrate the components of all frequencies. This approach helps us achieve better transfer learning results, especially for molecular classification tasks. Our main contributions can be summarized as follows:

- We introduce a new method that uses frequency decomposition to analyze molecular structures. This approach helps us better understand and transfer knowledge between different molecular domains by separating global patterns from local details. The method is especially useful for molecular property prediction tasks where overall structure and local features both matter.
- We propose a novel combination of contrastive learning and MMD alignment that helps solve the negative transfer problem in binary classification tasks. This combination maintains clear class boundaries while aligning different domains, leading to better classification results.
- We design a frequency-aware kernel that further enhances MMD-based domain alignment by separating and aligning molecular features at different frequencies, significantly outperforming traditional Gaussian kernels in capturing both global structural similarities and local molecular patterns.
- Our results demonstrate that understanding molecular structures through frequency decomposition and using contrastive learning can significantly improve domain adaptation performance.

## 2 Related Work

### 2.1 Domain Alignment

Domain alignment has emerged as a fundamental paradigm in transfer learning, particularly for scenarios with limited labeled data in the target domain [21,31]. Recent advances have focused on developing more sophisticated alignment strategies to handle complex domain shifts. [23] propose an adversarial framework with contrastive learning, while [28] present a unified framework that disentangles and aligns different aspects of the data distribution. In the context of structural data, [13] explore the synergy between internal feature exploration and external domain alignment. However, these methods typically rely on empirical objectives without rigorous theoretical guarantees on the optimality of alignment. Our work addresses this limitation by establishing theoretical connections between contrastive learning and Maximum Mean Discrepancy (MMD), providing provable bounds on alignment quality through frequency decomposition.

### 2.2 Graph Spectral Processing

Graph spectral processing has revolutionized the analysis of graph-structured data by leveraging frequency domain representations [2,14,15,37,38]. [3] introduce Specformer by incorporating spectral graph processing with transformers, while [26] bridge the gap between Weisfeiler-Leman algorithms and graph spectra. Recent work has focused on enhancing spectral methods' robustness, with [10] addressing heterophily through spectral analysis. While these methods demonstrate the effectiveness of spectral processing, they lack theoretical guarantees on the optimality of frequency decomposition in domain adaptation. Our framework addresses this limitation by proving that the proposed spectral decomposition achieves tighter mutual information bounds, with explicit guarantees on both local and global structural alignment.

## 3 Methodology

To achieve the domain adaptation considering both global and local patterns, we propose FracNet, a theoretically grounded spectral contrastive framework. The core of FracNet comprises two synergistic modules, a Spectral-guided Maximum Mutual Information (SMMI) module and a Frequency-aware Maximum Mean Discrepancy (FMMD) module, as illustrated in Fig. 3. Specifically, SMMI leverages spectral decomposition to disentangle graph signals into complementary frequency bands, enabling the model to capture both global topological invariants in low-frequency components and fine-grained structural variations in high-frequency components. FMMD proposed a new kernel to implement domain alignment in the frequency domain. Moreover, as FMMD is designed based on the most famous domain adaptation framework MMD, we integrate a contrastive framework in SMMI to further contribute to improving the blurring boundary problem of conventional MMD.

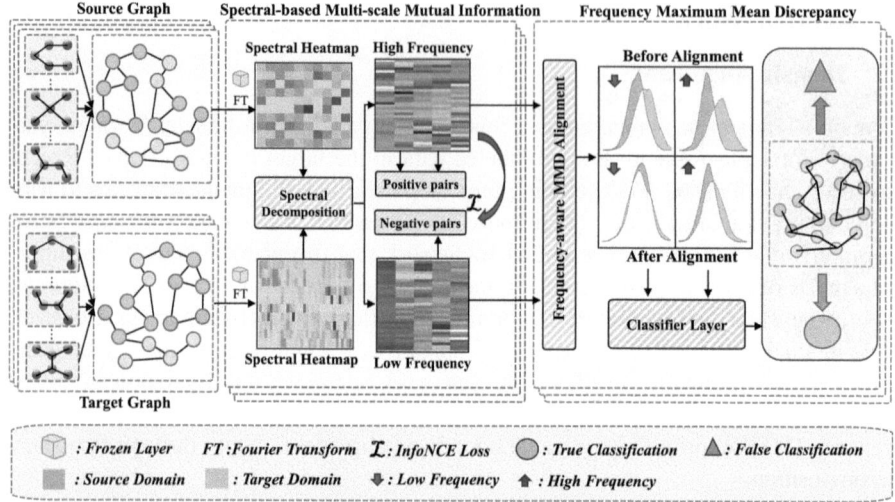

**Fig. 3.** Framework overview of FracNet. The model decomposes source and target graphs into high/low frequency components via Fourier Transform, followed by dual-stream processing with SMMI for contrastive learning and FMMD for domain alignment.

### 3.1 Problem Formulation

Given a graph $\mathcal{G} = (\mathcal{V}, \mathcal{E})$, where $\mathcal{V}$ is the set of nodes and $\mathcal{E} \subseteq V \times V$ denotes the set of edges. For each graph, we denote its Laplacian matrix by $L = D - A \in \mathbb{R}^{|\mathcal{V}| \times |\mathcal{V}|}$, where $D$ is the degree matrix and $A$ is the adjacency matrix. In our problem, we have access to a labeled source domain $D^S = \{(G_i^s, y_i^s)\}_{i=1}^{n_s}$ with $n_s$ samples and an unlabeled target domain $D^t = \{G_j^t\}_{j=1}^{n_t}$ with $n_t$ samples. $D^s$ and $D^t$ share the same label space $y = \{1, 2\}$ but with different distributions in the data space. Our objective is to train the graph classification model on both $D^s$ and $D^t$, and attain high accuracy on the test dataset of the target domain.

### 3.2 Spectral-Guided Maximum Mutual Information

Domain adaptation for graph-structured data faces unique challenges due to the complex interplay between node features and topological structures. Traditional methods often treat graphs as holistic entities, failing to capture the multi-scale nature of graph signals. Graph spectral transforms [27] project node features onto the eigenbasis of the graph Laplacian, where the eigenvectors reflect different patterns of node relationships: low-frequency components correspond to strongly connected nodes with similar features, while high-frequency components capture nodes with dissimilar features between local neighborhoods. This decomposition enables us to analyze and align domain shifts at different levels of node relationships. Although graph spectral transform has been well studied for years, integrating the decomposed components to further contribute to domain adaptation still remains challenging. To address this challenge, we propose a novel Spectral-guided Maximum Mutual Information (SMMI) mechanism.

Given source domain sample $z_s$, target domain sample $z_t$, and negative sample $z_n$, we decompose them into low-frequency and high-frequency components through graph Fourier transform while preserving the original graph structure:

$$z_s = \begin{pmatrix} \lambda_l z_{s,l} \\ \lambda_g z_{s_g} \end{pmatrix}, z_t = \begin{pmatrix} \lambda_l z_{t,l} \\ \lambda_g z_{t_g} \end{pmatrix}, z_n = \begin{pmatrix} \lambda_l z_{n,l} \\ \lambda_g z_{n_g} \end{pmatrix}, \quad (1)$$

where $\lambda_l$ and $\lambda_g$ are the weights for low-frequency and high-frequency components, respectively. Note that $z_n$ is defined here since we mainly focus on binary classification task and introduce a contrastive framework in the rest of this section. A For vectors $z_i = (\lambda_l z_{i,l}, \lambda_g z_{i,g})^T$, where $i \in \{s,t,n\}$, $z_{i,l}$ and $z_{i,g}$ are orthogonal $z_i^T z_j = \lambda_l^2 z_{i,l}^T z_{j,l} + \lambda_g^2 z_{i,g}^T z_{j,g}, j \in \{s,t,n\}$.

Based on this decomposition, we design the following contrastive learning objective to guarantee the discriminative representations for different frequencies:

$$\mathcal{L} = -\frac{1}{|P|} \sum_{(z_s, z_t) \in P} \left( \frac{Z_s^T z_t}{\tau} - \log \left( \sum_{z_n \in N} e^{\frac{z_s^T z_n}{\tau}} + \sum_{z_n \in N} e^{\frac{z_t^T z_t}{\tau}} \right) \right) \quad (2)$$

where $P$ is the set of positive pairs and $\tau$ is the temperature parameter. To better understand the behavior of this loss function, we introduce cosine similarity measures $\cos(\theta_{i,j,l}) = \frac{z_{i,l}^T z_{j,l}}{\|z_{i,l}\|\|z_{j,l}\|}$, $\cos(\theta_{i,j,g}) = \frac{z_{i,g}^T z_{j,g}}{\|z_{i,g}\|\|z_{j,g}\|}$, $i,j \in \{s,t,n\}$.

We assume that features are normalized, i.e., $\|z_{i,l}\| \approx \|z_{j,l}\| \approx K_l$, $\|z_{i,g}\| \approx \|z_{j,g}\| \approx K_g$, and define $\tilde{\lambda}_l^2 = \lambda_l^2 k_l^2, \tilde{\lambda}_g^2 = \lambda_g^2 k_g^2$. This normalization assumption is both theoretically motivated and practically beneficial. From a theoretical perspective, it ensures that the cosine similarities are well-defined and bounded. From a practical standpoint, it stabilizes training and makes the learning process more robust to numerical issues. Using these normalized features, we can rewrite our contrastive loss in a more interpretable form:

$$\mathcal{L}_{contrast} \approx -\frac{1}{|P|} \sum_{(z_s, z_t) \in P} \left( \frac{\tilde{\lambda}_l^2 \cos(\theta_{s,t,l}) + \tilde{\lambda}_g^2 \cos(\theta_{s,t,g})}{\tau} \right.$$
$$\left. - \log \left( \sum_{z_n \in N} \exp\left(\frac{\tilde{\lambda}_l^2 \cos(\theta_{s,n,l}) + \tilde{\lambda}_g^2 \cos(\theta_{s,n,g})}{\tau}\right) + \sum_{z_n \in N} \exp\left(\frac{\tilde{\lambda}_l^2 \cos(\theta_{t,n,l}) + \tilde{\lambda}_g^2 \cos(\theta_{t,n,g})}{\tau}\right) \right) \right) \quad (3)$$

To analyze this loss function rigorously, we employ Jensen's inequality*. Through algebraic manipulation, we can reorganize the terms to highlight the separate contributions of low and high-frequency components:

$$\mathcal{L}_{SMMI} \simeq -\frac{\tilde{\lambda}_l^2}{\tau} \left( \frac{1}{|P|} \sum_{(z_s, z_t) \in P} \cos(\theta_{s,t,l}) - \frac{1}{2}\mathbb{E}_{z_n \sim D_n}[\cos(\theta_{s,n,l}) + \cos(\theta_{t,n,l})] \right)$$
$$- \frac{\tilde{\lambda}_g^2}{\tau} \left( \frac{1}{|P|} \sum_{(z_s, z_t) \in P} \cos(\theta_{s,t,g}) - \frac{1}{2}\mathbb{E}_{z_n \sim D_n}[\cos(\theta_{s,n,g}) + \cos(\theta_{t,n,g})] \right) \quad (4)$$

This decomposition reveals two important properties of our SMMI mechanism: 1) The loss function naturally separates into low-frequency ($\tilde{\lambda}_l^2$) and high-frequency ($\tilde{\lambda}_g^2$) components, allowing for independent optimization of each frequency band; 2) Each frequency component maintains a balance between positive pair attraction (first term) and negative pair repulsion (second term).

### 3.3 Frequency-Aware Maximum Mean Discrepancy

Following the frequency decomposition, we propose a principled approach to measure and align the domain distributions across different frequency components. While Maximum Mean Discrepancy (MMD) has been widely adopted for distribution alignment, traditional MMD-based methods typically employ Gaussian kernels:

$$k_{gaussian}(x,y) = exp(-\frac{\|x-y\|^2}{2\sigma^2}) \tag{5}$$

where $\sigma$ is the bandwidth parameter. Though effective for general distribution alignment, Gaussian kernels treat all feature dimensions uniformly without considering the intrinsic spectral characteristics of graph-structured data. This limitation motivates us to design a frequency-aware kernel function. We propose a novel kernel function that explicitly measures similarities in both low and high-frequency components:

$$k(x,y) = \cos(\theta_{x,y,l}) + \cos(\theta_{x,y,g}) \tag{6}$$

where $\theta_{x,y,l}$ and $\theta_{x,y,g}$ represent the angles between samples in low- and high-frequency spaces, respectively. This design offers several key advantages over conventional Gaussian kernels: 1) Our kernel explicitly captures the angular relationships in different frequency bands, enabling more precise analysis of spectral distributional shifts; 2) Unlike Gaussian kernels that are sensitive to feature scaling, the cosine-based design is naturally invariant to the magnitude of features, making it more robust to frequency-specific variations; 3) The separation of frequency components provides clear geometric interpretation of distribution differences in the spectral domain, facilitating better understanding of domain gaps.

The proposed kernel satisfies several important theoretical properties. For random variables $X, X' \sim D$ independently sampled from distribution $D$, there exist $c_D \in \mathbb{R}$ and $\epsilon_D : \Theta \to \mathbb{R}$, such that:

$$\mathbb{E}_{X,X' \sim D}[k(X,X')] = c_D + \epsilon_D(\theta) \tag{7}$$

With the following properties:

1. $c_D$ depends only on distribution $D$
2. $\sup_{\theta \in \Theta} |\epsilon_D(\theta)| \leq \delta$ for some small constant $\delta > 0$
3. $\|\nabla_\theta \epsilon_D(\theta)\|_2 \leq \eta$ for some small constant $\eta > 0$

Furthermore, we prove that our kernel satisfies two crucial mathematical properties*:

1. **Lipschitz Continuity**: For any $x, y, x', y' \in X$:

$$|k(x,y) - k(x',y')| \leq L(\|x - x'\|_2 + \|y - y'\|_2) \tag{8}$$

2. **Boundedness**: For any $x, y \in X$:

$$|k(x,y)| \leq M \tag{9}$$

Where $L$ and $M$ are positive constants.

Based on this theoretically grounded kernel design, we can formulate the MMD between source and target domains as follows:

$$\begin{aligned} MMD^2(D_s, D_t) &= \mathbb{E}_{x,x' \sim D_s}[k(x,x')] + \mathbb{E}_{y,y' \sim D_t}[k(y,y')] - 2\mathbb{E}_{x \sim D_s, y \sim D_t}[k(x,y)] \\ &= c_{D_s} + c_{D_t} - \frac{2}{|P|} \sum_{(z_s, z_t) \in P} (\cos(\theta_{s,t,l}) + \cos(\theta_{s,t,g})) \end{aligned} \tag{10}$$

where $c_{D_s}$ and $c_{D_t}$ are distribution-specific constants.

To handle negative samples effectively, we extend our analysis to measure the distributional differences between positive and negative samples:

$$\begin{aligned} MMD^2(D_s, D_n) &= c_{D_s} + c_{D_n} - 2\mathbb{E}_{z_n \sim D_n}[\cos(\theta_{s,n,l}) + \cos(\theta_{s,n,g})] \\ MMD^2(D_t, D_n) &= c_{D_t} + c_{D_n} - 2\mathbb{E}_{z_n \sim D_n}[\cos(\theta_{t,n,l}) + \cos(\theta_{t,n,g})] \end{aligned} \tag{11}$$

where $D_n$ represents the negative sample distribution.

Furthermore, we can get $\mathcal{L}_{FMMD}$:

$$\mathcal{L}_{FMMD} = -[\mathbb{E}_{z_n \sim D_n}[\cos(\theta_{s,n,l}) + \cos(\theta_{s,n,g})] + \mathbb{E}_{z_n \sim D_n}[\cos(\theta_{t,n,l}) + \cos(\theta_{t,n,g})]] \tag{12}$$

### 3.4 Unified Spectral Contrastive Framework

A key theoretical insight of our work is that the SMMI objective and FMMD alignment are inherently connected through our frequency-aware kernel design. We get the final loss function $\mathcal{L} = \mathcal{L}_{CE} + \gamma_1 \mathcal{L}_{SMMI} + \gamma_2 \mathcal{L}_{FMMD}$ Where $\gamma_1$ and $\gamma_2$ are balance parameters. This integrative approach ensures that the learned representations are both discriminative within domains and transferable across domains, while preserving the multi-scale nature of graph-structured data.

## 4 Experiments

In this section, we conduct extensive experiments to evaluate the effectiveness of our proposed FracNet framework. Our experiments aim to answer the following key questions:

- **RQ1:** How does our FracNet perform compared to state-of-the-art domain adaptation methods for graph-structured data?

- **RQ2:** How do the spectral relationships between different domains (high- and low-frequency components) affect cross-domain classification accuracy?
- **RQ3:** What impact does the graph structure of molecules have on cross-domain classification performance?
- **RQ4:** How do different components and hyperparameters of our model contribute to the overall performance?

### 4.1 Experimental Settings

**Datasets.** We conduct extensive experiments on three widely-used benchmark datasets from TUDataset [25] in the setting of unsupervised domain adaptation. For convenience M, N, and P are short for Mutagenicity, NCI1, and PROTEINS, respectively. Their details are introduced as follows in Table 1. **Mutagenicity** [18] contains 4337 chemical compounds with corresponding Ames test data indicating their mutagenic effect. **NCI1** [30] consists of 4110 chemical compounds screened for activity against non-small cell lung cancer. **PROTEINS** [9] contains 1113 proteins where nodes represent amino acids and edges indicate spatial proximity (distance $<$ 6 Angstroms). Each of these datasets is divided into different domains based on node density. M0 represents the domain 0 of Mutagenicity dataset and the rest can be deduced by analogy.

Table 1. Statistics of the experimental datasets.

| Datasets | Graphs | Avg. Nodes | Avg. Edges | Classes |
|---|---|---|---|---|
| Mutagenicity | 4337 | 30.32 | 30.77 | 2 |
| NCI1 | 4110 | 29.87 | 32.30 | 2 |
| PROTEINS | 1113 | 39.1 | 72.8 | 2 |

**Baselines.** We compare FracNet with a wide range of existing methods. These baseline methods fall into three categories: (1) Graph neural networks, e.g., GCN [19], GIN [34], GMT [1], GAT [29], GraphSAGE [11] and DeSGDA [32]. These methods only use the source domain data for training and test on target domain data. (2) Unsupervised domain adaptation methods, e.g., CDAN [24] and ToAlign [33]. They leverage information from both source and target domains to reduce distribution discrepancy. (3) Unsupervised graph domain adaptation method, e.g., CoCo [35], which is the state-of-the-art source-free domain adaptation method designed for image classification.

**Implementation Details.** We employ a 3-layer GNN encoder (GIN by default) with an embedding dimension of 64. The model is optimized using Adam optimizer with a learning rate of 0.001 and a dropout rate of 0.3. We train the model for 200 epochs with a temperature parameter of 0.1 for contrastive learning. For baselines, we configure the methods with the same hyperparameters from their original papers and further fine-tune them to optimize performance. All experiments are conducted with PyTorch on NVIDIA A100-SXM4-80GB. To reduce randomness, we perform 5 runs with different random seeds and report the average accuracy (Tables 2 and 4).

**Table 2.** The results (in %) on Mutagenicity (source→target). The red and blue numbers denote the highest and second highest results.

| Methods | M0-M1 | M1-M0 | M0-M2 | M2-M0 | M0-M3 | M3-M0 | M1-M2 | M2-M1 | M1-M3 | M3-M1 | M2-M3 | M3-M2 | Avg. |
|---|---|---|---|---|---|---|---|---|---|---|---|---|---|
| GCN | 73.5 | 60.8 | 69.6 | 68.5 | 54.2 | 55.1 | 68.6 | 75.3 | 51.4 | 46.2 | 58.6 | 60.1 | 61.8 |
| GIN | 77.3 | 68.9 | 70.2 | 69.1 | 63.8 | 61.8 | 77.6 | 78.3 | 64.2 | 71.5 | 69.2 | 72.8 | 70.4 |
| GMT | 67.2 | 52.3 | 59.8 | 47.5 | 53.2 | 52.5 | 59.8 | 67.3 | 46.7 | 67.2 | 53.1 | 59.8 | 57.2 |
| GAT | 65.5 | 71.3 | 57.6 | 63.1 | 38.2 | 51.6 | 59.7 | 58.8 | 72.7 | 57.6 | 79.5 | 67.6 | 61.9 |
| GraphSAGE | 69.3 | 69.2 | 60.4 | 63.7 | 42.3 | 56.5 | 62.4 | 61.6 | 70.5 | 58.3 | 79.1 | 65.3 | 63.2 |
| DeSGDA | 76.5 | 72.3 | 71.4 | 71.5 | 60.7 | 67.3 | 75.2 | 79.4 | 62.7 | 75.8 | 65.5 | 72.1 | 70.9 |
| CDAN | 75.3 | 71.2 | 70.7 | 70.3 | 58.7 | 58.4 | 70.1 | 76.1 | 58.3 | 69.4 | 58.7 | 63.5 | 66.7 |
| ToAlign | 67.3 | 47.5 | 59.8 | 47.5 | 46.7 | 47.2 | 59.6 | 67.2 | 46.7 | 67.3 | 46.5 | 59.8 | 55.3 |
| CoCo | 75.4 | 71.7 | 68.7 | 69.2 | 60.8 | 65.7 | 79.2 | 76.8 | 63.4 | 73.6 | 64.6 | 70.1 | 69.9 |
| FracNet | 79.4 | 76.3 | 72.8 | 73.4 | 73.9 | 74.1 | 73.5 | 77.8 | 74.0 | 72.1 | 74.0 | 73.4 | 74.6 |

**Table 3.** The results (in %) on NCI1 (source→target). The red and blue numbers denote the highest and second highest results.

| Methods | N0-N1 | N1-N0 | N0-N2 | N2-N0 | N0-N3 | N3-N0 | N1-N2 | N2-N1 | N1-N3 | N3-N1 | N2-N3 | N3-N2 | Avg. |
|---|---|---|---|---|---|---|---|---|---|---|---|---|---|
| GCN | 51.2 | 70.2 | 42.7 | 27.6 | 32.1 | 27.1 | 55.2 | 50.6 | 50.9 | 49.1 | 67.3 | 57.5 | 48.5 |
| GIN | 66.8 | 78.4 | 60.2 | 72.3 | 51.1 | 68.6 | 63.5 | 67.8 | 65.9 | 60.3 | 71.1 | 67.2 | 66.1 |
| GMT | 50.6 | 72.9 | 57.3 | 72.8 | 66.4 | 73.1 | 72.4 | 50.8 | 66.5 | 58.3 | 66.3 | 72.6 | 65.0 |
| GAT | 67.2 | 62.5 | 63.6 | 70.1 | 61.4 | 59.7 | 63.9 | 68.5 | 66.3 | 64.9 | 64.6 | 68.1 | 65.1 |
| GraphSAGE | 67.5 | 70.6 | 61.3 | 69.2 | 65.8 | 64.7 | 68.5 | 66.2 | 64.2 | 59.4 | 63.9 | 68.4 | 65.8 |
| DeSGDA | 64.4 | 76.9 | 64.8 | 76.1 | 68.6 | 74.1 | 66.8 | 64.6 | 69.2 | 63.8 | 70.5 | 64.2 | 68.7 |
| CDAN | 57.1 | 74.7 | 61.2 | 73.7 | 68.2 | 73.3 | 60.2 | 56.5 | 68.2 | 53.9 | 68.4 | 59.6 | 64.6 |
| ToAlign | 49.1 | 27.2 | 57.3 | 27.1 | 66.4 | 27.1 | 57.2 | 49.1 | 66.4 | 49.1 | 66.5 | 57.3 | 50.0 |
| CoCo | 69.7 | 80.2 | 64.5 | 76.3 | 64.6 | 73.8 | 68.2 | 70.2 | 67.7 | 61.2 | 73.1 | 64.8 | 69.5 |
| FracNet | 74.1 | 75.6 | 72.4 | 74.2 | 69.3 | 68.9 | 74.1 | 73.9 | 74.0 | 69.5 | 74.1 | 71.2 | 72.6 |

## 4.2 Performance Comparison (RQ1)

We conduct extensive experiments across three benchmark datasets (Mutagenicity, NCI1, and PROTEINS) to evaluate FracNet against state-of-the-art baselines. The comprehensive results in Tables 1-3 demonstrate consistent superiority of our approach.

Traditional GNN methods (GCN, GIN, GAT, etc.) often struggle with domain adaptation tasks, particularly in challenging scenarios like Mutagenicity M0→M3 (54.2%) and PROTEINS P0→P3 (24.4%), where performance drops substantially. These methods fail to account for structural and distributional shifts between domains, leading to suboptimal transfer learning.

Domain adaptation approaches show improved but inconsistent performance. While DeSGDA achieves competitive results on PROTEINS (76.6% average accuracy), its effectiveness varies considerably across datasets (70.9% on Mutagenicity and 68.7% on NCI1). Similarly, CoCo performs well on certain transfer tasks (e.g., 80.2% on NCI1 N1→N0) but lacks robustness across broader evaluation settings. This instability stems from their monolithic treatment of graph representations, which fails to address the frequency-dependent nature of domain shifts.

**Table 4.** The results (in %) on PROTEINS (source→target). The red and blue numbers denote the highest and second highest results.

| Methods | P0-P1 | P1-P0 | P0-P2 | P2-P0 | P0-P3 | P3-P0 | P1-P2 | P2-P1 | P1-P3 | P3-P1 | P2-P3 | P3-P2 | Avg. |
|---|---|---|---|---|---|---|---|---|---|---|---|---|---|
| GCN | 73.7 | 82.6 | 57.5 | 83.9 | 24.4 | 17.3 | 57.6 | 70.8 | 24.5 | 26.3 | 37.5 | 42.4 | 49.9 |
| GIN | 71.6 | 70.2 | 58.4 | 56.9 | 74.2 | 78.2 | 63.3 | 67.1 | 35.8 | 60.8 | 71.6 | 65.2 | 64.4 |
| GMT | 73.6 | 82.5 | 57.6 | 83.1 | 75.6 | 17.3 | 57.6 | 73.5 | 75.4 | 26.3 | 75.5 | 42.3 | 61.7 |
| GAT | 67.2 | 66.3 | 68.5 | 71.4 | 70.6 | 53.5 | 65.1 | 64.6 | 58.2 | 57.5 | 70.9 | 68.1 | 65.2 |
| GraphSAGE | 70.5 | 66.8 | 66.4 | 72.3 | 71.7 | 63.7 | 64.7 | 68.1 | 59.6 | 60.1 | 71.6 | 69.2 | 67.1 |
| DeSGDA | 77.5 | 84.3 | 70.2 | 84.2 | 76.6 | 83.2 | 71.6 | 77.2 | 75.8 | 73.4 | 75.4 | 70.4 | 76.6 |
| CDAN | 75.8 | 83.1 | 60.6 | 82.6 | 75.8 | 70.5 | 64.7 | 77.4 | 73.1 | 75.4 | 75.6 | 67.1 | 73.5 |
| ToAlign | 73.2 | 82.5 | 57.4 | 82.3 | 24.3 | 82.6 | 57.5 | 73.7 | 24.3 | 73.6 | 24.2 | 57.6 | 59.4 |
| CoCo | 74.6 | 83.9 | 65.2 | 83.4 | 72.1 | 82.7 | 69.5 | 75.4 | 70.7 | 73.2 | 72.4 | 66.1 | 74.1 |
| FracNet | 76.4 | 87.5 | 70.7 | 87.9 | 74.7 | 72.4 | 74.5 | 74.3 | 77.2 | 73.7 | 77.3 | 73.7 | 76.9 |

FracNet demonstrates consistent state-of-the-art performance across all datasets, achieving the highest average accuracy on Mutagenicity (74.6%), NCI1 (72.6%), and PROTEINS (76.9%). The performance advantage is particularly pronounced in challenging transfer scenarios such as Mutagenicity M0→M3 (73.9% vs. next best 64.6%) and NCI1 N1→N3 (74.0% vs. next best 69.2%), where domain shifts are most severe. The significant improvement over strong baselines (+2.3% over DeSGDA on PROTEINS, +4.1% over CoCo on Mutagenicity, and +3.1% over CoCo on NCI1) validates the effectiveness of our approach.

### 4.3 Case Study (RQ2, RQ3)

#### 4.3.1 Spectral Shift Direction and Distance (RQ2)

We analyzed spectral properties of molecular domains by decomposing graph Laplacian eigenvalues into low and high-frequency components as illustrated in Fig. 4, where x-axis and y-axis represent the low-frequency energy and high-frequency energy for different domains, respectively.

Figure 4 maps domains in spectral energy space, revealing fundamental patterns governing transfer learning effectiveness. The *spectral distance* between domains influences adaptation quality, with the one of moderate distance typically outperforming the one of larger distance across all datasets. More importantly, we observe a consistent *directional asymmetry* in transfer performance: when high-frequency energy remains relatively low, knowledge transfer from domains with lower to higher low-frequency energy achieves superior performance (e.g., N1→N0 outperforms N0→N1). This establishes a key principle that when the high-frequency energy is low, adaptation along **ascending** low-frequency energy gradients facilitates more effective adaption between molecular domains.

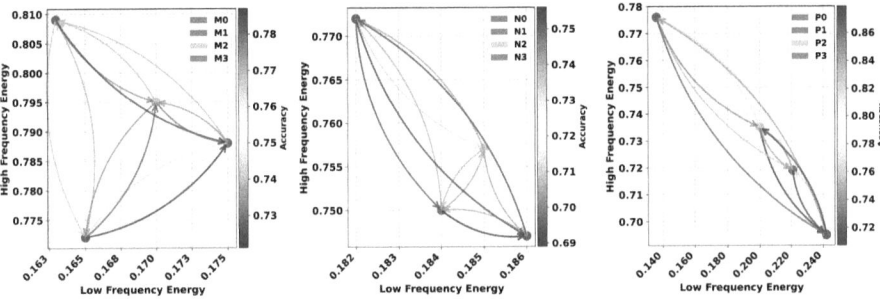

**Fig. 4.** Energy trajectories in frequency domain on three datasets.

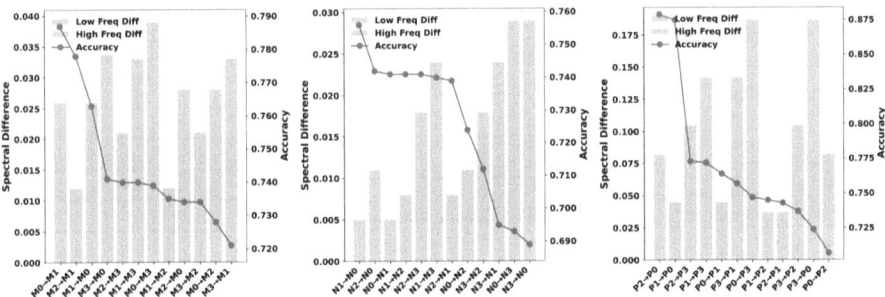

**Fig. 5.** Pairwise spectral differences, decomposed into low-frequency (blue) and high-frequency (pink) components. (Color figure online)

### 4.3.2 Proportion of Different Frequency Components (RQ2)

To further quantify spectral differences between molecular domains, we calculated the normalized energy distribution across frequency bands for each domain pair. For each transfer task, we decomposed the spectral energy difference into low-frequency and high-frequency components, visualizing their relative contributions as stacked bar charts, as shown in Fig. 5. Each rectangle is the difference between every two domains in terms of low-frequency (blue part) or high-frequency (pink part) regime, with a larger size indicating a larger difference.

Notably, Fig. 5 presents a distinctive pattern that explains FracNet's relatively smaller performance advantage on PROTEINS compared to other datasets. Unlike Mutagenicity and NCI1, PROTEINS transfer tasks exhibit substantially more balanced distributions between high and low-frequency differences, as evidenced by the more equal heights of pink and blue bars. Many PROTEINS transfer tasks show significant low-frequency contributions (larger blue portions). This balanced frequency profile in PROTEINS creates a unique challenge: when frequency differences are more evenly distributed across bands, conventional domain adaptation methods can partially compensate through their unified representation approach. The advantage of frequency-specific processing becomes less pronounced in such scenarios, explaining why FracNet shows a smaller margin of improvement (0.3% over DeSGDA) on PROTEINS compared to Mutagenicity (3.7% over CoCo) and NCI1 (3.1% over CoCo).

### 4.3.3 Graph Structure Analysis (RQ3)

Beyond spectral analysis, we examine graph structural properties to better understand how FracNet works. We chose cyclomatic numbers (count of independent cycles in a graph) as our structural metric because they directly influence spectral properties. Cycles create distinctive patterns in the Laplacian eigenvalue spectrum by introducing closed paths that alter graph connectivity structures. The distribution and density of cycles significantly shape the spectral energy profile: graphs with more cycles typically exhibit different eigenvalue distributions compared to sparser structures. This cycle distribution directly impacts how energy spreads across frequency bands in the graph spectrum, providing a concrete structural interpretation of our spectral observations.

Our cyclomatic distribution analysis reveals clear relationships between graph structural complexity and transfer performance. PROTEINS exhibits extreme cyclomatic variation (**maximum 539 cycles**) compared to Mutagenicity and NCI1 (**maxima of 16 and 18 cycles**). This structural disparity correlates with FracNet's performance patterns. While achieving high absolute accuracy (76.9%) on PROTEINS, FracNet shows minimal relative improvement (0.3% over DeSGDA). This suggests that excessive cycle distribution differences create spectral profiles too disparate for effective frequency-adaptive processing.

FracNet demonstrates its strongest performance advantages on Mutagenicity (3.7% over DeSGDA) and NCI1 (3.1% over CoCo), both characterized by moderate cyclomatic variations. These results identify an optimal efficacy zone for spectral adaptation methods where structural differences are significant enough to benefit from frequency-specific processing but not so extreme as to create fundamentally incompatible spectral distributions (Fig. 6).

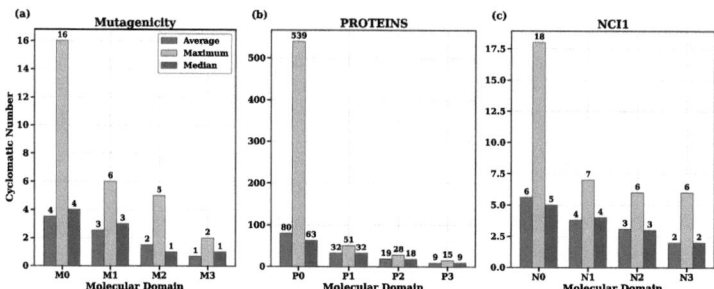

**Fig. 6.** Cyclomatic number distributions across molecular domains in three datasets.

### 4.4 Ablation Study (RQ4)

We evaluate each component's contribution through ablation studies on two datasets by creating variants: (1) **w/o SMMI**, removing the Spectral-guided Maximum Mutual Information module; and (2) **w/o FMMD**, removing the Frequency-aware Maximum Mean Discrepancy module.

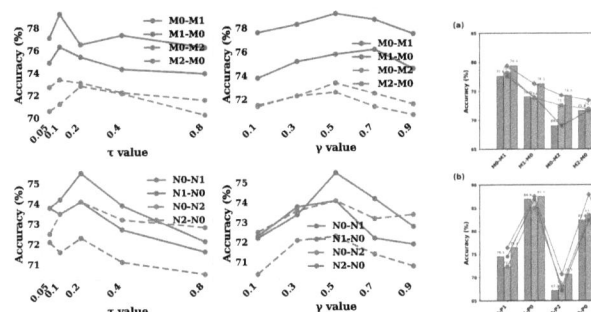 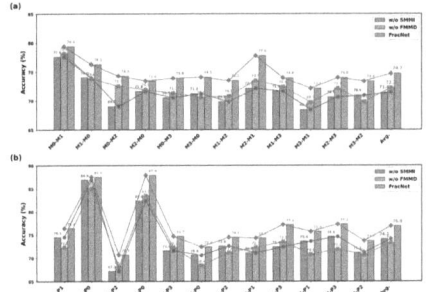

(a) Temperature coefficient ($\tau$) and balance parameter ($\gamma$). (The upper two represent the Mutagenicity dataset and the lower two the NCI1 dataset.)

(b) Ablation study results showing average accuracy on (a) Mutagenicity and (b) PROTEINS.

**Fig. 7.** (a) Hyperparameter sensitivity analysis; (b) Ablation study results.

As shown in Fig. 7(b), both components significantly enhance performance. On Mutagenicity, removing SMMI and FMMD reduces accuracy by 3.3% and 2.5% respectively, with similar patterns on PROTEINS (2.8% and 3.6% decreases). SMMI proves crucial for challenging transfers with significant domain shifts (M0→M2, P0→P2) by maintaining discriminative boundaries while aligning domains. FMMD contributes most to transfers involving structurally complex domains (M2→M1, P2→P0), validating its adaptive frequency-aware design for capturing domain-specific properties across frequency bands.

Interestingly, component contributions vary by dataset. In PROTEINS, with balanced high-low frequency differences, FMMD contributes more significantly. In Mutagenicity, where high-frequency differences dominate, SMMI plays a more critical role. These patterns confirm our spectral analysis: FMMD's adaptive frequency handling excels with balanced spectral differences, while SMMI's discriminative preservation becomes vital when high-frequency components dominate domain shifts. Together, these complementary components address domain adaptation's dual challenges: preserving discriminative information while effectively aligning domains across the spectral dimension.

### 4.5 Sensitivity Analysis

The sensitivity analysis of FracNet's critical hyperparameters reveals insightful patterns regarding the model's robustness and optimal configuration across different molecular domains (Fig. 7(a)). As shown in subfigures (a) and (c), the temperature parameter $\tau$, which governs the spectral filtering sharpness, demonstrates a consistent bell-shaped performance curve with optimal values centered around $\tau = 0.1 \sim 0.2$ across both Mutagenicity and NCI1 datasets. This moderate filtering threshold achieves an optimal balance between preserving essential structural information and eliminating domain-specific noise. Notably, performance degradation is more pronounced for larger $\tau$ values ($\tau > 0.4$), with accuracy dropping by up to 3.0% in M0→M1 and 2.5% in N1→N0 transfers, suggesting that excessive spectral compression eliminates crucial molecular structural signals. Similarly, the frequency modulation parameter $\gamma$, examined in subfigures (b) and (d), exhibits optimal performance at $\gamma = 0.5$ across most transfer tasks, with a more gradual performance decline toward extreme values.

## 5 Conclusion

We have presented FracNet with two synergic modules to decompose the original graph into high-frequency and low-frequency components and perform frequency-aware domain adaptation. The key insight is that domain shifts can be better understood through spectral analysis, where low-frequency components encode domain-invariant global patterns, and high-frequency components capture domain-specific local details. Moreover, the blurring boundary problem of domain adaptation is improved by integrating with a contrastive learning framework. Besides providing rigorous theoretical proof, we conducted extensive experiments across three benchmark datasets to demonstrate the significant performances of FracNet. Future work includes extending FracNet to multi-source domain adaptation scenarios and exploring applications in other graph domain adaptation tasks.

**Acknowledgments.** Wenqi FAN is partly supported by General Research Funds from the Hong Kong Research Grants Council (project no. PolyU 15207322, 15200023, 15206024, and 15224524), internal research funds from The Hong Kong Polytechnic University (project no. P0042693, P0048625, P0051361, P0052406, and P0052986).

## References

1. Baek, M., et al.: Accurate prediction of protein structures and interactions using a three-track neural network. Science **373**(6557), 871–876 (2021)
2. Bo, D., Fang, Y., Liu, Y., Shi, C.: Graph contrastive learning with stable and scalable spectral encoding. Adv. Neural Inf. Process. Syst. **36** (2024)
3. Bo, D., Shi, C., Wang, L., Liao, R.: Specformer: spectral graph neural networks meet transformers. arXiv preprint arXiv:2303.01028 (2023)
4. Butler, K.T., Davies, D.W., Cartwright, H., Isayev, O., Walsh, A.: Machine learning for molecular and materials science. Nature **559**(7715), 547–555 (2018)
5. Cai, R., Wu, F., Li, Z., Wei, P., Yi, L., Zhang, K.: Graph domain adaptation: a generative view. ACM Trans. Knowl. Discov. Data **18**(3), 1–24 (2024)
6. Chen, X., Wang, S., Long, M., Wang, J.: Transferability vs. discriminability: batch spectral penalization for adversarial domain adaptation. In: International Conference on Machine Learning, pp. 1081–1090. PMLR (2019)
7. Chen, Z., et al.: Bridging the gap between spatial and spectral domains: a unified framework for graph neural networks. ACM Comput. Surv. **56**(5), 1–42 (2023)
8. Choo, H.Y., Wee, J., Shen, C., Xia, K.: Fingerprint-enhanced graph attention network (fingat) model for antibiotic discovery. J. Chem. Inf. Model. **63**(10), 2928–2935 (2023)
9. Dobson, P.D., Doig, A.J.: Distinguishing enzyme structures from non-enzymes without alignments. J. Mol. Biol. **330**(4), 771–783 (2003)

10. Gao, Y., Wang, X., He, X., Liu, Z., Feng, H., Zhang, Y.: Addressing heterophily in graph anomaly detection: a perspective of graph spectrum. In: Proceedings of the ACM Web Conference 2023, pp. 1528–1538 (2023)
11. Hamilton, W., Ying, Z., Leskovec, J.: Inductive representation learning on large graphs. Adv. Neural Inf. Process. Syst. **30** (2017)
12. He, K., Fan, H., Wu, Y., Xie, S., Girshick, R.: Momentum contrast for unsupervised visual representation learning. In: Proceedings of the IEEE/CVF Conference on Computer Vision and Pattern Recognition, pp. 9729–9738 (2020)
13. Hu, J., Qi, L., Zhang, J., Shi, Y.: Domain generalization via inter-domain alignment and intra-domain expansion. Pattern Recogn. **146**, 110029 (2024)
14. Jiang, X., Qin, Z., Xu, J., Ao, X.: Incomplete graph learning via attribute-structure decoupled variational auto-encoder. In: WSDM Oral 2023, pp. 304–312. ACM (2023)
15. Jiang, X., et al.: Ragraph: a general retrieval-augmented graph learning framework. In: NeurIPS 2024 (2024)
16. Jiang, X., Zhuang, D., Zhang, X., Chen, H., Luo, J., Gao, X.: Uncertainty quantification via spatial-temporal tweedie model for zero-inflated and long-tail travel demand prediction. In: CIKM 2023, pp. 3983–3987. ACM (2023)
17. Ju, W., et al.: A comprehensive survey on deep graph representation learning. Neural Netw. 106207 (2024)
18. Kazius, J., McGuire, R., Bursi, R.: Derivation and validation of toxicophores for mutagenicity prediction. J. Med. Chem. **48**(1), 312–320 (2005)
19. Kipf, T.N., Welling, M.: Semi-supervised classification with graph convolutional networks. arXiv preprint arXiv:1609.02907 (2016)
20. Li, R., Jiang, X., Zhong, T., Trajcevski, G., Wu, J., Zhou, F.: Mining spatio-temporal relations via self-paced graph contrastive learning. In: SIGKDD 2022, pp. 936–944. ACM (2022)
21. Liu, F., Gao, W., Liu, J., Tang, X., Xiao, L.: Adversarial domain alignment with contrastive learning for hyperspectral image classification. IEEE Trans. Geosci. Remote Sens. (2023)
22. Liu, M., et al.: Rethinking propagation for unsupervised graph domain adaptation. In: Proceedings of the AAAI Conference on Artificial Intelligence, pp. 13963–13971 (2024)
23. Liu, W., et al.: Joint internal multi-interest exploration and external domain alignment for cross domain sequential recommendation. In: Proceedings of the ACM Web Conference 2023, pp. 383–394 (2023)
24. Long, M., Cao, Z., Wang, J., Jordan, M.I.: Conditional adversarial domain adaptation. Adv. Neural Inf. Process. Syst. **31** (2018)
25. Morris, C., Kriege, N.M., Bause, F., Kersting, K., Mutzel, P., Neumann, M.: Tudataset: A collection of benchmark datasets for learning with graphs. arXiv preprint arXiv:2007.08663 (2020)
26. Rattan, G., Seppelt, T.: Weisfeiler-leman and graph spectra. In: Proceedings of the 2023 Annual ACM-SIAM Symposium on Discrete Algorithms (SODA), pp. 2268–2285. SIAM (2023)
27. Sandryhaila, A., Moura, J.M.: Discrete signal processing on graphs: graph fourier transform. In: 2013 IEEE International Conference on Acoustics, Speech and Signal Processing, pp. 6167–6170. IEEE (2013)
28. Sun, Y., Liu, Y., Liu, X., Li, Y., Chu, W.S.: Rethinking domain generalization for face anti-spoofing: separability and alignment. In: Proceedings of the IEEE/CVF Conference on Computer Vision and Pattern Recognition, pp. 24563–24574 (2023)
29. Velickovic, P., Cucurull, G., Casanova, A., Romero, A., Lio, P., Bengio, Y., et al.: Graph attention networks. STAT **1050**(20), 10–48550 (2017)
30. Wale, N., Watson, I.A., Karypis, G.: Comparison of descriptor spaces for chemical compound retrieval and classification. Knowl. Inf. Syst. **14**, 347–375 (2008)

31. Wang, X., Peng, D., Yan, M., Hu, P.: Correspondence-free domain alignment for unsupervised cross-domain image retrieval. In: Proceedings of the AAAI Conference on Artificial Intelligence, pp. 10200–10208 (2023)
32. Wang, Y., Liu, S., Wang, M., Liang, S., Yin, N.: Degree distribution based spiking graph networks for domain adaptation. arXiv preprint arXiv:2410.06883 (2024)
33. Wei, G., Lan, C., Zeng, W., Chen, Z.: Metaalign: coordinating domain alignment and classification for unsupervised domain adaptation. In: Proceedings of the IEEE/CVF Conference on Computer Vision and Pattern Recognition, pp. 16643–16653 (2021)
34. Xu, K., Hu, W., Leskovec, J., Jegelka, S.: How powerful are graph neural networks? arXiv preprint arXiv:1810.00826 (2018)
35. Yin, N., et al.: Coco: a coupled contrastive framework for unsupervised domain adaptive graph classification. In: International Conference on Machine Learning, pp. 40040–40053. PMLR (2023)
36. Zhang, H., Zhang, W., Miao, H., Jiang, X., Fang, Y., Zhang, Y.: Strap: spatio-temporal pattern retrieval for out-of-distribution generalization. arXiv preprint arXiv:2505.19547 (2025)
37. Zhang, R., et al.: Infinite-horizon graph filters: leveraging power series to enhance sparse information aggregation. arXiv preprint arXiv:2401.09943 (2024)
38. Zhang, Y., Zhu, H., Song, Z., Koniusz, P., King, I.: Spectral feature augmentation for graph contrastive learning and beyond. In: Proceedings of the AAAI Conference on Artificial Intelligence, pp. 11289–11297 (2023)
39. Zhang, Z., Cui, P., Zhu, W.: Deep learning on graphs: a survey. IEEE Trans. Knowl. Data Eng. **34**(1), 249–270 (2020)
40. Zhou, Y., Zheng, H., Huang, X., Hao, S., Li, D., Zhao, J.: Graph neural networks: taxonomy, advances, and trends. ACM Trans. Intell. Syst. Technol. (TIST) **13**(1), 1–54 (2022)

# Grouped Discrete Representation for Object-Centric Learning

Rongzhen Zhao[1(✉)], Vivienne Wang[1], Juho Kannala[2,3], and Joni Pajarinen[1]

[1] Department of Electrical Engineering and Automation, Aalto University, Espoo, Finland
{rongzhen.zhao,vivienne.wang,joni.pajarinen}@aalto.fi
[2] Department of Computer Science, Aalto University, Espoo, Finland
juho.kannala@aalto.fi
[3] Center for Machine Vision and Signal Analysis, University of Oulu, Oulu, Finland

**Abstract.** Object-Centric Learning (OCL) aims to discover objects in images or videos by reconstructing the input. Representative methods achieve this by reconstructing the input as its Variational Autoencoder (VAE) discrete representations, which suppress (super-)pixel noise and enhance object separability. However, these methods treat features as indivisible units, overlooking their compositional attributes, and discretize features via scalar code indexes, losing attribute-level similarities and differences. We propose Grouped Discrete Representation (GDR) for OCL. For better generalization, features are decomposed into combinatorial attributes by organized channel grouping. For better convergence, features are quantized into discrete representations via tuple code indexes. Experiments demonstrate that GDR consistently improves both mainstream and state-of-the-art OCL methods across various datasets. Visualizations further highlight GDR's superior object separability and interpretability. The source code is available on https://github.com/Genera1Z/GroupedDiscreteRepresentation.

**Keywords:** Object-Centric Learning · Variational Autoencoder · Discrete Representation · Channel Grouping

## 1 Introduction

Under self or weak supervision, Object-Centric Learning (OCL) [5,10] represents dense image or video pixels as sparse object feature vectors, known as *slots*. These slots can be used for *set prediction* while their corresponding attention maps for *object discovery* [20]. OCL is bio-plausible, as humans perceive visual scenes as objects for visual cognition, like understanding, reasoning, planning, and decision-making [2,7,22]. OCL is versatile, as object-level representations of images or videos fit to tasks involving different modalities [31,34].

The training signal comes from reconstructing the input. Directly reconstructing input pixels [10,20] struggles with complex-textured objects. Mixture-based

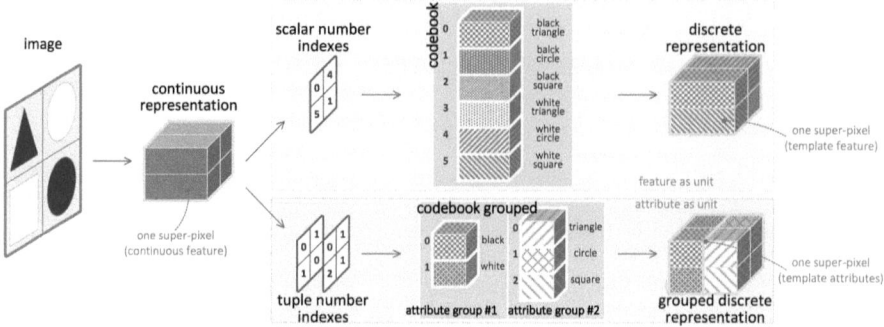

**Fig. 1.** Non-grouped vs grouped discrete representation. (*upper*) Existing methods treat features as units, selecting template features from a codebook by scalar indexes to discretize superpixels. (*lower*) We treat attributes as units, selecting template attributes from a grouped codebook by tuple indexes.

OCL methods [9,16] reconstruct more object-separable modalities, like optical flow and depth maps. Foundation-based methods [24,35] use the input's foundation model features as the target. Transformer-based [25,27] and Diffusion-based methods [14,32] reconstruct the input's Variational Autoencoder (VAE) intermediate representation. With a limited number of shared template features, i.e., codes in a codebook, continuous-valued superpixels in VAE representations are discretized [12,28]. This suppresses (super-)pixel noise and enhances object separability. Empirically, improved object separability in the reconstruction target offers OCL more effective training guidance.

However, these methods treat features as atomic units and entangle their composing attributes together, thus limiting model generalization. Moreover, the corresponding scalar code indexes fail to capture superpixels' attribute-level similarities and differences, thus hindering model convergence.

As illustrated in Fig. 1, consider a dataset characterized by two attribute groups: color (black, white) and shape (triangle, square, circle). An image in it contains four objects, each downsampled to a superpixel in the feature map. To select template features from a feature-level codebook, six scalar code indexes are needed, where digits 0–5 refer to black-triangle, black-circle, black-square, etc. Each code is reused with probability $\frac{1}{6}$. The feature map can thus be discretized as $\begin{bmatrix} 0 & 4 \\ 5 & 1 \end{bmatrix}$. But if decomposed, superpixels can be discretized as combinations of template attributes from two attribute groups, i.e., $\begin{bmatrix} 0,0 & 1,1 \\ 1,2 & 0,1 \end{bmatrix}$. The first and second numbers in these index tuples indicate whether superpixels' attributes are the same or different, facilitating model convergence. These codes are reused with higher probabilities $\frac{1}{2}$ and $\frac{1}{3}$ respectively, benefiting model generalization.

Our main contributions are as follows: (*i*) We propose *Grouped Discrete Representation* (GDR) for VAE discrete representation to guide OCL training better; (*ii*) GDR is compatible with mainstream OCL methods and boosts both their convergence and generalization; (*iii*) GDR captures attribute-level similarities and differences, also enhances object separability in VAE representations.

## 2 Related Work

**Object-Centric Learning** (OCL). Mainstream OCL obtains supervision from reconstruction using slots aggregated by SlotAttention [1,20] from the input's dense superpixels. SLATE [25] and STEVE [27], which are Transformer-based, generate input tokens from slots via a Transformer decoder [29], guided by dVAE [12] discrete representations. SlotDiffusion [32] and LSD [14], which are Diffusion-based, recover input noise from slots via a Diffusion model [23], guided by VQ-VAE [28] discrete representations. DINOSAUR [24] and VideoSAUR [35], which are foundation model-based, reconstruct input features from slots via a spatial broadcast decoder [30], guided by well-pretrained features of the foundation model DINO [6,21]. We focus on the VAE part of OCL.

**Variational Autoencoder** (VAE). Discrete representations of VAE have been shown to guide OCL better than direct input pixels as reconstruction targets. Transformer-based OCL methods [25,27] utilize dVAE [12] to discretize encoder representations by selecting template features from a codebook via Gumbel sampling [13]. Diffusion-based OCL methods [14,32] employ VQ-VAE [28] to achieve discretization by replacing features with their closest codebook codes. Similar to our idea, both [4] and [19] seek to decompose features into attributes, but their monolithic VAE representation is incompatible with OCL. Other VAE variants also offer techniques, like grouping [33], residual [3] and clustering [18], to enhance VAE representations. We borrow some for the OCL setting.

**Channel Grouping.** Splitting features along the channel dimension and transforming them separately is often used to diversify representations [8,11,17,36,37]. These solutions mainly perform grouping directly on feature maps [17] or on learnable parameters [36]. To the best of our knowledge, only one work has explored this idea in the OCL setting. SysBinder [26] groups slots along the channel dimension in the slot attention [20] to aggregate different attributes of objects, yielding better interpretability in object representation but limited performance gains. We group VAE intermediate representations along channels, yielding grouped discrete representations to guide OCL training better.

## 3 Proposed Method

We propose Grouped Discrete Representation (GDR), applicable to mainstream OCL methods, either Transformer-based [15,25,27,35] or Diffusion-based [14,32]. Simply modifying their VAE, our GDR improves them by providing reconstruction targets, or *guidance*, with better object separability.

**Notations:** As shown in Fig. 2, image or video frame $I$, continuous representation $Z$, discrete representation $X$, and noise $N$ are tensors in shape (height, width, channel); queries $Q$ and slots $S$ are tensors in shape (number-of-slots, channel); segmentation $M$ is a tensor in shape (height, width).

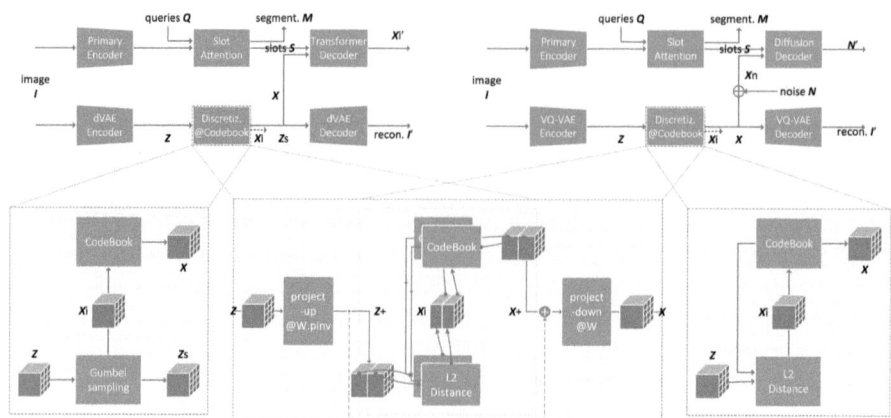

**Fig. 2.** Our GDR is applicable to mainstream OCL. First row: architectures of Transformer-based (*left*) and Diffusion-based (*right*) methods. Second row: non-grouped representation discretization in dVAE (*left*), non-grouped discretization in VQ-VAE (*right*), and grouped discretization (*center*) of our method.

### 3.1 Preliminary: Discrete Representation

Both Transformer-based and Diffusion-based methods learn to aggregate pixels into *slots* by reconstructing the input as its VAE discrete representation.

*Transformer-based* architecture is depicted in Fig. 2 first row left. The input image or video frame $I$ is encoded by a primary encoder and aggregated by SlotAttention [20] into slots $S$ under queries $Q$, with object (and background) segmentation masks $M$ as byproducts. Meanwhile, pretrained VAE represents $I$ as discrete representation $X$ and the corresponding code indexes $X_i$. Subsequently, using a Transformer decoder, $S$ is tasked with reconstructing $X_i$ as classification, guided by causal-masked $X$. For videos, current slots $S$ are transformed by a Transformer encoder block into queries for the next frame.

Specifically, discrete representations for Transformer-based OCL are obtained as shown in Fig. 2 second row left:

- Predefine a codebook $C$ containing $n$ $c$-dimensional learnable codes as template features;
- Transform input $I$ with a dVAE encoder into continuous intermediate representation $Z$;
- Sample $Z$ via Gumbel softmax, yielding one-hot indexes $X_i$ and soft sampling $Z_s$ for dVAE decoding;
- Select template features from $C$ by $X_i$ and compose the discrete representation $X$ to guide OCL training.

*Diffusion-based* architecture is drawn in Fig. 2 first row right. The key difference is that, with a conditional Diffusion model decoder, $S$ is tasked with reconstructing Gaussian noise $N$ added to $X$ as regression.

Specifically, discrete representations for Diffusion-based OCL are obtained as in Fig. 2 second row right:

- Predefine a codebook $C$ containing $n$ learnable codes as template features;
- Transform input $I$ via VQ-VAE encoder into continuous representation $Z$;
- Find the closest codes' indexes $X_i$ in $C$ for each superpixel in $Z$;
- Form discrete representation $X$ by selecting $C$ using $X_i$, for OCL training.

*Remark.* These methods' features as discretization units overlooks the composing attributes, thus impeding generalization. Their scalars as code indexes loses sub-feature similarities and differences, thus hindering convergence.

### 3.2 Naive Grouped Discrete Representation

Our naive GDR decomposes features into attributes via direct channel grouping in VQ-VAE for both Transformer- and Diffusion-based methods.

*Beforehand*, suppose a dataset is fully described by $n$ $c$-dimensional template features, which are further decomposed into $g$ attribute groups. Each group consists of $a$ $d$-dimensional template attributes, $n = a^g$ and $c = g \times d$. Thus, we predefine a set of attribute codebooks $C = \{C^{(1)}, C^{(2)}...C^{(g)}\}$, whose parameters are in shape $(g, a, d)$. The combinations of these codes are equivalent to the non-grouped feature-level codebook, whose parameters are in shape $(n, c)$.

*Afterwards*, we transform the input $I$ with a VAE encoder into continuous intermediate representation $Z$. In VQ-VAE, we sample distances between $Z$ and $C$ via Gumbel noise, yielding tuple code indexes $X_i$:

$$D = l2(Z^{(1)}, C^{(1)}) \circ l2(Z^{(2)}, C^{(2)}) ... \circ l2(Z^{(g)}, C^{(g)}) \tag{1}$$

$$D_s = \text{softmax}(\frac{D^{(1)} + G^{(1)}}{\tau}) \circ \text{softmax}(\frac{D^{(2)} + G^{(2)}}{\tau}) ... \circ \text{softmax}(\frac{D^{(g)} + G^{(g)}}{\tau}) \tag{2}$$

$$X_i = \text{argmin}(D_s^{(1)}) \circ \text{argmin}(D_s^{(2)}) ... \circ \text{argmin}(D_s^{(g)}) \tag{3}$$

where $Z^{(1)}...Z^{(g)}$ are channel groupings of $Z$; $G^{(1)}...G^{(g)}$ are Gumbel noises; $\circ$ is channel concatenation; $l2(\cdot, \cdot)$ denotes L2 distances between every vector pair in its two arguments; $D_s$ is soft Gumbel sampling of distances $D$ between continuous representations and codes; argmin$(\cdot)$ is along the code dimension. For our grouped VAE, multiple code indexes are selected from the attribute groups, forming "tuple indexes". In contrast, the non-grouped VAE selects only one index from a feature-level codebook, forming "scalar indexes".

*Subsequently*, we select template attributes by $X_i$ from $C$, forming grouped discrete representation $X$, which is the target of Diffusion decoding:

$$X = \text{select}(C^{(1)}, X_i^{(1)}) \circ \text{select}(C^{(2)}, X_i^{(2)}) ... \circ \text{select}(C^{(g)}, X_i^{(g)}) \tag{4}$$

where index$(\cdot, \cdot)$ selects codes from a codebook given indexes.

**Fig. 3.** Object discovery visualization of SLATE and SlotDiffusion plus GDR.

*Finally*, we transform $\boldsymbol{X}_i$ from tuple into scalar, which is the target of Transformer decoding:

$$\boldsymbol{X}_i := a^0 \times \boldsymbol{X}_i^{(1)} + a^1 \times \boldsymbol{X}_i^{(2)} + ... + a^{g-1} \times \boldsymbol{X}_i^{(g)} \tag{5}$$

where $\boldsymbol{X}_i^{(1)}...\boldsymbol{X}_i^{(g)}$ are the channel groupings of $\boldsymbol{X}_i$ from Eq. 3.

*Besides*, we introduce a mild loss to encourage code utilization after grouping

$$l_u = -\text{entropy}(\mathbb{E}[D_s^{(1)}]) - \text{entropy}(\mathbb{E}[D_s^{(2)}])... - \text{entropy}(\mathbb{E}[D_s^{(g)}]) \tag{6}$$

where $\mathbb{E}[\cdot]$ is computed along spatial dimensions while entropy$(\cdot)$ is computed along the channel dimension.

*Remark.* As illustrated in Fig. 1, by decomposing features into more reusable attributes, ideally any feature can be represented as a combination of these attributes, thus enhancing generalization. By indexing features with tuples rather than scalars, attribute-level similarities and differences can be captured for better object separability, thus benefiting convergence. Notably, when $g=1$, the above formulation except Eq. 6 reduces to the original non-grouped VAE.

However, directly grouping feature channels into different attributes may separate channels belonging to the same attribute apart or place channels belonging to different attributes together. This can degrade performance.

### 3.3 Organizing Channel Grouping

In case incorrect channel grouping, we further design a channel organizing mechanism. The key idea is: We use an *invertible projection* to organize the channel order of the continuous representation for grouped discretization, then apply this projection again to recover the (discretized) representation.

*Firstly*, we project continuous representation $\boldsymbol{Z}$ to a higher channel dimension using the pseudo-inverse of a learnable matrix $\boldsymbol{W}$:

$$\boldsymbol{Z}_+ = \boldsymbol{Z} \cdot \text{pinv}(\boldsymbol{W}) \tag{7}$$

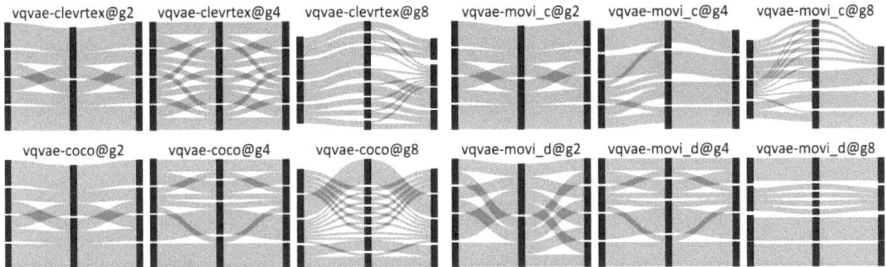

**Fig. 4.** GDR's invertible projection learns to organize channels' orders for grouped discretization. Every sub-plot has three columns of channels (black bars) and matrix weights among them (grey ribbons). The first column corresponds to continuous representation channels. Ribbons between the first and second columns are the project-up weights. The second column is discretization attribute groups. Ribbons between the second and third columns are the project-down weights. The third column is discretized representation channels.

where $Z$ is in shape (height, width, channel=$c$); pinv($\cdot$) is pseudo-inverse; and matrix pinv($W$) is in shape (channel=$c$, expanded channel=$8c$). This facilitates channels belonging to the same attribute to be placed together by ($i$) enabling channel reordering and ($ii$) generating extra channels to mitigate mis-grouping.

*Secondly*, we group $Z_+$ along the channel dimension and discretize it using the attribute-level codebooks $C$. This yields code indexes $X_i$ and the expanded discrete representation $X_+$. This follows the formulation in Eq. 1-5 above.

*Meanwhile*, we add $Z_+$ to $X_+$:

$$X_+ := Z_+ \times \alpha + X_+ \times (1 - \alpha) \tag{8}$$

where $\alpha$ decays via cosine annealing[1] from 0.5 to 0 in the first half of pretraining and is zeroed 0 afterward. With such residual preserving information through the discretization, VAE can be well pretrained even under mis-grouping.

*Thirdly*, we project $X_+$ back to obtain the final organized grouped discrete representation:

$$X = X_+ \cdot W \tag{9}$$

where $W$ is the previously introduced learnable matrix in shape (expanded channel=$8c$, channel=$c$).

*Fourthly*, to address potential numerical instability arising from matrix pseudo-inverse multiplcation, we normalize $X$:

$$X := \frac{X - \mathbb{E}[X]}{\sqrt{\mathbb{V}[X] + \epsilon}} \tag{10}$$

where $\mathbb{E}$ and $\mathbb{V}$ are the mean and variance over height, width and channel.

---

[1] https://pytorch.org/docs/stable/generated/torch.optim.lr_scheduler.CosineAnnealingLR.html.

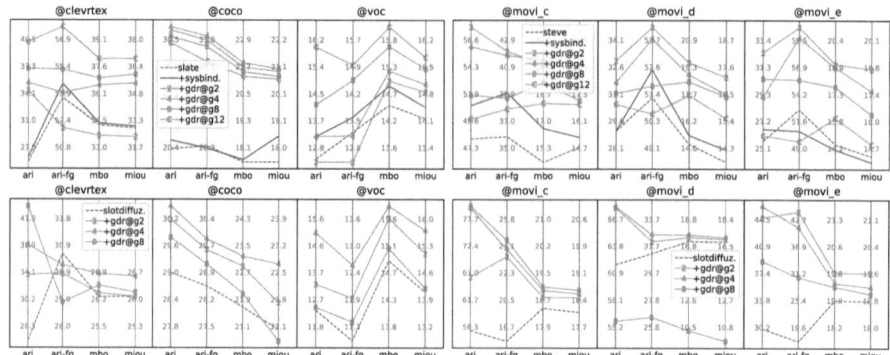

**Fig. 5.** GDR boosts object discovery performance of both Transformer- (*top*) and Diffusion-based (*bottom*) methods on images (*left*) and videos (*right*). A naive CNN is used as their primary encoder. Titles are datasets; x ticks are metrics while y ticks are metric values in adaptive scope. Higher values are better.

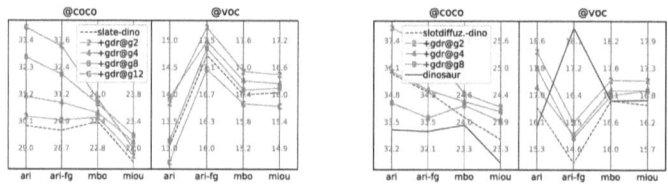

**Fig. 6.** With DINO1-B/8 for primary encoding, GDR still improves Transformer- (*left*) and Diffusion-based (*right*) methods. Higher values are better.

### 3.4 Grouped vs Non-Grouped

*Codebook Parameters.* Compared to the non-grouped, the number of parameters in our grouped codebook is significantly reduced to $\frac{agd}{a^g c} = \frac{ac}{a^g c} = \frac{1}{a^{g-1}}$. E.g., only $\frac{1}{64}$ when $a=64$, $g=2$, $c=256$ and $a^g=4096$. We increase $c$ to $8c$ and apply normalization plus linear to project it back to $c$, yielding $\frac{1}{1.6}$ the original number of codebook parameters – still 30% fewer.

*Codebook Computation.* Non-grouped computation only involves code matching using inner product for each continuous feature: $c \times n \times 1 = 256 \times 4096 = 2^{20}$. GDR computation involves two projections and code matching: $8c \times c \times 2 + 8c \times \sqrt[g]{n}$, which results in $2^{20} + 2^{17}$ for $g2$ and $2^{20} + 2^{14}$ for $g4$ – computation burden that is nearly identical to the original non-grouped case.

## 4 Experiments

We conduct experiments using three random seeds to evaluate: (*i*) How well GDR improves mainstream OCL, including Transformer- and Diffusion-based methods; (*ii*) What visual intuitions GDR exhibits in VAE representation; (*iii*) How designs of GDR contribute to its success in the OCL setting.

**Table 1.** Object discovery (*upper*) and set prediction (*lower*) of GDR upon state-of-the-arts, SPOT and VideoSAUR. DINO1-B/8 is used for primary encoding.

| COCO #slots=7 | ARI$_{fg}$↑ | mBO↑ | YTVIS #slots=7 | ARI$_{fg}$↑ | mBO↑ |
|---|---|---|---|---|---|
| SPOT | 37.5$_{\pm0.6}$ | 34.8$_{\pm0.1}$ | VideoSAUR | 39.5$_{\pm0.6}$ | 29.0$_{\pm0.4}$ |
| SPOT+GDR@$g2$ | 39.7$_{\pm0.5}$ | 35.1$_{\pm0.1}$ | VideoSAUR+GDR@$g2$ | 43.6$_{\pm0.5}$ | 31.7$_{\pm0.4}$ |

| COCO #slots=7 | class@top1↑ | bbox@R2↑ |
|---|---|---|
| SPOT + MLP | 0.59$_{\pm0.1}$ | 0.54$_{\pm0.1}$ |
| SPOT+GDR@$g2$ + MLP | 0.62$_{\pm0.1}$ | 0.56$_{\pm0.1}$ |

### 4.1 Experiment Overview

*Models.* We use both Transformer-based and Diffusion-based models as our GDR's basis. The former includes SLATE [25] for image and STEVE [27] for video. The latter includes SlotDiffusion [32] and its temporal variant. Upon such basis, we compare GDR against SysBinder@$g4$ [26]. We also apply GDR to state-of-the-art models, SPOT [15] and VideoSAUR [35], which are also Transformer-based. Methods such as SA [20] and SAVi [16] are excluded due to their low performance or reliance on additional modalities.

*Datasets.* We evaluate those models on ClevrTex[2] COCO[3] and VOC[4] for image OCL tasks, while MOVi-C/D/E[5] for video. We also use YTVIS[6] YouTube video instance segmentation. These encompass both synthetic and real-world cases, featuring multiple objects and complex textures. Except for those two state-of-the-arts, the input size is unified to 128×128 and other data processing follows the convention. Note that we use COCO panoptic instead of instance segmentation and the high-quality YTVIS[7] for strict evaluation.

*Hyperparameters.* The codebook size is $n=a^g=4096$ for all. GDR's group number is set to GDR@$g2$, $g4$, $g8$ and $g12$. Correspondingly, the attribute group sizes are (64, 64), (8, 8, 8, 8), (2, 2, 2, 2, 4, 4, 4, 4) and (2, 2, 2, 2, 2, 2, 2, 2, 2, 2, 2, 2), ensuring 4096 combinations. The number of slots is roughly set to the maximum/average object count plus one: 10+1 for ClevrTex, COCO, VOC and MOVi-C; 20+1 for MOVi-D; and 23+1 for MOVi-E. However, for those two state-of-the-arts, we strictly follow their official experiment settings.

---

[2] https://www.robots.ox.ac.uk/~vgg/data/clevrtex.
[3] https://cocodataset.org/#panoptic-2020.
[4] http://host.robots.ox.ac.uk/pascal/VOC.
[5] https://github.com/google-research/kubric/tree/main/challenges/movi.
[6] https://youtube-vos.org/dataset/vis.
[7] https://github.com/SysCV/vmt?tab=readme-ov-file#hq-ytvis-high-quality-video-instance-segmentation-dataset.

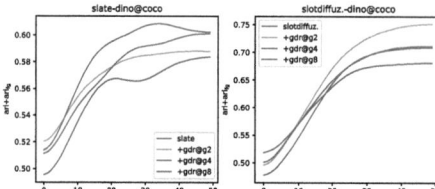 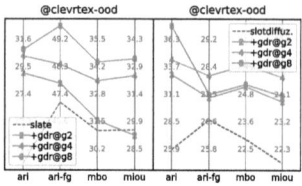

**Fig. 7.** (*left*) GDR accelerates model convergence. The x axis is val epochs while y is accuracy in ARI+ARI$_{fg}$. Smoothed with a Gaussian kernel size 5. (*right*) GDR improves model generalization. Models are trained on Clevrtex and tested on its out-of-distribution version. Higher values are better.

### 4.2 Performance

*Object Discovery.* We use common object discovery metrics: Adjusted Rand Index (ARI)[8] ARI foreground (ARI$_{fg}$), mean Best Overlap (mBO)[9] and mean Intersection-over-Union (mIoU)[10] As shown in Fig. 5, GDR significantly enhances accuracy across both synthetic and real-world images and videos. With the naive CNN [16] for primary encoding, it boosts both Transformer-based methods and Diffusion-based methods. GDR always outperforms the competitor SysBinder by a large margin. We further evaluate GDR's effectiveness with vision foundation model DINO1-B/8 [6] for strong primary encoding. As shown in Fig. 6 and 3, on both SLATE and SlotDiffusion, GDR improves accuracy across all metrics in most cases.

*Applying to State-of-the-Art.* Following the original settings, we apply GDR to SPOT [15] and VideoSAUR [35], by replacing SPOT's VAE with GDR and by replacing VideoSAUR's reconstruction target (continuous DINO features) with GDR discretized DINO features, respectively. As shown in Table 1 upper, GDR is still able to boost state-of-the-art methods' performance further.

*Set Prediction.* Following [24], we employ OCL to represent dataset COCO as slots, and use a small MLP to predict the object class and bounding box corresponding to each slot, with metrics of top-1 accuracy and the R2 score respectively. As shown in Table 1 lower, our GDR improves SLATE in set prediction, demonstrating is superior quality in object representation.

*Convergence.* The validation curves of ARI+ARI$_{fg}$ in Fig. 7 left demonstrate that GDR consistently accelerates the basis' convergence in OCL training. Along with Fig. 9, forming VAE discrete representation with tuple indexes captures attribute-level similarities and differences among super-pixels, thereby guiding OCL models to converge better.

---

[8] https://scikit-learn.org/stable/modules/generated/sklearn.metrics.adjusted_rand_score.html.
[9] https://ieeexplore.ieee.org/document/7423791.
[10] https://scikit-learn.org/stable/modules/generated/sklearn.metrics.jaccard_score.html.

*Generalization.* We transfer models from ClevrTex to its out-of-distribution version ClevrTex-OOD without finetuning. As shown in Fig. 7 right, GDR consistently improves basis methods' generalization. This confirms that GDR's decomposition from features into attributes helps the model learn more fundamental representations that are robust to distribution shifts.

### 4.3 Interpretability

*Decomposition from Features to Attributes.* Although without explicit supervision models can hardly learn concepts [26] as human-readable as in Fig. 1, we can still analyze GDR's decomposition from features to attributes as follows. Given GDR discrete representation $X$, we replace the attributes of objects' superpixels with arbitrary attribute codes then decode them into images to observe the changes. As shown in Fig. 8, under $g2$ setting, modifying one attribute group roughly alters the colors, whereas modifying the other destroys the textures. This suggests that the first group learns colors while the second learns textures.

**Fig. 8.** For GDR@$g2$, one attribute group roughly learns colors, while the other roughly learns textures. The original image is at the center. The left and right are images decoded from the modified VAE discrete representation.

*Attribute-Level Similarities and Differences.* Basis methods' scalar index tensor and GDR's tuple index tensor $X_i$ can be visualized by mapping different indexes to distinct colors. For our only competitor, SysBinder, we assign different colors to its different attention groups. As shown in Fig. 9, scalar indexes mix all attributes together, whereas our tuple indexes highlight similarities (identical colors) and differences (distinct colors) among superpixels in each attribute group. In contrast, SysBinder also captures such attribute-level information but with very limited diversity and details.

*Object Separability.* The visualization of $X$ for both the basis VQ-VAE and GDR can be achieved by coloring the different distances between each superpixel and the reference point (the average of all superpixels). As shown in Fig. 10, GDR consistently exhibits better object separability across all $g$ settings, suggesting GDR's superior guidance to OCL. However, using an excessive number of groups in GDR may result in the omission of certain objects.

### 4.4 Ablation

The effects of different designs in GDR are listed in Tab. 2. We use ARI+$\text{ARI}_{fg}$ since ARI largely indicates how well the background is segmented while $\text{ARI}_{fg}$ reflects the discovery quality of foreground objects.

*Number of groups*, formulated in Eq. 1-6: $g$=2, 4, 8 or 12. As shown in Fig. 5 and 6, the optimal $g$ depends on the specific dataset. However, $g$12 and $g$8 tend to result in suboptimal performance while $g$4 consistently leads to guaranteed performance gains over the basis methods.

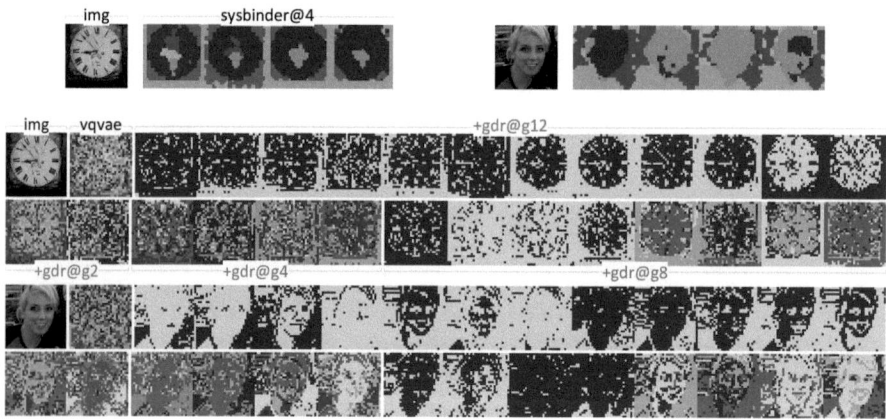

**Fig. 9.** SysBinder's attribute groups (*upper*), i.e., attention maps, and GDR's attribute groups (*lower*), i.e., tuple code indexes. GDR captures attribute-level similarities and differences among superpixels, whereas the non-grouped "vqvae" mixes all together. SysBinder lacks too much diversity and detail.

**Fig. 10.** GDR improves object separability in VAE discrete representation. More groups improve object separability but increase the risk of losing some objects.

*Channel expansion rate*, formulated in Eq. 7: $c$, $2c$, $4c$ or $8c$. Although $8c$ generally performs best, the expansion rate has a nearly saturated impact on GDR's performance. This suggests that our channel organizing mechanism is effective, reducing the necessity for a higher channel expansion rate.

The *channel organizing* based on our *invertible projection* designed in Sect. 3.3 is crucial for OCL model performance. If we disrupt it by replacing $W$ pseudo-inverse in project-up with specified weights, as formulated in Eq. 7, the object discovery accuracy drops significantly.

We also visualize how the invertible project-up and project-down organize channels for grouping. As shown in Fig. 4, some input channels are mixed, switched or split into different attributes for discretization, then the pseudo-inverse recovers them in the form of discrete representations. Such patterns are clearly observed across most datasets and grouping configurations.

Using *annealing residual connection* during training, formulated in Eq. 8, consistently yields better performance than without.

*Normalization at last*, formulated in Eq. 10, is generally beneficial, though its effect is not highly significant.

**Table 2.** Effects of expansion rate, utilization loss, invertible projection (and replacing $W$ pinv with specified weights), residual connection in training and final normalization. Experimented SLATE+GDR@$g4$ on ClevrTex.

| expansion rate | 8c | 4c | 2c | 1c |
|---|---|---|---|---|
| ARI+ARI$_{fg}$ | 89.47 | 89.29 | 88.93 | 88.16 |

| utilization loss | invertible projection | W pinv | residual connection | normalization | ARI+ARI$_{fg}$ |
|---|---|---|---|---|---|
| ✓ | ✓ | | ✓ | ✓ | 89.47 |
| ✗ | | | | | 84.78 |
| | ✗ | | | | 81.52 |
| | | ✗ Wpinv | | | 32.25 |
| | | | ✗ | | 88.84 |
| | | | | ✗ | 89.16 |

## 5 Conclusion

We propose grouped discrete representation in VAE to guide OCL training better. This technique improves the mainstream Transformer- and Diffusion-based OCL methods in both convergence and generalization. Although self-supervision cannot guarantee different groups learn different human-readable attributes, our method still exhibits interesting and interpretable patterns in attribute-level discrete representations. Fundamentally, we only modify the VAE part of OCL models, indicating broader applicability to other VAE-based models.

**Acknowledgment.** We acknowledge the support of the Finnish Center for Artificial Intelligence (FCAI) and the Research Council of Finland through its Flagship program. Additionally, we thank the Research Council of Finland for funding the projects ADEREHA (grant no. 353198), BERMUDA (362407) and PROFI7 (352788). We also appreciate CSC-IT Center for Science, Finland, for granting access to the LUMI supercomputer, owned by the EuroHPC Joint Undertaking and hosted by CSC (Finland) in collaboration with the LUMI consortium. Furthermore, we acknowledge the computational resources provided by the Aalto Science-IT project through the Triton cluster. Finally, the first author expresses his heartfelt gratitude to his wife for her unwavering support and companionship.

# References

1. Bahdanau, D., Cho, K.H., Bengio, Y.: Neural machine translation by jointly learning to align and translate. In: International Conference on Learning Representations (2015)
2. Bar, M.: Visual objects in context. Nat. Rev. Neurosci. **5**(8), 617–629 (2004)
3. Barnes, C., Rizvi, S., Nasrabadi, N.: Advances in residual vector quantization: a review. IEEE Trans. Image Process. **5**(2), 226–262 (1996)
4. Bouchacourt, D., Tomioka, R., Nowozin, S.: Multi-Level Variational autoencoder: learning disentangled representations from grouped observations. In: Proceedings of the AAAI Conference on Artificial Intelligence, vol. 32 (2018)
5. Burgess, C., Matthey, L., Watters, N., et al.: MONet: unsupervised scene decomposition and representation. arXiv preprint arXiv:1901.11390 (2019)
6. Caron, M., Touvron, H., Misra, I., et al.: Emerging properties in self-supervised vision transformers. In: Proceedings of the IEEE/CVF International Conference on Computer Vision, pp. 9650–9660 (2021)
7. Cavanagh, P.: Visual cognition. Vision. Res. **51**(13), 1538–1551 (2011)
8. Chen, Y., Fan, H., Xu, B., et al.: Drop an octave: reducing spatial redundancy in convolutional neural networks with octave convolution. In: Proceedings of the IEEE/CVF International Conference on Computer Vision, pp. 3435–3444 (2019)
9. Elsayed, G., Mahendran, A., Steenkiste, S., et al.: SAVi++: towards end-to-end object-centric learning from real-world videos. Adv. Neural. Inf. Process. Syst. **35**, 28940–28954 (2022)
10. Greff, K., Kaufman, R.L., Kabra, R., et al.: Multi-object representation learning with iterative variational inference. In: International Conference on Machine Learning, pp. 2424–2433. PMLR (2019)
11. Huang, G., Liu, S., Van der Maaten, L., Weinberger, K.: CondenseNet: an efficient densenet using learned group convolutions. In: Proceedings of the IEEE Conference on Computer Vision and Pattern Recognition, pp. 2752–2761 (2018)
12. Im Im, D., Ahn, S., Memisevic, R., Bengio, Y.: Denoising criterion for variational auto-encoding framework. In: Proceedings of the AAAI Conference on Artificial Intelligence, vol. 31 (2017)

13. Jang, E., Gu, S., Poole, B.: Categorical reparameterization with gumbel-softmax. In: International Conference on Learning Representations (2017)
14. Jiang, J., Deng, F., Singh, G., Ahn, S.: Object-centric slot diffusion. Adv. Neural Inf. Process. Syst. (2023)
15. Kakogeorgiou, I., Gidaris, S., Karantzalos, K., Komodakis, N.: SPOT: self-training with patch-order permutation for object-centric learning with autoregressive transformers. In: Proceedings of the IEEE/CVF Conference on Computer Vision and Pattern Recognition, pp. 22776–22786 (2024)
16. Kipf, T., Elsayed, G., Mahendran, A., et al.: Conditional object-centric learning from video. In: International Conference on Learning Representations (2022)
17. Krizhevsky, A., Sutskever, I., Hinton, G.: ImageNet classification with deep convolutional neural networks. Adv. Neural Inf. Process. Syst. **25** (2012)
18. Lim, K.L., Jiang, X., Yi, C.: Deep clustering with variational autoencoder. IEEE Signal Process. Lett. **27**, 231–235 (2020)
19. Liu, X., Yuan, J., An, B., Xu, Y., Yang, Y., Huang, F.: C-disentanglement: discovering causally-independent generative factors under an inductive bias of confounder. Adv. Neural. Inf. Process. Syst. **36**, 39566–39581 (2023)
20. Locatello, F., Weissenborn, D., Unterthiner, T., et al.: Object-centric learning with slot attention. Adv. Neural. Inf. Process. Syst. **33**, 11525–11538 (2020)
21. Oquab, M., Darcet, T., Moutakanni, T., et al.: DINOv2: learning robust visual features without supervision. Trans. Mach. Learn. Res. (2023)
22. Palmeri, T., Gauthier, I.: Visual object understanding. Nat. Rev. Neurosci. **5**(4), 291–303 (2004)
23. Rombach, R., Blattmann, A., Lorenz, D., Esser, P., Ommer, B.: High-resolution image synthesis with latent diffusion models. In: Proceedings of the IEEE/CVF Conference on Computer Vision and Pattern Recognition, pp. 10684–10695 (2022)
24. Seitzer, M., Horn, M., Zadaianchuk, A., et al.: Bridging the gap to real-world object-centric learning. In: International Conference on Learning Representations (2023)
25. Singh, G., Deng, F., Ahn, S.: Illiterate DALL-E learns to compose. In: International Conference on Learning Representations (2022)
26. Singh, G., Kim, Y., Ahn, S.: Neural systematic binder. In: International Conference on Learning Representations (2022)
27. Singh, G., Wu, Y.F., Ahn, S.: Simple unsupervised object-centric learning for complex and naturalistic videos. Adv. Neural. Inf. Process. Syst. **35**, 18181–18196 (2022)
28. Van Den Oord, A., Vinyals, O., Kavukcuoglu, K.: Neural discrete representation learning. Adv. Neural. Inf. Process. Syst. **30** (2017)
29. Vaswani, A., Shazeer, N., Parmar, N., et al.: Attention is all you need. Adv. Neural. Inf. Process. Syst. **30** (2017)
30. Watters, N., Matthey, L., Burgess, C., Alexander, L.: Spatial broadcast decoder: a simple architecture for disentangled representations in VAEs. In: ICLR 2019 Workshop LLD (2019)
31. Wu, Z., Dvornik, N., Greff, K., Kipf, T., Garg, A.: SlotFormer: unsupervised visual dynamics simulation with object-centric models. In: International Conference on Learning Representations (2023)
32. Wu, Z., Hu, J., Lu, W., Gilitschenski, I., Garg, A.: SlotDiffusion: object-centric generative modeling with diffusion models. Adv. Neural. Inf. Process. Syst. **36**, 50932–50958 (2023)
33. Yang, D., Liu, S., Huang, R., et al.: Hifi-codec: group-residual vector quantization for high fidelity audio codec. arXiv preprint arXiv:2305.02765 (2023)

34. Yi, K., Gan, C., Li, Y., Kohli, P., et al.: CLEVRER: CoLlision events for video REpresentation and reasoning. In: International Conference on Learning Representations (2020)
35. Zadaianchuk, A., Seitzer, M., Martius, G.: Object-centric learning for real-world videos by predicting temporal feature similarities. Adv. Neural Inf. Process. Syst. **36** (2024)
36. Zhao, R., Li, J., Wu, Z.: Convolution of convolution: let kernels spatially collaborate. In: Proceedings of the IEEE/CVF Conference on Computer Vision and Pattern Recognition, pp. 651–660 (2022)
37. Zhao, R., Wu, Z., Zhang, Q.: Learnable heterogeneous convolution: learning both topology and strength. Neural Netw. **141**, 270–280 (2021)

# ETT-CKGE: Efficient Task-Driven Tokens for Continual Knowledge Graph Embedding

Lijing Zhu[1], Qizhen Lan[6], Qing Tian[6], Wenbo Sun[3], Li Yang[4], Lu Xia[7], Yixin Xie[5], Xi Xiao[6], Tiehang Duan[2], Cui Tao[2], and Shuteng Niu[1,2(✉)]

[1] Bowling Green State University, Bowling Green, OH 43403, USA
niu.shuteng@mayo.edu
[2] Mayo Clinic, Jacksonville, FL 32066, USA
[3] University of Michigan, Ann Arbor, MI 48109, USA
[4] University of North Carolina, Charlotte, NC 28223, USA
[5] Kennesaw State University, Kennesaw, GA 30144, USA
[6] University of Alabama, Birmingham, AL 35294, USA
[7] Michigan State University, East Lansing, MI 48824, USA

**Abstract.** Continual Knowledge Graph Embedding (CKGE) seeks to integrate new knowledge while preserving past information. However, existing methods struggle with efficiency and scalability due to two key limitations: (1) suboptimal knowledge preservation between snapshots caused by manually designed node/relation importance scores that ignore graph dependencies relevant to the downstream task, and (2) computationally expensive graph traversal for node/relation importance calculation, leading to slow training and high memory overhead. To address these limitations, we introduce **ETT-CKGE** (**E**fficient, **T**askdriven, **T**okens for **C**ontinual **K**nowledge **G**raph **E**mbedding), a novel task-guided CKGE method that leverages efficient task-driven tokens for efficient and effective knowledge transfer between snapshots. Our method introduces a set of learnable tokens that directly capture taskrelevant signals, eliminating the need for explicit node scoring or traversal. These tokens serve as consistent and reusable guidance across snapshots, enabling efficient token-masked embedding alignment between snapshots. Importantly, knowledge transfer is achieved through simple matrix operations, significantly reducing training time and memory usage. Extensive experiments across six benchmark datasets demonstrate that ETT-CKGE consistently achieves superior or competitive predictive performance, while substantially improving training efficiency and scalability compared to state-of-the-art CKGE methods. The code is available at https://github.com/lijingzhu1/ETT-CKGE/tree/main.

**Keywords:** Graph Representation Learning · Continual Knowledge Graph Learning · Knowledge Graph · Graph Completion

## 1 Introduction

Knowledge graph embedding (KGE) aims to project nodes and relations into a continuous vector space to support downstream applications [5, 7, 10, 24] such as node classification, knowledge graphs (KGs) completion, and graph classification. While traditional KGE methods primarily focus on static KGs [23], real-world KGs are inherently dynamic, continuously evolving with emerging nodes, relations, and facts. In such settings, retraining KGE models from scratch becomes computationally expensive. To address this challenge, Continual Knowledge Graph Embedding (CKGE) [4] has been proposed as a practical paradigm that incrementally updates node and relation representations over a sequence of knowledge graph (KG) snapshots while mitigating catastrophic forgetting of previously learned knowledge.

Generally, previous research has explored approaches such as parameter isolation [15,18], replay-based [15,18], and regularization strategies [4,11,12,29]. Despite their effectiveness in mitigating catastrophic forgetting, these approaches still face fundamental limitations. Primarily, previous methods rely heavily on human-designed heuristics to estimate the importance of nodes and relations when transferring knowledge across evolving graph snapshots. Such handcrafted weighting schemes often do not align accurately with the true optimization objective, leading to suboptimal preservation and adaptation of knowledge between snapshots. Moreover, these methods typically require extensive computational resources due to explicit graph traversals or iterative importance computations for each node and relation. Consequently, they suffer from slow training times and substantial memory usage, rendering them inefficient and difficult to scale for large-scale KGs.

To address these limitations, we propose a novel **E**fficient **T**ask-driven **T**okens for **C**ontinual **K**nowledge **G**raph **E**mbedding (ETT-CKGE). Rather than relying on predefined node/relation importance ranking rules, we introduce task-driven tokens that learn to assess the importance of nodes and relations directly from the task loss. These tokens interact with the graph embeddings and subsequently generate a token-masked embedding, which is optimized during training. These learned tokens inherently capture the task-relevant components of the graph and produce an importance mask that can be seamlessly transferred to guide learning in future snapshots. This approach offers two key advantages: it aligns importance estimation with task objectives instead of human-designed importance heuristics, and it significantly reduces training time and memory usage by replacing the graph traversal with a single matrix multiplication.

**Table 1.** Comparison of regularization-based methods for graph search space

| Method | Graph Traversal | Weighting Metrics |
|---|---|---|
| LKGE | Full | Frequency |
| FMR | Full | Frequency & Gradient |
| IncDE | Partial | Centrality |
| FastKGE | Partial | Rank of centrality |
| **ETT-CKGE (Ours)** | **None** | **Task-driven** |

Moreover, Table 1 summarizes a comparison of advanced regularization-based methods. In particular, prior methods require either full or partial graph traver-

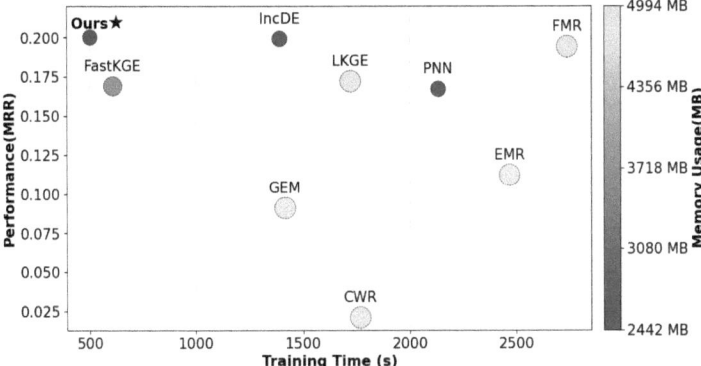

**Fig. 1.** (**Best view in color**) Comparison of performance(MRR), training time(S), and memory usage(MB) across CKGE methods on the RELATION data set. Our method achieves the best balance, delivering high accuracy with significantly reduced training time and memory consumption. The color scale indicates memory usage, with darker colors representing lower memory overhead.

sal and depend on handcrafted metrics to guide learning. In contrast, our proposed method removes the need for explicit graph traversal and human-designed metrics by introducing task-driven tokens. These tokens learn to identify critical entities and relations based solely on task loss, producing a token-masked embedding that adaptively highlights relevant knowledge.

As illustrated in Fig. 1, our method consistently outperforms CKGE baselines while requiring significantly less training time and memory usage. This improvement reflects not only computational efficiency but also enhanced scalability and smoother adaptation to evolving knowledge graphs, making our approach more practical for real-world, large-scale continual learning scenarios. The main contributions of this work are summarized as follows:

- We introduce a novel task-driven token module that learns to estimate the importance of nodes and relations directly from task loss. These task-guided tokens are then used to generate importance masks, enabling an effective knowledge transfer method that selectively preserves and adapts task-relevant information across growing KG snapshots without relying on human-crafted heuristics or static graph metrics.
- ETT-CKGE eliminates the need for graph traversal or iterative importance scoring by formulating importance estimation as a single matrix multiplication. This design significantly reduces computational overhead, achieves better scalability, and enables seamless integration with large-scale KGs, offering a practical and resource-efficient solution for CKGE settings.
- We conduct comprehensive experiments on six datasets with different data distributions, showing that ETT-CKGE consistently achieves competitive or superior performance in predictive accuracy while reducing training time and memory consumption compared to SOTA methods.

## 2   Related Work

Unlike standard KGE methods [1,8,20,22], which assume a static graph structure, CKGE is designed for dynamically evolving KGs. A recent survey [27] categorizes CKGE methods into three main strategies: parameter isolation methods, replay-based methods, and regularization-based methods.

Firstly, replay-based methods [16,28] replay past graph snapshots to retain information while learning new facts. However, these methods suffer from scalability issues as the memory required to store past knowledge increases significantly over time, making them impractical for large-scale applications. Secondly, parameter isolation methods, such as progressive neural networks (PNNs) [18] and dynamically expandable networks (DEN) [26], allocate separate parameter subsets to different tasks to prevent interference. While effective in avoiding catastrophic forgetting, these models require continuous expansion, leading to uncontrolled growth in model size. Lastly, regularization-based methods address catastrophic forgetting by constraining updates to critical parameters. Early approaches, such as elastic weight consolidation (EWC) [9], used parameter importance-based constraints, while R-EWC [13] improved knowledge consolidation through rotation-based constraints. More recent methods, such as FMR [29], leverage rotational techniques to enhance stability in CKGE, and IncDE [11] explicitly preserve graph structure to improve retention. Moreover, FastKGE [12] introduced low-rank adapters (LoRA) to CKGE, enabling efficient adaptation to new knowledge while reducing training time. However, FastKGE relies heavily on degree centrality within layers, requiring substantial memory to store layer information.

As shown in Table 1, other SOTA regularization-based methods, such as LKGE, FMR, IncDE, and FastKGE, also depend on graph traversal—some require full-graph traversal, while others operate on partitioned graphs. This reliance introduces considerable computational costs, particularly as the KG size increases. Unlike previous methods that rely on heuristic metrics to measure the informative knowledge to overcome the forgetting issues in CKGE, we propose a set of efficient and task-driven tokens to adaptively locate essential graph components without requiring exhaustive graph traversal. By leveraging pre-trained tokens to capture global knowledge with minimal overhead, our method achieves significantly better efficiency and scalability.

## 3   Continual Knowledge Graph Embedding

***Problem Definition:*** A growing knowledge graph is modeled as a sequence of snapshots: $\mathcal{G} = \{\mathcal{G}_1, \mathcal{G}_2, \ldots, \mathcal{G}_I\}$, where $I$ is the total number of snapshots. Each snapshot $\mathcal{G}_i$ represents a static KG at time step $i$, defined as $\mathcal{G}_i = \{\mathcal{T}_i, \mathcal{E}_i, \mathcal{R}_i\}$, where $\mathcal{T}_i$, $\mathcal{E}_i$, and $\mathcal{R}_i$ denote the sets of triplets, entities, and relations, respectively. In this context, entities represent the nodes of the graph, while relations define the semantic edges that connect them. The numbers of entities and relations in each snapshot are denoted as $N_E$ and $N_R$, respectively. A triplet

Efficient Task-Driven Tokens for Continual Knowledge Graph Embedding 485

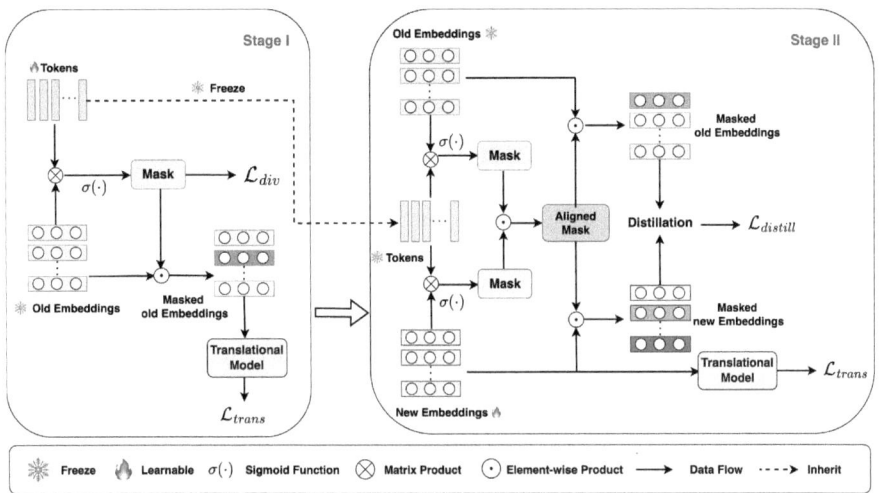

**Fig. 2.** An overview of the ETT-CKGE framework. Stage I focuses on token pre-training, where tokens interact with previous embeddings to capture and retain prior knowledge. In Stage II, the learned tokens mask both old and new knowledge, aligning them to facilitate knowledge distillation and ensure effective continual learning.

$(h, r, t)$ consists of a head entity $h$, a relation $r$, and a tail entity $t$, forming a directed semantic connection. The set of triplets in snapshot $\mathcal{G}_i$ is given by $\mathcal{T}_i = \{(h, r, t) \mid (h, r, t) \in \mathcal{E}_i \times \mathcal{R}_i \times \mathcal{E}_i\}$. Each snapshot $\mathcal{G}_i$ introduces incremental knowledge in the form of newly added entities, relations, and triplets compared to the previous snapshot $\mathcal{G}_{i-1}$.

***Inference:*** The primary task in this work is link prediction. We assess the model's accuracy within the dynamic context of evolving KGs. Specifically, for each test fact $(h, r, t)$ in a given snapshot $\mathcal{G}_i$, we construct two types of queries: $(h, r, ?)$ and $(?, r, t)$.

## 4 Our Approach: Efficient Task-Diven Tokens

The overall architecture of ETT-CKGE is illustrated in Fig. 2, consisting of two stages: Stage I for token learning and Stage II for knowledge transfer, which are detailed in Sects. 4.1 and 4.2, respectively.

In Stage I, we introduce a set of learnable tokens that act as task-driven representations, interacting with previously learned embeddings to capture task-relevant knowledge. Stage II focuses on continual knowledge transfer. In this stage, the previously learned embeddings and tokens are frozen to preserve historical knowledge, while only the embeddings of the new snapshot are updated. The learned tokens serve as task-driven guidance signals, promoting consistency across evolving graph snapshots. A distillation loss is applied to guide the transfer process and mitigate catastrophic forgetting. Importantly, our method achieves high computational efficiency by eliminating the need for graph traversal or iterative importance scoring, knowledge transfer is achieved through simple matrix multiplication and element-wise operations, enabling fast and scalable adaptation. Although we present the two stages separately for clarity, the token learning stage incurs negligible overhead, and the entire process can be seamlessly implemented as a single unified training pipeline in practice.

### 4.1 Task-Driven Token Learning

At snapshot $i$, we aim to extract and preserve critical structural knowledge from previously learned embeddings to guide future learning. Let the embedding matrix of entities or relations from snapshot $i-1$ be denoted as $\mathbf{E}_{i-1} \in \mathbb{R}^{N \times D}$, where $N$ corresponds to the number of entities ($N_E$) or relations ($N_R$), and $D$ is the embedding dimension.

To capture most task-relevant knowledge without relying on heuristic importance metrics in prior works [4,11], we introduce a set of learnable tokens $\mathbf{Z} \in \mathbb{R}^{T \times D}$, guided by the task objective, where $T$ denotes the number of tokens. These tokens serve as trainable attention mechanisms that interact with the old embeddings to identify salient components in the graph. The interaction between the tokens and the old embeddings is computed via inner product in the latent space, followed by a sigmoid activation which produces a soft importance mask. For matrix multiplication compatibility, we first transpose $\mathbf{E}_{i-1}$ resulting in:

$$\mathbf{M}_{i-1} = \sigma(\mathbf{Z}\mathbf{E}_{i-1}), \tag{1}$$

where $\mathbf{M}_{i-1} \in \mathbb{R}^{T \times N}$ represents the soft mask matrix indicating the importance of each entity (or relation) with respect to each token. $\sigma(\cdot)$ is the element-wise sigmoid function. Our approach achieves importance estimation through a single matrix multiplication, offering significantly improved computational efficiency and scalability. To propagate the mask signal into the learning process, we generate masked embeddings $\hat{\mathbf{E}}_{i-1}$ by applying a token-wise weighted sum over the original embeddings $\mathbf{E}_{i-1}$:

$$\hat{\mathbf{E}}_{i-1} = \sum_{t=1}^{T} \mathbf{M}_{i-1,t} \odot \mathbf{E}_{i-1}, \tag{2}$$

where $t$ indexes the $T$ token masks. The resulting $\hat{\mathbf{E}}_{i-1} \in \mathbb{R}^{N \times D}$ serves as the token-guided version of the embedding to replace $\mathbf{E}_{i-1} \in \mathbb{R}^{N \times D}$ for downstream optimization. The quality of the learned mask is implicitly guided by the translational loss $\mathcal{L}_{trans}$, which measures the effectiveness of the masked embeddings in modeling the knowledge graph structure. By freezing and optimizing only the task-driven tokens $Z$, we encourage these tokens to emphasize the most informative elements in $\mathbf{E}_{i-1}$ for task success. However, without explicit regularization, all tokens may converge to attend to the same substructures, resulting in redundant guidance. To address this, we introduce a diversity-promoting regularization based on the Dice coefficient which encourages the tokens to specialize in different graph components. Given two mask vectors $\mathbf{M}_j \in \mathbb{R}^N$ and $\mathbf{M}_k \in \mathbb{R}^N$, the diversity loss is defined as:

$$\mathcal{L}_{\text{div}} = \frac{1}{T(T-1)} \sum_{j=1}^{T} \sum_{k=1}^{T} \frac{2\sum_{n=1}^{N} \mathbf{M}_{j,n}\mathbf{M}_{k,n}}{\sum_{n=1}^{N} \mathbf{M}_{j,n}^2 + \sum_{n=1}^{N} \mathbf{M}_{k,n}^2}, \quad (3)$$

where $j \neq k$. The diversity loss $\mathcal{L}_{\text{div}} \in [0,1]$ penalizes high similarity between different tokens, encouraging each token to focus on distinct graph structures. By minimizing $\mathcal{L}_{\text{div}}$, we aim for the learned masks to distribute their attention across different substructures in the KG. This formulation penalizes high overlap between any two token masks, thereby enforcing diversity in their attention distributions.

To align token training with the predictive task, we adopt the TransE [1] as a translational model to learn the KGs in the current snapshot. The original TransE loss is defined as:

$$\mathcal{L}_{trans} = \sum_{(h,r,t) \in \mathcal{T}} \sum_{(h',r,t') \in \mathcal{T}'} \max(0, \gamma + f(\mathbf{h},\mathbf{r},\mathbf{t}) - f(\mathbf{h}',\mathbf{r},\mathbf{t}')), \quad (4)$$

where $\mathcal{T}$ represents the set of positive triplets, and $\mathcal{T}'$ denotes the set of negative triplets generated for negative sampling. The parameter $\gamma$ is a margin hyperparameter that controls the separation between positive and negative triplets. The score function is defined as: $f(\mathbf{h},\mathbf{r},\mathbf{t}) = ||\mathbf{h}+\mathbf{r}-\mathbf{t}||_2^2$. The final objective for token learning in Stage I is defined as:

$$\mathcal{L}_{\text{token}} = \mathcal{L}_{\text{trans}} + \lambda \mathcal{L}_{\text{div}}, \quad (5)$$

where $\lambda$ is a hyperparameter balancing the loss terms. This formulation enables tokens to capture both task-relevant and diverse structural patterns, serving as a lightweight mechanism to guide continual learning without expensive traversal or handcrafted rules.

### 4.2 Distillation via Learned Token Masks

Building on the effectiveness of the learned task-driven tokens in identifying key graph substructures, we further leverage these tokens to facilitate efficient and targeted knowledge distillation across growing knowledge graph snapshots. In this stage, we freeze the learned task-driven tokens $\mathbf{Z}$ and the old embeddings $\mathbf{E}_{i-1}$, thus preserving the saliency patterns learned from prior snapshots. Only the new embeddings $\mathbf{E}_i$ are updated during training, allowing it to align with task-relevant structural components identified by the learned tokens. To capture informative knowledge from both the old and new snapshots, we compute respective token-guided importance masks as:

$$\mathbf{M}_{i-1} = \sigma(\mathbf{Z}\mathbf{E}_{i-1}), \quad \mathbf{M}_i = \sigma(\mathbf{Z}\mathbf{E}_i), \quad (6)$$

where $\mathbf{M}_{i-1}, \mathbf{M}_i \in \mathbb{R}^{T \times N}$ represent the attention masks derived from previous and current embeddings, respectively. It is important to note that knowledge transfer is applied only to those transposed embeddings in $\mathbf{E}_i$ corresponding to entities and relations that also existed in the previous snapshot $\mathbf{E}_{i-1}$. In contrast, new entities and relations introduced in snapshot $i$ are learned purely through the task loss $\mathcal{L}_{\text{trans}}$, without any distillation guidance. This design ensures that distillation focuses solely on preserving previously acquired knowledge, while allowing the model to flexibly accommodate new information.

***Aligned Token Masks.*** Direct application of these independent masks may lead to structural misalignment, where salient components differ across snapshots. To address this, we introduce a token-level alignment mechanism, forming a joint mask $\mathbf{M} = \mathbf{M}_{i-1} \odot \mathbf{M}_i$. This aligned mask is applied to both $\mathbf{E}_{i-1}$ and $\mathbf{E}_i$ to emphasize consistently critical entity and relation embeddings across snapshots, ensuring that distillation focuses on components deemed important by both the previous and current knowledge, rather than on noisy or transient elements. Based on this, we formulate the knowledge distillation as:

$$\mathcal{L}_{distill} = \frac{1}{TN} \sum_{t=1}^{T} \mathbf{M}_t \odot \left\| \mathbf{E}_{i-1} - \mathbf{E}_i \right\|_2^2, \tag{7}$$

where the L2 norm quantifies the divergence between matched embeddings, and the aligned mask $\mathbf{M}$ selectively emphasizes structurally important graph components during distillation. In contrast to prior methods that require explicit graph traversal or iterative computations over all triples to estimate importance, our approach performs this step through a single matrix operation, yielding substantial improvements in computational efficiency.

***Overall Loss Function.*** The overall training loss in this stage combines the task-specific translational loss with the distillation loss:

$$\mathcal{L} = \mathcal{L}_{\text{trans}} + \alpha \mathcal{L}_{\text{distill}}, \tag{8}$$

where $\alpha$ is a hyperparameter controlling the strength of the distillation.

## 5 Experiment and Analysis

### 5.1 Datasets

We evaluate the proposed ETT-CKGE framework on six benchmark datasets: ENTITY, RELATION, FACT, HYBRID, FB-CKGE, and WN-CKGE. The first four datasets, introduced in [4], represent different types of knowledge growth in CKGE: ENTITY tracks increasing entities, RELATION focuses on evolving relations, FACT captures growing knowledge triples, and HYBRID combines all three. FB-CKGE and WN-CKGE were introduced by [12] as continual extensions of FB15K and WN18 [1]. We set the number of snapshots for all datasets to 5, with the train/validation/test split ratio fixed at 3:1:1. Dataset statistics are provided in Table 2.

**Table 2.** The statistics of datasets.

| Dataset | Snapshot 0 | | | Snapshot 1 | | | Snapshot 2 | | | Snapshot 3 | | | Snapshot 4 | | |
|---|---|---|---|---|---|---|---|---|---|---|---|---|---|---|---|
| | $N_E$ | $N_R$ | $N_T$ | $N_E$ | $N_R$ | $N_T$ | $N_E$ | $N_R$ | $N_T$ | $N_E$ | $N_R$ | $N_T$ | $N_E$ | $N_R$ | $N_T$ |
| ENTITY | 2909 | 233 | 46388 | 5817 | 236 | 72111 | 8275 | 236 | 73785 | 11633 | 237 | 70506 | 14541 | 237 | 47326 |
| RELATION | 11560 | 48 | 98819 | 13343 | 96 | 93535 | 13754 | 143 | 66136 | 14387 | 190 | 30032 | 14541 | 237 | 21594 |
| FACT | 10513 | 237 | 62024 | 12779 | 237 | 62023 | 13586 | 237 | 62023 | 13894 | 237 | 62023 | 14541 | 237 | 62023 |
| HYBRID | 8628 | 86 | 57561 | 10040 | 102 | 20873 | 12779 | 151 | 88017 | 14393 | 209 | 103339 | 14541 | 237 | 40326 |
| FB-CKGE | 7505 | 237 | 186070 | 11258 | 237 | 31012 | 13134 | 237 | 31012 | 14072 | 237 | 31012 | 14541 | 237 | 31010 |
| WN-CKGE | 24567 | 11 | 55801 | 28660 | 11 | 9300 | 32754 | 11 | 9300 | 36848 | 11 | 9300 | 40943 | 11 | 9302 |

$N_E$, $N_R$ and $N_T$ denote the number of cumulative entities and relations, and current triples in each snapshot $i$.

### 5.2 Baselines

We compare ETT-CKGE with a range of continual learning baselines, including **fine-tune**, **parameter-isolation**, **replay-based**, and **regularization-based** methods. Notably, the Fine-Tune baseline simply continues training the KGE model on new incoming data without any explicit mechanism to preserve previously learned knowledge. As a result, it is efficient in terms of training time but suffers from severe forgetting. The remaining baselines implement different strategies to mitigate catastrophic forgetting and preserve prior knowledge. Together, they provide a comprehensive framework to evaluate the effectiveness and efficiency of ETT-CKGE in continual knowledge graph embedding.

### 5.3 Experimental Setup

All experiments were conducted using PyTorch on a single NVIDIA A6000 GPU. Experiments were conducted using a batch size selected from {1024, 2048, 3072}, and a learning rate chosen from {0.01, 0.001, 0.0001, 0.00001}. The Adam optimizer is used for all experiments. The hyperparameter $\alpha$ varies across different datasets, ranging from 1,000 to 100,000, while $\lambda$ is selected from the range [0, 1]. The margin $\gamma$ is set to 9, and $D$ for all experiments is set to 200. In all experiments, the token number $T$ is set to different integer values within the range (0,10]. For fairness, we run all baseline models on each benchmark dataset five times to take their average performance and fine-tune their hyperparameters to report the best performance. The code and hyperparameter settings are available at Github.

### 5.4 Evaluation Metrics

We evaluate ETT-CKGE using three metrics: **Mean Reciprocal Rank (MRR)**, **Hits@$k$**, and **Training Time**. MRR measures the average inverse rank of the correct entity, while Hits@$k$ indicates the proportion of correct entities ranked in the top $k$ predictions. Training Time reflects the total time required to train the model across all snapshots. We report MRR, Hits@$k$ (with $k \in \{1, 10\}$), and training time to assess both performance and efficiency.

Table 3. Main experimental results

| Model | ENTITY | | | | RELATION | | | | FACT | | | |
|---|---|---|---|---|---|---|---|---|---|---|---|---|
| | MRR | H@1 | H@10 | Training Time (s) | MRR | H@1 | H@10 | Training Time (s) | MRR | H@1 | H@10 | Training Time (s) |
| Fine-Tune | 0.171 | 0.093 | 0.319 | 464 | 0.085 | 0.036 | 0.170 | 419 | 0.169 | 0.092 | 0.323 | 305 |
| PNN [18] | 0.229 | 0.130 | 0.425 | 2145 | 0.167 | 0.096 | 0.305 | 2134 | 0.157 | 0.084 | 0.290 | 1613 |
| CWR [15] | 0.087 | 0.028 | 0.200 | 2350 | 0.021 | 0.010 | 0.043 | 1768 | 0.082 | 0.028 | 0.194 | 2753 |
| GEM [16] | 0.165 | 0.085 | 0.321 | 1993 | 0.091 | 0.039 | 0.191 | 1417 | 0.174 | 0.091 | 0.344 | 1139 |
| EMR [21] | 0.173 | 0.065 | 0.333 | 4177 | 0.112 | 0.053 | 0.226 | 2740 | 0.170 | 0.090 | 0.335 | 1722 |
| LKGE [4] | 0.240 | 0.141 | 0.434 | 2374 | 0.172 | 0.093 | 0.343 | 1722 | 0.210 | 0.122 | 0.389 | 1090 |
| FMR [29] | 0.253 | 0.138 | 0.450 | 3094 | 0.194 | 0.107 | 0.367 | 2742 | 0.215 | 0.128 | 0.392 | 1661 |
| IncDE [11] | 0.253 | 0.151 | 0.448 | 1587 | 0.199 | 0.110 | 0.368 | 1392 | 0.216 | 0.128 | 0.391 | 1752 |
| FastKGE [12] | 0.230 | 0.140 | 0.404 | 821 | 0.169 | 0.101 | 0.296 | 610 | 0.171 | 0.105 | 0.291 | 583 |
| **ETT-CKGE** | **0.260** | **0.158** | **0.456** | **784** | **0.200** | **0.112** | **0.369** | **502** | **0.217** | **0.129** | **0.396** | **506** |

| Model | HYBRID | | | | FB-CKGE | | | | WN-CKGE | | | |
|---|---|---|---|---|---|---|---|---|---|---|---|---|
| | MRR | H@1 | H@10 | Training Time (s) | MRR | H@1 | H@10 | Training Time (s) | MRR | H@1 | H@10 | Training Time (s) |
| Fine-Tune | 0.137 | 0.074 | 0.256 | 559 | 0.182 | 0.098 | 0.344 | 277 | 0.1 | 0.004 | 0.259 | 392 |
| PNN [18] | 0.185 | 0.101 | 0.350 | 2039 | 0.215 | 0.122 | 0.402 | 1351 | 0.133 | 0.002 | 0.343 | 1429 |
| CWR [15] | 0.037 | 0.015 | 0.078 | 1986 | 0.072 | 0.011 | 0.187 | 2039 | 0.005 | 0.000 | 0.012 | 1265 |
| GEM [16] | 0.135 | 0.070 | 0.261 | 1804 | 0.183 | 0.098 | 0.352 | 1069 | 0.114 | 0.001 | 0.290 | 1049 |
| EMR [21] | 0.140 | 0.074 | 0.268 | 3154 | 0.181 | 0.097 | 0.347 | 1474 | 0.114 | 0.002 | 0.287 | 1160 |
| LKGE [4] | 0.179 | 0.111 | 0.372 | 1612 | 0.220 | 0.125 | 0.412 | 1197 | 0.139 | 0.070 | 0.333 | 1136 |
| FMR [29] | 0.206 | 0.121 | 0.375 | 3258 | 0.220 | 0.125 | 0.413 | 2086 | 0.132 | 0.003 | 0.324 | 1850 |
| IncDE [11] | 0.223 | 0.130 | 0.401 | 1675 | 0.232 | 0.133 | 0.425 | 1447 | 0.150 | 0.004 | 0.362 | 1087 |
| FastKGE [12] | 0.198 | 0.120 | 0.345 | 841 | 0.220 | 0.128 | 0.400 | 390 | 0.160 | 0.011 | 0.368 | 448 |
| **ETT-CKGE** | **0.224** | **0.131** | **0.402** | **535** | **0.236** | **0.137** | **0.428** | **413** | **0.153** | **0.080** | **0.385** | **369** |

Beyond performance, we assess efficiency and scalability using three metrics: **Cumulative Training time**, which reflects knowledge adaptation smoothness; **Peak Allocated memory**, which measures the maximum memory usage per snapshot; and **Updated Parameters**, which indicates the number of parameters updated during training and serves as an indicator of computational cost.

### 5.5 Experimental Results and Discussion

Table 3 presents the experimental results across six benchmark datasets. The results demonstrate that ETT-CKGE achieves competitive performance relative to state-of-the-art continual KGE methods, without overclaiming superiority. Compared to the Fine-Tune model, ETT-CKGE yields MRR improvements ranging from 30.1% to 135.3%, highlighting the severity of knowledge degradation in Fine-Tune as new snapshots are introduced. Notably, despite employing a more sophisticated architecture, ETT-CKGE achieves faster training time than Fine-Tune on the HYBRID dataset. This efficiency stems from the task-driven token design, which allows our model to selectively encode and transfer essential knowledge without relying on time-consuming graph traversal, thereby reducing computational overhead while maintaining strong performance.

Compared to the second-best performing models, ETT-CKGE achieves a 50% to 96% reduction in training time while maintaining comparable or superior MRR. This improvement stems from ETT-CKGE's token-guided, task-driven framework, which not only eliminates the need for expensive graph traversal and handcrafted heuristics, as seen in models like IncDE and FMR, but also enables the model to identify the most informative nodes and relations directly from task signals. This selective focus facilitates more efficient knowledge transfer and model

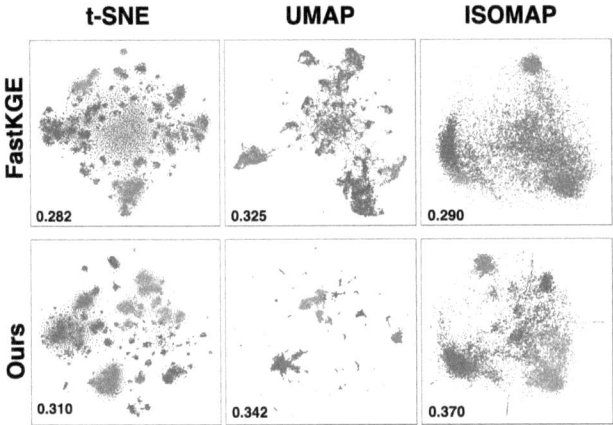

**Fig. 3.** Entity embedding visualization on the ENTITY dataset. The Silhouette Score, shown in the lower-left corner of each plot, quantitatively reflects the clustering quality of the entity embeddings; higher scores indicate more well-separated and compact clusters.

adaptation, resulting in a highly effective and scalable continual learning approach.

Compared to FastKGE, the second fastest model, ETT-CKGE consistently achieves 7.2% to 13% higher MRR across most datasets, demonstrating its superior accuracy in CKGE. While FastKGE relies on rank-based adapters and human-designed heuristics to integrate new knowledge, its optimization is not directly aligned with the task objective. In contrast, ETT-CKGE leverages task-driven tokens that are optimized adaptively through the training loss, enabling more effective and targeted knowledge transfer. Although FastKGE performs competitively on the WN-CKGE dataset, ETT-CKGE still achieves a shorter training time, offering a better balance between performance and efficiency.

While FastKGE sacrifices model expressiveness to speed up continual learning, our method maintains both efficiency and predictive quality, making it a more well-rounded choice. Furthermore, Fig. 3 presents entity embedding visualizations via three methods, t-SNE, UMAP, and ISOMAP. It is clear that the entity embeddings learned by ETT-CKGE have more separable patterns compared to embeddings learned by FastKGE.

Generally, ETT-CKGE achieves superior or comparable performance to complex, resource-intensive SOTA models while significantly reducing training time and memory consumption, as explained in Sect. 5.6. Compared to efficiency-focused approaches, ETT-CKGE demonstrates notable improvements in both accuracy and computational efficiency. Overall, ETT-CKGE offers an excellent balance between performance and efficiency, making it a practical and scalable solution for evolving knowledge graphs.

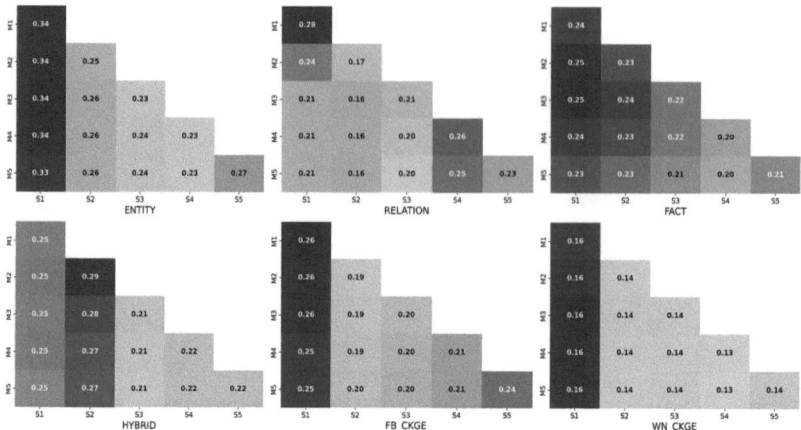

**Fig. 4.** MRR Changes.

### 5.6 Catastrophic Forgetting Analysis in Continual Learning

Since catastrophic forgetting is the main concern in CKGE, Fig. 4 illustrates how our model addresses catastrophic forgetting, showcasing its performance across six datasets during sequential learning. Each heatmap displays the MRR achieved by our model on each dataset over snapshots S1 to S5. Model stages are denoted as $Mi$, where $i$ represents the snapshot number. Warmer colors indicate higher MRR, while cooler colors suggest performance degradation and forgetting on that dataset.

In summary, it demonstrates our model's effective mitigation of catastrophic forgetting via robust knowledge preservation. Although some dataset-specific MRR variations appear, especially on the relation-centric RELATION dataset, ETT-CKGE generally maintains stable MRR across sequential snapshots. Notably, on FB-CKGE and WN-CKGE datasets, ETT-CKGE exhibits remarkable resilience to forgetting, indicating a strong capability to learn and adapt to evolving KGs without significantly compromising prior knowledge. This balance of knowledge preservation and sequential learning highlights the effectiveness of ETT-CKGE in addressing catastrophic forgetting in dynamic KG scenarios.

### 5.7 Efficiency and Scalability Analysis in Continual Learning

Figure 5 provides experimental validation of the efficiency and scalability on the RELATION dataset. For a model to scale well with evolving KGs, it must adapt to new information efficiently, meaning without a large increase in computational work. We analyze efficiency and stability metrics from snapshot 2 onward to focus on model behavior in dynamic scenarios.

- **Cumulative Training Time**: As shown in Fig. 5a, ETT-CKGE consistently achieves the lowest cumulative training time across all snapshots, outperforming even the second-fastest model, FastKGE, by 1.6 to 2.3x from S2 to S5.

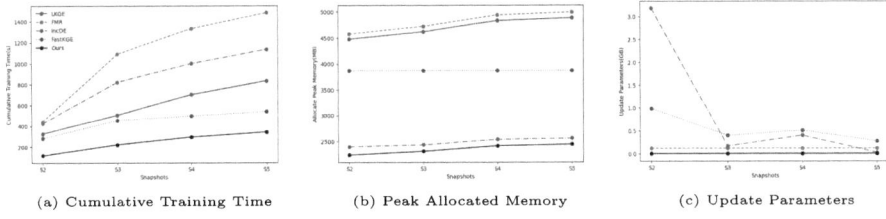

(a) Cumulative Training Time  (b) Peak Allocated Memory  (c) Update Parameters

**Fig. 5.** Model Scalability Analysis Over Time

Beyond the raw efficiency gain, training curves show smoother adaptation to evolving knowledge graphs, with stable incremental increases in training time. This indicates that ETT-CKGE facilitates more efficient knowledge transfer between snapshots, minimizing disruption and avoiding the sharp cost spikes observed in other models. Such smooth transitions suggest that the task-driven token mechanism effectively captures and reuses informative components without requiring heavy computational overhead. While training speed is a clear advantage, this stability in knowledge adaptation underscores the broader benefit of our design, ensuring efficient, consistent, and scalable continual learning.

- **Peak Allocated Memory**: Fig. 5b shows that ETT-CKGE achieves the lowest peak memory consumption among all baselines, reducing memory usage by 150MB to 2GB compared to memory-intensive models like FMR and LKGE. This efficiency comes from ETT-CKGE's fixed-size token design and lightweight architecture, which avoids storing additional structures like entity layers or replay buffers required in other methods.

**Updated Parameters:** As shown in Fig. 5c, ETT-CKGE consistently maintains a low number of updated parameters, around 2,000 across all snapshots. These parameters come from the fixed-size task-driven tokens, which are used solely to retain old knowledge and are not expanded when learning new snapshots. In contrast, models like IncDE introduce new parameters to learn additional knowledge at each snapshot, leading to significantly higher computational cost. This lightweight design allows ETT-CKGE to achieve faster training while still maintaining strong performance.

### 5.8 Ablation Study

Table 4 presents the ablation results of ETT-CKGE, evaluating the contribution of three key components: the distillation loss ($\mathcal{L}_{distill}$), Stage I training (SIT), and the diversity loss ($\mathcal{L}_{div}$), across various datasets.

**Effect of Distillation Loss**: The results clearly highlight that $\mathcal{L}_{distill}$ is the core driver of ETT-CKGE's effectiveness. Removing it leads to a significant performance drop across all datasets, underscoring its essential role in enabling task-relevant knowledge transfer. This task-driven loss directly optimizes the token-guided embedding space to capture critical information from both old and new knowledge without relying on handcrafted heuristics or traversal-based processing.

Table 4. Ablation results

| $\mathcal{L}_{distill}$ | Token Training SIT | $\mathcal{L}_{div}$ | ENTITY MRR | T(s) | RELATION MRR | T(s) | FACT MRR | T(s) | HYBRID MRR | T(s) | FB-CKGE MRR | T(s) | WN-CKGE MRR | T(s) |
|---|---|---|---|---|---|---|---|---|---|---|---|---|---|---|
| ✓ | ✓ | ✓ | 0.260 | 784 | 0.200 | 502 | 0.217 | 506 | 0.222 | 559 | 0.236 | 413 | 0.153 | 369 |
| ✓ | ✓ | ✗ | 0.258 | 722 | 0.194 | 496 | 0.215 | 461 | 0.220 | 567 | 0.233 | 405 | 0.152 | 343 |
| ✓ | ✗ | ✗ | 0.257 | 612 | 0.193 | 448 | 0.215 | 335 | 0.220 | 497 | 0.221 | 316 | 0.150 | 341 |
| ✗ | ✗ | ✗ | 0.170 | 528 | 0.085 | 417 | 0.161 | 287 | 0.138 | 406 | 0.178 | 275 | 0.102 | 410 |

**Effect of Stage I Training**: SIT plays an important supporting role. Eliminating Stage I training slightly reduces performance, especially in FB-CKGE, while reducing training time. This shows that although SIT introduces extra computation, it strengthens the quality of token learning and improves overall performance when paired with $\mathcal{L}_{distill}$.

**Effect of Diversity Loss**: Diversity loss helps ensure varied and effective token learning. Removing $\mathcal{L}_{div}$ causes a minor drop in MRR, indicating that it contributes to performance improvements but is not as crucial as $\mathcal{L}_{dist}$. Additionally, removing $\mathcal{L}_{div}$ reduces training time, confirming that its computation introduces extra overhead.

## 6 Conclusion Remarks and Future Work

This paper introduces a novel regularization-based CKGE model with a self-guided token mechanism for better efficiency and performance. The proposed model significantly reduces the adaptation time between snapshots and memory costs, thus opening the door to real-world applications with large data volumes. As evidenced by extensive comparative experiments and an ablation study, the proposed model outperforms the SOTA models in both predictive accuracy and model efficiency. In addition, our model can be adapted to downstream tasks at all levels, including link prediction, node classification, and graph classification.

In the future, while improving efficiency is critical for practical applications, enhancing robustness to noise and high sparsity in graphs is another challenge to be solved. With current advances in Large Language Models (LLMs) [2,3,19] and Multi-Modal Learning (MML) [6,17], leveraging knowledge foundations of built LLMs via MML has become a promising approach [14,25] to handle noisy and sparse graphs. Moreover, CKGE plays a vital role in graph foundation models in continually evolving domains, such as recommender systems, social networks, and biomedical knowledge reasoning.

**Acknowledgments.** The authors would like to thank the Department of Computer Science at Bowling Green State University, the Department of Artificial Intelligence & Informatics at Mayo Clinic, and the Department of Computer Science at University of Houston Clear Lake, and the Department of Ctr-Secure AI for Healthcare at The University of Texas Health Science, Houston, for the support and resources that contributed to this research. This work is supported by projects, R24ES036131, R01AT012871, and U24AI171008.

# References

1. Bordes, A., Usunier, N., Garcia-Duran, A., Weston, J., Yakhnenko, O.: Translating embeddings for modeling multi-relational data. In: Advances in Neural Information Processing Systems, **26** (2013)
2. Brown, T., et al.: Language models are few-shot learners. In: Advances in Neural Information Processing Systems, vol. 33, pp. 1877–1901 (2020)
3. Chowdhery, A., et al.: Palm: scaling language modeling with pathways. J. Mach. Learn. Res. **24**(240), 1–113 (2023)
4. Cui, Y., et al.: Lifelong embedding learning and transfer for growing knowledge graphs. In: Proceedings of the AAAI Conference on Artificial Intelligence, vol. 37, pp. 4217–4224 (2023)
5. Jeon, D.H., et al.: KGIF: optimizing relation-aware recommendations with knowledge graph information fusion. In: 2024 IEEE International Conference on Big Data (BigData), pp. 6021–6030 (2024). https://doi.org/10.1109/BigData62323.2024.10825929
6. Jia, C., et al.: Scaling up visual and vision-language representation learning with noisy text supervision. In: International Conference on Machine Learning, pp. 4904–4916. PMLR (2021)
7. Ju, W., et al.: A comprehensive survey on deep graph representation learning. Neural Networks 106207 (2024)
8. Kazemi, S.M., Poole, D.: Simple embedding for link prediction in knowledge graphs. In: Advances in Neural Information Processing Systems, vol. 31 (2018)
9. Kirkpatrick, J., et al.: Overcoming catastrophic forgetting in neural networks. Proc. Natl. Acad. Sci. **114**(13), 3521–3526 (2017)
10. Li, Y., et al.: Improving entity recognition using ensembles of deep learning and fine-tuned large language models: a case study on adverse event extraction from vaers and social media. J. Biomed. Inform. 104789 (2025)
11. Liu, J., et al.: Towards continual knowledge graph embedding via incremental distillation. In: Proceedings of the AAAI Conference on Artificial Intelligence, vol. 38, pp. 8759–8768 (2024)
12. Liu, J., et al.: Fast and continual knowledge graph embedding via incremental lora. arXiv preprint arXiv:2407.05705 (2024)
13. Liu, X., Masana, M., Herranz, L., Van de Weijer, J., Lopez, A.M., Bagdanov, A.D.: Rotate your networks: better weight consolidation and less catastrophic forgetting. In: 2018 24th International Conference on Pattern Recognition (ICPR), pp. 2262–2268. IEEE (2018)
14. Liu, Z., Yu, X., Fang, Y., Zhang, X.: Graphprompt: unifying pre-training and downstream tasks for graph neural networks. In: Proceedings of the ACM Web Conference 2023, pp. 417–428 (2023)
15. Lomonaco, V., Maltoni, D.: Core50: a new dataset and benchmark for continuous object recognition. In: Conference on Robot Learning, pp. 17–26. PMLR (2017)
16. Lopez-Paz, D., Ranzato, M.: Gradient episodic memory for continual learning. In: Advances in Neural Information Processing Systems, vol. 30 (2017)
17. Radford, A., et al.: Learning transferable visual models from natural language supervision. In: International Conference on Machine Learning, pp. 8748–8763. PMLR (2021)
18. Rusu, A.A., et al.: Progressive neural networks. arXiv preprint arXiv:1606.04671 (2016)

19. Touvron, H., et al.: Llama: Open and efficient foundation language models. arXiv preprint arXiv:2302.13971 (2023)
20. Trouillon, T., Welbl, J., Riedel, S., Gaussier, É., Bouchard, G.: Complex embeddings for simple link prediction. In: International Conference on Machine Learning, pp. 2071–2080. PMLR (2016)
21. Wang, H., Xiong, W., Yu, M., Guo, X., Chang, S., Wang, W.Y.: Sentence embedding alignment for lifelong relation extraction. arXiv preprint arXiv:1903.02588 (2019)
22. Wang, P., Han, J., Li, C., Pan, R.: Logic attention based neighborhood aggregation for inductive knowledge graph embedding. In: Proceedings of the AAAI Conference on Artificial Intelligence, vol. 33, pp. 7152–7159 (2019)
23. Wang, Q., Mao, Z., Wang, B., Guo, L.: Knowledge graph embedding: a survey of approaches and applications. IEEE Trans. Knowl. Data Eng. **29**(12), 2724–2743 (2017)
24. Xiao, X., et al.: HGTDP-DTA: hybrid graph-transformer with dynamic prompt for drug-target binding affinity prediction. arXiv preprint arXiv:2406.17697 (2024)
25. Yasunaga, M., Leskovec, J., Liang, P.: Linkbert: pretraining language models with document links. arXiv preprint arXiv:2203.15827 (2022)
26. Yoon, J., Yang, E., Lee, J., Hwang, S.J.: Lifelong learning with dynamically expandable networks. arXiv preprint arXiv:1708.01547 (2017)
27. Zhang, X., Song, D., Tao, D.: Continual learning on graphs: challenges, solutions, and opportunities. arXiv preprint arXiv:2402.11565 (2024)
28. Zhou, F., Cao, C.: Overcoming catastrophic forgetting in graph neural networks with experience replay. In: Proceedings of the AAAI Conference on Artificial Intelligence, vol. 35, pp. 4714–4722 (2021)
29. Zhu, L., Jeon, D.H., Sun, W., Yang, L., Xie, Y., Niu, S.: Flexible memory rotation (FMR): rotated representation with dynamic regularization to overcome catastrophic forgetting in continual knowledge graph learning. In: 2024 IEEE International Conference on Big Data (BigData), pp. 6180–6189 (2024). https://doi.org/10.1109/BigData62323.2024.10825244

# Resource Efficiency

# Unified Framework for Pre-trained Neural Network Compression via Decomposition and Optimized Rank Selection

Ali Aghababaei-Harandi[✉] and Massih-Reza Amini

Université Grenoble Alpes, CNRS, Computer Science Laboratory LIG,
Grenoble, France
{Ali.Aghababaei-Harandi,Massih-Reza.Amini}@univ-grenoble-alpes.fr

**Abstract.** Despite their high accuracy, complex neural networks demand significant computational resources, posing challenges for deployment on resource constrained devices such as mobile phones and embedded systems. Compression algorithms have been developed to address these challenges by reducing model size and computational demands while maintaining accuracy. Among these approaches, factorization methods based on tensor decomposition are theoretically sound and effective. However, they face difficulties in selecting the appropriate rank for decomposition. This paper tackles this issue by presenting a unified framework that simultaneously applies decomposition and rank selection, employing a composite compression loss within defined rank constraints. Our method includes an automatic rank search in a continuous space, efficiently identifying optimal rank configurations for the pre-trained model by eliminating the need for additional training data and reducing computational overhead in the search step. Combined with a subsequent fine-tuning step, our approach maintains the performance of highly compressed models on par with their original counterparts. Using various benchmark datasets and models, we demonstrate the efficacy of our method through a comprehensive analysis.

**Keywords:** Neural Network · Decomposition · Optimal Rank

## 1 Introduction

In recent years, deep learning has revolutionized various scientific fields, including computer vision and natural language processing [26]. Complex neural networks with millions or billions of parameters have achieved unprecedented accuracy. However, their size poses challenges for deployment on resource-limited devices like mobile phones and edge devices [27]. The storage, memory, and processing requirements of these models often prove to be unfeasible or excessively costly, thus limiting their practicality and accessibility.

Recent research has introduced various compression algorithms to address cost-effectiveness, scalability, and real-time responsiveness [22]. These approaches, which reduce a model's size and computational demands while preserving accuracy, can be classified into four primary categories. One straightforward method is *pruning*, which involves removing insignificant weights from the model [4]. *Quantization* reduces the precision of numerical values, typically transitioning from 32-bit floating-point numbers to lower bit-width fixed-point numbers [24]. *Knowledge distillation* trains a smaller "student" model to mimic a larger "teacher" model, resulting in a compact model with similar performance [3]. Lastly, *low-rank factorization* decomposes weight matrices or tensors into smaller components, reducing the number of parameters [2,35,36]. While effective, selecting the appropriate rank for decomposition remains a significant challenge.

Non-uniqueness in tensor rank is a major challenge in tensor decomposition research. Most tensor decomposition problems, especially CP decomposition, are NP-hard [13], and allow different decompositions of a same tensor even though some works tries to approximating the ranks of a tensor in a practical way [11,34]. Finding the ideal rank is an ongoing research topic, and determining multiple tensor ranks for deep neural network layers is not suitable for conventional hyperparameter selection methods like cross-validation. Typically, a single rank is chosen for the decomposition of layers based on a compression rate, but this can lead to significant performance degradation in complex models.

Recent studies propose automated methods for determining tensor decomposition ranks [5,20,33]. However, these approaches, including reinforcement learning, greedy search algorithms, and SuperNet search, can be computationally expensive and time-consuming, especially for large models and datasets. Their effectiveness often depends on hyperparameters like learning rates or regularization parameters, which are challenging to tune. Additionally, existing methods do not cover a wide enough search space to achieve ideal compression rates.

This paper introduces a unified framework that simultaneously addresses tensor decomposition and optimal rank selection using a composite compression loss within specified rank constraints. Also, when we combine this rank search with a subsequent fine-tuning step, our experiments show that the highly compressed model performs similarly to the original model. The key contributions of this paper are:

- Our proposed method allows to achieve maximum compression rates by covering all ranks in the search space through a simple and efficient multi-step search process that explores ranks from low to high resolution.
- The proposed search method involves an automatic rank search in a continuous space, which efficiently identifies the optimal rank configurations for layer decomposition without requiring training data.
- We perform a comprehensive analysis of the various components of our approach, highlighting its efficacy across various benchmark datasets and models such as convolution and transformer-based models. we achieved improvement in some experiments specifically improvement in all metrics in the case of ResNet-18, while in another experiment we had competitive results. Moreover, our method speeds up the search phase compared to other related work.

## 2 Related Work

Low-rank factorization techniques, particularly tensor decomposition, have gained attention in deep learning, especially in natural language processing (NLP) [22]. These methods provide an efficient means of fine-tuning large language models, offering advantages over alternative techniques such as quantization [24], knowledge distillation [3], and gradient-based pruning [37]. In this paper, we focus on tensor decomposition, which proved to be a robust compression tool with a high compression rate and a relatively lower computational cost. Their applications extend beyond NLP and have also been applied in computer vision [36]. However, selecting the appropriate rank for compressing deep neural models using decomposition techniques is NP-hard [13]. Research in this area falls into two main approaches.

The first approach relies on a rank-fixed setting, where the ranks of layers are determined based on a predefined compression rate target. Some work used a low-rank loss to substitute the weights of convolution layers with their low-rank approximations [38]. The two main low-rank approximation methods applied on pre-trained models are CP and Tucker decomposition [16]. Recent studies have revealed that fine-tuning after CP decomposition can be unstable and have addressed this issue by integrating a stability term into the decomposition process [25]. In addition, some work decomposed convolution and fully connected layers with tensor train, and trained the model from scratch [22]. However, tensor decomposition in a fixed-rank setting presents certain challenges. First, selecting the appropriate rank for different layers is complex and often relies on human expertise. Second, there is a lack of interpretable patterns between layer ranks, leading to inconsistencies among the chosen ranks between layers. Furthermore, the fixed rank strategy overlooks the varying importance of layers [19], which can result in suboptimal approximations that can lead to accuracy drops or insufficient compression rates.

The second approach involves determining the optimal ranks by setting the optimization problem on the basis of the ranks of layers. One technique consists in iteratively decreasing the ranks of the layers at each step of the search phase [12]. The discrete nature of rank search lends itself to discrete search algorithms, such as reinforcement learning and progressive search, to identify optimal ranks [20]. Other methods impose constraints on ranks and budget, using iterative optimization strategies [37]. More recent studies explore continuous search spaces to determine optimal ranks [6,8,32,33].

To address time complexity issues, these approaches depend on training data to search for ranks, restricting exploration to a limited search space, and thereby limiting the achievable compression rate. In contrast, we introduce a novel optimization problem that minimizes a decomposition loss while enforcing a rank loss constraint independent of the training data, which accelerates the search process for large models. For rank selection, we propose an efficient dichotomous search method that is both fast and allows for a broader range of rank exploration, ultimately enhancing the compression rate.

## 3 Background and Preliminaries

In the following, we represent indices using italicized letters and sets with italic calligraphic letters. For two-dimensional arrays (matrices) and one-dimensional arrays (vectors), we use bold capital letters and bold lowercase letters, respectively. Finally, tensors are represented as multidimensional arrays with bold calligraphic capital letters.

A fundamental technique for efficiently representing and processing tensors is tensor decomposition. This technique transforms a multidimensional array of data into a series of lower-dimensional tensors, thereby reducing both the representation size and computational complexity. The prevalent tensor decomposition techniques encompass canonical polyadic (CP) [10], Tucker [29], tensor train (TT) [23], and tensor ring (TR) decomposition [22].

In our work, we employ both the TT and CP decompositions. TT decomposition supports fast multilinear multiplication and integration while preserving structure, and CP decomposition has been shown to achieve high parameter reduction in CNNs with small performance drops [22]. In the following, we present the TT decomposition due to its structural advantages in capturing complex dependencies.

TT decomposition decomposes a tensor into smaller tensors with dimensions connected as a chain to each other. This decomposition mathematically can be represented as follows:

$$\hat{\mathcal{W}}^{(R_1,\ldots,R_{N-1})}(i_1, i_2, \ldots, i_N) = \sum_{j_1=1}^{R_1} \cdots \sum_{j_{N-1}=1}^{R_{N-1}} \mathcal{G}_1(i_1, j_1)\mathcal{G}_2(j_1, i_2, j_2) \cdots \mathcal{G}_N(j_{N-1}, i_N), \quad (1)$$

where the tuple $(R_1, R_2, \ldots, R_{N-1})$ represents the rank of the TT decomposition, and $\mathcal{G}_k$ are the TT cores with sizes $R_{k-1} \times I_k \times R_k$, and $R_0 = R_N = 1$. For a given convolutional layer with a weight tensor $\mathcal{W} \in R^{b \times h \times w \times c}$, the forward process for an input tensor $\mathcal{X} \in R^{k_1 \times k_2 \times k_3}$ can be expressed as:

$$\mathcal{Y} = \sum_{i_1=0}^{k_1-1} \sum_{i_2=0}^{k_2-1} \sum_{i_3=0}^{k_3-1} \mathcal{W}(t, x+i_1, y+i_2, z+i_3)\mathcal{X}(i_1, i_2, i_3). \quad (2)$$

Specifically, we investigate how the weight tensor of a convolutional layer can be decomposed into multiple smaller convolution operations. We utilize TT decomposition, as detailed in the following formulations:

$$\mathcal{Y} = \sum_{r_1=1}^{R_1} \sum_{r_2=1}^{R_2} \mathcal{G}_t(t, r_1) \left( \sum_{i_1=0}^{k_1-1} \sum_{i_2=0}^{k_2-1} \mathcal{G}_y(r_1, x+i_1, y+i_2, r_2) \right.$$
$$\left. \left( \sum_{i_3=0}^{k_3-1} \mathcal{G}_s(i_3, r_2)\mathcal{X}(i_1, i_2, i_3) \right) \right). \quad (3)$$

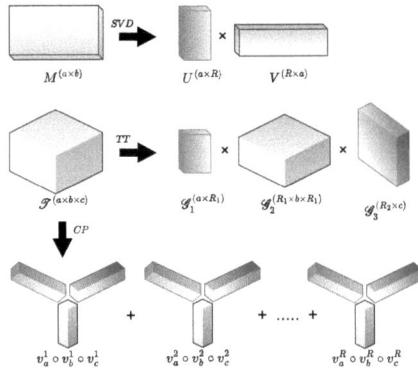

**Fig. 1.** An illustration of matrix decomposition (**upper row**) using SVD for a matrix $M \in \mathbb{R}^{a \times b}$, alongside Tensor Train decomposition (**middle row**), and CP decomposition (**bottom row**) for a tensor $\mathcal{T} \in \mathbb{R}^{a \times b \times c}$.

The CP decomposition expresses a multi-dimensional tensor into a sum of rank-one tensors. It follows a well-established factorization process that has been extensively studied in prior works [10]. Figure 1 illustrates TT decomposition and CP decomposition in relation to matrix decomposition using SVD.

## 4 Optimal Rank Tensor Decomposition

The proposed method, denoted as Rank adapt tENsor dEcomposition (RENE) and illustrated in Fig. 2, involves tensor decomposition with an automatic search for optimal ranks. The approach begins with a pre-trained neural network and aims to decompose its weight tensors layer by layer into lower-rank approximations while minimizing both decomposition and rank losses. This is achieved through an iterative optimization process that updates the decomposition weights and rank coefficients.

At each layer $i \in \{1, \ldots, n\}$, rank coefficients $(p_j^i)_j$ related to a set of ranks $\mathcal{R}_i$ for decomposition (Fig. 2 (left)) are found iteratively and progressively refined until a single optimal rank is determined. The decomposed network with this optimal rank is fine-tuned to align its outputs with the original model (Fig. 2 (right)), ensuring that the compressed model retains the performance of the original while being more efficient.

Equations (1) and (3) show that both the number of parameters and computation complexity are directly proportional to the rank of the layer. Consequently, selecting a lower rank results in a reduction in these computational costs. From this observation, we define the decomposition problem as the minimization of a decomposition error under a rank constraint.

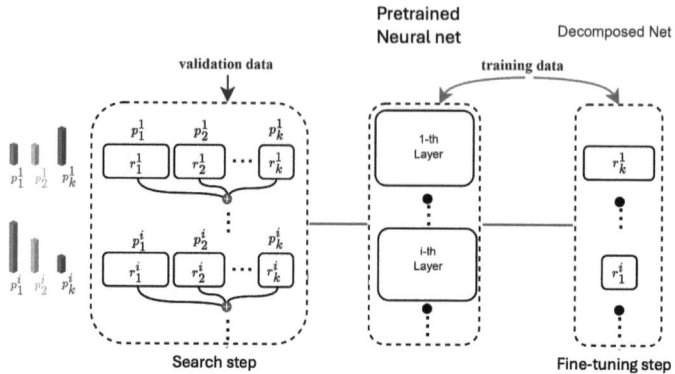

**Fig. 2.** Overview of RENE: Starting with a pre-trained neural network, weight tensors are decomposed layer by layer into lower-rank approximations. Rank coefficients for each layer are refined until optimal (left), followed by fine-tuning of the decomposed network (right).

### 4.1 Problem Formulation

Given a pre-trained neural network with $n$ hidden layers and weights $\{\mathcal{W}_i\}_{i=1}^n$, our objective is then to achieve a low-rank decomposition of these weights with the smallest possible ranks, formulated as the following optimization problem:

$$\min_{\widehat{\mathcal{W}}^\mathcal{R}} \mathcal{L}_d(\widehat{\mathcal{W}}^\mathcal{R}) \quad s.t. \quad \min_{\mathcal{R}} \mathcal{L}_r(\mathcal{R}), \qquad (4)$$

where $\mathcal{L}_d(.)$ and $\mathcal{L}_r(.)$ are a decomposition loss and a rank loss, respectively, and $\widehat{\mathcal{W}}^\mathcal{R} = \{\widehat{\mathcal{W}}_1^{(\mathcal{R}_1)}, \ldots, \widehat{\mathcal{W}}_n^{(\mathcal{R}_n)}\}$ is the set of decompositions to be found with $\mathcal{R} = \{\mathcal{R}_1, \ldots, \mathcal{R}_n\}$ the set of ranks, and $\widehat{\mathcal{W}}_i^{(\mathcal{R}_i)}$ are the weights of decomposition corresponding to the ranks $\mathcal{R}_i = \{r_i^1, \ldots, r_i^k\}$ of layer $i$.

For each layer $i \in \{1, \ldots, n\}$ of the network, we consider a set of decompositions $(\widehat{\mathcal{W}}_i^{(r)})_{r \in \mathcal{R}_i}$ of varying ranks defined in the set $\mathcal{R}_i$, for each weight tensor $\mathcal{W}_i$. To make the optimization problem under the rank constraint (4) continuous, we associate a rank coefficient $p_i^{(r)}$ with each decomposition of rank $r$ in layer $i$ based on a learnable parameter $\alpha_i^{(r)}$.

This rank coefficient, defined as $p_i^{(r)} = \text{softmax}(\alpha_i^{(r)})$, is adjusted via the parameter $\alpha_i^{(r)}$ to reflect the probability that the rank $r$ will be used in the decomposition of the weight tensor $\mathcal{W}_i$ for the layer $i$. Inspired by [31], we formalize the rank constraint in (4) using a normalized rank loss:

$$\mathcal{L}_r(\mathcal{R}) = \gamma \sum_{i=1}^n \left( \sum_{r \in \mathcal{R}_i} p_i^{(r)} \frac{r}{\max \mathcal{R}_i} \right)^\beta, \qquad (5)$$

where $\beta, \gamma \in [0, 1]$ are hyperparameters.

## 4.2 Tensor Decomposition and Rank Exploration

Building on the definition of $\mathcal{L}_r(\mathcal{R})$, we introduce two total losses to update weights and parameters $(\alpha_i^{(r)})_{i,r}$. The total weights loss for a neural network model with $n$ layers is defined as follows:

$$\mathcal{L}_{Tw}(\widehat{\mathcal{W}}^{\mathcal{R}}, \mathcal{P}^{\mathcal{R}}) = \sum_{i=1}^{n} \left\| \mathcal{W}_i - \sum_{r \in \mathcal{R}_i} p_i^{(r)} \hat{\mathcal{W}}_i^{(r)} \right\|_F^2 \times \gamma \left[ \sum_{i=1}^{n} \left( \sum_{r \in \mathcal{R}_i} p_i^{(r)} \frac{r}{\max \mathcal{R}_i} \right)^{\beta} \right], \quad (6)$$

and the total parameters loss for the same neural network can be formulated as:

$$\mathcal{L}_{T\alpha}(\widehat{\mathcal{W}}^{\mathcal{R}}, \mathcal{P}^{\mathcal{R}}) = \mathcal{L}_{val}(\widehat{\mathcal{W}}^{\mathcal{R}}, \mathcal{P}^{\mathcal{R}}) \times \gamma \left[ \sum_{i=1}^{n} \left( \sum_{r \in \mathcal{R}_i} p_i^{(r)} \frac{r}{\max \mathcal{R}_i} \right)^{\beta} \right], \quad (7)$$

The first term in (6) is referred to as the *decomposition loss*, while $\mathcal{L}_{val}$ in (7) denotes the cross-entropy loss on the validation data. The minimization of the losses, is tackled through a two-step iterative process. First, the weights of the decomposition, denoted as $\widehat{\mathcal{W}}^{\mathcal{R}}$, are updated by minimizing (6) while keeping the rank coefficients, denoted as $\mathcal{P}^{\mathcal{R}}$, fixed across all layers. Next, the parameters $(\alpha_i^{(r)})_{i,r}$, are updated using the newly updated weights $\widehat{\mathcal{W}}^{\mathcal{R}}$. This update is performed by minimizing the (7), where the weights between the layers are adjusted with the corresponding rank parameters. This two-steps updates ensures that each $\alpha$ update is based on well-trained weights, avoiding noisy signals from still-learning weights. This prevents the architecture from overfitting to transient weight states.

The updates of the decomposition weight parameters and rank coefficients are performed using stochastic gradient descent to ensure efficient and iterative optimization. The update rules are as follows:

$$\text{Weight update:} \quad \hat{\mathcal{W}}_i^{(r)} \leftarrow \hat{\mathcal{W}}_i^{(r)} - \eta_w \nabla_{\hat{\mathcal{W}}_i^{(r)}}(\mathcal{L}_{Tw}), \quad (8)$$

$$\text{Rank coefficient update:} \quad \alpha_i^{(r)} \leftarrow \alpha_i^{(r)} - \eta_\alpha \nabla_{\alpha_i^{(r)}}(\mathcal{L}_{T\alpha}). \quad (9)$$

For each layer $i$ and each rank $r \in \mathcal{R}_i$, the weight update (8) and rank coefficient update (9) are performed iteratively until a local minimum of the total loss (6) is reached. Each loss is a multiplication combination, where decomposition and validation losses are scaled by the rank loss (and vice versa). This scale-invariant feature balances both terms without requiring separate trade-off hyperparameters, enabling more stable training and better results compared to additive combinations.

## 4.3 Rank Search Space

Previous approaches to rank search in neural network compression typically rely on evaluating a small, fixed set of candidate ranks. While this strategy offers computational efficiency, it risks overlooking the most optimal rank configurations, as the true optimum may lie between the preselected candidates. To address this limitation, we propose a multi-step rank search method that systematically explores the entire rank space and progressively refines the search around the most promising solutions.

The process begins by defining a broad search space for each layer, denoted as $\mathcal{R}_i$, which spans all feasible rank values from $r_{\min}$ to $r_{\max}$. An initial step size $s^{(0)}$ is chosen to sample candidate ranks at regular intervals across this range, ensuring a coarse but complete coverage of the search space. For each sampled rank, the network weights and associated rank coefficients are updated, allowing the model to adapt to the current rank configuration. The quality of each candidate rank is assessed according to a loss function that may include both reconstruction error and a regularization term to encourage lower ranks.

After this initial exploration, the method identifies, for each layer $i$, the rank $\bar{r}_i$ that achieves the highest rank coefficient, indicating its potential as a promising candidate. To focus the search more precisely, the algorithm then defines new lower and upper bounds, $Lb_i$ and $Ub_i$, centered around $\bar{r}_i$ and separated by half the previous step size on either side. This effectively narrows the search space to a region most likely to contain the optimal rank. The step size is then reduced by a factor $f > 1$, yielding a finer sampling resolution for the next iteration. The new set of candidate ranks for layer $i$ is thus given by:

$$\mathcal{R}_i = \{r \mid r = Lb_i + ks, \text{ for } k \in \mathbb{N}, \text{ and } Lb_i \leq r \leq Ub_i\},$$

where $s$ denotes the updated step size. Before commencing the next iteration, the weights and rank coefficients are reinitialized for the refined search space. The process of sampling, updating, and selecting is then repeated. With each iteration, the search space contracts and the step size decreases, leading to an increasingly precise localization of the optimal rank. This iterative refinement continues until, for each layer, the candidate set $\mathcal{R}_i$ contains only a single element, signifying convergence to a unique rank selection.

Throughout this procedure, the weights and rank coefficients are jointly optimized, ensuring that both the model parameters and the rank configuration are adapted to minimize the overall loss. The loss function can incorporate not only the reconstruction or decomposition error but also a regularization component that penalizes higher ranks, thereby promoting model compression.

At the conclusion of the search, the final rank configuration $\bar{\mathbf{r}} = (\bar{r}_1, \ldots, \bar{r}_n)$ is validated using a cross-entropy loss or another appropriate metric on a held-out validation set. This step ensures that the selected ranks yield not only a compact model but also satisfactory predictive performance. The balance between compression and accuracy can be tuned by adjusting the regularization parameters $\gamma$ and $\beta$ in the loss formulation.

This multi-step, progressive rank search method offers several advantages over traditional approaches. By systematically narrowing the search space and refining the sampling granularity, it combines the thoroughness of exhaustive search with the efficiency of adaptive optimization. The method is capable of

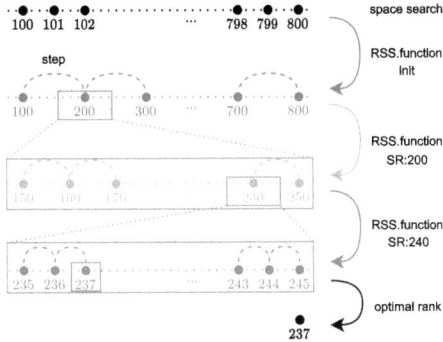

**Fig. 3.** A toy example illustrates the search for rank spaces. Initially, the search space includes integers from 100 to 800, with a step size of 100. After the first iteration, the selected rank is $\bar{r} = 200$, narrowing the search interval to $[150, 250]$ with a step size of 10. The second iteration selects $\bar{r} = 240$, refining the search space to $[235, 245]$ with a step size of 1. After 3 iterations, the optimal rank is identified within this interval.

escaping the limitations imposed by fixed candidate sets and can converge to globally optimal or near-optimal rank configurations. Figure 3 illustrates the evolution of the search space for a single layer: the process begins with a wide interval and large step size, then successively narrows and refines the search until the optimal rank is identified with maximal precision.

### 4.4 Final Decomposition and Fine-Tuning

The optimal ranks for decomposing the tensor weights for each layer, denoted as $\mathcal{R}^\star = \{r_1^\star, \ldots, r_n^\star\}$, are determined from these final sets and used to construct the decomposed network. To ensure the decomposed model replicates the behavior of the original model, it is crucial that the layers not only align their decomposed weights with the original weights but also produce the same outputs. To achieve this, our fine-tuning loss ($\mathcal{L}_f$) consists of two components: a cross entropy loss ($\mathcal{L}_{ce}$) and distillation loss ($\mathcal{L}_{diss}$). The cross entropy loss adjusts the model's weights based on the training data labels. Distillation loss aligns the decomposed weights with the original weights by minimized Frobenius distance, and enforces consistency between the outputs of the original and decomposed layers. The distillation and fine-tuning losses are defined as follows:

$$\mathcal{L}_{diss}(\widehat{\mathcal{W}}^{\mathcal{R}^\star}) = \sum_{i=1}^{n} \left\| \mathcal{W}_i - \widehat{\mathcal{W}}_i^{(r_i^\star)} \right\|_F^2 + \sum_{x \in X} \sum_{i=1}^{n} \|O_i(x) - D_i(x)\|_F^2, \quad (10)$$

$$\mathcal{L}_f(\widehat{\mathcal{W}}^{\mathcal{R}^\star}) = \mathcal{L}_{ce} + \lambda \mathcal{L}_{diss}, \quad (11)$$

where $X$ is the training set, $O_i(.)$ and $D_i(.)$ are the outputs of layer $i$ of the original model and the decomposed one, respectively and $\lambda$ is hyperparameter to control combination of losses. In this approach, the original model serves

---
**Algorithm 1:** Rank adapt tENsor dEcomposition (RENE)
---
1 **Input:** Pretrained model $M$, Training data $X$, Rank lower bounds $\boldsymbol{Lb} = \{Lb_1, \ldots, Lb_n\}$ and upper bounds $\boldsymbol{Ub} = \{Ub_1, \ldots, Ub_n\}$, Number of iterations $T$, Step size $s > 1$, Factor $f$;
2 **Initialize:** $\forall i, \mathcal{R}_i \leftarrow \{r \mid r = Lb_i + ks, \text{ for } k \in \mathbb{N}, \text{ and } Lb_i \leq r \leq Ub_i\}$;
3 **while** $s > 1$ **do**
4     **for** $i \in \{1, \ldots, n\}$ **do**
5         **for** $r \in \mathcal{R}_i$ **do**
6             **for** $t = 1$ **to** $T$ **do**
7                 $\hat{\boldsymbol{\mathcal{W}}}_i^{(r)} \leftarrow update(\hat{\boldsymbol{\mathcal{W}}}_i^{(r)})$;    // Eq. (8)
8                 $\alpha_i^{(r)} \leftarrow update(\alpha_i^{(r)})$;    // Eq. (9)

9     $s \leftarrow \lfloor \frac{s}{f} \rfloor$;
10     **for** $i \in \{1, \ldots, n\}$ **do**
11         $\bar{r}_i \leftarrow argmax_{r \in \mathcal{R}_i}(\text{softmax}(\alpha_i^{(r)}))$;
12         $Lb_i \leftarrow \bar{r}_i - \frac{s}{2}$;
13         $Ub_i \leftarrow \bar{r}_i + \frac{s}{2}$;
14         $\mathcal{R}_i \leftarrow \{r \mid r = Lb_i + ks, \text{ for } k \in \mathbb{N}, \text{ and } Lb_i \leq r \leq Ub_i\}$;

15 **Output:** Decomposed model $M^*$ by minimizing $\mathcal{L}_f(\widehat{\boldsymbol{\mathcal{W}}}^{\mathcal{R}^*})$ using $X$ ;
// Eq. (10)
---

as the teacher model and the decomposed model acts as the student model. The pseudocode for the overall procedure retracing these steps is presented in Algorithm 1.

## 5 Experiments

### 5.1 Experimental Setup

We evaluate RENE[1] on 3 datasets including CIFAR-10/100 [17] and ImageNet-1K [9]. To prevent convergence collapse during the updating of Eq.(6) and Eq.(7), we initially update only the weights for several iterations before jointly updating both weights and rank coefficients in an iterative manner. Each experiment is performed five times, and the best result from the fine-tuning step is reported. For TT decomposition, due to computational resource constraints, we assume that the two TT ranks are equal. In the search phase of RENE, for CIFAR-10/100, we set the initial rank space to $\{10, \ldots, 100\}$ with a step size of $s = 10$, which corresponds to 2 search steps. For ImageNet-1K, we set the initial rank space to $\{50, \ldots, 850\}$ with the step size $s = 100$, corresponding to 3 search steps. Across all datasets, we use $f = 10$. We used the standard SGD optimizer with Nesterov momentum set to 0.9, and hyperparameters $\lambda$, $\gamma$ and $\beta$ set to 0.5, 0.4 and 0.8, respectively. The initial learning rates were 0.001 for

---
[1] The code is available for research purposes at https://github.com/aah94/RENE.

CIFAR-10/100 and 0.0001 for ImageNet-1K. For the fine-tuning step we consider learning rate 0.00001 for all experiments and grid search with cross-validation is employed to select all hyperparameters, optimizing model performance based on validation accuracy. For comparing different approaches, the TOP-1 accuracy is used to compare the performance of the compressed model against the original uncompressed model. Additionally, we consider the gain in floating operations per second (FLOPs) and the compression rate.

## 5.2 Experimental Results

The following sections present a comprehensive analysis of RENE's performance and compression capabilities across various models and datasets.

**Performance and Compression Analysis.** For the initial evaluation, we tested RENE on CIFAR-10 using the ResNet-20 and VGG-16 models, with the results presented in Table 1. RENE with both CP and TT decomposition techniques yields competitive results compared to state-of-the-art methods. Using ResNet-20 as the original model, RENE with CP decomposition achieves 1.24% and 1.52% greater reduction of FLOPs and parameters, respectively, compared to the HALOC method [33]. Additionally, RENE with TT decomposition improves accuracy by 0.08% over the original uncompressed model. This suggests that our approach has effectively reduced the number of parameters of the original model, leading to a better generalization. Furthermore, with the VGG-16 model, RENE achieves significant compression rates while preserving performance. For instance, using RENE with CP decomposition reduces FLOPs by 85.23% and parameters by 98.6%. Furthermore, applying RENE with TT decomposition on VGG-16 improves generalization, resulting in a 0.04% increase in TOP-1 accuracy compared to the original uncompressed model.

The results on the ImageNet-1K dataset are presented in Table 2, where we evaluated RENE using ResNet-18 and MobileNetV2 models. For ResNet-18, our approach with CP decomposition yields competitive results, while TT decomposition outperformed other methods, achieving state-of-the-art performance across all metrics, including Top-1 accuracy, reduction in FLOPs, and parameters. With MobileNetV2, the CP method did not yield high performance, likely due to the model's reliance on depthwise convolution, which does not significantly benefit from decomposition in certain dimensions. However, RENE with TT decomposition demonstrated superior compression results, achieving 1.86% and 2.31% greater reductions in FLOPs and parameters, respectively, along with competitive Top-1 accuracy. Our results underscore the importance of selecting the appropriate decomposition method based on the model's complexity. Our experiments indicate that TT decomposition is more effective for compressing higher-complexity models, such as those trained on the ImageNet-1K dataset, while CP decomposition excels in compressing lower-complexity models, like those classically used on CIFAR-10.

**Table 1.** Results of different compression approaches for ResNet-20 and VGG-16 on CIFAR-10. C.T and A.R stand for *compression technique* and *automatic rank*, respectively.

| Method | C.T | A.R | Top-1 | FLOPs (↓%) | Comp. Rate |
|---|---|---|---|---|---|
| ResNet-20 | Original | - | 91.25 | - | - |
| RENE(CP) | Low-rank | ✓ | 90.82 | 73.44 | 77.62 |
| RENE(TT) | Low-rank | ✓ | 91.40 | 70.4 | 72.28 |
| HALOC [33] | Low-rank | ✓ | 91.32 | 72.20 | 76.10 |
| ALDS [21] | Low-rank | ✓ | 90.92 | 67.86 | 74.91 |
| LCNN [15] | Low-rank | ✓ | 90.13 | 66.78 | 65.38 |
| PSTR-S [20] | Low-rank | ✓ | 90.80 | 65.00 | 60.87 |
| Std. Tucker [16] | Low-rank | ✗ | 87.41 | 62.00 | 61.54 |
| VGG-16 | Original | - | 92.78 | - | - |
| RENE(CP) | Low-rank | ✓ | 92.51 | 86.23 | 98.60 |
| RENE(TT) | Low-rank | ✓ | 93.20 | 86.10 | 95.51 |
| HALOC [33] | Low-rank | ✓ | 93.16 | 86.44 | 98.56 |
| ALDS [21] | Low-rank | ✓ | 92.67 | 86.23 | 95.77 |
| LCNN [15] | Low-rank | ✓ | 92.72 | 85.47 | 91.14 |
| DECORE [1] | Pruning | - | 92.44 | 81.50 | 96.60 |
| Spike-Thrift [18] | Pruning | - | 91.79 | 80.00 | 97.01 |

**Table 2.** Results of different compression approaches for ResNet-18 and MobileNetV2 on ImageNet-1K.

| Method | C.T | A.R | Top-1 | FLOPs (↓%) | Comp. Rate |
|---|---|---|---|---|---|
| ResNet-18 | Original | - | 69.75 | - | - |
| RENE(CP) | Low-rank | ✓ | 68.46 | 57.1 | 66.2 |
| RENE(TT) | Low-rank | ✓ | 70.88 | 68.9 | 67.1 |
| HALOC [33] | Low-rank | ✓ | 70.65 | 66.16 | 63.64 |
| ALDS [21] | Low-rank | ✓ | 69.22 | 43.51 | 66.70 |
| TETD [37] | Low-rank | ✗ | 69.00 | 59.51 | 60.00 |
| Stable EPC [25] | Low-rank | ✓ | 68.50 | 59.51 | 61.00 |
| MUSCO [12] | Low-rank | ✗ | 69.29 | 58.67 | 60.50 |
| CHEX [14] | Pruning | - | 69.60 | 43.38 | 59.00 |
| EE [39] | Pruning | - | 68.27 | 46.60 | 58.00 |
| SCOP [28] | Pruning | - | 69.18 | 38.80 | 39.30 |
| MobileNetV2 | Original | - | 71.85 | - | - |
| RENE(CP) | Low-rank | ✓ | 65.39 | 11.78 | 51.6 |
| RENE(TT) | Low-rank | ✓ | 70.1 | 26.7 | 42.34 |
| HALOC [33] | Low-rank | ✓ | 70.98 | 24.24 | 40.03 |
| ALDS [21] | Low-rank | ✓ | 70.32 | 11.01 | 32.97 |
| HOSA [28] | Pruning | - | 64.43 | 43.65 | 91.14 |
| DCP [7] | Pruning | - | 64.22 | 44.75 | 96.60 |
| FT [40] | Pruning | - | 70.12 | 20.23 | 21.31 |

**Automatic vs. Manual Rank Selection.** We now examine the effectiveness of our rank search process compared to manual rank setting. In this experiment, we used pretrained ResNet18 and VGG16 models on the CIFAR-10 and CIFAR-100 datasets. For manual rank setting, we apply the TT decomposition and fix the rank across all layers to achieve a decomposed model with a specific percentage of the initial model's parameters, chosen from the set $\{1, 5, 10, 25, 50, 75\}$. All models are pre-trained on the ImageNet-1K dataset and fine-tuned for 20 epochs. Figure 4 presents these results. As shown, increasing the number of ranks (or equivalently, increasing the percentage of parameters of the decomposed model) improves the performance of both the decomposed VGG16 and ResNet18 models. When the decomposed models have 75% of the parame-

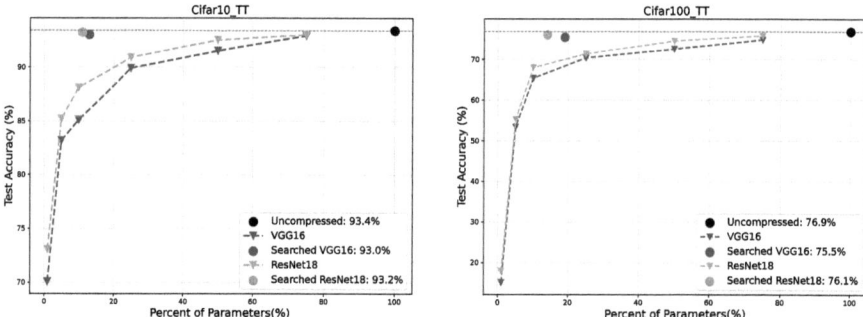

**Fig. 4.** Search vs Manual: Compression results for manual setting at different levels compression, compare to searched setting (left CIFAR10 and right CIFAR100).

ters of the initial models, the performance almost matches that of the original pretrained models. With RENE, We achieve comparable results while compressing the model by more than 80% on both ResNet18 and VGG16 across both datasets. These results indicate that fixing the ranks across layers is suboptimal. In contrast, RENE enables the automatic selection of ranks across different layers, achieving a good compression rate without significant performance loss.

**Rank Selection.** Figure 5 illustrates the selected ranks for both CP and TT decompositions using ResNet-18 as the original model on the ImageNet-1K dataset, highlighting that CP ranks are generally larger than those of TT.

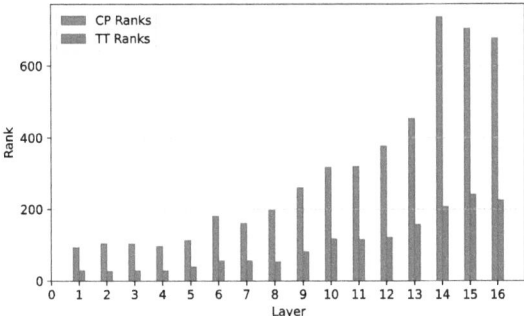

**Fig. 5.** Distribution of ranks achieved using CP and TT decompositions on ResNet-18 for the ImageNet-1K dataset.

This difference arises from the inherent characteristics of the decomposition methods: CP decomposition tends to produce larger ranks because it decomposes the tensor into a sum of rank-one tensors, capturing more detailed interactions but potentially leading to higher complexity. In contrast, TT decomposition typically results in smaller ranks due to its chain-like structure, which can lead to more compact representations and potentially better compression. The distribution of ranks reveals that even among layers of the same dimensions, the effective ranks can differ. This reflects the varying contributions of each layer to the model's performance. Some layers may capture more complex features, requiring higher ranks, while others may focus on simpler features, allowing for lower ranks. These results are in line with the case of selecting the ranks manually and the same over all layers that were been presented in the previous section.

**Double Compression.** In this experiment, we investigate the effects of double compression by applying RENE in conjunction with knowledge distillation. Our goal is to assess whether combining these two compression techniques can yield further reductions in model size and computational requirements without sacrificing performance. We focus on TT decomposition for this analysis, using two datasets: CIFAR-100 and ImageNet-1K.

For the CIFAR-100 dataset, we employ ResNet-56 as the teacher model and ResNet-20 as the student model. Similarly, for the ImageNet-1K dataset, ResNet-34 serves as the teacher model, while ResNet-18 acts as the student model. The distillation process involves training the student model to mimic the behavior of the larger, more complex teacher model, thereby transferring knowledge and improving performance.

**Table 3.** Double compression: RENE with distillation on CIFAR-100 and ImageNet-1K. The notations T and S denote the teacher and student, respectively.

| CIFAR-100 (T: ResNet56 (72.34%), S: ResNet20 (69.6%)) | | | |
|---|---|---|---|
| Method | Top-1 (%) | FLOPs (%) | Comp. rate (%) |
| Distillation [30] | **72.53** | 67.7 | 68.24 |
| RENE(Teacher) | 72.23 | 64.23 | 61.75 |
| RENE(Student) | 72.46 | **89.01** | **86.54** |
| ImageNet-1K (T: ResNet34 (73.31%), S: ResNet18 (69.76%)) | | | |
| Method | Top-1 (%) | FLOPs (%) | Params (%) |
| Distillation [30] | 71.98 | 50.27 | 46.33 |
| RENE(Teacher) | **73.23** | 59.91 | 63.46 |
| RENE(Student) | 71.9 | **76.77** | **78.69** |

After applying distillation, we further compress both the teacher and the distilled student models using RENE. The results, presented in Table 3, demonstrate that our decomposition method achieves competitive performance compared to distillation alone for both the teacher and student models. Notably, when applying RENE to the distilled student model, we achieve a significant reduction in both parameters and computational complexity. Specifically, on the ImageNet-1K dataset, the decomposed distilled student model reduces parameters by 78.69% and FLOPs by 76.77% compared to the original teacher model.

This double compression approach not only maintains the accuracy of the original model but also highlights the potential for substantial reductions in model size and computational requirements. These findings underscore the effectiveness of combining distillation with decomposition techniques to achieve efficient and high-performing compressed models.

## 6 Conclusion

In this paper, we presented an approach for compressing deep neural networks through decomposition and optimal rank selection. Our solution stands out with two key features: it considers all layers during the optimization process, aiming for high compression rates without compromising accuracy by identifying the optimal rank pattern across layers. This approach capitalizes on the varying contributions of different layers to the model's inference, allowing for smaller ranks in less critical layers and determining the most effective rank pattern for each. To achieve significant compression, we explore a broad range of ranks, addressing the substantial memory challenges of this extensive exploration with a multistage rank search strategy. This strategy enables comprehensive exploration while ensuring efficient memory usage. Our experimental results demonstrate that this approach effectively reduces the number of parameters and computational complexity, leading to better generalization and competitive performance across various models and datasets.

# References

1. Alwani, M., Wang, Y., Madhavan, V.: Decore: deep compression with reinforcement learning. In: Proceedings of the Conference on Computer Vision and Pattern Recognition, pp. 12349–12359 (2022)
2. Audibert, A., Amini, M.R., Usevich, K., Clausel, M.: Low-rank updates of pretrained weights for multi-task learning. In: Findings of the Association for Computational Linguistics: ACL, pp. 7544–7554 (2023)
3. Beyer, L., Zhai, X., Royer, A., Markeeva, L., Anil, R., Kolesnikov, A.: Knowledge distillation: a good teacher is patient and consistent. In: Proceedings of the Conference on Computer Vision and Pattern Recognition, pp. 10925–10934 (2022)
4. Blalock, D., Gonzalez Ortiz, J.J., Frankle, J., Guttag, J.: What is the state of neural network pruning? Proc. Mach. Learn. Syst. **2**, 129–146 (2020)
5. Cao, T., Sun, L., Nguyen, C.H., Mamitsuka, H.: Learning low-rank tensor cores with probabilistic $\ell_0$-regularized rank selection for model compression. In: Proceedings of the 33rd International Joint Conference on Artificial Intelligence, IJCAI, pp. 3780–3788 (2024)
6. Chang, C.C., Sung, Y.Y., Yu, S., Huang, N.C., Marculescu, D., Wu, K.C.: Flora: fine-grained low-rank architecture search for vision transformer. In: Proceedings of the IEEE/CVF Winter Conference on Applications of Computer Vision, pp. 2482–2491 (2024)
7. Chatzikonstantinou, C., Papadopoulos, G.T., Dimitropoulos, K., Daras, P.: Neural network compression using higher-order statistics and auxiliary reconstruction losses. In: Proceedings of the Conference on Computer Vision and Pattern Recognition Workshops, pp. 716–717 (2020)
8. Dai, W., Fan, J., Miao, Y., Hwang, K.: Deep learning model compression with rank reduction in tensor decomposition. IEEE Trans. Neural Netw. Learn. Syst. (2023)
9. Deng, J., Russakovsky, O., Krause, J., Bernstein, M., Berg, A.C., Fei-Fei, L.: Scalable multi-label annotation. In: ACM Conference on Human Factors in Computing Systems (CHI) (2014)
10. Domanov, I., Lathauwer, L.: Canonical polyadic decomposition of third-order tensors: relaxed uniqueness conditions and algebraic algorithm. Linear Algebra Appl. **513**, 342–375 (2017)
11. Goldfarb, D., Qin, Z.: Robust low-rank tensor recovery: models and algorithms. SIAM J. Matrix Anal. Appl. **35**(1), 225–253 (2014)

12. Gusak, J., et al.: Automated multi-stage compression of neural networks. In: Proceedings of the IEEE/CVF International Conference on Computer Vision Workshops (2019)
13. Hillar, C.J., Lim, L.H.: Most tensor problems are np-hard. J. ACM (JACM) 1–39 (2013)
14. Hou, Z., et al.: Chex: channel exploration for CNN model compression. In: Proceedings of the Conference on Computer Vision and Pattern Recognition, pp. 12287–12298 (2022)
15. Idelbayev, Y., Carreira-Perpinán, M.A.: Low-rank compression of neural nets: learning the rank of each layer. In: Proceedings of the IEEE/CVF Conference on Computer Vision and Pattern Recognition, pp. 8049–8059 (2020)
16. Kim, Y.D., Park, E., Yoo, S., Choi, T., Yang, L., Shin, D.: Compression of deep convolutional neural networks for fast and low power mobile applications. In: 4th International Conference on Learning Representations, ICLR (2016)
17. Krizhevsky, A., Hinton, G., et al.: Learning multiple layers of features from tiny images (2009)
18. Kundu, S., Datta, G., Pedram, M., Beerel, P.A.: Spike-thrift: towards energy-efficient deep spiking neural networks by limiting spiking activity via attention-guided compression. In: Proceedings of the IEEE/CVF Winter Conference on Applications of Computer Vision, pp. 3953–3962 (2021)
19. Li, H., Kadav, A., Durdanovic, I., Samet, H., Graf, H.P.: Pruning filters for efficient convnets. In: International Conference on Learning Representations, ICLR (2017)
20. Li, N., Pan, Yu., Chen, Y., Ding, Z., Zhao, D., Xu, Z.: Heuristic rank selection with progressively searching tensor ring network. Complex Intell. Syst. 1–15 (2021). https://doi.org/10.1007/s40747-021-00308-x
21. Liebenwein, L., Maalouf, A., Feldman, D., Rus, D.: Compressing neural networks: towards determining the optimal layer-wise decomposition. In: Advances in Neural Information Processing Systems (2021)
22. Novikov, A., Podoprikhin, D., Osokin, A., Vetrov, D.P.: Tensorizing neural networks. In: Advances in Neural Information Processing Systems, vol. 28 (2015)
23. Oseledets, I.V.: Tensor-train decomposition. SIAM J. Sci. Comput. **33**(5), 2295–2317 (2011)
24. Park, E., Ahn, J., Yoo, S.: Weighted-entropy-based quantization for deep neural networks. In: Proceedings of the IEEE Conference on Computer Vision and Pattern Recognition, pp. 5456–5464 (2017)
25. Phan, A.H., et al.: Stable low-rank tensor decomposition for compression of convolutional neural network. In: Computer Vision–ECCV, pp. 522–539 (2020)
26. Radford, A., et al.: Learning transferable visual models from natural language supervision. In: International Conference on Machine Learning (2021)
27. Sandler, M., Howard, A., Zhu, M., Zhmoginov, A., Chen, L.C.: Mobilenetv2: inverted residuals and linear bottlenecks. In: Proceedings of the IEEE Conference on Computer Vision and Pattern Recognition, pp. 4510–4520 (2018)
28. Tang, Y., et al.: Scop: scientific control for reliable neural network pruning. Adv. Neural. Inf. Process. Syst. **33**, 10936–10947 (2020)
29. Tucker, L.R.: Some mathematical notes on three-mode factor analysis. Psychometrika **31**(3), 279–311 (1966)
30. Wang, Y., Cheng, L., Duan, M., Wang, Y., Feng, Z., Kong, S.: Improving knowledge distillation via regularizing feature norm and direction. In: Computer Vision - ECCV, pp. 20–37 (2024)

31. Wu, B., et al.: Fbnet: hardware-aware efficient convnet design via differentiable neural architecture search. In: Proceedings of the IEEE/CVF Conference on Computer Vision and Pattern Recognition, pp. 10734–10742 (2019)
32. Xiao, J., Yin, M., Gong, Y., Zang, X., Ren, J., Yuan, B.: Comcat: towards efficient compression and customization of attention-based vision models. In: ICML, pp. 38125–38136 (2023). https://proceedings.mlr.press/v202/xiao23e.html
33. Xiao, J., et al.: Haloc: hardware-aware automatic low-rank compression for compact neural networks. In: Proceedings of the AAAI Conference on Artificial Intelligence, pp. 10464–10472 (2023)
34. Xu, L., Cheng, L., Wong, N., Wu, Y.C.: Tensor train factorization under noisy and incomplete data with automatic rank estimation. Pattern Recogn. **141**, 109650 (2023)
35. Yang, Y., Krompass, D., Tresp, V.: Tensor-train recurrent neural networks for video classification. In: International Conference on Machine Learning, pp. 3891–3900. PMLR (2017)
36. Yin, M., Phan, H., Zang, X., Liao, S., Yuan, B.: Batude: budget-aware neural network compression based on tucker decomposition. In: AAAI Conference on Artificial Intelligence, pp. 8874–8882 (2022)
37. Yin, M., Sui, Y., Liao, S., Yuan, B.: Towards efficient tensor decomposition-based DNN model compression with optimization framework. In: Proceedings of the IEEE/CVF Conference on Computer Vision and Pattern Recognition, pp. 10674–10683 (2021)
38. Yu, X., Liu, T., Wang, X., Tao, D.: On compressing deep models by low rank and sparse decomposition. In: Proceedings of the IEEE Conference on Computer Vision and Pattern Recognition, pp. 7370–7379 (2017)
39. Zhang, Y., Gao, S., Huang, H.: Exploration and estimation for model compression. In: Proceedings of the International Conference on Computer Vision, pp. 487–496 (2021)
40. Zhuang, Z., et al.: Discrimination-aware channel pruning for deep neural networks. In: Advances in Neural Information Processing Systems, vol. 31 (2018)

# Fine-Tune Smarter, Not Harder: Parameter-Efficient Fine-Tuning for Geospatial Foundation Models

Francesc Marti Escofet[1], Benedikt Blumenstiel[1(✉)], Linus Scheibenreif[2], Paolo Fraccaro[1], and Konrad Schindler[2]

[1] IBM Research Europe, Zurich, Switzerland
benedikt.blumenstiel@ibm.com
[2] ETH Zurich, Zürich, Switzerland

**Abstract.** Earth observation (EO) is crucial for monitoring environmental changes, responding to disasters, and managing natural resources. In this context, foundation models facilitate remote sensing image analysis to retrieve relevant geoinformation accurately and efficiently. However, as these models grow in size, fine-tuning becomes increasingly challenging due to the associated computational resources and costs, limiting their accessibility and scalability. Furthermore, full fine-tuning can lead to forgetting pre-trained features and even degrade model generalization. To address this, Parameter-Efficient Fine-Tuning (PEFT) techniques offer a promising solution. In this paper, we conduct extensive experiments with various foundation model architectures and PEFT techniques to evaluate their effectiveness on five different EO datasets. Our results provide a comprehensive comparison, offering insights into when and how PEFT methods support the adaptation of pre-trained geospatial models. We demonstrate that PEFT techniques match or even exceed full fine-tuning performance and enhance model generalisation to unseen geographic regions, while reducing training time and memory requirements. Additional experiments investigate the effect of architecture choices such as the decoder type or the use of metadata, suggesting UNet decoders and fine-tuning without metadata as the recommended configuration. We have integrated all evaluated foundation models and techniques into the open-source package TerraTorch to support quick, scalable, and cost-effective model adaptation.

**Keywords:** Foundation Models · Earth Observation · PEFT

## 1 Introduction

Earth observation (EO) is concerned with collecting information about the Earth using remote sensing, and it has become indispensable for monitoring environmental changes, managing natural resources, and enabling rapid responses to

---

F. Marti Escofet and B. Blumenstiel—Equal contribution.

**Supplementary Information** The online version contains supplementary material available at https://doi.org/10.1007/978-3-032-06106-5_30.

natural disasters [4,40]. The ever-growing volume and complexity of EO data pose substantial challenges for effective analysis and interpretation. Advances in deep learning have helped to mitigate these challenges by automating and improving the accuracy of EO data analysis across diverse applications, including flood detection, land use classification, and climate monitoring [40].

Foundation models (FMs), which leverage self-supervised learning, have recently emerged as powerful tools capable of capturing general-purpose representations from data. Domain-specific geospatial foundation models (GeoFMs), like Clay [9] or Prithvi [21,31], are pre-trained on large-scale satellite datasets. These models promise superior performance, improved generalization capabilities, and ease of use across geospatial tasks [13,24,31]. For instance, recent studies have demonstrated that GeoFMs outperform traditional deep learning baselines on tasks such as land cover mapping and crop classification [31].

However, as GeoFMs follow the general trend towards ever larger models [9,31], fine-tuning them becomes more expensive and requires substantial computational resources. This limitation restricts their broader application and adoption. Parameter-Efficient Fine-Tuning (PEFT) techniques provide a viable solution to this challenge. By updating only a small subset of the model parameters during training, PEFT significantly reduces computational demands and memory usage without sacrificing performance [15]. PEFT techniques have established themselves in natural language processing and computer vision [15], but to the best of our knowledge, they have not yet been systematically investigated in the context of GeoFMs.

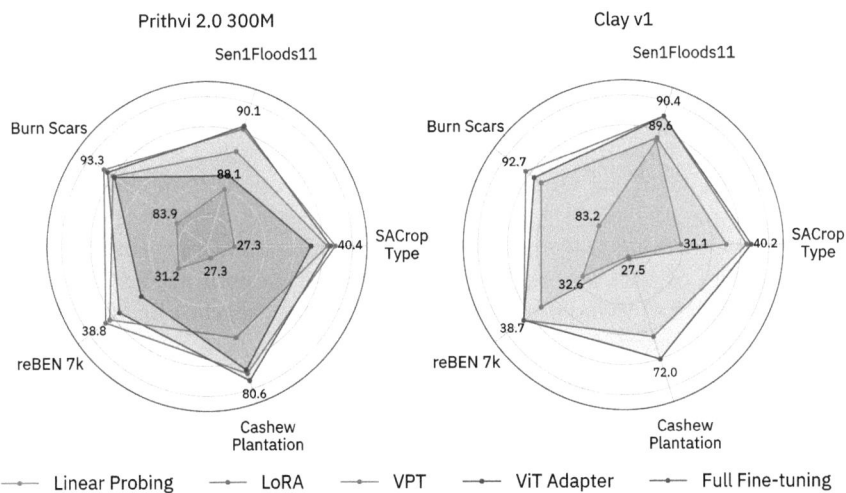

**Fig. 1.** Comparison between PEFT techniques for Prithvi 2.0 300M (left) and Clay v1 (right) with linear decoders. The test mIoU (%) ↑ is reported for all five datasets. Axes are scaled by min-max with dataset-specific buffers. The best and worst performance for each dataset is annotated.

Our work presents the first comprehensive evaluation of PEFT techniques applied to GeoFMs. Specifically, we investigate multiple GeoFM architectures and PEFT methods across five distinct EO datasets, providing insights into their effectiveness and limitations. Our experimental findings, illustrated in Fig. 1, indicate that the Low-Rank Adaptation (LoRA) method matches or even exceeds the performance of full fine-tuning, while enhancing generalization to unseen geographic regions.

Our key contributions can be summarized as follows: (1) we perform the first extensive comparative analysis of PEFT methods for GeoFMs across diverse EO tasks, (2) we explore the impact of architectural decisions, such as decoder choice and the inclusion of metadata, and (3) we evaluate model generalization to unseen geographical regions and inputs, demonstrating the robustness of PEFT. All evaluated models and techniques are integrated into the open-source package `TerraTorch` [13] to promote the application of efficient model adaptation techniques in Earth observation. The fine-tuning configs and code for our experiments are available at https://github.com/IBM/peft-geofm.

## 2 Related Work

Due to the growing volume of EO data available, machine learning techniques have become crucial to extract insights from these observations. A large body of work addresses the automated processing of EO data with deep learning techniques for a broad set of tasks, including, among others, environmental monitoring, land-cover mapping, and agricultural applications (see [40] for a review).

*Foundation Models in EO.* Foundation models are large neural network models pre-trained on vast datasets through self-supervised learning [3]. They have led to significant progress in domains such as natural language processing [5] or computer vision [6], and multiple foundation models for EO have recently been released [21,33,36]. They all leverage extensive collections of unlabelled remote sensing data to pre-train a generic data representation, using techniques such as contrastive learning [14] or masked autoencoding [16]. E.g., Prithvi 1.0 [21] uses time-series of remote sensing data in conjunction with masked autoencoding to create an EO foundation model. Similarly, approaches like Clay [9] and DOFA [36] leverage multi-modal remote sensing data with wavelength encodings to pre-train models for EO tasks. Contrastive GeoFM methods such as DeCUR [33] achieve strong performance on some downstream tasks with relatively small model architectures. Overall, foundation models owe their performance to large model capacity (resp., size) and massive amounts of unlabeled data for pre-training. In the EO domain, recent models like Prithvi 2.0 [31] demonstrate improved downstream performance by further scaling up both model size and data volume.

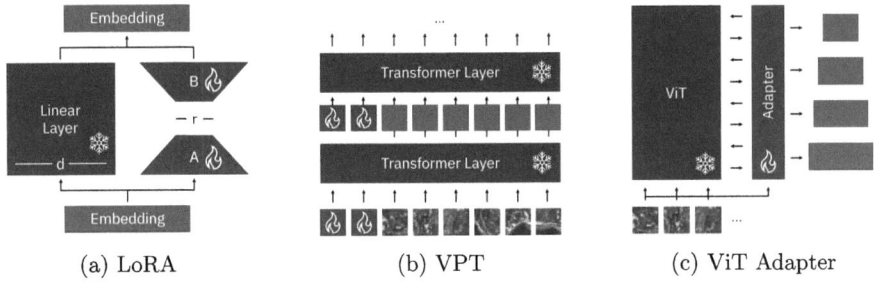

**Fig. 2.** Architectures of PEFT techniques, visualized with embeddings (blue), frozen (dark blue), and learnable layers (red). LoRA introduces small weight matrices that modulate linear layers. VPT adds learnable prompt tokens to each layer of a ViT. The ViT Adapter is a smaller parallel network that interacts with multiple transformer layers and maps their activations to a feature hierarchy. (Color figure online)

*PEFT Methods.* EO foundation models are typically adapted for a concrete downstream task by fine-tuning all model parameters in a supervised fashion for the target task [31,33]. With growing model size, such full fine-tuning incurs increasingly high computational costs and memory requirements. That bottleneck can be alleviated with PEFT methods, which drastically limit the number of fine-tuned parameters while still maintaining good downstream performance. The core idea of PEFT is to remain efficient by making an informed choice about which parameters of the pre-trained model to update during fine-tuning [38], or by introducing a small set of new parameters into the model [7] or its input space [22] and training only those. Several recent works introduce PEFT techniques specifically for EO data. For instance, methods like AiRs [19] and TEA [18] introduce adapters with additional residual connections for efficient fine-tuning of pre-trained transformers for EO. Similarly, UPetu [10] combines quantization with a learnable prompt to adapt pre-trained convolutional models to dense EO tasks. DEFLECT [32] further contributes to this direction by introducing a patch embedding layer (UPE) and an attention mechanism (uAtt) to adapt RGB-pretrained GeoFMs to multispectral images. Recent work also evaluates different PEFT methods on specific EO tasks, like the segmentation of winter-wheat fields [37], or employs PEFT for unsupervised domain adaptation in EO [30].
Unlike existing works, this work compares multiple PEFT methods across different multispectral EO foundation models and geospatial tasks.

## 3 Methods

We first introduce the different PEFT methods as well as the GeoFMs models and decoders used in our experiments.

*PEFT Techniques.* We combine three different PEFT methods with GeoFMs, see Fig. 2. Low-Rank Adaptation [17] (LoRA) introduces low-rank matrices into pre-trained transformer models ($A$ and $B$ in Fig. 2). Fine-tuning the low-rank matrices reduces the amount of trainable parameters for a pre-trained weight matrix $W \in \mathbb{R}^{d \times d}$ from $d^2$ to $2 \cdot d \cdot r$, where $r$ is the bottleneck dimension.

Instead of adapting the pre-trained model, visual prompt tuning [22] (VPT) introduces additional trainable prompt parameters into the input sequence of the embedded image patches before the GeoFM processes them. A variant of that idea introduces learnable prompts in all transformer layers (VPT-Deep), the configuration we adopted here.

ViT Adapters [7] address shortcomings of vision transformers (ViT) [11] in dense prediction tasks by introducing spatial inductive biases. A small convolutional model extracts spatial features from the input image, which are then injected into the ViT through cross-attention modules. Eventually, the ViT adapters extract multi-scale features from the transformer layers which are combined for a final dense prediction. As ViT Adapters involve integrating convolutional branches, cross-attention modules, and multi-scale feature fusion, their implementation is non-trivial. Due to this significant engineering overhead, we only study them for the Prithvi family of models.

**Table 1.** Overview of the EO backbones and their pre-training characteristics.

| Model | Archi. | # Params. | Sensors | # S-2 bands | # Samples | Metadata |
|---|---|---|---|---|---|---|
| DeCUR [33] | ResNet50 | 25M | S1, S2 | 13 | 1M | ✗ |
| Clay v1 [9] | ViT-B/8 | 92M | various | 10 | 70M | ✓ |
| Prithvi 1.0 [21] | ViT-B/16 | 86M | HLS | 6 | 250k × 3 | ✗ |
| Prithvi 2.0 [31] | ViT-L/16 | 304M | HLS | 6 | 4.2M × 4 | ✗/✓ |

*Foundation Models.* We evaluate the different PEFT schemes with four GeoFMs and provide an overview in Table 1. DeCUR [33] is pre-trained with contrastive learning. Specifically, the Decoupling Common and Unique Representations (DeCUR) approach separates shared and modality-specific features in the embedding. The model utilises per-modality ResNet-50 backbones and was pre-trained on the SSL4EO-S12 [34] dataset, using all 13 Sentinel-2 L1C bands and two Sentinel-1 GRD bands.

Prithvi 1.0 [21] employs masked autoencoder (MAE) [16] pre-training and is based on a ViT-B backbone with a patch size of 16. It is trained on Harmonized Landsat and Sentinel-2 data exclusively from the USA, limited to six spectral bands. The data consists of short time series with three timestamps to support multi-temporal inputs naturally. Like its predecessor, Prithvi 2.0 [31] employs MAE pre-training but uses a global dataset and includes larger backbones based on ViT-L/16 and ViT-H/14. While still training on HLS and covering six bands, optional temporal and location embeddings are introduced to enable better spatiotemporal reasoning. We evaluate the Prithvi 2.0 300M version, and do not use metadata unless specified otherwise.

Clay v1 [9] also pre-trains a ViT-B backbone, with a patch size of 8, by MAE augmented with DINO-style self-distillation [6]. It is trained on a diverse dataset that includes Landsat-8 and -9, Sentinel-1 and -2, NAIP, and LINZ imagery. It features dynamic patch embedding weights similar to DOFA [36], adjusted according to the input spectral bands. The model integrates additional metadata like latitude/longitude, ground sampling distance (GSD), and acquisition time into the positional embeddings.

*Decoder.* The downstream performance of a GeoFM depends on the quality of the encoder features and the decoder's capability to leverage them. We evaluate four decoder architectures: a linear decoder, Fully Convolutional Network (FCN) [26], UperNet [35], and UNet [29]. With its minimal complexity of a single transposed convolution without nonlinearities, the linear decoder serves as a way to evaluate the feature embeddings as directly as possible.

While the linear decoder is well-suited for controlled evaluations of the encoder, real-world applications require decoders capable of exploiting features in context. The FCN decoder [26] reconstructs spatial details through a sequence of convolutional blocks, each composed of a transposed convolution for upsampling, followed by a $3 \times 3$ convolution, Layer Normalization, and GeLU activation. The UperNet decoder [35] further improves upon this by combining multi-scale features through a Feature Pyramid Network (FPN) [25] and capturing global context with a Pyramid Pooling Module (PPM) [39]. Lastly, the UNet decoder [29] integrates multi-scale encoder features via skip connections, preserving detailed spatial information through decoder blocks consisting of interpolation, concatenation, and successive convolutional layers paired with Batch Normalization and ReLU activations.

The UperNet and UNet decoders require hierarchical, multi-scale features from multiple encoder layers. In our experiments, we use features from three intermediate encoder layers and the final one. While ResNet backbones naturally contain these hierarchical features, ViT embeddings require spatial upscaling. We therefore add learned upsampling layers that generate appropriate multi-scale features compatible with the UperNet and UNet decoders [13].

## 4 Experimental Setup

We have conducted extensive experiments to compare different PEFT techniques and GeoFMs. In the following, we describe the datasets used for evaluation and the fine-tuning protocol in detail.

*Datasets.* An overview of the data used for downstream evaluations is provided in Table 2. We restrict all experiments to multispectral optical inputs only.

**Table 2.** Overview of the evaluation datasets and their sample counts, including geographic hold-out sets (GHOS).

| Dataset | Sensors | Patch size | Classes | # Train | # Val. | # Test | # GHOS |
|---|---|---|---|---|---|---|---|
| Sen1Floods11 [4] | S1, S2 | 512 × 512 | 2 | 252 | 89 | 90 | 15 |
| Burn Scars [28] | HLS | 512 × 512 | 2 | 524 | 160 | 120 | – |
| reBEN 7k [8] | S1, S2 | 120 × 120 | 19 | 4690 | 946 | 945 | 807 |
| m-Cashew plant. [23] | S2 | 256 × 256 | 7 | 1350 | 400 | 50 | – |
| m-SA Crop type [12] | S2 | 256 × 256 | 10 | 3000 | 1000 | 1000 | – |

Sen1Floods11 [4] includes Sentinel-1 (S1) GRD and Sentinel-2 (S2) L1C satellite images at 10 m resolution covering eleven different flooding events on six different continents. The task is to segment surface water. In our evaluation, we use the 431 binary masks annotated by expert analysts. A hold-out set of 15 samples from Bolivia serves to test geographic generalization.

The Burn Scars dataset [28] contains images of wildfire scars, gathered with the help of the Monitoring Trends in Burn Severity (MTBS) historical fire database. Annotations from the continental US, from 2018 to 2021, were co-registered with Harmonized Landsat Sentinel-2 (HLS) observations at 30 m resolution. The 804 images include six spectral channels: Blue, Green, Red, NIR Narrow, SWIR 1, and SWIR 2. The original Burn Scars dataset provides a training and validation split. We propose new splits that include a test set. To further exclude the possibility of data leakage, we create the splits with a 5 km buffer between training and evaluation samples and ensure that close-by patches are assigned to the same split. We make the splits public at https://github.com/IBM/peft-geofm to ensure reproducibility.

reBEN 7k is a subset of the larger Refined BigEarthNet (reBEN) [8], sampled to preserve class balance. reBEN has over 400k samples, each consisting of S1 GRD and S2 L2A patches as well as land-use/land-cover annotations with 19 classes. While reBEN supports both semantic segmentation and multi-label classification, we only use the semantic segmentation task. Repeated fine-tuning on the full reBEN dataset would be computationally infeasible for our experiments. Therefore, we create a smaller subset following the example of BEN-ge 8k [27]. Compared to BEN-ge 8k, we derive our version from the latest edition of BigEarthNet [8] and introduce a geographic hold-out set (GHOS) for generalization experiments. Our subset is based on the land-cover multi-labels and designed to retain class diversity. To ensure fair representation of all classes, we draw 250 samples per class from the official training set and 50 samples per class for validation and testing, excluding Austria and Ireland. Then, up to 50 samples per class were drawn only from those countries' test sets to obtain an additional GHOS for testing model generalization to unseen geographic regions.

As further test cases, we include the m-Cashew Plantation [23] and m-SA Crop Type [12] datasets provided by GEO-bench [24]. The former provides labeled images of cashew plantations across a 120 km$^2$ region in central

Benin. Each pixel is assigned to one of seven classes, including *well-managed plantation*, *poorly-managed plantation*, and *no plantation*, enabling detailed land-use analysis. SA Crop Type [12] contains images and crop type labels for South Africa, with each pixel classified into one of ten categories, such as *weeds*, *wheat*, or *rooibos*. In both cases, we use the versions preprocessed by GEO-bench [24].

**Table 3.** Parameter counts for EO backbones and PEFT components. Percentages refer to the number of PEFT parameters relative to the encoder parameters.

| Model | # Encoder Params. | # VPT Params. | # LoRA Params. | # ViT Adapt. Params. |
|---|---|---|---|---|
| Clay v1 [9] | 92M | 0.9M (1.0%) | 2M (2.2%) | - |
| Prithvi 1.0 100M [21] | 86M | 0.9M (1.1%) | 2M (2.4%) | 12M (13.8%) |
| Prithvi 2.0 300M [31] | 304M | 2.5M (0.8%) | 5.5M (1.8%) | 20M (6.6%) |

*Fine-Tuning Procedure.* To ensure robust and reproducible results, we follow established experimental protocols [24,31] involving hyperparameter optimization (HPO) and repeated runs. For each combination of model architecture, dataset, and PEFT method, we carry out Bayesian hyperparameter optimization with 16 trials to select the optimal learning rate, implemented using TerraTorch Iterate [20]. With the best learning rate, we run the fine-tuning five times for each configuration, starting from different random seeds, and report the average.

Based on prior experiments, PEFT methods are configured as follows: For LoRA, adapters with bottleneck dimension $r = 16$ are added to the linear projections in the feed-forward layers, as well as to the query and value matrices of the attention layers of the GeoFMs. For VPT, we include 100 learnable prompts in all transformer layers (VPT-Deep). The specific parameter counts for each model and PEFT configuration are described in Table 3. VPT and LoRA increase the model parameters by only up to 2.4%. ViT Adapter introduces significantly more parameters, increasing the model parameter count by up to 13.8%.

For all experiments, we use the AdamW optimizer with $\beta_1 = 0.9$, $\beta_2 = 0.999$ and ReduceLROnPlateau scheduler (*patience* = 4 epochs, *factor* = 0.5). The batch size was set to 8, except for reBEN-7k, where we increased it to 32 to account for the smaller input size and higher number of images. We find that a small batch size with a correspondingly higher number of gradient updates leads to faster convergence on relatively small EO datasets. All models were trained on a single NVIDIA A100 GPU for up to 100 epochs, applying early stopping after 15 epochs without improvement. As far as possible, each GeoFM receives the Sentinel-2 bands it was pre-trained for: Ten bands for Clay, six for Prithvi, and all 13 L1C bands for DeCUR. If any bands are missing in a dataset (e.g., Burn Scars only has six bands), the patch embedding automatically adapts to the available subset via TerraTorch [13]. For reBEN-7k, the images are padded to 128 × 128 pixels with the *reflect* method to ensure compatibility across all architectures.

## 5 Experiments

We conduct a series of experiments to evaluate the effectiveness of PEFT methods for GeoFMs. Our analyses cover three aspects: (1) a comparison of PEFT techniques against full fine-tuning, (2) an assessment of generalization across unseen geographic regions, and (3) an evaluation of different decoder architectures.

### 5.1 Parameter-Efficient Fine-Tuning

Our experiments use a linear decoder to isolate the impact of PEFT techniques on geospatial foundation models. It ensures a controlled evaluation, as more complex decoders may obscure differences by significantly increasing model capacity. Table 4 presents the results of PEFT experiments, including three baseline models: a randomly initialized UNet [29] and a ViT-B/16 pre-trained on ImageNet-21k [11]. DeCUR [33], a ResNet-based GeoFM, is also considered a baseline since the selected PEFT methods are designed for ViTs. We perform five training runs with varying random seeds and report average performances for readability. Standard deviations are provided in the supplementary material. In most cases, the standard deviation is below 0.6pp, with some exceptions for the Cashew Plantation dataset.

**Table 4.** Test mIoU (%) ↑ for the evaluated models and PEFT techniques, averaged over five runs. We highlight the best-performing combination in bold and underline the second-best one.

| Model | Method | Sen1F11 | Burn Scars | reBEN 7k | Cashew Plant. | SACrop | Mean |
|---|---|---|---|---|---|---|---|
| UNet (Rand.) | Full FT | **90.75** | 89.34 | 34.62 | **81.81** | 34.99 | 66.30 |
| ViT (IN-21k) | Full FT | 89.19 | 92.31 | 36.15 | 80.05 | 37.98 | 67.14 |
| DeCUR | Linear Prob. | 80.83 | 78.17 | 28.29 | 16.05 | 20.93 | 44.85 |
|  | Full FT | 86.87 | 89.48 | 36.05 | 79.59 | 34.21 | 65.24 |
| Clay v1 | Linear Prob. | 89.57 | 83.17 | 32.65 | 27.50 | 31.10 | 52.80 |
|  | VPT | 89.67 | 90.67 | 36.87 | 28.38 | 36.89 | 56.50 |
|  | LoRA | <u>90.41</u> | 92.74 | <u>38.67</u> | 62.29 | 39.64 | 64.75 |
|  | Full FT | <u>90.41</u> | 91.58 | <u>38.67</u> | 72.03 | <u>40.22</u> | 66.58 |
| Prithvi 1.0 100M | Linear Prob. | 88.78 | 83.23 | 27.07 | 25.33 | 26.06 | 50.10 |
|  | VPT | 89.03 | 85.17 | 29.98 | 29.24 | 29.62 | 52.61 |
|  | LoRA | 89.33 | 89.34 | 30.60 | 53.00 | 31.58 | 58.77 |
|  | ViT Adapter | 87.72 | 89.47 | 32.90 | 73.31 | 32.34 | 63.15 |
|  | Full FT | 89.02 | 89.31 | 31.82 | 77.41 | 32.59 | 64.03 |
| Prithvi 2.0 300M | Linear Prob. | 88.08 | 83.90 | 31.25 | 27.29 | 27.26 | 51.55 |
|  | VPT | 89.31 | 92.16 | 38.40 | 62.00 | 39.33 | 64.24 |
|  | LoRA | 90.04 | **93.33** | **38.84** | 77.53 | **40.35** | <u>68.02</u> |
|  | ViT Adapter | 88.52 | 91.95 | 35.14 | 75.92 | 37.24 | 65.75 |
|  | Full FT | 90.13 | <u>92.85</u> | 37.42 | <u>80.58</u> | 39.74 | **68.14** |

While performance varies across datasets, Prithvi 2.0 300M is the best model overall, outperforming Clay v1 and the ImageNet-pre-trained ViT by +1pp. Notably, the randomly initialized UNet surpasses DeCUR and Prithvi 1.0. However, the superior UNet decoder may contribute to this advantage. Prithvi 1.0 exhibits the lowest fine-tuning performance, likely due to its limited pre-training data. In contrast, Prithvi 2.0, trained on a larger dataset, achieves +4pp improvement, reinforcing the importance of scaling both data and model size [31]. Among PEFT techniques, LoRA performs on par with, or better than, full fine-tuning for Clay and Prithvi 2.0. In contrast, VPT and ViT Adapter generally underperform full fine-tuning. On reBEN 7k, VPT and LoRA outperform full fine-tuning using Prithvi 2.0, while with the smaller Prithvi 1.0, ViT Adapter scores best. In general, PEFT methods are particularly performant when combined with large GeoFMs, like Prithvi 2.0.

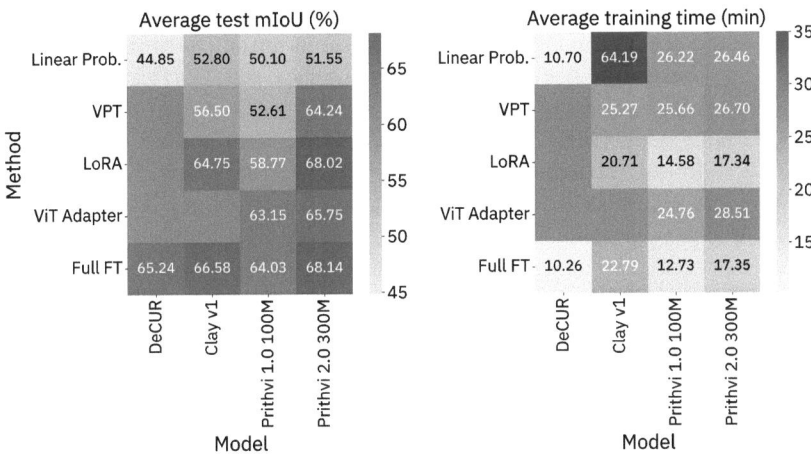

**Fig. 3.** Test mIoU ↑ and training time ↓ averaged over five datasets with five runs each. We trained all models up to 100 epochs and used early stopping after 15 epochs, resulting in best efficiencies for full fine-tuning and LoRA.

Figure 3 shows test performance compared with training time. LoRA and full fine-tuning require a similar training time for Prithvi 2.0, despite LoRA freezing most layers. This suggests that the fixed batch size for all experiments may limit LoRA's expected speedup. However, the lower memory footprint of LoRA makes it well-suited for GPUs with limited capacity and enables larger batch sizes for efficiency gains on larger datasets (see memory footprints in the supplementary material). Training time is also strongly influenced by model architecture. Clay, which uses a patch size of 8, must process four times more tokens than Prithvi 1.0 and takes more than twice as long, despite their similar parameter counts. Prithvi 2.0, being three times larger than Clay, still trains faster.

An interesting finding is the unexpectedly long training time of linear probing shown in Fig. 3, as the fitting of a less flexiblelinear function converges slower.

Notably, Clay outperforms Prithvi 2.0 by 1pp in linear probing, but ranks lower in all other settings. However, this trend does not hold for larger decoders, which can model non-linear patterns. Additional experiments with a UNet decoder showed training times comparable to full fine-tuning. When combined with larger decoders, our results suggest that freezing the encoder is viable for simple tasks like water mapping but leads to performance drops in more complex tasks like crop type classification.

Overall, our results indicate that PEFT techniques offer an effective trade-off between full fine-tuning and frozen encoders, particularly when memory efficiency is critical. Our findings further suggest that LoRA can match or surpass full fine-tuning, depending on the GeoFM and downstream task.

### 5.2 Model Generalization

We evaluate geographic generalization using geographic hold-out sets (GHOS). First, we compare Prithvi 2.0 300M embeddings after pre-training, full fine-tuning, and LoRA fine-tuning. Figure 4 visualizes the Sen1Floods11 embeddings, while reBEN 7k is provided in the supplementary material. The model trained without geographic metadata naturally clusters images by region. The geographic hold-out set from Bolivia forms two clusters after pre-training. Full fine-tuning disrupts this structure, suggesting that it forgets some pre-trained features. At the same time, LoRA better preserves geographic clustering, highlighting its potential to mitigate catastrophic forgetting, a key challenge in fine-tuning foundation models.

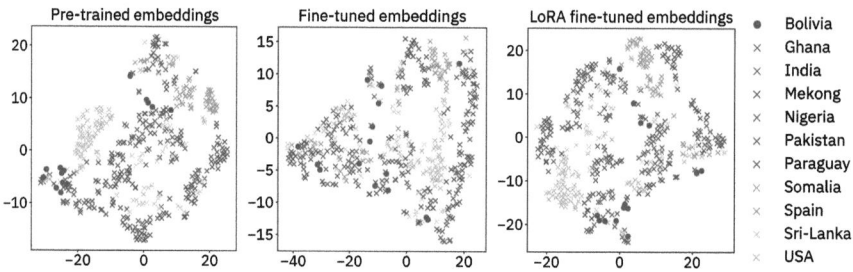

**Fig. 4.** Prithvi 2.0 300M embeddings of the Sen1Floods11 dataset colored by region. We averaged the patch embeddings per image and applied t-SNE.

To quantify these patterns, we compute the minimum Euclidean distance of each sample to the training set and average over validation, test, and hold-out splits. The results (see supplementary material) confirm that GHOS samples are significantly farther from training data than validation and test samples, which follow the training distribution. Full fine-tuning reduces distances for all Sen1Floods11 splits by a factor of two but unexpectedly increases them for reBEN 7k. LoRA fine-tuning increases distances for both datasets but maintains the pre-training embedding structure in the t-SNE plot. In all cases, GHOS distances remain higher than those of validation and test sets, highlighting the challenge of geographic generalization.

**Table 5.** Comparison between the in-distribution test set and the geographic holdout set (GHOS) using mIoU (%) ↑, averaged over five runs. We highlight the two best-performing combinations in bold and underlined.

| Model | Method | Sen1Floods11 | | reBEN 7k | |
|---|---|---|---|---|---|
| | | Test mIoU | GHOS mIoU | Test mIoU | GHOS mIoU |
| UNet (Rand.) | Full FT | **90.75** | 87.81 | 34.62 | 25.43 |
| ViT (IN-21K) | Full FT | 89.19 | 82.67 | 36.15 | 27.14 |
| DeCUR | Linear Prob. | 80.83 | 74.76 | 28.29 | 23.29 |
| | Full FT | 86.87 | 85.84 | 36.05 | 27.60 |
| Clay v1 | Linear Prob. | 89.57 | 84.88 | 32.65 | 24.38 |
| | VPT | 89.67 | 87.29 | 36.87 | 28.77 |
| | LoRA | <u>90.41</u> | **88.88** | <u>38.67</u> | 28.44 |
| | Full FT | <u>90.41</u> | <u>88.33</u> | <u>38.67</u> | 29.07 |
| Prithvi 1.0 100M | Linear Prob. | 88.78 | 79.57 | 27.07 | 24.04 |
| | VPT | 89.03 | 64.35 | 29.98 | 22.65 |
| | LoRA | 89.33 | 61.25 | 30.60 | 24.09 |
| | ViT Adapter | 87.72 | 82.31 | 32.90 | 25.66 |
| | Full FT | 89.02 | 74.16 | 31.82 | 24.53 |
| Prithvi 2.0 300M | Linear Prob. | 88.08 | 83.19 | 31.25 | 24.86 |
| | VPT | 89.31 | 86.19 | 38.40 | <u>29.83</u> |
| | LoRA | 90.04 | 87.57 | **38.84** | **30.21** |
| | ViT Adapter | 88.52 | 84.94 | 35.14 | 26.99 |
| | Full FT | 90.13 | 82.07 | 37.42 | 28.12 |

Table 5 quantifies the geographic generalization gaps: on average, mIoU drops by 7.79pp for reBEN 7k and 7.31pp for Sen1Floods11 across all settings and models. DeCUR exhibits the smallest drop with full fine-tuning (−4.74pp), while Prithvi 1.0 experiences the largest with LoRA (−17.30pp). The best-performing models across both in-distribution and GHOS sets are Prithvi 2.0 300M with LoRA, Clay (full fine-tuning), and Clay with LoRA. Notably, LoRA significantly improves geographic generalization for Prithvi 2.0 300M but has minimal impact for Clay. These results highlight that geographic generalization remains an open challenge for GeoFMs. However, they outperform a randomly initialized UNet (+2.2pp on GHOS) and an ImageNet-pretrained ViT (+3.7pp), with LoRA proving particularly beneficial for generalization which is in line with results from literature [2]. That being said, PEFT methods may struggle in scenarios with extreme distribution shifts, such as across sensor modalities (e.g., from optical to SAR) or when dealing with very high-resolution imagery. In such cases, pre-trained features are expected to transfer poorly, and PEFT's restricted capacity to adapt the encoder weights could become a bottleneck [1].

To assess model robustness to varying input bands, we conducted experiments with DeCUR and Clay using only six spectral bands (Prithvi bands) under both linear probing and full fine-tuning (results in the supplementary material). Reducing input channels resulted in a minor performance drop, typically within 1-2pp. No significant difference was observed between frozen encoder models and fully fine-tuned ones, suggesting that GeoFMs can adapt to missing bands without updating early layers. The performance loss is therefore attributed to the missing spectral information rather than to poor model adaptation.

### 5.3 Decoder Architecture

Figure 5 compares different decoder architectures across all evaluated foundation models using full fine-tuning. We also include Prithvi 2.0 300M TL, which incorporates additional metadata for reference. The decoder performance varies across GeoFMs, but the UNet decoder consistently achieves strong results, ranking within the top two across all architectures. FCN performs best for Prithvi 2.0 but lags behind UNet for other models. UperNet, despite having a similar parameter count, underperforms across most settings.

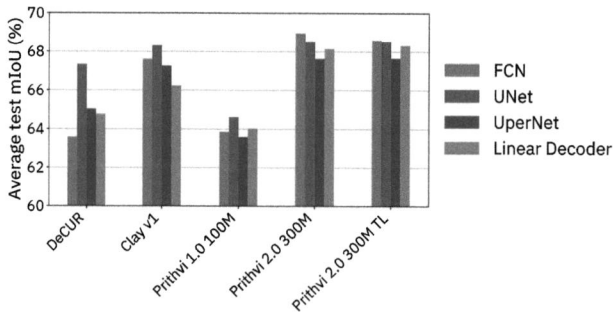

**Fig. 5.** Average test mIoU (%) ↑ over five datasets for each model and decoder combination with five runs each.

Surprisingly, with only a single layer, the linear decoder performs competitively and even outperforms UperNet for Prithvi models. However, this result is primarily influenced by a 5pp drop in UperNet's performance on the Cashew Plantation dataset. Combined with our findings from frozen encoder experiments, it suggests that GeoFMs can effectively learn non-linear functions within the encoder, reducing reliance on complex decoders for performance comparisons. However, the lower capacity of the linear decoder cannot capture small features, as shown in Fig. 6, and is unsuitable for applications.

While FCN achieves a high performance, it has a major drawback: Visual analysis of predictions reveals that FCN (and the linear decoder) produces patchy outputs, whereas UNet and UperNet generate more spatially consistent results (see Fig. 6). This is likely because UNet and UperNet access multi-scale feature maps, allowing them to preserve low-level spatial information, which helps with fine-grained segmentation. The visualized images are selected to show failures and do not fully represent the overall prediction quality. The UNet decoder leads to the best predictions, considering performance and visual quality.

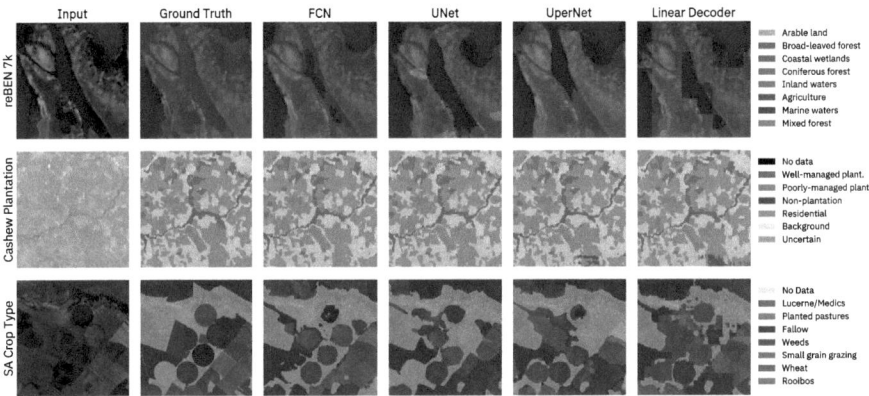

**Fig. 6.** Predictions of Prithvi 2.0 300M with different decoders and unfrozen backbone. The examples are selected to showcase patchy predictions from FCN and the linear decoder, while UperNet and UNet results are smoother.

## 6 Conclusion

We have extensively evaluated PEFT techniques for geospatial foundation models, analyzing different fine-tuning strategies, geographic generalization, and decoder architectures. Our results show that LoRA matches or exceeds full fine-tuning performance while significantly reducing memory and potentially training time, making it the most effective PEFT method. The decoder comparisons highlight UNet as the best-performing architecture, while metadata has minimal impact on fine-tuning. Geographic generalization remains an open challenge, though GeoFMs outperform standard baselines, especially when fine-tuned with LoRA. These findings suggest LoRA as a suitable fine-tuning strategy for EO applications, particularly in resource-constrained settings with large datasets. However, our study is limited to three models, and PEFT effectiveness may vary with architecture and data. Future work should explore more models and tasks, and assess additional PEFT variants like TEA [18] or DEFLECT [32] to identify robust strategies. All models and techniques are available in TerraTorch, enabling scalable adaptation for real-world use.

# References

1. Bafghi, R.A., Bagwell, C., Ravichandran, A., Shrivastava, A., Raissi, M.: Fine tuning without catastrophic forgetting via selective low rank adaptation. arXiv preprint arXiv:2501.15377 (2025)
2. Bafghi, R.A., Harilal, N., Monteleoni, C., Raissi, M.: Parameter efficient fine-tuning of self-supervised VITs without catastrophic forgetting. In: Proceedings of the IEEE/CVF Conference on Computer Vision and Pattern Recognition Workshops, pp. 3679–3684 (2024)
3. Bommasani, R., et al.: On the Opportunities and Risks of Foundation Models. arXiv preprint arXiv:2108.07258 (2021)
4. Bonafilia, D., Tellman, B., Anderson, T., Issenberg, E.: Sen1Floods11: a georeferenced dataset to train and test deep learning flood algorithms for sentinel-1. In: Proceedings of the IEEE/CVF Conference on Computer Vision and Pattern Recognition Workshops (2020)
5. Brown, T., et al.: Language Models are Few-shot learners. In: Advances in Neural Information Processing Systems, vol. 33 (2020)
6. Caron, M., et al.: Emerging properties in self-supervised vision transformers. In: Proceedings of the IEEE/CVF International Conference on Computer Vision (2021)
7. Chen, Z., et al.: Vision transformer adapter for dense predictions. In: The Eleventh International Conference on Learning Representations (2023)
8. Clasen, K.N., Hackel, L., Burgert, T., Sumbul, G., Demir, B., Markl, V.: reBEN: Refined BigEarthNet Dataset for Remote Sensing Image Analysis. arXiv preprint arXiv:2407.03653 (2024)
9. Clay Foundation: Clay Foundation Model (2024). https://huggingface.co/made-with-clay/Clay
10. Dong, Z., Gu, Y., Liu, T.: UPetu: a unified parameter-efficient fine-tuning framework for remote sensing foundation model. IEEE Trans. Geosci. Remote Sens. (2024)
11. Dosovitskiy, A., et al.: An image is worth 16x16 words: transformers for image recognition at scale. In: International Conference on Learning Representations (2020)
12. ESA: Fusion Competition (2023). https://source.coop/repositories/esa/fusion-competition/description
13. Gomes, C., et al.: TerraTorch: The Geospatial Foundation Models Toolkit. arXiv preprint arXiv:2503.20563 (2025)
14. Hadsell, R., Chopra, S., LeCun, Y.: Dimensionality reduction by learning an invariant mapping. In: IEEE Computer Society Conference on Computer Vision and Pattern Recognition, vol. 2. IEEE (2006)
15. Han, Z., Gao, C., Liu, J., Zhang, J., Zhang, S.Q.: Parameter-efficient fine-tuning for large models: a comprehensive survey. Trans. Mach. Learn. Res. (2024)
16. He, K., Chen, X., Xie, S., Li, Y., Dollár, P., Girshick, R.: Masked autoencoders are scalable vision learners. In: Proceedings of the IEEE/CVF Conference on Computer Vision and Pattern Recognition (2022)
17. Hu, E.J., et al.: LoRA: low-rank adaptation of large language models. In: Proceedings of the International Conference on Learning Representations, vol. 1, no. 2 (2022)
18. Hu, L., Lu, W., Yu, H., Yin, D., Sun, X., Fu, K.: TEA: a training-efficient adapting framework for tuning foundation models in remote sensing. IEEE Trans. Geosci. Remote Sens. (2024)

19. Hu, L., Yu, H., Lu, W., Yin, D., Sun, X., Fu, K.: AiRs: adapter in remote sensing for parameter-efficient transfer learning. IEEE Trans. Geosci. Remote Sens. **62** (2024)
20. IBM: TerraTorch Iterate (2025). https://github.com/IBM/terratorch-iterate
21. Jakubik, J., et al.: Foundation Models for Generalist Geospatial Artificial Intelligence. arXiv preprint arXiv:2310.18660 (2023)
22. Jia, M., et al.: Visual prompt tuning. In: Proceedings of the European Conference on Computer Vision. Springer (2022)
23. Jin, Z., Lin, C., Weigl, C., Obarowski, J., Hale, D.: Smallholder Cashew Plantations in Benin. Radiant MKHub (2021)
24. Lacoste, A., et al.: GEO-bench: toward foundation models for earth monitoring. In: Advances in Neural Information Processing Systems, vol. 36 (2023)
25. Lin, T.Y., Dollár, P., Girshick, R., He, K., Hariharan, B., Belongie, S.: Feature pyramid networks for object detection. In: Proceedings of the IEEE Conference on Computer Vision and Pattern Recognition (2017)
26. Long, J., Shelhamer, E., Darrell, T.: Fully convolutional networks for semantic segmentation. In: Proceedings of the IEEE Conference on Computer Vision and Pattern Recognition, pp. 3431–3440 (2015)
27. Mommert, M., Kesseli, N., Hanna, J., Scheibenreif, L., Borth, D., Demir, B.: BEN-GE: extending BigEarthNet with geographical and environmental data. In: IEEE International Geoscience and Remote Sensing Symposium. IEEE (2023)
28. Phillips, C., Roy, S., Ankur, K., Ramachandran, R.: HLS Foundation Burn-scars Dataset (2023). https://huggingface.co/datasets/ibm-nasa-geospatial/hls_burn_scars
29. Ronneberger, O., Fischer, P., Brox, T.: U-Net: convolutional networks for biomedical image segmentation. In: Medical Image Computing and Computer-Assisted Intervention–MICCAI. Springer (2015)
30. Scheibenreif, L., Mommert, M., Borth, D.: Parameter efficient self-supervised geospatial domain adaptation. In: Proceedings of the IEEE/CVF Conference on Computer Vision and Pattern Recognition (2024)
31. Szwarcman, D., et al.: Prithvi-EO-2.0: A Versatile Multi-Temporal Foundation Model for Earth Observation Applications. arXiv preprint arXiv:2412.02732 (2024)
32. Thoreau, R., Marsocci, V., Derksen, D.: Parameter-Efficient Adaptation of Geospatial Foundation Models through Embedding Deflection. arXiv preprint arXiv:2503.09493 (2025)
33. Wang, Y., Albrecht, C.M., Braham, N.A.A., Liu, C., Xiong, Z., Zhu, X.X.: Decoupling common and unique representations for multimodal self-supervised learning. In: Proceedings of the European Conference on Computer Vision (2024)
34. Wang, Y., Braham, N.A.A., Xiong, Z., Liu, C., Albrecht, C.M., Zhu, X.X.: SSL4EO-S12: a large-scale multi-modal, multi-temporal dataset for self-supervised learning in earth observation. IEEE Geosci. Remote Sens. Mag. **11**(3) (2023)
35. Xiao, T., Liu, Y., Zhou, B., Jiang, Y., Sun, J.: Unified perceptual parsing for scene understanding. In: Ferrari, V., Hebert, M., Sminchisescu, C., Weiss, Y. (eds.) ECCV 2018. LNCS, vol. 11209, pp. 432–448. Springer, Cham (2018). https://doi.org/10.1007/978-3-030-01228-1_26
36. Xiong, Z., et al.: Neural Plasticity-inspired Foundation Model for Observing the Earth Crossing Modalities. arXiv preprint arXiv:2403.15356 (2024)
37. Zahweh, M.H., Nasrallah, H., Shukor, M., Faour, G., Ghandour, A.J.: Empirical study of PEFT techniques for winter-wheat segmentation. Environ. Sci. Proc. **29**(1) (2023)

38. Zaken, E.B., Goldberg, Y., Ravfogel, S.: BitFit: simple parameter-efficient fine-tuning for transformer-based masked language-models. In: Proceedings of the 60th Annual Meeting of the Association for Computational Linguistics (2022)
39. Zhao, H., Shi, J., Qi, X., Wang, X., Jia, J.: Pyramid scene parsing network. In: Proceedings of the IEEE Conference on Computer Vision and Pattern Recognition (2017)
40. Zhu, X.X., et al.: Deep learning in remote sensing: a comprehensive review and list of resources. IEEE Geosci. Remote Sens. Mag. **5**(4) (2017)

# Transformer with Sparse Adaptive Mask for Network Dismantling

Yu Liu, Fanghao Hu, Haojun Huang, and Bang Wang[✉]

School of Electronic Information and Communications, Huazhong University of Science and Technology (HUST), Wuhan 430074, China
{yuliu_,hfh,hjhuang,wangbang}@hust.edu.cn

**Abstract.** The task of network dismantling aims to attack the least number of critical nodes to decompose a network into many small subnetworks. Recent approaches design task-oriented neural models to encode nodes' structural features for predicting their importance. Instead of crafting small models, an interesting question is about whether and how large models like Transformers can be exploited for this classic yet NP-hard task in the network science domain. This paper provides an affirmative answer. The key lies in how to enable a Transformer to encode nodes' representations based on comparisons over their importance to network integrity. In this paper, we propose to encode node egonet characteristics as well as internode spatial dependences from a global view. Furthermore, for each node encoding, we propose to include peer attention to enable networkwide importance comparison. A new fusion module with a sparse adaptive mask is designed into the Transformer architecture for encoding node comparative importance to network integrity. Experiments on real-world networks and synthetic networks validate the effectiveness of our design over the state-of-the-art schemes. The source code and datasets are available at: https://github.com/valyentine/TSAM.

**Keywords:** Network Dismantling · Transformer with Sparse Attention Mask · Network Science · Representation Learning and Ranking

## 1 Introduction

Numerous real-world physical systems can be abstracted as complex networks, where each network is represented by a graph $\mathcal{G} = (\mathcal{V}, \mathcal{E})$, with the node set $\mathcal{V}$ and edge set $\mathcal{E}$ defining its topology. Percolation theory [28] demonstrates that the failure of a small fraction of nodes can cause a large-scale network to disintegrate into numerous disconnected small subnetworks, leading to network instability or even collapse. A notable example is the Century Link outage in the United States on August 30, 2020, triggered by the malfunction of its critical backbone router AS3356 [19]. This incident highlights the significance of the *network dismantling* (ND) problem.

---

Y. Liu and F. Hu—Contributed equally to this work.

Following the literature [5,29,34], the ND problem can be formally defined as to find the smallest subset of nodes, termed the *target attack node set* (TAS), whose removal disintegrates a network into disconnected components such that the size of the *giant connected component* (GCC) falls below a predefined threshold $\theta$. Formally, the ND problem seeks to find the optimal TAS $\mathcal{V}^* \subseteq \mathcal{V}$:

$$\mathcal{V}^* = \underset{\mathcal{V}_t \subseteq \mathcal{V}}{\arg\min} \left\{ |\mathcal{V}_t| : |\mathcal{G}_t|/|\mathcal{G}| \leq \theta \right\}, \qquad (1)$$

where $|\mathcal{V}_t|$ is the cardinality of the TAS, $|\mathcal{G}_t|$ denotes the number of nodes in the GCC after removing $\mathcal{V}_t$, $|\mathcal{G}|$ is the original network size. The ND problem has been proven as non-deterministic polynomial hard (NP-hard) [5].

For tackling the ND problem, early efforts have proposed many centrality-based heuristic solutions, i.e., the degree centrality [1], collective influence [25], PageRank [26] and etc., to rank a node importance for constructing the TAS. However, they tend to be susceptible to interference from particular structures, while neglecting to compare the global competence among nodes. In the last few years, a few studies have employed *graph neural networks* (GNN) to learn nodes' representations from their local structures and/or global topologies for their comparison and ranking to the importance of network dismantling [22,23,37,38]. Compared to the centrality-based methods, these ND-oriented neural network approaches exhibit superior performance, yet they predominantly employ relatively small models with few parameters.

Recently, some researches have employed Transformers to address graph-related tasks, such as the node classification, link prediction and etc. [7,36,39]. The global attention mechanism of Transformer enables to encode nodes' representations with attentions to other nodes', thus can help discovering global relations in an encoding process for downstream tasks. However, due to the $\mathcal{O}(n^2)$ computation complexity of Transformer gradient backpropagation updates, it is difficult to extend them to large graphs. Some researches propose to apply a sparse attention mask in Transformers for reducing computation complexity [4,27], that is, the attention only takes care of an extended local structure of a node with its few hops away neighbors. Nevertheless, such approaches risk compromising latent dependencies in between far apart nodes.

To the best of our knowledge, we note that the application of large models such as Transformers to the ND problem remains unexplored. For the ND problem, the removal of a node and its associated edges directly impact on its local structure, however only local structure cannot necessarily reflect its global competence to the network integrity. That is, even two nodes are with the same local structure, they may play different role in dismantling a large network. For example, two such nodes are close to each other, so only one of them is necessary to be included in the target set. If two such nodes are far away, it is also necessary to compare which one, if with other target nodes, can contribute more to the network integrity.

Motivated from the aforementioned considerations, we are interested to explore potentials on exploiting a large model like Transformer to address the classic ND problem. The basic idea is to use a Transformer to encode nodes' representations for their ranking of importance to dismantle a network. For attribute-less nodes, we propose to iteratively encode the local structure of a node and its global relations to other nodes into its representation. For the dismantling task, we propose to compare the importance to network integrity for all nodes. A fusion model is designed to take care of both topological information and task importance for representation learning.

This paper proposes a *Transformer with Sparse Adaptive Mask* (TSAM) for network dismantling, where nodes' representations are iteratively updated with attention bias and mask for ranking their importance. In particular, the TSAM takes learnable degree ranking encodings and last round nodes' representations as input, and the output is the nodes' representations that are then converted to ranking scores via a linear layer. Top-ranked nodes are selected as the target attack ones. In the Transformer architecture, we propose to include a new fusion module, which fuses topological biases with a sparse adaptive mask to update the original Transformer attention matrix. The topological biases consists of local structural bias via degree ranking encodings and global relational bias via shortest-path encodings. The sparse adaptive mask consists of neighbor mask and peer mask. The peer mask is constructed by comparing nodes of similar representations, as they would score similar dismantling importance even if they are far apart in the input network. Experiments are conducted on eleven typical real-world networks and four synthetic network types. Results validate the superiority of our TSAM over the state-of-the-art schemes in terms of using fewer attack nodes in most cases.

## 2 Related Work and Preliminary

### 2.1 Network Dismantling

Most existing network dismantling methods evaluate node importance based on certain centrality measures and select the top-$K$ most critical nodes as the TAS. Commonly used approaches include degree centrality [1], betweenness centrality [12], closeness centrality [3], collective influence [25] and PageRank [26].

Recently, a few works have proposed neural network models to encode nodes' structural features for scoring their importance to network integrity [11,22,38]. For example, the FINDER [11] employs a reinforcement learning framework that incorporates a node reinsertion mechanism, i.e., strategically excluding some previously selected attack nodes from the target set and reinserting them back to the input network. In contrast, our work addresses the one-path dismantling approach excluding node reinsertion, where the simultaneous removal of all nodes in the TAS is executed in one iteration. The NIRM [37] encodes local structures and global topological signals via a neural model trained over small synthetic networks. The NEES [22] designs a graph neural network to extract the core structure of the network and transforms it into a smaller-scale structure with fewer nodes and edges. The DCRS [38] constructs a role graph based on the original graph, then encodes and integrates the nodes' propagation competitiveness and role importance to evaluate the nodes.

## 2.2 Transformer

We briefly introduce how one Transformer layer works, and multiple such layers can be stacked for complex tasks. Let the input to a layer be $\mathbf{H} \in \mathbb{R}^{n \times d}$, where $n$ is the sequence length and $d$ is the hidden dimension. Through learnable projection matrices $\mathbf{W}_q, \mathbf{W}_k, \mathbf{W}_v \in \mathbb{R}^{d \times d}$, the query $\mathbf{Q}$, key $\mathbf{K}$, and value $\mathbf{V}$ are generated:

$$\mathbf{Q} = \mathbf{H}\mathbf{W}_q, \quad \mathbf{K} = \mathbf{H}\mathbf{W}_k, \quad \mathbf{V} = \mathbf{H}\mathbf{W}_v.$$

The attention score matrix $\mathbf{A} \in \mathbb{R}^{n \times n}$ is computed via scaled dot-product of $\mathbf{Q}$ and $\mathbf{K}^\top$, which is then normalized by softmax. The layer output $\mathbf{H}'$ is obtained by the product of normalized $\mathbf{A}$ and $\mathbf{V}$:

$$\mathbf{A} = \frac{\mathbf{Q}\mathbf{K}^\top}{\sqrt{d}}, \quad \mathbf{H}' = \text{softmax}\left(\mathbf{A}\right)\mathbf{V}.$$

Note that the above single-head self-attention module can be generalized into a multi-head attention via the concatenation operation.

In recent years, a number of Transformer-inspired models have been developed for some graph tasks, like the node classification, link prediction, molecular property prediction and etc. [7,36,39]. For example, the GraphTransformer [7] uses positional encodings based on the Laplacian eigenvectors to learn nodes' representations for the node classification task. Gophormer [39] combines hierarchical pre-trained language models with GNNs through a hybrid architecture, enabling joint modeling of local neighborhood aggregation and global attention for knowledge graph completion tasks. Graphormer [36] integrates three structural encodings into Transformer layers to enhance structural awareness, achieving competitive performance in molecular property prediction. However, to the best of our knowledge, there are currently no Transformer-based methods for the ND problem.

## 3 Transformer with Sparse Adaptive Mask

### 3.1 The TSAM Framework

Consider an input network $\mathcal{G} = (\mathcal{V}, \mathcal{E})$ with $N$ nodes and $M$ edges. A Transformer can be used to iteratively encode nodes' representations $\mathbf{H} \in \mathbb{R}^{N \times d_h}$, where $d_h$ is the representation dimension. After training, the output of the Transformer $\mathbf{H}$ can be converted into dismantling scores via a linear layer for their ranking to construct the target set. During the Transformer encoding process, the attention mechanism necessitates computing pairwise attention scores in between all nodes. This imposes significant challenges for both parameter updates during backpropagation and memory consumption in large-scale networks, leading to $\mathcal{O}(n^2)$ computational complexity. Moreover, the fully-connected attention mechanism may degrade nodes' representational capacity by unnecessarily aggregating information from those nodes with few contribution to network dismantling.

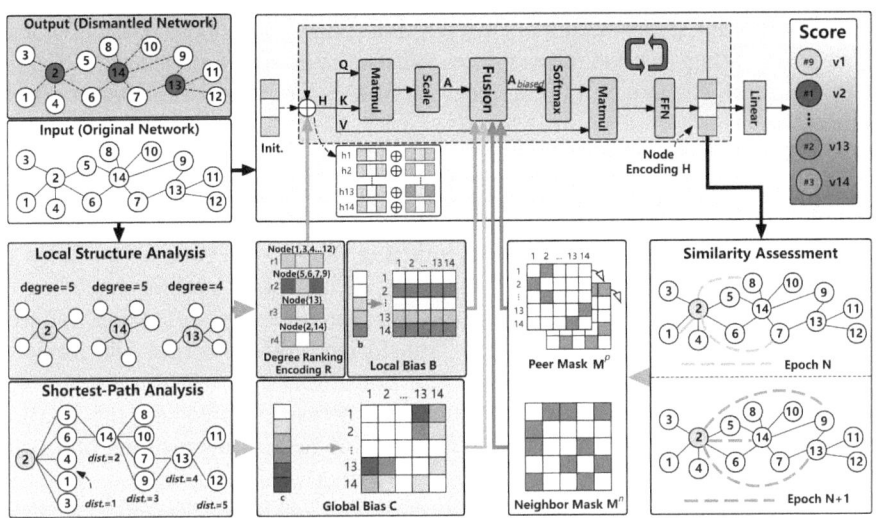

**Fig. 1.** The framework of Transformer with sparse adaptive mask (TSAM). The input is a connected network, and the output is nodes' dismantling scores which are used to compose the target attack node set (TAS). The TSAM includes a new fusion module in the Transformer architecture, which fuses the Transformer attention matrix with two biases a sparse adaptive mask.

Figure 1 presents the framework of our proposed Transformer with Sparse Adaptive Mask (TSAM) for network dismantling. In TSAM, the nodes' representations **H** are first randomly initialized, which will be aggregated with a learnable degree ranking matrix **R** as the Transformer input. The TSAM includes a new fusion module into a Transformer architecture. The fusion module first fuses the Transformer attention matrix **A** with a local attention bias **B** and a global bias **C** to obtain a biased attention matrix. It next selects for each node its peers with similar representations to construct a peer mask $\mathbf{M}^p$ in each iteration. The sparse adaptive mask **M** is the bitwise OR of the neighbor mask $\mathbf{M}^n$ and the peer mask $\mathbf{M}^p$, which is used to sparsify the biased attention matrix. During each training epoch, the updated nodes' representations **H** pass a linear layer to obtain dismantling scores for loss computation and dismantling evaluation.

## 3.2 Degree Ranking Encoding

Node degree centrality serves as an important indicator for local structures: The higher degree, the higher perturbation of structure stability caused by a single node removal, and such structural perturbation might propagate via neighbors to cause cascaded disconnections. We note that in many networks, node degree distribution is often not continuous, that is, some degrees are not associated with any node. For example, the network in Fig. 1 is without nodes of degree 3.

Encoding the value of degree centrality could lead to computational inefficiency. Moreover, topological heterogeneity across networks results in functional divergence among nodes with identical degrees. Thus, we propose to encode ordinal degree rankings instead of the degree values. For an input network $\mathcal{G} = (\mathcal{V}, \mathcal{E})$, let $d_i$ denote the degree of a node $v_i \in V$, and $\mathcal{D} = \{d_i\}$ denote the set of nodes' degrees, which is sorted in an increasing order. For example, in Fig. 1, we have $\mathcal{D} = \{1, 2, 4, 5\}$ as the sorted degree set of the input network, where $|\mathcal{D}| = 4$. We encode node degree ranking by a learnable matrix $\mathbf{R} \in \mathbb{R}^{|\mathcal{D}| \times d_h}$. Notice that the $i$-th row $\mathbf{R}_i$ indicates the encoding of the $i$-th element in $\mathcal{D}$. For a node $v_i$ with degree $d_i$, let $\mathsf{index}(\mathcal{D}, d_i)$ be an indexing function to return the index of $d_i$ in the set $\mathcal{D}$, denoted by $r_i = \mathsf{index}(\mathcal{D}, d_i)$. The degree ranking encoding of $v_i$ is denoted by $\mathbf{R}_{r_i}$, which is aggregated with the node representation updated in the last epoch as the input to the Transformer. We note that the iterative encoding process is expected to enable the Transformer for learning nodes' representations with the understanding about the network topological information as well as the node competence to the dismantling task. The encoding of a node $v_i$ is randomly initialized using the Xavier [13] method.

### 3.3 Topological Information as Attention Bias

The attention matrix $\mathbf{A} \in \mathbb{R}^{N \times N}$ is used to allocate an attention of $\mathbf{A}_{ij}$ by a node $v_i$ for a node $v_j$. For network dismantling, we propose two attention biases, a local bias $\mathbf{B}$ and a global bias $\mathbf{C}$ to update $\mathbf{A}$ into a biased attention matrix.

**Encoding Local Attention Bias.** When removing a node and its associated edges, its neighbors are the immediate sufferers, as they might be disconnected to the original network. Even worse, such disconnection might be propagated to incur cascaded disconnections of more other nodes. We propose to encode a learnable vector $\mathbf{b} \in \mathbb{R}^{1 \times |\mathcal{D}|}$ for each element in $\mathcal{D}$. That is, $\mathbf{b}_i$ is a learnable scalar indicating the $i$-th element in $\mathcal{D}$. Based on $\mathbf{b}$, we construct the local bias matrix $\mathbf{B} \in \mathbb{R}^{N \times N}$ as follows: The $i$-th row of $\mathbf{B}$ indicates the attention of node $v_i$ to other nodes. For $v_i$ with degree $d_i$, we also use $r_i = \mathsf{index}(\mathcal{D}, d_i)$ to return the index of $d_i$ in $\mathcal{D}$. Then we set all elements in the $i$-th row of $\mathbf{B}_i$ as $\mathbf{b}_{r_i}$. We note that although the degree ranking $\mathbf{R}$ and local bias $\mathbf{B}$ are with the same encoding rationale, they are encoded and used as two different matrices.

**Encoding Global Attention Bias.** The removal of a single node not only impacts on the connection of its neighbors to the input network, it could also impact on the connections of other far away nodes. However, capturing such long range influences may not be easy in the graph structure. We propose to use the shortest-path distance to measure the relation in between two nodes, as the shortest-path is the most efficient way for information dissemination in a network, which, we argue, could also be efficient to disconnect nodes from the network and critical for network integrity. We hence propose to encode shortest-paths in a network to represent the global relation of two nodes.

Let $c_{i,j}$ denote the shortest-path between two nodes $v_i$ and $v_j$. For example, in Fig. 1, we have $c_{2,5} = 1, c_{2,8} = 3$. For the input network $\mathcal{G}$, let $\mathcal{C}$ denote the set of all possible shortest-paths among two nodes, which is sorted in an increasing order. We propose to encode a learnable vector $\mathbf{c} \in \mathbb{R}^{1\times|\mathcal{C}|}$ for each element in $\mathcal{C}$. That is, $\mathbf{c}_i$ is a learnable scalar indicating the $i$-th element in $\mathcal{C}$. Based on $\mathbf{c}$, we construct the global bias matrix $\mathbf{C} \in \mathbb{R}^{N\times N}$ as follows: For a node $v_i$, we use an index function $r_{i,j} = \mathsf{index}(\mathcal{C}, v_i, v_j)$ to return the index of $c_{i,j}$ in $\mathcal{C}$. Then we set the element $\mathbf{C}_{ij} = \mathbf{c}_{r_{i,j}}$. Note that we set $\mathbf{C}_{ii} = 0$.

**Attention with Biases.** After obtaining $\mathbf{B}$ and $\mathbf{C}$, we input them into the fusion model to update the Transformer attention matrix $\mathbf{A}$ by

$$\mathbf{A}_{biased} = \mathbf{A} + \mathbf{B} + \mathbf{C},$$

to obtain a biased attention matrix $\mathbf{A}_{biased}$.

## 3.4 Fusion with Sparse Adaptive Mask

The biased attention matrix $\mathbf{A}_{biased}$ enables the Transformer to have a network-wide view on comparing and updating nodes' representations, that is, the attention of one node is computed based on the representations of itself and all other nodes. However, this network-wide computation is with exhibitive costs, sometimes causing the so-called over-globalization problem. That is, the attention of a node is unnecessarily allocated and normalized to those nodes without enough importance to network integrity. To address this issue, we propose to construct a sparse mask for each node only caring for its neighbors and peers. The peers of a node are regarded with similar importance to network integrity and so with similar encodings, even they are topologically far apart in the input network. Furthermore, as nodes' encodings are iteratively updated in each training epoch, the peers of a node can also change in different epochs. As such, we construct a sparse adaptive mask for the fusion module.

**Neighbor Mask.** A node should pay more attention to its neighbors, as they represent its local structure and would be directly impacted due to its removal. We use the adjacency matrix of the input network as the neighbor mask, denoted by $\mathbf{M}^n \in \{0,1\}^{N\times N}$. $\mathbf{M}^n_{ij} = 1$ indicates the existence of an edge between the node $v_i$ and $v_j$; Otherwise, $\mathbf{M}^n_{ij} = 0$. We note that the neighbor mask is not changed during the training epochs.

**Peer Mask.** The peer mask is used for a node to pay more attention to those nodes with similar importance to network integrity, even they could be topologically far away. By using a peer mask, the global competence to network integrity for two distant nodes can be compared. In order to enhance generalization capability, we propose to utilize the nodes' representations learned by the Transformer for competence evaluation (Fig. 2).

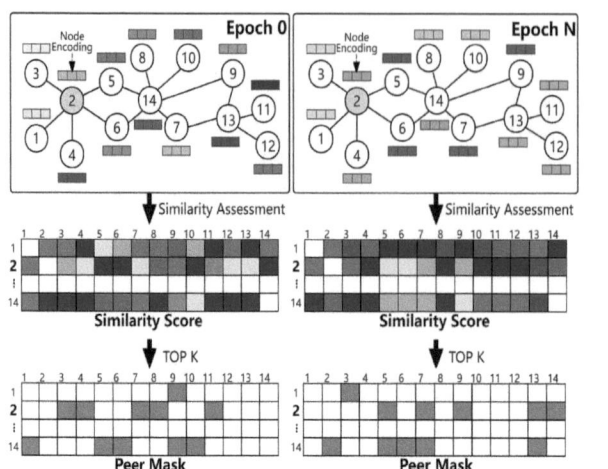

**Fig. 2.** Illustration of constructing a peer mask.

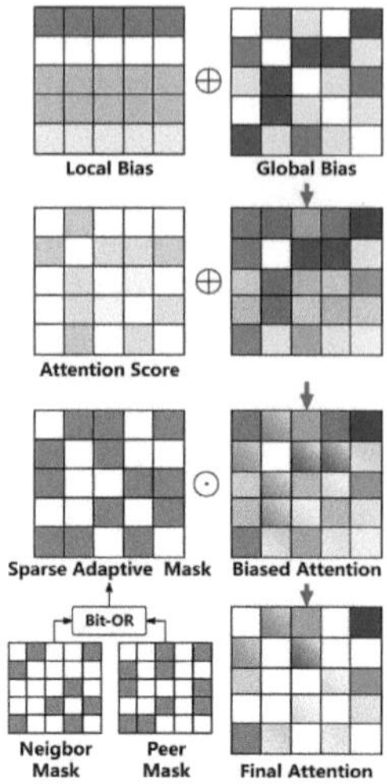

**Fig. 3.** Illustration of the fusion process.

Let $\mathbf{H} \in \mathbb{R}^{N \times d_h}$ denote the output of a Transformer layer, which will next pass a linear layer for scoring each node, as shown in Fig. 1. The $i$-th row of $\mathbf{H}$ is the representation of node $v_i$ learned by the Transformer. We compute the similarity between two nodes' representations, and construct a similarity matrix $\mathbf{S} \in \mathbb{R}^{N \times N}$ as follows:

$$\mathbf{S} = \left(\frac{\mathbf{H}}{\|\mathbf{H}\|_{\text{row}}}\right) \left(\frac{\mathbf{H}}{\|\mathbf{H}\|_{\text{row}}}\right)^\top,$$

where $\|\mathbf{H}\|_{\text{row}}$ denotes the L2 normalization applied to each row of the matrix $\mathbf{H}$. For a node $v_i$ with degree $d_i$, we only choose the top-$K_i$ similar nodes, where $K_i$ is computed by

$$K_i = \min\left(\max\left(d_i, \alpha_1\right), \alpha_2\right) \qquad (2)$$

where $\alpha_1$ and $\alpha_2$ are hyperparameters to denote the minimum and maximum sampling quantities respectively. We set the values of the top-$K_i$ elements in the $i$-th row of $\mathbf{S}$ to 1 and the rest to 0, to obtain the peer mask $\mathbf{M}^p$.

It is worth noting that, in contrast to the neighbor mask $\mathbf{M}^n$, the peer mask $\mathbf{M}^p$ is not fixed but subject to change in each training epoch. This ensures that the peer selection does not favor a specific type of nodes, but instead adaptively chooses more appropriate nodes as the Transformer gradually understands each node importance to network integrity.

**Fusion with Sparse Adaptive Mask.** The sparse adaptive mask $\mathbf{M}$ is the result of bitwise OR operation on the neighbor mask $\mathbf{M}^n$ and peer mask $\mathbf{M}^p$:

$$\mathbf{M} = \mathbf{M}^n \vee \mathbf{M}^p \qquad (3)$$

**Table 1.** Statistics of the real-world networks.

| Network | Nodes | Edges | Density | $\langle k \rangle$ | ClustCoeff. | Diameter | Category |
|---|---|---|---|---|---|---|---|
| Chicago [8] | 12,979 | 20,627 | 0.0002 | 3.18 | 0.0455 | 106 | Transport |
| Euroroads(Er) [32] | 1,039 | 1,305 | 0.0024 | 2.51 | 0.0339 | 62 | Transport |
| AirTraffic(AT) [21] | 1,226 | 2,408 | 0.0032 | 3.93 | 0.0639 | 17 | Airport |
| Gnutella [24] | 8,717 | 31,525 | 0.0008 | 7.23 | 0.0081 | 10 | Internet |
| FilmTrust(FT) [16] | 874 | 1,309 | 0.0034 | 2.99 | 0.1916 | 13 | Social |
| LastFM [30] | 7,624 | 27,806 | 0.0010 | 7.29 | 0.1786 | 15 | Social |
| RoviraVirgili(RV) [15] | 1,133 | 5,451 | 0.0085 | 9.62 | 0.1663 | 8 | Email |
| PPI [6] | 2,224 | 6,609 | 0.0027 | 5.94 | 0.1381 | 11 | Protein |
| Figeys [10] | 2,239 | 6,432 | 0.0026 | 5.75 | 0.0076 | 10 | Protein |
| Vidal [31] | 3,133 | 6,726 | 0.0014 | 4.29 | 0.0354 | 13 | Protein |
| Genefusion(Gf) [17] | 291 | 279 | 0.0066 | 1.92 | 0.0017 | 9 | Biology |

where $\vee$ denotes the bitwise OR operation. The fusion process applies the $\mathbf{M}$ to the biased attention matrix $\mathbf{A}_{biased}$ to obtain the final attention matrix $\mathbf{A}_{final}$:

$$\mathbf{A}_{final}(i,j) = \begin{cases} \mathbf{A}_{biased}(i,j) & \text{if } \mathbf{M}_{i,j} = 1, \\ -\infty & \text{if } \mathbf{M}_{i,j} = 0. \end{cases} \quad (4)$$

Note that the $(i,j)$-element of the final attention matrix represents the attention score of $v_i$ to $v_j$. In our experiments, we take negative infinity as a very small value ($-10^6$), so that after the softmax function, the attention score at this position will become 0. Figure 3 shows the full process of fusion module. By leveraging the two masks, we can achieve a balance between local and global information while significantly reducing computation costs.

### 3.5 Scoring and Loss Function

**Scoring.** After obtaining the nodes' representations $\mathbf{H}$, we evaluate a dismantling score $s_i$ for each node $v_i$ by a linear layer:

$$s_i = \mathbf{W}_s \mathbf{H}_i^\top \quad (5)$$

where $\mathbf{W}_s$ is the learnable matrix of the linear layer. The dismantling score $s_i$ can be understood as the importance of $v_i$ to network integrity. We finally select the top-$K$ nodes with highest dismantling scores to form the TAS $\mathcal{V}_t$.

**Loss Function.** To remove the least number of nodes while ensuring the remaining components in the network are small enough, we adopt the loss function defined in [38]:

$$\mathcal{L} = \sum_{v_i \in \mathcal{V}} \prod_{v_j \in \mathcal{N}(v_i)} \frac{1}{1+s_j} + \sum_{v_i \in \mathcal{V}} s_i, \quad (6)$$

**Table 2.** Comparison of normalized TAS sizes(%) on real-world networks with 0.01 dismantling threshold. The best is marked in bold green, the second best is marked in **bold**, while the third best is marked with underline.

| Datasets | DC | BC | CI | PR | NV | GAT | GCN | NIRM | NEES | DCRS | TSAM |
|---|---|---|---|---|---|---|---|---|---|---|---|
| Chi. | 50.8 | 55.58 | 60.42 | 51.56 | 70.74 | 77.73 | 76.65 | 46.58 | <u>42.15</u> | **35.3** | 33.03$_{+6.43\%}$ |
| Er | 41.29 | 48.99 | 82.19 | 33.69 | 46.2 | 87.78 | 89.51 | 38.11 | <u>28.1</u> | **23.39** | 22.42$_{+4.12\%}$ |
| AT | 32.79 | 50.98 | 68.03 | 28.14 | 73.82 | 76.59 | 98.04 | <u>25.61</u> | 26.43 | **23.57** | 21.70$_{+7.64\%}$ |
| Gnu. | 36.64 | 38.35 | 40.35 | 35.07 | 95.23 | 63.78 | 98.82 | <u>35.03</u> | 43.32 | 32.45 | **32.83**$_{-1.17\%}$ |
| FT | 22.77 | 33.75 | 42.68 | <u>22.20</u> | 64.87 | 81.69 | 98.74 | 44.39 | 25.97 | **19.11** | 14.53$_{+24.0\%}$ |
| Las. | 31.69 | 40.11 | 48.6 | <u>27.96</u> | 79.55 | 61.23 | 98.95 | 70.96 | 31.47 | **26.02** | 25.47$_{+2.17\%}$ |
| RV | 48.46 | 54.55 | 59.31 | <u>44.40</u> | 94.88 | 86.41 | 98.94 | 45.01 | 52.34 | **43.07** | 41.31$_{+4.10\%}$ |
| PPI | 27.34 | 35.7 | 34.67 | <u>24.19</u> | 41.32 | 61.38 | 98.88 | 25.49 | 24.82 | **21.67** | 21.04$_{+3.53\%}$ |
| Fig. | 18.89 | 18.89 | 25.9 | 16.03 | 86.02 | 54.27 | 30.64 | 39.53 | <u>10.05</u> | **8.93** | 8.84$_{+1.00\%}$ |
| Vid. | 20.84 | 23.46 | 31.6 | 20.14 | 89.59 | 54.23 | 98.82 | 31.38 | <u>17.3</u> | **16.02** | 14.20$_{+11.35\%}$ |
| Gf | 19.24 | 21.65 | 82.82 | **13.4** | 78.69 | 76.63 | 98.28 | <u>13.75</u> | 19.59 | 11.34 | 11.34$_{+0.00\%}$ |

**Table 3.** Average TAS and standard deviation results from twenty instances generated by four synthetic models.

| Datasets | DC | BC | CI | PR | NEES | DCRS | TSAM |
|---|---|---|---|---|---|---|---|
| PLC | 35.16±2.42 | 40.99±2.65 | 54.70±5.92 | <u>33.69±2.27</u> | 42.01±3.21 | **32.19±1.71** | 31.78±1.49 |
| BA | 45.30±1.76 | 47.60±2.32 | 64.17±3.58 | <u>43.23±1.88</u> | 53.40±2.78 | **41.47±1.60** | 40.56±1.79 |
| ER | 65.95±2.99 | 65.66±1.90 | 72.74±3.84 | <u>59.00±1.54</u> | 63.66±4.35 | **54.61±2.20** | 50.51±1.66 |
| WS | 77.13±2.53 | 76.92±2.36 | 82.04±3.18 | <u>73.01±3.66</u> | 76.65±3.30 | **63.98±1.30** | 63.80±1.34 |

where $\mathcal{N}(v_i)$ stands for the neighbor set of node $v_i$. The first term represents the expected number of unaffected nodes after the removal of a node. $\frac{1}{1+s_j}$ is inversely proportional to the importance of $v_j$ for network integrity. The number of unaffected nodes is estimated by evaluating the collective effect within the egonet after the removal of $v_i$. To minimize the number of targeted attack nodes, the sum of decomposition scores is used as a regularization term.

## 4 Experiments

### 4.1 Experimental Settings

**Datasets.** We evaluate the effectiveness of our TSAM on both real-world networks and synthetic networks.

*Real-world Networks.* We selected 11 real-world networks of diverse network scales and different topological structures spanning multiple domains, including society, internet, biology, collaboration and etc. Table 1 summarizes the statistics of these networks.

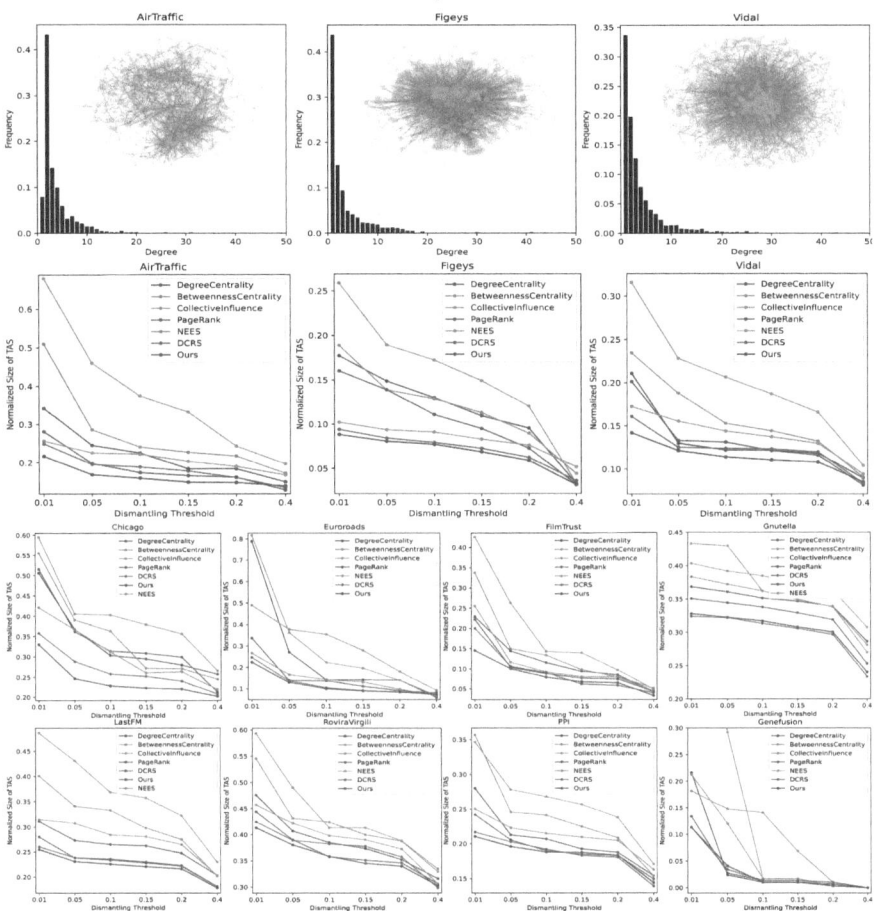

**Fig. 4.** Results of three real-world networks. Top: Network topology and degree distribution visualizations. Bottom: Dismantling performance of different models across varying dismantling thresholds on each network.

*Synthetic Networks.* We employ four standard generative models to get synthetic network data: the WS (Watts-Strogatz) [35], BA (Barabási-Albert) [2], PLC (Powerlaw-Cluster) [18], and ER (Erdös-Rényi) [9]. We use each model to generate 20 synthetic instances and average the results.

**Competitors.** We compare the TSAM with the two types of competitors: (1) four centrality-based schemes: DC (Degree Centrality) [1], BC (Betweeness Centrality) [12], CI (Collective Centrality) [25], and PR (PageRank) [26]; (2) six neural model-based schemes: the NV (Node2Vec) [14], GCN [20], GAT [33], NIRM [37], NEES [22], and DCRS [38].

**Implementation Details.** In our experiments, we use one Transformer layer and one attention head. All experiments are implemented in the Linux operating

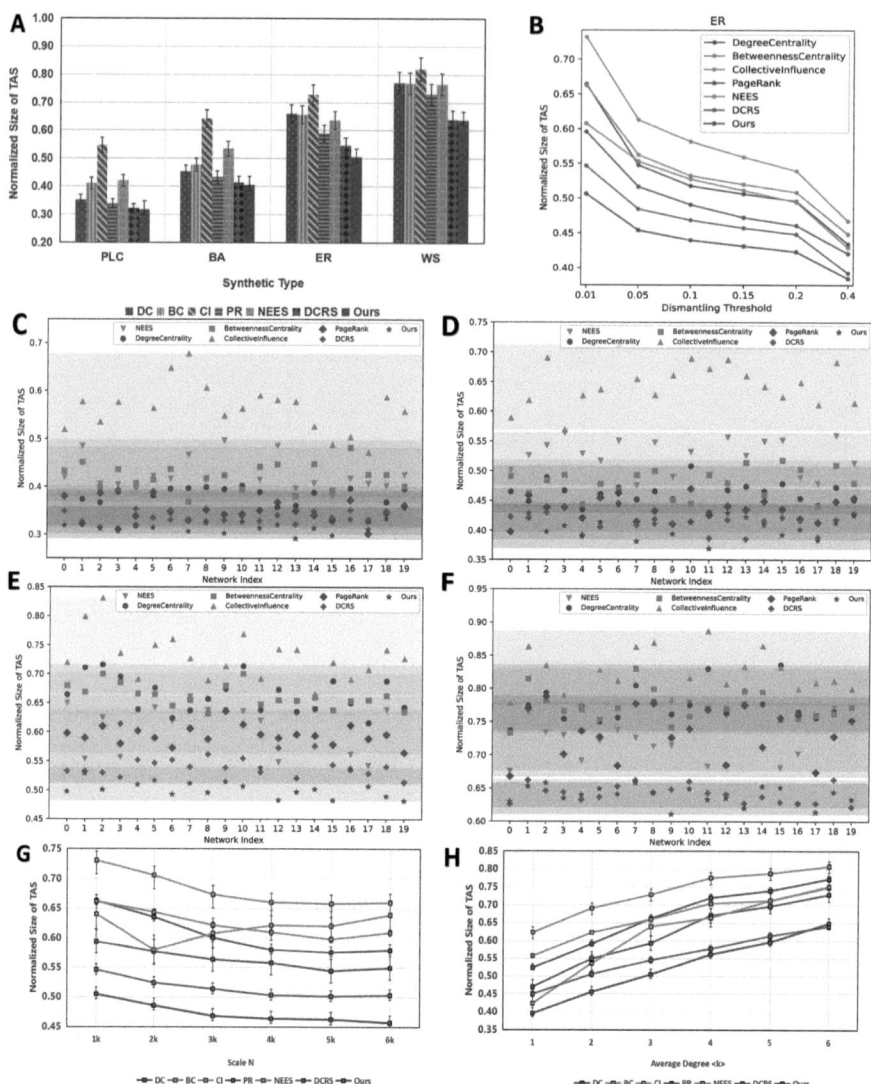

**Fig. 5.** Comparison of dismantling Performance on synthetic networks. (A): TAS comparison over four synthetic networks (network size $N = 1000$, dismantling threshold $\theta = 0.01$. (B): TAS against different dismantling thresholds on ER networks. (C,D,E,F): the result of the normalized TAS on PLC, BA, ER and WS models for the 20 experimented instances, respectively. (G): Dismantling performance on ER networks with fixed average degree $\langle k \rangle = 6$ and varying network sizes $N$ from 1000 to 6000. (H): TAS comparison on ER networks with fixed $N = 1000$ and varying $\langle k \rangle$ from 4 to 9.

system using an NVIDIA GeForce RTX 4090 with 24 GB memory, based on the Pytorch version 2.4.0, cuda 11.8, and Python 3.9.

## 4.2 Experimental Results

**Real-World Networks.** Table 2 presents the normalized TAS over network size for the real-world networks, when setting the dismantling threshold to 0.01. The smaller the normalized TAS, the more effective the network dismantling is, as it requires fewer target nodes to be removed. From the table, we can observe that our TSAM achieves the best performance in terms of the smallest normalized TAS in 10 out of 11 real-world networks, showing its superiority over the competitors. On the Gnu. real-world network, our model plays the second best, with a slightly more nodes than the best one.

Taking the real-world networks of the AirTraffic, Figeys and Vidal as examples, we visualize the network nodes and degree distribution in Fig. 4 to demonstrate the differences in their structures and characteristics. Facing these structurally heterogeneous real-world networks, achieving superior performance on all of them with a single model is highly challenging. The results demonstrate its generalization capability and resilience to topological differences. Figure 4 also plots the dismantling performance in terms of the normalized TAS under different dismantling threshold $\theta$ for the eleven real-world networks. It can be observed that our TSAM also outperforms the competitors in most cases.

**Synthetic Networks.** We select and compare six competitive methods with our TSAM on synthetic networks, as presented in Table 3. Figure 5 (A) plots the mean normalized TAS size and the standard deviation for the seven schemes, where each result is averaged over 20 generated network instances. Instances generated from the same synthetic model share similar network characteristics, while differences can exist across instances even using a same synthetic model with the same parameters. For example, the WS model generates networks with high clustering coefficients and small-world properties, whereas the PLC model produces networks exhibiting both scale-free degree distributions and hierarchical clustering structures. Results show that our TSAM achieves the best performance in synthetic networks.

Figure 5 (B) plots the normalized TAS size under different $\theta$ in ER networks as well, where our TSAM performs the best in terms of the smallest average results. Figure 5 (C,D,E,F) plot the normalized TAS for each experimented instances, where our TSAM achieves the smallest value in most instances and with a smaller variance. Note that although our TSAM outperforms the others in terms of averaged normalized TAS size, it may not be the best one in every network instance. We further investigate the dismantling performance of our TSAM on the ER networks generated with different parameters. Figure 5 (G) and (H) respectively plot the results for fixing the network average degree $\langle k \rangle = 6$ and increasing the network size $N$, and for fixed $N = 1000$ and varying $\langle k \rangle$ from 4 to 9. Our TSAM demonstrates robust performance in both scenarios, achieving competitive results comparable to state-of-the-art schemes.

## 4.3 Ablation Experiment

To verify the effectiveness of individual modules in TSAM, we conduct ablation experiments on the six key components, including the three structural encodings (w/o DRE: degree ranking encoding; w/o LB: local bias; w/o GB: global bias), two sparse masks (w/o NM: neighbor mask; w/o PM: peer mask), and the w/o IE: iterative encoding update mechanism. Table 4 presents the results of ablation experiments. It can be observed that removing any component degrades the model performance across all evaluated networks. This performance degradation validates the essential role of each module in the network dismantling task.

**Table 4.** Ablation study results on the real-world networks with $\theta = 0.01$.

| Methods | Chi. | Er | AT | Gnu. | FT | Las. | RV | PPI | Fig. | Vid. | Gf |
|---|---|---|---|---|---|---|---|---|---|---|---|
| w/o DRE | 49.65 | 56.02 | 69.17 | 79.86 | 46.68 | 60.99 | 77.05 | 57.06 | 52.30 | 40.82 | 49.83 |
| w/o LB | 33.31 | 22.51 | 22.43 | 33.04 | 14.53 | 25.47 | 42.81 | 21.17 | 9.20 | 16.69 | 11.34 |
| w/o GB | 35.52 | 23.10 | 22.84 | 36.07 | 19.45 | 33.85 | 41.40 | 22.71 | 13.04 | 17.30 | 11.68 |
| w/o NM | 43.58 | 35.51 | 37.93 | 57.80 | 28.15 | 67.92 | 77.67 | 41.95 | 53.37 | 43.47 | 19.59 |
| w/o PM | 33.28 | 26.37 | 23.90 | 32.93 | 18.88 | 31.22 | 41.57 | 23.56 | 14.92 | 17.34 | 11.34 |
| w/o IE | 34.86 | 29.45 | 22.43 | 35.31 | 16.13 | 29.11 | 43.51 | 24.37 | 9.78 | 15.19 | 11.34 |
| TSAM | **33.03** | **22.42** | **21.7** | **32.83** | **14.53** | **25.47** | **41.31** | **21.04** | **8.84** | **14.2** | **11.34** |

For the nodes' representations, the effect of eliminating the DRE (degree ranking encoding) part is generally lower than eliminating only the IE part. This may be due to the fact that by removing the DRE component, only global information is used for representations without taking into account local information, while local structural information usually plays a significant role in the ND problem. For similar reasons, the impact of eliminating the NM (neighbor mask) part has a greater effect than removing other bias or mask part in the fusion module. Although the local structure information is important, we note that the best performance is achieved when including global topology information (the global bias) and comparing node importance (the peer mask) in the TSAM scheme.

## 4.4 Efficiency Analysis

To validate the efficiency of our mask mechanism, we compare it with full global attention on several real-world networks and record the average runtime per epoch over 50 training epochs. Table 5 presents the detailed results. The results demonstrate that our mask mechanism achieves significant runtime reductions and operational efficiency improvements.

**Table 5.** Average runtime consumption per epoch (seconds).

| Methods | Er | AT | FT | RV | PPI | Fig. | Vid. | Gf |
|---|---|---|---|---|---|---|---|---|
| Full Att. | 93.06 | 137.14 | 32.78 | 107.51 | 433.52 | 424.68 | 663.71 | 4.83 |
| Masked Att. | 0.82 | 1.24 | 0.61 | 1.95 | 3.81 | 3.16 | 5.13 | 0.14 |

### 4.5 Hyperparameters Analysis

**Hyperparameter Configurations.** Our model incorporates two critical hyperparameters, $\alpha_1$ and $\alpha_2$, representing the minimum and maximum sample sizes respectively. These hyperparameters influence network dismantling performance to some extent, with their optimal values depending on network scale, average degree, and other topological characteristics. For reference, our hyperparameter configurations are provided in Table 6.

**Table 6.** Configurations of $\alpha_1$ and $\alpha_2$ in both real-world and sythetic networks.

| Datasets | Chi. | Er | AT | Gnu. | FT | Las. | RV | PPI | Fig. | Vid. | Gf | PLC | BA | ER | WS |
|---|---|---|---|---|---|---|---|---|---|---|---|---|---|---|---|
| $\alpha_1$ | 1 | 2 | 1 | 2 | 1 | 3 | 3 | 5 | 1 | 1 | 1 | 5 | 5 | 3 | 1 |
| $\alpha_2$ | 10 | 10 | 10 | 20 | 5 | 15 | 10 | 20 | 10 | 10 | 3 | 10 | 10 | 10 | 1 |

**Sensitivity Analysis.** To validate the sensitivity of our TSAM to hyperparameters, we configure $\alpha_1$ and $\alpha_2$ as four distinct pairs: $(1, \infty)$, $(5, 5)$, $(10, 10)$, and $(20, 20)$. These configurations represent sampling sizes equivalent to node degree, and fixed sizes of 5, 10, and 20 respectively. The comparative results on several real-world networks are presented in Table 7.

**Table 7.** Dismantling performance with different hyperparameters($\theta = 0.01$).

| Configurations | Er | AT | FT | RV | PPI | Fig. | Vid. | Gf |
|---|---|---|---|---|---|---|---|---|
| $(1, \infty)$ | 23.29 | 23.33 | 15.45 | 44.31 | 22.48 | 12.59 | 14.65 | 11.68 |
| $(5, 5)$ | 22.23 | 23.74 | 14.3 | 42.54 | 22.30 | 9.11 | 16.69 | 11.34 |
| $(10, 10)$ | 25.51 | 23.49 | 14.87 | 41.39 | 20.82 | 9.74 | 17.3 | 11.68 |
| $(20, 20)$ | 34.26 | 22.51 | 14.87 | 43.95 | 22.03 | 12.95 | 18.7 | 11.68 |
| TSAM | 22.42 | 21.7 | 14.53 | 41.31 | 21.04 | 8.84 | 14.2 | 11.34 |

The analysis reveals that the model performance exhibits measurable variations under different hyperparameter configurations. Nevertheless, our TSAM maintains robust dismantling efficacy across multiple networks, demonstrating competitive results relative to benchmark requirements.

## 5 Conclusion

This paper studies the potentials of using large models for the classic network dismantling problem. We have proposed the TSAM, a Transformer-based framework with a sparse adaptive mask, and experimented its superiority over the state-of-the-art competitors in real-world networks and synthetic networks. The performance superiority can be attributed to the large model encoding capabilities, but more important is from our design: The degree ranking encoding is to capture local structural biases, the shortest-path encoding is to encode global relations in terms of long-range dependencies, and a sparse mask combining static neighbor mask and adaptive peer mask. The adaptive mask helps to identify nodes of comparable importance to network integrity, enabling global comparisons while reducing computational overhead.

Despite the new state-of-the-art results, we acknowledge some limitations of our model. The TSAM does not fully exploit higher-order structural patterns (e.g., multi-hop egonet dynamics). While the peer mask reduces computation, scalability to billion-scale networks requires further optimization. Future work will explore hierarchical attention mechanisms for higher-order structures and large-scale networks.

**Acknowledgments.** This work is supported in part by National Natural Science Foundation of China (Grant No: 62172167).

## References

1. Albert, R., Jeong, H., Barabási, A.L.: Error and attack tolerance of complex networks. Nature **406**(6794), 378–382 (2000)
2. Barabási, A.L., Albert, R.: Emergence of scaling in random networks. Science **286**(5439), 509–512 (1999)
3. Bavelas, A.: Communication patterns in task-oriented groups. J. Acoust. Society America **22**(6), 725–730 (1950)
4. Beltagy, I., Peters, M.E., Cohan, A.: Longformer: The long-document transformer. arXiv preprint arXiv:2004.05150 (2020)
5. Braunstein, A., Dall'Asta, L., Semerjian, G., Zdeborová, L.: Network dismantling. Proc. Natl. Acad. Sci. **113**(44), 12368–12373 (2016)
6. Bu, D., et al.: Topological structure analysis of the protein-protein interaction network in budding yeast. Nucleic Acids Res. **31**(9), 2443–2450 (2003)
7. Dwivedi, V.P., Bresson, X.: A generalization of transformer networks to graphs. arXiv preprint arXiv:2012.09699 (2020)
8. Eash, R., Chon, K., Lee, Y., Boyce, D.: Equilibrium traffic assignment on an aggregated highway network for sketch planning. Transp. Res. **13**, 243–257 (1979)
9. Erdos, P., Rényi, A., et al.: On the evolution of random graphs. Publ. math. inst. hung. acad. sci **5**(1), 17–60 (1960)
10. Ewing, R.M., et al.: Large-scale mapping of human protein-protein interactions by mass spectrometry. Mol. Syst. Biol. **3**(1), 89 (2007)
11. Fan, C., Zeng, L., Sun, Y., Liu, Y.Y.: Finding key players in complex networks through deep reinforcement learning. Nature Mach. Intell. **2**(6), 317–324 (2020)

12. Freeman, L.: A set of measures of centrality based on betweenness. Sociometry (1977)
13. Glorot, X., Bengio, Y.: Understanding the difficulty of training deep feedforward neural networks. In: Proceedings of the Thirteenth International Conference on Artificial Intelligence and Statistics, pp. 249–256. JMLR Workshop and Conference Proceedings (2010)
14. Grover, A., Leskovec, J.: node2vec: Scalable feature learning for networks. In: Proceedings of the 22nd ACM SIGKDD International Conference on Knowledge Discovery And Data Mining, pp. 855–864 (2016)
15. Guimera, R., Danon, L., Diaz-Guilera, A., Giralt, F., Arenas, A.: Self-similar community structure in a network of human interactions. Phys. Rev. E **68**(6), 065103 (2003)
16. Guo, G., Zhang, J., Yorke-Smith, N.: A novel evidence-based Bayesian similarity measure for recommender systems. ACM Trans. Web (TWEB) **10**(2), 1–30 (2016)
17. Höglund, M., Frigyesi, A., Mitelman, F.: A gene fusion network in human neoplasia. Oncogene **25**(18), 2674–2678 (2006)
18. Holme, P., Kim, B.J.: Growing scale-free networks with tunable clustering. Phys. Rev. E **65**(2), 026107 (2002)
19. Jazmin, G.: Major internet outage: Dozens of websites and apps were down (2020)
20. Kipf, T.N., Welling, M.: Semi-supervised classification with graph convolutional networks. arXiv preprint arXiv:1609.02907 (2016)
21. Kunegis, J.: Konect: the Koblenz network collection. In: Proceedings of the 22nd International Conference on World Wide Web, pp. 1343–1350 (2013)
22. Liu, Q., Wang, B.: Neural extraction of multiscale essential structure for network dismantling. Neural Netw. **154**, 99–108 (2022)
23. Ma, S., Zeng, W., Xiao, W., Zhao, X.: Dismantling complex networks with graph contrastive learning and multi-hop aggregation. Inform. Sci. 120780 (2024)
24. Matei, R., Iamnitchi, A., Foster, P.: Mapping the gnutella network. IEEE Internet Comput. **6**(1), 50–57 (2002)
25. Morone, F., Makse, H.A.: Influence maximization in complex networks through optimal percolation. Nature **524**(7563), 65–68 (2015)
26. Page, L.: The Pagerank Citation Ranking: Bringing Order to the Web. Tech. rep, Technical Report (1999)
27. Park, J., et al.: Deformable graph transformer. arXiv preprint arXiv:2206.14337 (2022)
28. Radicchi, F.: Percolation in real interdependent networks. Nat. Phys. **11**(7), 597–602 (2015)
29. Ren, X.L., Gleinig, N., Helbing, D., Antulov-Fantulin, N.: Generalized network dismantling. Proc. Natl. Acad. Sci. **116**(14), 6554–6559 (2019)
30. Rozemberczki, B., Sarkar, R.: Characteristic functions on graphs: birds of a feather, from statistical descriptors to parametric models. In: Proceedings of the 29th ACM International Conference on Information and Knowledge Management, pp. 1325–1334 (2020)
31. Rual, J.F., et al.: Towards a proteome-scale map of the human protein-protein interaction network. Nature **437**(7062), 1173–1178 (2005)
32. Šubelj, L., Bajec, M.: Robust network community detection using balanced propagation. Europ. Phys. J. B **81**, 353–362 (2011)
33. Velickovic, P., Cucurull, G., Casanova, A., Romero, A., Lio, P., Bengio, Y., et al.: Graph attention networks. Stat **1050**(20), 10–48550 (2017)
34. Wandelt, S., Sun, X., Feng, D., Zanin, M., Havlin, S.: A comparative analysis of approaches to network-dismantling. Sci. Rep. **8**(1), 13513 (2018)

35. Watts, D.J., Strogatz, S.H.: Collective dynamics of 'small-world' networks. Nature **393**(6684), 440–442 (1998)
36. Ying, C., et al.: Do transformers really perform badly for graph representation? Adv. Neural. Inf. Process. Syst. **34**, 28877–28888 (2021)
37. Zhang, J., Wang, B.: Dismantling complex networks by a neural model trained from tiny networks. In: Proceedings of the 31st ACM International Conference on Information and Knowledge Management, pp. 2559–2568 (2022)
38. Zhang, J., Wang, B.: Encoding node diffusion competence and role significance for network dismantling. In: Proceedings of the ACM Web Conference 2023, pp. 111–121 (2023)
39. Zhao, J., et al.: Gophormer: ego-graph transformer for node classification. arXiv preprint arXiv:2110.13094 (2021)

# Author Index

**A**

Agapitos, Alexandros 163
Aghababaei-Harandi, Ali 499
Amini, Massih-Reza 499
Aria, Hadi Partovi 77
Arora, Chetan 289
Aslam, Muhammad Haseeb 235

**B**

Badam, Sriraj 59
Baktashmotlagh, Mahsa 272, 306
Beikmohammadi, Ali 41
Berg, Chris 59
Bewong, Michael 21
Birke, Robert 254
Blumenstiel, Benedikt 359, 516
Brunschwiler, Thomas 359

**C**

Chen, Geng 146
Chen, Jianyu 179
Chen, Lydia Y. 254
Chen, Minmin 59
Chen, Xiaoyu 179
Chen, Yulong 448
Cheng, Yuxuan 448
Chi, Ed H. 59
Christakopoulou, Konstantina 59
Christianos, Filippos 216
Chu, Tommy 322
Corazza, Jan 77
Cui, Xinyu 216

**D**

Dai, Tingting 376
Ding, LinLin 340
Dixon, Eric Bencomo 59
Dong, Xinyi 340

Doquet, Guillaume 395
Duan, Tiehang 481

**E**

Einizade, Aref 430
Etemad, Ali 235

**F**

Fan, Wenqi 448
Fekri, Faramarz 198
Feng, Zaiwen 21
Fraccaro, Paolo 516

**G**

Galjaard, Jeroen M. 254
Gan, Yanglei 376
Gao, Siyu 146
Giraldo, Jhony H. 430
Granger, Eric 235
Guo, Kaiyu 272
Gupta, Sunil 112

**H**

Haverbeck, Lukas 129
He, Bowei 3
Hebbalaguppe, Ramya 289
Hou, Junyu 95
Hu, Fanghao 533
Hu, Junwei 21
Huang, Haojun 533

**J**

Jakubik, Johannes 359

**K**

Kaddah, Rim 395
Kandar, Tamoghno 289
Kannala, Juho 465

© The Editor(s) (if applicable) and The Author(s), under exclusive license
to Springer Nature Switzerland AG 2026
R. P. Ribeiro et al. (Eds.): ECML PKDD 2025, LNAI 16018, pp. 551–553, 2026.
https://doi.org/10.1007/978-3-032-06106-5

Khirirat, Sarit 41
Khramtsova, Ekaterina 306
Kim, Hyohun 77
Koerich, Alessandro Lameiras 235
Kou, Yue 340
Kovalenko, Alexander 322
Kwashie, Selasi 21

**L**
Lan, Qizhen 481
Lan, Tian 376
Le, Hung 112
Le, Ya 59
Li, Daniel 59
Li, Dong 340
Li, Yongqiang 179
Liu, Qiao 376
Liu, Yao 376
Liu, Yu 533
Lovell, Brian C. 272
Lynch, David 163

**M**
Ma, Chen 3
Magnússon, Sindri 41
Marimo, Clive Tinashe 359
Marti Escofet, Francesc 516
Martinez, Clara 235
Massiani, Pierre-François 129
Mguni, David 216

**N**
Nagpal, Abhinav 289
Neider, Daniel 77
Nguyen, Hung Son 412
Nguyen, Minh Hoang 112
Nitsche, Maximilian 359
Niu, Shuteng 481

**P**
Pajarinen, Joni 465
Pan, Minting 146
Pang, Renning 376
Pedersoli, Marco 235

Pérez, Juan F. 254
Potter, Trevor 59

**R**
Read, Jesse 395
Richtárik, Peter 41

**S**
Salzmann, Mathieu 306
Scheibenreif, Linus 516
Schindler, Konrad 516
Shi, Xiaojun 376
Shi, Yucheng 163
Song, Yan 216
Sun, Jingyou 340
Sun, Wenbo 481
Sun, Zexu 3

**T**
Tang, Zuojin 179
Tao, Cui 481
Thil, Lucas 395
Tian, Qing 481
Tran, Hung The 112
Tran, Toan Van 412
Trimpe, Sebastian 129

**V**
Van, Linh Le Pham 112
von Rohr, Alexander 129

**W**
Wan, Hao 59
Wang, Bang 533
Wang, Jun 216
Wang, Vivienne 465
Wang, Xi 306
Wang, Yashen 376
Wang, Yunbo 146
Wang, Zijian 272
Wei, Yong 340
Wu, Haolun 3

**X**
Xia, Lu 481
Xiao, Xi 481

Xie, Shifeng   430
Xie, Yixin   481
Xu, Can   59
Xu, Duo   198
Xu, Zhe   77

## Y

Yan, Xue   216
Yang, Li   481
Yang, Xiaokang   146
Yi, Xinyang   59

## Z

Zhang, Haifeng   216
Zhang, Haoyu   448
Zhang, Sai   59
Zhang, Wendong   146
Zhang, Xiaokun   3
Zhang, Yansen   3
Zhang, Yifan   448
Zhao, Rongzhen   465
Zhao, Sibo   21
Zhu, Lijing   481
Zhu, Xiangming   146
Zuccon, Guido   306

MIX
Papier aus verantwortungsvollen Quellen
Paper from responsible sources
FSC® C105338

If you have any concerns about our products,
you can contact us on
**ProductSafety@springernature.com**

In case Publisher is established outside the EU,
the EU authorized representative is:
**Springer Nature Customer Service Center GmbH
Europaplatz 3, 69115 Heidelberg, Germany**

Printed by Libri Plureos GmbH
in Hamburg, Germany